An Introduction to
Health Psychology

Fourth edition
Val Morrison and Paul Bennett

Harlow, England • London • New York • Boston • San Francisco • Toronto • Sydney • Auckland • Singapore • Hong Kong
Tokyo • Seoul • Taipei • New Delhi • Cape Town • São Paulo • Mexico City • Madrid • Amsterdam • Munich • Paris • Milan

Pearson Education Limited
Edinburgh Gate
Harlow CM20 2JE
United Kingdom
Tel: +44 (0)1279 623623

Web: www.pearson.com/uk

First published 2006 (print)
Second edition published 2009 (print)
Third edition published 2012 (print)
Fourth edition published 2016 (print and electronic)

ISBN: 978–1-292–00313–9 (print)
         978–1-292–00314–6 (PDF)
         978–1-292–12944-0 (ePub)

British Library Cataloguing-in-Publication Data
A catalogue record for the print edition is available from the British Library

Library of Congress Cataloging-in-Publication Data
A catalog record for the print edition is available from the Library of Congress

10 9 8 7 6 5 4 3 2 1
19 18 17 16 15

Cover image: © Getty Images

Print edition typeset in 9.75/13 pt Times LT Pro by Lumina Datamatics, Inc.
Printed in Slovakia by Neografia
NOTE THAT ANY PAGE CROSS REFERENCES REFER TO THE PRINT EDITION

Contents

Preface   *xi*
Publisher's acknowledgements   *xv*

PART I   BEING AND STAYING HEALTHY   1

Chapter 1   What is health?   2

Learning outcomes   2
Chapter outline   4
What is health? Changing perspectives   4
Individual, cultural and lifespan perspectives on health   12
What is health psychology?   24
Summary   29
Further reading   29

Chapter 2   Health inequalities   30

Learning outcomes   30
Chapter outline   32
Health differentials   32
Minority status and health   43
Gender and health   46
Summary   48
Further reading   49

Chapter 3   Health-risk behaviour   50

Learning outcomes   50
Chapter outline   52
What is health behaviour?   52
Smoking, drinking and illicit drug use   55
Unprotected sexual behaviour   72
Unhealthy diet   78
Obesity   81
Summary   85
Further reading   85

Chapter 4   Health-protective behaviour   86

Learning outcomes   86
Chapter outline   88
Adherence behaviour   88

Healthy diet   95
Exercise   99
Health-screening behaviour   108
Immunisation behaviour   116
Summary   120
Further reading   120

Chapter 5   Explaining health behaviour   122

Learning outcomes   122
Chapter outline   124
Distal influences on health behaviour   124
Models of health behaviour   131
Sociocognitive models of behaviour change   134
Stage models of behaviour change   147
Summary   156
Further reading   157

Chapter 6   Changing behaviour: mechanisms and approaches   158

Learning outcomes   158
Chapter outline   160
Developing public health interventions   160
Strategies for changing risk behaviour   162
Summary   175
Further reading   176

Chapter 7   Preventing health problems   178

Learning outcomes   178
Chapter outline   180
Working with individuals   180
Using the mass media   184
Environmental interventions   188
Public health programmes   191
Using new technology   200
Summary   203
Further reading   204

PART II   BECOMING ILL   205

Chapter 8   The body in health and illness   206

Learning outcomes   206
Chapter outline   208
The behavioural anatomy of the brain   208
The autonomic nervous system   211
The immune system   214
The digestive system   221
The cardiovascular system   225
The respiratory system   232
Summary   235
Further reading   236

Chapter 9   Symptom perception, interpretation and response   238

Learning outcomes   238
Chapter outline   240
How do we become aware of the sensations of illness?   240
Symptom perception   242
Symptom interpretation   248
Planning and taking action: responding to symptoms   263
Summary   272
Further reading   272

Chapter 10   The consultation and beyond   274

Learning outcomes   274
Chapter outline   276
The medical consultation   276
Factors that influence the process of consultation   279
Moving beyond the consultation   286
Summary   298
Further reading   299

Chapter 11   Stress, health and illness: theory   302

Learning outcomes   302
Chapter outline   304
Concepts of stress   304
Types of stress   316
Stress as a physiological response   322
The stress and illness link   331
Summary   336
Further reading   336

Chapter 12   Stress and illness moderators   338

Learning outcomes   338
Chapter outline   340
Coping defined   340
Stress, personality and illness   346
Stress and cognitions   358
Stress and emotions   362
Social support and stress   364
Summary   370
Further reading   371

Chapter 13   Managing stress   372

Learning outcomes   372
Chapter outline   374
Stress theory: a quick review   374
Stress management training   375
The third wave therapies   379
Preventing stress   382
Minimising stress in hospital settings   388
Summary   391
Further reading   392

PART III BEING ILL393

Chapter 14 The impact and outcomes of illness: patient perspective394

Learning outcomes394
Chapter outline396
The impact of illness396
Coping with illness408
Illness and quality of life412
Measuring quality of life424
*Summary*431
*Further reading*431

Chapter 15 The impact and outcomes of illness: families and informal caregivers434

Learning outcomes434
Chapter outline436
Illness: a family affair436
Expectancies of care440
Family systems and family members443
Consequences of caring for the caregiver448
Influences on caring outcomes452
*Summary*464
*Further reading*464

Chapter 16 Pain466

Learning outcomes466
Chapter outline468
The experience of pain468
Biological models of pain472
A psychobiological theory of pain479
Future understandings of pain: the neuromatrix482
Helping people to cope with pain483
*Summary*492
*Further reading*493

Chapter 17 Improving health and quality of life496

Learning outcomes496
Chapter outline498
Coping with chronic illness498
Reducing distress499
Managing illness504
Preventing disease progression512
*Summary*517
*Further reading*517

PART IV   FUTURES

519

Chapter 18   Futures

520

Learning outcomes	520
Chapter outline	522
The need for theory-driven practice	522
Getting evidence into practice	525
Summary	534
Further reading	534
Glossary	535
References	547
Index	642

Supporting resources

Companion website

For open-access student resources specifically written to complement this textbook and support your learning, please visit **www.pearsoned.co.uk/morrison**

Lecturer resources

For password-protected online resources tailored to support the use of this textbook in teaching, please visit **www.pearsoned.co.uk/morrison**

Preface

Background to this book

Well, it's that time again . . . time to bring out another edition of the book. As always, this time provides an opportunity to update, revise and generally 'improve' the text. And this edition certainly achieves these goals. It is not just an update on previous editions, but has a number of significant revisions, reflecting changes in emphasis in both the practice of health psychology and its developing research base. Despite these changes, we remain true to our original goal and beliefs. We believe health psychology is an exciting and vibrant discipline to study at both undergraduate and postgraduate level. It has developed into an exciting professional discipline with a defined training pathway and increasing numbers of relevant jobs both in health-care systems and other contexts.

We wrote the first edition of the book because we believed that a comprehensive European-focused textbook was required that didn't predominantly focus on health behaviours, but gave equal attention to issues in health, in illness, and in health-care practice and intervention. In addition, we believed that health-care training textbooks should be led by psychological theory and constructs, as opposed to being led by behaviour or by disease. Diseases may vary clinically, but, psychologically speaking, they share many things in common; the potential for life or behaviour change, distress and emotional growth, challenges to coping, potential for recovery, involvement in health care and involvement with health professionals. We stick to this ideology; as clearly do many other people, because we have been asked to produce this fourth edition. We have maintained our comprehensive coverage of health, illness and health care, while updating and including reference to significant new studies, refining some sections, restructuring others, and basically working towards making this new edition distinctive and (even) stronger than the last! Our readership includes many medical students and therefore we have integrated several case studies to bring the human and clinical perspective even more to life.

Aims of this textbook

The overall aim of this textbook is to provide a balanced, informed and comprehensive UK/European textbook with sufficient breadth of material for introductory students, but which also provides sufficient research depth to benefit final year students or those conducting a health psychology project including at Masters level. In addition to covering mainstream health psychology topics such as health and illness beliefs, behaviour and outcomes, we include topics such as socio-economic influences on health, biological bases, individual and cultural differences, the impact on family and carers, and psychological interventions in health, illness and health care, as these are all essential to the study of health psychology.

In this edition, we have stuck to a format in which chapters follow the general principle of issue first, theory second, research evidence third, and finally the application of that theory and, where appropriate, the effectiveness of any intervention. We first examine factors that contribute to health, including societal, cognitive, emotional and behavioural factors, and how psychologists and others can improve or maintain individuals' health. We then examine the process of becoming ill: from the first perception of symptoms through their interpretation and presentation to health care. We examine the physiological systems that may fail in illness, psychosocial factors that may contribute to the development and impact of illness, how we and our friends and families cope with illness, and how the medical system copes with us when we become ill. Finally, we examine a number of psychological interventions that can improve the well-being and perhaps even health of those who experience health problems.

This text is intended to provide comprehensive coverage of the core themes in current health psychology but it also addresses the fact that many individuals neither stay healthy, nor live with illness, in isolation. The role of family is crucial and therefore while acknowledging the role of significant others in many chapters, for example in relation to influencing dietary or smoking behaviour, or in providing support during times of stress, in this 4th edition we devote all of Chapter 15 to the impact of illness on the family and caregivers of people who are ill. Another goal of ours in writing this textbook was to acknowledge that Western theorists should not assume cross-cultural similarity of health and illness perceptions or behaviours. Therefore from the first edition to this current edition we have integrated examples of theory and research from non-Westernised countries wherever possible. Throughout this text runs the theme of differentials, whether culture, gender, age/developmental stage, or socio-economic, and, as acknowledged by reviewers and readers of the first three editions, our commitment to this is clearly seen in the inclusion of a whole chapter devoted to socio-economic differentials in health.

Structure of this textbook

Key changes from earlier editions of this book include greater consideration of personality and cultural influences on health behaviour in Chapters 3–5, and the addition of a chapter focusing completely on theories and mechanisms of behavioural change. These developments are reflected in Chapter 6 of the new edition which is now devoted entirely to exploring the nature of these behavioural change strategies and the theories from which they are derived. Chapter 7 then considers how these strategies can be used in preventing disease both through working with individuals and at a population level. In terms of the chapters addressing the illness experience, in Chapter 14 we now consider the impact of illness on a range of outcomes directly impacting on the individual affected, while Chapter 15 is now devoted to the impact on the family and caregivers of these individuals. Chapter 17 considers the implementation of strategies of change or emotional regulation in people who have already developed disease. In addition to these structural changes, we have incorporated more discussion of health psychology in the context of younger people and more qualitative research.

The textbook continues to be structured into three broad sections. The first, *Being and Staying Healthy*, contains seven chapters, which first examine factors that contribute to health, including societal and behavioural factors, and then describe how psychologists and others

can improve or maintain individuals' health. Chapter 1 considers what we actually mean when we talk about 'health' or 'being healthy' and presents a brief history to the mind–body debate which underpins much of our research. We consider the important influence of current health status, lifespan, ageing and culture on health, and in doing so illustrate better the biopsychosocial model which underpins health psychology. Chapter 2 describes how factors such as social class, income and even postcode can affect one's health, behaviour and access to health care. Indeed, the health of the general population is influenced by the socio-economic environment in which we live and which differs both within and across countries and cultures. We have tried to reflect more of this diversity in the present volume.

Many of today's 'killer' illnesses, such as some cancers, heart disease and stroke, have a behavioural component. Chapters 3 and 4 describe how certain behaviours such as exercise have health-enhancing effects whereas others, such as non-adherence to medicines, smoking or the use of illicit drugs, have health-damaging effects. More detail has been added regarding two groups of behaviours – over-eating, and illicit drug use. As well as updating the epidemiological statistics regarding such health behaviours and outlining current health policy and targets where they exist, we continue to provide evidence of individual, lifespan, cultural and gender differentials in health behaviours. These behaviours have been examined by health and social psychologists over several decades, drawing on several key theories such as social learning theory and socio-cognitive theory. In Chapter 5 we describe several models which have been rigorously tested in an effort to identify which beliefs, expectancies, attitudes and normative factors contribute to health or risk behaviour. More coverage of adherence behaviour has been added as has greater discussion of some of the broader determinants of behaviour. This chapter has also been reworked to provide students with the opportunity for more critical reflection. This section of the book, therefore, presents evidence of the link between behaviour and health and illness, and highlights an area where health psychologists have much to offer in terms of understanding or advising on individual factors to target in interventions. The section ends with two chapters on intervention. Chapter 6 now focuses entirely on theories of behavioural change, while Chapter 7 considers how these may be applied, and with what success in interventions designed to prevent people developing illness and poor health. It addresses interventions targeted at both individuals and whole populations, in a strategy known as public health intervention.

The second section, *Becoming Ill*, contains six chapters which take the reader through the process of becoming ill: the physiological systems that may fail in illness, the psychosocial factors that may contribute to symptom perception, and report and how we communicate with the medical system. We start with a whole chapter dedicated to describing biological and bodily processes relevant to the physical experience of health and illness (Chapter 8). In this fourth edition, this chapter covers a broader range of illnesses as well as some individual case study examples and more signposts to relevant psychological content to be found elsewhere in the book. Chapter 9 describes how we perceive, interpret and respond to symptoms, highlighting individual, sociocultural and contextual factors that influence the process of health-care-seeking behaviour, including the use of lay and online referral systems (how many of us have not 'googled' our symptoms at some point?), and has seen general updating in order that the increasing number of studies addressing medically unexplained symptoms (MUS) are addressed and that studies of the dynamic and changing nature of illness perceptions and responses which more fully address the underlying theoretical assumptions are covered. In Chapter 10 presenting to, and communicating with, health professionals is reviewed with illustrations of 'good' and 'not so good' practice. The role of patient involvement in decision-making is an important one in current health policy and practice, and the evidence as to the benefits of patient involvement is reviewed here. The chapter also considers how health practitioners arrive at clinical decisions under time pressure and information poverty: and why they sometimes get them wrong.

Chapters 11 and 12 take us into the realm of stress, something that very few of us escape experiencing from time to time! We present an overview of stress theories, where stress is defined either as an event, a response or series of responses to an event, or as a transaction between the individual experiencing and appraising the event, and its actual characteristics. We also focus on aspects of stress beyond the individual, with consideration of occupational stress, and how stress impacts on health through consideration of the growing field of psychoneuroimmunology. In both this and the subsequent chapter greater consideration of gender, personality and lifespan issues are included. Chapter 12 presents the research evidence pertaining to factors shown to 'moderate' the potentially negative effect of seemingly stressful events, from distal antecedents such as socio-economic resources, social support and aspects of personality which we have increased coverage of (e.g. optimism, conscientiousness), to specific coping styles and strategies. We also include a more positive view of stress and well-being, focusing on the concepts of 'positive psychology'. In fact, positive beliefs become a recurring theme and also arise in Chapters 14 and 15. Chapter 13 turns to methods of alleviating stress, where it becomes clear that there is not one therapeutic 'hat' to fit all, as we describe a range of cognitive, behavioural and cognitive-behavioural approaches. The increasingly valued concept of mindfulness and mindfulness-based interventions is also introduced.

In the third section, *Being Ill*, we turn our attention to the impact of illness on the individual and their families across two chapters. Chapter 14 is devoted to the impact of illness on the ill individual, focusing on both negative and positive outcomes. Perhaps unique to this textbook, is a whole chapter, Chapter 15, devoted to the impact of providing care for a sick person within the family. This fourth edition further highlights research that considers the dyad (patient–spouse most typically) demonstrating how such studies can add to our understanding of illness experiences and health outcomes. Chapter 16 addresses a phenomenon that accounts for the majority of visits to a health professional – pain – which has been shown to be much more than a physical experience. This chapter is the only disease-specific chapter in our text, but we chose to contain a chapter on pain and place it at this point towards the end of our book because, by illustrating the multidimensional nature of pain, we draw together much of what has preceded (in terms of predictors and correlates of illness, health-care processes, etc.). Pain illustrates extremely well the biopsychosocial approach health psychologists endeavour to uphold. In a similarly holistic manner, Chapter 17 looks at ways of improving health-related quality of life by means of interventions such as stress management training, the use of social support, and illness management programmes.

Finally, we close the fourth edition of this text in the same way we closed the first, with Chapter 18, which we have called Futures. This chapter has changed significantly over time in that it now has three key foci: (i) how a number of psychological theories can be integrated to guide psychological interventions, (ii) how the profession of health psychology is developing in a variety of countries and the differing ways it is achieving growth, and (iii) how psychologists can foster the use of psychological interventions or psychologically informed practice in areas (both geographical and medical) where they are unused. This ends our book therefore by highlighting areas where health psychology research has or can perhaps in the future, 'make a difference'.

We hope you enjoy reading the book and learn from it as much as we learned while writing it. Enjoy!

Acknowledgements

This project has been a major one which has required the reading of literally thousands of empirical and review papers published by health, social and clinical psychologists around the globe, many books and book chapters, and many newspapers to help identify some hot health issues. The researchers behind all this work are thanked for their contribution to the field.

On a more personal level, several key researchers and senior academics also acted as reviewers for our chapters, some of whom have been with us from the first edition and have shown great commitment and forbearance! At each stage they have provided honest and constructive feedback and their informed suggestions have made this a better book than it might otherwise have been! They also spotted errors and inconsistencies that are inevitable with such a large project, and took their role seriously.

Many thanks also to the indomitable editorial team at Pearson Education, with several development editors having taken their turn at the helm and guided us through a few bad patches where academic demands and our own research prevented us from spending time on 'the book'. Particular thanks go to Lina Aboujieb who has been indomitable in her support and has pushed, pulled, advised and cajoled us up to the point where we hand over to the production team.

Paul Bennett and Val Morrison
June 2015

Publisher's acknowledgements

We are grateful to the following for permission to reproduce copyright material:

Figures

Figure 1.1 from *Towards a Common Language for Functioning, Disability and Health*, World Health Organization (ICF, 2002) p. 9, World Health Organization; Figure 1.2 from *EU Statistics on Income and Living Conditions* survey, OECD Health Data (2012), Health at a Glance: Europe 2012, OECD Publishing, Paris, http://dx.doi.org/10.1787/9789264183896-en; Figure 2.1 from Inequalities in health expectancies in England and Wales: small area analysis from 2001 Census, *Health Statistics Quarterly*, 34 (Rasulo, D., Bajekal, M. and Yar, M., 2007), contains public sector information licensed under the Open Government Licence (OGL) v3.0, http://www.nationalarchives.gov.uk/doc/open-government-licence, also reproduced with the permission of the author; Figure 2.2 from *Fair Shares for All*, Edinburgh: HMSO (Scottish Executive, 1999) Report of the National Review of Resource Allocation for the NHS in Scotland, chaired by Professor Sir John Arbuthnott, principal and vice-chancellor of Strathclyde University, contains public sector information licensed under the Open Government Licence (OGL) v3.0, http://www.nationalarchives.gov.uk/doc/open-government-licence; Figure 3.1 from *Alcohol in Europe: A Public Health Perspective*, Institute of Alcohol Studies (Anderson, P. and Baumberg, B., 2006); Figure 3.2 from *General Lifestyle Survey 2010*, Office for National Statistics (2010) p. 6, contains public sector information licensed under the Open Government Licence (OGL) v3.0, http://www.nationalarchives.gov.uk/doc/open-government-licence; Figure 3.3 from *Opinions and Lifestyle Survey, Drinking Habits Amongst Adults, 2012*, Office for National Statistics (2012), contains public sector information licensed under the Open Government Licence (OGL) v3.0, http://www.nationalarchives.gov.uk/doc/open-government-licence; Figure 3.4 from *Coronary Heart Disease Statistics: A Compendium of Health Statistics, 2012 Edition*, British Heart Foundation (2012) figure 4.9c, © British Heart Foundation 2012; Figure 3.5 from Overweight and obesity as determinants of cardiovascular risk, *Archives of Internal Medicine*, vol. 162, pp. 1867–72 (Wilson, P.W.F., D'Agostino, R.B., Sullivan, L., Parise, H. and Kannel, W.B., 2002), American Medical Association; Figure 4.1 from Increasing parental provision and children's consumption of lunchbox fruit and vegetables in Ireland: the Food Dudes intervention, *European Journal of Clinical Nutrition*, vol. 63, pp. 613–18 (Horne, P.J. et al. 2009), reprinted by permission from Macmillan Publishers Ltd; Figure 4.2 from World Health Organization (2004), www.euro.who.int; Figure 5.3 from http://www.hapa-model.de, Ralf Schwarzer; Figures 8.1, 8.2, 8.3 and 8.4 from *Physiology of Behaviour*, 8th ed., Allyn and Bacon (Carlson, N., 2005) © 2005, reproduced by permission of Pearson Education, Inc., Upper Saddle River, New Jersey; Figure 9.1 from Age- and gender-specific prevalence of self-reported symptoms in adults, *Central European Journal of Public Health*, 21, pp. 160–4 (Klemenc-Ketiš, Z., Krizmaric, M., and Kersnik, J., 2013), with permission from the National Institute of Health and the authors; Figure 9.2 adapted from A symptom perception approach to common physical symptoms, *Social Science and Medicine*, 57, pp. 2343–54 (Kolk, A.M., Hanewald, G.J.F.P., Schagen, S. and Gijsbers van Wijk, C.M.T., 2003), with permission from Elsevier; Figure 9.3 after *Making Sense of Illness: The Social Psychology of Health and Disease*, Sage Publications (Radley, A., 1994) p. 69, with the kind permission of Professor A. Radley, permission conveyed through Copyright Clearance Center, Inc.; Figure 9.4 from Illness cognition: using common sense to understand treatment adherence and effect cognitive interactions, *Cognitive Therapy and Research*, 16(2), p. 147 (Leventhal, H., Diefenbach, M. and Leventhal, E., 1992), with kind permission from Springer Science+Business Media and Howard Leventhal; Figure 9.5 adapted from Determinants of three stages of delay in seeking care at a medical setting, *Medical Care*, 7, pp. 11–29 (Safer,

M.A., Tharps, Q.J., Jackson, T.C. et al., 1979), Springer/Kluwer/Plenum; Figure 10.1 adapted from Breaking bad news: a review of the literature, *Journal of the American Medical Association*, 276, pp. 496–502 (Ptacek, J.T.P. and Eberhardt, T.L., 1996), American Medical Association; Figure 11.1 adapted from *Stress and Health: Biological and Psychological Interactions*, Sage (Lovallo, W.R., 1997) p. 77, Sage Publications, Inc.; Figure 11.2 from *Stress and Health*, Brooks/Cole (Rice, P.L. 1992) p. 5, Cengage Learning, Inc.; Figure 11.3 adapted from A delay-differential equation model of the feedback-controlled hypothalamus–pituitary–adrenal axis in humans, *Mathematical Medicine and Biology*, 22, pp. 15–33 (Lenbury, Y and Pornsawad, P., 2005), by permission of Oxford University Press and The Institute of Mathematics and its Applications; Figure 12.1 adapted from *Stress and Emotion: A New Synthesis*, Springer (Lazarus, R.S., 2006) p. 198, republished with permission of Springer Publishing Company, Inc., permission conveyed through Copyright Clearance Center, Inc.; Figure 12.2 from Conscientiousness and health-related behaviours: a meta-analysis of the leading behavioral contributors to mortality, *Psychological Bulletin*, 130, pp. 887–919 (Bogg, T. and Roberts, B.X. 2004), p. 908, American Psychological Association, reprinted with permission; Figure 12.3 adapted from Hardiness and health: a prospective study, *Journal of Personality and Social Psychology*, 42, pp. 168–77 (Kobasa, S.C., Maddi, S. and Kahn, S., 1982), American Psychological Association, reprinted with permission; Figure 14.1 from Positive effects of illness reported by myocardial infarction and breast cancer patients, *Journal of Psychosomatic Research*, 47, pp. 537–43 (Petrie, K.J., Buick, D.L., Weinman, J. and Booth, R.J., 1999), with permission from Elsevier; Figure 14.2 adapted from Turning the tide: benefit finding after cancer surgery, *Social Science and Medicine*, 59, pp. 653–62 (Schulz, U. and Mohamed, N.E., 2004), with permission from Elsevier; Figure 14.3 from Quality of life: a process view, *Psychology and Health*, 12, pp. 753–67 (Leventhal, H. and Coleman, S. 1997), with permission from Taylor & Francis; Figure 15.1 from Chronic illness and the life cycle: a conceptual framework, *Family Process*, 26(2), pp. 203–21 (Rolland, J.S., 1987), John Wiley & Sons, Inc.; Figure 15.2 from Interpersonal emotional processes in adjustment to chronic illness, in *Social Psychological Foundations of Health and Illness*, p. 263 (De Vellis, R.F., Lewis, M.A. and Sterba, K.R. (J. Suls and K.A. Wallston (eds)) 2003), Blackwell, reproduced with permission of Blackwell Publishing; Figure on p. 504 from Effect of mindfulness training on asthma quality of life and lung function: a randomised controlled trial, *Thorax*, 67, pp. 769–76 (Pbert, L., Madison, J.M., Druker, S. et al., 2012), with permission from BMJ Publishing Group Ltd.

Tables

Table 1.1 adapted from *World Health Statistics*, WHO (2013), World Health Organization; Table 1.2 adapted from *Health at a Glance: Europe 2012*, OECD (2012) p. 21, OECD Publishing, Paris, http://dx.doi.org/10.1787/9789264183896-en; Table 2.1 adapted from *Global Recommendations on Physical Activity for Health*, WHO (2013), World Health Organization; Table 3.1 from *Global Health Risks: Mortality and Burden of Disease Attributable to Selected Major Risks*, WHO (2009) p. 11, World Health Organization; Table 3.2 from Sensible Drinking Guidelines, http://www.drinkingandyou.com/site/pdf/Sensibledrinking.pdf, Alcohol in Moderation; Table 3.3 from *The 1971 The Misuse of Drugs Act*, HMSO (1971), contains public sector information licensed under the Open Government Licence (OGL) v3.0, http://www.nationalarchives.gov.uk/doc/open-government-licence; Table 3.4 from HIV/AIDS Surveillance in Europe reports, http://ecdc.europa.eu/en/healthtopics/aids/surveillance-reports/Pages/surveillance-reports.aspx, © European Centre for Disease Prevention and Control (ECDC); Table 4.1 from *Global Recommendations on Physical Activity for Health*, WHO (2010), World Health Organization; Table 4.2 adapted from *Health at a Glance: Europe 2012*, OECD (2012) p. 107, OECD Publishing, Paris, http://dx.doi.org/10.1787/9789264183896-en; Table on p. 174 adapted from Does theory influence the effectiveness of health behavior interventions? Meta-analysis, *Health Psychology*, 33(5), pp. 465–74 (Prestwich, A., Sniehotta, F.F., Whittington, C., Dombrowski, S.U., Rogers, L. and Michie, S., 2014), American Psychological Association, reprinted with permission; Table 7.2 from Effectiveness analysis on the physical activity and the health benefit of a community population based program, *Biomedical and Environmental Sciences*, 26(6), pp. 468–73 (Jiang, Y.Y., Yang, Z.X., Ni, R., Zhu, Y.Q., Li, Z.Y., Yang, L.C., Zhai, Y. and Zhao, W.H., 2013), with permission from Elsevier; Table on p. 203 adapted from A social media-based physical activity intervention: a randomized controlled trial, *American Journal of Preventive Medicine*, 43(5), pp. 527–32 (Cavallo, D.N., Tate, D.F., Ries, A.V., Brown, J.D., DeVellis, R.F. and Ammerman, A.S., 2012), Elsevier, Inc.; Table 11.1 from The social readjustment rating scale, *Journal of Psychosomatic Research*, 11, pp. 213–18 (Holmes, T.H. and Rahe, R.H. 1967), Elsevier, Inc.; Table 11.2 adapted from Investigating the cognitive precursors of emotional response to cancer stress: re-testing Lazarus's transactional model, *British Journal of Health Psychology*, 18, pp. 97–121 (Hulbert-Williams, N.J., Morrison, V., Wilkinson, C. and Neal, R.D., 2013), reproduced with permission of

Blackwell Publishing; Table 11.3 adapted from *Stress and Health*, Brooks/Cole (Rice, P.L., 1992) pp. 188–92, Cengage Learning, Inc.; Tables on pp. 387 and 388 adapted from Long-term effects of an intervention on psychosocial work factors among healthcare professionals in a hospital setting, *Occupational and Environmental Medicine*, 68, pp. 479–86 (Bourbonnais, R., Brisson, C. and Vézina, M., 2011), with permission from BMJ Publishing Group Ltd; Table 14.1 from EORTC QLQ-C30, http://groups.eortc.be/qol/eortc-qlq-c30, EORTC Quality of Life, for permission to use contact: Quality of Life Department, EORTC European Organisation for Research and Treatment of Cancer, AISBL-IVZW, Avenue E. Mounier, 83/11, 1200 Brussels, Belgium, website: http://groups.eortc.be/qol; Table 15.1 from Understanding the health impact of caregiving: a qualitative study of immigrant parents and single parents of a child with cancer, *Quality of Life Research*, 21, pp. 1595–605 (Klassen, A.F., Gulati, S., Granek, L., Rosenberg-Yunger, Z.R., Watt, L., Sung, L., Klaassen, R., Dix, D. and Shaw, N.T., 2012), with kind permission from Springer Science+Business Media and Anne Klassen; Table on p. 478 from Pain experience of Iraq and Afghanistan Veterans with comorbid chronic pain and posttraumatic stress, *Journal of Rehabilitation Research & Development*, 51(4), pp. 559–70 (Outcalt, S.D., Ang, D.C., Wu, J., Sargent, C., Yu, Z. and Bair, M.J., 2014), Journal of Rehabilitation Research and Development.

Text

Displayed text on p. 282 after SPIKES – A six-step protocol for delivering bad news: application to the patient with cancer, *The Oncologist*, 5(4), pp. 302–11 (Baile, W.F., Buckman, R., Lenzi. R., Glober, G., Beale, E.A. and Kudelka, A.P., 2000), *The Oncologist*, AlphaMed Press; Newspaper headline on page 467 from 'It's good for women to suffer the pain of a natural birth', says medical chief, *The Guardian*, 12/07/2009 (Campbell, D.), copyright Guardian News & Media Ltd, 2015.

Photos

The publisher would like to thank the following for their kind permission to reproduce their photographs:(Key: *b* – bottom; *t* – top) 2 Fotolia.com: godfer; 6 Fotolia.com: flysnow; 17 Alamy Images: Corbis Premium RF; 20 Fotolia.com: Robert Kneschke; 24 Alamy Images: Radius Images; 30 Fotolia.com: Halfpoint; 39 Photofusion Picture Library: Robert Brook; 50 Alamy Images: Agencja Fotograficzna Caro; 57 Photofusion Picture Library: Libby Welch; 63 Alamy Images: Ace Stock Limited; 74 Val Morrison; 86 Shutterstock.com: melis; 98 Bangor University: School of Psychology; 104 Change4Life; 112 Fotolia.com: Monkey Business; 118 Getty Images: Jacob Silberberg; 122 Tanya Louise Robinson; 129 Corbis: Ansgar Photography; 149 Fotolia.com: Chad McDermott; 155 Pearson Education Ltd; 158 Alamy Images: Juice Images; 161 Shutterstock.com: Rob Byron; 178 Fotolia.com: standardmixa; 187 Terence Higgins Trust; 192 Shutterstock.com: Veniamin Kraskov; 197 Shutterstock.com: CandyBox Images; 206 Fotolia.com: adimas; 216 Science Photo Library Ltd: Eye of Science (*b*); Dr Andrejs Liepins (*t*); 238 Fotolia.com: detailblick-foto; 242 Alamy Images: Bubbles Photo Library; 247 Val Morrison; 269 Corbis: Hero Images; 274 Fotolia.com: michaeljung; 280 Pearson Education Ltd; 289 Rex Shutterstock: TM & 20thC.Fox/Everett; 295 Shutterstock.com: Guzel Studio; 302 Fotolia.com: Focus Pocus LTD; 310 Pearson Education Ltd; 317 Shutterstock.com: Charlie Edward; 328 Shutterstock.com: Moriz; 338 Alamy Images: Peter Bowater; 353 Tanya Louise Robinson; 368 Val Morrison; 372 Fotolia.com: peshkova; 384 Shutterstock.com: Creativa; 389 Science Photo Library Ltd: John Cole; 394 Shutterstock.com: Wavebreak Premium; 410 Fotolia.com: sutichak; 416 Alamy Images: OJO Images Ltd; 423 Shutterstock.com: Featureflash; 434 Fotolia.com: chaiyon021; 439 Corbis: Reg Charity; 441 Fotolia.com: chuugo; 466 Science Photo Library Ltd: David Mack; 475 Getty Images: David Cannon; 487 Science Photo Library Ltd: Will and Deni McIntyre; 496 Shutterstock.com: Goodluz; 510 Getty Images: Alvis Upitis; 516 Paul Bennett; 520 Shutterstock.com: 2jenn; 527 Alamy Images: Tetra Images; 532 Shutterstock.com: hxdbzxy.

Part I
Being and staying healthy

Chapter 1
What is health?

Learning outcomes

By the end of this chapter, you should have an understanding of:

- key perspectives on health, illness and disability, including the biomedical and biopsychosocial models

- the influence of lifestage, culture and health status on health and illness concepts

- a range of influences on the domains of health considered important

- the role of psychology, and specifically the discipline of health psychology, in understanding health, illness and disability

- how health is more than simply the absence of physical disease or disability

Health is global

In August 2014 Rome was converged upon, not by tourists (although they were there too!), but by plane-loads of scientists from industry and academic institutions, those working in health informatics, and possibly some health psychologists, to attend the Third International Conference on Global Health Challenges. Of relevance here is that the Rome conference addresses how best to record and analyse global data relating to disease, death, lifestyle and population change, the 'big data' that helps guide public health policies for the future. In the conference, as in this chapter, it was essential to acknowledge inequities in these data within and between countries. The conference also addressed how health and mobile technologies can be best used to promote individual and population health through changes in clinical practice, increased health monitoring or behaviour change 'nudging', and how, globally, we can prepare for pandemics and an ageing population.

In 2011 the UK report 'Health is global: an outcomes framework for global health 2011–15' highlighted a need to promote health equity within and between countries through our foreign and domestic policies, particularly through action on the social determinants of health. There is a need to base our global health policies and practice on sound evidence, whether it is drawn from public health evidence or from psychological studies of human behaviour. We need to work with others to develop evidence where it does not exist. The attention being paid to global issues highlights that whilst we as individuals experience health and illness at a personal level, the cultural and social economic setting, the dominant government and its health policies, and even the time in which we live, all play a part. Health psychology contributes an important part to the jigsaw that is health and well-being.

Around the world many of us attend conferences such as that happening in Rome, in order to get a sense of what is 'new', what is cutting edge, what is the exciting science that can perhaps have an impact on future health. This textbook brings together evidence that can not only educate the aspiring health psychologist but can also hopefully help inform such policy and practice. Whether we achieve it will depend on what we as health psychologists 'do' with our evidence as described in the final chapter. Hopefully over the course of the next 18 chapters you will get a good sense of our successes, and the challenges ahead nationally and internationally.

Chapter outline

What do we mean by health, and do we all mean the same thing when we use the term? This chapter considers the different ways in which people have been found to define and think about health, illness and disability: first, by providing an historical overview of the health concept that introduces the debate over the influence of mind on body; and, second, by illustrating how health and illness belief systems vary according to factors such as age, culture and health status. We will introduce the issue of developmental differences in health perceptions and examine whether children define and think about health differently to a middle-aged or elderly person. Against this backdrop of defining health and related belief systems, we introduce the reader to key models on which our discipline is founded—the biomedical and the biopsychosocial models of illness. To conclude the chapter we introduce the field of health psychology and, by outlining the field's key areas of interest, highlight the questions health psychology research can address.

What is health? Changing perspectives

Health is a word that most people will use without realising that it may hold different meanings for different people, at different times in history, in different cultures, in different social classes, or even within the same family, depending, for example, on age or gender. Stone (1979) pointed out that until we can agree on the meaning of health and how it can be measured we are going to be unable to answer questions about how we can protect, enhance and restore health. The root word of health is 'wholeness', and indeed 'holy' and 'healthy' share the same root word in Anglo-Saxon, which is perhaps why so many cultures associate one with the other: e.g. medicine men have both roles. Having its roots in 'wholeness' also suggests the early existence of a broad view of health that included mental and physical aspects. This view has not held dominance throughout history, as described below.

Early understanding of illness is reflected in archaeological finds of human skulls from the Stone Age where small neat holes found in some skulls have been attributed

to the process of 'trephination' (or trepanation), whereby a hole is made in order to release evil spirits believed to have entered the body from outside and caused disease. Another early interpretation of disease seen in Ancient Hebrew texts is that disease was a punishment from the gods (1000–300 BC). As will be described in Chapter 9 ☞, similar beliefs remain today in some cultures, and understanding such variations in belief systems is extremely important to our understanding of individuals' response to illness ☞. Also important however is the shaping, over time, of our understanding of the association between mind and body.

Mind–body relationships

It is in the writings from Ancient Greece (*circa* 500 BC) that we see differing explanations of health and disease to that seen in earlier times. Instead of attributing illness to evil spirits or gods, the ancient Greek physician Hippocrates (*circa* 460–377 BC) attributed it to the balance between four circulating bodily fluids (called humours): yellow bile, phlegm, blood and black bile. It was thought that when a person was healthy the four humours were in balance, and when they were ill-balanced due to external 'pathogens', illness occurred.

The humours were attached to seasonal variations and to conditions of hot, cold, wet and dry, where phlegm was attached to winter (cold–wet), blood to spring (wet–hot), black bile to autumn (cold–dry), and yellow bile to summer (hot–dry). Hippocrates considered the mind and body as one unit, and thus it was thought that the level of specific bodily humours related to particular personalities: excessive yellow bile was linked to a choleric or angry temperament; black bile was attached to sadness; excessive blood was associated with an optimistic or sanguine personality; and excessive phlegm with a calm or phlegmatic temperament. Healing involved attempts to rebalance the humours, for example, through bleeding or starvation, or special diets and medicines. Even this far back in time, eating healthily was considered helpful to the balance of the humours (Helman 1978). This humoral **theory** of illness attributed disease states to bodily functions but also acknowledged that bodily factors impacted on the mind.

This view continued with Galen (*circa* AD 129–199), another influential Greek physician in Ancient Rome. Galen considered there to be a physical or pathological basis for all ill health (physical or mental) and believed not only that the four bodily humours underpinned the four dominant temperaments (the sanguine, the choleric, the phlegmatic and the melancholic) but also that these temperaments could contribute to the experience of specific illnesses. For example, he proposed that melancholic women were more likely to get breast cancer, offering not a psychological explanation but a physical one because melancholia was itself thought to be underpinned by high levels of black bile. This view was therefore that the mind and body were interrelated, but only in terms of physical and mental disturbances both having an underlying physical cause. The mind itself was not thought to play a role in illness **aetiology**. This view dominated thinking for many centuries to come but lost predominance in the eighteenth century when organic medicine, and in particular cellular pathology, developed and failed to support the humoral underpinnings. However, Galen's descriptions of personality types were still in use in the latter half of the twentieth century (Marks et al. 2000: 76–7).

During the early Middle Ages however (fifth–sixth century), Galen's theories had lost dominance when health became increasingly tied to faith and spirituality. At this time illness was seen as God's punishment for misdeeds or, similar to very early views, the result of evil spirits entering one's soul. Individuals were thought to have little control over their health, whereas priests, in their perceived ability to restore health by driving out demons, did. The Church was at the forefront of society at this time and so science developed slowly. The mind and body were generally viewed as working together, or at least in parallel. However the prohibition of scientific investigation such as dissection, limited medical progress and advancements in understanding and therefore mental and mystical explanations of illness predominated. Such causal explanations elicited treatment along the lines of self-punishment, abstinence from sin, prayer or hard work.

These religious views persisted until the early fourteenth and fifteenth centuries when a period of 'rebirth', a Renaissance, began. During the Renaissance, individual thinking became increasingly dominant and the religious perspective became only one among many. The scientific revolution of the early 1600s led to huge growth in scholarly and scientific study and developments in physical medicine. As a result, the understanding of the human body, and the explanations for illness, became increasingly organic and physiological, with little room for psychological explanations.

During the early seventeenth century, the French philosopher René Descartes (1596–1650), like the ancient Greeks, proposed that the mind and body were separate entities. However, Descartes also proposed that interaction between the two 'domains' was possible, although initially the understanding of how mind–body interactions could happen was limited. For example, how could a mental thought, with no physical properties, cause a bodily reaction (e.g. a neuron to fire) (Solmes and Turnbull 2002)? This is defined as **dualism**, where the mind is considered to be 'non-material' (i.e. not

---

theory

a general belief or beliefs about some aspect of the world we live in or those in it, which may or may not be supported by evidence. For example, women are worse drivers than men.

aetiology

(etiology): the cause of disease.

dualism

the idea that the mind and body are separate entities (cf. Descartes).

objective or visible, such as thoughts and feelings) and the body is 'material' (i.e. made up of real mechanical 'stuff', physical matter such as our brain, heart and cells). Dualistic thinking considers the material and the non-material to be independent. Physicians acted as guardians of the body – viewed as a machine amenable to scientific investigation and explanation – whereas theologians acted as guardians of the mind – a place not amenable to scientific investigation! The suggested communication between mind and body was thought to be under the control of the pineal gland in the midbrain (see Chapter 8 (☞)), but the process of this interaction was unclear. Because Descartes believed that the soul left humans at the time of death, dissection and autopsy study now became acceptable to the Church, and so the eighteenth and nineteenth centuries witnessed a huge growth in medical understanding. Anatomical research, autopsy work and cellular pathology concluded that disease was located in human cells, not in ill-balanced humours.

Dualists developed the notion of the body as a machine (a **mechanistic** viewpoint), understandable only in terms of its constituent parts (molecular, biological, biochemical, genetic), with illness understood through the study of cellular and physiological processes. Treatment during these centuries became more technical, diagnostic and focused on the physical evidence obtainable, with

> **mechanistic**
> a reductionist approach that reduces behaviour to the level of the organ or physical function. Associated with the *biomedical model*.
>
> **biomedical model**
> a view that diseases and symptoms have an underlying physiological explanation.

individuals perhaps more passively involved than previously (when at least they had been expected to pray or exorcise their demons in order to return to health). This approach underpins the **biomedical model** of illness.

Biomedical model of illness

In this model, health is defined as the absence of disease, and any symptom of illness is thought to have an underlying pathology that will hopefully, but not inevitably, be cured through medical intervention. Adhering rigidly to the biomedical model would lead to proponents dealing only with objective facts and assuming a direct causal relationship between illness or disability, its symptoms or underlying pathology (disease), and adjustment outcomes (see 'In the spotlight' for a discussion of changing models of disability). The assumption is that

Photo 1.1 Having a disability does not equate with a lack of health and fitness

Source: Fotolia.com/flysnow.

removal of the pathology through medical intervention will lead to restored health, i.e. illness or disability results from disease either originating outside the body (e.g. germs) or through involuntary internal changes (e.g. cell mutations). This relatively mechanistic view of how our bodies and its organs work, fail and can be treated allows little room for subjectivity. The biomedical view has been described as reductionist: i.e. the basic idea that mind, matter (body) and human behaviour can all be reduced to, and explained at, the level of cells, neural activity or biochemical activity. How then would we deal with evidence of debilitating, but medically unexplained symptoms? (see Chapter 9, ☞).

Reductionism also tends to ignore evidence that different people respond in different ways to the same underlying disease pathology because they vary in, for example, personality, cognition, social support resources or cultural beliefs (see later chapters).

Whilst the biomedical mode underpins many successful treatments including immunisation programmes which have contributed to the eradication of many life-threatening infectious diseases, significant challenges to a purely biomedical approach exist, as described below.

Challenging dualism: psychosocial models of health and illness

In terms of mind–body associations, what is perhaps closer to the 'truth', as we understand it today, is that there is one type of 'stuff' (monist) but that it can be perceived in two different ways: objectively and subjectively. For example, many illnesses have organic underlying causes, but also elicit uniquely individual responses due to the action of the mind, i.e. subjective responses. So, while aspects of reductionism and dualistic thinking have been useful, for example, in furthering our understanding of the aetiology and course of many acute and infectious diseases (Larson 1999), the role of the 'mind' in the manifestation of, and response to, illness is crucial to furthering our understanding of the complex nature of health and illness. Consider, for example, the extensive evidence of 'phantom limb pain' experienced in amputees – how can pain exist in an absent limb? Consider the widespread acknowledgement of the placebo effect – how can an inactive (dummy) substance lead to reported reductions in pain

or other symptoms which are equivalent to reductions described by those receiving an active pharmaceutical substance or treatment? (Chapter 16 ☞). Subjectivity in terms of beliefs, expectations and emotions interact with bodily reactions to play an important role in the illness or stress experience (see Chapter 9 in terms of symptom perception, and Chapter 11 in terms of stress reactivity ☞).

Evidence of changed thinking was illustrated in an editorial in the *British Medical Journal* (Bracken and Thomas 2002) suggesting a need to 'move beyond the mind–body split'. The authors note that simply because neuroscience enables us to explore the 'mind' and its workings 'objectively' by the use of increasingly sophisticated scanning devices and measurements, this does not mean we are furthering our understanding of the subjective 'mind' – the thoughts, feelings and the like that make up our lives and give it meaning. They comment that 'conceptualising our mental life as some sort of enclosed world living inside our skull does not do justice to the reality of human experience' (p. 1434). The fact that this editorial succeeded in being published in a medical journal with a traditionally biomedical stance is evidence of a weakened Descartian 'legacy'.

As our understanding of the bidirectional relationship between mind and body has grown, dualistic thinking has lessened, and psychology has played a significant role in this altering perspective. A key role was played by Sigmund Freud in the 1920s and 1930s when he redefined the mind–body problem as one of 'consciousness' and postulated the existence of an 'unconscious mind' seen in a condition he named 'conversion hysteria'. Following examination of patients with physical symptomatology but no identifiable cause, and by using hypnosis and free association techniques, he identified unconscious conflicts which had been repressed. These unconscious conflicts were considered to 'cause' the physical disturbances including paralysis and loss of sensation in some patients where no underlying physical explanation was present (i.e. hysterical paralysis, e.g. Freud and Breuer 1895).

Freud stimulated much work into unconscious conflict, personality and illness, which ultimately led to the development of the field of *psychosomatic medicine* (see later section). As a discipline, psychology has highlighted the need for medicine to consider the role played in the aetiology, course and outcomes of illness, by psychological and social factors.

IN THE SPOTLIGHT

Models of disability: from biomedical to biopsychosocial

Reflecting biomedical thinking, the World Health Organization's 1980 International Classification of Impairment, Disabilities and Handicaps (also the classification of the consequences of disease), introduced a hierarchical model which was utilised in a large body of research exploring responses to disease. In the WHO IC I-D-H model, impairments (abnormalities or losses at the level of a person's organs, tissues, structures or appearance), lead to disability (defined as a restriction or inability to function as 'normal for a human being') which in turn create individual handicap (whereby a person experiences disadvantage in fulfilling their normal social roles).

In this model, disability is placed within the individual and is considered an inevitable consequence of some form of impairment, and an inevitable precursor of handicap. How then, within this model, do we accommodate the Paralympian who in spite of sensory of physical impairments, functions at a level of physical performance many of us without such impairments perform? How do we describe the person with juvenile diabetes who has 'impairment' in terms of pancreatic dysfunction (see Chapter 8), but as long as they adhere to medication, function as any typical adolescent, without any evidence of disability? This same juvenile may, however, skip school as a result of perceived stigma and therefore miss out on the associated social relationships and potential long-term employment benefits (i.e 'handicap' without disability). What then are the implications of such a medical and positivistic/functionalistic view for the treatment of impairments (especially if we believe in a need to normalise)? For example, are cochlear implants for those with hearing impairments a more appropriate response than those around the individual with hearing difficulties learning sign language? Whose 'problem' is hearing impairment?

For some people, acquiring a disability signifies the end of life, an exclusion from normal function and roles, and, as many studies have shown, increased depression. For others, disability presents a challenge, a fact of life to be lived with, rather than something which prevents them living fully (see Chapter 14 ☛).

Yet again, as seen in relation to developing concepts of illness, evidence of individual variation in the response to impairment and disability challenges biomedical thinking and opens the door for biopsychosocial thought! People do not inevitably become equally or similarly 'disabled' or 'handicapped' even where impairment is similar (e.g. Johnston and Pollard 2001).

Reflecting this, the subsequent WHO model, the International Classification of Functioning, Disability and Health (WHO 2001), which emerged out of a series of studies including 2,000 live 'case' evaluations and 3,500 Case Summary evaluations conducted in 27 languages across 61 countries, takes a broader approach. The ICF presents a universal, dynamic and non-linear model whereby alterations in bodily structure or function (replaces impairment); activities and limitations therein (replaces disability), and participation or restrictions therein (replaces handicap) can potentially all affect each other. Furthermore, the ICF recognises that the relationship between structures, activities and participation are influenced by both environmental and personal factors. A person's ability to perform at 'capacity' i.e. at the best possible, given their physical status, is not solely due to the level of impairment. Disability no longer resides within the individual, but is a response to other factors including the physical, social and cultural environment the person is trying to function within, and on their own personal characteristics, behavioural and illness related beliefs and feelings (Quinn et al. 2013, and see Chapter 9 ☛).

---

biopsychosocial

a view that diseases and symptoms can be explained by a combination of physical, social, cultural and psychological factors (cf. Engel 1977).

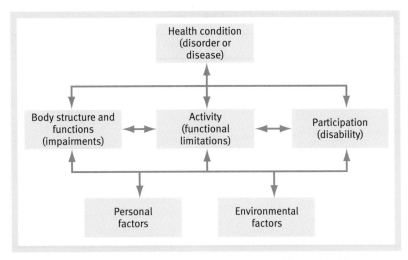

Figure 1.1 The international classification of functioning, disability and health.

Source: WHO (2002b).

As a result of these shifts in thinking, this textbook reflects a biopsychosocial perspective on health, illness AND disability/activity limitation which offer up opportunity for a range of interventions, not solely targeting the pathology or physical symptomatology.

Biopsychosocial model of illness

The biopsychosocial model signals a broadening of a disease or biomedical model of health to one encompassing and emphasising the interaction between body and mind, between biological processes and psychological and social influences (Engel 1977, 1980). In doing so, it offers a complex and multivariate, but potentially more comprehensive, model with which to examine the human experience of illness.

As a result of the many challenges to the biomedical approach described above, the biopsychosocial model is employed in health psychology as well as in several allied health professions, such as occupational therapy. Although also increasingly assimilated within the medical profession (Turner et al. 2001; Wade and Halligan 2004), there exists some pessimism that it is feasible, no matter how valuable, given constraints facing our healthcare systems (see editorial by Lane, 2014). Health is, however, more than simply the absence of disease and therefore this text will illustrate that psychological, behavioural and social factors can add to the biological or biomedical explanations and, rather than replacing these explanations of health and illness experiences, build on them.

In parallel with the above shifts in ways of thinking about health and illness is the increased recognition of the role individual behaviour plays in that experience. It is to that we turn attention now, with key behaviours explored more fully in Chapters 3 and 4 ☞.

Behaviour, death and disease

The dramatic increases in life expectancy witnessed in Western countries in the twentieth century, partially due to advances in medical technology and treatments, led to a general belief, in Western cultures at least, in the efficacy of traditional medicine and its power to eradicate disease. This was most notable following the introduction of antibiotics in the 1940s (although Fleming discovered penicillin in 1928, it was some years before it and other antibiotics were generally available). Such drug treatments, alongside increased control of infectious disease through vaccination and improved sanitation, are partial explanations of increases in life expectancy seen globally.

World Health Organization figures show that worldwide the average life expectancy at birth is 71 years (68.5 for males, 73.5 for females), with significant and sometimes shocking variation between countries. Table 1.1 presents a selection from the top and bottom of the 'league tables'. UK life expectancy at birth has increased from 47 years in 1900 to 81 years in 2013, which is a huge change in a relatively short period of time (WHO 2013). The most long-lived population is located in Japan with a small gender difference only, whereas in Australia,

Table 1.1 Life expectancy in selected global countries

	Overall (years)	Male (years)	Female (years)	Rank
Japan	86.5	85.3	89.0	1
Australia	83.0	80.5	85.5	9
Sweden	83.0	81.4	84.6	10
Netherlands	81.5	79.5	83.5	20
UK	81.0	79.5	83.5	29
USA	79.8	77.4	82.2	35
Jamaica	74.8	71.5	78.2	105
Iraq	69.0	65.0	72.0	131
Afghanistan	60.0	59.0	61.0	164
Malawi	58.0	57.5	58.5	170
Somalia	50.0	48.0	52.0	190
Sierra Leone	47.5	47.0	48.0	193

Source: WHO (2013).

also a long-lived population, the gender differential is 5 years. At the other end of this 'league table' average life expectancy drops dramatically from the low–mid 70s through to a fairly horrendous overall life expectancy of 47.5 years in Sierra Leone. Years of war account for many of those figures at the low end of the table.

Such life expectancy at birth statistics tell us that in some countries reaching a 60th birthday is not typical; furthermore country variations exist in *the additional years of life expected for those reaching the age of 60* between 2010 and 2015 (UN study of Population Ageing and Development, UN Dept of Economic & Social Affairs, 2013).

These cultural variations can be explained to a large extent by differences in lifestyle and diet, and the gender differences seen perhaps also due to variations in health behaviours (Chapter 3 ☞). There is some concern that, due to rising obesity in children and consequent health effects in adulthood, life expectancy may begin to show decreases in future generations, affecting disproportionately developed countries such as the UK and the USA which have high levels of obesity and inactivity (Chapter 3 ☞).

Much of the fall in **mortality** seen in the developed world preceded the major immunisation programmes and likely reflects public health successes following wider social and environmental changes over time. These include developments in education and agriculture, which led to changes in diet, or improvements in public hygiene and living standards (see also Chapter 2 ☞). Mortality rates within the European Union have also shown an overall 25 per cent reduction, with some vari-

ations seen between Western, Eastern and central regions, see Table 1.2 (which also includes 3 non- EU members, Iceland, Norway, Sweden). The significant decline in Ireland is attributed mainly to reductions in deaths from cardiovascular and respiratory disease, which in turn may reflect improved living standards and health-care investment. In countries where the decline is more modest, some, like Belgium, Greece and Sweden, had lower rates to start with, whereas in Eastern Europe changes are slow and mortality rates remain higher.

The physical causes of death have changed dramatically also. If people living in 1900 had been asked what they thought being healthy meant, they may have replied, 'avoiding infections, drinking clean water, living into my 50s/60s'. Death then frequently resulted from highly infectious disease such as pneumonia, influenza or tuberculosis becoming epidemic in communities unprotected by immunisation or adequate sanitary conditions. However, at least in developed countries over the last century, there has been a downturn in deaths resulting from infectious disease, and the 'league table' make no mention of tuberculosis (TB), typhoid, tetanus or measles. In contrast, diseases such as heart, lung and respiratory

> **mortality**
>
> (death): generally presented as mortality statistics, i.e. the number of deaths in a given population and/or in a given year ascribed to a given condition (e.g. number of cancer deaths among women in 2000).

Table 1.2 Decline in mortality rates from all causes, 1995–2010 (or nearest year)

	% decrease
Ireland	37
Estonia	35
Slovenia	33
Portugal	31
Malta	30
Czech Republic	29
Luxembourg	28
United Kingdom	27
Spain	27
Poland	27
Germany	26
Italy	26
Denmark	26
Hungary	26
Finland	26
Netherlands	26
Austria	24
France	23
Latvia	23
Greece	20
Sweden	20
Belgium	19
Lithuania	19
Bulgaria	17
Slovak Republic	16
Iceland	29
Norway	24
Switzerland	23

Source: Adapted from *Health at a Glance: Europe 2012,* OECD.

disease are the 'biggest killers' worldwide (along with 'accidents'). These causes have been relatively stable over the past few decades. The dementias are also attributed as the cause of death in significant numbers, e.g. 1 in 10 female deaths, 1 in 20 male deaths in 2011 in England and Wales (Office for National Statistics, 2012).

Worldwide in 2011, the top ten leading causes of death (all ages) were recorded as:

- Ischaemic heart disease (7 million)
- Stroke (6.2 million)
- Lower respiratory infection (3.2 million)
- COPD (3 million)
- Diarrhoeal diseases (1.9 million)
- HIV/AIDS(1.6 million)
- Lung diseases (including cancer) (1.5 million)

- Diabetes mellitus (1.4 million)
- Road injury (1.3 million)
- Prematurity (1.2 million)

These figures show large geographic variation, explained in part by AIDS, which in many African and Asian countries has a significant effect on life expectancy, possibly reducing it by as much as 15 years (WHO 2002a).

With the exception of lung cancer, cancer does not appear in the top ten globally. Within more developed countries, however, including Australia, USA, Europe, cancer is consistently placed in the top five causes of death. For example, recent England and Wales statistics (Office of National Statistics, 2014) show that 29 per cent of all deaths registered were as a result of cancer, followed closely by circulatory diseases including heart disease and stroke. For males, cancer was 'top' ranked in 2013, whereas for females circulatory diseases were.

What is notable is that the leading causes of death have a behavioural component, linked, for example, to behaviour such as smoking, excessive alcohol consumption, sedentary lifestyles and poor diet/obesity (Chapter 3 ☛). In fact, it has been estimated that up to three-quarters (Peto and Lopez 1990) of cancer deaths are attributable, in part at least, to our behaviour. The upturn in cancer deaths seen over the last century is also, however, due to people living longer with other illnesses they previously would have died from, thus they are reaching ages where cancer **incidence** is greater.

Projected worldwide mortality estimates placed heart disease, cerebrovascular disease including strokes, chronic lung disease (COPD), lower respiratory infections, and throat and lung cancers as the top five killers by 2020 (Murray and Lopez 1997), and certainly the WHO data above would suggest this projection is proving reliable. These authors also predicted, using sophisticated statistical modelling, that, worldwide, death from infectious diseases such as measles and malaria, and from perinatal (birth) and nutritional

> **incidence**
> the number of new cases of disease occurring during a defined time interval – not to be confused with **prevalence**, which refers to the number of established cases of a disease in a population at any one time.

diseases, will significantly decline, whereas tobacco-related diseases will increase almost three-fold. Encouragingly, UK statistics point to a decline (42 per cent for men, 40 per cent for women) in age-standardised deaths from circulatory (heart) diseases over the past 15–20 years and a lower but significant (13 per cent for females, 15 per cent for males) fall for cancer and for respiratory disease, (26 per cent for males, 20 per cent for females) (Office for National Statistics 2010).

So, if as a reader you have been asking yourself, 'why do all these figures matter?' the answer should now be clear! They matter because they demonstrate that our own behaviour contributes significantly to our health and mortality. As health psychologists, gaining an understanding of why we behave as we do and how behaviour can change or be changed, is a core part of our remit and therefore is something we discuss a lot in this and in the subsequent six chapters! Such links between individual behaviour, health and illness provide a key reason as to why health psychology has grown rapidly.

It is not therefore surprising, given evidence of the changes in what people are dying from, that views of what health is has also changed over time. In the eighteenth century, health was considered an 'egalitarian ideal', aspired to by all. Health was considered as potentially being under an individual's control; however, doctors were available to the wealthy as 'aids' to keeping oneself well, but less so to the poor. By the mid-twentieth century, accompanied or perhaps preceded by new laws regarding sickness benefit, and medical and technological advances in diagnostic and treatment procedures, health became increasingly and inextricably linked to 'fitness to work'. Doctors were required to declare whether individuals were 'fit to work' or whether they could adopt the 'sick role' (see also Chapter 10 ☞). Many today continue to see illness in terms of its effects on their working lives. However there is also evidence of the opposite direction of effects, i.e. the influence work role and conditions have on illness (see discussion of occupational stress in Chapter 11 ☞).

Also perhaps changing over time is the assumption that traditional medicine can, and will, cure us of all ills. Over recent decades, many more people have acknowledged the potential negative consequences of some treatments, particularly pharmacological ones (consider for example long-term use of anxiolytics such as Valium), and as a result the 'complementary' and 'alternative' medicine industry has burgeoned.

Most countries are seeking, in what is known as the 'post 2015 development agenda', to better measure their populations health and well-being, given the changing nature of disease (from acute infectious disease to chronic disease) and the population (an ageing one). Within the EU, targets have been recently set to gain an additional two 'healthy life years' in everyone living in their member states, with recognition that health is not simply about the absence of disease. Healthy life expectancy and subjective well-being are seen as key (WHO Report of a Technical Meeting, Geneva 10–11 December, 2012).

Individual, cultural and lifespan perspectives on health

Lay theories of health

If a fuller understanding of health and illness is to be attained, it is necessary to find out what people think health and illness are. The simplest way of doing this is to ask them. Here we explore lay perceptions of health.

In response to the question 'What does being healthy mean?' a classic early study by Bauman (1961) found that people with diagnoses of quite serious illness made three main types of response whereby being healthy was considered:

1. a 'general sense of well-being';
2. identified with 'the absence of symptoms of disease';
3. seen in 'the things that a person who is physically fit is able to do'.

She argued that these three types of response reveal health to be related to:

● feeling
● symptom orientation
● performance.

Respondents in this study did not answer in discrete categories however, with nearly half of the sample providing two of the above response types, and 12 per cent using all three types. This highlights the fact that the way we think about health is often multifaceted.

Furthermore, Bauman's sample consisted of those with quite serious illness, yet we now know that current health status influences subjective views of health and reports of what 'health is'. For example, amongst almost 500 elderly people asked to rate factors in order of importance to their subjective health judgements, the most important factors emerging related to physical functioning and vitality (being able to *do* what you need/want to do). However, the current health status of the sample (poor/fair; good; very good/excellent) influenced judgements; for example, those in poor/fair health based their health assessment on recent symptoms or indicators of poor health, whereas those in good health considered more positive indicators (being able to exercise, being happy). Consistent with this, subjective health judgements were more tied to **health behaviour** in 'healthier' individuals (Benyamini et al., 2003).

Although some people have been shown to find it hard to distinguish health from an absence of illness, health is generally viewed as a state of equilibrium across various aspects of the person, encompassing physical, psychological, emotional and social well-being (e.g. Herzlich, 1973). Bennett (2000: 67) considers these representations of health to distinguish between health as 'being', i.e. if not ill, then healthy; 'having', i.e. health as a positive resource or reserve; and 'doing', i.e. health as represented by physical fitness or function (as seen in Benyamini et al.'s study above). Bauman's respondents appear to have focused more on the 'being' healthy and 'doing' aspects, which may be in part because 'having' health as a resource was not prominent in the minds of her patient sample. Similarly, Krause and Jay (1994) found that older respondents more often referred to health *problems* when making their appraisals, whereas younger respondents referred to health *behaviour*. The frames of reference drawn on by people asked to evaluate their own health status therefore also differ.

It does seem that health is considered differently when it is no longer present, i.e. it is considered to be good when nothing is wrong (perhaps more commonly thought in older people) and when a person is behaving in a health-protective manner (perhaps more commonly thought in younger people).

A more representative picture of the health concept is perhaps obtained from a large, questionnaire-based *Health and Lifestyles* Survey of 9,003 members of the general public, of whom 5,352 also completed assessment seven years later (Cox, Huppert and Whichellow, 1993). This survey asked respondents to:

● Think of someone you know who is very healthy.

● Define who you are thinking of (friend/relative etc. – do not need specific name).

● Note how old they are.

● Consider what makes you call them healthy.

● Consider what it is like when you are healthy.

About 15 per cent could not think of *anyone* who was 'very healthy', and about 10 per cent could not describe what it was like for them to 'feel healthy'. This inability to describe what it is like to feel healthy was particularly evident in young males, who believed health to be a norm, a background condition so taken for granted that they could not put it into words. By comparison, a smaller group of mostly older women could not answer for exactly the opposite reason – they had been in poor health for so long that either they could not remember what it was like to feel well or they were expressing a pessimism about their condition to the interviewer (Radley 1994: 39).

The categories of health identified from the survey findings were:

● Health as not ill: i.e. no symptoms, no visits to doctor, therefore I am healthy.

● Health as reserve: i.e. come from strong family; recovered quickly from operation.

● Health as behaviour: i.e. usually applied to others rather than self; e.g. they are healthy because they look after themselves, exercise, etc.

● Health as physical fitness and vitality: used more often by younger respondents and often in reference to a male – male health concept more commonly tied to 'feeling fit', whereas females had a concept of 'feeling full of energy' and rooted health more in the social world in terms of being lively and having good relationships with others.

---

health behaviour

behaviour performed by an individual, regardless of their health status, as a means of protecting, promoting or maintaining health, e.g. diet.

● Health as *psychosocial* well-being: health defined in terms of a person's mental state; e.g. being in harmony, feeling proud, or, more specifically, enjoying others.

● Health as function: the idea of health as the ability to perform one's duties; i.e. being able to do what you want when you want without being handicapped in any way by ill health or physical limitation (relates to the World Health Organization's concept of handicap, now described as participation/participatory restriction, see 'In the spotlight': i.e. an inability to fulfil one's 'normal' social roles).

Such findings suggest that health concepts are perhaps even more complex than initially thought, with evidence that the presence of health is considered as something more than physical, i.e. as something encompassing psychosocial well-being. Categories found seem to fit with Herzlich's 'being' and 'doing' categorisations (see Bennett 2000: 66) and Bauman's findings of clusters of beliefs in 'health as not ill'. Generally, we can conclude that these dimensions of health are fairly robust (at least in Western culture; see later section for culture differences).

It is worth noting that subjective well-being ratings have been found to correlate strongly with objective health indicators (e.g. blood pressure and heart rate; Steptoe et al. (2012), English Longitudinal Study of Ageing) and also with wealth and educational levels (White 2007). We discuss the 'well-being' concept more fully in relation to quality of life in Chapter 14 ☞ and note that health is only one component of these typically self-rated concepts. What is relevant here, however, is that subjective evaluations are typically reached through comparison with others, and in this way one's concept of what health is, or is not, can be shaped. For example, Kaplan and Baron-Epel (2003) found that young Israelis reporting suboptimal health did not compare themselves with people of the same age, whereas many older people in suboptimal health did. When in optimal health, more young people than old compared themselves with people their age. This is interpreted as evidence that people try to get the best out of their evaluations – a young person

will tend to perceive their peers as generally healthy, so if they feel that they are not, they will be less likely to draw this comparison. In contrast, older people when in poorer health are more likely to compare themselves with same-aged peers, who may generally be thought to have normatively poorer health (thus their own health status seems less unusual). Asking a person to consider what it is that they would consider as 'being healthy' inevitably will lead people into making these types of comparison. Health is a relative state of being.

World Health Organization definition of health

The dimensions of health described in the preceding paragraphs are reflected in the WHO (1947) definition of health as a 'state of complete physical, mental and social well-being and. . . not merely the absence of disease or infirmity'. This definition saw individuals as ideally deserving of a positive state, an overall feeling of well-being, fully functioning. This standpoint informed and helped shape global health targets, including their own Global Strategy for Health for All by the Year 2000 (WHO 1981) and in 1998 the 'Health for all in the 21st Century' declarations. Each of these had the aim of securing health security for all, global health equity, increased life expectancy and access for all to essential health care. Many national policy documents followed, with the nature, specificity and time-frame of targets varying from country to country. In general, however, these set targets for reductions in deaths from the leading causes of cancers, heart disease, lung disease, strokes, or more explicitly targeted the associated behaviours. For example, in England The Health of the Nation White Paper,(Department of Health 1992) and the Saving Lives: Our Healthier Nation report, (Department of Health 1999) and in the Netherlands (Langer Gezond Leven – 'Towards a Longer and Healthier Life', Ministry of Health 2003) the targets were disease incidence reductions, whereas in Belgium the targets were more behavioural: reducing smoking behaviour, fat intake, fatal accidents, increasing uptake of vaccination programmes and increasing health screening in the over-50s. Some progress has been made. For example, reductions have been seen in mortality in developed countries from lung, colon and prostate cancers in men, and breast and colorectal cancers in

---

psychosocial

an approach that seeks to merge a psychological (more micro- and individually oriented) approach with a social approach (macro-, more community- and interaction-oriented), for example, to health.

women, and uptake of smoking is showing reductions amongst young males.

Some have questioned whether the WHO use of the term 'complete' in relation to physical well-being is unrealistic given the changing population age and prevalence of chronic disease and the likelihood that most of us will have some symptomatology as we age (Huber et al. 2011). What is clear, however, is that health policy, however health is defined, acknowledges the evidenced relationship between people's behaviour, lifestyles and their health. What they less clearly acknowledge and therefore often fail to explicitly address are the socio-economic and cultural influences on health, illness and health decisions. These important influences are addressed in the next chapter (see Chapter Two, ☛).

Other definitions of health do exist, for example Bircher (2005) describes a more context-aware view of health, defining it as 'a dynamic state of well-being characterized by a physical and mental potential, which satisfies the demands of life commensurate with age, culture, and personal responsibility'. Bircher's view places the individual centrally in the experience of health and illness whereas the WHO definition does not. Individual beliefs plays a major role in the experience of health and illness, and, as we discuss earlier, disability. (see 'In the spotlight'). The fascination for many health psychologists, quite simply, is why do some people respond in one way to health changes, illness or disability, and others respond quite differently.

Cross-cultural perspectives on health

What is considered to be 'normal' health varies across cultures and as a result of the economic, political and cultural climate of the era in which a person lives. Cultures vary in their health belief systems, health attributions and health practices. Think of how pregnancy is treated in most Western civilisations (i.e. medicalised) as opposed to many developing regions (naturalised). The stigma of physical disability, mental illness, or of dementia, among South Asian communities, and some Eastern European groups, may have consequences for the family which would not be considered in Caucasian families: for example, having a sibling with a disability, or a relative with dementia or depression, may affect siblings' marriage chances or even the social standing of

the family (Ahmad 2000; Mackenzie 2006; Moriarty et al. 2011). Such beliefs can influence disclosure of symptoms and health-seeking behaviour (Vaughn et al. 2009, and see Chapter 9, ☛).

Westernised views of health differ in various ways from conceptualisations of health in non-Westernised civilisations. Chalmers (1996) astutely notes that Westerners divide the mind, body and soul in terms of allocation of care between psychologists and psychiatrists, medical professions and the clergy, whereas in some African cultures, these three 'elements of human nature' are integrated in terms of how a person views them, and in how they are cared for. This **holistic** view is similar to that found in Eastern and in Aboriginal Australian cultures (e.g. Swami et al. 2009) where the social (e.g. social and community norms and rituals) as well as the biological, the spiritual and the interpersonal, are integral to explaining health and illness states.

Spiritual well-being as an aspect of health has gained credence following inclusion in many quality of life assessments (see Chapter 14 ☛), and, although faith or God's reward may sometimes be perceived as supporting health, attributing one's health to a satisfied ancestor may nonetheless raise a few eyebrows if stated aloud. Negative supernatural forces such as 'hexes' or the 'evil eye' sometimes share the blame for illness and disability: for example, Jobanputra and Furnham (2005) found that, when compared with British Caucasians, British Gujarati Indian immigrants more often endorsed such causes of illness. Among Hindus and Sikhs, in particular, it has been reported that disability, and even dementia may be considered a punishment for past sins within the family (Katbamna et al. 2000; Mackenzie 2006). Such belief systems can have profound effects on living with illness or, indeed, caring for someone with an illness or disability (see Chapter 15 ☛).

In addition to beliefs of spiritual influences on health, studies of some African regions consider that the community or family work together for the well-being

---

holistic

root word 'wholeness'; holistic approaches are concerned with the whole being and its well-being, rather than addressing the purely physical or observable.

of all. This **collectivist** approach to staying healthy and avoiding illness is far different from our **individualistic** approach to health (consider how long the passive smoking evidence was ignored). Generally speaking, Western European cultures are found to be more individualistic, with Eastern and African cultures exhibiting more holistic and collectivist approaches to health. For example, in a study of preventive behaviour to avoid endemic tropical disease in Malawians, the social actions to prevent infection (e.g. clearing reed beds) were adhered to more consistently than the personal preventive actions (e.g. bathing in piped water or taking one's dose of chloroquine) (Morrison et al. 1999). Collectivist cultures emphasise group needs and find meaning through links with others and one's community to a greater degree than individualistic ones, which emphasise the uniqueness and autonomy of its members i.e. promote and validate "independent selfs" (Morrison et al. 1999: 367).

Cultures that promote an interdependent self are more likely to view health in terms of social functioning rather than simply personal functioning, fitness, etc. For example studies by George Bishop and colleagues (e.g. Bishop and Teng 1992; Quah and Bishop 1996) have noted that Chinese Singaporean adults view health as a harmonious state where the internal and external systems are in balance, and, on occasions where they become imbalanced, health is compromised. Yin – the positive energy – needs to be kept in balance with the yang – the negative energy (also considered to be female!). Other Asian cultures, e.g. the Vietnamese, use mystical beliefs relating to maintaining balance between poles of 'hot' and 'cold'. In Eastern cultures illness or misfortune is commonly attributed to predestination; African Americans and Latinos are more likely than White Americans to attribute illness causes externally (e.g. to the will of God) (e.g. Vaughn et al. 2009).

Differences in collectivist values have also been shown in a study of 50 states within the USA (Vandello and Cohen 1999). In Hawaii and the Deep South states (e.g. Louisiana, Mississippi, Georgia) and New York State, there was greater collectivism than in the Midwest (e.g. Michigan, Ohio) or North East States (e.g. Maine, Massachusetts). Analyses found this to be associated with a higher percentage of ethnic minorities, whereby States with a higher population percentage of whites of a European ancestry were the most individualistic group, and those with higher proportions of Asians and Blacks had the highest collectivism levels. Adding in figures associated with former slavery made this correlation even stronger. Collectivism also correlated with poverty.

Clearly, therefore, to maximise effectiveness of health promotion efforts, it is important to acknowledge the existence and effects of such different underlying belief systems and resultant behaviours (see Chapters 6 and 7 ☞). It is also worth noting that variations exist within, not just between, cultures, especially where there may have been exposure to multiple cultural influences (Tov and Diener 2007). This is also reported by Wong et al. (2011) from studies in in Singapore where both Asian and Western influences coexist but have differential effects on subjective well-being ratings.

In the Western world, the perceived value of alternative remedies for health maintenance or treatment of symptoms is seen in the growth of alternative medicine and complementary therapy industries; however, Western medicine dominates. In contrast, in non-Western countries a mixture of Western and non-medical/traditional medicine can be found. For example in sub-Saharan Malawi, a person may visit a faith healer or a herbalist as well as a local Western clinic for antibiotics (Ager et al. 1996), and in Malaysia, while Western-style medicine is dominant, traditional medicine practice by 'bomohs' (faith healers) is still available (Swami et al. 2009). Similarly, among some Aboriginal tribes spiritual beliefs in illness causation coexist with the use of Western medicines for symptom control (Devanesen 2000), with traditional medicine and healing processes consistent with cultural and spiritual beliefs used by some still in the treatment of cancer (Shahid et al. 2010).

---

collectivist

a cultural philosophy that emphasises the individual as part of a wider unit and places emphasis on duties above rights, with actions motivated by interconnectedness, reciprocity and group membership, rather than individual needs and wants.

individualistic

a cultural philosophy that places responsibility at the feet of the individual and emphasises rights above duties; thus behaviour is often driven by individual needs and wants rather than by community needs or wants.

Photo 1.2 Visiting a herbalist to choose individually tailored remedies.

Source: Alamy Images/Corbis Premium RF.

These examples illustrate that the biomedical view is acknowledged and assimilated within different culture's belief systems, and show that, whilst access to and understanding of Western medicine and its methods and efficacy grows, better understanding of culturally relevant cognitions regarding illness and health behaviour is needed (see Kitayama and Cohen 2007; Vaughn et al. 2009). We need more research which considers the role religion plays in health across and within cultures. Swami et al. (2009) for example, in their study of 721 Malaysian adults, found that Muslim participants had higher beliefs in religious factors and fate as influences on recovering from illness than did Buddhist or Catholic participants and they were also more likely to believe that their likelihood of becoming ill was uncontrollable.

As we will discuss in a later chapter (Chapter 9 ☞), the use of health care, either traditional or Western, will in part be determined by the nature and strength of such cultural values and religious beliefs. Illness discourse will reflect the dominant conceptualisations of individual cultures and religions, and, in turn, how people think about health and illness will shape expectations, behaviour, and use of health promotion and health-care resources.

The way in which certain behaviour is viewed also differs across time. For example, alcohol dependence has shifted from being viewed as a legal and moral problem, with abusers seen as deviant, to a disease, with its patients treated in clinics; and smoking has shifted from being considered as glamorous, even desirable, to being socially undesirable and considered indicative of a weak will. Perhaps reflecting this latter shift, the prevalence of smoking behaviour is showing some decrease. Furthermore, what is normal (or deviant) and what is defined as sick (reflecting illness) in a given culture can have consequences for how others respond: consider how societal responses to illicit drug use have ranged from prohibition through criminalisation to an illness requiring treatment (see Chapter 3 ☞).

Lifespan, ageing and beliefs about health and illness

Psychological well-being, social and emotional health are affected by illness, disability and hospitalisation, which can be experienced at any age. Growing older may be associated with decreased functioning and increased disability or dependence; however, it is not of course only older people who live with chronic illness: think of childhood asthma, epilepsy and diabetes, for example.

There are developmental issues which health professionals should be aware of if they are to promote the physical, psychological, social and emotional well-being of their patient or client. While the subsequent section introduces lifespan issues in relation to health perceptions, it is recommended that interested readers also consult a developmental health psychology text, e.g. Resnick and Rozensky's (1997) edited collection or the newer text by Turner-Cobb (2014).

Developmental theories

The developmental process is a function of the interaction between three factors:

1. *Learning:* a relatively permanent change in knowledge, skill or ability as a result of experience.
2. *Experience:* what we do, see, hear, feel, think.
3. *Maturation:* thought, behaviour or physical growth, attributed to a genetically determined sequence of development and ageing rather than to experience.

Erik Erikson (Erikson 1959; Erikson et al. 1986) described eight major life stages (five related to childhood development, three related to adult development), which varied across different dimensions, including:

● cognitive and intellectual functioning;

● language and communication skills;

● the understanding of illness;

● health care and maintenance behaviour.

Each of these dimensions is important when examining health and illness perceptions or behaviour. Deficits or limitations in cognitive functioning (due to age, accident or illness) may, for example, influence the extent to which an individual can understand medical instructions, report their emotions or have their health-care needs assessed. Communication deficits or limited language skills can impair a person's willingness to place themselves in social situations, or impede their ability to express their pain or distress to health professionals or family members. The understanding an individual has of their symptoms or their illness is crucial to health-care-seeking behaviour and to adherence, and individual health behaviour influences one's perceived and/or actual risk of illness and varies hugely across the lifespan. All these aspects are covered in this textbook in the relevant chapters. We cannot, for example, assume that explanations or models of adult behaviour or adult decision-making can be applied to children, given normative cognitive development, or to adolescents, given variations in the salience of social influence (Holmbeck 2002).

A maturational framework for understanding cognitive development (Piaget, 1930, 1970) has provided a good basis for understanding the developmental course of concepts regarding health, illness and health procedures. Piaget proposed a staged structure to which, he considered, all individuals follow in sequence as below:

1. *Sensorimotor* (birth–2 years): an infant understands the world through sensations and movement, but lacks symbolic thought and moves from reflexive to voluntary action.

2. *Preoperational* (2–7 years): symbolic thought develops by around age 2, thereafter simple logical thinking and language develop, generally **egocentric**.

3. *Concrete operational* (7–11 years): abstract thought and logic develop hugely; can perform mental operations (e.g. mental arithmetic) and manipulate objects.

---

egocentric

self-centred, such as in the preoperational stage (age 2–7 years) of children, when they see things only from their own perspective (cf. Piaget).

---

4. *Formal operational* (age 12 to adulthood): abstract thought and imagination develop as does deductive reasoning. Not everyone may attain this level.

Piaget's work has been influential in terms of providing an overarching structure within which to view cognitive development. Of more relevance to a health psychology text, however, is work that more specifically addresses children's developing beliefs and understanding of health and illness constructs. We describe some of this work now, using Piagetian stages as a broad framework.

Sensorimotor and preoperational stage children

Little work with infants at the sensorimotor stage is possible in terms of identifying health and illness cognitions, as language is very limited until the end of this stage. At the preoperational stage, children develop linguistically and cognitively, and symbolic thought means that they develop awareness of how they can affect the external world through imitation and learning, although they remain very egocentric. In preoperational children, health and illness are considered in black and white, i.e. as two opposing states rather than as existing on a continuum. Children are slow to see or adopt other people's viewpoints or perspectives, which is crucial if one is to empathise with others. Thus a preoperational child is not very sympathetic to an ill family member, not understanding why this might mean they receive less attention.

Illness concept

It is important that children learn over time some responsibility for maintaining their own health; however, few studies have examined children's conception of health which would be likely to influence health behaviour. Research has focused more often on generating illness concepts. For example, Bibace and Walsh (1980) asked children aged 3–13 questions about health and illness, and suggested that an illness concept develops gradually. The questions were about knowledge – 'What is a cold?'; experience – 'Were you ever sick?'; attributions – 'How does someone get a cold?'; and recovery – 'How does someone get better?' Responses revealed a progression of understanding and attribution for causes of illness, and six developmentally ordered descriptions of how illness is defined, caused and treated emerged.

Under-7s generally explain illness on a 'magical' level – explanations are based on association:

- *Incomprehension:* child gives irrelevant answers or evades question: e.g. sun causes heart attacks.

- *Phenomenonism:* illness is usually a sign or sound that the child has at some time associated with the illness, but with little grasp of cause and effect: e.g. a cold is when you sniff a lot.

- *Contagion:* illness is usually from a person or object that is close by, but not necessarily touching the child; or it can be attributed to an activity that occurred before the illness: e.g: 'You get measles from people'. If asked *how*? 'Just by walking near them'.

Concrete operational stage children

Children over 7 are described by Piaget as capable of thinking logically about objects and events, although they are still unable to distinguish between mind and body until around age 11, when adolescence begins.

Illness concept

Bibace and Walsh describe explanations of illness at around 8 to 11 years as being more concrete and based on a causal sequence:

- *Contamination:* i.e. children at this stage understand that illness can have multiple symptoms, and they recognise that germs, or even their own behaviour, can cause illness: e.g. 'You get a cold if you get sneezed on, and it gets into your body'.

- *Internalisation:* i.e. illness is within the body, and the process by which symptoms occur can be partially understood. The cause of a cold may come from outside germs that are inhaled or swallowed and then enter the bloodstream. These children *can* differentiate between body organs and function and can understand specific, simple information about their illness. They can also see the role of treatment and/or personal action as returning them to health.

In this concrete operational stage, medical staff are still seen as having absolute authority, but their actions might be criticised/avoided: e.g. reluctance to give blood, accusations of hurting unnecessarily, etc. may appear as children can now begin to weigh up the pros and cons of actions. Children can be encouraged to take some personal control over their illness or treatment at this stage

in development which can help the child to cope. They also need to be encouraged to express their fears. Parents need to strike a balance between monitoring a sick child's health and behaviour and being overprotective, as this can detrimentally affect a child's social, cognitive and personal development and may encourage feelings of dependency and disability (see Chapter 15 ☞ for further discussion of coping with illness in a family).

Adolescence and formal operational thought

Adolescence is a socially and culturally created concept only a few generations old, and indeed many primitive societies do not acknowledge adolescence, and instead children move from childhood to adulthood with a ritual performance rather than the years of transition Western societies consider a distinct period in life. Puberty is a period of both physical and psychosocial change. During early adolescence (11–13 years), as individuals prepare for increased autonomy, independence and peers take on more credence than parents, much of life's health-damaging behaviour commences, e.g. smoking (see Chapter 3 ☞).

Illness concept

Bibace and Walsh describe illness concepts at this stage as being at an abstract level, based on interactions between the person and their environment:

- *Physiological:* children now reach a stage of physiological understanding where most can define illness in terms of specific bodily organs or functions (e.g. germs cause white blood cells to get active to try and fight them), and begin to appreciate multiple physical causes, e.g. genes plus pollution plus behaviour.

- *Psychophysiological:* in later adolescence (from around 14 years) and in adulthood, many people grasp the idea that mind and body interact, and understand or accept the role of stress, worry, etc. in the exacerbation and even the cause of illness. However, many people of all ages fail to achieve this level of understanding about illness and continue to use more cognitively simplistic explanations.

It should be noted that Bibace and Walsh's study focuses predominantly on the issue of illness causality, and these findings have been supported by more recent work of Koopman and colleagues (Koopman et al. 2004).

Extending illness cognitions further, other work has shown that children and young people are able to think about health and illness in terms of other dimensions, such as controllability and severity (e.g. Forrest et al. 2006; Gray and Rutter 2007; see Chapter 9 for fuller discussion of illness perceptions (☞).

Adolescents perceive more personal control over the onset and course of illness and are more aware that their actions can influence outcomes. Advice and interventions are more fully understood as are complex remedial and therapeutic procedures: e.g. they understand that taking blood can help monitor the progress of a disease or a treatment. They may, however, choose to be non-adherent if treatment is thought to disrupt one's goals or lose peer approval, and efforts to minimise a child's autonomy (from pre-adolescence) can be counterproductive (Holmbeck et al. 2002).

Overall, childhood sees the development of health and illness concepts and of attitudes and patterns of health behaviour which impact on the person's future health status (see Chapter 3 (☞). How children communicate their symptom experience to parents and health-care staff, their ability to act on health advice, and the level of personal responsibility for disease management taken is, according to such staged theories, determined by the level of cognitive development attained. This approach has not met with universal support whereby illness concepts are thought to derive from a range of influences, such as past experience and knowledge, rather than from relatively fixed stages of cognitive development. Illustrating this point, a large questionnaire and interview-based study with 1,674 Canadian children aged 5–12 years old (Normandeau et al. 1998) asked children to consider health in terms of their daily experiences (what signified good health in their friends; what behaviours are necessary to be healthy; what are the consequences of being healthy, and what things are dangerous to health). The children generally identified three main criteria for good health:

1. being functional (practising sports, absence of disease);

2. mental health (well-being, looking healthy, feeling good about oneself, good relationships with others);

3. lifestyle health behaviour (healthy diet, good hygiene, sleeping well).

Age influenced some components of these dimensions: for example, functionality in older children was more

Photo 1.3 Which of these are healthy? You can't always tell by looking. Neither would you know by looking which of these rated themselves as 'extremely healthy' would you? Health is more than objective symptoms.

Source: Fotolia.com/Robert Kneschke.

associated with sports participation and physiological functioning, whereas in younger children it was more related to 'going outside'. Older children also considered 'not being sick' as more important. In terms of lifestyle behaviour, older children more often referred to good diet than did younger children; and in terms of mental health, older children more often referred to self-concept, whereas younger children referred more to the quality of relationships with others. No effects were found in terms of gender or socio-economic background. In the context of this section on life stage and health concept, the important finding is that children as young as 5 elicited multidimensional concepts of health that were more complex than suggested by a shift from concrete to abstract thinking as described by stage theorists. Very early on, children's conceptions included a mental health dimension, which is contrary to that found in early research. Perhaps the methodology of inviting children to talk about their concepts in relation to their own lives and experience as opposed to more hypothetical questioning, accounts for this difference.

Adulthood 17/18

Adulthood tends to be divided between early (17–40), middle age (40–60) and elderly (60/65). Early adulthood blends out of adolescence as the person forges their identity and assumes the roles and responsibility of adulthood – a time of consolidation. In contrast to the years from 3–13 which Laslett (1996) describes as the '1st age', where dependency, childhood and education are key, adolescence and adulthood is considered as the '2nd age', a period of developing independence, maturity and responsibility. Early adulthood typically sees all sorts of transitions, such as graduating from school and college, taking on new careers, pregnancy, marriage, childbirth; many will divorce, some will lose a parent. Although Piaget did not describe further cognitive developments during adulthood, new perspectives develop from experience across the lifespan, and what is learned is ideally applied to achieving future life goals.

Adults are less likely than adolescents to adopt new health-risk behaviour and are generally more likely to engage in protective behaviour: e.g. screening, exercise, etc. for health reasons (see Chapter 4 ☞). Transitions in adulthood do not affect all sectors of the adult population in the same way: for example, marriage was found to benefit health in men – i.e. they have lower illness scores than men living alone, whereas for women, being married carries no such protection (Macintyre 1986; Blaxter 1987), suggesting differential social support perhaps (see Chapter 12 ☞ for a discussion of stress moderators). However changes in the work force, with more married women now also working than was the case in the 1980s when these studies were conducted, mean that such findings may not persist.

In contrast to generally positive views of early adulthood, middle age has been identified as a period of doubts and anxiety, reappraisal and change, some of it triggered by uncertainty of roles when children become adults and leave home, i.e. 'the empty nest' syndrome, some of it triggered by awareness of physical changes – greying hair, weight gain, stiff joints, etc. Positive health behaviour changes may follow (see Chapter 3 and 4).

WHAT DO YOU THINK?

Is middle age a state of mind? Are you 'as young as you feel'?

Think of your parents, aunts and uncles or of family friends in their 40s. Do they seem to share outlooks on life, expectancies and behaviours that are significantly different to those of you and your friends? How do you view growing older? Think about how it makes you feel and question these feelings.

Ageing and health

In the UK, as elsewhere in the world, the ageing population (accepting the cut-off age for 'older people' to be 60 or over) has burgeoned, but more particularly the percentage of persons living into their late 70s or 80s has increased and is projected to increase further. Worldwide 11.7 per cent of the population are aged over 60 years (compared to 8.6 per cent in 1980); 7 per cent over 65 years, and 1.7 per cent are over 80 years old – this latter percentage translates to 120,199,000 individuals (>120 million) (United Nations 2013). A worldwide increase is expected in the proportion of the populations aged over 65 from 5.2 % in 1950 to 10 per cent in 2025. Within the UK, projections are that the number of people aged 60 or older will rise from 22 per cent at present (Age Concern 2010, based on *National Population Projections, 2008-based*, Office for National Statistics 2009) to almost a third of the total population (31 per cent) by 2058. Globally the United Nations predict a 7.6 per cent increase in those aged 60+ by 2050, with older people outnumbering children by 2047 and representing half of those defined as 'dependants' by 2075.

The shift in proportions of older persons living in our society is underpinned by many factors including reduced birth numbers/slower population growth, as well as the reasons associated with longer life expectancy cited earlier. The implications for health and social care resources are obvious, given the **epidemiology** of illness: i.e. the fact that the incidence of many diseases increases with longevity.

Laslett (1996) describes the '3rd age' of those aged 65+ as a period of fulfilment as not all of course become ill or infirm at this point! The English Longitudinal Study of Ageing (see also Chapter 14 ☞, Steptoe et al. 2012/13), highlights that increased risk of dying prematurely is associated with poorer enjoyment of life, thus highlighting the role of subjective well-being, whatever the age. The '4th age', however, is more strongly

epidemiology

the study of patterns of disease in various populations and the association with other factors such as lifestyle factors. Key concepts include mortality, morbidity, prevalence, incidence, absolute risk and relative risk. Type of question: Who gets this disease? How common is it?

associated with disability and dependence, relating to the 'oldest old' those aged over 80 where health does decline more rapidly.

In an ageing society disability is common; 85 per cent may experience some chronic condition (Woods 2008), with the main problems being associated with memory loss, incontinence, depression, falls or immobility (UN 2013). Does the process of ageing influence how an older person thinks about themselves and their health?

Empirical research has shown that **self-concept** is relatively stable through ageing (e.g. Baltes and Baltes 1990; Coleman 1999) and that changes in self-concept are not an inevitable part of the ageing process. Whilst growing older may present an individual with new challenges, this should not be seen as implying that ageing is itself a problem, in spite of the ageist attitudes that exist in many industrialised countries.

The elderly often report expecting to have poor health. Such expectations can result in poor health-care checks and maintenance as they regard health protective behaviour as pointless. They may think loss of mobility, poor foot health and poor digestion is an inevitable and unavoidable part of ageing and so may not respond to symptoms as they should (e.g. Sarkisian et al. 2001). Exercise tends to decline in old age in the belief that it will overexert the joints, heart, etc. In fact, the elderly tend to underestimate their own physical capacities, yet as we shall see in Chapter 4 ☞, exercise is both possible and beneficial. Even in the face of 'objective' signs of illness, many older people retain a positive view of their health. If we can identify factors associated with 'successful ageing', then health promotion efforts can target the factors associated with this. What is 'successful ageing'?

Successful ageing

Bowling and Iliffe (2006) describe five progressively more inclusive 'models' of successful ageing and the variables considered within each model. Variables were

> ### self-concept
> that knowledge, conscious thoughts and beliefs about yourself that allow you to feel you are distinct from others and that you exist as a separate person.

all categorised or dichotomised: e.g. presence/absence of diagnosis; sense of purpose/no sense of purpose, etc., in order for each model to identify whether a person was 'successfully aged' or not:

Biomedical model: based on physical and psychiatric functioning – diagnoses and functional ability.

Broader biomedical model: as above but includes social engagement and activity.

Social functioning model: based on the nature and frequency of social functioning and networks, social support accessed.

Psychological resources model: based on personal characteristics of optimism and self-efficacy and on sense of purpose, coping and problem solving, self-confidence and self-worth (see Chapter 12 ☞ for a discussion of many of these positive cognitions).

Lay model: based on the above variables plus socio-economic variables of income and 'perceived social capital', which included access to resources and facilities, environmental quality and problems (e.g. crime, traffic, pollution, places to walk, feelings of safety).

The study assessed all the above variables in a sample of 999 individuals aged over 65 years and assigned them either as successfully aged or not based on achieving the 'good' score on each variable, e.g. no physical conditions versus one or more. The authors then tested which of these models 'best' distinguished those participants that rated quality of life (QoL) as 'Good' (included 'So good, could not be better', or 'Good') instead of 'Not good' (included 'Alright' or 'So bad, could not be worse').

Although each model could independently predict QoL (Chapter 15 ☞), the strongest prediction was achieved by the lay model. Those individuals who scored as 'successfully aged' on the basis of lay model variables were more than *five* times more likely to rate their QoL as 'Good' rather than 'Not good'. The odds of a 'good' QoL rating versus 'not good' was next best among those classified on the broader biomedical model (3.2 × more likely), than the biomedical model (2.6 × more likely), the psychological (2.4 × more likely) and social models (1.99 × more likely).

Such findings highlight the importance of multidimensional models of health in that medical or psychological or social variables are all important, but a more holistic model is 'better'. A broader model also opens up a range of opportunities for intervention; the challenge

IN THE SPOTLIGHT

Measuring self-rated or subjective health status

Health is commonly viewed in terms of how we feel and what we do. Our 'health status' is not simply whether we are alive or dead, nor is it defined simply on the basis of the presence or absence of symptoms – it is something we perceive for ourselves, sometimes referred to as 'subjective health status'. In fact, generally the relationship between subjective health and markers of 'objective' health is weak (e.g. Berg et al. 2006); however, self-ratings of health (SRH), often assessed as a simple single item (e.g. 'How is your health in general?'), have been found to predict major health outcomes, including mortality (e.g. Bond et al. 2006; Sargent-Cox et al. 2010). In almost all European countries a majority of the adult population will rate their health as good or very good, although this does not mean that the actual health within the countries depicted is 'objectively' better. These are self-reports, and with this type of data come some challenges.

For example, data are potentially influenced by the age composition of the sample, and furthermore the same associations are not always found for both genders. For example, Deeg and Kriegsman (2003) find a relationship between SRH and health outcomes only for men. Across all EU countries sampled for the data presented above (OECD Health at a Glance 2012), men were more likely to rate their health as good or better, and rating declined markedly after age 45 in many countries and then again after age 65. Socio-economic influences on reports are also reported (OECD 2012a) (see Chapter 2 ☞).

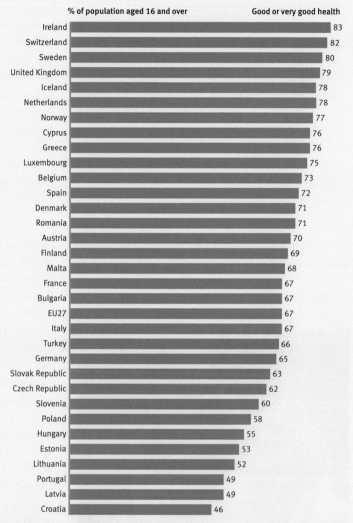

Figure 1.2 Adults' self-reported health status, 2010.

Source: EU Statistics on Income and Living Conditions, OECD Health Data 2012.

Addressing measurement issues, Sargent-Cox and colleagues conducted a study of over 2,000 Australian adults over the age of 65 assessed seven times between 1992 and 2004. They used three different measures of SRH – comparing self with previous self (a temporal comparison); comparing self with other people of the same age (an age-group comparison) and a no-comparison global rating (simply rated current health). They hypothesised that the age-group social comparison would show an increase as the sample increasingly engaged in downward social comparison (with those worse off) so as to enhance their self rating; and that the temporal comparison would show worsened SRH. In fact all three ratings worsened over time but the extent and rate of worsening varied: the global rating showed a steep decline over the 12 years; contrary to expectations, the age-group comparative ratings became more negative (in men but not the youngest i.e. those 65 on commencement), and self-comparative ratings became more negative although a ceiling effect is reported whereby, over time, they are more likely to rate self as having stayed the same as previously.

Findings such as this are important in highlighting that the measures we use can influence the results we find and thus the interpretations we make. For example, a self-comparison measure is seen to plateau in the context of an ageing population, perhaps out of a feeling that 'my health cannot get any worse' (and so, by scoring SRH as being 'same as the year previously', this could be misinterpreted as implying that health is better than expected given the passing of time – if we assume actual health deteriorates over time). Such findings also have relevance for other age groups, and for constructs other than self-rated health (for example, Chapter 5 ☞ describes how the comparator, made in questions regarding drinking behaviour, or disease risk, can also change responses).

now is to use such findings to develop and evaluate health promotion interventions with older populations

Photo 1.4 Many activities can be enjoyed at any age.

Source: Alamy Images/Radius Images.

(see Chapters 6 and 7). Of note, however, is that the sample in this study was 98 per cent white and thus the model of successful ageing best associated with QoL in this sample may not hold for non-white samples.

This chapter has described what is often meant by 'health'. In focusing on health, we have acknowledged that health is a continuum, not simply a dichotomy of sick versus healthy. Most of us will experience in our lifetime varying degrees of health and well-being, with periods of illness at one extreme and optimal wellness at the other. Some may never experience optimal wellness. 'Health refers to a state of being that is largely taken for granted' (Radley 1994: 5) and is often only appreciated when lost through illness. In the final section of this chapter we want to introduce what is broadly considered as the discipline of health psychology. The final chapter of this book addresses careers in health psychology (Chapter 18 ☞).

What is health psychology?

Before defining health psychology, let's first look at psychology as a discipline generally. Psychology can be defined as the scientific study of mental and behavioural functioning. Studying mental processes through behaviour is limited, however, in that not all behaviour is observable (for example, is thought not behaviour?) and thus for many aspects of human behaviour we have to rely on self-report, the problems of which are described elsewhere.

Psychology aims to describe, explain, predict and, where possible, intervene to control or modify behavioural and mental processes, from language, memory, attention and perception to emotions, social behaviour and health behaviour, to name just a few. The key to scientific methods employed by psychologists is the basic principle that the world may be known through observation = **empiricism**. Empirical methods go beyond speculation, inference and reasoning to actual and systematic analysis of data. Scientific research starts with a theory, which can be defined as a general set of assumptions about how things operate in the world. Theories can be vague and poorly defined (e.g. I have a theory about why sports science students generally sit together at the back of lectures) to very specific (e.g. sports science students sit at the back of lectures because they feel like 'outsiders' when placed with the large numbers of psychology majors). Psychologists scientifically test the validity of their hypotheses and theories. On an academic level this can increase understanding about a particular phenomenon, and on an applied level it can provide knowledge useful to the development of interventions.

Psychologists use scientific methods to investigate all kinds of behaviour and mental processes, from the response activity of a single nerve cell to the role adjustments required in old age, and the research method employed will depend on what specific questions are being asked. You obviously would not use the same methods to establish the extent of language in a two-year-old as you would to identify which areas of the brain were activated during speech. This text highlights those that are most commonly employed by health psychologists: for example, the use of questionnaires, interviews and psychometric assessments (such as of personality).

What connects psychology to health?

As introduced in this chapter, people have beliefs about health, are often emotional about it and have a behavioural role to play in maintaining their health and coping with illness. As such, we can address the underlying questions such as why some people behave in a healthy way and others do not. Is it all a matter of personality? Does a person who behaves in a healthy manner in one way, e.g. doesn't smoke, also behaves healthily in other ways, e.g. attend dental screening? Are we rational and consistent beings? Does gender, age or socio-economic status affect health either directly or indirectly via their effects on other things? Why do some people appear to get ill all the time while others stay healthy? What psychosocial factors can help a person adjust to, or recover from, illness? Health psychology integrates many cognitive, developmental and social theories and explanations, and applies them solely to health, illness and health care. Health psychology was described at an early stage in the emergence of this new field of study by Matarazzo as 'the aggregate of the specific educational, scientific and professional contribution of the discipline of psychology to the promotion and maintenance of health, the promotion and treatment of illness and related dysfunction' (1980: 815). This definition highlights the main goals of health psychology, i.e. we seek to develop our understanding of biopsychosocial factors involved in:

- the promotion and maintenance of health;
- improving health-care systems and health policy;
- the prevention and treatment of illness;
- the causes of illness: e.g. vulnerability/risk factors.

Unlike some other domains of psychology (such as cognitive science), health psychology can be considered as an applied science, although not all health psychology research is predictive. For example, some research aims only to *quantify* (e.g. what percentage of school pupils drink under age?) or *describe* (e.g. what are the beliefs of under-age drinkers regarding the effects of alcohol?). Descriptive research ideally provides the foundation for the generation of more causal questions: e.g. do beliefs about alcohol in primary schoolchildren predict age of onset of under-age drinking? By simply measuring health beliefs and attitudes, we can begin to grapple with the issue of predictors (see Chapters 3–5 ☞) before developing interventions.

> empiricism
> arising from a school of thought that all knowledge can be obtained through experience.

Health psychology and other fields

Health psychology has grown out of many fields within the social sciences. It has adopted and adapted models and theories originally found in social psychology, behaviourism, clinical psychology, cognitive psychology, etc. In fact you may also want to pick up an introductory psychology text and look at the learning, **motivation**, social, developmental and cognitive sections in more detail. Health psychology in Europe is, as in the USA and Australasia, linked with other health and social sciences (e.g. psychosomatic medicine, behavioural medicine, medical sociology and, increasingly, health economics) and with medicine and allied therapeutic disciplines. Few academic or practitioner health psychologists work alone; most are involved in an array of inter- and multidisciplinary work (see Chapter 18 ☞). In each of the above there exists a challenge to the dualist thinking regarding mind–body separation, but as well as similarity there are differences in theoretical underpinning (i.e. sociological, medical, psychological) and consequent differences in the methods of assessment, research and intervention suggested or employed.

Psychosomatic medicine

Developed in the 1930s this initially was the domain of now well-known psychoanalysts, e.g. Alexander, Freud, and offered an early challenge to biomedicine as discussed earlier in the chapter. 'Psycho-somatic' refers to the fact that the mind and body are both involved in illness, and where an organic cause is not easily identified the mind may offer the trigger of a physical response that is detectable and measurable. In other words, mind and body act together, not just the mind. Early work asserted that a certain personality would lead to a certain disease (e.g. Alexander's 'ulcer-prone personality', or Freud's

---

motivation

memories, thoughts, experiences, needs and preferences that act together to influence (drive) the type, strength and persistence of our actions.

operant conditioning

attributed to Skinner, this theory is based on the assumption that behaviour is directly influenced by its consequences (e.g. rewards, punishments, avoidance of negative outcomes).

'hysterical paralysis'), and while evidence for direct causality has proved limited, these developments in thinking certainly did set the groundwork for fascinating studies of physiological processes that may link personality type to disease (see Chapter 11's ☞ discussion of hostility and heart disease associations, for example). Until the 1960s, psychosomatic research was predominantly psychoanalytical in nature, focusing on psychoanalytic interpretations of illness causation, such as asthma, ulcers or migraine being triggered by repressed emotions. However, one negative by-product of this work is that among those with a biomedical viewpoint, illnesses with no identifiable organic cause were often dismissed as nervous disorders or psychosomatic conditions for which medical treatment was often not forthcoming. Illnesses with no physical evidence are known as psychogenic (see Chapter 9 for discussion of medically unexplained symptoms ☞).

Psychosomatic medicine today is more concerned with mixed psychological, social and biological/physiological explanations of illness. Illnesses are often viewed as 'psychophysiological', with increased acceptance that psychological factors can affect any physical condition. This notion in the 1970s led to the emergence of an integrated discipline known as behavioural medicine, and to health psychology itself.

Behavioural medicine

This is essentially an interdisciplinary field drawing on a range of behavioural sciences, including psychology, sociology and health education, in relation to medicine and medical conditions (Schwartz and Weiss 1977). Behavioural medicine developed in the 1970s and provided further challenge to the biomedical model dominant at the time. As its name suggests, behavioural principles (i.e. that behaviour results from learning through classical or **operant conditioning**) were applied to experimentally evaluate techniques of prevention and rehabilitation, and not solely treatment. Prevention does, however, receive less attention than rehabilitation and treatment of illness, which highlights one of the key differences between behavioural medicine and health psychology. In furthering the view that the mind had a direct link to the body (e.g. anxiety can raise blood pressure, fear can elevate heart rate), some of the therapies proposed, such as biofeedback (see Chapter 13 ☞) work on the principle of operant conditioning and feedback.

WHAT DO YOU THINK?

Think of some health behaviours you think you might have learned and consider the circumstances under which you learned them. Do different factors influence your maintenance of these behaviours?

Think of any health problem you have experienced and whether you consider a role for your behaviour in either avoiding that problem in the future or in helping recovery from it.

Matarazzo himself distinguished between 'behavioural health' and 'behavioural medicine', with the former being more concerned with health enhancement and disease prevention rather than focusing on those with illness as behavioural medicine does. 'Behavioural health' is not however, a stand-alone discipline but has been assimilated into others, including those areas of health psychology we describe in the following three chapters, i.e. behaviour and lifestyle factors associated with health and illness.

Medical psychology

In the UK, medical psychologists would now tend to be termed as health psychologists who do not dispute the biological basis of health and illness but who have adopted a more holistic model. In other parts of Europe, for example the Netherlands, the term 'medical psychologist' describes a professional working in a medical setting who has completed a psychology degree and Health Psychology Masters training (1 or 2 years), followed by a 2-year internship for generalist practitioner certification, or clinical psychology training (as for Health Psychology but adding a further 4 years to get full state specialist certification) (Soons and Denollet 2009). In the USA the term is used to describe a clinical psychologist who incorporates somatic (physical) medicine into their consideration of mental illness, and in some cases they can even prescribe medicines. Thus 'medical psychology' is a term more aligned to a profession than to a specific cognate discipline.

Medical sociology

Medical sociology exemplifies the close relationship between psychology and sociology, with health and illness being considered in terms of social factors that may influence individuals. It takes a wider (macro) approach to the individual in that they are considered within family, kinship, culture. While health psychology also considers external influences on health and illness, it has traditionally focused more on the individual's cognitions/beliefs and responses to the external world and obviously takes a psychological rather than a sociological perspective. The growth over time of a more critical and reflective health psychology may make the boundaries between medical sociology and health psychology more blurred.

Clinical psychology

Health psychology and health psychologists are often confused with clinical psychology and clinical psychologists! Clinical psychology is concerned with mental health and the diagnosis and treatment of mental health problems (e.g. personality disorders, phobias, anxiety and depression, eating disorders). Clinical psychologists are typically practitioners working within the health-care setting, delivering assessments, diagnoses and psychological interventions that are derived from behavioural and cognitive principles. Many of these principles inform health psychology research and practice (see the many examples of cognitive-behavioural interventions outlined in this text), but the difference fundamentally comes down to the populations with whom we work and the professional status of our discipline. Different countries differ on this and you are referred to your national psychological associations for more information and also to Chapter 18 ☞ where we have described health psychology careers.

Health psychology

Health psychology is fundamentally a discipline within the larger discipline of psychology, unlike behavioural medicine which integrates many disciplines, i.e. we are first and foremost psychologists. Health psychology emerged in the late 1970s as described above and takes a biopsychosocial approach to health and illness (Engel 1977, 1980). This means that it considers biological, social and psychological factors involved in the aetiology, prevention or treatment of physical illness, as well as in the promotion and maintenance of health. Health psychologists also need a basic (or greater!) understanding of body systems and their function including that of the nervous system, endocrine system, immune system, respiratory and digestive systems (see Chapter 8 ☞).

Unsurprisingly, health psychology has developed over time both academically and professionally, with different terminology and roles in different corners of the globe. For example, *clinical health psychology*, in the USA would describe a qualified health psychologist working in the clinical setting, in the UK this would be a qualified clinical psychologist working with physical health populations! Other health psychologists increasingly align themselves with *public health* to address issues such as immunisation, epidemics, and implications for health education and promotion (see McManus 2014, letter to *The Psychologist*); and others embrace *critical health psychology*, which addresses criticism that health psychology has been too individualistic in focus, at the expense of the social, although this is less valid now than ten years ago. In the UK we further distinguish between an *academic health psychologist* who has the same undergraduate academic training as a *professional health psychologist* but who focuses on research, teaching and supervision conducted from an academic base, in contrast to further training in 'consultancy', usually within the NHS and then working as a practitioner, for example in pain or rehabilitation clinics. Readers should refer to their own professional bodies for current roles and career opportunities.

The professional title 'health psychologist' is recognised now in many countries, including, for example, the British Psychological Society and the Health Professions Council UK, The American and Australian Psychological Societies. To address some of the concerns raised by critical health psychology, we have incorporated throughout this textbook a consideration of wider influences on health, and on illness, such as culture, lifespan and socio-economic **variables**.

> **variable**
>
> (noun): something that can be measured or is reported and recorded as data, such as age, mood, smoking frequency or physical functioning.

Humans do not operate in a vacuum but are interacting social beings shaped, modelled and reinforced in their thoughts, behaviour and emotions by people close to them, by less known people, by politicians, by their culture, and even by the era in which they live. Consider, for example, women and work stress – this was not an issue in the 1900s, when society neither expected nor particularly supported women to work, whereas in the twenty-first century we have a whole new arena of women's health issues that in part may relate to the way women's roles have shifted in society. Where in the early part of the twenty-first century the biopsychosocial model was more often treated by health psychologists as if the three components were simultaneous but separate influences (Crossley 2000), research today acknowledges the interplay and integration between the biological, social and psychological. Society (local, regional, national, global) and politics plays a significant role in the human experience of health and illness. There is a greater and growing acknowledgement of the rich diversity of cultures in the UK and the rest of Europe, and how variation in their beliefs and expectancies influence health and illness behaviour. Through review, critique and reflection, the still relatively new discipline of health psychology has developed and strengthened. As potential health psychologists of the future, readers should be aware of the risks of complacency and the importance of reflection and critique!

This text therefore considers cultural and social perspectives on health and illness in an integrated manner alongside mainstream psychological thinking. Moving from theory, through robust and methodologically rigorous research, we highlight the central goal of developing a theoretical and empirical *understanding* of human health and illness. Only then can we apply that understanding in shaping health policy or developing or leading interventions in health-care practice. For discussion of the importance of methodological and theoretical review and development see de Bruin and Johnston's commentary and proposal of a 'methods in health psychology' track convened within the European Health Psychology Society (2012).

SUMMARY

This chapter has introduced key areas of interest to health psychologists, including:

- What is health?
  - Health appears to consist broadly of domains of 'having', 'doing' and 'being', where health is a reserve, an absence of illness, a state of psychological and physical well-being; is evident in the ability to perform physical acts, as fitness, and is generally something that is taken for granted until it is challenged by illness.
- How has health and illness been viewed over time?
  - Views of health have shifted from fairly holistic views, where mind and body interact, to more dualist views, where the mind and body are thought to act independently of one another. This is shifting back towards holism, with the medical model being challenged by a more biopsychosocial approach.
- What influence does culture have on how health is perceived?

- Cultures can be grounded in collective or individualistic orientations, and these will influence explanations for health and illness as well as the behaviour of those within the culture.
- What influence might lifespan play on how health is perceived?
  - Children can explain health and illness in complex and multidimensional terms; and human expectations of health change over the lifespan as a function of background and experience as well as of cognitive development.
- What is health psychology?
  - Health psychology is the study of health, illness and health-care practices (professional and personal).
  - Health psychology aims to understand, explain and ideally predict health and illness behaviour in order that effective interventions can be developed to reduce the physical and emotional costs of risky behaviour and illness.
  - Health psychology offers a holistic but fundamentally psychological approach to issues in health, illness and health care.

Further reading

S. Kitayama and D. Cohen (eds) (2007). *Handbook of Cultural Psychology*. New York: Guilford Press.

As well as containing the Tov and Diener chapter referred to in this chapter, this 30-chapter text has become a leader and a landmark text for anyone interested in the role culture plays at all levels in terms of perceiving self and others, and in terms of cognition, emotion and motivation, and development. While not focusing on health specifically, it is worth a look.

Turner-Cobb, J. (2014). *Child Health Psychology*. London: Sage.

This new book goes a significant way towards filling a gap in the market of health psychology textbooks in that it focuses specifically on psychosocial and developmental aspects of child health and illness, including, as pertinent to this chapter, discussion of the health concept.

The British Psychology website is useful for defining health psychology as a discipline and as a profession in the UK (see also Chapter 18 (☞):

http://www.bps.org.uk/careers-in-psychology

The European Health Psychology Society website provides access to useful information about research across Europe, health psychology in practice, and access to the European health Psychologist Bulletin:

http://www.ehps.net/index.php?option=com_content&view=article&id=1&Itemid=118

Those interested in health psychology as applied to public health issues may find this link useful:

www.linkedin.com/groups/Health-Psychology-in-Public-Health-5182547

http://ec.europa.eu/health/ageing/policy/index_en.htm

If you have an interest in ageing and health issues, this site is worth a look at and is regularly updated.

For open-access student resources specifically written to complement this textbook and support your learning, please visit **www.pearsoned.co.uk/morrison**

Chapter 2
Health inequalities

Learning outcomes

By the end of this chapter, you should have an understanding of:

- the impact of poverty on health
- causes of variations in health between and within countries
- the impact of socio-economic deprivation on health and theories of why this occurs
- the relationship between work stress, unemployment and health
- the health impact of having a minority status in society
- the impact of gender on health

Bankers cause ill health throughout the world

Governments across the world are trying to make us healthier. We are urged to eat healthily, exercise and avoid drinking too much alcohol. But is this drive to healthy behaviours hiding an insidious fact – and one governments would like us to ignore? Perhaps the most important contributor to our health is not what we do, but who we are and where we are in society. A job is better for your health than no job at all. But better jobs are better for your health. People who live in deprived areas are likely to live 10 or more years less than those in less deprived areas. Women are more likely to experience work stress and its associated ill health than men. People in ethnic minorities may experience poorer working conditions and stress related to prejudice. These factors are easy to identify – difficult to change. And at a time of economic stringency, which most industrialised countries are now facing, health disparities due to work pressures, unemployment, and difficult economic conditions are likely to increase rather than decrease. The health as well as the wealth of the nation may suffer in the next decade as a result of the economic crisis of the late noughties.

Chapter outline

This chapter considers differences in health status that arise not as a result of individual behaviour but from the social context in which we live. Among other things, it considers why better-off people tend to live longer than those who are less well off, why women generally live longer than men, and why people from ethnic minorities are more likely to die earlier than those from majority populations. The greatest killer in the world is poverty, which is associated with poor nutrition, unhealthy water supplies, poor health care, and other factors that directly influence health. Among people who do not experience such poverty, more subtle social and psychological factors influence health. Men's health, for example, may be influenced by a general reluctance to seek medical help following the onset of illness. People who are economically deprived may experience poorer health because of problems of accessing health care, and greater levels of stress than the more economically well off. This chapter examines how social and psychological processes differentially influence health as a result of **socio-economic status (SES)**, ethnicity, gender and working environment.

Health differentials

Where we live can impact on our risk for disease as much, if not more, than how we live. The biomedical model and even health psychology have typically focused on individual risk factors such as personality, diet, and levels of exercise as risk factors for poor health. We discuss some of these issues in Chapters 3, 4, and 11 ☞. However, there is an emerging body of evidence that environmental and social factors may have an equal, if not greater, influence on our health. The better-off live longer than the less well off. People who occupy minority roles in society as a result of ethnic or other factors

socio-economic status
a measure of the social class of an individual. Different measures use different indicators, including income, job type or years of education. Higher status implies a higher salary or higher job status.

health differential
a term used to denote differences in health status and life expectancy across different groups.

may experience more illness or die earlier than the majority population; even findings that women live longer than men now appear to have psychosocial as well as biological explanations.

This chapter considers how people in various groups in society may experience differences in health and longevity as a result of their SES, ethnicity, gender and working conditions. It considers each factor separately, although in reality each of them may be intimately intertwined. People in ethnic minorities, for example, still tend to be less well off than the majority population and may suffer adverse health effects as a result of both their ethnicity and socio-economic position (although both may exert an influence through the common pathway of stress). Accordingly, although this chapter attempts to identify the specific health gains or risks associated with different social contexts, it should be remembered that many individuals face multiple advantages or disadvantages as a result of occupying several social contexts.

Evidence of health differentials

There are clear **health differentials** between countries. According to the World Health Organization (WHO),

Table 2.1 Life expectancy in years for the highest and lowest ranked countries in 2013

Top 10	Life expectancy	Bottom 10	Life expectancy
Japan	86.4	Sierra Leone	47.5
Italy	84.6	Central African Republic	48.5
Andorra	84.2	Democratic Republic of the Congo	48
Singapore	84	Somalia	50
Hong Kong	83.8	Swaziland	50
San Marino	83.5	Guinea Bissau	50
Iceland	83.3	Lesotho	51
Monaco	83.1	Mali	51
Australia	83	Chad	51
Sweden	83	Angola	52

Source: WHO (2013).

almost all the countries whose populations experience the shortest life expectancy are in Africa. The countries with the best health are scattered around the world. One may expect the populations of rich nations to live longer than those of the poor nations. This is generally, but not universally, true. Of note also is that the richest country in the world, the USA, fared rather badly in the WHO rankings, at only 35th place, with a life expectancy of 79.8 years. A number of explanations for this apparent anomaly include the following, some of which are considered in more depth later in the chapter:

● Some social groups within the USA, such as Native Americans and the inner-city poor, have health that is more characteristic of developing countries rather than rich industrialised ones.

● HIV has contributed to a higher proportion of death and disability to young and middle-aged Americans than in most other industrialised countries.

● The USA is one of the leading countries for cancers relating to tobacco use, especially lung cancer and chronic lung disease.

● The USA has high levels of violence, especially of homicides, compared to other industrialised countries.

Nearly one-third of deaths in the developing countries occur before the age of 5 years (http://www.who.int/health-info/global_burden_disease/), while a further third of deaths occur before the age of 65 years. This contrasts with the average two-thirds of deaths that occur *after* the age of 65 years within the industrialised countries. The factors that contribute to these differences are economic, environmental

and social. People in many developing countries experience significant health risks from lack of safe water, poor sanitation, inadequate diet, indoor smoke from solid fuels, and poor access to health care. The WHO estimates that poverty causes around 12 million deaths each year in children under the age of 5 living in the developing world, with the most common causes of death being diarrhoea, dysentery and **lower respiratory tract infections**. Major killers among the adult population include being underweight, tuberculosis and malaria. This high risk for death through infection contrasts markedly with the industrialised nations, where the key causes of death are chronic disease and abuse of drugs such as tobacco and alcohol. One particular problem now facing many countries in Africa results from HIV infection and AIDS. Botswana, Zimbabwe and Swaziland, for example, have HIV infection rates of 30 per cent or higher (UNAIDS 2008). In the early 2000s, there were over 11 million AIDS orphans in the region and this number was expected to rise to more than 20 million by the year 2010 (UNAIDS 2008). War is also a significant contributor to early mortality in many developing countries.

Even the 'haves' experience health differentials

While the industrialised world may not have the profound levels of poverty and illness found in the developing world, there are gradients of wealth within these countries, and differentials in health that match them. The richer people *within* most industrialised countries are likely to live longer than the less well off and be healthier while alive (Marmot 2005). One example of this can be found in data reported by Rasulo et al. (2007). They calculated the expected 'healthy life expectancy' of individuals living in 8,797 specified areas of the UK and the level of social deprivation of each area using a measure of deprivation known as the Carstair's deprivation score. This measures levels of household overcrowding, male unemployment, low social class and car ownership. They then calculated how long people were expected to live in good health across the varying levels of deprivation and found a

---

lower respiratory tract infection
infection of the parts of the respiratory system including the larynx, trachea, bronchi and lungs.

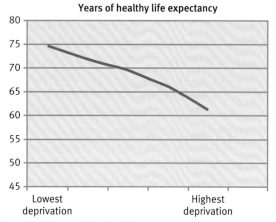

Figure 2.1 Years of healthy life expectancy according to Carstair's deprivation scores in the UK

Source: from 'Inequalities in health expectancies in England and Wales: small area analysis from 2001 Census', Health Statistics Quarterly, 34 (Rasulo, D., Bajekal, M. and Yar, M. 2007), © Crown copyright 2007; Crown copyright material is reproduced with the permission of the Controller, Office of Public Sector Information (OPSI), also reproduced with the permission of the author.

linear relationship between deprivation scores and expected 'healthy life expectancy' (see Figure 2.1). They reported a staggering 13.2 years difference between those in the least and most deprived areas.

Similar findings can be found across the industrialised world. It is important to note that the relationship between social deprivation and health is *linear*, indicating not just that the very poor die earlier than the very rich: instead, it indicates that quite modest differences in wealth can influence health throughout society. This effect can be subtle. Marmot et al. (1991), for example, reported that middle-class UK executives who owned one car were more likely to die earlier than their peers who had two cars.

WHAT DO YOU THINK?

While there is consistent evidence in industrialised countries that the better-off live longer, engage in less health-damaging behaviours, and experience less illness than those who are more economically deprived, this is not always the case in other countries. Singh et al. (1997), for example, reported that rates of heart disease were higher among Indian rural middle classes than among the lower social groups. What factors do you think may contribute to these differences? Are they likely to be a transient or permanent phenomenon? Do such findings indicate that we should be cautious in generalising any associations between socio-economic status and health across countries and cultures?

Explanations of socio-economic health inequalities

A number of explanations for health inequalities in the industrialised countries have been proposed, some of which attribute responsibility to the individual. Others suggest that factors related to occupying different socio-economic groups may directly impact on health. But, the first issue that has to be addressed is the causal direction between SES and health. Does SES influence health, or does health influence SES?

Social causation versus social drift

Explanation for socio-economic health differentials pits a social explanation against a more individual one. The first, the social causation model, suggests that low SES 'causes' health problems – that is, there is something about occupying a low socio-economic group that adversely influences the health of individuals. The opposing view, the social drift model, opposes this view. This suggests that when an individual develops a health problem, they may be unable to maintain a job or the levels of overtime required to maintain their standard of living. They therefore drift down the socio-economic scale: that is, health problems 'cause' low SES.

Longitudinal studies have provided evidence relevant to these hypotheses. These typically identify a representative population of several thousand healthy individuals who are then followed over a number of years to see what diseases they develop and from what causes they die. Differences in measures taken at baseline between those who do and do not develop disease indicate likely risk factors for disease: people who die of cancer, for example, are more likely to have smoked at baseline than those who did not, suggesting smoking contributes to risk for developing cancer. Each of the studies using this form of analysis has found that baseline measures of SES predict subsequent health status, while health status is less able to predict SES (e.g. Marmot et al. 1991). Socio-economic status is therefore generally seen as a *cause* of differences in health status rather than a consequence. Other data supporting the social causation model show that as people move from employment to unemployment as a result of factors unrelated to their health, many people's health deteriorates and mortality among older individuals increases (Montgomery et al. 2013). However, it should be noted that while such transient processes may significantly influence health, childhood factors continue to exert their influence well into adulthood. Kittleson et al. (2006), for example, reported a longitudinal study involving over a thousand male medical students and found that despite them all becoming doctors, and therefore occupying the same socio-economic group, those who came from economically deprived backgrounds were more than twice as likely to develop **coronary heart disease** (CHD: see Chapter 8 ☞) before the age of 50 years than those from more affluent backgrounds, even after adjusting for other risk factors including body mass index, cholesterol level, amount of exercise, smoking, hypertension, diabetes mellitus and parental history of heart disease.

Different health behaviours

We identified in Chapter 1 ☞ how a number of behaviours influence our health. With this in mind, one obvious potential explanation for the higher levels of ill health and **premature mortality** among people in the lower socio-economic groups is that they engage in more health-damaging and less health-promoting behaviours than those in the higher socio-economic groups. This does seem to be the case. People in lower socio-economic groups in industrialised countries tend to smoke, and drink more alcohol, eat a less healthy diet and take less leisure exercise than the better-off (e.g. Clare et al. 2014). However, there is consistent evidence that while differences in health-related behaviours account for some of the socio-economic differences in health, they do not provide the full story. In a study of over 8,000 US older men and women, for example, Nandi et al. (2014) found that people in lower SES groups were nearly three times more likely to die over a period of ten years. Two thirds of this variance was accounted for by diet, smoking, and so on. The other third was directly attributable to their SES. Thus low SES appears to exert an influence on health both by its association with less healthy eating habits and behaviours and also independently of behaviour.

What is perhaps worth considering here is *why* people in the lower socio-economic groups engage in more health-compromising behaviours. It does not appear to be the result of lack of knowledge (Narevic and Schoenberg 2002). Rather, it may be a deliberate choice based on a calculation of the costs and benefits of such behaviours.

Work by Graham (1994), for example, found that working-class women smokers were well aware of the adverse health consequences of smoking, but continued to do so as it helped them cope with the day-to-day stresses of running a family with low economic resources. More recently, Wood et al. (2010) found that many working-class mothers were aware of government guidelines on healthy eating, but this knowledge was often superficial and only formed part of their decision-making in relation to eating. Priority in food choice was often based on taste, being filling, hot and appetite-satisfying. Eating unhealthy foods was justified in various ways, and just like the smokers interviewed by Graham, many mothers considered their meals acted as a form of emotional support that could improve other aspects of family well-being. The type of health-behaviour choices we make, and in some cases the availability of such choices, may be constrained by the social context in which we live.

Access to health care

Access to health care is likely to differ according to both personal characteristics and the health-care system with which the individual is attempting to interact. The majority of studies of this phenomenon have been conducted in the USA, where different health-care systems operate for those with and without health insurance. Here, the less well off have clearly received poorer health care. Rahimi et al. (2007), for example, found that some individuals experienced substantial financial barriers to health care following a myocardial infarction (MI: see Chapter 8 ☞). Eighteen per cent of their large sample of patients, the majority of whom had health insurance, reported that financial barriers prevented them from having appropriate care: 13 per cent reported financial barriers to accessing appropriate medication. Poor access to health care or medication was associated

coronary heart disease
a narrowing of the blood vessels that supply blood and oxygen to the heart. Results from a build-up of fatty material and plaque (atherosclerosis). Can result in angina or myocardial infarction.

premature mortality
death before the age it is normally expected. Usually set at deaths under the age of 65 years.

with poorer quality of life, more hospitalisation and higher levels of angina.

By contrast, in the UK where the economic barriers to health care are less stark than in the USA, people in the lower socio-economic groups access health care more frequently than those in the higher SES groups (see Figure 2.2), suggesting that no such economic division is found in the UK. Unfortunately, these data do not address whether the increased use of health-care resources is sufficient to counter the additional levels of poor health associated with low economic status. What evidence there is suggests this is not the case. The Scottish Executive's (1999) report on health inequalities, for example, revealed considerable differences between the rates of a number of medical and surgical procedures across the poor and the more affluent areas of Scotland: rates of hip replacements, hernia repairs and varicose vein surgery were much higher per head of population among the better-off than those living in economically deprived areas. In addition, although a higher percentage of the most deprived sections of society received **coronary artery bypass grafts** for CHD than did those in the higher SES groups, the relative difference was not as great as the differences in the **prevalence** of CHD between the groups. Although more people received surgery, the poorer population remained relatively deprived of health care in comparison to those in the higher SES groups.

Unfortunately, these differences can be difficult to remedy. In 2003, the UK government (Department of Health 2003) established a high priority programme to

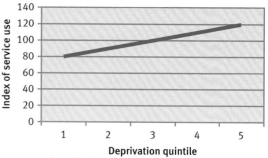

Figure 2.2 Health service use according to level of social deprivation in Scotland in 1999

Source: Scottish Executive (1999).

reduce health inequalities across England through a variety of social and health service interventions, including improvements in health service delivery in deprived areas, improving housing and reducing child poverty. A 2007 report (Department of Health 2007) identified an increase in inequalities in life expectancy over this time. There was also mixed evidence of the impact of this initiative on cancer and heart disease rates. Overall, differences in cancer rates over the social groups did lessen, but the differences in rates of heart disease actually increased. In addition, the gap between the quality of primary care services in middle-class and working-class areas increased. A further example of the differences in health provision in primary care can be found in an Australian study reported by Stocks et al. (2004) who found that patients from high socio-economic groups were more likely to be prescribed **statins** than people with the equivalent levels of cholesterol from low-income groups. People from lower socio-economic groups may also be less likely to seek appropriate medical care even when it is available (Wamala et al. 2007). Finally, even in contexts where treatment may be available without prescription, there may be inequalities in access. In the USA, for example, Bernstein et al. (2009) found that nicotine replacement therapy, a central element of any smoking cessation programme (see Chapter 6 (☛)), was less available and more expensive in pharmacies in the poorer suburbs of New York than the more affluent ones. Cigarettes were equally accessible throughout the city.

Environmental factors

A third explanation for differences in health across social groups suggests that people in lower socio-economic

---

coronary artery bypass graft

surgical procedure in which veins or arteries from elsewhere in the patient's body are grafted from the aorta to the coronary arteries to improve blood flow to the heart muscle.

prevalence

the percentage or total number of people to have a disease in a given population at any one time. Contrasts with **incidence**, which is the number or percentage of people who develop a particular disease within a particular time-frame. Prevalence is the number or percentage of existing cases, incidence is the number of new cases.

statins

drugs designed to reduce cholesterol levels.

groups are exposed to more health-damaging environments, including working in dangerous settings such as building sites, and have more accidents than those in the higher socio-economic groups throughout their working life. In addition, they may experience home conditions of low-quality housing, dampness and higher levels of air pollution than those in the higher socio-economic groups (World Health Organization 2010). The less economically well off are likely to live closer to main roads carrying high levels of traffic, airports, polluting industry, rubbish dumps and power stations. These risks may be particularly problematic for children as a consequence of their physical status and their chronic exposure to such pollutants. Schools, for example, tend to be close to children's homes, so if a child lives in a polluted environment, they are also likely to experience this adverse condition at school. Excessive exposure to adverse environments may interact with poor health behaviours and health status in a multiplicative risk to health (WHO 2010).

Environmental factors may also work through social and psychological pathways. Distance from exercise facilities, poor traffic safety, or poor environmental conditions may reduce levels of exercise (including walking to school; Panter et al. 2010) among both children and adults (e.g. Page et al. 2010). That said, only 3 per cent of respondents in a large US survey reported that environmental factors such as 'no safe place to ride or walk' prevented them from engaging in these sorts of exercise (DOT 2003).

A second pathway may be a direct consequence of poor living conditions. Both adults and children living in poor housing, for example, are more likely to suffer from poor respiratory health and asthma (e.g. Quinn et al. 2010). The overcrowding associated with poor housing may also have a more subtle and long-term impact, and is associated with high levels of stress hormones and, in animals, accelerated development of **atheroma** and CHD (Baum et al. 1999).

Other subtle processes may also be at work. One example of this can be found in research examining the effect of the type of housing we occupy. In Britain, premature mortality rates are about 25 per cent higher among tenants than owner-occupiers (Filakti and Fox 1995). Tenants also report higher rates of long-term illness than owner-occupiers. Woodward et al. (2003), for example, found that after adjusting for age, male renters were one-and-a-half times more at risk of developing

CHD than male owner-occupiers; women renters were over twice as likely to develop CHD as their owner-occupier counterparts. There are a number of explanations for these differentials:

● renters may experience more damp, poor ventilation, overcrowding and so on;

● rented occupation may be further away from amenities, making access to leisure facilities or good-quality shops more difficult;

● renters earn less than people who own their house;

● the psychological consequences of living in differing types of accommodation may directly impact on health.

Although the fourth pathway has received little attention, Macintyre and Ellaway (1998) found that a range of mental and physical health measures were significantly associated with housing tenure even after controlling for the quality of housing, and the age, sex, income and self-esteem of their occupiers. They interpreted these data to suggest that the type of tenure itself is directly associated with health. They suggested, for example, that the degree of control we have over our living environment may influence mood, levels of stress, and perceived control over a wider set of health behaviours – all of which may contribute to ill health. In addition, negative social comparisons – considering one's own house as worse than others – appears to have a direct effect on self-esteem, anxiety and depression, which may in turn influence health (Ellaway et al. 2004).

The stress hypothesis

The implication of the previous section is that poor housing leads to stress, which in turn leads to ill health. This argument can be widened to suggest that differences in stress experienced as a result of a variety of factors may contribute to differences in health across the social groups. This seems a reasonable hypothesis, as we know that people in lower SES groups experience more stress than their more affluent counterparts (e.g. Marmot et al. 1997), have less personal resources to help them cope with them

---

atheroma
fatty deposit in the intima (inner lining) of an artery.

IN THE SPOTLIGHT

Inequalities of health provision

There is consistent evidence that where we live contributes to the quality of the health care we can potentially receive. Some of these differences may be obvious. In the UK, for example, all medicine prescriptions are free in Wales but cost £8.20 per item in England. Other differences are less obvious, but still very real. In 2014, the Macmillan Cancer charity noted significant variation in cancer survival across England. The percentage of people dying from cancer following diagnosis in the areas with the worst prognosis (including much of South East England) were nearly 60 per cent higher than in the best areas (e.g. North East Hampshire): a 38 versus 24 per cent death rate. Scattered within the South East,

however, were areas such as Westminster and Richmond in Surrey with relatively good death rates (28 per cent). These differences may be attributable to a range of factors, not the least of which is the amount of money spent on cancer care in each area. Data published in the *Daily Telegraph* (2007) showed the highs and lows of spending on cancer (see table below).

Of course, it is possible that high levels of spending on cancer were to the detriment of treatment of other conditions, and may not represent the quality of service actually provided. However, the differences across the country on treatments considered to be a high priority by the national government is of concern, and may need to be addressed at a governmental level.

Most spent (per person)	Least spent (per person)
1 Nottingham City £17,028	Oxfordshire £5,182
2 Knowsley £16,819	Dorset £5,259
3 Manchester £14,999	Bedfordshire £5,262
4 Tower Hamlets, London £14,767	Cornwall and Isles of Scilly £5,749
5 Heart of Birmingham £14,511	Harrow, Middlesex £5,800
6 Salford Teaching £14,118	South Gloucester £5,902
7 City and Hackney, London £13,722	Herefordshire £5,967
8 Leicester City £13,217	West Sussex Teaching £6,038
9 Newham, London £12,753	Northumberland £6,108
10 Wakefield £12,454	Yorkshire, East Riding £6,379

(Finkelstein et al. 2007), and that stress can adversely impact on health (see Chapter 11 (☞). Some of the stresses and restricted life opportunities experienced more frequently by people in lower socio-economic groups than by the economically better off include:

● Childhood: family instability, overcrowding, poor diet, restricted educational opportunities;

● Adolescence: family strife, exposure to others' and own smoking, leaving school with poor qualifications, unemployment or low-paid and insecure jobs;

● Adulthood: working in hazardous conditions, financial insecurity, periods of unemployment, low levels of control over work or home life, negative social interactions;

● Older age: no or small occupational pension, inadequate heating and/or food.

Wilkinson (1990) took the stress hypothesis one stage further. He compared data on income distribution and life expectancy across nine Western countries and found that, while the overall wealth of each country was not associated with life expectancy, the income *distribution* across the various social groups (i.e. the size of the gap between the rich and poor) within each country was. The correlation between the two variables was a remarkable 0.86: the higher the income disparity across the population, the worse its overall health. Longitudinal studies provide further relevant data. Forwell (1993), for example, tracked average age of mortality and income distribution in Glasgow between the years 1981 and 1989. During this period, there was a significant increase in the income distribution within the population: the income of the richer section of society increased significantly more than that of the people in the lower SES groups. As these income disparities increased over this period, so did rates of premature mortality across the lower-income groups, despite their access to material goods (food, clothing and so on) remaining relatively constant over time, or even improving.

In his explanation of these phenomena, Wilkinson suggested a form of 'hierarchy-health hypothesis', which posits that simply being aware of one's position in the hierarchy influences health. According to Wilkinson, awareness of being low in the hierarchy and being 'aware' of one's relative lack of resources is itself stressful and may cause negative emotional responses, regardless of more objective measures of wealth or status. Support for this approach can be derived from the findings of Singh-Manoux et al. (2005), who found subjective SES was a better predictor of health than actual measured SES.

In a later explanation, Wilkinson suggested that wider wealth disparities within society were associated with lower levels of social cohesion and **social capital** (Wilkinson and Pickett 2010). Low social

capital is associated with both individual distrust and dissatisfaction, and social factors such as high levels of crime. It involves not feeling safe in the community in which you live: a perception that is inherently stressful. In one study of this phenomenon, Taylor et al. (2012) found that women with the highest levels of mental health problems included those who were single parents, unable to work or unemployed, had poor finances, and felt unsafe in their home and lacking in control over their life. Considering its effects on health, Scheffler et al. (2008) examined the association between social capital and the incidence of acute coronary events such as MI in different areas of California, and found that high levels of community-level social capital were associated with an 11 per cent lower rate of coronary events. This protective effect was largely confined to people whose household income was below $54,000 (around the 60th US income percentile). In reality, while low social capital is associated with low SES, it may exert an independent influence

> **social capital**
> feelings of social cohesion, solidarity and trust in one's neighbours.

Photo 2.1 Just kids hanging around. But how will their life circumstances affect their health (and perhaps that of others)?

Source: Photofusion Picture Library/Robert Brook.

on health. Aida et al. (2011), for example, found both SES and social capital to be a related and independent influence on health.

A further factor related to social capital that may co-vary with SES is the social support available to the individual. A large number of positive social relationships and few conflictual ones may buffer individuals against the adverse effects of the stress associated with low economic resources. Conversely, a poor social support system may increase risk for disease (Barth et al. 2010). Sadly, the potentially protective effect of good social support may be less available than previously. In contrast to research conducted in the 1950s, people in the higher social groups now appear to have more social support than those in the lower social groups, particularly where low socio-economic status is combined with high levels of social mobility and frequent changes of address (Chaix et al. 2007).

Work status and stress

Some of the excess mortality associated with low SES may be a consequence of the different work environments experienced by people across the socio-economic groups. Part of this difference may reflect the physical risks associated with particular jobs. Subtle work factors may also influence behaviour. Binge drinking, for example, has been associated with job alienation, job stress, inconsistent social controls, and a work drinking culture (e.g. Bacharach et al. 2004). Similarly, long work hours, lack of control over work and poor social support have been associated with high levels of smoking among blue-collar workers (e.g. Kouvonen et al. 2005). Other psychological research has focused on theories which suggest there is something intrinsic to different work environments that impacts directly on health–work stress.

One of the first theoretical models to systematically consider elements of the work environment that contributed to stress and illness was developed by Karasek and Theorell (1990). Their model identified three key factors that contribute to work stress:

1. the demands of the job;

2. the degree of freedom to make decisions about how best to cope with these demands (job autonomy);

3. the degree of available social support.

The theory differs markedly from previous theories that suggested occupational stress was an outcome of the demands placed on the person – the classic 'stressed executive'. Instead, it suggests that only when high levels of demands are combined with low levels of job autonomy, and perhaps low levels of social support (a situation referred to as high job strain), will the individual feel stressed and be at risk for disease. When an individual experiences high levels of demand combined with high levels of autonomy (e.g. being able to choose when and how to tackle a problem) and good social support, they will experience less stress. In contrast to the 'stressed executive' model, those in high-strain jobs are often blue-collar workers or people in relatively low-level supervisory posts (see Figure 2.3).

The majority of studies exploring the health outcomes of differing combinations of these work elements support Karasek's model. Kuper and Marmot (2003) found that within their cohort study of over 10,000 UK civil servants, those with low decision latitude and high demands were at the highest risk of developing coronary heart disease. Similarly, Clays et al. (2007) reported that average **ambulatory blood pressure** at work, home and while asleep was significantly higher in workers with

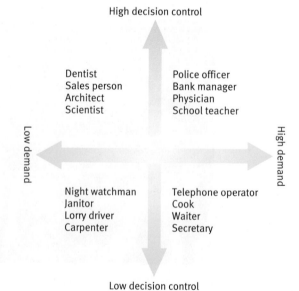

Figure 2.3 Some of the occupations that fit into the four quadrants of the Karasek and Theorell model

ambulatory blood pressure
blood pressure measured over a period of time using an automatic blood pressure monitor which can measure blood pressure while the individual wearing it engages in their everyday activities.

Ploubidis, G.B., Benova, L., Grundy, E. et al. (2014). Lifelong socio economic position and biomarkers of later life health: testing the contribution of competing hypotheses. *Social Science and Medicine* online 119, 258–65.

Background

Health differentials as a function of socio-economic status are smaller among older than younger individuals. Nevertheless, they exist, and this paper explored competing hypotheses about their causes. The four hypotheses they explored were:

1. the *critical life period hypothesis:* early socio-economic position (SEP) directly impacts on health in older age;

2. *chains of risk hypothesis:* early SEP exerts an influence indirectly through its influence on later SEP: SEP as a young person predicts SEP at an older age, which predicts health;

3. *accumulation of risk hypothesis:* early and late SEP, in combination, influence later life health, and

4. *social drift:* early life health predicts later life health and SEP.

Method

The study used data from the English Longitudinal Study of Ageing (ELSA). This measured personal and health data on a representative sample of individuals over the age of 50 years at baseline measurement in 1998, 1999 or 2001. Data in this study were obtained from similar measures made in 2007 and 2009. Measures taken at these time points were:

- ELSA life history interviews (2007): examined recall of early life SEP based on measures such as parental occupation, housing tenure, the number of people per room, and so on. Also included recall of early life health, including episodes of missing school for more than one month, restriction of activities for three months, and so on.

- Later life measures (2009): included later life income, total net wealth, physical health, including measurements of lung function, and self-report health. They also took measures of fibrinogen: a protein which influences the degree to which blood is likely to clot. High levels of fibrinogen contribute to risk for coronary heart disease. Other measures included age, gender, marital status and cognitive ability, all of which were seen as 'confounders': that is, they may influence the relationship between the key variables of the study: early and later life SEP and later health outcomes.

Analysis and results

The study used structural equation modelling to examine the relationships between the key variables under study. This allowed them to examine the strength of relationship between each of the variables they measured, to determine causal pathways between them (particularly early life variables predicting later life outcomes) and analysis of the overall 'fit' of the statistical models they derived. This was particularly important as each of the different hypothesis was associated with a different statistical model. The analyses tested the various hypotheses in order of simplest to most complex, and their results reflect this increase in complexity of modelling.

Men

- *Impact of early life SEP:* Early life SEP had a strong positive association with later health. This association was stronger for older groups (aged over 75 years) than younger groups (aged over 65 years). In the younger men, this relationship was largely indirect (mediated via early life health and later life SEP), supporting the causal chain hypothesis. In men over the age of 75 years, there was a direct association between early life SEP and later health, supporting the critical period hypothesis.

- *Impact of early life health:* Early life health did not predict later life SEP: rejecting the social drift hypothesis.

● *Impact of early life health:* Higher later life SEP had a positive direct effect on later life physical health in all age groups, but the relationship was weaker in the over-75 years age group. The combination of early and later life SEP made the strongest contribution to later life physical health, supporting the accumulation hypothesis.

Women

● *Impact of early life SEP:* Early life SEP had a strong positive association with later health. This association was stronger for older groups (aged over 75 years) than younger groups (aged over 65 years). Among all women, both direct and indirect routes of influence were found. As in men, among older women the direct route of influence was the strongest (and stronger than that found in men). In younger women, the statistical modelling found the dominant route was through the chains of risk route: that is, the influence of early SEP was largely mediated through late life SEP.

● *Impact of early life health:* Early life health did not predict later life SEP: rejecting the social drift hypothesis.

● *Impact of early life health:* The accumulation hypothesis (early life SEP and later life SEP effects combined) made the strongest contribution to later life physical health inequalities in all age groups, with later life SEP dominating the effect in women

up to 74 years old, but early life SEP in women over 75.

Discussion

Overall, the data show that SEP either in early or later life are independently predictive of later health. Conversely, early health does not predict SEP. The relationship between SEP and health is somewhat complex, with differences in effect dependent on gender (women are affected more than men by early SEP) and age (older participants were more influenced by early SEP than younger participants). This appears a somewhat anomalous finding: intuitively one would expect a stronger association between childhood events among younger rather than older participants. The researchers' explanation for this finding is that the 75-year-olds would have spent at least part of their childhood in the great depression in the 1930s, and those in the lower SEP groups may have experienced a profound and unusual impact on their health as a child and adult as a consequence. The most obvious weakness of the study is the very long-term recall of childhood events (and potentially exploration of issues such as housing tenure unknown to children). These may have been influenced by poor recall, and biased by poor health or depression in older adulthood. The researchers argue that while such biases did exist, they were not sufficient to bias the results to such a degree that they were no longer valid.

high job strain compared with others. Similar findings have been found across a range of European countries and studies (Kivimäki et al. 2012). By contrast, there is no evidence that job strain is related to the development of cancer (e.g. Gudbergsson et al. 2007).

WHAT DO YOU THINK?

One sentence in the discussion about job strain has led to a number of key questions: 'Those who are in high-strain jobs are often blue-collar workers or people in relatively low-level supervisory posts.' This has led critics of the Karasek model to question whether job strain is directly related to poor health, or whether the measure of job strain is simply a marker for occupying low SES.

Certainly, many of the jobs associated with high job strain are typically those considered to be 'working class'. So, Karasek and others have begun to explore whether job strain is simply a marker for social class (the third, hidden, variable), whether job strain impacts on health independently of social class, or whether job strain interacts with social class to determine risk of disease. The final model would suggest, for example, that a combination of being from a lower socio-economic group and in a high job-strain occupation would be particularly toxic, while having low-strain occupation would mitigate against the negative effects of being from a lower socio-economic group. How would you set about investigating this phenomenon, and what would you expect to find?

An alternative model of work stress has been proposed by Siegrist et al. (1990). They suggested that work stress is the result of an imbalance between perceived efforts and rewards. High effort with high reward is seen as acceptable; high effort with low reward combine to result in emotional distress and adverse health effects. This theory has received less attention than that of Karasek, and most studies of this theory (see de Lange et al. 2003) have focused on the impact of imbalance on well-being rather than physical health. Nevertheless, in a five-year longitudinal study tracking over ten thousand British civil servants (Stansfeld et al. 1998) both Karasek's and Siegrist's theories received some support: lack of autonomy, low levels of social support in work, and effort–reward imbalance each independently predicted poor self-report physical health. Even more impressively, Bosch et al. (2009) found that high levels of work stress, indicated by high workload, low social support, and high effort–reward imbalance were associated with increasingly impaired immune function, to the extent they considered work stress to 'contribute to immunological aging'.

Work–life balance and stress

Differing working conditions may differentially affect our health. But we only spend a proportion of our time at work, so how does this risk combine with other, out of work, factors to influence health? In a review of this issue, Kuper et al. (2002) considered the joint impact of a high-strain or high-reward imbalance job and either being in a low or higher SES group, and found a synergy between the two. A combination of low SES and high-stress job increased the risk of developing CHD more than having a high-stress job and being in a higher SES. This is probably because those in the high strain/low SES experience more stress both at home and at work than those in the high stress/higher SES group.

A particular example of this combined risk can be found in a phenomenon known as work–home spillover – the continuation of responsibilities within the home after work. Although there are some exceptions, this still affects more women than men (Krantz and Lundberg 2006), and where it occurs it can adversely impact on health. Hammig et al. (2009), for example, found that around 12.5 per cent of their sample of Swiss employees had a high work–life spillover, and those in this category were most likely to report poor health, anxiety and depression, lack of energy and optimism, serious backache, headaches, sleep disorders and fatigue. Spillover effects may also influence the health of the wider family. Devine et al. (2006) found that mothers experiencing work–home spillover, especially those from lower socio-economic groups, may compromise on things like the quality of food they cook to help cope with the time challenges of their work. More positively, when work practices are adjusted to reduce the frequency of spill-over, these changes may reduce smoking and excess drinking, increase levels of exercise and healthy eating, and improve sleep (Moen et al. 2013).

Unemployment

Having a stressful job impacts on health. But not having a job may also have adverse health consequences. The effects of unemployment appear to impact on both young and old. Gallo et al. (2006), for example, found that 51- to 61-year-olds who involuntarily lost their jobs were at particularly high health risk, experiencing significantly higher rates of heart attacks and stroke than those still in work. Not surprisingly, the impact of unemployment is worst for those with little savings or financial security. Ferrie et al. (2001), for example, found that people in good health reported increased numbers of minor health complaints after being made redundant, but noted that the key cause of their ill health appeared to be financial insecurity rather than the loss of job per se. The threat of unemployment may also be sufficient to adversely influence health. Dragano et al. (2005) found a combination of work stress (based on the effort–reward model) and the threat of redundancy was associated with a four-fold higher prevalence of self-reported poor health compared to individuals without these problems.

Minority status and health

A second factor that discriminates between people in society is whether or not they occupy majority or minority status within the general population. Perhaps the most obvious minority within any population are people who differ from the majority in terms of skin colour: often considered under the rubric of ethnic minorities. Nazroo (1998) pointed out that ethnicity encompasses a variety of issues, including language, religion, migration, culture, ancestry and forms of identity. Each of these may individually or together contribute to differences between the health of different ethnic groups. He therefore warned about considering all people in all ethnic minority groups as one single entity. These cautions are perhaps reflected in findings that in the UK, while rates of ill-health and premature mortality among people from ethnic minorities are generally higher than those of the indigenous population, people from the Caribbean experience better health (Wild and McKeigue 1997). The prevalence of different diseases also varies across ethnic groups. Rates of heart disease among British men from the Indian sub-continent, for example, are 36 per cent higher than the national average. The Afro-Caribbean population has particularly high rates of **hypertension** (Lane et al. 2002a) and **strokes**, while levels of diabetes are high among Asians (Mindell and Zaninotto 2006). By contrast, rates of many cancers are relatively low among people of Caribbean or West African origin (Mindell and Zaninotto 2006).

In searching for explanations of the relatively poor health among people in ethnic minorities, a number of issues have to be borne in mind. Perhaps the most important is that a disproportionate number of them also occupy low socio-economic groups. Before suggesting that being in an ethnic minority *alone* influences health, the effects of these socio-economic factors need to be excluded. This can be done by comparing disease rates between people in ethnic minorities and people from the majority population matched for income or other markers of SES, or by statistically partialling out the effects of SES in comparisons between majority and minority populations. Once this is done, any differences in mortality between the two groups lessen markedly. In one US study of ethnic disparities in risk for CHD, for example, Karlamangla et al. (2010) concluded that the majority of excess risk for coronary heart disease among Black and Hispanic men was largely related to their socio-economic status: the impact of ethnicity while of relevance was less strong. A similar direct association between poverty, low SES, and health problems experienced by many people in ethnic minorities has also been determined in the UK (Nazroo 1998).

Socio-economic status also exerts an influence *within* ethnic minorities. Just as for the majority population, people in the higher socio-economic groups generally live longer and have better health throughout their life than those with less economic resources (Karlamangla et al. 2010). However, again highlighting the dangers of considering people in different ethnic minorities as one single group, there are some exceptions to this rule. In the UK, there appears to be no SES-related differential risk for CHD among men born in the Caribbean or West or South Africa (e.g. Harding and Maxwell 1997). Similarly, while Tobias and Yeh (2006) found a strong relationship between SES and health among New Zealand Maoris, no such gradient was found among Pacific and Asian populations. Despite these cautionary notes, there is a general consensus that ethnicity impacts on health, and a number of explanations for these differences have been proposed.

Differential health behaviours

The behavioural hypothesis suggests that variations in health outcomes may be explained by differences in behaviour across ethnic groups. In the UK, for example, many Asian males of Punjabi origin consume high levels of alcohol and develop alcohol-related disorders; levels of consumption among Muslim people are minimal, with total abstinence being common. In a study of immigrants to the UK, Bhopal et al. (2002) reported that male Bangladeshi immigrants had a higher fat diet than most other ethnic groups, while Europeans were more physically active than Indians, Pakistanis or Bangladeshis (Hayes et al. 2002). In the USA, by comparison, Sharma et al. (2004) found that non-Hispanic Black men were twice as likely as the other ethnic groups they sampled (whites and Hispanics) to engage in a relatively high number of CHD-risk behaviours.

> **hypertension**
> a condition in which blood pressure is significantly above normal levels.
>
> **stroke**
> damage to the brain either as a result of a bleed into the brain tissue or a blockage in an artery, which prevents oxygen and other nutrients reaching parts of the brain. More scientifically known as a cerebrovascular accident (CVA).

Stress

A second explanation for the health disadvantages of people in minority groups focuses on the psychosocial impact of occupying minority status. People from ethnic minorities may experience wider sources of stress than majority populations as a consequence of specific stressors such as discrimination, racial harassment and the demands of maintaining or shifting culture. Two experimental studies (Clarke 2000; Clark and Gochett 2006) suggest mechanisms through which this may become manifest. In the first of these studies, Clarke found that among a sample of young African American women, the greater their experience of racism, the greater their increases in blood pressure during a task in which they talked about their views and feelings about animal rights. Clarke took this to indicate that these women had developed a stronger emotional and physiological reaction to general stress as a result of their long-term responses to racism.

In their second study, Clark and Gochett measured blood pressure, perceived racism, and the coping responses a sample of black American adolescents used in response to racism. They found blood pressure did not vary according to the level of racism the participants reported having experienced. However, blood pressure was highest among those individuals who were both subject to racism and whose coping response was not to 'accept it': individuals who perhaps became angry in response to racist behaviours. Accordingly, one contributor to high blood pressure in young black people may be chronically high arousal as part of a negative emotional or behavioural response to a variety of stressors, including racism. A related explanation is known as 'John Henryism'. This suggests that successful black individuals have to push harder than their white equivalents to achieve the same level of success, and that their higher blood pressure reflects the stress of such effort (Merritt et al. 2004; see also 'In the spotlight' in Chapter 8 ☞). By contrast, Todorova et al. (2010) identified depression, which has been associated with a range of chronic health problems, as a pathway through which discrimination towards Puerto Ricans living in the USA led to higher levels of a number of diseases.

Accessing health care

A third explanation for the relatively poor health among ethnic minorities may be found in the problems accessing health care. The situation in the USA was succinctly summarised in a report produced by the US Institute of Medicine (2002), which noted that:

- African Americans and Hispanics tend to receive lower quality of care across a range of diseases, including cancer, CHD, HIV/AIDS and diabetes;
- African Americans are more likely than whites to receive less desirable services, such as amputation of all or part of a limb;
- disparities are found even when clinical factors, such as severity of disease, are taken into account;
- disparities are found across a range of clinical settings, including public and private hospitals, and teaching and non-teaching hospitals;
- disparities in care are associated with higher mortality among minorities.

This situation is not limited to the USA, although it may be most evident there due to their clear records of the process of care for people of all ethnicities. In the UK, for example, there has been historically lower access to health-care provision by members of ethnic minorities, although increased ethnically sensitive record-keeping and legal requirement to provide equitable care are thought to prevent this now and in the future (Szcepura 2005).

Of course, whatever the provision of care, whether this is actually accessed is at the discretion of potential patients; not all of whom may choose to do so. The Health Utilisation Research Alliance (2006), for example, reported that New Zealand Maoris consulted their general practitioners at similar rates or less frequently than people of European origin, despite having significantly higher rates of disease. In the UK, black and Asian women appear to be less well informed of the risks of cervical cancer (www.cancerscreening.nhs.uk/cervical/news/013.html) than their white counterparts. They may also experience more barriers to attending screening. Low numbers of female family doctors in some areas of the UK with high ethnic minority populations have negatively impacted on Asian women's uptake of screening (Naish et al. 1994), while many Somali women do not access screening programmes as a result of a fatalistic attitude towards developing cancer (In sha' Allah: if it is God's will), embarrassment in relation to female circumcision, as well as more practical problems such as use of language, travel, and so on

(Abdullahi et al. 2009). Accordingly, differential use of health-care resources by people from ethnic minorities may result from a complex interaction between the types of health care available to them and choices they make on whether and how to access them.

Gender and health

An average woman's life expectancy in the industrialised countries is significantly greater than that of men. In the UK, for example, women have a life expectancy of around four years longer than men (81.6 years for women; 77.4 years for men: www.statistics.gov.uk). A large contributor to this difference is the earlier onset of CHD in men than women. Nearly three-quarters of those who die of a heart attack before the age of 65 years are men (American Heart Association 1995). However, of the men and women who do survive to the age of 65 years, women are still likely to live longer than men. Okamoto (2006), for example, reported data indicating that Japanese women aged 65 years were likely to live a further 22.5 years; men were likely to live an additional 17.4 years. Reddy et al. (1992) identified the male/female **risk ratios** for dying prematurely from a variety of diseases in the USA shown in Table 2.2.

These data indicate, for example, that men were nearly twice as likely to die before the age of 65 years of CHD than women, and over three times more likely to die from violence ('legal intervention' is a US euphemism for the death penalty). Despite these differences in disease rates and mortality, men typically report higher levels of self-rated health and contact medical services less frequently than women, while women report higher levels of physical symptoms and long-standing illnesses than men (Lahelma et al. 1999). It is worth noting that while this pattern of mortality is common among industrialised countries, the pattern of health advantage is

Table 2.2 Relative risk for men dying prematurely (before the age of 65) from various illnesses in comparison with women

Cause	Male/female ratio
Coronary heart disease	1.89
Cancer	1.47
Stroke	1.16
Accidents	2.04
Chronic lung disease	2.04
Pneumonia/flu	1.77
Diabetes	1.11
Suicide	3.90
Liver disease	2.32
Atherosclerosis	1.28
Renal disease	1.54
Homicide/legal intervention	3.22
Septicaemia	1.36

often different in industrialising countries. Here, differences in the life expectancy of men and women are smaller and in some cases are reversed (WHO 2008): women are more likely to experience higher rates of premature illness and mortality than men as a result of the experience of pregnancy and its associated health risks, as well as inadequate health services.

Biological differences

Perhaps the most obvious explanation for the health differences between men and women is that they are biologically different: being born female may bring with it a natural biological advantage in terms of longevity. Women, for example, appear to have greater resistance to infections than men across the lifespan. Other biological explanations have considered the role of sex hormones. For some years, it was thought that high levels of oestrogen in women delayed the onset of CHD by reducing the tendency of blood to clot and keeping blood cholesterol levels low. However, data from a variety of sources, including Lawlor et al. (2002) who reported rates of CHD in women living in the UK and Japan, have found no evidence of any reduction of risk prior to the menopause or increase in risk following it. Instead, the rates of CHD gradually rise as women get older, just as they do in men. Our understanding of the role of testosterone in men has also changed over time. High levels of testosterone were thought to increase risk levels of atheroma, and increase risk for MI. Now, the reverse appears to be true, and the majority of studies (e.g.

> **risk ratio**
>
> compares the probability of a certain event occurring in two groups. A risk ratio of 1 implies that the event is equally likely in both groups. A risk ratio greater than 1 implies that the event is more likely in the first group. A risk ratio less than 1 implies that the event is less likely in the first group.

Malkin et al. 2010) suggest high levels of testosterone are considered to be *protective* against CHD, probably as a consequence of its impact on lipids within the blood: high testosterone is associated with low levels of **HDL cholesterol**.

A second apparently biological cause of higher levels of disease in men involves their greater physiological response to stress than women. Men typically have greater increases in stress hormones and blood pressure in response to stressors than women, which may place them at more risk for CHD. However, there is increasing evidence these differences may not be the result of innate biological differences between the genders. Sieverding et al. (2005) found that blood pressure reactivity of men and women did not differ during a simulated job interview, but did vary according to the degree of stress they reported during the interview. Similarly, Newton et al. (2005) found no gender differences between men's and women's blood pressure and heart rate during discussions with previously unknown individuals. Dominance and not gender was consistently associated with blood pressure reactivity, with men who were challenged by a highly dominant male partner experiencing the greatest increase in blood pressure (and probably the most stress). It seems that it is not so much the gender of the individual that drives their physiological reactivity: rather, it is the type of stresses that the person is exposed to or the psychological response they evoke. Accordingly, any gender differences in stress reactivity may be more the result of long-term exposure to different stresses between the genders than biologically determined differences.

Behavioural differences

Further evidence that gender differences in health and mortality are not purely biological stems from studies that show clear and consistent health-related behavioural differences between men and women. Women consume less alcohol than men across a range of countries, are more likely to be abstinent, and less likely to engage in high volume drinking (Wilsnack et al. 2009). Although younger women may smoke at a similar or even greater levels than younger men (Pitel et al. 2010), by adulthood more men smoke than women (Kaplan et al. 2014). Men tend to eat more meat than women, who conversely tend to eat more vegetables and fruit (Arganini et al. 2012). The only health behaviour in which more men than women consistently engage in is work- or leisure-related exercise (Troiano et al. 2008).

Not only do men engage in more health-risking behaviours, but they are also less likely than women to seek medical help when necessary. Men visit their doctor less frequently than do women, even after excluding visits relating to children and 'reproductive care'. Socially disadvantaged men are half as likely to consult a doctor as their female counterparts when they are ill. High-earning men are even less likely to consult a doctor (Department of Health and Human Services 1998). The reasons for these behavioural differences may be social in origin. Courtenay (2000) contended that they arise from the different meanings given to health-related behaviours by men and women. According to Courtenay, men show their masculinity and power by engaging in health-risking behaviours and by not showing signs of weakness, even when ill. Traditional masculine beliefs endorse the idea that men are independent, self-reliant, strong and tough. Courtney suggested, for example, that when men say 'I haven't been to a doctor in years', they are both reporting a health practice and making a statement about their masculinity. Mahalik et al. (2007) found that masculine beliefs were stronger predictors of risky health behaviours including smoking and alcohol abuse than demographic variables such as education and income. These may be established relatively early in life: adolescents with traditional masculine beliefs are less likely to attend their doctor for a physical examination than those with less traditional beliefs (Marcell et al. 2007). We noted earlier that the one health-promoting behaviour that men consistently engage in more than women is leisure exercise. This may also act as a marker of masculinity and power and carry a social message as well as having implications for health.

Unfortunately, inequalities in power between the sexes may also adversely impact on women's health. One example of this can be found in the context of sexual behaviours, in which women are frequently less empowered than men. Abbott (1988), for example, found that 40 per cent of a sample of Australian women reported having had sexual intercourse on at least one occasion when they did not want to do so as a result of

---

HDL cholesterol

the so-called 'good cholesterol': see Chapter 8 ☛.

pressure from their sexual partner. This type of coerced sexual behaviour is associated with inconsistent condom use (Hoffman et al. 2006). Similarly, Chacham et al. (2007) found that Brazilian women aged between 15 and 24 years old who had been victims of physical violence by a partner or whose partners restricted their mobility were less likely to use condoms than those with more autonomy and control. Such behaviours clearly place them at risk of a variety of sexually transmitted diseases.

Economic and social factors

The negative impact of adverse socio-economic factors discussed earlier in the chapter does not affect men and women equally. In the UK, for example, nearly 30 per cent of women are economically inactive, and those in work are predominantly employed in clerical, personal and retail sectors in low-paid work. About two-thirds of adults in the poorest households in the UK are women, and women make up 60 per cent of adults in households dependent on Income Support (a marker of a particularly low income). Social isolation is also more frequent among women than men: women are less likely to drive or to have access to a car than men, and older women are more likely than older men to be widowed and to live alone. Women also appear more vulnerable to disrupted or poor social networks than men. Irregular social contact or dissatisfaction with a social network has been associated with both subjective health (Rennemark and Hagberg 1999) and mortality. Iwasaki et al. (2002), for example, found that in a population of older Japanese adults, women who were single and in irregular or no contact with close relatives were likely to die earlier than those with more relative contacts.

WHAT DO YOU THINK?

If health is, at least in part, a result of the social and environmental contexts in which we live, then how can society go about reducing them? Most health promotion has focused on changing individual behaviours, such as smoking, lack of exercise, and so on. But is this just tinkering at the edge? Should society work towards changing the health inequalities associated with low SES? Or should we adopt the American model of 'opportunity' to become upwardly economically mobile, and those left behind to fend for themselves? If society does take responsibility for reducing social inequalities, how can it set about doing so? And what about the health disadvantages of people in ethnic minorities and women with children at work? How much should society, and in particular psychologists and others involved in health care, involve itself in improving the health of these groups?

SUMMARY

Poverty is the main cause of ill health throughout the world. However, psychosocial factors may also influence health where the profound effects of poverty are not found.

One broad social factor that has been found to account for significant variations in health within societies is the socio-economic status of different groups. This relationship appears to be the result of a number of factors including:

● differential levels of behaviours, such as smoking and levels of exercise;

● differing levels of stress associated with the living environment, levels of day-to-day stress, and the presence or absence of uplifts;

● differential access to health care and differential uptake of health care that is provided;

● low levels of social capital and its associated stress in some communities.

The relationship between work and health is complex. Having a job is better for one's health than not having a job. However, if the strain of having a job is combined with significant demands away from the job, this can adversely impact on health. Many women, for example, appear to have high levels of work–home spillover, with its adverse effects on both mental and physical health.

● Jobs with high levels of demand and low levels of autonomy appear to be more stressful and more related to ill-health than other types of job.

- The financial uncertainties associated with unemployment also appear to have a negative impact on health.

A third factor that may influence health is being part of a social minority. The experience of prejudice may contribute significantly to levels of stress and disease.

As many people in minority ethnic groups may also occupy lower socio-economic groups, they may experience further stress as a result of this double inequity.

Gender may influence health, but not only because of biological differences between the sexes: indeed, many apparent biological differences may result from the different psychosocial experiences of men and women. In addition:

- men engage in more health-compromising behaviours than women;
- men are less likely to seek help following the onset of illness than women;
- many women are economically inactive or in lower-paid jobs than men. This makes them vulnerable to the problems associated with low socio-economic status.

Further reading

http://www.instituteofhealthequity.org/ Website of the University College, London Institute of Health Equity, which is aimed at 'reducing health inequalities on the social determinants of health'. An unashamedly activist site, intended to provide information to ensure improvements in health across the world. Its key publication is the 'Marmot Review', which is linked to the website.

http://www.sphsu.mrc.ac.uk/

Another resource website. The Medical Research Council's Social and Public Health Sciences Unit based at Glasgow University, with links to research on the impact on health of a range of social factors.

Wilkinson, R. and Pickett, K. (2010). *The Spirit Level: Why Equality is Better for Everyone.* Harlow: Penguin.

The most accessible psycho-socio-economic argument related to health inequalities, and its counterpart.

Snowdon, C.J. (2010). *The Spirit Level Delusion: Fact-checking the Left's New Theory of Everything*. London: Democracy Institute/Little Dice.

Courtenay, W.H. (2000). Constructions of masculinity and their influence on men's wellbeing: a theory of gender and health. *Social Science and Medicine*, 50: 1385–401.

An interesting critique of how men's attitudes towards their masculinity can influence their health-related behaviour and health.

Davidson, K.W., Trudeau, K.J., van Roosmalen, E. et al. (2006). Gender as a health determinant and implications for health education. *Health Education and Behavior*, 33: 731–4.

An interesting review of the impact of gender on health; which factors related to risk for disease associated with gender are modifiable, and suggestions about how to change them.

Arthur, M., Hedges, J.R., Newgard, C.D. et al. (2008). Racial disparities in mortality among adults hospitalized after injury. *Medical Care*, 46: 192–9.

We could have chosen so many papers showing racial disparities in health care. This paper shows that even when admitted to hospital as a consequence of trauma, white patients experience lower levels of mortality than black or Asian people.

Brondolo, E., Brady Ver Halen, N., Pencille, M. et al. (2009). Coping with racism: a selective review of the literature and a theoretical and methodological critique. *Journal of Behavioral Medicine,* 32: 64–88.

Kivimki, M., Ferrie, J.E., Brunner, E. et al. (2005). Justice at work and reduced risk of coronary heart disease among employees: the Whitehall II Study. *Archives of Internal Medicine*, 165: 2245–51.

A different take on stress and health.

For open-access student resources specifically written to complement this textbook and support your learning, please visit **www.pearsoned.co.uk/morrison**

Chapter 3
Health-risk behaviour

Learning outcomes

By the end of this chapter, you should have an understanding of:

- how to define and describe health behaviour

- the prevalence of key health behaviours associated with elevated disease risk

- the range and complexity of influences upon the uptake and maintenance of health-risk behaviour

- some of the challenges facing health behaviour research

The health costs of our behaviour

The World Health Organization (2009) demonstrates that the leading risks for death globally are high blood pressure (13 per cent of deaths), tobacco use (9 per cent), high blood glucose (6 per cent), physical inactivity (6 per cent) and being overweight or obese (5 per cent). Many of the most prevalent diseases – cancer, heart disease, stroke, respiratory diseases, diabetes – we could reduce significantly ourselves. In fact it is thought that approximately a third of deaths from such diseases could be eliminated by behaviour change. Patterns of behaviour are generally consistent with cancer statistics recorded in each country with variations, for example, between countries with continued high smoking rates (e.g. eastern Europe), or obesity and low activity rates (e.g. UK, Spain), Human behaviour plays a large part in human morbidity and mortality. Behaviours often set down in childhood, adolescence or in young adulthood play a major role in this, yet long-term consequences of some behaviours, for example, smoking, are rarely considered when we start them! As health psychologists, one of our primary goals is to gain better understanding of the factors that predict and maintain human behaviour, in order to help develop interventions to reduce behavioural risk factors for disease. This and the subsequent three chapters demonstrate the importance attached to this area of study.

Source: Boniol and Autier (2010) and see www.eurocadet.org

Chapter outline

Behaviour is linked to health. This has been shown over decades of painstaking research that has examined individual lifestyles and behaviour and identified relationships between these and the development of illness. For example, it has been estimated that up to three-quarters of cancer deaths are attributable to a person's behaviour. This chapter provides an overview of the evidence pertaining to an array of behaviour shown to increase an individual's risk of disease, such as unhealthy diet, smoking, excessive alcohol consumption, illicit drug use and unprotected sexual intercourse. Evidence regarding the negative health consequences of each type of behaviour is reviewed, and the prevalence of each behaviour considered. Both the health-risk behaviour described here and the health-enhancing behaviour described in Chapter 4 ☞ provide the impetus for many educational and public health initiatives worldwide.

What is health behaviour?

Kasl and Cobb (1966a: 246) defined health behaviour as 'any activity undertaken by a person believing themselves to be healthy for the purposes of preventing disease or detecting it at an asymptomatic stage'. This definition was influenced by a medical perspective in that it assumes that healthy people engage in particular behaviour, such as exercise or seeking medical attention, purely to prevent their chance of disease onset. Harris and Guten (1979), in contrast, defined health behaviour as 'behaviour performed by an individual, regardless of his/her perceived health status, with the purpose of protecting, promoting or maintaining his/her health'. According to this definition, health behaviour could include the behaviour of 'unhealthy' people. For example, an individual who has heart disease may change their diet to help to limit its progression, just as a healthy person may change their diet in order to reduce their future risk of heart disease.

However, these two definitions make a crucial assumption, i.e. that the behaviour is motivated by the goal of health. Many people engage in a variety of apparently health-related behaviour, such as exercise, motivated by reasons other than disease prevention.

For example, a person may exercise to lose weight and improve their appearance or as a means of making social contacts, or simply for pleasure (see also Chapter 5 ☞)! Nevertheless, whether intentional or not, engaging in health behaviour may prevent disease and may also prevent the progression of disease once it is established. Further elaboration of definitions of health behaviour was provided by Matarazzo (1984), who distinguished between what he termed '**behavioural pathogens**' and '**behavioural immunogens**', which in this text we call health-risk behaviours and health-protective behaviours respectively.

In spite of definitional differences, health behaviour research generally adopts the view that health behaviour is that which is associated with an individual's health status, regardless of current health or motivations.

The World Health Organization (2009) define 'health risk' as 'a factor that raises the probability of adverse

---

behavioural pathogen
a behavioural practice thought to be damaging to health, e.g. smoking.

behavioural immunogen
a behavioural practice considered to be health-protective, e.g. exercise.

health outcomes' (p. 6). As we will see in this chapter in the context of health risk, many of these risks are behavioural, although others are environmental, such as pollution or poverty, and so we address these where possible (see also Chapter 2 ☞).

It is worth bearing in mind history and generational change in perspectives on behaviour – what is considered health-risk behaviour has changed over the past century as medical understanding has developed: for example, we know now that smoking and excessive exposure to the sun carry significant risks for development of some cancers, whereas our ancestors did not. To further muddy the waters, there is also evidence of health benefits of some behaviours considered generally as 'risky'. Perhaps the best example is sun or ultraviolet radiation (UVR) exposure, including the use of indoor tanning machines, which is receiving growing attention in relation to skin cancer risk, a diagnosis with a significantly increased incidence in the past 50 years, particularly in younger females (Cancer Research UK, Lazovich and Forster 2005; Ferlay et al. 2013). In contrast, in the early twentieth century, sun exposure was considered useful in the treatment of skin tuberculosis, and today sunlight therapy may be offered in the treatment of skin disorders. Furthermore, there is evidence of beneficial effects of vitamin D levels (which are raised with sunlight exposure) to reduced risk of several diseases including osteoporosis, autoimmune disease, cardiovascular disease (and lower rates of several forms of cancer including of the breast, colon, prostate, ovary, lungs and pancreas (Holick 2004; Ingraham et al. 2008). Vitamin D from a typical diet is thought unlikely to be sufficient on its own to achieve these benefits: thus in this case a little bit of sunshine is beneficial. Later in this chapter we also raise the issue of beneficial effects of moderate alcohol consumption.

In order to test the nature and extent of associations between behaviour and health, longitudinal studies are necessary. One early and highly cited is the Alameda County study (Belloc and Breslow 1972), a large epidemiological study which collected data in 1965, 1973, 1985, 1988, 1994 and finally in 1999. This study followed 6,928 adults (aged over 20), all of whom were healthy at the beginning of the study, for over 30 years and compared the baseline behaviours of those people who developed disease and those who remained healthy. Key behavioural factors associated with health and longevity were identified, with a range of behaviours, later

named the 'Alameda seven', found to reduce subsequent development of disease and mortality. These were:

1. sleeping 7–8 hours a night;
2. not smoking;
3. consuming no more than 1–2 alcoholic drinks per day;
4. getting regular exercise;
5. not eating between meals;
6. eating breakfast;
7. being no more than 10 per cent overweight.

Men and women who performed 6 out of 7 of the above behaviours, in the final analysis, lived 7 and 11 years longer respectively than those performing <6, although in later re-analyses not snacking or not eating breakfast was not related to mortality. Overall, however, the Alameda findings contributed significantly to growing awareness of the associations between personal lifestyle behaviour and disease. The many publications (see Housman and Dorman 2005 for a chronological review of the survey and its findings) also concluded that the benefits of performing these activities were multiplicative and cumulative: in other words, not smoking as well as being active, conferred more than twice the benefit of only performing one of these behaviours, and furthermore the longer 'immunogens' (health-protective behaviours) were engaged in, the greater the benefits to our health and longevity (Breslow and Enstrom 1980).

Epidemiologists can clearly demonstrate that behaviour is predictive of mortality and that associations exist between specific behaviour and the onset of major illnesses such as heart disease or cancer. If, however, we are to prevent people from engaging in risk behaviour (the goal of health promotion – see Chapters 6 and 7 ☞), we also need to understand the psychological and social factors that contribute to the uptake and maintenance of risk behaviour or the avoidance of health-enhancing or preventive behaviour. Such studies are conducted by health and social psychologists rather than epidemiologists, and are referred to in this and the subsequent chapter, although addressed more fully in Chapter 5 ☞.

Health-risk behaviour

The message of the Director-General of the World Health Organization (WHO), in the opening to the *World*

Health Report (WHO 2002a: 3) was stark, but clear. It stated:

> *in many ways, the world is a safer place today. Safer from what were once deadly or incurable diseases. Safer from daily hazards of waterborne and food-related illnesses. Safer from dangerous consumer goods, from accidents at home, at work, or in hospitals. But in many other ways the world is becoming more dangerous. Too many of us are living dangerously – whether we are aware of that or not.*

This report by the WHO followed massive worldwide research into health risks in developed, developing and underdeveloped countries. Although specific health risks may vary across the world (for example, underconsumption of food in many African nations versus over-consumption in most Western countries), there are many commonalities such as the risk conferred by smoking tobacco. The WHO (WHO 2009) describes how (based on 2004 data) eight risk factors (alcohol use, tobacco use, high blood pressure, high body mass index, high cholesterol, high blood glucose, low fruit and vegetable intake, and physical inactivity) account for 61 per cent of cardiovascular deaths. In combination these same factors account for over three-quarters of ischaemic heart disease, which is the leading cause of death worldwide. More broadly defined, cardiovascular diseases (which includes heart disease, heart attacks, strokes) accounts for 36 per cent of all deaths in the EU Member States in 2010 (OECD 2012).

Table 3.1 list the 'top ten' risk factors for death globally according to income group (low, middle, high), which together account for more than a third of all deaths worldwide.

For reasons of length, we cannot address all risk factors in this chapter, even though the statistics attached to some are horrendous and thought-provoking: over two million childhood deaths occur *every year* in low-income countries as a result of being underweight, whereas in moderate- to high-income countries, including North America and Europe almost 2 million people die each year (based on 2004 figures) as a result of an obesity-related disease. Behaviour associated with high levels of **mortality** in developed countries are discussed in more detail here, as they have attracted the greatest attention from health psychologists to date:

- *heart disease*: smoking tobacco, high-cholesterol diet, lack of exercise;
- *cancer*: smoking tobacco, alcohol, diet, sexual behaviour;
- *stroke*: smoking tobacco, high-cholesterol diet, alcohol;
- *pneumonia, influenza*: smoking tobacco, lack of vaccination;
- *HIV/AIDS*: unsafe/unprotected sexual intercourse.

> **mortality**
>
> death. Generally presented as mortality statistics, i.e. the number of deaths in a given population and/or in a given year ascribed to a given condition (e.g. number of cancer deaths among women in 2000).

Table 3.1 Ranking of selected risk factors: 10 leading risk factor causes of death by income group, 2004

Overall	Low income[*] ranking	Middle income ranking	High income ranking
1. high blood pressure (12.8%);	2nd	1st	2nd
2. tobacco consumption (8.7%)	7th	2nd	1st
3. high blood glucose (5.8%);	5th	6th	5th
4. physical inactivity (5.5%)	8th	4th	4th
5. overweight and obesity (4.8%)	n/a[†]	3rd	3rd
6. high cholesterol (4.5%)	10th	7th	6th
7. unsafe sex (4.0%)	3rd	n/a[‡]	n/a[§]
8. alcohol consumption (3.8%);	n/a[†]	5th	9th
9. childhood underweight (3.8%)	1st	n/a[‡]	n/a[§]
10. indoor smoke from solid fuels (3.3%)	6th	9th	n/a[§]

[*] Countries grouped by **gross national income per capita** — low income USD 825m or less; high income USD 10,066m or more
[†] Low income countries have unsafe water, sanitation and hygiene ranked 4th, and suboptimal breastfeeding ranked 9th
[‡] Middle income countries have low fruit and vegetable intake in 8th and urban outdoor air pollution in 10th
[§] High income countries have low fruit and vegetable intake in 7th, urban outdoor air pollution in 8th and occupational risk in 10th

Source: WHO (2009).

With the exception of HIV/AIDS, these diseases are more common in middle age and beyond than in younger people. Given the worldwide increase in the proportion of the population aged 65 or above, the prevalence of such diseases in our communities will make increasingly significant demands on health-care systems. To illustrate this point further, approximately 5 per cent of the world population in 1950 were aged over 60; by 2012 this had increased to 11.11 per cent (approximately 810 million worldwide aged over 60, UN Dept of Economic and Social Affairs 2012). It is estimated that the over-60s will account for 20 per cent of the population by 2050 and, within this, those over 80 years old (the 'oldest-old') is likely to increase from 11 per cent in 1940 and 14 per cent in 2012 to 20 per cent by 2050 (United Nations Secretariat 2002). The rates of change vary across different regions of the world: for example, those over 65 has almost doubled in Australia over the past 50 years (from 10 to 20 per cent), whereas in the UK the change is less pronounced (from just over 15 per cent to 20 per cent). The implications of such statistics for health and social care services are clear, as is the need for health promotion directed at the elderly (see Chapter 7 ☛). Figure 3.1 shows the burden of ill health that can be attributed, in the EU at least, to behaviour or behaviour-related conditions. The data relate to DALYs – disability-adjusted life years – i.e. the number of years lost due to ill health or disability as well as due to early death, thus combining mortality and morbidity into one figure.

The next sections examine some of the major risk behaviours of importance in current times to those of all ages.

Smoking, drinking and illicit drug use

Smoking and alcohol consumption are leading risks for global deaths and disease (see also Lim et al, 2013), and along with illicit drug use also have significant addiction potential and social consequences.

Prevalence of smoking, drinking and illicit drug use

Globally the following behaviours contribute to a significant disease burden, including physical **morbidity** and

> ### morbidity
> costs associated with illness such as disability, injury.
>
> ### age-specific mortality
> typically presented as the number of deaths per 100,000, per annum, according to certain age groups: for example, comparing rates of death from cancer in 2001 between those aged 45–54 with those aged 55–64.

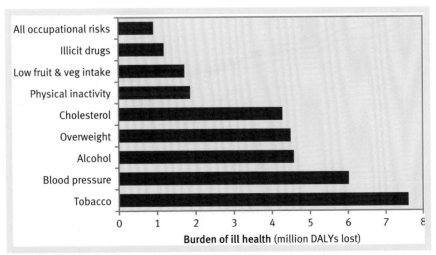

Figure 3.1 The burden of ill health that can be attributed to behaviour or behaviour-related conditions

Source: Anderson and Baumberg (2006).

death. It is perhaps not surprising that so much research attention has put them under scrutiny, and health policy has produced many guidelines and recommendations.

Smoking

After caffeine and alcohol, nicotine is the next most commonly used psychoactive drug in society today. While smoking behaviour receives a vast amount of negative publicity arising from the death toll attached to it, nicotine is a legal drug with sale of nicotine-based substances (cigarettes, e-cigarettes, cigars) providing many tobacco companies and governments with a vast income as a result of tobacco tax. Worldwide, almost 9 per cent of deaths (12 per cent of male deaths, 6 per cent of females; Global Health Risks report, 2009) are attributed to tobacco use, and as shown in Figure 3.2 tobacco creates the largest disease burden in developed countries. There have been some positive signs of a downturn in the prevalence and uptake of smoking over the past 50 years. Approximately 80 per cent of men and 40 per cent of women smoked in the UK during the 1950s, with this reducing significantly to 51 per cent of men but still 41 per cent of women by 1974 (Peto et al. 2000). Jumping forward three decades or so, 26 per cent of the English adult population (aged over 16 years)

smoked in 2002 and this has reduced further to just over 20 per cent in 2012 (ONS 2012; British Heart Foundation 2012; Health and Social Care Information Centre 2013). This pattern is reflected in the related figures presented in Figures 3.2 and 3.3 where you can see both gender and age group differences. Overall, these figures meet the target of 21 per cent by 2010 set out in 2004 (Public Service Agreements 2005–2008. Available at: www. hm-treasury.gov.uk/spend_sr04_psaindex.htm).

Currently concerns are growing regarding the burgeoning use of e-cigarettes amongst the under-25s, with as yet unclear evidence regarding long-term consequences (Pisinger and DØssing 2014) (see 'In the spotlight').

In the UK, legislation came into force in 2006 which prohibited smoking in enclosed work or public places, which may have contributed towards this downturn; however, as you will read here and in Chapter 5 ☞, the likely influences are many and varied.

While, overall, this reduced prevalence has been associated with a decrease in lung cancer rates, with the incidence, for example, in England and Wales dropping between 1999 and 2009 by 15 per cent for males and 13 per cent for females, actual female deaths increased by almost 5 per cent between 2004 and 2009 (Office for National Statistics 2010). The full benefits of decreased smoking, or negative consequences of any increase, will

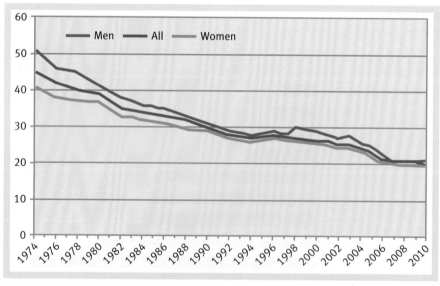

Figure 3.2 Adults smoking in Great Britain, trends for males and females 1974–2010.

1. For 1998 unweighted and weighted data are shown for comparison purposes. Weighted data are not available before this point.
2. The survey was not run in 1997/98 or 1999/00. A linear trend has been drawn between the data point before and after these years.

Source: General Lifestyle Survey 2010, Office for National Statistics 2012

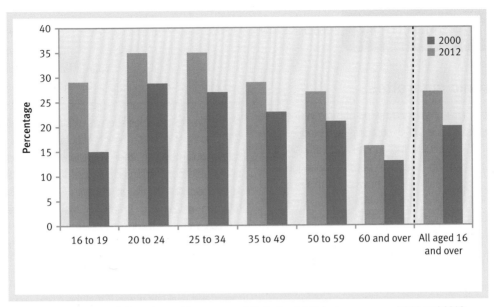

Figure 3.3 Prevalence of cigarette smoking among adults in Great Britain, by age group, 2000 and 2012

Source: *Opinions and Lifestyle Survey, Drinking Habits Amongst Adults, 2012*. Office for National Statistics (2012).

Photo 3.1 Do health warnings make a difference?

Source: Photofusion Picture Library/Libby Welch.

continue to be seen in mortality figures of future decades. The increased incidence of lung cancer among women over the past two decades is, in part, traceable to the increased prevalence of women smoking since the Second World War, and this worrying upturn looks likely to continue if recent survey figures are considered. Ethnic differences in smoking prevalence have also been reported and, whilst overall ethnic minority group figures suggest a lower smoking prevalence than among the total UK population, there are some subgroup exceptions (British Heart Foundation 2012, www.heartstats. org). In the 2004 Health Survey for England (these still remain the latest figures for ethnicity and smoking in the UK), 40 per cent of Bangladeshi men and 29 per cent of Pakistani men smoked compared to the then 24 per cent of White males. Bangladeshi men have also been found

Electronic cigarettes

Electronic nicotine delivery systems or e-cigarettes have been available since 2003 and are marketed as safe products which provide the sensation of smoking but without the known negative health consequences. However, do we really know yet whether this is a valid selling point? Analysis of the prevalence of use amongst young adult Americans aged 18–25 in three studies conducted over a five-year period, recorded significant increases in self-reported use of e-cigarettes in the past months – from 6 per cent in the 2009–10 study, to 19 per cent in 2010–11 to 41 per cent in the 2013 study, with particular increases amongst males in the first two studies (Ramo et al. 2015). Although, as this study showed, e-cigarettes are often used as an aid to quitting, we simply do not yet know conclusively as to whether these devices succeed in the long term or are better than alternative methods such as nicotine patches or gum (a recent meta-analysis suggests not, Grana et al. 2014).

A recent review of 76 studies (Pisinger and Døssing 2014) reports many findings of potential concern in terms of the content of the vapour (including carcinogenic compounds albeit at lower levels than tobacco cigarettes, and other chemicals and ultrafine harmful metal particles such as nickel). They also found 20 reports of adverse health effects including respiratory problems even after short-term usage, although no reliable conclusions could be drawn in that some study participants report benefits of use to cognitive function and even to breathing. Many of the reviewed studies were methodologically flawed, however, and significant conflicts of interest may be present in those studies conducted by e-cig manufacturers.

Needless to say, this behaviour requires long-term monitoring and evaluation and it may be many years before we know the full benefits (of their efficacy in smoking cessation) and risks. Whilst the health risks are likely to be significantly less than that of conventional tobacco smoking, the review authors conclude that 'Electronic cigarettes can hardly be considered harmless', particularly in those who were not previously smokers, a population which needs urgent further study before conclusions can be drawn as to whether e-cigarettes themselves act as a 'gateway' to conventional smoking behaviour. A story to watch over coming years.

to be at greater risk of coronary heart disease than other groups, and this has been attributed in part to their tendency to exercise less and smoke more than their white counterparts. In contrast, the percentage of Bangladeshi, Indian and Pakistani women smoking is significantly below the general population norm (Joint Health Surveys Unit 2005; BHF 2012). Aboriginal and Torres Strait islanders have been shown to have one of the highest prevalences of smoking recorded – with 51 per cent of these indigenous populations aged over 15 years smoking (Australian Bureau of Statistics 2005).

As well as culture, there are age differences in smoking prevalence: prevalence is highest in men aged 25 to 34 and women aged 20 to 24, with lowest levels seen, in the UK at least, in those over 60 (about 13 per cent). Amongst the more elderly, smoking was initiated before the medical evidence as to the health-damaging effects of smoking was clear and publicly available. Bratzler et al. (2002) review the evidence that smoking

in the elderly increases morbidity, disability and death, thus supporting the need for health promotion efforts to target smoking cessation in older people so as to enhance their quality of life and possibly their lifespan. The health gains of smoking cessation have been well documented. For instance, the ongoing American Cancer Society Cancer Prevention Study II, which has followed over a million American adults for over 24 years so far, reports significant decreases in **age-specific mortality** rates for former smokers compared with current smokers. This benefit is present in those aged over 60, and even in those who ceased smoking aged 70–74. Although elderly groups present particular challenges to health educators, due to the consistent finding that they

> **age-specific mortality**
> the mortality rate attributed to a specific age group

attribute many health consequences of smoking to general ageing processes, and that they are often highly dependent on the behaviour (psychologically and physically), interventions that combine age-relevant risk information and support are likely to be as effective in achieving smoking cessation as similar interventions in younger populations.

Alcohol consumption

Alcohol (ethanol) is the second most widely used psychoactive substance in the world (after caffeine) and in Westernised cultures at least it is considered an integral part of many life events, such as weddings, birthdays and even funerals. Social use of alcohol is widespread.

A significant increase in both the prevalence of drinking and the amount of alcohol consumed in the 11–15 years age group was seen between 1990 and 2000 (DOH 2000a, NatCen Social Research), although encouragingly, this seems to have changed in the subsequent decade. The 2010 General Lifestyle Survey (ONS 2011) reports a decline in prevalence amongst 11–15-year-olds from 27 per cent (boys) and 26 per cent (girls) in 1996 to 13 per cent of both in 2010. Data from the NatCen Social Research (NatCen) and the National Foundation for Educational Research (NFER) who repeated a survey of over 7,000 school children aged 11–15 in 2012 on behalf of the Health and Social Care Information Centre (2013) confirm this shift. Also, encouragingly, a decrease has been recorded in the prevalence of heavy drinking amongst 16- to 24-year-olds, there does, however, remain concern about adolescent drinking in many European countries due to its association with other behaviours (see also 'Issues').

In older age groups consumption over the past two decades has been relatively stable across Western Europe, although slow declines have been seen in countries where earlier levels were higher than average – including France, Spain, and more recent declines in countries with initially lower national levels, including the UK, Finland and Ireland (OECD Health Statistics 2014). Whilst the lowest prevalence of *heavy* drinking is seen in those over 65 years old (ONS 2011), recent trend data suggests that between 1994 and 2012, consumption in excess of UK recommended daily limits (see below) in those aged 65–74 years increased from 5.3 per cent to 14.0 per cent and from 6.0 per cent to 14.8 per cent in those aged 75 years or more, with this particularly evident among women (Health and Social Care Information Centre 2013). This is causing some public health concern, given physiological changes in older people, the likely presence of comorbidities and potential interactions with other medicines (Knott et al. 2015).

Recommended levels of drinking

Different individuals respond differently to the same amount of alcohol intake, depending on factors such as body weight, food intake and metabolism, the social context in which the drinking occurs, and the individual's cognitions and expectations. It is therefore difficult to determine 'safe' levels of drinking alcohol. While the recommended guidelines on 'safe' levels of alcohol consumption vary from country to country, the UK government's current recommended limit for weekly consumption is 28 units for males, and 21 units of alcohol for females. Some guidelines also recommend one or two alcohol-free days per week. For children, the guidance recommends that remaining alcohol free until 15+ is the healthiest option (Donaldson 2009), given evidence of longer-term consequences as described below.

There is some confusion internationally as to what constitutes a 'standard' measure or 'unit'. Typically, half a pint of normal-strength lager or a standard single measure of spirit (1/6 gill) or wine of average strength (11–12 per cent alcohol) = 1 unit. But what about the strength of the alcohol? For example, a standard drink in Japan is defined by government guidelines as 19.75 g alcohol, whereas in Europe a 'standard' drink would typically contain between 8 and 14 g of pure ethanol. The European Commission refer to safe levels as being under 40 g of alcohol a day for men (about 4 standard drinks) and under 20 g per day for women (about 2 standard drinks).

Many countries have specific national guidelines regarding the 'standard unit' of alcohol (Table 3.2), and guidelines regarding maximum 'gram per day'. The 'unit' size (grams of alcohol) vary as do the recommended weekly limits for males and females. Countries who do not have national guidelines (e.g. Belgium, China, Hungary and Russia) tend to follow WHO guidelines for sensible drinking:

● Women should not drink more than two drinks a day on average

● For men, not more than three drinks a day on average

Table 3.2 International 'Standard Unit' and daily limits where specified (selected countries only, based on 2015 data)

Country(ies)	Unit of alcohol (g)	Daily limits, (ranges where multiple countries)
France, Greece, Ireland, The Netherlands, Poland, Spain	10	Men 20g–30g, women 10–20g
Canada	13.6	Men 40g, women 27g
Denmark, Germany, Italy	12	Men 24g–36g, women 12g-24g
Japan	19.75	Men 19.75g–39.5g; women no guidance
Finland	11.0	Men 18.20g; women 10g
Portugal	14	Men 28g–42g, women 14g–28g
United Kingdom, Austria, Malta	8	Men 24g–32g, women 16g–24g
USA	14	Men 28g, women 14g

Source: http://www.drinkingandyou.com/site/pdf/Sensibledrinking.pdf (retrieved: November 2015).

- Try not to exceed four drinks on any one occasion
- Don't drink alcohol in some situations, such as when driving, if pregnant or in certain work situations and
- abstain from drinking at least once a week.

Illicit drug use

While about a third of UK resident individuals aged between 16 and 59 years old (British Crime Survey, Hoare and Flatley 2008) will try an illegal drug at least once in their lifetime, unlike what is seen with alcohol, very few go on to use such substances regularly. Between 3.5 and 7 per cent of the world's population will have used an illicit drug in the past year, with regular drug use tending to relate to cannabis use whereas dependent or problematic use classed as a drug abuse disorder tends to correspond to opiate use. About one-quarter of a per cent will have injected across the global population. Even cannabis, which is 'top' of the list of illicit drugs used, has a relatively low prevalence in terms of use 'in the past year' (7.6 per cent).

Amongst schoolchildren the use of Class A drugs (see Table 3.3) tends to relate to cannabis use, with a continuing downturn in prevalence reported over the past decade. In fact the prevalence in UK schoolchildren aged 11–15 years old was the lowest reported since

Table 3.3 Classification of drugs, UK

Drug	Mode of use	Classification
Amphetamines	Inject	A
Ecstacy	Oral	A
Cocaine	Sniff, inject	A
Crack	Inject, smoke	A
Heroin	Smoke, inject, sniff	A
LSD	Oral	A
Magic Mushrooms	Oral	A
Methadone	Oral	A
Amphetamines	Sniff, oral	B
Cannabis	Smoke, oral	B
Mephedrone	Sniff, inject	B
Tranquillisers	Oral, inject	B/C, depends on drug
Ketamine	Oral, sniff, inject	C
Poppers	Sniff	It is an offence for anyone other than a licensed outlet, such as a pharmacist, to supply amyl nitrite. Other types, e.g. butyl nitrite and isobutyl nitrite, are currently legal to possess and supply
Glue	Sniff	It is an offence to supply these if it is likely
Gas	Sniff	that the purpose is abuse

Source: The 1971 The Misuse of Drugs Act, HMSO, London (http://www.legislation.gov.uk/ukpga/1971/38/contents).
The 2005 Drugs Act amendments: http://www.opsi.gov.uk/acts/acts2005/ukpga_20050017_en_1

2001, with 12 per cent use in the last year, 7.5 per cent of which related to cannabis use and 3.6 per cent to volatile substance use including glue and gases. Less than 1 per cent had used any other illegal drug (Health and Social Care Information Centre 2013). This overall percentage for Class A drug usage other than cannabis is reflected in the adult population.

Negative health effects

Smoking

By 2008, smoking-attributable deaths had risen from approximately 3 million people worldwide in the late 1980s to approximately 5 million per year worldwide. It is predicted that over 1 billion people this century will die from tobacco-related causes (World Health Organization 2008). Such figures are staggering.

Tobacco products contain carcinogenic tars and carbon monoxide, which are thought to be responsible for approximately 30 per cent of cases of coronary heart disease, 70 per cent of lung cancer and 80 per cent of cases of **chronic obstructive airways disease**.

Carbon monoxide reduces circulating oxygen in the blood, which effectively reduces the amount of oxygen feeding the heart muscles; nicotine makes the heart work harder by increasing blood pressure and heart rate; and together these substances cause narrowing of the arteries and increase the likelihood of thrombosis (clot formation). Tars impair the respiratory system by congesting the lungs, and this is a major contributor to the highly prevalent chronic obstructive pulmonary disease (COPD: e.g. emphysema) (see also Chapter 8 (☞). Overall, the evidence as to the negative health effects of smoking tobacco is indisputable. Furthermore, the evidence as to the negative effects of passive smoking has grown over the past decade or so, with associations being shown between occupational exposure to smoke and significantly increased risk of developing a range of illnesses, including lung cancer and cardiovascular disease (US DHHS 2006). Passive smoking is considered to account for 25 per cent of lung cancer deaths among non-smokers. Passive smoking also carries risks to unborn babies; although many women will give up smoking during pregnancy, many do not.

Drinking alcohol

Although alcohol is commonly perceived as a stimulant, it is in fact a central nervous system depressant. Low doses cause behavioural disinhibition, while high levels of intoxication lead to a 25-fold increase in the likelihood of an accident, and extremely high doses severely affect respiratory rate, which can cause coma and even death. It is generally accepted that there is a linear relationship between the amount of alcohol consumed over time and the accumulation of alcohol-related illness, including diseases such as liver cirrhosis, liver and oesophageal cancer, stroke and epilepsy.

There is significant variation across Europe and elsewhere in terms of the volumes of alcohol consumed (World Health Organization 2002), and in the percentage of total liver cirrhosis mortality that is attributed to alcoholic liver cirrhosis. For example, between 1987 and 1995, a massive 90 per cent of Finnish male cirrhosis deaths were attributed to alcohol-related liver cirrhosis, as opposed to 56 per cent among French males, 45 per cent among UK males, and 10 per cent among Spanish males. Sadly for those of us based in the UK, in a comparison of 35 European countries, children in the UK still show the highest rates of alcohol consumption, and binge drinking (Hibell et al. 2012).

Liver cirrhosis is not the only cause of death attributed to alcohol. The European Commission estimates that 195,000 deaths across the EU each year are due to alcohol-related liver disease, accidents or violence, and in fact 1 in 4 deaths for young men aged 15–29 and 1 in 10 deaths for young women in this age range are attributed to alcohol (EC 2006). The WHO describe a selection of alcohol-related causes including: cancer of oesophagus and larynx, alcohol dependence syndrome, chronic liver disease and cirrhosis. The gradual increase in alcohol-related deaths seen in annual figures collated in the UK since the early 1990s reflects a doubling in deaths between 1991 and 2007 (ONS 2010). Males are twice as likely to die from alcohol-related causes generally defined than are females. It appears from national surveys that approximately a third of men and a quarter of women exceed national drinking guidelines.

Amongst young people, heavy or regular drinking has been associated with subsequent physical or mental

> ## chronic obstructive airways disease
> a persistent airway obstruction associated with combinations of chronic bronchitis, small airways disease, asthma and emphysema.

Photo 3.2 The increase in teenage binge drinking is of concern, particularly amongst females

Source: Alamy Limited/Ace Stock Limited.

health problems as well as being associated with behaviour problems or school performance (Viner and Taylor 2007). Rarely does a day go by in the media without reports of an association between antisocial behaviour and binge drinking. While the under-25s do tend to 'binge' drink more than older individuals, the social problems caused by drinking are by no means confined to this age group. A YouGov poll of 2,221 adults, commissioned by the British Society of Gastroenterology in 2010 and reported in the media in February 2011, points to a high degree of negative social consequences of drinking behaviour (loss of relationships, aggression, domestic violence, work absenteeism) and of personal injury: for example 27 per cent of 18–24-year-olds, and 31 per cent of 25–34-year-olds reported injuring themselves (including while driving or operating machinery) while drunk.

Also of concern is evidence of a relationship between alcohol consumption, and impaired judgements regarding (early) sexual activity and unprotected sexual intercourse (Wellings et al. 2001; Conner et al. 2008) which may result in teenage pregnancy or sexually transmitted disease (Hingson et al. 2003). Being 'drunk' is a commonly cited reason for first having sex when a teenager (e.g. Wellings et al. 2001). Apart from the risk of STDs or pregnancy, teenage substance use has the potential to create other significant long-term problems for the individual, in relation to substance use escalation and associated problem behaviours (Collado et al. 2014). Changing adolescent risk behaviour is often challenging, given the complexity of influences thereon, as we describe in the subsequent section. There is, however, some evidence that interventions which address self-esteem issues before addressing 'behaviour' problems, including under-age sex, smoking and drinking alcohol, seem to meet with greater success than those which do not (e.g. Health Development Agency Magazine 2005). (See also Chapters 6 and 7 ☞).

Amongst young adults of college or university age, drinking is primarily a social behaviour, which in excess has also been associated with poor academic performance, relationship breakdowns, unplanned and/or unprotected sexual activity. Heffernan and colleagues, speaking at the BPS annual conference in May 2014, concluded from their research that many undergraduate students drink at hazardous levels. At the same conference, Conroy reported findings that students held less favourable attitudes towards prototypical non-drinkers than protypical drinkers, including judgements that non-drinkers would be less sociable (personal communications). Such findings suggest that drinking alcohol is still 'normalised' in student culture, whereas developing more positive attitudes to healthy behaviours may well be beneficial. Drinking excessively in one context does not inevitably mean, however, that one 'progresses' to alcohol dependence or indeed to the use of other substances.

There is now also evidence that moderate alcohol consumption may be health-protective, with a J-shaped relationship found between alcohol consumption and CHD risk, i.e. abstinence confers a higher risk than moderate drinking, although not as high as risk conferred by heavy drinking (Doll et al. 1994; BHF 2012),

This surprising finding has emerged from both cross-sectional and prospective studies. It appears that light to moderate alcohol intake reduces circulating low-density lipoprotein (LDL, 'bad fat") levels (high levels are a known risk factor for CHD). If the amounts of alcohol consumed are low to moderate and the pattern of drinking does not include binges, the World Health Report states that alcohol's relationship to CHD, stroke and diabetes mellitus, is in fact a beneficial one (WHO 2002a), possibly even to reduced mortality (Klatsky 2008). There is some evidence also that moderate drinking amongst females may be more protective (of CHD) than amongst males (WHO 2002a).

Caution is advised before concluding from these reports, and from studies of non-drinkers where risk of CHD was higher than average, that not drinking conferred the increased risk. Non-drinkers may choose not to consume alcohol because they are already in poor health, or because they are members of particular religious or ethnic groups that forbid such use: these factors may hide some other 'cause' of CHD. It is safer to conclude only that heavy drinking has negative effects on health that increase in line with consumption; that moderate levels of drinking may not increase risk and may in fact be protective against CHD (although any protective effects are lost on people who smoke); and that the effects of not drinking at all need further exploration.

Continuing the theme of less negative aspects of drinking, moderate intake of red wine has been associated with reduced cardiovascular deaths, due to it being derived from red grapes which contain many different polyphenolic compounds including flavonol (e.g. German and Walzem 2000; Wollin and Jones 2001). It appears that by reducing oxidation these substances (derived from fruits, vegetables, but also from tea and ginger) protect arteries from the damaging effects of high levels of circulating serum cholesterol and can protect therefore against CHD (Engler and Engler 2006). More recently, it has been proposed that red wine polyphenols may also be beneficial by inhibiting the initiation of **carcinogenesis** due to their antioxidative or anti-inflammatory properties. Additionally, polyphenols may act as suppressing agents by inhibiting the growth of mutated cells or by inducing apoptosis, i.e. cell death. Laboratory and animal studies (e.g. Briviba et al. 2002) have shown that polyphenols isolated from red wine did in fact inhibit the growth of different colon carcinoma cells, but not breast cancer cells. Results of this nature naturally need to be carefully checked and double-checked before health recommendations follow. Individuals presenting to their GPs with health concerns around a family history of heart disease are unlikely to be told to increase their light alcohol consumption to moderate, and will probably be advised to follow a low-fat diet, yet the protection offered is similar. There does, however, remain a need for further research among human samples, with tight controls over other contributory factors. It will be some years before the evidence as to the effects of red wine drinking on people already with cancer becomes clear, whereas in relation to coronary heart disease, the evidence is of longer standing, and it would appear that moderate ingestion of alcohol, and not solely red wine, has health-protective effects.

The key term in experiencing any benefits from drinking is 'moderate ingestion of alcohol'. Heavy alcohol consumption in contrast is implicated in the above health effects and also in a range of social consequences as described.

Substance/illicit drug use

As Figure 3.1 shows, the 'burden' of disability-adjusted life years attributed to the use of **illicit drugs** is significantly less than that attributed to alcohol, smoking, or even to physical inactivity (see Chapter 4 ☞). Approximately 40 deaths per million of the population aged between 15 and 64 were attributed to illicit drug use in 2012, which was lower than in 2011 (United Nations 2014). The figures in terms of prevalence of use, as presented earlier, are small in comparison to

---

Carcinogenesis

the process by which normal cells become cancer cells (i.e. carcinoma).

Illicit drugs

includes illegal substances, but also legal substances that are used in ways other than intended e.g. sniffing glue, injecting valium.

alcohol or tobacco prevalence; however, the mere mention of illicit use of drugs (some legally obtained e.g. valium, some not e.g. heroin) can cause anxiety in teachers, parents, the police, the government, and in young people themselves. The statistics, however, at least for health and disease consequences perhaps do not support this.

The method of ingestion, perhaps more than the substance itself, has led people to associate some forms of drug use – injecting drug use – with serious diseases including HIV and Hepatitis C. It is estimated that, worldwide, approximately 12.7 million people (range 8.9 to 22.4 million depending on report) inject drugs, of whom approximately 13 per cent have an HIV diagnosis (range 0.9 to 4.8 million) and more than half have Hepatitis C (Aceijas and Rhodes 2007; Mathers et al. 2008; United Nations Office on Drugs Crime 2014). According to a report from the Centre for Social Justice in 2013, the UK is the 'addiction capital of Europe', in part due to increases in young people taking 'legal highs'. The health burden of addiction predominates amongst younger people, of whom 75 per cent are males (WHO 2009).

Why do people initiate potentially addictive substance use behaviours?

Smoking, drinking and substance use is generally adopted in youth. For example, the Norwegian Longitudinal Health Behaviour Study of over 1,000 participants followed from age 13 to age 30, found that smoking rates increased from 3 per cent to 31 per cent between age 13 and 18 (Tjora et al. 2011). There are a significant number of young people smoking and accumulating lung and airway damage, or drinking and promoting liver damage that will, for many, create significant health and social problems in the future. It has long been known that there is an increased risk of lung cancer in those that initiate smoking in childhood (about 66 per cent of smokers start before aged 18 years, 40 per cent before aged 16, (ONS 2012)) as opposed to in adulthood (about a third of smokers actually start smoking in early adulthood (19+ years)).

Culture and social policy are extremely important in predicting individual behaviour, including the use of alcohol, tobacco and illicit drugs. Consider, for example, Finland, where their previous strict legislation on alcohol sales and consumption was liberalised in the mid-1970s and where cirrhosis deaths showed subsequent increases in the 1980s and 1990s. In the UK the effects of the smoking ban in 2006 on smoking cessation and initiation is also being examined over time, and recent evidence of a downturn in prevalence partly ascribed to this legislative change.

As we have seen in Chapter 2 ☞, socio-economic correlates and predictors of initiating risky health behaviour exist, which some refer to as 'distal' or more 'macro' factors (e.g. Tjora et al. 2011). The reasons why generally young people start to smoke, drink alcohol, or take illicit drugs are, as with most social behaviours, many and varied, and reasons given for each of these behaviours show a significant degree of overlap, as you will see. We cover here only the key known factors:

● *Genetics*. With regards to smoking, there is some evidence of genetic factors and the reception and transport of the neurotransmitter dopamine being involved in initiation and possibly smoking maintenance, but it is unlikely that any genetic influences function in isolation (Munaf and Johnstone 2008).

● *Curiosity*. A commonly cited reason for having that first drink of alcohol, first cigarette, or first joint of cannabis is curiosity (Morrison and Plant 1991; Hecimovic et al. 2014). Wanting to know what 'it tastes like', 'how it feels', usually occurs when others have talked about the behaviour or been seen doing it.

● *Modelling, social learning and reinforcement*. Family behaviour and dynamics are important socialisation processes, with suggestions that observing such behaviour in parents increase the 'preparedness' of their children towards the behaviour by establishing positive attitudes towards it and by possibly reducing perceptions of risk (Tjora et al. 2011). Add to that the presence of smoking or drinking peers and this preparedness is more likely to turn into action. Children with peers (actual friends or even simply desired friends, elder siblings or parents who smoke or drink alcohol around them are more likely to imitate such behaviour than children not exposed to such models (e.g. Mercken et al. 2007, 2011; Johnston et al. 2009). Siblings who engage in such behaviours are perhaps even more influential than peers, although peer effects are also fairly robust, whether through modelling, or through perceived or actual peer pressure.

- *Social pressure.* Social or peer pressure, where smoking or drinking behaviour is positively encouraged (including portrayal in the media/TV) and reinforced by the responses of significant others, has commonly been cited as a reason for initiation of health risk behaviours, reflecting either social contagion or influence that a person conforms to. Interestingly, however, Denscombe (2001) reported that young people aged 15–16 years rejected the idea of 'peer pressure' being responsible for smoking initiation, preferring to see the behaviour as something they selected to do themselves. This fits with the notion of smoking initiation being tied up with seeking reputation and status. Motives given for cannabis use often include reasons of socialisation, with or without overt pressure (e.g. Hecimovic et al. 2014).

- *Image and reputation* is important during adolescence, and wanting to 'fit' in, be seen to be sociable (for drinking behaviour perhaps more so than smoking) and have status within one's social group is considered important to social functioning (Snow and Bruce 2003; Stewart-Knox et al. 2005). Gender differences may exist here. Michell and Amos (1997), for example, found that young males were more ambivalent than females about smoking, with their 'status' in the pecking order being conferred by fitness, whereas for girls high status was attached to appearing cool and sophisticated or rebellious, and for some, this may be achieved through smoking. Low family cohesion has also been associated with higher levels of smoking and drinking among adolescents and young adults aged 12 to 22 (Bourdeaudhuij 1997; Bourdeaudhuij and van Oost 1998), and although further longitudinal evidence is required, it may be that where parental or familial relationships are weaker, peers gain a stronger influence.

- *Self concept and self-esteem.* Studies of adolescent girls have pointed to the importance of self-concept (i.e. concept of what one 'is') and self-esteem (i.e.

concept of one's 'value' or 'worth') in determining involvement or non-involvement in risk behaviours. Some theorists further suggest that a significant amount of adolescent behaviour is motivated by the need to present oneself to others (primarily peers) in a way that enhances the individual's reputation, their social identity (Emler 1984). In some social groups the 'reputation' that will help the individual 'fit' with that social group will involve risk-taking behaviours (Odgers et al. 1996; Snow and Bruce 2003). Snow and Bruce (2003) found female smokers to have less self-confidence, to feel less liked by their families, and to have lower physical and social self-concepts, while their peer self-concept, i.e. what they thought their peers thought of them did not differ from that of non-smokers. Similarly, in relation to becoming pregnant as a teenager, low self-esteem and a negative self-concept may be implicated, as teenage mothers often show a history of dysfunctional relationships and social and financial strain.

- *Weight control.* Weight control has been identified as a motive for smoking initiation and maintenance more often among young girls than among young males (e.g. French et al. 1994; Crisp et al. 1999), although males are not immune from this strategy (Fulkerson and French 2003). In this American study, Native American and Asian American males cited weight control as a reason for smoking more often than males from other ethnic groups, highlighting the need to consider cultural and gender variation when examining or comparing national statistics. In contrast, alcohol is calorie dense and could contribute to weight gain and so this is not a factor cited for initiation, but could usefully be argued as a reason for cessation (see below!)

- *Risk-taking propensity.* Smoking, under-age drinking, and the first use of an illicit drug, typically cannabis, has been found to be a common feature of those engaged in a larger array of 'risk-taking' or problem behaviour, including truancy and petty theft (Johnston et al. 2009). Several disinhibitory-based traits have been associated with risk-taking in terms of substance use behaviours (e.g. Stautz and Cooper 2013, and see 'Research focus')

● *Health cognitions.* Many smokers, drinkers or substance users report expectancies of stress relief, anxiety reduction or other benefits to the behaviour. Users also often hold 'unrealistically optimistic' beliefs regarding the potential for controlling their behaviour and avoiding any negative health consequences: e.g. 'drinking will give me confidence', 'cannabis use will reduce my anxiety' or 'I won't smoke (tobacco, cannabis) as heavily as other people, so it won't affect my health' (see Chapter 5 for full coverage of health cognitions (☞).

● *Stress.* Stress is often cited as a factor which maintains both legal and illegal substance use behaviour (see below), and there is some evidence of a role for stress in smoking initiation. For example, in a longitudinal study of 2,600 Australian adolescents, Byrne and Mazanov (2003) confirmed their hypothesis that adolescent non-smokers at baseline who experienced stress in an intervening year would be more likely to become smokers than non-stressed non-smokers. Interestingly for boys, smoking uptake was only weakly associated with higher stress of attending school, but for girls smoking uptake was associated with higher stress from attending school, family conflict, parental control, and perceived educational irrelevance. These perceived stressors also distinguished those girls who started smoking from those who remained non-smokers. The National Longitudinal Study of Adolescent Health has also pointed to a role of depressive symptomatology in smoking onset (McCaffery et al. 2008).

The direction of effects of economic hardship on substance use amongst long-term unemployed has been a subject of much research, with some longitudinal studies reporting reduced smoking and alcohol consumption where finances are limited, but with most reporting the converse (see review by Henkel 2011). Low parental socio-economic status has also been positively associated with smoking initiation in their adolescent offspring (Tjora et al. 2011). Adding to the complexity of influences on alcohol use, a recent American study using the large Framingham Heart Study Offspring Cohort datasets of 1971–2008 found that unemployment affected consumption levels of women more than men, even when the unemployment was in the male spouse and not themselves (Arcaya et al. 2014).

Continuing unhealthy behaviour and developing dependency

While it has been reported (EC 2006) that 55 million adults drink at harmful levels in the EU, only a small number of people will become dependent on alcohol (perhaps one in ten). This challenges the dominant theory in this domain, which is that of a dependence model. It is not the case that all alcohol-related problems arise from situations of dependency: in fact the majority do not. In addition, the reasons for continuing to smoke, drink or take other drugs are not necessarily the same as reasons given for initiation. Patterns of the behaviour itself may change over time and thus the influences upon it may also change. Whilst some of the original reasons for a behaviour may persist, e.g. smoking or drinking for relaxation, other factors, including dependence, may emerge to maintain it. Unlike with tobacco smoking, for most people drinking alcohol does not become a daily occurrence and research has sought to distinguish individuals who maintain safe levels of drinking from those who develop problem drinking. The main aspects considered are:

● Genetics and family history: children of problem drinkers are more likely to develop problem drinking than children of non-problem drinkers (e.g. Heather and Robertson 1997). Evidence is inconclusive as parent–child drinking tendencies could also be socialised (see below), although adoptee studies support evidence of heredity to an extent.

● The pre-existence of certain psychopathology e.g. mood disorders, or personality risk factors, e.g. anxious **predisposition**, sensation-seeking or risk-taking propensities (e.g. Hittner and Swickert 2006; Khantzian 2003; Woicik et al. 2009; Zuckerman et al. 1978; Zuckerman and Kuhlman 2000), although personality's influence is not total and does change over time (Morrison 2003, and see Research focus).

● The social learning experience: social learning theory considers alcohol abuse or dependence to be a socially acquired and learned behaviour that has

---

predisposition

predisposing factors increase the likelihood of a person engaging in a particular behaviour, such as genetic influences on alcohol consumption.

endorphins

naturally occurring opiate-like chemicals released in the brain and spinal cord. They reduce the experience of pain and can induce feelings of relaxation or pleasure. Associated with the so-called 'runner's high'.

received reinforcement (internal or external, physical, social or emotional rewards). Addiction may result from repeatedly seeking the pleasurable effects of the substance itself or to avoid negative effects of withdrawal (e.g. Wise 1998).

For smoking, however, few people succeed in remaining casual or social smokers. The addictive potential of smoking arises from the biologically addictive properties of smoking. The active ingredient is the alkaloid nicotine, which acts as a brain stimulant, activates 'reward pathways' involving the neurotransmitter dopamine in the brain to release our natural opiates, beta-**endorphins**, thus perpetuating the need to repeatedly intake nicotine to avoid 'withdrawal' symptoms (Jarvis 2004). Physical dependence on a drug, whether legal or illegal, arises when an individual develops tolerance to its effects and therefore more consumption is required in order to attain the same effects or to avoid the withdrawal effects that follow a diminished bloodstream level of the substance. This withdrawal is manifest in both physical symptoms (e.g. cravings, insomnia, sweating, increased appetite (West 1992)) and psychological symptoms (e.g. anxiety, restlessness, irritability). In this way, drug use can become self-reinforcing as individuals seek to avoid these symptoms. Some individuals report that they relapse during an episode where they were trying to quit a substance, as a deliberate attempt to eliminate these symptoms, which are distressing not only for them but also for those around them! Resuming the behaviour then itself provides reinforcement in terms of the avoidance of any further withdrawal symptoms, thus a vicious cycle emerges.

Patterns of heavy drinking laid down in late childhood and early adulthood tend to set the pattern for heavy drinking in adulthood, and alcohol-related health problems such as liver cirrhosis tend to accumulate in middle age. It should not be assumed that heavy or problem drinking is more common in those less well educated or of lower socio-economic status, as evidence in this regard is quite mixed. The better educated have often been shown more likely to engage in various forms of risky behaviour but to be less likely to develop problem drinking (e.g. Caldwell et al. 2008). However, a recent study (Huerta and Borgonovi 2010) using a large sample of almost 10,000 individuals aged 34 years at the time of the study (all drawn from the British Cohort Study, which is a sample of all those born in a specific week in 1970) found that higher educational attainment *was* associated with increased odds of daily alcohol consumption and with problem drinking, particularly among females. However, this is a very specific cohort of those in their mid-30s and so we cannot assume from such findings that relationships do not exist at other ages, for example in teenage, or for other forms of drinking, such as binge drinking. More recently, the BHF (2012) confirmed a relationship between both drinking heavily and drinking more than recommended guidelines and a person's socio-economic status whereby males and females in the 'managerial or professional' classification engage in these behaviours more than those in either 'intermediate' or 'routine and manual' professions (see also Chapter 2, ☛). Access to alcohol by means of disposable income is an important consideration.

Among older people problem drinking has been shown to be influenced by physical health, access to social opportunities and financial status, with the affluent elderly having higher rates of drinking problems than those less well off (Health and Social Care Information Centre 2013). For some individuals, however, an increase in alcohol consumption can be attributed in part to loneliness, bereavement or physical ill health (e.g. Atkinson 1994).

In spite of clear evidence of physiological addiction to nicotine and other drugs including opiates, people who continue to use such substances typically also report psychological reasons for continuing such as:

- pleasure or enjoyment of the behaviour, and its effects reinforces positive attitudes towards it;

- 'simply a habit' (this could reflect psychological and/ or physical dependence): habit formation is a crucial barrier to behaviour change (see Chapter 5 ☛);

- a form of stress self-management, a method of coping/anxiety control; stress has been associated with the maintenance of adult substance use, but little work has explored this association in adolescence, although as described above there is some evidence of stress being associated with smoking initiation.

WHAT DO YOU THINK?

http://www.hscreformseries.co.uk/
community-care/18512-put-health-warnings-on-
alcoholic-drinks-say-mps

On 11 August 2014, it was reported that 'Alcoholic drinks should come with written health warnings similar to those that appear on tobacco products as part of a drive to tackle a "national crisis"', according to a group of MPs. The All-Party Parliamentary Group on Alcohol Misuse said that – along with other measures including the introduction of a minimum unit price and reducing the drink-drive limit – it would help encourage responsible drinking.

Would evidence-based labelling with messages regarding potential health risks of drinking change drinking behaviour amongst your peers? If not, why not? Are such approaches to changing health behaviour effective? Has smoking shown a downturn since graphic images appeared on cigarette packaging in the UK from 2011? Think about your own behaviour and that of others around you before you go on to read Chapters 5–7.

● a lack of belief in their ability to stop the behaviour; this belief, often referred to as self-efficacy is discussed in Chapter 5 ☞.

Cox and Klinger (2004) describe a motivational model of substance use based on consistent findings that people's decisions about substance use are not necessarily rational but involve a complex range of motivational and emotional components and depend also on the rewards and incentives received from the behaviour. For example, a person considering their smoking, drinking or drug use may do so in relation to other aspects of their lives that they may or may not derive satisfaction from. Individuals without commitment to healthy life goals or the motivation to work towards attaining them are less likely to perceive their substance use as a problem and consider themselves as less able to change the behaviour.

As with smoking or regular use of alcohol, it is not the case that the use of all illicit drugs leads to dependency. One example of this is recreational Ecstacy use, which is unlikely to lead to dependence, although there are health risks attached to use. Likewise, it is not the case that all those who engage in illicit drug use turn to theft or become violent as a result. Why then is so much negative feeling attached to illicit drug using behaviour? In part

this can be explained by perceptions of such drug use which are driven by one of two models – a dependence model where illicit drug users are thought to be addicted, possibly ill and out of control; or a criminal model, where they are seen as irresponsible, delinquent and even dangerous. These views have influenced how dependency has been treated and the treatments offered to those expressing a desire to stop.

Behaviour cessation

Even people who stop smoking when aged between 50 and 60 can avoid most of their subsequent risk of developing lung cancer or other smoking-related disease or disability such as Chronic Obstructive Pulmonary Disease, coronary artery disease, or stroke (Bratzler et al. 2002) and quitting at 55 can gain a male on average 5 life years (based on 50 years of follow-up of a sample of British male doctors, Doll et al. 2004). Better still, stopping when aged 30 leads to more than 90 per cent of lung cancer risk being avoided (Peto et al. 2000) and approximately 10 life years gained (Doll et al. 2004). Whilst older smokers may be less likely to try to stop smoking, there is some suggestion that they are more successful when they do (e.g. Ferguson et al. 2005).

Attempts to help people to stop smoking are generally viewed positively by the public, and in fact the majority of smokers themselves will report that they wish to stop smoking. It has been found that stopping smoking is more likely among individuals of a higher socio-economic status (dispelling expectations of significant downturns in smoking among those of lower socio-economic status caused by continual increases in cigarette prices) and is more successful in those with a higher level of education (Droomers et al. 2002). This may be directly attributable to higher levels of knowledge and understanding about potential health consequences, or it may be that quitters in higher social classes have fewer smoking acquaintances and friends than non-quitters.. Various studies have shown that smoking networks are associated with quitting to a larger degree than health beliefs, whereby not being part of a smoking network facilitates cessation (e.g. Rose et al. 1996). Barriers to cessation, including for some, a fear of weight gain (Pisinger and Jorgensen 2007; Schofield et al. 2007), are considered in Chapter 5 ☞. Chapters 6 and 7 ☞ describe interventions aimed at promoting smoking cessation.

RESEARCH FOCUS

PERSONALITY AND RISK BEHAVIOUR

Collado, A., Felton, J.W., MacPherson, L. and Lejuez, C.W. (2014) Longitudinal trajectories of sensation seeking, risk taking propensity, and impulsivity across early to middle adolescence. *Addictive Behaviors 39:1580–88.*

Hecimovic, K., Barrett, S.P., Darredea, C. and Stewart, S.H. (2014) Cannabis use motives and personality risk factors. *Addictive Behaviors*, 39: 729–732.

Hagger-Johnson, G.M. Bewick, B.M., Conner, M., O'Connor, D.B. and Shickle, D. (2011) Alcohol, conscientiousness and event-level condom use. *British Journal of Health Psychology* 16: 828–845.

Three papers caught my eye that explored the role personality played in a range of health risk behaviours: general risk behaviour in adolescence, cannabis use and condom use. In health psychology texts when presenting broad descriptions of behaviour such as in this chapter, it is quite typical to focus more on the demographic factors (age, gender, culture, etc.) and on the individual beliefs and attitudes, and forget about the underlying personality traits that potentially interact with these other factors.

In a recent study of adolescents followed annually for 5 years from early adolescence (9–13-year-olds) to age 13–18 years, the developmental trajectories of disinhibitory factors often associated with the onset of health-damaging behaviours, such as sensation-seeking, risk-taking propensity and impulsivity, were explored (Collado et al. 2014). Contrary to expectations of such factors being stable over time, interesting differences emerged: sensation-seeking scores did not change between Waves 1–2 (i.e. year 1–2) but increased between Waves 2–3, 3–4 and 4–5 in a linear fashion, with an effect of race (non-Blacks showing a greater increase); but no association with gender. In contrast, risk-taking propensity increased relatively steeply from Wave 1 onwards, but levelled out between Waves 4–5, with no gender or race effects. Impulsivity, assessed only from Wave 2, did

not change between Waves 2–3, or 3–4 where it peaked (aged 13–17), and then it decreased in the 5th Wave.

The authors interpret some of the differences by pointing out that where sensation-seeking is more a goal-directed construct (purposively seeking new or positive sensations and experience), impulsivity and risk-taking propensity are more related to behavioural control (or lack of!). The stabilisation of these latter characteristics may reflect age-related developments in neurologically mediated cognitive control (maturation of the prefrontal cortex, see Yurgelun-Todd 2007). What is needed now is a prospective study where actual risk behaviours are studied simultaneously over time with those disinhibitory variables, something Collado and colleagues do not do. What the findings suggest though is that, if such 'personality aspects' show a natural course of change over time, there are implications for the timings of any behaviour change interventions.

In the second study, focusing solely on cannabis users, Hecimovic and colleagues, found that different personality factors related to different *motives* for the cannabis use, i.e. the reasons given for using cannabis varied according to the extent to which the individual user scored on 4 personality 'risk' factors: sensation-seeking (SS), impulsivity (IMP), introversion/hopelessness (I/H), and anxiety sensitivity (AS). Whilst the sample studied varied in the frequency of cannabis use, all were able to report their motives for use, using a 29-item motive scale, which was then factor analysed to produce 4 Factors:

- 'Enhancement motives' i.e. to have fun; to enjoy the feeling;

- 'Expansion motives' i.e. to see things differently, to be more creative;

- 'Conformity motives' i.e. to fit in with peers, to help socialise; and

- 'Coping motives' i.e. as an escape, to forget about problems.

SS was significantly and positively associated with Expansion motives; AS was significantly and positively associated with Conformity motives and negatively and significantly associated with the Expansion motives (with a trend also towards association with Coping motives); and I/H was significantly and positively associated with Coping motives. Impulsivity overall was not associated with any of the 4 Factors but on analysis by item, impulsivity was significantly higher in those who endorsed the motive for cannabis use as 'because it was easier to get than the drugs' i.e. suggesting an availability motive.

These findings confirm previous evidence of substance use and coping motives but highlight that this may be a stronger motive in those who are introverted or have an anxious predisposition. Impulsive individuals by definition show less specific planning of behaviour, having more erratic motives perhaps, and hence why availability may simply create the environment for yielding to temptation in those impulsive folk. Notable is that those high on anxious sensitivity also reported using cannabis to conform and perhaps reduce social anxiety. This links us to the final study selected where personality is explored in relation to a fundamentally social behaviour – sex.

In the third study selected, non-use of condoms and risk-taking in term of risk of acquiring a sexually transmitted infection or unplanned pregnancy was examined. This risk behaviour has previously been associated with excessive alcohol consumption (see earlier), particularly for first partners (Leigh 2002). The broad trait of sensation-seeking has consistently been predictive of sexual risk-taking, as has low levels of Conscientiousness (one of the 'Big Five' personality traits see Chapter 12, ☞). Hagger-Johnson and colleagues (2011) explored the association between personality, drinking, and specific sexual encounters, to examine whether personality had a direct effect on condom use behaviour or whether alcohol use mediated this effect. In other words, does any effect of personality on condom use only operate VIA an effect on drinking behaviour? They found that Conscientiousness increased the likelihood of condom use during the most recent sexual event (when recency of event and partner type (casual/main) was controlled for), and did not confirm previous associations between alcohol consumption and non-condom use. The effect of personality therefore was a direct one, with low conscientiousness being the risk factor for unprotected sex.

All of these studies have limitations, and the interested student should read each paper as listed above; however, the take home message is this: studies of risk behaviour need to consider personality as well as the wider social and narrower cognitive factors that we more commonly attend to (see Chapter 5 ☞), because:

- Our personality may not be as fixed as initially thought, with some aspects associated with risk behaviour changing over time as we develop.
- Our personality likely influences our motivations to carry out certain risk behaviours.
- Low levels of conscientiousness affect sexual risk-taking directly and not necessarily via effects on other behaviour.

Things to think about and research yourself

How might some people interpret these kinds of findings – is there any room to intervene with personality? What would you try to work on if you recognised someone as being of a highly anxious predisposition, or introverted? What, if anything, can be done to increase conscientiousness or reduce impulsivity?

Thoughts about treating dependence

Dependency problems and how those with such problems are viewed by society have changed over time. In relation to alcohol and opiate taking, perspectives have shifted from viewing dependence, as the immoral behaviour of weak individuals, unable to exert personal control over their consumption during the seventeenth–eighteenth centuries, to being the behaviour of passive victims of an evil and powerful substance in the nineteenth century. The earlier 'moral' view considered individuals as responsible for their behaviour and therefore the ethos of treatment was punishment. The latter view considered the individual to have less control over their behaviour, and as such the prohibition of alcohol sales (as seen in the USA) was considered an appropriate societal response, and treatment was offered to those 'victims' who 'succumbed'. The medical treatment of individuals with alcohol problems reflects the beginnings of a disease concept of addiction where the drug was seen as being the problem. However, by the early twentieth century, it was clear that prohibition had failed and the model of alcoholism developed into one that placed responsibility back onto the individual. In 1960, Jellinek described alcoholism as a disease but considered both the nature of the substance and the pre-existing characteristics of the person who used it. While it became accepted that alcohol could be used by the majority without any resulting harm, a minority of individuals developed alcohol dependence, and for these individuals pre-existing genetic and psychological 'weaknesses' were acknowledged. Addiction was seen as an acquired, permanent state of being over which the individual could regain control only by means of abstinence, and treatment reflected this: for example, the self-help organisation, Alcoholics Anonymous, founded in 1935, had the primary goal of helping individuals to achieve lifelong abstinence.

However, in psychology during the early twentieth century, the growth of **behaviourism** brought with it new methods of treatment for those with addiction problems that drew from the principles of **social learning theory** and **conditioning theory**. These perspectives consider behaviour to result from learning and from the reinforcement that any behaviour receives. Excessive alcohol consumption, for example, according to these theories, can be 'unlearned' by applying behavioural principles to treatment. Such treatment would aim to identify the cues for an individual's drinking or drug use behaviour and the type of reinforcement individuals receive for it (see Chapter 6 ☞). These approaches therefore consider the individual, their behaviour and the social environment. Nowadays, at least in the UK and elsewhere in Europe, abstinence is considered as one possible treatment outcome among others, such as controlled drinking or opiate replacement therapies (e.g. methadone programmes). In controlled drinking, individuals are encouraged to restrict their consumption to certain occasions/settings/times of day, or to control the alcoholic content of drinks consumed by, for example,

switching to low-alcohol alternatives (Heather and Robertson 1997).

Health promotion efforts therefore have two targets: **primary prevention** in terms of educating children about the risks of smoking, drinking or drug use and about 'safe' levels of consumption; and secondary prevention in terms of changing the behaviour of those already engaged in such behaviours. Examples of these are described in Chapters 6 and 7 ☞.

Whether influenced by personality, cognitive development, peer behavioural norms, reacting to stress or availability, and whether motivated by a desire to escape negative thoughts, emotions or situations, the prevention of initiation to illicit drug use can and should be treated in the same way as alcohol use or smoking. In terms of reducing use among regular users, however, for a minority there will be, as with alcohol, issues of physical and psychological dependence to deal with. To a large extent the treatment of alcohol dependence can be the same as the treatment for opiate dependence, at least in terms of any cognitive or motivational therapy and given the social influences thereon (see Orford 2002 for a discussion of common themes supporting 'excessive appetites'). What will differ will have been people's responses to the individuals concerned and how, perhaps, they have been treated by health and social care services. In addition, the illegality of some substance use takes the user into contact with the legal system,

---

behaviourism

the belief that psychology is the study of observables and therefore that behaviour, not mental processes, is central.

social learning theory

a theory that has at its core the belief that a combination of outcome expectancy and outcome value will shape subsequent behaviour. Reinforcement is an important predictor of future behaviour.

conditioning theory

the theory that behaviour is directly influenced by its consequences, positive and negative.

primary prevention

intervention aimed at changing risk factors prior to disease development.

potentially the prison system, and all the ramifications of that. It is not the purpose of this book to do anything more than to raise, for the reader, the question of societal judgement. It is worth reflecting on whether greater attention and resources could be allocated towards the significantly more prevalent and more widely harmful behaviours such as alcohol misuse and tobacco smoking.

Unprotected sexual behaviour

Unlike the other behaviours described in this chapter, sexual practices are not inherently individual behaviour but behaviour that occurs in the context of an interaction between two individuals. Sex is fundamentally 'social' behaviour (although drinking behaviour may also be considered 'social', the actual physical act of drinking is down to the individual). As such, researchers studying sexual practices and the influences upon them (see 'Research focus' for one example), and health educators attempting to promote safer sexual practices such as condom use, face particular challenges. However, it is worth persevering, given the findings of a Cochrane Review of the evidence as to the effectiveness of condom use in reducing heterosexual transmission of HIV (Weller and Davis-Beaty 2007). This review concluded that consistent use of condoms (defined as use for all acts of penetrative vaginal intercourse) led to an 80 per cent reduction in HIV incidence.

Negative health consequences of unprotected sexual intercourse

Notwithstanding unwanted pregnancy, unprotected sexual intercourse carries with it several risks: infections such as chlamydia and HIV. Sexual behaviour as a risk factor for disease has received growing attention since the 'arrival' of the human immunodeficiency virus (HIV) in the early 1980s and the recognition that AIDS affects heterosexually active populations as well as homosexual populations and injecting drug users who share their injecting equipment.

HIV prevalence

From around 8 million cases in 1990, the most recent data produced by UNAIDS, UNICEF and WHO in 2015 which refers to cases up to the end of 2014 report that approximately 36.9 million people are currently living with HIV/AIDS. There were between 2.2 and 2.8 million new cases diagnosed and between 1.5 and 1.9 million AIDS deaths in 2011 alone, which may sound high, but encouragingly both these figures are down on previous years. This downturn in deaths is attributed to antiretroviral therapies; the downturn in diagnoses is more likely attributed to changes in individual risk behaviours including condom use and reductions in needle sharing amongst injecting drug users. While 69–70 per cent of HIV cases are concentrated in Sub-Saharan Africa (with a 4.9 per cent adult prevalence compared to an average 0.2 per cent prevalence in Western and 0.1 per cent prevalence in Central Europe), there is cause for concern in Eastern European and Central Asian countries where figures have tripled since 2000, and although some of this may be due to increased openness in reporting, this upturn is also attributed to increased 'unsafe' heterosexual sex, and needle sharing in drug users. (http://www.avert.org/worldwide-hiv-aids-statistics.htm; http://www.avert.org/european-hiv-aids-statistics.htm)

In Western Europe there is reasonable consistency in population prevalence of HIV: see Table 3.4, with the southern European countries of Spain, France, Portugal and Italy having higher infection figures, attributed in large part to the prevalence of injecting drug use. (See more at: http://www.avert.org/professionals/hiv-around-world/western-central-europe-north-america/overview)

Of the reported 27,325 people diagnosed with HIV in Europe in 2014:

● 33.7 per cent acquired HIV through heterosexual contact;

● 43.9 per cent became infected through male-to-male sexual contact;

● 3.1 per cent became infected through injecting drug use;

● 0.8 per cent was via mother-to-child transmission;

● 10.6 per cent were 15 to 24 years old;

● and for 18.1 per cent, transmission was unknown.

(http://ecdc.europa.eu/en/publications/Publications/hiv-aids-surveillance-in-Europe-2014.pdf)

Table 3.4 HIV/AIDS infection figures in Western Europe

Western Europe country	N living with HIV/AIDS 2014	Women N 2014	Adult prevalence % 2014	N AIDS-related deaths in 2014
Austria	8,400	2,000	0.1	29
Belgium	27,900	10,000	0.2	33
Denmark	6,800	1,900	0.1	0
Finland	3,400	900	0.1	N/A
France	65,900	23,500	0.1	70
Germany	53,800	10,300	0.1	60
Greece	14,400	2,500	0.2	44
Iceland	400	100	0.2	0
Ireland	7,300	2,200	0.2	0
Israel	8,500	2,800	0.1	26
Italy	33,300	8,100	0.1	N/A
Luxembourg	1,300	350	0.2	1
Malta	300	70	0.1	1
Netherlands	23,000	4,600	0.1	65
Norway	5,600	1,800	0.1	3
Portugal	52,700	14,600	0.5	126
Spain	34,700	6,500	0.1	143
Sweden	11,100	3,600	0.1	N/A
Switzerland	34,500	10,000	0.4	4
United Kingdom	139,800	42,300	0.2	131

Source: HIV/AIDS Surveillance in Europe, http://ecdc.europa.eu/en/publications/Publications/hiv-aids-surveillance-in-Europe-2014.pdf

In many countries, unprotected heterosexual sex has to a large extent taken over from homosexual sex and injecting drug use (IDU) as a route of infection, initially appearing to add weight to research findings of behaviour change among homosexual men (Katz 1997) and offering support to the effectiveness of syringe-exchange schemes for injecting drug users in some countries. Although needle sharing still occurs, in the UK diagnoses of HIV among IDUs have shown a steady decline over the past 30 years. In contrast, male homosexually acquired infection has increased gradually year on year since 2003, providing support for findings of an upturn in the practice of unprotected anal sex (e.g. Chen et al. 2002; Dodds and Mercey 2002). Part of this downturn in the practice of safer sex may be attributable to the fact that people consider AIDS a disease for which there are a growing number of treatments, and thus the perceived lethality of the disease, and the implicit requirement to practise safer sex, may have been undermined. Additionally, individuals' perceptions of their personal risk may be wrong.

Heterosexual infection has greater implications for women (as the 'receptors' of semen during sexual inter-course) than men, and in the USA this is evidenced in increased female HIV figures (e.g. Wortley and Fleming 1997; Logan et al. 2002). The prevalence of HIV infection in pregnant women is relatively low in Europe, but monitoring has found cases to have risen, suggesting an urgent need for development of further antenatal screening services.

Chlamydia, HPV and other sexually transmitted diseases

HIV infection is of course not the only STI that can result from unprotected sexual intercourse. There has been a significant increase in the prevalence of other sexually transmitted diseases or infections (STD/STIs) including chlamydia, genital herpes simplex and genital warts, most common among adolescents and young adults. Chlamydia is a curable disease and is also the most preventable cause of infertility: however, cases have doubled in the UK since 1999 (http://www.avert. org/stds-uk.htm). In contrast, new cases of gonorrhoea have shown a decline since peaking in 2002, and now show highest prevalence amongst males aged 19–24,

Photo 3.3 Education is needed about the health risks of the sun

Source: V. Morrison

females aged 16–19, black ethnic populations and homosexual males. Genital herpes hit a peak in 2008, with highest rates interestingly in males between 35 and 64 years old and females aged 16–24. New diagnoses of genital warts have tripled, and this most common STD in the UK was seen in over 92,000 cases in 2008 alone. Some of this increase may be due to increased uptake of screening checks offered in UK genito-urinary medicine (GUM) centres, and being tested may have become more normalised.

In terms of chlamydia, one UK national screening survey of prevalence in young people found that 13.8 per cent of those under 16 years old, 10.5 per cent of those aged 16–19 and 7.2 per cent of those aged 20–24 had this infection (Moens et al. 2003). Another large survey of sexual behaviour among 11,161 adults aged 16–44 urine-tested half of the sample and found that 10.8 per cent of men and 12.6 per cent of women had had a sexually transmitted infection, 3.6 per cent of men and 4.1 per cent of women had had genital warts, and 1.4 per cent of men and 3.1 per cent of women had chlamydia (Fenton et al. 2001). These are worrying figures, given that chlamydia could be avoided through the use of condoms.

A subgroup of a family of viruses known collectively as Human Papilloma Virus (HPV) have been associated with abnormal tissue and cell growth implicated in the development of genital warts and cervical cancer. The high-risk type viruses labelled HPV-16 and HPV-18 together cause over 70 per cent of squamous cell cancers (cancer develops in flat-type cells found on the outer surface of the cervix), and approximately 50 per cent of adenocarcinomas (the cancer develops in the glandular cells which line the cervix). About 95 per cent of cervical cancers are squamous cell type and about 5 per cent are adenocarcinomas. There are also low-risk type HPV viruses which are associated with the development of genital warts, which do not cause cervical cancer in themselves but which are a sexually transmitted infection which cause significant discomfort. HPV is not contagious as such, but can be transmitted from a single act of sexual intercourse with an infected person.

While condom use reduces the risk of infection, HPV 'lives' on the whole genital area and therefore a condom alone is insufficient to prevent transmission. HPV is startlingly prevalent and therefore the discovery of a vaccination against those types of HPV which cause 70 per cent of cervical cancers (but not genital warts) has been billed as a major public health discovery. This is discussed in Chapter 4 ☞.

It is likely that we will see a flurry of research into the predictors of uptake and non-uptake of vaccination and, therefore, from a health psychology perspective, this is quite an exciting time. Chapter 5 ☞ outlines key psychological factors and sociocognitive models of health behaviour and these models are likely to be tested in relation to HPV.

The use of condoms

Prior to HIV and AIDS, sexual behaviour was generally considered to be 'private' behaviour and somewhat under-researched (with the exception of clinical studies of individuals experiencing sexual difficulties). The lack of information as to the sexual practices of the general population made it initially extremely difficult to assess the potential for the spread of HIV infection. One notable survey that was triggered by this need for information was the National Survey of Sexual Attitudes and Lifestyles, conducted with nearly 19,000 adults (aged 16–59) living in Britain in 1990–91 (Wellings et al. 1994). It was found that:

- Young people use condoms more commonly than older people.

- Females tend to use condoms less often than males.

- Condom use is greatest with a 'new' sexual partner (34 and 41 per cent of males and females, respectively, used condoms on all occasions of sex with a single new partner).

- Condom use declined dramatically in those who reported having had multiple new partners.

- The rate of condom use was lowest in males who had multiple partners who were not new (only 5.7 per cent always used a condom).

- Female condom use was less affected by whether multiple partners were 'new' to them or not (14.3 per cent always used a condom with not new multiple partners).

This survey was repeated in 2001 with over 11,000 men and women aged 16–44 years and with a deliberate intention of boosting the cultural mix of the sample which also over-represented London (NATSAL II;

Erens et al. 2003). Non-white ethnicity and being of a non-Christian religion was also found to be associated with greater condom use, highlighting the importance of ensuring representation across differing cultural and religious groupings. Although not in fact as representative as the first survey, results regarding any use of condoms in the year prior to interview were encouraging (Cassell et al. 2006). A significant increase was reported in both males (from 43.3 per cent in 1990 to 51.4 per cent in 2000) and females (from 30.6 per cent in 1990 to 39.1 per cent in 2000). In both of these, and in subsequent national surveys (ONS 2010), condom use is highest among younger respondents (e.g. 18–24-year-olds) and for those for whom the last sexual partner was 'new'. One important finding is the rate of condom use among those with multiple partners – those 'high-risk' individuals are consistently more likely to report condom use. Among the heterosexual sample of Cassell's study, the prevention of pregnancy was given as the primary reason for condom use, although in those aged 16–24-years prevention of HIV and other STIs was of equal or greater concern. This may reflect increased awareness of HIV and sexual health in the decade between the two surveys, and provide support to those offering health education and health promotion (see Chapters 6 and 7 ☞).

Safer sex practices were not influenced solely by concerns about STIs but also by the type, number and length of sexually active relationships a person is engaged in. Condom use commonly begins to decline after six months within any given relationship. Many other factors have been reported to act as barriers against safer sex behaviour, as we describe in the next section (see also Chapter 5 ☞).

Barriers to condom use

Alcohol intake has been found to reduce condom use in both younger and older individuals, heterosexuals and homosexuals, an effect sometimes attributed to the disinhibitory effects of alcohol, as discussed earlier in the chapter. However, alcohol use may simply reflect a propensity towards general risk-taking behaviour which includes the non-use of condoms and so alcohol itself may not play a direct causal role but reflect underlying personality (see earlier 'Research focus').

The challenge of measuring health behaviour

The research tradition assumes that the objects of study, e.g. health, illness, or in the context of this chapter, behaviour, remain as fixed entities in people's minds. However, without a researcher actually being present and observing the individual behaving over long periods of time, it is difficult to know whether what a person reports to the researcher (or clinician) accurately reflects their actual behaviour. Obtaining valid measures of behaviour is made increasingly difficult when one is interested in behaviour that is perhaps considered 'undesirable' (e.g. excessive alcohol or drug use), or when it is private (e.g. sexual behaviour). Researchers also face the challenge of knowing how best to define the behaviours under study, and yet it is only through appropriate definition that measurement becomes possible. For example, rather than defining exercise in terms of organised activity, it could be defined as any physical activity that requires energy expenditure; or in terms of drinking alcohol, whether a 'drink' is defined and counted in terms of standard 'units' (see alcohol section), or size of glass, or strength of alcohol. The definition adopted will influence the questions asked and, furthermore, questions need to address not just the type of behaviour performed but also aspects such as the frequency, duration, intensity, and even social context in which it is performed.

Where direct observation and/or objective measurement (for example, taking blood or urine samples) are not possible, researchers have to rely on *self-report*. When studies are interested in the frequency with which certain behaviour is performed, it is commonplace to ask study participants to complete a diary, for example, of cigarettes/alcohol/foods consumed or activities undertaken. Participants in such studies are generally required to either record the relevant activity daily for a period of a week (any longer places high demand on participants), or to reflect back on the previous week's activity (a retrospective diary – RD). The latter has obvious memory demands – could you accurately recall how many units of alcohol you drank seven days ago? While there is no evidence of a systematic bias towards

overestimation or underestimation (Maisto and Connors 1992; Shakeshaft et al. 1999), some studies attempt to cross-validate behavioural self-reports by obtaining observer ratings or blood samples. However, observation is not always ethical, and biochemical tests are intrusive and costly. Other studies rely on asking participants about their 'typical or average' behaviour: for example, they report the typical amount of alcohol consumed (quantity), and the 'typical or average' number of days on which they consume alcohol (frequency) (e.g. Norman et al. 1998). This method known as a quantity/frequency index (QFI) may, however, provide over-general information. Shakeshaft and colleagues (1999) compared an RD method with a QFI, and found that the RD method elicited higher reported levels of weekly alcohol consumption than did the QFI. In fact, neither way may be totally accurate.

One way of minimising inaccuracies in reporting is by using continuous *self-monitoring techniques*, such as alcohol or food consumption diaries, with short recording periods, e.g. hourly. This can be a useful method of establishing patterns of behaviour and the circumstances in which they occur. For example, food diaries commonly instruct the person completing them to note not only the time at which each meal or snack is consumed but also the location, whether anyone else was present, whether any particular 'cue' existed and the reasons for consumption. Some studies invite the person to note also whether they are currently experiencing positive or negative emotions. A potential limitation of self-monitoring is that it can be reactive: in other words, it acts as an intervention itself, with participants modifying their consumption on the basis of their increased awareness of their intake. Behaviour that is seen as undesirable is likely to decrease while being monitored, whereas desirable behaviour is likely to increase. This may be useful in a clinical context, where the intention of self-monitoring *is* behaviour change, but in a research context it may be obstructive: for example, it may prevent researchers from obtaining reliable baseline measurement of behaviour against which to evaluate the efficacy of an intervention programme. Reliance on self-monitoring data can also create problems clinically: for example, Warren and Hixenbaugh (1998) reviewed evidence that people with diabetes make up their self-monitored blood glucose levels and found that, in some studies, individuals did so in order to present a more positive clinical profile to their medical practitioner (i.e. self-presentation bias/social desirability bias). This behaviour could potentially disadvantage treatment efficacy or disease management and outcomes.

Self-monitoring techniques are not the only data-collection technique which could potentially elicit self-presentation bias, as there is evidence that collecting data via *face-to-face interviews* can also elicit reporting bias. Face-to-face interviews enable researchers to seek more explanation for a person's behaviour by using open-ended questions such as 'Think back to your first under-age drink of alcohol. What would you say motivated it? How did you feel afterwards?' Interviews also facilitate the building of rapport with participants, which may be particularly important if the study requires participants to attend follow-up interviews or complete repeated assessments. Rapport may increase commitment to the study and improve retention rates; however, the interview process, content and style may also influence participants' responses. Some people may simply not report their 'risk

behaviour' practices (e.g. illicit drug use, unprotected sexual intercourse) or lack of preventive behaviour practices (e.g. toothbrushing, exercising) in the belief they will be judged to be 'deviant', in poor health, or simply as being careless with their health (e.g. Davies and Baker 1987). Impression management is common: i.e. people monitor and control (actively construct) what they say in order to give particular impressions of themselves (or to achieve certain effects) to particular audiences (Allport 1920 first noted this in the domain of social psychology).

So how can you tell whether health behaviour data that are collected provide a true representation of behaviour or simply the outcome of self-presentational processes? It is probably best to assume that they are a bit of both, and when reading statistics regarding the prevalence of particular behaviour, stop to consider the methods used in generating the data and ask yourself what biases, if any, may be present.

> **social desirability bias**
> the tendency to answer questions about oneself or one's behaviour in a way that is thought likely to meet with social (or interviewer) approval.

In terms of women and HIV prevention, many interpersonal, intrapersonal, cultural and contextual factors have been shown to interact and affect whether or not the woman feels able to control the use of condoms in sexual encounters (e.g. Bury et al. 1992; Sanderson and Jemmot 1996). In general, surveys of condom use among young women have found that while females share some of the negative attitudes towards condom use found among male samples (such as that condoms reduce spontaneity of behaviour or reduce sexual pleasure), and that they also tend to hold unrealistically optimistic estimates of personal risk of infection with STDs or HIV, women face additional barriers when considering condom use (Hobfoll et al. 1994; Bryan et al. 1996, 1997). These can include:

- anticipated male objection to a female suggesting condom use (denial of their pleasure);
- difficulty/embarrassment in raising the issue of condom use with a male partner;

- worry that suggesting use to a potential partner implies that either themselves or the partner is HIV-positive or has another STD;
- lack of self-efficacy or mastery in condom use.

These factors are not simply about the individual's own health beliefs and behavioural intentions regarding avoiding pregnancy, STDs or AIDS; they also highlight that sexual behaviour is a complex interpersonal interaction. Safer sexual behaviour perhaps requires multiple-level interventions that target not only individual health beliefs (such as those described in Chapter 5 ☞) but also their interpersonal, communication and negotiating skills (see Chapters 6 and 7 ☞). Individual behaviour, where positively or negatively associated with health, can be a sensitive issue, with some people preferring to keep their practices and motivations to themselves. This can create many challenges for those interested in measuring health or risk behaviour with a view to developing understanding of it. While measurement issues are not confined to studies of health behaviour, they are particularly pertinent in this domain (see Issues below).

Unhealthy diet

What and how we eat plays an important role in our long-term health. Heart disease and some forms of cancer have been directly associated with diet. Our dietary intake and behaviour (e.g. snacking, bingeing) may also confer an indirect risk of disease through its effect on weight and obesity – something we turn to later in the chapter. The degree of risk for cancer conferred by diet may be surprising. While many cancer deaths (approximately 30 per cent) are attributed to smoking cigarettes, it is perhaps a lesser-known and discussed fact that 35 per cent of cancer deaths are attributable, in part, to poor diet. A diet involving significant intake of high-fat foods, high levels of salt and low levels of fibre appears to be particularly implicated (American Cancer Society 2012). The World Health Report 2002 attributes over 7 per cent of the global disease burden to raised body mass index and about a third of heart disease and stroke and over 60 per cent of hypertension to people being overweight. Abdominal obesity, that is a high waist to hip ratio ('apple shape') is particularly implicated in heart attack, more so than BMI. Problems of overweight and obesity have been rising significantly amongst children as well as adults, with about a quarter of adults in many Western European countries, and the USA, being obese, and up to 60 per cent being overweight. Behaviours of poor or overeating and not exercising are central to this 'epidemic'.

Fat intake and cholesterol

Excessive fat intake has been found to be implicated in coronary heart disease and heart attacks (Yusuf et al. 2004) and to a lesser extent cancer, particularly colorectal, testicular and breast cancer (Freedman et al. 2008). (Chapter 8 discusses the relevant biological and chemical processes (☛).) Cholesterol is a lipid (fat) which is present in our own bodily cells. Normal circulating cholesterol (serum cholesterol) has a purpose in that it is synthesised to produce steroid hormones and is involved in the production of bile necessary for digestion.

Serum cholesterol levels can be increased by a fatty diet (and by other factors such as age). While there is not a perfect correlation between dietary cholesterol and serum cholesterol, they are related, which is why cholesterol is of interest to health psychologists concerned with behaviour change!

Fatty foods, particularly foods high in saturated fats (such as animal products and some vegetable oils), contain cholesterol, a fat-like substance which contains lipoproteins which vary in density. Those known as low-density lipoproteins (LDLs), when circulating in the bloodstream can lead to the formation of plaques in the arteries, and as a result cholesterol carried by LDLs is often called 'bad cholesterol'. LDL appears to be implicated in atherosclerosis (see below), whereas cholesterol carried by high density lipoproteins (HDLs) is called 'good cholesterol', as it appears to increase the processing and removal of LDLs by the liver. Some foods, such as polyunsaturated fats which can be more easily metabolised in the body, or foods such as oily fish which contain Omega-3 fatty acids and which have been found to raise HDL levels, are beneficial to one's health. What seems important to health is having a low ratio of total cholesterol (HDL + LDL + 20 per cent of even lower density triglycerides) to HDL, where the desirable ratio is less than 4.5:1. At that level people are thought to have a reduced risk of heart disease. However, it is still thought important to keep the actual LDL levels as low as possible, particularly in those with other risk factors for heart disease such as hypertension, family history, or smoking.

If fat molecules, a good store of energy in our bodies, are not metabolised during exercise or activity, then their circulating levels become high, and plaques (fatty layers) are laid down on the artery walls (**atherosclerosis**), causing them to thicken and restrict blood flow to the heart. An often related condition, **arteriosclerosis**, exists when increased blood pressure causes artery walls to lose elasticity and harden, with resulting effects on the ability of the cardiovascular system to adapt to increased blood flow (such as during exercise). These arterial diseases are together referred to as CAD (coronary artery

---

atherosclerosis
formation of fatty plaque in the arteries.

arteriosclerosis
loss of elasticity and hardening of the arteries.

disease) and form a major risk factor for angina pectoris (a painful sign of arterial obstruction restricting oxygen flow) and coronary heart disease (CHD).

Reduced fat intake is a target of health interventions, not solely because of its effects on body weight and, potentially, obesity (see later), but because of the links with CHD. Evidence for this link has come from many studies, including three large prospective studies (MRFIT study of 69,205 men followed over 16 years; CHA study of 11,017 men over 25 years; PG study of 1,266 men over 34 years) where a significant linear relationship between baseline cholesterol level and death from heart disease, stroke, or in fact mortality overall, was reported (Stamler et al. 2000). It has been shown that a 10 per cent reduction in serum (blood) cholesterol is associated at five-year follow-up with a 54 per cent reduction in the incidence of coronary heart disease at age 40, a 27 per cent reduction at age 60 and a 19 per cent reduction at age 80 (Law et al. 1994). This reduced association in older adults is a relatively consistent finding, suggesting that those over 65 need perhaps to worry less on their total cholesterol levels (Navas-Nacher et al. 2001). While there is some correlational evidence of higher breast cancer death rates in countries where high fat intake is common (e.g. the UK, the Netherlands, the USA) than in countries where dietary fat intake is lower (e.g. Japan, the Philippines), firm causal data is limited, both in terms of breast cancer (e.g. Löf et al. 2007) and prostate cancer risk (Crowe et al. 2008).

As a result of these and other data, governmental policy documents have been produced in many countries that provide guidelines for healthy eating and dietary targets. In the UK, for example, *The Health of the Nation* report (1992) recommended that a maximum of 35 per cent of food energy (calories) should be derived from fat intake, of which a maximum of only 11 per cent should come from saturated fats. Subsequently, the recommended percentage fat intake has decreased to 30 per cent (World Health Organization 1999; US Department of Health and Human Services 2000); however, there is evidence that, at least in Europe, average consumption figures remain around 40 per cent. In terms of grams per day, these recommendations convert to a maximum of 30g of saturated fat intake per day for males, 20g for females.

Ethnicity has been shown to have an effect on fat intake: for example, a study of ethnic minority males living in the UK found higher levels of fat intake among Bangladeshi males than among most other ethnic groups (2012 CHD Statistics; Bhopal et al. 1999). It is worth noting, however, that a systematic review (Cochrane Review) of evidence derived from four randomised controlled trials concluded that fat-restricted diets were no more effective than calorie-restricted diets in terms of long-term weight loss among overweight or obese individuals (Pirozzo et al. 2003), suggesting that dietary change should not focus solely on fat intake but on total intake. In relation to older populations, however, there is evidence that low rather than high levels of calorific intake are detrimental to health status and cognitive function, and older men living alone seem particularly vulnerable here (Hughes et al. 2004).

Salt

Salt intake is also a target of preventive health measures, with high salt (sodium chloride) intake, much of it coming from an increasing overreliance on processed foods, being implicated in those with persistent high blood pressure, i.e. hypertension. The detrimental effects of high salt intake on blood pressure appear to persist even when levels of physical activity, obesity and other health behaviour are controlled and thus educational interventions have attempted to modify intake.

A systematic review and meta-analysis of intervention trials assessed the impact of lowering salt intake in adults who were either normotensive (i.e. 'normal' blood pressure), who had high blood pressure that was not being treated, or who were hypertensive (i.e. had high blood pressure) and being treated using drug therapy (Hooper et al. 2002). Overall, the review is not conclusive in that salt reduction resulted in reduced **systolic** and **diastolic blood pressure**; however, the degree of reduction in blood pressure was not related to

---

systolic blood pressure
the maximum pressure of blood on the artery walls, which occurs at the end of the left ventricle output/contraction (measured in relation to *diastolic blood pressure*).

diastolic blood pressure
the minimum pressure of the blood on the walls of the arteries between heartbeats (measured in relation to *systolic blood pressure*).

the amount of salt reduction. In addition, the trials had no impact on the number of heart disease-related deaths seen in follow-ups ranging from seven months to seven years, with deaths equally distributed across the intervention and control groups. It seems therefore that interventions targeting salt intake provide only limited health benefits.

In spite of mixed findings, guidelines still exist as to recommended levels of salt intake. High salt intake is considered to be in excess of 6 g per day for adults, and

ISSUES

The changing messages

It is sometimes hard to keep up with health recommendations as new evidence or syntheses of evidence lead to new health messages, typically picked up by the media and summarised in a non-critical manner. There are two recent examples of this.

Saturated fats may not be as bad as we thought?

In March 2014 the *Daily Mail* picked up on the findings of a paper published in the *Annals of Internal Medicine*, a highly respected journal (Chowdury et al. 2014). In this the authors present findings from a meta-analysis of data pooled from 72 studies of fat intake and report that their findings do not fully support the risks attached to saturated fats in terms of heart disease risks. They point to a specific sub-component of saturated fats, trans-fatty acids, which do seem to confer the increased risk. So perhaps reducing all saturated fat is not the answer, but focusing on TFAs contained in processed oil-based products may be.

Coverage gives the suggestion that scientists do not really know what is best for us, but taken in the larger context of other published evidence, as responsibly reported in the *Guardian* (24.03.14), this new data is not that inconsistent with other evidence that concludes that focusing on reducing saturated fat is not the answer to reducing heart disease. Replacing fatty foods with more carbohydrates can increase obesity, eating the wrong polyunsaturated fats (from vegetable oils instead of, for example, from fish) can also carry risk. A balanced and more Mediterranean-style diet with a high amount of fruit and vegetables, nuts, beans and seeds, with a smattering of fish, meat and egg protein and dairy, is advocated. However, how many fruit and vegetables do we need to reap health gains . . .?

Fruit and Veg: 5, 7 or 10 a day?

Report from April 1st media coverage and paper from UCL BHF 2012 show that in Great Britain the average total grams of fresh fruit intake per week in 1942 was 197g; by 2010 this was 755g; for fresh vegetables (excluding potatoes) things were more stable (88g per week in 1942 to 757g in 2010), and potato consumption has also significantly decreased 1877g per week to 501g. Given that your average apple weighs about 100g, you can see how these weekly figures don't add up to average intake of 'five a day'.

Recent reports suggest, however, that 5 a day is not enough to obtain long-term health gains and that we should instead seek to consume a regular intake of 7 portions of fruit or veg a day. Add to that the debate over whether cooking destroys some of the potential beneficial ingredients and enzymes found in raw foods, or helps in their release (e.g. cooking may maximise the release of lycopene from tomatoes which has been associated with reduced risk of some cancers and heart disease), then it is understandable that people say they are confused. However, none are saying that fruit or vegetables are not good for you, and so whilst research progresses it would be advisable to just eat as many as you can, within a balanced diet and without putting your daily calorie intake above acceptable levels.

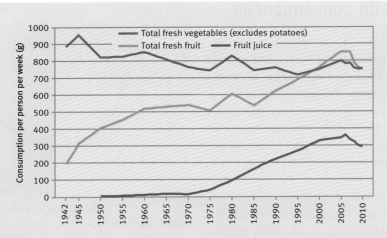

Figure 3.4 Consumption of fresh fruit and vegetables in adults aged 16 and over, United Kingdom 1942 to 2010

Source: Coronary Heart Disease Statistics: A Compendium of Health Statistics, 2012 Edition, © British Heart Foundation 2012

over 5 g per day for children aged 7 to 14 (British Medical Association 2003a), with BHF 2012 data showing a decline since 1975 from an adult average of 7g per day to a 2010 average of 6.3 g – still above recommendations. While it is perhaps difficult to establish the unique health benefits of a reduced-salt diet when examining individuals engaged in more general dietary change behaviour, the BMA guidelines raise awareness of the need to monitor salt intake from early childhood onwards.

WHAT DO YOU THINK?

Do you add before you taste? Why? Do you have any idea how much you consume a day?

Obesity

Even though obesity is not itself a behaviour, it is contributed to mainly by a combination of poor diet and a lack of exercise (Haslam and James 2005), both health behaviours which are the theme of this and the following chapter. Global concerns about the increasing prevalence of obesity, to epidemic proportions (WHO 2000), and its impact on morbidity (including disability and a range of diseases) and mortality justify our inclusion of this condition here.

How is obesity defined?

Obesity is generally measured in terms of an individual's body mass index (BMI), which is calculated as a person's weight in kilograms divided by their height in metres squared (weight/height^2). An individual is considered to be:

- 'normal weight' if their BMI is between 20 and 24.9;
- mildly obese or 'overweight' (grade 1) if their BMI is between 25 and 29.9;
- moderate or clinically obese (grade 2) if their BMI falls between 30 and 39.9;
- severely obese (grade 3) if their BMI is 40 or greater.

BMI does not, however, take age, gender or body frame/muscle build into consideration (although BMI cut-offs are based on being 20 per cent above the height–weight chart standards for a person of 'medium' frame), and so the index should only be used as a guide in context with these other factors. As well as considering BMI, it has become clear that waist circumference, ratio of waist to hip size, and fat deposited around the abdomen (often referred to as being 'apple-shaped') further increase the implications of overweight and obesity for heart attack in both men (Smith et al. 2005) and women (Iribarren et al. 2006), for type 2 diabetes and all-case mortality in women (Hu 2003) and for some forms of cancer (Williams and Hord 2005).

Negative health consequences of obesity

As noted earlier, being underweight is the largest global cause of mortality, yet a growing number of people, predominantly in Western or developed countries, are at risk from the opposite problem – obesity. Obesity is a major risk factor in a range of physical illnesses, including, for example, hypertension, heart disease, type 2 diabetes, osteoarthritis, respiratory problems, lower back pain, and some forms of cancer.

The relative risk of disease appears to increase proportionately in relation to the percentage overweight a person is, although evidence as to this linear relationship remains mixed. A recent meta-analysis published in the *Journal of the American Medical Association* (Flegal et al. 2013), concluded from review of 97 study datasets involving over 2.8 million individuals, that there was a raised risk (calculating Hazard Ratios (HR) relative to normal weight) of death for grade 2 and grade 3 obesity (combined HR 1.29), but not for those classed as overweight (HR 0.94) or grade 1 obese (HR 0.95). In fact, being just overweight was associated with lower risk of mortality than 'normal' weight. Although based only on BMI and not weight distribution, these are important findings, leading to some academic debate about potential health benefits to being a bit overweight, certainly compared to being underweight. In contrast, the longitudinal Framingham Heart Study shows a relationship between obesity and mortality which appears over two to three decades. In their data, being overweight confers slightly more risk than 'normal' weight. In both studies, however, a J-shaped curve exists (e.g. as in Figure 3.5) reminds us also of the risk of being underweight.

Apart from physical health problems, obesity is also implicated in psychological ill health including low self-esteem and social isolation, possibly arising from the experience of stigmatising behaviour (British Medical Association 2003a; Strauss 2000, Ogden and Clementi 2011). Being overweight as a child has been associated with poorer health-related quality of life (Williams et al. 2005) and even earlier mortality (Bjørge et al. 2008).

Prevalence of obesity

In 1999, The European Commission estimated that 31 per cent of the EU adult population was overweight,

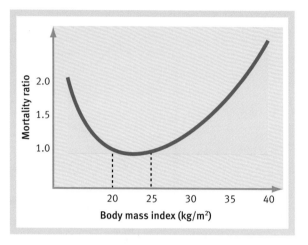

Figure 3.5 The relationship between body mass index and mortality at 23-year follow-up (Framingham heart study)
Source: Wilson et al. (2002).

with a further 10 per cent reaching weights defined as clinically obese. More recently, however, the proportions of adults defined as obese in England were as high as 26 per cent, among both adult men and women, with middle aged having the highest prevalence (BHF 2012). The World Health Organization collation of epidemiological data provides evidence of a three-fold increase in obesity rates in parts of North America, Australasia and China, and within the UK over the past three decades. Sadly this increase was predicted in the 1980s (Department of Health 1995). In England the prevalence of obesity in adult men has risen from 14 per cent to 26 per cent and for women over the same time period from 17 per cent to 26 per cent.

Alarmingly, excess body weight has been identified as the most common child disorder in Europe (International Obesity Taskforce and European Association for the Study of Obesity 2002) and within the English data reception class (aged 3–4) prevalence of obesity was at 9.4 per cent, rising to 19 per cent in year 6 (aged 10–11) (Department of Health Cross-Government Obesity Unit, 2011 and Lifestyle Statistics/ National Child Measurement Programme 2010/11). These data reflect the previous 9 per cent increase in the prevalence of overweight children aged between 2 and 10 years reported between 1995 and 2005 (Health Survey for England 2008). Obesity affects all age groups; however, in younger populations the particular concerns are about the early implications of obesity for psychological health and psychosocial development, whereas with ageing, as with middle-aged and older adults, the effects on physical health begin to be seen.

Lower social class has been related to increased obesity for young females, but not for males, and as obese children tend to grow up to be obese adults (Magarey et al. 2003), interventions need to start early. To be successful, interventions need to first understand the factors associated with the development of obesity, and to do this researchers have considered the influences on food choice, intake and, crucially, overeating behaviour. These factors fall within social learning theory, e.g. the powerful influence of significant others' behaviour or communications – peers, siblings, parents, the media – or within theories of associative learning where food choice and eating behaviours are associated with the receiving of intrinsic or extrinsic rewards or **reinforcers**, such as the pleasure attached to eating with family and friends, or the perceived stress reduction gained from 'comfort eating'. As well as considering these developmental theories which focus on social learning and modelling, health psychologists have also applied cognitive theories to behaviour change with regards to overeating (see Chapter 5 ☞). It is the case that many normal-weight women wish to weigh less, thus buying in to the idea of 'thinner is better' which is normalised in much media coverage (Wardle and Johnson 2002). In spite of this, we still face an obesity epidemic and those who are overweight face being judged against this perceived 'ideal'.

Obesity has a strong association with disease, but in considering the influences on it below you will see that it is not solely due to overeating.

What causes obesity?

A simple explanation of obesity is that it is a condition that results from an energy intake that grossly exceeds the energy output (Pinel 2003). However, early twin studies and studies of adopted children (who showed weight relationship with biological rather than adoptive mothers, e.g. Price and Gottesman 1991; Meyer and Stunkard 1993) proposed some genetic explanations to obesity, which are generally one of three types:

- Obese individuals are born with a greater number of fat cells: evidence of this is limited. For example, the number of fat cells in a person of average weight and

in many mildly obese individuals is typically 25–35 million. The number of cells is dramatically increased in a severely obese person, implying the formation of new fat cells.

- Obese individuals inherit lower metabolic rates and thus they burn calories more slowly and therefore they should require fewer calories to survive; however, if they don't know this and eat 'typically' they gain weight. However, research evidence shows that obese people do not consistently have lower metabolic rates than comparable thin persons, thus this common explanation seems unfounded.

- Obese individuals may have deficiencies in a hormone responsible for appetite regulation or control, or lack of control: more potential as a contributing factor.

This last explanation has received attention since the 1950s, when a gene mutation was identified in some laboratory mice that had become highly obese (Coleman 1979). Subsequent cloning of this mutated gene found that it was only expressed in fat cells and that it encoded a protein hormone called leptin (Zhang et al. 1994). Leptin is produced by fatty (adipose) tissue and is one of several signals to the hypothalamus of the central nervous system that help to regulate weight. Low leptin levels suggest low fat stores which then prompts a signal to the organism to eat, to re-establish fatty stores needed for energy (see Chapter 8 ☞). However, research has not found similar genetic mutation in all obese humans and increasing leptin by means of injection has not consistently reduced eating behaviour or body fat in the obese. More recently, exciting research showing the effects of common FTO (fat mass and obesity associated) gene variants on BMI, weight, waist circumference and body fat (e.g. Frayling et al. 2007) have been brought into the limelight by preliminary evidence that genetic susceptibility to obesity could be reduced or even negated by means of vigorous physical activity (Rampersaud et al. 2008).

> **reinforcers**
> factors that reward or provide a positive response following a particular behaviour or set of behaviours (positive reinforcer); or enable the removal or avoidance of an undesired state or response (negative reinforcer).

Another avenue of research has identified that serotonin, a neurotransmitter (see Chapter 8 ☞), is directly involved in producing satiety (the condition where hunger is no longer felt). Early animal experiments investigating the effects on hunger of administering a serotonin **agonist** have had their findings confirmed in humans, where the introduction of serotonin agonists into the body induced satiety, and reduced the frequency and quantity of food intake and body weight (Halford and Blundell 2000).

Such lines of research hold promise for future intervention; however, it is likely that such explanations are insufficient. Given the recent upsurge in obesity in developed countries, obesity is more plausibly attributed to an interaction between physiological and environmental factors such as sedentary lifestyle and behaviour patterns. People of all ages increasingly pass their time indoors, and there is evidence that activities such as watching television or computing can even reduce a person's metabolic rate, so that their bodies burn up existing calories more slowly. Lack of physical activity in combination with overeating or eating the wrong food types are associated with obesity, and it is unclear which is the primary causal factor.

People eat for different reasons and it may be that the obese differ from the non-obese in this regard. For many, eating carries positive incentives, such as the intrinsic rewards of taste enjoyment (sensory eating), and extrinsic rewards such as the pleasure of social eating (Pinel et al. 2000). Eating styles exist (van Strien et al. 1986; and see WHAT DO YOU THINK? below) whereby some people eat when they catch sight of food or food cues (external eating), or simply when their body signals hunger (internal eating); others eat when they are bored, irritated or stressed (emotional eating). There is some evidence that obese people and those who overeat are more external cue responsive and less led by internal hunger cues, and perhaps show more emotional eating (Snoek et al. 2007; van Strien et al. 2007; O'Connor et al. 2008). When eating when stressed, it seems that it is not only the amount of food that increases, but also the type of food selected, often that with high sugar or fat content (Oliver et al. 2000), and furthermore that the type of eating behaviour may differ depending on the nature of the stressor (O'Connor et al. 2008).

Effective interventions which aim to make what has been described as our 'obesogenic' environments (BMA 2003a) and behaviour more healthy need therefore to address a complexity of factors. Similarly, interventions to increase physical activity, the other major contributor to reduced obesity, are also high on the public health agenda (see Chapters 4, 6 and 7 ☞).

> ## WHAT DO YOU THINK?
>
> What style of eating do you have? Are you likely to eat when something looks or smells good even if you have recently eaten and don't actually feel hungry? ('external/sensory eating') Are you easily swayed by others simply eating in front of you? ('external eating') Can you exercise restraint over what and when you eat? For example, if you think you have eaten more than usual over the weekend, do you try to eat less the next day? ('restraint eating'). What about your mood: does that make a difference to when and what you eat? Some people eat less when depressed, others eat more and seek out certain food types – usually sweet or fatty foods. If you're angry, frustrated or impatient, do you snack or nibble more? ('emotional eating').
>
> Styles of eating reported by those with obesity have been 'matched' to different obesity treatments. If you are interested in reading further about this, use the references above and also Google the DEBQ (the Dutch Eating Behaviours Questionaire), a screening tool used in many studies of eating styles and which has been shown to have good construct validity and internal reliability.

A final thought on obesity

A word of caution is drawn from the BMA report (2003a) referred to previously: we as individuals, and as a society, must be careful not to over-focus on the weight of individual children – while obesity is on the increase, so too is extreme dietary behaviour and eating disorders; several recent studies point to increasing body dissatisfaction among children and adolescents, particularly females (e.g. Schur et al. 2000; O'Connor et al. 2008). Body dissatisfaction can lead to dietary restraint which can potentially have adverse physical and psychological consequences, including eating disorders (e.g. Stice et al. 2002).

> **agonist**
> a drug that simulates the effects of neurotransmitters, such as the serotonin agonist fluoxetine, which induces satiety (reduces hunger).

SUMMARY

This chapter has defined health behaviour as those behaviours associated with health status, whether or not they are performed with the explicit goal of health protection, promotion or maintenance in mind. The behaviours addressed in this chapter are sometimes referred to as 'behavioural pathogens' or health-risk behaviour and include smoking, heavy consumption of alcohol, unprotected sexual behaviour and an unhealthy diet. 'Behavioural immunogens' or health-enhancing behaviours, such as exercise, a balanced diet, health screening and immunisation behaviours, are discussed in the next chapter.

This chapter has described behaviours with clear associations with prevalent illnesses, and as such

they account for a vast amount of research enquiry within health psychology. A significant body of work has addressed the complexity of social, emotional and cognitive factors that contribute to the uptake and maintenance of health-damaging behaviour, and a range of theories and models of health behaviour which have been developed and tested are described in Chapter 5 ☞.

We concluded this chapter by bringing to the reader's attention some of the challenges to effective measurement of health behaviours and, as elsewhere in this text, we encourage readers to stop and think about the data on which a lot of the evidence we review is built, and to do this they may need some further individual reading.

Further reading

Knott, C.S., Coombs, N, Stamatakis, E., and Biddolph, J.P. (2015). All-cause mortality and the case for age-specific alcohol consumption guidelines: pooled analyses of up to 10 population based cohorts, *British Medical Journal*; 350 doi: http://dx.doi.org/10.1136/bmj.h384

A recent and important review of the different effects of alcohol by age, with calls for age-specific alcohol guidelines. It will be interesting to see whether these emerge.

West, R (2006). *Theory of Addiction*. Oxford, Blackwell.

Reading this as well as the above book by Knott et al. will give the interested reader an excellent and up-to-date grasp of both psychological and social models of addiction.

The World Drugs Report 2014, United Nations Office on Drugs and Crime, Vienna.

This report provides useful and up-to-date statistics regarding the health-risk behaviours reported in this chapter, particularly with regards to illicit substances. Other than making

recommendations for individual behaviour change, the report focuses on global strategies to reduce drug production and trafficking.

For a useful overview of current Department of Health survey statistics pertaining to health behaviour and illness (UK): www.doh.gov.uk/stats

For a copy of the recent UK survey of adolescent health and health behaviour, including recommendations for interventions: www.bma/org.uk

For information about the HPV vaccination programme, look at this website. It offers a health encyclopaedia to members of the public in order to provide up-to-date information about health conditions and their treatments: www.nhsdirect.nhs. uk/articles/article.aspx?articleId=2336

For a downloadable report of UK statistics (up to 2012) relating to heart disease, including behavioural and medical risk factors see: http://www.bhf.org.uk/publications/view-publication.aspx?ps=1002097

For information regarding worldwide HIV and AIDS figures, campaigns and news: http://www.avert.org/

For open-access student resources specifically written to complement this textbook and support your learning, please visit **www.pearsoned.co.uk/morrison**

Chapter 4
Health-protective behaviour

Learning outcomes

By the end of this chapter, you should have an understanding of:

- the behaviour found to have health-enhancing or health-protective effects

- the relevance of adherence to medicine and treatments, healthy diet, exercise, screening and immunisation to health across the lifespan

- the range and complexity of influences upon the uptake and maintenance of health-enhancing behaviour

Does your lifestyle affect your gene health?

BBC News of 3 December 2014 had a headline stating that 'Mediterranean diet keeps people genetically young'. A Mediterranean diet has long been associated with reduced risk of cardiovascular diseases and some forms of cancer, and likewise we know that being active and exercising is health protective. Those relationships are described in this chapter, but *how* does this work? What are the processes at play that result in behaviours influencing illness? To address such questions research has had to explore human biology, biochemistry and physiology. We are now beginning to get some answers that lie in the basic building blocks of life – our DNA!

The news headline and the coverage that followed was based on a well-conducted survey of 5,000 Boston nurses followed over a ten-year period. The findings reported in the *British Medical Journal*, suggest that healthy and well-rounded Mediterranean-style diets high in fresh fruit and vegetables, fish and white meat, for example, are associated with longer and healthier telomeres – these are little caps on the end of our chromosomes which store our DNA and when they shorten and weaken this is thought to be involved in a range of disease, and indeed general ageing. Diet may play a role in shortening and weakening them.

Whilst there remains a need for further controlled studies, as findings are often based on observational survey data, this new body of work is opening up exciting avenues of research that explore the *processes* that may underpin the reported associations between behaviour and health that we have described in the previous chapter with regards to health risk behaviour and in this chapter with regards to health-protective behaviour. We have described other routes where behaviours cause physiological changes, for example smoking and hardening of the arteries that increases the risk of heart disease, but we now should also consider 'gene health'. Scientific advances in genetic physiology are beyond the scope of detailed exploration in this psychology text; however, hopefully, this chapter whets your appetite for further understanding of 'how' these relationships might emerge!

Chapter outline

Behaviour is linked to health, and as shown in the previous chapter many of our behaviours have negative effects on our health; however, thankfully, other behaviours can benefit our health, and even protect against illness. These are sometimes called 'behavioural immunogens', and in this chapter we present an overview of the evidence surrounding a range of such behaviours, including medication or treatment adherence, healthy diet, exercise behaviour, health screening and immunisation. The scientific evidence pertaining to the health benefits of these behaviours is considered, and some national guidelines in relation to their practice will be provided. A broad array of influences on the uptake or maintenance of specific health-protective or enhancing behaviour is introduced to the reader here in order to provide a foundation for Chapter 5 ☞, where key psychosocial theories of health behaviour and health behaviour change are explored fully.

In a society where chronic disease is prevalent and where the population is ageing, it is increasingly important to take positive steps towards healthy living and healthy ageing. While media coverage and public health campaigns work towards increasing awareness of the beneficial effects of some behaviours on health, it is important to remember that people do not always behave as they do to protect their health or to reduce their risk of illness: for example, they exercise for fun or for social reasons. As health psychologists, it is important to develop an understanding not only of the consequences of certain behaviour for health but also of the many psychosocial factors that influence its performance. Individual behaviour can both undermine (see Chapter 3 ☞) and act to protect and maintain health (this chapter). The dominant psychosocial theories applied and tested in this regard are described in Chapter 5 ☞, and the manner in which such behaviours provide targets for educational and health promotion endeavours worldwide are discussed in Chapters 6 and 7 ☞.

We start the chapter with a look at adherence behaviour, focusing on medication and treatment adherence; however, the principles are relevant also to adhering to behaviours addressed in the preceding chapter (e.g. smoking cessation) or elsewhere in this chapter (e.g. healthy eating, exercise).

Adherence behaviour

Definition and measurement

Depending on whether you are reading from medical literature, pharmacological literature or psychological literature, you will come across the terms 'compliance', 'concordance' or 'adherence' being used to refer to the act of acquiring prescriptions and taking medicines appropriately, or carrying out other illness self-management behaviours such as rehabilitation exercises, as advised by a health-care professional. Although often used interchangeably, these terms are considered to suggest a different relationship between a patient and a health-care professional, as we illustrate with the brief definitions below:

● Compliance: most often used in medical literature, this term suggests patient medicine taking behaviour which conforms with 'doctor's orders', and thus non-compliance may be interpreted as wilful or even incompetent. The term 'patient compliance' was introduced in 1975 as an official Medical Subject Heading (MeSH term), used when conducting systematic literature reviews, something you may need to do at some point!

● Adherence: this terms suggest that a person sticks to, or cooperates with, advice about medication (or lifestyle changes, behaviours) (NICE 2009a) in a more collaborative practitioner–patient relationship (diMatteo et al. 2012; Vrijens et al. 2012). Adherence is viewed as a behaviour, a process influenced by individual and environmental factors including healthcare practices and system influences. 'Medication adherence' became a MeSH term only in 2009 (for electronic searches in systematic reviewing), and is the term most often used in health psychology and behavioural medicine although the newer term of concordance below overlaps significantly.

● Concordance: introduced by the Royal Pharmaceutical Society of Great Britain in 1995, this term is more often used in a pharmacological or therapeutic literature to describe a jointly determined agreement between physician and patient as to what is the appropriate treatement, following the patient having been fully informed of the costs and benefits of adhering to their particular treatment. It does not explicitly describe adherence behaviour, but more the conditions in which to encourage it (see also Chapter 10 for a discussion of shared decision-making (☞).

The World Health Organization's own definitions of adherence have changed from being 'the extent to which the patient's behaviour coincides with the clinical prescription' (suggesting accidental match rather than agreed behaviour) to one which emphasises partnership in terms of adherence being 'the extent to which the patient's behaviour corresponds with agreed recommendation from a health-care provider' (WHO 2009b).

Non-adherence behaviour, i.e. failing to follow recommended treatment or advice, can vary in extent, for example, from not filling a prescription in the first place (estimated occurrence in between 14–21 per cent), to skipping an occasional dose, through to skipping many doses or not taking at all. The various forms of non-adherence carry differing consequences, and as we describe below may occur for different reasons.

Thresholds, in terms of the amount of medicine taken, or behaviours performed appropriately in order *not* to be categorised as non-adherent, range from 70–100 per cent depending on the disease and the treatment concerned (as discussed below). This makes study comparison difficult. The consensus, however, is that a clinically relevant cut-off should be used wherever possible (Vitolins et al. 2000). In other words, if 60 per cent of a drug is needed to be taken daily for it to be effective, then any less than that should be defined as non-adherence. For example, Sherr et al. (2010) report that although as many as 57 per cent of their sample of HIV-infected adults in receipt of a prescription for HAART (Highly Active Antiretroviral Therapy, also known as ART) had taken a tablet at the wrong time in the previous week, it was the 10 per cent who reported having missed two or more dosages within the past week who risked a worse disease prognosis as a result. Thus in terms of setting clinically meaningful thresholds for defining non-adherence, in this instance adherence to HAART (once per day regimen) requires 70 per cent or better (i.e. 5 doses of 7 need be taken for optimal effect).

Why do definitions matter? They matter because if we are to measure the nature and extent of adherence or non-adherence, we have to know what it is we are assessing. Conceptual overlap and conceptual confusion is not helpful if one is to synthesise a literature, something some of you may discover if you carry out research in this domain. One attempt to assist in this was the work of the ABC (Ascertaining Barriers to Compliance) group, a multinational group of researchers from Poland, the UK, Belgium and Switzerland, where a systematic review of terminology as used in papers published prior to April 2009 led to the proposal of a new taxonomy of medication therapy management, where 'medication adherence' is the preferred term and, within that, initiation, implementation (the extent to which the patients actual dosing corresponds to the prescribed regimen) and discontinuation is specified (Vrijens et al. 2012). The work of this EU-funded group included a 12-country survey of health psychology and health economic predictors of adherence behaviour in people with hypertension

(See Chapter 5, Holmes et al. 2014; Morrison et al. 2015, and www.abcproject.eu).

In addition to the challenges of shared definitions described above, adherence researchers also face challenges when it comes to measuring adherence. Statistics are often derived from patient self-report that, while more reliable than asking the health professional involved in their care (who generally overestimate adherence), may be subject to recall and reporting bias. Some studies therefore gather data on adherence using mixed methods, combining self- and other-report, with biological measurements (e.g. urine or blood testing), or pill counts, including using electronic monitoring systems (MEMS, where counters are in the lids of pill bottles to record timing of openings). All methods have their limitations and, as it stands, no gold standard measure exists, although MEMS is often described as this (diMatteo 2004a). A recent meta-analysis of 11 studies (total of 1,684 participants), where both self-reported methods as well as electronic MEMS systems were used to record adherence, reassuringly found an overall moderate correlation between the two methods (0.46). Seven of the eleven studies were conducted with those receiving treatment for HIV, and within a separate meta-analysis of those studies the correlation was just slightly stronger (0.51) (Shi et al. 2010). Interestingly, there is also evidence that the method of dispensing medicines can itself affect adherence. For example, in a recent randomised controlled trial amongst adults with Type 2 diabetes (Sutton et al. 2014) participants provided with electronic packaging which records the date and time of each opening of the container (a MEMS device) were modestly more adherent than those whose oral glucose lowering medication was contained in standard paper packaging.

So, how well do people adhere and does it matter if they do?

Do people adhere?

Hippocrates (*c* 400 BC) was the first documented recorder of the finding that patients did not take medicines as prescribed, and that they even complained when they didn't seem to get better! Somewhat more recently (!) the WHO estimated that about a half of all medicines prescribed for chronic conditions are not taken as prescribed, and over all conditions, acute and chronic, about 25 per cent are non-adherent. However, adherence rates vary depending on many factors (di Matteo 2004a). DiMatteo's meta-analysis of data from 569 different study samples found some similarities across conditions; for example, adherence amongst those with cardiovascular disease averaged at 77 per cent, similar to the taking of essential immunosuppressant drugs amongst adult organ transplant patients, where 22.6 per cent were found to *not* adhere (Dew et al. 2007). However, variation was seen across many other conditions, attributed in part to treatment complexity (number, amount, type of administration, timing of medicines, etc.) and individual beliefs about, as well as actual, illness severity, and many other factors which we describe later in this section.

The costs of non-adherence

Patients themselves recognise the costs of non-adherence. For example, Annema et al. (2009) report that one-third of patients with heart failure described improvement in their adherence to their treatment regimes as the most important factor preventing hospital readmission. Few patients, however, probably realise the actual financial costs of non-adherence. For example, within the UK it has been estimated that individual non-adherence to prescribed medicines costs the UK NHS approximately £200 million *per year* due to repeat admissions to hospital, but a further £300 million may be wasted also due to not taking medicines as prescribed. This includes an estimated £90 million worth of unused and unwanted prescription medicines stored in individuals' homes, £110 million returned to pharmacies, and £50 million worth disposed within care homes (York Health Economics Consortium and University of London 2010). It is hard to ascertain what further costs can be attached to non-adherence to recommended behaviour change following illness events, such as dietary change or smoking cessation following a heart attack, but they are likely to add further to this huge figure.

Why do people not adhere to medical recommendations and treatments?

The reasons for non-adherence are many and varied, but they can be considered as falling into the following groupings (Sabaté 2003):

● *Patient-related factors*: e.g. culture, age, personality, knowledge, personal and cultural beliefs, attitudes towards illness and medicines (see 'Research focus'), self-**efficacy** beliefs (see Chapter 5 ☞).

● *Condition-related factors*: e.g. symptom type, perceived severity (NOT actual severity, diMatteo et al. 2007), presence or absence of pain, presence of comorbidities, prognosis.

● *Treatment-related factors*: e.g. the number, type, timing, frequency and duration of dosage of medications, presence and extent of side-effects, expense.

● *Socio-economic factors*: low educational level, costs of treatment (relates also to socio-economic equalities associated with ethnicity), access to dispensing pharmacy, social isolation.

● *System-related factors*: communications with healthcare provider regarding medicines, necessity or function, presence of traditional healing beliefs and systems (see 'Research focus').

For most people non-adherence will be influenced by a mixture of the above: not all non-adherence will be intentional, and not all non-adherence carries the same risks to health. Research tends to distinguish between intentional non-adherence (e.g. 'I stopped taking my pills as they made me feel sick/are too expensive') and unintentional non-adherence (e.g. 'Sometimes I forget to take a dose if I'm busy' as they are likely to have different predictors (Holmes et al. 2014; Morrison et al. 2015).

Influences on adherence can be considered as going from the micro level, which includes personality (for example, the association between neuroticism and medication non-adherence in older adults, Jerant et al. 2011), to the macro and meso level, such as culture and social systems. While a significant body of research has identified individual characteristics such as age or social class (Chapters 2 and 10 ☞), and psychological characteristics such as attitudes and expectancies (Chapter 5 ☞), which are associated with non-adherence, few studies have explored the wider 'structural' influences on adherence behaviour, such as social, cultural, economic and political influences. Few studies have in fact explored non-adherence in non-Western populations. Illustrating the importance of structural and system level influences Kagee and Deport (2010) describe barriers to adherence to Antiretroviral Therapy (ART) (a treatment which can significantly reduce AIDS deaths, but which needs to be taken fully and properly to be effective). Both micro- (the person's immediate environment, family, school, work), macro- (the cultural and political context) and meso- (social institutions such as health-care systems, transport systems, local economy) system influences were identified in qualitative interviews with 10 patient advocates, appointed to provide support, mentoring and counselling to patients with HIV in South Africa. This study highlights influences with specific relevance to the African cultural context: for example, poverty-related hunger was considered to increase the side effects of ART if taken on an empty stomach which reduced patient's willingness to take their medicines; the distance many needed to walk to clinics to receive treatments when feeling too fatigued to move was a further barrier, and taking medication was, by some, considered as reflecting a lack of faith in God's ability to heal, or in ancestral powers. These perceived barriers would be more unlikely if the sample had been recruited in a Western culture. The religious and spirituality factor identified adds a further dimension that interventions would need to address sensitively, possibly, the authors suggest, by building spiritual beliefs into adherence counselling. Finally, several of the identified barriers emerge in most HIV-related studies regardless of culture, such as waiting times at clinics, perceived stigma limiting the disclosure of diagnosis, health literacy and the challenge of understanding complex medical regimes, and other confounds such as drug injecting behaviour. Such findings highlight a need for greater education and more accessible, better staffed, and confidential services – structural and societal factors that may not fall within health psychology's remit per se, but due to their potential impact upon patient experience are factors we need consider. Micro-cultural variations exist also: for example, in a UK (Birmingham) study of adherence to oral pharmacotherapy for conditions including diabetes, those of Caribbean, African or 'Other Black' ethnicity, and also those whose first language was Urdu or Bengali, were the least adherent. The Birmingham primary care population constitutes 70 per cent from BME (Black and Minority Ethnic) groups (the highest in England) and so one would have hoped services were better equipped to support the adherence

efficacy
Bandura's technical term analogous to confidence.

RESEARCH FOCUS

Concerns about medication and medication adherence in patients with chronic pain recruited from general practice

Rosser, B.A., McCracken, L.M., Velleman, S.C., Boichat, C. and Ecceston, C. (2011). *Pain*, 152: 1201-1205.

A range of factors explain or predict individuals' adherence to medicines, ranging from the personal and individual through to the cultural and socio-economic. This study addresses patient concerns about their medication for chronic non-malignant pain. Pain, as described in Chapter 16 ☞, is one of the main reasons a person goes to, or is referred to, a doctor. Quite commonly, no clearly defined pathology (see medically unexplained symptoms in Chapter 9 ☞) presents itself but nonetheless pharmacological medication is a mainstay of treatment, with psychological and behavioural interventions also offered in some cases. Medication typically involves painkillers (analgesics) of varying strengths and also non-steroidal anti-inflammatory drugs which help to reduce inflammation around joints (NSAIDs). As noted already, patient adherence, which is necessary if treatment effectiveness is to be reliably judged and amended if found not to be working effectively, is not always optimal. This paper examines patient concerns with the expectation that they hold the key to why medications are often used inappropriately or not at all.

Aims and methods

The study focused on primary care patients (instead of chronic patients in specialist care). A total of 239 patients (58 per cent female, 61.5 per cent married, almost 96 per cent white, age range 25 to 94 years old, with a mean of 61.46 years (and a wide standard deviation of 13.73)) were recruited which represented 36 per cent of those initially contacted, following identification by 20 different GPs across 10 practices in southwest England. Issues of sample bias are acknowledged and discussed in the paper.

Participants were assessed at one timepoint. In addition to reporting their pain (intensity rated from 0 (no pain) to 11 (worst pain possible)) and treatment history, they provided information about the dosage and frequency of their use of prescribed and non-prescribed medication. The authors' Pain Medication Attitudes Questionnaire (McCracken et al. 2006) assessed concerns and beliefs about pain medication across seven concern subscales:

● Concerns about addiction
● Concerns about withdrawal (negative effects if stop using)
● Concerns about side effects
● Mistrust in doctors
● Perceived need for medication
● Concerns over scrutiny from others
● Worries about tolerance

The dependent variable was medication adherence (general adherence, underuse, overuse) using self-reports of general rather than specific medication use. This decision was primarily because of likely polypharmacy, i.e. chronic pain patients typically have varied and multiple medications and therefore assessing adherence only in terms of the patients' 'main' treatment would limit comparisons that could be drawn across the sample (e.g. some might respond in relation to paracetamol, others to morphine). Assessing general adherence therefore focuses on the populations' behaviour rather than the substance.

Underuse was assessed with regards to the frequency with which the individual (a) 'misses' a dose, and (b) 'takes less than prescribed'. Overuse was assessed in terms of the frequency with which the individual (a) takes an extra dose/s and (b) 'takes more than prescribed'. These four items were scored from 0=never, to 4=always, with a mean calculated for overuse and underuse separately, and total 'non-adherence' score computed from the score across all four items, described as 'general non-adherence'.

Participants also completed a checklist of 'side effects', consisting of 10 common adverse effects of painkilling analgesics, such as drowsiness, impaired concentration, agitation.

Results

Participant characteristics

Over a third of the sample were not working, worked part-time or had retired because of their pain, and 41.8 per cent were in receipt of state benefits. The median pain duration was 10 years (range 3-4 months to 50 years), and at the time of study 94 per cent judged their pain as chronic, 64 per cent saying it was constant. With a score of 11 referring to the 'worst pain imaginable', the mean present intensity was 5.2 (sd 2.5) with a slightly higher mean being 'usual' (6.1, sd 2.3). This suggests moderately high pain being experienced a lot of the time. Just over half of the sample (53 per cent) attributed their pain to osteoarthritis, and 37 per cent of the sample had had at least one pain-related surgery (e.g. likely joint replacements for those with osteoarthritis, i.e. hip or knee replacements).

Participant medications

Participants were in receipt of a modal N of two medications (this ranged from 1 to 21, suggesting a need for some outlier removal perhaps), with weak opioids being most common (67.4 per cent), (8.4 per cent were prescribed strong opioids), followed by NSAIDs (50.6 per cent), and then over-the-counter medications, mainly paracetamol (36.8 per cent). However, a significant minority (19.2 per cent) were in receipt of tricyclic antidepressants, a potentially important influence on results.

Adherence behaviour

Questions about adherence were asked in two ways, one very direct with a 'yes' or 'no' answer to 'do you take your medication exactly as prescribed?', the other more specific questions regarding over- or underuse. Interestingly these provide differing pictures. In response to the direct question, 75.6 per cent of participants answered 'yes', but subsequently 47.6 per cent report taking medication 'less than prescribed', 52 per cent 'miss a dose at least some of the

time, 23.4 per cent take 'more than prescribed' and 30.4 per cent 'take an extra dose at least some of the time'! This really illustrates the power of our questions to influence findings!

Overall, in this sample the average rate of general non-adherence was 38.4 per cent with almost a fifth of participants reporting instances of both over- and underuse – these behaviours are not therefore mutually exclusive.

Reasons for underuse included:

- low pain (31.8 per cent)
- forgetting (18.4 per cent)
- concern about side effects (13.4 per cent)
- worries about medication losing effectiveness (7 per cent)*
- worries about addiction or dependence (7 per cent)*.

(*These two reasons may be clinically meaningful, although not statistically so)

Reasons for overuse primarily included:

- having too much pain to tolerate (33.9 per cent)
- to help cope with a particular task (7.5 per cent).

Relating medication concerns to adherence patterns

Correlation analyses revealed a range of significant reasons for patterns of non-adherence as presented in the table below. Increased concerns about addiction were, unsurprisingly, reported by those who had some opioid-based medications.

In addition, frequency of side effects was positively and strongly associated with all the concern items, but ONLY to medication overuse. This finding is hard to disentangle in a cross-sectional study but by *controlling for* side effect frequency and reanalysing the association between adherence and medication concerns, overuse correlated only with perceived need for the medication, concerns about side effects, and concerns abut tolerance.

The final analyses conducted were multiple regression analyses, one for each adherence 'outcome'. It is unclear from the results described whether patient

Reason strength	Reasons for general non-adherence	Reasons for medication underuse	Reasons for medication overuse
Strong	Mistrust of doctor	Perceiving a low need for the medication Low concerns about withdrawal effects	Perceived need for the medication Concerns about side effects Concerns about tolerance
Moderate	Concerns about side effects Concerns about others' scrutiny	Mistrusting the doctor	Concerns about addiction Mistrust of doctor
Mild	Concerns about drug tolerance Concerns about addiction		Concerns about others' scrutiny

characteristics, (i.e. length of time living with pain, previous surgery, presence of current antidepression treatment and all sorts of other possible factors) were controlled for, although the level of pain was, however. The level of pain did not explain general non-adherence, nor overuse, although it was significant for underuse.

- 19.1 per cent of the variance in **general non-adherence** was explained by low concern over withdrawal, concern over side effects, and mistrust in the doctor.

- 19.6 per cent of the variance in **underuse** was explained by low level of pain, mistrust in doctor, and low concern over withdrawal.

- 18.9 per cent of the variance in **overuse** was explained by a high perceived need and concerns over side effects.

Discussion

What does this all mean? Certainly there are limitations to this study, including the relatively low response rate, the mixed sample in terms of pain and medication experience, and the fact that data is reported from one timepoint only. A strength, however, is that the study examines different forms of non-adherence, over- and underuse, and explicitly relates each to patient concerns. This is worthwhile when one looks at what emerges for each 'outcome'.

For example, mistrust of the prescribing doctor and reports of general non-adherence and underuse are important and need addressing through health professional communications training. Patient concerns about side effect and general non-adherence echoes this need.

However, some of these findings are surprisingly counter-intuitive and warrant greater consideration: why would someone overuse a medicine when so many medication concerns are present? Does the perceived need for medication outweigh concerns? Overuse was NOT explained by high pain level, where underuse was explained by low pain. Overuse in the face of so many reasons for non-use seems to me, as the authors suggest, to be a different kind of phenomenon. Although not sufficiently developed by the authors, the results strongly suggest conflicted behaviour: patients who have many concerns about what they continue to take. It would be useful to explore this in terms of implication for patients' emotional well-being, especially when analyses also idenitified a significant association between overuse non-adherence and side effect frequency, which did not emerge for general non-adherence or underuse.

The authors conclude 'Patient concerns appear more pivotal in determining non-adherence than both level of pain and frequency of side effects experienced'. Whilst making an interesting contribution, what is equally pivotal will be exploring these questions longitudinally in a more homogeneous sample – only then can we begin to understand the overuse findings as highlighted: does overuse cause the concerns, or are the concerns ignored in the face of a great perceived need for treatment?

Once again, human behaviour is complex and there will not be a straightforward explanation!

of the sub-populations therein (AMAS-Aston Medical Adherence Study 2012)

The contribution of both macro (societal) and micro (individual) influences on behaviour continues below in our exploration of influences on other health behaviours (Chapter 5 ☞). Chapter 10 ☞ describes some of the efforts made to maximise adherence and, given evidence of generally moderate impact (see Haynes et al. 2008 for a Cochrane review and meta-analysis), some of the challenges faced.

Healthy diet

As described in the previous chapter, what we eat plays an important role in our long-term health and illness status, with diet having both direct and indirect links with illness. For example, fat intake is directly linked to various forms of heart disease by a range of physiological mechanisms, and indirectly related to disease by virtue of its effects on weight control and, in particular, obesity. The World Health Organization (WHO 2002a) states that low intake of fruit and vegetables as part of diet is responsible for over three million deaths a year, worldwide, from cancer or cardiovascular disease. The World Health Organization attributes 16 million (1 per cent) disability adjusted life years and 1.7 million (2.8 per cent) deaths worldwide to low fruit and vegetable intake, with the highest percentage being in the developed world including Europe and America, and the lowest attributable percentage being in high-mortality developing countries including many parts of Africa. Furthermore, one-third of cancer deaths are attributable, in part, to poor diet, particularly high intake of fats, salt and sugar and low levels of fibre (American Cancer Society 2012; see also Chapter 3 ☞). Given these reports, it is no surprise that government bodies, health ministers and medical authorities are producing guidelines on how to eat healthily, and that health researchers are working towards identifying factors that facilitate the adoption of these guidelines in our daily lives.

The health benefits of fruit and vegetable consumption

Fruit and vegetables contain, among other things, vitamins, folic acid, antioxidants (for example, beta carotene, or lycopene in the red pigment of tomatoes, polyphenols in red grapes) and fibre, all of which are essential to a healthy body. They may also offer protection against diseases such as some forms of cancer, heart disease and stroke. For example, a recent large-scale review and meta-analysis of data from prospective studies found limited evidence of benefits of consumption for cancer risk, whereas all-cause mortality and cardiovascular disease risk was significantly reduced by higher fruit and vegetable intake (examining data from between 450,000 to over half a million study participants!) (Wang et al. 2014). Crucially these authors report a dose–response relationship whereby the reduced risk of cardiovascular mortality increase per additional portion of fruit and vegetable intake, up to a threshold of around 5 portions per day, after which no further reduced risk was observed. This finding is very important, given recent debates regarding 5,7, or even 10 portions of fruit and vegetables a day – see ISSUES below.

Such large-scale evidence calls into question earlier reports of associations between fruit and vegetable intake and risk of some forms of cancer (e.g Marmot et al. 2007). In 2005 Lock and colleagues estimated that worldwide, if people ate the recommended amounts of fruit and vegetables, the incidence of some forms of cancer, such as oesophageal and stomach cancers, would reduce significantly. Contrary to Wang's findings described above, however, a smaller, nationally representative study using the Health Survey for England dataset of over 65,000 adults aged over 35 (Oyebode et al. 2013) report a reduced cancer risk, as well as reduced all-cause and cardiovascular disease risk, with benefits gained from fruit and vegetable intake up to 7 portions a day. This study correctly controls for many risk factors such as age, alcohol consumption and levels of physical activity, but not, sadly, for smoking, a known risk for such mortality. It is, however, a nationally representative sample unlike many other databases, including the large 10 country European (EPIC) study, which recruited heavily from those accessing health-care services or systems and who are perhaps more likely to be health conscious.

It may also be that national variation exists depending on other lifestyle factors. For example, where fruit and vegetable intake is *combined* with a Mediterranean diet (e.g. low fat, fresh produce, more fish, less meat), there may be a stronger association between fruit and vegetable consumption and reduced disease risk. This was found within the Greek cohort of the EPIC study (Trichopoulou et al. 2009), whereas the pooled data across ten countries showed a weak relationship (Wang et al. 2014).

Further evidence of the beneficial effects of high fruit and vegetable intake comes from a large **meta-analysis** of data involving 124,706 men and women where vegetarians had significantly lower cancer incidence and significantly lower rates of **ischaemic heart disease** mortality (Huang et al. 2012) than non-vegetarians. However, vegetarians also reported lower rates of smoking and lower levels of alcohol consumption than non-vegetarians, risk behaviours which were not always controlled for in the analyses. It is crucial that these and other health risk behaviours are considered when comparing sub-populations as important sample differences may exist which may account for some of the health differences claimed. Such results should not lead one to conclude that vegetarianism is protective against such diseases (Katz and Meller 2014).

Overall, however, the research evidence is fairly consistent in finding positive health benefits of fruit and vegetable intake (e.g. Katz and Meller 2014). The benefits found are attributed to the presence of **antioxidant** compounds known as 'polyphenols', such as the flavonoids (specifically flavonol), and in the case of tomatoes, lycopene (more being released when cooked than when eaten raw).

In relation to reduced coronary heart disease risk, the effects of a healthy diet high in fruit and vegetable intake

---

meta-analysis

a review and re-analysis of pre-existing quantitative datasets that combines the analysis so as to provide large samples and high statistical power from which to draw reliable conclusions about specific effects.

ischaemic heart disease

a heart disease caused by a restriction of blood flow to the heart.

antioxidants

oxidation of low-density lipoprotein (LDL or 'bad') cholesterol has been shown to be important in the development of fatty deposits in the arteries; antioxidants are chemical properties (polyphenols) of some substances (e.g. red wine) thought to inhibit the process of oxidation.

---

may also be indirect via effects on weight, (see Chapter 3 ☛ for discussion of obesity) and there remains a need for further controlled nutritional trials to ascertain what and how any benefits are achieved (Dauchet et al. 2009; Katz and Meller 2014).

Why do people not eat sufficient fruit and vegetables?

Much of the research carried out with regards to healthy eating focuses on young people and their food choices and eating behaviours, and, while this makes sense in relation to the growing prevalence of obesity (see Chapter 3 ☛) and in light of the fact that health behaviours set down in childhood can contribute towards adult health state, our society is an increasingly ageing one and therefore a greater focus on 'healthy ageing' is also required. A loss of appetite and reduced energy is often associated with growing older, but are not inevitable consequences and may reflect social factors (such as experiencing a loss of interest in food caused by eating alone), physical factors (access to shops, physical mobility) or personal factors such as lack of skill. It may be that older males, when widowed, face a particular challenge when having to shop and cook for themselves, as among much of the older population such roles have commonly been adopted by women. Hughes et al. (2004) carried out a questionnaire and interview study of 39 older men and found that only five (13 per cent) consumed five portions of fruit and vegetables a day, that 64 per cent consumed less energy than appropriate even when controlling for BMI, activity and age, and most had lower intake of essential nutrients than they should. Interestingly, this study relates food intake to the individuals' cooking skills with perhaps unexpected findings. Those with good cooking skills reported higher vegetable intake but lower energy/calorie intake, whereas men with poorer cooking skills ate less vegetables but tended to eat more calorie-dense foods which, even if in line with calorie intake guidelines, is not necessarily a good thing as energy-dense foods are not always nutritious. The implications of such findings is that interventions should be quite practical, tying up cooking skills with both appropriately calorific and nutritious food (a new project for TV chef, Jamie Oliver, perhaps?!)

In spite of growing public awareness of the link between eating and health, fruit and vegetables tend not

IN THE SPOTLIGHT

Just how much fruit and veg is enough?!

In 1990 the WHO advised an intake of 400 grams of fruit and vegetables a day, with one portion equating to about 80 grams. This led to the UK launching its '5-a-day' campaign in 2003, which has also been embraced in other European countries, including France and Germany. Data from the Health Survey for England 2012 (The Health and Social Care Information Centre 2014) found that only 16 per cent of boys and 20 per cent of girls aged 5 to 15 were found to be eating at least 5 portions per day. While this is higher than in the 2001 and 2004 surveys, it is slightly lower than 2006 figures, and still reflects a small proportion of children. There is also substantial evidence that the majority of adults are also not following these recommendations, particularly young adults and males (e.g. Henderson et al. 2002; Baker and Wardle 2003) with only approximately 30 per cent reaching the recommended consumption.

Outside Europe, however, the campaign has differed, with higher guidelines existing, for example in Australia the 'GO for 2 + 5' campaign has, since 2005, provided recommendations currently for 2 servings of fruit (a serving being judged as 150 grams which is equivalent to your average apple) PLUS 5 servings of vegetables (with a serving being weighed in as 75 grams, about half a cup full of vegetables). It is notable that the Australian guidelines equate to 675 grams of daily intake, which in UK terms would be 8.5 portions, significantly more than the 5 portions currently recommended.

Do higher guidelines make for better consumption? Not if you consider that the 2007-08 National Health Survey in Australia revealed that 44 per cent of females and 54 per cent of males aged over 15 years were failing to meet the recommended intake for fruit, but even more worryingly, 90 per cent of females and 93 per cent of males failed to meet the recommended vegetable intake.

In the USA the '5 a day' approach was dropped in favour of a campaign simply promoting eating 'more' of both. Do health recommendations need to be precise and consistent in order to be taken seriously? In an article in the *Daily Mail* (2 April 2014), asking whether you should be eating 7 a day, two views of the new proposals were presented. The first is from a 'food writer' who argues that if we fail to meet the 5 portions currently recommended, there is no advantage in simply upping that to 7 without seriously addressing the barriers to behaviour change (costs, availability etc. and personal barriers, see Chapter 5 ☞). The second comment comes from a 'cancer expert' , a doctor who fully supports the need for higher intakes in the battle against increased cancer and heart disease risk , and who in fact advocates cramming in as much fruit and vegetables as we can.

So, what do you do? As students being trained in reviewing an evidence base, I would advise behaviour based on current knowledge. As reviewed in this chapter, two large studies, one multinational (Wang et al. 2014), one UK based (Oyebode et al. 2013) support 5–7 portions a day as being sufficient to accrue health benefits over time, but with the caveat that other risk factors should not go ignored.

to be the food of choice of many young people. For example, the National Diet and Nutrition Survey (Food Standards Agency 2009) found that the foods most frequently consumed by British young people (aged 4 to 18 years) were white bread, savoury snacks (e.g. crisps), biscuits, potatoes and confectionery, although an encouraging trend was seen in terms of increased fruit intake compared to previous years. Although the average

vitamin intake was not deficient, intake of some minerals was low. These food preferences can in part be understood by the findings of another survey of British young people (Haste 2004), which found that children gave 'It tastes good' (67 per cent) and 'It fills me up' (43 per cent) as the top two reasons for their favourite food choice, above 'Because it is healthy' (22 per cent) and 'It gives me energy' (17 per cent).

Unfortunately, tasting 'good' often appears to correlate with sugar and fat content rather than with healthy food, and preconceptions exist about healthy food that can work against a person making healthy food choices. For example, 37 per cent of Haste's sample agreed with the statement 'Healthy food usually doesn't taste as good as unhealthy food'. Where do these preferences and perceptions come from?

Food preferences

Whilst food preferences have a biological basis, they are also significantly determined by social and cultural factors (Pfeifer 2009). Parents play a major role in setting down patterns of eating, food choices and leisure activities inasmuch as they develop the rules and guidelines as to what is considered appropriate behaviour. Parental behaviours at mealtimes have been variously associated with child eating behaviour, for example, parental permissiveness was associated with less healthy eating behaviour among adolescents and young adults (Bourdeaudhuij 1997; Bourdeaudhuij and van Oost 1998), and child-centred feeding practices including

reasoning and praising related positively to fruit and vegetable intake in contrast to parent-centred feeding practices including warning or physically struggling to get a child to eat these food types (Vereecken et al. 2010). Food preferences are generally learned through socialisation within the family, with the food provided by parents to their children often setting the child's future preferences for:

- *cooking methods*: e.g. home-cooked/fresh vs. ready-made/processed;
- *products*: e.g. high-fat vs. low-fat, organic vs. non-organic;
- *tastes*: e.g. seasoned vs. bland, sweet vs. sour;
- *textures*: e.g. soft–crunchy, tender–chewy;
- *food components*: e.g. red/white meat, vegetables, fruit, grains, pulses and carbohydrates.

Various interventions have targeted the fruit and vegetable intake of young people, such as the Food Dudes programme developed in North Wales, which targets pre-school and primary-school children in the UK, Ireland and elsewhere in Europe (Tapper et al. 2003; Horne et al. 2004, 2009). This programme draws on established learning theory techniques of increased taste exposure to fruit and vegetables, modelling of healthy behaviour through cartoon youth characters (see Photo 4.1), and reinforcement by means of child-friendly rewards (e.g. stickers, crayons) for eating the fruit and vegetables provided at snack and meal times (Lowe et al. 2004). Long-term effectiveness of a peer-modelling and rewards-based intervention on the fruit and vegetable consumption of children was found (see Figure 4.1), with particular gains among those children who ate less fruit and vegetables at the study outset (Horne et al. 2009). These findings have also been replicated in the USA (Wengreen et al. 2013) where biophysical measurement methods were utilised alongside self-report measures to demonstrate effects of increased fruit and vegetable intake. Evidence suggests that simply increasing exposure to, or availability of, healthy food options, is insufficient: for example, a randomised controlled trial of having fruit 'tuck shops' in primary schools did not find an increase in fruit consumption (Moore et al. 2000; Moore 2001). In addition, there is reasonably strong evidence that the presence of factual knowledge that healthy eating is important, and even knowing what constitutes healthy eating, does not

Photo 4.1 'We are what we eat?' The importance of providing positive norms for healthy eating in children

Source: Bangor University, School of Psychology.

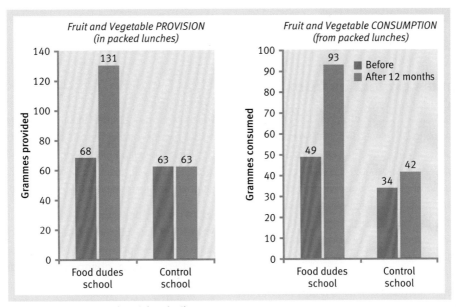

Figure 4.1 Ireland experimental evaluation

Source: Horne et al. (2009), reprinted by permission from Macmillan Publishers Ltd

guarantee healthy food choices in young people, as described in the next chapter where wider sociocognitive influences are described.

Given the challenge of increasing fruit and vegetable intake, ISSUES below raises the question of whether supplementing a person's diet with antioxidant vitamins (e.g. vitamins A, C and E; beta-carotene; folic acid) has benefits in terms of reducing disease risk.

Exercise

Physical inactivity has been identified by the World Health Organization as the fourth leading risk factor for global mortality. As we will describe here, regular exercise (physical activity) in contrast is generally considered as health-protective, reducing an individual's risk of developing diseases such as cardiovascular and coronary heart disease, type 2 diabetes mellitus, osteoporosis and obesity, and some forms of cancer, including colorectal and breast cancer (Department of Health 2004; Warburton et al. 2010; World Health Organization 2014: http://www.who.int/mediacentre/factsheets/fs385/).

As a result, most countries have guidelines as to what is considered the appropriate amount of exercise to gain health benefits.

Recommendations to exercise

Specific recommendations regarding physical activity for adults (aged 18–64 years) suggest at least 30 minutes of moderate intensity exercise on at least five days of each week (or as an alternative to this, 150 minutes of moderate exercise, 75 minutes of high-intensity exercise) and for children and young people (aged 5–17 years) the recommendations are higher, suggesting at least 60 minutes of at least moderate to vigorous intensity exercise a day, every day (e.g. World Health Organization 2010; Department of Health 2011). Within these guidelines are also recommendations for at least 2 exercise days to include muscles strengthening exercise (3 times a week for children), and for adults, the aerobic exercise should be done in bouts of 10 minutes plus duration. For those over 65 years of age, the WHO guidelines are the same as for younger adults although specific recommendations include balance-enhancing exercise for those with limited mobility. The aim of such guidelines is to set minimum activity targets with the

ISSUES

Do vitamins protect us from disease?

Research has suggested that a lack of vitamins A, C and E, beta-carotene and folic acid in a person's diet plays a role in blood vessel changes that potentially contribute to heart disease, and low beta-carotene has been linked with certain cancers. Beta-carotene is a form of vitamin A found in the cell wall of carrots and sweet potatoes, and we now understand that cooking these vegetables releases this more easily for absorption than eating them raw (see Bardia et al. 2008, for a systematic review and meta-analysis). Such associations are attributed to the antioxidant properties of these vitamins (i.e. they reduce the oxidated products of metabolism which can cause cell damage). Additionally, vitamins C and E have anti-inflammatory effects, and both inflammation and oxidation have been linked with cognitive decline and progression towards dementia. Naturally, such findings stimulate media and public interest, and taking vitamin supplements as a means of protecting one's health became commonplace in the USA and more recently across Europe. Vitamin supplementation has become a growth industry – just look at the shelves of your local supermarkets or pharmacist.

However, what is the evidence base as to their effectiveness? Do supplements work in the same way as when contained naturally in the foods we eat? The United States Preventive Services Task Force (USPSTF: an expert group formed to review research evidence in order to make informed health recommendations) conducted two large-scale reviews of studies of vitamin supplements, one in relation to reduced risk of cardiovascular disease (USPSTF 2003) and the other in relation to reduced risk of breast, lung, colon and prostate cancer (Morris and Carson 2003). They found that in terms of subsequent development of disease, even well-designed randomised controlled trials comparing vitamin supplements with an identical-looking placebo pill were inconclusive in their findings. Worryingly, they find 'compelling evidence' of an increase in lung cancer risk and subsequent death in smokers who take beta-carotene supplements. However, Bardia et al. (2008) concluded from their review of 12 randomised trials (9 with high methodological quality, overall related to 104,196 individuals) that even this evidence regarding mortality is limited because not all trials analysed mortality data by whether their sample smoked or not!

Furthermore, the stronger claims of associations between vitamin supplements and reduced disease risk come from more poorly designed and poorly controlled studies. For example, **observational studies** reporting an association between reduced breast cancer incidence and vitamin A intake generally failed to control for other relevant behaviours, such as general diet or levels of physical activity. Similarly, the reduced colon cancer risk reported amongst those taking folic acid supplements came from retrospective reports of those already diagnosed with colorectal cancer, rather than a prospective follow-up of initially healthy individuals.

Consistent with the USPSTF report, Bardia et al.'s review concludes that there was no effect of antioxidant supplementation in relation to primary cancer incidence and mortality. In making recommendations for vitamin usage, the USPSTF concluded that, with the exception of advising against smokers taking beta-carotene supplements, there was little evidence of vitamin supplements causing harm, BUT neither was their conclusive evidence of benefits in terms of reduced risk of heart disease or many forms of cancer.

Further study is, however, justified. As Bardia notes, these vitamins consist of several antioxidant components and also micro- and macro-nutrients, and studies so far focused on different compounds taken in

---

observational studies
research studies which evaluate the effects of an intervention (or a treatment) without comparison to a control group and thus such studies are more limited in their conclusions than randomised controlled trials.

differing amounts, rather than the interactions between components (for example, between selenium and lycopene).

In terms of vitamin C and E supplements and their potential in halting cognitive decline, the evidence is more preliminary. Well-designed randomised controlled trials (comparing vitamins with a placebo) are still required (Haan 2003). One study has pointed to beneficial effects of vitamins C and E on the verbal fluency and verbal memory scores of healthy elderly women (the loss of which are implicated in the development of dementia) (Grodstein et al. 2003). However, the benefits were found only when the two vitamins were taken together and not for either one taken alone, which raises interesting questions about interactions as noted above.

More recent evidence is less encouraging, however. Plassman et al. (2010) reviewed 127 observational studies, 22 randomised controlled trials and 16 systematic reviews in terms of a range of factors associated with cognitive decline, including the nutritional factors addressed here. They found insufficient evidence to support such an association, although nutritonal data were examined in only 7 of the studies reviewed. It may be that effects are confined to specific populations. For example, in women with pre-existing cardiovascular disease or cardiovascular disease risk factors, overall antioxidant supplementation did not slow cognitive change over a 5-year period, but an effect of vitamin C or beta-carotene intake was found among a sub-group who had low dietary intake levels (Kang et al. 2009). Given that cognitive decline and dementias are increasingly prevalent in an ageing society, more rigorous and focused studies with less varied populations are justified.

Overall, therefore, current research no longer supports the taking of antioxidant supplements, except perhaps where natural food sources are lacking. Eating a healthy diet with these vitamins contained within the foodstuffs and maintaining a healthy body weight is more relevant to reducing disease risk than relying on supplements.

potential to reduce the incidence of the diseases described above, including obesity, as well as improving general well-being. Guidelines are not intended to be set so high as to be beyond the reach of the average individual, and certainly the advice for a previously inactive individual is to build up their exercise levels gradually, rather than making dramatic changes to the frequency or intensity of exercise performance. Furthermore, where a pre-existing health complaint exists, plans to become more active should first be discussed with a medical professional.

In spite of obvious health benefits and active campaigning on the part of public health authorities to encourage people of all ages to become more active, exercise levels in some parts of Europe (as elsewhere) remain low.

Levels of exercise

There is some suggestion that levels of childhood activity influence adult health and disease risk although there is need for more longitudinal research to confirm the pathways through which any effects occur (Hallal et al. 2006; Mattocks et al. 2008). It may be that active youngsters maintain activity in adulthood, but it may also be that active youngsters' lifestyles vary in other (healthy) ways as they grow older – whichever explanation it may be, there is certainly no harm in setting down patterns of healthy behaviour early.

Less than half of the British adult population carry out some form of exercise at least once a month, and a similar percentage fail to exercise to current recommended levels, with percentages dropping with age. This pattern is not only evident in Britain: for example, Table 4.1 shows the prevalence of insufficient physical activity ranges from 71.9 per cent in Malta, through to 26 per cent in Hungary. Gender and age differences have also been reported, with women generally more inactive than men, and older women less active than younger women (e.g. Stephenson et al. 2000). Data on the behaviour of the 'very old' (i.e. 85+) are limited as many surveys simply compare people who are under 65 years of age with those aged over 65. In older populations exercise behaviour is likely to be influenced by factors such as current health status and physical functioning, access to facilities, and even personal safety

Table 4.1 Prevalence of insufficient physical activity in adults – Top and bottom 10 European countries

	European Country	Prevalence of insufficient physical activity (%)
1.	Malta	71.9
2.	Serbia	68.3
3.	United Kingdom	63.3
4.	Turkey	56
5.	Italy	54.7
6.	Ireland	53.2
7.	Portugal	51
8.	Spain	50.2
9.	Luxembourg	47.7
10.	Norway, Spain	44.2

	European Country	Prevalence of insufficient physical activity (%)
1.	Greece	15.6
2.	Estonia	17.2
3.	Netherlands	18.2
4.	Ukraine	18.4
5.	Russian Federation	20.8
6.	Slovakia	22.2
7.	Georgia	22.3
8.	Lithuania	22.6
9.	Cyprus	25.0
10.	Hungary	26.0

Source: WHO (2010).

concerns (in terms of walking alone, or of accidents at the gym). However, a person's lifespan (longevity) may be predicted by the extent to which a person is physically active as we describe in the next section.

While a greater percentage of younger adults (16 to 24 years) appear to meet current recommended physical activity levels compared with older adults, the prevalence of inactivity is high in child samples. For example, a World Health Organization study of 162,000 young people aged 11, 13 and 15 in 35 countries across Europe and North America found that only 35 per cent of 15-year-old boys and only 22 per cent of girls engage in at least one hour of moderate or heavier exercise five days a week, with huge geographical as well as gender differences (www.euro.who.int) (see Figure 4.2). In relation to even younger children, the Millenium Cohort study which is tracking the health of over 6,000 UK children born between 2000 and 2002 have recently reported (Griffiths et al. 2013) that when aged 7 years old, fewer than half were engaging in recommended levels of activity, with girls again less active than boys (38 per cent vs. 63 per cent

meeting guidelines). Many large-scale studies have reported similar gender differences, maintained through adolescence. Cultural differences have also been reported amongst both adults and children. For example, Bangladeshi, Pakistani and Indian (South Asian) participants are significantly less active than white participants (adults aged over 55 living in the UK in the Health Survey for England, Williams et al. 2011; adults screened for type 2 diabetes, Yates et al. 2010; and children aged 7, Griffiths et al. 2013). That ethnic variations in physical activity exist points also to wider influences on activity which have been described in Chapter 2 ☞ i.e. that of socio-economic inequalities in terms of access to sports and leisure facilities, and social inclusion for those of BME status, at least in the UK.

What are the physical health benefits of exercise?

We use the term 'exercise' broadly here, encompassing both planned physical activity such as going swimming or to the gym for an exercise 'class' and that which is simply physical activity generated by body movement in the pursuit of one's daily life such as going shopping, or walking the dog. The majority of research studies in this domain have focused on the presence of purposeful exercise. However, exercise does not have to be structured and formal; there is clear evidence from a meta-analysis of randomised controlled trials that simply regular walking can reduce the risk of cardiovascular disease, particularly among older people (Murphy et al. 2007).

An early pointer towards the benefits of moderate to high levels of exercise came from a longitudinal study of the lifestyles of 17,000 former graduates of Harvard University where significantly more deaths occurred between 1962 and 1978 among those who reported leading a sedentary life. Those who exercised the equivalent of 30–35 miles (48–56km) running/walking a week faced half the risk of premature death of those who exercised the equivalent of five miles (8km) or less per week. Moderate exercisers were defined as exercising the equivalent of 20 miles (32km) per week, and these individuals also showed health benefits in that on average they lived two years longer than the low-exercise group (<5 mile equivalent) (Paffenbarger et al. 1986). In a similar vein Hakim and colleagues (Hakim et al. 1998) followed a cohort of 61–81-year-old men over a period

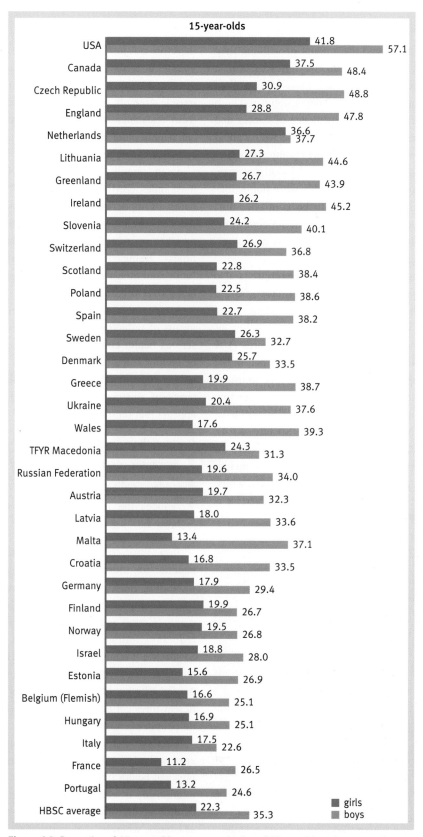

Figure 4.2 Proportion of 15-year-olds across a selection of 35 countries who engage in recommended exercise level, (at least an hour of moderate or high-intensity activity on five days per week)

Source: WHO (2004)

of 12 years and monitored the amount of walking they did. Men who walked more than two miles (3.2km) a day lived significantly longer than those who walked less (21.5 per cent died over the 12 years, compared with 43 per cent). Furthermore, the incidence of cancer and heart disease was also lower among those who walked more, even when controlling for other common risk factors such as alcohol consumption and blood pressure. All men who participated in this study were non-smokers, therefore this did not need to be controlled for; however, this otherwise careful study did not control for an individual's dietary behaviour, which may also play a role in the findings.

There is strong evidence that regular exercise is also protective against the development of osteoporosis, a disease characterised by a reduction in bone density due to calcium loss, which leads to brittle bones, a loss of bone strength and an increased risk of fractures (UK Department of Health 2004). It is estimated that, in the UK, someone experiences a bone fracture due to osteoporotic bones every two minutes, and that one in two women and one in five men over the age of 50 will have this condition (National Osteoporosis Society 2014). Regular exercise, particularly low-impact exercise or weight-bearing exercise such as walking and dancing, helps in the laying down of calcium in the bones, which helps to prevent bone thinning and fractures. Exercise is

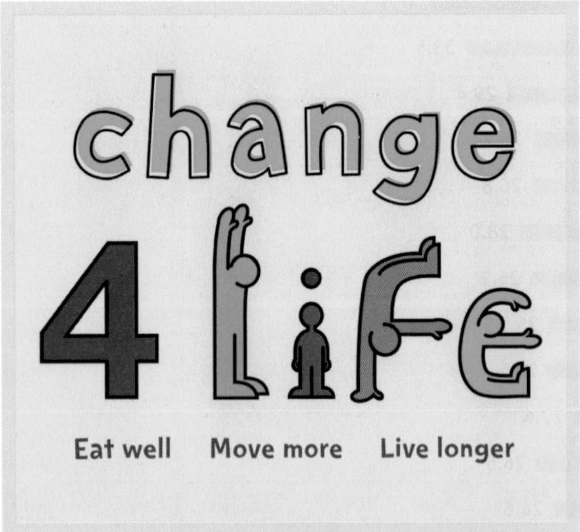

Photo 4.2 Public Health England's Change4Life initiative has become one of the most instantly recognisable brands in health improvement.

Source: Department of Health.

therefore not just important to bone development in the young but is also important for maintaining peak levels of bone density during adulthood. Additional benefits to muscle strength, coordination and balance can be gained from resistance-strengthening exercise, which in turn can benefit older individuals by reducing the risk of falls and subsequent bone fractures.

Even amongst overweight individuals with a body mass index (BMI, see Chapter 3 ☞) of 25.0 or more – being of moderate or high 'fitness' can significantly reduce overall mortality and heart attack incidence compared to overweight individuals who are also of 'low' fitness. Being 'fat' does not inevitably mean being 'unfit' and fitness may protect against negative effects of being overweight.

In general, therefore, regular exercise is an accepted means of reducing one's risk of developing a range of serious health conditions. Once a relationship between behaviour and a health outcome has been established, it is important to ask 'how' this relationship operates. In terms of exercise and reduced heart disease risk, it appears that regular performance of exercise:

● strengthens the heart muscles;

● increases cardiac and respiratory efficiency

● tends to reduce blood pressure;

● reduces the tendency of a person to accumulate body fat.

In addition to reducing risk of disease, exercise has benefits for those already with disease: for example, increasing muscular strength, function and quality of life, reducing fatigue and the side effects of cancer treatments (Cramp and Daniel 2008; Perna et al. 2008) and reducing fatigue in those with Chronic Fatigue Syndrome (White et al. 2011). However, as found amongst healthy individuals, a range of factors will predict whether clinical populations will engage in sufficient physical activity to reap the benefits (see 'Why do people exercise' below).

Exercise helps to maintain the balance between energy intake and energy output and works to protect physical health in a variety of ways. A 'dose–response' relationship is seen to exist in relation to reduced risk of cardiovascular disease, type 2 diabetes and some forms of cancer, whereby the greater the level (frequency and intensity) of exercise, the greater the benefits. There is some note of caution in relation to this dose–response association, however: extreme exercise dependence is sometimes associated with a poor body image and with other compulsive disorders including eating disorders (e.g. Hamer and Karageorghis 2007; Cook and Hausenblas 2008), and there is also the risk of injury and musculoskeletal damage (see later).

The psychological benefits of exercise

Exercise and mood

Exercise has been associated with psychological benefits in terms of elevated mood among clinical populations such as those suffering from depression (Craft and Landers 1998) and amongst some specific populations, for example the elderly (Sjösten and Kivelä 2006). Such findings, often from non-controlled, correlational studies, have contributed to recommendations that exercise be included as a treatment for depression, for example the National Service Framework for Mental Health (Donaghy and Durward 2000) and NICE (NICE 2007). There is much support for this. For example, a recent meta-analysis of data obtained from 23 randomised controlled trials where exercise was provided as an intervention to those with depression (compared to a control intervention or no treatment) found a large clinical benefit of exercise in terms of reduced depressive symptomatology. However, it is important to note that this effect reduced to a moderate and non-significant effect when the three most robust studies were meta-analysed, and exercise in these studies did no better than cognitive therapies (Mead et al. 2009), highlighting a need to draw conclusions from well-controlled, prospective studies rather than single correlational studies.

Regular exercise has also been associated with reduced anxiety and depression and improved self-esteem or body-image amongst non-clinical populations (Hausenblas and Fallon 2006; Lox et al. 2006). Single episodes or limited-frequency aerobic exercise appear beneficial also in terms of elevated mood, self-esteem and **prosocial behaviour** (Biddle et al. 2000; UK DoH 2005; Lox et al. 2006). These psychological benefits of exercise have been attributed to various biological mechanisms, including:

- exercise-induced release of the body's own natural opiates – endorphins – into the bloodstream, which produce a 'natural high' and act as a painkiller, and reductions in the stress hormone, cortisol (Duclos et al. 2003) (Chapter 12 ☞);

- stimulation of the release of **catecholamines** such as **noradrenaline** and **adrenaline**, which counter any stress response and enhance mood (Chapters 8 and 12 ☞);

- muscle relaxation, which reduces feelings of tension.

However, the relationship between exercise and positive mood states is not straightforward. Evidence exists of an inverse relationship between exercise intensity and adherence, whereby individuals are less likely to maintain intense exercise than moderate exercise, possibly because it is experienced as adversive (Brewer et al. 2000). This suggestion that, beyond a certain level, exercise may in fact be detrimental to mood was explored further by Hall et al. (2002) who examined the **affective** response of 30 volunteers to increasing levels of exercise intensity. Their results showed not only that intense exercise caused negative mood but also that the timing of mood assessments (pre- and post-exercise assessment, compared with

---

prosocial behaviour

behavioural acts that are positively valued by society and that may elicit positive social consequences.

catecholamines

these chemical substances are brain neurotransmitters and include adrenaline and noradrenaline.

noradrenaline

this **catecholamine** is a neurotransmitter found in the brain and in the **sympathetic nervous system**. Also known as norepinephrine.

adrenaline

a neurotransmitter and hormone secreted by the adrenal medulla that increases physiological activity in the body, including stimulation of heart action and an increase in blood pressure and metabolic rate. Also known as epinephrine.

sympathetic nervous system

the part of the autonomic nervous system involved in mobilising energy to activate and maintain arousal (e.g. increased heart rate).

repeated assessment during exercise) profoundly changed the nature of the relationship found. Studies measuring mood before exercise, and again after exercise has ended and the person has recovered, generally report positive affective responses. However, Hall and colleagues' data clearly show considerable mood deterioration as exercise intensity increases, with mood rising to more positive levels only on exercise completion. These authors propose that remembering the negative affective response experienced *during* exercise is likely to impair an individual's future adherence, and that this may explain why some studies report poor exercise adherence rates. Ekkekakis et al. (2008) replicated and extended these interesting findings, suggesting that methodological factors play a role in whether or not exercise is associated with positive mood. This is important as it highlights the need for researchers to consider both the timing of assessments and also that, because exercise is an event that typically takes time, a person's experience of it may also change over the course of its performance. Mood is a complex phenomenon!

Many other factors may combine with biological factors to influence the affective experience reported. Exercise may offer cognitive distraction or actual physical removal from life's problems, and as such provide a means of coping with stress. During exercise, a person may focus on aspects of the physical exertion or on the heart-rate monitor, they may distract themselves by listening to music or planning a holiday, or they may use the time to think through current stressors or demands and plan their coping responses (see Chapter 12 ☞). For others, the social support gained from exercising with friends plays an important role, particularly for females (Molloy et al. 2010). Even the exercise environment itself can play a role in mood outcomes, such as room temperature, the presence and type of music, and the presence of mirrors – the latter being associated with negative well-being (Martin Ginis et al. 2007).

For some individuals, self-image and self-esteem may be enhanced as a result of exercise contributing to weight loss and general fitness. Rightly or wrongly, we live in a society where trim figures are judged more positively (by others as well as by ourselves) than those that are considered to be overweight or unfit. However Mead and colleagues' (2009) meta-analysis found no significant linear relationship between the duration of exercise interventions and reduced depression (i.e. they did not find that longer exercise programmes showed greater reductions in depression), nor in fact was mood related to physical fitness in half of the trials analysed. This argues against concluding that mood benefits from increased *fitness*. However, the samples in this meta-analyses all fulfilled criteria for a depression diagnosis and so the findings may not generalise to those without this symptomatology.

Exercise and cognitive function

Exercise may have psychological benefits for those experiencing cognitive decline as a result of ageing or dementia. Cotman and Engesser-Cesar (2002) reported that physical activity was associated with delays in the age-related neuronal dysfunction and degeneration that underlies types of cognitive decline often associated with Alzheimer's disease, such as memory lapses and not paying attention. Physical activity may improve at least some aspects of cognitive funcion important for tasks of daily living (BHF National Centre for Physical Activity and Health 2007) by virtue of neuroprotective effects, although the evidence on this is relatively new. For example, reviewing evidence of the effects of exercise on those identified with mild cognitive impairment (MCI, defined as atypical cognitive decline given a person's age and educational level which confers risk for going on to develop dementia) Barber and colleagues conclude that the neurobiological and vascular processes (increased cerebral blood flow) attributed to exercise have some evidence base from anatomical studies using MRI brain scans, reasonable evidence from general population studies comparing cognitive decline in the active versus the inactive, and finally, encouraging but as yet limited evidence from randomised controlled trials of physical activity interventions (Barber et al. 2012).

In summary, regular physical activity is generally considered to be beneficial to physical and psychological health, and possibly even indirectly to survival, but, as with much behaviour, it may be that moderation is required.

---

affective
to do with affect or mood and emotions.

IN THE SPOTLIGHT

Exercise, our genes and ageing

A great example of health research moving from the laboratory run by cell biologists to potentially the interface with patients and health behaviour change interventions is the growing body of work exploring the association between our DNA and ageing. Telomeres are protective caps, made up of a combination of DNA and protein, based on the ends of chromosomes that affect how quickly cells age. As they become shorter, and as their structural integrity weakens, the cells age (lose their DNA) and die quicker. Telomerase is an enzyme that is involved in the repair and lengthening of telomeres which maintains the ability of cells to reproduce and maintain their DNA. Evidence from several prospective studies, both in animals and in humans, have found reduced telomerase levels and shorter telomeres to be associated with a broad range of diseases, including many forms of cancer, infectious diseases, stroke, vascular dementia, cardiovascular disease, obesity, osteoporosis and diabetes, and increased overall mortality risk . Elizabeth Blackburn, a Nobel prize winning scientist, and colleagues at University of California San Francisco have conducted many longitudinal studies amongst the healthy and patient groups, in both younger and older populations. Summaries of this exciting avenue of work conducted by themselves and by others is also available in a lectures series available on YouTube, making this science widely accessible (see for example, https://www.youtube.com/watch?v=-INR1xZS5GY)

In trying to establish WHY there may be an association between telomere length and disease, or even survival, several behavioural and psychosocial factors have been found to be associated, including perceived stress (including caregiving stress, see Chapter 15 ☞) and health behaviours. One recent example is a pilot study by Ornish and colleagues (2013) which followed 35 men with early stage, localised prostate cancer over five years, ten of whom were asked to make lifestyle changes in terms of their exercise levels, diet, use of social support and stress management. Compared to the 25 not making lifestyle changes, blood samples taken at five years found that their telomere length *grew* by approximately 10 per cent, compared to approximately 3 per cent shortening in the control group. In addition, a linear relationship was seen between the extent of lifestyle change and the percentage increase in length. No significant association was found between lifestyle change and telomorase enzyme levels, however.

Although a relatively small-scale pilot study, this study, published in *Lancet Oncology*, is adding to an exciting avenue of current work and larger-scale trials are needed within both patient and non-patient populations to explore further the interacting effects of genes, our behaviour and ageing.

The negative consequences of exercise

Paradoxically, for some people a reliance on exercise develops to the extent that exercise becomes a compulsion, interfering with other aspects of one's life and producing dependence (evidenced by, for example, experience of withdrawal effects, guilt and irritability when exercise is omitted) (e.g. Ogden et al. 1997; Hausenblaus and Symons Downs 2002). Experimental studies have shown that depriving regular exercisers of exercise can lead to mood reduction and irritability (e.g. review by Biddle and Murtrie 1991), with positive mood restored when exercise is reinstated. As with eating disorders, it may be that exercise affords an element of control to those who feel aspects of their lives are uncontrollable. The long-term physical consequences of excessive exercising relate to muscle wastage and weight loss rather than to any specific disease; however, these findings are a reminder that moderate levels of behaviour – even behaviour considered health-protective – are better than extreme levels.

Why do people exercise (or not)?

People who choose to exercise cite a variety of reasons for doing so, including, most commonly:

● desire for physical fitness;

● desire to lose weight, change body shape and appearance;

● desire to maintain or enhance health status;

● desire to improve self-image and mood;

● as a means of stress reduction;

● as a social activity.

However, it is not to be inferred that choosing *not* to exercise reflects an absence of the types of desire and goals listed above. Many perceived barriers exist that contribute to people's reasons for not exercising, even when they simultaneously report, for example, a desire to lose weight. Barriers commonly mentioned include:

● lack of time;

● cost;

● lack of access to appropriate facilities and equipment;

● embarrassment;

● lack of self-belief;

● lack of someone to go with to provide support.

Research has identified common clusters of reasons for choosing to exercise or not to exercise, although the extent to which this evidence is currently used to usefully inform intervention programmes has been questioned (e.g. Brunton et al. 2003). For example, busy routes, traffic congestion, and low cycle awareness in drivers, and no cycle paths are environmental barriers to a cycling commute that compound any personal or motivational barriers to exercise (e.g. Timperio et al. 2006), yet few countries have sufficiently adapted their towns and cities. Amongst older samples, having more positive views of ageing and what it means was associated with more regular walking and increased walking over time amongst adults aged 65–85 studied by Wurm and colleagues (Wurm et al. 2010), yet we continue to witness negative stereotypes of ageing. Importantly, differences have been found in the beliefs and attitudes towards exercise held by those who are active and those who are not active. Not surprisingly, individuals who exercise regularly are more likely to perceive (and report) positive outcomes of exercise than those who do not; perceive fewer barriers to exercising, and believe that exercising is under their own control. Such findings highlight the importance of 'getting people started'! There is also some evidence that parental activity during a child's preschool years influences the child's concurrent activity (Hinkley et al. 2008) and also has a modest effect on increased child activity by the age of 11–12 (Mattocks et al. 2008). However, the effect of parental activity on the concurrent activity of older children is less consistent as peer influence takes on more weight (Sallis et al. 2000; Heitzler et al. 2006, 2012). Such findings suggest a role for parental modelling and some scope for parental intervention for younger children, with different approaches taken for adolescents.

Of course, where there is a health-limiting condition, such as cancer , medical treatments and their side effects, the energy to exercise (Arroyave et al. 2008), and motivations and beliefs such as self efficacy for exercise (Gilliam and Schwebel 2013) may be reduced. These individual health cognitions are discussed in more detail in Chapter 5 ☛.

Health-screening behaviour

Screening is a growing part of preventive medicine across the industrialised world, with genetic testing becoming the 'hot issue' for the twenty-first century; however, screening is not without its challenges, as we shall describe below.

There are two broad purposes of health screening, each of which has implications for those involved:

1. identification of (behavioural and/or genetic) risk factors for illness to enable behaviour change, leading to required behaviour or lifestyle change, or, in the case of genetic risk, possibly prophylactic surgery;

2. to detect early asymptomatic signs of disease in order to treat, leading to the person possibly facing regular medication or further investigations.

Screening for risk factors

Screening for risk factors in those individuals thought to be healthy is based on the principle of susceptibility and, as such, it aims to identify an individual's personal level of risk for future illness (and in the case of genetic testing, also in their offspring) in order to offer advice and information as to how to minimise further health risk, or to plan further investigation and treatment. Examples of such primary prevention include:

- screening for cardiovascular risk (cholesterol and blood pressure assessment and monitoring);
- eye tests to screen for diabetes, glaucoma or myopia;
- prenatal genetic testing;
- genetic testing for carrier status of the cystic fibrosis, or Huntington's disease gene, or for breast, ovarian or colon cancer, in those with a family history.

Bearing testimony to the importance of primary prevention, some community or worksite-based programmes offer blood pressure and cholesterol testing, along with an assessment of lifestyle factors and family history of heart disease. These assessments generate an index of general susceptibility, or personal 'risk score' related to potential morbidity and, if a person's risk of disease is thought to be moderate or high, preventive measures can be suggested, such as dietary change or

smoking cessation. In order for screening to be of public health (societal) benefit as well as individual benefit, many of those identified as being at risk of future disease would be required to change their behaviour. It will become evident in later chapters that predicting behaviour change is highly complex (see Chapter 5 ☞), and thus interventions to change individuals' risk behaviour face many challenges (see Chapters 6 and 7 ☞).

Genetic screening

A range of diseases have a genetic component: for example, cystic fibrosis which results from mutation to a single gene; Downs syndrome which results from chromosomal disorder; type 1 diabetes, breast and ovarian cancer, which have a multifactorial cause in that genetic damage may have an acquired cause (e.g. diet) as well as being inherited. With advances in the diagnostic technology for carrier status of genes predisposing to a range of conditions, such as breast cancer (e.g. mutations to the genes BRCA1 and BRCA2) (Sivell et al. 2007; O'Donovan and Livingston 2010) or obesity (e.g. gene MC4R), arising from scientific research programmes such as the Human Genome Project (which ended in 2003), screening has perhaps become more controversial. Whilst BRCA1 or BRCA2 mutations are responsible for breast and ovarian cancer in approximately 45–65, and 17–39 per cent respectively *of those individuals with an inherited susceptibility* to the disease (National Cancer Institute 2009) such mutations are in fact relatively rare in the population, accounting for only 4-5 per cent of all breast cancer for example.

However, when compared to lifetime risk in those without the gene(s), of 12 per cent for breast cancer and 1.4 per cent for ovarian cancer, carrying these genes confers a significant increased risk (National Cancer Institute, *SEER Cancer Statistics Review*, 1975–2005, retrieved 20 April 2009 from: http://seer.cancer.gov/csr/1975_2005/index.html).

A review of studies of specific genetic testing for hereditary cancer found that between 60 and 80 per cent of the general population samples studied report high levels of interest in being tested (Braithwaite et al. 2002). Furthermore Ropka et al.'s (2006) systematic review of 18 studies of actual uptake decisions with regards to breast cancer screening as well as 40 hypothetical studies (of intention) found actual uptake to be just less than the hypothesised uptake (59 per cent vs. 66 per cent). An Australian study assessed interest in genetic testing for colorectal cancer among 300 Ashkenazi Jews, a population who have a higher risk of this multifactorial condition, and found that 94 per cent would have the predictive test, and a majority would make this decision out of a desire for information for their families as well as to decrease their own cancer risk through potentially changing lifestyle factors (Warner et al. 2005). Findings such as these show that interest in genetic testing has increased over time, is in fact high and this is perhaps not that unexpected given the increased risk such genes can carry.

Sivell and colleagues (2007) reviewed randomised controlled trials relating to the impact of genetic risk assessment in cancer and usefully summarised how genetic science had progressed over the preceding decade. Science never stops, however, and further advances in genetic testing for cancer susceptibility are being made. Developments in new technologies which enable simultanous testing of multiple susceptibilty genes (known as multiplex testing) are currently receiving attention (Domchek et al. 2013) and are exciting in their screening potential.

Screening for disease detection

Screening for the purpose of disease detection is based on a biomedical model, which states that by identifying abnormalities in cell or organ functioning as early as possible, treatments can be implemented prior to the onset or advancement of disease symptoms. This is basically secondary prevention in that a specific screening test is offered to individuals identified as being at moderate to high risk of a certain condition on the basis of family history or, in some forms of population screening, age. The best-known examples of this are:

● screening for breast cancer (**mammography**);
● screening for cervical cancer (cervical smear or Pap test);

---

mammography

a low-dose X-ray procedure that creates an image of the breast. The X-ray image can be used to identify early stages of tumours.

● antenatal screening, e.g. for Down's syndrome or spina bifida;
● bone density screening.

Population screening programmes for breast and cervical cancer are based on the fact that incidence of the former is high, and that although cervical cancer is less common than breast cancer (it is about the eighth most common form of cancer in women), identifying the disease at a pre-invasive stage, or at an early invasive stage can enable early treatment, with significant reductions to the associated mortality. For example, in the UK mammography is offered to woman aged 50–70 years old only (unless risk is identified in a younger woman), and amongst those screened less than 1 per cent are found to have an early cancer. However this itself can significantly reduce death rates associated with this disease (Hakama et al. 2008; Sarkeala et al. 2008). In Sarkeala's study there was a 22 per cent reduction in deaths from breast cancer among Finnish women who were invited to mammography compared to those who were not invited. Screening younger women, however, appears less effective (and therefore also less cost effective) partly because there is a reduced incidence of breast cancer in this population, and also because the greater density of breast tissue make it more difficult to identify lumps within it. Cervical cancer is the top-ranked cancer in females under the age of 35, with regular 'smear tests' (Pap tests) being advocated from early adulthood. The mortality rate associated with untreated cancer of the cervix is high (about 40 per cent). Most Western countries have a programme of routine invitation of women aged over 18 to cervical screening every five years, with women aged 60 or over being invited every three years in some countries. In some countries, however, more frequent screening is advised: for example, in Australia routine Pap smears (for all women) are recommended every two years, as is breast screening for women over 50. Recently, evidence has emerged that a large proportion of young, newly sexually active young women acquire a viral infection (HPV: human papilloma virus) which is itself a risk factor for cervical cancer. An HPV vaccination is now available and is discussed below.

For men prostate cancer is the most common form of cancer, with a lifetime risk of about 1:9 and with the majority (75 per cent) of UK cases seen in men aged over 65 years. Prostate cancer is treatable if detected early. Screening is available in the form of digital rectal examination, which can be uncomfortable, but also by means of a less invasive method, PSA testing: this involves a test to assess levels and density of a protein produced by the prostate and released into the bloodstream – Prostate Specific Antigen (PSA). Levels of PSA in the blood increase following the onset of prostate cancer. However, there are wide variations in normal levels of PSA and the test suffers from a lack of **sensitivity** (it fails to detect disease in about 15 per cent of cases where it is present) and **specificity** (about two-thirds of men with an elevated PSA won't have prostate cancer, but have other conditions which also influence PSA). In addition, results of a 20-year follow-up of a large Swedish trial (Sandblom et al. 2011) conclude that no survival advantage was found for men aged between 50 and 69 routinely screened every three years for 20 years. In spite of these limitations, men can access the PSA test if they wish to as long as they are given full information regarding the tests potential limitations as well as benefits. PSA screening is only available on a case-by-case basis and is not routinely available to the wider population (Cancer Research UK 2011). A qualitative study examining the influences on 20 men's uptake of PSA testing at their GPs, found that the GP's were perceived to have struggled to provide the men with balanced information (Rai et al. 2007). Recently, however, high-profile campaigns, including Movember, seeks to raise the profile of men's cancer and the need for screening, as males are generally found to have a lower uptake of health screening than women.

HIV (Human Immunodeficiency Virus) screening programmes are not routinely made available on invitation from a health authority, as is the case for breast screening but is instead generally requested by individuals who consider themselves as potentially at risk of having contracted this virus which leads on to the development of AIDS (either through unprotected sex or needle sharing). In certain populations, however, for example, known prostitutes, HIV screening is actively encouraged, as is screening amongst pregnant women. HIV screening falls between screening for risk detection as a form of primary prevention to encourage behaviour change perhaps, and disease detection to enable early secondary prevention of disease through antiretroviral therapies (i.e. HAART, highly active antiretroviral therapy) which involves the taking of a complex medication regimen to suppress the virus and progression to AIDS (see Chapter 10, ☞).

A few final examples of screening for disease detection include one predominantly used among the middle-aged

and one among pregnant women. The former is bone density screening which checks for bone deterioration and signs of osteoporosis, with screened individuals receiving a result indicating either early signs of bone disease (osteopenia) who can take action to prevent further bone loss, or osteoporosis; in both cases treatment involves increased calcium intake (daily medication in the case of osteoporosis) and increased weight-bearing exercise. At the other end of the age spectrum, antenatal screening procedures (amniocentesis) checks whether maternal serum alphafoetoprotein levels are indicative of spina bifida or Down's syndrome. In this instance, screening is routinely offered, at least in the UK, to pregnant women over the age of 30, and, if results are positive, there are no treatment options, but rather decisions to be made regarding continuation or termination of the pregnancy.

Where national population screening programmes exist, individuals are typically invited to screening while they generally consider themselves healthy, whereas being invited for screening on the basis of family history or age may mean that individuals already perceive themselves as being 'at risk'. As psychologists, the differences between these two groups are worthy of consideration.

In order to try to maximise the benefits of screening to both the individual and to society, criteria for effective screening programmes have been set out.

Criteria for establishing screening programmes

Austoker (1994: 315) described several criteria on which the introduction of screening programmes aimed

---

sensitivity (of a test)

the ratio of true positive tests to the total number of positive cases expressed as a percentage; for example, a sensitive test may have 95 per cent success in detecting a disease among patients known to have that disease. A test with high sensitivity has few false negatives.

specificity (of a test)

the ratio of true negative tests to the total number of negative cases expressed as a percentage; for example, healthy people are correctly identified as not having the condition being tested for. A test with high specificity has few false positives.

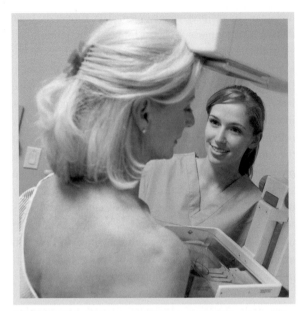

Photo 4.3 Mammogram: a routine experience for women aged 50+?

Source: Fotolia.com/Monkey Business.

at early detection of prostate, ovarian and testicular cancer should be based. These criteria have been developed over time (see Holland and Stewart 2005) and extended to consider the need for quality evidence drawn from randomised controlled trials before making screening recommendations (see the UK NHS National Screening Centre website (http://www.screening.nhs.uk/criteria)) for several additional criteria. The general criteria are that:

● The condition should be an important health problem: i.e. prevalent and/or serious.

● There should be a recognisable early stage to the condition, or, in the case of screening for risk factors, clear benefit to identifying changeable risks.

● Treatment at an early stage of a detected disease should have clear benefits to the individual (e.g. reduced mortality) compared with treatment at a later stage.

● A suitable (safe and validated) test with good sensitivity and specificity should be available.

● The test should be acceptable (clinically, socially and ethically) to the general population.

● Adequate facilities for diagnostic assessment and treatment should exist (including adequate staffing).

● Screening frequency and follow-up should be agreed.

● The individual and health-care costs should be considered in relation to the individual and public health benefits.

● Evidence-based information regarding the potential consequences of testing, any potential further investigations or treatment, should be provided to potential participants in order to enable informed choice re undertaking screening.

● Any particular sub-groups to target should be identified.

The costs and benefits of screening

While screening programmes for both disease detection and risk factor status have proliferated, questions remain as to whether there are as many benefits to the individuals undergoing screening as there are to wider society. Furthermore, some findings call into question whether the benefits of screening – in terms of eliciting behaviour change that reduces disease risk to the individual, or in terms of enabling early disease symptoms to be treated and subsequently the threat of disease progression to be reduced or removed – justify the financial costs of implementing large-scale screening programmes. Furthermore there are not always clear answers to screening results.

Marteau and Kinmouth (2002: 78) suggested that the effects of screening on the individual are not considered sufficiently. They highlight that information given to those invited for screening tends be brief, emphasising the public health benefits of participation in terms of reduced morbidity and mortality, rather than perhaps addressing the potential impact on the individual. For an individual to be fully informed prior to making a decision about screening uptake requires informing them about the possible adverse outcomes of screening and the limited prognostic benefits of some treatments (if any are available) for some individuals. This may of course affect the uptake of screening by some of those who would in fact have benefited from early detection and treatment, which creates a dilemma for screening professions who want to maximise screening uptake and public health gain. European statistics also highlight national variation in the rates of screening uptake, as presented with regards to cervical screening in Table 4.2. It should be noted also, however, that the highest rates of

Table 4.2 Cervical screening, percentage women screened aged 20-69, 2000 to 2010 (or nearest year)

Country	2000	2010
Austria[2]	n/a	81.52
Germany[2]	n/a	78.7
United Kingdom[1]	82.0	78.5
Sweden[1]	78.2	78.4
Switzerland[2]	76.5	74.9
France[2]	n/a	71.1
Finland[1]	70.3	69.8
Greece[2]	n/a	69.7
Poland[2]	n/a	69.1
Spain[2]	n/a	68.5
Denmark[1]	n/a	66.3
Netherlands[1]	65.6	66.1
Belgium[1]	58.6	63.2
EU24		62.1
Malta[2]	n/a	58.0
Czech Republic[1]	33.3	51.8
Bulgaria[2]	n/a	46.8
Italy[2]	n/a	40.0
Hungary[2]	28.4	23.7

[1] Programme
[2] Survey

Source: Health at a Glance: Europe 2012, OECD (2012).

cervical screening uptake do not translate into those countries having greater five-year relative survival rates. For example, the UK and Austria both have better uptake than the Netherlands and Belgium, but have poorer five-year survival figures (Health at a Glance Europe 2012). This raises inevitably questions of screening utility but also of the treatment availability and effectiveness variation across countries.

In the case of genetic testing, for example to identify whether an individual carries the gene that predisposes towards the development of Huntington's disease (an adult-onset disease), there is actually nothing that can be done to change the individual's risk, and therefore some question the value of screening other than as a means of preparing the individual for their future. In contrast, for those identified as carrying the BRCA1 or BRCA2 gene for breast cancer, there is an option of prophylactic surgery (i.e. breast removal) in order that disease cannot manifest itself (Lerman et al. 2000; Kauff et al. 2002) and in this group there is evidence of psychological benefit (Braithwaite et al. 2004). Hamilton et al. (2009) reviewed the evidence of negative psychological consequences of BRCA1 and BRCA2 testing in studies which assessed distress at a rage of timepoints following testing

and found that, whilst distress increased initially amongst those given a confirmed carrier status compared to non-carriers, this returned to baseline over time. This is consistent across many studies suggesting a null effect of testing in the longer term, with screening benefits reported regarding increased awareness of one's options for surveillance or prophylactic surgery and reduced uncertainty (Lim et al. 2004). Other authors have suggested that provision of a positive genetic risk result causes significant feelings of hopelessness about future health, which can persist for several years (Meiser 2005; Bennett et al. 2008, 2010).

Family members and partners are also affected by the identification of genetic risk as they may then also need to be tested, or share the responsibility for any identified children's risk. Results, for example, from a systematic review of male partners' response to women's ovarian/breast cancer risk suggests that the process causes significant distress in the partners of women identified as mutation carriers, although this was not all due to the result itself but to wider relationship and communication factors (Sherman et al. 2010).

Contrary to expectations, receipt of a negative test result does not inevitably reassure the individual (Bennett et al. 2008; Geirdal et al. 2005; Michie et al. 2003), possibly because the testing itself raises an issue into awareness, or because the genetic counsellor has then to explain that there may be other, unidentifiable risk factors, including as yet unknown gene carriers (Ropka et al. 2006), or other risks inherent in the individual's health behaviours or obesity, which mean that they should not consider themselves at 'no risk' whatsoever.

In terms of wider screening for disease detection, for example, mammography screening, the procedure itself appears to be preceded by some anxiety, particularly where the woman considers herself to be at high risk (Absetz et al. 2003; Montgomery and McCrone 2010). Even following a negative result, this anxiety can in fact prevent some from returning to subsequent screening. For example, amongst women screened for suspected breast cancer and showing distress during the screening phase, those receiving a benign result moved forward with remaining worries about their risk and an improvement to future screening, whereas, in those diagnosed with breast cancer, their distress was considered a risk to their treatment outcomes (Montgomery and McCrone 2010).

Making decisions about screening

Griffith et al. (2009) examined whether healthy adults formed an interest in, or intention to seek, genetic testing for breast cancer on the basis of the perceived pros and cons of such testing. Making decisions in this way is sometimes referred to as 'utility maximisation': i.e. it is assumed that a person weighs up the pros and cons of a choice and then selects the option that provides them either with the greatest perceived benefit, or, alternatively, the least undesirable consequences. To test whether or not utility maximisation occurs, this experimental study manipulated the understanding of genetic testing among 142 undergraduate students by providing information about testing in three different ways (Positive information only; Positive followed by Negative; Negative followed by Positive) compared to a control group who received information irrelevant to the genetic-testing decision questions. Beliefs about the pros and cons of testing, and the stated interest in, and likelihood of, testing were assessed pre- and post-manipulation. The experimental information in all three information groups influenced the ratio of pros to cons, and the interest in, and likelihood of, testing reported; however, there was a non-significant association between the weighted ratio of pros–cons and the post-manipulation interest and likelihood scores. This suggests that utility maximisation was *not* occurring and that models of decision-making need to look beyond simply the pros and cons of behaviour. This

can be seen in the many models of behaviour and health behaviour utilised by health psychologists (see Chapter 5 (☛).

Individuals considering any form of health screening will not just approach health professionals for information, using, for example, friends and family as sources of information, or, increasingly, the internet. Health professionals cannot control where individuals receive health information from nor the quality of the information provided. A review of studies of online health information seekers concluded that women, the more educated and those with greater income and faster internet speeds, made more use of this source of health-related information in general, with those aged 30–44 years being most active (European Centre for Disease Prevention and Control review by Higgins et al. 2011). A WHO study of e-health trends in seven European countries and over 9,000 respondents (Andreassen et al. 2007) found that 71 per cent of internet users had used the internet for health purposes, and, more specifically, further analysis found that 29 per cent had used information from the internet to decide whether or not they needed to see a doctor (Sorensen 2008). There is evidence of bias in e-health sources on the topic of health screening. For example a large-scale review of the nature of information about breast cancer screening mammography presented on the websites of international and national organisations found that in many cases the information presented was biased towards screening uptake, and provided limited clear information about the possibility of false positive and false negative results or about the adverse effects of screening, such as overdiagnosis and overtreatment (Jørgensen and Gøtzsche 2004). Few websites informed readers of the limited evidence of a reduction in risk of mortality in those screened compared with unscreened individuals (which is in fact only about 0.1 per cent reduction in relative risk of breast cancer over ten years). Overstating the benefits of screening, or understating potential risks or adverse consequences of screening results, is not providing the individual with fully informed choice, and while most people will cope with the screening process and its outcomes, for some the emotional and behavioural consequences are significant (Anderson et al. 2007).

Screening, for whatever risk factor or disease, is not compulsory. The generally low level of uptake of screening opportunities plays an important part in whether people go on to develop diseases that they may

---

WHAT DO YOU THINK?

What does it mean when a person has been tested for carrier status of a particular gene? Do you know? It has been found that the general public commonly do not understand the issues of heritability, recessive genes or gene penetrance. There is an obvious and growing need for education and information about these very issues as more and more genes are identified that predispose us to various diseases.

What thoughts do you have about genetic testing? Write down a list of pros and cons, for example in relation to breast or prostate cancer testing. Consider what your decision may be if testing were to become more widely available.

have been able to avoid or reduce their risk of developing. So far, we have described screening which involves an individual attending an appointment; however, other forms of health screening rely on an individual performing the screening themselves.

Self-screening behaviour

Although self-examination behaviour is most commonly advocated and studied in relation to early detection of breast cancer, there is a need for greater awareness and practice of testicular self-examination and skin self-examination. There has in fact been some controversy over the efficacy of breast self-examination (BSE) in saving lives. One study contributing to this controversy is a large randomised trial carried out in Shanghai, China (Thomas et al. 2002), whereby BSE was either taught or not taught to a huge sample (266, 064) of women factory workers aged 30+ to examine whether reduced breast cancer mortality could be found in those instructed in, monitored at least twice yearly in years 1–5, and reminded to keep practising BSE. Over a 10-year follow-up, rigorous data was gathered including factory records of a breast lump being found, referral to hospital, and medical confirmation of whether a cancer was present and at what stage of spread. All assessments were 'blind' as to whether the woman was in the control group (CG) or the intervention group (IG). Analyses also controlled for other known breast cancer risk factors. There was no effect on survival of the BSE training. An identical percentage of women developed breast cancer and died in both groups (0.10 per cent). What further adds to controversy about the value of BSE is that the women in the IG detected more lumps, with a larger number being found to be harmless (benign). The costs of health-care visits and biopsies for those individuals were significant and again counter the value of recommending BSE. One limitation of this otherwise rigorous study is that data on the specific frequency of BSE practice is absent; thus the study may attest more to the failure of teaching BSE than to the failure of BSE practice. However, this and other studies is cited as informing changes in national guidelines, with BSE no longer specifically recommended in Australia (Cancer Council Australia 2004).

Among men, testicular cancer is the most frequently occurring form of cancer and the second leading cause of death among those aged 15 to 35. Surviving testicular cancer is possible in 95–100 per cent of cases if the disease is detected early; however, over 50 per cent of cases present to health professionals after the early, treatable, stage has passed. Men are, however, less likely to engage in self-examination than women (Courtenay 2000; Evans et al. 2005). In fact, men have been found to be less willing to engage in cancer screening generally, although sharing women's beliefs in screening effectiveness (Davis et al. 2012).

Likewise, skin cancer incidence is also increasing, particularly in those aged 20 to 40, yet early detection of skin lesions of the more harmful type (malignant melanoma) can lead to high cure rates Whether self-examination is effective in this early detection has, however, been questioned and in fact is thought not to reduce morbidity or mortality. Perhaps surprisingly, even though the incidence of skin cancer is high in Australia with the population having one of the highest lifetime risks of melanoma, no specific techniques or frequency of self-examination is in current guidelines (Cancer Council Australia 2007).

A real challenge to health educators who seek to increase sun protection behaviours (e.g. use of sunscreen, avoidance of sunbeds) from an early age is what Ness et al. (1999) describe as a 'lay epidemiology' whereby the general perception within society is that sun exposure is healthy. Whilst in some instances this is correct and there is evidence of positive effects of sun exposure on well-being and mood, on vitamin D production and bone strengthening, there is a clear association between sun exposure and malignant melanoma, particularly in fair-haired, light-skinned and blue-eyed individuals. There is also some evidence of gender differences in tanning behaviours. For example, Scottish female adolescents were more likely to engage in riskier behaviours (e.g. sun-bathing/burning, using advancing tanning oils) than their male counterparts, despite reporting higher awareness of skin cancer. They were also more likely to hold pro-tanning beliefs suggesting that a tan made them feel better, healthier and more attractive (Kyle et al. 2014). Such differences suggests that interventions should address the value placed on a particular 'risk behaviour', as this will likely affect the intervention's effectiveness (see Chapter 3 ☞ for the same point in relation to smoking).

Uptake of screening behaviour

Psychology, particularly health and social psychology, has a large part to play in helping to identify predictors of the uptake of screening programmes, such as individual attitudes and beliefs about illness, about screening, and about preventive behaviour. (Chapter 5 ☞ considers attitudes and beliefs about behaviour more fully and Chapter 9 ☞ considers illness perceptions). While the increasing availability of screening programmes for many diseases and disease risk factors seems to have increased uptake, generally uptake remains at a lower level than is considered optimal in terms of disease reduction at a societal level.

Factors associated with screening behaviour

A range of factors have been found to be associated with the non-uptake of screening opportunities or self-examination behaviour, including:

- lower levels of education and income;
- age (e.g. younger women tend not to attend risk-factor screening);
- lack of knowledge about the condition;
- lack of knowledge about the purpose of screening;
- lack of knowledge about potential outcomes of screening;
- embarrassment regarding the procedures involved;
- fear that 'something bad' will be detected;
- fear of pain or discomfort during the procedure;
- lack of self-belief (self-efficacy, see Chapter 5 ☞) in terms of being able to practise self-examination correctly.

Ropka et al. (2006) conducted a systematic review of studies examining the uptake of breast cancer genetic testing and found that older age, being not married and having either a personal or family history of cancer increased actual uptake in several of the included studies, although findings were not unanimous.

In terms of self-screening behaviour, knowledge of testicular cancer and the practice of self-examination

have generally been found to be at a low level. Studies of breast self-examination have found that even among women who do perform it, many do not do so correctly (i.e. it should ideally be carried out mid-menstrual cycle, in an upright position as well as when lying down, and should include examination of all tissue in the breast, nipple and underarm areas). Worryingly, a study by Steadman and Quine (2004) confirmed low levels of knowledge among young adult males about testicular cancer and regarding the potential benefits of self- examination. This study went on to demonstrate that a simple intervention, which required half of the participants to write down and visualise when, where and how they would self-examine their testes over the forthcoming three weeks, led to a significantly higher proportion of them self-examining than that found in the control group who did not form such plans. This study demonstrates the relative ease with which behaviour can be changed, although a longer-term follow-up would be beneficial to check whether self-examination practices were maintained beyond the study period. This intervention focused specifically on making an individualised plan for action, referred to in health psychology as forming an 'implementation intention'. This construct, and further research supporting its practical utility in developing interventions, is described in the next chapter ☞.

Immunisation behaviour

The purpose of immunisation

Public health policy is to provide vaccinations that provide long-lasting protection against specific disease without adverse consequences to the individual, and with the costs of providing the vaccination being outweighed by the costs of having to treat the disease if no vaccination were to be provided. Vaccination is the oldest form of immunisation, in which immunity is provided to an individual by introducing a small amount of an **antigen** into their body (either orally, intramuscularly or intradermally (injecting into the skin)), which triggers the development of antibodies to that specific antigen. Some vaccinations, such as orally administered polio vaccine, measles, mumps and rubella, use live components, while others, such as hepatitis B or swine flu (available since 2009) use inactivated components. Although immunisation is offered to

> **antigen**
> unique process found on the surface of a pathogen that enables the immune system to recognise that pathogen as a foreign substance and therefore produce antibodies to fight it. Vaccinations introduce specially prepared viruses or bacteria into a body, and these have antigens.

various sub-groups in the population, such as influenza vaccination to the elderly or to those with pre-existing conditions that increase their vulnerability to infection (e.g. asthma), the main emphasis of immunisation has been on the prevention of childhood disease.

All EU Member States have established child vaccination programmes which are considered to be highly cost effective; where the uptake of immunisation against infectious disease is widespread, it is beneficial to the wider community when 'herd immunity' is achieved. The UK policy with regards to child immunisation is shown in Table 4.3.

Public health specialists consider vaccines both safe and successful and, at least in developed countries, vaccinations against infectious disease have been credited with the virtual eradication of diseases that in previous centuries caused widespread morbidity and mortality, such as smallpox, diptheria and polio (e.g. Woolf 1996). However, the European Centre for Disease Control reports that Europe has not met the target of eliminating measles by 2010. Furthermore, outside Europe and in developing countries, immunisation coverage is even more variable and there is growing concern that some diseases, such as whooping cough and measles, may re-emerge as uptake has not reached saturation level. Infectious diseases still account for approximately 17 million deaths in developing countries and half a million deaths in industrialised countries (BMA 2003a). Compulsory administration of any vaccine is generally not supported (Blume 2006).

A new vaccine has emerged which targets a sub-group of a family of viruses known collectively as **human papillomavirus (HPV)** which is present in 70–95 per cent of cervical cancers (Kuper at al. 2000; Health at a Glance, Europe 2012), although only a small percentage of HPV infections do develop into a cancer. The discovery of a vaccination against those types of HPV was billed as a major public health discovery in 2006, with clinical trials finding the vaccine to be effective in both adults and children, with 90 per cent effectiveness in those who have not already acquired infection (Lo 2006, 2007; Steinbrook 2006). As a result, in September 2008 the UK government began a vaccination programme targeted initially at girls aged 12–13 years, on the basis that the vaccination needs to be given before sexual activity commences, with a 'catch-up' programme in 2009/10 targeting 15–17-year-olds. In 2014, the original vaccine was replaced with one which also protects against genital warts (Gardasil) and which is believed to provide protection for at least 20 years. The vaccination requires two injections given at least six months apart and is available in secondary schools as part of the NHS childhood vaccination programme. Parental permission will of course be required in order for the vaccination to be given, which has been controversial given the implicit acknowledgement of sexual activity.

WHAT DO YOU THINK?

Some US parenting groups have voiced concerns that offering vaccination against a sexually transmitted infection such as this is condoning sexual activity. What do you think? What about sex education more generally? Is offering a vaccination programme through schools the most appropriate way of reaching the population concerned? What young people might be missed? How might parents react to this vaccination programme? In many states of the USA, adolescents can provide consent for treatments of STIs (sexually transmitted infections) without that of their parents. Do you think the offering of this vaccine to under-18s is likely to achieve a high uptake?

Table 4.3 Immunisation policy in the United Kingdom*

Age	Vaccine	Means of administration
2–4 months	Polio	By mouth Combined injection Injection
12–15 months	Measles, mumps and rubella (MMR)	Combined injection
3–5 years	Polio	By mouth Combined injection
	Measles, mumps and rubella (MMR)	Combined injection
10–14 years	Rubella (girls)	Injection
12-13 years	HPV (girls)	2 injections over 6-24 months
15–18 years	Tetanus booster	Injection

* HPV: Human Papilloma Virus

human papillomavirus (HPV)

a family of over 100 viruses, of which 30 types can cause genital warts and be transmitted by sexual contact. While most genital HPV come and go over the course of a few years, two specific HPV types markedly elevate the risk for cancer of the cervix.

Costs and benefits of immunisation

Over the past century, the widescale benefits of child-hood vaccination programmes have become apparent. It is now rare for a child living in the Western world, and increasingly in developing countries where vacci-nation programmes are being promoted, to die from measles, diphtheria or polio. High hopes of achieving population immunity against measles following the introduction of a vaccine in 1988, and high initial uptake (97 per cent), have not quite been achieved, in part due to a now fully discredited 1998 study that reported adverse effects of the combined MMR vacci-nation and received widespread publicity, leading to a downturn in immunisation uptake, to an average 81 per cent in 2004. Although there was huge regional variation, for example from 59 to 98 per cent between 2002 and 2004 in one study of 257 general medical practices in one region of England (Lamden and Gemmell 2008), the lack of public confidence in this vaccine was significant. Thankfully, however, there are encouraging signs of change: a recent measles out-break among 10–16 year-olds in the UK encouraged a national catch-up campaign in 2013, which went on to reach its target of having 95 per cent of 10–16 year-olds in England immunised with at least one dose of the MMR vaccine (Public Health England 2014).

While socio-economic variables such as low educa-tional attainment have sometimes been found to influence the uptake of vaccination (see Chapter 2 ☞), not all studies report this (Lamden and Gemmell 2008). Evidence more consistently points to emotional and cognitive predictors of uptake: for example, Bennett and Smith (1992) studied the vaccination status of 300 children aged 2 to $2^{1}/_{2}$ in Wales and found that those parents who did not have their child vaccinated exhib-ited anxiety about the risks of vaccination as well as low perceptions of the potential benefits of vaccina-tion. Risk perceptions and outcome expectancies and the research evidence as to their utility in explaining health behaviour are examined in Chapter 5 ☞.

Photo 4.4 Immunisation behaviour is crucial to public health, yet is influenced by many cultural, social, emotional and cognitive factors. Here, a queue of mothers take up the first opportunity of vaccination for their child against measles to be offered in their village

Source: Getty Images/Jacob Silberberg.

IN THE SPOTLIGHT

Immunisation

In order to achieve population immunity, the required uptake of a measles vaccine is between 92 and 95 per cent (BMA 2003b). In the UK, at least, General Practitioners are financially rewarded if they hit the World Health Organization target of 95 per cent. While an upturn in UK MMR uptake has been reported since 2008, it is still lower than that recorded for other vaccinations. Data for 2009–10 show that in England the proportion of children having at least one dose of the vaccine by the time they reach the age of 2 increased from 79.9 per cent to 88.2 per cent between 2004 and 2010; in Wales 92.2 per cent of children have been vaccinated, in Scotland 93.7 per cent and in Northern Ireland it's 92.2 per cent. However, to varying extents all countries fall short of target (NHS Information Centre 2010).

Drawing from data presented in the useful Europe at a Glance (2012) report, there is evidence both of national differences but also variation in uptake depending on the vaccination. Across Europe in 2010 measles vaccination rates for children aged around 1 year old ranged from 99 per cent in Greece and Hungary, through 9 per cent in the UK overall, and to a worrying 73 per cent in Malta. The rates for the diptheria, tetanus and pertussis combined vaccination for these same selected countries are again 99 per cent in Greece and Hungary, and to a better 96 per cent in the UK (target met) and 76 per cent in Malta. At the other end of the age spectrum, the average EU rate of vaccination uptake for influenza amongst those aged over 65 years was 45 per cent, yet the target set for 2010 was 75 per cent. There is evidence that appropriate vaccination can reduce the risk of serious complications or death from influenza by 70–85 per cent, and so the low uptake is disappointing. Again, this ranges by country, with the Netherlands 'top' with 74 per cent, the UK at 70.3, through to only 12.1 per cent in Poland.

Why is one immunisation being taken up less commonly than another? There are many explanations, including variation in national data recording which makes contrasting statistics at times difficult; however, differing perceptions of the illnesses concerned are likely to play a role. For example, meningitis is almost universally feared, whereas measles, or flu/influenza may be considered a less serious illness. Other influences include the manner in which health professionals advocate the different vaccines and the nature of publicity attracted by the different diseases/vaccines. As referred to earlier, a 1998 study (Wakefield et al. 1998) which suggested a link between the measles, mumps and rubella (MMR) vaccine and autism, and to inflammatory bowel disease (IBD), has been blamed for the decline in the uptake of the MMR vaccination. Although published over 16 years ago, and in spite of several larger-scale and more rigorous studies finding no such evidence (Peltola et al. 1998; Taylor et al. 1999, 2002), and in spite of the General Medical Council ruling in May 2010 that Wakefield had acted 'dishonestly and irresponsibly' before striking him off the medical register, this perceived association is still cited as a contributing factor in parental anxiety about this combined vaccination!

Parental fears, once raised, are hard to reduce, and lay perceptions of risks attached to vaccinations need to be addressed through informed and balanced communication. More recently, there has been anxiety about the HPV vaccination offered to young girls. HPV is one of the most commonly diagnosed sexually transmitted viruses, spread through oral, vaginal or anal sex, and also from genital skin to skin contact. This virus has been found to be stigmatising itself and wrongly associated with promiscuity; however, it is strongly implicated in the development of cervical, and, more recently, oral cancers, and therefore vaccination holds important benefits. Concerns that vaccination would confer feelings of global protection to sexually transmitted diseases, or increase sexual activity amongst teenagers, have not been confirmed (see Chapter 5 ☞).

What the immunisation debates referred to above highlight is the power of the media. While it is indeed important that the media stimulate debate, it is important that the general public are informed objectively and in an evidence-based manner. Health professionals also, in communicating with their patients, need to present both sides of the evidence so as to enable informed decisions.

Things to think about and research yourself

Do you think that you would provide your child(ren) in the future with vaccination protection? Would you consider all vaccines as equally important or would you weigh up the pros and cons for each one independently? Where can people find reliable evidence of the pros and cons of immunisation?

How do you think health professionals could better convince the public as to the benefits of immunisation? Where do policy makers and public health speakers go 'wrong' in communicating the need for immunisation?

SUMMARY

This chapter has provided an overview of a range of behaviour often described as 'behavioural immunogens': behaviour that acts in ways that protect or enhance an individual's health status. The evidence as to the associations between a healthy diet, being physically active, adhering to any necessary medications or treatments and taking preventive measures with regards to screening or immunisation uptake is clear. In addition, a lack or low level of 'immunogens' is health damaging, as seen, for example, in the contribution of low levels of physical activity to the global obesity figures which in turn carries its own health consequences (see Chapter 3 ☛). Given the convincing evidence of a behaviour–disease association reviewed in this and the previous chapter, we could perhaps be forgiven for expecting that the majority of people would behave in a manner that protects their health. However, we have shown that this is not borne out by statistics. It is increasingly evident that there is a complexity of influences on health behaviour practices and so this is what we turn to next. Chapter 5 ☛ will describe the key psychosocial theories and models of health behaviour employed in health psychology research.

Further reading

Di Matteo, M.R (2004a). Variations in patients' adherence to medical recommendations: a quantitative review of 50 years of research. *Medical Care*, 42: 200–9.

A useful review of over 500 studies, this provides a summary of the relative contributions made by individual and illness-related factors.

Domchek, S.M., Bradbury, A., Garber, J.E. et al. (2013). Multiplex genetic testing for cancer susceptibility: out on the high wire without a net? *Journal of Clinical Oncology*, 31: 1267–1270.

This paper offers an informed and balanced account of the exciting new technology of multiple susceptibility testing in cancer genetics, with important words of caution as to the need to ensure these tests are only offered in a manner that fully informs and supports patients both before and after testing.

Biddle S.J.H. and Mutrie, N. (2008). *Psychology of Physical Activity: Determinants, Wellbeing and Interventions*, 2nd edn, London:Routledge.

This books provides thorough coverage of the evidence with regards to influences on, and benefits of, physical activity and introduces the reader to intervention studies relevant to subsequent chapters in our textbook.

This link will take you to other useful downloads, including Department of Health documents referred to in the chapter: www.dh.gov.uk/en/Publicationsandstatistics/Publications/PublicationsPolicyandGuidance/DH_4094550

Aluttis, C., Krafft, T. and Brand, H. (2014) Global health in the European Union – a review from an agenda-setting perspective, *Global Health Action*, 7: 10.3402/gha.v7.23610.

This paper reflects on progress made following the Commission of the European Communities (2007) White Paper. *Together for Health: A Strategic Approach for the EU*

2008–2013 (http://ec.europa.eu/health/ph_overview/strategy/health_strategy_en.htm).

This strategy aimed to place the EU at the centre of a global health agenda spanning core issues in relation to ageing, child health, health behaviours, infectious disease. Aluttis and colleagues review its successes and importantly the social, political and financial challenges the implementation of any strategy and policy has faced.

Visit the website at **www.pearsoned.co.uk/morrison** for additional resources to help you with your study, including multiple choice questions, weblinks and flashcards.

Chapter 5
Explaining health behaviour

Learning outcomes

By the end of this chapter, you should understand and be able to describe:

- how demographic, social, cognitive and motivational factors influence the uptake of health or risk behaviour

- key psychosocial models of health behaviour and health behaviour change

- how 'continuum' or 'static' models differ from 'stage' models in terms of how they consider behaviour change processes

- the research evidence that supports or refutes the models in terms of which factors are predictive of health behaviour and health behaviour change

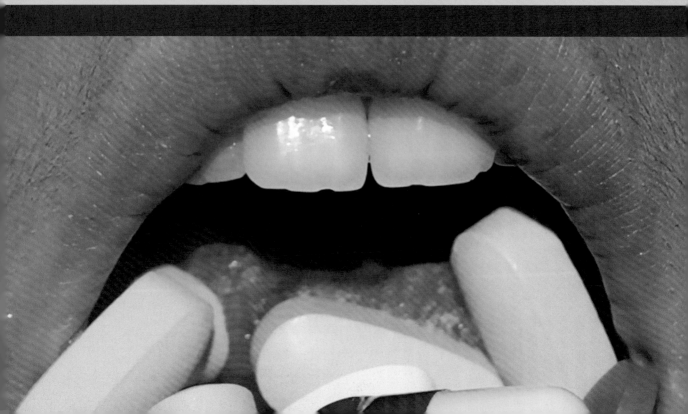

HPV vaccinations do not encourage risky sexual behaviour, *Lancet Oncology*, News, 7 February 2014 http://dx.doi.org/10.1016/S1470-2045(14)70053-1

When the UK government brought about vaccination to provide protection against infection with the Human Papilloma Virus (HPV), a virus known to cause about 70 per cent of cervical cancers, there was widespread concern amongst clinicians as well as parents that vaccination would be viewed by teenage girls as a form of wider protection against other STIs (sexually transmitted infections), potentially increasing their sexual activity and exposure to risk. The above *Lancet* news item highlights findings obtained from a study published in the journal *Pediatrics* of 339 girls and women aged between 13 and 21 who were either sexually experienced or inexperienced at the time of vaccination (Mayhew et al. 2014). Amongst the sexually inexperienced there was no association between post-vaccination risk perceptions and sexual behaviour initiation in the subsequent six months, and amongst the sexually experienced there was no increase in the number of sexual partners, nor a change in condom use behaviour. When looking at age stratified groups it emerged that sexually inexperienced women aged 16–21 with inappropriately low perceptions of risk of other STIs, were in fact *less* likely to initiate sexual activity after vaccination. This study's findings that beliefs about HPV vaccination are not a significant influence on behaviour counters concerns and possible barriers to being vaccinated. It must be noted, however, that as the sample consisted of those who *DID* present for vaccination, more work is needed to answer the question of beliefs and behaviour in those who choose not to present for vaccination. We will show in this, and subsequent chapters, that there is not just one but many personal and social influences on human behaviour, including sexual behaviour.

Chapter outline

The previous two chapters have described behaviour that is associated with health and illness: positive or health-protective behaviours such as exercise and health screening, and health-risk behaviours, such as smoking or unsafe sex. This chapter aims to describe the key theoretical models that have been proposed and tested in terms of their ability to explain and predict why people engage in health-risk or health-protective behaviour. Personality, beliefs and attitudes play an important role in motivating behaviour, as do our goals and intentions, social circumstances and social norms. The key psychological models and their components are described and critiqued, drawing on evidence from studies of an array of health behaviours. While our understanding of health behaviour remains incomplete due to the complexity of influences upon human behaviour generally, the empirical studies described have identified many significant and modifiable influences upon health and health behaviour that offer potential targets for future health promotion and health education, as described in Chapters 6 and 7 ☞.

Distal influences on health behaviour

One way of considering the factors predictive of health behaviour generally is to view some influences as 'distal', such as culture, environment, ethnicity, socio-economic status, age, gender and personality, and others as 'proximal' in their influence, such as specific beliefs and attitudes towards health-risk and health-protective behaviour. This division is somewhat arbitrary but is intended to reflect the fact that some distal influences, such as socio-economic status, operate on behaviour indirectly, by means of their effects on other more proximal factors, such as a person's attitudes, beliefs or goals. These proximal factors therefore potentially **mediate** the effect of socio-economic status on health. To illustrate this further, there is reasonably consistent evidence that people in the lower socio-economic groups drink more, smoke more, exercise less and eat less healthy diets than those in the higher socio-economic groups (e.g. Health and Social Care Information Centre 2013; Clare et al. 2014). Evidence of such a distal influence does not, however, explain 'how' or 'why' this is the case, (see Chapter 2 ☞ for a full discussion of

socio-economic inequalities in health). Further explanation can be offered from evidence showing that social class affects health beliefs (see Chapter 1 ☞), which in turn may then affect behaviour. These health beliefs can be considered 'closer' to the behaviour (more proximal) and offer a more feasible target for intervention than would an intervention aimed at altering a person's social class. Beliefs may therefore mediate the effects of more distal influences, and this hypothesis can be tested statistically. Another term you may come across when reading about relationships between variables is **moderation**. Moderating

---

mediate/mediator

mediating variables explain how or why a relationship exists between two other variables: for example, the effects of age upon behaviour may be mediated by health beliefs; thus age effects would be said to be indirect, rather than direct.

moderator/moderation

moderating variables explain the conditions under which a relationship between two other variables may exist: for example, the relationship between individual beliefs and behaviour may be different depending on gender or health status.

variables explain the conditions under which a relationship exists, for example the relationship between a potential predictor (such as social class) and an outcome (for example screening uptake) may vary according to categories of another variable (e.g. male/female, under 65/over 66). The models described in this chapter all acknowledge the role of these 'distal' influences, but vary in the extent to which they hypothesise or test specific associations between these and the more proximal factors. Before turning to the models, we therefore present some of the evidence regarding the specific distal influences of demographic characteristics of age, gender and personality. For a fuller discussion of socio-economic and cultural influences on health behaviour, see Chapter 2 ☞.

Demographic influences

In terms of age, the health behaviours that receive the majority of attention from educational, medical and public health specialists (i.e. smoking, alcohol consumption, unprotected sexual activity, exercise and diet) are patterns of behaviour set down in childhood or early adulthood. For instance, according to the Global Youth Tobacco Survey Collaborative Group (2002) the majority of smokers took up the habit as teenagers. Attitudes also change at this time when adolescents generally begin to seek autonomy (independence) from their parents. This may include making health-related decisions for themselves: for example, whether or not to start smoking or drinking alcohol, whether or not to brush their teeth before bed. Influences on decisional processes, attitudes and behaviour change during these years, with more credence being given to the attitudes, beliefs, values and behaviour of one's peers (and in fact siblings) than to the advice or attitudes of parents or teachers (e.g. Chassin et al. 1996; Hendry and Kloep 2002; Mercken et al. 2007). While establishing a sense of identity among one's peer group and attempting to 'fit in', it is perhaps not surprising that, for some adolescents, this will include the initiation of 'risk' behaviour as part of rebelling against authority or because the behaviour is considered to be 'cool' and grown-up (Michell and Amos 1997; Health and Social Care Information Centre 2013). Gender has been shown to exert a significant influence on the nature and performance of health-protective or health-risk behaviours, as we have described in the two preceding chapters. Perceptions of health and the meanings attached to health and health behaviours offer a partial explanation for gender differences in health behaviour. For example,

studies have suggested that drinking alcohol excessively, or avoiding seeking health care, are projections of their masculinity and desire to be seen as 'strong' (Addis and Mahalik 2003; Marcell et al. 2007; Visser and Smith 2007). Conversely, constructions of masculinity may also contribute to health-enhancing activity – exercise (Steffen et al. 2006). Visser and Smith (2007) present qualitative material from a study of males aged 18–21, which illustrates the linkages made between health-risk behaviour and social constructions of masculinity. Some of the material quoted highlights how other factors, such as sporting success, can 'compensate' for the reduced perceived masculinity attributed to an individual who drinks less:

> … really icons of masculinity who go out and booze, and get in fights, and get lots of women and stuff like that, they are regarded as … the prime kind of, you know, specimens of maleness … (but) because I was better than most of the players, they didn't, like, pressure me into drinking, because … you know, it was kind of like I could say to them 'Forget it' or whatever. Um … that was, that's personally me, but then I have friends who … weren't quite as experienced as me at hockey, but just to kind of get into the group I think they felt the need to partake in that [drinking].

Exceptions to the masculinity and drinking behaviour association were seen amongst some black and Asian Muslim interviewees whose religion exerted stronger influences on their behaviour than did the need to be seen as 'masculine'.

The broader influences of age, gender and ethnicity need to be acknowledged to a greater extent than is often the case in studies of health behaviour and health behaviour change. Individuals operate in varying social worlds, each with their own systems and norms, which exert influence on individual beliefs and behaviours. We try to highlight these wider influences wherever possible.

A further influence on behaviour that is not consistently operationalised or tested in studies of health behaviour change, although usually included in the diagrammatic representation of the models (see below), is that of personality.

Personality

Personality is, generally speaking, what makes individuals different from one another, in that each of us thinks and behaves in a characteristic manner, showing traits that are particularly enduring regardless of situation. Different scientists have proposed different numbers of key traits or dimensions of personality; two of the major examples are presented here.

Eysenck's three-factor model

According to Eysenck (1970, 1991), individual personality is reflected in an individual's scores along three dimensions:

1. *Extroversion* (outgoing social nature): dimensionally opposite to introversion (shy, solitary nature).

2. *Neuroticism* (anxious, worried, guilt-ridden nature): dimensionally opposite to emotional stability (relaxed, contented nature).

3. *Psychoticism* (egocentric, aggressive, antisocial nature): dimensionally opposite to self-control (kind, considerate, obedient nature).

For example, one individual may score positively and high on neuroticism and extroversion but negatively on psychoticism, whereas another may score positively and high on neuroticism, and negatively and high on extroversion and psychoticism. These three factors have received significant empirical support and are considered to be valid and robust personality factors (Kline 1993). However, another model exists, often referred to as the 'big five' (McCrae and Costa 1987, 1990), which identifies five primary dimensions of personality — and, within health psychology, it is this model which has received the most attention (see also Chapter 12 ☞ for more detailed discussion of personality and responses to stress).

McCrae and Costa's five-factor model

The Big Five traits include:

1. neuroticism

2. extroversion

3. openness (to experience)

4. agreeableness

5. conscientiousness.

Four of these five have been validated in different cultures (with the exception of conscientiousness) and at different points in the lifespan from age 14 to 50+ (McCrae et al. 2000), and are considered therefore relatively stable and enduring. Many associations between these personality traits and health have been reported

(see Vollrath's 2006 review); however, less attention has been directed at whether individual behaviours mediate this association. There is some evidence that high extroversion, neuroticism or openness increases risk-taking behaviour whereas less risk-taking is seen among those scoring higher on agreeableness and conscientiousness (e.g. Terracciano and Costa 2004; Nicholson et al. 2005). Similar directional associations have been reported with health-protective behaviours. For example, Magee and Heaven (2011) found that extroversion predicted two-year weight gain amongst Australian adults, and Goldberg and Strycker (2002) found that openness predicted low meat fat consumption and high fibre intake of those taking part in a large-scale community survey. These support the earlier findings of Steptoe et al. (1995), where openness was associated with a willingness to try novel situations, including new food tastes and types. In general, conscientiousness is associated with health-protective behaviour (for a meta-analysis see Bogg and Roberts 2004) whereas neuroticism tends to associate with health-risk behaviour (Booth-Kewley and Vickers 1994; Goldberg and Strycker 2002), including dietary 'pickiness' (fussiness) and **neophobia** among a sample of 451 Scottish children aged between 11 and 15 (MacNicol et al. 2003).

In seeming contradiction to this negative influence of neuroticism, it has also been associated with greater health-care use. This is attributed to the tendency of highly neurotic individuals to report greater attention to bodily sensations and to label them as a potential threat or 'symptom' of disease more than people lower in neuroticism (Jerram and Coleman 1999; Cameron and Leventhal 2003 and see Chapter 9 ☞). However, Friedman (2003) concluded that there is no consistent evidence that people scoring high on neuroticism engage in a greater range or frequency of health-protective behaviour or in less damaging health behaviour than those people with low neuroticism, and that 'healthy neurotics' may exist as well as 'unhealthy neurotics'. This suggests therefore that personality traits such as neuroticism offer insufficient explanation for health or risk behaviour.

> **neophobia**
> a persistent and chronic fear of anything new (places, events, people, objects).

Other aspects of personality

Another commonly investigated aspect of personality is generalised **locus of control** (LoC) beliefs (Rotter 1966). Rotter originally considered individuals to have either an internal LoC orientation (i.e. they place responsibility for outcomes on themselves and consider that their actions affect outcomes) or an external orientation, which suggests that they place responsibility for outcomes at the door of external factors such as luck. A sense of internal control was thought to be adaptive in that individuals believe they have some control over their lives. There is some evidence of this: for example, working adults with high locus of control perceive their job more positively and report greater job satisfaction (Judge et al. 2000). Why this may be the case (i.e. do individuals high in LoC behave or cope with stress differently, for example?) is discussed more in Chapter 11 ☞.

Testing this assumption in relation to health outcomes, Kenneth Wallston and colleagues (Wallston et al. 1978) developed the MHLC (multidimensional **health locus of control**) scale, an LoC scale specific to health beliefs, which identified three statistically independent dimensions:

1. *Internal*: strong internal beliefs consider the individual themselves as the prime determinant of their health state. Theoretically associated with high levels of health-protective behaviour and with Bandura's self-efficacy construct (see below).

2. *External/chance*: strong external beliefs consider that external forces such as luck, fate or chance determine an individual's health state, rather than their own behaviour.

3. *Powerful others*: strong beliefs on this scale consider health state to be determined by the actions of powerful others such as health and medical professionals.

Wallston argued that these dimensions become relevant only if an individual values their health. This reflects the theoretical underpinning to locus of control, that of social learning or social cognitive theory (Bandura 1986), whereby an individual acts on the expectancy of certain valued outcomes. If individuals do not value their health, it is thought that they are unlikely to engage in health-protective behaviour (even if they believe in personal control over health), simply because health is not prioritised (e.g. Wallston and Smith 1994). Individuals with an internal, or even a powerful others

HLC who do value their health are therefore more likely to behave in a health-protective manner. In the case of internal LoC, this might be seen in a person commencing a healthy eating programme, or in the case of a powerful others HLC, going to a local health clinic to request appetite suppression medication. Powerful others beliefs can, however, detract from an individual taking active responsibility for behaviour, with such individuals being overreliant on a medical 'fix'.

Such generalised LoC dimensions have proven, however, to be modest, or indeed weak, predictors of behaviour. For example, a large-scale survey of over 13,000 healthy individuals found that positive health behaviour was weakly correlated with higher internal control, and even more weakly associated with lower external and powerful others control beliefs (Norman et al. 1998). Given consistently modest findings, researchers turned their attention to more behaviourally specific and proximal constructs, such as **perceived behavioural control** (see theory of planned behaviour on p. 317) and **self-efficacy** (Bandura 1977 and see the health action process approach model on p. 153). Armitage (2003) has suggested that dispositional or generic control beliefs might in fact influence these more specific proximal control beliefs, based on his findings that generalised internal control beliefs independently predicted the relationship between perceived behavioural control and intention. In other words, the ability of perceived behavioural control beliefs to explain intention was strongest among those

---

locus of control

a personality trait thought to distinguish between those who attribute responsibility for events to themselves (i.e. internal LoC) or to external factors (external LoC).

health locus of control

the perception that one's health is under personal control; controlled by powerful others such as health professionals; or under the control of external factors such as fate or luck.

perceived behavioural control

one's belief in personal control over a certain specific action or behaviour.

self-efficacy

the belief that one can perform particular behaviour in a given set of circumstances.

individuals with high generalised internal LoC. Such findings suggest that interventions aiming to enhance specific perceived behavioural control beliefs may work better if targeted at those with an internal locus of control.

Further evidence that personality characteristics affect proximal predictors of behaviour includes findings that beliefs in low personal control over cure of skin cancer were associated with higher perceived risk / likelihood of developing skin cancer but lower intention to engage in prevention (Cameron 2008). She suggested that this may reflect underlying personality such as **dispositional pessimism** or anxiety, as other studies have found these to influence susceptibility beliefs (e.g. Gerend et al. 2004).

Overall, findings highlighted in this section support suggestions that the personality–health behaviour relationship is one which warrants further consideration (O'Connor 2014). Perhaps one reason why health psychologists have paid relatively less attention to personological predictors of behaviour than cognitive, emotional or even social factors is that personality is considered fixed and unchangeable (as the definition of 'trait' suggests). Whilst in principle correct, personality shapes the beliefs which cognitive interventions address and thus contributes to the whole picture.

Self-determination theory

What may add to the predictive utility of personality factors is some exploration of how personality traits effect the motivations for carrying out behaviour. **Self-determination theory** (Deci and Ryan 2000) distinguishes between intrinsic and extrinsic motivation. In the first of those, a person is motivated to behave in a certain way for the inherent personal satisfaction or rewards it produces, such as feelings of increased competence, autonomy, or relatedness to others. On the other hand, extrinsically motivated behaviour arises from perceived externally situated rewards, such as a need for peer approval. Testing this theory in relation to the safer sexual behaviour of students, Ingledew and Ferguson (2007) found that students scoring high on agreeableness or conscientiousness had intrinsic, autonomous or self-determined motivations to perform safer sex (e.g. 'Personally, I would practise safe sex because… I personally believe it is the best thing for my health'), rather than extrinsic, external or controlled motivations (e.g. 'Personally, I would practise safe sex because… I feel pressure from others'). Further evidence of a relationship between personality and behavioural motives is provided by Cooper et al. (2000), who found that neurotic individuals drank to reduce negative mood states whereas extroverted individuals drank to enhance their positive mood. Such studies make useful contributions to an area of research where understanding of the processes by which personality achieves its effects on health behaviour, and ultimately health, remains limited.

Social influences

Humans are fundamentally social beings. Our behaviour is a result of many influences: the general culture and environment into which we are born; the day-to-day culture in which we live and work which generally has a set of shared norms and expectations; the groups, sub-groups and individuals with whom we interact; and our own personal emotions, beliefs, values and attitudes, all of which are influenced by these wider factors. We learn from our own positive and negative experiences, but we also learn 'vicariously' through exposure to, and observation of, other people's expectancies, behaviour and experiences. The behaviour of other people in our culture or smaller social groups creates a perceived 'social norm', which suggests implicit (or explicit) approval for certain behaviours, values and beliefs (Aronson et al. 2005). For example, a four-year follow-up study of nearly 10,000 American high school students (Choi et al. 2003) found clear differences in the factors that explained initiation to smoking from non-smoking, and progression from experimental (defined as irregular, social, short-term) smoking to current smoker. Those who initiated smoking were typically white rebellious students who did not like school, and who perceived greater parental approval for smoking. Those who progressed in their smoking behaviour perceived peer approval for

> **dispositional pessimism**
> having a generally negative outlook on life and a tendency to anticipate negative outcomes (as opposed to dispositional optimism).
>
> **self-determination theory**
> this theory considers the extent to which behaviour is self motivated (i.e. by intrinsic factors) and influenced by the core needs of autonomy, competence and psychological relatedness.

their smoking and perceived experimental smoking as safe. College and university students similarly have been found to make assumptions about what constitutes 'typical' alcohol intake, and thus, for some, their problematic drinking can be judged as 'normal' when it may not be (Perkins et al. 2005). These assumptions of what relevant others 'do' have been described as 'descriptive norms', and differ from norms which 'proscribe' how others want you to behave in a certain situation, which have been referred to as 'injunctive norms' (Aronson et al. 2005; Stok et al. 2014). In 'Research focus' we describe a study which suggests that both types of norms may influence behaviour but in different ways.

In relation to health-risk behaviour, broader social influence is seen in the many sources of information that a person is exposed to: for example, televised advertisements graphically illustrating the negative consequences of smoking; an older sibling or parent appearing to be healthy in spite of regular binge-drinking episodes; a classroom workshop on how to 'just say no' to the first offer of a cigarette or other drug; a friend who smokes telling you that smoking is cool. There is consistent evidence to show that the credibility, similarity to self and even the attractiveness of the source of information influences whether or not attitudinal change or behaviour change occurs as a consequence (e.g. Petty and Cacioppo

1986, 1996). Evidence also exists that we respond to persuasive messages differently depending on whether the message source is seen to be numerically a minority or majority source. We may explore a message more when it is advocated by a majority, even when the recommendation is against our own self-interest (Martin and Hewstone 2003). However, as we discuss below, changed attitude is only part of the story!

Goals and self-regulation of behaviour

Health-protective and risk behaviours are generally performed for a reason; people have **outcome expectancies** attached to them as described in **social cognition theory** (SCT) and thus behaviour tends to be goal-directed (both

> **outcome expectancies**
> the outcome that is expected to result from behaviour, e.g. exercise will make me fitter.
>
> **social cognition theory**
> a model of social knowledge and behaviour that highlights the explanatory role of cognitive factors (e.g. beliefs and attitudes).

Photo 5.1 Social norms have been found to be important predictors of whether or not a person initiates specific health behaviours, in this instance smoking and drinking alcohol

Source: Corbis/Ansgar Photography.

short- and long-term goals) (e.g. Fiske and Taylor 1991; Carver and Scheier 1998). Ingledew and McDonagh (1998) have shown that health behaviour serves coping functions (which may be considered as short-term goals of the behaviour): for example, for some individuals smoking may serve the function of coping with stress. These authors identified five coping functions attached to health behaviour: problem solving, feeling better, avoidance, time out and prevention – for example, exercise behaviour loaded onto a 'prevention with problem-solving' function, but also on to a 'time out with problem-solving' function. Such findings highlight that there are many reasons why individuals behave in the way that they do; in this case, individuals exercised as a means of preventive health behaviour but also as a means of time out or relaxation. The implication therefore is that interventions designed to reduce 'unhealthy' behaviour need to take account of the coping functions or goals that individual behaviour serves for each individual – it is these goals that will motivate the behaviour (see also Chapter 6 ☞).

Processes of **self-regulation**, the cognitive and behavioural processes by which individuals guide, control, modify or adapt his or her responses, enable an individual to achieve desired outcomes or reduce undesired outcomes, i.e. their goals. Goals focus our attention and direct our efforts. More valued, and more specific, goals lead to greater and more persistent effort than general 'do your best' goals (Locke and Latham 2002, 2004). Goal-setting is closely related to behaviour-change techniques advocated by Abraham and Michie (2008), with setting SMART (specific, measurable, attainable, realistic and timely) goals a core component (see Chapter 6, ☞)

Cognitive regulation (i.e. controlling or modifying our thoughts) is required as well as emotion regulation (controlling or modifying our emotions) if we are to successfully organise and execute goal-directed activity: in other words, if we are to turn our intentions into actions (Mann et al. 2013). An inability to control thoughts and evaluate decision options and potential outcomes or to regulate our emotions (for example, when drunk!) may increase impulsivity and risk-taking behaviour (Magar et al. 2008). There is some suggestion that women use such self-regulation more than men: for example, in relation to planning for exercise uptake (Hankonen et al. 2010) and healthy eating (Renner et al. 2008). Attentional control is defined as the extent to which a person can focus on activities and goals and avoid being distracted by competing goals, demands, or negative arising emotions (such as anxiety about failure) that might interfere with goal attainment or, at least, be able to return to goal-directed activity after the distraction has passed or been dealt with (e.g. Luszczynska et al. 2004). Note that this is different from *action control* which refers to self-regulation of behaviour, i.e. action (Sniehotta et al. 2005), As a behaviour change technique (Chapter 6 ☞), encouraging attentional control could translate into statements such as 'If you feel the urge to smoke, focus your attention on other things happening around you – not on your desire for a cigarette'.

Thinking more broadly about our goal-directed behaviour, existential theory (Frankl 1946/2006) states that individuals need to be able to find meaning in their lives if they are to achieve mental health or even happiness (Diener and Seligman 2002; Diener et al. 2009). A sense of meaning or purpose in life is derived from achieving one's goals and feeling that one's activities are worthwhile. Having a weak sense of meaning or purpose in life has been associated with greater likelihood of risk behaviours such as smoking (Konkolÿ Thege et al. 2009) and drinking alcohol (Marsh et al. 2003).

---

self-regulation

the process by which individuals monitor and adjust their behaviour, thoughts and emotions in order to maintain a balance or a sense of normal function.

WHAT DO YOU THINK?

Think of three aspects of your life that are important to you and that you currently value highly. Why do you value them? What meaning do they have? What function do they serve?

What goals do you hope to achieve over the next six months? Over the next five years? If you engage in any specific health or risk behaviour, how does it 'fit' with your current values? How does it fit with your short- and long-term goals?

Now, think ahead to when you reach middle age (or if you have already reached this, think of your post-retirement years!). What do you think will be important to you then? Will the areas of importance change? Why? Do you think your values will have changed, or your goals, or your behaviour? If so, in what way and why?

The next part of the chapter addresses a range of psychological theories and models that have been developed in an attempt to explain and thereby predict health behaviour.

Models of health behaviour

First, it is important to remind the reader that by adopting healthy habits, we are only reducing the statistical risks of ill health, not guaranteeing that we will lead a long, healthy life. Furthermore, examination of human behaviour and the motives for it will never provide a full explanation for the huge variations in people's health. This is true for two broad reasons. Firstly, behaviour is not the only factor that causes disease. Secondly, humans, and the influence upon them, are inconsistent. For example:

- Different health behaviours are controlled by different external factors: for example, smoking may be socially discouraged, while exercise may be supported; however, cigarettes are readily available, whereas access to exercise facilities may be limited.

- Attitudes towards health behaviour vary within and between individuals. In the same individual, health behaviour may be motivated by different expectations: for example, a person may smoke to relax, exercise to lose weight and consume alcohol to socialise.

- Individual differences are in part explained by life stage: for example, a teenager may diet for fashion reasons, while a middle-aged man may diet to reduce the risk of having a heart attack.

- Motivating factors may change over time: for example, drinking alcohol when under age may be a form of rebellion but may later be considered an aid to social interaction.

- The social context can trigger or alternatively limit behaviour: for example, alcohol consumption may be lower when with parents or colleagues than when drinking with friends.

Given those caveats, we can only ever hope to offer a partial (social, cognitive and behavioural) explanation of behaviour and of any resulting illness. The evidence gathered can inform the content of interventions seeking to prevent or reduce the likelihood of illness in some individuals, even if we are unlikely to succeed with all!

Early theories as to why we changed our behaviour were based on the simplistic, implicit assumption that:

Information → Attitude change → Behaviour change

These were found to be naive. Although many past, and sometimes current, health education campaigns still draw upon this simplistic premise, the evidence regarding predictors of behaviour change show that things are much more complex. Eccles and colleagues (2012) conducted an important comparison of this implicit model of behavioural prediction with other theory-led models (Social Cognition Theory, the TPB, Learning Theory, the Precaution Adoption Process Model, and Implementation Intentions), which we consider in this chapter, and the Common Sense Model of Illness (see Chapter 9 ☞). In relation to the five health-care professional behaviours examined, the implicit model performed poorly. In fact they conclude that it would be '…. sensible to suggest that this is not a viable model for promoting the uptake of evidence-based practice'. Within patient or general public populations it has also been shown that simply having information or knowledge, for example about the value of a low-cholesterol diet or the health risks of sun-tanning behaviour (see Chapters 3 and 4 ☞), is not inevitably associated with healthy attitudes towards the behaviour (e.g. Ruiter and Kok 2005; Kyle *et al.* 2014). For example, in Kyle's study of more than 2000 Scottish adolescents, although more females than males knew of the association between sun exposure and skin cancer risk, they also held more positive attitudes towards tanning behaviour, and sun bathed more often. More than information and knowledge about a health threat is required to motivate behaviour change. Attitudes and risk perceptions do, however, play a significant role, as you will see in the models presented in the following sections.

Attitudes

What is an attitude? Attitudes are thought to be the common-sense representations that individuals hold in relation to objects, people and events (Eagly and Chaiken 1993). Some early theorists described attitudes as a single component based on affective evaluation of an object/event (i.e. you either like something/someone or you do not; e.g. Thurstone 1928); others presented a two-component model, where attitude is defined as an unobservable and stable predisposition or state of mental readiness that influences evaluative judgements (e.g. Allport 1935). From the 1960s onwards, a three-component model of attitude gained acceptance, whereby attitudes are considered as relatively enduring and generalisable and made up of three related parts – thought (cognition), feeling (emotion) and behaviour:

1. *Cognitive*: beliefs about the attitude-object – for example, cigarette smoking is a good way to relieve stress; cigarette smoking is a sign of weakness.

2. *Emotional*: feelings towards the attitude-object – for example, cigarette smoking is disgusting/pleasurable.

3. *Behavioural* (or intentional): intended action towards the attitude-object – for example, I am/am not going to smoke.

The three components of such explicit attitudes were considered to be generally consistent with each other and likely to predict behaviour; however, the empirical evidence to support a direct association between attitudes and behaviour is inconclusive. Even if attitudes become more negative towards a health-risk behaviour, increased perceived personal risk and behaviour change may not follow (e.g. Ruiter and Kok 2005; Kyle et al. 2014). This may be because an individual may hold several different, sometimes conflicting, attitudes towards a particular attitude-object, depending on social context and many other factors.

> **ambivalence**
>
> the simultaneous existence of both positive and negative evaluations of an attitude-object, which could be both cognitive and emotional.
>
> **social desirability bias**
>
> the tendency to answer questions about oneself or one's behaviour in a way that is thought likely to meet with social (or interviewer) approval.
>
> **implicit attitude**
>
> attitudes that activate unintentionally in response to actual or symbolic presence of an attitude-object (stimulus) and which therefore don't require the cognitive effort of explicit attitudes.

I may, for example, enjoy the taste of chocolate but be worried about the implications of high fat/high calorie intake. Such contradictory thoughts can produce what is known as 'dissonance', which many people will attempt to resolve by bringing their thoughts into line with one another. However, others maintain a dissociation between attitudes and behaviour: for example, so-called dissonant smokers or sun-bed users, who continue to smoke or use sun-beds despite holding a number of negative attitudes towards the behaviours. This conflict is sometimes referred to as **ambivalence**, where a person's motivation to change could potentially be undermined by the holding of ambivalent attitudes or competing goals (e.g. Sparks et al. 2001). Attitudes alone are insufficient.

Furthermore, measuring explicit attitudes brings with it criticisms of creating a **social desirability bias,** i.e. will people report that they hold positive attitudes towards behaviours they know are held in negative esteem socially, for example, illicit drug use or, increasingly, smoking? Recent technological developments in reaction time testing enables measurement of **implicit attitudes,** i.e. attitudes that activate unintentionally in response to actual or symbolic presence of an attitude-object (stimulus) and which therefore don't require the cognitive effort of explicit attitudes (Fishbein and Ajzen 2010). This effect can be achieved, for example, with experimental presentation of images of different faces or body genders or colours, or different food types, where the speed with which individuals can categorise these computer-presented images according to attitudinal criteria such as 'good/bad' 'attractive/not attractive', tasty/not tasty', member of etc. as conducted in social and cognitive psychology (e.g. studies of racial prejudice using the implicit association test of Greenwald et al. 1998). One advantage of implicit attitudes is that they are considered less prone to social desirability bias, but, because they are not under our conscious control, they may also be harder to change (Wilson et al. 2000; Fazio and Olson 2003). It is therefore unclear as yet whether their assessment will be of benefit to the development of health behaviour change interventions.

Many factors can shape, challenge or change initial attitudes, cause them to be ignored, or increase the likelihood of them being acted upon. An important influence on attitude is that of personal relevance and perceived risk.

Risk perceptions and unrealistic optimism

People often engage in risky or unhealthy behaviour because they do not consider themselves to be at risk or facing limited understanding or acceptance of any threat information received. While some of us may process threat information systematically and rationally, there is evidence that, for many, information is processed in a way that best fits with how one sees oneself: i.e. any information has to have relevance, and thus some information processing is defensive and self-affirming (Good and Abraham 2007; Wright 2010).

For some, their risk perceptions may be inaccurate, with individuals believing, for example, that 'I do not smoke as much as "person X" and therefore won't be at risk of cancer compared with them'. Weinstein (1984) named this biased risk perception, which he found to be common '**unrealistic optimism**' – 'unrealistic' because quite obviously not everyone can be at low risk. He noted that individuals engage in forms of social comparison that reflect best on themselves (comparative optimism/optimistic bias) (Weinstein and Klein 1996; Weinstein 2003): for example, in relation to HIV risk, 'I may sometimes forget to use a condom, but at least I use them more than my friends do'. He found that the negative behaviour of peers is focused on more when making these judgements than is the same peers' positive health behaviour. Such selective attention can lead to unrealistically positive appraisals regarding personal risk.

Weinstein (1987) identified four factors associated with unrealistic optimism:

1. a lack of personal experience with the behaviour or problem concerned;

2. a belief that their individual actions can prevent the problem;

3. the belief that if the problem has not emerged already, it is unlikely to do so in the future: for example, 'I have smoked for years and my health is fine, so why would it change now?';

4. the belief that the problem is rare: for example, 'Cancer is quite rare compared with how common smoking is, so it is pretty unlikely I'll develop it'.

There is some evidence that unrealistic optimism is associated with greater belief in control over events (e.g. 'I am at less risk than others because I know when to stop drinking') and that such beliefs are associated with risk-reducing behaviour (Weinstein 1987; Hoorens and Buunk 1993). However, Schwarzer (1994) suggests instead that the relationship between such optimism and behaviour is likely to be negative because individuals underestimate their risk and thus do not take precautions against the risk occurrence. There remains a need to test this empirically.

Within health psychology, risk perceptions are generally defined and assessed as individually generated cognitions, i.e. the extent to which a person considers themselves as facing potential harm, (see, for example, the health belief model below). However, risk perceptions are also influenced by the current social and cultural context: for example, if I were to perceive my risk of contracting TB (tuberculosis) as high while living in North Wales, this would likely be considered as being unrealistically pessimistic, whereas if I work with homeless populations where TB is still present, or make regular trips to countries where the incidence is high, then my beliefs may be more realistic (for an example of 'realistic pessimism' in a malaria endemic country, see Morrison et al. 1999). The mass media is also a primary source of information about health and associated behaviours and risks, whether it uses the scientific evidence appropriately or not. Assessing the context in which beliefs arise, wax and wane is important if interventions to change beliefs are to have optimal effect.

Self-efficacy

Self-efficacy is defined as 'the belief in one's capabilities to organise and execute the sources of action required to manage prospective situations' (Bandura 1986), or more simply, 'beliefs about whether one can produce certain actions' (Bandura 1997: 29). For example, believing that a future action (e.g. weight loss) is within your capabilities is likely to generate other cognitive and emotional activity, such as the setting of high personal goals (losing a stone rather than half a stone), positive outcome

> **unrealistic optimism**
> also known as 'optimistic bias', whereby a person considers themselves as being less likely than comparable others to develop an illness or experience a negative event.

expectancies and reduced anxiety about failure. These cognitions and emotions in turn affect actions, such as dietary change and exercise, in order to achieve the goal. As Bandura (1997: 24) states: 'It is because people see outcomes as contingent on the adequacy of their performance, and care about those outcomes, that they rely on efficacy beliefs in deciding which course of action to pursue and how long to pursue it'. Efficacy beliefs promote perseverance. Success in reaching a goal feeds back in a self-regulatory manner to further a person's sense of self-efficacy and to further efforts to attain goals (Schwarzer 1992). In situations where competence of one's own performance is unrelated or less closely tied to outcome, self-efficacy, as with other control constructs, will be less predictive of outcome (for example, physical recovery following a head injury will also depend to a large degree on the extent of neurological damage).

Self-efficacy beliefs often emerge as an important and strong predictor of individual health behaviour (e.g. predicting medication adherence in nine European countries, see Morrison et al. 2015), and behaviour change (Eccles et al. 2012), although it is not sufficient alone. Its effects are moderated by outcome expectancies and the value placed on the behavioural goal (French 2013).

Whilst not all influences on health behaviour are psychological, health and social psychologists have developed theoretical models to examine which factors combine empirically to explain a wide range of behaviour. The main models currently applied to behaviour change (initiation, maintenance or cessation) are presented below.

Sociocognitive models of behaviour change

Social cognition is a broad term used to describe how people encode, process, interpret, remember and then learn from and use information in social interactions in order to make sense of the behaviour of others and make sense of the world in which they operate. Social cognition shapes our judgements (including prejudices and stereotypes), attitudes and responses, and in turn these can shape our behaviour.

Social Cognitive Theory (SCT)

According to Bandura (1977, 1986) behaviour is determined by three types of individual expectancies:

● *Situation-outcomes expectancies* whereby a person connects a situation to an outcome: for example, smoking to heart attack;

● *outcome expectancies*: for example, believing that stopping smoking would reduce the risk of heart attack;

● *self efficacy beliefs*: for example, the extent to which the person believes they can stop smoking.

SCT proposes that these expectancies may or may not provide lasting incentives to change: for example, if the outcome of changing one's diet is weight loss that may incentivise behaviour change maintenance; however, if weight remains the same, behaviour change may be undermined. SCT also considers the facilitators and barriers to behaviour change, including social support and environmental factors.

Defined further by Maddux (2009) as 'what I believe I can do with my skills under certain conditions' (p:336) self efficacy beliefs are incorporated into several of the core models of behaviour described below. Bandura highlights interventions based on providing mastery experiences, or modelling of successes (Chapter 6 and 7 ☛) to enhance self-efficacy.

The health belief model

One of the first and best known models of health behaviour change is the health belief model (HBM) (Rosenstock 1974; Becker 1974; Becker and Rosenstock 1984). The HBM proposes that the likelihood that a person will engage in particular health behaviour depends on demographic factors: for example, social class, gender, age and four beliefs that may arise following a particular internal or external cue to action (see Figure 5.1). These beliefs encompass perceptions of threat (or risk perception, discussed above) and evaluation of the behaviour in question, with cues to action and health motivation added at a later date.

Specific examples best illustrate how the various components fit together:

● Perception of threat:

  ● I believe that coronary heart disease (CHD) is a serious illness contributed to by being overweight: *perceived severity*.

  ● I believe that I am overweight: *perceived susceptibility*.

- Behavioural evaluation:
  - If I lose weight, my health will improve: *perceived benefits* (of change).
  - Changing my cooking and dietary habits when I also have a family to feed will be difficult, and possibly more expensive: *perceived barriers* (to change).
- Cues to action (added in 1975; Becker and Maiman):
  - That recent television programme on the health risks of obesity worried me (*external*).
  - I am regularly feeling breathless when I climb stairs, so maybe I should lose some weight (*internal*).
- Health motivation (added in 1977; Becker et al.):
  - It is important to me to maintain my health.

The HBM has been applied to a wide range of behaviour over many years, as illustrated below.

The HBM and preventive behaviour

The HBM predicts that preventative behaviour follows from beliefs of susceptibility to serious health threats, and beliefs that the perceived benefits of behaviour outweigh any perceived barriers to that behaviour. In addition, an internal or external cue to action, being motivated by health gain and being confident that you could perform the behaviour in question will all increase the likelihood of that behaviour. But is this the case?

Taking the example of breast self-examination (BSE), there is evidence that many people do not practise it at all, adherence rates are low and practice decreases with age, even though the incidence of breast cancer increases with age. When exploring why this may be the case using the HBM, perceiving benefits of self-examination and few barriers to its performance are most consistently and most highly correlated with both intention to perform BSE and actual behaviour. Perceived seriousness of breast cancer, perceived susceptibility and being motivated towards health (e.g. seeking health information and generally engaging in health-promoting activity) are also found to be predictive (e.g. Champion 1990; Savage and Clarke 1996; Ashton et al. 2001). In fact, the level of health motivation distinguished between low, medium and high BSE performers, and predicted BSE over a one-year follow-up period (Champion and Miller 1992). This supports the need to assess health motivation rather than assume that all people value health or are equally motivated to pursue it. Parents are likely to be universally motivated to achieve health for their child; however, this alone may be insufficient when it comes to making decisions about vaccinations (Painter et al. 2010, 2011). For example, whilst perceiving benefits to vaccination of their 24-35-month-old child was associated with greater parental uptake in a large National Immunisation Survey conducted in the USA, uptake fell in those who perceived greater side effects and who had a poor relationship with the health-care practitioner (Smith et al. 2011).

Perceiving barriers is generally associated with low levels of preventive behaviour, such as low medication adherence (Holmes et al. 2014) or low dental flossing

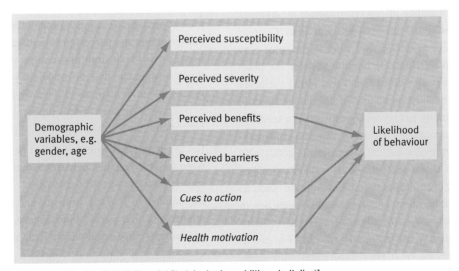

Figure 5.1 The health belief model [(original, plus additions in italics)]

(Buglar et al. 2010). Norman and Brain (2005) found, more specifically, low emotional barriers and low self-efficacy barriers to be predictive of breast self-examination. In spite of the relative consistency of findings regarding perceived barriers and failure to carry out the behaviour in question, removing barriers is not always sufficient to increase behaviour. For example, a lifestyle intervention which reduced perceived barriers to exercise amongst older couples with hypertension did not predict exercise initiation nor maintenance (Burke et al. 2007).

Components of the HBM and their salience to individuals in explaining behaviour may be influenced by ethnicity. For example, an American study (Chen et al. 2007) found that, while uptake of an influenza vaccination was strongly related to beliefs in influenza seriousness and personal susceptibility in the whole sample, these factors were much more strongly associated among African American and European American adults than among Hispanic Americans who were more influenced by perceived barriers to vaccination.

The HBM and risk behaviour

In terms of HBM components predicting a reduction in risk behaviour such as smoking, or increased condom use to avoid HIV infection, one would hypothesise that positive behaviour change would occur when the perceived benefits of change outweigh the perceived benefits of continued risk-taking; however, the evidence of this is mixed. In relation to smoking, this is likely to be because smoking is a dependency-producing behaviour and thus the impulse to smoke can occur independent of our conscious cognitive efforts (Hofmann et al. 2008; as cited in Sutton 2010 see Issues, and also Chapter 3 (☞) – thus our models do not work in the same way (Vangeli and West 2008). In relation to safer sex practices, Abraham et al. (1996) found that HBM variables were not significantly predictive of consistent condom use among sexually active adolescents once a measure of previous condom use had been taken into consideration. In a later review he (Abraham et al. 2002) also concluded that 'threat perceptions are weaker correlates of condom use than action-specific cognitions, such as attitudes towards condom use, perceived self-efficacy in relation to condom use, the social acceptability of condom use and condom use intentions' (p. 228). For example, failed condoms or a poor experience with them, similar to previous failed attempts to quit smoking, can

become barriers to future change, possibly because this elicits poor self-efficacy beliefs for future attempts. This all highlights that an important predictor of what we do in the future is what we have done in the past. Past behaviour is consistently found to be predictive, not only in relation to safer sexual behaviour (Yzer et al. 2001), but also, for example, in relation to breast self-examination (Norman and Brain 2005), or objective and self-report physical activity (Plotnikoff et al. 2014). Nowadays, research studies using the HBM and the other models described in this chapter tend to include a measure of previous behaviour in their design.

Limitations of HBM

The HBM components appear to be more relevant to predicting the initiation of health preventive behaviours than perhaps reducing health-risk behaviour. Other limitations include:

● Older studies did not include assessment of cues to action and health motivation which we now know are important.

● Rosenstock (1966) did not specify how the different variables interact with one another or combine to influence behaviour, although he implied that components could usefully be summed. Many studies examine components independently and few examine the interrelationships between them.

● Strecher and Rosenstock (1997) suggested that adding or multiplying susceptibility X severity scores to get an overall 'perceived threat' score may enable greater prediction than using each independently; that cues to action and perceived benefits and barriers may better predict behaviour in situations where perceived threat is high; and that the model may be better tested against intention than actual behaviour. Few of these hypotheses have been tested empirically, although the latter point has received empirical support.

● Becker et al. (1977) suggested that perceived benefits were weighted against perceived barriers, but did not specify how this was to be calculated - Do you subtract the number of barriers from the number of benefits reported, or vice versa? Furthermore, do all benefits and barriers carry equal weight to an individual?

● Steadman and colleagues (2002) have shown that highly salient beliefs (i.e. those of high importance to the individual) may predict outcomes better than a model which employs modal beliefs.

- The HBM may overestimate the role of 'threat', given findings that perceived susceptibility inconsistently predicts health behaviour change. Health promotion messages should not overuse fear arousal as this can be counter-productive to behaviour change (Albarracín et al. 2005), particularly among those who lack the resource to change (e.g. Ruiter and Kok 2006).

- The HBM takes limited account of social influences or contexts in which behaviour occurs: For example, there is more than one person present when considering condom use.

- The HBM fails to consider whether the individual feels able to initiate the behaviour or behaviour change required, i.e. their perceived behavioural control and self-efficacy beliefs (as do the Theory of Planned Behaviour (TPB) and the Health Action Process Approach (HAPA) – see below).

- Insufficient attention is paid to the role played by mood or negative affect, found, for example, to be inversely associated with exercise behaviour among women with breast cancer (Perna et al. 2008).

- The HBM is a static model, suggesting that beliefs occur simultaneously: this does not allow for staged or dynamic processes such as changing or oscillating beliefs over time.

Given the limitations and more recent improvements to models of behaviour change which we present in this chapter, it is perhaps not surprising that studies using the HBM components have only accounted for a small proportion of variance in behaviour change. Protection motivation theory (PMT) (Rogers 1983; Rogers and Prentice-Dunn 1997) expanded on the HBM to include response-efficacy and costs, and self-efficacy to the 'coping appraisal' factors they consider influence behaviour change, as well as adding the emotion of fear as part of threat appraisal. However, by also failing to consider the interactions between its components and the role of social norms and influences, the PMT also provides only a limited account of human action, and thus more extensive models were adopted.

The theory of planned behaviour

While the HBM is predominantly a cognitive model derived from **subjective expected utility theory** (i.e.

individuals are active and generally rational decision makers who are influenced by the perceived utility (usefulness to them) of certain actions or behaviour (cf. Edwards 1954), the Theory of Reasoned Action (TRA) and its successor, the Theory of Planned Behaviour (TPB), derive from social cognition theory (SCT, described earlier). These models assume that social behaviour is determined by a person's beliefs about behaviour in given social contexts and by their social perceptions and outcome expectations and not simply by their cognitions or attitudes.

Underlying the development of these models is the assumption (Fishbein 1967; Ajzen and Fishbein 1970) that individuals behave in a goal-directed manner and that the implications of their actions (outcome expectations) are weighed up in a *reasoned* manner (not necessarily rational, Fishbein and Ajzen 2010) before the decision is taken whether to engage in the behaviour or not. The TPB explores and develops the psychological processes linking between attitude and behaviour by incorporating wider social influences, beliefs in personal behavioural control, and the necessity of intention formation. Behaviour is thought to be proximally determined by intention, which in turn is influenced by a person's attitude towards the object behaviour (outcome expectancy beliefs, e.g. positive outcome expectancy: if I stop smoking, exercising will become easier for me; negative outcome expectancy: if I stop smoking, I will perhaps gain weight; and outcome value: it is important for me to be healthier) and their perception of social norms and pressures regarding the behaviour (e.g. my friends and parents do not smoke and really want me to stop smoking) (known as a **subjective norm**). The extent to which they wish to comply or fall into line with the preferences

---

subjective expected utility (seu) theory

a decision-making model where an individual evaluates the expected utility (cf. desirability) of certain actions and their outcomes and selects the action with the highest seu.

subjective norm

a person's beliefs regarding whether important others (referents) would think that they should or should not carry out a particular action. An index of social pressure, weighted generally by the individual's motivation to comply with the wishes of others.

or norms of others is known as motivation to comply (I would like to please my parents and friends). The model states that the importance of the person's attitudes towards the behaviour is weighted against the subjective norm beliefs, whereby a person holding a negative attitude towards behaviour change (I don't really like dieting) may still develop a positive intention to change in situations where their subjective norm promotes dieting and they wish to comply with their significant others (e.g. all my friends eat more healthily than I do, and I would like to be more like them).

The third influence on intention is that of perceived behavioural control, added to the TRA to create the TPB (Ajzen 1985, 1991; see Figure 5.2). Perceived behavioural control (PBC) is defined as a person's belief that they have control over their own behaviour in certain situations, even when facing particular barriers (e.g. I believe it will be possible for me to breastfeed even if I go to the supermarket café). The model proposes that PBC will directly influence intention and thus, indirectly, behaviour. A direct relationship between PBC and behaviour is also considered possible if perceptions of control were accurate, meaning that if a person believes that they have control over their diet, they may well intend to change it and subsequently do so, but if the preparation of food is in fact under someone else's control, behavioural change is less likely even if a positive intention had been formed (Rutter and Quine 2002: 12). PBC beliefs themselves are influenced by many factors, including past behaviour and past successes or failures in relation to the behaviour in question, and in this way the PBC construct is very similar to that of self-efficacy. For example, a person who has never tried to stop smoking

before may have lower PBC beliefs than a person who has succeeded in stopping previously and who may believe that it is within their control to do so again.

It is clear that this construct has been an important addition, with most studies using the TPB reporting significant correlations between PBC and intention, although intention remains a stronger predictor of subsequent behaviour than PBC is directly (Sheeran and Orbell 1999). It has been suggested that PBC may be most powerful when it is considered in interaction with the other components of the model, such as attitudes and motivations (Eagly and Chaiken 1993) and even more dispositional measures of locus of control (e.g. Armitage 2003). Armitage et al. (1999) compared the predictive utility of self-efficacy beliefs (which address perceived confidence and competence and not simply control) with perceived behavioural control beliefs in relation to the use of legal and illegal drugs and found that self-efficacy beliefs were more strongly associated with behaviour than were PBC beliefs. Self-efficacy is central to the HAPA model (see later section).

In a large-scale meta-analysis of studies employing the TPB, its variables accounted for between 35 and 50 per cent of variance in intentions, and between 26 and 35 per cent of the variance in behaviour (Sutton 2004). Intention is considered to be the proximal determinant of behaviour, and it reflects both the individual's motivation to behave in a certain manner and how hard they are prepared to try to carry out that behaviour (Ajzen 1991: 199). This compares favourably with the HBM, which simply stated that a combination of motivational beliefs predicted a greater or lesser likelihood of action, without a statement of intent ever having been formed.

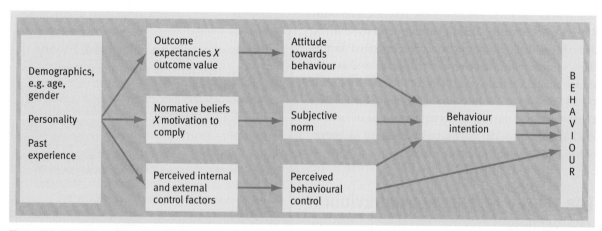

Figure 5.2 The theory of planned behaviour

The TPB and preventive behaviour

The TPB has been used in numerous studies in relation to both intention and actual preventative behaviour amongst both healthy and unhealthy populations, and across a wide range of behaviours. Some examples include eating breakfast (Wong and Mullan 2009), breastfeeding intentions (Giles et al. 2014), chlamydia-testing intentions (Booth et al. 2014), physical activity (PA, many references below), medication adherence (Morrison et al. 2015), or mothers' behaviours to encourage an active versus a sedentary lifestyle in their children (Hamilton et al. 2013). Only a few can be described here.

In relation to physical activity of children, Hagger et al. (2001) found that attitudes, perceived behavioural control (PBC) and intention were significant influences on exercise behaviour assessed a week later. PBC and attitude both predicted intention, but subjective norm did not. In contrast, subjective norm (as well as attitudes and PBC) were significant predictors of Canadian adolescents' intention to engage in regular physical activity, eat fruit and vegetables daily, and be smoke-free over a one-month period (Murnaghan et al. 2010). Such inconsistency of findings regarding the strength of influence played by normative beliefs may be partly explained by the age of the children (the Canadian sample were older than Hagger's sample (12–16 years compared to 12–14 years) and thus perhaps more responsive to social influence (Conner and Sparks 2005). Social influence is also seen in children with chronic health conditions such as those with cancer, where physical activity is an important part of health and quality of life maintenance. A recent review (Gilliam and Schwebel 2013) found that parental engagement in PA was an important influence on the child's levels of physical activity, although indirect parental support via encouragement and transportation (!) was more important than engagement when adolescents were considered and when peer influence takes on more salience. Amongst adults with type 2 diabetes, the prediction of PA over 12 months from TPB components was significant (49 per cent for objective PA, 27 per cent for self-reported PA), with past PA being the main predictor, followed by PBC and not, surprisingly, intention (Plotnikoff et al. 2014).

Exploring these relationships among individuals with chronic diseases, Eng and Martin-Ginis (2007) found that the leisure time physical activity of 80 men and women with chronic kidney disease was predicted by

PBC assessed a week previously. Among adolescent survivors of cancer, intentions to be physically active on a regular basis were predicted by affective attitudes towards physical activity (e.g. seeing it as enjoyable–unenjoyable) and instrumental attitudes (seeing it as useful–useless), but not by any of the other TPB components (34 per cent of variance explained in total). Physical activity itself was explained by intention (19 per cent variance explained) and by self-efficacy (added a further 10 per cent). This study assessed both PBC and self-efficacy and note that it is the latter that emerged significant (Keats et al. 2007). That different components of the TPB explain intention than predict actual exercise behaviour is consistent with findings of a meta-analysis of exercise behaviour among healthy populations (Hagger et al. 2002) and also from studies of the uptake of screening opportunities for cervical cancer and breast cancer. With regards to the latter, Rutter (2000) found that intention to attend screening was predicted by attitude, PBC and subjective norm, although only attitude and subjective norm were predictive of actual uptake of screening. Studies of self-screening, in terms of breast or testicular self-examination, report similar differences in predictors, but more longitudinal studies are crucial if causal relationships are to be confirmed.

One prospective longitudinal study of predictors of mammography uptake among 1,000 women examined the influence of different measures of 'norms', comparing individual normative belief with modal beliefs (Steadman et al. 2002). Generally, subjective norm has been assessed by asking individuals to state what they believe the norms and expectancies of a range of listed other people are in relation to the behaviour in question. In this method of questioning, an individual is prompted to think of many people or many influences and a 'modal' belief is what is analysed. The same applies to calculations of attitudes, as totals are used rather than examining the strength and **salience** of individual attitudes therein. Steadman and colleagues argue that in modal beliefs there may be one or more highly salient belief that holds high importance to the individual, and that prediction of outcomes may be improved if such salient individual beliefs are analysed rather than modal

> **salience**
> strength and importance.

beliefs. The results only partially confirmed the authors' hypotheses. There was not a stronger association between individual beliefs and intention or attendance behaviour than between modal beliefs and intention or attendance. However, there was evidence of individual beliefs *adding to* the prediction of attendance, a result not found in terms of modal SN (subjective norm) beliefs. Earlier studies had not reported an effect of SN on mammography uptake behaviour, which may be, as the authors conclude, because 'an individually generated subjective norm is a more sensitive and accurate estimate of the true effect of normative pressure' (p. 327). It is worth noting that the data of women who could not identify a normative influence on their behaviour was necessarily removed for this study; such women are an interesting group worthy of separate investigation in that their decisions about screening uptake (or any other behaviours potentially) are likely to be made on a very individual basis.

Hunter et al. (2003) examined the predictors of intention to seek help from a GP for breast cancer symptoms among a general population sample of women. Attitudes towards help seeking (e.g. 'Making an appointment to see my doctor for a symptom that might be cancer would be good/bad, beneficial/harmful, pleasant/unpleasant, wise/foolish, necessary/unnecessary') and perceived behavioural control (e.g. 'There is nothing I could do to make sure I got help for a breast cancer symptom': agree–disagree (seven-point scale)) explained a small but significant amount of variance in intention (7.1 per cent).

Subjective norms were not predictive of intention to seek help for such symptoms. Given the point above about measuring individual and not modal subjective norm beliefs, this is perhaps not surprising; furthermore, we see in the 'Research Focus' box how descriptive norms (i.e. describe what others do) may operate in a different way than injunctive norms (i.e. those that proscribe what you should do because others do and think it appropriate you do too). It is important to note that Hunter and colleagues also examined participants' perceptions of cancer (**illness representations**; see Chapter 9 ☛) and entered these variables into the regression analysis before the TPB variables. Illness representations explained 22 per cent of the variance in intention, with the TPB variables adding a further 7.1 per cent thereafter. This highlights the importance of considering individuals' perceptions of the illness that the behaviour in question is related to. For example, when examining smoking behaviour, perhaps perceptions of cancer or COPD should be more fully addressed.

Additionally, perceptions of treatment may influence the health behaviour of adherence, as suggested in studies

> ### illness representations
>
> beliefs about a particular illness and state of ill health – commonly ascribed to the five domains described by Leventhal: identity, timeline, cause, consequences and control/cure.

RESEARCH FOCUS

Don't tell me what I should do, but what others do: the influence of descriptive and injunctive peer norms on fruit consumption in adolescents.

Stok, F.M., de Ridder, D.T.D., de Vet, E. and de Wit, J.B.F. (2014) *British Journal of Health Psychology*, 19: 52–64.

As we have described in Chapter 4 ☛, having a healthy diet is important to weight management and

also to the prevention of a range of diseases such as cardiovascular disease and some forms of cancer. Patterns of fruit and vegetable consumption are generally developed in childhood or adolescence and this paper has been selected to illustrate the role adolescent beliefs about what is 'normative' plays in such behaviour. Evidence suggests that adolescents know about the importance of healthy eating, but that many fail to follow nutritional guidance. The authors explore whether perceived social norms that are unsupportive of healthy eating intervene between putting available knowledge into action. This study employs an

(continued)

experimental method to manipulate normative beliefs of two broad kinds: those *descriptive norms* which describe what others 'do' in a certain situation, and *injunctive norms* which proscribe behaviour and indicate what others think is appropriate for an individual to do in a certain situation. Following on from recent findings (Lally et al. 2011) that adolescents underestimate peers' actual consumption (descriptive norm) and overestimate peers' negative attitudes towards fruit and vegetable consumption (injunctive norm), this is a timely study, given concerns about adolescent health, obesity and poor nutritional practices.

Aims and method

By manipulating perceived norms experimentally and recording participants' actual behaviour in terms of their subsequent fruit consumption, this study offers a prospective test of an important question, with relevance to the development of real-world health promotion.

The authors hypothesise that:

● receiving normative information will increase both intended and actual fruit consumption relative to participants not receiving normative information;

● participants receiving the descriptive norm message will report higher intended and actual fruit consumption than those receiving an injunctive norm message.

To test these, 96 adolescents aged between 14 and 17 years old were recruited from a Dutch high school, and 80 completed both the initial pre-intervention and the follow-up assessments. Those who dropped out were no different in terms of their age, gender, BMI (body mass index), motivation nor tendency towards social comparison, nor did more drop out of one of the experimental conditions than the other. Thus we can be reasonably confident that the final sample of 80 is representative of the initial sample.

Participants randomly received one of three booklets: descriptive norm text, injunctive norm text, control condition text. Each booklet also contained the demographic, motivation, social comparison, and intention to eat fruit measures. Three days later participants completed an assessment of fruit consumption over the past two days.

Results

The paper does not clearly describe the intention to eat fruit reported by participants in each of the three experimental groups *before* the intervention message – most likely because the assessments were delivered simultaneously with the normative message and it would be difficult to control for the order in which participants completed the booklet. The data that is presented describes the correlations between likely predictor variables and intention and reveals that females and those high on autonomous motivation reported higher intention to eat fruit. These factors were therefore controlled for when looking at actual fruit intake reported in the follow-up assessment. In doing this, a significant effect of experimental group was found whereby those adolescents receiving the injunctive norm message reported significantly lower intention to eat fruit than those in both the descriptive norm and the control group. Those in the descriptive norm condition did not differ from those in the control condition.

In terms of subsequent reported behaviour, age was associated with eating more fruit (older adolescents ate more). Controlling for this and for autonomous motivation (it is unclear whether gender is again controlled for), greater fruit consumption was found in these who received the descriptive norm information (average 2.3 pieces of fruit per day, sd 1.6) compared to the injunctive norm group (average 1.5 pieces, sd 0.9), or the controls (average 1.7, sd 1.0). The injunctive norm group did not differ from participants in the control group.

Discussion

This paper describes an interesting experimental study with valued hypotheses if we are to further develop our understanding of the role of perceived norms in health behaviour, perhaps more important in adolescence than in older adults.

The findings demonstrate differential effects of injunctive and descriptive social norms. Injunctive norms (i.e. 'the majority of high school students think other high school students *should* eat sufficient fruit') affected intention negatively, and descriptive norms (i.e. 'the majority of high school students try to eat sufficient fruit

(continued)

themselves'), in contrast, affected behaviour positively. As such, the findings partially confirm the study hypotheses. However, the interest lies more in what was *not* associated. Firstly, the descriptive norm message affected behaviour but not intention, which is contrary to theoretically driven, TPB-led hypotheses where intention is the proximal determinant of behaviour. The authors suggest that this is because the broad description of others' behaviour acts as a quick and easy 'heuristic' – a rule of thumb that can guide behaviour without the need for much conscious cognitive effort nor need to form explicit intentions to eat fruit. They just 'did' (or rather, report that they did). This has important implications for brief interventions.

Secondly, amongst this adolescent sample, presentation of an injunctive message had a negative effect by reducing intentions to eat fruit. The authors suggest this may reflect adolescent resistance to a message suggesting how they should be behaving, although it is important to note that this negative effect did not emerge in relation to subsequent behaviour. Further study of the presence and duration of any resistance to injunctive messages would be useful.

There are, however, some methodological limitations that undermine the full theoretical importance of these two main findings. The obvious limitation is that unfortunately the study did not measure actual fruit consumption nor that reported by participants in the two days prior to the intervention study; therefore no 'change' data is provided, only a comparison in amounts reportedly consumed at follow-up between the three groups. This limits conclusions that can be drawn, as the group may have had behavioural differences to start with.

The issue of relying on self-report when it comes to behaviour that is viewed as having social norms and expectations is a common limitation in such studies, and socially acceptable answers are possible. The authors, however, do try to address this by simultaneously assessing participants' tendency to indulge in social comparison and find that social comparison tendency was not in fact associated with reported intention or consumption.

Finally, there was only a two-day gap between assessments and so any longer-term effects are unclear.

Limitations aside, the issues raised in this experimental study lend themselves to fairly straightforward replication and extension and, with the potential to inform effective and brief interventions, it is likely we will see more such studies in the coming years.

of the beliefs in the necessity of medicine and concerns about taking them (e.g. Clifford et al. 2008; Morrison et al. 2014). Ethnic differences in how certain conditions are perceived may also affect help-seeking behaviour; in our multicultural society it should not be assumed that beliefs about conditions, or about relevant preventive health behaviours, are the same (see also Chapter 9 ☞).

Another behaviour that is considered health protective is that of vaccination, and the TPB has been employed in several studies in this regard. One example is a study conducted in the UK among the 317 parents of 11–12-year-olds. Results revealed a low level of intention to have their child vaccinated against HPV infection (see also Chapter 3, ☞). In this study only 38 per cent 'certainly' agreed to vaccination, although a further 43 per cent stated they would probably agree (Brabin et al. 2006). A more recent study focused on predicting intention found that the method of presenting (visual vs. textual) risk/benefit information to parents is important (Cox et al. 2010). Crucially, however, studies that assess actual uptake behaviours are needed if health promotion efforts are to be targeted effectively. Intention is also not sufficient to motivate behaviour, as we discuss below.

The TPB and risk behaviour

Two different examples of behaviour will be illustrated here: smoking and unprotected sexual intercourse. Smoking is fundamentally an individual behaviour requiring one person only for its performance, whereas unprotected sexual intercourse is a behaviour that involves two people in a social encounter or interaction. Smoking is talked about frequently but as a behaviour is increasingly becoming marginalised, whereas unprotected sexual intercourse is rarely discussed in public! As described in Chapter 3 ☞ smoking also carries significant potential for dependence, whereas this is rare in relation to sexual behaviour (although sexual addiction does exist; see Orford 2001). There are sufficient differences between these behaviours to perhaps expect that the predictors of each may differ.

Godin et al. (1992) reported that the frequency of smoking behaviour over a six-month period among a general population sample could be explained primarily by low perceived behavioural control over quitting beliefs. Norman et al. (1999) applied the TPB to smoking cessation and found that the best predictor of intention to quit was not only perceived behavioural control, but also beliefs in one's susceptibility to the negative health consequences of continued smoking. Few studies have actually applied the TPB to smoking cessation, acknowledging that addictive behaviour is subject to different controlling and contributing factors than is behaviour of a more **volitional** nature (see ISSUES). In saying that, however, beliefs in control over the behaviour, and in particular self-efficacy beliefs (as defined in the HAPA, below), have been found to be salient. Social influence is also seen in studies of child smoking uptake where parental influence is strong (see Chapter 3 ☛, and also Hiemstra 2012).

In terms of sexual risk behaviour, research has predominantly focused on identifying factors associated with increased condom use. A meta-analysis of studies has demonstrated that previous use of condoms, a positive attitude towards use, subjective norms of use by others, partner support of use, self-efficacy in relation to both the purchase and use of condoms, and intentions are important (see Albarracin et al. 2001). One limitation of this area of research is that many studies have been conducted with educated young adult populations (e.g. students) rather than in more 'chaotic' populations for whom behaviour change is crucial. Interestingly, perceiving a risk of not using a condom (HIV, STDs) does not necessarily follow actual risky practices: for example, MacKellar et al. (2007) found that young men who had sex with men were overly optimistic about their HIV risk. It is important to address also whether sexual partners are long-term or casual, as this will also affect real and possibly perceived risk as well as, potentially, attitudes towards the need for, and importance of, 'safe sex'. These factors are likely to influence whether or not the issue of using condoms is raised with a potential partner. It has been suggested that for some individuals the non-use or the use of condoms is less governed by intention

(and by implication the cognitive processes that the TPB claims precede intention) than by habit, and, as such, interventions should be targeted very early in a sexual career so as to facilitate the development of 'safer sex' habits (cf. Yzer et al. 2001). For further discussion of the challenge to health behaviour change interventions when dealing with 'habits', see 'In the spotlight'.

Limitations of the TPB

The TPB does not acknowledge likely bi-directional relationships between predictor variables (attitudes and subjective norms) and outcome variables, either intention or behaviour. Behaviour may shape attitudes as well as vice versa. Only prospective longitudinal studies enable the changing relationships between variables over time to be examined.

The evidence supporting a link between intention and subsequent behaviour has been limited by an overreliance on cross-sectional studies. A recent meta-analysis of experimental changes in intention-behaviour relationship, at least with regards to physical activity, finds that medium-sized changes in intention only resulted in trivial-sized changes in behaviour (Rhodes and Dickau 2012). This is known as the 'intention–behaviour gap'.

When the prediction of behaviour from TPB variables is significantly lower than the prediction of intention, this provides strong evidence for the need to identify further variables that move an individual from intention to action. These are described below.

The TPB, as with most models of health behaviours, assumes that the same factors and processes predict the initiation of a behaviour/behaviour change and its maintenance. In fact the majority of studies focus on behaviour initiation. This may be why interventions based on such findings fail to have long-term effects on behaviour change maintenance (van Stralen et al. 2009).

Extending the TPB

From rigorous review and evaluation of the limitations of the TPB over the past four decades, several other potential

---

Volitional

behaviour following deliberate or reflective processes rather than those which are automatic or impulsive.

predictors of behaviour have emerged, including past behaviour as alluded to earlier. Others include affective (emotional) variables (e.g. anticipatory regret), those that relate to planning processes involved in the initiation of action following intention formation (e.g. implementation intentions), self-regulatory processes including self-efficacy, attentional control and those that acknowledge automaticity or habit. As noted by the TPB authors (Fishbein and Ajzen 2010: 282) ' for the sake of parsimony, additional predictors should be proposed and added to the theory with caution, and only after careful deliberation and empirical exploration. They also suggest that any additions should be 'conceptually independent of the theory's existing predictors'. Over the past 15 years or so, this has taken place with several components emerging as adding to the explanation of behaviour change:

● *Past behaviour*: The best predictor of what you do today is likely to be what you have done in the past. For example, trying to stop smoking is influenced by whether or not you have tried to before. Hoie et al. (2010) found, in a Norwegian study of 357 daily smoking students, that the original TPB components accounted for 12.3 per cent of the variance in quitting intentions, while the addition of past behaviour (more specifically, past quitting attempts), moral norms, self-identity and group identity added 16.5 per cent to the explained variance in intentions. When the students were split into categories according to whether they had tried to stop smoking before or not, the predictive utility of the TPB in fact increased with the number of quit attempts. Importantly, PBC and group commitment were significantly stronger predictors of intention among those who had several previous quit attempts compared with those who never had tried to stop smoking. The extended TPB model explained 1 per cent and 28 per cent of the variance in intentions among those with no and several previous quit attempts, respectively. However, as noted by Fishbein and Ajzen (2010: 286), examining past behaviour tells us what we did and predicts what we now do, but it does not tell us 'why'. Interestingly, the effect of past behaviour on intention is not fully mediated by the core TPB components – attitudes, norms, PBC— suggesting that other factors are at play which to date are not clearly understood. Past behaviour, if frequent, can also develop into habit, which brings further challenges to those seeking to explain behaviour.

● *Habits and automaticity:* see 'In The Spotlight'

● *'Moral norms'*: rather than a behaviour being influenced by subjective social norms, it has been recognised that some intentions and behaviour may be partially motivated by moral norms, particularly behaviours that directly involve others, such as condom use or drink driving (e.g. Armitage and Conner 1998; Manstead 2000; Evans and Norman 2002).

● *Anticipatory regret* (Triandis 1977; Bell 1982): Many have criticised sociocognitive models, such as the TPB, for insufficient consideration of how emotion or affect might influence attitudes, perceived norms and PBC and thus behavioural intention and behaviour, or examining whether in fact emotions have direct effects on intention or behaviour. Perugini and Bagozzi (2001) propose that anticipatory emotions arise from a person's consideration of the likelihood of attaining (success) or not attaining (failure) the desirable outcomes of the behaviour. Studies examining anticipatory regret, (anticipated when a certain behavioural decision is thought to have an undesireable future outcome) have found significant improvements to the prediction of a range of behaviour, including, for example, unprotected sexual intercourse. Anticipatory regret (i.e. 'I would really regret it if she got pregnant/If I got an STD') increased an individual's intention to use condoms (e.g. Richard et al. 1996; van der Pligt and de Vries 1998). A meta-analysis of 24 datasets (Sandberg and Conner 2008) found that anticipated affect (some studies assess regret, but others assess anticipatory sadness, worry, and some assess positive affect such as feeling proud or exhilarated) added 7 per cent to the explanation of a range of behavioural intentions, but only 1 per cent of behaviour. Akin to SCT's outcome expectancies (but generally assessed in relation to an expectancy if a behaviour is NOT performed) it seems to be the case that anticipated affective reactions to behaviour change (or non-change) make a small but significant contribution. When anticipating negative affect is not associated with behaviour change (for example, when anticipating a hangover does not reduce a night's drinking, Murgraff et al. 1999), this may suggest that the perception of the behaviour concerned (e.g. risky unprotected sex/less risky drinking) may moderate the effect of anticipatory regret. Anticipatory affect is likely linked to attitude formation.

- *Self-identity*: how one perceives and labels oneself using socially meaningful categories, roles and traits (Turner 1991) has been shown to influence intention above and beyond the effect of core TPB variables, and the normative components specifically. For example, self-identifying as a 'health conscious green consumer' and valuing this self increased intention to eat organic vegetables (Sparks and Shepherd 1992), and increased young adults' intentions to seek chlamydia testing (Booth et al. 2014). A meta-analysis of 24 sets of data examining the prediction of behavioural intention found that including self-identity increased the variance explained by 13 per cent, which is considerable (Rise et al. 2006). We tend to behave in a manner that affirms our self-image. For self-affirmation as an intervention tool, whereby people are encouraged to reflect on cherished values or attributes of themselves as a means of enhancing risk information processing and acceptance, in order to promote behaviour change, see Epton and Harris (2008) (fruit and vegetable intake),

or van Koningsbruggen et al. (2009) (caffeine intake).

- Behaviour change tends to occur in contexts where social support is important (Greaves et al. 2011), yet more attention needs to be paid to the *type* of support that social networks exert, in terms of their social and action control (persuasive and encouraging, versus, critical and undermining, for example)(Rook et al. 2011; Sorkin et al. 2014).

- *Planning*: Coping planning involves anticipating and planning for how to deal with barriers to behaviour (Sniehotta et al. 2005), which has shown to be important in predicting behaviour change and maintenance. Action planning refers to making a mental note of when, where and how one intends to perform a behaviour and is most often operationalised as forming an *implementation intention* (II) (see below). Forming an II is thought to be part of the process involved in turning an intention into action, i.e. filling the intention–behaviour gap highlighted by limitations in behavioural prediction by TPB studies.

IN THE SPOTLIGHT

The problem of non-reflective action – good and bad habits!

Every morning you wake up, you probably have a routine: toilet, wash hands, shower, dress, go downstairs for breakfast. Oops, did you forget something? Did you forget to brush your teeth? Or was this routinely sandwiched in between showering and dressing, and, if so, were you barely conscious of doing it perhaps, the action triggered by facing the mirror when washing one's hands rather than conscious decision-making? How long did it last? Did you do the top row for as long as the bottom? Front and back?(!)

The point of these silly questions is actually serious. Habits form through repeated performance in relatively stable contexts which often then become automatic triggers of the behaviour. Habits don't use up cognitive resource, as described in relation to attitude for-

mation, for example, and therefore they can override competing intentions in determining behaviour. If something becomes automatic and habitual, awareness of doing it is only attained on being presented with the consequences— 'I don't recall doing my teeth, yet I have white paste all over my chin: therefore I must have done so automatically!' (adapted from smoking example of Sniehotta and Presteau 2012, as cited in Gardner and Tang 2014). Thus self-reports of a habitual behaviour may be unreliable. How do we accurately assess characteristics of a behaviour when its performance is automatic and therefore lacking the cognitive processes rational or motivated behaviour demand? Several recent papers have debated this issue and interesting alternatives to assessment proposed. One example is a recent think-aloud study carried out at University College London by Gardner and Tang, whereby students spoke their thoughts

(continued)

aloud whilst completing habit measures relating to snacking, commuting using public transport, and context-free and context-specific alcohol consumption (Gardner and Tang 2014). A total of 90 per cent of participants in this necessarily small qualitative study (N=20) reported at least one problematic response, with difficulties relating to recalling their behaviour or the cues for them, or lacking confidence answering questions about the extent to which their behaviour was performed automatically. So the validity and usefulness of measuring habit is questioned.

Why does this matter? What if you have a 'bad' habit? Intervening to reduce 'automatic', negative health behaviours, such as that cigarette you light without thinking whilst waiting for the kettle to boil or when you answer the telephone, may not lend itself to interventions if those carrying out the behaviours find it difficult to accurately report their behaviour characteristics or its cues. If we seek to increase healthy habitual behaviours (e.g. routine exercise) and reduce unhealthy habitual behaviours (e.g. smoking), we need to better understand what regulates them. A lack of this understanding may explain why the dominant models described in this chapter, each of which is underpinned by an assumption of conscious awareness and cognitive effort, do less well than theorised when it comes to habits … good or bad!

Implementation intentions

One of the reasons why people may not always translate their good intentions into action (the 'inclined abstainers' as described by Sheeran 2002) is that they have not made adequate plans as to how, when and where they will implement their intention. Gollwitzer suggests that individuals need to shift from a mindset typical of the motivation (pre doing) phase towards an implementational mindset, which is found in the **volition** (doing) phase (Gollwitzer 1993, 1999; Gollwitzer and Oettingen 1998; Gollwitzer and Schaal 1998). Gollwitzer describes how individuals need to make a specific 'If–Then' statement , for example, 'If I go out with my friends, then I will not drink'; however, others prefer more detailed planning statement of intention, i.e. 'when, where and how' plan that commits them to a certain time and place and to using a particular method of action. For example, rather than stating, as is typical in the TPB measures, how strongly I intend to stop smoking, an implementation intention would require me to state that I intend to stop smoking first thing next Sunday morning, at home, using a nicotine replacement patch. Although Ogden (2003) argues that this method of questioning is manipulative rather than descriptive (i.e. it has the purpose of intervention), studies now generally include a measure of II.

Implementation intentions have been shown to increase a person's commitment to their decision and the likelihood of their attaining a wide variety of specified health-related goals by carrying out the intended action (meta-analysis of varied behavioural studies, Gollwitzer and Sheeran 2006; meta-analysis of studies of physical activity, Belanger Gravel et al. 2013). In one of the first studies on II, Orbell et al. (1997) assessed the attitudes, social norms, PBC and intentions of female students and staff to perform breast self-examination in the next month and then instructed half of the sample to form an II as to when and where they would carry it out. A month later, those receiving the II intervention showed a significantly higher rate of subsequent self-examination (64 per cent) than the control group (14 per cent). Such findings have been replicated in studies across a wide range of health behaviours. It appears that commonly reported barriers to attaining goals or implementing intended behaviour, such as forgetting or being distracted from it, can be overcome by committing the individual to a specific course of action when the environmental conditions specified in their II are encountered (Rutter and Quine 2002: 15). Gollwitzer and Brandstätter (1997) describe how an II creates a mental link between the specified situation (e.g. next Monday) and the behaviour (e.g. starting a diet) and suggest that IIs obtain their effects by making action more automatic, i.e. in response to a situational stimuli set down in the II. This reflexive action control is automatic initiation of goal-directed behaviour – an 'intention activiation' (Sheeran et al. 2005) , which can be contrasted with deliberative and reflective processes in which a person might procrastinate and think

> **volition**
>
> action or doing (the post-intentional stage highlighted in the HAPA model of health behaviour change).

'When will I do this?' type thoughts that prevent many intentions being put into action (Mendoza et al. 2010).

Gollwitzer (1999) also notes that, while forming proximal (more immediate) goals leads to better goal attainment than forming distal (long-term) goals, IIs do show persistence over time. For example, with regards to physical activity, (Belanger-Gravel et al. 2013) a meta-analysis of 26 datasets found that a consistent small-to-medium effect of forming IIs on physical activity was not reduced in studies with longer follow-up periods: i.e the effect sizes were similar. They did find that student and clinical samples responded better to the II intervention than studies which recruited from the general population. Such findings have implications for a wide range of groups where brief interventions are more feasible than prolonged intervention; for example, hospitalised patients could be encouraged to form IIs about their home-based rehabilitation in order to improve exercise adherence (and hence recovery) post-discharge. Some people spontaneously form IIs when they form a motivational intention ('I intend to exercise every morning after breakfast'); however, many others do not and could benefit from such an intervention (see Chapter 6 ☞). De Vet and colleagues (de Vet et al. 2011) rightly point out that much of the evidence of positive effects of II formation on behaviour comes from research studies where individuals were helped to form their II. This face-to-face assistance is not always available in real life: for example, when considering safer sex practices. They examined the quality of IIs developed independently by young single females aged between 16 and 30 years regarding 'preparing' to buy a condom and actually 'using' the condom. Results showed that IIs were of better quality (sufficiently complete and precise) in relation to preparation (buying) than for actual sexual activity, but in fact IIs were not predictive of all preparatory behaviours (buying, having at home, discussing with potential partner). In spite of some sample restrictions, such findings serve to highlight that effective planning for condom-use behaviour is complex. In general, perhaps IIs for preparatory action should be encouraged rather than targeting IIs for the behaviour directly. This is similar to conclusions of Belanger-Gravel and colleagues with regards to physical activity where they suggest the need also to formulate plans for barrier management: for example, 'IF I encounter a friend who smokes, THEN I will tell them straight away that I have stopped'. This has been described as 'coping planning'. For example, Molloy and colleagues (Molloy et al. 2010) examined predictors of university students' physical activity. They found that females in particular benefited from social support for physical activity but that the influence of social support on subsequent physical activity was partially mediated by both PBC and coping planning.

Importantly, however, there is evidence that forming an II may not be so effective in changing habitual behaviour (Webb et al. 2009; Wood and Neale, 2009). This relates to 'In The Spotlight' where we describe how habits may not be subject to the same conscious controls. Webb and colleagues, for example, found that forming an II was effective in reducing smoking behaviour amongst adolescent smokers ONLY when smoking was light–moderate rather than heavy. In a later, useful review, specific to attempts to change addictive behaviour, Webb et al. (2010) describe how interventions with addictive behaviours may require greater consideration of issues around self-control.

Generally, we succeed in achieving our goal when we value the likely outcome; believe that the goal is attainable through our actions, i.e. self-efficacy; and when we receive feedback on progress made (this is particularly important where long-term goals, such as weight loss, are involved). So far this chapter has reviewed static or continuum models with additive components whereby beliefs (or sets of them) are combined to try to predict where an individual will lie on an outcome continuum, i.e. the level of intention or behaviour. We turn our attention now to stage models, i.e. models of behaviour change which consider individuals as being at 'discrete ordered stages', each one denoting a greater inclination to change outcome than the previous stage (Rutter and Quine 2002: 16).

Stage models of behaviour change

Weinstein (Weinstein et al. 1998; Weinstein and Sandman 2002) suggested that a stage theory requires four properties:

1. *A classification system to define stages*: stage classifications are theoretical constructs, and, although a prototype is defined for each stage, it is accepted that few people will perfectly match this ideal.

ISSUES

How the wording and ordering of questions may influence the data obtained

The effect of question ordering has been studied in many domains, and will be referred to at a few points in this textbook. It is important that we consider whether the data we generate (or read about) are as 'real' as can possibly be captured, or whether they reflect a measurement artefact.

One example is in the assessment of 'unrealistic optimism' (UO) – the belief that I am at less risk of something than others … but which others? Weinstein (1982, 1984) originally asked one simple question to establish the presence of UO: 'Compared with others of my sex/age … my chances of developing "disease x" are … (great/average/low)'. Other studies, however, ask two questions: the first generating a rating for personal risk, the second generating a rating for the risk of similar others, and UO is considered to be present when the second rating is higher than the first (e.g. van der Velde et al. 1992). Hoorens and Buunk (1993) manipulated the ordering of these two questions and also the comparison group that their sample of adolescents were required to think of when making their risk judgements. Doing this changed the results: those rating personal risk first, and then comparative others' risk, exhibited lower levels of UO than those receiving the questions in the opposite order!

Furthermore, Budd (1987) had previously found that muddling the order of theory of reasoned action items in different versions of a questionnaire significantly altered the inter-correlations between perceptions of threat, attitude, normative beliefs and intention to either smoke, brush teeth three times per day, or exercise for 20 minutes. Sheeran and Orbell (1996) partially replicated this using protection motivation theory (PMT) components in relation to condom use and dental flossing and, while fewer effects of ordering emerged, correlation strengths between some key variables did change.

Furthermore, the very questions we ask may effect subsequent behaviour, sometimes referred to as 'mere measurement effects' (Morwitz et al. 1993, as cited in Godin et al. 2008: 179). For example, a questionnaire assessing perceived susceptibility to a illness may increase awareness of the illness, cause the individual to reflect on their own behaviour, change their belief structure, or, potentially, even their behaviour. In one study examining beliefs and intentions about hypothetical genetic testing uptake for breast cancer (Morrison et al. 2010), participants rated their attitudes towards genetic testing, their outcome expectancies, perceived benefits of, or barriers to testing, and their intention to undertake testing were it to become available. For some individuals, such questions may have caused them to think about something they had not thought of previously. The questions also provide information to the participant about the behaviour: for example, 'To what extent do you think that genetic testing will: reduce uncertainty about my long-term risk of breast cancer?; enable me to make positive decisions about my future?', which could potentially change beliefs and attitudes. This has been reported in a study of intention to donate blood (Godin et al. 2008) whereby 2,900 adults who completed a TPB-derived questionnaire were significantly more likely to register for donation and subsequently donate blood than a control group of 1,772 adults who did not receive a questionnaire. In effect, the questionnaire itself acted as an intervention – and a relatively cheap one at that! Perhaps the direction of behaviour change could be manipulated by changing the wording of the questions used, in the same way as other studies attempt to change beliefs by manipulating the nature of information provided. This may be desirable in certain circumstances; however, the issue of questions as interventions requires greater attention in research designs and greater acknowledgement in the discussion of findings.

Photo 5.2 How questions are asked and how they are scored may influence the responses obtained.

Source: Fotolia.com/Chad McDermott.

2. *Ordering of stages*: people must pass through all the stages to reach the end point of action or maintenance, but progression to the end point is neither inevitable nor irreversible. For example, a person may decide to quit smoking but not do so; or may quit smoking but lapse back into the habit sometime thereafter.

3. *Similar barriers to change facing people within the same stage*: this would be helpful in encouraging progression through the stages: for example, if low self-efficacy acted as a common barrier to peoples' *initiation* of dietary change, but a lack of social support acts as a barrier to *maintenance*.

4. *Different barriers to change facing people in different stages*: if the factors (e.g. self-efficacy) producing movement to the next stage were the same regardless of starting stage, then the concept of stages would be redundant. Ample evidence exists that barriers are different in the different stages (see below).

The transtheoretical model (TTM or 'Stages of Change' model)

This model was developed by Prochaska and di Clemente (1984) to describe processes of elicitation and maintenance of *intentional* behavioural change. Initially applied mostly to smoking cessation (e.g. di Clemente et al.

1991), 'stages of change' have been reported in many other behaviours, including for example, cocaine use, alcohol use, exercise, condom use, sunscreen use, dietary fat intake, and mammography screening (Prochaska 1994; Prochaska et al. 1994; Armitage 2009). The model makes two broad assumptions: that people move through stages of change; and that the processes involved at each stage differ and are independent; thus it meets several of Weinstein's requirements.

Stages of change

The stages of change proposed by the TTM are stages of motivational readiness. These are outlined below, using dietary behaviour as an illustration:

- *Pre-contemplation*: a person is not currently thinking of dieting, no intention to change food intake in next six months, may not consider that they have a weight problem.

- *Contemplation*: a person demonstrates awareness of a need to lose weight and consideration of doing so: for example, 'I think I need to lose a bit of weight, but not quite yet'. Generally assessed as planning to change within the next six months.

- *Preparation:* a person is ready to change and sets goals. Stage includes thoughts and action, such as planning a start date for the diet (within three months) or stocking up on healthy options.

● *Action*: overt behaviour change: for example, a person starts eating fruit instead of biscuits.

● *Maintenance*: keeps up with the dietary change, resists temptation.

While the above stages are the five most commonly referred to, there are also:

● *Termination*: behaviour change has been maintained for adequate time so the person feels no temptation to lapse and believes in their total self-efficacy to maintain the change.

● *Relapse*: A person may lapse into earlier behaviour patterns and return to a previous stage. This is common and can occur at any stage, i.e. it is not a final stage or alternative to termination (di Clemente and Velicer 1997).

People do not necessarily move smoothly from one stage to another. For example, some individuals may go from preparation back to contemplation and stay there for months or years before re-entering the preparation phase and successfully moving on to action. For others action can fail, maintenance may never be achieved, and relapse is common. The model therefore allows for 'recycling' from one stage to another and is sometimes referred to as a 'spiral' model (e.g. Prochaska et al. 1992).

The first two stages are generally considered defined by intention or motivation; the preparation stage combines intentional and behavioural (volitional) criteria, whereas the action and maintenance stages are purely behavioural (Prochaska and Marcus 1994).

To help understand factors that influence progression through the stages, the model outlines independent psychological 'processes of change' that are considered to be at play in the different stages (with some being important in more than one stage). These processes include the covert or overt activities that people engage in to help them to progress: for example, seeking social support and avoiding settings that 'trigger' the behaviour, as well as more 'experiential' processes that individuals may go through emotionally and cognitively, such as weighing up pros and cons of changing; self re-evaluation or consciousness raising. These cognitive and behavioural processes are the targets of intervention efforts to firstly motivate individuals to change and then 'move' individuals through the stages towards effective and maintained behaviour change (see Chapter 6 (☛)).

● In the pre-contemplation stage, individuals may be using denial about the health issues' relevance to them and their goals, and/or may report lower self-efficacy (to change) beliefs and more barriers to change.

● In the contemplation stage, people are more likely to seek information and may report reduced barriers ('cons') to change and increased benefits, although they may still underestimate their susceptibility to the health threat concerned.

● In the preparation stage, people start to set their goals and priorities, and some will make concrete plans (similar to IIs described earlier) and small changes in behaviour (e.g. joining a gym). Some may be setting unrealistic goals for success, or underestimating their own ability to succeed. Motivation and self-efficacy are crucial if action is to be elicited.

● In the action stage, realistic goal setting is crucial and perception of 'cons' lower. The use of social support provides reinforcement that will help to maintain the lifestyle change.

● Many individuals will not succeed in maintaining behavioural change and will relapse or 'recycle' back to contemplating a future attempt to change. Maintenance can be enhanced by self-monitoring and reinforcement.

There is evidence that several motivational factors vary across these stages: for example, perceived behavioural control and attitudes to activity (Lorentzen et al. 2007), outcome expectancies and anticipated affective consequences (Dunton and Vaughan 2008), and the perception of barriers and benefits, or 'pros and cons'. For example, one meta-analysis of the pros and cons relative to 48 different behaviours found that there were more 'pros' in the action stage than in the pre-contemplation stage, and less 'cons' in the action stage than in the contemplation stage (Hall and Rossi 2008). An individual in the contemplation stage is likely to focus on both the pros and cons of change, but the 'cons' or barriers may be weighted more heavily (e.g. 'Even if I get healthier in the long term, I am probably going to gain weight if I stop smoking'), whereas someone in the preparation stage is likely to focus more on the pros of change (e.g. 'Even if I gain weight in the short term, it will be worth it to start feeling healthier'). The relative weight between pros and

> **decisional balance**
> where the costs of behaviour are weighed up
> against the benefits of that behaviour.

cons is referred to as **decisional balance**. This factor, as well as self-efficacy, is thought to mediate the relationship between the processes of change and progress through the stages (cf. Prochaska and Velicer 1997).

The TTM and behaviour change

De Vet and colleagues (2007) compared whether a previously described 'static' model variable of 'intention' (TPB) was more or less predictive of fruit intake (action) than the stages of change, and in fact intention did better. However, much support for interventions based on staged models exists (Dijkstra et al. 2006; Armitage 2009). For example, studies of physical activity uptake, both among general public and patient populations, offer support to the TTM. A longitudinal trial of an exercise behaviour change programme, delivered either at an exercise centre or at home, and promoting either 'moderate' or 'intense' exercise, found that sedentary Australian women aged 40–65 benefited from either intervention (Cox et al. 2003). Notably, the role of self-efficacy and decisional balance in relation to changes in exercise behaviour were observed. When reassessed after 18 months, increases were seen in self-efficacy in line with the 'stage of change' achieved (i.e. self-efficacy increased as the stage progressed towards action) and appeared to be critical, whereas decisional balance findings were inconclusive. Similar support for the TTM comes from a study of adults with type 1 or type 2 diabetes, where progression through stages of change with regards to physical activity was found to be associated with self-efficacy beliefs, the reported pros for behaviour change, and the behavioural processes outlined above.

Limitations of the TTM

Several studies have questioned whether these change processes are in fact useful predictors of change. For example, Segan et al. (2002) examined the changes in specific behavioural and experiential processes, self-efficacy and decisional balance amongst 193 individuals who were preparing to stop smoking and making the transition to the action stage. Results suggested that some changes in TTM processes resulted *from* the transition to action, rather than preceded it: for example, increases in situational confidence and counter-conditioning (where positive behaviour is substituted for smoking). The main findings for the effect of behavioural and experiential processes were not reported, even though the TTM claims that these act as 'catalysts' for change. Furthermore, although self-efficacy was associated with making a quit attempt, it did not predict the success or failure of that attempt. As with Cox's study of exercise prediction described above, decisional balance was not predictive of any behaviour change. Although a relatively small study, these findings have further questioned the validity of the TTM stages and processes as a model of change, whilst at the same time further reinforcing the central role of self-efficacy. Self-efficacy is central to the next model we discuss below, the HAPA.

Other limitations include:

- Prochaska and di Clemente suggested a time-frame within which they distinguish contemplaters from preparers (i.e. thinking of changing but not in the next six months versus thinking of changing within the next three months). There is, however, little empirical evidence that these are qualitatively different or differ in terms of the attitudes or intentions of stage members (e.g. Kraft et al. 1999; Godin et al. 2004). This has implications for the likely effectiveness of stage-tailored interventions (Herzog 2008).

- As described already past behaviour is a powerful predictor of future behaviour, yet the stage model assumes that readiness or intentions to change are key (Sutton 1996, 2001). Godin et al. (2004) present a model which combines recent past behaviour with future intentions to produce four 'clusters' of individuals with different attributes in terms of current behaviour and future exercise intention. They find that attitudes and perceived behavioural control associate more strongly with membership of these staged clusters than with membership of the five stages of change that do not consider past behaviour. This suggests that we should be assessing both intentions and current or recent behaviour.

- The validity of five independent stages is challenged by data that did not succeed in allocating all participants to one specific stage (e.g. Budd and Rollnick 1996). Perhaps a continuous variable of 'readiness' may be more useful than discrete stages of readiness (Sutton 2000).

● The model, as with many psychological models, insufficiently addresses the social aspects of much health behaviour (Marks et al. 2000).

● The model does not allow for some people not knowing about the behaviour or the issue in question. This is likely when a rare or new illness is being considered (such as when HIV/AIDS or BSE (bovine spongiform encephalopathy) emerged); when the risk concerned is related to a new behaviour, for example mobile phone use, or newly identified risk factors, for example human papillomavirus or HPV. Lack of awareness is acknowledged in a less commonly employed model, the precaution adoption process model addressed below.

Some of the proposed limitations of the TTM have been tested in intervention studies (see Chapter 6 ☞), where targeting the processes of change has not consistently resulted in the anticipated movement between stages. A systematic review of the findings of 37 controlled interventions studies provided limited support for stage appropriate interventions (Bridle et al. 2005), thus leading to calls for an end to TTM based interventions (e.g. Sutton 2005; West 2005); however, other studies do continue to provide support (Dijkstra et al. 2006; Hall and Rossi 2008). The debate continues!

The precaution adoption process model (PAPM)

Weinstein and colleagues (Weinstein 1988; Weinstein and Sandman 1992) developed the PAPM as a framework for understanding deliberate actions taken to reduce health risks which meet Weinstein's criteria for a stage theory (see above). The PAPM has seven stages, and highlights important omissions in the TTM (Table 5.1). Factors that 'move' people from one stage to another are proposed and, similar to the TTM, the model asserts that people pass through stages in sequences, but no time limit within which to reach the action stage is specified. The major difference between this model and the TTM is that the PAPM gives greater consideration to the pre-action stages.

● *Stage 1*: a person has no knowledge/is basically *'unaware'* of the threat to health posed by a certain risk behaviour or the absence of a protective behaviour, (e.g. unaware of HIV transmission routes);

● *Stage 2*: termed *'unengaged'*, a person has become aware of the risks attached to a certain behaviour but believes that the levels at which they engage in it is

Table 5.1 Stages in the transtheoretical model and the precaution adoption process model

Stage	Transtheoretical model	Precaution adoption process model
1	Pre-contemplation	Unaware of issue
2	Contemplation	Unengaged
3	Preparation	Considering whether to act
4	Action	Deciding not to act (and exit the model)
5	Maintenance	Deciding to act (and proceed to next stage)
6		Action
7		Maintenance

insufficient to pose a threat to their health ('I know smoking causes various diseases, but I don't smoke enough for them to be a threat'). This is seen as 'optimistic bias' and led to Weinstein's development of the construct of unrealistic optimism (see earlier).

● *Stage 3*: people become engaged for some reason (includes internal and external triggers). They enter a *'consideration'* stage, akin to pre-contemplation and are deciding whether or not to act. So many things compete for our attention that knowledge about a hazard can be significant before this decision-making phase is even entered. Three decisions can be reached: they can remain at stage 3, or make one of two opposing decisions taking them to either stage 4 or 5.

● *Stage 4*: although perceived threat and susceptibility may be high, some people actively *'decide not to act'*, which is very different from intending to act but then not doing so. These individuals may not progress further, or may do so at a later date.

● *Stage 5*: some enter a *'decide to act'* stage, similar to intention/preparation. There are important differences between people who have decided to act or not act and those who are undecided/considering action (stage 3). Those at stage 3 may be more open to information and persuasion than those with a definite stance (as in stage 4 or stage 5). As noted previously, stating an intention to act does not inevitably lead to action. Perceived susceptibility beliefs are considered necessary here to motivate progression to action. Moving from stage 5 to stage 6 relates to moving from motivation to volition.

● *Stage 6*: the *action stage*, when a person has initiated what is necessary to reduce their risk.

Stage 7: this final stage is not always required/relevant as it is about *maintenance* and, unlike with smoking cessation, some health behaviour processess are not long-lasting: for example, deciding whether or not to have a vaccination or a mammogram.

Weinstein applied the PAPM to studies of home testing for radon, an invisible odourless radioactive gas produced by the decay of naturally occurring uranium in soil in some geographical areas. It enters homes through cracks in foundations, and, although little heard of, it is the second leading cause of lung cancer after smoking (Weinstein and Sandman 2002). Perceived susceptibility (or vulnerability) was found to be crucial in the transition between stage 3 (trying to decide) and stage 5 (deciding to act). A stage-matched intervention (as with interventions based on the TTM) was not as successful in moving 'decided to act' stage 5 participants into action (e.g. buying a home radon testing kit) as it was in shifting undecided participants into making a decision to act (not necessarily action). However, participants receiving either of these stage-matched interventions did do significantly better than control participants (Weinstein et al. 1998), showing support for matched interventions.

Limitations of the PAPM

The PAPM has been tested less extensively than the TTM, although both models suffer from a lack of longitudinal testing. However, the PAPM does progress thinking to include the issue of awareness and pre-decisional processes.

The health action process approach (HAPA)

The HAPA is a hybrid model having both 'static' and staged qualities. The HAPA has really taken on board the issue of stages and attempts to fill the 'intention–behaviour gap' by highlighting the role of post-motivational (or volitional) self-efficacy and action planning, factors not addressed by the TPB or PMT (Schwarzer 1992; Schwarzer et al. 2008). The HAPA model has been influential because it suggests that the adoption, initiation and maintenance of health behaviour must be explicitly viewed as a process that consists of at least a pre-intentional motivation phase and a post-intentional volition phase (where a conscious choice or decision is made) which leads to the actual behaviour (Figure 5.3). Schwarzer (2001) further divided self-regulatory processes into sequences of planning, initiation, maintenance, relapse management and disengagement; however, only the first three of these are where the model has been best tested.

Motivation phase

As proposed in models such as the TPB, individuals form an intention to either adopt a precautionary measure (e.g. use a condom during sexual intercourse) or change

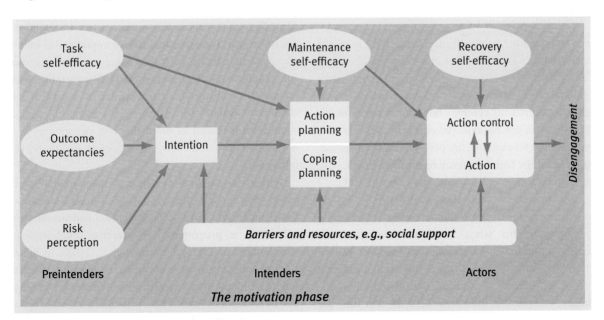

Figure 5.3 The health action process approach model

Source: Schwarzer (1992); http://www.hapa-model.de

risk behaviour (e.g. stop smoking) as a result of various attitudes, cognitions and social factors. The HAPA proposes that self-efficacy and outcome expectancies are important predictors of goal intention (akin to TPB perceived behavioural control). Perceptions of threat severity and personal susceptibility (perceived risk) are considered a distal influence on actual behaviour, playing a role only in the motivation phase and likely to be of limited importance for some behaviours, such as fruit and vegetable intake (Schwarzer et al. 2007). In terms of 'ordering' of self-efficacy and outcome expectancies, the latter may precede the former (e.g. an individual probably thinks of the consequences of their action before working out whether they can do what is required). Under conditions where individuals have no previous experience with the behaviour they are contemplating, the authors suggest that outcome expectancies may have a stronger influence on behaviour than efficacy beliefs.

Intention in the motivation phases is considered as a goal intention: for example, 'I intend to stop smoking to become healthier'. Schwarzer also proposes *phase-specific self-efficacy* beliefs, consistent with Bandura's findings (1997). Self-efficacy in the motivational stage is defined as 'task/pre-action self-efficacy': for example, 'I can succeed in eating a healthy diet even if I have to change my lifestyle a bit'. At this stage, it is important for an individual to imagine successful outcomes and be confident in their ability to achieve them.

Volition phase

Once an intention has been formed, the HAPA proposes that in order to turn intention into action, a conscious decision to act is made which involves planning. Such volitional processes are thought to be particularly important in the context of complex behaviours where multiple barriers might be anticipated. Fruit and vegetable consumption, for example, has perceived barriers including the need for high frequency to obtain benefits, cost, access, preparation, etc. (e.g. Adriaanse et al. 2011).

The model incorporates Gollwitzer's (1999; Gollwitzer and Oettingen 2000) concept of implementation intentions: the 'when, where and how' plans are thought to turn the goal intention into a specific plan of action. Schwarzer proposes that at this stage a different kind of self-efficacy is required, that of initiative self-efficacy, whereby an individual believes that they are able to take the initiative when the planned circum-

stances arise (e.g. the individual needs to believe that they can implement their plan when the morning of the planned diet arrives). Once the action has been initiated, the individual next needs to try to maintain the new, healthier behaviour. At this stage, coping (or maintenance) self-efficacy is considered important to success (e.g. 'I need to keep going with this diet even if it is hard at first'). This form of self-efficacy describes a belief in one's ability to overcome barriers and temptations (such as being faced with a birthday celebration) and is akin to the self-regulatory processes described earlier in the chapter. Such beliefs enhance resilience, positive coping (such as drawing upon social support) and greater persistence. If, as many do, the individual gives in to temptation and relapses – as often reported in the case of addictive behaviours – the model proposes that 'recovery self-efficacy' is necessary to get the individual back on track (Renner and Schwarzer 2003).

Support for the role of self-efficacy at different stages in behaviour change was seen in a longitudinal study of breast self-examination behaviour among 418 women. Pre-actional self-efficacy and positive outcome expectancies (but not risk perception) were significant predictors of (goal) intention. Self-efficacy beliefs also predicted planning. In terms of actual BSE behaviour at follow-up 12–15 weeks later, planning was, as hypothesised, highly predictive, with maintenance and recovery self-efficacy also predicting greater behaviour frequency (Luszczynska and Schwarzer 2003). Although it is perhaps surprising that risk perception regarding breast cancer was not predictive of intention nor behaviour, it may be that risk perceptions had influenced participants *before* they were assessed for the study, and therefore effects on the HAPA variables had passed. It is always hard in research to establish an absolute 'baseline' for measurement, and such results should not be taken as proof that risk perceptions are not important – the body of evidence would prove otherwise.

Further longitudinal evidence of the importance of phase-specific self-efficacy has been found amongst those undergoing cardiac rehabilitation and needing to adhere to a programme of exercise rehabilitation (Sniehotta et al. 2005; Schwarzer et al. 2008). In these studies, believing in one's ability to resume activity after failure or illness was a significant predictor of planning and of actual behaviour. These proximal predictors open up avenues to quite different intervention than those that address risk perceptions, generally not found to be significant in studies employing the HAPA. Findings from studies using the HAPA have made a strong contribution to the field with volitional processes receiving ever-increasing attention.

Limitations of the HAPA

The limitations of this model could in fact be attributed to any of the preceding models and thus are raised only briefly here as they are discussed in the chapter conclusions.

Renner et al. (2007) found that the HAPA modelled the behaviour of middle-aged and older people better than it did that of younger people (although this could be culture specific as their sample was composed of South Koreans).

More was still needed in terms of our understanding of volition-action processes and, indeed, this has been the focus of much work (e.g. Gollwitzer and Sheeran

Photo 5.3 Preparing for healthy eating by making the purchases will increase the likelihood of action

Source: Pearson Education Ltd.

2006; Schwarzer and Luszczynska 2008; Rhodes and de Bruijn 2013). Volitional processes regarding action planning, coping planning and action control have received significant empirical support. De Vries and colleagues (2006) describe these as proximal post motivational determinants (e.g. action planning and control, goal setting, coping planning and control, implementation intentions).

Insufficient attention is again given to non-conscious processes.

The need to consider self-regulatory processes

The models described in this chapter differ in some aspects but share a common goal – to aid our understanding of correlates and predictors of behaviours associated with health, whether positively or negatively. Increasingly, researchers are considering sociocognitive models of health behaviour within a wider body of work concerning behavioural (and emotional) self-regulation, i.e. what we do deliberately, reflectively and consciously in order to achieve goals or desired outcomes (Hofmann et al. 2008 as cited in Sutton 2010: 58; Hagger et al. 2009; Hagger 2010). self-regulation requires self-control, and individuals likely vary in that regard (Cameron and Leventhal 2003)!

As we have described in this chapter, newer constructs such as 'action control', 'implementation intentions' and behavioural monitoring are highly pertinent. Research adopting a self-regulatory perspective in relation to health behaviour change includes that described by Hall and Fong (2007) as 'temporal self-regulation', where dynamic changes in regulatory thoughts and emotions are seen to influence behaviour (see also the commentaries published in a Special Issue of *Health Psychology Review*, September 2010). In another newer development Hagger et al. (2010a) discuss a 'strength' model of self-regulatory failure (i.e. when an individual fails to elicit an intended change or relapses following change). It may be that for behaviours that require daily performance, daily maintenance, such as reduced fat intake or increased fruit and vegetable consumption, self-monitoring of one's behaviour against one's goals becomes increasingly important if relapse is to be avoided. Challenges to behaviour change are discussed further in Chapters 6 and 7 ☞ where intervention successes and failures are described.

SUMMARY

As shown in this chapter, many proximal and distal factors influence our behaviour and health behaviour. Are models of health behaviour therefore globally useful? Certainly, the models described have brought our understanding of behaviour a long way, but we are still far from being able to predict all behaviour (perhaps thankfully). Continuum models like the HBM and the TPB have demonstrated the importance of social and cognitive factors in predicting both intention to act and action, although the static nature of these models does not facilitate understanding of the processes of change. Stage models like the TTM, PMT and the HAPA address processes of change, and the growing focus on volitional planning and action control processes goes some way towards filling the gap between intention and behaviour.

It has proven important to acknowledge that different factors determine behaviour initiation than behaviour maintenance or change (see van Stralen et al. 2009 for a review of the differential determinants of physical activity initiation and maintenance in the over-40s). We do not yet fully understand the differential influences, partly because most studies employing the models described in this chapter focus on behaviour change initiation (e.g. starting a low-fat diet) rather than behaviour maintenance. Perceived susceptibility and self-efficacy are identified as relatively important and consistent predictors of change and, as such, carry intervention potential. Evidence of the efficacy of tailored interventions for different stages (which are more costly than a 'one size fits all' approach) is more mixed. Interventions, such as described in Chapter 6 ☞ need to acknowledge this.

Furthermore, IN THE SPOTLIGHT has highlighted the particular challenges faced when trying to motivate change in habitual behaviour such as smoking, which can occur independently of our conscious cognitive efforts, using models which rely on conscious processes and decision-making (Hofmann et al. 2008; Vangeli and West 2008).

It is worth noting (cf. Renner et al. 2007) that models and their components might 'work better' in some samples than do others. Many studies have been conducted among young healthy populations. The prolific use of student samples, for example, enabled theories to be tested and built, and interesting questions to be addressed such as: what influences students' drinking behaviour and, given its normative function, can it be changed? What factors influence non-regular use of condoms, and does drinking alcohol interfere with even the best of intentions? However, the findings of such studies may not translate across to prediction of behaviour among older populations, less educated individuals, or to those leading less structured lives, such as the homeless drinker or drug user; or even to those who are attempting to change behaviour as a response to a life-threatening condition, such as dietary change following a heart attack, or physical activity among those with diabetes (e.g. Plotnikoff et al. 2010). Other social, environmental, cognitive and emotional factors are likely to play a role in these populations. Sallis et al. (2007), for example, highlight the importance of environmental influences, such as perceived crime and traffic safety or perceived access to facilities, on the initiation and maintenance of physical activity among the over-50s. Perceived safety is not often cited as an exercise determinant among student samples. The models of health behaviour primarily used in health psychology research perhaps focus more on individual cognitions than is warranted. Behaviour is influenced hugely by environmental context, by socio-economic resources, by culture and by laws, sanctions and habits. We have highlighted these at various points in most chapters, but also in detail in Chapters 1 and 2 ☞.

Therefore, whether reviewing research or planning some of your own, you should consider:

● The salience of potential predictors of behaviour may differ by behaviour (for example, subjective norm may be more important to smoking initiation than vitamin intake).

● The salience of potential predictors may vary by age or gender (e.g. attitude to medicines may predict intention to adhere to medication in adults, but not in children, where adherence is more under parental control).

● The role of culture, ethnicity and religion may significantly influence beliefs about health and preventive health. For example, an individual of the Muslim faith who drinks heavily will likely face very different emotional and normative pressures than someone of Christian faith.

- Cognitive models do not account very well for habitual behaviours driven more by non-conscious processes, nor for dependency-producing behaviours where physiological cues take on salience and create impulses which may override rational thought (where present).

- There may be bias in self-reports of illegal or socially undesireable behaviour or of behaviour perceived to be unconventional. For example, the incidence of teenage drug use as self-reported was significantly discrepant from that 'proven' in hair sample bioassays (Delaney-Black et al. 2010).

- We need to take much more account of non-rational processes, such as impulsivity (Strack and Deutsch 2004). People differ in the extent to which they can, or even wish to, control their impulses. When drunk, angry or tired, for example, we may reflect less on our behaviours or on the decision-making process, or be biased in what cues we attend to (Wiers and Hofmann 2010). Health psychologists perhaps need to consider more the influence of context on the shifting balance between reflection, attentional processes and impulse.

Finally, research which examines the social cognitive, emotional and behavioural processes that occur once a person has engaged in health behaviour change will better inform interventions that seek to maximise maintained change (see Chapters 6 and 7 for examples ☞).

Further reading

Conner, M. and Norman, P. (eds) (2015). *Predicting Health Behaviour: Research and Practice with Social Cognition Models*, 3rd edn. Buckingham: Open University Press.

An excellent updated text that provides comprehensive coverage of social cognition theory and all the models described in this chapter (with the exception of the HAPA). A useful resource for sourcing measurement items for components of the models if you are designing a questionnaire.

Fishbein, M. and Ajzen, I. (2010). *Predicting and Changing Behavior: The Reasoned Action Approach*. Psychology Press: New York.

An in-depth review of both of reasoned action theories and their constituent parts as described in this chapter– (the TRA and the TPB), their theoretical and methodological development, the empirical evidence that has amassed over the past 40 years, the challenges and resultant extensions to the models, and suggestions for the likely future direction of behavioural prediction. A great read.

Eccles, M.P., Grimshaw, J.M., MacLennan, G. et al. (2012). Explaining clinical behaviours using multiple theoretical models. *Implementation Science*, 7: 99-112.

Health behaviour is not just about the individuals engaged in behaviours like smoking, excessive eating, etc. It is also about the health-promoting behaviours carried out by our health-care practitioners. This makes for an interesting read.

Plotnikoff, R.C., Lubans, D.R., Penfold, C.M. and Courneya, K.S. (2014). Testing the utility of three social-cognitive models for predicting objective and self-report physical activity in adults with type 2 diabetes. *British Journal of Health Psychology*, 19: 329-346.

This paper is well worth a read as, in addition to the TPB findings referred to in this chapter, this study compares the predictive utility of social cognitive theory and another model, protection motivation theory, with that of the TPB. It highlights issues of conceptual overlap as well as presenting interesting longitudinal findings in a patient sample – clinical samples are often overlooked in relation to studying physical activity prediction.

Visser, de R.O. and Smith, J.A. (2007). Alcohol consumption and masculine identity among young men. *Psychology and Health*, 22: 595 – 614.

In addition to highlighting masculinity as an 'explanation' of drinking behaviour, this qualitative paper raises the important influence of culture and/or religous norms.

For open-access student resources specifically written to complement this textbook and support your learning, please visit **www.pearsoned.co.uk/morrison**

Chapter 6
Changing behaviour: mechanisms and approaches

Learning outcomes

By the end of this chapter, you should have an understanding of:

- the process of working with communities to determine the targets of public health programmes

- strategies used to increase motivation to change

- strategies used to change behaviour

- when and how best to use these interventions

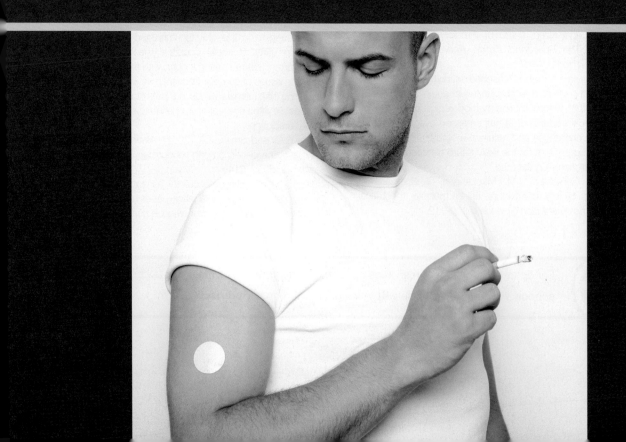

Health education doesn't work!

Doctors have reported that many health education programmes fail to achieve any impact on behaviours including safer sex, smoking and attending hospital health clinics. Resorting to scare tactics made things even worse. There is an interesting assumption implicit in many government or health service strategies designed to change our behaviour - that if they tell us what to do, then we are likely to do it, especially if the message carries a slightly worrying health message. Yet, there is repeated evidence that simple factual or scary information does not work. One example of this failure can be found in the repeated information campaigns about AIDS, the prevention of AIDS, and scary (indeed, terrifying) videos depicting death and hell as a consequence of enjoying unprotected sex broadcast in the UK in the late 1980s and 90s. Reported measures of condom use over this time revealed absolutely no change in response to any of these programmes. The public appeared utterly impervious to the potentially catastrophic consequences of AIDS and remained obstinately fixed in their old behaviours. Clearly, relevant information is necessary to instigate change, but many other factors contribute to the likelihood of change, and the simple repetition of health information (scary or otherwise), however accurate, is proven unlikely to significantly influence change.

Chapter outline

This chapter outlines a range of strategies designed to motivate and support changes in health-related behaviours at both an individual and whole population level. It starts by examining the process through which health professionals can begin to consider what behavioural change may benefit whole communities or individuals within them, and how these can be supported by using or increasing resources from within that community. It then considers how to motivate change at an individual level and how to support the process of behavioural change.

The effectiveness of interventions discussed in this chapter are considered in Chapters 7 and 17 ☞. Chapter 7 ☞ examines their effectiveness in the context of reducing risk for disease among healthy individuals; Chapter 17 ☞ considers interventions in those who have already become ill.

Developing public health interventions

Public health interventions are designed to change health behaviours within whole populations. The technology of behaviour change they use must therefore range from widely accessible approaches such as the mass media to smaller, more focused, interventions addressing individual needs. Despite their apparent differences, these approaches may have many commonalities. New skills, for example, may be taught using the mass media or working one-to-one with individuals, using the same principles of modelling and rewarding appropriate change. But before any intervention is developed, those involved need to determine which behaviours to address and how best to address them.

The best known framework for making these sorts of decisions is known as the PRECEDE–PROCEED model (Green and Kreuter 2005). The PRECEDE element identifies a range of psychosocial variables that could be the target of any intervention:

- *Predisposing factors*: knowledge, attitudes, beliefs, personal preferences, existing skills and self-efficacy in relation to desired behaviour change.
- *Enabling factors:* characteristics of the environment that may facilitate behavioural change and the skills or

resources required to achieve change. These include environmental factors such as the availability and accessibility of resources or services, such as exercise facilities, cookery classes or crèches to allow young parents to exercise, that could facilitate behavioural change.

- *Reinforcing factors*: factors that reward or reinforce desired behaviour change, including social support, economic rewards and social norms.

The PRECEDE model also takes into account any political, social and environmental influences that may facilitate behaviour change, including changes in health, education, or social policy. It is implemented in five phases:

- *Phase 1: social diagnosis*
  - Planners gain an understanding of the health problems that affect the quality of life of a community and its members, their strengths, weaknesses, resources and readiness to change. This may stem from community forums, focus groups, surveys and/or interviews. If the model is fully implemented, local people are involved in the planning process and the planners are able to see the issues from the community's perspective.
- *Phase 2: epidemiological, behaviour and environmental diagnosis*
  - Epidemiological assessment involves identification and assessment of health issue(s) specific to

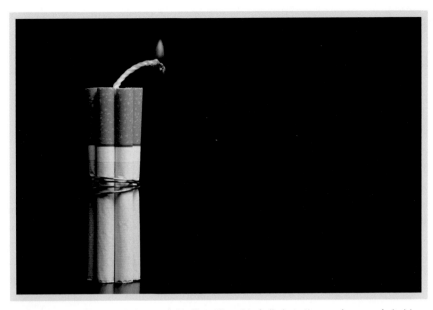

Photo 6.1 Choosing a quit date and ritually getting rid of all cigarettes can be a good start to stopping smoking.

Source: Shutterstock.com/Rob Byron.

the community, and their related behavioural and environmental influences. These may involve a range of factors. Poor nutrition may be related to poor cooking skills, low nutritional knowledge, social norms that support the use of snacks and ready meals, and so on. Environmental diagnosis involves an analysis of social and physical environmental factors that could be linked to target behaviours. Dietary choice, for example, may be influenced by education or difficulties (physical or economic) in accessing healthy food. Interventions here may require policy changes.

- *Phase 3: educational and ecological diagnosis*
  - This phase involves prioritising and determining how to change any behaviours identified in phase 2, and identifying predisposing factors, enabling factors and reinforcing factors of relevance. Consideration is also given to the likely impact of any behavioural change, the likelihood of any changes being made and how acceptable to the target community any strategies of change are likely to be.
- *Phase 4: administrative and policy diagnosis*
  - This administrative phase is designed to ensure that the programme is consistent with the policies of the organisation in which it is situated and which it wishes to address.

- *Phase 5: programme implementation*

The PROCEED phase is just that: the implementation of the planned intervention with three elements of evaluation:

- *Process*: did the programme do what was intended?
- *Impact*: what impact did the intervention have on the target behaviours/outcomes?
- *Outcome*: what long-term effects on health were achieved?

WHAT DO YOU THINK?

Before reading on, it may be interesting to consider how you would develop a public health programme and how you would evaluate it. Consider one key health behaviour, such as a healthy diet, or a target group you may want to address, such as overweight individuals. How would you facilitate change using a combination of large-scale (such as the mass media), environmental, and individually based interventions? And how would you set about deciding whether you have actually achieved your goals? These are not easy issues; if they were, our health problems would be resolved. So, good luck!

Strategies for changing risk behaviour

What the PRECEDE process does not consider in any detail are the optimal interventions to bring about change in each domain. How do we increase motivation, change beliefs and attitudes, encourage people to work towards desired goals, and so on? It is to these issues we now turn.

One way of addressing this issue is to consider the psychological state of the individuals any programme hopes to influence. One helpful model from this perspective is the 'stages of change' model of Prochaska and di Clemente (1986). This identified a series of five stages through which an individual may pass when considering change:

1. *pre-contemplation*: not considering change;
2. *contemplation*: considering change but without thought about its exact nature or how it can be achieved;
3. *preparation*: planning *how* to achieve change;
4. *change*: actively engaged in change;
5. *maintenance or relapse:* maintaining change (for longer than six months) or relapsing.

Prochaska and di Clemente noted the factors that may shift an individual from one stage to another (and they can move back and forth along the change continuum or even skip stages) can differ markedly. A smoker may shift from pre-contemplation to contemplation as a result of developing a chest infection, move to preparation and action after seeing a book on giving up smoking in the local library, and relapse after being tempted to smoke while out for a beer with friends. As a consequence, the model does not attempt to specify what these factors are; merely that they occur and that they can shift the individual from stage to stage. Although the transtheoretical model is not without its critics (e.g. Weinstein et al. 1998), the model does appear to predict behaviour with some degree of accuracy.

The stages of change approach has been particularly useful from an intervention perspective in that it has focused consideration on what is the best type of intervention to conduct within each stage of change. The most obvious implication of the model is that there is little point in trying to show people *how* to achieve change if they are in the pre-contemplation or possibly the contemplation stage. Such individuals are unlikely to be sufficiently motivated to attempt change, and will benefit little from being shown how to do so. By contrast, an individual in the planning or action stage may benefit from this type of approach.

Motivating change
Information provision

One apparently simple approach to increasing motivation to change involves the provision of information. If individuals are unaware of the advantages of change, they are unlikely to be motivated to attempt to make change. The logic is clear. Unfortunately, while clear information may be of benefit when it is completely novel, does not contradict previous understandings of issues, is highly relevant to the individual, and is relatively easy to act on, health-related information rarely meets all these criteria. And even when it does, it may well not impact on behaviour. Early information films on the risk of HIV infection and how to counter it had remarkably little impact on sexual behaviour, even when the messages were absolutely novel, highly threatening, and the behaviour required to reduce risk of infection was (apparently) simple to implement.

Reasons for these failures are complex and involve social, psychological and situational factors. Many men and women used to unprotected sex found negotiation of the use of condoms, as well as their actual use, complex and embarrassing. More complex cultural factors include the positive embracing of risk in sexual relations and the meaning of condom use within a sexual relationship. Some HIV-positive women were reported to use a condom if having casual sex, but not with their regular partner, as this was seen as a sign of lack of trust and would result in a loss of pleasure for their partner.

Clearly, encouraging behaviour change in less critical circumstances, and when information is neither new nor dramatic (healthy eating, stop smoking), presents significant challenges. For this reason, a number of specific strategies have been used in attempts to influence motivation both at an individual and population level. Many informational approaches have provided information about the negative consequences of health-damaging behaviour: damaged lungs, obesity and so on. But a wider set of influences may also be considered in any information that intends to increase motivation to change. Information about the ease of behavioural change and relevant norms may also be of value. The NICE guidelines on behavioural change (NICE 2014), for example, identified several ways of presenting information in order to increase the motivation of smokers to quit. Key messages should influence:

- *outcome expectancies*: Smoking causes people to die on average eight years earlier than the average.

- *personal relevance*: If you were to stop smoking, you could add six years to your life, and be fitter over that time.

- *positive attitude*: Life is good and worth living. Better to be fit as you get older than unable to engage in things you would like to do.

- *self-efficacy*: You have managed to quit before. With some support there is no reason why you cannot sustain change now.

- *descriptive norms*: Around 30 per cent of people of your age have successfully given up smoking.

- *subjective norms*: Your wife and kids will appreciate it if you were to give up smoking.

- *personal and moral norms*: Smoking is anti-social and you do not want your kids to start smoking.

The elaboration likelihood approach

Even this sophisticated information may have less impact than is optimal. However clever the informational message, it may be ignored or filtered out. One approach particularly relevant to the mass media, known as the elaboration likelihood model (ELM; Petty and Cacioppo 1986; see Figure 7.1 on p. 185), acknowledges these problems and considers how to work around them. The model suggests that attempts to motivate people who are not interested in a particular issue using rational argument will not work; nor will they succeed if the arguments for change are weak. Only those individuals with a pre-existing interest in the issue are likely to attend to such information and, perhaps, act on it. In their jargon, individuals are more likely to 'centrally process' messages if they are 'motivated to receive an argument' when:

- it is congruent with their pre-existing beliefs;

- it has personal relevance to them;

- recipients have the intellectual capacity to understand the message.

Such processing involves evaluation of arguments, assessment of conclusions, and their integration into existing belief structures. According to the ELM, any attitude change resulting from such deliberative processes is likely to be enduring and predictive of behaviour. But what about those individuals who are less motivated to engage with logical arguments? According to the ELM, influence here is less reliable but still possible. The model suggests that this can be achieved through what it terms 'peripheral processing'. This is likely to occur when individuals:

- are not motivated to receive an argument;

- have low issue involvement;

- hold incongruent beliefs.

Peripheral processing involves maximising the credibility and attractiveness of the source of the message using indirect cues and information. Attempts, for example, to influence middle-aged women to take part in exercise may involve a technical message about health gains that can be achieved following exercise (the central route) and also include images associated with exercise that will appeal to the target audience, such as making friends while engaging in gentle exercise and wearing attractive clothes in the gym (the peripheral route). Similarly, the importance of a message can be emphasised by a senior person, such as a medical professor presenting information. More cautiously, Petty and Cacioppo noted that any attitude change fostered by the peripheral route may well be transient and not predictive of behaviour.

A number of UK television advertisements targeted at smokers provide good examples of this approach. These involved real people who had serious smoking-related illnesses – we were told that one person died soon after filming – talking about the adverse outcomes of their smoking. The film was black and white, and the images involved the people sitting in a chair against a very sparse background. The message was that smoking kills, and the peripheral cues associated with the image were downbeat and gloomy. It did not encourage the viewer to take up smoking! Of course, one danger of this negative portrayal is that viewers may find it too depressing and simply disengage from the adverts – either mentally by thinking about something else, or physically by switching the television to another channel (see discussion of fear appeals in the next section). To avoid such an outcome, the PRECEDE model states it is necessary to develop media campaigns based on sound psychological theory and also to include a testing process, discussing the nature of the interventions with their target population – perhaps through the use of focus groups – to fine-tune the finished product.

The use of fear

A second potential approach to increasing the influence of both mass media and interpersonal communication is through the use of fear messages. Many health professionals consider this a key strategy to motivate change, and the approach has also proven popular among health promoters, politicians, and those involved in the mass media, including its recipients. Biener et al. (2000), for example, found the general public considered fear-engendering advertisements to be more effective than humour. Despite this support, high levels of threat have proven relatively ineffective in engendering behavioural change.

R.W Rogers' (1983) protection motivation theory provides one explanation for these findings. This suggests that individuals will respond to information in either an adaptive or maladaptive manner depending on their appraisal of both threat *and* their own ability to minimise that threat (their self-efficacy judgements). The theory suggests that an individual is most likely to behave in an adaptive manner in response to a fear-arousing health message if they have evidence that engaging in certain behaviours will reduce any threat and they believe they are capable of engaging in them. This approach has been further developed by Witte's (1992) extended parallel process model which states that individuals who are threatened will take one of two courses of action: danger control or fear control. Danger control involves reducing the threat, usually by actively focusing on solutions. Fear control seeks to reduce the perception of the risk, often by avoiding thinking about the threat. For danger control to be selected, a person needs to consider that an effective response is available (response efficacy) and that they are capable of engaging in this response (self-efficacy). If danger control is not selected, then fear control becomes the dominant coping strategy. Fear control, in this context, involves withdrawal from the message, not the health threat, as it is too overwhelming. People may turn the television off, try to avoid thinking about an issue, and so on. Any

intervention which triggers fear control may make people even less likely to consider change than before, as their immediate response to the health threat becomes one of avoidance.

Both these theories suggest that the most persuasive messages are those that:

● arouse some degree of fear: 'Unsafe sex increases your risk of getting HIV';

● increase a sense of severity if no change is made: 'HIV is a serious condition';

● emphasise the ability of the individual to prevent the feared outcome (efficacy): 'Here are some simple safer sex practices you can use to reduce your risk of getting HIV'.

Information framing

A less threatening approach to the development of health messages involves 'framing' the message. Health messages can be framed in either positive (stressing positive outcomes associated with action) or negative terms (emphasising negative outcomes associated with failure to act). Smoking cessation, for example, can be framed as either the positive gain of being more able to exercise, looking and smelling better, or the negative effects of not dying of cancer or other lung diseases. The use of sun screen can be influenced by messages that urge you to use sun screen to maintain a healthy skin, or to reduce the risk of skin cancer. Negative framing often gets quite close to the fear arousal discussed in the previous section, which has struggled to prove effective. However, both positive and negative framing of information have proven effective at times. Unfortunately, there is no consistent benefit from either approach, and the optimal approach will depend on the behaviour and target population. For this reason, as in any intervention, some degree of pilot work – testing out early versions of the intervention – may be necessary before its implementation.

Motivational interviewing

The most effective form of persuasion in one-to-one interventions is known as motivational interviewing (Miller and Rollnick 2002). Its goal is to increase an individual's motivation to consider change, not to show them how to change. If the interview succeeds in motivating change, only then can any intervention proceed to considering ways of achieving it.

Motivational interviewing is designed to help people explore and resolve any ambivalence they may have about changing their behaviour. The approach assumes that when an individual is facing the need to change, they may have beliefs and attitudes that both support and counter change. Prior to the interview, thoughts that counter change probably predominate; or else the person would be actively seeking help to achieve change. Nevertheless, the goal of the interview is to elicit both sets of beliefs and attitudes and to bring them into sharp focus ('I know smoking does damage my health', 'I enjoy smoking', and so on). This is thought to place the individual in a state of **cognitive dissonance** (Festinger 1957), which is resolved by rejecting one set of beliefs in favour of the other. These may (or may not) favour behavioural change. If an individual decides to change their behaviour, the intervention then focuses on consideration of how to achieve change. If the individual still rejects the possibility of change, they would typically not continue in any programme of behavioural change.

The motivational interview is deliberately non-confrontational. Miller and Rollnick (2002) considered it to be a 'philosophy of supporting individual change' and not attempting to persuade an individual to go against their own wishes. Nevertheless, a few key strategies can be identified. The key questions in the interview are:

● What are some of the good things about your present behaviour?

● What are the not so good things about your present behaviour?

The first question is perhaps slightly surprising but important, as it acknowledges the individual is gaining something from their present behaviour. It is intended to reduce the potential for resistance to any discussion of change. Once the individual has considered each issue, both for and against change, these are summarised by the counsellor in a way that highlights the dissonance between the two sets of issues. Following this feedback, the

individual is invited to consider their reaction to this information. Only if they express some interest in change should the interview then go on to consider how to change.

Since its original conception, the motivational interview process has been further developed (Miller and Rollnick 2012) and now incorporates a strong element of planned behaviour change, much as promulgated by Egan in the next section. It has also developed a number of additional strategies of motivating change, which make it a more explicit process of persuasion. These include:

● Consideration of the disadvantages of the status quo:
 – What worries you about your current situation?
 – What makes you think that you need to do something about your blood pressure?
 – What difficulties or hassles have you had in relation to your drug use?
 – What is there about your drinking that you or other people might see as reasons for concern?
 – What do you think will happen if you don't change anything?

● Consideration of the advantages of change:
 – How would you like for things to be different?
 – What would be the good things about losing weight?
 – What would you like your life to be like five years from now?
 – If you could make this change immediately, by magic, how might things be better for you?
 – What are the main reasons you see for making a change? What would be the advantages of making this change?

● Evoking the intention to change:
 – I can see that you're feeling stuck at the moment. What's going to have to change?
 – How important is this to you? How much do you want to do this?
 – Of the options I've mentioned, which one sounds like it fits you best?
 – Never mind the 'how' for right now – what do you want to have happen?
 – So what do you intend to do?

● Evoking optimism about change:
 – What makes you think that if you did decide to make a change, you could do it?

Cognitive dissonance
A state of discomfort resulting from holding two sets of opposing beliefs. Usually resolved by rejecting one set in favour of the other

– What do you think would work for you, if you decided to change?

– When else in your life have you made a significant change like this? How did you do it?

– How confident are you that you can make this change?

– What personal strengths do you have that will help you succeed?

– Who could offer you helpful support in making this change?

Changing behaviour

Following the rubric of the stages of change model, if individuals are motivated to change their behaviour, then any intervention should focus on helping them *achieve* the changes they wish to make. This may not be easy. How does a busy working mother find time to exercise or cook healthily? How does an addicted smoker quit? Some changes, such as moving from full-fat to semi-skimmed milk are easy to make. But more complex behaviours, embedded in busy and demanding lives, may be much more difficult to change even if we are motivated to do so. It is estimated, for example, that around 70 per cent of smokers have made at least one attempt to quit smoking over any one-year period. Simply exhorting such individuals to change is likely to be of little benefit. They have tried and failed.

The reasons for failures to change can be complex and lie both within and beyond the individual. They may be a result of fluctuating motivation, lack of knowledge of how to change, obstacles to change that may be difficult to overcome, and so on. For this reason, the best approaches to changing behaviour support the individual in negotiating these issues.

Problem-solving approaches

Problem-focused interventions involve considering *how*, rather than *whether*, to change and are best suited to individuals who want to change their behaviour but need help working out how to do this. Perhaps the most clearly explicated problem-focused counselling approach has been developed by Egan (e.g. 2013). His form of problem-focused counselling is complex in parts but has an elegantly simple basic framework. It emphasises the importance of appropriate analysis of the problem the individual is facing as a critical element of the counselling process. Only when this has been achieved can an appropriate solution to the problem be identified. A further element of Egan's approach is that the job of the counsellor is not to act as an expert solving the person's problems. Instead, their role is to mobilise the individual's own resources both to identify problems accurately and to arrive at strategies of solution. Counselling is problem-oriented. It is focused specifically on the issues at hand and in the 'here and now', and has three distinct phases:

1. *problem exploration and clarification*: a detailed and thorough exploration of the problems an individual is facing: breaking 'global insolvable problems' into carefully defined soluble elements;

2. *goal setting*: identifying how the individual would like things to be different; setting clear, behaviourally defined and achievable goals (or sub-goals);

3. *facilitating action*: developing plans and strategies through which these goals can be achieved.

Case history Mrs T

Mrs T provides a good example of how the problem-solving approach may lead to issues and interventions far from those that might be expected. Mrs T took part in a regular screening clinic held at her local GP's surgery, where she was found to be obese and to have a raised serum cholesterol level. Following standard dietary advice, Mrs T agreed to a goal of losing two pounds a week over the following months. She was given a leaflet providing information about the fat and calorific content of a variety of foods and a leaflet describing a number of 'healthy' recipes.

On her follow-up visits, her cholesterol level and weight remained unchanged – so she saw a counsellor to provide her with more help. The counsellor used the problem-focused approach of Egan. In the first session, she explored why Mrs T had not made use of the advice she had previously been given. Mrs T explained that she already knew which were 'healthy' and 'unhealthy' foods. Indeed, she had been on many diets before – without much success. Together, she and her counsellor began to explore why this was the case. At this point, a number of problems became apparent. One important issue was that she was not receiving support from her family, and in particular her two grown-up sons. Mrs T was the family cook, in a family that often demanded 'fry-ups'. She accepted this role but had difficulty in not nibbling the food as she cooked it. Although she actually ate quite small (and low-fat) meals, her nibbling while cooking significantly increased her calorie and cholesterol intake.

Mrs T's husband supported her attempts to lose weight and was prepared to change his diet to help her. However, her sons often demanded meals when they got back from the pub, late at night and often the worse for drink. The upshot of this was that Mrs T often started to cook late at night at the end of what may have been a successful day of dieting. She then nibbled high-calorie food while cooking. This had two outcomes. First, she increased her calorie input at a time when she did not need calories. Second, she sometimes catastrophised ('I've eaten so much, I may as well abandon my diet for today') and ate a full meal at this time. It also reduced her motivation to follow her diet the following day.

Once this specific problem had been identified, Mrs T set a goal of not cooking late night fry-ups for her sons. She decided that, in future, if her sons wanted this they could cook it themselves. Once the goal was established, Mrs T felt a little concerned about how her sons would react to her no longer cooking for them, so she and the counsellor explored ways in which she could set about telling them – and sticking to her resolution. She finally decided she would tell them in the coming week, explaining why she felt she could no longer cook for them at that time of night. She even rehearsed how she would say it. This she did, with some effect, as she did start to lose weight.

Some people may not need to work through each stage of the counselling process. Others may be able to work through all the phases in one session. Still others may require several counselling sessions. However, it is important to deal with each stage sequentially and thoroughly. Flitting from stage to stage serves only to confuse both the counsellor and the individual being counselled.

IN THE SPOTLIGHT

There is now a whole community of people involved in the provision and training of motivational interviewing. So-called MINTers (members of the Motivational Interview Network of Trainers) are spreading the word about the benefits of motivational interview. Many YouTube videos are also available through which interested individuals may gain the skills more informally. This is probably the most focused training programme of any single intervention strategy ever developed. The programme is also now incorporating not just motivational aspects, but some of the classic problem-focused skills of Egan. It is a long way from its origins as a simple one-off strategy of motivation change. As such, it has the potential to 'skill up' a whole work force of health professionals. The challenge for health-care providers for whom such people work is to provide the time for these intervention strategies to be used appropriately. Appointment times during which health professionals see their clients may too often not be long enough to allow the effective (and probably cost-effective) use of these counselling skills. The system in which health professionals work has still to catch up with the potential for change brought about by this (and other) approaches to behavioural change. Without both working together, care of people with lifestyle-related diseases or those at risk for them is unlikely to be optimal.

Smoking cessation as a form of problem solving

Although they may not explicitly state it, many behavioural change programmes have within them an element of problem identification and resolution. The example of smoking cessation can illustrate this point. Smoking is driven by two processes:

- a conditioned response to a variety of cues in the environment – picking up the telephone, having a cup of coffee, and so on – the so-called habit cigarette;

- a physiological need for nicotine – to top up levels of nicotine and prevent the onset of withdrawal symptoms.

Nicotine is an extremely powerful drug. It acts on the **acetylcholine** system in the central nervous system, and mediates levels of attention and muscle activity throughout the body. Its activity is bi-phasic.

Short, sharp inhalations increase activity in this system as the nicotine bonds with the acetylcholine receptors and activates the neurons – resulting in increased alertness. Long inhalations, by contrast, result in the nicotine remaining in the post synaptic acetylcholine receptors, preventing further uptake of nicotine or acetylcholine by the receptors – leading to feelings of relaxation. Accordingly, when an individual stops smoking, they may have to deal with:

- the loss of a powerful means of altering mood and level of attention;

- withdrawal symptoms as a consequence of a biological dependence on nicotine;

- the urge to smoke triggered by environmental cues.

The best smoking cessation programmes address each of these issues. Following a 'quit day', most call for complete cessation of smoking, following which the individual may have to cope with varying degrees of urges to smoke as a result of withdrawal symptoms or encountering cues that previously were associated with smoking. Any withdrawal symptoms may take up to two or three weeks to subside, and be at their worst in the first two to three days following cessation. Accordingly, there is an acute period of high risk for relapse following cessation which may be driven by the immediate psychological and physiological discomfort associated with quitting.

Many programmes prepare ex-smokers to cope with these problems. Each set of strategies involves a degree of problem solving, as the smoker has to identify both the particular problems they may face and individual solutions to those problems (see Table 6.1). The strategies may involve:

- coping with cues to smoking – this may involve avoiding them completely or working out ways of coping with temptation triggered by smoking cues;

- reducing the possibility of giving in to cravings should they occur;

- coping with any withdrawal symptoms.

Table 6.1 Some strategies that smokers may use to help them to cope in the period immediately following cessation

Avoidant strategies	Coping strategies
Sit with non-smoking friends at coffee breaks	If you feel the urge to smoke, focus attention on things happening around you – not on your desire for a cigarette
Drink something different at coffee breaks – to break your routine and not light up automatically	Think distracting thoughts – count backwards in sevens from 100
Go for a walk instead of smoking	Remember your reasons for stopping smoking – carry them on flashcards and look at them if this helps
Chew sugar-free gum or sweets at times you would normally smoke	
Move ashtrays out of sight	
Try to keep busy, so you won't have time to think of cigarettes	

Make it difficult to smoke	Cognitive re-labelling
Don't carry money – so you can't buy cigarettes	Cognitive re-labelling: 'These horrible symptoms are signs of recovery.'
Avoid passing the tobacconist where you usually buy your cigarettes	

acetylcholine
a neurotransmitter that is released at the ends of nerve fibres in the parasympathetic nervous system and is involved in the transmission of nerve impulses in the body.

One strategy for coping with any withdrawal symptoms involves the use of nicotine replacement therapy (NRT), either as a gum, spray, patch on the skin, or e-cigarette. The development of NRT was initially seen as a major breakthrough that would prevent the need for any psychological intervention to help people to stop smoking. This has not proved to be the case. Indeed, most manufacturers of nicotine replacement products now recommend using a number of problem-solving strategies along with the NRT – a recommendation clearly supported by the outcome of clinical trials of their use.

Implementing plans and intentions

A simpler, but potentially highly effective, approach to changing behaviour involves simply planning change. According to Gollwitzer (1999), we often fail to translate goal intentions into goal attainment. This may occur for a number of reasons:

- *Failing to start*: the individual does not remember to start, they do not seize the opportunity to act, or they have second thoughts at the critical moment.

- *Becoming 'derailed' from goal striving*: the individual is derailed by enticing stimuli, they find it difficult to suppress habitual behavioural responses, or may be adversely affected by negative mood states or the expectation of negative mood if they implement change.

To overcome these obstacles, a relatively simple procedure known as implementation intentions may be utilised. This involves a so-called 'if–then' approach: 'If I find myself bored and hungry, then I will try to find something active to do.' The ideal is that the action is specified in terms of when, where and how. Although simple, the premise of this approach is that this process will result in a mental association between representations of specified cues (feeling bored) and means of attaining goals (engaging in non-boring activities; not eating), which will become activated when the cue is encountered. Developing appropriate implementations is simple in practice, particularly for one-off simple behaviours. Sheeran and Orbell (2000) suggested the following implementation plan to increase uptake of cervical screening: 'If it is [time and place], then I will [make an appointment, e.g., by phone]!'. More complex if–then links may be made as part of changing more complex behaviours: 'If I have an urge to smoke in the house, I will play a game on the X-box to take my mind off it'; 'If I am offered a

cigarette by a friend …', and so on. Establishing these if–then associations may promote the initiation of goal striving behaviours, stabilise them over time and shield the individual from alternatives and obstacles. Here are some typical implementation intentions, linked to potential problems they are trying to combat:

- Failing to get started — If it is 8 am on Friday, I will ride my bike to work.

- Missing opportunities — As soon as I hear from the doctor, I will book my health check-up.

- Initial reluctance — If it is Saturday 10 am, I will prepare five healthy meals to eat during the week.

- Unwanted attention to distractors — If I start to think about snacking, I will focus on alternative things to do.

- Stopping old habits — If I see the stairs, I will tell myself how good I will feel if I walk up the stairs – and do it.

Modelling and practice

Problem-focused and implementation-intention based interventions can help individuals develop strategies of change and determine when such changes can be enacted. However, achieving change can still be difficult, particularly where an individual lacks the skills or confidence in their ability to make them. Egan himself noted that it may be necessary to teach people the skills required to achieve any goals they have set or to change the social norms in which such behaviours occur.

One way to remedy these deficits is by learning skills from observation of others performing them: a process known as vicarious learning. Bandura's (2001) social cognitive theory suggests that both skills and confidence in the ability to change (self-efficacy) can be increased through a number of simple procedures, including observation of others performing relevant tasks, practice of tasks in a graded programme of skills development, and active persuasion. Bandura identifies three basic models of observational learning:

- A *live model*, which involves an actual individual demonstrating or acting out a behaviour

- A *verbal instructional model*, which involves descriptions and explanations of a behaviour

● *A symbolic model*, which involves real or fictional characters displaying behaviours in books, films, television programmes, or online media.

The effectiveness of learning from observation of others can be influenced by a number of factors. However, optimal learning and increases in self-efficacy are often achieved through observation of people similar to the learner succeeding in relevant tasks. This provides a 'coping model', which does not leave the observer feeling de-skilled or incapable of gaining the skills. Indeed, it gives them confidence they can achieve them ('If they can do it, so can I'). Complex skills can be taught through observation models learning skills over time and through various stages.

A further addition to problem-solving or implementation-based strategies involves the practice of new behaviours. Here, solutions to problems as well as the skills needed to achieve change can be worked out and taught in an educational programme, increasing both skills and self-efficacy. Cookery, purchasing and negotiating the use of condoms, the skills required to refuse a proffered cigarette, for example, can all be taught and practised. Differing approaches can be planned, rehearsed, and feedback may be given within educational or counselling sessions in order to develop skills before their use in the 'real world'. Modelling change has the advantage that it can be done remotely, through the use of mass media and other large interventions, or at a more individual level.

Cognitive interventions

The interventions so far considered can be thought of as behavioural interventions, in that they attempt to directly influence behaviour. They may also result in cognitive change: increasing an individual's confidence in their ability to make and maintain any lifestyle changes, and so on. But this is an indirect effect. By contrast, cognitive strategies attempt to change cognitions directly and, in particular, those that drive an individual to engage in behaviours that may be harmful to their health or prevent them making appropriate behavioural changes. From a health psychology perspective, various categories of relevant cognitions have been identified, including attitudes towards the behaviour and relevant social norms (Ajzen 1985), beliefs about the costs and benefits of disease prevention and behavioural change (Becker 1974), self-efficacy expectations (Bandura 2001) and beliefs about an illness or condition and the ability to manage it (Leventhal et al. 1984; see Chapter 9 (☛). The need to change cognitions is based on the premise that individuals may not have relevant information or have developed distorted or inappropriate beliefs about a relevant issue, and that changing these beliefs will result in more

Photo 6.2 Cycling can be fun and healthy, but only in a safe and pollution-free environment.

Source: Pearson Education Ltd/123rf.com

appropriate (and health-promoting) behaviour. The simplest form of intervention may involve the provision of appropriate education – particularly when an individual is facing a new health threat or is unaware of information that may encourage appropriate behavioural change. Such education is likely to be optimal if it targets factors known to influence health-related behaviours. It can educate individuals about the nature of their risk, show them how to change their behaviour, and so on. This approach has been considered earlier in the chapter.

More complex interventions may be required to change inappropriate beliefs that have been developed and reinforced over time. Beliefs that encourage substance use or abuse, for example, may include 'I cannot cope with going to a party without a hit' or 'Drinking makes me a more sociable person'. At the beginning of a history of drug use, positive beliefs such as 'It will be fun to get high' may predominate. As the individual begins to rely on the drug to counteract feelings of distress, more dependent beliefs may predominate: 'I need a drink to get me through the day'. Cognitive interventions may be of benefit where such thoughts interfere with any behavioural change. Key to any intervention is that the beliefs we hold about illnesses, our health, events that have happened or will happen in the future, and so on, are *hypothetical*. Some of these guesses may be correct; some may be wrong. In some cases, because maladaptive beliefs ('I need a shot of whisky to get through this') come readily to mind, they are taken as facts, and alternative thoughts ('Well, I might be able to cope without') are not considered. The role of cognitive therapy is to teach the individual to treat their beliefs as hypotheses and not facts, to try out alternative ways of looking at the situation and to have different responses to it based on these new ways of thinking ('Well, I used to cope in this situation before without having a drink. Perhaps I can do the same this time').

One way in which this can be achieved involves a process known as Socratic dialogue or guided discovery (Beck 1976). In this, beliefs about particular issues are identified and questioned by the therapist in order to help the individual to identify distorted thinking patterns that are contributing to their problems. It encourages them to consider and evaluate different sources of information that provide evidence of the reality or unreality of the beliefs they hold. Once they can do this in the therapy session, they can be taught to identify and challenge these automatic thoughts in the real world and to replace thoughts that drive inappropriate behaviour with those that support more appropriate behaviour. An example of their use is provided by this extract from a session adapted from Beck et al. (1993) using a technique known as the downward arrow technique designed to question the very core of an individual's beliefs – in this case their assumptions about their drinking.

Health professional You feel quite strongly that you need to be 'relaxed' by alcohol when you go to a party. What is your concern about being sober?

John I wouldn't enjoy myself and I wouldn't be much fun to be with.

Health professional What would be the implications of that?

John Well, people wouldn't talk to me.

Health professional And what would be the consequence of that?

John I need to have people like me. My job depends on it. If I can't entertain people at a party, then I'm no good at my job.

Health professional So, what happens if that is the case?

John Well, I guess I lose my job!

Health professional So, you lose your job because you didn't get drunk at a party?

John Well, put like that, perhaps I was exaggerating things in my head.

Here, the downward arrow technique has been used both to identify some of the client's core beliefs and to get them to reconsider the accuracy of those beliefs.

A second strategy is to set up homework tasks that directly challenge any inappropriate cognitive beliefs that individuals may hold. An example of this can be found in the case of the individual who believes that they cannot go to a party without drinking, and who may be set the homework task of trying to remain sober at a party – directly challenging their belief that they need to drink alcohol to be socially engaging (and the exaggerated ultimate belief that they will lose their job if they remain sober). Clearly, such challenges should be realistic. If a person attempts a task that is too hard and fails to achieve it, this may maintain or even strengthen the pre-existing beliefs. Accordingly, they have to be chosen with care and mutually agreed by both the individual concerned and the therapist. However, success in these tasks can bring about long-term cognitive and behavioural changes.

Changing the environment

Almost all the interventions considered so far involve attempts to change the behaviour of individuals by directly interacting with their target audiences. However, health behaviours occur in a social and economic context. Individual dietary choice is often limited by family dynamics: children may baulk at being asked to eat lots of vegetables, partners may not wish to be meat-free, and so on. The level of exercise we can realistically engage in may be determined by our economic situation: can we afford gym membership, how long is our working week, and so on? It may also be moderated by the environment in which we live. Cycling in inner London, for example, may be a very different experience to cycling in the country; people may feel cautious about jogging close to busy roads with poor street lighting, and so on.

Because of the wide number of people affected by these issues, the social, economic and environmental constraints on behavioural change may become targets for change. The health belief model (Becker et al. 1977; see Chapter 5 (☛) provides a simple guide to key environmental factors that can be influenced in order to encourage behavioural change. In particular, the model suggests that an environment that encourages healthy behaviour should:

● provide cues to engage in healthy behaviours or remove cues to unhealthy behaviour: for example, signs reminding people to use the stairs, nutritional information on food packaging, removal of cigarette advertising from shops;

● minimise the costs and barriers associated with engaging in healthy behaviours: for example, increasing the number of public recreation areas, cheap gym membership, building safe cycle paths, selling healthy food close to centres of economic deprivation;

● maximise the costs of engaging in health-damaging behaviour: for example, increasing taxation of alcohol and cigarettes, not allowing smoking in public places, increasing the geographical distance between alcohol outlets.

Environmental strategies are widely used by governments, both national and local, to influence behaviour and are central to the PRECEDE model. A number of projects, under the rubric of the 'Healthy Cities movement' (World Health Organization 1988), for example, have attempted to design city environments in ways that promote the mental and physical health of their inhabitants. The movement initially involved cities in industrialised countries, but is now expanding to include cities in industrialising countries such as Bangladesh, Tanzania, Nicaragua and Pakistan. To be a member of the movement, cities have to develop a city health profile and involve citizen and community groups. Priorities for action include attempts to reduce health inequalities as a result of socio-economic factors, traffic control, tobacco control, and care of the elderly and those with mental health problems (Kickbusch 2003). The complexity of these goals means they often *remain* goals, with large-scale behavioural change difficult to achieve. Nevertheless, the health cities movement provides an aspirational target for all cities.

Spreading the word

A key approach that has been used to disseminate new behaviours through the general population involves the use of individuals or groups within the population to actively promote any targeted changes, such as healthy eating, smoking cessation, and so on. It is based on a theory of the spread of new behaviours through society known as 'diffusion of innovations' (Rogers 1983) see Figure 7.2 page 187. In this, Rogers segmented the population in terms of their responses to innovation and their influence on the behaviour of others:

● *Innovators*: a small group of individuals, usually of high status. They seek out and gain ideas from a wide range of sources and are willing and able to test out new ideas gained from them. This group is relatively isolated from the 'mainstream'. However, they bring innovations to a group with wider links to the general population and with wider influence: early adopters.

● *Early adopters*: this larger group of people has a wider sphere of influence than innovators. They are often described as 'opinion leaders'. Potential adopters look to this group for information about an innovation, and they serve as role models for the wider population. Adoption of an innovation by this group is crucial to its adoption by the wider population.

● *Early majority*: this group adopts ideas reasonably early, but does not have the power to influence the wider population.

● *Late majority*: these people adopt the innovation only after adopting by the early majority. They are a fairly cautious group, and are only likely to adopt an innovation after it has been well tested by the previous groups.

● *Laggards*: this group of people are the last to adopt, or may never adopt, an innovation.

Rogers also noted a number of characteristics of any innovation that may influence its likely uptake by each group:

● Its advantage over other behaviours: the bigger the advantage the more likely it is to be adopted.

● Its compatibility with the values and norms of the social system it is trying to influence: if the innovation is too radical, it will be rejected.

● Ease of uptake: if the innovation is easy to adopt, it is more likely to be adopted than if it is difficult to understand or engage in.

● Evidence of effectiveness: the more any effectiveness can be seen, the more likely it is to be adopted.

The model has a number of implications for the active diffusion of health-enhancing behaviours by any public health intervention. It suggests key target groups that may be addressed in any public health information intervention. Early adopters, for example, may usefully be identified and targeted in any advertising of an innovation. Early adopters, or opinion leaders, may also become actively involved in an intervention. Interventions discussed in the next chapter, for example, have actively recruited gay men of some standing in their local community to lead interventions designed to increase condom use among their peers.

Getting it right

The chapter so far has outlined a number of theoretically driven approaches to behaviour change. But these approaches only work when they are used. An obvious point, you may reasonably cry. But not all, or even most, behavioural change programmes do so at present. One reason for this is that many people who develop interventions designed to change behaviour are not familiar with the relevant theories or fail to integrate them into any intervention. Another reason is that understanding of research into the effectiveness of interventions is often hampered by a lack of detail when describing the intervention used. Terms such as 'psycho-educational programme' or 'motivational programme' frequently used in reporting interventions convey little to the reader and prevent them

understanding the mechanisms of change. In order to address both these issues, there have recently been a number of calls to form a list of intervention approaches to be considered when developing a behavioural change intervention. The chapter has already referred to the NICE guidelines on behavioural change. An example of the use of these types of guideline is afforded by Michie et al. (2012) who broke down the optimal approach to encouraging smoking cessation into considerable detail.

Information provision should include information about:

● The consequences of the behaviour in general: smoking causes people to die on average eight years earlier than the average.

● The consequence of behaviour to the individual: if you were to stop smoking, you are likely to add six years to your life, and be fitter over that time.

● Others' approval of behavioural change: your wife will appreciate it if you were to give up smoking.

● Normative information about others' behaviour: around 30 per cent of people of your age I see have successfully given up smoking.

Problem-focused approaches include:

● Goal setting
  – Establishing goals of behavioural change: I will give up smoking after I finish this packet.
  – Establishing non-behavioural goals: I will not get out of breath when I run for a bus.

● Action planning
  – This is usually linked to goal setting and involves developing a plan by which to achieve goals. As a minimum, these should involve a 'when statement': 'When I have the urge to smoke I will eat some fruit'.

● Barrier planning/problem solving
  – As part of a plan, consideration is given to how to deal with challenges or barriers to the plan. These may form competing goals in specified situations: 'I will not carry money, so even if I am tempted to smoke, I will not be able to. I will ask my friends not to offer me a cigarette, however desperate I am.'

● Set graded tasks
  – Breaking a large target behaviour into smaller achievable tasks: I will cut out five cigarettes each day for one week.

● Prompt review of behavioural goals

- Involves review and reflection of behavioural goal achievement on a regular basis.

● Prompt review of outcome goals

- Involves review and reflection of outcome goal achievement on a regular basis.

● Prompt rewards contingent on effort or progress towards behaviour

- This can involve self-reward (a treat for successfully cutting down smoking) or praise or rewards given by a health professional.

● Prompt rewards contingent on successful behaviour

- This can involve self-reward (a treat for successfully stopping smoking) or praise or rewards given by a health professional.

As you can see, the detail by which interventions are broken down and described is enormously detailed. This should allow researchers and practitioners to determine which elements of interventions are most useful, and those involved in developing interventions to ensure they include all possible active interventions. A combination of planning using the PRECEDE model combined with the use of behavioural change taxonomies should ensure that future interventions whether targeted at individuals or whole populations should prove more effective than those used so far.

RESEARCH FOCUS

Prestwich, A., Sniehotta, F. F., Whittington, C., Dombrowski, S. U., Rogers, L. and Michie, S. (2014). Does theory influence the effectiveness of health behavior interventions? Meta-Analysis. *Health Psychology* 33: 465–74.

This chapter has emphasised the need to develop theory-led interventions, with close ties between theory and each element of the intervention. The meta-analysis reported in this study provided systematic reviews of the links between theory and practice reported in the literature relating to physical activity and health eating interventions. It then went on to consider the comparative effectiveness of theory-led interventions and any links between specific intervention types and behavioural outcomes.

Method

The study group identified papers for selection into their analysis from two previous meta-analyses. The first of the two previous papers reported studies involving adults 18 years or over, interventions targeting physical activity or healthy eating, use of experimental design, clear validated outcome measures and use of cognitive or behavioural strategies beyond simple provision of information. The second included studies of individuals over 40, obese and with at least one health-related problem. Again, the interventions targeted healthy eating or exercise, and behaviour change was assessed using self-report or behavioural measures.

The Theory Coding Scheme of Michie and Prestwich (2010) was used to code the reported use of behaviour change theory. This is a list of intervention strategies, each linked to a specific theory. The raters rated the interventions reported in the studies and the degree to which these interventions were linked to theory in the paper's text.

Results

A range of further analyses were conducted by descriptive links between the mention of theory in the text, explicit use of theory and linking this to the intervention, and a number of other relevant variables. Some key findings were:

● The paper mentions a theoretical approach on which the intervention was based   61%
● Intervention based on single theory   27%
● Theory used to develop intervention techniques   56%

- Theory used to tailor the intervention to individual participants   22%

- At least one intervention technique is explicitly linked to a theory   25%

- All theory constructs are linked to at least one intervention strategy   5%

- Results are discussed in relation to theory   29%

- Results are used to refine theory   2%

Perhaps the most salient issue related to effectiveness is that when 'tests of mediation' measuring whether changes in apparently theoretically relevant constructs were associated with behavioural change, only 4 per cent of these analyses found a significant relationship.

A second set of analyses considered whether reported theory use was associated with intervention effectiveness. The interventions reported in the studies were based on the trans-theoretical model (TTM) and social cognitive theory (SCT). Overall, the effect size of the interventions based on one theory, whether it was the TTM or SCT (Hedge's g = .33: small–medium), was larger than those based on multiple theories (Hedge's g = .21: small). More disappointingly, studies reporting interventions specifically tailored to individuals had lower effect sizes than those that did not report this tailoring (.21 versus .33). In addition, there was no evidence that theoretically based interventions proved more effective than those that did not explicitly link to a theory.

Discussion and comment

Coming from a group of psychologists with a particular interest in advocating the use of theoretically driven interventions, the finding that there was no association between the use of theory and intervention outcome must have been particularly disappointing, as it will be for most readers of the paper. The authors note the importance of this finding, but suggest a few factors may have contributed to this finding. Although the studies examined the association between the use of theoretically informed interventions, those used may not have been optimal, and differing combinations to those used may have been more effective. Perhaps more important may be the common finding that the design of interventions frequently does not match well to their actual delivery. Future studies need to consider not only the theoretical base of any intervention but use 'fidelity assessments' to ensure the interventions as applied are those stated in any intervention plan. Nevertheless, the findings suggest that the effect of interventions such as those assessed in these analyses may not be consistently stronger than atheoretical interventions, suggesting the need to either improve the quality of these interventions or to move to different theoretical intervention models.

SUMMARY

1. The PRECEDE–PROCEED model provides a strong framework for the development of public health programmes. Key stages to their development include: social diagnosis; epidemiological, behaviour, and environmental diagnosis; educational and ecological diagnosis; and programme implementation.
2. A number of approaches can be used to motivate behavioural change:
   - Information provision: ideally based round theoretically driven models of behavioural change and guidelines such as those developed by NICE

   - The central and peripheral routes of the elaboration likelihood model
   - Appropriate informational framing: based on 'test' studies to identify the optimal framing for a particular intervention
   - Motivational interviewing.
3. Similarly, a number of approaches can be used to change behaviour:
   - Problem-solving approaches
   - Implementation plans
   - Modelling and practice
   - Cognitive interventions

4. A third approach to changing behaviour involves adopting the environment to facilitate or reward behavioural change and to inhibit engagement in health-damaging behaviours.

5. Some change may filter through society in a natural way, known as 'diffusion of innovation'. This process may be facilitated through the use of early adopters or opinion leaders as advocates of appropriate behavioural change.

Further reading

http://www.nice.org.uk/Guidance/PH49/chapter/glossary#individual-level-behaviour-change-interventions

A range of internet links to the NICE guidelines on behaviour change, behaviour change competency frameworks, brief interventions, and much much more.

Michie, S., Ashford, S., Sniehotta, F.F. et al. (2011). A refined taxonomy of behaviour change techniques to help people change their physical activity and health eating behaviours: the CALO-RE. *Psychology and Health*, 26 1479–98.

An example of the development of behaviour change taxonomies by one of the leading groups in their development.

Miller W.R. and Rollnick S. (2012). *Motivational Interviewing: Helping People Change* (Applications of Motivational Interviewing). Third edition. Guilford Press.

The latest iteration of the classic text on motivational interviewing.

Li, Y., Cao, J., Lin, H. et al. (2009). Community health needs assessment with precede–proceed model: a mixed methods study. *BMC Health Service Research*, 9:181.

A nice example of the assessment phase of the PRECEDE–PROCEED model

Hagger, M.S. and Luszczynska A. (2014). Implementation intention and action planning interventions in health contexts: state of the research and proposals for the way forward. *Applied Psychology: Health and Well Being*, 6, 1–47.

A recent critical consideration of the state of the art of implementation and planning-based interventions.

Li J., Weeks M.R., Borgatti S.P. et al. (2012). A social network approach to demonstrate the diffusion and change process of intervention from peer health advocates to the drug-using community. *Substance Use and Misuse*, 47, 474–90.

An example of a diffusion-based approach focusing on the process of its implementation.

For open-access student resources specifically written to complement this textbook and support your learning, please visit **www.pearsoned.co.uk/morrison**

Chapter 7
Preventing health problems

Learning outcomes

By the end of the chapter you should have an understanding of the effectiveness of the following approaches to changing health-damaging behaviours:

- individually based interventions, including risk factor screening programmes, motivational interview-based interventions, and problem-focused approaches

- using the mass media, including information framing, population targeting and the use of fear

- environmental interventions, including increasing cues to action, minimising the costs of healthy behaviour and increasing the costs of unhealthy behaviour

- public health programmes focusing on reducing risk for coronary heart disease and increasing safer sex

- worksite public health

- school-based interventions

- using new technologies

An apple a day keeps the doctor away

Well, there is no evidence that eating one apple a day will provide any health advantage: although eating five portions of vegetables and fruit may. But the point of the title addresses a key issue in modern health care. In their report, *The Growing Danger of Non-Communicable Diseases: Acting Now to Reverse Course,* the World Bank concludes that Africa, Eastern Europe and Asia face alarming increases in chronic disease levels as a consequence of poor lifestyle, and suggests that if left unchecked these prevalence rates could increase from an already high 51 per cent to an alarming 72 per cent of all deaths. More than a third of these deaths will be preventable through appropriate changes in lifestyle. Western European countries, meanwhile, cannot afford to relax. The cost of caring for people with diabetes (1 and 2) in the UK may eventually soak up half the NHS budget, with present estimates of £14 billion a year being spent on treating diabetes and its complications. Lifestyle-related diseases, and in particular, type 2 diabetes and various manifestations of coronary heart disease and hypertension, carry a massive financial toll as well as a personal one. Lowering these costs can only be achieved by significant lifestyle change among apparently healthy individuals.

Chapter outline

The previous chapter identified a number of strategies of behavioural change that can be used in interventions designed to prevent the onset of disease. This chapter examines the effectiveness of a range of interventions designed to reduce the health risk associated with health-damaging behaviours such as smoking, poor diet and low levels of exercise. It considers interventions that involve working directly with individuals and also those that target whole populations. This chapter also considers the anxiety that may be associated with some risk change programmes and how this can be addressed within the context of such programmes.

Working with individuals

Individually targeted interventions in public health frequently involve working with people identified as being at risk for disease and attempting to change any health-damaging behaviours in which they are engaging. The most basic approach to motivating and facilitating this type of behaviour change involves simply informing people of their risk for disease. This approach assumes that if individuals are identified as being at increased risk of disease, knowledge of this risk will evoke appropriate behavioural change. The most common context in which this approach has been adopted involves screening for risk of coronary heart disease (CHD) as a consequence of high cholesterol, blood pressure, or behavioural risk factors such as smoking or low levels of exercise.

Risk-factor screening programmes

Many of the early CHD screening programmes were established in the UK during the 1990s; perhaps the best known was developed by the OXCHECK Study Group (1994). In this, all adults in participating primary care practices around Oxford who went to their doctor for any reason were invited to attend a 'health check' conducted by a nurse. This involved an interview to identify risk behaviours, blood pressure, and cholesterol levels. Where appropriate, participants were advised to stop smoking, eat a low-cholesterol diet and/or increase their

exercise levels, or received medical treatment for hypertension and high cholesterol levels. By one-year follow-up, participants' blood pressure levels were lower than those of people who did not take part in the screening programme, as were the cholesterol levels of women, but not men. There were no differences between the groups on measures of smoking or **body mass index**.

By the three-year follow-up, cholesterol levels, systolic blood pressure and body mass index of both men and women who took part in the programme were lower than those of the controls. Smoking levels remained the same in both groups. Despite these gains and those in some other studies (e.g., Finkelstein et al. 2006), not all studies have found behavioural change following screening, and even when this does occur its impact on health may be small: so much so that a recent meta-analysis found no long-term health gains following screening and counselling for coronary risk factors. Across 55 studies and data on over 139,000 individuals, the risks of having a cardiac event were the same for those who did or did not go through a primary prevention screening programme (Ebrahim et al. 2011).

More specific interventions have perhaps met with more gains. For instance, Stead et al.'s (2008) review of

> ### body mass index
> a measurement of the relative percentages of fat and muscle mass in the human body, in which weight in kilograms is divided by height in metres squared and the result used as an index of obesity.

relevant literature found that smoking cessation rates with no intervention were around two to three per cent each year and that advice to stop smoking by a doctor could increase them by an additional one to three per cent. Although a relatively small difference, if considered over the potentially thousands of smokers who could receive such advice, the health impact of this approach could be significant. Of note also, are the findings of Gilpin et al. (1993) who found that the first instance of advice was the most important determinant of quitting. Giving advice in further sessions did not result in further quit attempts. In addition, despite many years of smoking, people over 50 years old still appear to both benefit from, and to have positive attitudes towards, physician advice (Ossip-Klein et al. 2000). Of course, this type of intervention only works if physicians actually provide the impetus to quit smoking; but this may not always be the case. This was certainly the finding of Unrod et al. (2007) who found that most of their sample of general practitioners were neither actively encouraging their patients to stop smoking nor following simple guidelines on how this may be achieved. However, when these doctors were given specific training in smoking cessation techniques and used a one-page leaflet suggesting personalised strategies of how to stop smoking with their patients, they found abstinence rates of 12 per cent among the intervention group and 8 per cent among those who received standard advice to quit.

Motivational interviewing

A more sophisticated approach to triggering behavioural change, particularly for those with low motivation or in the pre-contemplation stage of change, involves the use of motivational interviewing. These techniques were initially used to help people who presented with substance misuse problems but more recently the approach has been used with a range of other behaviours. In the context of smoking, Lai et al.'s (2010) meta-analysis comparing the effectiveness of motivational interviewing against brief advice revealed a 25 per cent higher quit rate among those receiving motivational interviewing. The approach was most beneficial when delivered by primary care physicians, who achieved a three times higher quit rate following the use of motivational interviewing than simple advice or no intervention.

Addressing other behaviours – consumption of fruit and vegetables and exercise levels among older adults (aged over 66 years) – Campbell et al. (2009) examined the effectiveness of either written information or information combined with a brief motivational telephone contact in two groups: people who had survived cancer and a group with no evidence of disease. They found that the combined intervention was more effective than the simple provision of information in facilitating changes in diet, but only in the healthy group. The intervention had no impact on exercise levels. Dawson et al. (2014) also found limited effects of a one-off motivational interview. In their study, children aged 4–8 years took part in a health-screening programme following which their parents either received feedback on the health consequences of their child's weight using a simple 'traffic light' visual aid or received a motivational interview designed to encourage their participation in a family-based weight loss programme for their child. Both interventions were equally effective.

The relatively modest gains reported in these studies may be attributed to a failure to target appropriate participants. Neither group, for example, targeted individuals identified as having low levels of motivation. Addressing this issue, Steptoe et al. (1999) adjusted their intervention to suit the stage of change of participants in a screening programme aimed at identifying and reducing risk for CHD. They identified individuals at risk of CHD as a consequence of one or more modifiable risk factors: regular cigarette smoking, high cholesterol levels, and high body mass index combined with low physical activity. Practice nurses then provided brief behavioural counselling on the basis of the stages of change model, using elements of motivational interviews for those who were in pre-contemplation and by developing strategies of change for participants who were considering the possibility of change. Compared to no intervention, some benefits were achieved, with modest reductions in dietary fat intake and cigarettes smoked per day, and increased regular exercise at 4- and 12-month follow-up assessments.

A second approach to increasing the effectiveness of motivational interviewing has been to integrate it within more complex programmes of change. Resnicow et al. (2001), for example, examined the impact of the 'Eat for Life' programme conducted among church-attending African Americans. They compared the effect of two interventions intending to increase fruit and vegetable intake in the target group. These involved either a self-help intervention with a telephone call to encourage use of the programme, or this approach combined with three telephone calls using motivational interviewing techniques. At one-year follow-up, participants in the second group were eating more fruit and vegetables than those in the self-help only group, who in turn were eating more than a no-treatment control group. Integration of motivational interviewing or similar techniques within more complex intervention programmes also seems to add to the effectiveness of the programme (e.g. Carels et al. 2007).

Problem-focused approaches

The previous chapter argued that problem-focused interventions are likely to be more effective than those simply providing information. Surprisingly, very few studies have explicitly compared a simple information provision intervention with one inviting people to actively think through how they will change their behaviour, at least in the context of public health. However, those that have been reported have favoured the latter approach. Gomel et al. (1993), for example, screened hundreds of factory workers for risk factors for CHD, assigning them to one

of three groups if at least one risk factor was found: (i) risk factor education, (ii) problem-focused counselling and (iii) no intervention control. Participants in the educational programme received standard advice on the lifestyle changes needed to reduce their risk of CHD and videos showing how to modify these risk factors. Participants in the problem-solving programme first went through an exercise based on motivational interviewing techniques. Following this, they identified a number of high-risk situations in which they were likely to engage in CHD-risk behaviour (such as smoking or eating high-fat meals) or which would prevent them from engaging in health-promoting behaviours (such as lack of planning, leaving no time for exercise). They were then encouraged to think through how they could minimise their effect. This more complex intervention proved the most effective. Participants in this condition had greater reductions in blood pressure, body mass index and smoking than those in either the education-only intervention or no-intervention control.

In a study targeted more specifically at reducing blood pressure, Elmer et al. (1995) also reported the outcome of

Case history: Mr JB

A more personal account of the benefits of motivational interviewing in an unlikely context can be found in a one-off engagement with a smoker experienced by PB early in his career as a health psychologist. He was asked to see a smoker, JB, who had refused to give up smoking despite several requests by his cardiologist. He was experiencing significant health problems as a consequence of his smoking, the most critical of which were significant reductions in the diameter of the arteries supplying blood to his lower legs due to significant atheroma. Their diameter was so reduced that when he walked he was unable to get enough blood to the muscles in his lower legs and he experienced **ischaemic pain** in his calves. He was also experiencing mild angina due to similar processes in the cardiac arteries (see Chapter 8 ☞). Continued smoking, it was feared, would result in his need to have his lower legs amputated and a myocardial infarction (see Chapter 8 ☞). Repeated requests by his clinicians were met with blunt refusals to quit

smoking despite his knowledge of the health risks he was running.

PB was asked to see him in order to persuade him to stop smoking. This meeting was well before motivational interviewing was well known. Nevertheless, in somewhat of a panic (How do you persuade people to stop smoking when they don't want to?), he simply asked JB why, given the number of people who had asked him to stop smoking, he continued to do so. This question, which neatly fits the first of the original motivational interview questions of 'what are the good things . . . ' elicited a somewhat surprising response. JB was somewhat startled by the question, and was very responsive to it. Rather than adopt a defensive response to yet another attempt at persuasion, he immediately began to ask himself this question, and concluded that actually he *did* want to stop smoking – but was frightened that he was unable to do so, as several previous attempts had ended in failure. This revelation shifted the entire meeting to one of consideration of how to stop, and application of strategies of change similar to those described later in the chapter– with a highly successful outcome.

a problem-solving based intervention. Participants were taught to recognise environmental or psychological cues that led to overeating and to plan how to change or cope with them, as well as considering how to begin and maintain an exercise programme. They also worked with their partners to develop a joint strategy to support any lifestyle changes they made. One year after the programme started, the intervention appeared to be a success. By this time, 70 per cent of the participants had significantly reduced their alcohol intake and increased their exercise levels. As a consequence, they had achieved significant weight loss over the year, and their blood pressure had fallen significantly.

A number of other intervention types have identified the last of Egan's stages as the key therapeutic element. Based on the social cognitive models of the health action process approach (HAPA; Schwarzer and Renner 2000) and implementation intentions (Gollwitzer and Schaal 1998; see Chapters 5 and 6 ☛), both of which identified planning as an important determinant of behavioural change, these approaches have simply encouraged individuals to plan when, how, or under what circumstances they will engage in their behaviour of choice. Some interventions have targeted relatively simple or short-term behavioural change. De Nooijer et al. (2006) found that writing plans to eat an extra serving of fruit per day for one week resulted in a higher intake of fruit than a no-treatment condition. Sheeran and Orbell (2000) found implementation plans resulted in a higher attendance at a cervical screening clinic than a no-treatment condition. Even more impressively, Conner and Higgins (2010) found forming implementation plans resulted in a higher rate of quitting smoking than no intervention among adolescents, while Luszczynska et al. (2007) found that they significantly enhanced the effectiveness of a weight loss programme for obese women. Women who were on a standard commercial weight loss programme achieved a weight loss of 2.1 kilograms over a two-month period, while those given the implementation-planning intervention achieved a weight loss of 4.2 kilograms over the same period. Gratton et al. (2007) found an intervention based on implementation plans to be equally effective as one designed to enhance motivation in relation to children's fruit and vegetable consumption.

Reducing anxiety

One of the barriers to attending screening for risk of disease is anxiety about its outcome: what will be found?

Do I really want to know? Fear may both prevent people engaging in any screening programme (Ackerson and Preston 2009), and be the result of screening (see Chapter 10 ☛). An early example of how easily health anxieties can be evoked can be seen in the findings of Stoate (1989), who reported that around a third of men taking part in a screening programme to detect high blood pressure found to have slightly raised blood pressure on their first assessment, and then found to have normal levels of blood pressure on subsequent measurements, reported significant levels of health anxiety in the subsequent months. This anxiety has been found in a range of subsequent screening programmes, even when screening has found individuals to carry no or low additional risk of disease (e.g. Bolejko et al. 2013; Korfage et al. 2014).

Unfortunately, these anxieties are only now receiving the attention they deserve. However, the best approach to reducing them may involve teaching coping or anxiety management skills (see Chapter 13 ☛). Phelps et al. (2005), for example, found that providing women undergoing assessment of their genetic risk for breast cancer with a leaflet providing simple distraction techniques to help them cope with any worries they may have been experiencing was sufficient to reduce anxiety during the risk assessment process. In another context a study by Marteau et al. (1996) considered the very specific effectiveness of two booklets given to women referred for **colposcopy** following an abnormal **cervical smear**:

1. A coping booklet provided brief information about the procedure they were about to experience, information on the likely outcomes of the procedure, and instructions on relaxation and distraction techniques (see Chapter 13 ☛) they could use to help them to cope before and during the procedure.

> ### colposcopy
> a method used to identify cells that may develop into cancer of the cervix. Sometimes follows a cervical smear if abnormalities are found. A colposcope is a low-power microscope.
>
> ### cervical smear
> smear of cells taken from the cervix to examine for the presence of cell changes indicating risk of cancer.

2. A medical information booklet provided more details on the nature of cervical abnormalities, the procedure and its likely outcomes than the standard information booklet. However, it did not suggest any coping strategies that the women might use.

The results suggested a specific effect of each aspect of the information given. All patients who received the booklets knew more about issues around the colposcopy than a group of patients who received the standard level of information. However, the women who received the medical booklet did not experience any reductions in anxiety as a consequence. By contrast, those patients given the coping booklet were less anxious when they attended the hospital for their operation than those who received either the medical or no booklet.

Using the mass media

Psychology also has much to offer public health initiatives targeted at whole populations, using the mass media. The earliest media campaigns adopted a 'hypodermic' model of behavioural change, which assumed a relatively stable link between knowledge, attitudes and behaviour (something we now know to be somewhat optimistic: see Chapter 5 (☛). The approach assumed that if we could 'inject' appropriate information into the recipients, this would change their attitudes and in turn influence their behaviour. This approach, led by people such as McGuire (e.g. 1985), suggested that the key to success was to make the information persuasive and for it to come from appropriate sources. Defining each of these elements is not easy. What is persuasive for one person may not be for another. Good sources of information may be an 'expert', 'someone like you', a neutral individual or someone clearly linked to the issue, such as a doctor providing health information. Seeing someone affected by a particular condition or who has achieved significant behavioural change can be a much more potent source of information than a neutral person or even an expert. It is much more powerful to see a 34-year-old man explain how smoking caused his lung cancer, for example, than to have the risks of developing lung cancer explained by a doctor who has not been personally affected by the condition. In one study of this phenomenon, Scollay et al. (1992) reported that a lecture to a school audience about the risks of unsafe sex by someone known to be HIV-positive resulted in greater increases in knowledge, less risky attitudes and safer behavioural intentions than a neutral source.

Despite the popularity of media campaigns, a key question is whether they result in any behavioural change. This cannot be taken for granted – nor can the fact that the target audience even notices the campaign. Isolated health campaigns may have little impact. In a typical programme, focusing on attempting to increase levels of exercise in the community, Wimbush et al. (1998) assessed the effect of a mass media campaign in Scotland designed to promote walking. Although 70 per cent of those asked about the campaign were aware of its existence, it had no impact on behaviour. Such limited outcomes have led some to argue that media campaigns are best used to raise awareness of health issues rather than attempts to engender significant behavioural change (Huberty et al. 2012), and that behavioural change is most likely when media campaigns form one element of a multi-modal intervention or when the target behaviour is a one-off or episodic behaviour, such as attending a vaccination or screening clinic (Wakefield et al. 2010).

More positively, the cumulative effects of repeated media campaigns may influence attitudes and behaviour. One example of this can be found in US anti-smoking media advertising which has campaigned against smoking consistently over many years. Such advertising has two key goals: first, to be noticed and, second, to influence knowledge, attitudes and behaviour. The programmes seem to have achieved both goals (Bala et al. 2008). In Massachusetts, for example, over half the population noticed anti-smoking advertisements at least weekly for a period of three years (Biener et al. 2000). Exposure to anti-smoking advertising at this level was associated with increases in the perceived harm of smoking, and stronger intentions not to smoke (Emery et al. 2007). It may also impact on smoking rates. McVey and Stapleton (2000) calculated that an 18-month-long British anti-smoking advertising campaign resulted in a 1.2 per cent reduction in smoking levels. Again showing the benefits of long-term advertising, Hyland et al. (2006) found a 10 per cent increase in the likelihood that people would quit smoking for every '5000 units of exposure' to anti-smoking television advertising over a two-year period. Even more dramatic results have been reported in programmes specifically targeted at young people and which place the advertising within a more complex intervention. Zucker et al. (2000) reported that their US 'truth'

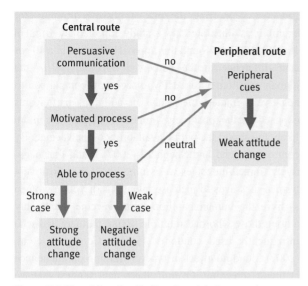

Figure 7.1 The elaboration likelihood model of persuasive communication

(anti-tobacco marketing) campaign, which involved 'in-school education, enforcement, a school-based youth organisation, community based organisations, and [...] an aggressive, well funded, counter-advertising programme' resulted in a 19 per cent reduction in smoking among middle-school students, and an 8 per cent reduction among high-school students. It seems that the level of exposure is highly influential in terms of its impact.

Despite, or perhaps because of, these successes, those involved in using the media to influence behaviour have adopted a number of methods to maximise its effectiveness, including:

- refining communication to maximise its influence on attitudes;
- the use of fear messages;
- information framing;
- specific targeting of interventions.

Refining the message

The elaboration likelihood model discussed in the previous chapter has been subject to a number of experimental tests. The majority of these (e.g. Flynn et al. 2011) have shown that information containing carefully chosen peripheral cues can facilitate attitudinal change in people who are relatively unmotivated to consider particular issues, or that combining central processing with peripheral cues can enhance the effectiveness of some

interventions. Kirby et al. (1998), for example, showed women two health messages about mammography involving both central and peripheral cues. They systematically varied the number of each type of cue over four messages embedded as advertisements in a television talk show. Women who reported a high involvement in the issue reported stronger intentions to seek mammography than those with low involvement, regardless of the presence of central arguments or peripheral cues. By contrast, women with a low involvement in the issue were more likely to report strong intentions to seek mammography if they had been exposed to high levels of favourable peripheral cues than if they had not.

Whether these attitudinal changes result in behavioural change is less clear. Drossaert et al. (1996) found this not to be the case. Again, in the context of attempts to increase attendance at mammography, they made two versions of a leaflet designed to increase attendance. The main arguments were the same in each leaflet, but one leaflet had low levels of peripheral cues and the other had high levels. Attendance rates of women exposed to the differing leaflets sent out with the invitation to attend did not differ, suggesting that there was little or no benefit from adding peripheral cues to their leaflets. Perhaps this is the real limitation of the ELM and other models of attitude change. They can suggest means of maximising attitudinal change, but many other factors will influence whether any attitudinal change or even behavioural intentions are translated into action (see Chapter 5 ☞ for a discussion of the relationship between attitudes and behaviour).

The use of fear

There are good theoretical and empirical reasons to suggest that interventions based entirely on fear arousal are likely to be of little benefit (see Chapter 6 ☞). The limitations of this approach can be demonstrated in both the UK and Australian governments' early attempts to change sexual practices in response to the development of HIV/AIDS. Both countries used high-fear messages, including visual images of the chipping of a gravestone with the words AIDS (in the UK) and a celestial bowling alley in which a 'grim reaper' representing HIV bowled down families and children (in Australia). These were associated with portentous messages declaring the need to avoid HIV infection and to use safer sex practices. The Australian advert can be watched on YouTube (www.youtube.com/watch?v=U219eUIZ7Qo). Both campaigns increased HIV-related anxiety in audiences that saw them, but they neither increased knowledge about HIV/AIDS nor triggered any behavioural change (Sherr 1987; Rigby et al. 1989). Subsequent fear-based messages have also failed to promote appropriate behavioural change, and may even increase feelings of shame and scepticism relating to the issues being addressed (Slavin et al. 2007).

If fear messages *are* used, they need to be accompanied with simple, easily accessible strategies of reducing the fear. A simple example of this can be found in warnings of risk for skin cancer on Australian beaches being accompanied by access to free sunscreen. Witte and Allen (2000), for example, concluded that high threat/fear appeal should be accompanied by an equally high-efficacy message, and that the stronger the levels of fear evoked, the more likely the individual is to produce strong fear-defensive responses – the outcome of which is the maintenance of the old behaviour rather than behavioural change. Further cautionary data stem from Earl and Albarracin's (2007) meta-analysis of HIV-specific fear appeals from a sample including 150 treatment groups. These data indicated that receiving fear-inducing arguments increased perceptions of risk but decreased knowledge and condom use. By contrast, resolving fear through HIV counselling and testing both decreased perceptions of risk and increased knowledge and condom use. More subtly, Brengman et al. (2010) found that different groups of individuals responded differentially to different elements of fear-based messages designed to increase physical exercise in sedentary employees. One group was responsive to both threat and efficacy appeals, one to threat alone, and one to efficacy alone.

Information framing

A more neutral approach to the development of health messages involves 'framing' the message. Health messages can be framed in either positive (stressing positive outcomes associated with action) or negative terms (emphasising negative outcomes associated with failure to act). While some have argued that negative frames are more memorable, others have suggested that positive messages enhance information processing. This may particularly be the case when time is short and individuals are not highly motivated to receive a message. But the evidence can be conflicting, and complex to interpret.

Evidence supporting the use of positive framing, for example, is illustrated by a study reported by Bigman et al. (2010), who found this approach resulted in a 40 per cent difference in the perceived effectiveness of the human papillomavirus (HPV) vaccine in comparison to negatively framed messages. In addition, participants exposed to the positively framed message were more likely to support the public availability of the vaccine. By contrast, Gerend and Shepherd (2007) found that negatively framed messages were more likely than positively framed messages to increase intentions of young women to have the human papillomavirus vaccine – but only among those who had multiple sexual partners and who infrequently used condoms. Finally, Consedine et al. (2007) found no effect of type of framing on attendance at breast screening. Overall, these data suggest that we can make no strong *a priori* judgements about what type of framing will affect particular populations – emphasising the need to test out any intervention as a pilot before it is finally aired in public. These conclusions have been supported by a number of meta-analyses that have found non-significant differences in the effectiveness of either loss- or gain-framed approaches in changing behaviours as varied as safer-sex behaviours, skin cancer prevention behaviours, or diet and nutrition behaviours (e.g. O'Keefe and Jensen 2007).

Audience targeting

Early attempts to influence behaviour via the mass media frequently targeted whole populations, whether their targets or messages were relevant or not. Media attempts to influence sexual behaviour illustrate the point. Early media approaches promoting safer sex, as noted above, were based on fear messages, and the same messages were received by all, whether they were elderly, non-sexually active widows and widowers or young sexually active gay men enjoying multiple partners. The outcome of such an approach was the raising of unnecessary fears among a group of people for whom HIV/AIDS had little immediate relevance, while not speaking the language of, or giving relevant advice to, the groups for whom it was most relevant. Now, media messages on sexual behaviour are more carefully targeted and use the language of their differing target audiences, making them much more effective.

Audience targeting can be based on a number of factors, including behaviour, age, gender and socio-economic status – each of which is likely to influence the impact of any message (Flynn et al. 2007). The change4life (https://smarttools.change4life.co.uk) campaign in the UK, for example, has targeted several thousand families with children aged 5–11 years, sending each family a questionnaire and sending back an individual action plan to enhance their children's health. Interventions may even be developed by the target audience. Bethune and Lewis (2009) aimed to increase Maori women's use of cervical screening services and used focus groups with 'priority women' and other key informants to identify the key messages likely to influence their behaviour. The intervention worked, and resulted in an increase from 7 to 13 per cent in screening uptake over a one-year period. The relative cost-effectiveness of this intervention is clear. A simple example of the social targeting process is afforded by the Terrence Higgins Trust leaflet in Photo 7.1, which would be considered outrageous by many, but fits the profile of its target audience – young, sexually active gay men – well.

Audiences may also be segmented along more psychological factors, such as their motivation to consider change. A worksite exercise programme reported by Peterson and Aldana (1999), for example, involved attempts to increase levels of participation in exercise among 527 corporate employees who either received written messages tailored to their reported stage of change or general information about exercise. Six weeks after the material was received, participants who received the tailored, stage-based messages increased their activity by 13 per cent and were more likely to shift towards contemplating change than those receiving general

Photo 7.1 An example of a health promotion leaflet targeted at gay men – with a sense of humour – encouraging them to have three vaccinations against hepatitis, produced by the Terrence Higgins Trust

Source: Terrence Higgins Trust.

information. A similar intervention reported a comparable effect one year after the intervention, but only in women (Plotnikoff et al. 2007). An interesting study reported by Griffin-Blake and DeJoy (2006) compared a

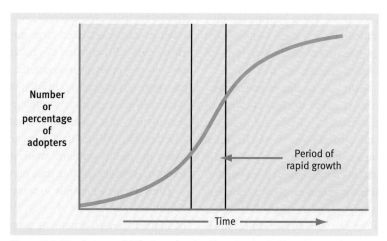

Figure 7.2 The S curve of diffusion, showing the rate of adoption of innovations over time

stage-matched intervention and a social cognitive intervention focusing on self-efficacy, outcome expectancies and goal satisfaction (see Chapter 5 ☛). Both interventions proved equally effective in increasing physical activity within their target group of college employees.

Environmental interventions

Behaviour and behaviour change do not occur in isolation from the environment in which they occur. The health belief model (Becker et al. 1977; see Chapter 5 ☛) provides a simple guide to key environmental factors that can be influenced in order to encourage behavioural change. In particular, the model suggests that an environment that encourages healthy behaviour should:

● provide cues to action or remove cues to unhealthy behaviour;

● enable healthy behaviour by minimising the costs and barriers associated with it;

● maximise the costs of engaging in health-damaging behaviour.

Cues to action

Two key areas where cues have been used to either decrease unhealthy behaviour or increase health-promoting behaviour involve information provided at the time of purchase: health warnings on cigarettes and nutritional information on food. These approaches may be of some benefit, although the evidence suggests that they reinforce existing behaviour rather than prompt consideration of behavioural change.

Part of this lack of effect may be due to poor understanding of the issues raised and/or the low visibility of such cues. Cowburn and Stockley (2005), for example, in a review of over a hundred relevant papers, reported that many people in the general public, and particularly those on low incomes, did not understand or were uninterested in the nutritional information on food packaging. One South African study (Jacobs et al. 2010), for example, reported that the vast majority of the respondents to their survey only took notice of the expiry date of the food. Nutritional information was considered far less

important, with participants favouring taste and price over nutritional content. In addition, many participants did not understand the information provided and were therefore unable to use it to inform health-related decisions. Similarly, Krukowski et al. (2006) found that just under half their sample of US college students looked at food labels, or said they would not use the information of food labels even if available. It is possible that the information provided on food packaging is now simply too complex to be of value in triggering appropriate behaviours for most people: simpler messages (low fat, high fibre, and so on) may be much more effective.

Much of the literature on smoking advertising is now historical, due to the increasing bans on smoking advertising and changes in cigarette packaging in many countries. However, it provides a good example of what may or may not work in other countries and contexts. Borland (1997) evaluated the effect of the introduction of larger and clearer health warnings on cigarette packets in Australia by comparing self-reported responses to health warnings in two surveys between which the new warnings were introduced. Before the changes were initiated, 37 per cent of respondents reported noticing the health warning. Following increases in its size, 66 per cent reported noticing it. The numbers refraining from smoking as a result of the warning rose from 7 to 14 per cent. A significant impact can also be obtained by using graphic imagery rather than written text (Thrasher et al. 2007). The present trend across some countries to enforce standard packaging of cigarettes also appears to be of benefit. Its relatively recent enforcement means that its health consequences are yet to be determined. However, it does appear to have reduced the appeal of cigarettes. In December 2012, for example, Australia introduced drab olive green packets with large graphic health warnings. Brose et al. (2014) found this packaging was less appealing and less likely to motivate the purchase of cigarettes than previous packaging. In addition, smokers using them were seen as less attractive, and the taste of cigarettes was considered less pleasant. Similarly, Moodie and Mackintosh (2013) found smokers were less likely to avoid the health warning, smoked less, and were more likely to consider quitting than previously.

Cues reminding people to engage in health-promoting behaviours may also be of value. One simple example can be found in posters reminding people to use stairs instead of lifts or escalators. Webb and Eves (2007) found that posters encouraging people to use the stairs instead of a nearby escalator in a shopping centre resulted in a near doubling of stair use. The same research team found that overweight individuals were more likely to respond to the signs than individuals of more average weight, suggesting this may be a simple but effective way of increasing fitness among this group. These individuals may also act as models, encouraging others to climb the stairs rather than use the escalator, while those who do walk up the stairs are more likely to continue walking up subsequent stairs (e.g. Webb et al. 2011).

Environmental cues not only act as prompts to healthy behaviour, conversely they can also act as reminders to behave in unhealthy ways. Frequent exposure to relevant advertising, for example, has been shown to increase perceptions of the prevalence of smoking (Burton et al. 2010) as well as increase cigarette (Sargent et al. 2000) and alcohol use (Smith and Foxcroft 2009) among young people. Accordingly, those involved in public health frequently strive to limit and legislate against such things as tobacco and alcohol advertising. The UK government, for example, banned television advertising of tobacco in 1965 and totally banned its advertising from 2003. How effective this approach has been appears to differ across countries. Quentin et al. (2007) reported that total bans on advertising of tobacco products were associated with mixed reductions in consumption. Of the 18 studies they reviewed from various countries, only 10 reported a significant reduction in smoking following the ban; two studies suggested a partial ban on advertising had little or no effect. Of course, advertising is not the only media influence on attitudes about health-related behaviour, some of which may be less supportive of appropriate behavioural change. The portrayal of alcohol consumption in films, music videos and soap operas, for example, has been shown to influence the onset and progression of consumption among young people (Koorderman et al. 2012). The net impact of these images and messages is that any health advertising is competing against a background of complex and influential processes. Any gains should therefore be applauded.

Minimising the costs of healthy behaviour

The environment in which we live can either facilitate or inhibit our level of engagement in health-related behaviour. Poor street lighting, busy roads and high levels of pollution may inhibit some inner-city dwellers from taking exercise such as jogging or cycling; shops that sell healthy foods but which are a long way from housing estates may result in more use of local shops that sell less healthy foodstuffs, and so on. Making the environment safe and supportive of healthy activity presents a challenge to town planners and governments. Such an environment should promote safety, provide opportunities for social integration and give the population control over key aspects of their lives.

A number of projects, under the rubric of the 'Healthy Cities movement' (World Health Organization 1988), have attempted to design city environments in ways that promote the mental and physical health of their inhabitants. The movement initially involved cities in industrialised countries, but is now expanding to include cities in industrialising countries such as Bangladesh, Tanzania, Nicaragua and Pakistan. To be a member of the movement, cities have to develop a city health profile and involve citizen and community groups. Priorities for action include attempts to reduce health inequalities as a result of socio-economic factors (see Chapter 2 ☞), traffic control, tobacco control, and care of the elderly and those with mental health problems (Kickbusch 2003). Unfortunately, while very laudable, this rather broad set of strategies has proved difficult to translate into measurable and concrete action. Indeed, as recently as 2006, O'Neill and Simard (2006) were still writing discussion papers on how to evaluate the effectiveness of the, by then, 20-year-old programme, while Ison (2009) reported the recent introduction of a common measure of health impact to be used in its assessment. Nevertheless, where appropriate measures have been used and appropriate environmental changes made, this does seem to influence health behaviour. Jago et al. (2005), for example, found that levels of low-intensity exercise were greater among male adolescents when there was good street lighting, safe areas for jogging or walking, well-maintained pavements, and the presence of trees.

More specific studies have shown that environmental manipulations aimed at minimising the costs of engaging in exercise may result in significant change. Linegar et al. (1991), for example, took advantage of the unusual context of a completely closed community of a naval base to manipulate both its physical and organisational environment. They established cycle paths, provided exercise equipment and organised exercise clubs and competitions within the base. In addition, they gave workers 'release time' from other duties while they participated in exercise. Not surprisingly, perhaps, this combination of interventions resulted in significant increases in exercise, even among people who had not previously exercised. This combination of approaches is rarely possible, but the results indicate what is possible when there is the freedom to manipulate a wide range of environmental factors.

A more realistic programme, intended to increase levels of exercise among women in a suburb of Sydney, was reported by Wen et al. (2002). It targeted women aged between 20 and 50 through a marketing campaign and increasing opportunities for participation in exercise. The marketing included establishing community walking events, and initiating walking groups and community physical activity classes. Local council members were invited onto the project group to raise the profile of the project with council members and to ensure that the project fitted within the council's social and environmental plans. Pre- and post-project telephone surveys indicated a 6.4 per cent reduction in the proportion of sedentary women in the local population, as well as an increased commitment to promoting physical activity by the local council. Overall, programmes including those establishing and improving cycle lanes, alone or in combination with high-profile cycling initiatives, do seem to achieve modest increases in the level of cycling across many countries (Yang et al. 2010).

Another area where the costs of healthy behaviour have been considered is that of needle-exchange schemes for injecting drug users. Needle-exchange schemes exchange old for new needles, preventing the need for sharing and reducing the risk of cross-infection of blood-borne viruses, including HIV and hepatitis. Where syringes cannot legally be obtained elsewhere, they are effective. Kerr et al. (2010), for example, reported reductions in needle borrowing from 20 to 9 per cent of respondents in a sample of 1,228 injecting drug users in British Columbia, which was associated with a significantly lower risk of contracting HIV. This reduction in the use of shared needles has been associated with a reduction in risk of disease transmission. Bramson et al. (2015), for example, reported significantly lower rates of HIV infection among intravenous drug users in areas of the USA where they could access needle-exchange programmes than where they were unavailable.

Increasing the costs of unhealthy behaviour

Making unhealthy behaviour difficult in some way (often through pricing) can act as a barrier to unhealthy behaviour and a facilitator of healthy behaviour. Economic measures related to public health have been largely confined to taxation on tobacco and alcohol. The

---

IN THE SPOTLIGHT

The binge drinking epidemic

Despite some reductions in the consumption of alcohol throughout the population, many countries have significant levels of binge drinking, particularly among young people. This phenomenon has been reported, for example, in the UK, New Zealand, Australia, an area known as the vodka belt (Russia and other countries where vodka is the primary drink), but is less prevalent in South America and southern Europe. The causes of this behaviour are not fully understood, but the availability of cheap alcohol in supermarkets, clubs and pubs – and the culture of drinking while standing – is widely recognised as

contributing to the phenomenon. The drinking culture contributes to significant personal harm, as well as having a substantial economic and social impact on the affected communities. Some cities have increased policing in response to the social problems. Some have made bars contribute to the cost of this policing. But one French town took their approach a stage further. They bought the bars! The city of Renne, in Brittany, has bought two bars in the centre of town and converted one into a DVD shop, and one into a restaurant in an attempt to reduce alcohol consumption in its centre. Time will tell whether this impacts on alcohol consumption . . . but you have to admit, it's a pretty bold approach to health promotion!

price of alcohol impacts on levels of consumption, although its impact is greater among moderate than heavy drinkers – nevertheless, even among this group, price still does have a modest impact on consumption (Wagenaar et al. 2009).

Increases in tobacco taxation may also be the most effective measure in reducing levels of cigarette smoking. Hu et al. (1995) modelled the relative effectiveness of taxation and media campaigns on tobacco consumption in California. They estimated that a 25 per cent tax increase would result in a reduction in sales of 819 million cigarette packs, compared with 232 million packs likely to result from media influences. Taxation seems to be a particularly effective deterrent among young people, who are three times more likely to be affected by price rises than older adults (Ding 2003).

While prohibition may be seen as a necessary barrier by some, others have called for more modest barriers to availability. One approach involves restricting the number of outlets for drugs such as alcohol. This increases transaction 'costs' as people have to travel further and make more effort to purchase their alcohol, and in reduced cues to consumption from advertising in shop windows and other signs. Connor et al. (2010) found this approach to achieve modest gains, with more geographically widespread off-sales outlets across New Zealand being associated with less binge drinking and alcohol-related harm; there was no association between outlet density and frequency of 'sensible' drinking. By contrast, increasing availability – as occurred in Sweden after stopping its restriction of Saturday opening of alcohol retail shops – may result in an increase in consumption (Norström and Skog 2005).

A more direct form of control over smoking has been the introduction of smoke-free work and social areas. These clearly reduce smoking in public places – and may impact on smoking elsewhere. Heloma and Jaakalo (2003) found that secondary smoke inhalation levels fell among non-smokers, while smoking prevalence rates at work fell from 30 per cent to 25 per cent following a national smoke-free workplace law. Following a ban on smoking in Norwegian bars and restaurants, Braverman et al. (2007) reported significant reductions in the prevalence of daily smoking, daily smoking at work by bar workers, number of cigarettes smoked by continuing smokers, and the number of cigarettes smoked at work by continuing smokers.

Even more encouraging are emerging data suggesting that such bans can positively impact on health. Although they do not provide absolute proof of an association between reduced smoking and reduced disease, a number of studies have now shown reductions in the number of admissions to hospital with myocardial infarction both in the USA (e.g. Herman and Walsh 2010) and Europe (Cesaroni et al. 2008) since the ban was implemented. Of particular note is that there appears to be a reduction in smoking-related conditions among people, such as bar staff directly affected by the ban (e.g. Larsson et al. 2008), and even those indirectly affected by it. Been et al. (2014), for example, reviewed eleven recent studies of the effects of second-hand smoke exposure by children, and found significant reductions in premature births, low birth-weight children and asthma directly attributable to smoke-free legislation.

Public health programmes

So far, we have looked at some broad approaches to behavioural change in large populations, and some of the underlying principles that underpin them. The next sections of this chapter examine how these, and some other, approaches have been used in public health programmes targeted at whole populations and more specific target groups within them. We consider a number of differing target populations, the approaches that have been used to change their behaviour, the theoretical models that have guided the interventions, and their effectiveness.

Community intervention programmes

Some of the first public health programmes targeted at whole towns aimed to reduce the prevalence of key risk factors for CHD (smoking, low levels of exercise, high fat consumption and high blood pressure) across the entire adult population. The first of these, known as the Stanford Three Towns project (Farquhar et al. 1977), provided three towns in California with three levels of intervention.

The first town received no intervention. The second received a year-long media campaign targeting CHD-related behaviour. Although the media programme

Photo 7.2 Making ways of achieving exercise easy and cheap to access may both increase health and save the environment

Source: Shutterstock.com/Veniamin Kraskov.

preceded the stages of change model (Prochaska and di Clemente 1984; see Chapter 6 ☞) by some years, it followed a programme very similar to that suggested by that model. It started by alerting people to the need to change their behaviour (itself a relatively novel message in the early 1970s). This was followed by a series of programmes modelling behaviour change – for example, by broadcasting films of people attending a smoking-cessation group or showing cooking skills. These were based on social learning theory (Bandura 1977; see Chapters 5 and 6 ☞) and were aimed at teaching skills and increasing recipients' confidence in their ability to change and maintain change of their own behaviour. This phase was followed by further slots reminding people to maintain any behavioural changes they had made, and showing images of people enjoying the benefits of behavioural change, such as a family enjoying a healthy picnic (potentially impacting on attitudes and perceived social norms). In the third town, this media intervention was targeted at a group of individuals at particularly high risk of developing CHD and their partners. They received one-to-one education on risk behaviour change and were asked to disseminate their knowledge through their social networks. This strategy provided another channel for disseminating information – through the use of people given the role of opinion leaders – and aimed

at increasing motivation in both people at high risk of disease and the general public.

Accordingly, there were three levels of intervention, each of which was expected to result in a stepwise increase in effectiveness (see Table 7.1). The expected outcomes were found. By the end of the one-year programme, scores on a measure of CHD-risk status based on factors including blood pressure, smoking and cholesterol level indicated that average risk scores among the general population actually rose in the control town, while they fell significantly among the general population who received the media campaign alone, and fell to an even greater extent among those who lived in the town that received the combined intervention. After a further year, risk scores in the intervention towns were still significantly lower than those of the control town, although because scores in the media-only town continued to improve, ultimately there was no difference between the scores of the two intervention towns (Farquhar et al. 1990a).

The European equivalent of this programme was established in North Karelia in Finland (Puska et al. 1985). This five-year programme differed slightly from the Stanford approach in that, in addition to a media approach, it also changed environmental factors, encouraging local meat manufacturers and butchers to promote

Table 7.1 The three levels of intervention in the Stanford Three Towns project

Approach	What it involved	Expected effect
Ongoing public health activity	A minimal intervention 'comparison' town	+/−
Year-long media campaign	Phase 1: alerting people to the need to change Phase 2: modelling change Phase 3: modelling continued change	+
Media campaign + high-risk intervention	Media as influence combined with dissemination of knowledge from lay experts	++

low-fat products, encouraging 'no smoking' restaurants, and so on. It was generally considered to be a success, with reductions in a number of risk factors including blood pressure, cholesterol levels and smoking among men. However, its final summary paper showed that these reductions in risk factors were not consistently better than those in a control area, which received no intervention.

Unfortunately, this apparent lack of success has been repeated in a number of subsequent large-scale interventions. A second study conducted around Stanford, called the Five City project (Farquhar et al. 1990b), for example, combined its previous media approach with an increased emphasis on community-initiated education and environmental interventions similar to the Karelia intervention. In a cohort followed for the duration of the intervention, the general population in the intervention area showed improvements in cholesterol levels, fitness and rates of obesity in the early stages of the intervention. However, by its end, the only differences between a comparison area that did not receive the intervention and the intervention areas were on measures of blood pressure and smoking (the latter being perhaps the most important risk behaviour due to its links with so many other diseases). On this criterion, the intervention could be considered a modest success. But unfortunately, a series of cross-sectional studies comparing the control and intervention areas over time found no difference in smoking and risk levels for CHD at any time during the course of the programme, calling into question the programme's success.

A final US intervention to be considered here used virtually all the approaches so far considered in this and the previous chapter. The Minnesota Heart Health programme (Jacobs et al. 1986) used the mass media to promote awareness and to reinforce other educational approaches. In addition, the programme established large-scale screening programmes in primary care settings, as well as a number of other interventions including telephone support, classes in the community and worksite, self help materials and home correspondence programmes. Environmental interventions included healthy food labelling (low fat, high fibre, etc.), establishing healthy menus in restaurants, smoke-free areas in public and work areas, and increased physical recreation facilities. Despite this complex and sophisticated approach, the programme had surprisingly little impact on health and health behaviour. Levels of smoking in the intervention differed little from those in the control areas, while the average adult weight in both control and intervention areas rose over the course of the study by seven pounds. Similar findings were found for another intervention known as the Community Intervention Trial for Smoking Cessation (COMMIT Research Group 1995), which did not change heavy smokers' behaviour and had only a marginal effect on light smokers.

At first glance, these data are clearly disappointing. Indeed, they provide little encouragement to suggest that the approaches they used should be continued. However, before they are dismissed, it is important to contextualise their findings. First, apart from the original Stanford study, they occurred at a time when there were significant changes in health behaviour and disease throughout the countries in which the studies were conducted. Rates of CHD fell by 20 per cent over the time they were running (Lefkowitz and Willerson 2001), and there was a general increase in health-promoting behaviour and a concomitant fall in health-damaging behaviour such as smoking. Why did these changes occur, and what implications do they have for interpretation of the results of the large-scale programmes considered above?

Perhaps the experiences of the five-year Heartbeat Wales programme (Tudor-Smith et al. 1998) sum up those of all the programmes so far considered. This programme combined health education via the media with health screening and environmental changes designed to promote behavioural change. These included some of the first food labelling (low fat, low sugar, etc.) in the UK, establishing exercise trails in local parks, no-smoking areas in restaurants, the promotion of low-alcohol beers in bars, and so on. It also used doctors and nurses as opinion leaders within their own communities to argue the case for adopting healthy lifestyles. Remember that the interventions in each programme were compared with 'control' areas: areas that did not receive the intervention. However, these were not true 'control' areas in the sense that they received no intervention at all; rather they received whatever local health education programmes were being conducted at the time. In addition, any innovations conducted by these major research programmes could not be guaranteed to remain only in the intervention area. In the case of Heartbeat Wales, for example, its 'control' area was in the northeast of England, which itself was subject to large-scale heart health programmes conducted in England at the same time as Heartbeat Wales. It was certainly not a 'no intervention' control. In addition, innovations such as food labelling, originally conducted just in Wales, spread through to England via supermarkets such as Tesco over the course of the programme. It is perhaps not surprising, therefore, that although levels of risk factors for CHD fell in Wales over the five-year period of Heartbeat Wales, they did not fall any further than levels in the control area. The research programme essentially compared the effectiveness of two fairly similar interventions.

The majority of information about heart disease is now probably provided by the mass media as part of its general reporting: discussion of healthy diets, issues such as men's health, and so on. It is therefore increasingly difficult for any public health programme to add further to this information and result in a meaningful reduction in risk for CHD. Interestingly, however, when community interventions are run in countries with a relatively short or limited experience of public health programmes, the same positive results are found as in the initial Stanford Study. Jiang et al. (2013), for example, found a two-year community-based intervention in China which involved interventions including those identified in Table 7.2 reduced levels of smoking, and increased levels of exercise compared with those in a control area. Significant gains in healthy eating were made in both intervention and control areas. It appears this type of intervention can be effective, but only in certain contexts and at certain times in the cycle of population knowledge of CHD and the background availability of health-promoting environmental factors.

Reducing risk of HIV infection

In contrast to interventions targeted at CHD, those targeted at sexual behaviour in relation to HIV and AIDS appear to have been more successful across industrialised (Simoni et al. 2011) and developing (Medley et al. 2009) countries. Johnson et al. (2008), for example, reported reductions of between 40 and 54 per cent on

Table 7.2 Examples of multilevel interventions used by Jiang et al. (2013)

Level	Examples of interventions
Individual	● Distributing health-related messages through various channels; ● Distributing tools for a healthy lifestyle including salt spoons and oil pots; ● Providing free disease screening and risk assessment for cardiovascular disease; ● Providing physical fitness testing;
Social environment	● Encouraging health professionals to screen and give prescriptions for health; ● Starting a walking club; Increasing positive interaction between parents and children to promote healthy lifestyle;
Physical environment	● Implementing a smoke-free worksite initiative; ● Implementing and enforcing smoking bans and restrictions in public areas; ● Using point-of-decision prompts to increase stair use; ● Organising work-break exercises, sports competitions, mountain-climbing events and sports interest groups; ● Building walking trails with stone distance markers along the canal and in the community park; ● Building health theme parks; Initiation of a public bicycle service system; ● Healthy cooking intervention in restaurants and workplace cafeteria; ● Making health-related or calorie information of foods available to consumers;
Policy environment	● Smoke control ordinance in public places; ● Policy and planning for healthy city movement and enhancing public transportation.

Source: Jiang et al. (2013).

IN THE SPOTLIGHT

To vaccinate or not vaccinate? That should not have been the question

All too frequently, uncontrollable forces may actively interfere with public health programmes . Despite multiple medical information campaigns, South Wales experienced a child measles epidemic in 2013 because many parents were reluctant to vaccinate their child. They believed this would increase his or her risk for autism, following publicity given to spurious findings of a now discredited researcher and their promulgation by a local activist. But this experience is hardly unique. Sensible drinking messages are countered by portrayal of alcohol as glamorous or a means of stress reduction from adverts, television programmes, and the media in general. Healthy eating messages can be confused and confusing: Fat is bad for you; fat is not that bad for you;

don't substitute fat for sugar; sugar kills, cholesterol is less problematic than we used to think; eat five portions of fruit and vegetable a day; eat seven portions, but mostly vegetables. Information on the contents of food are also often complex and difficult to understand. Recommendations of healthy exercise levels are gradually shifting lower and lower: because of changing evidence, or because of the failure to encourage appropriate levels of the higher exercise demands? Those involved in public health are caught between a range of influences: new research that may change health recommendations, the need to make complex messages simple and doable, or the additional demands of more sophisticated recipients of health information. How all these various factors are integrated into the development of public health campaigns is a complex and demanding process and one that is clearly difficult to achieve.

measures of the frequency of unprotected sex following community-level interventions targeted at gay men.

Many of these positive outcomes have been achieved using an approach called peer education which has successfully been used across the world (Simoni et al. 2011). In this approach, opinion leaders and other key players within specific communities are involved in projects and form a key part of the programme. The approach draws upon social learning and diffusion theory, as these individuals provide particularly strong role models of change within a specific community. Using people known and respected within a particular community makes their message salient and shows that appropriate change can be achieved. In one of the first studies using this approach, Kelly et al. (1992) tried to increase levels of safer sexual behaviour among patrons of gay bars in three small southern US cities. They identified and recruited key individuals in these bars and trained them to talk to patrons on issues of risk behaviour change and to distribute relevant health education literature. Following this intervention, levels of high-risk sexual behaviour fell by between 15 and 29 per cent. In a larger community trial conducted by the same team

in eight US cities (Kelly et al. 1997), levels of unprotected anal intercourse fell from 32 to 20 per cent among men frequenting gay bars in the intervention group – in contrast to a 2 per cent rise among those in the control cities. Amirkhanian et al. (2005) found this approach translated to East Europe, examining its impact in Russia and Bulgaria, with similar results to those found in the USA. In addition, more formal peer counselling, within clinics and involving a formal referral process has also been found to reduce sexually risky behaviour (McKirnan et al. 2010).

Merzel and D'Afflitti (2003) noted that the HIV/AIDS prevention programmes have been markedly more successful than those targeted at CHD. Why this should be the case is unclear. Perhaps the most obvious difference between the interventions was the use of peers by those involved in HIV prevention; working *with* specific groups of people rather than trying to impose change from without. This may have been a crucial factor. Janz et al. (1996), for example, conducted a process evaluation of 37 AIDS prevention programmes and concluded that the use of trained community peers whose life circumstances closely resembled those of the target population was one of the most important factors influencing acceptance of health messages. Merzel and D'Afflitti speculated that a second reason for these differences may lie in the natural history of the diseases that each programme was trying to influence. Coronary heart disease develops over time, and there is no marked increase in risk as a result of particular action: 'One bar of chocolate won't do me any harm'. It is therefore relatively easy to minimise risk and put off behaviour change. By contrast, the risks associated with unsafe sex are highly salient. It can take just one unsafe sexual encounter to contract HIV, and the consequences can be catastrophic, so the imperatives of change are much more salient than in CHD.

While the above studies allow comparison of interventions within the same culture, it should not be forgotten that AIDS is a global issue. Given the devastating impact of HIV/AIDS in Africa, interventions here and in other parts of the developing world are of paramount importance. Some approaches mirror those in other countries. Galavotti et al. (2001), for example, described an approach known as the Modeling and Reinforcement to Combat HIV (MARCH), which was used in Africa and was modified from a pre-existing US media approach. The intervention model had two main components: (i) use of the media and (ii) local influences of change. It used the media to provide role models in 'entertainment that educates' by providing information on how to change, and modelling appropriate changes in sexual behaviour. Serial dramas on television were also used to educate, because they involved the viewer emotionally with the action on the screen. This was thought to increase its personal relevance and encouraged viewing. Interpersonal support involved the following: creation of small media materials such as flyers depicting role models progressing through stages of behaviour change for key risk behaviour; the mobilisation of members of the affected community to distribute media materials and reinforce prevention messages, and the increased availability of condoms and bleacher kits for injecting drug users.

In one study of effectiveness of media approaches using these strategies (Vaughan et al. 2000), Radio Tanzania aired a radio soap opera called *Twende Na Wakati* ('Let's go with the times'). This soap played twice weekly for two years with the intention of promoting reproductive health and family planning, and preventing HIV infection. In comparison with an area of Tanzania that did not receive national radio at the time of the study, people who lived in areas where the radio programme was received reported greater commitment to family planning and higher uptake of safer sex practices. In addition, attendance at family planning clinics increased more in the intervention than control area.

Other approaches, both in Africa and other countries, have gone beyond using the media. Asamoah-Adu et al. (1994) engaged prostitutes in Ghana to provide peer education and distribute condoms to their fellow prostitutes, resulting in a significant reduction in unsafe sex. Overall, the women who took part in the intervention were more likely to use a condom than they were prior to the intervention. In addition, three years after the end of the formal programme, women who maintained contact with the project staff were more likely to continue using condoms than those who did not maintain contact. Other, varied, interventions have included legal interventions including the mandatory use of condoms in brothels in Thailand, and economic measures enhancing empowerment of women in a number of African countries in order to reduce their economic dependence on men and increase their ability to negotiate decisions such as the use of contraceptives (see Ross et al. 2006).

Worksite public health

One response to the problems encountered by large-scale population interventions has been to target smaller, more easily accessible and 'controllable' target groups. As such, the past few decades have seen the development of many impressive public health programmes in the workplace. The majority of these have been conducted in the USA, perhaps because enhancing the health of the workforce reduces the cost of workers' health insurance, often paid by the employer, and therefore benefits the company as well as the individuals in it. Interestingly, these interventions may also provide other benefits to the employers: Jensen (2011) concluded that diet-related worksite interventions improved labour efficiency by 1-2 per cent as a result of reduced absenteeism.

Worksite programmes have targeted a range of health-related behaviour, including diet, exercise, smoking and stress (generally focusing on risk factors for CHD and cancer). Because the worksite offers a wide possibility of interventions, a variety of formats have been utilised, including some innovative approaches:

● screening for risk factors for disease;
● providing health education;

- provision of healthy options, such as healthy food in eating areas;
- providing economic incentives for risk behaviour change;
- manipulating social support to facilitate individual risk behaviour change;
- provision of no-smoking areas (and, more recently, smoking rooms) in the work environment.

More succinctly, these may be thought of as interventions which reward healthy lifestyles or punish unhealthy ones. Mujtaba and Cavico (2013) boldly outlined a range of interventions that have been applied in the workplace, placing them into the categories of 'carrot' or 'stick'. Carrots included: (i) providing gyms at work and/or free gym membership, (ii) providing low-fat meals in the cafeteria, or (iii) making employer contributions to health insurance if people have or adopt a healthy lifestyle, have markers of good health (appropriate weight, low cholesterol, and so on), or engage with some sort of behavioural programme in order to improve health. Sticks include: (i) higher health-care insurance premiums for unhealthy employees, (ii) increasing 'deductibles' for employees with unhealthy lifestyles who fail to meet health-care standards, and (iii) not hiring job applicants who are smokers, overweight or otherwise unhealthy.

Mirroring the lack of effectiveness found in primary care, screening employees for CHD risk factors has proven of no real benefit. In a more complex intervention, Sorensen et al. (2010) achieved some success when they provided a bespoke four-month-long education plus telephone counselling programme designed to reduce tobacco use and enhance weight management among blue-collar workers at risk for CHD in 17 US ports. Before running the programme, they ran a number of focus groups to identify particular issues relevant to their work environment which were then incorporated into recruitment materials, intervention messages and, where possible, in the counselling. Of 542 workers invited to participate, half agreed to participate and received at least the first telephone call. By ten-month follow-up, the quit rate was significantly higher among those in the counselling programme than those who did not participate (39 versus 9 per cent). However, they did not make concomitant gains in the weight management programme.

Other, more contextual, programmes have met with mixed success. Perhaps the simplest intervention has been to provide information on the nutritional and calorific content of food provided in dining areas; however, there is no evidence that this simple approach is likely to be successful (Engbers et al. 2006). Accordingly, a number of studies have developed more complex interventions. The Well

Photo 7.3 Attractive healthy food served in the workplace can increase healthy eating rates

Source: Shutterstock.com/CandyBox Images.

Works programme reported by Sorensen et al. (1998) recorded modest improvements in fat, and fruit and vegetable consumption, following a programme in which they combined health education programmes with providing healthy food options. Similarly, the Health Works for Women programme (Campbell et al. 2002) targeted blue-collar women employed in small- to medium-sized workplaces. They provided information on healthy lifestyle behaviour and suggestions on how to change to it, using information tailored to individual participants' needs, determined by questionnaires completed before the intervention. The programme also worked at developing peer support from social networks among the workforce. Despite these complex interventions, they found no long-term changes in fat intake, smoking or physical activity levels among the intervention group. Their only gain was modest increases in self-reported fruit and vegetable intake.

Acknowledging the potential influence of the home as well as work on diet and health, the Treatwell programme (Sorensen et al. 1999) compared two interventions with a minimal intervention control group. An in-work programme involved classes and food demonstrations open to factory workers to teach them about healthy eating, and provided healthy options and food labelling in their worksite eating areas. A second approach combined the in-work programme with a family intervention designed to encourage healthy eating within the home. Total fruit and vegetable intake increased by 19 per cent in the worksite-plus-family group, 7 per cent in the worksite intervention group and 0 per cent in the control group.

The worksite provides more than a simple opportunity for the provision of health education and healthy food options. It gives the opportunity to exert more influence over behaviour than can be achieved elsewhere. One way that employers can influence their workforce is to provide financial incentives for change; to provide an external reward system for appropriate behavioural change rather than relying on employees' personal motivation. These have proven reasonably successful. Glasgow et al. (1993), for example, offered monthly lottery prizes to people in a factory workforce who quit and maintained their no-smoking status for up to one year: 19 per cent of smokers in the workforce took part in the intervention, 20 per cent of whom remained abstinent by the end of the programme. By contrast, Hennrikus et al. (2002) found that financial incentives alone increased levels of entry into a smoking cessation programme, but successful quitting was only achieved if participants could access further support, such as telephone counselling.

The worksite can also provide strong social support for those involved in behavioural change. Koffman et al. (1998) compared a multi-component smoking cessation programme (see Chapter 6 ☞) alone, or combined with either financial incentives for abstinence or a team competition in which groups supported each other in the months following cessation. Six months after initiation of the programme, 23 per cent of those in the multi-component group were abstinent. This contrasted with 41 per cent cessation rates among those who also received the incentive and competition programme. By the one-year follow-up, the equivalent figures were 30 and 37 per cent, respectively. Summarising the data so far, Leeks et al. (2010) found this type of multi-component intervention that combines incentives with other approaches, such as education, smoking-cessation groups and telephone support, to be more successful than incentives alone – and cost-effective for the companies that ran the projects as they reduced the costs of tobacco-related illnesses.

Just as preventing smoking in bars appears to reduce smoking-related harm, preventing people smoking at the worksite will necessarily reduce levels of secondary exposure to cigarette smoke among non-smokers. In addition, the discomfort associated with smoking outside buildings may provide a disincentive for many smokers, which may impact on smoking levels. Longo et al. (2001) certainly found such an effect. They studied the smoking habits of employees in hospitals that became smoke-free and those that continued to permit smoking over a period of three years, and found that twice as many smokers in the non-smoking hospitals quit smoking than did in the hospitals that continued to allow smoking.

WHAT DO YOU THINK?

Worksite health promotion programmes clearly aim to support appropriate health behaviours. But the very nature of some working environments may provide a more complex challenge to our health. Shift work, night shifts, stressful and traumatic incidents as a routine part of work, and the increasing shift towards 'precarious employment', with its inherent financial and time insecurities may all prove deleterious to health. So, we have two competing interests: business, which says such practices are inevitable and necessary, and the health imperative of minimising any negative health impact of work. These type of work structures impact most on workers in the lower socio-economic groups, who may have little choice of where and how they work. So, should employers have a responsibility to consider the health of their workforce when establishing jobs? Or is this a case of 'employee beware': the employees know the risks and choose to take on the jobs; It's their choice, and their health is not their employer's responsibility?

School-based interventions

School brings to mind traditional lessons: passively listening to the teacher providing information relevant to the topic under consideration and a number of public health initiatives have used this type of model. James et al. (2007) reported short- but not long-term gains following educational lessons targeted at health nutrition and weight control. School also provides a context in which health professionals can access students and act as agents of change. Pbert et al. (2006), for example, found that a smoking cessation intervention involving school nurses working with school students resulted in greater (self-report) abstinence rates than with no intervention. School also brings connotations of discipline and control; but whether attempts at control, however harsh, impact on health behaviours is questionable. Evans-Whipp et al. (2010) found that school policies that incorporated a comprehensive smoking ban, harsh and remedial penalties for those caught smoking, as well as more positive strategies had no impact on smoking levels in schools in the USA and Australia.

At a higher, systemic level, simple one-target interventions may be effective, particularly if they target pupils early in school life. In the Netherlands, for example, the *Schoolgruiten* project (Moore et al. 2010) gave 9–10-year-old pupils a free piece of fruit or ready-to-eat vegetables (tomatoes or baby carrots) twice a week in their mid-morning break (thereby not competing with the unhealthy foods that are often preferred by children and available at mealtimes). The aim of this regular exposure was to both increase consumption and encourage a taste preference for fruit. A year after the inception of the project, children in the intervention group, but not their parents, reported they had a higher vegetable intake. By two-year follow-up (Tak et al. 2009), both

children and parents reported higher levels of fruit intake among children in the intervention condition, although there were no differences in vegetable intake. Finally, the children in the intervention condition were more knowledgeable than those in the control condition.

A more complex systemic approach, advocated by the World Health Organization (1996) has produced more mixed results. The WHO health-promoting schools initiative states that schools should prioritise the health of their pupils and develop an integrated approach to enhancing health, preventing uptake of unhealthy behaviour and educating pupils about health-promoting activities. This stops health education from simply being a taught part of the curriculum to something that is central to the aims of the school, and around which school activities and infrastructure are based. The framework which schools involved in this sort of programme typically adopt includes:

- 'healthy policies', such as a 'no helmet, no bike at school' policy for cycle safety or an Australian 'no hat, no play' policy (to avoid sunburn), as well as more traditional policies such as no smoking on school premises and no tolerance of bullying;
- establishing a safe, healthy physical and social environment;
- teaching health-related skills;
- providing adequate health services within the school;
- providing healthy food;
- school-site health-promotion programmes for staff;
- availability of school counselling or psychology programmes;
- a school physical education programme.

This approach has met with limited success, partly perhaps as a result of its complexity and limited uptake and implementation in schools where it has been advocated. In Hong Kong, Lee et al. (2006a) found that schools which had most successfully implemented the various elements of the healthy schools evidenced the greatest improvements in diet and antisocial behaviour. Of particular note was that the scheme was more influential in primary rather than secondary schools. Less optimistically, Schofield et al. (2003) established an intervention involving formal education addressing the health risks associated with smoking. Information leaflets and bi-weekly school newsletters for parents, letters to tobacco retailers, a smoke-free school policy development, encouragement of non-smoking parents, peers and teachers as role models, peer influence programmes and incentive programmes were all utilised. But when compared to schools that had not implemented these elements, no differences in smoking rates were found over a period of two years.

WHAT DO YOU THINK?

Effective sex education provides a powerful influence on sexual behaviour. Countries where sex education is central to the curriculum, starts early and focuses on the social as well as physical aspects of sexual relations have lower unwanted pregnancy rates than countries where the sex education is less central and starts later in the academic curriculum. In the UK, sex education is not compulsory, occurs late in the curriculum and is often taught in one or two lessons independently of the wider curriculum by teachers lacking in relevant expertise. The UK has one of the highest teenage pregnancy rates in Europe. Are these two factors related? Or is there a third (or fourth) hidden factor that explains this association? How would you teach sex education?

Peer education

One final approach to health education in schools involves peer education. As in the social interventions to reduce the spread of HIV described earlier in the chapter, this typically involves training influential pupils in a school about a particular health issue such as smoking, alcohol consumption or HIV education and encouraging them to educate their peers about the issues, hopefully in a way that encourages healthy behaviour. The methods used vary considerably. They may involve teaching whole classes, informal tutoring in unstructured settings, or one-to-one discussion and counselling. In one study of this approach, Lotrean et al. (2010) examined the impact of combining peer-led discussions with teaching cigarette refusal skills in their smoking-prevention programme targeted at 13–14-year-old Romanian school pupils. Compared to a control group who did not receive the intervention, the percentage of pupils to take up smoking was halved in the nine months following the intervention (4.5 versus 9.5 per cent).

A more informal approach to peer education in the context of smoking was reported by Campbell et al. (2008). In their study, pupils aged 12–13 years were asked to identify particularly influential people within their social group. From this list, the intervention team identified a group of people who were particularly influential among the target population: some of whom may not have been the choice of their form teachers! Volunteers from this group were then taken to a hotel for two days, where they were given training in their peer education role. The training gave them information about short-term risks to young people of smoking, and the health, environmental and economic benefits of remaining smoke-free. It also used role-play and small group work to enhance their communication skills, including verbal and non-verbal communication skills and conflict resolution. It aimed to enhance students' personal development, including their confidence and self-esteem, empathy and sensitivity to others, and assertiveness. Following their training days, the peer educators were asked to talk to their friends and anyone else they felt appropriate about smoking, sharing information and advice over a period of 10 weeks. This model of uncontrolled dissemination contrasts strongly with some of the more formal methods adopted by other programmes. Campbell et al. found that students in the control condition were significantly more likely to become a smoker at one- and two-year follow-up, than those who received the intervention and a sub-group of pupils they considered particularly at risk of taking up smoking.

A subsequent unpublished study of the approach used by Campbell et al. focusing on alcohol consumption, unfortunately, failed to have any positive impact. More positively, Cui et al. (2012) reported that, compared to a control condition, peer-led exercise classes led to increases of 20 minutes less sedentary time on each week day and 15 minutes less sedentary time at each weekend day. However, there was no evidence of any changes in moderate to high levels of exercise. In addition, the control condition received no intervention. It is therefore not clear how effective a non-peer intervention would be and how strongly the peer-led intervention would match up to this.

Using new technology

The internet and smart phone technology provide a simple means of communicating with vast numbers of individuals, and have been eagerly appropriated by many of those involved in public health. The difficulties in measuring outcomes and conducting randomised controlled trials in this research context means that many papers simply report usage rather than outcomes. Skov-Ettrup et al. (2014), for example, examined the uptake of a Danish smoking-cessation intervention provided through (i) an internet-based smoking-cessation programme, (ii) 'proactive' telephone counselling (i.e. participants had to call the line themselves), (iii) 'reactive' telephone counselling (i.e. potential participants were called by counsellors) and (iv) a self-help booklet. Uptake of any programme was highest among people aged 40-59 years, women, heavy smokers and those with tertiary education. The most used intervention was the self-help leaflet, accessed by 84 per cent of participants. Uptake of the other interventions was: proactive telephone counselling, 74 per cent; internet, 69 per cent; reactive telephone counselling, 9 per cent. Not surprisingly, younger participants were most likely to access the internet intervention.

Analysis of the effectiveness of internet interventions shows both their reach in terms of the number of people they can potentially access and their effectiveness. Schulz et al. (2014), for example, reported a study with over 5,000 participants in which participants received feedback via the internet on how well they complied with the Dutch guidelines for physical activity, vegetable consumption, fruit consumption, alcohol intake and smoking. They then received tailored motivational feedback on all relevant behaviours, the same feedback but in a sequential flow addressing one behaviour at a time, or no further intervention. The results were presented as a summary statistic of health behaviour, which showed significant gains compared to the control condition for both interventions, and in particular the sequential approach. Importantly, greater gains were made following sequential feedback on difficult to change behaviours: cigarette smoking, alcohol consumption.

In contrast to the previous study, which based its evidence on self-report data, Dallery et al. (2013) based their intervention and its outcome on behaviourally validated outcomes. In a much smaller study, they asked participants in an online smoking cessation intervention to use internet video to confirm that the level of carbon dioxide in their breath was low enough to indicate they were not smoking cigarettes. In their 'contingent reinforcement' condition, those that achieved this criterion received a small monetary voucher. In their 'non-contingent reinforcement' condition, participants received the same monetary voucher simply for continuing to take part in the intervention. Validated non-smoking rates during the intervention were 68 and 25 per cent respectively. There were continued gains at three- and six-month follow-up, although neither intervention proved superior by this time. Other exciting approaches that show the flexibility of the internet include an Australian study that allowed people to 'photoage' a photograph of themselves to see how they would look in the future as a smoker and a non-smoker (Burford et al. 2013) and asking school students (as part of the intervention) to develop health-promoting videos that were 'novel and more effective interventions promoting healthy lifestyle behaviours' for inclusion in a website (Simmons et al. 2013).

A second increasingly used technology is that of texting. Text messages can be used to remind people of the need to change, provide skills and prompts to engage in change, and record any behavioural change; these interventions have proven effective. In a meta-analysis on data from 19 studies across a range of countries, Head et al. (2013) concluded that text messaging was broadly successful in engendering behavioural change. They were most effective for smoking cessation and increasing physical activity, and when they were personalised to the individuals involved. A more recent study to explore the benefits of text messaging was reported by Naughton et al. (2014). This considered whether personalised text messages could add to the gains made in a primary-care smoking-cessation intervention. Interestingly, there were no immediate benefits to the texting, but at six-month follow-up those who had received the texts were nearly twice as likely to remain non-smoking than those that attended the smoking-cessation groups only. By this time, quit rates in the control group were 9 per cent, while in the text group, 15 per cent of the group were non-smoking. More cautiously, Stanczyk et al. (2014) compared the effects of tailored videos that could be accessed via the internet versus tailored text messages and a comparison condition involving short generic text advice. The negative scenario accessed through the internet was more effective than texts on measures of total number of cigarettes smoked and the percentage of people to quit smoking. Video computer tailoring also resulted in five-fold greater odds of achieving prolonged abstinence rates among smokers with a low readiness to quit.

Technology can be attractive for modern health promoters, but the temptation to ignore more traditional approaches must be met with caution. The chapter earlier noted one study that found uptake of written self-help materials to be higher than those that are electronically available. And this is not the only relevant evidence. Cook et al. (2007) compared the effectiveness of a web- and paper-based intervention designed to improve dietary practices, reduce stress and increase physical activity. The web-based programme was more effective than print materials in producing improvements in the areas of diet and nutrition but was no more effective in reducing stress or increasing physical activity.

Marshall et al. (2003) found no difference in the effectiveness of written or internet-based programmes designed to increase physical activity, while Marks et al. (2006) found that printed materials were more effective than the internet in changing exercise levels. It should be noted, however, that none of these programmes utilised the Web and its potential interactivity to its maximum. There was no interaction between the users and the programme and no use of prompts or other strategies that can be used with modern multimedia approaches. More complex and interactive interventions using the internet may be more engaging and more likely to engage its recipients (Plotnikoff et al. 2005).

RESEARCH FOCUS

Cavallo, D.N., Tate, D.F. Ries, A.V. et al. (2012) A social media-based physical activity intervention: a randomised controlled trial. *American Journal of Preventive Medicine,* 43: 527-32.

Introduction

The use of *Facebook* is almost ubiquitous in many countries, and this study examined whether use of a *Facebook* group aiming to enhance physical activity among young women would add to the effectiveness of an internet-based programme. The authors note that around one-third of adults (and a much higher percentage of younger adults) have online social network accounts, and they have a number of features that allow them to enhance interventions, including the ability to share information such as levels of exercise in real time that may encourage others to increase their exercise levels.

Method

Participants were 134 female undergraduates at a large US public university. Over three hundred were screened to ensure they met the criteria for entry into the study: < 25 years, < 30 minutes of daily exercise,

> 30 minutes on *Facebook* a day. Potential participants were excluded if their responses to a screening questionnaire revealed evidence of an eating disorder. Participants were randomly allocated to one of two conditions:

● *Self-monitoring and education:* provided education about exercise and a self-monitoring programme that allowed participants to set exercise goals, monitor their daily activity and view a chart comparing their activity compared with national recommendations.

● *Self-monitoring and education plus membership of a* Facebook *exercise support group*: the same intervention combined with membership of a *Facebook* group which allowed participants, amongst other things, to access a discussion board, connect with other group members using a Wall and dedicated discussion boards, post pictures and share relevant information.

Key measures taken online included the Paffenbarger Activity Questionnaire and Chogahara's Social Influence on Activity Questionnaire, measuring social support in achieving behavioural change. Measures were also taken of the use of *Facebook*.

Results

Calorie expenditure on three levels of physical activity before and after the interventions

		Baseline mean	Post-study survey mean	Group X time interaction	Time
Overall activity	Control	1706	2248		
	Intervention	1646	2394	p = .52	p < .001
Heavy activity	Control	155	378		
	Intervention	151	298	p = .55	p = .003
Moderate activity	Control	166	272		
	Intervention	81	253	p = .61	p = .01
Light activity	Control	25	61		
	Intervention	76	81	p = .41	p = .11

As you can see in the table, participants in both conditions significantly increased the amount of physical activity, and particularly moderate and 'heavy' calorie expenditure exercise. These levels include exercise that involves planning and is more than incidental exercise. Importantly, the ANOVA interaction terms are all non-significant, indicating that there were no differences between the two groups: the addition of *Facebook* had no significant effect. The cause of this lack of effectiveness may be reflected in the Social Influence on Activity Questionnaire findings, which indicated no effect of *Facebook* on the degree to which participants felt socially supported in any changes they were trying to make.

Discussion and commentary

A clear weakness of the study, and one which is common in this form of study, is the use of self-report measures of exercise. Exercise levels are notoriously difficult to measure, and all approaches have limitations. However, the use of accelerometers or pedometers, which provide a measure of actual activity, exercise diaries, and even 'live' measures of activity via smartphones may all increase the accuracy of measures. Nevertheless, the demand characteristics of both interventions are likely to be similar and the comparative levels of activity likely to be reasonably accurate. The study is therefore disappointing in that the addition of a *Facebook*-based support failed to add to the already relatively successful programme in a group of regular *Facebook* users. Clearly, while these approaches can be beneficial, any benefits cannot be automatically assumed, particularly in people with already existing social support networks. The approach may be more useful in less socially embedded individuals.

SUMMARY

1. Risk factor screening may be of benefit to some individuals, but has not consistently been found to reduce risk for disease. And it may contribute to health anxieties.
2. Motivational interviewing may be more beneficial in both motivating and maintaining health behaviour change, although its impact is not guaranteed.
3. Problem-focused approaches are significantly more effective than those that simply provide health information.
4. Screening for health risk can result in significant anxieties. For some individuals, these may be alleviated by teaching simple coping strategies.
5. Simple media campaigns have proven of little benefit in achieving behavioural change. Augmentation through refining communication

based on theories such as the elaboration likelihood model, combining fear and fear reduction messages, appropriate information framing, and audience segmentation may be of benefit.

6. Environmental interventions may also be of benefit. These may provide cues to action or remove cues to unhealthy behaviour; enable healthy behaviour by minimising the costs and barriers associated with it; or maximise the costs of engaging in health-damaging behaviour.

7. Traditional CHD prevention programmes have achieved only modest health gains in the population targeted unless aimed at relatively naive populations.

8. Peer-led interventions have proven more successful across a range of behaviours.

9. The worksite offers a key environment to foster and facilitate health behaviour change.

Further reading

White, J. and Bero, L.A. (2004). Public health under attack: the American Stop Smoking Intervention Study (ASSIST) and the tobacco industry. *American Journal of Public Health*, 94: 240–50.

A reminder that the public health agenda is not adopted by all.

http://www.kingsfund.org.uk/health_topics/public_health.html

The King's Fund is a UK 'think tank' that considers health policy in a number of arenas. This link takes you to their public health web page, where there is a wealth of information about community and environmental approaches to public health.

Gielen, A.C., McDonald, E.M., Gary, T.L. and Bone, L.R. (2008). Using the PRECEDE/PROCEED model to apply health behavior theories. In K. Glanz, F.M. B. K. Rimer and K. Viswanath, (eds.), *Health Behavior and Health Education:* *Theory, Research and Practice*. 4th edition, pp. 407-433. San Francisco: Jossey-Bass.

A short but useful introduction to the PRECEDE/PROCEED framework.

Webb, T.L., Joseph, J., Yardley, L. and Michie, S. (2010)

Using the internet to promote health behaviour change: a systematic review and meta-analysis of the impact of theoretical basis, use of behaviour change techniques, and mode of delivery on efficacy.

Journal of Medical Internet Research, 12, (1) (doi:10.2196/jmir.1376).

An all-encompassing review of behavioural interventions delivered via the internet.

http://cancercontrol.cancer.gov/brp/constructs/implementation_intentions/ii5.html

An internet site providing details of implementation intentions. Of interest not just because of its content, but its source: the American National Cancer Institute.

For open-access student resources specifically written to complement this textbook and support your learning, please visit **www.pearsoned.co.uk/morrison**

Part II
Becoming ill

Chapter 8
The body in health and illness

Learning outcomes

In this chapter, we outline the physiology and pathology underpinning a number of chronic diseases, as well as the experiences of people who develop them. This is intended to support the chapters considering the personal and psychological impact of disease on the individual (Chapters 14 and 16 ☞) and their family (Chapter 15 ☞) as well as interventions designed to help people cope more effectively with any symptoms and psychological sequelae of chronic illness they may experience (Chapter 17 ☞). Readers who already have an understanding of the nature of the illnesses described here may choose to skip the chapter. For those that do read the chapter, it should provide an understanding of:

- the basic anatomy and disorders of:
  - the brain
  - the autonomic nervous system

- the basic anatomy, physiology and disorders of:
  - the digestive system
  - the immune system
  - the cardiovascular system
  - the respiratory system

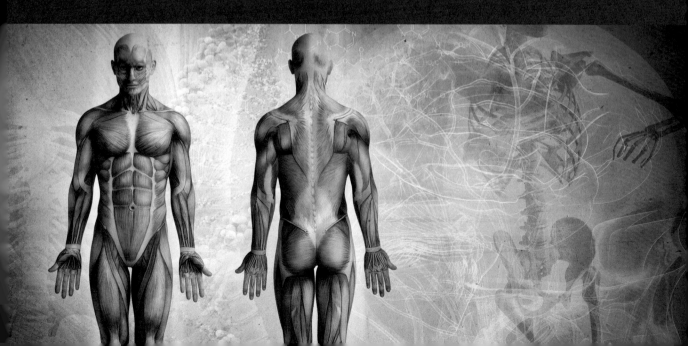

Bad health costs money!

In the UK, over two million people either have or have recovered from cancer, and a further 3 per cent of the population develops cancer each year. Over 6 per cent of men and 4 per cent of women have heart disease – and treating these individuals costs around £3.5 billion a year, with additional economic costs due to absence from work, caring for others with the disease, and so on adding a further cost of £3.1 billion to the economy. In the USA, an astonishing 17 per cent of individuals within the country have some type of lung disease. A further 4 per cent have some form of cancer or diabetes, and nearly 7 per cent have heart disease. Together, these chronic diseases cost the nation around $1.5 trillion each year as a consequence of treatment costs and lost productivity. Clearly, chronic diseases are highly prevalent and extremely costly to the nation. Oh, and the personal experience of long-term illness can be emotionally and physically 'costly' as well.

Chapter outline

This chapter provides an introduction to the key organ systems within the body. Each section considers the basic anatomy and physiology of each system, and describes some of the disease processes and their treatment that may occur within them. Later chapters consider how people can prevent or cope with these diseases, and in some cases the psychological interventions that may help them do this. As well as being a chapter to read on its own, it also forms a reference providing basic information on the illnesses and treatments we refer to in other chapters of the book.

We start by examining two systems that influence the whole body:

1. the brain and autonomic nervous system

2. the immune system.

We then go on to examine three other organ systems:

1. the digestive system

2. the cardiovascular system

3. the respiratory system.

The behavioural anatomy of the brain

The brain is an intricately patterned complex of nerve cell bodies. It is divided into four anatomical areas (see Figures 8.1 and 8.2):

1. *Hindbrain*: contains the parts of the brain necessary for life – the medulla oblongata, which controls blood pressure, heart rate and respiration; the reticular formation, which controls alertness and wakefulness; and the pons and cerebellum, which integrate muscular and positional information.

2. *Midbrain*: contains part of the reticular system and both sensory and motor correlation centres, which integrate reflex and automatic responses involving the visual and auditory systems and are involved in the integration of muscle movements.

3. *Forebrain*: contains key structures that influence mood and behaviour, including:

- *Thalamus*: links the basic functions of the hindbrain and midbrain with the higher centres of processing, the cerebral cortex. Regulates attention and contributes to memory functions. The portion that enters the limbic system (see below) is involved in the experience of emotions.

- *Hypothalamus*: regulates appetite, sexual arousal and thirst. Also appears to have some control over emotions.

- *Limbic system*: (Figure 8.3) a series of structures including a linked group of brain areas known as the Circuit of Papez (the hippocampus–fornix–mammillary bodies–thalamus–cingulate cortex–hippocampus). The hippocampus–fornix–mammillary bodies circuit is involved in memory. The hippocampus is one site of interaction between the perceptual and memory systems. A further part of the system, known as the amygdala, links sensory information to emotionally relevant behaviour, particularly responses to fear and anger. It has been called the 'emotional computer' because of its role in coordinating the

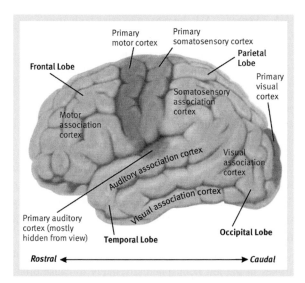

Figure 8.1 A cross-section through the cerebral cortex of the human brain

Source: Carlson, N. (2005), © 2005, reproduced by permission of Pearson Education, Inc.

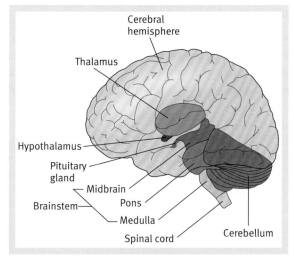

Figure 8.2 A lateral view of the left side of a semi-transparent human brain with the brainstem 'ghosted' in

Source: Carlson, N. (2005), © 2005, reproduced by permission of Pearson Education, Inc.

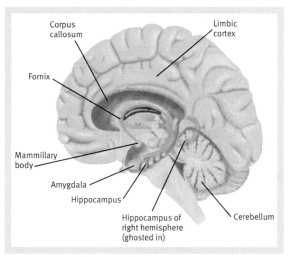

Figure 8.3 The major components of the limbic system. All of the left hemisphere apart from the limbic system has been removed

Source: Carlson, N. (2005), © 2005, reproduced by permission of Pearson Education, Inc.

process that begins with the evaluation of sensory information for significance (i.e. threat) and then controls the resulting behavioural and autonomic responses (see below).

4. *Cerebrum*: the most recently evolved part of the brain includes:

- *Basal ganglia*: responsible for complex motor coordination.

- *Cortex*: the convoluted outer layer of grey matter comprising nerve cell bodies and their synaptic connections. It is divided into two functional hemispheres linked by the *corpus callosum*, a series of interconnecting neural fibres, at its base and is divided into four lobes: frontal, temporal, occipital and parietal:
  - *The frontal lobe* has an 'executive' function, as it coordinates a number of complex processes, including speech, motor coordination and behavioural planning. The frontal lobes also influence motivation. The pre-frontal lobes are connected to the limbic system via the thalamus and motor system within the cortex. Links between the pre-frontal cortex and the limbic system are activated during rewarding behaviour.
  - *The temporal lobes* have a number of functions. In right-handed people, at the risk of oversimplification, the main language centre is generally located in the left hemisphere, and visuo-spatial processing is located in the right. In left-handed individuals, there is less localisation within the hemispheres. The temporal lobes are also involved in the systems of smell and hearing. They integrate the visual experience with those of the other senses to make meaningful wholes. The temporal lobes have an important role in memory and contain systems that

preserve the record of conscious experience. Finally, they connect to the limbic system and link emotions to events and memories.

○ *The occipital and parietal lobes* are involved in the integration of sensory information. The occipital lobe is primarily involved in visual perception. Links to the cortex permit interpretation of visual stimuli.

Problems of neurological functioning

There are many causes of neurological dysfunction, including brain trauma and neural degeneration as a consequence of a range of types of dementia. However, the neurological problem most frequently encountered by health psychologists is variously known as a 'stroke' or, more technically, a cerebrovascular accident (CVA). The primary cause of a CVA is the disruption of blood supply to part of the brain, causing the death of neurons previously provided with oxygen and other nutrients by the affected blood vessel(s). This can result from one of two causes: a clot (thrombosis) developing in, and blocking the blood flow through a blood vessel or rupture in a blood vessel's wall causing a bleed into the neural tissue. A temporary restriction of blood supply which may also result in the short-term and reversible experience of symptoms similar to a CVA is referred to as a transient ischaemic attack (TIA) (ischaemia meaning lack of blood supply).

The location of the stroke within the brain will determine the type of symptoms experienced. However, there are now some internationally acknowledged signs of the onset of a stroke and how to respond to them:

● Sudden numbness or weakness in the face, arm, or leg, especially on one side of the body.

● Sudden confusion, trouble speaking, or difficulty understanding speech.

● Sudden trouble seeing in one or both eyes.

● Sudden trouble walking, dizziness, loss of balance, or lack of coordination.

● Sudden severe headache with no known cause.

If these symptoms are identified, the acronym F.A.S.T. guides a response:

F - Face: Ask the person to smile. Does one side of the face droop?

A - Arms: Ask the person to raise both arms. Does one arm drift downward?

S - Speech: Ask the person to repeat a simple phrase. Is their speech slurred or strange?

T - Time: If you observe any of these signs, call for emergency medical help immediately.

If the stroke is a result of a blood clot, immediate treatment using **thrombolytic** drugs can dissolve the clot and reduce or eliminate any neural damage. Delay will negatively influence the likely effectiveness of such treatment.

As a rough and ready guide, one rule of thumb is that strokes in the left hemisphere are likely to cause problems in language and communication as they may impact on the language centres in the right side of the brain in right-handed individuals. Those in the right hemisphere will result in problems of muscular weakness or even paralysis of limbs as the motor cortex is often involved. However, the long-term symptoms can be more subtle than this crude dichotomy (which also does not apply to left-handed individuals), and include a whole dictionary of symptoms, including: **hemiplegia** or **hemiparesis, dysphasia** and **dysarthria, aphasia** and

---

thrombolytic

drugs that affect the blood clotting. Usually involves drugs that reduce the risk of clots forming.

hemiplegia

paralysis of one side of the body.

hemiparesis

weakness of one side of the body.

dysphasia

an inability to generate speech, and sometimes to understand speech.

dysarthria

poor articulation of speech due to muscular problems.

aphasia

impaired ability to understand or produce speech due to brain damage.

apraxia, **visual field loss**, and **hemianopia**. The affected individual may also experience problems in learning, concentration, and recall from long- or short-term memory, fatigue, and inappropriate emotional responses. While any one individual will only experience some of these symptoms, the condition can clearly be problematic in the long term and patients may require significant input from a range of health professionals, including speech therapists, neuropsychologists and physiotherapists to aid their long-term recovery.

The autonomic nervous system

The autonomic nervous system is responsible for control over levels of activity in key organs and organ systems in the body. Many organs have some degree of control over their functioning. The heart, for example, has an intrinsic rhythm of 110 beats per minute. However, this level of activity may not be appropriate at all times. The heart may have to beat more at times of exercise, less at times of rest. The autonomic nervous system overrides local control to provide a higher level of coordinated control across most of the bodily systems in response to the varying demands being placed on the body. Its activity is controlled by a number of brain areas, the most important of which is the hypothalamus. The hypothalamus receives information about the demands being placed on the body from a variety of sources, including:

- information about skin temperature from the reticular formation in the brainstem;
- information about light and darkness from the optic nerves;
- receptors in the hypothalamus itself provide information about the ion balance and temperature of the blood.

The hypothalamus also has links to the cortex and limbic systems of the brain, which are involved in the processing of cognitive and emotional demands. This allows the autonomic system to respond to psychological factors as well as physical demands being placed on the body. Accordingly, the autonomic nervous system can initiate sweating in high temperatures, increase blood pressure and heart rate during exercise, and also make us physiologically responsive at times of stress, distress or excitement (we discuss these responses further in Chapters 11 and 13 ☞).

The autonomic nervous system controls these varying levels of activity through two opposing networks of nerves (see Figure 8.4):

1. the **sympathetic nervous system**: involved in activation and arousal – the fight–flight response;
2. the **parasympathetic nervous system**: involved in relaxation – the rest–recover response.

Both sets of nerves arise in an area in the brainstem known as the medulla oblongata (which is linked to the hypothalamus). From this, they pass down the spinal cord to various **synapses**, where they link to a second series of nerves that are linked to all the key body organs, including the heart, arteries and muscles (Figure 8.4). For the sympathetic arm, the **neurotransmitter** involved at the

---

apraxia

an inability to execute purposive actions due to brain damage.

visual field loss

a loss of part of the usual field of vision. Does not include complete blindness in either one or two eyes.

hemianopia

loss of half the visual field, usually on one side of a vertical midline. People with the disorder may, for example, when asked only see or draw half a clock.

sympathetic nervous system

the part of the autonomic nervous system involved in mobilising energy to activate and maintain arousal (e.g. increased heart rate).

parasympathetic nervous system

arm of the autonomic nervous system that is responsible for rest and recuperation.

synapse

junction between two neurons or between a neuron and target organ. Nerve impulses cross a synapse through the action of neurotransmitters.

neurotransmitter

a chemical messenger (e.g. adrenaline, acetylcholine) used to communicate between neurons and other neurons and other types of cell.

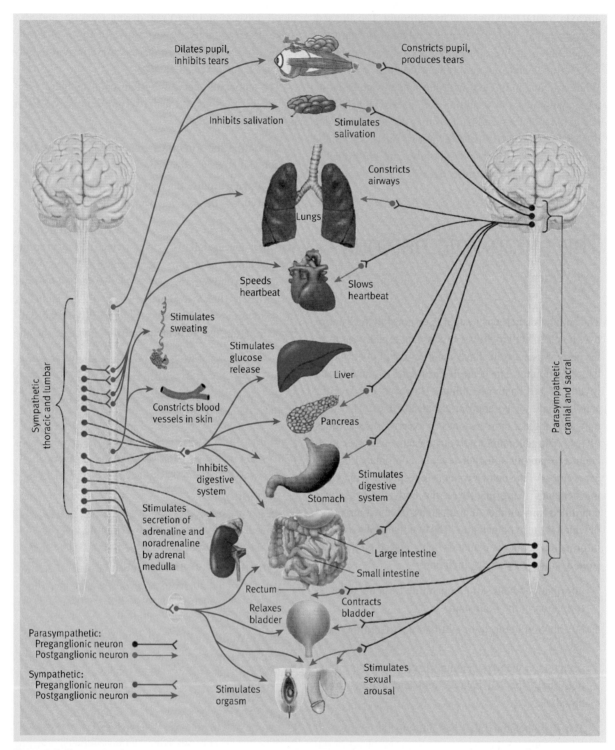

Figure 8.4 The autonomic nervous system, with the target organs and functions served by the sympathetic and parasympathetic branches

Table 8.1 Summary of responses of the autonomic nervous system to sympathetic and parasympathetic activity

Structure	Sympathetic stimulation	Parasympathetic stimulation
Iris (eye muscle)	Pupil dilation	Pupil constriction
Salivary glands	Saliva production reduced	Saliva production increased
Heart	Heart rate and force increased	Heart rate and force decreased
Lung	Bronchial muscle relaxed	Bronchial muscle contracted
Stomach	Peristalsis reduced	Gastric juice secreted; motility increased
Small intestine	Motility reduced	Digestion increased
Large intestine	Motility reduced	Secretions and motility increased
Liver	Increased conversion of glycogen to glucose	
Kidney	Decreased urine secretion	Increased urine secretion
Bladder	Wall relaxed	Wall contracted
	Sphincter closed	Sphincter relaxed

synapse between the spinal cord nerves and the nerve to the target organ is acetylcholine. Activity at the synapse between this second nerve and the end organ mainly involves a neurotransmitter known as norepinephrine, and to a lesser extent epinephrine (confusingly, also often called noradrenaline adrenaline). The parasympathetic system uses acetylcholine at both synapses. The activity in each of the organs depends on the relative activity in the sympathetic and parasympathetic nervous systems. When activity in the sympathetic system dominates, the body is activated; when the parasympathetic system is dominant, the body is resting and relatively inactive, allowing basic functions such as digestion and the production of urine to occur more easily (see Table 8.1).

the neurotransmitter noradrenaline into the bloodstream, in which it is transported to the organs in the body. Receptors in the target organs respond to the hormone and maintain their activation. Because the hormone can be released for a longer period than the neurotransmitter, this extends the period of activation.

A second activating system involves the pituitary gland, the activity of which is also controlled by the hypothalamus. This lies immediately under the brain (see Figure 8.2), and, when stimulated by the hypothalamus, it releases a number of hormones into the bloodstream, the most important of which is adrenocorticotrophic hormone (ACTH). When the ACTH reaches the adrenal cortex, it causes it to release hormones known as **corticosteroids**, the most important of

Endocrine processes

The activity initiated by the sympathetic nervous system is short-lived. A second system is therefore used to provide longer-term arousal. This system uses **endocrine glands**, which communicate with their target organs by releasing hormones into the bloodstream. The endocrine glands that extend the activity of the sympathetic nervous system are the **adrenal glands**, which are situated above the kidneys. These have two functional areas, each of which is activated in different ways:

1. the centre or *adrenal medulla*;

2. the surrounding tissues, known as the *adrenal cortex*.

The adrenal medulla is innervated by the sympathetic nervous system. Activity in this system stimulates the adrenal medulla to release the hormonal equivalent of

endocrine glands

glands that produce and secrete hormones into the blood or lymph systems. Includes the pituitary and adrenal glands, and the islets of Langerhans in the pancreas. These hormones may affect one organ or tissue, or the entire body.

adrenal glands

endocrine glands, located above each kidney. Comprises the cortex, which secretes several steroid hormones, and the medulla, which secretes noradrenaline.

corticosteroids

powerful anti-inflammatory hormones (including cortisol) made naturally in the body or synthetically for use as drugs.

which is **cortisol** – also known as hydrocortisone. Cortisol increases the availability of energy stores and fats to fuel periods of high physiological activity. It also inhibits inflammation of damaged tissue. The sympathetic nervous system is central to our stress response, and we discuss this again in Chapter 11 ☞.

The immune system

Components of the immune system

The immune system provides a variety of protective mechanisms that respond to attacks from bacteria, viruses, infectious diseases and other sources (collectively known as **antigens**) from outside the body. In this section, we briefly describe the role of different elements of the immune system. We then go on to look at the links between them and how they combine to combat invading pathogens and the development of cancers.

A number of organs and chemicals form the front line of the system. These include:

---

cortisol
a stress hormone that increases the availability of energy stores and fats to fuel periods of high physiological activity. It also inhibits inflammation of damaged tissue.

antigens
a collective name for a variety of challenges to our health and immune system, including bacteria and viruses.

antibodies
immunoglobulins produced in response to an antigen.

lymphocyte
a type of white blood cell. Lymphocytes have a number of roles in the immune system, including the production of antibodies and other substances that fight infection and disease. Includes T and B cells.

phagocyte
an immune system cell that can surround and kill micro-organisms and remove dead cells. Phagocytes include macrophages.

- *Physical barriers*: provided by the skin.
- *Mechanical barriers*: cilia (small hairs in the lining of the lungs) propel pathogens out of the lungs and respiratory tract – coughs and sneezes achieve the same goal more dramatically. Tears, saliva and urine also push pathogens out of the body.
- *Chemical barriers*: acid from the stomach provides an obvious chemical barrier against pathogens. Sebum, which coats body hairs, inhibits the growth of bacteria and fungi on the skin. Saliva, tears, sweat and nasal secretions contain lysozyme, which destroys bacteria. Saliva and the walls of the gastrointestinal tract also contain an **antibody** known as immunoglobulin A (IgA).
- *'Harmless pathogens'*: a variety of bacteria live within the body and have no harmful effects on us. However, they defend their territory and can destroy other bacteria that invade it.
- *Lymph nodes*: secondary organs at or near possible points of entry for pathogens. This system includes the tonsils, Peyer's patches in the intestines, and appendix. They contain high levels of **lymphocytes** (see below), ready to attack any invading pathogens.

As well as these relatively static defences against attack, there are a number of cells that circulate around the body. This can be through the circulatory system or a parallel system known as the lymphatic system. This carries a fluid called lymph and transports cells important to the destruction of antigens to the sites of cellular damage, and the waste products of their destruction away from them.

Two groups of cells in the circulatory and lymphatic systems provide protection against a variety of pathogens. **Phagocytes** (sometimes called white blood cells) circulate within the circulatory system. They are created in the bone marrow and attract, adhere to and then engulf and destroy antigens in a process known as phagocytosis. The immune system has a number of phagocytes, including:

- *Neutrophils* have a short life of a few hours to days. They provide the major defence against bacteria and the initial fight against infection by engulfing and digesting them.
- *Macrophages* are long-lived and are best at attacking dead cells and pathogens capable of living within cells. Once a macrophage destroys a cell, it places

some of its own proteins on its surface. This allows other immune cells to identify cells as invaders and to attack them.

A second group of cells known as lymphocytes circulate in the blood (where they are also known as white blood cells) and lymph system. These include **T cells** and **B cells**:

- *Cytotoxic T cells* bind onto antigens, including virus-infected cells and tumour cells. They form pores in the target cell's plasma membrane, allowing ions and water to flow into the target cell, making it expand, then collapse and die.

- *Helper T cells* trigger or increase an immune response. They identify and bind to antigens, then release chemicals that stimulate the proliferation of cytotoxic T and plasma B cells (see below). Helper T cells are also known as **CD4+ cells** because of their chemical structure.

- *Plasma B cells* destroy antigens by binding to them and making them easier targets for phagocytes. They attack antigens in the blood system before they enter body cells.

- *Memory B cells* live indefinitely in the blood and lymphatic systems. They result from an initial attack by a novel antigen. In their initial response to such attacks, memory B cells 'learn' the chemical nature of the antigens they attack and are able to deal with them more effectively should they encounter them again.

A third group of attacking cells are **natural killer (NK) cells**, which move in the blood and attack cancer cells and virus-infected body cells.

Central nervous system links with the immune system

The immune system is intimately linked to the central nervous system. The influence of these two interacting systems affects the development and activity of phago-cytes, B, T and NK cells. Lymphocytes also have epinephrine and cortisol receptors, which are affected by hormones from both the adrenal cortex and medulla (see above). The influence of these neurotransmitters and hormones is complex. Increased epinephrine in response to short-term stress can stimulate the spleen to release phagocytes into the bloodstream and increase NK cell counts, but decrease the number of T cells. Cortisol release decreases the production of helper T cells and ingestion of cells by macrophages. These issues are complex and differ over the time course of stress and the nature of the stressor. However, it is generally recognised that chronic stress significantly impairs the effectiveness of the immune system, leaving us less able to ward off infection (see Chapter 11 ☞ for further discussion of this issue).

Immune dysfunction

Human Immunodeficiency Virus infection

The human immunodeficiency virus (HIV) is the cause of a potentially fatal condition known as Acquired ImmunoDeficiency Syndrome (AIDS). The virus belongs to a subgroup of viruses known as 'slow viruses', which have a long interval between initial infection and the onset of serious symptoms – potentially up to 10 years and beyond. The virus affects the T helper (CD4+) cells. In response to a virus or other pathogens, healthy CD4+ cells replicate and send messages to B and T cells to also replicate and attack the pathogen. When infected with HIV, CD4+ cells still replicate in response to pathogens, but the replicated CD4+ cells are infected with the virus, are unable to activate their target B and T cells, and eventually die. Initially, the non-infected CD4+

T cell

a cell that recognises antigens on the surface of a virus-infected cell, binds to that cell and destroys it.

B cell

a form of lymphocyte involved in destruction of antigens. Memory B cells provide long-term immunity against previously encountered pathogens.

CD4+ cells

otherwise known as helper T cells, these are involved in the proliferation of cytotoxic T cells as part of the immune response. HIV infection impairs their ability to provide this function.

natural killer (NK) cells

cells that move in the blood and attack cancer cells and virus-infected body cells.

cells still provide an effective response against pathogens. However, over time, proliferation of infected CD4+ cells in response to pathogens results in an increase in infected CD4+ cells in circulation. These will eventually die, but before doing so may bind with healthy CD4+ cells, resulting in their death. In addition, the immune system may recognise the virus-laden cells as invasive, and begin to attack its own CD4+ cells. Together, these processes result in a gradual reduction in the number of circulating CD4+ cells, reducing the immune system's ability to defend itself effectively against viruses, bacteria and some cancers. When the CD4+ cell count falls below 500/mm^3, approximately half the immune system reserve has been destroyed. At this point minor infection such as cold sores and fungal infections begin to appear. Once the CD4+ cell count falls below 200/mm^3, life-threatening opportunistic infections and cancers typically occur. AIDS, the end point of HIV disease, occurs when the CD4+ cell count is less than 200/mm^3 or when the individual develops potentially life-threatening infections such as pneumonia or cancers such as **Kaposi's sarcoma**.

Treatment for HIV infection involves three classes of drugs:

● *Reverse transcriptase inhibitors*: HIV uses reverse transcriptase to copy its genetic material and generate new viruses. Reverse transcriptase inhibitors disrupt the process and thereby suppress its growth.

● *Protease inhibitors*: these interfere with the protease enzyme that HIV uses to produce infectious viral particles.

● *Fusion inhibitors*: these interfere with the virus's ability to fuse with the cellular membrane of other CD4+ cells, blocking entry into the host cell.

These drugs do not cure HIV infection or AIDS, although life expectancy for some groups of individuals

> ### Kaposi's sarcoma
> a malignant tumour of the connective tissue, often associated with AIDS. The tumours consist of bluish-red or purple lesions on the skin. They often appear first on the feet or ankles, thighs, arms, hands and face.

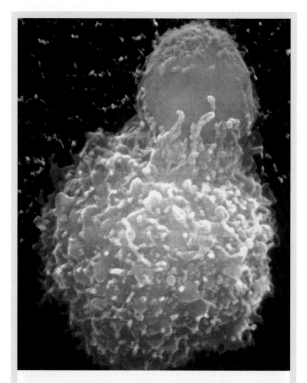

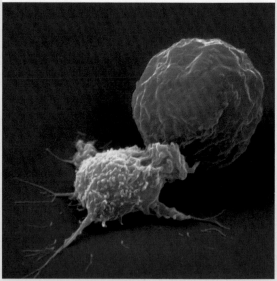

Photo 8.1 and Photo 8.2 Here we see two cells, a virus and cancer cell, being attacked and either engulfed by B cells (8.1) or rendered inert by NK cells (8.2)

Source: Dr Andrejs Liepins/Science Photo Library (8.1) and Eye of Science/Science Photo Library (8.2).

treated early in the infection may now achieve or exceed population norms (Samji et al. 2013). They can suppress the virus, even to undetectable levels, but are unable to completely eliminate HIV from the body. Accordingly, infected individuals still need to take **antiretroviral drugs**. In addition, as HIV replicates itself, different strains of the virus emerge, some of which are resistant to antiretroviral drugs. For this reason, treatment guidelines state that HIV-positive individuals take a combination of antiretroviral drugs known as Highly Active Antiretroviral Therapy (HAART or ART). This strategy, which typically combines two different classes of antiretroviral drugs, has been shown to effectively suppress the virus when used appropriately. Unfortunately, strict adherence to the HAART regimen presents a significant challenge to the individual taking the medication, both in terms of taking the medication at the correct time and the side effects that they may experience (see Chapters 10 and 17 ☞). The relatively recent development of complex single drugs that include up to three different types of antiretrovirals (e.g. Atripla, Complera) and which need to be taken only once daily, herald the promise of much simpler drug regimens, better adherence to medication regimens, and lower risk of progression to AIDS (Rao et al. 2013).

Autoimmune conditions

The immune system is able to identify cells that are part of the body ('self') and those that are 'non-self': antigens, developing cancers, and so on. On occasion, this process breaks down and the immune system treats cells within the body as non-self and begins to attack them. This can result in a number of **autoimmune conditions**, including diabetes, rheumatoid arthritis and multiple sclerosis.

Diabetes

Two types of **diabetes** have been identified. In **type 1 diabetes**, the body does not produce sufficient insulin within the islets of Langerhans in the **pancreas**. Its onset is frequently triggered by an infection, often by one from the Coxsackie virus family. This virus expresses a protein similar in structure to an enzyme involved in the production of insulin, and the immune response to this virus can also destroy the insulin-producing cells within the pancreas. Insulin normally attaches itself to glucose molecules in the circulatory system, permitting it to be taken up by the various body organs which need it to provide them with energy. Without insulin, these glucose molecules cannot be absorbed, leading to high levels of glucose within the blood which the body cannot use. This can lead to a life-threatening coma known as diabetic

ketoacidosis, which requires hospitalisation and immediate treatment to avoid death. Less dramatic symptoms include increased thirst and urination, constant hunger, weight loss, blurred vision and extreme fatigue.

Treatment typically involves between one and four injections of insulin a day, meal planning to avoid sudden peaks of glucose being released into the bloodstream, weight control and exercise. Treatment is a balancing act, aimed at achieving appropriate levels of circulating blood glucose. Too much food and/or too little insulin can result in ketoacidosis. Too little food and/or too much insulin can result in a condition known as hypoglycaemia, characterised by symptoms including a period of confusion and irritability, followed by a fairly rapid loss of consciousness. Immediate treatment is to give oral glucose where possible, or intravenously if the individual has lost consciousness. Good day-to-day control over diabetes reduces but does not obviate long-term complications, including poor circulation which can lead to loss of sight, heart disease, skin ulcers, loss of limbs and nerve damage.

A second form of the condition is known as **type 2 diabetes**. In this, the body produces sufficient insulin (or

antiretroviral drugs

drugs that prevent the reproduction of a type of virus known as a retrovirus. Most well known in the treatment of the HIV.

autoimmune conditions

a group of diseases, including type 1 diabetes, Crohn's disease and rheumatoid arthritis, characterised by abnormal functioning of the immune system in which it produces antibodies against its own tissues – it treats 'self' as 'non-self'.

diabetes (type 1 and 2)

a lifelong disease marked by high levels of sugar in the blood and a failure to transfer this to organs that need it. It can be caused by too little insulin (type 1), resistance to insulin (type 2), or both.

type 1 diabetes

see **diabetes**.

pancreas

gland in which the islets of Langerhans produce insulin. Also produces and secretes digestive enzymes. Located behind the stomach.

type 2 diabetes

see **diabetes.**

close to sufficient), but the cells that take up the glucose insulin molecules become 'resistant', and no longer absorb them. Type 2 diabetes often develops later in life, and is associated with obesity – a person's chances of developing type 2 diabetes roughly increases by 4 per cent for every pound of excess weight. The symptoms of type 2 diabetes develop gradually, and their onset is not as sudden as in type 1 diabetes. They may include fatigue or nausea, frequent urination, unusual thirst, weight loss, blurred vision, frequent infections and slow healing of wounds or sores. Some people have no symptoms. First-line treatment involves weight loss and exercise – although many people find it hard to adhere to such regimens (Vermeire et al. 2007). Second-line treatment involves treatment with oral medication designed to variously stimulate the beta cells in the pancreas to release more insulin, decrease the amount of glucose produced by the liver and enhance the effectiveness of naturally produced insulin, and lower glucose levels by blocking the breakdown of starches in the gut. We discuss the impact of diabetes on the individual and family in Chapter 15 ☞ and interventions designed to increase adherence to insulin and appropriate behavioural change in Chapter 17 ☞.

Rheumatoid arthritis

Rheumatoid arthritis (RA) may be triggered by viruses in individuals with a genetic tendency for the disease. It is a systemic disease that affects the entire body (and can impact on internal organs including lungs, heart and eyes) characterised by inflammation of the membrane lining the joints (the synovium). Any joint may be affected, but the hands, feet and wrists are the most frequently involved. It is a chronic, episodic condition, with 'flare-ups' and periods of remission. During flare-ups, people with the condition experience significant pain, stiffness, warmth, redness and swelling

rheumatoid arthritis
a chronic autoimmune disease with inflammation of the joints and marked deformities.

multiple sclerosis
a disorder of the brain and spinal cord caused by progressive damage to the myelin sheath covering of nerve cells.

in affected joints – as well as fatigue, loss of appetite, fever and loss of energy. Over the long term, inflammatory cells in the synovium release enzymes that digest bone and cartilage, leading to joints losing their shape and alignment, and pain and restricted movement within the joint. Rheumatoid arthritis is more common in women than in men, and affects relatively young people: the age of onset is usually between 25 and 50 years.

There is no known cure for RA although its symptoms can be managed. The goal of treatment is to reduce joint inflammation and pain, maximise joint function, and prevent joint destruction and deformity. Treatment involves both medication and self care: rest, joint strengthening exercises and joint protection. Two types of medications are used: fast-acting 'first-line drugs' and slow-acting 'second-line drugs'. First-line drugs, such as aspirin and cortisone (corticosteroids), are used to reduce pain and inflammation. Slow-acting second-line drugs, such as gold, methotrexate and hydroxychloroquine promote disease remission and prevent progressive joint destruction. As can be seen in the example of Mrs K (see p. 219), people with RA may also benefit from a number of aids to help them engage in many everyday behaviours. Mrs K recounts a typical day which may not be different to many people's day, but which is characterised by small (and not so small) frustrations due to her condition.

We examine the impact of arthritis on the individual and their family in Chapters 14 and 15 ☞, treatment of the pain associated with arthritis in Chapter 16 ☞, and self-management programmes to help people minimise the negative impact of arthritis on their lives in Chapter 17 ☞.

Multiple sclerosis

Multiple sclerosis (MS) is a neurological condition involving repeated episodes of inflammation of the central nervous system (brain and spinal cord). This results in the slowing or blocking of the transmission of nerve impulses. As this may occur in any part of the brain or spinal cord, symptoms can differ markedly across individuals, and include loss of limb function, loss of bowel and/or bladder control, blindness due to inflammation of the optic nerve, and cognitive impairment. Muscular spasticity is a common feature, particularly in the upper limbs. Around 95 per cent of people with MS experience debilitating fatigue, which can be so severe that about 40 per cent of people with the condition are unable to engage in sustained physical activity, while 30 to 50 per cent require walking aids or a wheelchair for mobility. During acute symptomatic episodes, patients may be hospitalised.

The course of MS differs across individuals. Twenty per cent of people with the condition have a benign form of the disease in which symptoms show little or no progression after the initial episode. A few people experience malignant MS, resulting in a swift and relentless decline, with significant disability or even death occurring shortly after disease onset. Onset of this type of MS is usually after the age of 40 years. The majority of people have an episodic condition, known as remitting–relapsing MS, with acute flare-ups followed by periods of remission. Each flare-up, however, is usually followed by a failure to recover to previous levels of function, resulting in a slowly deteriorating condition. Death is usually due to complications of MS including choking, pneumonia and renal failure. As well as physical problems, nearly half the people with MS experience some degree of cognitive impairment and memory problems. In addition, around half will be clinically depressed at some time during the course of the illness (Siegert and Abernethy 2005). Whether this is a direct result of neuronal damage or a reaction to the experience of the disease is not clear. It may, of course, be both.

One chemical within the immune system, called gamma-interferon, is particularly implicated in MS. This stimulates production of cytotoxic T cells, which are responsible for attacking and destroying diseased or damaged body cells. In MS, the activated cytotoxic T cells

Case history: Mrs K

I am a 42-year-old wife and mother of two young children. I have had severe rheumatoid arthritis for nearly eight years. This has caused deformities in my hands and feet. My fingers are gnarled. My wrists have nearly fused. My toes have bent upwards. My knees and many of the small joints of my knuckles are swollen.

I am usually very stiff when I wake up, so I get up slowly. After sitting at the side of the bed, I stand slowly, then slowly walk to the kitchen to prepare breakfast and school lunches for my children. Because my grip has been impaired with my deformities, I use a knife with an oversized grip handle to make sandwiches. I use a lid gripper pad to open jars. I take my tablets with my breakfast.

After breakfast, it's time for my morning washing routine. I have a raised toilet seat to avoid straining my joints sitting down and getting up. I shower while waiting for the morning tablets to start working. Washing my hair is difficult with my hands and I have adapted a scrubbing brush to help me wash it. I am careful getting in and out of the shower because the instability of my legs puts me at risk of falling.

Getting dressed is not easy. I am too clumsy to use buttons, so most of my shirts are pullover or have velcro attachments. My bra can be fastened in front and reversed or I ask my husband to fasten it for me. Most of my trousers have elastic waistbands and do not require buttoning or zipping. My shoes are especially wide and I usually wear running shoes for comfort. I dress for comfort – not for 'fashion'!

I drive the kids to school. Getting into and out of the car is painful and slow. I have a special key enlarger attachment for my car and house keys, which makes it easier to turn them. I can drive, but it makes my wrists hurt.

I try to exercise every day. I start with stretching exercises, then either ride a stationary bike or go on a walk. Once a week, I go for a swim. Exercise makes me feel good and gives me a sense of control over my body. Housework also always needs doing. I make good use of attachments to the vacuum cleaner that help me get to places that are hard to reach. Our door handles are levers instead of knobs so that it is easier for me to turn them. I can't do the ironing. When I cook, I use special grippers to hold the handles of pots and pans, and an electric can opener.

At bedtime, undressing can be as challenging as dressing. My husband frequently assists me with the undressing. My wrists are frequently painful by the evening, so I strap on my wrist splints before reading a few chapters of my novel, and calling it a night.

wrongly identify the **myelin sheath** of nerve cells within the brain and spinal column as 'non-self', and attempt to destroy it. Viral infections may act as a trigger to the production of gamma-interferon, and the onset of MS may follow a viral infection. One approach to the treatment of MS involves a different type of interferon. Beta interferon appears to inhibit the action of gamma interferon and prevents the T cells attacking the myelin sheath. Unfortunately, interferons have to be regularly

> **myelin sheath**
>
> a substance that contains both protein and fat (lipid) and surrounds all nerves outside the brain. It acts as a nerve insulator and helps in the transmission of nerve signals.

injected, and are responsible for the fever, muscle aches, fatigue and headache experienced during illnesses such

Case history: Ms F

I developed MS about four years ago. It was odd to start with. I didn't think I had anything serious, although you do worry about symptoms you don't understand. It started when I had some problems with my sight. I couldn't see as well as I used to be able to – it came on suddenly so I didn't think it was age or anything normal. I think at the time I was also a bit more clumsy than I had been – nothing obvious, but I dropped things a bit more than before. Nothing really that you'd notice unless other things were happening as well. I went to my GP about my eyes and he sent me to see a neurologist. He tried to reassure me that there was nothing too badly wrong and that he wanted to check out a few symptoms. But I began to worry then … you don't get sent on to see the hospital doctors unless there is anything really wrong with you. He suggested that he thought it might be MS, which was why he was not sending me to an eye specialist.

I got to see the neurologist pretty quickly and she ran a few tests over a few weeks – testing my muscle strength, coordination, scans and so on … sticking needles into me at various times. The upshot of this was that I was diagnosed as having MS. My consultant told me and my husband together, and allowed us to ask questions about things. We also got to speak to a specialist nurse who has helped us over the years. She was able to take the time to tell us more than the doctor about what to expect and what support we could have. Although I think it was nice to hear the diagnosis from the doctor.

I must admit that I found it really hard to deal with things at the beginning – you don't know what to expect and perhaps you expect the worst. You hear all sorts of horror stories about people dying with MS and that. And

no one can really reassure you that you won't have problems … Over the last few years, I've got to know my body and seen things getting worse. But it happens gradually and a lot of the time there are no changes. So that is reassuring – that things aren't going to collapse too quickly and I won't be left incontinent and unable to feed myself for a long time – hopefully not ever!

The worse thing is the tiredness and clumsiness. My eyes have actually got better, thank goodness. I use sticks to get around the house. Sometimes I can walk a little out of the house. Often I have to take the wheel-chair. I just get exhausted too quickly, there isn't a lot of point trying to walk, because I cannot go far …

I hate having MS. I used to take part in sports, go out, be lively. Now I can't do any of that. I'm tired … down a lot of the time. I think the two often go together. My memory was never that good, but now it seems to be worse than ever. I can hold conversations, but keeping my concentration up for a long time is difficult. So, people find you difficult to deal with. I know my husband feels that way. He married a lively, sporty, slim woman … now I'm lethargic, down, putting on weight because I eat and don't exercise – even though they tell me not to, so I can keep mobile and not develop skin problems. I don't go out very much because it's such a hassle in my wheelchair … cities were not designed for people in wheelchairs … and people don't like people in wheelchairs. You are ignored … and just want to say, 'Hey, I'm here. I have a brain you know … ' I know this sounds sorry for myself. And sometimes I feel more positive. But I find living with uncertainty difficult. Will I have a bad day today? Will I have a flare-up – have to go to hospital, take mega-steroids, come out worse than when I went in? I guess you have to live for the day … but it can be difficult.

as influenza. These also form the side effects of taking them as medication, and as a consequence many patients avoid their use. There is increasing evidence that cannabis can be effective in reducing pain and muscle spasticity associated with MS. But the treatment has to counter the problems of its legal status. It is legally prescribed, for example, in the Netherlands and Canada and several states in the USA but is not legally available, for example, in the UK or Australia.

Ms F provides an insight into what it feels like to have MS. At the time of our talk she was taking antidepressants for her depression and, as you can read, was having problems coming to terms with her illness.

We examine the impact of multiple sclerosis on caregivers in Chapter 15 ☞ and some interventions designed to reduce the problems of living with MS in Chapter 17 ☞.

The digestive system

The digestive tract (see Figure 8.5) is the system of organs responsible for the ingestion of food, absorption of nutrients from that food, and finally the expulsion of waste products from the body. It comprises a number of connected organs, each with a different role:

- *Mouth*: here, food is masticated by chewing, causing the release of enzymes in the saliva and beginning the process of digestion.
- *Oesophagus*: this transports food from the mouth to the stomach, compressing it in the process.
- *Stomach*: here, food is churned and mixed with acid to decompose it chemically.
- *Small intestine*: this is responsible for mixing the bowel contents with chemicals to break it into its constituent parts and then absorbing them into the bloodstream for transportation to other organs. Chemicals involved in this process include **bile**, which is made by the liver and stored in the **gallbladder** and digests fats, and enzyme-rich juices released from the pancreas.

> ### bile
> a digestive juice, made in the liver and stored in the gallbladder. Involved in the digestion of fats in the small intestine.
>
> ### gallbladder
> a structure on the underside of the liver on the right side of the abdomen. It stores the bile that is produced in the liver before it is secreted into the intestines. This helps the body to digest fats.

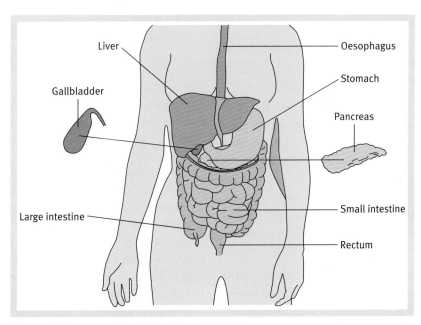

Figure 8.5 The large and small intestine and related organs.

● *The large bowel* (colon): this is largely responsible for reabsorption of water from the bowel contents and expulsion of the unused bowel contents.

Movement between and along these various organs is controlled by a process known as peristalsis. This involves smooth muscle within the walls of the organs narrowing and the narrow sections moving slowly along the length of the organ in a series of waves, pushing the bowel contents forward with each wave.

Controlling digestion

Each of these digestion processes is controlled by both hormone and nerve regulators. Hormones are produced and released by cells in the mucosa (lining) of the stomach and small intestine at key stages in the digestive process. Among other roles:

● Gastrin causes the stomach to produce its acid.

● Secretin causes the pancreas to produce a fluid that is rich in bicarbonate and enzymes to break down food into its constituent proteins, sugars and so on. The bicarbonate is alkaline and prevents the bowel wall from being damaged as the highly acidic stomach contents are released into the small intestine. Secretin also stimulates the liver to produce bile, the acid that aids fat digestion.

● Cholesystokinin triggers the gallbladder to discharge its bile into the small intestine.

Activity in the digestive system is also controlled by a complex local nervous system known as the enteric nervous system, in which:

● Sensory neurons receive information from receptors in the mucosa and muscle. Chemoreceptors monitor levels of acid, glucose and amino acids. Sensory receptors respond to stretch and tension within the wall of the gut.

● Motor neurons, whose key role is to control gastrointestinal motility (including peristalsis and stomach motility) and secretion, control the action of smooth muscle in the wall of the gut.

Key neurotransmitters involved in the activity of the enteric nervous system are norepinephrine and acetylcholine: the former provides an activating role, the second an inhibitory role. The enteric nervous system works independently of the central nervous system. However, the gut also has links to the central nervous system, providing sensory information (such as fullness) to the hypothalamus and allowing the gut to respond to the various excitatory or inhibitory processes of the autonomic nervous system. In general, sympathetic stimulation inhibits digestive activities, inhibiting gastrointestinal secretion and motor activity, and contracting gastrointestinal sphincters and blood vessels. The latter may be experienced as feelings of 'butterflies in the stomach' – and also some other, perhaps even more obvious, symptoms! Conversely, parasympathetic activity typically stimulates digestive activities.

Disorders of the digestive system
Gastric ulcer

Gastric ulcers are ulceration of the lining of the stomach (mucosa), which can result in a number of symptoms, the most common of which is abdominal discomfort or pain. This typically comes and goes for several days or weeks, occurs two to three hours after eating, is relieved by eating, and may be at its worst during the night – when the stomach is empty following a meal. Other symptoms include poor appetite, weight loss, bloating, nausea and vomiting. If the disease process is not treated, the ulcer may erode through the stomach wall, resulting in the potentially fatal outflow of its contents into the abdomen.

Until relatively recently, gastric ulcers were thought to be a consequence of stress, which was thought to increase acid secretion in the stomach. More recent evidence, however, has shown that a bacterium known as *Helicobacter pylori* is responsible for 70 per cent of cases of the disorder. *Helicobacter pylori* infection is thought to weaken the protective mucous coating of the stomach and duodenum, and allow acid to reach the sensitive lining beneath. It may also increase the amount of stomach acid secreted. Both acid and bacteria irritate the stomach lining and cause the ulcer. Stress may, nevertheless, still be implicated in the development and maintenance of gastric ulcers as it may increase risk behaviours such as smoking or alcohol consumption, as well as adversely affecting the immune system's ability to influence levels of *H. pylori* in the gut.

Treatment involves suppressing acid secretion and, if appropriate, eradicating the *H. pylori* bacteria. Various types of drugs may be used to achieve this effect. Reductions in acid production can be achieved by histamine blockers (e.g. Cimetidine) and drugs known as hydrogen pump antagonists (e.g. Omeprazol). Drugs which eradicate *H. pylori* include antibiotics such as tetracycline or amoxicillin which are frequently given in combination with histamine blockers or hydrogen pump antagonists. Only rarely is surgery used in the treatment of gastric ulcers, and this usually when the ulcer has eroded through the stomach wall and has led to life-threatening haemorrhage.

Inflammatory bowel disease

Inflammatory bowel disease (IBD) is a group of inflammatory conditions of the large and, in some cases, small intestine. The main forms of IBD are:

* Crohn's disease
* ulcerative colitis.

Crohn's disease

Crohn's disease can involve any part of the gastrointestinal tract. It is an inflammatory condition characterised by episodes of severe symptoms followed by periods of remission. Its key symptoms are chronic, and occasionally severe, diarrhoea and disrupted digestion. Over time, the inflammation process can result in a thickening of the bowel wall, which may result in the diameter of the bowel becoming so constricted that food cannot pass through these damaged sections. These may require surgical excision. Unfortunately, as the disease tends to recur at these sites, the constriction may reoccur and require further surgery within a few years. For this reason, surgery is often considered the treatment of last resort. There is some evidence that the condition may have a genetic basis, although a diet high in sugar and fats, smoking and stress have also been implicated in its aetiology. The usual age of onset is between 15 and 30 years of age, with no difference in prevalence between men and women. Its symptoms include:

* abdominal pain;
* changes in bowel movements – faeces may vary between solid and watery;
* periods of mild fever, sometimes with blood in the stools, and pain in the lower right abdomen;
* loss of appetite;

* unintentional weight loss;
* boils and **fistulas**;
* general malaise.

At times of acute symptoms, individuals become severely dehydrated and are unable to digest food and absorb necessary nutrients, resulting in the need for significant medical care. At such times, a number of drugs designed to reduce inflammation and antibiotics may be necessary.

Ulcerative colitis

Ulcerative colitis is similar to Crohn's disease, but usually affects the terminal part of the large intestine and rectum. It may develop into cancer after many years of the disease. For this reason, patients have regular checkups for the beginning of cancer or even have preventive removal of segments of the bowel. This may result in the affected individual needing a **colostomy**. Its severity can be graded as:

* *Mild*: fewer than four stools daily, with or without blood. There may be mild abdominal pain or cramping.

---

inflammatory bowel disease

a group of inflammatory conditions of the large intestine and, in some cases, the small intestine. The main forms of IBD are **Crohn's disease** and **ulcerative colitis**.

Crohn's disease

autoimmune disease that can affect any part of the gastrointestinal tract but most commonly occurs in the ileum (the area where the small and large intestine meet).

fistulas

formation of small passages that connect the intestine with other organs or the skin.

ulcerative colitis

a chronic inflammatory disease of the large intestine, characterised by recurrent episodes of abdominal pain, fever and severe diarrhoea.

colostomy

a surgical procedure that creates an opening (stoma) in the abdomen for the drainage of stool from the large intestine (colon). It may be temporary or permanent.

● *Moderate*: more than four stools daily. Patients may be anaemic and have moderate abdominal pain and low-grade fever.

● *Severe*: more than six bloody stools a day, and evidence of systemic disease such as fever, **tachycardia**, or anaemia.

● *Fulminant*: ten bowel movements daily, continuous bleeding, abdominal tenderness and distension. Patients will require blood transfusion and their colon may perforate, resulting in the gut content being released into the abdomen. Unless treated, fulminant disease will soon lead to death.

The goals of treatment with medication are to treat acute episodes and to maintain remission once achieved. Treatment is similar to that of Crohn's disease, and involves steroids to reduce inflammation and immunomodulators which suppress the body's immune processes that are contributing to the condition. An interesting fact is that risk of developing ulcerative colitis appears to be higher in non-smokers and in ex-smokers, and some patients may actually improve when treated with nicotine.

Irritable bowel syndrome

Irritable bowel syndrome (IBS) is a condition of the bowel involving a period of at least three months abdominal discomfort or pain, with two or more of the following features:

● pain, relieved by defaecation;

● pain associated with a change in the frequency of bowel movements;

● change in the form of the stool (loose, watery, or pellet-like).

> ### tachycardia
> high heart rate – usually defined as greater than 100 beats per minute.
>
> ### irritable bowel syndrome
> a disorder of the lower intestinal tract. Symptoms include pain combined with altered bowel habits resulting in diarrhoea, constipation or both. It has no obvious physiological abnormalities, so diagnosis is by the presence and pattern of symptoms.

Also central to a diagnosis of IBS is that these symptoms occur in the absence of any obvious physical pathology. Because of this lack of physical pathology, IBS was at one time considered to be the archetypal psychosomatic disorder. Indeed, Latimer (1981) went so far as to suggest that anxiety and IBS were one and the same, with IBS symptoms reported by people who were unwilling or unable to attribute their anxiety symptoms to psychological factors. However, evidence of this link to stress is not as strong as was previously thought, and other factors have now been linked with IBS. These include food hypersensitivities and the presence of bacteria such as *Blastocystishominis* and *Helicobacter pylori* (see Singh et al. 2003). Spence and Moss-Morris (2007) argued that the initial trigger to IBS may be an infection (an episode of gastroenteritis), with the condition maintained in the longer term by high levels of anxiety and/or stress. Whatever its cause, psychological treatment using cognitive-behavioural therapy or a form of relaxation known as autogenic training, in which patients are given specific instructions of visualising and feeling warm and relaxed in the gut appear to be effective forms of treatment (see Chapter 17 ☞). Medical treatment involves the use of smooth muscle relaxants to reduce gut motility, adding or reducing fibre to the diet (depending on the level of fibre already in the diet), drugs which 'bulk' up stools to reduce diarrhoea and, on occasion, anxiolytic or anti-depressant drugs. While IBS may be unpleasant, and some people may be restricted by the pain they experience or the fear of not being able to get to a toilet in time if they were to have diarrhoea, it is not a life-threatening condition nor as debilitating as the previously described conditions. We examine psychological treatments for IBS in Chapter 17 ☞, and the role of stress in the development of bowel disorders in Chapter 11 ☞.

Colorectal cancer

Colorectal cancer is the third most common cancer in men and women. Risk for the condition is increased by both biological and behavioural factors, including genetic factors, pre-existing inflammatory conditions including ulcerative colitis, and a diet high in fat and low in fibre. Symptoms of the disorder are often unnoticed because they are relatively mild, and include: bleeding, constipation or diarrhoea, and unformed stool. One early symptom may be a general tiredness and shortness of breath as a consequence of anaemia caused by long-term, but unnoticed, bleeding within the gut. For this reason, the cancer may be quite advanced before people seek medical help. It is nevertheless generally treatable with a combination of surgery to remove the cancer followed by chemotherapy. Radiotherapy is rarely used except in cases of rectal cancer. As with many cancers, the condition can be described in terms of its stages, with the higher stage being more difficult to treat and having a poorer **prognosis**:

- *Stage 1*: the cancer is limited to the inside of the bowel.
- *Stage 2*: the cancer penetrates through the wall of the bowel to the outside layers.
- *Stage 3*: the cancer involves the lymph glands in the abdomen.
- *Stage 4*: the cancer has metastasised to other organs.

The cardiovascular system

The main function of the cardiovascular system is to transport nutrients, immune cells and oxygen to the body's organs and to remove waste products from them. It also moves hormones from their point of production within the body to their site of action. The transport medium used in this process is the blood; the pumping system that pushes the blood around the body involves the heart and various types of blood vessel:

- *Arteries*: transport blood away from the heart. These vessels have a muscular sheath that allows them to

> **prognosis**
> the predicted outcome of a disease.

IN THE SPOTLIGHT

Cancer

Hundreds of genes play a role in the growth and division of cells. Three classes of gene control this process and may contribute to the uncontrolled proliferation of cells, which is cancer:

1. *Oncogenes* control the sequence of events by which a cell enlarges, replicates its DNA, divides and passes a complete set of genes to each daughter cell. When mutated, they can drive excessive proliferation by producing too much, or an overactive form, of a growth stimulating protein.
2. *Tumour suppressor genes* inhibit cell growth. Loss or inactivation of this gene may produce inappropriate growth by losing this inhibitory control.
3. *Checkpoint genes* monitor and repair DNA, which is often damaged prior to reproduction and needs to be repaired before cell division. Without these checking mechanisms, a damaged gene will become replicated as a permanent mutation. One of the most notable checkpoint proteins is known as p53, which prevents replication of damaged DNA in

the normal cell and promotes **cell suicide** in cells with abnormal DNA. Faulty p53 allows cells carrying damaged DNA to replicate and survive and has been found to be defective in most human cancers.

Other factors are also important in tumour development. Growing tumours are dependent on a good blood supply. To promote this, local tissues may be transformed into blood vessel cells, allowing the tumour to establish its own blood supply. Some modern treatments of cancer attack this blood supply as well as the tumour mass itself. Tumours also acquire the ability to migrate and invade other tissues, forming tumour masses at different sites in the body. This process is known as metastasis – and in some cases these secondary tumours may be more deadly than the original tumour.

> **cell suicide**
> a form of cell death in which a controlled sequence of events (or programme) leads to the elimination of cells without releasing harmful substances into the surrounding area.

contract or expand slightly. This activity is controlled by the autonomic nervous system.

● *Arterioles*: these are small arteries, linking the large arteries to the organs of the body.

● *Veins*: these transport blood back to the heart once the oxygen and nutrients have been absorbed from it and replaced by carbon dioxide, and a variety of waste products. They are thinner than arteries, and because they are so far from the heart have much lower pressures than the arteries. Blood is pushed through them partly by the pressure of the pulse of blood from the heart, partly through the action of the moving muscles. As large muscle groups contract during everyday

activities, they push blood through the veins. To prevent back flow of blood they have a series of valves, which allow the blood to flow in only one direction. When the muscles are inactive, blood may no longer flow freely in the veins and may even stagnate and begin to clot – a deep vein thrombosis that may occur after long-haul flights or other periods of inactivity in some susceptible individuals.

The heart

The heart has two separate pumps operating in parallel. The right side of the heart is involved in the transportation of blood to the lungs; the left side pumps blood to the rest of the body (Figure 8.6). Each side of the heart has two chambers (Figure 8.7), known as atria and ventricles. The right atrium takes deoxygenated blood from veins known as the superior and inferior venae cavae and pumps it into the right ventricle. Blood is then pumped into the pulmonary artery, taking it to the lungs, where it picks up oxygen in its **haemoglobin** cells. Oxygen-laden blood then returns to the heart, entering through the left atrium. It is then pumped into the left ventricle, and then into the main artery, known as the **aorta**, which carries blood to the rest of the body.

> ### haemoglobin
> the main substance of the red blood cell. When oxygenated in the lungs, it is converted to oxyhaemoglobin, thus allowing the red blood cells to carry oxygen from the air in our lungs to all parts of the body.
>
> ### aorta
> the main trunk of the systemic arteries, carrying blood from the left side of the heart to the arteries of all limbs and organs except the lungs.

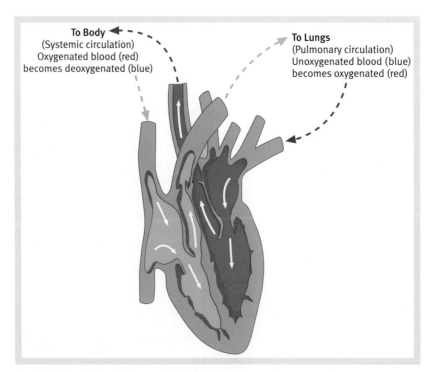

To Body
(Systemic circulation)
Oxygenated blood (red)
becomes deoxygenated (blue)

To Lungs
(Pulmonary circulation)
Unoxygenated blood (blue)
becomes oxygenated (red)

Figure 8.6 The flow of blood through the heart

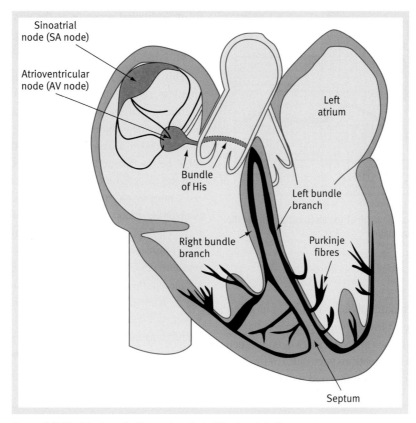

Figure 8.7 Electrical conduction and control of the heart rhythm

The rhythm of the heart is controlled by an electrical system. It is initiated by an electrical impulse generated in a region of the right atrium called the sinoatrial node. This impulse causes the muscles of both atria to contract. As the wave of electricity progresses through the heart muscle and nerves, it reaches an area at the junction of the atria and ventricles known as the atrioventricular node. This second node then fires a further electrical discharge along a system of nerves including the Bundle of His and Purkinje fibres (see Figure 8.7), triggering the muscles of both ventricles to contract, completing the cycle. Although the sinoatrial node has an intrinsic rhythm, its activity is largely influenced by the autonomic nervous system.

An electrocardiogram (ECG) is used to measure the activity of the heart. Electrodes are placed over the heart and can detect each of the nodes firing and recharging. Figure 8.8 shows an ECG of a normal heart, indicating the electrical activity at each stage of the heart's cycle.

The P wave indicates the electrical activity of the atria firing – the time needed for an electrical impulse from the sinoatrial node to spread throughout the atrial musculature.

- The QRS complex represents the electrical activity of the ventricles compressing.

- The T wave represents the repolarisation of the ventricles.

When the heart stops beating or its electrical rhythm is completely irregular and no blood is being pushed around the body, doctors may use a **defibrillator** to stimulate a normal (sinusoidal) rhythm.

> **defibrillator**
>
> a machine that uses an electric current to stop any irregular and dangerous activity of the heart's muscles. It can be used when the heart has stopped (**cardiac arrest**) or when it is beating in a highly irregular (and ineffective) manner.

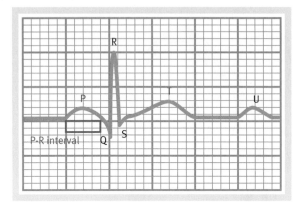

Figure 8.8 An electrocardiograph of the electrical activity of the heart (see text for explanation)

Blood

The body usually contains about five litres of blood. Its constituents include a fluid known as plasma and a variety of cells. As well as the various **exogenous** cells carried in the blood (nutrients, oxygen, etc.), it produces its own cells. These are manufactured by **stem cells** in the bone marrow. Three different types of cell are produced:

1. **Erythrocytes** (or red blood cells) transport oxygen around the body. In them, oxygen combines with haemoglobin in the lungs and is transported to cells in need of oxygen, where it is released, allowing cell respiration.

2. Phagocytes and lymphocytes (or white blood cells; see above) include the immune system's B cells and T cells described earlier in the chapter.

3. **Platelets** are cells that respond to damage to the circulatory system. They aggregate (form a clot) around the site of any damage and prevent loss of blood from the system. They are also involved in repair to damage within the arteries themselves and contribute to the development of atheroma. We consider this process later in the chapter.

Blood pressure

Blood pressure has two components:

1. the degree of pressure imposed on the blood as a result of its constriction within the arteries and veins – known as the diastolic blood pressure (DBP);

2. an additional pressure as the wave of blood pushed out from the heart flows through the system (our pulse) – known as the systolic blood pressure (SBP).

This pressure is measured in millimetres of mercury (mmHg), representing the height of a tube of mercury in millilitres that the pressure can push up (using a now old-fashioned sphygmomanometer). Healthy levels of blood pressure are an SBP below 130–140 mmHg and a DBP below 90 mmHg (written as 130/90 mmHg: see also the discussion of hypertension later in the chapter).

A number of physiological processes are involved in controlling blood pressure. Those of particular interest to psychologists involve the autonomic nervous system. The brainstem receives continuous information from pressure-sensitive nerve endings called **baroreceptors** situated in the **carotid arteries** and aorta. This information is relayed to a centre in the brainstem known as the vasomotor centre, and then on to the hypothalamus. Reductions in blood pressure or physical demands such as exercise that require increased blood pressure causes activation of the sympathetic nervous system.

---

exogenous
relating to things outside the body.

stem cell
a 'generic' cell that can make exact copies of itself indefinitely. In addition, such cells have the ability to produce specialised cells for various tissues in the body, including blood, heart muscle, brain and liver tissue. Found in the bone marrow.

erythrocyte
a mature blood cell that contains haemoglobin to carry oxygen to the bodily tissues.

platelets
tiny bits of protoplasm found in the blood that are essential for blood clotting. These cells bind together to form a clot and prevent bleeding at the site of injury.

baroreceptors
sensory nerve endings that are stimulated by changes in pressure. Located in the walls of blood vessels such as the carotid sinus.

carotid artery
the main artery that takes blood from the heart via the neck to the brain.

Sympathetic activation results in an increase in the strength and frequency of heart contractions (via the activity of the sinoatrial and atrioventricular nodes) and a contraction of the smooth muscle in the arteries. Together, these actions increase blood pressure, and allow sustained flow of blood to organs such as the muscles at times of high activity. Parasympathetic activity results in an opposing reaction.

Diseases of the cardiovascular system

Hypertension

Hypertension is a condition in which resting blood pressure is significantly above normal levels (see Table 8.2).

Two broad causes of hypertension have been identified:

1. *Secondary hypertension*: here, hypertension is the result of a disease process usually involving the kidneys, adrenal glands or aorta. This type of hypertension accounts for about 5 per cent of cases.

2. *Essential (primary) hypertension*: in the majority of cases, there is no known disease process that causes the problem. It seems to be the 'normal' consequence of a number of risk factors, such as obesity, lack of exercise and a high salt intake. It is a progressive condition, and people with the condition usually experience a gradual rise in blood pressure over a period of years, with no obvious symptoms.

Psychological stress may also contribute to the development of essential hypertension. At times of stress, sympathetic activity increases muscle tone in the arteries and the strength of the heart's contractions – both of which contribute to short-term increases in blood pressure, which then falls as parasympathetic activity follows a period of stress. If the stress is sustained or frequent, however, the activity of the sympathetic nervous system begins to dominate and gradually pushes blood pressure up for longer periods until the individual develops chronically raised blood pressure.

Hypertension may be present and remain unnoticed for many years, or even decades. It is usually considered to be a syndrome with few if any symptoms, and many cases of hypertension are detected during routine screening (see Chapter 6 ☞). If high blood pressure has no symptoms, why bother treating it? At low levels of high blood pressure – mild hypertension – some have argued that medical treatment may actually be of little benefit, and that the side effects of treatment may outweigh its benefits (although this position is now being challenged as new drugs are used to treat the condition: see Weber and Julius 1998). However, as blood pressure rises, so too does the amount of damage it can do. High blood pressure increases the risk of a heart attack (myocardial infarction (MI) – see below), stroke, kidney failure, eye damage and **heart failure**. It also contributes to the development of atheroma. Hypertension is usually treated with anti-hypertensive drugs with a variety of actions, including **ACE inhibitors**, **diuretics** and **beta-blockers**, all of which have been proven effective in reducing blood pressure.

---

heart failure

a state in which the heart muscle is damaged or weakened and is unable to generate a cardiac output sufficient to meet the demands of the body.

ACE inhibitors

angiotensin II causes the muscles surrounding blood vessels to contract and thereby narrows the blood vessels. Angiotensin Converting Enzyme (ACE) inhibitors decrease the production of angiotensin II, allowing blood vessels to dilate, and reduce blood pressure.

diuretics

elevates the rate of bodily urine excretion, reducing the amount of fluid within the cardiovascular system, and reducing pressure within it.

beta-blockers

block the action of adrenaline and noradrenaline on b-adrenergic receptors, which mediate the 'fight or flight' response, within the heart and in muscles surrounding the arteries. In doing so, they reduce increases in blood pressure associated with sympathetic activation.

Table 8.2 Typical blood pressure readings in normal and hypertensive individuals

	Diastolic (mmHg)	Systolic (mmHg)
Normal	90	140
Mild hypertension	90–99	140–159
Hypertension	100	160

Coronary heart disease

Like hypertension, coronary heart disease (CHD) may develop over many years before becoming evident. Indeed, people may have quite significant CHD and never be aware of their condition. The long-term, and silent, element of CHD is the development of atheroma in the blood vessels. This may eventually cause more obvious manifestations of CHD, including an MI and angina (see below).

Atherosclerosis

Atherosclerosis is a disease in which atheroma builds up on the lining of the arteries. The main constituent of atheroma is cholesterol. This is a waxy substance that is present in blood plasma and in all the body's cells. Without it, cells could not maintain the integrity of their walls, and we would become seriously ill or die. Too much cholesterol, on the other hand, may be harmful. To get to cell walls in order to repair and maintain them, cholesterol must be transported through the body via the bloodstream attached to groups of proteins called lipoproteins. **Low-density lipoproteins** (LDLs) transport cholesterol to the various tissues and body cells, where it is separated from the lipoprotein and is used by the cell. It can also be absorbed into atheroma on the inner surface of the blood vessels. **High-density lipoproteins** (HDLs) transport excess or unused cholesterol from the tissues back to the liver, where it is broken down to bile acids and then excreted. LDLs are therefore characterised as 'harmful' cholesterol; HDLs are considered to be health-protective. Although some cholesterol is absorbed

from our food through the gut, about 80 per cent of cholesterol in our bodies is produced by the liver. The development of atherosclerosis involves a series of stages:

● *Early processes*: atheroma usually occurs at sites of disturbed blood flow, such as bifurcations of the arteries. It forms as part of the repair process to damage of the artery wall caused by the disturbed blood flow. In this process, inflammatory monocytes, which are precursors to macrophages (see the section on the immune system earlier in the chapter), absorb LDL cholesterol from the circulating blood to become what are known as foam cells. These form a coat over the lining of the damaged artery. As the foam cells die, they lose their contents of LDL, resulting in pools of cholesterol forming between the foam cells and the artery wall. The presence of foam cells may trigger the growth of smooth muscle cells from the artery wall to cover them. In this way, the walls of the artery become lined with lipids, foam cells and finally a wall of smooth muscle. This repeated process results in a gradual reduction of the diameter of the artery.

● *Acute events*: at times, more acute events may occur, and clots of cholesterol and foam cells may be pulled out of the artery wall. This may result in a clot blocking an artery in a key organ such as the heart, resulting in an MI (see below).

The distribution of atheroma within the circulatory system is not uniform throughout the body. It is most developed around the junctions of arteries because disturbances in blood flow at such points can facilitate these processes, but the heart arteries are also one of the areas most likely to be affected. High levels of cholesterol may be treated with drugs known as statins, if dietary changes are insufficient to lower cholesterol to safe levels. They work by blocking an enzyme (HMG-CoA reductase) the liver needs to make cholesterol. They may also help reabsorb cholesterol that has accumulated in atheroma on the artery walls.

Myocardial infarction

As we noted in the last section, an important end point of CHD is when a clot is pulled off an artery wall and enters the circulating blood. This may prove a harmless event, with no health implications for the individual. However, if the circulating clot has a greater diameter than the blood vessels it is passing through, it will inevitably block the blood vessel and prevent the flow of

---

low-density lipoprotein (LDL)

the main function of LDL seems to be to carry cholesterol to various tissues throughout the body. LDL is sometimes referred to as 'bad' cholesterol because elevated levels of LDL correlate most directly with coronary heart disease.

high-density lipoprotein (HDL)

lipoproteins are fat protein complexes in the blood that transport cholesterol, triglycerides and other lipids to various tissues. The main function of HDL appears to be to carry excess cholesterol to the liver for 're-packaging' or excretion in the bile. Higher levels of HDL seem to be protective against CHD, so HDL is sometimes referred to as 'good' cholesterol.

IN THE SPOTLIGHT

The life and (heroic) death of John Henry

John Henry was born a slave in the USA in the 1840s or 1850s. So what has he got to do with modern-day psychology? Well, legend has it that he was a giant of a man, who rose to any challenge he faced – a characteristic that eventually resulted in his death. He died while working as a labourer on the railroad tunnelling through a mountain in West Virginia. One of his jobs was to pound holes into rock, which were then filled with explosives and used to blast through tunnels. When the railroad owners brought in steam drills to do the same job more quickly and cheaply, he challenged the steam drill to a contest. He won the contest but died of exhaustion soon after. His name has now become synonymous with a process, initially at least, thought to drive hypertension in black males – John Henryism.

Hypertension is particularly prevalent among African Americans. Black people in the USA are significantly more likely than whites to develop hypertension by the age of 50 (see, e.g. Fuchs 2011). One of the reasons for this is thought to be that they are more frequently placed in situations in which they have to respond to difficult psychological stressors – poverty, racism, and so on – than their white counterparts (see Chapter 2 ☞). Those people who have emotional or behavioural responses to such stressors experience sustained increases in heart rate and blood pressure. This overcomes the body's homeostatic processes and pushes their resting blood pressure increasingly up until they develop long-term hypertension. Although initially viewed as an issue for black men, the process is increasingly being seen as the outcome of the stresses associated with a low socio-economic position – and may account for some of the more general health inequalities considered in Chapter 2 ☞.

blood beyond this blockage. This occlusion may result in significant health problems if it occurs in the arteries supplying oxygen and nutrients to the heart. Unless rapidly treated, the cells of the heart muscle beyond the occlusion no longer receive their nutrients and oxygen and die – a myocardial infarction (MI). The severity of the MI is determined by how large a blood vessel is affected (larger is worse) and which parts of the heart are damaged.

The classic symptoms of an MI include what is often described as 'crushing chest pain'. The affected individual may feel like their chest is trapped in a vice. Other symptoms include shortness of breath, coughing, pain radiating down the left arm, dizziness and/or collapse, nausea or vomiting, and sweating. However, an MI may also be much less dramatic. Indeed, many people delay seeking help for an MI as their symptoms are vague, may be confused with heartburn or indigestion, and the affected individual hopes they will go away without treatment. Perhaps the strangest symptom that can rarely be indicative of an MI is toothache – although we would not recommend you visit your local hospital complaining

of a heart attack should you be unfortunate enough to develop this problem!

Depending on the site of the infarction within the heart, around 2.5 to 10 per cent of people will die of their MI immediately or in the month or so following the event (e.g. Rosamond et al. 2012). The majority go on to make a good recovery. This may be aided by treatment with drugs known as '**clot busters**'. These drugs dissolve the clot causing the blocked artery and, if given within an hour or so of the infarction, can prevent permanent muscle damage. Longer-term treatment now frequently involves a procedure known as an angioplasty (or its longer formal name, Percutaneous Transluminal Coronary Angioplasty: PTCA) in which a long narrow catheter is inserted into the femoral artery (near the

> **clot busters**
> drugs which dissolve clots associated with myocardial infarction and can prevent damage to the heart following such an event. Are best used within one hour of the infarction.

groin) and, guided by X-rays, is pushed along the arteries until it reaches the coronary arteries. After reaching the site of the MI, a small balloon is inflated which pushes against the occluded artery wall, increasing the diameter of the artery and allowing normal blood flow through it. A small wire mesh tube (known as a stent) is then frequently left in position at the site to maintain the patency of the artery. Long-term contributors to CHD, including high cholesterol or blood pressure, are treated with appropriate lifestyle changes (see Chapters 6, 7 and 17 ☞) and medication if necessary.

Angina

The key symptom of **angina** is similar to that of an MI. It is a central chest pain that may radiate to the left shoulder, jaw, arm or other areas of the chest. Some patients may confuse arm or shoulder pain with arthritis or indigestion pain. Unlike an MI, however, it is a temporary condition which occurs when the heart muscle needs more oxygen than can be provided by the heart arteries, and stops once these demands are reduced. It is frequently precipitated by exertion or stress, and may result from two underlying causes:

1. atheromatous lesions of the coronary arteries reduce their diameter and limit the blood flow through them;

2. **vasospasm** of the coronary arteries results in a temporary reduction in their diameter;

3. a combination of both.

Classic angina (or angina pectoris) is associated with high levels of atheroma in the coronary arteries which limits the amount of blood they can carry to the heart

muscle. Physical exertion, emotional stress and exposure to cold are among the triggers for this type of angina. In a second type of angina known as unstable angina, people with the condition experience angina symptoms after relatively little effort (such as just taking a few steps) or even when they are resting. It is usually the result of a severe narrowing in a coronary artery, and may lead to an MI if it is not treated. As with an MI, treatment involves interventions to reduce the immediate symptoms of angina and to prevent the underlying disease progress. Symptomatic relief can be achieved through the use of GlycerylTrinitrate (GTN: otherwise known as nitroglycerin!). This comes as a spray (sprayed into the mouth) or tablets (placed under the tongue) to take when an angina episode starts, and results in an immediate widening of the arteries and relief from symptoms. If the level of disease warrants it, patients with angina may also be given PTCA, or a **coronary artery bypass graft** (CABG), in which blood vessels are taken from the legs or the chest and used to bypass the diseased artery. Treatment of underlying conditions may involve the use of statins or hypertensive medication. In Chapter 17 ☞, we describe the case of Mr Jones, whose angina was so severe that on two occasions he believed he was having an MI and went to the emergency department of the local hospital. We also show how we helped him adjust better to his condition.

The respiratory system

The respiratory system delivers oxygen to and removes carbon dioxide from the blood. The exchange of oxygen and carbon dioxide occurs in the lungs. The system comprises:

● the *upper respiratory tract*, including the nose, mouth, larynx and trachea;

● the *lower respiratory tract*, including the lungs, bronchi, bronchioles and alveoli. Each lung is divided into upper and lower lobes – the upper lobe of the right lung contains a third subdivision known as the right middle lobe.

The bronchi carry air from the mouth to the lungs. As they enter the lungs, they divide into smaller bronchi, then into smaller tubes called bronchioles (see Figure 8.9). The bronchioles contain minute hairs called cilia, which beat

---

angina
severe pain in the chest associated with a temporary insufficient supply of blood to the heart.

vasospasm
a situation in which the muscles of artery walls in the heart contract and relax rapidly, resulting in a reduction of the flow of blood through the artery.

coronary artery bypass graft
surgical procedure in which veins or arteries from elsewhere in the patient's body are grafted from the aorta to the coronary arteries, bypassing blockages caused by atheroma in the cardiac arteries and improving the blood supply to the heart muscle.

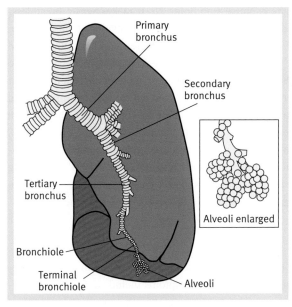

Figure 8.9 Diagram of the lungs, showing the bronchi, bronchioles and alveoli. As we breathe out, carbon dioxide concentration in the blood is greater than that in the alveoli, so it passes from the blood into the alveoli and is then exhaled.

rhythmically to sweep debris out of the lungs towards the pharynx for expulsion and thus form part of the mechanical element of the immune system – see earlier in the chapter. Bronchioles end in air sacs called alveoli – small, thin-walled 'balloons', which are surrounded by tiny blood capillaries. As we breathe in, the concentration of oxygen is greater in the alveoli than in the haemoglobin in the blood travelling through the capillaries. As a result, oxygen diffuses across the alveolar walls into the haemoglobin.

Respiration is the act of breathing:

- *Inspiration*: two sets of muscles are involved in inhalation. The main muscle involved is the diaphragm. This is a sheet of muscle that divides the abdomen and is found immediately below the lungs. Contraction of this muscle pulls the lungs down and sucks air into them. The second set of muscles is known as the intercostal muscles. These are found between the ribs and can expand the chest – again pulling air into the lungs.

- *Expiration*: relaxation of the diaphragm and intercostal muscles allows the lungs to contract, decreases lung volume, and pushes air out of them. The air then passively flows out.

The rate of breathing is controlled by respiratory centres in the brainstem. These respond to:

- the concentration of carbon dioxide in the blood (high carbon dioxide concentrations initiate deeper, more rapid breathing);

- air pressure in lung tissue. Expansion of the lungs stimulates nerve receptors to signal the brain to 'turn off' inspiration. When the lungs collapse, the receptors give the 'turn on' signal, known as the Hering–Breuer inspiratory reflex.

Other automatic regulators include increases in blood pressure, which slows down respiration; a fall in blood acidity, which stimulates respiration; and a sudden drop in blood pressure, which increases the rate and depth of respiration.

Diseases of the respiratory system

Chronic obstructive airways disease

Chronic obstructive pulmonary disease (COPD) is a group of lung diseases characterised by limited airflow through the airways resulting from damage to the alveoli. Its most common manifestations are **emphysema** and **chronic bronchitis**.

Emphysema

Emphysema results from the destruction of the alveoli, resulting in reduced lung elasticity and reductions in the surface area on which the exchange of oxygen and carbon dioxide can occur. People with the condition experience chronic shortness of breath, an unproductive cough

---

emphysema

a late effect of chronic infection or irritation of the bronchial tubes. When the bronchi become irritated, some of the airways may become obstructed or the walls of the tiny air sacs may tear, trapping air in the lung beyond them. As a result, the lungs may become enlarged, at the same time becoming less efficient in exchanging oxygen for carbon dioxide.

chronic bronchitis

an inflammation of the bronchi, the main air passages in the lungs, which persists for a long period or repeatedly recurs. Characterised by excessive bronchial mucus and a cough that produces sputum for three months or more in at least two consecutive years.

(which produces no phlegm), and a marked reduction in exercise capacity. The condition typically results from exposing the alveoli to irritants, whether as a result of direct or passive smoking or living or working in a polluted environment. About 15 per cent of long-term smokers will develop COPD (Mannino 2003). More rarely, an enzyme deficiency called alpha-1 anti-trypsin deficiency can cause emphysema in non-smokers. Treatment of emphysema involves a number of approaches: drugs known as bronchodilators widen the air passages and relax smooth muscle tissue in the lungs. Some individuals may need continuous oxygen therapy. Finally, as people with emphysema are prone to lung infections, they may require treatment with antibiotics. What is it like to live with emphysema? Well, here is a quote from someone (Gary Bain) with the condition taken from a self-help website (www.emphysema.org):

> Sit down somewhere and relax a little and when you feel comfortable, take your right or left hand and with your thumb and forefinger, hold your nose shut. While holding your nose shut, cover your mouth tightly with the rest of your hand so you can just barely breathe through your fingers. Now, walk for about 40 steps and turn around and come back while still breathing through your hand. Now, do you see how hard it is to breathe? Especially when you try to walk around? That is what emphysema is …

Chronic bronchitis

Chronic bronchitis results from inflammation and a consequent narrowing of the airways. Bronchitis is considered to be chronic when it persists for three months or more for at least two consecutive years. People with the condition experience shortness of breath and have excessive mucus within the bronchial tree and a 'wet' cough. They may also experience wheezing and fatigue. As with emphysema, it is caused predominantly by smoking and second-hand smoke. Allergies, outdoor and indoor air pollution, and infection may exacerbate the condition. Treatment involves the use of bronchodilators, and, for some people, oxygen therapy. Corticosteroids may also be used at times of acute severe episodes of breathing difficulty when other treatments are ineffective.

Self-help for people with COPD

Unfortunately, the way many people cope with their COPD may inadvertently add to their problems. Understandably, people who become out of breath when they exercise stop doing so. It makes sense: breathlessness is both unpleasant and frightening. Unfortunately, this avoidance results in a decrease in lung function and a worsening of symptoms. As patients' contribution to their lung health has become more evident, a number of programmes have now been developed and implemented to teach people how best to cope with COPD. Often referred to as pulmonary rehabilitation (see, for example, http://www.patient.co.uk/doctor/pulmonary-rehabilitation) , these provide advice on 'lung health' and coping with breathlessness, and a gentle physical exercise programme designed to increase fitness and lung capacity.

Lung cancer

Lung cancer is the second most common cancer affecting both sexes. Its symptoms include a dry non-productive cough, shortness of breath, coughing up sputum with signs of blood in it, an ache or pain when breathing, loss of appetite, fatigue and losing weight. The main cause of lung cancer is smoking, and as women have taken up smoking following the Second World War, rates of lung cancer among this group have risen, while those among men have fallen (Tyczynski et al. 2004). Other risk factors involve exposure to carcinogens, including asbestos and radon, and scarring from tuberculosis. There is some evidence of a genetic risk also.

Two different types of lung cancer have been identified:

1. *Small cell cancer*: the main treatment is radiotherapy or chemotherapy. The overall survival rate depends on the stage of the disease. For limited-stage small cell cancer, cure rates may be as high as 25 per cent, while cure rates for extensive-stage disease are less than 5 per cent.

2. *Non-small cell cancer* (between 70 and 80 per cent of cases): the main treatment for this type of cancer involves removal of the cancer through surgery. Where the tumour is small and has not spread, up to 50 per cent of people with the condition may survive. The prognosis is worse the larger the tumour. Where the tumour has spread and lymph nodes are involved, the disease is almost never cured, and the goals of therapy are to extend life and improve quality of life (Beadsmoore and Screaton 2003).

We examine how people respond to having lung cancer in Chapter 9 ☛, and some interventions designed to help people with lung diseases in Chapter 17 ☛.

SUMMARY

- This chapter reviewed some of the anatomy and physiology relevant to health psychology and other chapters of this book. In the first section, it briefly described key functions of the brain and their situation within it. Key functional areas include:
  - the medulla oblongata, which controls respiration, blood pressure and heartbeat;
  - the hypothalamus, which controls appetite, sexual arousal and thirst. It also exerts some control over our emotions;
  - the amygdala, which links situations of threat and relevant emotions such as fear or anxiety, and controls the autonomic nervous system response to such threats.

- One of the key systems controlled by the brain is the autonomic nervous system. This comprises two parallel sets of nerves:
  - The sympathetic nervous system is responsible for activation of many organs of the body.
  - The parasympathetic nervous system is responsible for rest and recuperation.

- The highest level of control of the autonomic nervous system within the brain is the hypothalamus, which coordinates reflexive changes in response to a variety of physical changes, including movement, temperature and blood pressure. It also responds to emotional and cognitive demands, providing a link between physiological systems and psychological stress.

- Activation of the sympathetic nervous system involves two neurotransmitters – norepinephrine and epinephrine – which stimulate organs via the sympathetic nerves themselves. Sustained activation is maintained by their hormonal equivalents, released from the adrenal medulla. A second system, controlled by the hypothalamus and pituitary gland, triggers the release of corticosteroids from the adrenal cortex. These increase the energy available to sustain physiological activation and inhibit inflammation of damaged tissue.

- The immune system provides a barrier to infection by viruses and other biological threats to our health. Key elements of the system include phagocytes, such as macrophages and neutrophils, which engulf and destroy invading pathogens. A second group of cells, known as lymphocytes, including cytotoxic T cells and B cells, respond particularly to attacks by viruses and developing tumour cells. Both groups of cells can collaborate in the destruction of pathogens through a complex series of chemical reactions.

- Slow viruses, including HIV, attack the immune system – by infecting CD4+ cells – and prevent the T and B cell systems from responding effectively. This leaves the body open to attack from viruses and cancers, either of which may result in life-threatening conditions.

- The immune system may, itself, cause problems by treating its own cells as external invading agents. This can result in diseases such as multiple sclerosis, rheumatoid arthritis and type 1 diabetes.

- The digestive tract is responsible for the ingestion, absorption and expulsion of food. Activity within it is controlled by the enteric nervous system, which is linked to the autonomic nervous system. Activity in the system is therefore responsive to stress and other psychological states. That said, some conditions thought to be the result of stress are now thought to be the result of physical as well as psychological factors. Gastric ulcers are thought to result from infection by *Helicobacter pylori*, while irritable bowel syndrome is no longer seen as entirely the result of stress but as having a multi-factor aetiology of which stress is but one strand.

- The cardiovascular system is responsible for carrying oxygen, nutrients and various other materials around the body. Its activity is influenced by the autonomic nervous system. Two long-term 'silent' conditions that may lead to acute illnesses such as myocardial infarction or stroke are hypertension and atheroma. Both involve long-term processes. One way in which long-term hypertension may develop is by repeated short-term increases in blood pressure through the action of the autonomic nervous system in response to stress. Atheroma develops as a result of repair processes to the artery wall. Two obvious outcomes of this process are myocardial infarction, in which an artery supplying the heart muscle is blocked and dies. Angina presents with similar symptoms but is the result of spasm of the arteries and is reversible.

● Finally, the respiratory system is responsible for inspiring and carrying oxygen around the body, and the expulsion of carbon dioxide. It is prone to a number of disease processes, including chronic obstructive airways disease and lung cancer, all of which are significantly exacerbated by cigarette smoking.

Further reading

Lovallo, W.R. (2005). *Stress and Health. Biological and Psychological Interactions*. Thousand Oaks, CA: Sage.

A relatively easy introduction to the autonomic and immune systems, as well as how stress can influence their activity.

Kumar, P.J. and Clark, K.L. (2012). *Clinical Medicine*. Oxford: W.B. Saunders.

At 1,304 pages, this is not a textbook you may want to buy (although shorter versions are available). But if you want to know more about the development of various diseases, this is an excellent starting point.

Vedhara, K. and Irwin, M. (eds) (2005). *Human Psychoneuroimmunology*. Oxford: Oxford University Press.

A readable guide to psychoneuroimmunology, written for those people who do not want to plough through £250, 400-page tomes (or so say the editors).

You can also find a wealth of information about illnesses and their treatment from the internet. Three excellent sites are:

medlineplus.gov/ – this is a free service provided by the US National Library of Medicine and the National Institutes of Health.

www.netdoctor.co.uk/ – provides similar information and is also free.

www.patient.co.uk/ – as does this site.

In addition, many sites provide information on specific illnesses, including:

www.heartfoundation.org.au/index.htm – the Australian Heart Foundation

www.ulcerativecolitis.org.uk/ – the Ulcerative Colitis Information Centre

www.lunguk.org/ – the British Lung Foundation.

In fact, simply using the name of an illness as a search term in any search engine will undoubtedly allow you to access all the information you are likely to need about that illness and its treatment.

For open-access student resources specifically written to complement this textbook and support your learning, please visit **www.pearsoned.co.uk/morrison**

Chapter 9
Symptom perception, interpretation and response

Learning outcomes

By the end of this chapter, you should have an understanding of:

- key theoretical models of symptom perception, interpretation and response
- contextual, cultural and individual influences upon symptom perception
- the core dimensions upon which illness can be represented
- the measurement of illness perceptions and their relationship with illness outcomes
- a broad range of influences upon symptom interpretation
- factors that influence delay in seeking health-care advice for symptoms

'Being a man – putting life before death'

This strong title, coined by Martin Seager and David Wilkins, the former an Honorary Consultant Psychologist with a branch of the Samaritans, the latter Policy Officer for the UK Men's Health Forum, opened a special feature on the issue of 'male psychology' in *The Psychologist*, June 2014. Do men really put life before death? Do women not also? Most of us, whatever our gender, probably get on with living on a daily basis without thinking about dying. However, what the title taps into is a large body of evidence pointing to gender differences in health-related behaviours. Men are certainly overrepresented in most figures attached to health and behavioural risks (as addressed in Chapters 3 to 5 ☞ of this textbook), and they are also overrepresented in suicide and crime figures. As we will see in this chapter, men generally also perceive, respond and act on bodily signs and symptoms differently to women and delay longer in, or avoid altogether, communicating health concerns or seeking health care. Is health - valued by men through 'doing', as described in Chapter 1 ☞- more important to them than issues around dying or increasing one's risk of doing so? None of the empirical differences noted above confirm that issues of health, or indeed death, are *less important* to men – we cannot infer that from such behavioural data. The difference may lie in how men express their needs or how they are supported in (not) doing so. *The Psychologist's* special feature addresses a gender inequality which, it is proposed, society may ignore. At many and various points throughout this textbook, we highlight gender *differences* where they exist; however, that is not quite the same as highlighting gender inequalities. Certainly if we do that, we should ensure we look at inequalities in both directions – male and female. Are health and social care services in effect 'gender-blind' in a way that is more disenfranchising for men than they are for women? Are such services male-friendly? Are men 'allowed' to express feelings of vulnerability or concern about any physical (or mental) health symptoms they experience? The series of articles Seager and Wilkins introduce are thought provoking and well worth a read as we encourage more critical thinking around gendered identities and roles in an evolving discipline of health psychology.

Chapter outline

How do we know if we are getting ill? Do we all react in the same way to symptoms? What influences how we perceive and interpret symptoms of illness? Do beliefs about illness differ across the lifespan? Do illness perceptions and their interpretation influence health-care seeking? These types of question are important to our understanding of how people cope with illness and of differentials in health-care-seeking behaviour. They are questions that you need to ask yourself when thinking about the study of health and illness, whether as a future health psychologist or health-care practitioner.

How do we become aware of the sensations of illness?

Illness generates changes in bodily sensations and functions that a person may perceive themselves or perhaps have pointed out to them by another person who says, for example, 'You look pale'. The kind of sign that is likely to be noticed by the individual themselves includes changes in bodily functions (e.g. increased frequency of urination, heartbeat irregularities), emissions (such as blood in one's urine), sensations (e.g. numbness, loss of vision) and unpleasant sensations (e.g. fever, pain, nausea). Other people may not notice these changes but would perhaps notice changes in bodily appearance (weight loss, skin pallor) or function (e.g. paralysis, limping, tremor). Radley (1994) distinguishes, as did MacBryde and Blacklow in a key early paper (1970), between 'bodily signs' and 'symptoms of illness'. The former can be objectively recognised, but the latter requires interpretation: for example, a person has to decide whether a raised temperature (a bodily sign) is symptomatic of illness (e.g. influenza) or simply a sign of physical exertion.

While some diseases have visible symptoms, others do not and instead involve a subjectively sensed component of bodily responses, e.g. feeling sick, feeling tired, being in pain, which cannot be seen per se. A recent study of the prevalence of physical (and some emotional) symptoms in a representative sample of Slovenian adults (defined as 16+ years; Klemenc-Ketis et al. 2013) found that 71.4 per cent of men and 84.6 per cent of women had experienced at least one physical symptom in the past month, with the three most common symptoms overall being back pain, joint pain or fatigue, although the distribution of other symptoms varied by gender sexes, with irritability next most prevalent for men, and headache next most prevalent for women (see Figure 9.1). Many people regularly experience such symptoms, but there is huge variability between individuals when it comes to attending to, or reporting, symptoms. Although 70 to 90 per cent of us have, at some time, a condition that could be diagnosed and treated by a health professional, only about one-third will actually seek medical attention. Health psychologists are interested in why this is the case.

As described in Chapter 1 ☛, people's views about health are shaped by both their prior experience of illness and their understanding of medical knowledge, whether expert or lay. People therefore learn about health in the same way as they learn about everything else – through experience, either their own or of other people's. People 'fall ill against a background of beliefs about good and poor health' (Radley 1994: 61). Furthermore, Radley notes, people's lives are 'grounded in *activity*', i.e. on the everyday activities or behaviour that depends upon the body, whether they be instrumental activities such as being able to run for a bus, or expressive activities like being able to look attractive. Illness can therefore challenge a person at a fundamental level.

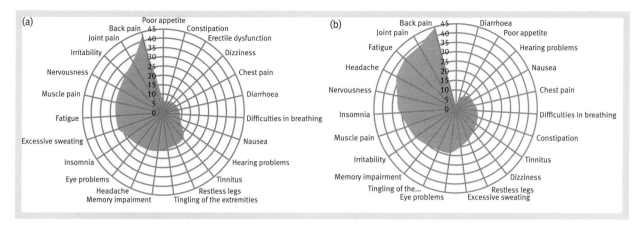

Figure 9.1 The prevalence of self-reported symptoms (a) by men and (b) by women in the past month within a representative adult Slovenian sample

Source: Klemenc-Ketiš, Krizmaric and Kersnik (2013: 162).

Illness or disease?

Cassell (1976) used the word 'illness' to stand for 'what the patient feels when he goes to the doctor', i.e. the experience of not feeling quite right as compared with one's normal state; and 'disease' to stand for 'what he has on the way home from the doctor's office'. Disease, then, is considered as being something of the organ, cell or tissue that suggests a physical disorder or underlying pathology, whereas illness is what the person experiences. People can feel ill without having an identifiable disease (think of a hangover!), and, importantly, people can have a disease and not feel ill (for example, well-controlled asthma or diabetes, early-stage cancer). A routine medical check-up may lead to a person who thought themselves healthy finding out that they are in fact 'officially' ill as indicated by the result of some routine test. By providing a diagnosis, doctors mark the entry of a person into the health-care system.

How does a person know if they are getting ill? This chapter will attempt to answer this by describing the processes underlying three stages of response:

1. perceiving symptoms;

2. interpreting symptoms as illness;

3. planning and taking action.

WHAT DO YOU THINK?

How many of the symptoms below have you experienced in the last two weeks? Of those experienced, how many have you seen a health professional about? Think of the reasons why you did, or did not, seek medical advice about your symptoms.

- fever
- nausea
- headache
- tremor
- joint stiffness
- excessive fatigue
- back pain
- dizziness
- stomach pains
- visual disturbance
- chesty cough
- sore throat
- breathlessness
- chest pain.

Symptom perception

Many different stimuli compete for our attention at any given moment, so why do certain sensations become more salient than others? Why do we seek medical attention for some symptoms when we perceive them and not for others? An early study of American college students found that they had experienced an average of 17 different symptoms per month (Pennebaker and Skelton 1981). More recently, amongst a broader age range adult sample the average symptoms reported in the past month for women was 4.9±3.9 compared to men, 3.6±3.8 (a significant difference reflecting a commonly reported gender effect; Klemenc-Ketiš et al. 2013). In both samples, however, independent of age and culture, few will have sought medical attention – partly because most symptoms are transient and pass before we think too much about them, but also because people are not necessarily the best judges of whether their own perceived symptoms are in fact signs of illness.

There are several models of symptom perception. The attentional model of Pennebaker (1982) describes how competition for attention between multiple internal or external cues or stimuli leads to the same physical sign or physiological change going unnoticed in some contexts but not in others. The cognitive–perceptual model of Cioffi (1991) focuses more on the processes of interpretation of physical signs and influences upon their attribution as symptoms while also acknowledging the role of selective attention (Cioffi 1991). Overall, research has highlighted an array of biological, psychological and contextual influences upon symptom perception (see Figure 9.2), with bottom–up influences upon perception arising from the physical properties of a bodily sensation, and top–down influences being seen in the influence of attentional processes or mood.

Characteristics of bodily signs that increase likelihood of symptom perception

Bodily signs are physical sensations that may or may not be symptoms of illness: for example, sweating is a bodily sign, but it may not indicate fever if the person has simply been exerting themselves. Signs can be detected and identified, for example, blood pressure, whereas symptoms have been defined as what is experienced and,

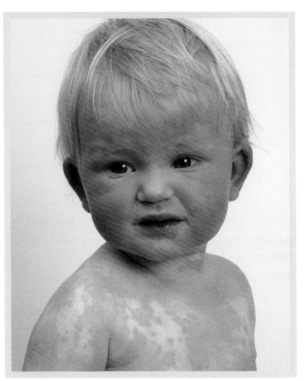

Photo 9.1 This rash looks unpleasant, but is it a heat rash or something more serious?

Source: Alamy Images/Bubbles Photo Library.

as such, they are more **subjective**, e.g. nausea (MacBryde and Blacklow 1970). Symptoms generally result from physiological changes with physical (somatic) properties, but the fact that only some will be detected by the individual highlights that biological explanations of symptom perception are insufficient. Those receiving attention and interpretation as a symptom are likely to be:

● *Painful or disruptive*: if a bodily sign has consequences for the person, e.g. they cannot sit comfortably, their

---

subjective

personal, i.e. what a person thinks and reports (e.g. excitement) as opposed to what is **objective**. Subjective is generally related to internal interpretations of events rather than observable features.

objective

i.e. real, visible or systematically measurable (e.g. adrenaline levels). Generally pertains to something that can be seen, or recorded, by others (as opposed to subjective).

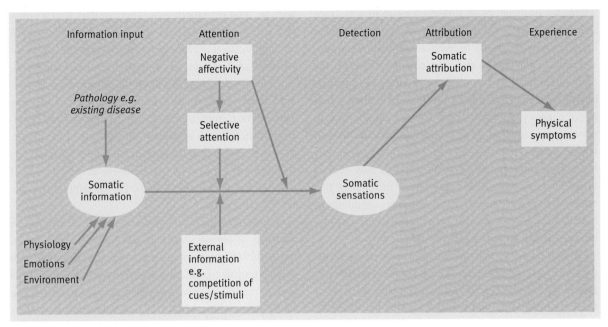

Figure 9.2 A simplified symptom perception model

Source: adapted from Kolk et al. (2003).

vision is impaired, or they can no longer perform a routine activity, then they are more likely to perceive this as a symptom (Cacioppo et al. 1986, 1989).

- *Novel*: subjective estimates of prevalence significantly influence (1) the perceived severity of a symptom and (2) whether the person will seek medical attention (e.g. Jemmott et al. 1988; Ditto and Jemmott 1989). Experiencing a 'novel' symptom (new to oneself or believed not to have been experienced by others) is likely to be considered indicative of something rare and serious, whereas experiencing a symptom thought to be common leads to assumptions of lower severity and a reduced likelihood to seek out health information or care. For example, tiredness among students may be normalised and interpreted as a sign of late nights studying or partying, where it may, for some, reflect underlying disease.

- *Persistent*: a bodily sign is more likely to be perceived as a symptom if it persists for longer than is considered usual, or if it persists in spite of self-medication.

- *Pre-existing chronic disease*: past or current illness experience has a strong influence upon somatisation (i.e. attention to bodily states) and increases the number of other symptoms perceived and reported (e.g. Kolk et al. 2003; Chapman and Martin 2011).

There are many trivial symptoms which do not require medical attention and which can be self-managed successfully without the costs associated with seeking health care (e.g. most flu episodes), but there are also some illnesses with few initial symptoms, such as cancer where seeking health care would confer significant advantage. Symptoms alone are therefore 'unreliable indicators of the need for medical attention' (Martin et al. 2003: 203).

Attentional states and symptom perception

Individual differences exist in the amount of **attention** people give to their internal state and external states (Pennebaker and Skelton 1981; Pennebaker 1982, 1992). Pennebaker discovered that somatic sensations are less likely to be noticed when a person's attention is engaged externally than when they are not otherwise distracted.

> **attention**
> generally refers to the selection of some stimuli over others for internal processing.

Think, for example, of an athlete going on to win a race in spite of having sustained a leg injury. On the other hand, individuals are more likely to notice tickling sensations in their throats and start coughing towards the end, rather than at the start, of lectures as attention begins to wane! Individuals are limited in their attentional capacity, so internal and external stimuli have to compete for attention. This 'competition of cues theory' (Pennebaker 1982) explains why a bodily sign that may be noticed immediately in some contexts may remain undetected in others. (This also points to findings that manipulating attentional focus, through cognitive or behavioural distraction, can be a useful form of symptom management; see Chapter 13 (☛).)

A high degree of attention increases a person's sensitivity to new, or different, bodily signs. Consider the effects of well-publicised outbreaks of illnesses, infections or toxins on symptom perception: for example, outbreaks of Ebola virus in 2014-15, or of Swine flu, identification of new diseases such as SARS in 2003, or chemical leaks. Attendance at doctors' increases massively at such times, and in extreme circumstances can lead to what is called 'mass psychogenic illness'. This response illustrates the powerful effect of anxiety and suggestion on our perceptions and behaviour. Worry about even tenuous links to the source of infection heightens a person's attention to their own bodily signs and can produce the belief that they have contracted the illness. However, many people who seek medical attention at such times will find that there is no organic explanation for their symptoms. Another example of external stimuli altering attention to, and processing of, bodily signs can be seen in what has been described as 'medical student's disease' (Mechanic 1962). In this case the increased knowledge about disease-specific symptoms obtained during medical lectures increased the self-reported experience of exactly these symptoms among over two-thirds of the medical students studied!

Brown (2004), using chronic fatigue syndrome (CFS) as an example (a condition where there is currently no medically identified pathology to explain the reported symptoms, see 'Issues'), distinguished between two attentional systems which are proposed to influence how symptom information is processed. The first, the primary attentional system (PAS), is proposed to operate below the level of consciousness and acts on stored representations, such as illness schema which it automatically selects from when a person for whatever reasons, over-attends to

somatic (bodily) experiences. This can thus lead a symptom to be wrongly matched to a pre-existing schema, such as might happen in cases of 'mass psychogenic illness' or 'medical student's disease' referred to above. The secondary attentional system (SAS) on the other hand is considered more amenable to executive control, i.e. attention here can be manipulated by conscious thoughts and cognitive processes, such as rational weighing up of likelihood. However, this process is hampered if the PAS has already dictated where the person's attention is focused on, and, if a 'label' has already been assigned to the symptoms, it can be difficult to shift.

Furthermore, previous experience with an illness can increase a person's attentional bias, as seen in an experimental study using an emotional Stroop task with threatening words relating to coronary heart disease as well as neutral, positive and other negative words. Those participants with a history of CHD showed clear attentional bias to CHD words and greater interference of such words on their response times, when compared to healthy controls (Ginting et al. 2013). The interference of CHD words was heightened in those CHD participants who also had higher anxiety, and, as described below, anxiety is commonly implicated in enhanced attention to potential or actual health threats.

Finally, attentional processes may be at play in the extent to which people manifest a placebo response, i.e where a person reports a changed physical or psychological experience in the face of receiving an inert, inactive or non-specific intervention. Described more fully in relation to pain (see Chapter 16, (☛)), the placebo response is quite fascinating in its demonstration of the power of expectation. Does the expectation of pain relief alter the attention paid to pain signals by virtue of a reduction in an individual's anxiety or does altered expectations reduce pain by some other, more physiological route? These are empirical questions, which warrant further investigation if we are to better understand how placebos work.

Social influences on symptom perception

It has been shown that people hold stereotypical notions about 'who gets' certain diseases and that this can interfere with perception and response to initial symptoms. For example, Martin et al. (2003) describe studies showing that the general public associate males with vulnerability to heart disease and not females, and that among heart attack patients, females less often recognised their initial bodily signs as symptoms of heart disease. The implications for health-care-seeking behaviour are obvious.

Our motivation to attend to and detect signs or symptoms of illness will depend on the context at the time the symptom presents itself. As referred to above, people tend not to notice internal sensations when their environment is exciting or absorbing, but a lack of alternative distraction may increase perception of symptoms. Furthermore, situations bring with them varying expectations of physical involvement, as illustrated in Figure 9.3. Bodily signs, for example muscle spasms, when running a marathon or giving birth are expected and thus would not generally be considered symptomatic of illness; however, these two situations differ in the extent to which they would expect a person to either express or suppress the pain caused by the spasms (very few people give birth silently!). In a similar vein, few bodily signs are expected when sitting in lectures or watching TV, and unless a bodily sign (e.g. lower back pain) can be attributed to posture or bad seating, it may be interpreted as a symptom of illness. In terms of expression, setting also plays a role, with suppression of physical discomfort by means of motivated distraction being more likely in the lecture setting (e.g. listening to learn) than at home where pain may be expressed (e.g. moaning out loud). Amongst children and adolescents there is also evidence that peer presence can influence

the willingness to express symptoms, referred to as 'social display rules' by Hatchette et al. (2008). These authors conducted focus groups with Canadian adolescents aged 12–15 years old and found that reluctance to be removed from a social activity with peers, on account of a minor injury, led to concealment of pain and delayed symptom reporting. In addition, empathy from peers for expressing pain depended on whether, for example, a sports injury, was considered 'real' and severe, or a means of attention seeking.

Individual differences affecting symptom perception

The same bodily sign may or may not be perceived as a symptom due to individual differences in factors such as gender, life stage, emotional state or personality traits, and the effect these have on attentional states. Understanding whether differences in symptom perception exist may help us understand differences seen in health-seeking behaviour (see later section).

Gender

It is often proposed that gender **socialisation** provides women with a greater readiness to attend to and perceive bodily signs and symptoms; however, the evidence appears to vary according to the symptoms explored (Macintyre et al. 1996; Young 2004). A qualitative study of symptom perception and reporting behaviour of men with prostate disease found that four themes emerged from interviews: 'living up to the image'; 'normal or illness?' (re symptom interpretation); 'protecting the image'; 'engaging with the system'. These themes encompass men's accounts of learning to ignore symptoms out of a need to be seen to be strong and masculine, point to a lack of understanding about prostate problems being symptoms of illness as opposed to part of ageing, and highlight men's unwillingness or anxiety about taking 'embarrassing' symptoms to a health-care professional (Hale et al. 2007). In keeping with this, Gijsbers van Wijk and Kolk

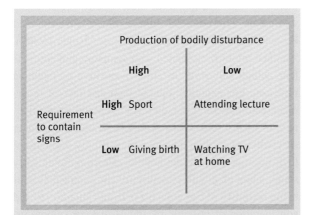

Figure 9.3 Situational differences in the production and containment of physical symptoms

Source: adapted from Radley (1994: 69).

> **socialisation**
>
> the process by which a person learns – from family, teachers, peers – the rules, norms and moral codes of behaviour expected of them.

(1997) suggest that as male-directed media is less inclined to provide health advice than women's media, less developed illness cognitions may exist in males which reduces the likelihood of them perceiving a bodily sign as a 'symptom' and limits their reporting behaviour (see later). Hale and colleagues' studies also find evidence of men 'avoiding' information about illness even when they are faced with it in the media.

Such gender differences are not confined to adults – the focus group study of adolescents, reported by Hatchette and colleagues (described above) revealed similar differences, whereby female adolescents felt 'freer' to discuss pain symptoms than did males who expressed pain more cautiously.

In considering gender differences in symptom perception, there are many overlapping explanations, although it is generally acknowledged that differences exist in the extent to which males and females are 'allowed' to respond to bodily signs. It may also be that physiological differences arising from puberty and menstruation influence **pain thresholds** in the first place, or perhaps the evidence that women talk about symptoms more and attend health care more does not reflect so much a gender difference in symptom perception as one in reporting behaviour (see later section).

Life stage

With age comes experience and typically an increasing awareness of one's internal organs, their functions and sensations. While there are age differentials in concepts of health and illness (Chapter 1 (☛), do age differences in symptom perception contribute to identified differentials in health-care-seeking behaviour (Ramirez et al. 1999; Grunfeld et al. 2003; see Chapter 2 (☛)? Ageing populations certainly bear the burden of many chronic or life-threatening diseases, such as heart disease, stroke, arthritis and breast cancer, but does this mean they pay less attention to their bodily states and perceive fewer symptoms? There is little evidence of this: in fact, increasing age tends to be associated with increased symptom self-report (e.g Bardel et al. 2009). As we will

see later, however, older adults may *interpret* and respond differently to symptoms when perceived.

As described in Chapter 1 (☛ children develop a conceptual understanding of illness during the course of their cognitive development and socialisation, but whether children perceive specific symptoms differently to adults is unclear. The limited language of very young children presents challenges to parents, researchers and health professionals alike. In the absence of language, crying, rubbing or other nonverbal behaviour is relied upon by adults as indicating symptom experience in the very young, with pain, for example, being exhibited rather than reported. It is likely, however, that the child's own symptom perception is influenced by similar attentional, contextual, individual and emotional influences as seen in adults, Indeed, it has been shown that the presence of problems in attention, concentration and impulsivity may be related to symptom perception and asthma outcomes (McQuaid et al. 2007; Koinis-Mitchell et al. 2009).

Emotions and personality traits

Generally, mood is crucial. People who are in a positive mood tend to rate themselves as more healthy and indicate fewer symptoms, whereas people in negative moods report more symptoms, are more pessimistic about their ability to act to relieve their symptoms and believe themselves to be more susceptible to illness (Leventhal et al. 1996). Negative emotional states, particularly anxiety or depression, may increase symptom perception by means of its effect on attention, as well as by increasing rumination and recall of prior negative health events, which increases the likelihood of new bodily signs being viewed as symptoms of further illness (Watson and Pennebaker 1989; Cohen et al. 1995; see Chapter 16 (☛). Another emotion associated with symptom perception is fear, which can work in either a positive or negative direction. For example, fear of pain and fear of recurrence can increase a person's attention and responsiveness to bodily signs, seen among heart attack or cancer survivors who often become increasingly vigilant of their internal states in the hope of detecting, at an early stage, signs of possible recurrence. In contrast, fear of being seriously ill can reduce a person's attention to and consideration of possible meanings of their symptoms, such as reported among men with prostate problems who downplayed symptoms out of fear of finding disease (Hale et al. 2007).

> **pain threshold**
> the minimum amount of pain intensity required before it is detected (individual variation).

Photo 9.2 Making screening accessible by means of mobile screening units in city centres such as this one on Sydney may increase the likelihood of screening uptake.

Source: V. Morrison.

Neuroticism (N) is described as a trait-like tendency to experience negative emotional states and is related to the broader construct '**negative affectivity**' (NA). NA can manifest itself either as a state (situation-specific) or a trait (generalised). State NA can incorporate a range of emotions, including anger, sadness and fear. Trait NA, like neuroticism, has been found to affect the perception, interpretation and reporting of symptoms. In terms of perceptual style, neurotics and those high in trait NA are more introspective and attend more negatively to somatic information and thus they perceive more frequent symptoms and are more likely to misattribute them to underlying disease (Williams 2006). It is worth noting that, while such traits appear associated with retrospectively reported symptom experience, the support for longitudinal effects of negative affectivity on symptom perception is mixed (e.g. Diefenbach et al. 1995; Leventhal et al. 1996). Quite often, studies examining such relationships have implied a link between N and hypochondriasis, where there is a preoccupation with being ill based on misattributions and misinterpretations of bodily signs as symptoms (Ferguson 2000). This suggests that the symptom perception is unfounded in terms of actual physical symptoms; however, Williams (2006) points to

> **neuroticism**
>
> a personality trait reflected in the tendency to be anxious, feel guilty and experience generally negative thought patterns.
>
> **negative affectivity**
>
> a dispositional tendency to experience persistent and pervasive negative or low mood and self-concept (related to **neuroticism**).

a body of evidence where neuroticism is in fact associated with greater physiological reactivity to stress, including elevated levels of stress hormones such as cortisol (see Chapter 11 ☞). In some circumstances, therefore, there may be a 'real' or objective pathway between N and increased symptom experience.

Cognitions and coping style

How people characteristically think and respond to external or internal events can also influence symptom perception. For example, there is some evidence that individuals characterised by time urgency, impatience, hostility and competitive drive (i.e. **type A behaviour**, see Chapter 11 (☞) are less likely to perceive symptoms, perhaps because they are highly task-focused or because they avoid paying attention to signs of self-weakness. In contrast, their desire for control, is associated with prompt health-care-seeking behaviour once a severe health threat is acknowledged (Matthews et al. 1983). There is also evidence that people who cope with aversive events by using the cognitive defence mechanism of **repression** are less likely to experience symptoms than non-repressors (Ward 1988; Myers 1998), with repression being associated with higher levels of **comparative optimism** regarding controllable health threats, such as tooth decay (Myers and Reynolds 2000). Both repressive coping and comparative optimism have previously been related to poor physical health (Weinstein and Klein 1996).

A further distinction has been drawn between monitoring and blunting coping styles (Miller et al. 1987). **Monitors** deal with threat by monitoring their situation for threat-relevant information, whereas **blunters** ignore or minimise external and internal stimuli. Where one stands on this dimension will influence symptom perception as well as determine how quickly a person uses health services (see below).

Symptom interpretation

Once a symptom has been perceived, people do not generally consider it in isolation but relate it to other aspects of their experience and to their wider concepts of illness. Symptoms are more than labels for the various changes that happen to the body; they not only derive from medical classifications of disease but can also influence how we think, feel and behave. Culture will influence the meanings and labels that individuals ascribe to symptoms (Stainton Rogers 1991; Vaughn et al. 2009), as will gender, life stage, past experience, illness beliefs and representations. While information about illness and symptoms are increasingly woven into popular television programmes and other media, we know little about how this information is processed by children.

Cultural influences

We have heard in earlier chapters about cultural variations in health behaviours and in the incidence of certain

---

type A behaviour (TAB)

a constellation of characteristics, mannerisms and behaviour including competitiveness, time urgency, impatience, easily aroused hostility, rapid and vigorous speech patterns and expressive behaviour. Extensively studied in relation to the aetiology of coronary heart disease, where hostility seems central.

repression

a defensive coping style that serves to protect the person from negative memories or anxiety-producing thoughts by preventing their gaining access to consciousness.

comparative optimism

initially termed 'unrealistic optimism', this term describes an individual's estimate of their risk of experiencing a negative event compared with similar others (Weinstein and Klein 1996).

monitors

this generalised coping style involves attending to the source of stress or threat and trying to deal with it directly, e.g. through information-gathering/attending to threat-relevant information (as opposed to **blunters**).

blunters

this general coping style involves minimising or avoiding the source of threat or stress, i.e. avoiding threat-relevant information (as opposed to **monitors**).

---

diseases, (for example, a four times higher incidence of diabetes among South Asian populations, Dreyer et al. 2009). Cultural variation also exists in the extent to which individuals respond to perceived physical symptoms, although the extent to which differences can truly be ascribed to culture is not always clear, given that the range of other influences (e.g. age, illness experience) are not always controlled for in studies. For example, several American studies have compared samples of pain patients by virtue of their Jewish, Italian, Irish or 'old' American (those of Anglo-Saxon descent) origin. Stereotypic explanations were often provided whereby Jewish and Italian American men expressed pain more readily than Irish or 'old' Americans, with further difference found in terms of willingness to complain about pain at home: Italian Americans felt less free to do so as they wanted to project the image of being the strong 'head of the family', whereas Jewish American men did not consider pain expression at home as a sign of weakness. Such differences were further associated with group differences in willingness to accept treatment (Italian American men more likely to accept pain medication than Jewish American men). The 'old' Americans differed in pain expression by removing emotional content and instead reported their pain in a factual way - these men saw emotional expression as a likely hindrance to the doctor's knowledge, skill and efficiency in treating them. At home, 'old' American men withdrew from other people if their pain got too severe, and their wives reacted with either embarrassment or concern if their husbands expressed emotional responses to their pain. Finally, Irish Americans stoically accepted or denied their pain, again reflecting a socialised gender phenomenon. Zborowski (1952) states that such cultural variations are learned during socialisation, where people's ideas about what is acceptable pain to bear and express is shaped. This lengthy illustration shows that not only do pain perception and expression differ, but that they also have a social function (see also Chapter 16 ☞).

Individual difference influences

Some individuals maintain their everyday activities even when experiencing symptoms which would be perceived as debilitating to another person. Why? Because **individual differences** exist in how symptoms are interpreted.

Gender

Somatisation disorder, i.e. the experience of multiple or medically unexplained symptoms (see 'In the spotlight'), is more common in females (Noyes 2001). Women tend also to score higher on measures of neuroticism (Williams 2006). This, and the presence of gender socialisation, suggests that women will interpret a bodily sign as

> **individual differences**
> aspects of an individual that distinguish them from other individuals or groups (e.g. age, personality).

IN THE SPOTLIGHT

Medically unexplained (physical) symptoms MU(P)S

It is thought that between 30 per cent and 50 per cent and between 40 per cent and 60 per cent of symptoms presenting to primary or secondary care respectively are unexplainable (Nimnuan et al. 2001; Khan et al. 2003). The estimated health-care cost of this, in England alone, is around £3 billion per *year*, with roughly 42 million work days lost due to these health complaints (Bermingham et al. 2010). A whole special issue of the journal *Clinical Psychology Review* addressed the issue of 'medically unexplained symptoms' in 2007, and articles point to an array of influences including genetic, psychophysiological and social as well as those cognitive processes of attention and memory described in this chapter. There are many different symptoms that cluster to make up unexplained conditions, and, where not attributed to anxiety, depression, or other psychiatric disturbance,

MUS are often described as functional somatic symptoms. Many of these symptoms, including fatigue, gastrointestinal discomfort, pain, are common to a range of disorders, with a range of labels emerging – for example, Chronic Fatigue Syndrome, Irritable Bowel Syndrome, Fibromyalgia. In fact the same symptoms, for example persistent pain and fatigue (lasting 3– 6 months typically, an arbitrary cut-off) presented to a different specialty depending on where your GP (general practitioner) has referred you to, will result in a different diagnosis – for example, a referral to internal medicine = CFS; a referral to rheumatology = fibromyalgia; a referral to psychology or psychiatry = Somatoform Disorder (Judith Rosmalen 2014, personal communication).

Explanations of MUS include psychodynamic accounts of dissociation, poor attachment and early conflict; cognitive behavioural theories of attention and misinterpretation; and more integrated theories drawing on both these (see Brown 2004, 2013). What is clear is that MUS can be highly distressing and debilitating to a person's physical functioning and global quality of life. Furthermore, medical professionals, communications to patients about their 'unexplainable' symptoms can undermine a patient's sense of satisfaction in the HCP's competence, whilst also failing to validate their concerns. This can contribute to further distress (Weiland et al. 2012; Stone 2014). Dealing with MUS can also in fact be highly frustrating for the HCP themselves, given their preference for providing a positive explanation or diagnosis. Stone (2014) emotively describes how these patients can elicit feelings of 'heartsink" in the family practitioner.

Indeed, the label of MUS itself is 'dualistic' (see Chapter 1, ☛) in its suggestion that the mind and the body are separate and that medicine has nothing to offer these symptoms. However, the label has become more or less accepted in both psychology and medicine, and even by patients themselves (Creed et al. 2010), although current debate concerns whether the term 'multiple somatic symptoms' may be a more preferable biopsychosocial term (Creed et al. 2012). Whatever the label, given the prevalence and the huge personal and social cost attached to these symptoms and symptom clusters, it should come as no surprise that the need for improved health-care professional training in how to best manage those affected by MUS has been highlighted. For example, in 2011, the UK Royal College of General Practitioners and the Royal College of Psychiatrists highlighted the following key learning points in their guidance for health professionals on MUS:

● People want to be taken seriously – show you believe them.
  ○ Ask yourself and the patient 'Am I hearing and understanding what you are trying to tell me?'
● Doctors can make a difference to the patient's well-being even when their symptoms are unexplained.
  ○ Concentrate on helping to manage symptoms and improve functionality
● Sometimes the only 'therapy' needed may be the strength of your doctor–patient relationship
  ○ continuity of care and a long-term relationship helps.
● Be pre-emptively reassuring, yet show you have an open mind and will continue to reassess
  ○ Explain rather than just 'normalise'
● Be explicit about your thoughts, your uncertainties and your expectations of referrals to specialist care.
● Proactively communicate with other clinicians
● Recognising that MUS exist and treating any symptoms that can be treated using a combination of medical (e.g. pain medication) and behavioural (e.g. exercise, relaxation) approaches can work to the benefit of both patient and HCP.

symptomatic of underlying illness more than men. Evidence bears this out inasmuch as women are seen to present to health services more frequently (Eurostat 2007); however, few studies have explicitly compared men and women who have been matched in terms of other influences on symptom interpretation (such as personality, social context, etc.), with gender often being controlled for in analysis rather than explicitly examined. Where gender differences are highlighted, such as in some studies of illness perceptions, we have included them.

Life stage

It is likely that young children are distinct from adolescents in their cognitive awareness of illness and its implications by virtue of the stage of cognitive development attained (Bibace and Walsh 1980; see Chapter 1 ☛) but also by virtue of the difference in life or illness experience and knowledge accumulated (Eiser 1990). Studying the illness perceptions and interpretations of very young ill children is challenging, for various reasons, including ethical issues in submitting sick children to the demands of face-to-face interviews, methodological issues such as the limited availability of child validated assessment tools, or the challenges of limited linguistic and cognitive skills.

Young people with diabetes, both pre-adolescent and adolescent, were described as having 'a basic understanding of the nature, cause and timeline of their illness and treatment recommended' (Standiford et al. 1997, cited in Griva et al. 2000); however, there is convincing evidence that children have similar multidimensional illness representations to adults, with perceived illness consequences and issues of control being highlighted in both quantitative and qualitative studies. Multidimensional illness constructs have been reported among children and young adults considering acute and less serious conditions (e.g the common cold, Koopman et al. 2004), their own serious and chronic conditions, such as CFS (Gray and Rutter 2007), asthma and eczema (Walker et al. 2006), and illness in others, such as their mother's cancer (Forrest et al. 2006). In this latter study, children aged 6 to 18 years talked about their mother's breast cancer, and mothers also talked about how they thought their child perceived the cancer and its treatment. Children's ideas about cancer included seeing it as common, as rare, as a killer, as treatable, as something that can be genetic, caused by smoking, worsened by stress; and ideas about treatment included thinking that the more treatment received the worse the cancer, but the less likely it would be to come back. Mothers were not always aware of how much their child understood about the illness and its treatment and, indeed, many found communicating about treatment implications or potential life-threatening consequences of the cancer difficult. When illness is in the family (Chapter 15 ☞), communication and shared understanding of symptoms or treatment is an important factor in aiding adaptive coping with illness, both for the 'ill' person and for those affected by it.

Personality

As well as influencing symptom perception, personality and emotional characteristics can affect how symptoms are interpreted. For example, as described earlier, those high in Neuroticism or NA commonly exhibit heightened symptom perception. Such individuals not only over attend to their internal states but they also exaggerate the meaning and implications of perceived symptoms and, as a result of their negative interpretations of symptoms, they are more likely to seek health care than those low in N. However, neuroticism is not all bad: there is evidence that moderate levels of neuroticism can benefit health: for example, in terms of better adherence to treatment or quicker presentation to medical services following actual illness events (see Williams 2006 for a fuller discussion).

Self-identity

It has been suggested that the medical sociological tradition of assessing lay models of health and illness (e.g. Blaxter's study – see Chapter 1 ☞) – which takes a broader view of beliefs and knowledge shaped by social factors such as social class, culture or economic environment – and the health psychological model of individual cognitions (illness perceptions, as described in later sections) should be merged. Levine and Reicher (1996) proposed an account of symptom evaluation based on self-categorisation theory (e.g. Turner et al. 1987), which highlights the importance of **social identity**. Most people have several social identities depending on context (e.g. student/partner/daughter), and it is proposed that the interpretation of symptoms differs depending on a person's current salient social identity. For example, they found that female teacher-training students specialising in PE (physical education) evaluated illness and injury scenarios differently depending on whether they were in a condition that identified them by gender or as a PE student. The extent to which the illness scenario details were perceived as threatening their salient identity was important. These findings were explored in two further studies, one involving female secretaries and the other involving rugby-playing males. In the secretary sample, different scenarios (based around threat to attractiveness, occupation or emotionality) elicited different responses depending on whether the women were in the 'gender-identity' group or the 'secretary-identity' group. Perceived illness severity was highest when the scenario posed an attractiveness threat to the gender-identity group, or an occupational performance threat (e.g. hand injury) to the secretary-identity group. The study of male rugby players introduced two hypothetical comparison groups, telling the men that their results would be compared with either females or 'new men'. This allowed the research team to explore the effect of context on symptom representations and self-identity. The scenarios presented threatened physical attractiveness, emotionality or physicality. Attractiveness threat led to greater illness severity perceptions when the

> **social identity**
> a person's sense of who they are at a group, rather than personal and individual, level (e.g. you are a student, possibly a female).

comparator group was females, and the threat to emotionality led to less serious perceptions of the illness when compared with 'new men'. There was no difference in the perceived severity of illness when the threat was to physicality.

Although participants in Levine's studies were dealing with hypothetical illness/injuries in an artificial experimental setting, the reality is that most people fulfill a variety of social roles, and therefore it is logical to suppose that salient identity may differ in different contexts, with potential effects upon symptom perception and interpretation.

Illness experience

Prior experience affects interpretation of and response to symptoms in that having a history of particular symptoms or vicarious experience (e.g. experience of illness in others) leads to assumptions about the meaning and implications of some symptoms. Also, as previously stated, symptoms considered to be rare in either one's own experience, or in that of others, are more likely to be interpreted as serious than a previously experienced or widespread symptom (Croyle and Ditto 1990). Believing symptoms to be 'just a bug that's going round' can mean that people sometimes ignore potentially dangerous 'warning signals'. A knowledge of which bodily signs are associated with particular behaviour or illnesses (e.g. sweats and flu, sweats and exercise) will enable interpretation and attachment of a meaning to the symptom. These reserves of knowledge are known as 'disease prototypes'.

Illness/disease prototypes

Even when a physical sensation or bodily sign is perceived as a 'symptom', what is it that leads a person to believe they are sick? This arises when the symptoms a person is experiencing 'fit' a model of illness retrieved from their memory and it is here that health psychology draws from models dominant in cognitive psychology. People have disease prototypes that help them to organise and evaluate information about physical sensations that might not otherwise be interpretable. Symptoms are placed in the context of a person's past knowledge and experience, which has led to the development of protypical expectations of certain illnesses. Matching or not matching symptoms to a disease prototype (also referred

to as cognitive 'schemata') shapes how a person perceives and responds to bodily signs, influences whether bodily signs are perceived to be symptoms of illness or not, and influences how it is then interpreted and responded to.

Illnesses that have clear sign-sets (symptoms) associated with them are more likely to be easily recognised in self-diagnosis: for example, a person experiencing serious abdominal pains may quickly consider appendicitis, and another person experiencing mild chest pain may quickly consider indigestion. It would be easy to assume therefore that a lump found in the breast would, generally, prompt concerns that it may signify cancer and result in health-care seeking, and this is generally the case (see Chapter 4 ☛ for a discussion of influences on breast-screening behaviour). However, there are other symptoms of breast cancer, such as breast pain or skin scaling around the nipple, that may not be in a person's 'prototype', and thus such symptoms may go unidentified. This inability to correctly identify various potential breast cancer symptoms predicted help-seeking delay among a general population sample of 546 women (Grunfeld et al. 2003). Relevant to this, Cacioppo et al. (1989) pointed to the notion of 'salience', i.e. some symptoms will be 'tagged' to strong and emotive labels in our memory stores, e.g. cancer, heart attack, whereas others will be less so, e.g. menstrual cramps, indigestion. He reports data whereby women with gynaecological cancers had initially been more likely to consider less-threatening explanations for their symptoms, e.g. menopause, than they were the most negative interpretation of their symptoms, i.e. cancer, and had only accepted cancer as a possibility (leading them to seek health care) when symptoms had worsened. In this early, influential paper Cacioppo also notes that the 'more non-descript the sign or symptom, the greater the number of potential matches in long-term memory and the greater tends to be the likelihood of making errors when linking these bodily events to a particular physiological condition' (p. 260). Similarly, Perry et al. (2001) report that when heart attack symptoms do not 'match' the existing illness prototype in terms of severity, delay in seeking medical attention is greatest. Furthermore, there is evidence that a failure of a symptom to fit a protypical image of the 'likely victim' of one possible explanation for the symptom can lead to misinterpretation or delay. For example, Martin and colleagues (2004) found that women were less likely to attribute chest pain to a possible heart

Table 9.1 Disease prototypes

	Influenza	AIDS
Identity	Runny nose, fever, shivery, sneezing, aching limbs	Weight loss, swollen glands, fever, skin lesions, pneumonia
Cause	Virus	Virus
Consequences	Rarely long-term or serious (except if new 'strain')	Long-term ill health, death, uncertainty, stigma
Timeline	24 hours to a week	Months to years
Cure	Time and self-medication	None, multiple treatments to delay progression
Type of person	Anybody	High-risk groups of injecting drug users; increasingly anyone via unprotected sexual intercourse

attack, as their stereotypical image of a heart attack victim was male.

These prototypes have given rise to what is often described as 'common-sense models of illness', examples of which are contained in Table 9.1. A vast amount of health psychology research has developed this thinking into what is often referred to as 'illness representation' research.

Illness representations and the 'common-sense model' of illness

Many different terms are employed, sometimes interchangeably, by authors discussing illness models: for example, cognitive schemata (Pennebaker 1982); **illness cognition** (Croyle and Ditto 1990); common-sense models of illness and illness representations (Lau and Hartman 1983; Lau et al. 1989; Leventhal et al. 1980; Leventhal et al. 1984); personal models (Hampson et al. 1990; Lawson et al. 2007) and illness perceptions (Weinman et al. 1996). One well-known model is the self-regulatory model of illness and illness behaviour proposed by Howard Leventhal and colleagues (see Figure 9.4). In this model, illness cognitions are defined as 'a patient's own implicit common-sense beliefs about their illness' (e.g. Leventhal et al. 1980, 1992). This 'common-sense model' states that mental representations provide a framework for understanding and coping with illness, and help a person to recognise what to look out for. What Leventhal and his colleagues proposed is a dual-processing model, which considers in parallel the objective

> **illness cognition**
>
> the cognitive processes involved in a person's perception or interpretation of symptoms or illness and how they represent it to themselves (or to others) (cf. Croyle and Ditto 1990).

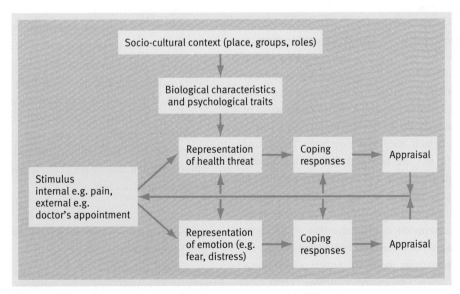

Figure 9.4 The self-regulation model: the 'common-sense model of illness'

Source: Leventhal, Diefenbach and Leventhal (1992: 147).

components of the stimuli, e.g. the symptom is painful (cognitive), and the subjective response to that stimulus, e.g. anxiety (emotional). This model suggests that people actively process this information, which then elicits a coping response thought to be appropriate. Coping efforts, if subsequently appraised as being unsuccessful, can be amended, or alternatively the initial representation of the stimuli/health threat can be revisited and amended. For example, if a person experiences a headache that they believe is a hangover, they are unlikely to be too worried about it and may simply self-medicate and wait for the symptoms to pass. If the symptoms persist, however, they may rethink their coping response (e.g. go to bed), or rethink their initial perception (e.g. maybe this isn't a hangover) and thus alter their coping response (e.g. go to the doctor's). The existence of feedback loops from coping to representations and back again contributes to the model being called 'self-regulatory', with self-regulation simply meaning that an individual makes efforts to alter their responses in order to achieve a desired outcome. Feedback loops enable responsiveness to changes in situations, appraisals or coping responses and thus maximise the likelihood of coping in a way that facilitates a return to a state of 'normality' (for that individual). Initially research studies tended not to assess the dynamic nature of such beliefs and their interaction with illness and associated treatments, and reported instead the associations between components, both cross-sectionally and longitudinally. Following the description of the model we summarise this literature and then introduce more methodologically advanced studies.

Mental representations of illness (illness representations – IRs – as they are called by those working within Leventhal's framework) emerge as soon as a person experiences a symptom or receives a diagnostic label. At this point they start a memory search to try to make sense of the current situation by retrieving pre-existing illness schemata with which they can compare (Petrie and Weinman 2003). IRs are acquired through the media, through personal experience and from family and friends and, as prototypes, they can be vague, inaccurate, extensive or detailed. IRs are thought to exist in memory from previous illness experience, generally that of common illness such as a cold or flu, and the new symptom may be matched to a pre-existing model or 'prototype' of illness that the person holds. Obviously, 'matching' chest pain erroneously to previously experienced indigestion could be dangerous if it is in fact a heart attack.

Early development work asked open-ended questions of people suffering from a range of common conditions, including the common cold (Lau et al. 1989), cancer or diabetes (Leventhal et al. 1980) and found five consistent themes in the content of IRs reported. These were:

1. *Identity*: variables that identify the presence or absence of the illness. Illnesses are identified by label, concrete signs and concrete symptoms. For example, 'I feel shivery and my joints ache, I think I have flu'.

2. *Consequences*: the perceived effect of illness on life: physical, emotional, social, economic impact or a combination of factors. May be short-term or long-term. For example, 'Because of my illness I won't be able to go to the gym today' or 'Because of my illness I will have to take early retirement'.

3. *Cause*: the perceived cause(s) of illness. May be biological (e.g. germs), emotional (e.g. stress, depression), psychological (e.g. mental attitude, personality), genetic or environmental (e.g. pollution), or as a result of an individual's own behaviour (e.g. overwork, smoking). Some of these causes may overlap, e.g. stress and smoking behaviour, and may overlap with **attributions** of cause made after the onset of illness (e.g. French et al. 2001, 2002).

4. *Timeline*: the perceived time-frame for the development and duration of the illness. Can be acute (or short-term, with no long-term consequences), chronic (or long term) or episodic (or cyclical). For example, 'I think my flu will last only three or four days' or 'My pain comes and goes'.

5. *Curability or controllability*: Lau and Hartman (1983) added questions to assess the extent to which individuals perceive they, or others, can control, treat or limit progression of their illness. For example, 'If I take this medicine it will help to reduce my symptoms' or 'The doctor will be able to cure this'. This dimension may be particularly relevant for those facing chronic disease.

---

attributions

a person's perceptions of what causes beliefs, feelings, behaviour and actions (based on attribution theory).

Opinions vary about how best to elicit and assess individuals' privately held illness perceptions and beliefs. The use of open-ended interviews as a method of eliciting illness representations (as used in Leventhal and colleagues' early work) led to the criticism that questions such as 'To what extent when thinking about your illness do you think about its consequences?' may well be leading. Furthermore, interviews are very time consuming and generally restrict sample size, although some studies have managed to successfully employ open-ended questioning (using prompts where necessary) (e.g. Hampson et al. 1990, 1994; Forrest et al. 2006).

While Leventhal's model provides a useful framework on which to base studies of illness perceptions, many early studies focused on specific component beliefs, for example perceived control over illness (e.g. Multidimensional Health Locus of Control Scale, Wallston et al. 1978). The ability to assess all five constructs was made easier with the development of a quantitative scale by a team of UK- and New Zealand-based researchers, (Weinman et al. 1996), the illness perception questionnaire (IPQ).

The Illness Perception Questionnaire (IPQ and IPQ-R (revised))

The IPQ has had significant uptake in the 20 years since its developement; has been validated in a wide range of illness populations across varying time-spans; and has significant support from meta-analyses in terms of the construct and predictive validity of the components (see Hagger and Orbell's 2003 meta-analysis of 45 studies across 23 different health conditions). The multitude of overlapping causal attributions, given the range of conditions studied, however, made meta-analysis of this component problematic.

A child-specific version (CIPQ, Walker et al. 2006) was piloted amongst children aged 7–12 with asthma and eczema, and, although overall it performed satisfactorily, the cure–control scale did not show acceptable internal consistency, suggesting that perhaps children of this age did not fully understand the concept of personal control or potential for cure. Interestingly, this subscale had also performed less consistently in several adult studies and thus the control/cure items were a main target of IPQ revisions (Moss-Morris et al. 2002; Moss-Morris and Chalder 2003).

The revised scale, the IPQ-R distinguishes between beliefs about personal control over illness from outcome expectancies and from perceived treatment control; strengthens the timeline component by adding items regarding cyclical illnesses as well as acute/chronic timeline items; assesses a new dimension of emotional responses to illness such as fear and anxiety (part of Leventhal's self-regulatory model not well addressed in the original IPQ) and finally, examines the extent to which a person feels they understand their condition, defined as illness coherence. Initially tested across eight different illness conditions and shown to have a reliable and valid dimensional structure, not all conditions could of course be included, for example, cancer. This has subsequently been rectified within the burgeoning field of psycho-oncology research, with confirmation of the IPQ-R structure having a 'good fit' to an oesophageal cancer population (Dempster and McCorry 2011). Researchers should, however, seek to confirm the domains of IRs held in the illness they are themselves studying.

Both Leventhal's theory and the empirical findings demonstrate that there are logical interrelationships between component IRs: for example, strongly believing that an illness can be controlled or cured is likely to be associated with fewer perceived serious consequences of the illness and a short expected duration. Most studies using the IPQ-R, including those in non-Western populations (e.g. Chen et al. 2008) have found that emotional representations are highly correlated with perceived consequences (high perceived negative consequences associated with high anxiety representation). The clustering and relationships between the component parts of an illness representation may be as important in fact than the individual components, in that overall this reflects illness understanding (in addition to the IPQ-R's illness coherence subscale); however, few studies test this statistically and most tend to correlate the individual components with outcomes separately. Chen's findings also highlight that cognitions and emotions are hard to disentangle causally, as acknowledged by Lazarus and colleagues (Chapter 11 ☞). Perhaps our dominant models (Lazarus's stress appraisal-coping theory, Leventhal's self-regulation of illness model) could benefit from working together when exploring predictors of stress or illness outcome.

There is evidence also, that while the domains of IR hold true in many different groups, their salience can vary. For example, when the IRs of patients with either chronic fatigue syndrome (CFS) or Addison's disease (AD) (both chronic illnesses with common symptoms of fatigue and weakness, but with clearer treatment for AD) were compared, although within each disease group the illness perceptions were similarly interrelated, differences existed *between* illness groups: CFS patients viewed their illness more negatively than AD patients and reported more frequent and serious consequences and less positive future expectation of control or cure (Heijmans and de Ridder 1998). Therefore, although IR components were robust in terms of how they related to each other, illnesses differed in the specific strengths of each component. In a similar vein, a recent confirmatory factor analysis of the IPQ-R completed by a large sample (N = 587) of oesophageal cancer patients found that the domains of the IPQ-R model 'fitted' the data adequately but that some of the questionnaire items, in particular those relating to timeline beliefs, needed further consideration (Dempster and McCorry 2011). For example, one timeline factor was more closely aligned to the treatment control factor, suggesting that believing the illness will improve in time is, quite intuitively perhaps, related to treatment beliefs in this cancer sample. In addition, two acute/chronic items acted independently, suggesting that these patients can believe in both an acute illness model (it will last only a short time) but also in a chronic or permanent illness (i.e. perhaps something that will be with them till an imminent death). Such differences highlight the need for communications or interventions with patients to have specific focus, and not rely solely on generic observations drawn from other populations.

With specific populations in mind, the IPQ-R has also been tested in children: for example, in a small study of 15 children with juvenile idiopathic arthritis (Barsdorf, et al. 2009), where it operated satisfactorily with the exception of Timeline Cyclical and one of the Treatment Control items, and where children under 12 needed more of the terms explained (e.g. permanent, hereditary, immune system).

As described, the content and organisation of IRs can vary between individuals and even within the same individual over time, and can be attributed to underlying beliefs about disease. Furthermore, one's own health status will affect one's beliefs regarding illness. This is clearly illustrated by Buick and Petrie (2002) who compared perceptions of breast cancer and post-surgical treatment, mood and coping responses held by 78 women who had received surgery for breast cancer with the perceptions and anticipated responses of 78 healthy

women, matched on age, marital status and educational attainment. Healthy women overestimated the number, severity and frequency of patient symptoms (identity component), rated patient health as poorer, believed more strongly in chance, patient-related internal (e.g. behaviour), genetic and environmental causes of breast cancer, believed that breast cancer had a longer timeline, that its consequences were worse and that treatment offered less cure or control. Healthy women also had more negative perceptions of how a woman with breast cancer would cope, thinking, for example, that patients would engage in generally avoidant coping such as mentally and behaviourally disengaging from treatment, venting emotion, using denial, alcohol and drugs, religion and restraint coping to a higher degree than patients themselves reported. The healthy women thought that patients were less likely to use positive reappraisal and acceptance than other strategies, yet in reality these were the two most common strategies reported by patients (who also did not report using alcohol or drugs!). Given these differences, it was not surprising that healthy women also overestimated the emotional impact of breast cancer treatment. It is a sad fact that most people will encounter cancer at some point in their lives, either personally or through a family member or friend, and thus most of us non-oncologists have, to varying extents, a 'lay model' of this condition. Perceiving internal causes, or more specifically the person's behaviour, to be the cause of the illness may limit a healthy person's expression or provision of support for the ill person. Furthermore, if a societal perception of cancer is that patients' best cope by avoidance, then healthy members of that society may consider any attempts to discuss the illness with the affected person to be unhelpful. Mismatched perceptions have obvious implications in terms of responses to people with cancer (see Chapter 15 ☞), but they also hold implications for healthy individuals. For example, if the lay perception is that treatments offer little hope of cure, preventive health practices such as screening behaviour may be undermined. Therefore, identifying the illness perceptions of healthy individuals is highly relevant, not only due to their influences on their own behaviour but also as a means of increasing professionals' understanding of supportive behaviours towards those affected by illness.

Finally, the existence of reasonably well-validated quantitative assessment tools should not detract from the important contribution made by more open-ended methods of eliciting illness perceptions. For example, whilst existing studies confirm statistical associations between the variables (i.e. illness representations, coping, illness outcomes) specified in the common-sense model of illness, it could be said that they are limited in the extent to which they develop our understanding of what lies *within or behind* the representations presented. Understanding the sources and salience of beliefs and perceptions, and the reasons behind these, could be crucial to the development of targeted interventions. The value of qualitative enquiry can be highlighted by the findings of a study exploring cultural differences in illness perceptions regarding 'fatigue' between European American women and South Asian immigrant women (Karasz and McKinley 2007). Using a case vignette of a woman suffering from fatigue, conceptions were elicited which revealed that, while some conceptions of fatigue were shared (e.g. perceiving both physical and psychological general causes), there were significant differences. For example, European Americans referred more often to genetic causes, medicalised/somatised the condition more and considered it a chronic condition, whereas South Asian women tended to think fatigue was temporary, caused by something transient and less needing of medical treatment. In exploring reasons for these differences, the qualitative accounts exemplify differing models of illness – a biomedical 'disease' model (European Americans), and a more socially oriented 'depletion' model (South Asians) that also drew on traditional 'humoral' concepts of illness (see Chapter 1 ☞). The similarities and differences between groups as described here may not of course hold for other symptoms or, indeed, for other comparison groups. Culture, these authors note, is more than simply a demographic variable, and it is only through this type of study that we can begin to explore 'the structures, contexts, conditions, ideologies, and processes through which culture shapes illness cognition and illness behaviour' (p. 614). One limitation of this study, however, is that participants were invited to respond to the vignette in a way that addressed predetermined IR dimensions whereas allowing more spontaneous responses to the vignette scenario would have helped ascertain whether the dimensions outlined by Leventhal and others were actually implicit in the models of illness portrayed.

This more spontaneous elicitation method was used in the following studies. Consider, for example, the following quotes from cancer patients, one regarding cause and the other regarding consequences:

> … to begin with, it just didn't sink in that I was really sick. I had a lot of difficulty in grasping it, because… we have lived pretty – soundly I think… outdoors a lot. And that, that I have heart problems also. I just don't really understand that it has turned out like this… And just that one should exercise a lot and try to eat properly and I've done that, largely because you don't want to gain weight either, but no – I don't understand it.

> (woman with lung cancer reflecting on the onset of her condition, Leveälahti et al. 2007: 468)

> … I don't feel a proper man. I feel… completely emasculated and it's difficult to explain but I still have a problem wearing jeans. I still have a problem wearing shorts. Because I think that people know.

> (man aged 48, diagnosed with penile cancer when aged 46; Branney et al. 2014: 411)

The depth of emotion in these words would be hard to capture quantitatively. Furthermore, our measures of illness perceptions (and in fact illness impact and outcomes, see Chapters 14 and 15 ☞) have tended to focus on the negatives, where we must not forget that illness can bring about positive experience also. Consider this final quote,

> I remember sitting in this mound of grass overlooking the bay and just feeling completely in the moment, and completely at peace; this is wonderful, this is one of the best times in my life… so in some ways it (the cancer) has given me quite a lot because it's given me that appreciation of living now, living every day… I still hold onto that kernel, of this is the only life I've got, today may be the only day I've got, so I think that's a very valuable thing to come from it, a positive thing, and I don't think I've ever had that before, that appreciation.

> (woman with breast cancer talking about the consequences of her condition, Ingram et al. 2008)

What we hope to have shown in this section is that a person's perceptions of illness 'make sense' to them and can be elicited in various ways. Whilst individual researchers should decide which is most suited to their questions and their population, perhaps mixed methods can be more informative than either method alone?

Illness representations and outcomes

While proposed in Leventhal's theoretical model to affect illness outcome via effects on coping (i.e. a mediated effect of IRs), illness representations have also been shown to have direct effects on a wide range of outcomes, including, for example:

● seeking and using/adhering to medical treatment (Scharloo et al. 1998; Horne and Weinman 2002; Kim and Evangelista 2010);

● engagement in self-care behaviour or behaviour change (Costanzo et al. 2011; Hudson et al. 2013; D. B. O'Connor et al. 2008; Petrie et al. 2007) and see RESEARCH FOCUS;

● attitudes towards the use of brand-specific vs. generic medicines, and treatment choices (Figueiras et al. 2010);

● illness-related disability and return to work (Heijmans 1998; Petrie et al. 2002);

● caregiver anxiety and depression (Parveen et al. 2013);

● quality of life (Gray and Rutter 2007 (child and young adult sample); Scharloo et al. 2005).

RESEARCH FOCUS

Hudson, J.L., Bundy, C., Coventry, P.A., and Dickens, C. (2013). Exploring the relationship between cognitive illness representations and poor emotional health and their combined association with diabetes self-care. A systematic review with meta-analysis. *Journal of Psychosomatic Research*, 76: 265–274.

One likely route through which illness perceptions affect illness outcomes, both physical and emotional, is through their effect on coping responses, as described in Leventhal's self-regulation model of illness described in this chapter. One aspect of coping with illness is the need to engage in illness self management – whether by adherence to medication or through other health-enhancing behaviours. The paper described here reviews the evidence of association between illness representations and emotional distress and explores whether together these are associated with self-care amongst adults diagnosed with type 1 or type 2 diabetes.

Aims

To review the literature in relation to the relationships described in the figure below (adapted):

Methods

Empirical papers published in English were identified from systematic electronic searches of four common databases: Medline, Psycinfo, EMBASE and CINAHL. Study samples were to be adults in receipt of a diagnosis of diabetes and each had to include quantitative assessment of illness perceptions (including beliefs about medicines), a continuous (not categorical) measure of depression, anxiety or mixed depression and anxiety symptoms, and had to examine the bivariate association between illness perceptions and emotion.

Results

Nine studies were retained after the usual process of screening. Of those only two had conducted regression analyses (or equivalent) with diabetes self-care as the outcome (dependent) variable (one longitudinally).

The total sample represented in these nine studies comprised 2,480 participants (age range 24–68 years), with six studies recruiting those with type 2 diabetes only, one study recruiting those with type 1 diabetes only, and two having both diagnostic groupings.

Overall, the revealed associations between illness perceptions and emotional health had small to large effect sizes. More specifically, in the meta-analysis of eight studies examining IRs and depression cross-sectionally, depression was associated with higher beliefs in the unpredictable nature of diabetes (r=0.25, timeline cyclical), its impact (r=0.41, consequences), its threatening nature (r=0.38, seriousness), and lower appraisals of control in terms of personal (r=-0.27) and treatment resources (r=-0.10) were associated with increased depression scores (all p values ≤0.01). Other IRs were either not assessed across sufficient studies to enable meta-analyses or were non-significant.

Only one study conducted longitudinal analyses whereby greater perceived diabetes consequences and increased illness understanding at 4 months, predicted increased depression at 12 months.

In meta-analysis of the only two studies examining IRs and anxiety only two IRs were assessed in both and, in both, timeline chronic associated with higher anxiety (r=.20), as did greater consequences (r=.44). One further study only examined mixed anxiety and depressive symptoms and therefore was not meta-analysed.

Within the two studies analysing, perhaps the more interesting question, of the effects of illness perception and mood on diabetes self-care, both found independent effects of IRs but only one found an independent effect of mood. Self-care was assessed in terms of diet in one study, and diet, exercise, foot care, and blood glucose monitoring in the other. In the cross-sectional study with more detailed measures of self-care, increased depression and greater perceived unpredictability of diabetes (timeline cyclical) was associated with lower diabetes self-care, and increased perceived control was associated with better self-care. However, the perceptions of control did not mediate the effect of depression as was hypothesised. In the longitudinal study assessing dietary self-care only, there was no effect of depression and only greater beliefs in treatment effectiveness was associated with lower high-fat eating patterns.

Finally and importantly, the authors conduct reanalyses taking into account the quality of the studies and their inherent risk of bias (due to sampling, N design, etc.), with effect sizes found to be smaller in the lower quality studies: i.e effect sizes were larger when poorer quality studies were removed. They also examine heterogeneity in the associated measures and point to significant heterogeneity in the identity-

depression and the seriousness–depression relationships, which limits the conclusions one can draw from these specific findings.

Discussion

Overall, this paper provides a focused and rigorous review of key theorised associations between illness perceptions, depression or anxiety, and self-care. Self-care is not only relevant but crucial to diabetic samples as addressed here, but also in other conditions where personal health behaviours combine with medical treatments to help control symptoms, e.g. asthma, hypertension. It is unfortunate, however, that only two studies explored the relationships with self-care, focusing instead on the IR–mood relationship itself. In addition, only two studies provide longitudinal data. Furthermore, the quality of studies included (when judged on risk of bias) was predominantly moderate (seven studies), with two considered weak.

In spite of such limitations, consistent findings related to higher timeline cyclical, consequences, and seriousness beliefs, and lower personal control beliefs, all of which were associated with poorer emotional health symptoms. Inconsistent findings were found regarding identity and timeline chronic beliefs, which emerged only with anxiety. The authors relate this to associations with somatisation and anxiety (i.e. anxious people tend to attribute non-specific symptoms to their condition, i.e. greater identity) and where a chronic timeline belief would support the need for symptom vigilance.

In conclusion, this review points to the potential for certain cognitive representations to become the target of clinical communications and intervention, although the cross-sectional nature of the data contained in the studies reviewed does not enable conclusions regarding whether IRs 'cause' the negative mood states or vice versa; nor can it conclude whether enhancing mood in this way will benefit subsequent self-care although the longitudinal findings were encouraging. As is the case in so many health psychology contexts, longitudinal data are needed if we are to take the next step towards evidence-based intervention.

Further to the meta-analytic support for the contribution of illness representations to coping and illness outcomes across 23 health conditions reported by Hagger and Orbell (2003), there have been several disease-specific reviews, including the one related to distress and diabetes self-management presented in 'Research focus' (Hudson et al. 2013). Generally speaking, perceived controllability has been associated with adaptive outcomes including psychological well-being and social functioning, whereas perceptions of high symptom identity, chronicity and serious consequences are negatively associated with such outcomes. However, many of the studies reviewed are **cross-sectional** and thus limited to providing evidence only of concurrent associations.

The past decade has, however, seen growth in the number of longitudinal studies. For example, amongst head and neck cancer patients (Llewellyn et al. 2007) illness and treatment beliefs prior to treatment were *not* predictive of health-related QoL, generic QoL or mood, although they were associated with coping one month and six to eight months later. Chronic timeline beliefs held at baseline also directly predicted depression 6–8 months after treatment, i.e. there was no indirect relationship via one-month coping strategies. In final predictive analyses, coping and satisfaction with information received pretreatment were more predictive of these outcomes than IRs; however, the sample size prevented statistical tests of the effects of change in key variables over time. This was possible, however, in a larger longitudinal study of 241 osteoarthritis patients (Kaptein et al. 2010) followed over an impressive six years. Those participants whose perceived illness timeline, personal control and illness coherence reduced over time and whose chronic timeline, identity, emotional representations and consequence beliefs increased (described as having a negative illness model) exhibited less positive change/ greater deterioration in two of three pain and function measures used. Similarly, amongst a sample of informal caregivers assessed over a nine-month period, perceptions of illness consequence also increased, and this 'change' was predictive of emotional outcomes – in this case, caregiver anxiety. Furthermore, decreases in perceived control beliefs and increased emotional representations predicted caregiver depression (Parveen et al. 2014) and increased illness coherence predicted caregiver gains (Parveen and Morrison 2012).

Finally, there is longitudinal evidence that the experience of being rehabilitated can affect illness beliefs, as seen in a study of 87 patients with COPD (mean age 63.3 years, 50 males, 37 females) who were taking part in a 12-week rehabilitation programme (Fischer et al. 2010). Timeline cyclical (not chronic) and personal control beliefs significantly increased between baseline and a follow-up assessment conducted within one month of completing rehabilitation. In both cases the higher levels could be partially explained not only by baseline timeline or control beliefs but also by patient perceptions of having achieved their desired goals through taking part in the rehabilitation programme. A longer time since diagnosis also predicted less perceived control. In addition, beliefs changed in a coherent manner. For example, a reduced perception of consequences was associated with a reduced illness identity and a lowered emotional response; increased illness coherence was associated with a lowered emotional response, and increased perceptions of control were associated with increased belief in treatment control.

These four studies, three of patients and one of caregivers, provide good examples of the importance of examining the interrelations between components and outcomes over a changing illness course, i.e. the dynamic nature of Leventhal's model explored (as intended).

The impact of treatment changes on illness perceptions

This issue of change in illness representation is also relevant where there is change possible in the nature of treatments patients undergo. For example, although beliefs in treatment control specifically were not assessed in a rare seven-year follow-up of kidney dialysis and transplant patients, Griva and colleagues (2012) found there were significant influences of actual treatment transitions on patients, illness perceptions. For end-stage renal disease patients moving from dialysis to the receipt of a kidney transplant (if they are lucky), or back to dialysis if the transplant fails (if they are unlucky), this represents a series of significant transitions, in illness and treatment expectancies and experiences. A large

> **cross-sectional design**
> a study that collects data from a sample on one occasion only. Ideally, the sample should be selected to be representative of the population under study.

cohort study of 262 patients identified 60 who received a transplant and 28 who experienced transplant failure. In these two subgroups clear differences in IR changes were seen. Between pre- to post-transplantation, reported QoL increased as did illness identity (symptoms) and perceived consequence beliefs, whereas illness intrusiveness reduced and acute timeline and perceived control beliefs increased. For those who experienced transplant failure the converse was seen – QoL reduced, perceived identity, timeline, consequences and intrusiveness increased, and perceived control decreased. Importantly, these changes in IRs showed consistent association with QoL either negatively or positively, even though that actual underlying condition remained the same and only the treatment modality changed. The effects of treatment have been confirmed in another study of kidney disease patients, although using a chronic population, rather than all end-stage population as in Griva et al.'s study. This more recent study (Jansen et al. 2013) compares the illness and treatment perceptions of those at different treatment stages – either pre-dialysis, or receiving either haemodialysis (where the blood is purified externally via a dialysis machine) or peritoneal dialysis (where the blood is purified internally via the patient's own peritoneal membrane which acts as a filter). Perhaps unsurprisingly, those who were pre-dialysis had lower treatment control beliefs and fewer perceived illness consequences than both the dialysis groups, who did not differ from each other. Those on haemodialysis perceived more treatment consequences than both other groups, with the length of time on dialysis increasing this further. On examining longitudinal associations between specific IRs within the dialysis patient sub-group, with the exception of perceived treatment consequences, correlations over an eight-month period were only moderate, indicating that changes in illness perceptions had taken place within that time period.

Taken together, these studies highlight a need to consider patient's perceptions at important treatment transition points in order to best 'manage' their perceptions and optimise patient QoL and adaptation.

It is worth noting to conclude this section that, while Leventhal's framework dominates this area of research within health psychology, other models do exist: for example, the implicit models of illness approach which also utilises a questionnaire (IMIQ; Turk et al. 1986). They report four slightly different dimensions to those described by Leventhal: seriousness, personal responsibility,

controllability and changeability; however, these results emerged when asking participants (diabetic patients, diabetic educators, college students) to *compare* two diseases. This may suggest that the identified dimensions are more what discriminates *between* illnesses, rather than domains like Leventhal's and assessed with the IPQ-R, which relate to perceptions of individual illnesses. It may in fact be impossible to have a model or measure to fit all illnesses: for example, potential for cure or treatment simply does not exist for all conditions and in such cases this dimension would likely lack validity. In contrast, most illnesses bring with them some perception of 'cause', as we discuss next.

Causal attributions

Attributional models are all about where a person locates the 'cause' of an event (Heider 1958) or, as here, symptoms and/or illness. We make attributions in order to attempt to make unexpected events more understandable or to try and gain some sense of control – if we know 'why' something has happened, we can elicit coping efforts. Of course, attributions can be wrong and thus coping efforts misguided, as we will discuss later.

The majority of attributional research in health psychology has addressed 'ill populations', such as those who have suffered a heart attack (myocardial infarction) (e.g. Affleck et al. 1987; Gudmunsdsdottir et al. 2001), or those diagnosed with cancer (Costanzo et al. 2005, 2011; Salander 2007). In relation to heart attack, attributions of cause – stress, work, it being in the family, smoking, eating fatty foods – were recorded regardless of whether attributions were *spontaneous* (patients asked to describe what they think about their illness), *elicited* (asked directly about their ideas of what may have caused their heart attack) or *cued* (asked to respond 'yes', 'no' or 'might have' to a list of 34 causes) (Gudmundsdottir et al. 2001). A review of studies of attributions for heart disease concluded that lifestyle factors and stress were the most common attributions made, with the latter more likely to come from heart attack patients than from healthy individuals, suggesting a form of self-preservation bias (French et al. 2001). This bias in perceived cause is also reported in a rare longitudinal study of lung cancer patients (Salander 2007). It is a relatively well-established fact that smoking accounts for about 80 per cent of the incidence of lung cancer (Chapter 3 ☛), yet among the 16 smokers interviewed repeatedly (of a sample of 23), the two most common attributions of 'cause of their illness' was 'don't know' and 'environmental toxins/pollution'. A total of 14 did not consider smoking as a probable cause, and the author points to this as a defence mechanism or 'disavowal', potentially useful for a sample at a relatively late stage in their illness. Lung cancer patients in other studies have been found to attribute partial cause to their smoking behaviour (e.g. Faller et al. 1995), but studies of this patient group are rare, and methodologies and timing of sampling generally differ. Another disease with a strong association to smoking is COPD (chronic obstructive pulmonary disease) and, in contrast to Salander's study of lung cancer patients, the vast majority of this sample (93 per cent of 394 patients with a smoking history) agreed or strongly agreed with smoking as a cause, with workplace/environmental pollution, and infection/pneumonia also common (48.5 and 36.5 per cent respectively). These patients, however, were not newly diagnosed (Hoth et al. 2011).

When attributions were examined at an earlier stage in illness experience, i.e. at the time of symptom perception, Swartzman and Lees (1996) found that the dimensions of controllability, locus (internal physical/external non-physical cause) and stability described by attributional theorist Weiner (1986), and consistently reported in studies of illness attribution and coping (Roesch and Weiner 2001), were only partially supported. Symptoms addressed primarily reflected physical discomfort and were attributed to either a physical (e.g. age, exertion)–non-physical (e.g. stress, mood) dimension; a high–low personal controllability dimension; and a dimension thought to reflect controllability by health professional/treatable versus stability/not treatable, although this dimension was less clear. Attributions of causes of symptoms (rather than attributions of cause of a confirmed illness) may be an area worth further exploration, given cultural and other influences thereon (see below). Perceiving a cause of fatigue as being physical, under high personal control and stable/not treatable may lead to very different interpretation, response and health-care-seeking behaviour than a cause of fatigue with external, supernatural attribution.

As described in this chapter, attributions of cause can be affected by one's own illness experience and can potentially affect how we respond to illness in others; they can also influence how we respond to our own illness: for example, perceiving diet as a causal factor in breast cancer increases the likelihood of dietary change following treatment (Costanzo et al. 2011). Unfortunately however, they can sometimes be wrong. For example, a woman may attribute joint pain to excessively high-heeled shoes rather than to the first signs of arthritis, and she may fail to seek medical advice. Other risks of misattributed cause is failure to adhere to essential medication: for example, a study of women with HIV infection found that drug treatment was wrongly attributed as causing their symptoms, leading to reductions in, or cessation of, medication adherence (Siegel and Gorey 1997).

Culture and causal attributions

Culture influences illness at many levels in that it shapes both how it is perceived, understood and experienced (Adams and Salter 2009). For example, as described above, and in Chapter 1 ☞, there is significant variation in the extent to which members of specific cultures believe in supernatural causes of illness: e.g. evil spirits, divine punishment or in spiritual explanations (Vaughn et al. 2009). In terms of the latter, it has been described how Chinese women made sense of their cancer experiences by attributing their cancer to '*tien ming*' (the will of Heaven, a concept from the Chinese Confucian and Daoist traditions) and to 'karma' (a Buddhist concept of cause and effect that cannot be changed through human effort) and as a result showed acceptance and 'going with the flow' ('*ping chang xin*') (Leung et al. 2007).

Culture and other perceptions

Cultural differences have also been reported in terms of other illness representation dimensions. For example, a study of perceptions of diabetes held by South Asians, Europeans and Pacific Islanders found that the Pacific Islanders perceived more symptoms of diabetes, greater consequences and were affected more emotionally by the condition, and that the Europeans differed from the other two groups only in terms of perceiving a longer timeline (Bean et al. 2007). The differences in beliefs identified related to poorer metabolic control and aspects of self-care, highlighting a need for health professionals to address illness perceptions when trying to improve a person's self-management of symptoms or health condition such as diabetes, or indeed many other controllable conditions such as hypertension, epilepsy or asthma.

Beliefs about treatment have themselves been shown to be associated with culture, race and ethnicity. For example, concerns about understanding treatments were higher among non-Caucasian cancer patients than

Caucasian patients (Jean-Pierre et al. 2010), and African-American patients with end-stage kidney disease held more negative perceptions of illness control via either personal or medical treatments than Hispanic, Filipino or Korean patients (Kim et al. 2012). In this same study, whilst illness coherence beliefs did not differ between the aforementioned groups, there were some gender differences within racial groups: for example, female Filipinos had lower personal control beliefs than male Filipinos, and female Hispanics and female Koreans both had lower illness coherence scores than their male counterparts.

It is likely that cultural and religious factors will indirectly influence health and illness outcomes via their effects on health and illness beliefs and behaviours, for example as examined by Kim and Evangelista (2010) in their study of adherence to kidney dialysis. However, longitudinal research evidence from cross- and within-culture comparisons is relatively limited, particularly within Western Europe. One study pointing to within-culture differences is that of Swami et al (2009), where Malaysian Muslim participants believed more strongly than Malaysian Buddhist or Malaysian Catholic participants that their likelihood of becoming ill was uncontrollable and that fate played a role in recovery. If pursued into a longitudinal study, such differences may well be reflected in different health behaviours (such as health-risk behaviours or seeking health care) and personal engagement in recovery from illness (cf. French et al. 2006). We turn now to consideration of the responding to symptom perception in the form of health-care-seeking behaviour.

Planning and taking action: responding to symptoms

As this chapter has described, the first step towards seeking medical care begins with a person recognising that they have symptoms of an illness, and it may take some time for this step to occur. In many cases, people choose to treat an illness themselves by self-medicating with pharmaceutical, herbal or non-proprietary products, and others will rest or go to bed and wait to see whether they recover naturally. A number of surveys have suggested that less than one-quarter of illnesses are seen by a doctor.

Kasl and Cobb (1966a) refer to the behaviour of those who are experiencing symptoms but who have not yet sought medical advice and received a diagnosis as **illness behaviour**. Illness behaviour includes lying down and resting, self-medication and seeking sympathy, support and informal advice in an attempt to determine one's health status. Many people are reluctant to go to the doctor on the initial experience of a symptom and instead first seek advice from a **lay referral system**, generally including friends, relatives or colleagues (Croyle and Barger 1993). Symptoms are therefore not always sufficient to motivate a visit to the doctor (see ISSUES).

Once people recognise a set of symptoms, label them and realise that they could indicate a medical problem, they therefore have the option of:

- ignoring the symptoms and hoping they recede;
- seeking advice from others;
- presenting themselves to a health professional.

Some people will do all three over time.

One might expect that the recognition that one has symptoms would be a sufficient condition for deciding that one is sick, but Radley (1994: 71) suggests that one must question that assumption. Think of your own experience – symptoms do not necessarily precede sickness – sometimes being deemed to be sick (by virtue of receiving a diagnosis) is an important element in appearing symptomatic, and perhaps adopting what is termed **sick role behaviour** (Parsons 1951; Kasl and Cobb 1966b).

---

illness behaviour

behaviour that characterises a person who is sick and who seeks a remedy, e.g. taking medication. Usually precedes formal diagnosis, when behaviour is described as **sick role behaviour**.

lay referral system

an informal network of individuals (e.g. friends, family, colleagues) turned to for advice or information about symptoms and other health-related matters. Often but not solely used prior to seeking a formal medical opinion.

sick role behaviour

the activities undertaken by a person diagnosed as sick in order to try to get well.

ISSUES

Where do you go to with your symptoms?

Increasingly we are using online search engines such as Google to identify health organisations and symptom checkers to refer ourselves to when something doesn't 'feel right' but when we are as yet unsure as to whether or not the bodily sign is symptomatic of something worthy of making an appointment at a doctor's for! Many official health organisations, such as the national health services in the UK and Australia have symptom checkers (see **https://www.nhs.uk/symptom-checker**; **www.healthdirect.gov.au/symptom-checker**), as do many other countries (for example, in the Netherlands or Germany **http://www.gezondheidsplein.nl/symptomenchecker/**, **http://www.netdoktor.de/service/symptom-checker/**

It is estimated that approximately 60 per cent of internet users will use the internet for health-related purposes (particularly younger populations and those with chronic disease), primarily seeking information about a condition or a treatment using health-professional sites, but also to read health-related patient blogs, or join patient forums (Thackeray et al. 2013). However, not all health websites are underpinned by professional bodies or expert regulation. Whilst many websites have become more sophisticated and gather information about your age, body mass, risk factors, etc. first, before asking what symptoms you are currently experiencing and making a tentative diagnosis, many less informed sites do not, and instead just take your symptoms and then present you with a long list of alternative diagnoses, from the mildly inconvenient to the life threatening!

Symptom checkers carry risks of being misinformed – relaxing when one should not; over-reacting when one should not – but they do provide an extension to what is known as our 'lay referral system' as described in this chapter and therefore should be treated as a modern extension to information sources people will likely use when first detecting a symptom.

Once ill, we can also use online forums and various forms of social media to compare our experiences with that of similar others. For example, at **healthtalkonline.org** interviews with a wide range of people about their health and illness experiences are shared in a series of over 70 modules that are underpinned by rigorous qualitative research. This website has attained registration with the Information Standard (UK) and is increasingly recognised as a useful educational resource, not just for patients and their families but also for students in health care, and health psychology!

The world of social media and access to online resources (not just in health) is expanding, with inherent risks as well as potential benefits. Public health research could perhaps better explore the role such health-relevant resources play in patient decision-making regarding health-care-seeking behaviour. It is also plausible that the growth of online health-information-seeking behaviour, and in mobile technologies more generally, has contributed to the increased use of electronically delivered interventions: for example, the use of text messages to prompt behaviour change (see meta-analysis by Head et al. 2013) or even Facebook (these intervention methods are discussed in Chapter 7, ☞).

Our response even to serious symptoms may still involve some delay to see whether things improve or whether attempts at self-care will improve the situation. A dramatic example of this was reported by Kentsch et al. (2002), who found that over 40 per cent of patients who thought they were having a heart attack, *and who* *considered this to be potentially fatal*, waited over one hour before calling for medical help. This delay would have had a significant impact on the outcome of their illness. Treatment with 'clot-busting' drugs, which dissolve the clot that causes an MI and minimise damage to the heart, are at their most effective when given within an hour of the onset of problems. An example of delay in a more chronic but equally serious condition was reported by Prohaska et al. (1990), who found that the first response of over 80 per cent of their sample of patients with colorectal cancer was the use of over-the-counter medication. Patients waited an average of seven months before seeking medical help. Cockburn et al. (2003) also found significant evidence of our ability to ignore important symptoms. In a survey of over a thousand adults, they found that 23 per cent of their sample reported having had blood in their stools (a potential symptom of bowel cancer) – but only one-third had ever reported these symptoms to a doctor. Perhaps more encouraging was the reporting of breast lumps by women in a study by Meechan et al. (2002). They found that of their sample of women who identified breast lumps following breast self-examination, 40 per cent had seen their doctor within seven days, 52 per cent within fourteen days, 69 per cent within thirty days, and only 14 per cent had waited over ninety days. However, it should be noted that even among this group of health-aware women who took active steps to identify and prevent disease, a significant proportion still delayed significantly in reporting their symptoms to their doctor.

WHAT DO YOU THINK?

Health is one of our most precious attributes. Yet many people who fear they have an illness – in some cases one they think may be fatal – delay in seeking medical help. Interestingly, people who are in the presence of someone else when their symptoms occur are more likely to call for help than people who are alone at the time. It seems that by talking with this person they are given 'permission' to call for medical aid. Why should this be necessary? Think of your own illness experience and consider what you do when experiencing symptoms and whether you seek validation by others before seeking help. Factors influencing delay are discussed next.

Delay behaviour

Delay behaviour in this instance refers to an individual's delay in seeking health advice as opposed to delays inherent in the health-care system itself. In many conditions, including cancer and heart attack, for example, delay in presenting symptoms for medical attention is highly related to outcomes of **morbidity** and mortality (e.g. Richards et al. 1999; Henriksson et al. 2011), and thus it is important to gain an understanding of the factors that influence delay behaviour.

Safer et al. (1979) developed a model of delay behaviour, defined as the time between recognising a symptom and seeking help for it. They described three decision-making stages (see Figure 9.5) and point out that a person will enter treatment only after all three stages have been gone through and the questions in each stage have been answered positively.

In the first stage, a person infers that they are ill on the basis of perceiving a symptom or symptoms – the delay in reaching this decision is termed 'appraisal delay'. Next, the person considers whether or not they need medical attention, and the time taken to decide this is termed 'illness delay'. The final stage covers the time taken between deciding one needs medical attention and actually acting on that decision by making an appointment or presenting to a hospital. This is termed 'utilisation delay'.

To illustrate these three stages, let us imagine that on Sunday you wake up with a sore throat (recognise symptoms); by Tuesday you decide you are sick (appraisal delay); on Wednesday you decide to see your doctor (illness delay); on Friday you actually see the doctor (utilisation delay). The latter delay may not be under the individual's control if it includes time to the actual appointment (referred to as a 'scheduling delay'), as opposed to the time taken to *make* the appointment. The length of each delay period is likely to vary for different symptoms and illnesses, with, for example, appraisal delays being long for embarrassing personal symptoms such as rectal bleeding but scheduling delays likely to be short. It becomes obvious therefore that appraisals are crucial in getting the help-seeking process moving along, particularly when symptoms are potentially lethal. It follows therefore that if the potential for the appropriate cognitive appraisal is diminished through intellectual or cognitive impairment, appraisal and illness delays are likely to be exacerbated.

Many factors influence whether a person will or will not seek medical help above and beyond reasons of socioeconomics (the lower one's level of education and income, the greater the delay), demographic characteristics (age, gender, see Chapter 2, ☞), or personality as described above. Personal beliefs about illness, treatments

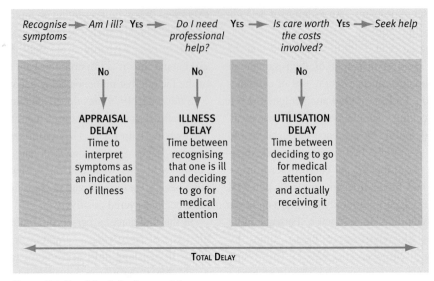

Figure 9.5 The delay behaviour model

Source: adapted from Safer et al. (1979).

and expectations of health care and health-care professionals interact with a range of emotional factors, and external influences such as social network expectations. For example, among patients with type 1 diabetes, perceived treatment effectiveness was a significant predictor of attendance at health-care clinics along with the coping strategy of seeking instrumental support (Lawson et al. 2007). Table 9.2 summarises common practical, emotional and social reasons for seeking or not seeking medical attention, drawing from a range of studies across a range of conditions (including, for example Cheng, 2000; Lawson et al. 2007; Hale et al. 2010; Henriksson et al. 2011).

Symptom type, location, perceived prevalence

As described in the symptom perception section, symptoms that are visible, painful, disruptive, frequent and persistent generally (not always) lead to action. If the symptom is easily visible to oneself and others, for example a rash, then one will delay less in seeking treatment. When people believe that their symptoms are serious (whether or not subsequently confirmed by the doctor), unusual (e.g. no one else seems to have had them) and that they can be controlled or treated through medical intervention, they are more likely to take action. The effects of symptoms are also important. When symptoms threaten normal relations with friends and family, or when they disrupt regular activity or interaction, people usually seek help (Peay and Peay 1998; Ringström et al. 2007). However, Grunfeld and colleagues (2003) found that even when a potential symptom of breast cancer had been self-identified, a significant number of women aged 35–54 delayed seeking health care in the belief that seeking help and potentially entering protracted treatment would be disruptive to their lifestyle! Not seeking help for such symptoms could result in an illness and treatment regime significantly more disruptive than presenting to health care early.

The location of the symptom also influences use of a lay referral system and/or going to a doctor: for example, persistent headaches may be discussed with friends and family before seeking medical help, whereas detection of a lump in the genital region, or irritable bowel symptoms, may not be – certain parts of the body seem more open to discussion than others. The attributes associated with some diseases may also influence ease of reporting; Hale et al. (2007), for example, noted that shame or embarrassment about the likely need for rectal examinations contributed significantly to delayed reporting of symptoms subsequently found to be associated with prostate cancer. This is also one of the reasons that many testicular cancers are diagnosed late, with potentially serious consequences (for cancer screening issues, see Chapter 4 (☞).

Table 9.2 Reasons for seeking, delaying in or not seeking a medical consultation

Reason
Seekers
Believe their symptom to be serious
Are experiencing life disruption as a result of their symptoms
Want information about symptoms and their cause
Want reassurance about symptoms
Want legitimisation of their concerns
Believe there is a treatment with the potential to manage or cure symptoms
Were encouraged to attend by a loved one or lay referral
Want to avoid the risk of symptoms progressing or things 'getting worse'
Delayers or non-seekers
Think they do not have time
Do not want to take sick leave from work or family responsibilities
Do not like clinics or hospital settings/ Do not trust the medical profession
Are worried about possible costs of treatment
Think the symptoms are 'just a bug going round', i.e. transient
Think the symptoms are not serious enough, i.e. are afraid of being 'a nuisance' or wasting doctor's time
Are unaware of the potential meaning of their symptoms
Are reassured by friends/lay referral that their symptoms are not a cause for concern
Hold non-medical views of illness experience (see cultural influences below)
Are worried about appearing 'weak' (particularly in males)
Believe there is nothing that can be done, no treatment potential
Are worried or scared of the result and implications
Are fearful of possible tests and examinations
Are afraid of being judged negatively by the health-care professional for some behaviour they believe is associated with their symptoms (e.g. smoking)

Furthermore, people make judgements about the prevalence of symptoms and disease that influence their interpretation and whether they seek medical attention. Diseases that a person has experience of have been found to be judged as more prevalent by both patients *and* by physicians, and diseases considered prevalent tend to become normalised and viewed as less serious or life-threatening (Jemmott et al. 1988). Thankfully, however, it has been shown that presenting with symptoms of a condition that one reports a family history for predisposes the emergency services to respond in an urgent manner (Hedges et al. 1998).

Financial reasons for delay

For some, seeking refuge in the sick role following a formal diagnosis might be an attractive option as it can allow a person time out from normal duties and responsibilities. However, some people do not want to be declared sick because of the implications it may have for them socially ('If I am sick how can I attend that party?'); occupationally ('If I am off sick my work will pile up and await my return or will someone else get my job?'); or financially ('I cannot afford to lose wages or overtime payments by being sick.' 'I cannot afford to pay for tests or medicines'). In the USA, some people delay seeking medical care when money for the anticipated treatment is limited; or where they do not have sufficient health insurance (USBC 1999), although even when people have medical insurance, delay is present, for example, following a heart attack (Rahimi et al. 2007, see Chapter 2 (☞). Treatment cost concerns are particularly highlighted within some minority groupings: for example, one American focus group study found that African-Americans were more likely than White or Hispanic American participants to report delaying calls to emergency services out of concerns about the costs and location of care (Finnegan et al. 2000). Luckily, many countries have health-care systems that make personal finance less of a barrier to treatment, for example the National Health Service in the UK.

Cultural influences on delay behaviour

Westernised cultures have been found to promote an independent sense of responsibility, i.e. the individual has supreme importance, whereas African cultures (e.g. Chalmers 1996; Morrison et al. 1999; Vaughn et al. 2009), and Chinese and Japanese cultures (e.g. Heine and Lehman 1995; Tan and Bishop 1996) have been shown to perceive health and illness more collectively and interdependently, in terms of the effects of health and illness on group function. As a result, different cultures may exhibit broadly different belief systems and different attitudes towards, and responses to, illness. To illustrate this, Bishop and Teng's (1992) study of Singaporean Chinese students found that, while severity and contagiousness were commonly used dimensions of illness perception (consistent with Western students), an additional dimension existed whereby illness was tied to behaviour and to blocked *qi* – the source of life and energy. These beliefs were associated with either the use of traditional or Western health care. It appears that when dual health-care systems operate in parallel in a society, they are used differentially depending on the specific illness and illness perceptions (Heine and Lehman 1995; Quah and Bishop 1996; Lim and Bishop 2000). African studies (Chalmers 1996) have shown that the use of traditional medicine such as faith healers remains strong even as Westernised health-care availability increases. These kind of findings suggest that delays in seeking professional medical help may in part result from holding

specific cultural beliefs about illness causation that do not 'fit' biomedical views of illness and treatment (Pachter 1994; Mir and Tovey 2002). In these cases, individuals will seek culturally relevant cures, including, for example, herbal or animal-based treatments, acupuncture, faith healing, and so on. In some cases, this may be associated with a parallel seeking of medical help – in others, seeking Westernised medical treatment may be considered only if the condition fails to respond to the more traditional remedies (Chalmers 1996; Heine and Lehman 1995; Lim and Bishop 2000; Quah and Bishop 1996).

Minority status, which includes ethnicity, but also gender, sexuality and so forth, may also contribute to delayed help-seeking where health-care consultations are seen as holding potential for humiliation or discrimination (Wamala et al. 2007). A fuller discussion of the influence of ethnicity on health-care-seeking behaviour, and access to services, is covered in Chapter 2 (☞).

Age and delay behaviour

The young and the elderly use health services more often than other age groups (see Chapter 2 (☞)). Acute onset of severe symptoms tends to result in quicker seeking of medical attention by everyone, although particularly among the middle-aged. Elderly people generally present to their doctors more quickly regardless of symptom severity and in spite of the fact that many symptoms are commonly attributed initially to ageing (Prohaska et al. 1987). The quicker presentation of older individuals to health-care professionals has been interpreted as a need to remove uncertainty, whereas middle-aged individuals may attempt to minimise their problems, often relying on self-medication, until they worsen or fail to disappear naturally (Leventhal and Diefenbach 1991). In terms of a symptomatic child, the responsibility for acting on, interpreting symptoms and subsequently seeking health care (or not) lies often with the parent or guardian, and it may be expected that delay would be minimal. However, this is not inevitable, and presenting a child to health care may be subject to similar influences as presenting oneself. For example, a Nepalese study found that, even when presenting a child to health care, the speed of seeking health care depended on maternal educational level, family income, and the number and perceived severity of symptoms

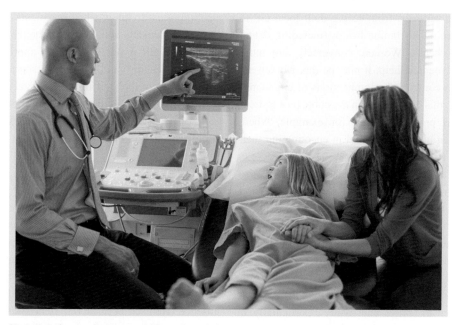

Photo 9.3 Communicating to children about their symptoms presents additional challenges

Source: Corbis/Hero Images

(Sreeramareddy et al. 2006). In late adolescence the decision to attend moves away from some parents and these young people can become reluctant to seek medical attention, particularly if their symptoms are something they wish to conceal from their parents. For example Meyer-Weitz et al. (2000) interviewed 292 South African adolescent and young adults (aged under 20 years) about the influences on their seeking health care for a sexually transmitted disease. The majority presented within six days of symptoms (56 per cent), 23 per cent waited seven to ten days, and 21 per cent waited more than ten days. The reasons given by those seeking health care early were perceived seriousness of the symptoms, absence of any self-treatments and positive attitudes to autonomy and, perhaps surprisingly, to condoms. Adolescents may also delay in seeking health care out of a sense of invulnerability and a resulting optimism about susceptibility to health problems (see Chapter 3 ☞).

Gender and delay behaviour

Women generally use health services more than men and we have already explored whether this may reflect greater attention being paid to internal states and bodily signals or gender socialisation. Perhaps women

make better use of their social support and lay referral networks, which promote health-care-seeking behaviour (Krantz and Orth 2000). However, a study conducted in France (Melchior et al. 2003) found that occupational status, and not gender, influenced social support usage, with those with low social status reporting better support. This contradicts American and British findings (Marmot et al. 1998; Stansfeld et al. 1998), where low socio-economic status was associated with less social support. The interaction between gender, socio-economic status, social support and health-care use is not yet fully understood (see Chapter 2 ☞) and any explanation is likely to be multifaceted, given the range of potential influences described in this section.

Gender differences in seeking medical help may occur as a result of different meanings given to health-related behaviour by the two sexes (Courtenay 2000). The differences, they propose, and as reflected on at the start of this chapter, reflect issues of masculinity, femininity and power. Men show their masculinity and power by engaging in health-risking behaviour, by presenting late in the course of illness to add to a notion of not fussing or not malingering, and by not showing signs of weakness – even when ill. A key explanation for men's poorer longevity is likely to be their lower rate of usage of health services, from seeing their local GP to attending screening or routine health (including dental and eyesight) checks. Women, conversely, are more willing to seek medical help. It may be that women are more willing to confront the implications of any symptoms than men; this can be seen in the context of testicular, bowel and prostate cancer, for example, where women are often highly influential in encouraging their male partners to attend for doctor consultations (e.g. Gascoigne et al. 1999; Hale et al. 2007). It is also reported that by presenting because 'someone else said I should come' men can preserve their masculine image as someone who 'doesn't fuss about his health' (Hale et al. 2010). This point arose in their interesting qualitative study of the perceptions of men entering health care as judged by ten GPs. Interviews revealed that all GPs attributed the lower self-referral rate among men to their need to be seen as 'brave and manly', particularly in those of lower socio-economic status. Interestingly, GPs felt this group only presented when perhaps the need was genuine – saying, for example: 'Working men, for instance, we don't see as many of them, unless they've got a real health problem . . . ' suggesting that other patient groups, including non-working men, and women, may present with non-real problems! In addition, self-referral seemed to be considered by some as a feminine behaviour. Furthermore, there was some indication that male GPs are more understanding of males who do not present than those who do, even though we know from, for example, cancer statistics that late presentation causes significant morbidity and increased mortality!

Finally, there may be preferences in who we see when we go to a GP. Previously it has been shown that both male and female patients prefer to see female GPs when presenting with 'personal' or 'sexual' problems, although the evidence is inconsistent. Certainly findings from Hale's study suggests that male doctors may be unsympathetic to a regularly presenting male patient. It is speculated that female doctors are more empathic and reassuring in their communications with male patients than male doctors, consistent with gender differences in health-care professional communications (see Chapter 10 ☛). Further research needs to compare these attitudes with those held by female GPs – they too may judge male patients differently to female patients, and they too may make judgements about who over-attends and why. Inappropriate attendance is a challenge to medical services whatever the gender of the patient. It is

also important to know whether patients' perceptions of critical judgements being made of them by GPs is borne out, as the GP is our first line of approach for many critical screening and treatment services. Are GPs ambivalent to the self-referrals of certain types of patient? If so, does it affect any aspects of their communication or treatment actions? These issues are controversial, but nonetheless need to be addressed.

Influence of others on delay behaviour

People often take action only when they are encouraged to do so by others in their lay referral network or when they realise that others with the same problem sought help in the past. It appears that many people look for 'permission' to call for help from their friends or family members – and are more reluctant to call for help in its absence (Kentsch et al. 2002; Henriksson et al. 2011). Related to this are delays as a result of 'not wanting to bother anybody'.

Discussing symptoms with others can be helpful. For example, Turk et al. (1985) found that discovering the presence of a family history of the symptoms currently being experienced led to health-care contact being made. Such disclosures of family history or of others' illness experiences are a likely outcome of conversations within a lay referral network, and having a family history is associated with seeking health care (Weinman and Petrie 1997). However, not all social networks are helpful: some people consulted may distrust doctors after negative experiences of their own; others may believe in alternative treatment or therapies rather than traditional medical routes; yet others may decide that the symptoms reflect something else going on, their friend/relative being stressed for example (Leventhal and Crouch 1997). The use of lay referral networks, including online networks (see ISSUES) can therefore work for or against delays in the seeking of health care.

Treatment beliefs and delay behaviour

Horne (Horne 1999; Horne and Weinman 1999) suggests an extension to Leventhal's self-regulation model (described earlier in the chapter) whereby, in addition to illness perceptions predicting illness responses, the perceived benefits that an individual foresees of any treatments they may obtain as a result of seeking medical help are also predictive. For example, believing that one has a serious illness but that it can be cured with treatment is more likely to result in seeking medical help than the opposite cluster of beliefs. The identification of treatment representations (Horne and Weinman 1999) highlights perceptions of medicines as restorative, as symptom relievers, or as disruptive, harmful or addictive. Representations of medication and knowledge about treatment rationale have been associated with treatment adherence among adult populations (e.g. McElnay and McCallion 1998; Horne and Weinman 1999, 2002), and a further effect of beliefs about treatment – perhaps obtained online (see ISSUES) – might be their influence on decisions to seek or not seek health-professional advice for a symptom.

Perhaps due to growing concerns about some traditional medical treatments (e.g. antibiotics, steroids, HRT – hormone replacement therapy), Western populations are increasingly turning to complementary therapies, involving both physical and non-traditional pharmaceutical interventions, such as acupuncture, chiropractice, homeopathy and alternative therapies such as traditional Chinese herbal medicine or Indian Ayurvedic medicine (Vaughn et al. 2009). Interestingly, those using such treatments tend to be from more highly educated and more economically well-off groups (Astin 1998).

Emotions, traits and delay behaviour

Neurotics and those high in trait NA are more likely to report symptoms (Watson and Pennebaker 1989, 1991; Bennett et al. 1996; Deary et al. 1997); however, fear and anxiety have been inconsistently associated with delay in seeking health care. O'Carroll et al. (2001), for example, found that people who had relatively high scores on a measure of dispositional anxiety were more likely to seek help quickly following the onset of symptoms than their less anxious counterparts. While fear of doctors, treatment procedures or medical environments can delay health-care-seeking, and trait anxiety, neuroticism and negative affectivity have generally been found to increase non-emergency health-care utilisation, illness-specific anxiety appears to be less influential. For example, delay in seeking medical care was not significantly associated with anxiety among a study of individuals with head and neck cancer (Tromp et al. 2004). Furthermore, with regards to seeking future *urgent* health care, a recent meta-analysis of studies examining the prospective relationship between this behaviour and anxiety in patients diagnosed either with CHD, asthma, diabetes or COPD,

found no relationship (Blakely et al. 2014), unlike studies of the predictive role of depression (Dickens et al. 2012). In interpreting the anxiety finding, Blakely suggests that many previously reported associations were limited by being cross-sectional concurrent associations only.

Emotion itself may be insufficient to determine health-care-seeking behaviour, given the previously described importance of illness prototypes, symptom perception and interpretations and treatment beliefs, all of which act together to shape a person's response to a health threat. For example, a person who is highly anxious about a symptom and believes it signifies a terminal illness for which there is no treatment is less likely to seek medical attention quickly than someone who is equally anxious but believes that the symptom may be an early warning sign of a condition for which preventive or curative treatment is available.

One further response to health threats is that of denial. It has been shown that people who engage in denial generally show reduced symptom perception and report, and greater delay in seeking help (Jones 1990; Zervas et al. 1993). Unrealistically optimistic beliefs about health status or illness outcomes were thought to reduce symptom report and preventive health behaviour by means of increasing the presence of denial. However, neither of these relationships was upheld in a study of symptom report among those with either multiple sclerosis or insulin-dependent diabetes (de Ridder et al. 2004). Aspinwall and Brunhart (1996) have pointed out that optimism is not necessarily unrealistic and maladaptive, but that optimistic beliefs may actually benefit symptom report by enabling people to attend to symptoms without perceiving them as a threat. Tromp et al. (2004) offer support for this from a study of predictors of delay among patients with head and neck cancer, where delay was found to be greater (> three months) in those scoring low on optimism, as well as low on active coping, the use of social support and low **health hardiness**.

There is a limited literature examining the influence of personality traits on health-care-seeking behaviour

---

health hardiness

the extent to which a person is committed to and involved in health-relevant activities, perceives control over their health and responds to health stressors as challenges or opportunities for growth.

(Williams 2006), and what there is tends to focus on optimism, as discussed above, or neuroticism. Neurotic individuals, as described earlier, tend to over-attend to internal bodily signs and over-interpret and over-report symptoms; this means that they generally exhibit shorter delays in seeking help than those less neurotic individuals (O'Carroll et al. 2001). However, it has been suggested that their consulting style, of elaborate symptom description, for example, works against them being seen as credible and potentially undermines the medical care they receive (Ellington and Wiebe 1999).

Finally, following diagnosis, Kasl and Cobb describe how people engage in sick role behaviour, as the symptoms have been validated (and may increase once a label has been attached to them; Kasl and Cobb 1966b). People are then working towards getting better, adjusting to changed circumstances, or preserving health such as avoiding activity or further injury. Seeking health care does not inevitably lead a person into the sick role, however, as effective treatment may be provided that rids them of their symptoms and enables them to carry on as usual. For those, however, who face ongoing illness, there is a further set of challenges to be met, and we turn to this in later chapters, firstly in terms of impact and outcomes for the patient (Chapter 14 ☞), and secondly in terms of the illness impact upon family and friends (Chapter 15 ☞).

SUMMARY

This chapter has described the various processes that people go through before deciding that they might be getting ill. We have described how people may or may not become aware of certain bodily signs, depending upon the context or upon individual characteristics. Both internal and external factors influence the extent to which a person attends to their own bodily states, and how they subsequently interpret bodily signs as symptoms. We have described how, upon interpreting bodily signs as symptoms of some underlying illness, a person compares them with pre-existing illness prototypes derived from their personal experience or from external sources of information. People's beliefs about illness have commonly been found to cluster around five domains: perceived identity (label), timeline, consequences, cure–control and cause and

research has shown that ways of thinking about illness are relatively stable across various patient groups, but may differ from that of a healthy person. Finally, we have described health-care-seeking behaviour. The journey from a bodily sign perceived as a symptom to the doctor's door is often a long one, and delay in seeking health care can itself be damaging to one's health.

At each stage a range of relevant individual, cultural, social and emotional influences have been summarised. Health psychology has an important role to play in identifying the factors that contribute to this journey in order to maximise the likelihood of positive health outcomes for patients. How people communicate with health professionals and engage in their treatment is discussed in the following chapter.

Further reading

Brown, R. (2004). Psychological mechanisms of medically unexplained symptoms: an integrative conceptual mode. *Psychological Bulletin*, 130: 793–813.

An interesting model of cognitive and attentional processes is presented that brings cognitive psychology thinking to the domain of medically unexplained symptoms, such as those seen in chronic fatigue syndrome. See also his editorial in a Special Issue of *Clinical Psychology Review*: Brown, R.J. (2007). Introduction to The special issue on medically unexplained symptoms: background and future directions. *Clinical Psychology Review*, 27: 769–80.

Griva, K., Davenport, A., Harrison, M. and Newman, S.P. (2012). The impact of treatment transitions between dialysis and transplantation on illness cognitions and quality of life: a prospective study. *British Journal of Health Psychology*, 17: 812–27.

This paper acknowledges the important influence of treatment and transitions into and out of treatment on the illness representation components of Leventhal's Self Regulation model of illness. Whilst restricted to end-stage renal disease patients, the relevance of the approach taken to those with any health condition with varying treatment options or illness trajectory is clear.

Martin, R. and Leventhal, H. (2004). Symptom perception and health-care-seeking behaviour. In J.M. Raczynski and L.C. Leviton (eds), *Handbook of Clinical Health Pschology*, Vol. 2. Washington, DC: American Psychological Association, pp. 299–328.

This chapter, contained in an excellent and well-resourced text, provides a clear overview of theory and findings regarding the illness-related and personal influences on how people interpret and act upon symptoms.

Williams, P.G. (2006). Personality and illness behaviour. In M.E. Vollrath (ed.), *Handbook of Personality and Health*. Chichester: Wiley, pp. 157–73.

This chapter provides an overview of evidence regarding the role of personality in illness behaviour, from symptom perception to health-care-seeking behaviour. It also highlights key gaps in current knowledge and highlights why personality research offers exciting opportunities to develop our theoretical models of illness behaviour.

www.healthtalkonline.org

Visit www.healthtalkonline.org for video and interview material derived from a wide range of rigorous research interviews with people who have direct experience with a wide range of health conditions. Qualitative material such as provided here from study can be both insightful and helpful when developing your own research ideas.

For open-access student resources specifically written to complement this textbook and support your learning, please visit **www.pearsoned.co.uk/morrison**

Chapter 10
The consultation and beyond

Learning outcomes

By the end of the chapter, you should have an understanding of:

- the process of the medical consultation
- the movement towards 'shared decision making' and the issues it creates
- factors that contribute to effective and ineffective consultations with health professionals
- issues related to 'breaking bad news' and medical decision-making
- factors that influence adherence to medical treatments and behavioural change programmes
- interventions to improve adherence to medication and behavioural regimens

Doctor error causes heart attack death

This is a headline that could probably be written in the newspapers every day. But this error was not the fault of long waiting lists, giving the wrong drugs, or poor surgery. Rather, it was the result of the doctor's communication with the patient – or rather their lack of it. Mr Jones who had a history of anxiety went to his General Practitioner about a mild pain in his chest that had been going on for some hours. Unfortunately, for him, Mr Jones was what doctors sometimes call a 'heart sink' patient – the doctor's heart sinks when they see them come in the door, because they know the patient will make several complaints of a very general nature that they will not be able to treat, and the patient will return in the next few weeks with new complaints – which will again be untreatable. Even more unfortunately, the doctor then acted on her assumption that this was the case rather than trying to get a full picture of Mr Jones's symptoms and without conducting relevant tests. The doctor took charge of the consultation, asking closed questions about the symptoms, and confirmed to her satisfaction that the symptoms were psychosomatic in nature. She gave some reassuring words to Mr Jones, who left feeling somewhat disappointed by the relatively brief consultation and still doubtful that his symptoms were not more serious. However, he followed the doctor's advice and did not seek further medical help. Later that day, he died of a heart attack at home. In this chapter we cover the two key issues that may have contributed to this outcome: the doctor adopting a medically led interview style that did not allow the patient to volunteer information they considered relevant to the case, and their use of faulty diagnostic heuristics. Together, they proved fatal.

Chapter outline

Conversations between health-care providers and patients are one of the most important means through which both groups give and receive information relevant to medical decisions, treatment and self-care. As such, the consultation remains one of the most important aspects of medical care. Good communication enhances the effectiveness of care; poor communication can lead doctors to make poor diagnoses and treatment decisions and leave patients feeling dissatisfied and unwilling or unable to engage appropriately in their own treatment. This chapter considers a number of factors that contribute to the quality of the consultation, and how doctors, other health-care workers, and patients act on information gained from it. It starts by examining the process of the consultation – what makes a 'good' or a 'bad' consultation. It then considers how doctors use the information given in the consultation to inform their diagnostic decisions. Finally, the chapter considers how factors in the consultation and beyond influence whether and how much patients follow medical treatments or behavioural programmes recommended in it.

The medical consultation

The nature of the encounter

Consultations are a time in which doctors and other health professionals can obtain information to inform their diagnostic and treatment decisions, and patients can gain information about their condition, its treatment, and discuss issues relevant to them. They typically include five phases:

1. The doctor establishes a relationship with the patient.

2. The doctor attempts to discover the reason for the patient's attendance.

3. The doctor conducts a verbal or physical examination or both.

4. The doctor, or the doctor and the patient, or the patient (in that order of probability) considers the condition.

5. The doctor, and occasionally the patient, considers further treatment or further investigation.

These phases appear to hold for most consultations, although, as we consider later, what happens within each 'stage' can vary significantly. Another way of exploring the consultation is to consider the key elements that make for a successful interview. Ford et al. (2003) identified six factors considered to be important to a 'good' medical consultation by a variety of informants including general practitioners, hospital doctors, nurses and lay people. They involve the health professional:

1. having a good knowledge of research or medical information and being able to communicate this to the patient;

2. achieving a good relationship with the patient;

3. establishing the nature of the patient's medical problem;

4. gaining an understanding of the patient's understanding of their problem and its ramifications;

5. engaging the patient in any decision-making process – treatment choices, for example, are discussed with the patient;

6. managing time so that the consultation does not appear rushed.

Who has the power?

The consultation involves both patient and health professional: and both can contribute to its outcome. The nature of the meeting, however, means that the health professional usually has more power over the consultation than the patient. This power differential can be exacerbated by the patient's behaviour and expectations within the consultation. They may often defer to the professional and be reluctant to ask questions or challenge any conclusions they may make. Such behaviour is more likely to occur in consultations with doctors than with other health professionals, such as nurses. Nevertheless, all health professionals have significant responsibility for determining the style and outcome of the consultation. This can result in approaches differing from 'doctor knows best', the professional-centred approach identified by Byrne and Long (1976), to a more patient-centred approach pioneered by Pendleton (1983) and others.

Characteristics of the professional-centred approach include:

- The health professional keeps control over the interview.
- They ask questions in order to gain information. These are direct, closed (allow yes/no answers), and refer to medical or other relevant facts.
- The health professional makes the decision.
- The patient passively accepts this decision.

Characteristics of the patient-centred approach include:

- The professional identifies and works with the patient's agenda as well as their own.
- The health professional actively listens to the patient and responds appropriately.
- Communication is characterised by the professional encouraging engagement and seeking the patient's ideas about what is wrong with them and how their condition may be treated.
- The patient is an active participant in the process.

Over the past decade, there has been a gradual shift from the professional-centred model to the patient-centred approach. Increasingly, both health professionals and patients are seen as collaborators in decisions concerning patient health care. This is perhaps most strongly expressed in a movement among health professionals towards a process of 'shared decision making' (Elwyn et al. 2012), in which the patient and health professional have an equal share (and responsibility) in many treatment decisions. Its advocates note that this approach is

not relevant to all medical encounters, and may only truly occur where there is no dominant choice of treatment – a situation referred to as equipoise. This may occur in the context of very important health issues – such as a woman with breast cancer deciding whether or not to conserve a breast with a **lumpectomy** or to have more radical surgery and remove the whole affected breast. Here, there is no differential medical benefit from either approach (i.e. equipoise), and the choice may be more determined by factors such as the patient's concerns over their appearance or their desire to minimise the risk of recurrence.

The process of shared decision-making is illustrated by Elwyn et al.'s (2012) consultation approach which involves the following steps: choice, option, decision.

- *Choice* refers to the step of making sure that patients know that reasonable treatment options are available. The health professional 'conveys awareness' that a choice exists.
- *Option* refers to providing more detailed information about options. Patients are informed about treatment options in more detail.
- *Decision* refers to supporting the work of considering preferences and deciding what is best. The patient is encouraged to determine their initial choice, based on their existing knowledge and then shift this to informed preferences based on 'what matters most to patients' based on an understanding of the most relevant benefits and harms.

To facilitate this process, a number of clinicians (e.g. Lee et al. 2010) have developed written or computer-based 'decision aids' to help patients make decisions about their treatment in the light of complex health information. These typically provide patients with information both for and against a number of treatment options, encouraging them to score each item of information in terms of its desirability or lack of desirability, and to achieve a total plus or minus score in relation to each potential treatment.

> **lumpectomy**
>
> a surgical procedure in which only the tumour and a small area of surrounding tissue are removed. Contrasts with mastectomy in which the whole breast is removed.

In this process, although the health professional may provide information to inform patient choice, or even offer an opinion about that choice, the final decision should be reached jointly. By contrast, where equipoise does not exist, for example, in the case of a request for antibiotics for the treatment of a viral condition (where they will be of no benefit), the health professional may educate the patient to help them understand or accept the health professional's choice of treatment, and so arrive at a 'joint decision', but not a truly shared decision.

Both shared and joint decision-making approaches are now advocated by, among others, the British National Health Service (NHS) which has called for 'active partnerships' between health professionals and patients (NHS England 2013; http://www.england.nhs.uk/wp-content/uploads/2013/09/trans-part-hc-guid1.pdf). Despite this enthusiasm, there are often power differentials between high status health professionals (particularly doctors) and patients within the consultation. The health professional, for example, typically has more relevant knowledge than the patient. The appearance of equality can therefore be an illusion rather than reality, and both health professionals and patients may find it difficult to move away from this implicit power structure. Indeed, many patients *prefer* this asymmetry and resist moves to 'empower' them into a decision-making role. Some patients may be distressed and worried if a health-care professional admits there is no clear evidence about the best choice of intervention, or that the evidence is mixed or premised on poor methodology. By contrast, being prescribed a particular treatment by an expert health professional may confer certainty and reassurance in the treatment of disease that cannot be found when the patient is asked to make choices about a number of uncertain treatment options.

Empirical research confirms some of these cautions. Lee et al. (2002) asked over a thousand patients with either breast cancer or who were receiving **stem cell transplants** to identify their preferred consultation style. Only a minority of individuals opted for the shared

decision-making approach. Patients' preferred decision-making processes were:

- Physician makes treatment decisions   10 per cent
- Physician makes decisions following discussion with patient   21 per cent
- Shared decision-making   42 per cent
- Patient makes decision following discussion with doctor   22 per cent
- Patient makes decision   5 per cent

Women, older people, those with an active coping style, and people with more education and a severe health problem are most likely to want to be engaged in the decision-making process (Arora and McHorney 2000). Paradoxically, Arora and McHorney found that people who placed the highest value on their health were least likely to want to be engaged in the decision-making process – perhaps because they considered this to be such an important issue that they did not want to question the expert opinion of the doctor.

Whatever the preferences of patients, the stated preferences of doctors are shifting from doctor-led to patient-based communication styles. In a survey of over a thousand US physicians, for example, Murray et al. (2007) found that 75 per cent preferred to share decision-making with their patients, 14 per cent preferred paternalism, and 11 per cent preferred consumerism (patient knows best). Nearly 90 per cent considered themselves to be practising their preferred style.

Despite these stated preferences for shared or joint decision-making, the majority of patients do not report this experience. Keating et al. (2002), for example, found that 64 per cent of their sample of over a thousand women with breast cancer desired a collaborative role in decision-making, but only 33 per cent reported having had such an experience. Worse, Bensing et al.'s (2006) analysis of Dutch family doctors' consulting styles revealed that over the 15 years before their report, consultations had become increasingly medically led and interrupted by frequent recording of information on computer. In addition, Robertson et al.'s (2011) discourse analysis of treatment decisions made in general practice found that so-called 'partnership talk' which was designed to engage patients in decision-making was actually used to minimise resistance to medically suggested treatment approaches, and doctors worked to achieve (medically led) consensus rather than

---

stem cell transplant

procedure in which stem cells are replaced within the bone marrow following radiotherapy or chemotherapy or diseases such as leukaemia where they may be damaged.

involvement. Finally, there are data suggesting that patients are demanding increasingly complex communication with their doctor, and some are finding this difficult to provide. In 2012, the General Medical Council reported the number of complaints regarding doctors had increased by 23 per cent, with complaints focusing primarily on how doctors interacted with their patients. Allegations about poor and inappropriate communication in particular increased by 69 per cent. Clearly, some doctors are struggling to communicate effectively in an increasing patient-oriented environment.

Consultations which *do* involve patients in decision-making are likely to result in high levels of patient satisfaction, confidence in health-care recommendations, improvements in self-care and well-being, and, on occasion, fewer drug prescriptions and less demand for inappropriate surgical treatments. They also appear to have similar, but no better, medical outcomes to more traditional consultation approaches (e.g. Bieber et al. 2006; Krones et al. 2008). Indeed, medical outcomes may not always be optimal. Kinmonth et al. (1998), for example, found that patients who were given a patient-centred approach to the treatment of their type 2 diabetes expressed higher levels of satisfaction with their communication with health professionals, greater treatment satisfaction, and greater well-being than patients who received a standard health-professional-led consultation. However, they were less careful in sticking to the calorie-controlled diet necessary to maximise control over their condition. This may not be a bad outcome, of course. Rather, it suggests that patients may have knowingly opted to have a higher day-to-day quality of life rather than one constrained by medical 'necessities'. Ultimately, it is their life, and fully informed decisions such as this need to be supported.

patients they liked than those they disliked. Encounters may also be influenced by the time available, the type of problem being dealt with, and so on. Patients and health professionals may also hold different agendas and expectations of the consultation. Patients are frequently concerned about issues such as pain and how an illness may interfere with their everyday lives. Health professionals are often more concerned with understanding the severity of the patient's condition and developing their treatment plan. These differing agendas may mean that health professionals and patient fail to appreciate important aspects of any information given and received. They may also impact on the outcome of the consultation.

In one study of this phenomenon, Langewitz et al. (2009) found some elements of doctor behaviour that actively benefited the consultation. The use of **reflection** and **mirroring** patient communications, for example, resulted in higher levels of patient disclosure of information related both to their medical condition and its psychosocial consequences. However, this increase in information led to a recording of medical information only in the doctors' notes: personal, non-medical information was disregarded. Patients tell physicians about things they deem important for the physician to know; physicians filter this out, and essentially record medical information they deem appropriate. Whether this affects subsequent care is as yet unknown.

The findings of Zachariae et al. (2003) are also relevant here. They found that patients' ratings of how well they considered the physician understood their feelings during the consultation, whether they attempted to gain an understanding of their viewpoint, and the quality of their contact with the doctor were as important as their confidence in their doctor's ability to handle the medical aspects of their care in predicting satisfaction with the

Factors that influence the process of consultation

Working together

A variety of factors may influence the behaviour of health professionals, some of which may be of no immediate medical relevance. Gerbert (1984), for example, found that health professionals gave more information to

reflection

the process of paraphrasing and restating both the feelings and words of the speaker in order to show empathy and understanding of what they are saying.

mirroring

a key strategy in the process of reflection in which a health professional repeats key words or the last words spoken by a patient, which both show understanding and prompts further information provision.

interview, their confidence in their ability to cope with their illness, and levels of emotional distress. Of note also was that doctors who evidenced poor communication skills were least aware of the patients' responses and level of dissatisfaction with the interview.

The type of health professional

As well as these subtle differences in skills and personal characteristics, more obvious factors may also influence the style of the encounter. The style of interaction appears to differ across professions. Nurses, for example, are generally seen as more nurturing, easier to talk to and better listeners than doctors. These different roles were highlighted by Nichols (2003) who suggested that doctors may find it difficult to become emotionally involved or to know their patients as people when they are involved in life and death decisions or actions such as surgery. With this in mind, he suggested that nurses should provide the main 'caring' role and be more involved in holistic care of the individual. For this reason, nurses typically address more psychosocial concerns than doctors, and have different styles of talking to patients. Collins (2005), for example, found that nurses' communication frequently involved responding to patients' contributions: doctors' communication involved leading the consultation and addressing matters important to them. In addition, nurses' explanations began from the viewpoint of patients' responsibilities and behaviour; doctors' explanations began from the viewpoint of biomedical intervention.

Gender of the health professional

The gender of the health professional may have a significant influence on the nature of the consultation. Roter and Hall (2004), for example, determined that medical visits with female physicians were, on average, two minutes (10 per cent) longer than those of male physicians. During this time, female physicians engaged in significantly more patient-centred communication: active partnership behaviours, positive talk, psychosocial counselling, psychosocial question asking, and emotionally focused talk. In addition, the patients of female physicians spoke more overall, disclosed more biomedical and psychosocial information, and made more positive statements to their physicians than did the patients of male physicians. Interestingly, satisfaction with female doctors is likely to be high only when they adopt what are perceived to be gender-role congruent

Photo 10.1 Being a friendly face and expressing empathy can help patients cope with bad news. Here an occupational therapist discusses therapy options with someone with a progressive muscular disorder in a completely informal and 'non-medical' manner

Source: Pearson Education Ltd.

communication styles (Schmid Mast et al. 2007). What may also be important is the concordance or lack of it between the gender of health professionals and patients. Beran et al. (2007), for example, found that both men and women were more likely to report being treated disrespectfully by doctors of the opposite gender than when they saw someone of the same gender.

Culture and language

Culture and language are inextricably linked in the context of the consultation, and there is clear evidence that people from differing cultures and languages will experience differing styles of consultation (see also Chapter 2 (☛)). The optimal consultation appears to occur when patients consider themselves to be similar to the health professional on a range of characteristics, including values in life and spiritual beliefs. These assumptions may be inferred, at least in part, from the ethnicity (and gender) of the health-care professional. Accordingly, the most highly rated consultations tend to occur when patient and health-care professional are ethnically similar (Street et al. 2008). This may be facilitated by the potential for mutual understandings of culture, language and health priorities.

Where patient and health-care provider are discordant, difficulties may arise. One UK research group (Neal et al. 2006), for example, found that South Asians fluent in English had the shortest consultations with their family doctors; South Asians not fluent in English had the longest. White patients discuss more emotional problems than the South Asian patients, and are more active during the consultations than either of the Asian groups. In the Netherlands, consultations with immigrant patients (especially those from Turkey and Morocco) are likely to be significantly briefer, and the power distance between patient and doctor greater than those with Dutch patients. Doctors invest more effort in trying to understand immigrant patients, while they show more involvement and empathy with those that are Dutch (Meeuwesen et al. 2006). Problems in communication may result in doctors experiencing difficulties in reaching appropriate diagnoses (e.g. Okelo et al. 2007) and patients misunderstanding information given in the consultation (e.g. B. Jones et al. 2007). The likelihood of these communication errors may be increased as a consequence of many health professionals' overestimation of the level of language understanding these patients have (Kelly and Haidet 2007), and exacerbated further

by many health professionals' expectations of how patients expect to be treated. Fagerli et al. (2007), for example, found that their sample of Norwegian health professionals thought that Pakistani-born patients preferred an authoritarian health-worker style. In fact, they preferred empathy and care. This disparity resulted in a lack of trust between patients and professionals.

The type of information and the way it is given

One obvious factor that will influence the degree to which patients understand what is said in a consultation is the language used within it. Technical or medical language can be confusing unless appropriately explained. Even relatively simple technical language can be confusing. Dua et al. (2013), for example, found that 60 per cent of their patients thought a bone fracture was a crack in the bone, and less severe than a broken bone (it isn't). Lobb et al. (1999) found significant misunderstandings of information given to women diagnosed with breast cancer. Not surprisingly, perhaps, 73 per cent of their sample did not understand the term 'median survival'; but the reassuring term 'good prognosis' also did not carry a clear meaning. In a study of patients' understandings of words used to describe 'lumps', Chadha and Repanos (2006) found that a majority were unaware of the meaning of words such as 'sarcoma' and 'lipoma'. While this confusion may be expected, 19 per cent of patients thought that a 'benign' lump was a malignant cancer, a serious misunderstanding. Not surprisingly, the use of jargon may result in significant anxiety. Finally, Abramsky and Fletcher (2002) found that the words rare, abnormal, syndrome, disorder, anomaly and high risk in the context of genetic screening were particularly worrying to patients. They also found that risk for developing a disorder expressed as '1 in X' evoked more worry than when the same information was expressed as a percentage. These subtle uses of language show how careful health-care professionals need to be when talking to patients.

The way information is given within consultations is also important. Of particular importance may be whether information is 'framed' or reported in a positive (not smoking will improve your health) or negative (smoking causes cancer) way. Edwards et al. (2001) noted the 'paucity of evidence' relating to the effects of framing of information and health behaviour but noted that some early evidence suggested framing may form an important influence on patient and even health professional behaviour. Subsequent studies have found information framing may influence a range of behaviours and factors that influence behaviour, but not always in a consistent manner (see Akl et al. 2011). Berenbaum and Latimer-Cheung (2014), for example, found that positive framed communication about exercise was more influential in a group of women than negative framed communication on outcomes as diverse as recall, attitudes, intentions and actual behaviour. By contrast, Carling et al. (2010) found that both positive *and* negative framing resulted in higher uptake of anti-hypertensive medication than neutrally framed information. In addition, while framing may influence intentions, it may not always impact on behaviour. Van't Riet et al. (2010) found that computer-generated feedback on fitness plus gain-framed messages resulted in stronger intentions to be physically active than the same feedback with loss-framed messages, but did not result in greater levels of exercise. Similarly, P. Park et al. (2010) found message framing had no effect on attendance for screening for type 2 diabetes. Accordingly, any interventions using message framing need to assess their impact on behaviour in pre-intervention pilot studies, to ensure the optimal approach is being used.

Patient factors

Patient factors will also significantly influence the consultation. High levels of anxiety or distress during the interview, a lack of familiarity with the information discussed, a failure to actively engage with the interview, and not having considered issues to be discussed within the consultation may minimise patients' level of engagement. Patients may not think through what information they want, or realise only after the interview what they could have asked. They may also be reluctant to ask questions of doctors and other health professionals who are still frequently seen as of a higher status than them (Schouten et al. 2003). Perhaps for these reasons, people who are well educated and of high socio-economic status tend to gain more information and to have longer consultations than people with low levels of education and less economic status (Stirling et al. 2001).

Breaking bad news

One type of consultation for which the necessary skills have received particular attention is called the 'bad news' interview. As its name implies, these interactions are typically those in which patients and/or their partners are told that they have a serious illness or that they may die of their illness. Clearly, such interviews are stressful for both patients and health-care professionals. Historically, information about the likelihood of dying has frequently been withheld from patients – although their relatives were frequently told, placing a significant burden of knowledge on these people. However, this is no longer considered ethical – patients are now considered to have the right to be told their prognosis.

There is consistent evidence that the way in which bad news is given will impact on patient well-being (P. Schofield et al. 2003). Unfortunately, there is little evidence about the best methods of doing so, and most guidelines are based on opinion and basic principles of good communication rather than empirical data. One of the best known process models of this approach is the six stage SPIKES model of Baile et al. (2000):

● **Step 1: S – SETTING UP the interview**

This involves mentally rehearsing the likely plan of how the interview will proceed and setting up the physical setting in an appropriate way.

– *Arrange for privacy*. Ideally, a private room; certainly a place where no one can overhear the meeting or intrude on it.

– *Involve significant others*. Most patients want to have someone with them at this time, whether it be friend or family member. However, this should be their choice.

– *Sit down*. Sitting down relaxes the patient and is a sign you will not rush. Avoid barriers between you and the patient.

– *Make connection with the patient*. This may be enhanced by appropriate eye contact and touching or holding an arm or hand.

– *Manage time constraints and interruptions*. Inform the patient of any time constraints you may have.

● **Step 2: P – Assessing the patient's PERCEPTION**

The clinician uses open-ended questions, such as 'What have you been told about your medical situation so far?', to gain an understanding of how the patient perceives their medical situation: what it is and whether it is serious. It can also allow the clinician to determine whether the patient is engaging in any denial of their situation or has unrealistic expectations of treatment.

● **Step 3: I – Obtaining the patient's INVITATION**

The goal of this stage is to determine how much the patient wants to know about their diagnosis. They may be asked questions such as 'How much information would you like to know about your test results? Would you like me to give all the information, or just look at the treatment plan?' If patients do not want to know the details of their condition or prognosis, the clinician may offer to answer any questions they have in the future or to talk to a relative or friend.

● **Step 4: K – Giving KNOWLEDGE and information to the patient**

This is the stage in which the 'bad news' is given. Some verbal warning of the message may lessen any shock the patient may experience: "I'm sorry to say, but I have some bad news to tell you…. 'Information should then be given in non-technical language ('your cancer has spread' rather than 'your cancer has metastasised'), avoiding phrases such as "You have very bad cancer and unless you get treatment immediately you are going to die.' Information should be given in small 'chunks', with checks that the patient has understood the information given at regular intervals. Finally, phrases such as 'There is nothing more we can do for you.' should be avoided. Such phrases are inconsistent with possible patient therapeutic goals such as good pain control and symptom relief.

● **Step 5: E – Addressing the patient's EMOTIONS with empathic responses**

Responding to the patient's emotions is perhaps the most difficult challenges of breaking bad news. Patients' emotional reactions may vary from silence to disbelief, crying, denial, or anger. The clinician can be supportive through the use of empathic responses, which themselves involve a series of processes:

1. Observe for any emotion on the part of the patient.
2. Try to follow and identify the emotions experienced by the patient. If they appear sad but silent, the clinician should use open questions (see Chapter 13 (☛) to find what they are thinking or feeling.
3. The reason for the emotion should be identified. It is easy to assume this is due to the bad news, but it may not be clear which issue is of concern.

4. After the patient has been given a brief period of time to express his or her feelings, the clinician should respond to their distress through empathic feedback: 'I can understand that the test result was not what you were hoping for.' The clinician may also move closer to the patient and provide some physical comfort by, for example, touching their arm or hand.
5. Any further medical dialogue needs to be suspended until the patient is able to reengage with it. This may take some time, during which the clinician may provide more empathic responses ('I too wish the news had been better'), and respond to issues raised by the patient in an empathic and non-technical manner.

● **Step 6: S – STRATEGY and SUMMARY**

Having, and knowing, a clear treatment plan will reduce anxiety and uncertainty but should be discussed only after patients are ready to address these issues. Where possible, a shared decision approach should be taken so that patients feel involved in their care, and understand their clinician considers their wishes to be important. As before, it is important to check the patient's understanding of the issues as discussion continues to ensure they do not become inappropriately optimistic (or pessimistic) about the likely outcome of any treatment plan.

When these, or similar, guidelines are followed, patients appear to benefit. M. Schofield et al. (2003), for example, asked patients to recall a **bad news interview** in which they received information about a 'life threatening' **melanoma**. They were asked questions about how their diagnosis was given, whether they received as much information as they wanted about their diagnosis, its treatment options, and its prognosis, and how the interview was conducted. They examined the relationship between their responses and levels of anxiety and depression at the time of diagnosis, 4 and 13 months

---

bad news interview
conversation between health professional (usually a doctor) and patient in which they are told 'bad news', usually that their illness has a very poor prognosis and they may die.

melanoma
a form of skin cancer. Usually begins in a mole and has a poor prognosis unless treated early.

later. Factors associated with low levels of anxiety included the health professional preparing the patient for their diagnosis, giving as much information as required, providing written information, talking about the patient's feelings, being reassuring, and the presence of other (supportive) people while being given the diagnosis. Practices associated with low levels of depression included encouraging the patient to be involved in treatment-related decisions and discussing the severity of the diagnosis and how it may affect other aspects of their life. The importance of non-specific factors within the interview was highlighted by the findings of Roberts et al. (1994), who found that the physician's caring attitude was more important in aiding psychological adjustment to a diagnosis of breast cancer than the information given during the interview.

WHAT DO YOU THINK?

Many doctors considered it a kindness not to tell patients when they were dying: a belief that also obviated *their* need to go through this painful process. Indeed, so common was this practice that a rule of thirds was often cited as relevant to this situation. That is, two-thirds of patients were assumed to wish to know their prognosis, and two-thirds of doctors did not want to tell them. It is now considered a patient's right to know they are dying, and the practice of telling the relatives and not the patient is no longer acceptable (although the SPIKES protocol outlined above does allow for this).

Patients may be upset, or even distraught, when given such information. However, knowledge of a poor prognosis can allow them to prepare for death: from the most prosaic preparation such as making sure bills are paid to dealing with relationship issues and more existential aspects of their lives. When death is not immediate, patients may prepare life goals that they wish to achieve before they die, and so on. So there are both positive and negative issues to be considered. Do the benefits outweigh the costs? Perhaps this decision can only be made on an individual basis. But on what grounds? Or perhaps all patients should be told whatever their circumstances?

Having identified 'best practice', a number of studies have examined how well physicians actually give bad news. Farber et al. (2002) found that over half their sample of junior doctors reported always or frequently performing 10 of 11 emotionally supportive strategies (e.g. ask about patients' worries, fears and concerns) and engaging 6 of 9

environmental supports (e.g. ensure that the patient has a support person present). Similarly, Chadha and Repanos (2006) found that 64 per cent of their sample of surgeons felt confident in their ability to break bad news (compared to 91 per cent who felt confident in gaining consent to surgery and 40 per cent who felt confident in discussing 'do not resuscitate' decisions). These optimistic self-ratings may be contrasted with the findings of Ford et al. (1996), who used audiotapes of consultations to analyse cancer specialists' bad news interviews with their patients and found that the majority of time was spent giving biomedical information with relatively little emphasis on empathic responses or acknowledgment of distress. In addition, the doctors exerted significant levels of control over the interview, moving away from the patient-led interview that the guidelines indicate as being optimal. Another observational study by the same group (Fallowfield et al. 1990) found that surgeons did not detect 70 per cent of instances of emotional distress in women being diagnosed with breast cancer.

Despite the clear need for skills in breaking bad news, many senior doctors (around one-half of consultants surveyed in the UK by Barnett et al. (2007)) receive no formal training in doing so. Most considered such training to be of value: an expectation that is justified by empirical studies. Back et al. (2007), for example, measured bad news skills in what they termed standardised patient encounters, which involved the use of actors playing patients. They found that physicians made significant gains in their ability to give bad news following a four-day workshop. Most changes were substantial: for example, 16 per cent of participants used the word 'cancer' when giving bad news before the workshop; 54 per cent used it at the end of the workshop. However, it is not clear how these skills translated to their day-to-day work. The findings of Curtis et al. (2014) in the 'Research focus' box consider this issue.

Before ending this section, it should be acknowledged that the bad news interview is stressful for health professionals as well as patients. Ptacek and Eberhardt (1996) mapped out patient and doctor stress in relation to the interview (see Figure 10.1), suggesting that doctors experience significant anticipatory stress before the consultation, peaking during the 'clinical encounter', while patients' levels of stress typically peak following the interview. Many clinicians experience a range of emotions including sorrow, guilt, and feeling a failure (Fallowfield and Jenkins 2004). The stress associated with giving bad news can last as long as three days or more (Ptacek et al. 2001), and can result in significant increases in blood pressure and impaired immune (NK cell) response (Cohen et al. 2003).

RESEARCH FOCUS

Curtis, J.R., Back, A.L., Ford, D.W. et al. (2014). Effect of communication skills training for residents and nurse practitioners on quality of communication with patients with serious illness: a randomized trial. *Journal of the American Medical Association*, 310, 2271–81.

Introduction

Studies such as Back et al. (2007) suggest that communication skills relevant to the care of people with serious and terminal disease can be taught. However, so far the effectiveness of these teaching programmes has largely been evaluated through role-play with simulated patients: actors who play the role of the sick patient. This is very different to the experience of real patients with real emotions and complex needs, when seen in the context of real-life pressures of doctor workload and limitations on time. This study addressed this issue, by considering patient ratings of the communication skills of doctors and nurse practitioners (who see patients largely in a consultant, advisory role) involved in their care, and the overall quality of the care they received. Participating doctors and nurses had either gone through a skills-based training programme or a control condition.

Method

Participants

● *Trainees*: 391 junior doctors involved in the care of patients from a range of medical specialties and 81 nurse practitioners with training in the care of patients with life-threatening or chronic illnesses.

● *Patient-evaluators:* identified as having had contact with a study participant from their medical notes. Those involved had a high likelihood of having a discussion about end-of-life care, could remember the doctor well enough to rate their medical encounters.

● *Family-evaluators:* family members were identified by participating patients and could provide reports on participant communication.

● *Clinician-evaluators*: Senior nurses and physicians who observed care provided by the trainee.

The intervention

Participants were randomly allocated to either a skills-based intervention or 'usual education'. The skills-based intervention involved eight four-hour sessions led by a senior doctor and nurse. Each session included (1) a brief didactic overview, including a demonstration role-play (2) skills practice using simulation (simulated patients, family, or clinicians); and (3) reflective discussions. Each addressed a specific topic including building rapport; giving bad news; nurse–physician conflict; conducting a family conference; and talking about dying. Assessment during the course, involving role-play with simulated patients, showed significant gains on communication skills in relation to giving bad news and responding to emotion. Unfortunately, there was no description of what, if any, relevant education, the control condition received.

Measures

Measures were taken in the six months prior to the workshop and the six months following it.

1. Quality of Communication (QOC): the primary outcome measure was patient- and family-reported quality of communication within medical encounters, rated from 0-10, with 0 = poor and 10 = perfect.

2. Quality of end-of-life care (QEOLC): patient- and family-reported quality of end-of-life care, again rated from 0–10.

3. Personal Health Questionnaire [PHQ-8] depressive symptoms assessed using the 8-item questionnaire with a range of possible scores from 0–24. Higher scores were indicative of higher levels of depression.

Results

The study obtained 1,866 patient ratings (from 44 per cent of those approached) and 936 family ratings (68 per cent of those approached). The mean QOC score for the intervention group was 6.5 (95 per cent CI, 6.2 to 6.8). That of the control condition was 6.3 (95 per cent CI, 6.2 to 6.5). The mean score for the QEOLC for the intervention group was 8.3 (95 per cent CI, 8.1 to 8.5). The score for the control condition was 8.3 (95 per cent CI, 8.1 to 8.4). There was no difference between the scores of either group nor was there any differential change over time. QOC scores on the intervention group rose by a mean of 0.4, and those in the control condition rose by 0.1. This difference was not significant. The scores for the family-rated measures were remarkably similar, and again showed no benefit of the training programme. Finally, and even more concerning, patients who were seen by the workshop attenders were more likely to be depressed than either patients seen by the control condition doctors or the same doctors prior to them attending the training. The mean PHQ-8 score for post-intervention trainees was 10.00. That of the non-attenders was 8.8: a highly significant difference (p 0.006). Sub-group analysis revealed this overall finding to be largely a consequence of the interactions of the most junior doctors.

Discussion

This was a very large study, and had a definitive finding. Neither physicians nor nurses who attended a simulation-based communication skills training programme showed any evidence of having greater communication skills in their day-to-day work than non-attenders. The authors suggest that one explanation of the findings is a failure of generalisation of skills from training room to clinic. A second possibility, and one that cannot easily be dismissed, is that the measure was insensitive to subtle differences in skills, particularly when completed by patients often some time after they were seen by the health professional they were rating, and who were one of several people who provided care. More sensitive measures, and measures taken closer to the time of the clinical encounter, may have provided better quality results.

The finding of higher levels of depression in the patients they saw is interesting, and adds some intrigue to these findings. It is difficult to explain why this should be the case. The skills evident in the intervention group may not have been better than those in the control group – but they were also no worse – and there were no more junior doctors in the intervention group than control group, which may have differentially affected the findings. One possible explanation is that participating in the training encouraged a greater proportion of these junior doctors to discuss difficult issues such as dying (the bad news interview) with their patients, and may have evoked more distress than more experienced doctors, whether or not they had participated in the training course.

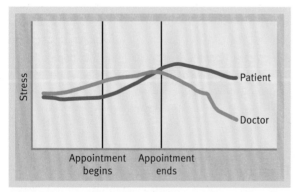

Figure 10.1 The timescale of stress experienced by health-care professionals and patients in relation to the bad news interview

Source: adapted from Ptacek and Eberhardt (1996).

Moving beyond the consultation

A key goal of the consultation is to allow health-care professionals and patients to receive and provide information relevant to medical decision-making and treatment. The next part of the chapter considers two outcomes of this process: one involving the health-care professional, and one involving the patient.

Medical decision-making

Health-care decisions do not happen in a neutral context – and may be influenced by a wide variety of factors. They may be biased by health-care professionals' expectations of their patients, their fellow professionals, and the sheer pressure of making decisions in a short time – often without all the information necessary to make a fully informed decision. Doctors' own views about the nature of health care may also influence their decisions. Some doctors, for example, may only be willing to treat patients who are actively involved in maintaining their own health. Such doctors may refuse to provide expensive curative treatment for smoking-related diseases in patients who are unwilling to give up smoking. Other biases may be less conscious, or may be motivated by non-health-related issues. Mitchell et al. (2000), for example, found that, even after adjusting for demographic factors, the presence of other serious diseases and ability to pay, African American patients with **transient ischaemic attacks** were significantly less likely to receive specialist diagnostic tests or to see a specialist doctor than white patients (see Chapter 2 ☞ for an extended discussion of this issue). Gender differences may also influence the care people receive in hospital. Nurses are more likely to offer pain medication to women than to men, at least in casualty departments (Raftery et al. 1995). By contrast, proportionately more men than women are likely to be offered a place on cardiac rehabilitation programmes (see Chapter 17 ☞) following an MI (British Heart Foundation 2010).

A key area of medical decision-making involves diagnosing the illness with which patients present. Elstein and Schwarz (2002) identified a number of ways that doctors achieve this:

- *Hypothesis testing*: the so-called 'gold star' level of decision-making. This involves a logical sequencing of establishing and testing hypotheses about the nature of the diagnosis. Hypotheses are established, tested, and when they fail are replaced by further hypotheses until a final 'correct' hypothesis is established.

> **transient ischaemic attacks**
> short periods of reduced blood flow to the brain resulting in symptoms including short periods of confusion, weakness and other minor neurological symptoms.

- *Pattern recognition*: compares patterns of symptoms with disease prototypes. This may be a good way of reaching easy diagnoses, with the hypothesis-testing approach being utilised for more complex decisions.

- *Opinion revision or 'heuristics and biases'*: perhaps the least reliable approach to making diagnoses: involves making decisions based on partial evidence as a result of using rules of thumb or heuristics.

Clearly, most of the diagnoses assigned by doctors are accurate. However, their decision-making may be prone to error, particularly when decisions are made by heuristics. Indeed, cognitive errors contributed to 74 per cent of the diagnostic errors resulting in injury or death investigated by Graber et al. (2005). The use of heuristics may be inevitable in the context of medical decisions made at times of crisis or when optimal information may not be available. But the use of these short-cuts can also happen in other, less demanding, situations as well. The most commonly used heuristics are often those termed 'fast and frugal' (Marewski and Gigerenzer 2012): that is, they aid quick decision-making on the basis of minimal information. They allow doctors and other health professionals to make decisions at times of uncertainty but may lead to errors because they are based on assumptions which may or may not be relevant to particular situations, and even more importantly may prevent clinicians from investigating further to obtain information that is. In a qualitative study of this process, André et al. (2002) asked a number of family doctors to describe some of their decision-making processes. One doctor stated that she was so used to 40-year-old men who presented with chest pain being diagnosed with an MI, she no longer tested for alternative diagnoses (as is recommended practice). Another doctor stated that if he thought a condition was psychosomatic, 'I begin to try to tie down the idea right away. I won't start with physical examination before talking about the possibility that it could be something emotional...' – a process that may miss a physical disease process.

A key problem with the use of heuristics is that they limit thinking through the full diagnostic possibilities, and may be biased by a number of factors (Marewski and Gigerenzer 2012): These include:

- *Availability*: diseases that receive considerable media attention are frequently thought to be more common than they actually are, even by doctors. Assuming a high probability of finding a condition may lead to it being diagnosed in error. A similar factor may occur if the diagnosing doctor has knowledge of previous diagnoses given by colleagues.

● *Representativeness*: this involves comparing a patient's symptoms to symptom prototypes of a number of conditions. The closer to the symptom prototype, the more likely the diagnosis. This seems a logical process, and is generally successful. However, it may fail because clinicians may have inaccurate prototypes of common conditions, because they see many atypical as well as typical cases, and uncommon diseases as a result of their rarity.

● *Potential 'pay off' of differing diagnoses*: if a diagnosis is unclear, the diagnosis assigned may be the one that carries the least cost and most benefit for the individual. When doctors are presented with a young child complaining of abdominal pain of no obvious origin, for example, a diagnosis of appendicitis and treatment of appendicectomy may be made, as treating the appendicitis successfully may be considered to outweigh the risks associated with an unnecessary operation.

Examples of these types of heuristic errors were provided by Vickrey et al. (2010) who described several cases of misdiagnosis by a number of neurologists. One occurred as a result of the doctor inappropriately focusing on the onset of a disease in Mexico – excluding alternatives that were not based on the place of onset (a framing effect of geography); a repeated misdiagnosis of depression-related neurological difficulties that was made as an initial diagnosis but was then repeated by several clinicians despite evidence of no benefit from antidepressant medication (bias as a result of the 'anchoring' effect of the first diagnosis), and a diagnosis of cobalamin deficiency made as a result of a superficial similarity of the presenting symptoms to a recently treated case of this very rare problem (the availability heuristic).

One method of improving decision-making involves the use of computerised programmes that support doctors in their decision-making. One such web-based programme was evaluated by Ramnarayan et al. (2006). This comprised a 'diagnostic reminder system that provided rapid advice with free text data entry' that participants could access if they were unsure of a diagnosis. To evaluate its impact, trainee doctors who used the system to diagnose children with acute disorders noted the initial diagnosis they made without the programme and then (when they felt necessary) following its use.

These diagnoses were then compared to the diagnosis the child was given prior to discharge from hospital. Before using the programme, 45 per cent of their diagnoses were considered 'unsafe'; following its use, this figure fell to 33 per cent. In an analogue study of a similar programme, using simulated patients, the same team (Ramnarayan et al. 2006) found that the diagnostic accuracy of all grades of doctors, including experienced hospital consultants, improved following the use of such a system. To be of use, however, these programmes need to be user friendly. Where they are not, they rapidly fall into misuse and clinicians retreat back to the use of familiar heuristics (Marewski and Gigerenzer 2012).

Compliance, adherence and concordance

A key determinant of the success of any medical intervention is whether patients actually follow the recommended medical regime – whether this involves taking tablets or making more complex behavioural changes. Initially, research into this issue focused on what was termed treatment compliance, which implied a doctor- or health-professional-led process in which the patient was expected to comply with whatever instructions they were given. After several years, the more politically correct term 'adherence' was introduced, implying that patients were more involved in the decision-making process – although how this increase in patient independence was achieved was not always clear. More recently still, the term 'concordance' has been introduced reflecting a further development in this process. Here, both health professional and patient reach a jointly determined agreement concerning the treatment regimen. This joint decision requires a patient to be fully informed of the benefits and costs (in terms of side effects, treatment benefits, etc.) of following a particular treatment regimen. Full concordance between health professional and patient is assumed to increase the likelihood of patients following a treatment plan; although patients may of course change their decision or not follow the agreed treatment for a number of other reasons.

Take the tablets

The most frequent medical treatment involves patients taking prescribed medication at times and in sufficient

More heads make worse decisions

Decisions may be affected by a number of factors beyond the consultation. Christensen et al. (2000) examined the effect of group diagnostic decision-making involving small teams of junior doctors and medical students. Information given to the groups was manipulated by asking the physicians to individually watch videos of actors acting as patients, offering the same information to all those in the group, and some information unique to each viewer, including one viewer who was given information crucial to making a correct diagnosis.

Their results were interesting in that, once convened, the groups discussed the information common to all those involved more than they discussed the unique information held by each group member. As a result they actually made *more* diagnostic errors than a control group of individual doctors given the same information. These data are particularly pertinent to making difficult diagnoses that may involve discussion by several doctors with information gleaned from a variety of different consultations or to some medical specialties (particularly those involved in mental health) where information from many sources may be used to arrive at a diagnosis.

quantities to provide a therapeutic dose. This may not be a simple task. Taking HIV antiretroviral medication known as HAART (Highly Active Antiretroviral Therapy, or ART as it is frequently now called: see Chapter 8 ☞), for example, is an extremely important and complex

issue. People taking this medication not only have to take tablets on a daily basis, but they also have to take them within very tight time limits during the day. HAART medications may require different dosing schedules – some at twelve-, eight-, six-, or four-hour

Photo 10.2 Some decision-making contexts are more difficult than others. Joint decisions, particularly if led by a powerful consultant, may not always be correct

Source: Rex Features/TM & 20th Century Fox/Everett.

intervals. Some tablets need to be taken with food, some with fatty foods, some with non-fatty foods and some on an empty stomach. Many result in serious side effects that require taking further medication, and other medications may be required to treat secondary opportunistic infections. Not only is the required regimen for taking HAART complex, but it may also take place in the absence of symptoms. Indeed, it may cause more short-term symptoms than it appears to prevent. Failure to keep to this regime, however, can result in the virus mutating, with serious implications for both the individual involved and any person to whom they may pass the mutated virus. Nevertheless, adherence levels may be far from ideal. Sherr et al. (2010), for example, found that 57 per cent of their UK sample had taken a tablet at the wrong time in the previous week, 21 per cent had missed one dosage, and 10 per cent had missed two or more dosages within the previous week. Using measures of viral status, they determined that the third level of non-adherence was sufficient to worsen these people's prognosis.

The complexity of taking the anti-HIV regimen perhaps makes this a special case. However, the percentage of people to follow the optimal medical regimen required in many chronic illnesses can be low. It has been estimated that, on average, only half of those prescribed pharmacological therapies take sufficient medication to experience a therapeutic benefit (Haynes et al. 1996), resulting in about 10 per cent of hospital admissions (Schlenk et al. 2004). Looking at more specific disorders, Cramer (2004) reported that between 36 and 93 per cent of patients with type 2 diabetes followed the recommended regimen of **oral hypoglycaemic agents** for between 6 and 24 months. Between 30 and 50 per cent of people are thought to not take all their anti-hypertensive medication (Caro et al. 1999), placing them at a nearly six-fold higher risk of dying from a stroke than their more adherent counterparts (Herttua et al. 2013). Krigsman et al. (2007) reported that 42 per cent of their sample were underusing their asthma medication, while 23 per cent were overusing it. Finally, Bernal et al. (2006) reported that 43 per cent of patients with inflammatory bowel disease admitted to missing

medication; 20 per cent of patients admitted to self-medicating.

Given the importance of taking these medications, one may wonder why people fail to do so. One simple explanation is that many people forget to take their medication or find their treatment regimen too complicated to cope with effectively. This may be particularly pertinent in the case of complex medical regimes, such as those associated with the treatment of HIV (see also Chapter 17 ☞). A wide range of other factors have been found to predict sub-optimal use of medication in general (e.g. Krueger et al. 2005), including:

- *social factors*: including low levels of education, unemployment, concomitant drug use, low levels of social support;
- *psychological factors*: including high levels of anxiety and depression, use of emotion focused coping strategies such as denial, a belief that continued use of a drug will reduce its effectiveness, taking drug holidays to prevent 'harm' as a consequence of long-term drug use;
- *treatment factors*: including misunderstandings regarding treatment, complexity of the treatment regimen, high numbers or fear of side effects, little obvious benefit from taking medication, poor relationship between patient and health-care provider, poor health professional–patient communication.

To these issues, patients prescribed HAART medication may add those of fear of disclosure, suspicions of treatment, the sheer number of pills required, decreased quality of life, and problems of access to medication (Mills et al. 2006). Another contextual factor that may affect adherence with medical regimens, particularly in children, involves the family system. While parental illness beliefs are important determinants of children's adherence to medication (Drotar and Bonner 2009), disease-specific family issues have also been determined as important. Tubiana-Rufi et al. (1998), for example, found that diabetic children from families characterised as rigid, with low levels of cooperation and communication between family members, were more than six times less likely to adhere to their insulin regimes than children from families with more positive dynamics. From a different perspective, Mellins et al. (2004) found that children's non-adherence with HAART was significantly associated with high caregiver stress, and poor parent–child communication,

---

oral hypoglycaemic agents
various drug types, all of which reduce circulating blood glucose levels.

caregiver quality of life and caregiver cognitive functioning. Older people also appear less adherent to recommended treatment regimens than younger people. However, any age issues may be more apparent than real. Edelmann (1999) contended that because older people tend to have more chronic diseases than younger people, apparent differences in medication adherence may reflect the problems of taking multiple prescriptions rather than being purely an age-related phenomenon.

A more theoretical perspective on adherence to medication is based on a combination of the illness representation (Leventhal et al. 1992; see Chapter 9 (☞) and health belief (Rosenstock 1974; see Chapter 5 (☞) models (Horne and Weinman 1999). Illness beliefs include understandings of the nature of the illness, its severity, cause, time-frame, likely prognosis, and its 'treatability'. Illnesses that are seen as minor, short-term and likely to self-remit may result in less use of active treatments than conditions which are seen as long-term and likely to benefit from treatment. The second arm of this deliberation involves an evaluation of the costs and benefits of taking any medication. These include consideration of how likely the treatment is to cure the condition and how 'costly' this is likely to be. Cost here includes, but is not limited to, consideration of the likely side effects of the medication.

Applying this model to a condition such as hypertension may explain why adherence to anti-hypertensive medication is frequently so low. Many people believe hypertension to be a short-term condition. It is symptom-free, so it is not clear to the patient that it is present for much of the time. Accordingly, people prescribed such medication may not see the necessity to take any medication over a long period of time. Add in a number of side effects associated with this type of medication, such as dizziness or light-headedness, dry mouth, constipation, drowsiness, headache and impotence, and the result is a scenario that involves patients taking medication for a condition they are not aware of having, which provides no obvious benefit, and which brings with it some unpleasant side effects. Little wonder that adherence to such medication can be so low. Even in severe conditions such as HIV infection, these issues also hold. Siegel et al. (1999) found that HIV-positive men and women stopped taking their antiretroviral medication if they considered it either made them sicker than their condition itself or carried greater risks than benefits. Reassuringly, a subsequent study by the same research group found that HAART medication was viewed more positively than the older antiretroviral treatments being given at the time of the initial study, and its benefits were usually seen as outweighing any problems it caused (Schrimshaw et al. 2005).

Interestingly, the Horne model may not hold in all circumstances. When a medical condition is severe, some patients may actually welcome a treatment that brings high levels of side effects. Leventhal et al. (1986) found that some women who received chemotherapy for the treatment of breast cancer found the *absence* of side effects distressing: their expectation was that treatment of serious illnesses involved serious side effects, and the lack of them implied that the drug used was not sufficiently potent to cure their condition. Other factors may be quite idiosyncratic to the individual. Gamble et al. (2007), for example, found that adherence to asthma medication was largely influenced by the fear of side effects such as weight gain, anxiety, irritability and depression. However, participants also described feelings of 'not being themselves' and personality changes, resulting in a loss of their role within relationships when taking the medication.

Maximising medication use

The chances of an individual taking the medication they are prescribed can be increased by a few simple strategies within the consultation.

Achieving concordance

One key factor that may increase adherence to a recommended regimen is that both patient and prescriber have discussed the various treatment options and agreed to follow a treatment regimen. The discussion of shared decision-making earlier in this chapter provided an outline of the steps within the consultation that will lead to shared decisions/concordance between doctor and patient. A number of factors that enhance this process can also be identified from the previous discussion, including the doctor providing relevant information in a language understandable to the patient, and the doctor listening and responding to the patient in ways that encourage engagement in the decision-making process. Concordance is unlikely to be achieved by health professionals who adopt a strong biomedical stance within the consultation and who pay little regard for the social and emotional concerns that patients may bring to the consultation.

Maximising understanding

A further key aspect of both achieving concordance and, more generally, ensuring patients fully understand the nature and implications of any medication they are being prescribed involves the health professional using language appropriate to the particular patient. However, patients can also improve their understanding of an issue by preparing questions to ask in the consultation. Many patients leave a consultation without the information they want – for a variety of reasons discussed earlier in the chapter. To avoid this occurring, a number of studies have examined whether preparing patients before a consultation can help them ask relevant questions within it.

In one study of this approach, Clayton et al. (2007) randomly allocated patients with advanced cancer to either a standard consultation or a consultation augmented by a prompt sheet. This comprised a list of questions prepared by the patient before the consultation that they wanted to ask within it. Patients took the prompt sheet into the consultation to remind them which questions to ask as it progressed. Clayton and colleagues evaluated the programme by examining audiotapes of the consultation as well as by patient-completed questionnaires. Their results were impressive. Patients given the prompt sheet asked more than twice as many questions than patients in the control group. In addition, they discussed 23 per cent more issues, asked more prognostic questions and discussed more end-of-life issues. Their consultations with the doctors were longer, and they left the consultation with fewer unmet-information needs. In a similar study population of patients with oesophageal cancer, Smets et al. (2012) also found patients asked significantly more questions following the use of prompts (an average of 12 versus 8 in a non-prompt condition), although their interviews did not differ in length and patients in both conditions reported equal satisfaction with the consultation.

Maximising memory

Memory for information given in consultations is often surprisingly poor. Summing up the relevant evidence, Ley (1997) suggested that 75 per cent of information given in four statements is likely to be retained : only 50 per cent of information given in ten statements will be. In time, patients may even forget their own actions. Montgomery et al. (1999), for example, reported that nearly a quarter of patients undergoing radiotherapy for the treatment of cancer did not recall having signed a consent form to permit the treatment, despite there being clear evidence that they had. Of those who did remember providing consent, a quarter could not remember being told about the side effects of the treatment, while half could not remember its most frequent side effect of feelings of exhaustion. Such poor outcomes are not always found, though. In a study of this phenomenon in the African country of Benin, Kelly et al. (2007) reported very high retention of information given during consultations, even when the amount of information given was high and the majority of the recipients were illiterate. People in the study were given an average of 39 points of information designed to improve their management of their child's illness. Immediately following the consultation, they were able to accurately recall an average of 90 per cent of the information points given. One day later, this had fallen to 82 per cent of the information points.

Despite this optimistic finding, there is a need for health professionals to help maximise patients' memories of information they are given during the consultation. A number of strategies have been found to be useful in achieving this aim (Watson and McKinstry 2009), including: providing written information, providing audiotapes of consultations, using prompt sheets, direct questioning of patients to ensure they process the information they have been given, using visual aids during the consultation, minimising the amount of medical jargon, simplifying the language used, emphasising and the patient repeating (rehearsing) essential information, and personalised action plans.

One simple strategy involves giving information in a structured manner. According to Ley (1997), the most important information should be given early or late in the flow of information to maximise primacy and recency effects, and its importance should be emphasised. Further strategies include repetition and the use of specific rather than general statements. This may be augmented by asking patients to repeat key messages during the consultation to ensure understanding and increase memory consolidation.

A second strategy involves providing some form of permanent record of key information. This may involve pre-prepared information or a record of the information given during a consultation. In one examination of the latter approach, Stephens et al. (2008) provided patients with oesophageal cancer a tape-recording of the consultation in which they were given their diagnosis. Patients in this group were more likely to retain information given in the consultation, but were no more likely to be depressed or anxious than those in a comparison group who did not receive the tape.

When information is given in written form, many people read it: Nathan et al. (2007), for example, found that 70 per cent of patients read patient-information leaflets when given new medication. Of course, written information should take into account the same issues as those that relate to spoken information – it needs to be clear, jargon-free, and not so complex that readers will be unable to understand it. Unfortunately, this requirement is not always met. Less than 30 per cent of the population would understand the leaflets given to patients with head injuries in Scotland (Macdonald et al. 2010). Similarly, Freda (2005) found that 41 of 74 patient education brochures produced by the American Academy of Pediatrics had readability levels beyond the majority of their readers. At the other end of the scale, some innovative methods have been used to increase the readability of leaflets. One approach has involved the use of pictograms in addition to text to help people with limited literacy skills. This has proven surprisingly difficult to do. Knapp et al. (2005), for example, found that only 30 per cent of pictograms used in medication leaflets were understood by 85 per cent of the population.

Keep taking the tablets

Whatever transpires within the consultation, patients have to be motivated and remember to take their medication or follow other advice in the hurly-burly of their everyday life. Any intervention designed to maximise adherence has also to take these contextual issues into account. McDonald et al. (2002) examined the effectiveness of 39 interventions which did so and were designed to enhance adherence to medication in a variety of chronic health problems including CHD, hypertension, asthma, chronic obstructive pulmonary disease (COPD: see Chapter 8 ☞), HIV infection, rheumatoid arthritis and epilepsy. They concluded that the most effective interventions were generally complex and involved combinations of:

- convenient timing of drug taking;
- providing relevant information;
- reminders to take medications;
- self-monitoring (i.e. noting down when and where medication is taken);

- reinforcement of appropriate use of medication;
- family therapy.

They also noted that even the most effective interventions had 'modest' effects.

The simplest methods involve ensuring that the prescribed medical regimen places as little demand on memory as possible. Nachega et al. (2010), for example, noted significant increases in adherence and measures of viral load in people with HIV whose HAART regimen was simplified to one tablet a day. While this approach may not provide the optimal medical treatment, it is much more effective than intermittent use of a more effective therapeutic regimen. Accordingly, it may be the best treatment approach for people with a history of poor medication adherence. Other approaches involve helping patients to select contextual cues to help them remember to take medication (take with food or other daily routines) or placing medicine in plastic medication boxes with compartments that are filled with the tablets to be taken at each time during the week. These are often used by older people, and can be filled by health-care professionals or family members.

More complex procedures involve the use of reminders sent via the post, text or telephone. Overall, these have proven reasonably successful in the treatment of conditions as varied as asthma, diabetes, glaucoma and heart disease (see, for example, de Jongh et al. 2012). In one study following people with asthma, for example, Chatkin et al. (2006) found that 74 per cent of people receiving bi-weekly reminders followed the recommended regimen; 52 per cent of those in a standard treatment (no reminders) group achieved the same level of adherence. In a study showing both the benefits and potential short-comings of texting reminders to take medication, Puccio et al. (2006) contacted young people newly diagnosed with HIV by telephone when their medication was required. While the calls continued, adherence remained high. However, as the calls were tapered and then stopped over a period of several weeks, so did levels of adherence, and levels of viral suppression decreased. It seems that once initiated, prompting may need to continue in the long term. This may be because a dependency on prompts has been established; it may reflect a lack of carryover effect following cessation. One even more hi-tech approach has involved the use of microelectronic devices in tablet containers that measure whether the container is moved or opened (e.g. Wu et al. 2006). Failure to do so within certain time limits can result in electronic notification of health-care providers who then contact the patient to remind to take their medication.

One of the more complex therapeutic regimens to follow, and also the most critical to life, involves the use of HAART medication in the treatment of HIV infection. A range of interventions have struggled to achieve significant benefits in this context (e.g., Mathes et al. 2013), partly because of the complexity of the required regimen, partly because many of the people required to take the medication, such as drug users, may lead chaotic and disorganised lives with low levels of contact with medical services (e.g. Fogarty et al. 2002). Accordingly, either the simplification of treatment regimens or more encompassing interventions may be appropriate in this context. In one study of the latter approach, Safren et al. (2001) compared two quite complex but very different interventions. The first involved self-monitoring and use of a pill diary to record when each tablet was taken, combined with visits to the clinic to provide feedback on medication usage. A more active intervention, known as Life-Steps, involved a single-session intervention involving an educational video, motivational interview (see Chapter 6 (☞)), training in planning medication schedules, cues to pill taking, and the use of imagery involving successful adherence in response to daily cues. This may seem an overly complex process. However, it should be remembered that taking HAART medication can involve planning different types of meals and being in particular places at set times. Patients may even be taught skills to take pills surreptitiously so that no one knows they are taking

them. With this in mind, this sort of training programme may not seem so excessive. Adherence was measured at 2 and 12 weeks following the intervention. The researchers also examined a number of personal and social predictors of adherence. Both interventions led to improvements in adherence. However, among people with low levels of adherence, the Life-Steps programme achieved these more quickly than the self-monitoring condition. It also appeared to improve adherence more than the self-monitoring programme in those people who were depressed – a particularly important finding, as depression was the one person-factor they found to be independently associated with non-adherence.

In contrast to these positive results, a warning that some people can be particularly difficult to influence was provided by Martin et al. (2001). They compared the effect of an educational plus counselling intervention with counselling alone to enhance adherence to HAART therapy. A total of 74 per cent of those approached (many of whom were injecting drug users) refused to take part in the programme: 59 per cent of those who refused to take part did so for 'personal reasons', while 33 per cent did so because of trouble in their jobs. Those who were poor adherers to their HAART were most likely to decline to take part in the programme. Similar null effects have been reported elsewhere, including a report by Simoni et al. (2007) in an intervention involving providing peer support to a group largely comprising 'indigent' men and women from the Bronx. Despite the dire effects of non-adherence, there are many societal groups who find it difficult to follow recommended treatment programmes, and who are not helped by even quite substantial and sophisticated interventions.

Case history: Mr F

Many older adults fail to take their medication at appropriate times or forget to take it at all. As noted in the main text, this may be because of the complexity of their medication regime, rather than failing memory. But, where memory is fading, adherence to appropriate medication regimens may become particularly problematic and responsibility for this may fall to others rather than the individual involved. Mr F was one such person who at the age of 73 years had a variety

of health problems, many of which may well have contributed to his failing memory, but all of which required appropriate medication dosage. His tablets included treatment for rheumatoid arthritis using painkillers and non-steroidal anti-inflammatory medication, high blood pressure using anti-hypertensive medication, and type 2 diabetes using tablets to lower his blood sugar levels. Importantly, with this not unusual combination of medical problems, Mr F was taking a carefully prescribed medication regimen that was designed to maximise its effectiveness while avoiding

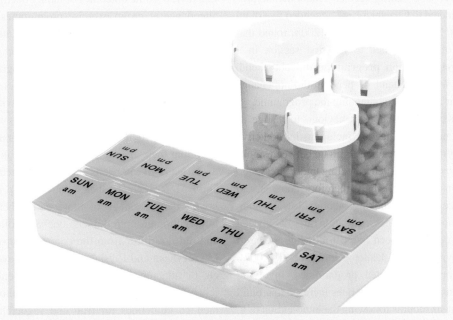

Figure 1 A pill organiser that can be used to facilitate adherence to complex medical regimens

Source: Shutterstock.com/Guzel Studio.

problematic combinations of drugs that may have had a serious impact on his health.

Neither Mr F nor his wife proved effective in adhering or ensuring adherence to his medication regimen and he was increasingly affected by painful joints, which restricted the activity he should have been engaging in to help his diabetes. Regular check-ups with his doctor revealed that his blood pressure was much higher than it should have been and his visiting nurse regularly found higher blood sugar levels than were ideal. Clear labelling of bottles, written instructions when each tablet should be taken, and repeat visits by a district nurse had failed to improve his or his wife's adherence to his medication regimen. The nurse therefore initiated a simple, but highly effective, approach that did prove of benefit: a pill organiser (see Figure 1). The timing of his medication was simplified to either morning or evening. Then, his district nurse visited the home each week and placed the relevant medication in each box within the organiser. The organiser was then kept on display in an obvious position in the kitchen to ensure that it was seen and acted as a cue to take medication. With this regimen, neither Mr F nor his wife had to remember which drugs were taken at any one time. He simply took the drugs in each box at the time stipulated. The nurse who set the scheme up visited each day at the beginning of his use of the pill organiser to check all was well, and then visited briefly each week to refill it. As a consequence, Mr F did not experience a 'miracle cure', but his blood pressure and blood glucose levels did fall significantly, reducing his risk of further medical complications.

Changing behaviour

Many medical interventions require more significant behavioural change than taking medication, and it is to these we turn now. Measuring adherence to behavioural change programmes can be difficult. Measurement of daily diet, smoking or exercise levels is notoriously difficult to achieve accurately. However, one measure of adherence is relatively simple to measure accurately: whether patients attend clinics and other appointments. In this context, non-attendance can be high, and rises as the demands on the patient increase. Kosminder et al. (2009), for example, reported that 21 per cent of patients treated for colorectal cancer failed to attend one or more outpatient appointments. More complex programmes typically have lower attendance rates. Only 56 per cent of the patients taking part in Jolly et al.'s (2007) cardiac rehabilitation programme considered in Chapter 17 (☞ attended five of up to 21 sessions. Similarly, Al-Moamary (2008) found that 26 per cent of those invited to the first session in a **pulmonary rehabilitation programme** did not attend. Among those who did attend, 43 per cent did not change their behaviour as a result of attending the programme.

Smoking is one of the hardest behaviours to change, as a result of a number of factors including its addictive nature and the strong associations built up between smoking, and various contexts such as feeling under stress, and social occasions. Not surprisingly, therefore, adherence to medical advice to stop smoking is often low. Among patients with no evident illness, cessation rates of between 3 and 12 per cent have been found following advice to quit and provision of a leaflet (Unrod et al. 2007). Following more sophisticated programmes, involving drug plus counselling, adherence rates increase to around 30–35 per cent six months following the intervention (e.g. Swan et al. 2010). Among people with smoking-related diseases, initial quit rates may be higher, but these fall over time and are no higher than among the healthy population. Hajek et al. (2002), for example, found that six weeks following a myocardial infarction (MI), 60 per cent of previous smokers reported not smoking. One year after their MI, this figure had dropped to 37 per cent.

Changes in exercise levels may also be modest and reduce over time in both patient and non-patient populations. Lear et al. (2003) reported that few cardiac patients had achieved any changes on measures of leisure-time exercise and treadmill performance one year after a standard cardiac rehabilitation programme (see Chapter 17 (☞) which gave recommended exercise levels. In a more extended programme, involving monthly prompts to exercise and the provision of heart rate monitors and exercise diaries, Dolansky et al. (2010) reported that less than 37 per cent of their sample of cardiac patients adhered to a three-times-a-week exercise programme one year following attending a cardiac rehabilitation programme. Planned exercise programmes in sedentary individuals are also likely to have low attendance rates.

> **pulmonary rehabilitation programme**
> a course attended by patients with chronic lung disease teaching strategies of disease management: relaxation, deep breathing, managing activity, and so on.

In a review of the outcomes of family doctors prescribing attendance at group exercise programmes to sedentary but otherwise healthy individuals, Williams et al. (2007) reported that only between 12 and 42 per cent of those starting completed their 10–12-week programmes.

Maintaining dietary change is also not easy, both in patient populations and those people without evident disease who would benefit from losing weight. Leslie et al. (2004) found that 65 per cent of cardiac patients attending their dietary counselling programme achieved the target of five portions of fruit and vegetables per day. Only 31 per cent of their control group achieved this goal. The percentage of those eating healthily in the intervention group fell over a one-year follow-up period and did not differ from the control group by this time. Luszczynska and Cieslak (2009) found even lower levels of adherence in their cardiac patients: following rehabilitation, only 20 per cent were following recommended guidelines for fruit and vegetable intake, and this figure fell to 12 per cent at one-year follow-up. Long-term intervention programmes also show significant declines in adherence over time. An example of this can be found in a detailed study of a one-year behavioural weight loss programme in healthy but overweight individuals reported by Acharya et al. (2009). They made weekly records of the percentage of overweight patients who attended their group sessions, monitored their food intake, set an exercise plan, and limited fat and calorie intake. In the first session after goals had been set, 90 per cent of the people attended the session, 82 per cent had adhered to the self-monitoring element, 72 per cent had exercised, while only 28 per cent had kept to the calorie and fat requirements. At the six-month mark, the respective percentages were 50 per cent (attendance), 45 per cent (self-monitor), 30 per cent (exercise and calorie target) and 20 per cent (fat intake). By one year, these figures had fallen to 50 per cent attendance, 25 per cent self-monitoring, 20 per cent calorie target and exercise, and 5 per cent fat intake. Overall, just as in adherence to medication, adherence to behavioural programmes is far below optimal, and may benefit from programmes designed to enhance them.

Reasons for non-adherence

Reasons for poor or non-adherence vary considerably across behaviour and contexts. A number of studies have assessed non-adherence from an atheoretical perspective.

Low adherence with the leg exercises and elevation required in the treatment of leg ulcer, for example, was found to be associated with pain, discomfort and lack of clarity concerning what exercises and other precautionary behaviours patients could engage in to improve their ulcers (Van Hecke et al. 2009). A study of Kuwaiti patients (Serour et al. 2007) at high risk of cardiac disease revealed some interesting and culturally idiosyncratic reasons for non-adherence to a number of lifestyle changes. The main predictors of non-adherence to a low-fat diet were lack of motivation, difficulties in adhering to a diet different to that of the rest of the family, and social gatherings. The main barriers to adherence to exercise were lack of time, coexisting diseases and adverse weather conditions (presumably heat, not rain!). Factors influencing adherence to lifestyle measures in general were the high fat and calorie content of traditional Kuwaiti food, stress, a high consumption of fast food, high frequency of social gatherings, an 'abundance of maids' and excessive use of cars.

One key issue of relevance is that of motivation, or lack of motivation, and competing demands on time. In the context of exercise, for example, both Jones et al. (2007) in cardiac patients and Casey et al. (2010) in people with type 2 diabetes, found this to be the primary reason for non-adherence. Both found that the presence of other health problems also impacted on engagement with the exercise programme. Family and social support, whether from friends or professionals, are also important factors. In the context of diet, Luszczynska and Cieslak (2009) found that intake of fruit and vegetables in cardiac patients was predicted by the presence of family support, while the type 2 diabetics of Casey et al. (2010) appreciated the monitoring, encouragement and accountability provided by programme staff, and, when this was withdrawn, frequently reduced the levels of exercise they took. From a series of qualitative studies, Huberty et al. (2008) found that the key factors associated with continuing physical activity following completion of a structured exercise programme were participants' self-worth, motivation, activity enjoyment, priorities, body image, ability to access support, and self-regulation skills such as planning and/or coping with obstacles to exercise and so on.

From a more theoretical perspective, the illness perceptions model of Leventhal or Horne's extension of this model also appear relevant to prescribed behavioural change. MacInnes (2013a), for example, found that 46 per cent of the variance in self-care of patients with heart failure was predicted by their illness representations and

treatment beliefs. Bourbeau and Bartlett (2008) found adherence to exercises to improve lung function and smoking cessation in patients with COPD were predicted by their perceptions of the disease, their confidence in their ability to control their health, and anticipating serious consequences should they not adhere to the treatment programme. In the context of adhering to appropriate self-care behaviours such as taking medication, meal planning, regular exercise, and testing blood glucose by type 2 diabetics (see Chapter 8 ☞), Daly et al. (2009) found that key predictors of adherence to an appropriate regime were cost, the belief that diabetes was a serious problem, being married, and greater self-reported satisfaction linked to taking medication and testing blood glucose. Depression was independently predictive of non-adherence.

More extended theoretical models may also be useful in this context. In a review of the psychological factors that contributed to adherence to exercise programmes by cardiac patients, Petter et al. (2009) found the most consistent predictors were: confidence in the ability to exercise (including dealing with obstacles to exercise and other indirect issues), intentions to exercise, perceived control over exercise, belief in the benefits of previous physical activity, perceived barriers to exercise, and action planning, all of which fall within the self-regulation (Leventhal and Diefenbach. 1991) or Health Action Process models discussed in Chapters 5 and 9 ☞ (see Sniehotta 2009).

Improving adherence to behavioural programmes

The work of Petter et al. suggests that programmes aimed at increasing adherence to behavioural programmes may advantageously be based on the self-regulation or health action process models. In a test of whether such an approach could be more effective than a standard educational approach in the context of exercise, Sniehotta et al. (2006) allocated patients who had already completed a cardiac rehabilitation programme into one of three conditions:

1. standard care involving check-ups with physicians but with no therapeutic input;

2. developing action plans on when, where and how to exercise; or

3. action planning plus developing coping plans on how to deal with anticipated barriers to exercise.

Participants in the combined planning group did significantly more physical exercise two months post-discharge than those in the other groups. An alternative, and perhaps simpler, intervention reported by Arrigo et al. (2008) involved patients writing a diary of physical activities complemented by quarterly group meetings. In comparison to a standard care group, significantly more patients adhered to regular physical activity (73 vs. 40 per cent) at one-year follow-up (see also discussion of implementation intentions in the context of preventive interventions in Chapter 6 ☞).

A differing approach, based on social cognitive theory (Bandura 1986), involves a structured and gradual increase in the degree of behavioural change achieved. Steps in behaviour change should be sufficient to leave the participant feeling they are making acceptable progress, but small enough to ensure that they are achievable. This approach should result in increases in change self-efficacy and be sufficiently rewarding to maintain or enhance motivation. An example of this approach was reported by Pisters et al. (2010), who compared the effectiveness of graded increases in activity against usual care involving less structured advice to exercise in patients with osteoarthritis of the hip or knee. The active intervention group received 18 sessions of behavioural graded activity over 12 weeks and up to 7 booster sessions over the next year. The control group received 18 sessions of usual care over 12 weeks. So, there was some inequality of input between the two groups. However, 13 weeks after the start of the programme, when both groups had received a similar level of professional input, those in the active intervention were more likely to adhere to the recommended exercise regimen.

Based on evidence such as this, the ERIC database (www.ericdigests.org/pre-9219/exercise.htm) suggested a number of components that should be central to any programme of behavioural change. These can be divided into self-regulation and motivational strategies (although there are fuzzy edges to these categories, and some strategies may achieve both goals).

● *Self-control strategies*: participants are more likely to adhere to a programme if they attribute any successful behavioural change to their own efforts rather than those of health professionals. This can be enhanced by teaching self-management skills such as self-monitoring, goal setting, planning, and so on. Early goals should be relatively easy to achieve so that there is immediate success and the rewards and confidence that come from success. Goals should be both behaviourally ('I will run for 20 minutes after work on Monday, Wednesday and on Saturday morning') and outcome ('I will lose 2lbs a week') defined. Participants should write plans down where they will act as regular reminders, and make visible measures of progress.

● *Relapse prevention:* this involves identifying high-risk situations that may result in 'relapse' back to previous behaviours, and planning how to avoid or cope with them. It may also involve planning how to re-engage with any behavioural change following a 'relapse'.

● *Motivational strategies:* these may include a stepwise progression in the degree of behaviour change made, using social support where available, using a structured but flexible approach, setting achievable personal goals and measuring successes in reaching them, rewarding oneself for success – with concrete rewards, not simply the satisfaction of having achieved change.

● *Make change habitual:* change should be continuous and sustained, not intermittent. Rewarding appropriate dietary choice with, for example, an occasional high-calorie 'take way' meal prevents the establishment of long-term habits, which are the key to long-term change.

We consider more of the evidence related to these and similar interventions designed to maximise adherence to behavioural change programmes in Chapters 5 and 17 ☞.

SUMMARY

The chapter has reviewed a number of issues related to how health professionals interact with patients, and how this can influence the outcome of any treatment they may recommend.

1. There has been a shift from the paternal 'doctor knows best' type of consultation to more patient-centred approaches, and the ultimate outcome of this shift – shared decision-making. It was noted that while this has many benefits, many patients are cautious in adopting it, as it raises concerns over the apparent expertise of health professionals and may place a responsibility on

patients for their treatment that they are unwilling to carry.

2. Some other elements of the consultation that may influence its outcome, including:
   - the gender of the health professional – women appear more empathic and caring, factors usually associated with greater satisfaction with the interview;
   - the 'spin' given to information;
   - the input of the patient: people who ask more questions tend to gain more information from the consultation.

3. Breaking bad news involves telling patients that they have a serious illness, and that they may die from it. It is a stressful process for both patient and health professional. Key factors in optimising this process include:
   - Give the news in person, in private, with enough time and without interruptions.
   - Find out what the patient knows about their diagnosis.
   - Find out what the patient wants to know.
   - Share the information, starting with a 'warning shot'.
   - Respond to the patient's feelings.
   - Plan and follow through.

4. Medical decision-making can be influenced by a number of factors. Doctors often employ heuristics to help them arrive at a diagnosis. This can speed the process up, but increases the risk of diagnostic errors. Typical errors are those of:
   - availability;
   - representativeness;
   - differing pay-offs of differing diagnoses.

5. Adherence to recommended medical treatments is influenced by a number of factors, including:
   - social factors;
   - psychological factors;
   - treatment factors;
   - family dynamics;
   - beliefs about the nature of the illness and its treatment regimen.

6. Adherence may be enhanced by:
   - the use of patient-centred approaches and shared decision-making;
   - maximising satisfaction with the process of treatment;
   - maximising understanding of the condition and its treatment;
   - maximising memory for information given.

7. Beyond the consultation, these factors may be added to be a number of strategies, including:
   - convenient timing of drug taking;
   - relevant information;
   - reminders to take medications;
   - self-monitoring (i.e. noting down when and where medication is taken);
   - reinforcement of appropriate use of medication.

8. Adherence to behavioural programmes is also far from maximal. This may result from a variety of factors, including cost–benefit analysis of change, low motivation, and difficulties in planning or executing consistent change. Key theoretical variables associated with adherence to behavioural programmes are:
   - confidence in the ability to exercise;
   - intentions to exercise;
   - perceived control over exercise;
   - belief in the benefits of previous physical activity;
   - perceived barriers to exercise;
   - action planning.

9. Self-regulation-based interventions that take these factors into account appear to be the most effective means of achieving sustained behavioural change.

Further reading

Here are a number of reviews of issues dealt with in the chapter. Most of them are 'as it says on the tin', in that the title shows the content of the paper.

Committee on Patient Safety and Quality Improvement and Committee on Health Care and Underserved Women (2014). Committee Opinion. No. 587. Effective patient–physician communication. *Obstetrics and Gynecology*, 123: 389-93.

A US Physician College's recommendations for how to talk to patients.

Marewski J.N. and Gigerenzer G. (2012). Heuristic decision making in medicine. *Dialogues in Clinical Neuroscience*, 14: 77-89.

Free; and an interesting article supporting the use of heuristics in medical decision-making

Elwyn, G., Dehlendorf, C., Epstein, R.M. et al. (2014). Shared decision making and motivational interviewing: achieving patient-centered care across the spectrum of health care problems. *Annals of Family Medicine,* 12:270-5.

A paper on the process of shared decision-making and an apparently rival approach (motivational interview) by one the leading UK researchers in shared decision-making.

Mast, M.S. (2007). On the importance of nonverbal communication in the physician–patient interaction. *Patient Education and Counseling*, 67: 315–18.

Tackles an important issue not looked at in the chapter – the role of non-verbal behaviour during the doctor consultation.

van Dulmen, S., Sluijs, E., van Dijk, L. et al. (2007). Patient adherence to medical treatment: a review of reviews. *BMC Health Service Research*, 7: 55.

Free on the internet, and a good review to boot.

Prestwich, A., Sniehotta, F.F., Whittington, C. et al. (2014) . Does theory influence the effectiveness of health behavior interventions? Meta-analysis. *Health Psychology*, 33: 465-74.

Having argued in the chapter that theory-led interventions are likely to most effective, this papers considers what theories have actually been used to develop interventions – and concludes that more could be done.

For open-access student resources specifically written to complement this textbook and support your learning, please visit **www.pearsoned.co.uk/morrison**

Chapter 11
Stress, health and illness: theory

Learning outcomes

By the end of this chapter, you should have an understanding of:

- stress as a stimulus (stressors)
- stress as a result of an interaction between an event and an individual
- the critical role of cognitive appraisal
- the nature of acute and chronic stress
- physiological processes invoked by the stress experience
- how stress manifests itself in various diseases

Are you sleeping like a baby or is stress getting in the way?

Why is it that, for many people, getting to bed and letting your head hit that cosy soft pillow is exactly when your brain kicks in with an unconscious determination to run through all the good, and more often, the less good events of the day?! And more than revisiting the day past, it decides to work through all the options for the day or days to come. Worrying about things that have already happened, e.g. 'Why did I say "this" instead of "that"?', 'Did I take the right decision in that meeting today?', can lead to excessive worrying about things now outside our control. Likewise, worrying about future work-related events, e.g. 'Have I prepared enough for tomorrow's big test/meeting?' and working your way through possible outcomes, e.g. 'If I fail it then that's it, I surely won't graduate/ get promotion', or 'Will I get the job if I make a mess of this presentation?' or worrying about financial pressures and meeting the costs of everyday life (one of the most commonly reported stressors) can take up a lot of thinking, planning and rehearsing time, before the event and its outcome is even known! All the while the clock moves slowly through the night. Ruminating over even simple things like 'What will the weather be like?' may lead to the small hours of the night being spent considering what to wear! If only we had a switch to turn off our minds at the same time as turning out the lights!

Such thoughts and scenarios playing out in our heads when we should be trying to get the beneficial six hours sleep are not unusual – the 2014 American Psychological Association annual survey of Stress in America (APA 2015) revealed that 25 per cent of men and 35 per cent of women report that stressful thoughts interfere with their sleep – whether it's getting to sleep in the first place, or waking them up at repeated intervals in the night.

Sleep is essential to our cognitive, emotional and behavioural functioning. Waking up exhausted and anxious is unlikely to help you get through the day ahead in an optimal way. There are behavioural risks of exhaustion, for yourself through having that extra two or three coffees, drinks or cigarettes, possibly becoming snappy with friends or colleagues; and for others, for example, if the sleepy-head's job requires dexterity or handling machinery, or responsibility for making decisions affecting the health of others, such as prescribing medicines. So, best to pay attention to stress so as to help our sleep!

This chapter and Chapter 12 ☞ consider what factors contribute to events being described and experienced as 'stressful', and highlights how thoughts and appraisals of events can have a range of negative consequences for health and well-being, via effects on coping responses and behaviours, but also on physiological systems.

Chapter outline

The beginning of this chapter outlines the main thinking about stress in terms of nature and definition, and highlights three main ways in which stress is studied: as a stimulus, as a transaction between a stimulus event and an individual's appraisal of it, and as a biological and physiological response. The second of these reflects a psychological model of stress proposed by Richard Lazarus and his colleagues and is described in detail to illustrate the central role of cognitive appraisal. This is done by examining how stress impacts upon us all in our living and working lives, and by examining acute and chronic stressors. The final part of the chapter provides evidence as to the physiological processes by which stress and our responses to it exert an influence on physical health, focusing particularly, but not solely, on cancer, CHD and HIV. By the end of the chapter, the nature of stress and the processes by which it may impact on illness should be clear.

Concepts of stress

The term 'stress' is used very widely and with several meanings: everyone probably thinks they know what the term means, but few people define it in exactly the same way.

Stress has generally been examined in one of three ways: as a stimulus or event external to the individual; as a psychological transaction between the stimulus event and the cognitive and emotional characteristics of the individual; or as a physical or biological reaction. Each of these perspectives and their accompanying methodologies have their own strengths and weaknesses, which are outlined in the forthcoming sections.

WHAT DO YOU THINK?

What does stress mean to you? What causes you to feel stressed?

Think of some recent events that you have experienced as stressful. Why was this? Reflect on your answers to these questions as the chapter progresses.

Stress as a stimulus

In thinking of stress as a stimulus, researchers focus on stressful events themselves and on the external environment: i.e. a person will attribute their tension to an event or events such as moving house or getting married. The event and its properties are considered amenable to objective definition and measurement: for example, the event can be labelled (e.g. wedding) and aspects of it such as its proximity (e.g. next week, next year) can be assessed. Researchers taking this approach have studied the impact of a wide variety of stressors on individuals or groups, including *catastrophic events* such as earthquakes, floods or plane crashes, and, more commonly, *major life events* such as losing one's job or starting a new job, getting married or divorced, giving birth, being bereaved, or even going on holiday. Life events such as these are considered to require significant adjustment on the part of the person experiencing them, and can include both positive and negative events.

Life events theory

The major proponents of this approach were Holmes and Rahe, who in 1967 proposed their **life events** theory. They proposed that naturally occurring life events did not simply have unitary consequences for a person but cumulative effects; in other words, the more life events one experienced, for example within the past year, the greater the likelihood of physical health problems. Furthermore, they claimed that specific kinds of event could be weighted against each other. To make these claims, Holmes and Rahe had carried out a series of interesting studies. First, they invited over 5,000 participants to generate a list of events that they found most stressful; from this, they generated a representative list of 43 commonly mentioned events, including positive, negative, frequent and rare events. Holmes and Rahe then asked a new sample of almost 400 people to rank the listed events in order of the degree of disruption the event, if experienced, had caused them. Furthermore, they asked participants to rate each event against marriage, which had arbitrarily been given a value of 500 by the researchers. For example, if a participant considered divorce as requiring twice as much adjustment as

> **life events**
>
> a term used to describe occurrences in a person's life which may be viewed positively or negatively but which inherently require some adjustment on the part of the person (e.g. marriage, loss of job). Such events are implicated in the experience of stress.

marriage, it was given a value of 1,000. By averaging the ratings received for each event item and then ranking them, Holmes and Rahe produced a scale known as the social readjustment rating scale (SRRS; Holmes and Rahe 1967; see Table 11.1), with values ranging from 11 (minor violations of law) to 100 (this maximum value was assigned to death of a spouse, which averaged out as the event requiring greatest adjustment). The values were called life change units (LCU). Social readjustment was defined as 'the intensity and length of time necessary to accommodate to a life event, *regardless of the desirability of this event*' (Holmes and Masuda 1974: 49), highlighting the fact that both positive events (e.g. marriage) and negative events (e.g. redundancy) would require some adjustment on the part of the individual. A subsequent study of 88 physicians (Rahe 1974) found that the greater the LCU score the higher the risk of ill health. Of the 96 major health changes reported by the participants, 89 took place in individuals scoring over 150 LCUs; and when LCU scores exceeded 300, over

Table 11.1 Representative life event items from the social readjustment rating scale and their LCUs

Event	LCU rating (1–100)
Death of a spouse	100
Divorce	75
Death of a close family member	63
Personal injury or illness	53
Marriage	50
Being fired from work	47
Retirement	45
Sex difficulties	39
Death of a close friend	37
Change to a different job	36
Foreclosure of mortgage or loan	30
Son or daughter leaving home	29
Outstanding personal achievement	28
Begin or end school	26
Trouble with boss	23
Change in residence	20
Change in social activities	18
Vacation	13
Christmas	12

Source: Holmes and Rahe (1967).

70 per cent of the physicians reported subsequent ill health. Those individuals scoring less than 150 LCUs tended to report good health. Holmes and Masuda (1974) defined a *mild life crisis* as scoring between 150 and 199 LCUs, a *moderate life crisis* as scoring between 200 and 299 and a *major life crisis* as scoring over 300. They drew not only on their own work but also on that of other researchers of the time to support their hypothesis that life change could cause ill health (see review by Tennant 2002). For example, more recently, Lorenz et al. (2006) found negative health impacts of divorce upon women divorcees both in the short term but also in the decade following, Feldman et al. (2007) report health consequences of stress, prejudice and change experienced by refugees in the Netherlands.

Limitations of life events measurement

The evidence of the associations between LCUs and ill health (physical and/or mental) has been questioned as a result of various methodological or sampling limitations. For example:

● Many studies reporting moderate to strong associations between LCUs, health and illness (including many of Holmes and colleagues') relied on retrospective assessment: i.e. participants who were already ill were asked to report whether or not they had experienced any life events prior to the onset of illness. We know (see Chapter 14 ☞) that ill people search for explanations for illness, which may include misattributions to past events. Studies employing prospective designs found much weaker or non-existent relationships.

● Items included in the scale are not globally appropriate, nor commonplace. For example, depending on your age, many of the listed events may not be applicable (divorce, childbirth, etc.). Some of the listed events may simply not occur with sufficient frequency to enable many individuals to report them or for their effects on health to be experienced (e.g. moving house). See IN THE SPOTLIGHT for stress in children.

● Items may be intertwined/interrelated and may cancel out or enhance the effects of one another (for example, marriage requires positive adjustments but may coincide with a negatively perceived house move).

● Some of the listed events are vague and ambiguous: for example, reporting a 'change in social activities' could mean many things brought about for many different reasons, from taking up dancing with a new partner, to giving up dancing due to ill health.

● Allocating LCUs to events assumes that all people rank events in a similar way. However, as psychologists, we know this is unlikely! Think of moving house. For some people this will be the desired outcome of increased financial resources, while for others it will be the unwanted consequence of repossession by a bank following prolonged failure to pay a mortgage.

● Finally, inconsistencies have been reported between events rated as 'severe' using the checklist approach, but then not rated as severe in a subsequent interview (Brown and Harris 1989), raising questions about the SRRS's reliability. Addressing this, Brown and Harris developed a more rigorous approach using the LEDS (Life Events and Difficulties Scale) in a semi-structured interview carried out by a trained interviewer. Interviews were recorded and then events described to an independent rater along with details of the individual's biography and context. The rater then rated the events on the basis of its severity in terms of 'threat' or 'loss' and the event's context, but without any emotional inference. This method of assessing the severity of life events has led to a reduction in the incidence of reporting 'serious' life events, which may impact on reported relationships between life events and health (e.g. cancer study of Butow et al. 2000).

In spite of many measurement limitations, major life events can and do impact on people's lives, whatever their age. For example, children experiencing stressful life events have been found to show increased fear emotions in the future, suggesting a future social influence of stress experiences (Laceulle et al. 2014). As well as the number of events experienced, the 'type of event' is also important. For example health-related life events (for example, receiving a serious illness diagnosis, having an operation) significantly predicted mortality amongst a middle-aged sample followed for 17 years even after controlling for other risk factors such as sex, BMI, systolic blood pressure, MI and occupational status, whereas health-unrelated life events, such as moving house or divorce, were not predictive (Phillips et al. 2008). Many prospective longitudinal studies now assess the frequency and nature of life event experience of study samples on the basis also that life events may influence other variables of interest: for example, adjustment to disability may be undermined by the occurrence of other major life changes.

The life events approach to stress does not, however, systematically address the many internal and external factors that may moderate the relationship between the event and its outcomes. With regards to internal factors, attention has turned to a possible environmental-sensitivity gene which influences a person's emotional or behavioural response to exposure to stressful life events (e.g. parental divorce and conduct disorder, childhood stress and later depression (e.g. Belsky and Pluess 2009)). Although a fascinating avenue of research, it is early days to draw any firm conclusions and, in fact, recent evidence from a longitudinal study of children and adolescents offer little support for measures of gene sensitivity moderating the effects of prior stressful life events on temperament change (Laceulle et al. 2014).

In contrast, psychological theories of stress illustrated in this chapter have aided the identification of many other consistent internal and external moderators of the stress experience which are described in Chapter 12 ☞.

Life hassles

In addition to major and often rare life events, research has highlighted the stressful nature of daily *hassles*. Kanner et al. (1981: 3) defined hassles as 'irritating, frustrating, distressing demands that to some degree characterize everyday transactions with the environment' and measured such things as not having enough money for food or clothing, losing things, being overloaded with responsibilities, making silly practical mistakes, or having a row with a partner. Unlike major life events, hassles do not generally require major adjustment on the part of the person experiencing them but their impact was thought to be particularly evident if they were frequent, chronic or repeated over a particular period of time. To test this proposal, Kanner and colleagues developed a tool to assess daily hassles and found that they strongly associated with negative mental and physical outcomes even when controlling for major life events. This association has been confirmed in many studies using either Kanner's original scale or a shorter version developed by De Longis et al. (1997) (e.g. Bouteyre et al. 2007 – a study of first-year psychology students!). Stronger associations are often found between hassles and health outcomes (including psychological

health) than between life events and health outcomes (e.g. Kanner et al. 1981; Lazarus 1984; Searle and Bennett 2001).

Positively rated events, described as 'uplifts' (e.g. getting away with something, completing a task, getting or giving a compliment, having a laugh) were acknowledged more thoroughly in those taking a 'hassles' approach than in life events theory. Kanner found effects of life stage/role and gender on how both hassles and uplifts were perceived and appraised. For example, Kanner studied middle-aged individuals, professionals and students – and found that these three groups differed in the importance they attached to particular events, in particular economic concerns, work and time pressures, and social hassles. In terms of uplifts, the groups differed in their weighting of having good health, spending time with family, and hedonistic items such as socialising and having fun. Kanner also found that women experienced psychological symptoms following uplifts as well as hassles, whereas men were unaffected by uplifts, suggesting perhaps that women are affected by 'change' in either a positive or negative direction. Such findings highlight that two people could experience the same number of events, weight them equally, but experience very different health outcomes. Why could this be? This question obviously moves us away from considering stress simply in terms of the stimulus. We return to this later and also in Chapter 12 ☞ where moderators of the stress experience are discussed.

It has also been suggested that only negatively rated events or hassles lead to adverse outcomes and that positive events or uplifts may 'moderate' the impact of negative events (e.g. Thoits 1995), which is consistent with both stress theory and positive psychology thinking whereby the experience of positive emotions (a likely consequence of experiencing an uplift such as receiving a compliment, getting a good grade) enhances coping appraisals (e.g. Lazarus et al. 1980; Fredrikson 1998, 2001; Folkman 2008). However, the evidence for this is inconclusive, as few studies explore the prospective interactions between positive and negative events. For example, in one study of schoolchildren, only a weak association existed between hassles and uplifts, and uplifts were only weakly associated with mental health outcomes (Barrett and Heubeck 2000).

If health outcomes are indeed affected by major events or an accumulation of minor events (for example, regular teasing at school), what are the processes

IN THE SPOTLIGHT

Stress in children

Most studies of stress have been conducted with adults, and most stress assessments have been developed with adult populations, in part due to concerns about the language competence of particularly young children. However, a preliminary study conducted by Valentine (2010) demonstrated that the majority (78 per cent) of schoolchildren aged 4–11 knew the word stress, and with age, more could define it: Knowledge ranged from 45 per cent of the 4–5-year-olds, to 62 per cent of the 6–7-year-olds and up to 100 per cent of those aged 8 or more. Although a relatively small sample took part in this study (50 children ranging from 4–11 years old), the finding that children have a stress concept, which becomes increasingly complex with age is important. The challenge of friendships and 'fitting in', being separated from parents (particularly in younger children), balancing school demands of continuous assessment with social interests and the increasing expectations placed on children, all contribute to stress, as do the child's response to family events — household tensions are picked up on by a child, such as moving home, parental unemployment, financial pressures and, increasingly, parental divorce.

A child's coping response when faced with stress are important to their health and behavioural outcomes, to their future ability to cope and even to their future outlook on life. Whilst child and adolescent appropriate measures exist, such as the Children's Hassles Scale (Kanner et al. 1987) which includes items such as being teased at school or having to talk in front of the class, we perhaps need updated measures to incorporate modern pressures such as those emerging from social network usage and incidences of cyber bullying (e.g. Chapin 2014).

For more detailed consideration of issues related to child stress concepts and measurement challenges more generally, see Turner-Cobb (2014).

(psychophysiological or behavioural) by which this occurs? For example, studies of the effects of unemployment have been carried out in terms of the morbidity and mortality of a general population (e.g. House et al. 1982) as well as among refugees (e.g. Schwarzer et al. 1994). However, such studies do not tell us *how* unemployment affects illness or even death rates, or *why* it may in some people but not others (Marmot and Madge 1987). To answer the 'how' question leads us to consider physiological theories of stress (stress manifest in biological responses, see later section), whereas to answer the 'why' question requires consideration of sociological explanations (see, in part, Chapter 2's ☞ discussion of social inequalities in health) and psychological theories of stress involving cognitive appraisal and emotion. We turn here to the psychological explanations.

Stress as a transaction

According to psychological theory, stress is a subjective experience, an internal state of being that may or may not be considered by an outside observer as being appropriate to the situation that evoked the response. As John Milton (1608–74) put it when he wrote *Paradise Lost*: 'The mind is its own place, and in itself can make a heaven of hell, a hell of heaven'. This points to what has become the central tenet of psychological theories of stress: that appraisal is central to whether or not an event is deemed to be a stressor or not.

The key figure in this domain is Richard Lazarus, who with colleagues (e.g. Lazarus and Launier 1978; Lazarus and Folkman 1984) proposed what is called a cognitive transactional model of stress (Figure 11.1). Evidence of the importance of psychological processes was drawn from early experimental studies of Lazarus and colleagues (e.g. Speisman et al. 1964), which quite simply exposed student participants to stressful films while monitoring self-reported stress levels and physiological arousal (i.e. heart rate and skin conductance). One example included a gruesome video about tribal initiation rites that included genital surgery. Before the film, participants were divided into four experimental

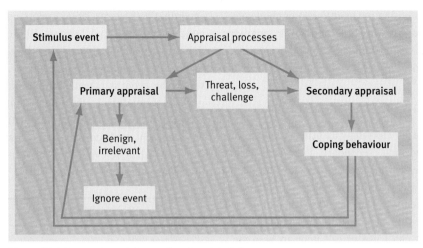

Figure 11.1 Lazarus's early transactional model of stress

Source: adapted from Lovallo (1997: 77).

conditions, each of which received different introductions and soundtracks. One group heard an intellectual description of the rites from a cultural perspective (to mimic a **distancing response**); another heard a lecture that de-emphasised the pain the 'willing' initiates were experiencing and emphasised the excitement they were feeling (to mimic a **denial response**); another heard a narrative that emphasised the pain and trauma the initiates were undergoing (to emphasise the perceived threat); and a control group received no information or soundtrack. Results showed quite clearly that the introductions influenced the way in which the film was seen, reflected in both self-reported stress and skin conductance, with the first and second groups (distancing and denial) showing significantly less stress than group 3. While these classic studies were initially intended to address the idea of 'ego defences' (i.e. what people do to protect themselves from threat), Lazarus realised that appraisal processes were mediating stress responses, and hence he subsequently developed a theory of stress that remains one of the most influential in health psychology.

According to Lazarus, stress is a result of an interaction between an individual's characteristics and appraisals, the external or internal event (stressor) environment, and the internal or external resources a person has available to them. Motivational and cognitive variables are considered central. Lazarus's initial model maintained that when individuals confront a new or changing environment, they engage in a process of **appraisal**, which is of two types: primary and secondary.

Primary appraisal processes

In primary appraisal, a person considers the quality and nature of the stimulus event. Lazarus distinguished three kinds of possible stressor: those that pose harm, those that threaten and those that set a challenge. Harm is considered as damage that has already been done, i.e. a loss or failure; threat is the expectation of future harm; and challenge results from demands that are appraised as opportunities for personal growth or opportunities that a person is confident about dealing with. Events that are not appraised as either harm, threat or challenge are considered to be benign events that require no further action. The questions asked of oneself are along the lines of 'Is this event something I have to deal with?' 'Is it relevant to me?' 'If so, what is at stake?' 'Is it a positive, negative or neutral event? If potentially or actually

distancing response

taking a detached view, often a scientific view, of an event or stimulus in order to reduce emotional activation.

denial response

taking a view that denies any negative implications of an event or stimulus. If subconscious, it is considered a defence mechanism.

appraisals

interpretations of situations, events or behaviour that a person makes.

negative, then is it posing me harm/threat or challenge?' Simultaneously to making these appraisals, emotions may arise that, as well as influencing coping, may elicit various physiological responses (see later).

Secondary appraisal processes

At the same time as carrying out primary appraisals, Lazarus proposed that secondary appraisals occur whereby one assesses one's resources and abilities to cope with the stressor (problem-focused or emotion-focused coping potential). The questions asked of oneself at this stage are of the type: 'How am I going to deal with this?' 'What can I use or call upon to help me?' Resources can be either internal (e.g. strength, determination) or external (e.g. social support, money).

Using forthcoming exams as an example, various appraisal judgments may be made, for example:

● 'There is no way I can possibly deal with this. I simply know I will fail' (threat + no resources = stress).

● 'This will be really hard. I just am not as clever as the other students' (threat + limited internal resources = stress).

● 'Maybe I can manage this if I revise really hard' (challenge + possible internal resources = less stress).

● 'I could perhaps do it if I get some help from my friends' (challenge + external resources = less stress).

● 'This isn't a problem. I know the material really well' (benign).

● 'I managed to pass the last time, I'll be okay this time' (benign).

Lazarus maintained that stress would be experienced when perceived harm or threat was high but perceived coping ability was low, whereas when perceived coping ability was appraised to be high (i.e. resources were considered to be available to deal with the threat), then stress was likely to be minimal. In other words, stress arose from a mismatch between perceived demands and resources, both of which could change over time. It is important that stress is viewed as a dynamic process.

Developments in Lazarus's framework

In the 1990s, Lazarus increasingly considered the stress process as part of the wider domain of emotions and modified his cognitive appraisal theory of stress

accordingly (Lazarus 1991a), working with an eminent colleague (Smith and Lazarus 1993). Smith proposed that primary appraisal consists of two sequential assessments: one of *motivational relevance*, i.e. the extent to which the event is considered relevant to one's current goals or commitments; the other of *motivational congruence*, i.e. the extent to which the situation is perceived to be congruent with current goals. Stress was likely in situations where relevance was high and congruence was low. This is illustrated below:

APPRAISAL	
motivational relevance	motivational congruence
'The proposed class test is important to my studies'	*'I would prefer to party'*
high relevance	low congruence

Photo 11.1 This is a good example of 'eustress', something positive and controlled, but nonetheless often considered stressful

Source: Pearson Education Ltd.

Lazarus also included in primary appraisal an appraisal of *ego involvement*, whereby appraisals of threat to one's sense of self or social esteem would elicit anger, events violating one's moral codes would result in guilt, and any existential threat would create anxiety.

Removing threat/challenge and harm/loss appraisals from the core cognitive definition of primary appraisal and instead attaching them to emotion types is important to how we think about stress. Prior to this, it had often been overlooked that appraisals associate with emotions, yet it makes intuitive sense. For example, appraising an event as a threat to, or incongruent to, one's life goals is likely to precede the emotion of anxiety, whereas a loss appraisal is likely to precede the emotion of sadness (Smith and Lazarus 1993). Less well articulated are the appraisals associated with positive emotions, but positive appraisals such as that of benefit, gain or challenge may precede emotions such as joy or hope (Snyder et al. 1991; Folkman 2008; Hulbert-Williams et al. 2013). An early stress researcher, Hans Selye (1974), generally known for his work on physiological responses to stressful stimuli (see later), distinguished between good and bad stress; between 'eustress', i.e. stress associated with positive feelings or healthy states (seen perhaps in sporting activities or in the performing arts, where the stress gives you focus or a competitive edge perhaps), and 'distress', i.e. the bad kind of stress associated with negative feelings and disturbed bodily states. Although he did not detail how these two types of stress differed in terms of physiological response, their distinction remains an important one, and research attempts such as those examining the emotions attached to different forms of stress appraisal (e.g. nursing students on placement described experiential learning as eustress in a recent study by Gibbons et al. 2008) go some way towards addressing this distinction.

Also in working with Smith, secondary appraisal became more complex, consisting of the following:

1. *Internal/external accountability ('blame/credit')*: concerned with attributing responsibility for the event; is seen to distinguish between emotions of anger (other-blame) and guilt (self-blame). Credit is less often studied but may associate with emotions such as pride.

2. *Problem-focused coping potential*: considers the extent to which the situation is perceived as changeable by instrumental (practical, problem-focused) coping options. If the situation is perceived as changeable, hope or optimism will exist; if not then the emotions of sadness or helplessness will be elicited.

3. *Emotion-focused coping potential*: concerned with perceiving an ability to cope emotionally with the situation. Perceptions of not being able to cope are associated with fear or anxiety.

4. *Future expectancy concerning situational change*: refers to perceived possibilities of the situation being changeable, with perceptions of unchangeability also associating with sadness.

Lazarus merged the second and third assessment, referring simply to 'coping potential'.

The important factor arising from these developments in Lazarus's theory is that the role of emotions was being addressed as well as the cognitions (see Table 11.2), with both aspects interlinked in ongoing and dynamic transactions. Furthermore, this theory proposes that emotional impressions of events are stored in

Table 11.2 Appraisals, core-related themes and emotions

Appraisal components	Core-relational theme	Emotion
Motivationally incongruent, motivationally relevant, other-accountability	Other-blame	Anger
Motivationally relevant, self-accountability	Self-blame	Guilt
Motivationally incongruent, motivationally relevant, low emotion-focused coping potential	Danger/threat	Fear/anxiety
Motivationally incongruent, motivationally relevant, low problem-focused coping potential, low future expectancy	Loss, helplessness	Sadness
Motivational relevance, motivational incongruence, problem-focused coping potential	Optimism	Hope/challenge
Motivational congruence	Success	Happiness

Source: adapted from Hulbert-Williams et al. (2013).

memory and will influence how we appraise the same event in any future encounters.

Criticism of Lazarus's framework

Amongst the many advantages of the transactional approach and its cognitive appraisal theory is that it is compatible with both biological and social models, acknowledging as it does the role of the stimulus, of emotional and behavioural responses, of individual differences and of the external environment. There is a large body of supporting empirical evidence, and few studies of coping with stress or illness are conducted without acknowledging the central role of individual difference variables and appraisals, as will become quite evident in the subsequent chapter. (See Chapter 12 ☞). However, no model or theory escapes without criticism, as this is one way in which academic understanding is advanced. Some criticisms include:

- Lazarus's framework has an inherent circularity and little research has attempted to examine the nature of interaction between primary and secondary appraisals, i.e. between perceived demands and perceived coping resources. Perceived demand and perceived coping capacity are not defined separately, leading to claims of the model being tautological (Hobfoll 1989) – put simply, this means that whether an event is demanding or not depends on perceived coping capacity, and whether coping capacity is perceived as adequate or not is dependent on perceived demand!

- It is unclear whether both primary and secondary appraisals are necessary; for example, Zohar and Dayan (1999) found positive mood outcomes in their sample to be affected mainly by coping potential variables and not by primary appraisal variables. Additionally, stress arose and increased as the stakes or motivational relevance of an event increased, even in situations where coping potential was unlimited. Any slight uncertainty about coping potential modified the effect of 'stakes' (primary appraisal) on stress. For example, imagine a situation where you believe that a forthcoming mid-term examination is a 'mock' and does not count towards your final grade, but on turning up to the exam you are told that it is not a 'mock' but a 'real' exam. In spite of having revised the subject seriously and having no major concerns about your ability to answer the questions,

this new situation is likely to be appraised differently because its value has changed (raised stakes), and the stress experience will therefore also change (increase), even though your resources (secondary appraisals of coping potential) have not.

This relates to the next section where it is noted that unexpected and uncontrollable events increase the likelihood of a stress response. Future research should investigate the interaction between primary and secondary appraisals, and test the assumption that perceived demands need to outweigh perceived resources in order for stress to be experienced. In 'Research focus' we describe one longitudinal study, which investigates the often ignored relationship between cognitive appraisals and emotions and demonstrates the complexity of Lazarus's model.

WHAT DO YOU THINK?

Which do you think comes first – the thought (appraisal) or the emotion? Is it possible to order them? Think of a recent event that you were unhappy about – what thoughts were 'attached' to that unhappiness? Did your feelings about the event change over time and, if so, did your thoughts also change? What about an event that made you happy – WHY did it make you happy? Consider the thought processes. Does Lazarus's model make sense to you?

What factors influence appraisal?

While the nature of stimulus events/potential stressors varies hugely – from, for example, receiving a final demand for an unpaid bill to being a victim of a natural disaster, from having a head cold to receiving a diagnosis of a life-threatening illness – certain features of events have been found to increase the likelihood of their being appraised as stressful. These are events that:

- are *imminent* (e.g. medical results due the next day; driving test that afternoon);

- occur at an *unexpected time* in life (e.g. being widowed in one's 40s compared with when in one's 70s; the death of a child);

- are *unpredictable* in nature (e.g. being made redundant; sudden bereavement);

- are *ambiguous* in terms of:

  ○ personal role (e.g. starting a new job);

○ potential risk or harm involved (e.g. undergoing surgery, taking new medication);

○ events are undesirable (e.g. having to move house because of financial loss);

● the individual perceives *no control* over (behavioural or cognitive, e.g. noisy neighbours);

● events that elicit high amounts of *life change* (e.g. childbirth, relocation).

Further distinction has been drawn (e.g. Sapolsky 1994: 5) between:

● acute physical stressors, which demand immediate physiological adaptation (e.g. being attacked);

● chronic physical stressors (e.g. being ill or surviving in a hostile environment);

● long-term physiological demands that we are not so good at dealing with, such as pain;

● psychosocial stressors, which involve our cognitions, emotions and behavioural responses as well as the physiological arousal that will be triggered.

Many psychologists would argue that all these are in fact psychosocial as they involve more than simply the event or stimulus. Chapter 12 ☞ will deal with the personal and inter-personal influences on appraisals and stress responses.

RESEARCH FOCUS

Appraisals and emotions in cancer patient

Hulbert-Williams, N.J., Morrison, V., Wilkinson, C. and Neal, R.D. (2013). Investigating the cognitive precursors of emotional response to cancer stress: Re-testing Lazarus's transactional model. *British Journal of Health Psychology*, 18:97–121.

Introduction

Lazarus's model, as described earlier, links appraisals with stress outcomes, via their effects on coping. Developments in the model included the relationship between appraisals, their relational meaning and emotions and suggest that, in combination, these influence individual coping responses. For example, if I consider my life goals to be threatened by an injury received at work, I may blame others (core relational theme, CRT) and in doing so I may experience the emotion of anger. If in contrast my life goals are threatened by injury from a car accident, and I blame my bad driving, I am more likely to experience the emotion of guilt. Different coping responses are likely in these two scenarios. Not all emotions have been fully theorised, although the six emotions of anger, guilt, fear/anxiety, sadness, hope/challenge and happiness have been, and therefore the few studies that exist have addressed those.

This study seeks to test a fuller set of emotions using a longitudinal design which acknowledges that Lazarus's model is intended to be one which is dynamic: i.e stress is a process, therefore appraisals and emotions are not fixed at one point in time. By focusing on a sample of cancer patients followed over six months it is hoped that change in core appraisals will occur which can be examined in relation to changes in the theoretically associated emotions.

Whilst a relatively complex theoretical paper to read, the purpose of presenting it here is less to describe the theoretical detail and challenges to Lazarus's theory that the findings present (the theoreticians amongst you can read it for this purpose at leisure!) than to highlight the empirical findings regarding the relationship between cognition and emotion amongst those in the first six months following a cancer diagnosis. The paper tests two hypotheses: (1) that change scores on any emotion will be more highly correlated with the theoretically proposed CRT or appraisals than any other cognitions and (2) that the findings would verify Lazarus and Smith's model. This RESEARCH FOCUS addresses hypothesis (1). Exploring changes in appraisals and emotions, and the relationships between them is crucial to our understanding of the illness experience and to the development of effective interventions (see later chapters).

Methods

A total of 160 recently diagnosed adult cancer patients (mixed cancer sites, 63 men, 97 women, mean age 64.2 years) were recruited to a longitudinal questionnaire-based study by a clinical nurse specialist at one of three hospitals. Patients were not invited to take part if they were in a palliative, rather than a curative, treatment regime, or expected to have less than six months, life expectancy.

Questionnaires assessed self-reported appraisals, core relational themes and emotions at baseline and, to assess change, the same assessments were completed three and six months subsequently. Participants also completed demographic and clinical questions and a range of other measures not reported in this paper, including mood and quality of life outcomes (see Hulbert Williams et al. 2013).

Eight items assessed primary appraisals (motivational relevance, irrelevance, congruence) and secondary appraisals (self-accountability, other accountability, problem-focused coping potential, emotion-focused coping potential, future expectancy). Twelve CRTs described by Smith and Lazarus were assessed: other-blame; self-blame; threat; loss-helplessness; effortful optimism; success; self-consciousness; relevance; unexpectedness; irrelevance; lack of concern; removal of threat. Sixteen emotions—surprise, guilt, resignation, frustration, tranquillity, self-directed anger, challenge/hope, regret, sadness, shame/humiliation, interest, happiness, boredom/detachment, anger, anxiety/fear, relief – were assessed using adjectival clusters.

All questions were anchored towards the participants' experiences of having cancer.

Results

The response rate for this study, although low at 34.6 per cent is reasonably consistent with many other psycho-oncology studies which recruit within the first couple of months from diagnosis. Retention in the study to six months was high (76.8 per cent), with 123 participants completing the six-month analysis.

Change scores were calculated for appraisals, core relational themes and emotions by subtracting baseline scores from those either at three or six months.

Between baseline and three-month assessment patient cognitions and emotions were relatively stable, with a few interesting exceptions. Motivational incongruence appraisals decreased, whereby participants in general perceived slightly less incongruence between cancer and other aspects of their lives. Four CRTs changed - irrelevance decreased, and threat removal, lack of concern and success increased.

Between baseline and six months motivational incongruence appraisals decreased, as did the irrelevance CRT. Threat removal, lack of concern and success increased plus also perceived relevance, and threat decreased. By six months two emotions shame/humiliation and relief decreased.

In relation to testing the theoretically driven hypothesis that changes in certain appraisals or CRTS should be associated with changes in the theoretically corresponding emotion, the evidence was mixed. For example, if the theory were upheld, change in anger emotion should correlate with changes in the CRT of other-blame and in the appraisals of motivational relevance, motivational congruence and other-responsibility.

Analyses found that at three months, with the exception of change in emotion-focused coping potential appraisals being associated with changes in fear/anxiety, *no* other changed appraisals correlated with the theorised change in emotion, nor at six months.

There was more evidence of association between changes in CRTs and changes in the corresponding emotion with, for example, at three months, an increase in loss/helplessness associating with sadness, and decreased threat removal correlating with relief. Unexpectedly an increase in threat was associated with a decrease in fear/anxiety. At six months, increased self-blame corresponded with increased guilt, threat removal again associated with increased relief, and increased self-consciousness associated with increased shame/humiliation.

What was also surprising was that stronger associations emerged between emotions, CRTs and appraisals that were NOT theorised by Smith or Lazarus. For example, at three months low emotion-focused coping potential was associated with anger (not fear/anxiety), and high self-blame was strongly associated with fear/anxiety (not guilt). At six months a high threat CRT was associated with guilt.

In addition, many directions of association were unexpected: for example, increased motivational incongruence was associated at six months with decreased anger and sadness rather than more, and, as noted above, an increase in threat was associated with a decrease in fear/anxiety.

Discussion and conclusion

From a theoretical perspective the findings of this study with regards to the first hypothesis raise more questions than answers. Changes in appraisals over the six months following a cancer diagnosis were not consistent or even matched by change in the theorised emotions. In fact, stronger associations were found between those not theorised to be associated! There are several possible explanations offered. Firstly, in this sample there was not a huge amount of change in appraisal or emotion by three or six months and thus correlations between change scores are undermined. Secondly, the very nature of the sample, recruited at

a time when both practical, experiential, existential and emotional life has likely been challenged by a cancer diagnosis, may mean that simply too much is happening too quickly for three-month gaps between assessment to operate reliably. Furthermore, the study anchored questions to the 'current cancer-related experience' and, within our sample, this varied with differences in the treatments undergone by patients. Perhaps anchoring responses to the fixed point of diagnosis (although this introduces issues of retrospective reporting), or repeating the assessments more regularly, could address these issues.

In spite of these challenges, this paper highlights that appraisals are associated with many more emotions than typically addressed in the study of illness experience. Few studies examine feelings of relief, shame/humiliation or anger that, in these data, are associated with certain cognitions. Similarly, the core relational themes of self-blame, threat and loss/helplessness emerged as the most commonly associated with emotions. These cognitions and emotions often emerge in qualitative studies and are potentially powerful drivers of coping responses, as will be described in Chapter 12 ☞. This paper therefore serves to highlight the need to widen our scope. Living with cancer and its associated treatments (as well as living with other chronic conditions) is not just about anxiety or depression.

Lay theories of stress

Before moving on to describing types and potential sources of stress, it is worth stopping to reflect on what has been made clear in the above review of scientific study of stress. Stress is the subject of significant scientific enquiry, yet as a subjective construct it is hard to define. As discussed in Chapter 9 ☞, in relation to symptom perception and interpretation, lay models of illness are important to understanding what occurs between symptom perception and response. Similarly in relation to stress, we need to acknowledge the role played by what the layperson considers to be the causes and consequences of stress – stress as a concept exists not only in scientific study but also in our everyday language. Several authors have studied these understandings in relation to work stress (e.g. Chartered Institute of

Personnel Directors 2011; Rystedt et al. 2004; Kinman and Jones 2005; Jones et al. 2006; William and Copper. 2002) and some have studied understanding of stress in relation to specific illnesses, such as heart attack (e.g. Clark 2003). In Clark's study of 14 Scottish heart attack survivors, while the understanding of social, personal and situational influences on what was considered to be 'stress' varied significantly between individuals, there was a common view that the stress was a more salient cause of their heart attack than even smoking or diet. This type of understanding and attribution could of course be self-serving! In relation to work stress, lay theories were similarly multifaceted and variable. Interestingly in Kinman and Jones's (2005) study, we find an example of rank or position in a company making a difference. In this instance it is seen in the differential understanding of the impact of stress – lower-level workers considered the impact of occupational stress to be more personal and requiring of joint efforts by themselves and the organisation if stress is to be managed, whereas managerial workers considered that the responsibility for stress management lay at the feet of the individual workers – in spite of agreeing that many causes of stress were organisational! Such lay beliefs are important, given that evidence of their longitudinal effects on worker stress, including mental strain (Rystedt et al. 2004), and certainly lay theorising about why stress has occurred and what its likely consequences are, holds implications for stress management interventions (Chapter 13 ☞).

Now, we turn our attention to potential sources of stress: 'potential' sources because, as described above, the role of appraisal is brought to bear on the stimulus and it is this situation – person interaction – that determines whether stress, as a response, results.

Types of stress

Stress and resource loss

Hobfoll (1989) proposed a 'conservation of resources' model of stress whereby individuals are assumed to work to conserve or protect their valued resources (e.g. objects, roles, personal characteristics such as self-esteem, energy, time, money, skills). Hobfoll suggests that stress will result when there is actual or threatened loss of resources or a lack of gain after investing resources. Resources are thought to be quantifiable and 'real' and therefore 'mean' the same to all people when they are lost. This therefore de-emphasises the role of individual appraisal, central to Lazarus's model. Hobfoll states that the more resources are lost, the more difficult it becomes to replace them, and the greater the resulting stress. This quantification of resources fits with the kind of evidence discussed in Chapter 2 ☞, i.e. that of socio-economic deprivation, unemployment and poverty, all of which are found to associate with illness, independent of the individual's appraisals. By focusing on loss of quantifiable entities rather than appraisals, this model avoids any difficulties in distinguishing appraisals from responses. However, Marks et al. (2000) point out that the loss and resource constructs are not particularly well defined or easy to measure, and that many questions remain unanswered by this model. For example, how permanent must loss be for a person to experience stress? Does the speed and extent of resource loss

matter? Is resource gain never stressful? (Some lottery winners would perhaps challenge this.)

Hobfoll (1991) found that rapid and extensive depletion of valued resources, such as that experienced following a natural disaster, was associated with traumatic stress responses. Natural disasters are generally acute-onset stressors, but many may have long-term consequences. Examples of other acute stressors are given below.

Acute stress

Studies of acute-onset stress generally distinguish between stimulus events that are rare but cataclysmic and more common acute stressors, such as exams.

Cataclysmic events

Earthquakes, hurricanes and air disasters are rare events that allow a person little or no preparation time. Natural catastrophes, such as the Asian tsunami in 2004, Hurricane Katrina in 2005, and technological disasters such as the nuclear meltdown at Chernobyl in 1986 and Japan in 2011, produce intense physical and psychosocial suffering for victims and for the 'worried well', i.e. those not actually in the disaster but affected by it in that it raises issues for them about their own personal safety and future. Environmental stress theory (Fisher et al. 1984; Baum 1990) considers stress to be a combined psychological and physiological response to demands, and support for this can be found in the many psychological and physical symptoms reported in survivors of a natural calamity.

These include:

- initial panic
- anxiety
- phobic fear
- vulnerability
- guilt (survivor guilt)
- isolation
- withdrawal (including some suicide attempts)
- anger and frustration
- interpersonal and marital problems
- disorientation
- lack of attachment
- loss of sense of security
- sleep disturbances
- eating disturbances.

The severity and duration of these effects seem to depend on the magnitude of the loss. In addition to this long list of possible outcomes, some people continuously relive the event in distressing dreams and/or suffer from 'flashbacks'. Such symptoms may lead to the individual being diagnosed as suffering from **post-traumatic stress disorder** (PTSD; see Chapter 13 ☛).

Hobfoll's 'conservation of resources' model of stress was applied in a study of lost resources or 'losses' among 135 individuals assessed following Hurricane Andrew in the United States (Benight et al. 1999). This study also investigated the extent to which **coping self-efficacy** (cf. Bandura 1986) determined stress responses and the ability of individuals to recover from their losses by employing their remaining coping resources. Coping self-efficacy was specific to the ability to meet needs following the hurricane, and losses were focused on loss of material resources rather than psychological resources, although both were assessed. Overall, the results confirmed a positive association between loss of resource, coping self-efficacy and subsequent distress. Resource loss was positively associated with long-term distress,

with active coping efforts mediating this relationship and reducing the distress experienced (see Chapter 12 ☛).

This study highlights that quantifiable resource loss is in itself distressing, but that appraisals related to coping ability also play a significant role: thus the conservation of resources model need extend to consider such factors. It is clear that acute-onset stressors can have chronic effects on a person's psychological well-being. Interventions to minimise distress therefore need to be targeted appropriately. For example, in the case of hurricane survivors, interventions may maximise their effectiveness if they

---

post-traumatic stress disorder

a disorder that forms a response to experiencing a traumatic event. The key elements are unwanted repetitive memories of the event, often in the form of flashbacks, attempts at avoidance of such memories, and a generally raised level of arousal.

coping self-efficacy

the belief that one can carry out a particular coping response in a given set of circumstances.

Photo 11.2 Floods in UK have cost many families much more than money – their home, possessions and memories are often lost in mud.

Source: Shutterstock.com/Charlie Edward.

target both the lost resources (e.g. restoration of housing, water, clothing) and the emotions and cognitions (e.g. self-efficacy) of the victims. Stress management and coping-based interventions are discussed fully in Chapter 13 ☞.

Exam stress

Cohen et al. (1986) found that high levels of perceived stress can impair people's memory and attention during cognitive activities. For example, many students report the experience of having the answer to questions on the tip of their tongue, and even memories of revising it the night before, but being unable to remember it once in the exam setting. Others will misread and misinterpret clearly written questions. It has been found that there is an optimum level of arousal necessary to maintain attention and memory, but that too little arousal, or too much, can be detrimental to one's performance. This is known as the Yerkes–Dodson law, first described in 1908 (see Figure 11.2). An exam in a subject where the result is desired and valued will generally elicit more arousal than an exam that is not valued, and the key to good performance lies in not becoming over-aroused so that all the learning goes to waste and the mind empties in the exam room!

Exam stress has been associated with increased smoking, increased alcohol consumption, poor eating, increased caffeine intake, and less physical activity, and was attributed to a breakdown in self-control, particularly among those with poor study skills, as evidenced in a study of Australian students (Oaten and Cheng 2006). This association between stress and behaviour is an indirect route by which stress can be considered to influence illness status. Exam stress has also been found to affect bodily responses, such as blood pressure. The repeated assessment of physical indices of **stress reactivity** (such as blood pressure, see later section on physiological responses) is necessary so that researchers have multiple baselines against which to assess increases and decreases in blood pressure over time when the individual is performing different activities. For example, Sausen and colleagues (Sausen et al. 1992) attached ambulatory (mobile) monitoring devices to medical students which activated at set and regular intervals to read blood pressure, and recorded increases in blood pressure on exam days. Regular national testing in our schools has also been associated with stress in children and adolescents. Some individuals seem to inherently be more stress-reactive than others, which may underlie an increased susceptibility to disease (see later).

A link between acute stressors such as exams and actual illness (rather than focusing on physiological reactivity, which poses no danger to the individual unless it is maintained; Brosschot et al. 2005) has been proposed following findings that students exhibit increased prevalence of infections at exam periods compared with during non-assessment periods. These studies often include blood sampling to identify immunological markers, and findings suggest that for many individuals, exams and the build-up to them (which is often accompanied by anxiety and changed behaviours) are sufficiently stressful to increase susceptibility to illness, via immunosuppressant effects (e.g. Kiecolt-Glaser et al. 2002; Vedhara and Irwin 2005; see also the later section on stress as a physiological response).

Chronic stress

Occupational stress

The workplace is a good environment in which to study the chronic effects of stress, although many other environmental situations have been studied, for example traffic jams and

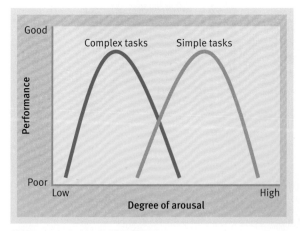

Figure 11.2 The Yerkes–Dodson law

Source: Rice (1992: 5).

> **stress reactivity**
> the physiological arousal, such as increased heart rate or blood pressure, experienced during a potentially stressful encounter.

road rage, noise pollution and overcrowding on public transport (Fisher et al. 1984; Evans and Stecker 2004). Loss of control in these situations, particularly when demands are also high, appears to play a crucial role in the stress experienced (e.g. Wang et al. 2007, 2008) (for discussion of this construct see Chapter 12 ☞). Most working individuals will experience workplace stress at some point, and while for many it is short-lived or manageable, for others it is chronic and damaging, being accompanied, for example, by changes in eating or sleep patterns, fatigue or relationship strain.

What is it about some jobs which makes them so stressful? One possible explanation is offered by person–environment fit theories (cf. French et al. 1982), or the 'goodness-of-fit' approach described by Lazarus (1991b). Such approaches suggest that stress arises because of a mismatch between environmental variables (demands) and person variables (resources). 'Fit' is considered as dynamic rather than static, in that demands and resources can change over time. Early work focused more on environmental features of the workplace than on individual difference variables, a primary example of this being the job demand–control (JDC) model of occupational stress, or job strain, put forward by Karasek and colleagues (1979, 1981, 1990). The job features identified as leading to stress included:

- demand
- controllability
- predictability
- ambiguity.

Each of these broad features can be assessed with specific questions, as illustrated in Table 11.3.

Chronic ongoing stressors such as permanently excessive workload demands are thought to create stress in employees, as are sudden, unexpected requests or interruptions, being pushed to make a decision, not having the latitude to take decisions, or being unclear as to what is expected of one. Interestingly, underload, as well as overload, has been found stressful, with frustration and boredom proving as stressful for some employees as overload. This highlights a point central to the study of stress: it is subjective and each individual will construct their own definition of what is stressful 'for them'. This is seen in the findings of an idiographic study of the meaning of stress to five health professionals (neurological consultant – NC, ophthalmology assistant – OA, paediatrician – P, psychiatrist – PS and theatre nurse – TN) where aspects listed as most stressful included work environment factors such as monotonous tasks (NC), maintaining cleanliness (TN), time pressures (NC, TN), full waiting room (P), overload (NC), poor pay or conditions (OA) as well as external factors such as family pressure (PS, P) (Kirkcaldy et al. 2000).

Karasek's model proposed that a combination of demand and control would determine whether or not the employee experienced stress (high demand and low control contributing to higher stress–strain than would situations of high demand and high control) (Karasek and Theorell 1990). Karasek's model has been tested and proven useful in many studies. However, whilst initially thought that perceived or actual control acted as

Table 11.3 Examples of items to assess work-related stress

	Never	Rarely	Sometimes	Often	Most times
Demand					
☒ My workload is never-ending					
☒ Job deadlines are constant					
☒ My job is very exciting					
Control					
☒ I have autonomy in carrying out my duties					
☒ There are too many bosses					
Predictability					
☒ My job consists of responding to emergencies					
☒ I am never sure what will be expected of me					
Ambiguity					
☒ My job is not very well defined					
☒ I am not sure about what is expected of me					

Source: adapted from Rice (1992: 188–92).

a moderator of demand (in other words, that control 'buffered' the negative effects of demands), reviews of studies using the JDC model between 1979 and 1997 (van der Doef and Maes 1998, 1999) found only minimal evidence that control moderated the negative impact of high work demands upon well-being, or burn-out (Rafferty et al. 2001). It appears that demand and control have independent and direct effects on stress outcomes.

As well as better specifying the control component, it was proposed that social support, or lack of it, needed to be added to the model (see Van der Doef and Maes 1999; Searle et al. 2001;). Others have suggested adding a more general 'resources' component to the model , i.e the JD-R model (Demerouti et al. 2001) whereby resources could include social support, or aspects of personal control, etc. A further alternative model to that of Karasek's is the Effort/Reward Imbalance model (Siegrist et al. 2004) which highlights what the individual 'puts in' to their work and notes how a lack of recognition or return for effort can be stressful (for a review of studies using this model see van Vegchel et al. 2005). For example, an over-commitment to work has been associated with increased blood pressure (Steptoe et al. 2004a); job strain and an effort/reward imbalance significantly predicted risk of CVD mortality over 25 years of the Whitehall 11 Study (Kivimäki et al. 2002); and along with low levels of support was associated with reduced immune function in a study of German factory workers (Bosch et al. 2009).

Many studies have addressed stress within teaching or health-care sectors. For example, teachers report stress arising from a range of factors, including poor classroom conditions and lack of materials or equipment, frequent reorganization in school policy or practice both internally and externally imposed, challenging pupil conduct, and excessive workload/job demands carried over to home (e.g. Griva and Joekes 2003; Skaalvik and Skaalvik 2009). The impact of austerity measures on staff recruitment or facilities is felt at many levels, including in applied psychology within our health service. For example, clinical psychologists report unhappiness with their work environments, changing systems and the impact these can have on their clients (Webb 2013). Undergraduate students are of course not exempt from stress; in fact, undergraduates have a higher prevalence of mental health

problems than age-matched non-students, and these problems disrupt performance (Royal College of Psychiatrists 2003). Given the current climate of austerity across Europe, including changes to fee structures in British universities, more of us may be experiencing mental, emotional and physical ill health, given evidence of their higher levels among those experiencing financial pressures (e.g. Jessop et al. 2005, and see Chapter 2 (☞).

One possible outcome of prolonged chronic occupational stress has been described as 'burn-out' (Maslach 1982, 1997). Burn-out is similar to the final stage of Selye's general adaptation syndrome: i.e. exhaustion, both mental and physical (see later section on stress response). Maslach (1997) defined burn-out as a three-part syndrome of gradually developing emotional exhaustion, depersonalisation and reduced personal accomplishment that occurs among individuals who work with people in some capacity, and which can be associated with both physical and mental ill health. For example, hospital consultants (e.g. Taylor et al. 2005), nurses (e.g. Jones and Johnston 2000; McVicar 2003; Allan et al. 2009), and those working with cancer patients (e.g. Isikhan et al. 2004; Barnard et al. 2006; Trufelli *et al.* 2008) have shown a high incidence of burn-out and stress. Related to burn-out is the concept of carer strain or carer burden, identified among many individuals whose 'job' is to provide care for dependent relatives (due to chronic illness or disability). Chapter 15 (☞) addresses the impact of illness on family and friends in full.

However, it is worth noting that not all studies have found an association between workload itself and levels of burn-out, (e.g. Healy and McKay 2000; Payne 2001, and see McVicar 2003 for a review). Several reasons might exist for such differences in study findings:

- sample or setting differences (e.g. registered general nurses vs. palliative or hospice nurses);
- varying individual characteristcs and responses made to the demands;
- whether demands, resources or both were assessed.

Considering these in turn, different job types are likely to contain different objective demands: shift workers or factory workers, for example have particular challenges to face (unsocial hours, repetition), as do those working in a high-risk environment (e.g. firefighters, prison officers) or those having to deal with the public (see Park et al. 2014). Secondly, individual characteristics and coping responses show variable associations with job stress: for example, teachers with a stronger sense of competence report less stress and appear to cope more effectively (e.g. Schwarzer and Hallum 2008) (see Chapter 12 ☛ for further discussion of coping). In fact, one study which found that workload-specific stress factors were more strongly associated with mood disturbance than nurses' coping responses (Healy and McKay 2000) would suggest that organisational interventions aimed at reducing workload may be appropriate and of more benefit than interventions targeting individuals' coping strategies. This contrasts with the conclusion of McVicar following a review of 21 studies, where he states (p. 640) that 'Development of preventative strategies will be hindered until employers enable individualized coping strategies, and research enables understanding of personal and workplace interactions and provides a means of assessing the intensity of distress experienced by individuals.' Finally, with regards to the third point, it has been proposed that job demands are more likely to predict emotional exhaustion, whereas job resources, or lack of them (e.g. low perceived control), would be associated with disengagement and lack of accomplishment. In a recent meta-analysis of 71 independent samples with over 48,000 participants where job control was considered as a resource within the Conservation of Resources model (see earlier), this hypothesis was confirmed (Park et al. 2014).

It has been suggested that men would benefit more than women from work-based interventions to reduce stress and improve well-being, following reasonably consistent findings that men are less likely to seek out support for stress elsewhere and that a sense of identity and self-worth arising from positive work experience is more salient to men's experience (World Economic Forum 2008). In 2014 a core topic of the annual Men's Health week, organised in England and Wales by the Men's Health Forum, was work, stress and unemployment, with the government Minister for Care and Support highlighting the need for better integration and communication between workplace and social care facilities to recognise and support workers who are experiencing stress (important, regardless of gender).

WHAT DO YOU THINK?

Are you stressed? If not, then that is good news! If you are though, what do you think is currently contributing to your feelings of stress? Are there aspects of your workload as a student in your list? If so, what are the features of your workload that are making it stressful? Is it that the demands (real or perceived) are too great and your resources (real or perceived) too low? Is it about ambiguity of expectations or a lack of control? Is it that you have other things you would rather be doing, other goals and desires distracting or competing for your attention? Once you have a better sense of what features your stress triggers have, it becomes easier to work out the appropriate solution (see Chapter 13 ☛).

Several studies carried out among staff in the police force (in a range of countries, e.g. Germany: Kirkcaldy and Cooper 1992; Britain: Brown et al. 1996; Wales: V. Morrison et al. 2002; New Zealand: Stephens et al. 1997; Scotland: Biggam et al. 1997; the Netherlands: Kop et al. 1999) have also highlighted the role of contextual and personal factors on the stress experience. Policing is an occupation considered to be inherently stressful due to operational, bureaucratic and interpersonal demands. For example Morrison et al.'s (2002) study of 699 police officers and 230 police support personnel in North Wales found bureaucracy-associated stressors (increased paperwork, poor communication with managers) were reported, particularly among mid–low-ranked staff and amongst the higher ranked personnel, job-overload in terms of increasing levels of unpaid overtime and the need to take work home were common. There are many factors which influence the nature of the stress experienced, with personal resource variables of self-efficacy and optimism, the rank of the employee, and access to and use of home- and workplace-based support emerging as moderators of stress and distress in this study. These factors are fully addressed in the next chapter. Some occupations, such as the police force, or in health-care professions, may also have strong internal sanctions against exhibiting symptoms of stress, given the level of contact required with the public. This may present additional challenges. While rank may not be so explicit in other occupations, except perhaps the Armed Forces, an implicit hierarchy exists in most workforces. The effects of status on interactions between personnel is a factor that needs considering in any studies of occupational stress. Illustrating this, conflict with or harassment by other colleagues has been associated with a significant level of staff absenteeism, to the stage where the Royal College of Nursing (RCN 2002) has acknowledged a need to improve interprofessional and intraprofessional communication and management style.

The commonly employed models of occupational stress described here have therefore succeeded in integrating what the individual brings to the workplace (personal characteristics, cognitions, effort), their support resources and the environmental features. Depending on which contributing factor one addresses, interventions have potentially different targets to attempt stress reduction and management (see Chapter 13 ☞). Aspects of the individual such as their resources, their coping strategies, their health-damaging behaviours such as increased smoking or alcohol consumption (APA 2015), or their use of social support are potentially more amenable to intervention that attempts to challenge or resolve issues of job control, decision latitude, overload, underload or ambiguity of role with one's employer! Training of management or supervisory staff can, however, help them to better communicate to their workforce, to delegate responsibility and to bolster worker confidence (see Park et al.'s meta-analysis, 2014). Better still are combined workplace-based interventions which target both the work environment and individual's stress responses for the benefit of physical and emotional well-being and also productivity – outcomes of importance to both employee and employer (e.g. Brabantia Work Health Program, Maes and van der Doef 2004). For those who avoid stress through sickness and absenteeism, early workplace interventions have huge potential gain. Stress responses carry huge costs for employers in terms of loss of productivity, staffing shortages and accidents in the workplace (Cooper and Payne 1988).

So far we have established that stress responses arise from events and from appraisals of these events, but we have not yet described what happens following these cognitive or emotional processes. Lazarus's transactional model of stress posits that appraisals and their attached emotions lead to cognitive and behavioural coping efforts, and in Chapter 12 ☞ coping theory and the role of coping in moderating stress outcomes is discussed fully. However, in addition to these psychological stress responses, stress can also trigger biological and physiological responses, and it is to these that we now turn our attention.

Stress as a physiological response

Thinking of stress as a response takes us into the domain of seeking biological or physiological explanations of how stress affects the body and potentially illness; the assumption here is that stressors place demands on the person that are manifested in some response; in physics, this response would be termed 'strain'. Proponents of the 'response' model of stress describe how individuals react to danger or potentially harmful situations or even pleasant demands with a coordinated physiological and behavioural response (e.g. Cassel 1974, cited in Leventhal and Tomarken 1987). Initially, an event has to be appraised, and this involves the **central nervous system** (CNS). The sensory information and the appraisal of the event combine to initiate autonomic and endocrine (hormone) responses. The autonomic nervous system is part of the peripheral nervous system and contains both the sympathetic and the parasympathetic NS (see below). These responses in turn feed back to the cortex and limbic system, which in turn links with the hypothalamus and brainstem. It has been found that, for example, appraising an event as *unpredictable* in nature affects various aspects of physiological activation (Zakowski 1995).

These processes are summarised below, although Chapter 8 ☞ provides greater physiological definition and detail.

Early work on the stress response

An early researcher, Walter Cannon (1932), outlined the role of catecholamines (adrenaline and noradrenaline), which, when released from the adrenal glands of the sympathetic nervous system as hormones, heighten arousal in order to facilitate the 'fight or flight' response. When faced with imminent danger or a high level of threat (such as when being charged at by an angry dog), the options are to face the challenge or escape it. This

---

central nervous system
that part of the nervous system consisting of the brain and spinal cord.

natural response of physical arousal – dry mouth, increased heart rate, rapid breathing – signifies the release of adrenaline, a hormone that enlarges the autonomic responses (e.g. breathing deeply, a rapid heart rate) and facilitates the release of stored fuels for energy, which enables either running away or fighting the threat. This 'fight or flight syndrome', Cannon reasoned, was *adaptive* because it enabled quick responses to threat but also *harmful* because it disrupted emotional and physiological functioning. If prolonged, such responses were thought to contribute to many medical problems, (based on early animal studies whereby dogs and monkeys were exposed to prolonged periods of stress causing excessive hydrochloric acid to build up in the stomach, thus contributing to ulcer formation). In other words, in situations of chronic or ongoing stress, this fight–flight response would not be adaptive.

Subsequent to Cannon, another physiologist, Hans Selye (1956), discovered (quite accidentally while conducting animal research into the sex hormones) that a triad of responses commonly followed the unpleasant injecting procedures used – the adrenal glands enlarged, the thymus gland shrank and ulcers developed in the digestive tract. He followed up his early findings with over forty years of research using different aversive stimuli (injections, heat, cold, exercise), and came to the conclusion that there were universal and non-specific responses to stress: i.e. the same physiological responses followed a range of stimuli, whether pleasant or unpleasant, and that the 'fight–flight' response was only the first stage of response to stress (e.g. Selye 1974). Selye's model of stress is known as the **general adaptation syndrome**. The response to stress was seen to be an innate drive of living organisms to maintain internal balance, i.e. homeostasis, and he proposed that it did so in a three-stage process:

1. *Alarm reaction:* awareness of a stressor can cause a downturn in bodily defences, as blood pressure and heart rate may initially fall before rising to higher than normal levels. Once raised, Selye noted, this arousal could not be maintained for long periods. He attributed his stress response to activitation of the anterior–pituitary–adrenal

cortex system, although exact physiological processes only became clear some years later (Selye 1991; Pinel 2003; and see later section).

2. *Stage of resistance:* the next stage is where the body mobilises its bodily defences to try to adapt to a stressor that has not subsided in spite of resistance efforts made during the alarm stage. Whilst physiological arousal is less than during the alarm stage it is still higher than normal. Selye noted that this stage could not last indefinitely without the organism becoming vulnerable to illness.

3. *Stage of exhaustion:* if the resistance stage lasts too long, a depletion of bodily resources and energy would result in exhaustion. At this stage, the ability to resist the stress declines and at this point, Selye proposed, the increased likelihood of 'diseases of adaptation' such as cardiovascular disease, arthritis and asthma.

Later work on stress responses

Whilst Cannon's and Selye's work stimulated a huge amount of research into the physiology of stress, much of it has not confirmed the presence of a consistent 'non-specific response'. Different physiological responses have been found to be associated with different kinds of stressor as evidenced in a wide range of experimental studies carried out in the 1980s: for example, participants exposed to mental challenge showed higher blood levels of adrenaline than those exposed to a physical stress task, whereas noradrenaline increased during physical stress (Ward et al. 1983, cited in Rice 1992).

There is no doubt, however, that adverse events (and positive events) produce physiological changes. A large and growing body of evidence show that typical stress responses (e.g. rapid and deeper breathing, increased heart rate, sweating or shaking) result not just from activation of the anterior–pituitary–adrenal cortex system (as Selye thought) but also from increased activity of the sympathetic branch of the autonomic nervous system (ANS). The ANS can be divided into two connected systems – the sympathetic nervous system (SNS) and the parasympathetic nervous system (PNS) – which 'exist in a state of dynamic but antagonistic tension' (Rice 1992: 126). The SNS is involved in arousal and expenditure of energy (such as during a 'fight–flight' response), whereas the PNS is involved in reducing arousal and in restoring and conserving the body's energy stores (such as during rest) (see Chapter 8 ☛).

---

general adaptation syndrome
a sequence of physiological responses to prolonged stress, from the alarm stage through the resistance stage to exhaustion.

Both neural systems control the actions of many internal organs, such as the heart and skeletal muscles, with their activity initially mediated by the neurotransmitter acetylcholine. Acetylcholine links the neurons of the spinal synapse to the brainstem, where the nerves then act on their target organs. Mediation in the sympathetic branch is provided by noradrenaline (adrenergic fibres) and, to a lesser degree, adrenaline; whereas in the parasympathetic branch, acetylcholine (cholinergic fibres) makes this final link.

Activation of the sympathetic–adrenomedullary system (SAM) results in release of the catecholamines adrenaline and noradrenaline (epinephrine and norepinephrine being the US terms) from the adrenal medulla (the adrenal medulla and the adrenal cortex comprise the adrenal glands). This activation which is triggered from the hypothalamus, which sends nerves signals down to the adrenal medulla via the spinal cord, enables a person to make an immediate response to a stressor, such as 'flight or fight' enabled by adrenalin being released into the bloodstream.

However, the stress response following sympathetic arousal is short-lived and therefore the endocrine (hormonal) system, in fact neuroendocrine (combining the nervous and the endocrine systems, i.e. electrical/chemical and hormonal), responses follow. This second system, the hypothalamic–pituitary–adrenocortical (HPA) system (see Figure 11.3), enables our bodily organs to alter their usual function to facilitate a longer lasting adaptive response to both internal and external stresses.

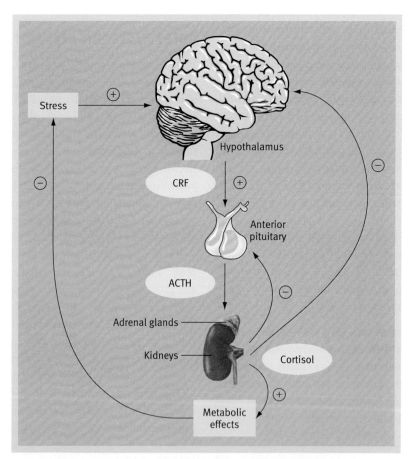

Figure 11.3 Schematic diagram of the hypothalamus-pituitary-adrenal (HPA) axis. Stimulatory and inhibitory paths are indicated by the arrows and + or − signs respectively. CRF represents corticotropin releasing factor and ACTH represents adrenocorticotropic hormone.

Source: Adapted from Lenbury and Pornsawad (2005).

This system also originates in the hypothalamus, which releases its own hormone, corticotrophin-releasing factor (CRF), which controls the anterior pituitary gland at the base of the brain in its secreting of adrenocorticotrophic hormone (ACTH). ACTH then travels to the adrenal cortex, which then secretes glucocorticoids, particularly the hormone cortisol, which is stimulated from the adrenal cortex.

While Cannon's early model described the role of adrenaline, Selye was more interested in such adrenocortical responses, and in fact it is the HPA system that has received most research attention over the past 30 years. We now know that circulating glucocorticoids provide energy for the 'alarm phase' as the release of glucocorticoids into the bloodstream regulates the levels of glucose in the blood from which energy can be drawn. Almost every cell in the human body contains glucocorticoid receptors, and hormones such as cortisol affect every major organ system in the body. For example, cortisol inhibits glucose and fat uptake by tissue cells so that more can be drawn on for immediate energy; it increases blood flow, it suppresses immune function by inhibiting the action of phagocytes and lymphocytes, and it inhibits inflammation of any damaged tissue that is sustained during the fight or 'flight' (e.g. Antoni 1987; Kemeny 2003). Blood cortisol levels are at their peak 20–40 minutes after a stressor and thus their levels have been used as stress indices in many studies.

The duration of some of the physiological responses to stress, such as the release of cortisol, influences whether the responses are beneficial to the organism or not. Prolonged release of cortisol can actually have negative effects as the suppression of the immune system caused by increased blood-circulating cortisol (serum or s-cortisol) can make a person vulnerable to infection. Abnormally high levels of cortisol as a result of an overactive pituitary gland are seen in people with Cushing's disease (typified by bloating, atypical facial hair). Cortisol levels are also known to be elevated in those with sleep deprivation. Interestingly, also, there is some suggestion of an association between cortisol and processses central to ageing. Animal research has shown that long-term exposure to such glucocorticoids damaged neurons in the hippocampal formation (Sapolsky 1996; Antoni 1987; Coburn-Litvak et al. 2003), an area of the brain crucial to learning and memory, hence a link being proposed with ageing (Sapolsky et al. 1986; Magri et al. 2006). Magri and

colleagues interpret the increased cortisol levels found in older individuals as evidence of a reduced ability to adapt to stress, and possibly related to cognitive declines associated with dementia. Although more research with humans is required to address such associations. Prolonged chronically elevated cortisol is seen in those with both major depression and Cushing's disease; however, in both of these conditions, the duration of the illness and not the age of the subjects predicted a progressive reduction in the volume of the hippocampus, determined by structural magnetic resonance imaging (McEwen 2008).

Prolonged release of adrenaline and noradrenaline can also have negative results, including suppressed cellular immune function, increases in heart rate and blood pressure, heartbeat irregularities (arrhythmia) and, potentially, hypertension and heart disease (Fredrickson and Matthews 1990; Clow 2001).

There may be positive steps that can be taken to reduce cortisol levels: for example, Steptoe and colleagues (2005) presented evidence of a relationship between positive psychology and lower (better) cortisol levels. They gathered data on daily 'moments' where positive affect had been experienced and found an association between the aggregated experiences, lower cortisol production and higher heart rate variability (showing higher parasympathetic activity), in response to a mental stress test. In contrast, in an earlier study the same group (Steptoe et al. 2004b) found that people with low self-esteem had larger cortisol responses to wakening in the morning, and higher natural killer (NK) cell responses to a mental stress test, as well as sleep problems.

Some people may indeed be more prone to physiological responses such as this, which again opens up opportunities for interventions (see Chapter 13 ☛). Others may experience an accumulation of stress, with consequences for their neuroendocrine and immune responses. This 'wear and tear' resulting from chronic or repeated stress has been described by McEwen (2008) as 'allostatic load'. In this the process of 'allostasis' (coined by Sterling and Eyer 1988) – a process of physiological response and adaptation to changes in our environment (e.g. noise, heat, overcrowding) or in our own physical states (due to illness, for example) – is overloaded, challenged and ultimately fails. Our physiological systems overrun due to repeated acute stressors perhaps or fail to shut off as we fail to adapt to chronic stress. It is the stress response that is creating the illness here, NOT the initial stressor, and in this regard psychological and social factors also play a role. Increased or dysregulated allostasis, referred to by McEwen as being 'stressed out' can indirectly lead to illness by virtue of behavioural and physiological responses to this state: e.g. health-damaging behaviour such as smoking, excessive comfort eating, sleep loss (e.g. Segestrom and Miller 2004). For a discussion of studies exploring physiological stress responses, including allostatic load, amongst child or adolescent samples, see Turner-Cobb (2014: 121–131),

HPA activation also elevates the production of growth hormones and prolactin, beta endorphins and encephalin, which are also found in the brain in response to stress. Beta endorphins have a useful analgesic (pain-killing) function and, as such, may explain why people can endure high levels of pain until they succeed in escaping stressful situations or completing demanding tasks: for example, soldiers with extreme injuries have been known to crawl long distances to receive help, and athletes can complete races in spite of damaged muscles (e.g. see Chapter 16 ☞ for a discussion of psychobiological theories of pain).

Overall, SAM and HPA systems can be thought of as providing total coverage with regards to the stress response, one via adrenaline for acute responses such as fight or flight, and one via cortisol for more sustained responses. These responses within the autonomic nervous system and the endocrine system work together to prepare our bodies to meet the demands of our environment. Our autonomic nervous system may work 'behind the scenes', but its functions are essential to basic human responses. Further understanding of the physical effects of stress are also seen in studies of immune responses where, as we will see below, cortisol again plays a crucial role.

Stress and immune function dysregulation

Declines or alterations in immune function have frequently been associated with the experience of stressful life events (e.g. Salovey et al. 2000; Ader 2001; Glaser and Kiecolt-Glaser 2005). As described in Chapter 8 ☞, the immune system is the body's defence against disease. Beyond the physical barrier of the skin, we contain certain types of cell that work to protect us from foreign organisms (e.g. bacteria, poisons, viruses, parasites) and abnormal cells (e.g. cancer cells) in the blood and lymphatic systems. These potential threats are known as antigens, and their threat can be met by either a general and rapid-response first line of defence (natural immunity), or a slower, more specifically targeted defence (specific immunity).

Immune cells are white blood cells of two major types, lymphocytes and phagocytes, which can be found in the lymphatic system, in the lymph nodes, spleen and in the blood circulation. The second of these, phagocytes, are attracted to sites of infection due to tissue releasing chemical messengers, and when they reach their destination they destroy abnormal cells or antigens by engulfing and consuming them. Phagocytes provide what is known as *non-specific immunity* in that they offer a first general line of defence, whereas lymphocytes offer *specific immunity* which follows the first natural responses. This consists of *cell-mediated immunity* via lymphocyte action which involves T cells made in the thymus (CD4+ T cells or helper T cells, and CD8+ cells or cytoxic T cells) and also *humoral-mediated immunity* involving B cells (memory and plasma cells). B cells label invading antigens in order to identify them for destruction and also, cleverly, 'remember' the antigen to enable early detection of future attacks. Their plasma produces antibodies, which remain in the blood circulation until the germ or disease is no longer present.

Natural killer (NK) cells also occur in body plasma and slow down the growth of abnormal cells (in cancer, for example) so that other immune responses can form an attack. As with phagocyte action, the NK cells provide non-specific natural immunity in that they defend against a wide variety of antigens, whereas the specific and acquired immunity provided by B and T cells is to those antigens to which they have been sensitised to (see Table 11.4 for a summary of T and B cell roles). Both the natural and the specific systems, involving NK, B and T cells, interact and help one another in the fight against infection or the growth of abnormal cells (see Chapter 8 ☞ for further details of the action of these cell types, and for consideration of some conditions associated with 'faulty' immune system function, i.e. diabetes, rheumatoid arthritis, multiple sclerosis).

T-helper cells also produce the chemical messengers (between the nervous and the immune system) known as pro-inflammatory and anti-inflammatory cytokines. Pro-inflammatory cytokines (for example interleukin-1 (IL-1)) are thought to signal to the brain when injury or infection has occurred and play a role in triggering

Table 11.4 Specific immunity and cell types

Humoral immunity: B cells	Cell-mediated immunity: T cells
Operate in the bloodstream	Operate at level of the cell
Work by releasing antibodies, which then destroy the antigen	Include memory, killer (NK), helper (CD4+) and suppressor T cells
Include memory cells	Mature in the thymus and not the bone marrow as other white blood cells do

inflammatory responses that facilitate, for example, wound repair. The SAM and HPA systems are involved here as catecholamines increase pro-inflammatory cytokine production, and glucocorticoids such as cortisol are known to inhibit it.

Therefore, the immune system is affected by the workings of the sympathetic nervous system and the endocrine responses: for example, the HPA system causes the release of hormones such as cortisol from the adrenal glands, and these hormones are thought to stimulate the immune system. Pro- and anti-inflammatory cytokines are produced by many cells in the body, for example B and T-helper cells of the immune system, and they are part of the signalling process to the brain that enables the stress responses. Their production is regulated by glucocorticoids and catecholamines, but while catecholamines increase pro-inflammatory cytokine production, glucocorticoids are known to inhibit it, with consequences of reducing immunity, i.e increasing susceptibility to infection or impairing wound healing (Sapolsky et al. 2000; Gouin et al. 2008). It is now generally accepted that there is communication both within and between the neuroendocrine and immune systems, with the brain providing an immuno-regulatory role (e.g. Blalock 1994).

What is important to health psychologists is that studies have found a link between the proliferation of B, T and NK cells and the subjective experience of stress; in other words, they have shown that psychological stress interferes with the workings of our body. One early study by Kiecolt-Glaser et al. (1984) found a significant reduction in NK cell activity among students prior to important end-of-term exams compared with those tested in mid-term. In addition, those students who reported feelings of loneliness plus a high number of recent stressful life events showed significantly less NK cell activity at both times than those students who were low in life events and low in loneliness. The findings of such experimental studies took a long time to be accepted, because they necessitated a paradigm shift from where the body was thought to operate independently of the mind to acceptance of the fact that psychological factors could influence immuno-competence (i.e. the degree to which our immune system functions effectively). Since the late 1970s, work in the area of psycho-neuroimmunology (the study of how psychosocial factors interact with the central and peripheral nervous system and the immune system) has gone from strength to strength, with improvements in technologies leading to even greater developments in the twenty-first century (compare the classic reviews of Herbert and Cohen 1993 and Cohen and Herbert 1996 with more recent work, e.g. Vingerhoets and Perski 2000; Vedhara and Irwin 2005; Ader 2007).

Age and immune function

It is generally accepted that immune function declines with age. This is sometimes referred to as 'immuno-senescence' whereby the innate system of an immediate immune response to invading germs, and also the slower-acting immune resistance response, declines (Gomez et al. 2008). There is evidence, from animal and human studies, suggesting that NK cell function becomes less efficient even though they are increased in number in older people, and that pro-inflammatory cytokine activity is also increased. The importance of these findings lies in the fact that they place older people at greater risk of severe reactions to infections, as seen in the influenza mortality statistics, for example, or in the complications of inflammation following wounds or surgery and slower healing. Additionally, Graham et al. (2006), in a review of the current evidence, suggested that in young adults stress can mimic the effects of ageing, and in older adults stress can exaggerate the effects of ageing on immune competence. While this is a relatively under-researched area, studies of caregivers are certainly pointing to significant associations, with Alzheimer's caregivers, for example, showing slower wound healing than age-matched non-caregivers, and reduced antibody responses to immunisation (Kiecolt Glaser et al. 1995; Damjanovic et al. 2007; Pederson-Fischer et al. 2009) (see also Chapter 15 ☞).

IN THE SPOTLIGHT

Can stress prevent your wounds healing?

Janice Kiecolt-Glaser and Ronald Glaser have spent many years researching the mind–body relationship, in particular the relationship between the experience of stress and immune function. While this chapter has presented evidence of the physiological pathways underlying stress responses, you may not have stopped to consider how stress might affect you, not just in terms of potentially increasing your risk of diseases such as heart disease but also in terms of more day-to-day health challenges, such as wounds received while participating in sporting activities. The Glasers have shown in many studies of elderly carers of people with Alzheimer's disease that healing of experimentally induced tissue wounds took significantly longer among carers than among healthy age-matched control participants. However, this may in part be due to coexisting ageing processes, so further studies have explored whether similar effects can be found in younger samples. Vedhara and colleagues in Bristol (2003) examined the healing rates of foot ulcers among 60 adults with type 2 diabetes. They found that healing was reduced in those who had shown high anxiety, depression or stress. Importantly, similar effects of stress have been found on the healing rates of otherwise healthy students who are given a small experimental skin wound at two different times, one during the summer holiday, the other prior to sitting exams. The wound inflicted before exams took on average three days longer to heal, and this was reflected by decreases in immunological status (Marucha et al. 1998). Broadbent et al. (2003) have confirmed the impairing effects of high stress and worry levels on wound healing where wounds were not experimental but real, i.e. participants were recovering from hernia surgery.

Why do such findings matter? Think of your own stress levels; think of your likelihood of becoming wounded in sport or other activity; or of the potential of facing surgery in the future. Think of current concern about MRSA (methicillin-resistant *Staphylococcus aureus*) and *C. difficile* infections in hospitals and in the community. Effectively dealing with your own stress is important, not only in keeping you healthy but also in helping you to heal and recover when and if you become ill or injured or require surgery.

Photo 11.3 Stress has been shown to influence the healing process

Source: Shutterstock.com/Moriz.

Stress and cardiovascular reactivity

There is also a reasonably consistent body of psychobiological evidence showing that stress can cause alterations in physiological responses, with arousal of the sympathetic nervous system (*and* deactivation of the parasympathetic response, see Brindle et al.'s 2014 review) being greater in some people than in others. This 'reactivity hypothesis' first proposed by Krantz and Manuck (1984) describes how genetic or environmental factors combine to influence a person's vulnerability to a physiological response following stress and to negative emotions that can be detrimental to their health, particularly their arterial health, implicated in heart disease. Reactivity, for example periods of elevated heart rate or blood pressure, has been observed both in laboratory settings where individuals are exposed to acute or repeated stress, such as mental arithmetic tasks or public speaking, and in real-life settings where people face occupational challenge or marital conflict, for example. There are some pointers towards ethnic variations in reactivity, for example, that African Americans tend to show greater reactivity where Asian or European Americans may not, although whether this is biologically or environmentally explained remains unclear. Whether or not this CVR (cardiovascular reactivity) is related to the development of disease, or indeed disease progression, is something of great interest to psychobiologists and psychologists alike (e.g. Linden et al. 2003; Johnston 2007; Brindle et al. 2014). The whole process of physiological arousal, from before an event (e.g. anticipatory responses), during (as suggested by reactivity work), and after, in terms of perseverative thoughts or ruminative responses that may maintain physiological changes, warrants further attention (Brosschot et al. 2006). Reactivity, which is thought to occur during an event (laboratory or real-life stressor), is perhaps only part of the physiological story, given also findings that under-activation can be harmful also (Brindle et al. 2014).

Evidence of the influence of psychological stress upon immune function, or upon cardiovascular reactivity has given scientists the opportunity to assess 'objective' indices of the stress response alongside, and in relation to, subjective stress reports. For example, V. Burns et al. (2003) examined the effects of minor and major life events on the antibody response to influenza vaccination among a sample of undergraduate students. Students were followed up over five months, and results found that participants with low antibody levels at five months reported having experienced significantly more life events in the intervening time following vaccination. Similar findings have been reported among those caring for a spouse with Alzheimer's disease (a chronic stressor), whereby their antibody responses to flu vaccination are lower than that of non-carer controls (e.g. Kiecolt-Glaser et al. 1996; Vedhara et al. 1999), although studies of younger carers have not consistently supported such findings (e.g. Vedhara et al. 2002).

Evidence of physiological correlates of occupational stress have also been reported: for example, Clays et al. (2007) found that ambulatory blood pressure at work, home and even while asleep was significantly higher in workers with high job strain than in those with lower strain.

Students are often used as participants in stress research due to the 'occupational hazard' of exposure to potentially stressful patterns of assessment and examinations. Chandrashekara et al. (2007), for example, found that medical students with high anxiety and poorer emotional adaptability about end-of-term exams showed lower levels of an inflammatory cytokine (tumour necrosis factor alpha – TNF-α) than students with lower anxiety and greater emotional adaptability. The effect was not seen for mid-term exams, similar to that reported in the 1984 study of Kiecolt-Glaser et al. mentioned above. Such situation-specific responses contrasts with other findings where exposure to non-academic stressors contributed to a delayed *increase* in circulating cytokine levels (Steptoe et al. 2001). More research on these responses is warranted, particularly studies which contrast stressor types and contexts, as well as consider other individual difference variables that may contribute to stress reactivity (see Chapter 12 ☞). Importantly, it appears that extreme cardiovascular responses at either end of the spectrum, i.e. blunted or exaggerated, signal system dysregulation that can negatively impact upon health and behavioral outcomes (Lovallo 2011). In terms of the implications of such findings for psychological intervention (see Chapter 13 ☞), there is some evidence that individuals can be 'trained' using classical or operant conditioning procedures to alter their immune response to threat (see Miller and Cohen 2001 for a meta-analytic review of 85 studies of psychological interventions and immune functioning). However, further work, including better controlled studies that also address potential mediators of any shown effects, is needed.

It should have become clear during the course of this chapter that stress is not a unitary process but a highly complex one. The experience of stress is, to varying degrees, dependent on stimulus events (acute or chronic, physical or psychological), on internal representations of events, including a person's appraisals and emotional responses, and on the nature and extent of physiological and behavioural activation that follows. Stress indisputably has a strong psychological component, and furthermore stress responses change over time as a person adjusts (or not) to their situation. Given all the evidence reviewed above, it is hardly surprising that measuring stress is complex, as described in ISSUES below.

ISSUES

Can stress be measured?

As with any concept, how stress is defined influences how it is measured. We have described three broad ways of thinking about stress – as a stimulus, as the result of cognitive appraisal and as a physiological response – and each of these views leads to different forms of assessment.

Measuring stress as a stimulus is problematic, given what was described earlier as weaknesses in the life events approach to stress – if many of the life events are irrelevant to the responder because of their age or life stage, does this mean that they are less stressed because their potential total scores are reduced? Additionally, people generally search for explanations for how they feel or for events that have happened to them – it is common, for example, for people to report many life events in the lead up to a heart attack – so measuring retrospective accounts of life events or even smaller 'hassles' may in this instance lead to inflated estimates of the role that stress plays in illness. Some researchers argue for greater validity of measures, taking a daily hassles (and uplifts) approach rather than a time-lagged retrospective. However, daily assessment places many demands on respondents, and in fact reviews of findings from studies using a life events approach has found the SSRS to have good predictive utility in terms of stress-related symptoms (Scully et al. 2000).

Stress is based upon appraisal, which involves stimulus, cognition and emotion, and therefore it is necessary to measure, not only the events, but also people's appraisals of the event, their emotions, their perceived resources and their perceived coping potential. Stress appraisals tend to be assessed by simply asking people how they feel or getting them to complete a standardised psychometric assessment. One commonly employed example is the Perceived Stress Scale, which assesses the degree to which life situations are appraised as stressful (Cohen et al. 1983). Examples include 'In the last month, how often have you been upset because of something that happened unexpectedly?' and 'In the last month, how often have you found that you could not cope with all the things you had to do?' (scored as 0 = never; 1 = almost never; 2 = sometimes; 3 = fairly often; 4 = very often). Higher scores are indicative of greater perceived stress. The stressor, or the event being considered, is not specified in the standard wording of this scale, thus general appraisals are assessed only. Some studies, however, reword the PSS to record event-specific stress appraisals, e.g. 'In the last weeks since receiving your diagnosis…'.

In order to assess secondary appraisal processes central to Lazarus's model, measures of personal resource, such as perceived control, self-efficacy or perceived social support, which are thought to moderate, mediate or 'buffer' the stress–outcome relationship, can be employed (see Chapter 12 ☞). Regardless of the number of assessment tools used, however, there are inherent limitations in assessing an experience as subjective as stress. For example, distress is likely to bias the answers one gives to questions regarding the nature of the stressor, or regarding the number of recent life events experienced, and is also likely to influence the resources one considers to have available. Stress is also quite circular – our mood and appraisals may increase our feelings of stress, which in turn will influence our appraisals and our mood! Aspects of the stress experience interact, therefore research studies need well-designed, well-controlled longitudinal studies if they are to disentangle precursors of a stress response from the stress response itself.

In terms of assessing individual responses considered to be indicative of stress, a measure of distress or more specific mood states (e.g. anger, depression or anxiety), for example, the general health questionnaire (GHQ; Goldberg and Williams 1988) is a commonly used tool available in different validated lengths. The 28-item version measures a combination of emotional states (anxiety, insomnia, social dysfunction, severe depression and somatic symptoms), whereas the more common, and perhaps more user-friendly in terms of time demands, 12-item version does not distinguish between each of these, although the GHQ-12, still provides a sensitive measure of psychiatric disorder. Respondents indicate whether they have experienced a particular symptom or behaviour 'less than usual', 'no more than usual', 'rather more than usual' or 'much more than usual', and example items include 'have you recently... been able to concentrate on whatever you're doing? been feeling unhappy and depressed?. . . felt constantly under strain?'.

Stress as a response can be measured using physiological and physical indices such as heart rate, blood pressure, galvanic skin response, levels of adrenaline, noradrenaline and cortisol levels in the blood, urine, or saliva, other indicators of increased cortisol levels such as reflected decreases in salivary secretory immunoglobulins (Sig-A), or other immune responses such as described earlier in relation to helper T cells, B or NK cell activity. Measurement of these aspects of the stress experience require specific skills and expertise in their collection, storage, analysis and interpretation and are more often gathered in laboratory-based stress research than perhaps in naturalistic settings, although ambulatory measures of blood pressure or heart rate are available. Even these so-called 'objective' measures of stress are open to question, however, as some people may be more 'stress-responsive' or 'stress-reactive' than others (Felsten 2004; Johnston 2007) and thus, for example, the extent of heart-rate or blood-pressure increase seen in response to threat is not universal, due to genetic differences, variations in central nervous system activity (Lovallo 2011) or individual differences such as those described in Chapter 12 ☞.

In spite of challenges of measurement, a vast amount of research is conducted in this field that acknowledges that since stress is a subjective experience, measuring it cannot be expected to be an exact science. As Kasl (1996: 21) stated: 'What we have, at best, are indirect and partial indicators of the stress process, and these indicators tend to measure both too much and not enough'. As an illustration of this, he refers to the perceived stress scale, which measures 'too much' in that it correlates significantly with depression and measures 'not enough' in that it does not assess secondary appraisal processes, emotions or indicators of physiological reactivity. It is hard to satisfy all the needs of 'sufficient' assessment in the stress domain as hopefully this chapter has shown. Many empirical research studies have acknowledged the challenge and employ multiple methods of assessment; however, this has costs in terms of participant demands and potentially response rates. A further challenge to researchers therefore is deciding which part of the picture to examine!

The final challenge in the domain of stress research is that of establishing causality between stressful events and illness, ideally via immune or other physiological pathways. In the final section of this chapter therefore we introduce you to some of the evidence of such associations.

The stress and illness link

In Chapter 8 ☞, the workings of the nervous, respiratory, digestive, cardiovascular and immunological systems were described in some detail and the reader was introduced to common diseases associated with these bodily systems. This final section takes a closer look at the role of stress in activating these systems with resulting implications for the development of illness. First, however, it is worth reminding ourselves that there are different ways of viewing the relationship between stress and illness.

The direct route

As described above, stress can produce physiological changes that may lead to the development of illness, particularly in instances where the stress is chronic

(Cacioppo et al. 1998; Smith et al. 2003; Johnston 2007). However, there is so much individual variation in responding to stressors that the direct route is not a straightforward one, as reviewed below.

The indirect routes

People, by virtue of their behavioural responses to stress such as smoking, eating habits and drinking, predispose themselves to disease (see Chapter 3 ☞).

People, by virtue of certain personality traits, predispose themselves to disease by the manner in which they respond to stress (see Chapter 12 ☞).

People experiencing stress are more likely to use health services than people who are not under stress. Stress can produce symptoms such as anxiety, fatigue, insomnia and shakiness, which people seek treatment for but which are not in themselves illnesses (see Chapter 12 ☞).

However, we should bear in mind a quote of Sapolsky's while reading the next sections: 'everything bad in human health now is not caused by stress, nor is it in our power to cure ourselves of our worst medical nightmares merely by reducing stress and thinking healthy thoughts full of courage and spirit and love. Would it were so. And shame on those who sell this view' (1994).

There is a moderate relationship between stress and illness. We address a selection of the many illnesses that have been found to have an association with stress below, with the psychosocial influences upon, or moderators of, the stress response being discussed in Chapter 12 ☞.

Stress and the common cold

Various researchers (Cohen et al. 1993a, 1993b; Stone et al. 1993; Cohen 2005) have conducted experiments where volunteers submit themselves to artificial exposure to respiratory rhinoviruses of the common cold (using nasal drops mainly). Participants then remain in a controlled environment for varying lengths of time while researchers wait to see whether colds or infections develop more often among those who received viral drops than among the control subjects, who received saline drops. Volunteers who had reported more chronic negative life events, perceived stress, negative affect and poor coping responses prior to the experiment were more likely to develop signs of respiratory infection and

subsequent colds than both control subjects and experimental subjects with low-level life stress. This is known as a dose–response relationship. In Cohen's studies perceived stress and negative affect predicted infection rates, whereas negative life events did not predict infection itself but predicted the probability of illness among those who became infected. These associations persisted when health behaviour such as smoking and alcohol consumption or personality variable such as self-esteem and introversion–extroversion were controlled for (Cohen et al. 2003). It also emerged that longer duration of the event was more likely to be followed by infection than severe but short-lived stress (Cohen et al. 1998).

Although the studies above were predominantly lab-based using artificially induced viruses, there is reasonably convincing evidence of a relationship between chronic stress (as opposed to severity) and upper respiratory infections – the common cold, and influenza (Takkouche et al. 2001; Marsland et al. 2002). Takkouche and colleagues importantly considered the naturally acquired common cold in a one-year prospective cohort study among the faculty and staff of a Spanish university (N = 1,149). Like the laboratory-based work before it, they found that the occurrence of stressful life events, perceived stress, and positive and negative affect were all related to the occurrence of common cold. Prospective studies with clinical populations facing 'natural' stressors will inevitably improve our understanding of the stress–immune function–illness link.

Stress and coronary heart disease

Coronary heart disease (CHD) is a disease of the **cardiovascular** system that develops over time in response to a range of factors, such as family history and lifestyle factors (e.g. smoking and diet; see Chapter 3 ☞). As described in Chapter 8 ☞, the cause of CHD is a gradual narrowing of blood vessels that supply the heart. In situations of acute stress, activation of the sympathetic nervous system causes increased cardiac output and the blood vessels to constrict, thus restricting blood flow, so blood pressure increases. This can cause

> **cardiovascular**
> pertaining to the heart and blood vessels.

damage to the artery walls, a process that is contributed to further by stress-induced adrenaline and noradrenaline output. If blood pressure remains raised for prolonged periods of time, a person is said to have hypertension, a contributory factor in CHD.

Repeated or chronic stress also activates the sympathetic nervous system's release of fatty acids into the bloodstream, which, if not utilised for energy expenditure, are metabolised by the liver into cholesterol. A build-up of cholesterol is highly implicated in the 'furring up' of arteries or atheroma (the laying down of fatty plaques on artery walls), and a key feature of heart disease is this atherosclerosis. Furthermore, the release of catecholamines during the stress process also increases the stickiness of blood platelets (thrombocytes), which elevates the risk of a clot forming or thrombosis as they adhere to the artery walls with the fatty plaques, thus making the 'passageway' even narrower for blood to flow through. Inflammatory processes, involving pro-inflammatory cytokines such as IL-6 (interleukin-6), are also implicated in this process (see Chapter 12 ☞ in relation to hostility). If reduced blood flow causes a clot to form, it could then travel through a person's arteries until it becomes so big as to form a blockage (occlusion) and, depending on whether it blocks an artery to the brain or to the heart, this will lead to either a stroke or a heart attack – both major causes of mortality worldwide. In terms of acute coronary syndromes such as heart attack and stroke, the evidence that stress plays a role in precipitating the event is good. For example, work and home stress, financial problems and past year major life events were significantly associated with heart attack in a huge cross-cultural, 52-country study of more than 11,000 heart attack survivors and over 13,000 controls, the INTER-HEART study (Rosengren et al. 2004). In terms of processes by which this may be achieved, other studies have found that among those with pre-existing CVD, an acute stressor – for example, an anger outburst, or a depressive episode – may trigger the rupture of atherosclerotic plaques, which disrupt blood flow and cause a heart attack or a stroke (Sheps 2007).

In terms of the development of CHD, stress does appear to contribute to various related conditions, such as hypertension, elevated serum lipids (fats in the blood) and smoking behaviour, an acknowledged risk factor (e.g. Ming et al. 2004). Cardiovascular reactivity during acute stress (i.e. increased heart rate or blood pressure) has been implicated in various disease processes, such as

the extent and progression of carotid artery atherosclerosis, and the emergence of coronary heart disease itself (Smith et al. 2003). Reactivity, however, in itself is not 'disease', but a risk factor (Johnston 2007). Experimental studies of reactivity in response to aversive or rewarding stimuli have speculated that the individuals who responded to aversive tasks with sizeable heart-rate and blood pressure increases (high reactives) but who showed no difference from controls in subjective ratings of the tasks, had greater activation of the hypothalamic system and neuroendocrine responses such as those described earlier. Indeed, high-reactive participants showed larger noradrenaline increases in response to both types of task than low-reactive participants, and larger cortisol increases to the aversive task but not to the reward task (Lovallo et al. 1990). This highlights the importance of considering the type of task. Also important is finding that effects persist outwith the artificial laboratory setting, as found, for example, by Johnston and colleagues (Johnston 2007). In this study laboratory-based reactivity was reflected in similar increases in heart-rate reactivity when individuals were exposed to the real-life stressor of public speaking. Furthermore, in relation to ongoing stress of an occupational nature, job strain was linked to progression of coronary atherosclerosis over a three-year period in a large sample of women employees (Wang et al. 2007). In another study, ambulatory blood pressure at work and at home (and even while asleep!) was significantly higher in workers with high job strain than in those with lower strain (Clays et al. 2007). It is worth noting that most research into the physical consequences of carer stress (see also Chapter 15 ☞) have examined the increased vulnerability to disease resulting from immune changes rather than actual disease development; however, raised levels of the pro-inflammatory cytokine interleukin-6 found among caregivers is actually at a level considered a risk factor for cardiovascular disease (Kiecolt-Glaser et al. 2003).

The findings reviewed here point to a need to distinguish between the role stress plays in triggering or maintaining certain risk behaviours which provide the 'indirect' link with chronic manifestations of CHD, e.g. smoking and arterial disease; the role chronic stress plays in the activation of physiological risk factors and in progression of existing disease; and the role played perhaps by more acute stress events in the potentiating of acute coronary events, such as heart attacks (Johnston 2002, 2007; Strike and Steptoe 2005; Sheps 2007).

Speculation as to the role of stress in the development of actual disease has abounded for many years: for example, Rosch (1994), in an editorial in the journal *Stress Medicine*, pointed to the importance of distinguishing between causal factors and contributing factors when considering disease, arguing that the 'true cause' of any disease is biomedical and that behavioural or social factors such as smoking or stress are not 'true' causes but contributors. This conclusion has received some challenges from longitudinal research in the years since – with some evidence of a causal role for stress reactivity, inflammatory responses, and also negative emotions (depression primarily) in relation to acute coronary events and to CHD. For example, in the field of occupational stress, Kuper and Marmot (2003) found, within a cohort of over 10,000 UK civil servants, that those with low decision latitude and high demands were at the highest risk of developing CHD over 11 years. However, an American study with a ten-year follow-up found no association between job strain and CHD (Eaker et al. 2004). A review of studies (including those two referred to above) with long-term follow-ups ranging from 5 to almost 20 years (Byrne and Espnes 2008) suggests that overall findings are persuasive, but that more rigorous and prospective research is required.

Finally, just as reactivity can be considered as a 'psychophysiological trait' that is stable within any given individual across time and events, it can also be considered as a moderator, in that evidence suggests that being reactive or not will moderate any effect of stress upon disease risk (Segerstrom and Smith 2006). Furthermore, as discussed in Chapter 12 (☛), stress reactivity can itself be influenced by other traits, such as anger, and therefore reactivity is considered within a broader personological model. However reactivity is considered, it is a factor that seems unwise to ignore. We know nowadays that the mind and body interact, and if into this we add individual 'risk' or 'protective' behaviours (see Chapters 3–4 (☛)), we can begin to understand the complexity of influences upon disease processes such as those subsumed under the broad heading of 'heart disease'.

Stress and cancer

Cancer, like heart disease, develops slowly and begins with mutation of cells and the development of generally undetectable neoplasms, which eventually develop into spreadable tumours (i.e. the cells metastasise).

Predominantly animal research has demonstrated associations between environmental stressors (electric shocks, surgery) and increased susceptibility to tumour development; however, human evidence is limited. Forms of cancer vary hugely in terms of rates of growth, spread and prognosis; in terms of their sensitivity to neuroendocrine or immune system changes (Greer 1999), and in terms of available treatment options. Accordingly, it is perhaps unwise to expect stress to exert uniform effects, if any, on different forms of cancer and in fact the general consensus is that there is no clear link. For example a meta-analysis of 46 studies investigating the association between psychosocial factors, including life event stress, and the development of breast cancer concluded that life events were not predictive, but rather a combination of risk factors and psychosocial factors were (McKenna et al. 1999). This is consistent with findings of a meta-analysis specifically examining the predictive role of life events in breast cancer development (Petticrew et al. 1999).

However, caution is needed regarding the role of the individual and their cognitions, emotions and stress or coping responses in cancer progression although there is some evidence of direct and indirect effects. For example, stress may directly affect tumour cell mutation by slowing down the cell repair process, possibly by virtue of stress effects on hormonal activation and the release of glucocorticoids, or by influences on the immune system's production of lymphocytes (see Rosch 1996 for a review of both animal and human research). Furthermore, a review of 24 studies reported that 19 studies showed an association between depression and faster breast cancer progression (Spiegel and Giese-Davis 2003), although note therefore that 5 did not. In terms of life events and progression, Palesh et al. (2007) presented data from 94 women with metastatic or recurrent breast cancer tumours and found that those with no retrospective reports of traumatic life events, or lesser stressful events, had a significantly longer disease-free interval than women with experience of traumatic events, or of stressful events (median of 62 months as compared to median of 31 months). The women who had experienced traumatic events, or lesser stressful events, did not significantly differ from those reporting no stress events, in terms of current age, age at diagnosis, medical history, relationship status, cortisol levels, site of metastases, and disease status indicators that may have offered alternative explanations for the findings. It is worth noting, however, that the reported events had not necessarily occurred in the intervening time period (i.e. between first diagnosis and recurrence) and therefore some had potentially played a role in the initial cancer. The authors had hypothesised that the mechanisms through which stress exerted any effect on recurrence was likely to relate to HPA function, yet cortisol did not differ between groups. This study is limited by its retrospective nature and challenged by the findings of a five-year prospective study of women diagnosed with breast cancer where recurrence was not increased in those who had experienced one or more extremely stressful events in the year prior to diagnosis or in the five years subsequently (Graham et al. 2002). This latter finding is more robust: it involves a larger sample of women, is prospective in nature, and more clearly controls for biological prognostic indicators such as tumour size and the extent to which the cancer involved the lymph nodes.

Many other studies have explored whether personality, coping style (particularly one that is passive and indicative of helplessness and hopelessness) and mood affect cancer outcome and have provoked some controversy. These are addressed in Chapter 12 (☞).

Stress and bowel disease

Two diseases of the bowel have been investigated in terms of their association with stress, whereby stress is examined as an exacerbating factor rather than one involved in the condition's aetiology (see also Chapter 8 (☞). First, *irritable bowel syndrome* (IBS) is a disorder of the lower large intestine characterised by abdominal pain and prolonged periods of either diarrhoea or constipation, although no organic disease or obvious physical cause is identifiable. During stressful episodes, the reactivity of the gut is greater and symptoms such as bloatedness, pain or diarrhoea increase and may be maintained by stress or anxiety (Naliboff *et al*, 1998; Spence and Moss-Morris 2007). A second bowel disease is *inflammatory bowel disease* (IBD), which can be subdivided into Crohn's disease (CD) and ulcerative colitis (UC). Both these diseases are typified by pain and diarrhoea, which worsen and improve in an alternating and disruptive manner, but UC typically involves inflammation of the lower colon, whereas CD can occur anywhere in the gastrointestinal tract and is seen as inflammation of the outer intestinal wall. Both diseases, as with IBS, were originally thought to be psychosomatic, with some

limited evidence that stress plays a role in their aetiology. More likely, however, is that stress may exacerbate the condition. For example, Duffy et al. (1991) examined exposure to stressful events among 124 individuals with IBD and found that over a period of six months, those exposed to stress showed a two- to fourfold increase in clinical disease episodes compared with those participants who did not report stressful incidents. When disease-related and disease-unrelated events were distinguished (on the basis of patient report), the relationship between stress and illness was clearest when the reported events were health-related but not necessarily IBD-specific. However, when the authors examined the time lag between the event and disease activity (i.e. a stressful event preceding disease activity), they found that concurrent relationships were strongest and, in fact, disease activity was predictive of subsequent levels of stress rather than vice versa. Such bidirectional relationships between variables makes the disentangling of issues of cause and effect difficult, although other evidence of stress being associated with symptom 'flare-ups' does exist (Searle and Bennett 2001).

As previously mentioned, individual variation in stress-responsivity/reactivity may explain mixed research findings. For example, in a study of 31 IBS patients who provided repeated measures of daily stress and daily symptomatology (so that the associations between stress and symptoms over time could be examined), an association between stress and the onset or exacerbation of symptoms only emerged in half of the sample (Dancey et al. 1998). If there were a direct stress–symptomatology link the proportion showing this relationship would have been higher. Symptom perception and reactivity can also be influenced by personal characteristics of somatisation and attention to internal organs, features often associated with neuroticism (see Chapter 9 (☞).

Stress and HIV/AIDS

Over the past 30 years, AIDS has spread throughout the world to become a major cause of death in Africa and a leading cause of death elsewhere (see Chapter 3 (☞). AIDS (acquired immune deficiency syndrome) is a syndrome characterised by opportunistic infections and other malignant diseases, caused by acquisition of HIV (human immunodeficiency virus) which was first identified in 1984. The nature of the HIV virus and how it infiltrates the body is described in Chapter 8 ☞, but, crucially, in terms of potential stress for the sufferer, as a lentivirus (i.e. slow-acting), it can be many years before an HIV-infected individual develops AIDS. As well as being life-threatening, the disease label itself can be psychologically stressful due to the continued social stigma attached to the disease (due primarily to its early associations with homosexuality, drug abuse and sexual promiscuity). Petrak et al. (2001) found that self-disclosure of HIV status to family (53 per cent of sample had told their family) and to friends (79 per cent had told close friends) was significantly influenced by wanting to protect others from distress and out of fear of discrimination. Living with this illness is inherently stressful, and there is evidence that stress plays an influential role in disease progression, particularly when moderating variables such as depression, social support and coping responses are taken into consideration. For example, a meta-analysis (Zorrilla et al. 1996) suggested that depressive symptoms, but not stress experience, were associated with increased speed of symptom onset in HIV-positive individuals, and that stress, but not depressive symptoms, was associated with reduced NK cell count. Similarly, progression to AIDS was found to be quicker in those experiencing a build-up of stressful life events, depressive symptoms and low social support (Leserman et al. 1999). In a meta-analysis of cognitive behavioural interventions targeting negative emotions, benefits were obtained for individual immune status (Crepaz et al. 2008), which is an important finding for those working with this population. For many within this disease group, the loss of a partner through AIDS is a reality. This itself has been found to impact upon disease progression over subsequent years (Kemeny et al. 1994). Social support, or lack or loss of it, is discussed in Chapter 12 ☞; however, social support in the form of providing care to a loved one is considered in Chapter 15 ☞.

SUMMARY

This chapter set out to provide a definition of stress in order to show that there is no such thing as a simple definition! Stress is generally examined in one of three ways: as a stimulus that focuses on the external event (stressors); as a transaction between the external event and the individual experiencing it; and as an array of physiological responses that are manifested when an individual faces demanding events. The transactional psychological model of stress highlights the crucial role of appraisal, and points to the importance of considering the individual in the stress experience. Many different events may be appraised as stressful; stressor events can be acute or chronic in their manifestation and the responses they require highly variable.

We provided examples of these, drawing both from studies of occupational stress, something that most of us will experience at some time, and of chronic health conditions (which many of us will also experience at some point!). The physiological pathways by which stress has been shown to affect health status were examined. While some evidence of a direct effect of stress on the development of illness exists, many of stress's effects are either indirect, for example via an influence on behaviour, or are more evident during the illness experience, when individual differences in personality, cognitions and social resources become important to outcome. These moderating variables are the focus of the next chapter.

Further reading

Key texts

Sapolsky, R.M. (2004). *Why Zebras Don't Get Ulcers*. New York: Henry Holt & Co.

Although dated in terms of empirical material covered, this remains an engaging read with excellent coverage of both physiological and psychological theories of stress. You will, however, need to supplement reading of this book with reading of up-to-date empirical studies such as those referred to in this chapter!

Ader, R. (2007). *Psychoneuroimmunology*, 4th edn. New York: Academic Press.

An essential read for any student wanting to get to grips with the fundamental science of psychoneuroimmunology (the processes, mechanisms and effects of behavioural, neural, endocrine and immune responses) while not getting put off by hard-core biological language. Written for an interdisciplinary audience including behavioural scientists, psychobiologists, neuroscientists and immunologists, this book is an accessible review of the current state of knowledge.

Anisman, H. (2014). *An Introduction to Stress and Health*. London: Sage.

This recent addition to my bookshelf is a very useful and informed one. It addresses the psychosocial aspects of stress but particularly focused on the (neuro)biological correlates of stress and their association with physical health conditions, emotional well-being and mood, drawing from a large, up-to-date body of research.

Key articles

Lazarus, R.S. (1993). From psychological stress to the emotions: a history of changing outlooks. *Annual Review of Psychology*, 44: 1–21.

This article provides a useful account of the transactional model of stress and the developments in thinking about appraisal in terms of relations with emotions. Although from the 1990s, this remains a key theoretical paper.

Byrne, D.G. and Espnes, G.A. (2008). Occupational stress and cardiovascular disease. *Stress & Health*, 24: 231–8.

This review paper is found in a special issue addressing 'Stress and the Heart'. This paper reviews evidence of the role played by work stress and coronary risk, hypertension and heart disease and concludes that 'Taken broadly, the evidence is supportive of postulated links', although further prospective evidence would be welcome.

Brindle, R.C., Ginty, A.T., Phillips, A.C. and Carroll, D. (2014). A tale of two mechanisms: A meta-analytic approach toward understanding the autonomic basis of cardiovascular reactivity to acute psychological stress. *Psychophysiology*, 51: 964-976.

Kiecolt-Glaser, J.K. (2006). Stress, age and immune function: toward a lifespan approach. *Journal of Behavioral Medicine*, 29: 389–400.

This well-written paper catalogues the key findings relating to the relationship between age and immune function, stress and immune function (considering both acute and chronic stressors), and the interaction between stress, age and the immune function, with a particular, but not exclusive, focus on older adults.

www.stressinamerica.org

This useful website, although drawing from annual USA surveys of Stress, describes and presents a wealth of material relevant to this and the subsequent chapter in terms of: changing life pressures and stress, responses to stress and how they differ by age, gender, or even whether a parent or not; the effects of stress on health behaviours such as drinking or smoking, and also factors that moderate stress, such as social support (see also Chapter 12 ☞).

For open-access student resources specifically written to complement this textbook and support your learning, please visit **www.pearsoned.co.uk/morrison**

Chapter 12
Stress and illness moderators

Learning outcomes

By the end of this chapter, you should have an understanding of:

- coping theory, definitions and the distinction between coping styles, strategies and goals
- how coping responses influence the manner in which stress may affect health outcomes
- aspects of personality which influence stress appraisal, coping response and illness outcomes
- aspects of individual cognitions which influence stress appraisal, coping response and illness outcomes
- aspects of emotion, which influence stress appraisal, coping response and illness outcomes
- the nature and function of social support and how it influences stress appraisal, coping responses and illness outcomes

Millions of Britons have no close friends
(*The Guardian*, 12 August 2014)

A survey, 'The Way We Are Now 2014' conducted by Relate of 5,778 people aged 16 or over and living in England, Wales, Northern Ireland or Scotland, found that one in ten reported not having a close friend. Extrapolating from that to the UK population, that equates to about 4.7 million people. That's a lot of people. Furthermore, almost one in five (19 per cent) had never or rarely 'felt loved' in the two weeks before completing the survey. Whilst it is obviously encouraging that the vast majority of those surveyed *did* have a close friend or felt loved, the findings suggest that there is a significant and sizeable minority who feel – what for many of us would be unimaginable – lonely and unloved. We know from many studies that social support and feeling loved is a powerful predictor of well-being, both from data gathered from couples, and from single people talking about their family relationships and friendships. More people who were married or cohabiting felt 'good about themselves' (81 per cent) compared to those who were single (69 per cent), (although the quality of any relationship significantly influences this first figure). Another factor influencing satisfaction with friendship is gender, with females more likely to describe their friendships as good or very good (81 per cent) than men (73 per cent).

As we describe in this chapter many factors influence our response to stress and our coping ability, but social support is an important one, whatever your age, gender or culture, with effects not only on emotional well-being but also potentially, as we will report below, physical well-being.

Chapter outline

The preceding chapter established that stress can be considered as both an objective and subjective experience, and evidence was provided as to physiological and immunological pathways by which stress may influence health and illness status. However, not all people will become ill when exposed to stressful events, which raises questions of great fascination to health psychologists. What aspects of the individual, their stress responses, or their stress-coping resources and actions moderate or influence the negative impact of stress on health? This chapter will provide some answers to this question by providing evidence of psychosocial influences on stress outcomes. Individual differences in personality, cognitions and emotions (both positive and negative) have direct and indirect effects on stress outcomes. Indirectly, they affect outcome by influencing our cognitive and behavioural responses to any stressful demand placed on us – these responses are known as coping. In addition, aspects of social relationships and social support act as external resource variables, which also directly and indirectly influence the negative impact of stress. By the end of the chapter, the complexities of the relationship between stress, health and illness should be clear.

In Chapter 11 ☞ we described stress theories, acute and chronic stressors and the broad theoretical links between stress and disease. We also presented evidence relating to direct pathways by which physiological and immune processes affect the stress–disease relationship. As there is so much individual variation in responding to stressors, this chapter focuses more on the indirect routes introduced in Chapter 11 ☞, i.e. how different personalities, beliefs and emotions, and social relationships influence the stress–illness relationship, either directly, or via an effect on cognitive and behavioural coping responses.

It is unlikely that anyone can avoid stress and, certainly, as indicated previously, some stress is good for us in that it enhances performance (eustress e.g. Gibbons et al. 2008). However, stress is more commonly considered as negative appraisals and negative emotions, which elicit a desire to reduce such thoughts and feelings in order to restore a sense of harmony or balance in our lives. Lazarus's transactional model of stress and coping (Lazarus 1966; Lazarus and Folkman 1984) was introduced in the previous chapter and highlights the crucial role of appraisal of events. Individual differences in

appraisal in turn influences the cognitive, emotional and behavioural response to them, i.e. the coping response. What exactly do we mean by coping?

Coping defined

Although over thirty definitions of coping exist, Lazarus's transactional model (see Figure 11.1) has had the most profound impact on the conceptualisation of coping (cf. Lazarus 1993a, 1993b; Lazarus and Folkman 1984). According to this model, psychological stress results from an unfavourable person–environment fit: in other words, when there is a perceived mismatch between demands and resources as perceived by an individual in a specific situation (Lazarus and Folkman 1984; Lazarus 1993a). Individuals are required to alter either the stressor or how they interpret it in order to make it appear more favourable. This volitional (purposeful) effort is called coping.

Coping involves a constellation of cognitions and behaviour that arise from the primary and secondary appraisals of events, and the emotions attached to them (see Chapter 11 ☞). In turn, our appraisals are influenced by many factors, not least of which is the extent to which we perceive the event as interfering with our personal life goals (e.g. to succeed in school, to avoid conflict, to be independent, Elliot et al. 1997, 2011). Coping is *anything* a person does to reduce the impact of a perceived or actual stressor, and, because appraisals elicit emotions, coping can operate to either alter or reduce the negative emotions, or it can directly target the 'objective' stressor. Coping does not inevitably succeed in eliminating the stressor, but it may manage the stressor by various means: for example, through mastering new skills to deal with it, tolerating it, reappraising it or minimising it. Coping therefore is volitional because it has the aim of trying to achieve adaptation: it is consequently a dynamic, learned (we hopefully learn from past coping successes and failures) and purposeful process.

Cohen and Lazarus (1979) described five main coping functions, each of which contribute to successful adaptation to a stressor:

1. reducing harmful external conditions;

2. tolerating or adjusting to negative events;

3. maintaining a positive self-image;

4. maintaining emotional equilibrium and decreasing emotional stress;

5. maintaining a satisfactory relationship with the environment or with others.

Coping responses may succeed in one or more of these, but coping in a certain way will not be universally effective or ineffective (Taylor and Stanton 2008) as it very much depends on the 'goodness of fit' between the situation and the coping response selected (Chapter 11 ☞). For example, coping with the flu will likely require different coping responses from coping with the diagnosis of cancer.

Coping can be cognitive or behavioural, active or passive, with many different, often overlapping, terms being used in the coping literature. Two of the main taxonomies are summarised in Table 12.1: firstly, those which differentiate between problem-focused and emotion-focused coping (cf. Folkman and Lazarus 1980, 1985); and secondly those which distinguish between approach-oriented coping and avoidance (cf. Roth and Cohen 1986; Suls and Fletcher 1985). In addition, amongst those studying child coping a distinction has been drawn between primary control coping which acts on the stressor or the emotions elicited by either problem- or emotion-focused coping; secondary control coping which involves efforts to adapt to the stressor such as distraction, cognitive restructuring or acceptance; and disengagement coping which involves efforts to withdraw from the stressor or the emotions it elicits, through the use of denial, avoidance or wishful thinking (Compas et al. 2012; Connor-Smith et al. 2000; Miller et al. 2009; Zimmer-Gembeck and Skinner 2011).

Within each of the broad dimensions described in Table 12.1 are a variety of coping subscales, generally

Table 12.1 Coping dimensions

---

1. **Problem-focused coping (problem-solving function)**, i.e. instrumental coping efforts (cognitive and/or behavioural) directed at the stressor in order to either reduce the demands of it or increase one's resources. Strategies include: planning how to change the stressor or how to behave in order to control it; suppressing competing activities in order to focus on ways of dealing with the stressor; seeking practical or informational support in order to alter the stressor; confronting the source of stress; or showing restraint.

   +/or

   Emotion-focused coping (emotion-regulating function), i.e. mainly, but not solely, cognitive coping efforts directed at managing the emotional response to the stressor: for example, positively reappraising the stressor in order to see it in a more positive light; acceptance; seeking emotional support; venting anger; praying.

2. **Attentional/approach, monitoring, vigilant, active,** i.e. concerned with attending to the source of stress and trying to deal with the problem by, for example, seeking information about it, or making active cognitive or behavioural efforts to manage the stressor (see also coping styles).

   +/or

   Avoidant, blunting, passive, i.e. concerned with avoiding or minimising the threat of the stressor; sometimes emotion-focused, sometimes involves avoiding the actual situation: for example, distraction by thinking of pleasant thoughts or distraction by engaging in other activities to keep one's mind off the stressor; disengagement through substance use.

> **Factor analysis**
> A method of analysis which seeks to reduce relationships between a wide set of correlated items into meaningful groups, or factors.

derived from **factor analysis** of a large number of coping items in an attempt to identify statistically meaningful 'clusters' of items that can then be used in a new measurement scale.

Folkman and Lazarus (1988), in the popular Ways of Coping scale, distinguish eight subscales that address the two dimensions of problem-focused and emotion-focused coping: confrontive coping, distancing, self-controlling, seeking social support, accepting responsibility, escape–avoidance, planned problem solving and positive reappraisal. Carver and colleagues (1989) distinguish 13, and subsequently 15, subscales: planning, active coping, suppressing competing activities, acceptance, turning to religion, venting emotions, seeking instrumental support, seeking emotional support, humour, positive reinterpretation, restraint coping, denial, mental disengagement, behavioural disengagement, alcohol or drug use (COPE scale). In contrast, Endler and colleagues (Endler and Parker 1993; Endler et al. 1998) assess across three dimensions: *emotion-oriented* (person-oriented strategies such as daydreaming, emotional response or self-preoccupation); *task-oriented* (strategies to solve, minimise or reconceptualise the problem) and *avoidance-oriented* (includes distraction or social diversion (CISS scale)). In contrast to situational specific coping 'strategies', Krohne's (1993) proposal, that vigilance and cognitive avoidance responses were two coping 'superstrategies' on orthogonal dimensions of attention orientation which were likely to reflect underlying personality, has led to considerations of coping 'style'.

Coping styles or strategies

Coping styles are generally considered as unrelated to the specific context or stressor stimulus; instead, they are trait-like forms of coping that people have a tendency to adopt when facing a potentially difficult situation. If you think about your own behaviour, you will probably know whether you tend to duck and avoid stressors or whether you face them head-on! One example of a coping style dimension is that of 'monitoring versus blunting' (Miller

1987; Miller et al. 1987). Monitoring reflects an approach style of coping, where threat-relevant information is sought out and processed, for example, asking about treatments and side effects, or seeking information about forthcoming exam content. Blunting reflects a general tendency to avoid or distract oneself from threat-relevant information, such as by sleeping or daydreaming, or engaging in other activities to avoid thinking about forthcoming exams. Van Zuuren and Dooper (1999) examined the relationship between monitoring and blunting coping styles and engagement in disease detection (e.g. attending doctor if frequently feeling tired, having blood pressure checked) and preventive behaviour (e.g. eating low-fat diet, exercising regularly). Monitoring was modestly, but significantly, associated with both detection and preventive behaviour, and individuals with a dominant blunting style were less likely to engage in protective behaviour than those where blunting was less dominant. In contrast, in a review of 63 separate studies of monitoring and blunting amongst those at risk of, or diagnosed with, cancer, results revealed that, although monitoring increased a person's knowledge of health threat, monitors experienced lower information satisfaction, greater perceived risk and higher negative affect (Roussi and Miller 2014). The conflicting outcomes of a monitoring style of coping highlights the importance of context – a person's coping style may not 'fit' the situation and as a result may be counter-adaptive. This is where the adoption of situation-specific coping strategies is important.

Coping strategies (see Table 12.1 for examples of commonly employed coping subscales) derive from an approach that considers stress and coping as a dynamic process that varies according to context, event and the person's personal goals, resources, mood, and so on (see Figure 12.1). Coping at any one time might include a range of seemingly oppositional strategies, i.e it is not the case that a person may cope solely in a problem-focused way. For example, Lowe et al. (2000) found that in the months following a heart attack, people used both passive coping (e.g. acceptance, positive reappraisal) and active, **problem-focused coping** simultaneously. In a similar vein, Macrodimitris and Endler (2001) found that both

> **problem-focused coping**
> coping that seeks to reduce the demands of the stressor or increase one's resources to deal with it.

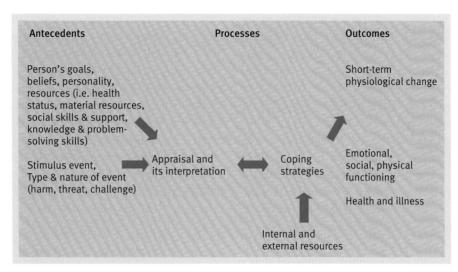

Figure 12.1 The coping process

Source: adapted from Lazarus (1999: 198).

instrumental and distraction coping strategies were employed by people with diabetes. Also, in a rarely studied population of people aged over 85 years old living in the community (i.e. not in institutions), Johnson and Barer (1997) found that both acceptance of change (in oneself cf. dependency) as well as disengagement from stressful roles were common. This study also highlighted that for the oldest-old, giving up some control was beneficial, whereas this is not the case in studies of the younger-old where fighting to retain aspects of self and independence are common (Rothermund and Brandstädter 2003).

While coping research in the field of health psychology more commonly assesses coping strategies than styles, the two approaches can be addressed simultaneously. For example, studies adopting repeated assessment periods can examine the nature and consistency of coping strategies over time, with consistent use of specific strategies suggesting a 'style' of coping (e.g. Tennen et al. 2000). Individual differences in aspects of personality influence the extent to which people are flexible in their choice of coping strategy, and, furthermore, explicit associations between aspects of trait personality, such as neuroticism and extroversion (D. Watson et al. 1999) or of optimism (e.g. Carver and Scheier 2005) and specific coping responses have been reported. These issues are addressed later in this chapter.

What is adaptive coping?

Generally, it is considered that problem-focused approach or attentional coping is more likely to be adaptive when there is something that can be done to alter or control the stressor event. Focusing one's thoughts on aspects of the situation and planning how to deal with each would be an example of a cognitive problem-focused coping strategy, whereas seeking helpful information about the event would be a behavioural problem-focused coping strategy. Behavioural examples of **emotion-focused coping** include venting and displaying emotion, or seeking emotional support. This latter strategy is generally considered to be adaptive.

Being responsive

Lazarus's model of coping suggests that it is hard to predict which coping strategies will be effective in which situations, as both problem-focused and emotion-focused strategies are interdependent and work together to create the overall coping response in any situation (Lazarus 1993b). Tennen et al. (2000) confirmed this in an impressive longitudinal study of pain patients where daily measures of coping were taken. They found that emotion-focused coping strategies were 4.4 times more likely to be used on a day when problem-focused strategies were also used than on days where problem-focused

> **Emotion-focused coping**
> Coping that seeks to manage the emotional response to the stressor.

strategies were not used. They also report that day-to-day pain symptomatology influenced the coping strategies used on a daily basis: for example, 'an increase in pain over yesterday's pain increased the likelihood that problem-focused coping yesterday would be followed by emotion-focused coping today' (p. 632). This highlights the role of appraisal and reappraisal of coping efforts: modifications are made depending on whether previous coping efforts are thought to have been successful or not. Troy et al. (2010) further highlight the critical role of cognitive reappraisal as a means of emotional regulation, i.e. regulating the emotional coping (such as getting upset or venting anger) that often exists in situations of high stress. They found that at high, but not low, levels of stress, women with high cognitive reappraisal ability experienced fewer depressive symptoms than those low in this ability. This individual difference factor may explain why in highly stressful situations some people appear to adjust emotionally better than others (see later section for further discussion of such (di)stress moderators).

Coping flexibility

Coping is highly contextual – to be effective it has to be amenable to change (see Figure 11.1 in the previous chapter, where there are arrows feeding back from coping to (re)appraisal, and also Figure 12.1). If the stressor event is starting a new job and this is eliciting anxiety, coping can either deal with the 'job' (make contacts with new colleagues, research the company and its products), or it can deal with the anxiety (engage in meditation, talk with a friend, get drunk). The person may in fact do all the above and thus it should not be assumed that coping in a way which addresses the problem directly (researching the new role) is inherently more adaptive than coping which does not (talking to a friend). Maintaining distinctions between emotion-focused and problem-focused coping is sometimes difficult, as movement between them is ever-present.

Individuals who are typically problem-focused, vigilant or attentional in their coping with stress may find that in some circumstances this is counter-productive. For example, when receiving a diagnosis of a life-threatening illness emotion-focused coping may be more adaptive because in such events the individual has little control. For example, the cognitive emotion-focused coping strategy of denial was found to be an effective coping response among women with a recent breast cancer diagnosis (Greer et al. 1990; Carver et al. 1993) although, among Greer's sample, ongoing denial was associated with poorer 15-year survival outcomes, suggesting that denial may have a good 'fit' (Lazarus and Folkman 1984; Lazarus 1999) to the situation in the short term but not long term. Demonstrating this further, a review of children coping with cancer found that in the first 6–12 months following diagnosis, approach coping (a control-oriented, problem-focused coping) was associated with poorer adjustment, whereas it predicted better adjustment when patients were 5–6 years after diagnosis (Aldridge and Roesch, 2007).

Emotional-approach coping

In relation to coping and adaptation, Stanton et al. (2000) have pointed out that emotions can have adaptive coping functions rather than disruptive functions (as often implied in the emotion-focused coping distinction). In a series of studies, they examined 'emotional-approach coping' and distinguished between 'emotional processing' (active attempts to understand the emotions experienced) and 'emotional expression'. Both forms of coping associated with indicators of positive psychological adjustment (see later section on emotional expression). In support of this, emotion-focused coping is shown to be adaptive: for example, positive reappraisal of one's responses to an event (e.g. 'It could have been worse, at least I did my best') can elicit positive emotion (e.g. pride, satisfaction) (Fredrickson 1998; Folkman and Moskowitz 2004). Positive emotions in turn, according to Fredrickson (2001), 'broaden' what a person feels like doing at that time, i.e. it expands their desired possibilities, whereas negative emotions shut off our thinking of possibilities, and also 'build' our resources, for example problem-solving abilities and adaptive-coping responses. This upward spiral of positive emotions is also called the *'broaden and build model'* of positive emotions (Cohn and Fredrickson 2009).

As well as positive emotions, positive coping response have been identified: for example, 'fighting spirit' (e.g. 'I am determined to beat this disease') was found to be associated with improved outcomes and long-term survival among breast cancer patients (Greer et al. 1979, 1990). In contrast, feelings of hopelessness and helplessness (e.g. 'I feel there is nothing I can do to help myself') were associated with poorer survival among this same population (M. Watson et al. 1999a) and among stroke patients (Lewis et al. 2001). These coping responses of fighting spirit and helplessness differentially associated with either active, problem-focused or passive, **avoidant coping** behaviour. Fighting spirit was thought to reflect a kind of realistic optimism and determination, with people high in fighting spirit facing illness head-on rather than avoiding it (Spiegel 2001). These early findings elicited hope for interventions that could enhance disease outcomes by targeting such attitudes and coping responses: for example, increasing fighting spirit while decreasing feelings of helplessness. However, a review and meta-analysis of 26 studies investigating the effects of fighting spirit or hopelessness/helplessness and cancer survival or recurrence concluded that many of the reported predictive associations between these variables were limited by restricted sample sizes or poor methodological quality of the studies (Petticrew et al. 2002). Furthermore, a later ten-year follow-up of 578 women with early-stage breast cancer conducted by the original research team also failed to replicate long-term predictive associations for fighting spirit, although helpless/hopelessness coping remained predictive of survival outcome (Watson et al. 2005).

Finally, in relation to forms of coping, Folkman and Moskowitch describe what they call a 'previously unaddressed aspects of coping', that of *meaning-focused coping*. This is typified by coping strategies which draw on a person's values and beliefs and encompasses goal revision, reordering priorities and focusing on strengths in order to obtain personal and possibly existential meaning within a negative and stressful situation (Park and Folkman 1997). Meaning-focused coping was thought to regulate the experience of positive emotion, such as hope (Folkman 2010), and is akin to the growing literature on benefit-finding and growth (see Chapter 14 ☛, and also Helgeson et al. 2006). However, following findings from an admittedly small and select sample, it has recently been suggested (Baumeister et al. 2013) that a meaningful life is not necessarily a happier one! Perhaps more research is needed as to whether there are in fact adaptational benefits to meaning-focused coping.

---

avoidant coping

a style of coping that involves emotional regulation by avoiding confrontation with a stressful situation. Analagous to emotion-focused coping.

Most people will experience stress at some point in their life. Think of a recent stressful experience you have faced. What strategies did you adopt in order to deal with this event? What were you hoping to achieve through the use of these strategies? Would you describe some of the strategies you adopted as 'problem-focused' and others as 'emotion-focused' or did you rely on one form of coping only? If you tried several different strategies, did they each have a different goal and, if so, which were effective and which were not?

In revisiting that experience, can you think of anything in your personal background, your character or outlook on life that influenced how you responded to that event? Keep the experience you have just been thinking about in mind as you continue reading this chapter and consider whether any of the influences on stress and coping that we describe are relevant to how you dealt with that event in particular, or with stress generally.

Coping goals

Coping intentions or goals (cf. Cohen and Lazarus 1979 (see earlier); Laux and Weber 1991) are likely to influence the coping strategies employed in any given situation and their likely success. Few studies have explicitly addressed goals (such as a desire to return to 'normalcy' after a trauma or illness) in relation to the specific strategies which are selected in an attempt to achieve that goal.

Why do people choose to cope in the way that they do? The reason for selecting one (or more) strategy to deal with a perceived stressor is related to past experience with that coping response, but more importantly it is related to the anticipated outcomes of that coping response, i.e. coping is a purposeful or motivational process (Lazarus 1993b). The general purpose or goal of coping, i.e. to manage or understand a situation so as to make it less distressing, brings with it an inherent need to maintain one's self-esteem and self-image, and to maintain good relations with others. To illustrate this, a study of arguments between married couples found that anger and attack coping responses arose when one or the other party felt that their self-esteem was under threat and their coping goal was therefore one of self-defence. In contrast, when couples were in a situation where there was a shared anxiety about some external event, anger was more often suppressed and supportive forms of coping used instead, as the goal in such instances was that of resolving shared concerns (Laux and Weber 1991).

As Coyne and Racioppo note (2000: 658) 'Coping checklist research has paid scant attention to differences in goals and agendas across situations and persons, and coping effectiveness cannot be evaluated without attention to these considerations.' In other words, unless we know 'why' a person choses to cope in a particular way in terms of what they hoped to achieve – reduced distress, more support, less pain etc., etc. – we cannot tell whether or not that particular coping strategy has been effective. People use different coping strategies, often simultaneously, perhaps because each one is aiming for a different goal. Furthermore, some goals may be short-term (e.g. reduce pain) and others may be longer-term (e.g. to manage to walk independently, to resolve the problem). Perceived social support was found to be more related to the attainment of resolution-focused coping than it was to coping goals that focused on attaining understanding (Siewert et al. 2013), demonstrating again the important role of personal resources on coping and its outcomes. More research is needed if we are to progress our understanding of coping goals, and influences on and how and why they may change over time, as this will also be beneficial to the shaping of interventions to individuals' coping.

Stress, personality and illness

What is personality? Personality can be defined as the 'dynamic organization within the individual of those psychophysical systems that determine his characteristic behavior and thought' (Allport 1961: 28). This definition reflects a trait approach to personality (see also Chapter 5 ☛), which considers a person's personality profile in terms of stable and enduring dimensions such as sensitivity, conscientiousness or neuroticism. Personality traits provide a helpful means for us to typify behaviour patterns, with clusters of traits often providing 'typologies'; for example, an extroverted 'type' of person will generally exhibit sociable, adventurous and impulsive traits, while a psychotic 'type' will exhibit egocentric, aggressive, cold and impulsive characteristics (Eysenck 1982). Note that impulsivity features in both 'types', yet overall the two types differ in terms of clustered traits.

Eysenck (1970) argued for two dimensions, neuroticism and extroversion, with psychoticism added at a later stage; however, over fifty years of work has confirmed that five superordinate factors provided a better description of the structure of personality (see Wrosch and Scheier's overview, 2003). The model adopted most widely in health psychology is therefore a five-factor model, often referred to as the 'Big Five' theory, which conceptualises and assesses personality using the following dimensions (Costa and McCrae 1992a, 1992b):

● agreeableness, i.e. cooperative, trusting, compliant;

● conscientiousness, i.e. responsible and striving;

● extroversion, i.e. positive, assertive, active, sociable;

● neuroticism, i.e. tense, anxious, pessimistic;

● openness, i.e. imaginative, curious, open to new experiences.

Each of these factors are superordinate traits which include various facets (see Costa and McCrae's 1992 measure, the NEO-FFI). Many associations between these relatively stable personality traits, stress, coping and health outcomes have been reported (see Vollrath 2006; Semmer 2006). In fact, a recent association has been found between conscientiousness and all-cause mortality in a large epidemiological study of over 76,000 individuals where 3,947 individual deaths were examined (Jokela et al. 2013), and, similarly, in another meta-analysis, openness to experience was also a protective factor in relation to all-cause mortality (Ferguson and Bibby 2012). Arguably, health psychology needs to pay more attention to personality and its influence on stress–health processes (see Ferguson 2013).

There are various possible models of association between personality variables and health and illness that have differing degrees of 'directness':

Personality may promote unhealthy behaviour predictive of disease (e.g. drug use, see Figure 12.2), thereby having an indirect effect on disease risk (e.g. Bogg and Roberts, 2004) (see Chapter 5 ☛).

General aspects of personality may influence the manner in which an individual appraises or copes with stress or illness events (e.g. neurotic individuals may overattend to the stressor; stress may be more damaging for those low in conscientiousness), thereby having an indirect effect on illness progression or outcomes (e.g. Penley and Tomaka 2002; Ferguson 2013).

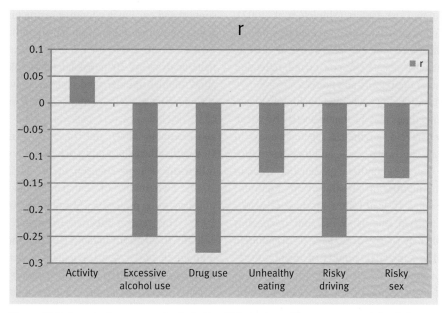

Figure 12.2 Conscientiousness and selected health behaviours. The average correlation between conscientiousness and selected health behaviours, meta-analysis. NB The number of studies and sample N included for each behaviour differed, ranging from 14 studies of unhealthy eating (N 6,356), to 65 studies of excessive alcohol use (N 32, 137).

Source: Adapted from Bogg and Roberts (2004: 908).

Personality may simply be predictive of disease onset (e.g. Friedman and Booth-Kewley 1987). This is the notion of a generic 'disease-prone personality' which underpins the psychosomatic tradition.

Specific clusters of personality traits may predispose to specific illnesses (e.g. Type A behaviour pattern and heart disease, Type C and cancer, see later section). One likely route of such effects is physiological: for example, angry personalities may be more physiologically stress-reactive (see Chapter 11 ☞). Thus this route is also indirect.

Studies employing five-factor models have found that each has differential associations with health behaviour (e.g. Booth-Kewley and Vickers 1994; Goldberg and Strycker 2002; Terraciano and Costa 2004; Nicholson et al. 2005), symptom perception (Feldman et al. 1999; Cameron and Leventhal 2003), coping (e.g. David and Suls 1996; Cooper et al. 2000) and illness behaviour (e.g. Korotkov and Hannah 2004).

Neuroticism and negative affectivity

As one of the three personality dimensions identified by Eysenck (1982), and one of the 'Big Five', neuroticism (N)

has received a lot of research attention in relation to stress and to illness. Trait N is considered to be relatively unchangeable and is a broad dimension characterised by the tendency to experience negative emotions and to exhibit associated beliefs and behaviours, including withdrawal or apprehensiveness (Costa and McCrae 1987; McCrae 1990). Individuals high on neuroticism often display anxious beliefs and behaviour disproportionate to the situation (Suls and Martin 2005, and see also Chapter 9 ☞ in terms of attention to internal states and increased somatic complaints). Related to neuroticism is a pervasive trait known as negative affectivity (NA), proposed by Watson and Clark (1984) to play a central role in the stress–health relationship. High-NA individuals are characterised by a generalised negative outlook, greater introspection, low affect (mood) and low self-concept. In studies of a range of adult samples, NA has been associated with lower self-rated health, greater health complaints, but generally not with objective ill-health indicators (Watson and Pennebaker 1989; Cohen et al. 1995; Evers et al. 2003). In terms of the ultimate health indicator – death – this was predicted by neuroticism in a 21-year prospective cohort of 5,424 UK adults, specifically death from cardiovascular diseases, even when controlling for known risk factors (Shipley et al. 2007). This effect was found to be partially mediated by sociodemographic, health behaviour and physiological factors, and lessened when mood state was considered, reflecting the close association between N and mood.

Another explanation for such relationships between N and negative outcomes may be that neurotics by virtue of their character have a heightened responsiveness to negative situations, e.g. work stress, and that this in turn can increase the degree of conflict experienced, which in turn increases the number of stressful events reported! This was reported in a 15-year follow-up study of work–family conflict carried out by Wille and colleagues (Wille et al. 2013). It is, however, hard to disentangle actual events from subjective reports of events, especially since most studies rely on self-report. In terms of responding to events appraised as stressful, neurotic individuals are commonly found to employ a greater variety of coping strategies (perhaps searching for one that works), although these tend to be maladaptive and emotion-focused coping strategies (see Semmer 2006).

Without fully understanding the mechanisms by which N and NA affect outcomes, these variables are sometimes described as 'nuisance factors' (Watson and Pennebaker 1989: 248), whereby researchers interpret self-reported outcomes of health complaints, stress or distress, with caution, because any relationship 'found' between stress and illness may be inflated by reporting bias of participants high in N/NA. There is, however, some evidence that neuroticism and NA have a direct route to negative health outcomes via immune suppression. For example, NA has been associated with cortisol production (e.g. van Eck et al. 1996); and neuroticism associated with interleukin-6 (Il-6) in older samples (implicated in depression also) (e.g. Bouhuys et al. 2004). Given that stress has also been shown to have immune effects as we have described in Chapter 11 ☞, it may be that personality adds to this already negative relationship.

Conscientiousness and the other Big Five traits

Conscientiousness (C), defined as being of a responsible and dependable character, following social norms, having foresight, being persistent and self-disciplined, has shown a consistent relationship to positive outcomes both in relation to stress and to health. Conscientious individuals may be more likely to problem-solve effectively, seek support and engage in cognitive restructuring factors useful in reducing work–life/family conflict, for example (Michel et al. 2011). In relation to health outcomes, a meta-analysis of 20 independent samples, representing child samples, middle-aged samples, as well as those with chronic disease, found a modest, but nonetheless significant correlation of 0.11 between C and longevity (Kern and Friedman 2008), and conscientiousness was associated with reduced mortality risk in studies with long-term follow-up (Hagger-Johnson et al. 2012; Jokela et al. 2013). Two studies of centenarians also find conscientiousness to be protective (Masui et al. 2006; Martin et al. 2006). This general effect across a range of samples and cultures is therefore notable and may be attributable to findings of fairly robust associations between conscientiousness and positive health behaviours (e.g. Bogg and Roberts 2004 (see Figure 12.2 for a summary of their findings); Nicholson et al. 2005; O'Connor et al. 2009: Paunonen and Ashton 2001), including medication adherence (Molloy et al. 2014). In addition to influencing health behaviours, those high in conscientiousness have been shown to use problem-focused coping when responding to stress (Bartley and Roesch 2011), and their characteristic persistence is considered beneficial to self-regulatory efforts, such as when trying to control one's response to stress (Hagger et al. 2010; Solberg Nes et al. 2011). It has also been suggested that while extraversion and neuroticism are more closely associated with emotional well-being (e.g. happiness), conscientiousness is more closely aligned to cognitive and evaluative aspects of well-being (e.g. satisfaction) (De Neve and Cooper 1998; Hayes and Joseph 2003). The 'Research focus' below considers further the ways in which conscientiousness may moderate the effects of stress appraisals on affect and physical symptoms.

Of the other 'Big Five' personality traits, agreeableness is generally considered adaptive in terms of flexible coping response to stressors, including using their affiliative skills to build social support networks known to be beneficial for an array of outcomes (see later). In relation to work–family conflict, agreeableness has been found both beneficial in some studies and not so in others (see Michel at al.'s 2011 review), suggesting that being agreeable to others may not always be in your own best interests perhaps! Extraversion, that tendency to have a positive and active attitude and behavioural style, has been found to be positive in some regards, e.g. appraisal, active coping, and emotional well-being (Hayes and

Joseph 2003), not significant in relation to work–life conflict contrary to hypotheses (Wille et al. 2013), and more negative in relation to health-risk behaviours, given extroverts' tendency to seek stimulation (see Chapter 5 (☞)). Extraversion has also emerged as protective for mortality generally among centenarians (Masui et al. 2006; Martin et al. 2006) and also for specifically respiratory-disease-related death (Shipley et al. 2007), possibly explained by enhanced immune function by way of increased Natural Killer cells (Bouhuys et al. 2004). These positive effects contradict associations with risk behaviours such as smoking (see Chapter 3 (☞)); however, it is worth noting that Shipley's study controlled for such risk factors, and therefore the mechanism through which extraversion operates remains unclear.

Besides the Big Five, other personality traits have been identified that have 'general' positive effects on stress responses and health, and we turn attention now to these 'personal resource' variables.

Optimism

One 'protective' resource is that of dispositional optimism, i.e. having a generally stable positive outlook and positive outcome expectations. Scheier and colleagues (Scheier et al. 1986; Scheier and Carver 1992) proposed that dispositional optimists are predisposed towards believing that desired outcomes are possible, and that this motivates optimistic individuals to cope more effectively and persistently with stress or illness events, thus reducing their risk of negative outcomes. Dispositionally optimistic persons are less likely to make internal ('It is my fault'), stable ('It is an aspect of my personality that I cannot change') and global attributions for negative

---

RESEARCH FOCUS

BEING CONSCIENTIOUS IS GOOD FOR YOU

Gartland, N., O'Connor, D.B., Lawton, R. and Ferguson, E. (2014). Investigating the effects of conscientiousness on daily stress, affect and physical symptom processes: a daily diary study. *British Journal of Health Psychology*, 19: 311–328.

Background aims

Consistent evidence of an association between conscientiousness (C) and health behaviour (high C and health protective/enhancing behaviours, low C and risk behaviours such as smoking, see also Chapter 5 (☞)) suggests that this may be the route through which C exerts the reported positive effects on health status and even lifespan. However, these authors note that in longitudinal studies, health behaviour does not provide a full explanation for this influence, which leads these authors to ask, how else might C work?

This paper briefly reviews evidence whereby studies considering the facets of conscientiousness (identified as order, virtue, traditionalism, self-control, responsibility and industriousness) in some detail highlight that, as well as being associated with health behaviours, aspects of C, such as self-discipline, influence stress appraisals or the reporting of daily hassles (e.g. O'Connor et al. 2009; Gartland et al. 2012). The current study seeks to take this further by examining the moderating effect of C on the impact of daily hassles on daily positive and negative affect and on reported physical symptoms. Instead of focusing on a single event they record multiple hassles over a two-week period using an innovative diary methodology. They hypothesise specifically that 'the relationship between a high appraisal ratio of hassles (where perceived demands outweigh perceived resources) and more symptoms/negative affect or less positive affect will be stronger in lower C individuals compared with higher C individuals' (p. 314).

Method

A total of 103 adults (73 women, 30 men, mean age 35.26 years (sd 14.75)) were recruited from local organisations including a university, and consented to completing:

- a baseline questionnaire assessing their conscientiousness (the Chernyshenko Consciousness Scale which assesses all 6 facets identified above)*;
- a 14-day daily diary administered online or on paper if preferred, completed at the end of each day before going to bed to record
  - daily hassles description and appraisals (using an 8-item Stressor Appraisal Scale, which assesses both perceived demands and resources)
  - 10 items assessing positive (e.g. excited, alert) and negative affect (e.g. nervous, distressed);
  - 12 items assessing experience of a range of physical symptoms (e.g. headache) over the past 24-hour period.

The performance reliability of all scales/facets was good or very good (Cronbachs alpha > .70) with the exception of the Responsibility facet of C, results from which therefore need to be interpreted with caution. Although an initial sample of 175 completed the baseline measures, attrition before completing diary day 1 was high (22.6 per cent), and of the remaining 136 only 103 completed >4 days of diaries to be used in subsequent analysis. The low completion threshold was to enable, hopefully, the capture of low C individuals, who by definition might be those least likely to complete the 14-day task! Whilst there was no difference in the baseline Conscientiousness scores of study drop-outs compared to the completers, completers had significantly lower scores on the Order facet which reflects an ability to plan or organise tasks and activities, and thus this direction of effect is surprising.

Results

Both within-person variations (Level 1) and between-person variations (Level 2) are explored. The analysis presented looks complex; however, you will find it systematically explained, with a good description of moderation and a clear test of the study hypotheses.

*the authors also assess Neuroticism which they use as a control variable only and do not report fully in the paper as the effects of C were statistically significant when N is controlled for.

Conscientiousness was higher in older participants and amongst females. Older age was also found to influence primary appraisals and physical symptom frequency (they made lower than average 'hassles' appraisals and reported less frequent symptoms). Gender did not influence appraisals nor outcomes. Age and gender were controlled for in subsequent analyses.

In within-subject analysis, total Conscientiousness and the six separate facets, were not found to be associated *directly* with primary or secondary appraisals or with the ratio between them. When analysing the main effects of C and appraisals on outcome variables, there were both within-person (Level 1) and between-person (Level 2) effects of C on outcome.

When C is average, the relationship between perceiving demands to outweigh resources (appraisal ratio) and having less positive affect was as expected, and also higher hassles appraisals predicted negative affect. There was no relationship with the physical symptoms measure. Conscientiousness levels moderated the relationship between appraisal ratio and positive affect – for those individuals with higher C there was no relationship between demands outweighing resources and lower positive affect. In contrast, amongst those with low or medium C, demands outweighing resources significantly reduced positive affect.

Carrying out the same moderation analyses but using the C-facets revealed similar findings only for Order and Industriousness – those with low or medium levels were significantly affected (in positive affect) by considering that their demands outweighed their resources, whereas those scoring high on these facets were not affected by this stress-appraisal ratio.

Discussion

The moderating effects of low or medium total Conscientiousness, and low or medium Order and Industriousness demonstrate that an imbalance between perceived hassles/demands and resources does not inevitably lead to negative outcomes as having high levels of C and these two facets seem to buffer this effect.

Sadly, no such findings emerged for either negative affect or physical health/symptom reporting, which is interesting – why does a situation where you feel demands outweigh your resources challenge and reduce your positive affect, but not increase your negative affect? Furthermore why should low or medium C (and the two facets above) make any difference – is it because these individuals cope differently? The current study sadly did not integrate an assessment of daily coping, but perhaps this is something for the future – although there is of course a limit to how many measures you can expect participants to complete on a daily basis for two weeks!

In addition, perhaps further research using clinical populations would generate different findings in the hypothesised direction between personality and physical health. The current sample actually report a low level of physical symptoms with little variance (mean 1.91, sd 2, with a maximum possible score of 12) and thus this part of the analysis is biased against finding anything significant.

In their conclusions the authors stress the importance of positive affect for health and well-being, pointing to developments in the field of 'positive psychology' – see later section in this chapter and 'Issues'. Positive affect may buffer against the negative effects of stress, or stress itself may lead to coping and a sense of mastery which then enhances positive affect. The current findings suggest that those low or moderate in conscientiousness would not benefit from the stress-buffering effects of positive affect.

In spite of some challenges regarding diary completion rates and the reliance on self-report measures, this study confirms the importance of general Conscientiousness and specific facets within it, to the stress experience. However, as acknowledged, much remains to be understood in terms of the over-time interactions of personality, stress appraisals and outcomes. To date, the various options for causality have not been fully explored in longitudinal studies exploring multiple outcomes in relation to multiple predictors. Furthermore, we cannot even conclude for sure that personality facets such as C are in fact fixed and immune to change as a result of experience – the current study only measures C at baseline and therefore cannot test this hypothesis. If it emerges that C can in fact be changed, a whole new avenue of interventions become possible. Watch this space!

events: i.e. they are more likely to appraise stress as changeable and specific and coming from external sources that are potentially more changeable or ignorable than internal ones. Pessimism, on the other hand, is a generalised and stable negative outlook associated with denial and distancing responses to stress. Pessimism among cancer patients, for example, was found to have independent effects to optimism and was associated with mortality among younger patients even when controlling for the related construct of depression (Schulz et al. 1996). Optimism and pessimism, however, are measured on a continuum, not a dichotomy, as seen in the Life Orientation Test (LOT, the measure of optimism developed by Scheier and Carver 1985; see Table 12.2) or the LOT-R (revised, Scheier et al. 1994).

In a meta-analysis of studies, Andersson (1996) reports that optimism was significantly associated with active coping, with reduced symptom reporting and with reduced negative mood or depression, with this latter relationship being strongest. This was confirmed in a later meta-analysis where optimism was positively associated with approach coping and negatively associated with avoidance coping (Solberg Nes and Segestrom 2006). Optimism has been found to benefit both healthy populations dealing with stressful events (e.g. Steptoe et al. 2008) and patient populations dealing with various aspects of their illness (e.g. Carver et al. 1993; Fournier et al. 2002).

It appears that optimism promotes better functioning and outcomes because optimistic people expect positive outcomes and appraise events in a way that increases their likelihood of adopting problem-focused coping strategies, and if that is not an option they use adaptive emotion-focused coping strategies such as positive reframing, humour or acceptance (Wrosch and Scheier 2003). For example:

- Optimistic patients with fibromyalgia were less likely to give up on goals even when pain made this challenging (Affleck et al. 2001).

Table 12.2 Measuring optimism: the Life Orientation Test

Please be as honest and accurate as you can be throughout. Try not to let your response to one statement influence your responses to other statements. There are no 'correct' or 'incorrect' answers. Answer according to your *own* feelings rather than how you think 'most people' would answer. Using the scale below, write the appropriate letter in the box beside each statement.

	A I agree a lot	B I agree a little	C I neither agree nor disagree	D I disagree a little	E I disagree a lot
1. In uncertain times, I usually expect the best					☐
2. It's easy for me to relax*					☐
3. If something can go wrong for me, it will					☐
4. I always look on the bright side					☐
5. I'm always optimistic about my future					☐
6. I enjoy my friends a lot*					☐
7. It's important for me to keep busy*					☐
8. I hardly ever expect things to go my way					☐
9. Things never work out the way I want them to					☐
10. I don't get upset easily*					☐
11. I'm a believer in the idea that 'every cloud has a silver lining'					☐
12. I rarely count on good things happening to me					☐

*These are 'filter' items, which have the function of disguising the focus of the test.

● Optimism following cancer diagnosis predicted more positive adjustment in the subsequent 12 months, possibly by reducing disease-related threat appraisals and avoidant coping (Schou et al. 2005).

● Optimistic children (as assessed using the Youth-Life Orientation Test) reported more hope in relation to goal attainment, greater global and social self-competence, and fewer depressive symptoms (Ey et al. 2005).

● Optimistic law students exhibited less avoidance coping than non-optimistic students (Segerstrom et al. 1998).

It is worth noting that in this latter study optimists also reported lower perceived stress; however, this association was with situationally specific optimism rather than the general trait, or dispositional optimism. Further highlighting this important distinction, these different measures of optimism predicted different outcomes – situational optimism predicted elevated mood and immune function, whereas dispositional optimism did not.

Another construct related to dispositional optimism is that of unrealistic optimism, i.e. the view that unpleasant events are more likely to happen to others than to oneself, and that pleasant events are more likely to happen to oneself than to others (Weinstein 1982; see Chapter 5 (☞). Sometimes referred to as 'defensive optimism' (Schwarzer 1994), this way of thinking may operate as an emotional buffer against the recognition or acceptance of possible negative outcomes, i.e. it may protect people from a depressing reality.

The effects of an optimistic disposition do, however, vary, depending on context and the controllability of the disease, with evidence that in controllable conditions, such as self-management of insulin-dependent diabetes, dispositional optimism is beneficial, whereas in less controllable conditions, such as multiple sclerosis, it is not (Fournier et al. 2002). In saying this, however, higher optimism was associated with subsequent higher QoL in a sample of 217 women in the terminal phases (last year of life) of ovarian cancer (Price et al. 2013). Whilst stable, dispositional variables such as optimism offer more limited opportunity for intervention than do situational cognitions, such as unrealistic optimism or perceptions of control. Price also found that higher minimisation and less hopelessness/helplessness predicted QoL. This finding suggests perhaps that optimism is akin to denial in this context, which has adaptive benefits in such an uncontrollable situation, i.e. impending death.

Photo 12.1 How optimistic are you? Is this glass half-empty or half-full?

Source: Tanya Louise Robinson.

Another study suggests, however, that the beneficial effects of optimism may be more complex in chronically or multiply challenging situations. Solberg Nes et al. (2011) found that while there were beneficial effects of optimism on task persistence of those with chronic multi-symptom illness (and also control participants), the association was weakened in the patient sample when self-regulatory fatigue was experienced. Perhaps when facing multiple challenges to self-regulation and where 'self-regulatory fatigue' is present, optimism may struggle to maintain its positive influence. Further research is needed to explore this interesting finding.

Although generally considered to be a trait, Folkman and Moskowitz (2000) have suggested that optimistic beliefs can be maintained by successful coping outcomes. This suggests that coping-skills training and positive feedback on successful efforts may build optimism. If so, optimism would then become closer to self-efficacy.

Hardiness and resilience

When searching for factors that might differentiate those who respond to stress by becoming ill from those who stay healthy, Kobasa (1979) identified a belief system arising from a person having experienced rich, varied and rewarding experiences in childhood, and manifest in feelings of:

- *Commitment*: a person's sense of purpose or involvement in events, activities and with people in their lives. Committed individuals would view potentially stressful situations as meaningful and interesting.

- *Control*: a person's belief that they can influence events in their lives. Individuals high on control were thought to view stressors as potentially changeable.

- *Challenge*: a person's tendency to view change as a normal aspect of life and as something that can be positive. Individuals scoring high on the challenge dimension would view change as an opportunity for growth rather than as a threat to security.

Rather than exerting a direct effect on health, it is thought that by possessing each of these characteristics, a hardy person would be buffered against the experience of stress, thus enabling them to remain healthy. Kobasa's first study reported correlations between the scores of male executives on the Holmes and Rahe's life events scale (see Chapter 11 ☞) and their self-reported checklist of symptoms and illness events, and these findings were upheld in subsequent longitudinal prospective studies (Kobasa et al. 1982). The buffering effects are presented in Figure 12.3, where it is evident that hardiness has more effect in situations of high stress than in situations of low stress, i.e. a 'buffering' effect. This was supported by findings of Beasley et al. (2003) in a study of 187 university students who retrospectively reported life stress. In addition to a direct relationship between hardiness and reduced distress, hardiness buffered the effects of negative life events on the psychological health of female participants, i.e. the effects of negative life events were less for females higher in hardiness. For both genders, the negative effect of emotion-oriented coping on distress was less in those scoring high on the hardiness measure. However, such cross-sectional findings of buffering effects of hardiness have not been consistently replicated in prospective studies leading to some concluding that a lack of hardiness is important, rather than the presence of it, in terms of how this might

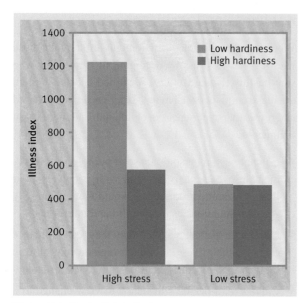

Figure 12.3 The buffering effects of hardiness

Source: adapted from Kobasa et al. (1982).

affect appraisals. This has led to suggestions that non-hardiness may reflect underlying trait neuroticism (Funk 1992), and certainly there is a relationship between the two (see review by Semmer 2006).

Attention has turned to the concept of resilience – the ability to 'bounce back' in times of adversity, first identified in the 1980s by Smith (Werner and Smith 1982, 1992) following her 40-year study following a birth cohort of 700 Hawaiian babies and examining their social and academic outcomes in relation to childhood adversity factors such as impoverished home environments or parental addiction. Smith identified two facets to those who 'bounced back' – an outgoing disposition, and an ability to access several sources of social support (possibly reflecting a sense of challenge and commitment as described in hardiness), leading to questions as to whether resilience is a fixed trait held by a person regardless of stress being present, or an adaptive response that emerges only in times of stress. Those considering resilience as a personality resource provide evidence both of benefits to stress adaptation, positive psychological health and health outcomes (Smith 2006), and even adolescent health behaviours (Mistry et al. 2009).

Trait views dominated research until the late 1960s, but when traits failed to explain observed behaviour sufficiently well, attention turned to the role of external or situational variables and the existence of state-like characteristics (e.g. anxiety specific to a situation). Some of these are described next.

Type A behaviour and personality

Coronary heart disease (CHD) and its outcomes (heart attack, angina, cardiac death) have been studied extensively in relation to personality variables and to emotion (see later section). The search for a coronary-prone personality led to the discovery of a constellation of behaviour labelled Type A behaviour (TAB) (Friedman and Rosenman 1959, 1974; Rosenman 1978). TAB is a multidimensional concept combining action and emotion (see Chapter 9 ☞ definition) and is manifest in individuals showing the following:

● competitiveness;

● time-urgent behaviour (trying to do too much in too little time);

● easily annoyed/aroused hostility and anger;

● impatience;

● achievement-oriented behaviour;

● a 'vigorous' speech pattern characterised by being rapid, loud, tense and clipped, with much interrupting of others.

In the 1960s and 1970s, TAB was found to modestly but consistently increase the risk of CHD and MI (heart attack) mortality when compared with persons showing a Type B behaviour pattern (the converse of Type A, i.e. relaxed with little aggressive drive) (e.g. the Western Collaborative Group study (WCGS) – Rosenman et al. 1976; and the Framingham heart study – Haynes et al. 1980). Yet most subsequent research, including longer-term (22 years) follow-up of the WCGS participants, has failed to confirm these early associations (e.g. Booth-Kewley and Friedman 1987; Hollis et al. 1990; Orth-Gomér and Undén 1990; Ragland and Brand 1988). In fact, some of these studies found very different results to what was expected: for example, Ragland and Brand's 22-year follow-up of the WCGS cohort found that Type Bs with prior CHD experienced a second heart attack sooner than Type As with prior CHD, and healthy Type As were no more likely than healthy Type Bs to have experienced a fatal heart attack. Some of these contradictory findings may be explained by differences in the methods of assessment of TAB (for example, structured face-to-face interviews versus self-completed questionnaires) or by sampling differences (some studies used healthy samples, others used heart attack survivors or those with other risk factors, such as smoking). Or perhaps, as a meta-analysis of studies suggests (Myrtek 2001), contradictory findings arise from differences in the heart disease outcome assessed (e.g. heart attack event, heart attack death, angina, arterial disease), with studies reporting positive findings predominantly using *self-reported angina* as the indice of CHD, with obvious limitations.

While evidence of a TAB–coronary illness link may be less consistent than it was once considered, there is some evidence suggesting that Type As respond more quickly and in a stronger emotional manner to stress, and that they exhibit a greater need for control than non-Type A individuals (Furnham 1990). These features of Type A may actually increase the person's likelihood of encountering stress, as they are likely to influence their interactions with others (Smith 1994) and result in the individual experiencing a more 'stressful' environment. Type As also show greater physiological reactivity than Type Bs, although this appears to be task-dependent and evident when tasks are competitive or challenging rather than in tasks that are irrelevant to the TAB character, such as simple perceptuo-motor tasks (e.g. Krantz et al. 1982). As described in Chapter 11 ☞, cardiovascular reactivity during stress has been implicated in various disease processes, such as the extent and progression of carotid artery atherosclerosis and the emergence of coronary heart disease (Smith et al. 2003), and therefore it is this reactivity that may provide the mechanism by which personality or Type A characteristics influence disease. Part of Type A personality therefore is seen in behavioural responses to provocative situations where the core component appears to be antagonistic, or hostile attitudes and behaviour. This likely key trait of hostility emerged from a review where the collapsing of findings across 83 different studies of the links between Type A and CHD found small but consistently significant correlations between the hostility component and total CHD outcomes (Booth-Kewley and Friedman 1987). In fact, hostility was the only aspect of TAB that showed this association, although anger showed some associations with subcategories of outcomes. After a subsequent review almost a decade later confirmed this conclusion (T. Miller et al. 1996), Type A research had all but been replaced by hostility and anger research.

Hostility and anger

Hostility emerged as an important predictor of illness from various large-scale studies (see T. Miller et al. 1996 for a meta-analysis of findings from 45 studies, including the highly cited MRFIT and Western Collaborative Group studies) with interest then turning to investigations of the pathways through which hostility might be having its effects. Several possible mechanisms have been explored:

1. Hostile individuals may be more likely to engage in health-risk behaviour which are risk factors for illnesses such as heart disease, for example excessive smoking or alcohol intake (Whiteman 2006). Studies investigating the hostility–disease link therefore must control for such risk factors in order that the actual extent to which hostility independently contributes to disease outcomes becomes clear.

2. Hostile individuals have a lower capacity to benefit from psychosocial resources or interpersonal support and thus are less 'buffered' against the negative effects of stressful or challenging events (T. Miller et al. 1996). Described as a 'psychosocial vulnerability hypothesis', whereby hostility is considered to moderate the relationship between stressful environmental characteristics and health problems, Kivimäki's (Kivimäki et al. 2003) large-scale study of Finnish adults found that, for men only, hostility influenced the relationship between unemployment and ill health, with hostile men having a high prevalence of health problems regardless of employment status, whereas non-hostile men had better health if employed. (This paper also highlights a commonly reported but insufficiently explored gender difference in the associations between hostility and health outcomes (many earlier studies did not include women)).

3. Experimental studies suggest that hostile individuals are generally more stress-reactive than non-hostile individuals. Reduced 'buffers' plus a tendency to greater stress reactivity among hostile individuals makes them vulnerable to coronary heart disease, and even acute events such as heart attack (Strike and Steptoe 2005). For example, in a series of experimental studies, Suarez and colleagues (e.g. Suarez and Williams 1989; Suarez et al. 1998) found that persons scoring high in cynical hostility on the Cook–Medley hostility scale produced larger blood-pressure responses

and greater neuroendocrine responses (e.g. raised cortisol levels) than non-hostile participants did when performing a task either during or immediately after an encounter with a rude and harassing laboratory assistant. Similar evidence from Everson et al. (1995) showed that individuals scoring high in hostility had increased cardiovascular activation during a task performed after a staged interruption and that, furthermore, hostile individuals differed in their evaluations of the experiment and the person who interrupted them than did low-hostility participants (e.g. they manifest more irritation and anger, and feelings of being personally insulted). As described in Chapter 11 ☞, prolonged or repeated episodes of elevated blood pressure may cause damage to the walls of vessels carrying blood to the heart (the coronary arteries).

Enough evidence was amassed from systematic reviews and meta-analyses to conclude that hostility is a likely risk factor for development of CHD, with several studies suggesting that the association is most evident in younger samples (aged 60 or under) (e.g. Smith et al. 2003; and see Myrtek 2001; and Whiteman 2006 for reviews). However, there have been inconsistencies in findings and so, similar to that which happened with Type A research, studies have also addressed the component parts to try and establish whether there is a key component.

Hostility itself has shown to be made up of emotional, cognitive and behavioural components. Trait anger is the central emotional component that is both experienced by the individual and manifested in aggressive or antagonistic actions or expressions; cognitive components include having a cynical view of the world, a negative general attitude and negative expectations (cynicism, mistrust and denigration) about the motives of others; and behaviourally, hostile individuals may appear overtly aggressive or angry. In investigating the pathways through which hostility affected health status, trait anger has emerged consistently. For example, studies have consistently identified associations between both inhibited anger (anger-in) and anger expression (anger-out) and blood pressure and hypertension, and interventions to reduce hostility have been associated with reductions in blood pressure (e.g. Davidson et al. 2007). Some studies have reported an increased CHD risk among participants with high anger expression (e.g. Suls et al. 1995; Rosenman 1996; Williams et al. 2000), with anger inhibition or suppression more associated with hypertension risk (Vögele and Steptoe 1993; Vögele et al. 1997). The UK-based Caerphilly study, however, found that low anger expression and suppressed anger significantly increased CHD risk (Gallacher et al. 1999). As with much research, such mixed findings are probably largely due to differences in measures and methods used. There do seem to be physiological correlates of hostility: for example, in addition to heightened stress reactivity, there is some evidence of of an association with pro- and anti-inflammatory cytokines, discussed previously in relation to stress responses and potential associations with heart disease (e.g. among healthy male military personnel, Mommersteeg et al. 2008).

One final thought on hostility. It has been suggested that risk 'characteristics' such as hostility may be created by certain social contexts that undermine an individual's ability to attain goals or financial security, and that hostility may be less of a trait than a coping response (e.g. Taylor et al. 1997). Perhaps hostility is indirectly associated with disease by virtue of a relationship with social deprivation (e.g. Siegman et al. 2000) (see Chapter 2 ☞).

Type C personality

The search for a disease-prone personality in relation to CHD, which led to identification and examination of Type A and hostility, stimulated research into whether or not there was a cancer-prone personality type. Earlier work that considered the existence of disease-prone personality types (e.g. Eysenck 1985; Grossarth-Maticek et al. 1985) had identified four personality 'types'. Their 'cancer-prone personality', type 1, was characterised by suppression of emotion and inability to cope with interpersonal stress, leading to feelings of hopelessness, helplessness and finally depression, whereas a CHD-prone personality, type 2, was characterised by strong reactions of frustration, anger, hostility and emotional arousal (similar to TAB described above). Eysenck and Grossarth-Maticek (1989), following a large-scale community survey in Yugoslavia, reported evidence to show that type 1 increased individual risk of cancer by 120 times and type 2 increased CHD risk 25 times. These figures suggest that phenomenal amounts of risk can be conferred on personality variables, for example greater risk than that elicited even by smoking. Their claims inevitably led to much scrutiny of their work by scientists worldwide, resulting in their findings being heavily criticised on the grounds of inappropriate analyses, insufficient methodological detail being provided in their paper, and a general inability of others to replicate their findings in either CHD studies or cancer studies (Pelosi and Appleby 1992, 1993; Amelang and Schmidt-Rathjens 1996; Smedslund and Rundmo 1999).

In contrast, Temoshok's typology (Temoshok and Fox 1984; Temoshok 1987), following a 15-year follow-up of women with breast cancer, did generate a robust finding of an association between passive and helpless coping style and poor disease prognosis. They described a **Type C personality** as having the following characteristics:

- cooperative and appeasing;
- compliant and passive;
- stoic;
- unassertive and self-sacrificing;
- tendency to inhibit or repress negative emotions, particularly anger.

However, reviews of the role of Type C characteristics (and in fact any psychosocial factor) and cancer onset suggest that effects are limited and weak (e.g. Garssen 2004; Stürmer et al. 2006).

Personality as a factor that influences appraisal of, and response to, cancer has also been explored in terms of outcomes such as recurrence and survival. Generally, support for the predictiveness of characteristics of Type C is limited (Garssen 2004; Stephen et al. 2007), and this is true also of studies examining effects of other personality characteristics such as neuroticism or extroversion (e.g. Canada et al. 2005). There is mixed evidence of survival benefits of aspects of personality best described as 'coping styles', for example of 'fighting spirit' (see 'What is adaptive coping?' above), and of helplessness–hopelessness.

Type D personality

Another construct has been examined in relation to CHD risk and that is a **Type D personality**, best described as a 'distressed' personality, with individuals scoring highly on negative affectivity (NA) and social inhibition (SI, defined as 'the avoidance of potential dangers involved in social inter-action such as disapproval or nonreward by others', Denollet 1998: 209). Type D individuals by definition experience negative emotions but inhibit them while also avoiding social contact. These

researchers have presented evidence of associations between Type D and cardiovascular disease prognosis and outcomes, including mortality after a heart attack or other **cardiac event**, (Denollet and Potter 1992; Denollet et al. 1996, 2006; Denollet 1998; Denollet et al. 2006) even when controlling for other biomedical risk factors, or for concurrent symptoms of stress. The effect was found in both women and men who had pre-existing heart disease. A meta-analysis of six studies (Reich and Schatzberg 2010) found that Type D was associated with worse cardiac outcomes in all cases (two studies related to heart transplant surgery) although the extent to which risk factors were controlled for is unclear.

In an attempt to identify physiological correlates of Type D personality so as to better understand the process by which Type D may achieve its reported effects, Habra et al. (2003) examined cardiovascular reactivity (blood pressure, heart rate, salivary cortisol levels) of students completing a mental arithmetic task while being harassed. Socially inhibited males showed heightened blood pressure reactivity; negative affectivity associated with dampened heart-rate changes during the task in males; and salivary cortisol levels positively associated with both Type D dimensions (but not in final, more stringent analyses). Unlike Denollet's studies, where NA and SI were only predictive jointly, Habra's findings suggested that NA and SI operated independently. These differences may be due to clear differences in the samples (older adults with CHD versus healthy undergraduate students); however, they also point to a need to further explore what this construct is. A final point regarding the process through which any effect of Type D may be achieved is preliminary evidence relating to psychoneuroimmunological

---

Type C personality

a cluster of personality characteristics manifested in stoic, passive and non-emotionally expressive coping responses. Thought to be associated with an elevated cancer risk.

Type D personality

a personality type characterised by high negative affectivity and social inhibition.

cardiac event

generic term for a variety of end points of coronary heart disease, including a myocardial infarction, angina and cardiac arrest.

responses, including that of increased pro-inflammatory cytokine activity (see Chapter 11 ☞).

Some controversy, however, exists around the Type D findings, with failure to confirm associations between Type D and mortality in a study which included a larger number of death events than many of the earlier studies (Coyne et al. 2011), and inconsistent findings depending on sample sizes highlighted in a recent meta-analysis, which itself has been subject to methodological challenge (Grande et al. 2012 as cited in de Voogd et al. 2012). The future of Type D research therefore remains open to discussion.

Generally therefore, as described in this section, whilst there is reasonably good evidence that aspects of our personality influences the appraisals of events and even the cognitive, behavioural and physiological responses made to them, which may confer increased risk of some diseases, the influence of personality on disease outcomes such as survival is limited.

Stress and cognitions

Perceived control

Early work on the construct of control considered it to be a personality trait, for example, locus of control. Derived from Rotter's social learning theory, LoC was proposed as a generalised belief that would influence behaviour, as greater reinforcements (e.g. rewarding outcomes) were expected when responsibility for events was placed internally rather than externally (Rotter 1966). Furthermore, internal locus of control beliefs would only predict behaviour in situations where the rewards/outcomes were valued. LoC therefore refers to the trait-like expectation that personal actions will be effective in controlling or mastering the environment, with individuals falling on the side of either internality or externality. An 'internal' individual would take responsibility for what happens to them: for example, they would attribute successes to their own efforts and their failures to their own laziness! An 'external' individual would be more likely to believe that outside forces or chance circumstances control their lives, and both success and failures would be likely to be attributed to luck or chance. These beliefs would therefore influence a person's behaviour. It is considered that internal individuals have more efficient

cognitive systems and that they expend energy on obtaining information that will enable them to influence events of personal importance. In other words, internally oriented individuals would engage in more problem-focused coping efforts when faced with personal or social stressors. Highlighting this, Henselmans et al. (2010) demonstrated in a longitudinal study of breast cancer patients that threat appraisals (primary appraisal) were greater, and secondary appraisals of coping ability were lower in women who reported low perceptions of control over events and situations in life (using Pearlin and Schoolers 1978 mastery measure) pre-diagnosis, and that this impacted on these women's greater distress. This shows how internal resources/beliefs and appraisals interact in a dynamic manner, and, furthermore, suggests a protective role for a general sense of personal control, or mastery (as assessed in this study).

There is a large body of evidence relating locus of control to physical and psychological health, and much of it has employed a scale specific to health developed by Kenneth Wallston and colleagues (e.g. Wallston et al. 1978) – the multidimensional health locus of control scale. The MHLC assesses the extent to which a person believes that they themselves, external factors or 'powerful others' (e.g. friends, health professionals) are responsible for their health and health outcomes. This measure therefore has three subscales and includes items such as:

● 'I am in control of my health' – internal;

● 'No matter what I do, if I am going to get sick I will get sick' – external;

● 'Regarding my health, I can only do what my doctor tells me to do' – powerful others.

Scores on these subscales have been found to be associated with a range of coping, emotional and behavioural outcomes (including health behaviour itself). For example, among two longitudinal studies of patients with lower back pain, internal HLC was associated with reduced physical disability at follow-up, and patients with stronger internal control beliefs gained more from their treatment and exercised more often (distress was associated with poorer exercise behaviour) (Härkäpää et al. 1991; Fisher and Johnston 1998). Using an HLC measure specific to recovery from disability (the recovery locus of control scale; Partridge and Johnston 1989), Johnston et al. (1999) also found that perceptions of internal control predicted better recovery from disability (measured in terms of the ability to perform a range of activities such as walking, dressing and toileting) six months after an acute stroke, although this was not achieved by means of an influence on exercise behaviours, as reported by the Finnish study (Härkäpää et al. 1991). Importantly, Johnston and colleagues reassessed their stroke survivors after three years to examine whether the beneficial effects of perceived control persisted long term, and confirmed that perceived-control beliefs, as assessed at baseline (10–20 days post-stroke onset) were significantly predictive of long-term physical recovery, but not emotional recovery in terms of reduced distress (Johnston et al. 2004; Morrison et al. 2005). The importance of this type of finding is that, unlike neurological impairment or age (both predictors of outcome following stroke), control beliefs can be modified with simple (e.g. Fisher and Johnston 1996b) or more intensive (e.g. Johnston et al. 2007) intervention.

Few studies have found perceived control to be predictive of disease course, for example cancer relapse or survival (DeBoer et al. 1999). Furthermore, there is evidence that encouraging patients or research participants to increase internal control may not always be popular (e.g. Joice et al. 2010) nor adaptive, given that unrealistic perceptions of control could potentially lead to unrealistic optimism. However, the direction of causality is unclear here – do optimists perceive control, or does perceiving control make you optimistic – only prospective studies can explore this (see Klein and Helweg-Larsen 2002 for a meta-analytic review). Furthermore, maintaining beliefs in internal control in situations where such beliefs are unrealistic (e.g. severe and permanent disability following traumatic brain injury) may lead to problem-focused coping efforts that fail. This perceived failure may contribute to feelings of depression and helplessness, whereas accepting the reality of having no control could encourage more adaptive emotion-focused coping responses (Thompson 1981; Folkman 1984). However, rather than accept an absence of control, Folkman (2010) notes that by revising one's goals a sense of hope can be maintained for new, more realistic or attainable goals and that this may help provide a sense of control and sustain a person's well-being.

This highlights the importance of asking ourselves what we are trying to measure, i.e. 'Control over what?' Various types of control have been described:

- *Behavioural:* the belief that one can perform behaviours likely to reduce the negative impact of a

stressor, e.g. using controlled breathing techniques prior to and during a painful dental procedure.

- *Cognitive:* the belief that one has certain thought processes or strategies available that would reduce the negative impact of a stressor, e.g. distracting oneself from surgical pain by focusing on pleasant thoughts of a forthcoming holiday.

- *Decisional:* having the opportunity to choose between options, e.g. having a local anaesthetic prior to a tooth extraction (bearing in mind that the after-effects can last for hours!) or having the tooth removed without anaesthetic.

- *Informational:* having the opportunity to find out about the stressor; i.e. the what, why, when, where, likely outcomes, possibilities, etc. Information allows preparation (see Chapter 13 (☞).

- *Retrospective:* attributions of cause or control of an event made after it happens, i.e. searching for the meaning of an event can give some sense of order in life: e.g. blaming a birth defect on a defective gene (internal) may be more adaptive than attributing blame externally, although this is not clear-cut.

Each of these types of control can reduce the stressfulness of an event by altering the appraisal a person makes of the stressor, by reducing emotional arousal or by influencing the coping responses adopted. Even in generally uncontrollable circumstances, for example in terms of disease progression, believing in control over one's day-to-day symptoms rather than over the disease as a whole, has been associated with better adjustment (Schiaffino and Revenson 1992) and reduced distress (Thompson et al. 1993; Stanton et al. 2007). Therefore, while control over outcome may not be realistic, finding or retaining control over some aspects of an event or one's responses to it is generally considered beneficial (Montpetit and Bergeman 2007).

In a study of cancer caregivers however, Fitzell and Pakenham (2010) found that perceived control over caregiving demands was not a significant predictor of any outcome, positive or negative (in spite of modest correlations with positive affect and subjective health status). They investigated caregiver appraisals of demand (stress, challenge) and resources (personal control, social support) in relation to both positive, and negative, caregiver adjustment. While perceived control was not predictive in the final regression analyses, perceived stress (assessed as a single item) was a significant predictor of all outcomes in the expected direction; a more robust five-item measure of perceived challenge was predictive only of life satisfaction; and the 'resource' variable of satisfaction with social support also added significantly to the prediction of all outcomes. The authors suggest the lack of prediction of control beliefs (and also in fact of most of the coping subscales) may be due to using items which referred to control over caregiving challenges generally, rather than specific demands/caregiving tasks. This important issue of whether to assess constructs generically or specifically is one which we address at various points throughout this text.

Self-efficacy and perceived locus of control are the two main control concepts used in health psychology, and they could be considered as spanning different phases of the coping process: for example, locus of control is an appraisal of the extent to which an individual believes they can control outcomes, whereas self-efficacy addresses appraisal of the resources and skills an individual believes they can use in order to achieve desired outcomes. For example, the finding that academic demands are more likely to be appraised as challenges than threats where self-efficacy is high was shown across five different national samples (Luszczynska et al. 2005).

Another control-related construct is that of personal mastery (e.g. 'I can do just about anything I really set my mind to'). In a study examining mastery and another control-related construct perceptions of constraints in one's life (e.g. 'Other people determine most of what I can and cannot do') in a large sample of adults aged 25–75 years, personal mastery beliefs were lower and constraints higher among those with lower incomes (used as an indice of social class). However, when lowest-income participants reported a high sense of control, their health and well-being became comparable with the higher-income groups (Lachmann and Weaver 1998). This finding suggests that control moderated the effect of low income on both physical (self-rated health, functional limitations) and psychological (life satisfaction, depressed mood) outcomes. Providing further evidence about how such beliefs may be beneficial, a study of 2,471 Norwegian adults aged 40–79 years who were followed up over five years found high mastery beliefs be a significant predictor of youthful self-perceived age, with particular effects in those aged 60–69 years, rather than 40–49 or 70–79 (Bergland et al. 2013). Thus, rather than demonstrating a linear relationship with age, mastery seems to have particular effects, at least with regards to subjective or self-perceived age, in late middle age – when perhaps ageing begins to become a concern with regards to changes in physical or mental health.

WHAT DO YOU THINK?

While findings such as those described above make general conclusions, there are obviously individuals who differ from the mean (in other words, some people of low socio-economic status (SES) will report high mastery, and some of high SES will report low mastery). However, thinking of the overall picture, stop and ask yourself why many people of a lower SES have a lower sense of control and greater perceptions of constraints in their lives than people of higher SES. Do you think they are right in having such views, i.e. might such beliefs be adaptive in certain circumstances? Refer back to Chapter 2 ☞ when thinking about these issues.

Finally, also related to control beliefs are **causal attributions**. In a review of 64 datasets exploring associations between attributions of cause in a wide range of conditions (including arthritis, cancer, heart disease, burns, AIDS, infertility, stroke and pregnancy loss) and adjustment (Hall and Marteau 2003), contrary to expectations 80 per cent of studies reported no association between internal (behavioural self-blame) attributions or external (other-blame) attributions and adjustment. In fact, no particular attribution was strongly associated with achieving a better outcome. Characterological self-blame (e.g. 'It is something in my nature that I can't change that caused me to become ill') was, however, most often associated with poorer outcomes, which fits with previous reports of associations between this type of self-blame and depression.

Hope

Snyder and colleagues (1991a) introduced hope and its measurement to the study of cognitive–motivational

---

causal attribution
where a person attributes the cause of an event, feeling or action to themselves, to others, to chance or to some other causal agent.

processes involved in explaining human behaviour. Relevant to the study of stress and coping, hope was defined as 'a positive motivational state that is based on an interactively derived sense of successful (a) agency (goal-directed energy) and (b) pathways (planning to meet goals)' (Snyder et al. 1991b: 287). For Snyder, hope was fundamentally the person's belief that they can set, plan and attain goals – hope emphasises goal-directed thinking and was believed to have both trait and state-like aspects. There is some conceptual overlap between the hope construct and other constructs, such as dispositional optimism and self-efficacy, both of which have also been associated with persistence in the face of goal challenges and positive physical and emotional well-being. Snyder et al. (2006) acknowledge that all three constructs focus on individual 'resources', but explain that hope is about the motivation (agency) and route (pathway) to achieving goals (outcomes), whereas optimism reflects a generalised positive outcome expectancy that is not founded solely on agency and pathway thinking, and self-efficacy is less a generalised belief than a situational and goal-specific belief that depends on various contingencies (i.e. I can do 'a' even if the situation is 'b'). (Some might question this, given that self-efficacy theories do also propose a more generalised construct.) Snyder further supports his argument by describing how a hope-based intervention would differ from an optimism- or a self-efficacy-based intervention, although the differences have not been fully tested. However, in their recent book, Snyder's colleagues (Lopez et al. 2014) suggest that together 'self efficacy, optimism and hope provide the momentum needed to pursue a good life' (p. 210), suggesting perhaps that interventions may be less concerned with their separation.

Folkman (2010) described how 'Hope, like stress, is appraisal based, it waxes and wanes, is contextual, and is complex' (p. 902). For Folkman, hope is about more than goals; it is motivational but it is also in a bidirectional and active relationship with coping and is about emotion and finding meaning (Folkman and Moskowitz 2000). For example, when faced with a life-threatening illness, people may revise their goals in order to find one which falls more easily within their control which they can then imbue with hope. Hope in some contexts can have faith-like or existential qualities, for example, when coping with an uncertain future or a changing reality following an HIV or terminal cancer diagnosis (e.g. hope to find peace). Whether closely tied to goals, or more broadly defined, the construct of hope is hard to capture empirically. As Folkman acknowledges, we, as behavioural and social scientists 'cannot capture all of its aspects. However, what we do learn from those aspects we are able to study can be used to help people sustain well-being through difficult times' (p. 907). There does, however, still remain a need for empirical studies to establish whether the measurable aspects of hope adds any 'unique' explanation in terms of health outcomes, compared to that offered by assessment of other personal 'resource' variables such as optimism and personal control.

The constructs reviewed in this section are often referred to within a field of study known as 'positive psychology', i.e. where a person's strengths, resources and abilities are focused on and harnessed rather than their pathology, limitations or negative cognitions and emotions. 'In the spotlight' further highlights this area of work. In the subsequent section, however, we return to addressing the more negative emotions found to be associated with stress responses and outcomes.

IN THE SPOTLIGHT

Positivity and meaningful lives vs. happiness from low expectations!

There has been a growth in what is being called 'positive psychology' (Folkman and Moskowitz 2000; Seligman and Csikszentmihalyi 2000; Snyder and Lopez 2005). Basically, positive psychologists suggest that, as a discipline, we need to move away from a focus on the negatives (inability as a result of illness pathology, lack of resources, negative thoughts and emotions) and address the benefits to health and well-being offered by thinking and acting positively. Increasingly, this also addresses exploration of meaning-based coping and benefit-finding. The premise of positive psychology is that 'positive affect in the context of stress has important adaptational significance of its own' (Folkman and Moskowitch 2000: 648). For example, in addition to optimism and hope, discussed earlier, happiness and joy are thought to contribute to what Seligman, in a special edition on positive psychology in *The Psychologist* (2003), calls desirable lives: the pleasant life, the good life and the meaningful life. A pleasant life arises from one that pursues positive emotions about present, past and future experiences and involves the simple pleasures and gratifications or rewards that we get out of life. A good life arises from 'being' as well as 'doing' and by being involved in life and all its activities, in order to get the best out of it. A meaningful life is when we use our strengths and skills to benefit more than just ourselves.

To feel that life is pleasant, good or meaningful would imply that a person would therefore be happy. However, scant research has addressed positive emotions such as happiness in relation to health outcomes, with subjective 'well-being' (which may not be quite the same), often being used as a proxy (Diener et al. 2009). Ryan and Deci (2001) in fact distinguish between 'hedonic' well-being which focuses on happiness, pleasure attainment or the avoidance of pain, and 'eudaimonic' well-being which is more concerned with finding meaning and self-realisation. This latter consideration to well-being sits well with recent growth in mindfulness and compassion-based interventions (see Chapter 13 ☞).

Veenhoven (2003) believes that happiness is a subjective construct best measured by simply asking people, using questions such as: How happy are you on a scale of 1 to 10? What makes you happy? What makes your life good? For some it may be the reduction of tension, for others it will be attaining a desired goal, both which reflect a sense of being satisfied. For others, happiness is seen as resulting from meaningful engagement in life and its activities, with the experience of 'flow' (when engagement is successfully matched by your skills) making us even happier (Csikszentmihalyi, 1997). For others, the ability to be happy is possibly genetic, or at least personality-based: for example, happiness has been found to be associated with extroversion (Lucas and Fujita 2000).

Think about your own life and what makes you happy – some would suggest it may help you live longer, but while that is yet to be proven, it seems reasonable to expect that it won't do you any harm! However, the *Daily Telegraph* reported in August 2015 that, following an experimental study of gambling researchers from the University of London (Rutledge et al. 2014) it had 'concluded that the key to happiness is having low expectations'. Not such a positive spin, but perhaps a note of cautio:-)

Stress and emotions

Depression and anxiety

The role of depression in increasing the incidence/ likelihood of disease experience is controversial and depends on the disease concerned. The Alameda County study discussed in Chapter 3 ☞ (where we listed the seven types of 'healthy behaviour') did not find any effect of depressed mood upon CHD incidence; however, other studies have associated depression with hypertension, even when taking other risk factors into consideration. As early examples, the Framingham Heart Study found that depression, as well as anxiety, predicted 20-year incidence of hypertension even controlling for age, smoking and obesity (Markovitz et al. 1993), and, in relation to cancer, a major study showed that recurrent major depression among an elderly sample predicted a higher incidence of breast cancer (Penninx et al. 1998).

In relation to CHD, several reviews and meta-analyses have reported significant association between depression and CHD outcomes (heart attack, angina, cardiac death, as well as global CHD) (e.g. Booth-Kewley and Friedman 1987; Hemingway and Marmot 1999). In the latter review, 11 out of 11 longitudinal prospective studies in healthy populations presented results supportive of a role of depression and/or anxiety in the aetiology (development) of CHD, and 6 out of 6 prospective studies among CHD patients reported a significant prognostic role for depression. More recently, a large UK study (Surtees et al. 2008) found that of almost 20,000 CHD-free participants followed up on average 8.5 years, those diagnosed as having major depression were 2.7 times more likely to die from ischaemic heart disease than those who were not. This relationship existed even after all behavioural and demographic risk factors were controlled for.

A significant association between depressed mood and mortality from heart attack (myocardial infarction, MI) has also been reported (Bush et al. 2001). Frasure-Smith et al. (1995) concluded that depression was more predictive of death than either the degree of heart damage or having had a previous heart attack. This was confirmed in a longitudinal study of 237 healthy men where 45 per cent of those with a depressive episode at or before the baseline assessment were dead by the time of follow-up – a massive 55 years later – compared with only 5 per cent of those who had not experienced such an episode (Vaillant 1998). Neither depression nor anxiety predicted (non-) survival in two longitudinal studies of Scottish stroke patients (Lewis et al. 2001; Johnston et al. 2004; Morrison et al. 2005), although other studies with longer follow-ups have found a significant relationship (Morris et al. 1993).

Depressed mood may reflect an underlying state of negative affectivity and it is likely that, for some individuals, psychosocial risk factors cluster together: for example, stress plus hostility plus depression plus social isolation would confer compounded risk. It is also notable that anxiety and depression themselves are interrelated (Suls and Bunde 2005) and, although depression is perhaps more commonly found to be associated with CHD, and in fact all-cause mortality, anxiety also plays a role (Grossardt et al. 2009).

The evidence of a role of depression on CHD onset is relatively consistent when compared to the evidence of emotions associated with increased cancer risk. For example, the large-scale longitudinal Alameda County study found no relationship (Kaplan and Reynolds 1988). In the 1990s, two longitudinal studies of healthy, but older, samples followed over six years found inconsistent results, one finding an association between chronic depression and cancer incidence (Penninx et al. 1998), the other, finding no relationship (Whooley and Browner 1998). Notably, the latter study was conducted in a women-only sample and an association was in fact found with CHD and all-cause mortality. It is worth noting of course that findings revealed among older individuals may not hold for middle-aged or younger samples. Overall, the evidence appears to be, as with CHD, more

strongly in support of depression influencing outcomes rather than aetiology (Petticrew et al. 2002). Depression as an outcome of illness is addressed in Chapter 14 ☛.

When considering pathways by which depression may affect health outcomes, there are, as with personality, various possible routes. First, depression and anxiety have been shown to influence the appraisals that individuals make when facing stressful events (appraisals of threat, as opposed to appraisals of challenge), thus influencing the coping actions a person engages in. For example, for many, stress and distress may be maintained in those with the stable coping style/trait known as rumination, whereby a person will repeatedly rethink past events and worry about future ones (e.g. Nolen-Hoeksema 1991; Nolen-Hoeksema et al. 2008). Rumination has been related to many 'negative' states including anxiety and depression, has been shown to exacerbate negative future thinking and contribute to poorer problem-solving and is thought to be 'stress-reactive' (Alloy et al. 1999; Robinson and Alloy 2003). Although consistently associated with negative emotions, cognitive models of emotional distress in chronic physical illness rarely include rumination (Soo et al. 2009), with some exceptions, for example with cancer patients (Morris and Shakespeare-Finch 2010). It is likely that different aspects of rumination exist which have different effects: for example, a deliberate reflective rumination reappraises the situation to seek benefits and may be associated with post-traumatic growth, whereas life purpose rumination which revisits past events and losses and ponders one's purpose in life, and an intrusive rumination which is when unwanted thoughts of the negative experience regularly intrude into consciousness, are associated with negative emotions and coping responses. Brosschot et al. (2006) describe rumination as perseverative cognition and report further effects on physiological stress responses. Rumination is, however, amenable to intervention (e.g. Segal et al. 2002), using, for example, mindfulness-based interventions (e.g. Ramel et al. 2004; Foley et al. 2010; and see Chapter 13 ☛).

The second route in considering pathways by which depression may affect health outcomes is also indirect, i.e. via a person's behaviour. Depression is seen to reduce the likelihood of healthy behaviour or cessation of unhealthy behaviour. For example, people who had experienced a heart attack (MI) and who exhibited subsequent depression had lower rates of smoking cessation than those who did not show signs of depression five months after the MI (Huijbrechts et al. 1996). Depressed individuals were also less likely to attend cardiac rehabilitation classes than non-depressed individuals (Lane et al. 2001), and generally research findings suggest that adherence to therapeutic interventions or treatments such as exercise or medication is lower among depressed individuals than those who are not depressed (e.g. DiMatteo et al. 2000; Wing et al. 2002). Such non-adherent behaviour can expose individuals to adverse health outcomes, such as future illness, poorer recovery from illness, or even mortality.

Thirdly, there may be physiological pathways through which depression exerts its effects. Pointing to this, individuals with elevated depressive symptoms but without a history of coronary disease were twice as likely as their non-depressed counterparts to have **carotid plaques** (a significant risk factor for CHD), and this association also controlled for baseline risk factors (Haas et al. 2005), suggesting that this association was not solely attributable to behaviours such as smoking. A link has also been made between depression and increased pro-inflammatory cytokines in older people with cancer (Spolentini et al. 2008), suggesting a further possible mechanism of effect.

Finally, depression may also interfere with a person's ability to seek, or benefit from, social support and supportive interactions (see later section).

Emotional disclosure

One possible moderator of coping receiving increased attentions in recent years is that of emotional disclosure – the opposite of emotional suppression, or repressive coping, commonly found to be detrimental to health (see earlier 'Type C personality' section). A leading figure in this area is Pennebaker (e.g. Pennebaker et al. 1988; Pennebaker 1993), who with various colleagues has developed a paradigm whereby writing about one's feelings regarding a recent trauma (typically for 15 minutes, for several consecutive days) is shown to have long-term benefits in terms of reduced stress (Zakowski et al. 2004), immune functioning, including wound healing (Pennebaker et al. 1988; Petrie et al. 2004; Weinman et al. 2008) and health-care use (Pennebaker and Beall 1986). A large meta-analysis of 146 such studies supports the potential of this low-cost intervention (Frattaroli 2006).

Disclosure of emotional experiences is not to be confused with work on **expressed emotion** (EE; can include the venting of negative as well as positive emotion) which, although studied using a similar writing paradigm,

has been associated with poorer prognosis among psychiatric populations and is showing contradictory findings among the physically ill (interested readers can see a meta-analysis by Panagopoulou et al. 2002). It is thought that venting negative emotion may maintain the emotion by virtue of increasing the attention paid to it; it can also interfere with the potential to receive social support (Semmer 2006). For example, Coyne and colleagues (2003) found that EE among couples where one had experienced **congestive heart failure** was associated with poorer marital quality and increased distress. Other authors suggest that EE assists in emotional self-regulation by allowing the person to develop greater mental control over the stressor and a coherent narrative of events in their head, which facilitates 'closure' and reduces distress (Niederhoffer and Pennebaker 2005). There is evidence that the style of expression (antagonistic vs. constructive expression of anger) influences whether the outcome of expression is positive or not (e.g. Davidson et al. 2000).

Social support and stress

So far in this chapter we have focused on aspects of the individual that influence how they respond to stress. We now turn attention to include those beyond the individual – to social support. Evidence exists that people who have strong (in both size and usage) networks of social support

---

carotid plaque

a plaque is a thick waxy coating which forms on blood vessel walls and restricts blood flow, in this instance in the carotid artery.

expressed emotion

the disclosure of emotional experiences as a means of reducing stress; often achieved by describing the experience in writing.

congestive heart failure

a disorder in which the heart loses its ability to pump blood efficiently. As a consequence, many organs do not receive enough oxygen and nutrients, leading to the potential for them to become damaged and, therefore, not work effectively.

are healthier and live longer than the socially isolated (Cohen 2004; Cacioppo and Patrick 2008). Being in a social network and receiving support from it is available to most people at some points in their lives, but is not experienced by all people at all times (see also Chapter 15 ☞). What is meant by the term 'social support'?

Definition, types and functions of social support

Social support can be actual (received support) or perceived. People with social support believe they are loved and cared for, esteemed and valued, and part of a social network of communication and mutual obligation, such as that often shared with family, friends or members of a social organisation. Sources of support can include anyone from partners, close family and friends, to colleagues, to health and social-care professionals and support groups.

Social support is generally considered in terms of two interacting components – its structure (i.e. type of support, size of networks) and the function(s) they serve (Uchino 2006). The social network facilitates the provision of goods, services and mutual defence in times of need or danger (Cobb 1976). However, people may vary in the extent to which they participate in these networks – how 'tied' they are to those within them, and what they offer, for example. People also differ in how they perceive the quality of relationships within their social networks and how satisfied they are with the support they receive from them (Rokach 2011).

A lack of integration with one's supportive resources is often referred to as social isolation, which is a recognised risk factor for poor well-being; however, a lack of satisfaction, or meaningful connection with one's relationships, no matter how many the person has, is more likely to be associated with, as Utz and colleagues describe (Utz et al. 2013) a 'state of mind' called loneliness. In studying social support, therefore, one must not only be aware of the interconnectedness of the common terms of 'social support', social networks' and 'social integration' (Gottlieb and Bergen 2010), but furthermore, consider the individual's appraisals of their support, as this distinguishes two qualitatively different experiences, that of being alone, and that of feeling alone/lonely.

Table 12.3 presents examples of types of social support and their functions in terms of what the social support provider provides and in terms of what is received by the recipient. Some support may be global (i.e. from people generally) or specific to one event or support person. Five basic types have been described, although the most common distinction is between instrumental, emotional and informational. Most studies do not attempt to record what the recipient actually 'gets' from the support but instead assume that it is all helpful. (Chapter 15 ☞ challenges this assumption when care-giver and care-receiver relationships are examined in terms of whether support given 'matches' what is needed or desired, cf Cutrona and Russell 1990). Furthermore, some studies assess perceived support which is a person's belief that support is available to them, whereas others address actual received support, and there is evidence that this is an important distinction, particularly where there is a mismatch between what is expected and what is received. Perceived support is often more predictive of outcome than actual received

Table 12.3 Types and functions of social support

	Provider	Recipient
Emotional support	Empathy Caring Concern	Reassurance Sense of comfort and belongingness
Esteem support	Positive regard Encouraging person Positively comparing	Builds self-worth Sense of competence Being valued
Tangible/instrumental support	Direct assistance financial/practical aid	Reduces strain/worry
Informational support	Advice, suggestions feedback	Communication self-efficacy/self-worth
Network (or 'companionate', cf. Gottlieb and Bergen 2010) support	Welcoming Shared experiences	Sense of belonging Affiliation

support, and in fact having to seek it out rather than receive what was anticipated spontaneously can have a negative impact (E. Lawrence et al. 2008).

Social support is considered within Lazarus's stress and coping framework as a resource variable that when perceived as being available will affect how individuals appraise and respond to, i.e. cope with, events. Individuals who perceive support levels as high are likely to appraise events as less stressful than individuals who do not perceive they have any support (i.e. social support acts as a 'buffer' against stress). Evidence of the association between social support and health outcomes is reviewed below, followed by consideration of some of the likely mechanisms of action. First, however, it is worth highlighting that social support may show different patterns in different people. For example, there is evidence that socio-economic and cultural factors shape the extent to which individuals can access social networks which facilitate support provision and receipt (Chaix et al. 2007; Parveen et al. 2011). A gender difference has also been reported whereby friends were found to benefit men's and women's well-being equally, but for men, family support had a stronger effect (Cable et al. 2013). In addition, although the size of one's social network has been generally found to reduce with age and become proportionally more composed of family than non-kin friendships, this does not inevitably mean the quality of support is less (Soulsby and Bennett 2015).

Social support and mortality

Many years have been spent trying to establish whether receiving social support is causally implicated in mortality. Early support was obtained from the Alameda County study (Berkman and Syme 1979), showing almost a twofold increased risk of mortality for both men and women with fewest social ties, even when health status and self-reported health-risk behaviour were controlled for. Social isolation (low social support and social activity) was associated with heart disease mortality among middle-aged men followed up for ten years (Orth-Gomér et al. 1988), and in a 15-year follow-up of 2,603 adults (Vogt et al. 1992), social 'networks' (size, number of supportive domains, frequency of use) strongly predicted mortality from ischaemic heart disease, cancer and stroke. More recently support has come from a meta-analysis of data from 148 studies by Holt-Lunstad et al. (2010) where it was shown that people

with adequate social relationships (size and function) had a 50 per cent lower mortality risk compared to those reporting poor social relationships (p. 14).

Social support and disease

Evidence of a relationship between life stress and health status has pointed to social support as a moderator (for a review, see Taylor 2007). For example, among individuals suffering from rheumatoid arthritis, social support in terms of a limited social network was predictive of disease activity three years later, even when coping behaviour was controlled for (Evers et al. 2003). Among healthy samples, a large sample of French employees (Melchior et al. 2003), a lack of social support and dissatisfaction with social relationships predicted poor health status. It has further been suggested that social relationships are particularly important in diseases where physical dependence on others and decreased social activity resulting from the disease are present (Penninx et al. 1999). One measure of social support commonly used amongst older samples is the Duke Social Support Index (23-item version or an abbreviated 11-item version, e.g. Koenig et al. 1993) which assesses both satisfaction with support (e.g. 'Does it seem that your family and friends (i.e. people who are important to you) understand you'?) and social interaction (e.g. 'How many times did you talk to someone, friends, relatives or others on the phone in the past week (either they called you or you called them')?). Used in a large (1,2000) nationally representative sample of Australian women aged 70–75 years (the Womens Health Australia cohort) (Powers et al. 2004), the association between social support and both physical and mental health was confirmed. In particular, the 'satisfaction' rather than the 'interaction' factor was significant, demonstrating the importance of quality over quantity. Within older adults where loss of social relationships is common, it may be important to balance a need for solitude with a need for contact with others. Social conflict within one's reduced social network can be detrimental to emotional well-being (Rook et al. 2011; Rook 2015).

How does social support influence health status?

We all need support. There is ample evidence that social support effectively reduces distress during times of stress, and furthermore the lack of social support during times of need can itself be very stressful, particularly for people with high needs for social support but insufficient or altered opportunities to obtain it, e.g. the elderly, the recently widowed and other victims of sudden, severe or uncontrollable life events (e.g. Penninx et al. 1999; Balaswamy et al. 2004; Stroebe et al. 2005, Utz et al. 2013). There is, however, more evidence for the benefit of social support in reducing stress and distress during illness than there is on actually preventing it occurring. Greenwood et al. (1996), following a review of empirical studies, also concluded that poor social support had a stronger effect on CHD incidence than did stressful life events.

Two broad theories as to how social support might operate have been proposed (Cohen 1988):

1. *Direct effects hypothesis:* social support is beneficial regardless of the amount of stress people experience, and a lack of social support is detrimental to health even in the absence of stress. High levels of social support provide greater 'ties' to others and a greater sense of belonging and self-esteem than low levels, thus producing a positive outlook and healthier life-styles. Alternatively, social support has a physiological route to health by virtue of either reduced blood pressure reactivity, thought to arise from positive stress appraisals and emotions, or possibly via enhanced endocrine or immune system functions, although there are less consistent findings in this area. (For a comprehensive review, see Uchino 2006.)

2. *Buffering hypothesis:* social support protects the person against negative effects of high stress. Social support acts as a buffer by either (a) influencing the person's *cognitive appraisals* of a situation so they perceive their resources as being greater to meet threat; or (b) modifying the person's *coping response* to a stressor after it has been appraised as stressful (e.g. social support encourages positive thinking or behaviour) (Cohen and Wills 1985; Badr et al. 2010).

Evidence for direct effect of social support

In terms of direct effects on healthy behaviour, there is reasonably consistent evidence that social support facilitates healthy behaviours such as not smoking and adhering to medication, although, as discussed in Chapter 5 ☞, social influence can also be negative.

It is likely that social support enables the individual, for example, by promoting their self-efficacy (see Chapter 5 ☞) beliefs. For example, when stopping smoking, a supportive person, perhaps someone who has already quit smoking themselves, can provide assurances and enhance the other person's confidence and self-efficacy for change (Schwarzer and Knoll 2007). Many studies have pointed to beneficial effects of social support for psychosocial well-being among both healthy and ill populations. For example, marital support has been shown to benefit partner mental and physical well-being, although some studies show stronger effects for male partners than for females (Kiecolt-Glaser and Newton 2001), possibly reflecting gender differences in ability to seek or provide needed support, and also in the response to it (see also Chapter 15 ☞). Here we consider more the direct effects of social support on physiological rather than behavioural processes.

Uchino (2006) reviews the evidence regarding physiological pathways affected by social support, and highlights both reduced stress reactivity seen in typical measures of cardiovascular reactivity (see Chapter 11 ☞) and also some evidence of neuroendocrine and immune responses, the latter particularly important among older samples. However, this review primarily addresses experimentally manipulated support and we need to consider 'real-world' evidence also. Turner-Cobb et al. (2000) found that breast cancer patients who assessed social support as being present and helpful had lower morning cortisol levels than those who did not assess social support in this way, suggesting a physiological route by which social support may enact its benefits. As described in Chapter 8 ☞ and Chapter 11 ☞ cortisol has been implicated in immune down-regulation and is perhaps implicated in tumour growth. Cognitive-behavioural interventions that have provided breast cancer patients with group support have also reported reduced cortisol levels (e.g. Creuss et al. 2000). A recent review of social support and cardiovascular disease and cancer risk has also highlighted a role for the immune system and biochemical processes of inflammation, involving pro-inflammatory cytokines and interleukins (see also Chapter 11 ☞; Penwell and Larkin 2010). While the evidence is not conclusive, such reviews certainly offer exciting insights into some of the potential mechanisms through which social support achieves its beneficial effects on health.

ISSUES

Is giving support to others good for your health?

Studies by Poulin and colleagues (e.g. Poulin and Holman 2013; Poulin et al. 2013) have suggested a physiological route to well-being offered by being helpful to others. In a series of studies adults were assessed in relation to:

- stressful life events exposure;
- 'prosocial behaviour' whereby a person is involved in their communities e.g. giving blood donations, giving money or time to charity, being involved in a community action;
- group membership, e.g. of religious, community or social groups such as youth clubs;
- lifetime self-reported physical and mental health ailments (diagnosed) and
- their oxytocin receptor genotype (OXTR).

The first four of these have been described at various points throughout this textbook; however, the latter, OXTR, needs further mention. This neurohormone has been found to motivate parental caregiving behaviour in animal research, as referred to in Chapter 11 ☞ in humans, has been shown to modulate HPA (hypothalamic–pituitary–adrenal) pathway activity as well as cardiovascular reactivity in response to stress. In addition prosocial behaviour has been associated with positive health outcomes.

Following on from what these findings suggest, Poulin's studies sought to identify whether oxytocin was the mechanism behind these effects. They confirmed this hypothesis, finding that oxytocin mediated the negative effects of stressful life events on the onset of new health conditions experienced over a two-year period, in those with a specific type of oxytocin receptor genotype. This effect was further mediated by prosocial behaviour, suggesting that charitable behaviour may have boosted the compromised oxytocin release that characterises those with the genotype. Although this does not mean that acting in a charitable manner benefits everyone's health (only those with this specific genotype) and instead suggests perhaps that being charitable is underpinned by genetics (hence Poulin's research being described as the 'neurogenics of niceness'), it is a fascinating new line of research which needs extension and replication.

Photo 12.2 From an early age, social support is a powerful moderator of stress response

Evidence for indirect or 'buffering' effect of social support

The effect of perceived and actual social support on the appraisal of stressful events has not perhaps been rigorously studied to date, although there is some evidence that perceiving social support as being available contributes to more positive outcome expectancies and appraisals of control over the event. Furthermore, perceptions of control in relation to illness outcomes were positively associated with seeking social support in a meta-analysis of 45 empirical studies, albeit not as strongly as might have been expected (Hagger and Orbell 2003). This may in part be because social support was often assessed as part of a generic measure of coping, rather than by a specific assessment of the different types and function of social support.

Generally speaking, seeking social support is considered an active coping strategy, whether the support is sought for informational and practical reasons or with the goal of emotional support. When examining the coping strategies of young people within two months of developing cancer, Kyngaes et al. (2001) found that emotion-, appraisal- and problem-focused coping strategies were all used, but accessing social support was one of the most common strategies. Different 'functions' of support were seen, i.e. they sought information about their disease and its treatment from health professionals, and emotional support from their families. Seeking information about one's condition or about what lies ahead in order that one can plan is considered a form of **proactive coping**, as opposed to reactive coping. Other skills that reflect proactive coping are goal setting, organisation and mental stimulation (cf. Aspinwall and Taylor 1997). In proactive coping, a person's efforts are aimed at goal management, with altered events or demands seen more as challenges than threats, and it appears that social support promotes proactive coping because resources from one's social network help shape one's choice of coping strategy. Greenglass and colleagues (2006) examined proactive coping amongst an elderly sample of community-residing older adults (mean age 75 years), in order to examine

> **proactive coping**
> the process of anticipating potential stressors and acting in advance either to prevent them or to minimise their impact.

its direct or indirect effects on functional disability (FD). Given the global ageing population, there is a growing number of people living, in the community, with functional limitations and disability. Functional ability or disability is predicted by factors described in this chapter, including personal resources of health status, age and social support, and by the manner in which the individual copes with stressful events. Whilst the hypothesis that proactive coping would predict less FD was supported, the hypothesised direct association between social support and low FD was not supported, and an association (positive) between depression and FD was. Social support enhanced the proactive coping efforts these elderly participants engaged in and, as such, proactive coping can be described as mediating the effects of social support on functional disability and on depression. Proactive coping was associated with both less depression and less functional disability. The measure used did, however, suggest some overlap with self-efficacy, for example, items such as 'I always find a way around obstacles, nothing really stops me' and so potential opportunities for intervention to enhance proactive coping might operate via self-efficacy training.

Gender and cultural influences on seeking support

Gender is considered to be a robust predictor of the use of social support, with many empirical studies finding that females have a greater tendency both to seek and provide social support, and as a result tend to report larger social networks than males. Taylor (2006) suggests that female socialisation may generate a 'tend and befriend' response in times of stress, whereby nurturing loved ones or seeking and maintaining supportive networks are characteristic coping behaviours. Within spousal relationships, male partners tend to receive their support from female spouses, whereas female partners tend to receive support from female friends and relatives.

There are consistent findings that cultural differences exist in the norms of support-seeking behaviour and in the perceptions of available support, where Asian cultures, which have a collectivist rather than individualist orientation, tend not to seek or expect support (V. Lawrence et al. 2008; Kim et al. 2009). As Kim et al. state, 'people in the more collectivistic cultures may be relatively more cautious about bringing personal problems to the attention of others for the purpose of enlisting their help because they share the cultural assumption that individuals should not burden their social networks and that others share the same sense of social obligation' (p. 519). In contrast, Europeans, and Americans, use friends for support as much as, if not sometimes more than, family (Taylor et al. 2004; Chun et al. 2007; and see review by Parveen 2011). It is consistently found that in Asian samples (including Chinese, Korean, Japanese), for example, carers of those with chronic or disabling illness (see Chapter 15 ☞) report receiving significantly less social support than that reported by white American carers (e.g. Chun et al. 2007; McCabe et al. 2005; Katbamna et al. 2004). Interestingly, however, this difference may only be between Asian and non-Asian; Lincoln et al. (2003), for example, found in contrast that African Americans turned to family for support to a greater extent than did European Americans. The difference seems to lie in the 'seeking' of support, with Asian individuals exhibiting reluctance to disrupt relationships by talking of personal problems and seeking explicit support. Taylor et al. (2007) found that in Asian cultures the perception of having the 'implicit support' of others was more acceptable than explicitly seeking or receiving support, as it does not necessitate any disclosure of problems to others. Implicit support was both biologically (seen in reduced cortisol responses) and psychologically (seen in reduced stress scores) more beneficial to their Asian American participants, with the reverse actually being true for European Americans for whom explicit support is preferred and more beneficial. A review of studies relating to this important cultural difference is found in Kim et al.'s (2009) paper, and strongly highlights the need for cultural norms to be taken into account when, for example, considering any intervention which aims to deliver explicit support.

Can social support be bad for you?

There are some instances where high levels of social support can be detrimental. For example, among pain patients, it was found that high social support in terms of providing practical assistance with everyday tasks caused poor adaptation through operant conditioning (e.g. Gil et al. 1987). Over-caring can cause the care recipient to become overly dependent on the carer and overly passive in terms of their own recovery (see Chapter 15 ☞). In Chapter 15 ☞ we will describe a more systemic extension of Lazarus's transactional stress-coping model which has been described in this and the previous chapter, where the interdependence between the support provider and the support receiver is considered more fully (e.g. Falconier et al. 2013). The type of social support provided may not always be received as supportive, or, more importantly, the help offered may not match the needs of the patient (Rook et al. 2011). For example, instrumental support is helpful if aspects of the event are controllable; emotional support may be more helpful when things are uncontrollable, e.g. after a death (e.g. Cutrona and Russell 1990; Cutrona et al. 2007).

Finally, there is a caveat in social support research. Given the subjectivity of the construct, studies have to rely on self-report. As noted elsewhere, there are inherent biases in gathering self-report data, and it is likely that individual difference variables, such as neuroticism, may influence not only an individual's perceptions of the nature and level of social support they have received but also their satisfaction with it. Additionally, personality or emotional state might interfere with social resources and in effect prevent or enhance a person's ability to access support, or gain from it (see discussion of hostility or depression). These confounding factors therefore need consideration in any social support enhancing interventions.

SUMMARY

The evidence reviewed in Chapter 11 ☞ suggested that stress can increase the risk of artery damage, which in turn encourages the development of CHD. This is a direct effect proposal, which implies that simply reducing stress exposure would reduce the likelihood of that disease. However, this chapter has shown this to be overly simplistic. Many factors moderate the impact of stress on health, or the impact of stressful illness upon longer-term outcomes such as disability, distress and survival. This chapter has described how factors attributed to a person's personal profile (age, gender, ethnicity), personality, beliefs, emotions (both positive and negative), and social support can affect stress responses in terms of coping or in terms of physiological responses, which in turn influence health outcomes. Such variables can be studied in terms of the direct relationships they have with stress and illness outcomes, or as variables that need to be controlled for when examining other predictors. For example, one study might examine whether trait neuroticism predicts psychological distress following surgery, where another study might control for neuroticism in examining the effects of a pre-surgical information sheet on patient distress following surgery. Whatever the research question, it has become increasingly clear that many variables influence our appraisals of events and how we cope with them, and that biological, psychological and sociocultural factors work together in the stress–health–illness experience.

Further reading

Snyder, C. and Lopez, S.J. (2005). *Handbook of Positive Psychology*. New York: Oxford University Press.

A comprehensive collection of chapters from eminent research academics such as Martin Seligman (positive psychology), Ed Diener (science of happiness), Howard Tennen and Glenn Affleck (benefit-finding). The chapters address the cognitive, emotional, interpersonal, behavioural and biological aspects of positive strengths such as seen in appraisals, coping or social support mechanisms.

Key papers

Lopez, S.J., Pedrotti, J.T. and Snyder, C.R. (eds) (2014). *Positive Psychology: The Scientific and Practical Exploration of Human Strengths*. 3rd edition, Los Angeles: Sage.

Given the burgeoning field of positive psychology, this textbook presents a useful and informed review of the history of the field, the evidence surrounding concepts such as personal strengths, resilience, pleasure, positive emotions (including happiness), optimism and hope, and the opportunities for intervention some of the evidence points to.

Semmer, N.K. (2006). Personality, stress, and coping. In M.E. Vollrath (ed.), *Handbook of Personality and Health*. London: Wiley, pp. 73–113.

A clear account of the various processes and mechanisms through which personality may influence stress and coping responses and disease risk, progression or other outcomes.

Taylor, S.E., Welch, W., Kim, H.S. and Sherman, D.K. (2007). Cultural differences in the impact of social support on psychological and biological stress responses. *Psychological Science*, 18: 831–7.

A fascinating and important review of a strong body of evidence pointing to cultural variations in support-seeking coping – read this if you are planning a social support intervention!

Weblinks

For personality assessment items based on a scientific collaboration to develop advanced measures of personality and other individual difference variables, go to the International Personality Item Pool at:

http://ipip.ori.org/ipip

For open-access student resources specifically written to complement this textbook and support your learning, please visit **www.pearsoned.co.uk/morrison**

Chapter 13
Managing stress

Learning outcomes

By the end of this chapter, you should have an understanding of:

- cognitive-behavioural and mindfulness approaches to stress management
- ways of intervening at a population or organisational level to reduce work stress
- interventions of value in helping people to cope with the stress associated with a surgical operation

Stress costs the National Health Service millions of pounds

No surprise in that, we hear you think. And, indeed, stress-related diseases do cost the British National Health Service (NHS) millions of pounds. But these are not the only cause of stress-related financial drain on valuable NHS resources – some can be directly influenced by the health-care system itself. Staff sickness due to stress is estimated to cost the NHS in excess of £400 million a year. Less measurable is the impact of stress on patient recovery. Being in hospital and having an operation are both inherently stressful events: stress that may impact on patients' experience of pain, their use of pain medication, and even the time taken to recover from surgery. Conversely, simple interventions to reduce stress prior to an operation or giving patients control over pain medication have been shown to reduce the amount of pain medication used, and even reduce the time patients spend in hospital. Stress may be an ambiguous term; it may even be inherent in the experience of being a health-care worker or patient, but reducing the stress of both hospital staff and their patients may not only make their lives better but also actually save money.

Chapter outline

Stress, they say, is all around us. Indeed, one of the most frequently reported problems in general practitioners' surgeries is tiredness as a symptom of stress. Other chapters in this book comment on the role of stress in the development or response to illness (Chapters 11 and 12 ☞) or how learning to manage stress can enhance mood, improve disease outcomes and reduce the experience of pain (Chapters 16 and 17 ☞). What they do not consider in any detail is how any changes can be achieved. This chapter addresses this issue from a number of perspectives. It starts by reviewing the basic cognitive-behavioural model of stress, before building on this and more complex models to introduce two distinct treatment approaches. The first, known as stress management training, adopts a traditional cognitive-behavioural approach. The second involves the use of mindfulness approaches to managing negative emotions. The chapter then considers approaches used to minimise stress in healthy individuals, both in the public at large and in the workplace. In this, it complements Chapters 5 and 6 ☞ and their consideration of health-promotion strategies. Finally, we consider how stress may be minimised when people face a specific stressor, surgical intervention in hospital, using relatively simple interventions.

Stress theory: a quick review

In this first section, we examine components of interventions collectively referred to as **stress management training**. They are based on cognitive-behavioural theories of stress, which consider stress to be the outcome of a variety of environmental and cognitive processes. Stress is seen as a negative emotional and physiological state resulting from our cognitive responses to events that occur around us: that is, stress can be seen as a process rather than an outcome. We discussed appraisal and transactional theories of stress in Chapter 11 ☞. Stress

management approaches are in part based on these theories and in part based on more clinical theories, the two most prominent of which are those of Aaron Beck (1976) and Albert Ellis (1977). Both assumed that our cognitive response to events – not the events themselves – determines our mood, and that feelings of distress or other negative emotional states are a consequence of 'faulty' or 'irrational' thinking (see Figure 13.1). That is, they considered stress to be the result of *misinterpretations* of environmental events or cognitions that exaggerate the negative elements within them and lose focus on any positive aspects of the situation.

Beck referred to the thoughts that drive negative emotions as automatic negative thoughts (ANTs). They come to mind automatically as the individual's first response to a particular situation and are without logic or grounding in reality. Despite this, their automaticity means they are unchallenged and taken as true. He identified two levels of cognition. Surface cognitions are those we are aware of. We can access them and report them relatively easily. Underlying them are a set of

---

stress management training

a generic term for interventions designed to teach participants how to cope with stress.

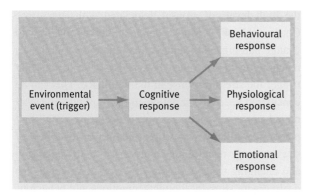

Figure 13.1 A simplified representation of the event–stress process suggested by Beck and other cognitive therapists

unconscious beliefs about ourselves and the world, known as **cognitive schemata** (singular, schema) which influence our surface cognitions and, in turn, our emotions, behaviour and physiological arousal. Stress-evoking thoughts, for example, result in an increase in sympathetic nervous system arousal (see Chapter 8 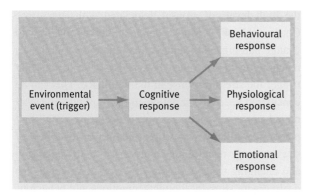), behaviour that may be more or less helpful in resolving the problem an individual is facing, and feelings of anxiety. Beck identified a number of categories of thought that lead to negative emotions, including:

- *Catastrophic thinking:* considering an event as completely negative, and potentially disastrous: 'That's it – I've had a heart attack. I'm bound to lose my job, and I won't be able to earn enough to pay the mortgage.'

- *Over-generalisation:* drawing a general (negative) conclusion on the basis of a single incident: 'That's it – my pain stopped me going to the cinema – that's something else I can't do.'

- *Arbitrary inference:* drawing a conclusion without sufficient evidence to support it: 'The pain means I have a tumour. I just know it.'

- *Selective abstraction:* focusing on a detail taken out of context: 'OK, I know I was able to cope with going out, but my joints ached all the time, and I know that will stop me going out in future.'

---

cognitive schemata

set of unconscious beliefs about the world and ourselves that shape more conscious cognitive responses to events that impinge on us.

A good example of how long-term schemata drive very stressful ways of responding to external events is provided by Price's (1988) cognitive model of Type A behaviour (see Chapter 12). From her clinical work with Type A men, she concluded that the schemata underlying Type A behaviour were low self-esteem and a belief that one can gain the esteem of others only by continually proving oneself as an 'achiever' and a capable individual. These underlying beliefs underpinned more conscious competitive, time-urgent or hostile thoughts.

Surface cognitions associated with Type A behaviour include:

- *Time-urgent thoughts:* 'Come on – we haven't got all day – I'm going to be late! Why is he so slow? Am I the only person who gets things done around here?'

- *Hostile thoughts:* 'That person cut me up deliberately! I'll sort him out. Why is everyone else so incompetent – they really are pretty stupid.'

Deeper (unconscious) schemata include:

- 'I can't say no to her request or I will look incompetent and I will lose her respect.'

- 'I must get to the meeting on time – whatever the cost – or people will think I'm incompetent and I will lose their respect.'

- 'People only respect me for what I do for them – not for who I am.'

So, somewhat ironically, behaviours that are generally seen as aggressive, confident and self-serving may actually be driven by negative beliefs about the self and low self-esteem.

Stress management training

The model of the stress response described above suggests a series of factors that can be changed in order to reduce an individual's stress. These include:

- environmental events that trigger the stress response – or a series of triggers to longer-term stress;

- inappropriate behavioural, physiological or cognitive responses that occur in response to this event.

The cognitive-behavioural model of stress assumes that stress lies within the individual. Stress arises from the misinterpretation of events that happen to us. But is this really true? It is possible to argue that, while some stress may be the result of faulty thinking, stress can also be triggered by truly stressful circumstances. Most people would consider having a surgical operation, for example, to be a stressful event. Theorists such as Hobfoll have argued that many more general factors, such as being a single mother or holding down a demanding job, are universally stressful events. Arguments that socio-economic status influences health through psychological processes discussed in Chapter 2 ☛ also suggest that there are broad differences in the degree of stress experienced across different social groups.

If these assertions are true, then, at least in some cases, stress truly may result from the environmental circumstances an individual is facing. Such arguments may lead us to question how relevant stress management techniques can be in these contexts.

The argument cognitive-behavioural therapists would marshal against this critique is that, while acknowledging the role of environmental factors as a cause of stress, some people cope with them better than others. There is individual variability in our ability to cope with the demands placed on us. The role of stress management is not to deny the role of the environment but to help people to cope with stressful circumstances they face as effectively as they can and with the least possible emotional distress.

This seems to be a reasonable argument, but it leaves a number of questions for health psychologists. One particularly pertinent issue is how much effort we should put into changing the sources of stress and how much into changing people's responses to potentially stressful environments? Should we help some people to cope better with operations, for example, or try to make the processes before and after an operation less stressful for all? Often, teaching people to cope better with stressful situations is easier and cheaper than changing the causes of stress. But is it the best approach?

Most stress management programmes focus on changing people's reactions to events that happen around them or to them. Many simply teach relaxation to minimise the high levels of arousal associated with stress (see Chapter 11 ☛). More complex interventions try to change participants' cognitive (and therefore emotional) reactions to these events. Few address the factors that trigger the stress response in the first place. This can be considered a serious limitation, as the most effective way of reducing stress is to prevent it occurring in the first place. Accordingly, we incorporate into our overview of stress management training a process of both identifying and changing triggers to stress as well as strategies for dealing with stressful thoughts, emotions and behaviour once initiated:

● Triggers can be identified and modified using problem-solving strategies.

● Cognitive distortions can be identified and changed through a number of cognitive techniques, such as **cognitive restructuring** (see below).

● High levels of muscular tension and other signs of physiological arousal can be reduced through relaxation techniques.

● 'Stressed' behaviour can be changed through consideration and rehearsal of alternative behavioural responses.

Changing triggers

This is an often neglected part of stress management training, perhaps because there is no standard intervention that can be applied. The triggers to each person's stress necessarily differ, as will any strategies they develop to reduce their frequency. Changing them involves first identifying situations that contribute to an individual's stress and then either changing their nature or reducing the frequency with which they occur. A simple strategy to reduce an individual's level of stress or anger while driving to work, for example, may be to start the journey earlier than previously so they feel less pressure during the journey.

One of the most frequently used approaches to identifying and changing triggers to stress was developed by Gerard

> **cognitive restructuring**
> a reconsideration of automatic negative or catastrophic thoughts to make them more in line with reality.

Egan (1998). His model of problem-focused counselling introduced in Chapter 6 ☞ can be adapted to coping with stress, so stress triggers are dealt with in three stages:

1. *Problem exploration and clarification:* what are the triggers to stress?

2. *Goal setting:* which stress triggers does the individual want to change?

3. *Facilitating action:* how do they set about changing these stress triggers?

Stress may have multiple sources, and some may be easier to change than others. It can be helpful to change relatively easy stress triggers before working towards those that are more difficult to change as the individual gains skills or confidence in their ability to effect change. Some changes can be achieved using personal resources already available to the individual. Others may require the individual to learn new skills in order to manage their stress more effectively. They may also benefit from learning to relax or reducing the frequency or type of any stress-provoking thoughts that contribute to their stress. It is to these taught skills that we now turn.

Relaxation training

The goal of relaxation is to enable the individual to relax as much as is possible and appropriate while dealing with any stress they may be experiencing. This contrasts with procedures such as meditation, which often provide a period of deep relaxation or 'time out' as sufficient in themselves. As well as the physical benefits, effective use of relaxation techniques can lead to an increase in actual and perceived control over the stress response. This can be a valuable outcome in itself. Relaxation may also increase access to calm and constructive thought processes, reflecting the reciprocity between each of the different stress components. Relaxation skills are best learned through three phases:

1. learning basic relaxation skills;

2. monitoring tension in daily life;

3. using relaxation at times of stress.

Learning relaxation skills

The first stage involves learning to relax under optimal conditions: a comfortable and fully supportive chair in a quiet room. Ideally, a trained practitioner should teach the process of deep relaxation live. This can be augmented by continued practice at home, typically using taped instructions. Regular practice over a period of days, and sometimes weeks, is important at this stage, as the skills need to be well practised and relatively automatic before they can be used effectively in 'real life' contexts.

The relaxation process most commonly taught is based on Jacobson's (1938) deep muscle relaxation technique. This involves alternately tensing and relaxing muscle groups throughout the body in an ordered sequence. Over time, the emphasis of practice shifts towards relaxation without prior tension, or relaxing specific muscle groups while using others, to mimic the use of relaxation in the 'real world'. While practising their relaxation skills, individuals can begin to monitor their levels of physical tension throughout the day. Initially, this serves as a learning process, helping them to identify how tense they are at particular times and what triggered any excessive tension. This process may also help identify likely future triggers to stress and suggest when the relaxation procedures may be particularly useful. This frequently involves the use of a 'tension diary', in which the individual records their level of tension on some form of numerical scale (0 = no tension, 100 = the highest tension possible) at regular intervals throughout the day or at times of particular stress. As a prelude to cognitive or behavioural interventions, such diaries may also focus on the thoughts, emotions or behaviour experienced at such times. Figure 13.2 provides an excerpt from a typical stress diary. As the individual begins to use additional strategies to combat their stress, they may add columns measuring their level of tension after the use of relaxation, the strategies they used to deal with their stressful thoughts, and so on.

After a period of monitoring tension and learning relaxation techniques, individuals can begin to integrate relaxation into their daily lives. At this stage, relaxation involves reducing tension to appropriate levels while engaging in everyday activities. Initially, this may involve trying to keep as relaxed as possible and appropriate at times of relatively low stress and then, as the individual becomes more skilled, using relaxation at times of increasing stress. The goal is not to escape from the cause of stress but to remain as relaxed as possible while dealing with the particular stressor.

Time	Situation	Tension	Behaviours	Thoughts
8.32	Driving to work – late!	62	Tense – gripping steering wheel Cutting up other drivers Cursing at traffic lights	Late again!! . . . the boss is bound to notice . . . Come on – hurry up – I haven't got all day! Why do these bloody traffic lights always take so long to change?!
10.00	Presenting work to colleagues	75	Spoke too quickly Rushed	I'm not looking good here . . . why can I never do this properly? They must think I'm a fool! I feel a wreck!

Figure 13.2 Excerpt from a stress diary noting stress triggers, levels of tension and related behaviours and thoughts

Cognitive interventions

Two strategies for changing cognitions are frequently employed. The simplest, known as self-instruction training, was developed by Meichenbaum (1985) and is targeted at surface cognitions. It involves interrupting the flow of stress-provoking thoughts and replacing them with pre-rehearsed stress reducing or 'coping' thoughts: so-called 'positive **self-talk'**. These typically fall into one of two categories: (i) reminders to use any stress-coping techniques the person has learned ('You're winding yourself up here – remember to relax, deep breaths, relax your muscles') and (ii) reassurance that the individual has previously coped effectively with their feelings of distress ('Come on, you've dealt with this before – you can again – keep calm – things will stay in control'). To make sure these are relevant to the individual, and to help to actually evoke these thoughts at times of stress, Meichenbaum suggested that self-talk should be rehearsed, wherever possible, before the stressful events occur, whether in a therapy session or minutes before an anticipated stressor.

A more complex intervention, known as cognitive restructuring, involves first identifying and then challenging the accuracy of stress-evoking thoughts. It asks the individual to consider their beliefs as hypotheses, not facts, and to assess their validity without bias. This process may involve consideration of both surface cognitions and cognitive schemata, although the latter requires

significant insight. Learning this skill often involves a process known as the Socratic method or 'guided discovery' (Beck 1976). In this, the client often identifies a number of stress-provoking thoughts that have recently occurred, and then challenges their accuracy under the guidance of their therapist. They may challenge their stressful assumptions by asking key questions such as:

● What evidence is there that supports or denies my assumption?

● Are there any other ways I can think about this situation?

● Could I be making a mistake in the way I am thinking?

Once the individual can engage in this process within the therapy session, they are encouraged to use the Socratic process at times when they experience stress in their daily lives (see also the discussion of the downward-arrow technique in Chapter 6 (☛)).

Behavioural interventions

The goal of behavioural change is to help the individual respond to any stress triggers in ways that maximise their effectiveness in dealing with the trigger and cause them minimal stress. Some behavioural changes may be relatively simple. Behaviour that reduces the stress of driving may involve driving within the speed limits, putting the handbrake on when stopped at traffic lights and taking time to relax, not cutting in front of other cars, and so on. Others may take practise: a person who becomes excessively angry, for example, may need to practise appropriately assertive responses in therapy sessions to prepare them for doing the same in 'real life'. Still others may have to be thought through at the time of the stress. The goal of stress management training is

> **self-talk**
> talking to oneself (internally). Can be negative and thus add to stress. Therapeutically, individuals are taught to use self-talk in a way that helps them to keep calm.

to teach individuals to plan and ensure their response to any potential stressor is one that minimises their personal stress. A simple rule of thumb is to encourage individuals to stop and plan what they are going to do – even if this takes a few seconds – rather than to jump into action without thought, as this typically leads to more rather than less stress.

Stress inoculation training

In his approach called **stress inoculation training**, Meichenbaum (1985) suggested that the various strands of cognitive therapy described above could be combined so that, when an individual is facing a stressor, they concentrate on:

- checking that their behaviour is appropriate to the circumstances;
- maintaining relaxation;
- giving themselves appropriate self-talk.

In addition, he suggested that, when a particular stressor can be anticipated, the opportunity should be taken to rehearse these actions before the event itself. Once in the situation, the planned strategies should be enacted. Finally, after the situation has occurred, time should be given to review what occurred and how any successes or failures can be learned from, rather than treated as triumphs or disasters that should be soon forgotten.

The third wave therapies

Historically, the stress management approach outlined above falls into what has become known as the second wave of cognitive-behavioural therapies. The first wave theories and treatments were based on Pavlov and Skinner's conditioning theories, and did not consider

stress inoculation training

a form of stress-reducing intervention in which participants are taught to control stress by rehearsing prior to going into stressful situations. Participants are taught to relax and use calming self-talk. The approach was developed by Donald Meichenbaum.

changing cognitions to be relevant to behavioural change. The second wave adopted a much more cognitive approach, viewing cognitions as central to both the development and treatment of emotional problems. Although most stress management interventions are still based on this approach, a so-called third wave of therapies is now gaining increasing empirical validation and use in the treatment of emotional disorders. The key characteristic of this approach can be characterised by the phrase 'Feel the fear, but do it anyway'. It adopts a more behavioural stance, shifting the focus from changing cognitions back to directly changing behaviour.

Proponents of this approach (e.g. Hayes et al. 2004) state that one way in which we become inappropriately anxious or distressed is through the avoidance of difficult or feared situations. As a consequence, we fail to learn that many of our fears are exaggerated, and that we could actually cope more effectively in the avoided situation than we believe. The goal of therapy is therefore to encourage the individual to engage in a feared behaviour, cope with the emotional or physiological responses they may experience while doing so, and through successful negotiation of the situation come to learn that there is actually nothing to fear.

The treatment of someone with agoraphobia using second and third wave therapies may illustrate the contrasting principles of the two approaches. Treatment using second wave therapies would initially involve the use of Socratic dialogue to identify and challenge the catastrophic beliefs they may hold about leaving the house. They may be taught to use coping skills such as relaxation and cognitive challenge when they leave the house, and engage in a behavioural programme involving going into increasingly challenging situations. On these occasions, they would monitor their arousal levels and try to reduce them through the use of relaxation. At the same time, they would monitor and challenge the veracity of any stressogenic thoughts using cognitive challenge. By contrast, third wave therapies would not teach individuals to challenge any negative thoughts they may have. Quite the opposite. Rather than challenge them, the individual learns to tolerate them and to understand that such thoughts have no power and cannot harm them. To help them achieve this, they may use mindfulness meditation (see below) to minimise their emotional impact. Success is measured by increasing engagement in previously avoided or fearful behaviours.

Mindfulness-based interventions

According to Buddhist learning, mindfulness is necessary on the road to enlightenment, and is achieved through the meditative process of focusing one's awareness on the present; not memories of the past or possible creations of the future. Through meditation, we learn that 'thoughts are just thoughts' that may or may not be true. We can also learn to ignore particular thoughts or to be aware of them without them evoking an emotional reaction. Bishop et al. (2004) proposed a two-component model of mindfulness:

● *Self-regulation of attention:* this involves being fully aware of current experience: observing and attending to thoughts, feelings and sensations as they occur, but not elaborating on these experiences. Rather than getting caught up in ruminative thoughts, mindfulness involves a direct non-judgemental experience of events in the mind and body as they occur. This leads to a feeling of being very alert and 'alive'.

● *An orientation toward one's experiences in the present moment characterised by curiosity, openness and acceptance:* the lack of cognitive effort given to the elaboration of the meanings and associations linked to our various experiences allows the individual to focus more on their present experience. Rather than observing experience through the filter of our beliefs and assumptions, mindfulness involves a direct, unfiltered awareness of our experiences.

Clearly, learning mindfulness is not simple, and most teaching programmes involve attending a number of classes spread over many weeks or months. During meditation, participants learn to focus on a particular physical stimulus, such as a picture, or a sensory stimulus such as the sound of a repeated mantra, and to be aware of, but not focused on, unwanted intrusive sensations, thoughts or emotions. Participants also practise mindfulness during ordinary activities like walking, standing and eating. This process can help people to become aware of their thoughts but not be overwhelmed by them. Rather than challenge such thoughts, practitioners of mindfulness learn to be aware of them, but only as a small, unattended part of their perceptual awareness which is still largely focused on the immediate experiences of the moment.

The most frequently cited method of mindfulness training is the mindfulness-based stress reduction programme of Kabat-Zinn (e.g. 2013). The programme comprises an 8–10-week course for groups who meet weekly for around two hours for instruction and practice in mindfulness meditation skills, together with discussion of stress, coping and homework assignments. An all-day (7–8-hr) intensive mindfulness session is usually held around the sixth week. Several mindfulness meditation skills are taught. For example, the 'body scan' is a 45-minute exercise in which attention is directed sequentially to numerous areas of the body while the participant is lying down with eyes closed. Sensations in each area are carefully observed. In sitting meditation, participants are instructed to sit in a relaxed and wakeful posture with eyes closed and to direct attention to the sensations of breathing. Hatha yoga postures are used to teach mindfulness of bodily sensations during gentle movements and stretching. Participants also practise mindfulness during ordinary activities like walking, standing and eating. Participants are instructed to practise these skills outside group meetings for at least 45 minutes a day, for six days per week. Audiotapes are used early in treatment, but participants are encouraged to practise without tapes after a few weeks. For all mindfulness exercises, participants are instructed to focus attention on the target of observation (e.g. breathing or walking), and to be aware of it in each moment. When emotions, sensations, or cognitions arise, they are observed non-judgementally. When the participant notices that their mind has wandered into thoughts, memories or fantasies, their nature or content is briefly noted, if possible, and then attention is returned to the present moment. Even judgemental thoughts (e.g. 'This is a waste of time') are to be observed non judgementally! An important consequence of mindfulness practice is the realisation that most sensations, thoughts and emotions fluctuate, or are transient, passing by 'like waves in the sea'.

Mindfulness

Mindfulness can form a stand-alone intervention or be combined with other stress management approaches. Wells (2000) argued that emotional distress arises following an appraisal of a disjunction between an actual and desired state ('If I stay here I am going to get really stressed', 'My angina is going to be triggered if I do any exercise'), and the development of plans to reduce or prevent this discrepancy from occurring. In the case of stress or anxiety (or the perceived health risk of exercising), these plans usually involve avoiding the situation that causes or contributes to these negative emotional states. This may reduce the immediate discrepancy between feeling fearful and the desired state of not being fearful. However, continued use of avoidance prevents the individual learning that the feared situation will not result in the expected harm. The goals of therapy include encouraging participants to engage in feared behaviours or enter feared situations in a graduated process, using skills such as mindfulness to help them cope with difficult thoughts or emotions that may occur at this time.

Acceptance and Commitment Therapy

A second mindfulness-based approach is known as Acceptance and Commitment Therapy (ACT; pronounced 'act'). According to Hayes et al. (2004: 143), ACT is a therapy approach that uses acceptance and mindfulness as well as commitment and behaviour change processes to teach increased psychological flexibility. ACT is rooted in radical behaviourism, as it assumes that psychological events (thoughts, emotions, behaviour) are the result of classical and operant conditioning processes. In addition, ACT does not consider thoughts or feelings as directing behaviour. Change can be achieved through changing contextual variables or direct behavioural change rather than attempts to change internal processes such as cognitions, emotions, sensations, and so on.

ACT teaches the individual to be aware of ongoing private events (thoughts), but not to be driven by them: to be in touch with the present moment as fully as possible, and to either change or persist in behaviours in order to achieve valued goals. All ACT interventions aim to increase the individual's flexibility in responding to situations they face. This flexibility is established through a focus on five related core processes: acceptance, defusion, contact with the present moment, values and committed action.

- *Acceptance:* allowing oneself to be aware of thoughts, feelings and bodily sensations as they occur, but not to be driven by them. The aim is to experience non-judgemental awareness of these events and actively embrace the experience. Therapy emphasises that attempts at inappropriate control are themselves stressful and maintain the distress one is trying to control: 'control is the problem, not the solution'.

Acceptance is taught through a variety of techniques, including mindfulness. Clients learn through graded exercises that it is possible to feel intense emotions or notice intense and bodily sensations without harm.

- *Cognitive defusion:* teaching clients to see that 'thoughts are simply thoughts, feelings are simply feelings, memories are memories, and physical sensations are physical sensations'. None of these experiences are inherently damaging. Just as in the second wave of cognitive therapy, clients are taught that our thoughts form just one interpretation of events, and there are many others that may be equally appropriate to any situation. However, rather than attempt to identify incorrect thoughts and change them to a 'correct' interpretation of events, clients are encouraged to accept their presence, and not to try to change or control them.

- *Contact with the present moment:* contact comprises effective, open and undefended contact with the present moment. There are two features to this process. First, clients are trained to observe and notice what is present in the environment and in 'private experience' (i.e. their thoughts and emotions). Second, they are taught to label and describe what is present without excessive judgements or evaluation. Together, these help establish a sense of 'self as a process of ongoing awareness' of events and experiences. Mindfulness is one technique through which this can be achieved.

- *Values:* the motivation for change. In order for a client to face feared psychological obstacles, there needs to be a purpose for doing so. The aim of ACT is not simply to rid the person of their problems, but to help them build a more vital, purposeful life. This is a central element of ACT. Its goal is to enable the individual to progress towards valued life goals without being prevented from doing so by worries, emotions and other private events.

- *Committed action:* developing strategies for achieving desired goals. Individuals are encouraged to define goals in specific areas and to progress towards them. Progress, or lack of it, towards these goals becomes a key part of therapy.

Strosahl et al. (2004) identified a number of broad strategies to help people make changes in each of these domains. These included:

- helping the individual make direct contact with the paradoxical effect of emotional control strategies: i.e. the more you try to avoid painful thoughts, the more they may be experienced, and avoidance of feared situations leads to continued fear;

● using a graded and structured approach to acceptance as assignments: a form of systematic desensitisation in which participants learn acceptance of painful emotions (and other factors) in gradually more demanding situations;

● using various interventions, including mindfulness, to reveal that unwanted private experiences are not toxic and can be accepted without judgement;

● showing the client how to pull away from worries or ruminations and come back to the present moment.

ACT is a complex therapy involving a variety of behavioural methods as well as the use of stories, metaphors and mental exercises to encourage change. As such, the approach cannot be fully considered within the present chapter. Interested readers may find the book edited by Strosahl et al. (2004), and listed at the end of the chapter, a useful further reader. However, the key underpinning of their approach is that the primary process of change is to engage in previously avoided behaviours or refrain from previous ineffective and problematic coping behaviours, to learn to cope or reduce the distress involved in doing this through the use of mindfulness, and thereby learn that the feared consequences will not occur. As such, despite many differences in philosophy and approach, both the cognitive approach of Wells and the behavioural approach of the ACT therapists have much in common.

Preventing stress

Teaching stress management strategies

There is clear evidence that second wave stress management programmes can significantly reduce stress and improve well-being. In addition, they have been shown to impact on a variety of biological processes known to be affected by stress. Both Storch et al. (2007) and Hammerfald et al. (2006), for example, found differing stress management programmes to be effective in reducing both perceived stress and levels of the stress hormone, cortisol (see Chapters 8 and 11 ☞). There is also increasing evidence that mindfulness-based interventions

can reduce stress. Shapiro et al. (2008), for example, randomly allocated college undergraduates with no evidence of mental health problems to either a mindfulness intervention or a waiting-list control group. Those in the mindfulness group achieved greater reductions in mindfulness as well as greater gains on measures of perceived stress and rumination. Nyklícek and Kuijpers (2008) also found mindfulness to be more effective in changing measures of well-being, perceived stress and exhaustion than a no-treatment control condition. Of course, comparison with a no-treatment group in both studies allows the possibility that any gains were a consequence of seeing a therapist or group dynamics rather than the therapy. However, the results are indicative of the potential for mindfulness to be an effective intervention. This is substantiated by the findings of Smith et al. (2008), who compared the effectiveness of an eight-week mindfulness-based intervention with a second wave CBT intervention for people recruited from the community. The mindfulness intervention appeared to be most effective, achieving the same level of benefit as second wave CBT on the core measures of well-being, perceived stress and depression, but performing better on measures of mindfulness (perhaps not surprisingly), energy and pain.

We consider the impact of stress management on well-being and biological processes in people with health problems in more detail in Chapter 17 ☞. The next sections, however, examine stress management interventions conducted with healthy individuals in a specific context – the workplace.

Stress management in the workplace

Stress management interventions clearly have the potential to provide significant benefit to those who take part – but only a very small proportion of the public who have the potential to benefit are likely to take the time and trouble to attend workshops or other training programmes. Health psychologists and others have therefore turned to other methods of reaching out to those who may benefit from stress management. One of the most important approaches they have adopted is to develop strategies for reducing stress in more 'captive audiences', the most important of which has been people at work.

There is significant and rising pressure on employers to provide staff with the skills to manage stress effectively. In the UK, this has become increasingly important as the Health and Safety Executive, which determines safety standards in the workplace, gives employers a legal obligation to protect the emotional as well as physical well-being of their employees. Their reasons for this policy include data indicating that:

- over half a million individuals in Britain experience work-related stress at a level that is making them ill, while nearly one in five think their job is very or extremely stressful;

- work-related stress, depression or anxiety accounts for an estimated 13.5 million lost working days per year in Britain;

- levels of work stress are rising;

- teachers and nurses have particularly high prevalence of work-related stress.

Most published attempts to reduce stress in the workplace have involved running stress management training at the workplace using similar methods to those described earlier in the chapter (with the majority involving relaxation training): that is, they have tried to help attenders to cope more effectively with the demands placed upon them. These appear to be effective. Summarising the relevant data in their meta-analysis, Richardson and Rothstein (2008) reported a limited but significant benefit. In one such study, Eriksen et al. (2002) randomly allocated a large group of employees to one of three intervention conditions: physical exercise, stress management training, or an integrated health programme involving physical exercise and health information. None of the interventions influenced health complaints, sick leave or job stress. However, each of the interventions did appear to impact on its target. Participants in the physical activity intervention showed improvements in general health and physical fitness, while the stress management group

reported reductions in their levels of general stress. A similar result was reported by Mino et al. (2006) who found improvements in general mood following a stress management programme, but little effect on the specific stress associated with work.

There have been a number of criticisms of individually targeted stress management programmes within the workplace. Oldenburg and Harris (1996), for example, noted that this type of programme usually attracts only between 10 and 40 per cent of the workforce – and even less if it is not given a 'high profile' in the workplace. In addition, the majority of people who do attend seem to have relatively few stress-related problems, while many anxious individuals do not attend, perhaps because they feel that they will gain little from such courses or do not want to air their problems in front of their colleagues. Noblet and Lamontagne (2006) had more philosophical concerns, as they suggested that the approach can be seen as labelling those with high stress as somehow not coping, and avoids employers having to modify any work-related causes of stress. The failure of Eriksen et al. and Mino et al. to influence either work-related stress or levels of sick leave highlights the need to influence these issues more directly – by addressing the *causes* of stress.

Identifying organisational causes of stress is more complex than providing stress management classes and can have more significant implications for an organisation. Table 13.1 indicates the variety of potential stressors that may influence the stress of people working in a hospital, some of which are common to many work situations, some of which are unique to working in health-care settings.

Case history

Changing any organisational factors may impact on the stress of hospital workers; but working out where and how to intervene at an organisational level is not easy.

Table 13.1 Some of the sources of stress for hospital workers

Professional issues	Patient issues	Work issues
Over-promotion	Distressed patients or relatives	Shift work
Under-promotion	'Difficult' patients or relatives	Poor working conditions
Interactions with colleagues	Dying patients	Too high a workload
Interactions with management	Complaints made against staff	Work intruding on home time
Working beyond knowledge level		Lack of social support
Lack of management support		Inadequate equipment

Photo 13.1 Sometimes even students can experience stress!

Source: Shutterstock.com/Creativa.

However, the process used by one of the authors (PB) to reduce stress in a group of hospitals provides an example of how this might be done. The process involved:

● identifying causes of stress in the working environment;

● identifying solutions to this stress from those most involved;

● developing a process of change to address the issues raised.

The first two stages of the intervention involved running a series of focus groups with different staff throughout the organisation. These were led by a health psychologist, who worked with the management of the hospital but who was not part of the management team. Many focus groups were run with key hospital staff, including cleaners and porters, nurses, managers, clerical workers, and people from the paramedical professions such as occupational therapists and physiotherapists. In each of these meetings, comprising about six people, attenders were invited to identify factors in their working environments that adversely affected their 'quality of life' at work. If problems were identified – and they inevitably were – they were also asked to identify any solutions to those problems. These meetings were intended to last up

to one hour but often went on longer, and were extremely productive.

Each of the issues and solutions put forward in the groups were then arranged into a set of common problems (and perhaps solutions) in a document that formed the basis of the next phase of the intervention. Problems raised included major systemic problems, such as:

● a poor computer network system;

● poor timing of the hospital bus provision (it did not fit in with shift times);

● very poor parking facilities, making transport to and from work difficult;

● inadequate crèche facilities;

● the organisation of various groups of wards in the hospital into competing rather than cooperating units;

● a working culture among management that punished people who did not work significant overtime.

Interestingly, the solutions that some workers had used to manage their stress impacted on other workers by increasing their dissatisfaction and stress. One example of this was that the management team in one hospital had moved its offices away from the wards to avoid what they thought of as too much day-to-day contact with the ward staff and to allow them to concentrate on more long-term planning. As a result, the management group felt less stressed and more able to get on with their job effectively. By contrast, and unbeknown to the management team, the ward nurses were angry and disillusioned as they felt this was an example of management blocking off contact they felt vital to their effective running of the wards.

Once the problems and solutions were documented, these were taken to a small committee of senior managers, which formed a response to the needs. It did so by grouping the issues raised into three broad categories:

1. those likely to have minimal effect, but relatively easy to instigate;
2. those likely to have a significant effect, but more difficult to instigate;
3. those likely to have a significant effect, but impossible to instigate.

Clearly, the interventions focused on the first two of these categories. Changes made included increasing the size of the crèche and lengthening its opening hours so that it was more useful for shift workers, changing the times of the hospital buses to make them more user-friendly, and initiating a new hospital computer system – over a number of years. However, any interventions need not necessarily be on such a large scale. One example of this was provided by a nurse manager, who noted that her staff often arrived late or very close to the time of their morning shift. When she asked them why, she found that these were predominantly single mothers who had to leave their child with a childminder on their way to work. Because childminders would only take children from a time close to the beginning of the shift, this put these nurses under significant time pressure. If the traffic was good between the childminder's and hospital, they got to work on time; if the traffic was busy or delayed, they were late to work. The simple solution to the problem was to start the shift 15 minutes later.

Do organisational interventions work?

The effectiveness of this systemic approach to reducing stress was summarised by Montano et al. (2014) in their meta-analysis of the effectiveness of interventions designed to improve the health of workers reported in 39 intervention studies. The studies addressed a range of stress outcomes, including mental and physical

> **burnout**
> a psychological state characterised by long-term exhaustion and diminished interest in work.

health measures as well as some musculo-skeletal measures more relevant to changes in physical working conditions. Those addressing mental health issues reported outcomes such as mental distress and sleep, mental health, stress-related health problems and '**burnout**'. Nineteen of the 39 studies reported significant benefits of the interventions, and those with multiple targets including issues such as working hours and the intensity of work, organisational stressors including the degree of control over the job, the structure of work hierarchies, and 'material conditions' (noise, vibrations, ergonomics) were nearly three times more effective than those with limited targets. Reasons for the failure of interventions were often organisational constraints on change, including a lack of enthusiasm for change among relevant management and workers, external events such as job turnover, organisational restructuring and merging of companies, and a failure to establish the intervention properly within the workplace. These ubiquitous problems illustrate well the challenge of establishing organisational change in any large organisation.

A report by Mikkelsen and Saksvik (1999) illustrates both the types of intervention and problems encountered in these studies. They intervened in two offices in the Norwegian Post Office. The intention of their intervention was to increase employees' learning opportunities and decision-making authority in order to improve the work environment and health. In order to decide what changes to make, they ran discussion groups with the workers, which 'diagnosed' any problems, then planned and enacted changes to the working environment to remedy them. They reported that work conditions in the larger organisation actually deteriorated over the course of the study, a process that was reversed in one but not both intervention offices. They attribute the failure of the latter to organisational restructuring and turbulence interfering with potential benefits of the intervention. A second, and much simpler, intervention was reported by Dababneh et al. (2001). They evaluated the impact of short rest breaks on productivity and well-being in a meat-processing factory. In one condition, workers were given 36 minutes of extra breaks by adding to their present breaks – one by adding 49-minute break schedules distributed evenly throughout the day, the other by adding 12 3-minute breaks. Neither additional break lowered production, but both resulted in significant reductions in psychological discomfort. Workers preferred the 9-minute rest interval. A further intervention is reported in the 'Research focus box'.

RESEARCH FOCUS

Bourbonnais, R., Brisson, C. and Vézina, M. (2011). Long-term effects of an intervention on psychosocial work factors among healthcare professionals in a hospital setting. *Journal of Occupational and Environmental Medicine*, 68: 479-486.

Introduction

This study provides an example of a systemic intervention designed to reduce stress in the workplace. The intervention was premised on the Karasek model of work stress that states that work-related stress is the outcome of the demands placed on an individual, the degree of control they have over them (high stress comes from high demands and low control), and the degree of social support available to the individual; and Siegrist's model of stress as an imbalance between the demands of a job and the rewards (largely financial) from that job. It reports the three-year outcomes of the intervention.

Method

Participants

The study involved a comparison of a control and intervention condition. The respondents to questionnaires were all 'care-providing personnel' in an 'experimental' (n=674) and 'control' (n=894) hospital.

The intervention

In the intervention group, an intervention team met with health-care workers and other 'stakeholders' in three care units within the hospital. The goals of these meetings were to determine what changes should be introduced to reduce psychosocial stressors in the care units and hospital in general. Eight meetings, each of around three hours, were held over a four-month period. Numerous target issues were determined in these meetings, which were categorised into six themes: team work and team spirit, staffing processes, work organisation, training, communication and ergonomics. Changes were monitored through the minutes of intervention team meetings and follow-up interviews with key informants. Issues and solutions included:

Measures

Measures were taken before the intervention and three years after its implementation using a 30 minute telephone survey in which the researcher was unaware of the condition the participants had experienced. Measures included: *Karasek's Job Content Questionnaire* measuring job demand, control, and social support; *Siegrist's measure of job effort–reward*; the *Psychiatric Symptom Index*, measuring the frequency of symptoms of anxiety, depression, aggressiveness and cognitive problems; the *Copenhagen Burnout Inventory* measured job-related exhaustion; and the *Nottingham Health Profile* to estimate sleep disturbance.

Results

Only data from participants working in the hospital at both measurement times was analysed in the reported analysis. Even these data were somewhat confounded by events in the various hospitals. Changes that may have affected the findings included senior nurses leaving and not being replaced, the appointment of a new hospital director, increases in very difficult to treat infections within the hospital, one (private; this is a US study) hospital experiencing significant financial problems, and a further reorganisation of the hospital staff.

Issue	Solution(s)
Lack of recognition and respect between trained and untrained nurses	Teams were instituted to discuss problems and solutions, adapt the workload and manage conflict
Lack of mutual assistance	
Overly large workload for untrained nurses	'Twinning' and 'task rotation' organised between untrained and trained nurses in one unit
Lack of control over workload of untrained nurses	
Lack of nurse confidence in dealing with negative attitudes of doctors	Recommendation made by the intervention team to the chief nurses to write a letter to the physicians addressing the issues. Chief nurses preferred to tackle the problem in an informal way, and organised meetings with groups of physicians who worked in their specific departments.
Lack of cooperation of physicians, especially when woken in the night	
Physicians sometimes leave it to nurses to give 'bad news'	
Lack of stability in care teams	Implementation of replacement self management in each care unit allowed unit heads to select replacements from among their regular unit staff, thereby enhancing team stability
Frequent replacement of skilled with unskilled task	
Lack of space in nursing station	Ergonomic rearrangements made
Unsafe disposal of televisions in patient rooms	
Difficult access to patients' bathrooms	

Reprinted with permission from BMJ Publishing Group Ltd

Despite these various challenges to the veracity of the study, over the three-year follow-up, scores in the intervention hospital psychosocial measures all improved expect for the measure of social support (which fell markedly in the control condition). The improvement was statistically significant for 5/9 factors: psychological demands, effort–reward imbalance, quality of work, and physical and emotional demands. All health indicators improved and 2/5 significantly: work-related and personal burnout. The equivalent figures of statistically significant improvement in the control hospital were 3/9 psychosocial measures, and 0/5 health indicators. As can be seen in Table 1, several mean scores were statistically higher in the intervention group than the control group after adjusting for baseline differences at three-year follow-up.

Discussion

The results are impressive in that they suggest long-term benefits on staff stress and work demands as long as three years following a complex, but doable, intervention. An impressive 80 per cent of solutions proposed by the intervention team were implemented. It is difficult to determine which interventions proved more or less effective, and are likely to be highly specific to the context and hospitals in which they were implemented. The study has a number of strengths, including a strong developmental phase to ensure an appropriate intervention was established. In addition, the interventions were strongly grounded on theory specific to work stress. Limitations obviously include the uncontrolled working environment in which the study was implemented. Perhaps, though, while this may result in some variation in outcomes beyond the influence of the intervention itself, that the effects are still apparent despite all this 'noise' may indicate the robustness of effects of the intervention. The lack of a intervention in the control hospital (ideally they would have received some form of 'attentional placebo') also allows the possibility that the effects found were a result of the attention given to the hospital staff and its engagement in active research rather than the intervention per se. Countering this, the active phase of the research was conducted three years before the final measures were taken, so any Hawthorne effect may have been minimal.

Table 1 Selected comparisons of psychosocial work factors and health problems between the experimental and control hospitals at three-year follow-up

	Mean scores at 3 years Experimental Control		p Value
Supervisor support	11.2	10.6	0.007
Co-worker support	12.5	12.4	0.279
Total support	23.7	23.0	0.011
Reward	31.2	30.2	0.003
Effort–reward imbalance	1.01	1.1	<0.001
Emotional demands	16.5	16.3	0.525
Psychological distress	20.4	22.4	0.083
Sleeping problems	1.0	1.2	0.169
Work-related burnout	43.2	48.3	<0.0001
Personal burnout	40.3	44.2	0.003

Reprinted with permission from BMJ Publishing Group Ltd

IN THE SPOTLIGHT

Ban football . . . save a life!

There may be one stress management approach not detailed in the chapter that could save many lives. Ban football! Or at least, ban watching football. There is now accumulating evidence that high levels of excitement and stress associated with important games of football can trigger a heart attack in vulnerable individuals. Wilbert-Lampen and colleagues (2008), for example, reported in the *New England Journal of Medicine* that three times as many German men had a myocardial infarction (MI) on the days that Germany was playing in the 2008 World Cup than on days they were not playing. Women were also at increased risk, but slightly less so than men. The peak admission time was in the first two hours after the beginning of each match. But this is not an isolated finding, and it is not restricted to German fans. Similar findings were reported by Carroll and colleagues (2002) among English fans during the 1998 World Cup. They found that the risk of admission to hospital with an MI increased by 25 per cent on 30 June 1998 – the day England lost to Argentina in a penalty shoot-out – and the following two days. Dutch, Australian and other fans have also been similarly affected. The moral of the story? If banning football can save one life, it has to be considered!

Minimising stress in hospital settings

Preoperational preparation

Having an operation is a stressful event, whether it is a small operation conducted under local anaesthetic or a larger one involving a period of unconsciousness and a significant period of recovery. It should not be surprising, therefore, that levels of anxiety can be high both before and after an operation. This anxiety is both unpleasant for the individual concerned and can add to the complications they experience. It may increase the amount of painkilling medication they take, the degree to which they need reassurance both before and after the operation,

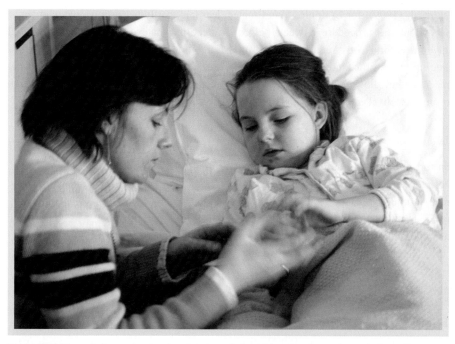

Photo 13.2 The calming presence of a parent can help children to relax and cope better with any concerns they may have about their operation

Source: Science Photo Library Ltd/John Cole.

and even the time necessary for them to stay in hospital (Johnston and Vogele 1993). As a consequence, a number of researchers have attempted to identify ways of minimising this distress. While the stress management approaches described above may be appropriate under such circumstances, health-care staff and patients rarely have the time to teach or learn these strategies (although hypnosis has been used with some effect with adults (Montgomery et al. 2007) and children (Liossi et al. 2006)). Accordingly, a very different approach has been taken to help people to cope with this specific type of stress.

Many studies have shown that we feel less anxiety when faced with potentially stressful circumstances if we can be given some degree of control over them (e.g. Lok and Bishop 1999). These findings have led health psychologists to examine whether giving patients undergoing surgery some degree of control over their situation will reduce the amount of stress they experience. Clearly, patients cannot have much control over their anaesthetics or surgery – such things really should be left to the experts! So, in this case, 'giving control' has been interpreted as 'keeping people informed about what is happening to them'. This is thought to reduce anxiety

by minimising the fear of the unknown. If patients know what to expect, they may understand better and be less alarmed by any experiences they have. If patients are told, for example, that they will experience some pain after their surgery they will be less alarmed and less likely to think that things have gone wrong if they do experience pain. A number of studies have examined the effectiveness of providing two sorts of information to patients prior to them having surgery:

1. *Procedural information:* telling patients about the events that will occur before and after surgery; having a pre-medication injection, waking in the recovery room and having a drip in their arm, and so on.

2. *Sensory information:* telling patients what they will feel before and after surgery: that it is normal to feel some pain following surgery, they may feel confused when they come round from the anaesthetic, and so on.

The overall picture is that these interventions usually work, and may both reduce anxiety and improve rehabilitation outcomes such as pain management, ambulation, engagement in physiotherapy and even day of discharge (e.g. Ong et al. 2009). Despite a generally positive story, such interventions are not always successful. Luck et al. (1999), for example, found that showing a video about the procedure a week before patients were given a **colonoscopy** reduced anxiety in the period leading up to the procedure. In a subsequent study of the same procedure, however, the same research group found no such benefit (Pearson et al. 2005).

Matching patient needs

One explanation for these mixed findings could be that the effect of the intervention is relatively weak, and is not always found. Another explanation could be that the intervention works for some people, and not others. What may be as important as the type of intervention is matching it to the characteristics of the patients receiving it. Patients who typically cope with stress by using avoidant coping strategies may benefit, for example, from receiving less information than those who typically cope through the use of problem-focused strategies (see Chapter 11 ☛), and vice-versa. This hypothesis was tested by Morgan et al. (1998), who gave people identified as primarily 'information seekers' or 'avoiders' either sensory information about the nature of a forthcoming colonoscopy or no information. Patients who were given information congruent with their coping style (i.e. no information for 'avoiders'; information for 'seekers') reported less anxiety prior to the procedure than those who were given incongruent information. They also scored lower on a measure of 'pain behaviour' made by nursing staff during the procedure, although participants did not report any differences in pain during the procedure, or differ in their use of sedative drugs. These data suggest that:

- People who usually cope using problem-focused strategies benefit from information that helps them to understand their experience and to actively interpret their experience in relation to information they are given.

- People who usually cope using avoidant, emotion-focused strategies benefit most from not being told what to expect, and perhaps being helped to develop strategies that help them distract from the situation.

Levels of anxiety may also influence the impact of preoperative preparation. Hathaway (1986), for example, concluded from a meta-analysis that patients with low levels of anxiety benefited most from the provision of procedural information, while those with high levels of anxiety gained most from unstructured discussion. Anxiety inhibits new learning, partly because people who are anxious may not attend to whatever they are being told, partly as a direct inhibition of memory processes. It is possible, therefore, that anxious patients may benefit most when they are given relatively little information, but the information they are given matches their needs.

Working with children and parents

Much of the recent work in preparing people for surgery has focused on helping children and their parents. Studies that have focused on children have shown that a variety of techniques may be of benefit. Perhaps the simplest has simply been the provision of storybooks while awaiting surgery, which has achieved particularly successful outcomes in relatively young girls (Tunney and Boore 2013). In a more complex intervention, Hatava et al. (2000) randomly assigned children and parents to one of two interventions designed to reduce anxiety before an ear, nose or throat (ENT) operation. In the first condition, they were given written or verbal information by a nurse two weeks prior to surgery. This included information about general hospital rules, routines and the date of the operation. This acted as a form of **placebo intervention** as there is little here that would have been expected to reduce anxiety other than meeting the nurse that may be involved in their care. The second group was given a more complex intervention comprising the same information two weeks prior to the operation followed by a visit to the ENT department the day before surgery. During this visit, each child and parent met the anaesthetist who would be at the operation and took part in a group session led by a nurse in which they were shown the operating theatre and lay on the operating table. They were also shown the equipment that would be used during anaesthesia and were encouraged to play with it in order to minimise its threat and increase

> **colonoscopy**
> a minor surgical procedure in which a small piece of bowel wall is cut from the colon. This can then be tested for the presence of malignant cells.
>
> **placebo intervention**
> an intervention designed to simulate a psychological intervention but not believed to be a specific therapy for the target condition.

familiarity. They were then shown the procedure that would occur on the day through role-play using a doll. This complex intervention resulted in significant benefits. Both younger and older children reported less fear and anxiety prior to the surgery. In addition, their parents reported more satisfaction and less anxiety than those who did not receive the intervention.

Jay et al. (1995) provided an unusual comparison between medical and psychological methods of reducing distress in children undergoing **bone marrow biopsy** – an excruciatingly painful procedure. It can also be distressing for both the children and parents involved. They compared two approaches to minimising this distress in a sample of children aged between 3 and 12 years. The first was simply to fully anaesthetise the children during the procedure. While this approach evokes some degree of anxiety, they reasoned that it may be less distressing than experiencing the process while under local anaesthetic. They compared this approach with conducting the procedure under local anaesthetic after teaching the children both relaxation and cognitive restructuring as a means of controlling their distress. One can only imagine

> ### bone marrow biopsy
> usually performed under local anaesthetic by making a small incision into the skin. A biopsy needle is then pushed through the bone and takes a sample of marrow from the centre of the bone. Marrow contains platelets, phagocytes and lymphocytes.

that this was taught at a very simple level, particularly to the younger children. Perhaps not surprisingly, the children who received training in stress management methods experienced more distress than those who were anaesthetised at the beginning of the procedure. However, their parents' ratings suggested that they were the least distressed in the following days. Interestingly, neither the children nor their parents showed any preference for either intervention. One final approach used by Liossi et al. (2009) compared the effects of a local skin cream anaesthetic alone or combined with the use of self-hypnosis involving suggestions including numbness, topical anaesthesia, and glove anaesthesia (pain-free area mirroring that of a glove over a hand) prior to a painful procedure (in this case taking blood). This combined intervention proved superior on measures of anxiety and procedure-related pain.

Tackling the issue from another perspective, interventions that target parents may benefit both parent and child. Kain et al. (2007), for example, compared the effectiveness of standard care, parental presence alone prior to surgery, a complex family-based preparation including a parental training package on supporting their child prior to and during anaesthesia induction, and oral anti-anxiety medication. Parents who received the family intervention were less anxious than those in the other conditions. In addition, children of these parents were less likely to experience delirium following surgery, required less anaesthesia in the recovery room, and were discharged from the recovery room more quickly than children in the other conditions.

SUMMARY

This chapter has examined a variety of approaches to stress management and contexts in which it has been conducted. Systemic interventions that target whole organisations can be used as a preventive approach. More individual approaches based around specific therapeutic approaches may benefit people experiencing general stress. Finally, simple procedural information may benefit people facing the stress of an operation where there is little time (or need) to use these more complex interventions.

1. Stress management 'classes' based around second and third wave interventions provide a potentially useful intervention, attendance is likely to be limited, and health psychologists and others have targeted larger and more 'captive audiences' in organisations.
2. Managing stress at this level can involve a variety of approaches depending on the organisational causes of stress. Stress management interventions should follow an audit of stressors, and target environmental issues that both contribute to stress and can realistically be changed in the context of the particular workplace.

3. Cognitive-behavioural interventions targeted at reducing stress involve changing:
   - triggers to stress, using, for example, the problem-focused approach of Egan;
   - the cognitive precursors to stress, using the self-instruction and cognitive restructuring approaches of Beck, Meichenbaum and Ellis;
   - the physiological response to stress using relaxation methods, including the modified Jacobsen technique;
   - the behavioural reactions to stressful situations using Meichenbaum's stress inoculation and role-play techniques.
4. Mindfulness-based, third wave approaches to stress management take an opposing view. Rather than directly attempting to change cognitions, they teach participants to acknowledge any stress-engendering thoughts they may have, but not to make these the focus of their attention. This can be achieved using mindfulness or acceptance techniques, and allows the individual to engage in previously stressful behaviours, and learn through experience that they can cope while doing so.
5. Finally, providing relevant information to help people to understand and cope with the stress of hospital procedures such as operations may reduce distress and pain and facilitate rehabilitation following surgery. However, its benefits vary according to individual differences in coping style.
   - Patients who are typically problem solvers benefit most from the provision of information.
   - Patients who typically cope with stress using avoidant strategies may be helped best by teaching them distraction techniques.

Further reading

Elkin, A. (2013). *Stress Management for Dummies*. New York: Wiley.

A fairly irreverent but useful guide to managing your own stress.

Carlson, R. (2011). *Don't Sweat the Small Stuff . . . and It's All Small Stuff*. London: Hodder Mobius.

Latest version of a classic. Not an academic text, but it gives good insight into cognitive and other elements of stress management.

Wells, A. (2011). *Metacognitive Therapy for Anxiety and Depression*. New York: Guilford Press.

Harris, R. (2009). *ACT Made Simple: An Easy-to-read Primer on Acceptance and Commitment Therapy*. Oakland, CA: New Harbinger Publications.

Kabat-Zinn, J. (2013). *Full Catastrophe Living, revised edition: How to Cope with Stress, Pain and Illness Using Mindfulness*. London: Piatkus.

Cooper, C. (2002). *Organisational Stress Management: A Strategic Approach*. London: Palgrave Macmillan.

Examines both the consequences of organisational stress and how these may be reduced. Looks at organisations rather than individuals.

Jain, S., Shapiro, S.L., Swanick, S. et al. (2007). A randomized controlled trial of mindfulness meditation versus relaxation training: effects on distress, positive states of mind, rumination and distraction. *Annals of Behavioral Medicine*, 33: 11–21.

An interesting study showing a specific effect of meditation on levels of intrusive worries.

Type 'stress management' or 'stress management training' into any search engine, and you will get thousands of hits. Few are useful resources though, as most are links to commercial sites who want your money before you can access information. You could try this site, though (although no promises!):

http://www.mindtools.com/

For open-access student resources specifically written to complement this textbook and support your learning, please visit **www.pearsoned.co.uk/morrison**

Part III
Being ill

Chapter 14
The impact and outcomes of illness: patient perspective

Learning outcomes

By the end of this chapter, you should have an understanding of:

- the physical and emotional impact of illness
- the diverse nature of coping responses in the face of illness
- demographic, clinical and psychosocial influences on patient outcomes
- QoL as a multidimensional, dynamic and subjective construct
- typical models of patient adjustment to illness
- challenges to assessing subjective health status and quality of life

Physical health problems have more than a physical impact

At the crux of health psychology is the simple fact that we, as humans, respond in complex and varied ways to the experience of symptoms, illness, communication with health-care professionals and treatments. Whilst our individuality is what makes life exciting, it also presents challenges to traditional health-care systems and personnel. Health-care professionals seek to treat the illness but are faced with not just physical symptoms but an array of emotional, behavioural and social correlates and consequences, which they may feel less equipped to deal with. As highlighted in *The Psychologist* in 2012, 'physical health services and psychological health services have traditionally been provided by different organisations. . .' (Jacobs et al. 2012: 190). These authors highlight where inroads are being made into integrated care in the UK using pediatric clinical psychology as an example, where clinical psychologists are increasingly embedded within a hospital multidisciplinary team, for example in a pediatric pain service. The goal of such multidisciplinary teams goes beyond treating the physical health problem to minimising the impact it has on the individual's (and hopefully their families') quality of life. National guidelines commonly make recommendations for the commissioning of psychological services alongside medical services; however, this does not yet happen consistently across all age groups and all health conditions. As this chapter and the next will show, the psychosocial impact of illness has implications not only for emotional well-being and quality of life, but also for future physical health. Therefore, current or future health psychologists must continue to demonstrate the 'added value' to health outcomes, of recognising the psychosocial impact of illness and the resulting needs of patients and their families.

Chapter outline

Illness is a dynamic process, beginning with perception of symptoms or a diagnosis which continues or changes over time as a function of the disease pathology, treatment possibilities and the responses to illness by the person affected and those around them. In previous chapters we described the many individual and social factors that influence a person's responses to life stresses, and here we consider a specific potential stressor - illness. We consider the impact of illness not only on physical functioning but on emotional well-being, adjustment and quality of life (QoL). These broad constructs are defined before we explore the range of factors that influence perceptions and experience of them.

We highlight illness-specific, personal, psychological and social factors that play a role in adjustment to illness, with coping theorised, and often evidenced, as playing a key role. The wide range of coping responses made by individuals facing the challenge of illness and the functions these serve is described. Rather than focusing only on negative responses or outcomes of illness, this chapter will present evidence of personal growth or benefit-finding in the illness experience and consider how positive appraisals and emotions may influence the perception of gain.

Given the subjectivity of many of the concepts described in this chapter, we close it by turning attention to issues of how to measure illness outcomes, and in particular the multidimensional, dynamic and subjective concept of quality of life.

Many of those affected by illness do not cope alone and so this chapter leads nicely into the subsequent one which addresses the impact of illness on significant others, and on the relationship between patients' and carers' beliefs, experiences, and outcomes.

The impact of illness

Illness presents individuals with many challenges that may change over time, depending upon the illness, the treatment, the individual's cognitive, behavioural and emotional responses, and the social and cultural context in which the illness occurs. Illness is a complex process, illustrated by Morse and Johnson's (1991) generic model of emotional and coping responses from the onset of symptoms through to living with a chronic illness. Individuals are considered as having to deal with:

1. *Uncertainty:* in this period the individual tries to understand the meaning and severity of the first symptoms.

2. *Disruption:* this occurs when it becomes evident to the individual that they have a significant illness. They experience a crisis characterised by intense stress and a high level of dependence on health professionals and/or other people who are emotionally close to them.

3. *Striving for recovery:* this period is typified by the individual attempting to gain some form of control over their illness by means of active coping.

4. *Restoration of well-being:* in this phase, the individual achieves a new emotional equilibrium based on an acceptance of the illness and its consequences.

A similar series of stages of response to a cancer diagnosis was proposed by Holland and Gooen-Piels (2000). Initial feelings of disbelief, denial and shock, where some people challenge the health professional's ability or diagnosis and try to defend themselves from the implications of the diagnosis are followed by a one-to two-week period of *dysphoria* where individuals gradually come to terms with the reality of their diagnosis. At this time significant distress and related symptoms such as insomnia, reduced appetite, poor concentration, anxiety and depression may be experienced; but as information given about treatment is gradually processed, hope and optimism may emerge to compete with the more distressing thoughts. After this, adaptation emerges and the person develops long-term coping strategies in order to maintain equilibrium.

Although these models propose a staged adaptive process, not all individuals will move through stages smoothly nor achieve emotional equilibrium or a stage of acceptance and adaptation. Elements from different 'stages' may co-occur: for example, a person may experience significant distress even when actively coping with their illness. Individuals may also move backwards and forwards between stages and reactions, for example shifting their focus from one of cure to one of 'healing', in which they try to resolve life issues and achieve some completion of their life's achievements. They may still maintain hope at this time, but rather than hope for a cure they may shift towards hope for a 'good' or pain-free death (Little and Sayers 2004).

'Staged' approaches have been criticised for the manner in which they categorise patients and create expectations of responses to serious illness events (e.g. Hale 1996; Crossley 2000). Whilst staged theories provide a useful starting point for those working with the ill or the dying, recognition that individuals may not neatly 'fit' into any one defined stage and that caring responses may need to be individually tailored is required. The nature of an illnesses impact will determine the well-being, quality of life and adjustment outcomes an individual experiences, but there are personal, cultural, cognitive and emotional influences on this relationship, as we outline in this chapter.

Illness and physical outcomes

It is estimated that, in Europe, approximately 40 per cent of the population aged over 15 years old have at least one chronic health condition, with roughly 65 per cent of older adults having at least two such conditions (http://ec.europa.eu/research/innovation-union/pdf/active-healthy-ageing/steering-group/operational_plan.pdf and European Chronic Disease Alliance, WHO Europe 2012). Worryingly, the rising obesity in childhood figures will also cause future increases in chronic disease incidence in adulthood. In addition to personal impact, physical illness and its consequences carry significant societal costs, including people working less, earning less and retiring earlier (see Busse et al. 2010 Report for Europe).

The physical consequences of illness for individual functioning, disability, social integration and role performance are discussed in this text, with a whole chapter also dedicated to discussing the experience of pain Chapter 16 ☞. The ultimate physical outcome of illness is of course death, and many research studies therefore assess survival rates. However, of perhaps more interest to psychologists is the *variation* in the physical and psychosocial morbidity associated with illness – the ability and disability, the quality of life survivors experience, and the extent to which a person is able to function independently rather than relying on others for aspects of their care (see Chapter 15 ☞ for a discussion of caregiving).

Fatigue

One physical aspect of illness or associated treatments, which is pervasive in many chronic conditions, is that of fatigue: for example, post-viral fatigue, post-stroke fatigue, post-chemotherapy fatigue, post-surgical fatigue. Fatigue is common in neurological conditions such as stroke (prevalence ranging from 36 to 77 per cent) and was recently found to be particularly prevalent in those with Multiple Sclerosis (reported in up to 83 per cent of patients) (Kluger et al. 2013). Whilst fatigue is likely due in large part to the neurological, immunological, hormonal and inflammatory processes of MS, the consequent emotional demands of the symptoms and associated negative affect are also thought to play a role.

Fatigue can be assessed by evaluating performance such as the speed and strength of physical movement (motor function), or derived from indices of sleep amount and quality, but is also often recorded through subjective reports, such as the Fatigue Assessment Scale (Michielsen et al. 2003). This subjective fatigue has also been explored in those diagnosed with CFS – Chronic Fatigue Syndrome which, unlike in stroke and MS populations, is characterised by pervasive and persistent fatigue in the absence of any identified pathology. Several studies within this population (e.g. Moss-Morris and Chalder 2003; Wearden et al. 2012) and other conditions, including cancer (see Brown and Kroenke's review 2009), lung disease, diabetes, CHD and rheumatoid arthritis (Katon et al. 2007), have found associations between fatigue, depression and anxiety. Such negative emotional correlates of fatigue can increase the detrimental impact of illness on a person's life, and of course any relationship is likely to be bidirectional. Fatigue is consistently associated with impaired quality of life, with inactivity as a result of fatigue contributing to further weakness: i.e. it can become a 'self perpetuating cycle where physiological changes, illness beliefs, reduced and inconsistent activity, sleep disturbance, medical uncertainty and lack of guidance interact to maintain symptoms' (Moss-Morris et al. 2013: 303). In addition, as described in the next chapter, the responses of significant others to a loved one's illness, or in this case, persistent fatigue, may influence other patient outcomes (Band et al. 2015).

Immune changes

Also, just as we know from studies of responses to acute stress such as examinations that immune changes are provoked such as reduced NK cell activity or slowed wound healing (see Chapter 11☞), studies of those experiencing acute pain or undergoing surgery have reported immune changes of a similar nature (see review by Graham et al. 2006).

Physical responses to illness therefore have wider consequences, emotional and social, and it is to the first of these that we now turn.

Illness and negative emotions
Reactions to diagnosis

In terms of the response to diagnosis, perhaps because of the perceived threat to life, but also due to its prevalence,

the majority of studies seem to address those receiving a cancer diagnosis, with reactions typically described as catastrophic and highly emotional. One qualitative study reports how one woman, recently diagnosed with breast cancer, described herself as standing 'with one foot in the grave, the other on the edge' (p. 115), with other individuals describing themselves quite literally as 'fighting for their life' (Landmark and Wahl 2002). In a rare study of men diagnosed with penile cancer (Bullen et al. 2010) one man describes how, on being told of his diagnosis he 'just broke down and I don't know what he was talking about 'cos when you mention cancer, well you have got six weeks to live'. Whilst for some the stark reality of the health threat led to quick acceptance of the need for a positive decision about treatment, including surgery (e.g. 'if they do not amputate this penis you are dead, all right, so you have two choices: you live or you die. I said "cut it off"'), beyond the reassurance surgery offered regarding cancer removal, longer-term negative consequences were seen in terms of self-concept, 'it starts to dawn on you then: you are no longer . . . you're half a man'.

Negative emotional reactions commonly follow diagnosis of many other conditions, including those with sudden-onset brain injury (Gracey et al. 2008), heart disease (e.g. Lane et al. 2002b; Polsky et al. 2005), stroke (e.g. Astrom 1996; Robinson 1998; Morrison et al. 1999, 2005), or following a positive HIV diagnosis (Valente 2003; Moskowitz et al. 2009). Polsky and colleagues (2005), for example, followed over eight thousand adults aged 51 to 61 for over six years and found that those diagnosed with cancer or heart disease in that time had more than twice the risk of developing depression than those not getting such a diagnosis. For some conditions, the response of those diagnosed today possibly differs from that of those diagnosed in earlier decades or centuries. For example, receiving an HIV diagnosis today compared to when the virus was first identified in the 1980s when no antiretroviral treatment was available, or receiving a TB (tuberculosis) diagnosis now compared to in the nineteenth century before the discovery of antibiotics. Different responses to diagnosis may be due to the changes in personal and social expectancies attached to such conditions as much perhaps as to the improved prognosis of those examples.

Emotional reactions to illness

In this chapter we can only cover a selection of more common and potentially life-changing health conditions.

As a general principle, it is important to distinguish between illness with a sudden onset, such as a stroke or heart attack, and those with a less acute and more insidious development such as cancer, multiple sclerosis or dementia, as the speed in which life is changed can have important consequences.

Depression and anxiety

In terms of two of the major killers in Western society, heart disease and heart attack, it is estimated that one-third or more of sufferers will experience levels of depression above cut-offs indicating clinical disorder, with depression and anxiety often persisting for up to a year following hospital discharge (Lane et al. 2002b). Among stroke patients the figures reported range from 10 to around 40 per cent, depending on whether samples are assessed in hospital or at home or in the community (Robinson 1998). For many stroke patients, the significant levels of emotional distress (anxiety and/or depression) persist for many months, with psychosocial factors in addition to disease features predicting long-term emotional outcome: for example, patient satisfaction with health care and confidence in recovery predicted depression at six months and three years following acute stroke (Morrison et al. 2000b, 2005). Further dramatic change is experienced by those experiencing other forms of brain injury, for example traumatic brain injury (TBI) following an accident, with the multiple losses (cognitive, emotional and behavioural) often also resulting in depression (prevalence up to 33 per cent) and generalised anxiety (prevalence up to 41 per cent, see review by Schwarzbold et al. 2008).

The overall prevalence rates of emotional distress in cancer patients have been reported as high as 70 per cent, with both depression and anxiety considered to be present in the majority of patients at some point (e.g. Fallowfield et al. 2001; Zabora et al. 2001). However, this depends on whether global distress or more specific mood states are assessed, and on the stage of the disease of the specific patients assessed. For example, a diagnosis of clinical levels of depression is seen in between 8 and 25 per cent of cancer patients with advanced disease (Hotopf et al. 2002) (NB. stage of disease is not *inevitably* a predictor of greater distress, as reported in a review of 100 studies, Massie 2004). Some cancers do, however, consistently associate with higher distress: for example,

among 304 pancreatic cancer patients - a cancer carrying a high mortality risk – almost 29 per cent reported elevated depression compared to 18.5 per cent of 7,749 patients with other cancers, even when controlling for gender and age (Clark et al. 2010).

Interestingly Burgess et al. (2005) found that whilst almost 50 per cent of early-stage breast cancer patients had depression, anxiety or both in the first year following diagnosis, that incidence dropped to 25 per cent at two-, three- and four-year follow-ups, and further to 15 per cent at a five-year follow-up. These levels are not inconsistent with the general population.

While depression may be less common among cancer 'survivors' (a term generally referring to those 5+ years post-treatment completion), these individuals face the uncertainties that survivorship brings: recurrence, the possibility of developing other cancers, lasting effects of treatment, and the potential of a shortened life expectancy, thus anxiety or worry remains prevalent (e.g. Deimling et al. 2006).

A systematic review of studies comparing adults with diabetes with healthy control participants found significantly more emotional distress, generalised anxiety disorder, and anxiety symptoms in those with diabetes, with the latter being seen in 40 per cent of the diabetic sample (Grigsby et al. 2002). For those living with this chronic, controllable, but potentially life-threatening illness, daily self-management is required. Diabetes self-management includes seven domains (Greenhalgh et al. 2011): having knowledge of one's condition controlling diet taking insulin foot care exercise testing and monitoring glucose levels daily attending check-ups. This therefore requires a significant investment of time and effort by the diabetic patient. Greenhalgh's qualitative analysis highlighted that diabetes self-management generated several 'storylines': for example, 'becoming sick'; 'rebuilding a spoiled identity'; 'living a disciplined and balanced life'; 'mobilizing a care network' and 'navigating and negotiating in the health care system'. These emotional and behavioural tasks, elicited by the person's illness, can take on a life of their own, above and beyond symptom management. In addition, some treatment interventions can create not just health benefits but also significant challenges: consider, for example, undergoing chemotherapy, or a kidney transplant (See RESEARCH FOCUS).

RESEARCH FOCUS

The experience of kidney transplantation

Schipper, K., Abma, T.A., Koops, C. et al. (2014). Sweet and sour after renal transplantation: A qualitative study about the positive and negative consequences of renal transplantation. *British Journal of Health Psychology*, 19: 580-591.

Introduction

In this chapter we consider the impact of illness at the point of diagnosis and beyond, acknowledging that illness and associated treatments can exert a range of effects on the person affected. This paper has been selected because it addresses a serious and life-threatening condition, which often requires a serious and life-threatening surgical procedure – renal (kidney) transplant – to increase an individual's chances of survival. For those in end-stage renal disease, kidney transplantation has been found, in quantitative studies, to benefit survival over the alternative treatment of (haemo)dialysis. Evidence of benefits to psychosocial outcome is less clear, however, and patient QoL tends to remain lower than that of healthy comparators. This study seeks to identify both the emotional impact of kidney transplant surgery and the coping behaviours that are used whilst living with a donated kidney. Recognising that emotions can be positive or negative, and that they interact with coping to influence patient adaptation, the authors selected a qualitative method to better enable exploration of these factors within the reflected patient experience.

Method

Purposive sampling using a range of recruitment methods: via a patient organisation using digital or personal invitation, or by health professional invitation during a hospital clinic appointment. This achieved a sample of 30 including both genders (16 males, 14 females), a range of ages (17-70 years), time since transplantation (2-9 years) and two transplant methods (i.e. 14 deceased donor, 16 living-related donor). Eighteen individuals were first interviewed using a topic list covering the following issues: positive and negative changes following transplantation; coping with changes and factors helping or hindering this; use of support and satisfaction with it in terms of meeting need, and suggestions for improved psychosocial support. These interviews were recorded, transcribed and analysed using inductive content analysis (emerging themes and subthemes were identified across all interviews, then individual interviews analysed in more depth, with final themes emerging in an iterative process). Participants were then asked to confirm whether the interpretation of their interview was recognisable and to add further clarification if they wished. Between-interview analysis then followed, with interpretations being checked by several project team members to enhance theme reliability, and field notes being integrated to enhance validity.

Secondly, the issues arising from these interviews were taken into a second phase, with focus groups held with the 12 other participants, and data from these used to expand and triangulate the interview data. The focus groups followed a discussion protocol addressing the identified themes of:

- freedom
- QoL improvement
- Physical improvement
- Different roles and relations
- Expectations and dealing with them
- Tiredness
- Side effects
- Body image
- Fear and other emotions
- Sexuality
- Learning to live a new life
- Attitude – being a victim or not
- Relationship with donor
- Practical issues

Results

Four final themes (*sub themes paraphrased in italics*) emerged from the two methods of data collection and their triangulation:

- **Experiences before transplantation:** participants described the *limitations and lack of freedom* during dialysis and the dependency on it and the *range of emotions* dialysis and the waiting for a kidney donor invoked: fear (of the wait, of missing the donation), doubt (about outcome), anger and even jealousy of those who got a transplant before them. For some, the positive emotion of hope was challenged by the long wait for a suitable donor.

- **Positive improvements but with adaptation problems:** whilst many *positive improvements in participants' physical condition* were reported and valued, such as increased independence and sense of control over one's life, these *changes had required time to adapt to*. 'Feeling better is sometimes scary' said one participant. Being able to relearn how to live a normal life meant leaving behind the 'patient role' to which participants had become accustomed. As the illness no longer plays a central role in their life or in their relationships with others, some roles and relationships were challenged. One woman described how 'My husband saw me changing – from being dependent to becoming independent. We had to find a new balance. I wasn't the woman I was before'. This fascinating theme really highlights how even treatment or interventions with positive intent and outcome presents challenges to those affected – patient and family. Overwhelmingly, patients felt *grateful* for their transplant and to the donor, and whilst some had *faith in their new kidney*, others worried it may not last. Where the donor was considered, there was some *guilt* attached, particularly in the case of the suffering of non-live donors. There was also guilt for those still awaiting transplants, and guilt about not knowing how best to express one's gratitude to living donors. Guilt is a complex emotion.

- **Less positive improvements and adaptation problems:** *Negative experiences* included ongoing feelings of fatigue and, for some, concern around sexual functioning, appearance and weight gain. Their *expectations* varied and the more positively

transplantation and its likely outcomes had been viewed, they found they still faced some restrictions. This led to further *guilt and feeling ungrateful,* and these complex feelings couldn't always be expressed to others. With regards to the *responses of others*, sometimes their expectations of the 'patient' post-transplant caused problems: e.g. '. . . and since then I've lost all the support from my surroundings. They think it's gone, I can do it by myself'.

- **Adaptation and resilience:** This final theme describes the coping strategies participants used with the goal of helping them adapt to their changed circumstances, and to be resilient. These included positive refocusing and benefit-finding, appreciation and a shift in priorities, and developing an ability to take responsibility for one's own life and behaviour, '. . . You should not be a victim . . . It's not a good thing to give in too much to your illness. . . .' For some, retaining control was achieved through healthy behaviours, medication adherence and being more symptom aware. Others highlighted the importance of expressing emotions and being honest with oneself and others.

Discussion

Whilst the data in this study showed many adaptive coping responses of these patients who had undergone life-transforming surgery, data also highlight that physical gains present significant adjustment challenges to the recipients. Furthermore, the complexity of emotions experienced, from gratitude to guilt, is tied up with prior expectations. This has important implications for how transplantations are 'sold' to these patients as a positive option to kidney dialysis. Even successful transplantation can elicit negative emotions if the reality of the situation is not what was anticipated – by themselves or by significant others. Changing lives, roles within them and changing values as a result of living with a new kidney opens up opportunities for communication. Some emotions, such as disillusionment, are hard to express if they are thought to reflect a lack of gratitude. The authors conclude this interesting paper with suggestions as to how psychological interventions based on cognitive-behavioural principles could help this patient group, and their loved ones, address the emotional consequences of renal transplantation.

In illnesses where a certain degree of stigma is attached, for example those with HIV infection and AIDS, the social meanings surrounding the illness can be associated with the higher levels of reported distress. Valente's (2003) review concluded that between 20 and 30 per cent of people with HIV are clinically depressed at some stage in their illness, and among women with HIV, M. Morrison et al. (2002) reported depression levels four times higher than that expected among age-matched control subjects. Although anxiety levels were not raised significantly in this all-female sample, other studies of both genders have reported 70 per cent having moderate to high anxiety (Cohen et al. 2002). Perhaps unique to those with HIV infection, the presence of what have been identified as 'punishment beliefs' (i.e. where HIV infection is considered by the individual to be a 'punishment' for 'inappropriate' behaviour) have been associated with relatively high levels of depression and relatively low self-esteem (Safren et al. 2002). Such beliefs reflect possible internalisation of early beliefs or prejudices about HIV and likely routes of infection, such as injecting drug use or unprotected homosexual sex. As with depression among physically healthy individuals, high levels of background stress, low levels of personal resources and social support, and poor coping skills also contribute to depression (e.g. Catz et al. 2002).

Both among children and adults, chronic illness typically increases the prevalence of depression and anxiety approximately two-fold in comparison to healthy comparators. Amongst children, distress is created by both acute events (e.g. a fracture, tonsilitis) and chronic and more serious illnesses (e.g. juvenile arthritis, acute lymphoblastic leukemia) (Jacobs et al. 2012). Studies of pediatric psychology highlight the impact of disruption to a child's routine, altered environments (e.g. hospitalisation, removal from parents or school) and changes in role, function and ability, on aspects of a child's sense of self, as well as their well-being (e.g. Coyne 2006; Gannoni and Shute 2010; Christie and Khatun 2012; Compas et al. 2012 (review)).

Loss of 'self'

As suggested above, chronic illness can also bring about a sense of 'loss of self' (Charmaz 1983, 1991) to the sufferer. This is exacerbated by the necessity of living a restricted life due to symptoms, by social isolation due to physical limitations, by struggling to function in the world as previously or by fears of others' response to their 'new state'. Negative responses of others can sometimes lead to perceptions of the self being discredited, or to perceiving oneself as being a burden on others by being unable to fulfil one's 'normal' social roles and tasks (Cloute et al. 2008; Band et al. 2015). As Radley (1994: 148) notes: 'The problems of chronic illness are to do with retention and loss, not just of "self" but of a way of life'. Illness often forces the person to redefine themselves, from a 'healthy' person to one with limitations, and this can reduce feelings of self-worth or self-esteem. There is evidence that enabling a person to hold on to their pre-illness sense of identity rather than having an identity consumed by a serious or chronic illness can be beneficial. Aujoulat et al. (2008) describes how patient empowerment requires two processes: one of being able to 'hold on' to earlier ideas of 'self' (identity and worth, different roles) and learning to control the illness as something separate to these, and another process of 'letting go' where patients accept that they cannot control everything and that they have boundaries, and in effect this requires them accommodating the illness. In engaging in both processes, the authors suggest, patients will experience greater adjustment and ability to value oneself. Such a distinction has implications for those working with patients with a view to enhancing control – there are aspects to hold on to, and others to let go, and, as stated previously in this textbook, perceived control beliefs have to be realistic if they are to be most helpful. In a similar vein, Jones et al. (2011) found that, among those with acquired brain injury, personal change in terms of developing a strong sense of self-identity encompassing a sense of survivorship, and strong social networks, mediated the negative effects of severe head injury on life satisfaction. Curiously, those with more severe head injury had higher life satisfaction and well-being which was explained by their having done greater 'identity work' resulting in a stronger self-identity, and improved social relationships. These factors likely interact, and, although this was not a longitudinal study, such data point to the importance of gaining positives from adversity. Related to this sense of identity and separation from the illness is the notion of 'illness centrality', i.e. the extent to which a person incorporates an illness into their self-concept. Helgeson and Novak (2007) found illness centrality to be higher amongst female adolescents with type 1 diabetes than males, and related to poorer psychological well-being, and also, in a later study, illness centrality was related to poorer adjustment among women with breast cancer (Helgeson 2010). It has been proposed that adopting high illness centrality will have further negative consequences for those where there is associated stigma, with implications for disclosure, support-seeking and the like (Fisher and Chaudoir 2010).

WHAT DO YOU THINK?

There is reasonable evidence, as described in various chapters, that gender differences exist in our health behaviours, responses to symptom, presentation to health care and coping with illness. It also appears, as described above, that females take on an illness identity more than males. Does this mean females value their health more, or communicate about it more, or both? Simultaneously, does taking on an illness identity carry risks for their well-being? We need to know more about the influences on illness centrality and its outcomes.

Emotional reactions to treatment and hospitalisation

Not everyone will willingly submit themselves to hospital care if it is necessary, nor take on the 'sick role' and the depersonalisation and loss of control that can often accompany entering large institutions such as hospitals (Koenig et al. 1995). Fear of anaesthetic, of treatments which confine (e.g. MRI scanners; Bolejko et al. 2008) or which involve pain and discomfort, all require sensitive pre-procedural information (e.g. Uman et al. 2008; Smolderen and Vingerhoets 2010) (see Chapter 13 ☞). Pre-surgical anxiety in both adults and children is high and has been shown to influence post-surgical outcomes such as wound healing (Rokach and Parvini, 2011) and where treatments are repeated and ongoing: for example, courses of chemotherapy or dialysis, patients report feelings of anticipatory anxiety and anticipatory nausea (i.e. feeling worried and unwell just at the thought of entering hospital for the treatments) (Pandey et al. 2006; Rosco et al. 2010).

While initial levels of distress among cancer patients generally fall over time to levels comparable with healthy populations (e.g. Burgess et al. 2005), levels increase at certain points during treatment, when awaiting test results, or when end-stage illness is reached and treatment concludes with no further hope for a cure. During the active treatment phase of their illness, cancer patients may have to cope with a variety of stressors, including significant side effects such as nausea, fatigue and weight loss. Distress at this time is complex: individuals may weigh up the unwanted effects of treatment against the benefits of symptom reduction and survival gains, and patient perceptions and expectancies of the treatment, as well as the perceived severity of symptoms, play a role (Thuné-Boyle et al. 2006).

While the majority of cancer-affected individuals choose to continue with treatment, a small minority do opt to withdraw from treatment. Even when *at risk* of illness, some will decline treatment. For example, Lovegrove et al. (2000) found that, of 106 women at high familial risk of breast cancer attending a breast care clinic and asked to take part in a trial of tamoxifen (a synthetic, non-steroidal agent with tumour-limiting benefits in an unaffected breast), half refused to participate. Those refusing tended to be younger, found the information about tamoxifen as a potential preventive treatment harder to understand than those who took part, knew more about lifestyle risk factors, and saw fewer benefits of the drug. If a demanding treatment is not thought to have significant benefits, then saying no to it is a patient's right.

At all stages of treatment, health professional communication is key to whether a patient feels informed, cared for, and able to make choices about their treatment that address their needs and their goals (Brataas et al. 2009). It is not uncommon for needs regarding open, sincere and clear communications to be high on cancer patients' lists of salient needs, although many (but not all) studies do, thankfully, find these needs to have been met satisfactorily (Morrison et al. 2011).

Reactions at the end of treatment

In the immediate period following treatment, patients and their families may experience a degree of emotional ambivalence: on the one hand, the treatment and any side effects have stopped, but on the other hand, a sense of vulnerability and of being abandoned can result from decreased contact with the health professional staff, with whom relationships have inevitably built up during treatment. This feeling of 'abandonment' following treatment discharge has been reported in various patient groups, for example, among cancer patients (Costanzo et al. 2007) and stroke patients (e.g. Pound et al. 1994). It may be that when cancer survivors no longer need to focus so much of their attention on medical treatment, room is left for a psychological struggle to begin (Schnipper 2001), and at this time some of the support available during treatment recedes, from friends and family, as well as from the health professionals, which can contribute to feelings of distress (Stanton et al. 2005). However, increased distress at this time is not inevitable if patient expectations are managed. For example, Wiles et al.'s (2004) qualitative study of stroke patients' experience found that, where discharge expectations were 'managed well', distress and disappointment was contained to the cessation of physiotherapy rather than disappointment in terms of lost expectations of further potential recovery. Costanzo (Costanzo et al. 2005) in considering conflicting findings of the effect of treatment ending for cancer studies suggests that distress specific to worry or anxiety regarding recurrence may increase, where more global negative mood, or depression, may not.

A transition from curative to palliative treatment, if the former is unsuccessful, can be extremely distressing for patients, if they understand this transition. The rates of depression are moderate among people who are dying, ranging in a review of ten years of research, from 12.2 to 26 per cent (Massie 2004); however, anxiety levels can be higher. The certainty of death commonly brings with it emotional and existential crises alongside concerns about the process of dying and about pain control (Strang and Strang 2002), and fears about a loss of dignity, which can raise distress and even lower the will to live (Chochinov et al. 2002). Kubler-Ross (1969) described a staged reactive process to dying, with initial shock and numbness following a terminal diagnosis being followed by a stage of denial and feelings of isolation, at which point individuals may become angry, blame others or even attempt to 'bargain' for goals they wish to meet before dying. Kubler-Ross describes the final stage as one of acceptance. However, acceptance is not always reached, highlighting as we have previously, that the proposed 'stages' do not hold for all cases. For example, Hinton (1999) found that only half of the terminal-phase cancer patients followed in their study were 'accepting' of death, and 18 per cent of patients and 24 per cent of relatives actually became less accepting of death as they moved towards it.

The effect of negative emotional reactions to illness

Depressed people are less likely than non-depressed people to engage in illness self-management, for example, to adhere to medication (Lin et al. 2004), cease smoking following a heart attack (Huijbrechts et al. 1996), or engage in cardiac or orthopaedic rehabilitation exercise (Lane et al. 2001; Pomp et al. 2012). The effect of depressed mood may also extend to risk-taking. For example, depressed HIV-positive homosexual males reported twice the rate of engagement in unprotected anal sex with partners than did non-depressed men (Rogers et al. 2003).

Although less often studied than depression, anxiety is also associated with poorer illness self-management: for example, control of blood glucose levels among those with diabetes (e.g. Niemcryk et al. 1990), and poorer response to haematological cancer treatments in those undergoing stem cell transplants (e.g. Park et al. 2010). Evidence for an influence on disease course has also been reported: for example, the experience of distressing events preceded exacerbation of symptoms and relapse in those with multiple sclerosis (Ackerman et al. 2002).

Depression also exerts a significant influence on whether such patients resume pre-illness functioning, particularly in terms of return to work and social activities. This could be due to the symptom inflation commonly witnessed among depressed people, or to reduced expectancies of positive outcomes leading to disengagement (Bjärehaed et al. 2010; Pomp et al. 2012) (see Chapter 9 ☛). There is consistent evidence that depressive illness is a significant cause of morbidity and disability and even reduced survival, for example, following a stroke (see review of 28 prospective studies conducted by Pan et al. 2011). Furthermore, a meta-analysis of 17 studies of the impact of emotional well-being (primarily measures of positive affect as indicated by depression or mood scores) found significant effects on recovery and survival amongst individuals with a range of physical conditions. This led the authors to conclude that positive emotional well-being has prognostic significance, albeit small, for the recovery and survival of those with physical illness (Lamers et al. 2012).

Emotion regulation is important to illness outcomes. In other words, how a person experiences, processes and copes with their emotions can impact on their adjustment, with avoidance and repression of one's emotions generally maladaptive, and acknowledgement and expression of how one feels, generally adaptive (see review by de Ridder et al. 2008). Although positive emotions were not assessed explicitly in this review, the results point to a growing area of research, which we therefore turn to next.

Positive responses to illness

There is consistent evidence that positive dispositional characteristics and positive appraisals can influence illness outcomes either directly or indirectly, and that illness itself can bring about positive changes.

Positive appraisals

Having a positive or optimistic outlook has been consistently associated either directly or indirectly (via effects on coping responses) with positive outcomes (see also Chapter 12 ☞). Being optimistic and having higher mastery beliefs was associated with less severe pain and reduced fatigue among cancer patients followed up over ten weeks from receiving chemotherapy (Kurtz et al. 2008). Conversely, pessimists endorsed more maladaptive coping strategies, which predicted emotional morbidity, amongst the post-surgical breast cancer patients assessed by Schou and colleagues (Schou et al. 2004).

Positive emotions

Fredrickson (1998, 2001) summarised the key benefits of maintaining positive emotions as:

● the promotion of psychological resilience and more effective problem solving;

● the dispelling of negative emotions;

● the triggering of an upward spiral of positive feelings.

Illustrating the benefits of positive emotions, Fredman and colleagues (Fredman et al. 2006) found that elderly patients with a hip fracture who had high levels of positive affect during initial hospitalisation had better functional recovery as seen in standing and walking speeds at 2-, 6-, 12-, 18- and 24-month follow-up, than those with low levels of positive affect. Those with consistently high levels, i.e. high positive affect at each time point, had the best functional recovery. Furthermore, positive emotions may have beneficial effects on inflammatory responses associated with heart disease (see, for example, Dockray and Steptoe 2010), as also discussed in the chapter on stress (Chapter 12 ☞). However, maintaining positive emotions form only part of a person's response to illness: the coping strategies that a person adopts to help them to cope with the disease and its consequences are also important in determining illness outcomes (see below, but also Chapters 9, 11 and 12 ☞ for a discussion of Leventhal's self-regulation model of illness and Lazarus's stress-coping theory).

Finding benefit and post-traumatic growth

There are increasing reports that those facing significant health or life stressors often report gains from their experience – this is not a new phenomenon but more a reflection of a shift in research attention. Commonly referred to as benefit-finding, studies of this phenomenon fit within a larger framework described as 'post-traumatic growth', whereby individuals experience positive psychological change as a result of a struggle with stressful life circumstance(s) (Tedeschi and Calhoun 2004; and see the handbook of Calhoun and Tedeschi 2007 for a discussion of post-traumatic growth following a range of stressors).

Five domains of positive change as a result of stress or trauma have generally been identified:

1. enhanced personal relationships;
2. greater appreciation for life;
3. a sense of increased personal strength;
4. greater spirituality;
5. a valued change in life priorities and goals.

The strength of these possible dimensions of growth varies across studies depending on the event and sample under consideration, but there is reasonable consistency from quantitative studies (e.g. Park and Helgesen 2006 – general stress; Fromm et al. 1996 – bone marrow transplant; Petrie et al. 1999 – heart attack and breast cancer; Tomich and Helgeson 2004 – breast

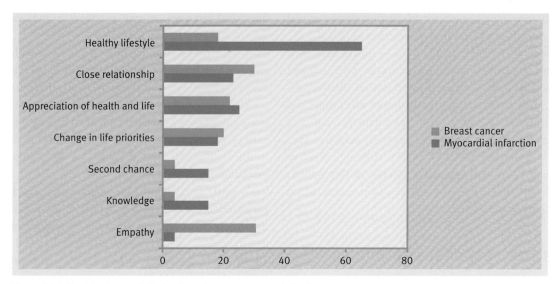

Figure 14.1 Perceived gains following breast cancer or a heart attack

Source: Petrie et al. (1999).

cancer; Danoff-Burg and Revenson 2005 – rheumatoid arthritis) and from qualitative studies (e.g. Gall and Cornblatt 2002; Ingram et al. 2008 (both cancer)). Carver and Antoni (2004) report long-term advantage to benefit-finding in that women who found benefit in the first year following a breast cancer diagnosis showed improved psychological adjustment five to eight years after treatment, compared to those who did not find benefit. However and crucially, Tomich and Helgeson (2004) found a subgroup of women for whom benefit-finding was associated with higher distress over time – those with advanced disease. They suggest that benefit-finding may have reflected early unrealistic hope which, when unmatched by outcomes, became a cause of distress. This points to the importance of realism.

How common is benefit-finding and what form does it take? Petrie et al. (1999) found that 60 per cent of those who had had a heart attack or had developed breast cancer reported some personal gains over the first three months following illness onset, and 58 per cent reported specific positive effects of their illness (see Figure 14.1). The most commonly endorsed benefits were improved close relationships, increased empathy among women with breast cancer, and a healthier lifestyle for men following a heart attack. In a qualitative study of women with breast cancer, Gall and Cornblatt (2002) revealed a spiritual aspect to growth, with women reporting an increased inner strength, spirituality and sense of peace, a sense of becoming a better person and being more

thoughtful, compassionate, understanding and accepting, and increased confidence. Improved relationships with significant others is also commonly reported (e.g. Danoff-Burg and Revenson 2005), and it has been suggested that good relationships between couples may work towards the creation and maintenance of positive emotions (in patients and/or caregivers), which may benefit adjustment (de Vellis et al. 2003). Becoming more accepting of things in life or having closer relationships with family or friends may in fact lead to reported QoL levels higher than those reported by healthy individuals (as reported by Tempelaar et al. 1989, cited in Schulz and Mohamed 2004).

Benefit-finding can be considered as a potential predictor of outcomes, such as improved mood, better adjustment or QoL, but it has also been considered by some as an outcome in its own right. In these instances, as with predicting negative consequences of illness, personal characteristics and psychosocial resources, including coping responses, are potential influences. Stanton et al. (2007) and de Ridder et al. (2008) in their reviews note that younger age is commonly associated with benefit-finding, minority ethnic status and lower socio-economic status have variable effects and gender tends not to exert a significant effect. So what other factors might influence the experience of benefits? A prospective study of 105 cancer patients, interviewed at one, six and twelve months following tumour surgery found that finding benefit at twelve months was directly

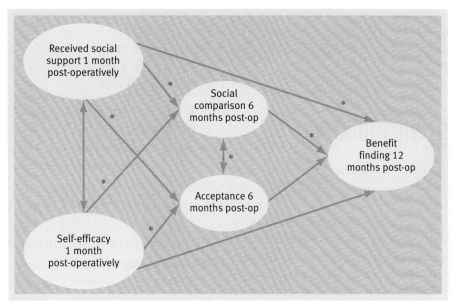

Figure 14.2 The direct and indirect effects of internal (self-efficacy) and external (social support) resources upon benefit-finding in the twelve months following cancer surgery

Source: adapted from Schulz and Mohamed (2004: 659).

predicted by levels of self-efficacy (a personal resource) and social resources (amount of social support received) at one month (Schulz and Mohamed 2004). However, as can be seen in Figure 14.2 (in which the arrowed lines with asterisks reflect significant associations), when examining whether coping mediated the relationship between such personal and external resources and benefit-finding, individuals with high social support resources exhibited greater benefit-finding regardless of whether **acceptance coping** or **social comparison** coping was used, whereas the beneficial effect of self-efficacy appeared to be mediated by coping (as the direct association between self-efficacy and finding benefit was insignificant). These are important prospective findings, because assessing such variables retrospectively (as many studies have done) runs the risk of, as Stanton et al. (2007) point out, the time since the event influencing the extent to which growth is reported. People may reconstruct their past experiences in order to make them more congruent with current experience. Benefit-finding, or the reporting of gains (see Chapter 15 ☞ on caregivers) could therefore be considered a form of coping. Optimism is also a factor that could influence reported benefit, as we know that optimists tend to reappraise events in positive ways, and also tend to cope in a more problem-focused way. In addition, searching for

'meaning' via finding a sense of order or purpose in one's new situation is a form of cognitive restructuring that may help a person deal with or adapt to the challenge of illness (Sharpe and Curran 2006; Park 2010).

Benefit-finding and 'post-traumatic growth', as it has also been described, may be an integral part of 'normal' life experience. To address this, Park and Lechner (2007) note the importance of including control groups in research studies – this is not as common as it should perhaps be.

The final point worth considering here is that cultural variations may exist in the nature of personal growth or benefit-finding. Ho et al. (2004) suggest that individuals from Asian cultures which are more 'collectivist' in approach to health and illness (see Chapters 1 and 9 ☞) may not make changes to their personal outlook, goals

---

acceptance coping

accepting the reality of a situation and that it cannot easily be changed.

social comparison

the process by which a person or group of people compare themselves (their behaviour or characteristics) with others.

or priorities to the same extent as individuals from more 'individualistic' cultures. We return to this issue in the next chapter with regards to reported caregiver gains (Chapter 15 ☞).

Coping with illness

Moos and Schaefer (1984) described the experience of illness as a 'crisis' (crisis theory), whereby individuals face potential changes in identity (healthy person to sick person, for example), location (home to hospital or nursing home), role (e.g. independent to dependent), and changes to aspects of social support (e.g. from socially integrated to socially isolated). The coping strategies used to cope with illness do not differ from those used to cope with any other problem that an individual faces: in other words, illness does not trigger unique coping strategies, and, as such, the theory and concepts of coping outlined in Chapter 11 ☞ are as relevant here as they are to consideration of stress coping. However, as with stress, there needs to be a distinction between acute illness events (e.g. flu, minor surgery) and chronic illnesses, as these present the individual with a different set of challenges. The accepted 'cut-off' for becoming 'chronic' tends to be where an illness and its symptoms or effects last for greater than six months, or where there may be no potential for cure. Some, but not all, chronic diseases are progressive, for example asthma is not, whereas many forms of cancer or arthritis are.

Moos and Schaefer (1984) identified three processes that resulted from the crisis of illness:

1. *Cognitive appraisal:* the individual appraises the implications of the illness for their lives.
2. *Adaptive tasks:* the individual is required to perform illness-specific tasks such as dealing with symptoms, and general tasks such as preserving emotional balance, or relationships with others (see below).
3. *Coping skills:* the individual engages in coping strategies defined as either appraisal-focused (e.g. denial or minimising, positive reappraisal, mental preparation/planning); problem-focused (e.g. information and support-seeking, taking direct action to deal with a problem, identifying alternative goals and rewards); and emotion-focused (e.g. mood regulation, emotional discharge such as venting anger, or passive and resigned acceptance).

Full discussion of cognitive appraisals of stress and illness can be found in Chapters 9 and 11 ☞. Here we explore further Moos and Schaefer's second and third processes. The adaptive tasks required as a result of chronic illness include:

● dealing with the symptoms of the disease and the possibility of pain;
● maintaining control over illness, including aspects of symptom management, treatment, or prevention of progression;
● managing communicative relationships with health professionals;
● facing and preparing for an uncertain future;
● preserving self-image and possibly self-esteem when challenged (e.g. by altered appearance or function);
● maintaining control and emotional balance over health and life in general;
● dealing with changes in relationships with family and friends.

These challenges are generic to many different conditions, although aspects may vary in strength and salience depending on the condition: for example, dealing with treatments may present greater challenges to adaptation in those with painful arthritis than among those with asthma. How a person chooses to deal (cope) with these challenges may vary, as described elsewhere (Chapters 11 and 12 ☞); however, here we focus on illness stressors.

Coping by denial or avoidance

A common initial response to diagnosis or illness onset is either conscious or unconscious denial of its occurrence. Denial appears to be adaptive in the short term as it enables the individual to minimise any threat and cope with the distress felt. In the longer term, however, denial and the related strategy of avoidance tend to interfere with active coping efforts and are associated with increased long-term distress (Stanton et al. 2007). Many, but not all, studies report negative outcomes of avoidant coping and denial – for example:

● Avoidant coping and emotion-focused strategies were associated with greater depression than problem-focused coping among a sample of HIV-positive homosexual men (Safren et al. 2002).

- In a meta-analysis of studies of coping among men with prostate cancer, avoidant coping was generally associated with maladjustment (Roesch et al. 2005).

- Cognitive avoidance coping, including passive acceptance and resignation, among women with breast cancer was associated with a significant risk of poor long-term psychological adjustment at a three-year follow-up (Hack and Degner 2004).

- Among adolescents with chronic disease (asthma, juvenile arthritis, cystic fibrosis, eczema), positive adjustment was predicted by seeking social support and confrontational coping; negative adjustment was predicted by depressive coping (e.g. passivity), but avoidance coping was not a strong predictor (Meijer et al. 2002).

- Among patients with rheumatoid arthritis, passive and disengaging strategies were associated with poor adjustment over time (Covic et al. 2003); although scoring highly on an avoidance/denial pain coping subscale was positively correlated with active coping and positive outcomes (Smith et al. 1997). This unusual finding is thought to reflect the specific context of coping with pain (see Chapter 16 ☞).

Problem-focused and acceptance coping

Generally speaking, after the initial period following illness onset or diagnosis has passed, problem-focused coping, such as making use of social support resources or planning how to deal with the problems faced, and acceptance coping are associated with more positive adaptation (Stanton et al. 2007). Lowe et al. (2000) found that acceptance-focused coping (e.g. accepting things as they are, reinterpreting things in a positive light) was the most prevalent form of coping in hospital and at two months following a heart attack, followed by problem-focused, emotion-focused and, least of all, avoidance coping. At a six-month follow-up, acceptance coping was associated with lower levels of distress, problem-focused coping was associated with high levels of positive mood, and emotion-focused coping was associated with low mood. A prospective relationship existed between problem-focused coping and improved health outcomes, suggesting that effort directed to changeable aspects of the situation resulted in improved health outcomes (either perceived or actual).

People engage in all sorts of coping efforts and do not generally use strategies defined as only emotion-focused, only problem-focused or only avoidant. This is because situations are generally dynamic and multidimensional, and therefore responses also need to be dynamic and multidimensional. As evidence of this, a study of young people within two months of developing cancer (Kyngaes et al. 2001) found that emotion-focused, appraisal-focused and problem-focused strategies were all employed, with the most frequently used being accessing social support (seeking information from health professionals as well as emotional support from families), believing in recovery, and returning to 'normal' life (positive reframing). Some authors point to a 'time X strategy interaction' whereby different strategies are adopted at different periods in the illness 'crisis'. For example, Heim et al. (1987) suggested that cancer patients use more active and problem-focused strategies earlier in the disease, with a shift to more passive and avoidant strategies as the disease progresses. This shift may be highly functional. Stanton et al. (2002a) reported a complex relationship between positive future expectancies, coping and outcomes of women with early-stage breast cancer. Active acceptance at the time of diagnosis predicted better adjustment in terms of mood and reduced fear of recurrence than did avoidant strategies. Pessimism about the future was associated with coping by turning to religion, whereas those women who retained high amounts of hope for the future generally benefited from the use of more active coping strategies.

The nature of coping responses to illness may also be influenced by culture, as suggested by Roy et al. (2005) when their study of an ethnically diverse British cancer population revealed that UK Asians who were more depressed than the Caucasian sample endorsed helplessness and hopelessness and a greater fatalistic attitude to coping.

Religious coping and spirituality

Ethnic and cultural variations have also been found in the extent to which individuals are actively religious, or use religious coping. For example, according to a Gallup survey 83 per cent of Americans felt that a God was important in their lives, whereas in Western and Eastern Europe this figure reduced to 49 per cent , and in the UK, 12 per cent of the population attend a place of worship in contrast to 47 per cent of North Americans (Gallup International online millenium survey 2000).

Religious beliefs have been associated with higher perceived challenge appraisals, greater optimism, hope, meaning-making (positive appraisals of events, personal growth (cf. V. Lee et al. 2006b)), and better emotional and physical adjustment in older adults' response to general stress (Park 2006). Such beliefs are reflected also in coping behaviours adopted across a range of illnesses (e.g. breast cancer, Gall et al. 2000; rheumatoid arthritis, van de Creek et al. 2007; cardiac surgery patients, Ai et al. 2004), although the benefits are not consistently reported. This may be in part due to measurement differences, although most studies distinguish cognitive and behavioural religious coping (RC) strategies and their functions, with some further distinguishing positive or supportive RC where God is seen as 'supportive' and comforting, negative RC where a less secure relationship exists with a more distant and 'punishing' God, and between active and passive RC. (e.g. Pargament et al. 2000; Loewenthal 2007). Loewenthal (2007) described how a belief in a 'punishing' God was associated with poorer mental health than beliefs in a benign 'supportive' God. Where religious coping may often be considered passive, it is not necessarily so: consider, for example, attending prayer groups as a form of seeking support from like-minded others, or of setting out to help others (Harrison et al. 2001), both could be considered as active coping. A review of 17 studies (Thuné-Boyle et al. 2006) concerning adjustment to cancer found that religious coping benefited distress and adjustment in 7 studies (3 found benefits only for specific sub-groups according to race, extent of 'hope'), 7 studies found no beneficial effects, and 3 studies in fact found religious coping to be harmful.

In the Western world many people will describe themselves as spiritual, but not religious (Csof et al. 2009) and, although empirical evidence is typically sought in psychological science, interest in human spirituality has grown (Collicutt 2011). Spirituality can be contrasted with religion in that it tends to be more personal and individualistic rather than institutional or collectivist; more emotion-focused than problem-focused; directed inwards more than outwards; more concerned with self-actualisation than sacrificial demands or duties, and more anti-authoritarian than religion (e.g. Koenig et al. 2001). Many of the third-generation therapies have a 'spiritual' element, for example mindfulness-based practice and meditation (See Chapter 16 ☞). It appears likely that religiosity or also spirituality affect illness experience by influencing appraisals of meaning, by maintaining hope, or by influencing coping, although there remains a need for further research into the role such beliefs play in illness outcomes.

Photo 14.1 Buddhist monks at a meditation

Source: Fotolia.com/sutichak.

Examining whether coping responses change as expectancies around and understanding of a condition changes, Siegel and Schrimshaw (2005) compared women with HIV pre-HAART (Highly Active Antiretroviral Therapy) in the mid-1990s with a matched sample of women living with HIV after HAART had been introduced. Perhaps surprisingly, well-being did not differ but the coping of the later cohort did. HIV-positive women diagnosed in an era where treatment options were available showed more self-controlling, acceptance and escape–avoidance coping than those diagnosed pre-HAART. Moskowitz et al. (2009) meta-analysed these data and data from other studies and found some fascinating differences in coping as a result of which treatment era a person had had the fortune or misfortune to be living in. Overall, this meta-analysis found a general effect of length of time since diagnosis on the adaptiveness of coping in terms of affect and physical health by means of distancing (e.g. 'I went on as if nothing had happened'), seeking social support, and direct action (e.g. 'I concentrated my efforts on doing something about it'), with self-controlling coping (e.g. 'I tried not to act too hastily or follow my first hunch') becoming more adaptive over time. Regardless of time since diagnosis or whether pre- or post-HAART, two forms of coping stood out as being adaptive in this population as a whole – *direct action*, which was associated with more positive affect, less negative affect, better health behaviour and better physical health; and *positive reappraisal coping* (e.g. 'I looked for something good in what was happening'), which was associated with increased positive affect, decreased negative affect and better physical health. In contrast, behavioural disengagement, alcohol or drug use, distancing, and social isolation were found to be maladaptive. The effect of historical context on disease adjustment, or in the effectiveness of coping generally, makes for a novel research study.

As described, the coping responses of people facing illness are individual and influenced by many factors, and they are also dynamic and changeable, as a result of changing demands, resources and coping appraisal (what seems to work best for the person). This reflects Lazarus's transactional model of stress and coping (see Chapter 11 ☞), as does evidence that the factors that moderate this illness-coping relationship may also change over time: for example, social support may fluctuate. Crisis theory (see above) assumes that individuals cope out of a motivation to restore equilibrium and

normality to their lives, and certainly one of the key resources that most individuals draw upon is that of family support. Since illness also impacts on these supporting individuals, we devote the whole of the next chapter to the impact of illness on family – see Chapter 15 ☞.

Illness acceptance

Part of the process of adjusting to illness is the individual process of evaluating its impact on their lives and that of those around them, and a central part of this is thought to be the extent to which the person 'accepts' their illness. This is not to suggest passivity, but rather, acceptance is considered as beneficial to both patient mood and coping and to a range of key health outcomes including, for example reduced pain-related disability (McCracken and Eccleston 2003) and improved physical functioning or enhanced well-being, such as that found amongst adolescents with cystic fibrosis (CF) (Casier et al. 2011, 2013). Acceptance of illness has been defined as 'recognizing the need to adapt to chronic illness while perceiving the ability to tolerate the unpredictable, uncontrollable nature of the disease and handle its adverse consequences' (Evers et al. 2001: 1027, as cited in Casier et al. 2013) and is also associated with a continued engagement in life goals other than illness-related ones. In a study of 38 Belgian adolescents with CF (N=22) or diabetes (N=16), Casier and colleagues (2013) found that negative mood was higher and positive mood was lower in those with diabetes compared to CF, but in both groups acceptance of illness was associated with better daily mood as recorded on daily diaries kept for a period of three consecutive weeks.

Generally, acceptance is considered to be necessary if a patient is to 'move on' with their treatment or with their life more broadly, and is thought to benefit wider adjustment and quality of life. In a study of cardiac patients who had experienced heart failure for example (Obieglo et al. 2015), those with lower illness acceptance were more likely to report less energy, more severe pain, negative emotional reactions, sleep disorders and limited mobility, and were socially isolated. This wide-ranging effect on indices of quality of life have led to suggestions of acceptance-enhancing interventions (Chapter 16 ☞).

Acceptance of one's illness or condition may be challenged where there is a high degree of visibility: for example, in burns or injury victims, those born with congenital disfigurement or those left with post surgical scarring (Rumsey and Harcourt 2005). The reactions of others to one's appearance is an added challenge, with often negative consequences for self-confidence and self-esteem, social interaction and emotional well-being of the person affected. As Partridge and Pearson (2008) describe in a moving article in *The Psychologist* about their own experience of disfigurement, 'liking and living with 'different' outsides can be very challenging' (p. 490) and how 'the first step was getting to like myself.' As a society we perhaps do not support 'difference' in a way that bests supports those that, for whatever reason, are judged to be different (whether it be obesity or a genetic or acquired disfigurement or disability).

Illness and quality of life

While the primary goal of medicine and health care is to improve health and/or treat and cure illness and its symptoms, in order to reduce morbidity and premature mortality, there is a need to address more global outcomes of health-care treatments and services. While clinical outcomes can be assessed in an objective manner (such as observing improved physical functioning, reduced symptomatology), assessing patient well-being requires that the view of the patient be sought, i.e. it is subjective. For example, in clinical trials such as those conducted to test the efficacy of a new drug and intervention studies based on either psychological or clinical principles and practices, it is important to evaluate not only clinical outcomes but also the individual's perceptions of how the treatment or intervention has influenced their illness experience and their general psychosocial functioning. Technological advances in medicine can effectively treat conditions that previously people would have died from (e.g. major strokes, heart attacks, many forms of cancer) and people are living longer, often with some dependency needs or with some aspect of their life restricted. As a result, the importance of knowing about and understanding the psychosocial outcomes of treatments or interventions (as well as the clinical) has been recognised, along with the implications such knowledge has for future care, treatment and service provision. The significant growth in quality of life (QoL) research reflects Boini et al.'s (2004: 4) observation that 'physicians now have the opportunity to add life to years, as well as adding years to life'. However, as highlighted in IN THE SPOTLIGHT (on p. 414),

patients may derive great benefit from certain treatments or interventions in terms of enhanced quality of life, even though these same treatments or interventions may not extend survival or quantity of life.

What is quality of life?

In general terms, quality of life (QoL) can be referred to as an individual's evaluation of their overall life experience (their situation, experiences, states and perceptions) at a given time (global quality of life), with the term 'health-related QoL' (HRQoL) emerging to refer to evaluations of this life experience and how it is affected by symptoms, disease, accidents or treatments, and also by health policy. HRQoL is associated with 'optimal levels of mental, physical, role (e.g. work, parent, carer) and social functioning, including relationships, and perceptions of health, fitness, life satisfaction and wellbeing. It should also include some assessment of the patient's level of satisfaction with treatment, outcome and health status and with future prospects' (Bowling 1995a: 3).

According to the World Health Organization Quality of Life (WHOQOL) working group (1993, 1994), QoL is a person's perceptions of their position in life in relation to their cultural context and the value systems of that context in relation to their own goals, standards and expectations. Quality of life is a broad concept affected by an individual's physical and mental health, level of independence, quality of social relationships, social integration and, added subsequently (WHOQOL 1998), their personal, religious and spiritual beliefs. This working group produced the generic and cross culturally valid assessment tool (WHOQOL-100), which addresses 25 different facets of QoL grouped into one of six domains:

1. *physical health:* pain and discomfort; energy and fatigue; sleep and rest;

2. *psychological:* positive feelings; self-esteem; thinking, memory, learning and concentration; bodily image and appearance; negative feelings;

3. *level of independence:* activities of daily living (e.g. self-care); mobility; medication and treatment dependence; work capacity;

4. *social relationships:* personal relationships; practical social support; sexual activity;

5. *relation to environment:* physical safety and security; financial resources; home environment; availability

and quality of health/social care; learning opportunities; leisure participation and opportunities; transport; physical environment;

6. *spirituality, religion and personal beliefs.*

This generic tool provides core items for use across all conditions, with disease- and population-specific versions being developed subsequently (see later). Most of the available QoL measures are composite scales which address the multiple dimensions described above, which seems to hold face validity – in other words if you asked someone what their 'quality of life' was, their answer would likely reflect many differing aspects of their life.

However, early studies tended to focus more keenly on physical function as if QoL was reflected fundamentally in this, and certainly ascertaining the impact of disease on an individual's functioning is crucial. Many studies use measures of disease or symptom severity, disability or physical functioning as outcome measures considered to be indicative of quality of life. However, the WHO model of impairment, disability and handicap (see Chapter 1 ☞; WHO 1980) described how illness had more than just physical consequences, by defining handicap as disadvantages and limitations in performing social roles that resulted directly from impairment and/or disability. However, the linear relationship between impairment, disability and handicap, or, between impairment, activity limitations and participation restrictions, as defined in the WHO's revised model of disability (International Classification of Functioning, Disability and Health WHO 2001), is not inevitable but depends on psychological and social factors (e.g. Johnston and Pollard 2001). Support for this is seen, for example, among individuals suffering from rheumatoid arthritis, where the link between pathophysiology and disability outcomes is often indirect and moderated by psychosocial and environmental factors (see Walker et al. 2004 for a review), or in stroke patients receiving a workbook intervention targeting their beliefs in control over their recovery, where disability was reduced relative to a control group (Johnston et al. 2007). Rather than considering disease or disability as indicative *of* quality of life, they could therefore be considered as potential influences *upon* it (McKenna et al. 2000; McKenna 2004) that may or may not affect a person's perceived QoL, depending on the extent to which that individual rates them as important to that judgement (e.g. Cox 2003).

What influences quality of life?

For some individuals, the inability to perform valued activities as a result of impairment or disability may be considered a 'fate worse than death' (e.g. Ditto et al. 1996); however, for others they will continue to find meaning and purpose in life in spite of disablement (e.g. life-threatening disease such as cancer or HIV infection; Tsarenko and Polonsky 2011). As noted by Carr et al. (2001), 'health-related quality of life is the gap between our expectations of health and our experience of it' (p. 1240), yet 'existing measures of quality of life do not account for expectations of health'. Not everyone *expects* good health, and thus poor health may not be judged as impacting on their QoL, and vice versa, with illness considered more damaging to QoL in those who expect good health. 'In the spotlight' (below) raises the question of patient preferences in health care and in making quality-of-life judgements and introduces the reader to one approach taken by health economists.

Many factors influence QoL including:

- demographics: e.g. age, culture;
- the health condition: e.g. symptoms, presence or absence of pain, functional disability; neurological damage with associated motor, emotional or cognitive impairment, sensory or communicative impairment;
- treatment: e.g. its availability, nature, extent, toxicity, side effects, etc.;
- psychosocial factors: e.g. emotions (anxiety, depression), coping, social context, goals and support.

Age and quality of life

Age has been shown to influence the aspects of life considered to be important to people. Research is becoming more aware of some of the unique challenges of working with populations at different ends of the life trajectory – children, and those at the end of life.

In terms of children, it is necessary to understand the different contexts which may mediate the impact of illness and its treatments on the child (Matza et al. 2004), as any effects of impaired QoL in childhood may be cumulative and affect later development (Jirojanakul et al. 2003). For example, cancer treatments commonly impact upon school attendance and participation in school activities important to a child's social development

IN THE SPOTLIGHT

Which health outcomes are important to whom?

For most people, the choice between a treatment without major side effects and a treatment with major side effects would be an easy decision, i.e. that without the side effects. However, the decision becomes more complex if the choice is now between a treatment without major side effects but with only moderate proven success in eradicating or controlling the illness concerned, and a treatment with significant side effects but with excellent success rates. Which would you choose? These types of decision are faced daily by many cancer patients, who are fighting for survival but facing often toxic treatments in terms of their side effects. The quantity of life may be added to by these treatments, but what about life quality? These questions raise the issue of which outcomes are best for the individual being treated.

If economics also enters the debate, as it increasingly does in terms of treatment costs, costs of hospital stays, costs of follow-up care, etc., then decisions about which treatment outcomes are best often fall into the hands of doctors and hospital managers who are responsible for the spending. The outcome of mortality has little health-care cost, whereas prolonged morbidity does and therefore treatment efficacy is central to these decisions. The ideal outcome from a medical standpoint is likely to be optimal functioning of the patient, but few treatments come with that guarantee and, if they do, then they are likely to be very expensive! Decisions are generally made by weighing up the costs of treatment (e.g. financial costs, costs to the person in terms of side effects) against the objective benefits (e.g. financial savings from reduced need for further treatment, projected quantity of life gain for the individual).

Health economists increasingly work alongside health psychologists, and using 'time trade-off techniques' can examine the utility (importance) attached to health states. Patients are asked, for example, to compare living with a certain condition for a couple of years, to living in better health for a shorter length of time if given a certain treatment, although they may die or be very ill after this time. The actual periods in normal health are adjusted until the person can no longer choose between the states. For example, if you were indifferent as to whether you lived in poor health for six months or in optimal health for three months with treatment, then this would indicate the utility of that treatment for that individual. Basically, these kinds of judgement require individuals to consider how much time in terms of current QoL they would be willing to trade for post-treatment QoL: for example, how many days of treatment would you willingly trade for how many months of improved health? (See Bowling 1995a: 12–14 for a fuller discussion of the complexities of such techniques.)

Health professionals differ in their ability to communicate with patients about such issues and, furthermore, they may underestimate patients' HRQoL (Detmar et al. 2000). Furthermore, what is valued may change over the lifespan. For example, will a 75-year-old cancer patient consider the treatment option of six three-weekly doses of chemotherapy, its anticipated benefits in terms of extended lifespan, and likely side effects (nausea, achey limbs, hair loss, etc.) in the same way as a 35–45-year-old? It is important to assess individuals' perceptions of what makes *their* life 'quality'.

(Eiser 2004); childhood epilepsy can impede social functioning, independence and relationships with peers as well as, in some cases, self-esteem and mood (McEwan et al. 2004). Studies of aggression or of oppositional behaviour and noncompliance have been less commonly addressed but hold important implications for both the child patient and their families (Compas et al. 2012).

Do children with chronic disease modify their future life expectations as a result of QoL being compromised in their childhood? We simply do not know this for sure. Logically, however, we might expect so, given evidence that negative experiences such as social rejection in childhood (a possible consequence of the non-participation some physical illnesses or disabilities may create) can have long-term effects (Maddern et al. 2006). In terms of adolescents, often considered to be a particularly challenging time to be diagnosed with a chronic or serious illness, the evidence is mixed regarding whether or not illness such as cancer has long-term effects on quality of life. For example, Larsson et al. (2010) conducted a longitudinal study of 61 individuals diagnosed with cancer in adolescence (mean age 15.5), and compared their QoL over four years with age- and gender-matched controls. While initially (up to 6 months post diagnosis), the cancer group had significantly lower mental health and vitality and greater depression than controls, at 18 and 48 months this was reversed and the cancer group actually reported greater vitality and lower anxiety and depression. Although a small study, such findings confirm other large studies of cancer survivorship following a childhood diagnosis (e.g. Hudson et al. 2003) and suggest perhaps that the early experience of illness and its associated treatments lead to a maturation and heightened appreciation of life, and what is sometimes referred to as **post-traumatic growth** (Tedeschi and Calhoun 2004).

While many studies with younger children have relied on parental 'proxy' reports of their child's QoL (see the section on measuring quality of life, below), several interesting studies using **qualitative methods** to elicit domains of importance in QoL and factors that influence it have identified a broad range of influences on quality of life. For example, focus-group discussions among adolescents (aged 11–17) with epilepsy (Cramer et al. 1999, cited in McEwan et al. 2004) identified eight subscales related to health-related QoL:

1. general epilepsy impact;
2. memory/concentration problems;
3. attitudes towards epilepsy;
4. physical functioning;
5. stigma;
6. social support;
7. school behaviour;
8. general health perceptions.

Quantitative results from the same study found that seizure severity was the main predictor of health-related quality of life, independent of age of onset of the illness. In other words, the length of time that the child had had the illness did not reduce the impact of severe seizures on QoL. In another focus-group study that examined health-related QoL and its relation to distress among younger children (aged 6–12) with epilepsy, distress was mainly associated with loss of independence and restrictions in daily activities, concern about the reactions of others to their illness and seizures, treatment by peers, and concerns about the side effects of medication (Ronen et al. 1999, as cited in McEwan et al. 2004).

The effect of age on QoL ratings is not inevitable. For example, age was not predictive of quality of life in a one-year longitudinal study of stroke survivors ranging from 32 to 90 years old, where other factors, such as physical disability, depressed mood and gender (females had poorer QoL) were (Carod-Artal et al. 2000). It may be that age is less important than 'life stage': i.e. the impact of a disabling illness on QoL might vary according to whether or not it occurs at a time in life when a person is still professionally or reproductively active. Among younger people who have suffered an acute stroke, being unable to return to work has been associated with reduced life satisfaction and subjective well-being (e.g. Vestling et al. 2003), whereas this would not concern the majority of stroke patients who are post-retirement age. Referred to as the 'third age', the period of life after retirement can continue to be full of enjoyment and opportunity, whereas the 'fourth age' is when illness and disability present challenges to an older person's independence (Woods 2008). Maintaining QoL and promoting healthy, positive and successful ageing has become increasingly important, given the ageing population of most societies (Baltes and Baltes 1990; Grundy and Bowling 1999). The goal of healthy ageing approaches is to minimise dependency (physical and/or emotional), which, in turn, it is hoped, will reduce the 'costs' to society of health-care provision for an

---

post-traumatic growth
following a traumatic event, including serious illness, a person may experience positive psychological change, e.g. increased life appreciation, improved relations to self and others, new life values and priorities.

qualitative methods
concerned with describing (qualifying) the experience, beliefs and behaviour of a particular group of people.

> **well-being**
> the subjective evaluation of a person's overall life.

increasingly ageing population. Studies of older people have found the life domains of importance to be good physical functioning, having relationships with others, and maintaining health and social activity. Compared with younger samples, older people are more likely to mention independence, or the fear of losing it and becoming dependent (Bowling 1995b). **Well-being** has also been studied as a subjective evaluation of a person's overall life which reflects in part objective circumstances, including one's health status, employment status and financial security, relationships, etc. Assumptions of declines in subjective well-being with age have been challenged by findings that life satisfaction does not change hugely over adulthood, and in fact increases between early 40s through to early 70s (in British but not German data reviewed by Baird et al. 2010), with a decrease then in later life as hypothesised. However Baird summarises findings from two national population surveys and not chronic illness populations and therefore cannot account for the effect of illness on such judgements.

WHAT DO YOU THINK?

Have you ever experienced a challenge to your quality of life? If so, in what way, and how did you deal with it? Did one domain of QoL take on greater importance than it had previously and if so, why? Have the 'weightings' you attach to the different domains returned to their pre-challenge levels or has the event had a long-lasting impact on how you evaluate life and opportunities? Think about you 'now' compared perhaps with your parents. Do you think you see 'quality of life' differently to them? Consider what may change your judgements of quality of life in the future.

Bowling and Iliffe's (2006) study of the relationship between five 'models' of successful ageing and QoL among 999 adults aged over 65 years found that the broadest model of understanding of what it meant to have 'aged successfully' was most predictive of a person reporting they had a good quality of life, or not 'a not good' one. This broad 'lay model' encompassed biomedical (function), broader biomedical (e.g. roles and function), social functioning (social networks and support), and psychological resources (e.g. self-efficacy, optimism, coping) models, but added in socio-economic (income, capital) and environmental (safety, services, access) factors.

Photo 14.2 Social participation can benefit healthy ageing.

Source: Alamy Images/OJO Images Ltd

Therefore, while having a limiting illness influences the domains of importance in terms of judging one's own QoL in that they become more focused on physical functioning and activity, social support and social contact, feeling that you have 'successfully aged' is about a lot more than that. Furthermore, illness type appears less important than the level of any resultant physical disability, most likely because physical disability challenges many of these other important domains – a person's social, emotional, cognitive, economic, social and environmental functioning. For example, Blane et al. (2004) found that serious and limiting health problems were most strongly predictive of QoL in over three hundred individuals aged between 65 and 75, whereas non-limiting chronic disease did not affect QoL. They also found housing security, receipt of welfare or non-pension income and (for men only) years out of work to be predictive.

Being limited in terms of one's activities or roles, whilst commonly predictive of poorer mental and physical QoL, quality of life is about more than this. For example, over half of the older people with long-standing limiting illness surveyed by Evandrou (2006) self-rated their health as good or fairly good. In fact Berg et al. (2006) highlights, that while subjective health ratings of the oldest-old (85 years +) correlate with other self-evaluations including general well-being or quality of life, anxiety and depression, they tend to be more weakly associated with objective health-related measures. While a key global aim of interventions to enhance QoL, regardless of disease type, is the improvement and maintenance of physical and role functioning at all ages, QoL continues to be multidimensional. As Windle and Woods (2004) point out, it is a person's subjective appraisal of their situation which mediates objective circumstances into experienced life quality.

Expectancies and adaptation

One possible explanation for why some people with chronic illness report higher than expected QoL, sometimes at levels similar to that of healthy comparator groups, can be found in studies of adaptation which suggest that, when a situation is clear-cut and understood to be a permanent feature of one's life (e.g. bereavement, loss of a limb, an incurable illness), adaptation is easier and better than when one believes their circumstances are temporary and may change (Herrman and Wortman 1985). This paradoxical suggestion led to a fascinating study of life satisfaction conducted by Smith and

colleagues (Smith et al. 2009). They compared patients who had all had surgery resulting in the bowel being bypassed so bodily waste was passed via a tube to an external receptacle (therefore the 'disability' is the same), but one group had a temporary and reversible colostomy (also known as an ileostomy, reversed if the condition improves), the others, a permanent colostomy. Following patients to one and six months post-surgery, and controlling for the underlying condition, the main hypothesis that QoL would increase more over time for those with permanent colostomy than for those with a temporary colostomy was strongly supported. Those with a reversible colostomy reported higher initial life satisfaction (although not significantly so), but it did significantly decline over time, whereas the permanent group's life satisfaction increased. Such findings are not consistent with models of adaptation that assume that negative reactions fade with time merely because of continued exposure to a negative stimulus (Diener et al. 2006). Crucially, the authors suggest that such findings highlight a role for cognitions, particularly expectancies of an improvement in circumstances, which paradoxically may impede adaptation. They argue that the motivation to cope may vary in these two groups and that looking forward to the potential of surgery being reversed at some point in the future may deter the person from adapting positively to current circumstances, as they are constantly comparing their current state with one yet to be achieved. Unfortunately the study does not explicitly assess these expectations, for example by assessing hope, nor does it assess the other possible illness-specific beliefs that may also explain differences in life satisfaction and quality of life ratings. In spite of this, however, findings suggest that health professionals' communications about prognosis which may improve should avoid being unduly optimistic about change, as this may instill false hope that is detrimental to patient adjustment. Hopefully, more and larger studies will pursue this research question further before we turn away from the newly burgeoning field of positive psychology (see Chapters 11 and 12 ☞) and accept that no hope may be better than hope!

In 'Issues' (below) we address the question of whether or not QoL is attainable at the end of life, as a result of either ageing or terminal illness.

Culture and quality of life

Chapter 1 ☞ described how health itself is viewed slightly differently in Western and non-Western cultures, with individualistic Western views and more collectivist Eastern views of health being identified. In comparing data from studies of Chinese patients with Western data samples, Yan and Sellick (2004) noted cultural influences on many factors relevant to quality of life judgements, such as responses to pain, attitudes towards and use of traditional versus Western medicines and treatments, concepts of dependency, the use of social support and the culture of communication. As Bullinger (1997: 816) observed: 'If disease, as anthropological research suggests, is so very much culture-bound, how could quality of life be culture free?' The meaning of health and illness is affected by cultural norms and experiences of health, illness and health care, as well as by different belief systems, such as the Chinese belief in the need to maintain a balance between *yin* and *yang*, or as in some tribal beliefs in the supernatural. Differences also exist in the extent to which Europeans, Americans, Asians, Africans and Latinas use religious-based coping, with religious beliefs and spirituality also being a component of quality of life for some more than others (e.g. Culver et al. 2004). We described many such different beliefs in the opening chapter (see Chapter 1 ☞). Cultural differences also affect how QoL can be assessed (see the section on measuring quality of life, below).

Aspects of the illness and quality of life

There is a reasonably strong body of evidence showing that physical illness has an impact on a person's reported QoL. For example, a review of the pooled data of 118 studies of health-related QoL in adults with type 2 diabetes (Norris et al. 2011) concluded that diabetes had a negative effect, particularly on physical function and general health domains of QoL, although of course pooled effects obscure the many individual different factors that influence individual experience of QoL. Aspects of the illness also matter: for example, pervasive and persistent pain and disability are generally found to be associated with a lower QoL, for example as reflected in depression levels, disability and use of health care (see Chapter 16 ☞). Ferrucci et al. (2000) investigated the extent to which disease severity in stroke, Parkinson's disease (PD) or coronary heart disease (CHD) patients was associated with their health-related QoL and found, interestingly, that the relationship was non-linear in the stroke and CHD patients, and that only in the least severe stroke and most severe CHD cases was QoL in

fact associated. In Parkinson's disease, however, there was a linear relationship whereby severe PD associated with lower health-related QoL. In other words, severity of illness is not inevitably or consistently associated with lower health-related QoL, and disease-specific relationships need to be explored.

In those with neurological illnesses such as Parkinson's disease, cognitive dysfunction such as memory impairment or attentional deficits can disrupt key QoL domains. Furthermore, memory deficits can make it hard for some individuals to evaluate their current status against their former status in order to make meaningful QoL judgements (Murrell 2001). Perhaps for this reason, patients with cognitive impairments have been the subject of less research attention.

Aspects of treatment and quality of life

Treatment itself also influences QoL. Most studies examining the effects of treatment on QoL do so in order to either determine its impact on specific populations or compare which of several treatment alternatives is associated with the greatest QoL outcomes. In cancer, for example, scores on the POQOLS (pediatric oncology (child cancer) QoL scale; Goodwin et al. 1994) differed across groups receiving different treatments: for example, children undergoing intensive treatment showed poorer QoL than those in remission (Bijttebier et al. 2001).

Many treatment evaluations carried out as part of randomised controlled trials of new or comparable treatments include some indicator of QoL, such as symptomatology, physical functioning or return to work. Increasingly 'patient-centred' measures, PROMS (Patient-reported Outcome Measures) which invite patients to describe outcomes important to them in terms of their QoL, are being used (Carr and Higginson 2001). In a UK study, for example, Watson et al. (2004a) examined the QoL outcomes of a large number (481) of leukae-mia patients who had participated in a randomised trial of one of two types of bone marrow transplantation (BMT) (both preceded by intensive chemotherapy) compared with a course of intensive chemotherapy alone. At a one-year follow-up, those patients who received BMT reported greater fatigue, more problems in sexual and social relationships, and disruptions to work and leisure activities. In addition, having BMT from a related sibling had a greater negative impact on the QoL indices than either unrelated

ISSUES

End-of-life QoL

While the majority of deaths take place in hospitals, the care of the dying more often takes place in patients' homes, until the point is reached where some home carers can no longer provide the necessary care or medication, and hospitalisation in nursing homes or hospices ensues. Among others, Elizabeth Kubler-Ross (1969) highlighted the psychological and emotional aspects of dying and the need to 'listen to the dying patient'. The hospice movement developed in the late 1960s out of recognition that traditional hospitals with their routines, emphasis on treatment and depersonalised atmosphere were not best placed to provide care to the dying (Saunders and Baines 1983). Hospices seek to provide care that facilitates an optimal QoL for both patients and their families as death approaches. This requires that patients are pain-free, experience little distress, maintain some dignity and control, and can maintain relationships with loved ones in a caring and compassionate environment. A good QoL at the end of life has also been found to encompass patients' need to remain as independent as possible so as not to 'burden' their carer (e.g. Gill et al. 2003). It is also important for carers' needs to be supported in order that they are able to provide the patient with whatever support is needed during the final days and weeks of their life (World Health Organization Expert Committee 1990). Importantly, such settings need to acknowledge cultural variations in the 'rituals' that accompany dying and the resultant expectancies family and friends may have. For example, positioning of the deceased to face Mecca is important to those of Muslim faith; the burning of sage by American Indians is an important ritual to prepare a dying person's soul for the afterlife. As Emanuel et al. (2007) note, the dying 'role' encompasses practical, relational and personal elements, all of which are necessary if the person is to move from a 'sick' role to the 'dying' role and adjust to it. Although taking on this role is emotional and accompanied by feelings of loss and grief, focusing only on the physical needs is insufficient. Do hospices achieve this?

Carers of patients who had died in hospices reported that 'their' patients were more aware that they were dying than did carers of those who had died in hospital, perhaps reflecting the ethos of openness encouraged in hospices (ibid.). This openness regarding dying may enable greater preparation for death and bereavement among patients and spouse carers, which has, in turn, been associated with reduced levels of emotional distress (e.g. Chochinov et al. 2000). However, Seale and Kelly (1997) did not find a difference between hospice and hospital care in terms of the care and support provided to spouses. Thinking positively, this may reflect the changing nature of standard hospital care towards more holistic, psychosocial care, or, thinking less positively, perhaps a growing medicalisation of hospices (Crossley and Small 1998). With increasing emphasis on specialist nurses in hospitals, at least in the UK, we can perhaps infer that hospital care is becoming more holistic. Certainly, within England and Wales the National Institute for Clinical Excellence (NICE) guidance on Improving Supportive and Palliative Care for Adults with Cancer (2004) recommends that 'assessment and discussion of patients' needs for physical, psychological, social, spiritual and financial support should be undertaken at key points (such as at diagnosis; at commencement, during, and at the end of treatment; at relapse; and when death is approaching)' (Key recommendation 2).

Whenever a person is facing death, issues such as 'a good death' and 'dying with dignity' become salient and bring with them many ethical and moral debates. Research has consistently shown that older people do not fear death itself, as younger people do, but are more concerned about the process of dying and the fear of dying in pain or without dignity and self-control (e.g. McKiernan 1996; Chochinov et al. 2002; Strang and Strang 2002). Difficult questions arise, such as: When should treatment be stopped? How much can, or should a person endure, and for how long? Should a dying person who has been experiencing great pain or severe dyspnoea (breathlessness) be resuscitated if they become unconscious? Should a person facing a terminal illness and inevitable decline towards death (such as the highly publicised case of Diane Petty, who faced full physical paralysis while remaining mentally intact as a result of motor neurone disease) be allowed to invite assisted suicide? How, and even where, an ill person chooses to die is inevitably a personal decision. Choosing 'when' to die is altogether more contentious, and even when an 'advance directive' from a patient is in place indicating their wishes for medical intervention (or not) when and if the time comes that they cannot communicate their wishes, health professionals may give priority to family members' preferences regarding end-of life care (Mowery 2007).

The practice of non-treatment of a dying person – passive euthanasia – is generally acknowledged as an inevitable part of medicine; however, active euthanasia in terms of carrying out an action that effectively ends that life (such as administering a fatal dose of adrenaline) is much less common and varies by country (e.g. Van der Heide et al's review in six European countries 2003) reflecting in part national differences in the legality of assisted suicide or euthanasia. This varies from being fully prohibited (e.g. Italy) to prohibited except in specific circumstances (e.g. Belgium, the Netherlands). In the Netherlands, GPs have been able to carry out these practices since 1991 (Onwuteaka-Phillipsen et al. 2003), while other countries have yet to make policy on this issue. For example, a study conducted in Wales (Pasterfield et al. 2006) asked GPs 'Do you think that the law on intentional killing should be changed to allow (a) physician assisted suicide and (b) voluntary euthanasia?' Of the 1,025 doctors who responded (a very reasonable 65 per cent of those invited to respond), 62.4 per cent did not favour a change in law regarding (a), and 55.8 per cent similarly did not favour a change of law regarding (b). In the face of such findings, it is likely to be some time before this contentious issue is resolved in terms of any legislation, at least in the UK, although public support is reported to be high in the case of those suffering from painful, terminal illness (House of Lords 2005).

Human rights legislation, the desire for control over our lives and the fact that the world is facing an ageing population, many of whom will live many years with chronic ill health, suggests that issues regarding euthanasia are going to remain, and possibly grow, in most parts of the ageing world (Zucker 2007). It is worth noting that a 'good death' in terms of the quality of the death experience is also important to the bereaved, to reduce any lingering anger or resentment and enable the grief process to be a more positive one (Tedeschi and Calhoun 2008).

Have your own personal experiences of death, if you have experienced any, influenced your thoughts on how you would choose to die, if that choice were available? What do you think would provide 'quality of life' at the end of life?

donor transplantation or the chemotherapy group. A significant number of BMT patients may continue to experience significant functional limitations in the longer term, although the vast majority report their quality of life to be good to excellent (Broers et al. 2000). Supporting this, another Dutch study (Helder et al. 2004) found that the majority of QoL domain scores in young adults who had been children at the time of their BMT were in fact not significantly lower than that found in a comparison group of healthy young adults (although their general health was rated lower). This would suggest that the childhood experience of a serious illness requiring intensive treatment and a prolonged period of adjustment does not have long-lasting effects into adulthood, although larger-scale prospective studies which also assess a number of other possible influences on the QoL of BMT survivors, such as social support resources, are required.

The use of PROMS is becoming more widespread, particularly in studies of cancer treatments, although being more accepting of their use does not automatically equate with their having influence on clinical decision-making (Meldahl et al. 2012).

Psychosocial influences on quality of life

The presence of anxiety symptoms or disorder has been associated with poor QoL among the physically healthy (e.g. Mendlowicz and Stein 2001), and among those with physical illness, emotional responses unsurprisingly also have an impact. For example, depression and anxiety symptoms measured within 15 days of a heart attack both predicted low QoL at four months, with depression being the strongest predictor (Lane et al. 2000). Similarly, among 568 cancer patients, anxiety and depression were both related to the QoL dimensions of emotional, physical and social functioning, pain, fatigue (depression only), and global QoL, although as in Lane's study, depression was more strongly associated (Skarstein et al. 2000).

Leventhal and Coleman (1997) state that as well as being examined as an outcome, QoL needs to be considered as a process, itself influenced by various life domains, including the experience and perceptions of illness, symptoms and its treatment (see Chapter 9 ☞), and the importance attached to those perceptions at any given point in time. Changes in any of these determinants will influence changes in QoL (see Figure 14.3).

This process model has generally been accepted in psychological research studies where multiple determinants are assessed, as well as generic or specific QoL 'outcome' measures (see discussion of measures below).

One example of this is drawn from studies of pain (see Chapter 16 ☞), which is commonly found to be strongly associated with depressed mood, and also with lower QoL. For example, Rosenfeld et al. (1996) conducted a prospective survey of over four hundred AIDS patients in New York, 63 per cent of whom reported frequent or persistent pain in the preceding two weeks. Comparing scores across a range of QoL indices between those who were and those who were not currently experiencing pain revealed significant differences between the groups in terms of psychological distress, depression, feelings of hopelessness and global QoL. The analyses controlled for other possible influences on the QoL indices, such as age or gender, and social support, and confirm that pain affects a broad range of psychosocial functioning. Another

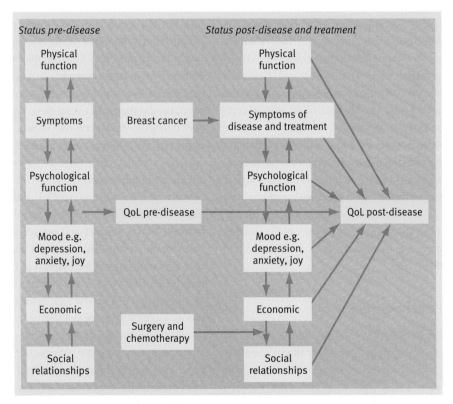

Figure 14.3 The quality-of-life process prior to and subsequent to breast cancer. Baseline QoL is changed by the impact of the disease and treatment upon each of the domains. Changes in functioning post-disease are weighted and will lead to changes in post-disease onset QoL

Source: Leventhal and Coleman (1997: 759).

important finding is that race was significantly related to QoL and distress, with non-white patients reporting poorer QoL and more distress. The authors suggest this may be due to differences in access to pain management, or to other factors not assessed in their study, such as socio-economic or life stress, which may negatively impact on QoL evaluations. It is clear that various factors need to be taken into account when attempting to establish what 'predicts' QoL: the presence or absence of pain; the presence or absence of depressed mood; levels of social support, ethnicity and other background stressors that may be happening independently of the disease process under study.

Coping and QoL

In terms of coping response, Carver et al. (1992) point out that avoidant coping is likely to be beneficial to QoL in situations where a person is unable to exert control, and they suggest that approach coping in these situations could lead to frustration when control is not forthcoming. Others suggest that maintaining a good QoL in relatively unalterable situations, such as that faced by individuals with chronic pain, may require individuals to cope by means of acceptance coping or positive reinterpretation. Supporting this, McCracken and Eccleston (2003), in a study of 230 adults with chronic pain, found that, whilst coping was weakly related to pain acceptance and unreliably associated with adjustment, those who *did* show acceptance of their pain reported higher QoL, including reduced pain symptomatology and disability, less depression and pain-related anxiety, a higher amount of time per day spent up and about, and a greater likelihood to be working. Such findings underscore the importance of the 'goodness of fit' of the coping strategy adopted to the current context, as also discussed in Chapter 12 ☞.

Social support and QoL

In terms of resources upon which individuals may draw when faced with stress or the demands of illness, previous chapters have highlighted the crucial role of social support (Chapter 12 ☞). Many positive relationships between perceived social support, coping and adjustment to chronic disease have been reported. However, the direction of causality between variables is not always clear. For exam-

ple, in a study of 210 outpatients receiving treatment for epilepsy, regression analyses found that, independent of current physical health status, psychological distress, loneliness, coping and stigma perception contributed most significantly to the measures of QoL (Suurmeijer et al. 2001). However, disentangling the direction of relationships between mood, resources (or lack of resource if considering loneliness), coping variables and illness outcomes such as QoL requires studies with several waves of data collection, where change in the levels of support and adjustment, changes in coping responses, etc. can be assessed. In an attempt to do this, Burgoyne and Renwick (2004) assessed 41 Canadian adults with HIV three times over a four-year period and examined whether changes or stability in social support was associated with changes or stability in QoL. Although having a relatively small sample size, this study considers the dynamic associations between disease symptomatology, social support and QoL and explores the direction of causality between these factors. Do changes in social support lead to changes in QoL, or do changes in QoL lead to changes in social support? Slightly contrary to expectations, analyses revealed that both social support and QoL remained relatively stable over the four-year period. It did, however, decrease significantly for 40 per cent of the sample. If this finding were obtained in a larger sample, it would warrant further exploration to try and ascertain 'who' these 40 per cent were: i.e. did they differ from those for whom social support remained stable in terms of any personal or illness characteristics? Poorer mental functioning QoL scores tended to predict subsequent lower perceived emotional and informational support, but the directional relationship between physical functioning QoL and social support was unclear. Importantly, no strong longitudinal association between social support and subsequent QoL emerged. Furthermore, results did not reveal that changes in either QoL or social support were linked in the longer term (i.e. from year one to year four), although there was evidence of a link between the first and second year. Certainly the two measures were associated *within* each time point, with positive or negative changes in social support corresponding to positive or negative changes in QoL domains; however, the disappointing longitudinal predictive results means that social support and its effects on QoL, at least in this disease group, remains open to debate and in need of a similarly designed study to be conducted with a much larger sample.

Goals and QoL

QoL research has sometimes been criticised for the absence of a theoretical model around which to develop and test the QoL concept. One attempt to bring theory to bear has employed Scheier and Carver's self-regulation theory (see Chapter 9 ☞), which describes a process of goal attainment in the face of a disturbance such as illness (1992). It is proposed that the disturbance of personal goal attainment caused by chronic illness and its consequences is likely to influence a person's perceived QoL (e.g. Echteld et al. 1998). Within the self-regulatory framework, event appraisal, appraisals of goal disturbance, outcome expectancies, appraisals of resources and coping processes all combine to influence QoL (e.g. Maes et al. 1996). Echteld et al. (2003), for example, found that among 158 patients who had undergone **coronary angioplasty**, disease-specific quality of life and positive affect three months after surgery were predicted by pre-surgery QoL, low stress appraisals and avoidant coping. Goal disturbance predicted disease-specific QoL and negative affect. Boersma *et al.* (2005b) also found that, following a heart attack, disturbance in 'higher-order' goals such as fulfilling duties to others, or having fun, was associated with anxiety, depression and a lower health-related quality of life. It may be that goals indirectly influence QoL outcomes by altering the 'meaning' a person attaches to their illness (Taylor 1983; theory of cognitive adaptation to illness, see below). The 'meaning' of illness has been defined as 'an individual's understanding of the implications an illness has on self, relationships with others, priorities, and future goals', and as such has been shown to influence well-being and adjustment (e.g. Fife 1995, cited in Walker et al. 2004: 467). Examining personal goals (both day-to-day and higher-order goals) and their attainment or non-attainment as a result of ill health is important if we are to better understand why people rate their QoL in the way that they do when given standardised QoL assessment tools.

---

coronary angioplasty

a procedure where a small balloon is inserted into the blocked coronary artery of a person with atheroma.

WHAT DO YOU THINK?

When Christopher Reeve, aka Superman, was asked 'How would you rate your quality of life?' having been confined to a wheelchair following a horrific spinal injury, he replied 'I would say better than good. I would say it's, you know, good plus. I wouldn't say excellent because there are limitations . . .'

Illness or even being totally paralysed from the neck down in the case of Christopher Reeve does not inevitably lead to a poor evaluation of one's QoL. QoL is based on many things other than subjective health factors, including, for example environmental indicators, such as traffic, pollution, the housing market, and social statistics regarding leisure activities, consumer-good ownership, crime, educational attainment and unemployment. Using such data to provide an 'objective' estimate of 'quality of life, the *Economist* (2008 PocketWorld in Figures) found Norway, Iceland and Australia ranked in the top three for QoL, where the Netherlands, Finland and Switzerland tie for 9th, and Italy and the UK tie for 17th! In this chapter we argue that QoL is a subjective construct - should we pay much attention to such rankings? Are such 'league tables' there purely to feed the media with buckshot to fire at our politicians, or do they raise real concerns about the health and social care systems and environmental policies of our countries?

Supporting this latter stance, a study of 5–8-year-old children either attending school or working alongside construction worker parents in Thailand found, that generic QoL (health-related QoL is not assessed) was less affected by health states (chronic, acute or severe illness) than by parental income, education and occupational status, type of housing and extent of child's extracurricular activities (Jirojanaku/ et al. 2003). Although conducted in Thailand among predominantly healthy children and where work practices and cultural variations in health and illness perceptions exist (see Chapters 1 and 9 ☞), the findings support those of Western child populations, where current life circumstances (and the expectations they bring with them) are important to QoL (e.g. Eiser and Morse 2001).

Think about aspects of your own living environment and whether it affects your QoL judgements or what might change to make it different.

Measuring quality of life

There are several reasons as to why QoL assessment is a useful clinical practice (e.g. Higginson and Carr 2001), including:

- *Measure to inform:* increased understanding about the multidimensional impact of illness and factors that moderate impact will (a) inform interventions and best practice, and (b) inform patients about treatment outcomes or possible side effects in order that they are 'prepared' for them, or so that supportive resources can be put in place. Descriptive data from QoL studies can also be used to inform patients and their families about likely treatment experiences so that treatment choices can be made. For example, Cocquyt et al. (2003) reported inconclusive evidence that breast-sparing procedures have better QoL and psychosocial outcomes than mastectomy (although some studies find better body image and sexual functioning in those with breast-conserving therapy) - such information can be presented by health-care providers to help patient decision-making.

- *Measure to evaluate alternatives:* QoL measures may be used as a form of clinical 'audit' to identify which interventions have the 'best' outcomes – for the patient, but also often in relation to costs. Medicine often employs the health economics concept of quality-adjusted life years, or QALYs (number of years or proportion of year achieved with a good QoL following a given intervention). Different treatments may increase length of life and its quality to varying degrees, and when calculated these weightings can be assessed against the actual treatment cost (i.e. value for money). QALYs can inform medical treatment decisions: for example, two cancer treatments may offer the same survival benefits, but different QoL and QALYs during and after treatment.

- *Measure to promote communication*: whilst unlikely to be the primary motive for conducting QoL assessments in a clinical setting, doing such assessments may enable health professionals to address areas that they may not otherwise have done: for example, about treatment satisfaction, treatment or illness impact on family interactions, social or sexual functioning. Taking a more holistic view of the impact of illness or treatment upon patients can help health care to be responsive to individual patient circumstances or needs.

Whatever the motive for assessing QoL, a major issue faced by researchers or clinicians is which instrument or method of assessment to use. As noted by Carr and Higginson (2001: 1,359): 'if they [standardised measures] do not cover domains that are important to individual patients they may not be valid measures for those patients'. Also, clinicians need to feel confident in their interpretation and potential benefit to their practice, which evidence suggests they are not (e.g. Meldahl et al. 2013). If we accept that QoL is a multidimensional, dynamic and subjective construct, measurement is inevitably going to face many challenges!

Generic versus specific QoL measures

The global domains of QoL described by the WHOQOL group and outlined earlier have received empirical

Photo 14.3 Christopher Reeve aka Superman, rated his quality of life an 'better than good' in spite of being confined to a wheelchair.

Source: Shutterstock.com/Featureflash.

support; however, a question remains as to whether to adopt a generic, or global, measure of QoL which assesses concepts relevant to all illness groups or to adopt a measure specific to the illness being studied. As well as the WHOQOL-100 or WHOQol-Brev, commonly employed generic measures include the Medical Outcome study short form 36 (SF36, Stewart and Ware 1992); the Nottingham Health Profile (NHP; Hunt et al. 1986); and the EUROQOL (Euroqol group 1990). In terms of disease-specific measures, an increasing number are available (see Bowling 2005), including for people with cancer (e.g. EORTC QLQ-C30; Aaronson et al. 1993; Cocks et al. 2008, or the FACT-G, Cella et al. 1993; Holzner et al. 2004), asthma (e.g. Hyland et al. 1996), arthritis (e.g. AIMS-1, 2; Meenan and Mason 1990) or Parkinson's disease (see review by Marinus et al. 2002).

There are disadvantages and advantages to both types of measure. Generic measures allow for comparison between different illness groups, but may fail to address some unique QoL issues for that illness. For example, the European Organisation for Research and Treatment of Cancer (EORTC) developed a cancer-specific tool (EORTC QLQ-C30) not only to assess quality of life issues relevant to most people (see Table 14.1) but also

Table 14.1 Assessing quality of life – examples from the EORTC QLQ-C30 (version 3)

(NB: This is NOT the full scale: do not use in research)

We are interested in some things about you and your health. Please answer all of the questions yourself by circling the number that best applies to you. There are no 'right' or 'wrong' answers. The information that you provide will remain strictly confidential.

	Not at all	A little	Quite a bit	Very much
(2 examples of 5)				
Do you have any trouble taking a *long* walk?	1	2	3	4
Do you need to stay in bed or a chair during the day?	1	2	3	4
DURING THE PAST WEEK:				
(10 examples of 23)				
Were you limited in doing either your work or other daily activities?	1	2	3	4
Were you limited in pursuing your hobbies or other leisure-time activities?	1	2	3	4
Have you had pain?	1	2	3	4
Have you had trouble sleeping?	1	2	3	4
Have you lacked appetite?	1	2	3	4
Did you feel tense?	1	2	3	4
Have you had difficulty remembering things?	1	2	3	4
Has your physical condition or medical treatment interfered with your family life?	1	2	3	4
Has your physical condition or medical treatment interfered with your *social* activities?	1	2	3	4
Has your physical condition or medical treatment caused you financial difficulties?	1	2	3	4

FOR THE FOLLOWING QUESTIONS PLEASE CIRCLE THE NUMBER BETWEEN 1 AND 7 THAT BEST APPLIES TO YOU

How would you rate your overall health during the past week?

1   2   3   4   5   6   7

very poor   excellent

How would you rate your overall quality of life during the past week?

1   2   3   4   5   6   7

very poor   excellent

Source: from EORTC Quality of Life group http://groups.eortc.be/qol/questionnaires_qlqc30.htm For permission to use contact: Quality of Life Department, EORTC European Organisation for Research and Treatment of Cancer, AISBL IVZW, Avenue E. Mounier, 83/11, 1200 Brussels, BelgiumWebsite: http://groups.eortc.be/qol.

included cancer-specific supplementary modules concerning fears of recurrence or of treatment side effects (Aaronson et al. 1993). In HIV infection and AIDS, issues such as HIV testing and the results process, and disclosure of a positive diagnosis to others, are addressed in a tool developed out of the previously mentioned WHOQOL (the WHOQOL-HIV) (O'Connell et al. on behalf of WHOQOL-HIV group 2003).

Disease-specific measures therefore have 'added value', but they do not allow for the same amount of between-illness comparability which considers, 'Is the quality of life reduced more by cancer than by heart disease?' – a question of interest perhaps to those considering funding allocations or developing community support resources, for example.

Individualised QoL measures

Another option is to take an individualised approach to assessing QoL which allows respondents to choose the dimensions and concerns relevant and of value to them – not everyone will rate health, social life or work highly, for example! Demonstrating that QoL ratings can be obtained without using a questionnaire, Stenner et al. (2003) adopted a technique known as 'Q-sort' whereby 90 healthy participants (white, employed adults under 65 years old) sorted a collection of 52 statements about QoL into piles according to their importance to them (least important, neutral, most important). Within these three piles they then sort each item on a scale ranging from −5 least important, through 0 neutral, to +5 extremely important. Participants then examine their unique 'Q-sort' and discuss why they ranked items as they did, and whether they believe their ranking accurately reflects their personal view about QoL. Eight significant factors emerged that were interpreted as reflecting distinct constructs of the meaning and personal relevance of QoL *for this sample*: happy families; standing on my own two feet; emotional independence; just do it; life as a positive challenge; in God we trust; staying healthy enough to 'bring home the bacon', and 'You can't choose your family'. Demographic influences on these emergent factors included younger participants rating standing on their own two feet and being independent and in control more highly than older participants; whereas older participants, more often married, rated happy familes and their relationships and support more highly. Many other differences existed, for example, in the extent to which

mental well-being was valued in comparison to physical health. Furthermore, study findings highlight that different strands of QoL interact, and that causal sequencing seems likely: in other words, psychological aspects may influence the reported social, financial and physical aspects, and vice versa.

This 'idiographic' approach is also taken in specific assessment instruments: for example, the schedule for the evaluation of individual quality of life (SEIQoL; O'Boyle et al. 1993; Joyce et al. 2003). This is not specific to health and invites individuals to identify five aspects of life that are important to them (i.e. 'What are the five most important areas of your life at present – the things that make your life a relatively happy or sad one at the moment. . . the things that you feel determine your quality of life?'). Individuals rate their current level of functioning on each, attach a weighting of importance to each aspect and rate how satisfied they are currently with that aspect of life. The aspects of life mentioned most often by the hip replacement patients in the original study were family, leisure activities, independence, happiness, finances and religion. Health control subjects provided similar rating, although nominated health more often than patients, suggesting perhaps the importance of retaining health to those currently having – whereas amongst the patient sample who perhaps had had to readjust their life goals and values and downplay health as one of the most important domains in their lives, health featured less strongly. This, however, was not explored in the study.

Another individualised measure, specific to those with a health condition, is the PGI – the Patient Generated Index (Martin et al. 2007). This also asks individuals to name the (five) most important areas of their life, but unlike in the SEIQoL, the five *are* to be those that are affected by their health condition. These are then rated on a 0–100 scale (worst imaginable, to no effect, exactly as they would like it to be). This measure also allows for other aspects additonal to the five listed to be noted. Finally, in a novel addition, participants are given 60 points to 'spend' on buying improvement in any of their listed domains, and this spend is multiplied with the rating to provide a final score for the weight attached to that QoL domain. This really highlights the subjective value of different domains to different people. Whilst the PGI is popular, it was not found to be concurrently associated in the hypothesised manner with illness perceptions in head and neck cancer patients (see Chapter 9 ☞; Llewelyn et al. 2007), and PGI scores showed only moderate reproducabilty, responsiveness to change and correlation with other QoL measures amongst older heart failure patients (Witham et al. 2007). Perhaps further validation work with this measure is required.

While individualised methods of assessment acknowledge the subjectivity of QoL, such methods are time-consuming and relatively complex processes. Addressing the point that this could have excluded their use in certain populations, Jenkinson et al. (2001) adopted technology to make QoL assessment quicker, portable and possibly more adaptable to clinical situations. They presented the dynamic health assessment (DYNHA) system (see www.qualitymetric.com), which offers a short computer-based assessment where items are selected from a pool, dependent upon participants' prior responses to global questions. Currently on offer are assessments for generic Qol based on the SF36, as well as specific measures of the impact of headache, arthritis, pain and paediatric asthma. Such methods benefit from being more adapted to uniquely individual problems, while the use of SF36 items still enables comparison with other SF36 assessed populations. More studies are required using this method, but results from Jenkinson's study with neurological populations are encouraging.

Measuring illness experience and outcomes

Where circumstances allow, most studies use multiple measures and, as well as assessing generic and/or illness-specific multidimensional QoL, will generally also include unidimensional outcome measures such as assessments of mood, pain or disability. There is a natural limit to how many questionnaires can be 'inflicted' on an ill individual, and it is important for researchers to be sensitive to this. Furthermore, a good research tool may not be an appropriate tool to administer in a clinical setting. For example, the functional limitations profile (Patrick and Peach 1989), while a well-validated and commonly employed outcome measure, includes 136 items assessing 12 domains of potential illness impact (e.g. self-care, mobility, social functioning, communication and emotion). The FLP takes 20–30 minutes to complete, which is simply impossible in many clinical settings! In fact, the detection of mood disorders in hospitalised patients, such as clinical levels of depression, was often difficult for front-line nurses (see meta-analysis by Mitchell and Kakkadasam 2011), which in part was

due to the complexity of assessment instruments. The use of the simple Distress Thermometer has addressed this somewhat, although this is a screening tool only and not a full assessment (Mitchell and Kakkadasam 2011).

In addition, illnesses that elicit a communication deficit, such as the receptive and expressive aphasias that are common following a stroke, make it difficult to carry out assessments of subjective perceptions, which often results in aphasic patients being excluded from self-report studies (e.g. Morrison et al. 2005). In these situations the other option is the use of proxy measures, the limitations of which are described below.

There is a proliferation of measures available to assess illness outcomes. These have been developed predominantly in the English language, meaning that for use in non-English-speaking countries, measures have to be translated. Bowden and Fox-Rushby (2003) reviewed the process of translating measures, in 23 countries across Africa, Asia, Eastern Europe, the Middle East and South America and concluded that in this process the meaning of items may be lost. In addition, using measures that have been generated predominantly from samples of Western populations assumes that words and concepts hold equivalent meaning across cultures, and that domains have equal salience. The fact that the incidence of disease and morbidity and mortality outcomes vary considerably between countries creates differences in disease experiences which likely affect illness perceptions and QoL expectations. For example, in Europe only 6 per cent of mortality is attributable to communicable diseases (such as HIV, TB), whereas in Africa and South-east Asia communicable diseases account for 71 and 39 per cent of deaths, respectively.

The WHOQOL group addressed the issue of cultural equivalence in developing its measure, and similarly the cancer-specific QoL measure, the FACT-G (Cella et al. 1993) has received cross-cultural validation: for example, in a Korean sample (e.g. Lee et al. 2004). While Chapter 9 ☞ described cultural variations in perceptions of illness and health-care-seeking behaviour, few studies have addressed specific differences in understanding of QoL. In conducting factor analysis with the FACT-G items, Lee et al. found that the physical, emotional and functional well-being dimensions had good construct validity, but that the social/family well-being subscale was problematic with items not loading together onto a coherent factor. This subscale assesses closeness to friends and partners, seeking of emotional support from family or friends, family communication, accepting illness on the part of the family, and sex life. The authors interpret these findings as evidence that the Korean women separated out family from friends in terms of what they offered to their well-being, with family communication and closeness fundamental, whereas the cancer was often kept from friends. This focus on familial support rather than that external to the family has been reported amongst Asian cultures also (e.g. Parveen and Morrison 2009; Parveen et al. 2013). Such influences need to be borne in mind and the pooling of data obtained using multidimensional measures within mixed cultural samples avoided.

The choice of which outcome to address in a research study and which measure(s) to use will necessarily be determined by a study's aims and by the practicalities offered by the research situation and the population in question. This ultimately introduces a lot of heterogeneity into the empirical literature which can make it quite difficult to compare across studies, or to translate research findings into clinical practice. While the dominance of some measures i.e. those considered gold-standard measures (e.g. for mood, for function, for QoL) may go some way towards achieving consistency in measurement, such standardisation bring with it the risk of losing information as to the very personal and individualised experience of illness, hence perhaps why qualitative methods are increasingly incorporated into large quantitative studies.

ISSUES

Allowing for response shift and social comparison

Consideration needs to be given to when and how often illness outcomes are assessed, and by whom. As described in this chapter, medical professionals are increasingly recognising the scientific evidence regarding the importance of psychosocial outcomes; however, there is a limit to how many outcomes and how often we can feasibly assess patients within the clinical context. In addition, findings can sometimes appear inconsistent with QoL, function or mood scores improving in patient reports over time even where no objective change in the condition has occurred. In fact, some authors have found individuals with limiting illness to rate their QoL higher than do healthy people (e.g. in diabetes; Hart et al. 2003). In trying to interpret this counterintuitive finding, we can either consider simply that it reflects the subjectivity of our measurements, or that illnesses do not inevitably limit a person's perceived quality of life. Alternatively, illness may itself create what is described as a **response shift**, i.e. illness causes people to recalibrate their internal standards, reprioritise expectations and perhaps change their life values (Schwartz et al. 2004) or reconstruct their identity to accommodate and take ownership of an illness identity (Jones et al. 2011; Tsarenko and Polonsky 2011).

> **response shift**
> changes in subjective reports that may result from a reprioritisation of life expectations or recalibration of internal standards so that the construct being assessed is reconceptualised.

Yardley and Dibb (2007) nicely illustrated this in their longitudinal study of 301 individuals with Meniere's disease, a chronic although not life-threatening condition characterised by severe disabling vertigo, tinnitus and progressive hearing loss. When the scores obtained on the SF36 quality of life measure obtained at the first study time point were compared with the score given 10 months later when participants were asked to look back to that first time point and score their quality of life 'then', there was a significant reduction in the reported level of general health, mental health, role-physical, and role-emotional attributed to the first time point. In other words, when looking back, these participants attributed poorer QoL across all SF36 subscales, except the 'physical health' one, to 'then' than they had reported at the time. The *'then test'* was significant whereas the difference between the first time point and the second time point was not, i.e. the ten-month follow-up scores themselves did not differ from the baseline scores. This is response shift and is worth bearing in mind when conducting longitudinal studies. Yardley offers some explanation for this response shift by also showing that scores on a measure of goal orientation relevant to five broad domains of QoL *did* change over time with an improvement in participants' approach. Others have suggested that, when facing a serious or life-threatening condition, patients may 'scale-back' goals (Carver and Scheier 2000; Sharpe and Curran 2006). Qualitative studies support this by highlighting changes in life expectations, meanings, goals and priorities following diagnosis or during illness (e.g. Ingram et al. 2008). To better understand 'change' over the course of illness, the 'then-test' needs to be incorporated into many more future studies, including where the stressors are not necessarily life-threatening so as to ascertain whether response shift exists only in serious circumstances. We should not be surprised to find that such 'shifts' in perspective affects how questionnaire items are interpreted and scored at different time points, and, although there is likely to be an adaptive function, more evidence is needed in this regard.

Related to this, an interesting study by Sargent-Cox and colleagues (2010) assessed self-rated health in the large Australian Longitudinal Study on Ageing and identified that these judgements are often made in comparisons to others and that ratings can vary depending on who the comparator is. They found that self-comparative ratings ('Is your health now, better, about the same, or not as good as it was 12 months ago?') declined over a ten-year follow-up period, whereas age-comparative ratings (i.e. 'Would you say your health is better, about the same, or worse than most people your age?') stayed roughly stable for women but became more negative for men. This goes against the expected downward social comparisons (Festinger 1954), whereby contrasting oneself to those worse off at the same age could be helpful in enabling one to dissociate from the 'ageing' stereotype and increase one's self-esteem (Wills 1981) or contribute to adaptive coping (Buunk et al. 2006). *Identifying* downwards (as opposed to *contrasting* downwards), seen particularly amongst oldest-old men (85+ years) who compared themselves negatively against age-similar peers, is likely to create feelings of threat or anxiety. In contrast, young-old men (65 years) showed the expected increasingly positive age-comparative ratings. A global rating ('How would you rate your overall health at the present time?') which is commonly found to be predictive of many health outcomes, including mortality, significantly declined over time. Such findings have implications for the conclusions drawn. Unlike in this study where participants are *explicitly* invited to make comparative ratings, how are we to know whether social comparisons are *implicitly* enacted in the responses people make to our questions?

Assessing illness experience and outcomes in children

McEwan et al. (2004) point out that adapting an adult questionnaire into a child version needs to consider cognitive limitations that make it difficult for young children to understand abstract questions such as those concerning life satisfaction or global well-being. Developmentally, and consistent with Piagetian thinking (see Chapter 1 ☞), the understanding of the more concrete domains of QoL (such as pain) may emerge as early as between four and six years of age, for example the Childhood Asthma Questionnaire Form A (French et al. 1994), whereas the more abstract domains (such as feelings) emerge from around age seven. In addition, as Matza's very useful review of conceptual, methodological and regulatory issues highlights (Matza et al. 2004): 'When designing a pediatric HRQoL instrument, it is important to ensure that items correspond to experiences, activities, and contexts that are directly relevant to the age of the sample' (p. 80). There is little to be gained from asking children about the impact of illness on general functioning where a distinction between school, play, at home, and with peers is likely to be needed.

Although some measures have been developed specifically to assess QoL in child populations, few have been fully validated (see Matza et al. 2004). This fact, alongside a common assumption of cognitive limitation in children, has led to many studies using parents to complete questionnaires on behalf of their children - this is known as proxy measurement. However, parental 'proxy' reports in effect go against the principle of QoL being a personal subjective belief, as a parent may not share the same views as their child (Matza et al. 2004). This point was well illustrated by Eiser and Morse's (2001) review of studies of chronically ill samples where both child reports and parental proxy reports were generated. Parent–child agreement was greater for observable aspects of QoL, such as physical functioning, but less for emotional or perceived social functioning. Supporting this, a study of 100 children with congenital heart disease and their parents found that, while both parents and children reported reduced child motor functioning and autonomy when compared with healthy children, the children reported lower levels of emotional QoL than did their parents. In addition, parents reported that their child faced more problems than the children themselves reported (Krol et al. 2003).

By assessing 'visible' emotional distress, perhaps the reliability of parent proxy is increased. For example, a study of QoL among young cancer patients (using parental proxy reports, Bijttebier et al. 2001)) assessed predominantly observable aspects of QoL, including those related to emotions:

● *physical restriction:* e.g. my child has been able to perform as usual;

● *emotional distress:* e.g. my child has anger outbursts;

● *discomfort from medical treatment:* e.g. my child complained of pain after a medical procedure.

However, not all emotion is reflected in overt behaviour.

Healthy children, by contrast, have been reported to show less agreement with their parents regarding their physical status than they do in other domains (e.g. Theunissen et al. 1998). Furthermore , a review of six studies where two sets of ratings were obtained found significant discrepancies between a physician's perceptions of patient well-being and QoL during the course of long-term (primarily cancer) treatment and that reported by the patients or, in the case of children, a parent (Janse et al. 2004). Given the above evidence of divergence in reports, it is unclear who researchers should direct their questions to: it may be that assessing both the 'patient' and a significant other will give a more complete picture of the illness experience.

Models of adjustment

Adjustment or adaptation in fact means different things depending on the perspective taken. For example,

adaptation from a medical viewpoint will consider pathology, symptom reduction or physical adjustment; from a psychological viewpoint it may well consider emotional well-being or lack of distress, cognitive adaptation (see below) or psychiatric morbidity; and from a biopsychosocial perspective (that adopted by health psychology as outlined in Chapter 1 (☞) adaptation is likely to consider pathology, emotions, cognitions and coping responses, and also the nature and extent of social adjustment or functioning. Walker et al. (2004) review these three approaches or paradigms in relation to adjustment to rheumatoid arthritis, which has a clear pathology and is a typically painful and disabling chronic inflammatory disease of the joints with significant repercussions for both the sufferer and their families. All three models of adjustment have relevance to this condition. However, following an informed review and critique, Walker and colleagues conclude that the biopsychosocial approach best 'fits' the chronic disease experience (not just of rheumatoid arthritis), given evidence of the critical role of personal characteristics (e.g. optimism), appraisals (e.g. control), mood (e.g. anxiety) and coping responses in predicting symptom experience and disease outcomes. Support for this can be seen in a study of the disabling conditions of stroke and chronic idiopathic axonal polyneuropathy (CIAP) where the extent of disease impairment explained variance in control beliefs, and activity limitations explained variance in mood and in control beliefs (Schröder et al. 2007). Social factors such as the nature and availability of social support also play a significant role in the illness experience as described in Chapter 12 (☞ and in relation to caregiving (Chapter 15 (☞).

A well-cited example of a psychological model of adjustment was provided by Shelley Taylor (1983), who argued that the process of adjustment to threatening events, whether illness or not, centred around three themes:

● searching for meaning in the experience;

● attempting to gain a sense of control or mastery over the experience;

● making efforts to restore self-esteem.

This is known as a cognitive adaptational model in that, following a stressful event (challenge or threat), a person is motivated to face the challenges and be proactive in finding ways to deal with them in order to restore equilibrium in one's life. Unlike the stage models of response to illness described earlier, Taylor does not impose any sequencing on these three themes of adjustment, although it is likely that finding meaning in the experience will facilitate attempts to gain some control or enhance self-esteem.

Five related conceptualisations of adjustment to chronic disease have also been outlined by Stanton et al. (2001), where the latter two reflect outcomes rather than cognitive adaptational tasks or processes, and where adjustment is usually defined as the absence of these negative mood states:

- mastery of disease-related adaptive tasks;
- preservation of functional status;
- perceived quality of life in several domains;
- absence of psychological disorder;
- low negative affect.

Both these writers acknowledge that adjustment is dynamic and, to achieve it, finding meaning in one's situation and achieving some degree of control or mastery over it are necessary. Finding meaning implies a degree of acceptance of the situation, but not to the extent that it produces passivity, but rather to the extent that it promotes adjustments being made (to expectations and goals, to behaviours) that enable life to carry on (cf. Folkman and Moskowitch 2004). Gaining a realistic sense of control need not mean actual control over the illness, but may simply mean control over some aspects of that illness: for example, over symptom medications or over dietary change. In fact, Taylor describes how the meaning, sense of control and restoring self-esteem may be 'illusions' which are nonetheless essential if adjustment is to take place. Much of adjustment is tied up with beliefs and coping, although the relationship is likely to be bidirectional, as seen in Chapter 9 ☞ in relation to illness self-regulation where the crucial role of illness representations and coping responses was highlighted.

Increasingly, positive indicators of adjustment, such as maintaining positive mood, finding meaning and retaining purpose in life are being studied, and, as described in this chapter, it is possible to attain good adjustment in the face of challenging conditions. This may be in part due to the 'response shift' described in Issues, where individuals 'recalibrate' what is important to them and shift their priorities, but this is not necessarily a problem – perhaps this is at the crux of adjustment to changed circumstances, whether work or life stress (see Chapters 11 and 12 ☞) or a health threat – we need to be flexible and respond to changing circumstances. Our theories acknowledge this, but our empirical evidence needs to catch up with many more studies assessing change in beliefs, expectances and responses over the course of an illness than do currently.

SUMMARY

This chapter has provided evidence that illness can have a multitude of impacts on a person's life, whether physical, emotional or social, or a combination of these, as seen in multidimensional assessments of QoL. In addition, positive outcomes are possible. In this chapter we have described a range of illness outcomes and a range of influences on them, from aspects of the disease and its treatment, to aspects of the individual such as their age, ethnicity, mood or levels of social support. We have hopefully demonstrated that, in spite of difficulties in measuring health outcomes, there is clear need for research and practice to look beyond clinical outcomes of illness, such as symptomatology and mortality, to more holistic psychosocial outcomes. This shift is seen in the growing inclusion of QoL assessment in clinical trials of treatments or in psychosocial interventions.

For outcomes research, there is also the need to be sensitive to the needs of specific populations: for example children, or those from different cultures. As with beauty, mood or quality of life are in 'the eye of the beholder', which presents challenges to interventions based on identified predictors of such outcomes, as it is unlikely that 'one size will fit all'. However, the evidence presented in this chapter offers a starting point from which to develop interventions.

Further reading

Suls, J. and Wallston, K.A. (eds) (2003). *Social Psychological Foundations of Health and Illness*. Malden, MA: Blackwell.

This comprehensive text presents material that is central to many chapters in our textbook. For this and the subsequent chapter, you could look particularly at Chapters 16–19, where psychological, social and relationship influences on adjustment to illness are described.

Stanton, A.L., Bower, J.E. and Low, C.A. (2007). Post-traumatic growth after cancer. In L.G. Calhoun and R.G. Tedeschi (eds) (2007). *Handbook of Post-traumatic Growth: Research and Practice*. London: Lawrence Erlbaum Associates, pp. 138–75.

This excellent handbook contains many chapters relevant to topics addressed in this textbook, but for this chapter I recommend you look at Stanton and colleagues' chapter for an up-to-date account of how some good can come from what is often perceived as all bad.

Key papers

Park, C.L. (2010). Making sense of the meaning literature: an integrative review of meaning making and its effects on adjustment to stressful life events. *Psychological Bulletin*, 136: 257-301

This paper usefully distinguishes between *searching* for meaning, a common response to stress and illness, and *finding* meaning, and the differential effects these two processes have for adjustment.

Compas, B.E., Jaser, S.S., Dunn, M.J. and Rodriguez, E.M. (2012). Coping with chronic illness in childhood and adolescence, *Annual Review of Clinical Psychology*, 8: 455-480.

This review highlights the importance of understanding processes of coping and adaptation to illness in children and adolescents. The paper focuses on control-based coping efforts.

Moss-Morris, R., Deary, V. and Castell, B. (2013). Chapter 25: Chronic fatigue syndrome, *Handbook of Clinical Neurology*, 110: 303-14.

This chapter presents an up-to-date summary of evidence relating to the experience of CFS in all its complexity and provides a good example of where cognitions and emotions interact with the experience of physical symptoms, and the implications this has for interventions.

Stanton, A.L., Revenson, T.A. and Tennen, H. (2007), Health psychology: psychological adjustment to chronic disease. *Annual Review of Psychology*, 58: 565–92.

A useful review of key proximal and distal factors shown in empirical study to be associated with adjustment to cancer, cardiovascular disease and rheumatic disease: for example, sociocultural factors, personality attributes, beliefs and coping responses.

Matza, L.S., Swensen, A.R., Flood, E.M. *et al.* (2004). Assessment of health-related quality of life in children: a review of conceptual, methodological, and regulatory issues. *Value in Health*, 7: 79–92.

For anyone considering a research project involving assessment of children, this paper is a must, whether you are assessing QoL or some other construct. Matza and colleagues clearly describe issues regarding the timing, content and scoring of QoL measures in children, and debate the issues of proxy measurement and response bias. They also provide a useful table of selected child QoL measures.

Weblink

Type 'quality of life' into any search engine and you will get thousands of hits, some from health-professional pages, some from academia, while others will be papers from economists, policy makers and even governmental bodies. It is clear that QoL is a term in use in many domains outside psychology! Christopher Reeve (1952-2004), aka Superman, talking of his experience of spinal injury on the Muppet Show: http://www.youtube.com/watch?v=OzHvV.UGTOM

The Association for Death Education and Counseling website is produced by one of the oldest multidisciplinary organisations studying policy, practice and related evidence in the field of death and dying:

www.adec.org

For open-access student resources specifically written to complement this textbook and support your learning, please visit **www.pearsoned.co.uk/morrison**

Chapter 15
The impact and outcomes of illness: families and informal caregivers

Learning outcomes

By the end of this chapter, you should have an understanding of:

- the prevalence and nature of informal caregiving within family systems

- expectations of care and caregivers, and the issue of willingness to care

- the consequences of informal caregiving, including caregiving benefits

- key personal, social and cognitive influences on caregiver outcomes

- coping responses in the face of caregiving

- forms of caregiving which can be detrimental to the *recipient*

- the importance of dyadic and relational factors to psychosocial outcomes of patients and their caregivers

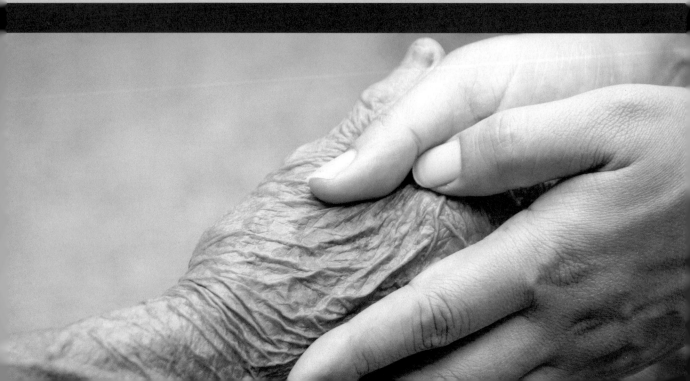

In sickness and in health . . .

Would you willingly provide care for a loved one if they became chronically ill or disabled? According to the United Nations World Population Ageing report 2013, there is 'a need for all societies to address the significant consequences of population ageing in the coming decades' (p xi). Globally the population of those aged over 60 has increased from 9.2 per cent in 1990 to 11.7 per cent in 2013, with further projections to 2050 predicting that by then this age group will constitute over a fifth (21.1 per cent) of the population. The actual numbers of people this relates to is from 840 million in 2013 to over 2 BILLION by 2050. This is a huge shift in the composition of society. Why does all this matter in the opening of a chapter on caregiving? It matters because three in every five of us will likely experience someone in their family, whether parent or partner, becoming chronically ill and in need of support with aspects of day-to-day living where they did not before. Whilst it is certainly the case also that many people younger than 60 experience illness, disease and disability, it is a simple fact that, as described in preceding chapters, the prevalence of chronic diseases and disability increases with age. Because women globally tend to live longer than men, it is likely that the need for care of older widows will fall to their adult children, whereas when both members of a couple are living it is likely to be the female partner who needs to provide care to her male partner. This chapter focuses on the nature of this caregiving and the potential impact it can have on the care provider, and in turn the quality of care provided to the recipient. Healthy, happy and supported caregivers are likely to offer a better quality of care.

Chapter outline

In previous chapters, although describing many individual and social factors that influence responses to a stressful experience such as illness, the focus has predominantly been on the person experiencing the stress or suffering the illness. In this chapter, we turn our attention to those who are the providers of social support that, in the preceding chapter, we described as buffering the stress of those with illness. We consider the impact of illness on the physical and emotional well-being of family members, many of whom act as informal caregivers. Who are these caregivers? What is the nature of caring tasks that they face and are they willing and able to take up the role when required or does society place unavoidable expectations on family members?

We describe evidence of personal and cultural influences on the uptake of caring and introduce the readers to concepts of filial obligation and reciprocity. We next describe a significant body of evidence showing detrimental physical and emotional consequences of caregiving, before presenting a growing and equally significant body of evidence describing positive outcomes of caregiving. We conclude the chapter by reviewing the individual, cognitive, social and cultural factors that make it more or less likely for a caregiver to experience gain or strain. This takes us into exploring factors concerning relationship quality, dyadic relationships and systemic transactions; shared perceptions and experiences; and on the value of matched support. Whilst increasingly relying on family caregivers to bolster deficient health and social care systems, government policy and health and social care services still have a long way to go in supporting the valuable contribution informal caregivers make. Health psychology and health services research is, however, increasingly addressing those affected by illness other than the 'patient', and, by dedicating a whole chapter to their experience, we seek to further the core teaching of the psychosocial impact of informal caregiving within a health psychology programme.

Illness: a family affair

People do not get ill in a vacuum: their illness exists within their immediate personal context and within their larger social network and culture. Not surprisingly, many of the wide-ranging effects of illness on the 'sufferer' described in the previous chapter (Chapter 14 (☛)) can also be experienced by those closest to the ill person. The growing trend towards home care and day treatments places further pressures on families.

Formal and informal care

Alongside care provided by a professional or trained individual working in health and social care, typically paid for a certain amount of time and a specified role and on some form of employment contract (typically described as formal care), it is an assumption of many European health and social care policies that unpaid, informal care, will supplement formal care provision with regards to the management of those with long-term conditions (Triantafillou et al. 2010: 43). The extent to which informal care is relied upon varies from one country to another dependent on their national welfare systems, and an individual's ability to access private care will aid in determining the degree to which there is choice involved for the potential caregiver and recipient. We return to the issue of choice later. Unlike formal carers, informal carers tend to be untrained family members or friends of the person with the illness or disability, who have no contractual 'hours' per se, no clearly defined limits to their role and variable financial recompense (European Commission 2008).

While family members are generally involved in providing support to a family member if they become ill, some also become that person's primary (main) caregiver: i.e. they are required to provide assistance above and beyond that which is 'normal' for their role (preparing a meal for a partner may be usual, whereas helping them to bathe may not be) (e.g. Schulz and Quittner 1998).

Approximately 70 per cent of care recipients are aged over 65 years and thus the 'problems' caregivers are providing care for are predominantly those of chronic diseases, with significant proportions caring for problems relating to ageing: dementia, problems of mobility, and mental, emotional or neurological problems. Typical tasks of caregiving, as identified in the Carers UK State of Caring Survey (2014) include providing:

- practical help, e.g. with cooking, doing laundry, shopping (93 per cent)
- emotional support, encouragement, and general watching over (by phone or in person) (87 per cent)
- help arranging or coordinating medical/ care appointments (85 per cent)
- management of paperwork or financial matters (83 per cent)
- help with personal care tasks, e.g. dressing, bathing, eating and toileting (71 per cent)
- help with mobility, help to get in and out of bed, move around the house (57 per cent)

The different tasks place varying demands on informal carers' own physical, practical, emotional and time resource (for example, caregivers report finding the cognitive and behavioural changes associated with many dementias more 'burdensome' than providing practical support) The nature and extent of caregiving tasks will also depend on whether the caregiver lives with the care recipient or not. Caring tasks also vary according to the nature of the condition, its symptoms and any associated level of dependency, and as described later can have different impacts on the caregivers (for example, caregivers

report finding the cognitive and behavioural changes associated with many dementias more 'burdensome' than providing practical support). Kalra et al. (2004) presented findings of positive effects of training caregivers in providing physical care to their care recipient (stroke survivor), in terms of reduced caregiver burden, reduced anxiety and depression, and improved QoL for both the caregivers and their patients, highlighting that caregiver interventions are beneficial for both parties. National policy to assess caregiver needs in order to direct appropriate interventions to them is growing.

Prevalence of informal care

Given the prevalence of chronic disease and disability, the need for informal care is growing as health and social care systems struggle to keep up with demand. For example, in Ireland it is anticipated that the oldest-old population (aged 80+) will treble between 2008 and 2031 (Central Statistics Office Dublin, 2008). Ireland is not atypical. Whilst globally, it is estimated that over a fifth of the population will be aged over 60 by 2050, it is even higher in some regions of the world. For example, in China it is predicted that a third of the population will be aged over 60 by 2050, with the population of the oldest-old (80 years plus) multiplying five-fold to almost eight per cent of the population, both facts with implications for informal care provision in a vast country where families assume the primary responsibility (Feng et al. 2013). It is also estimated that, in Europe, two-thirds of those over retirement age will have at least two chronic conditions (European Chronic Disease Alliance; WHO Europe 2011). In the long term, many of these conditions will be managed in the home environment: for example, in Italy it estimated that two-thirds of the help needed by older people with care needs is provided by families (Triantafillou et al. 2010).

In the UK currently it is estimated that there are approximately 6.5 million informal caregivers, a figure which has grown by 11 per cent between the 2001 and 2011 census, and which is expected to increase further to over 9 million by 2037 (Carers UK 2014). The turnover in caregiving is high, with an annual increase of over two million informal caregivers in the UK being matched by those who give up the role, for reasons of the care recipients' recovery, relocation into residential care, or death. Owing to population changes it is now estimated that three in every five people will be providing care for a family member or friend at some point in their lives.

It is estimated that informal caregivers save the UK NHS and social services approximately £119 billion per year and a further £1 billion by virtue of the community-based self-help groups they offer! However, as noted by Kalra et al. (2004: 1,099) in relation to stroke management: 'Although the physical, psychological, emotional, and social consequences of care-giving and its economic benefit to society are well recognised, care-givers' needs are often given low priority'. Addressing caregiver needs is crucial to both patient and caregiver outcomes, hence the reason we dedicate a whole chapter to their experience, influences on it, and the importance of the relationship with the person they care for.

What does being a caregiver mean?

Definitional issues exist in the literature as to who 'qualifies' as a caregiver, or as some prefer, 'carer' – for example, if you become ill is your co-resident partner or spouse, or your adult child who happens to live with you or close at hand, and who seems willing to support you, automatically become labelled as your 'caregiver' or 'carer'? Or does their identity remain as your spouse or child, as support is an 'expected' part of that loving relationship, with its characteristics of mutual reciprocity of care? Does this person only become a caregiver if they perform specific tasks for you that they would otherwise not have done, for example, help you to dress, or feed you, and do so with regularity? The latter is the approach taken more typically (e.g. Roth et al. 2015). However, although we researchers 'label' those who are providing, generally unpaid, care to a loved one, it does not automatically imply that the label is an accepted one. We use the term(s) (carer/caregiver) in this chapter for ease of describing and contextualising our discussion with a literature that also uses one or other of the term(s), but we highlight the importance of considering the implications of terminology we use in ISSUES.

Demographic characteristics of informal caregivers

In a study of six European countries – Germany, Greece, Italy, Poland, Sweden and the UK (EUROFAMCARE

ISSUES

What's in a word – the issue of 'carer'

Looking after a parent –who previously looked after you – may not mean that you consider yourself their 'carer' or 'caregiver'. The element of reciprocity arising from the nature of most (if not all) parent–child relationships can lead to some participants in caregiving research rejecting such a label. The term 'carer' has been described as arising from the loving concern that constitutes part of a natural loving relationship – it has an 'affective' character – whereas 'caregiver' is thought to reflect more the 'doing' actions that naturally follow from caring (Pearlin et al. 1990). For child carers, a sick or disabled parent may be what they have grown up with, and therefore helping out is not labelled as anything other than 'looking after Mum, or Dad, because that's what I've always done'. Something that is considered to be the family norm doesn't need a special label.

Does labelling people who take part in our studies, or for use in policy documents, actually help? Certainly, criteria are needed if society is to establish who is eligible for financial or practical support from the more formal care systems. For carer needs to be identified and carer policy implemented (e.g. the National Carers Strategy in England, Department of Health 2010), we need to be able to identify who they are, what care they are providing and how often, and quantify what financial or social assistance may be required (Arksey and Glendinning 2008).

However, does labelling the 'caregiver' change the nature of the relationship between, for example, the healthy spouse and the one unlucky enough to have physical care needs? Molyneux and colleagues (Molyneaux et al. 2011) argue that it does; that it fundamentally devalues the care recipient in that the term 'carer' fails to recognise the nature and quality of the relationship between the provider and the recipient and what the recipient themselves may be bringing to the reciprocal relationship. To my knowledge, we do not have a study of the perception of the label from the care recipients' perspective.

Examining the caregivers' perspective, Hughes et al. (2013) interviewed 40 'carers' of either a family member or a friend with multiple sclerosis about their experiences of MS from the point where the illness became apparent to them. Using identity theory to analyse the interview transcripts, these authors found four, sometimes overlapping, categories of self identification with the label 'carer':

- those who *'embraced'* the carer identity as congruent with their other identities (regardless of whether support provided was more emotional or practical in nature);

- those who *enforced* the identity but in discord with their other identities (e.g. partner, sibling, child) with an acknowledged loss of self and of the spousal role;

- those who *absorbed* a partial carer identity but with ambivalence, pragmatism and flexibility depending on the needs of the day ('I'm just my dad's son looking after him. But if I'm speaking to somebody I'll say I'm his carer because that's what I'm doing. It's a role that I'm playing');

- those who *rejected* the carer identity in favour of holding on to their relationship identity: i.e. whilst acknowledging they may be described as a carer by others, they did not internalise this identity.

It was clear in this paper that identification with a label and a role is not straightforward: different identities took on different saliences, depending on both the relationship type, the gender of the caregiver, and the nature of the caregiving tasks – which in multiple sclerosis can fluctuate considerably. In fact those less 'typical' caregivers – adult child, sibling, appeared to embrace the role more than those more typical caregivers – spouses. This may relate to feelings of social obligation and assumptions regarding willingness to care which we return to later in the chapter.

Photo 15.1 Having more time to spend with a partner as a result of illness can lead to a sharing of activities previously lost to the other demands of life. Spending 'quality time' together can strengthen some relationships

Source: Corbis/Reg Charity.

2006) – over half (56 per cent) of the almost 6,000 informal caregivers shared the same household or building as the care recipient, three-quarters (76 per cent) were female (although this is 58 per cent in the UK), and the mean age was 55 years. Most national surveys find that informal caregivers are aged predominantly between 45 and 64 (peak age 50–59 years). Gender variation is also seen in the number of hours care is provided, with women even more highly represented in those providing care for 50 hours a week or more (Carers UK 2014). In fact, in the UK, one in every four women aged 50–64 have caring responsibilities, compared to one in six men of this age. For many women this means they are in the 'sandwich' generation, providing care for young adult children (often students!) whilst providing care to a parent. Women at this point, more often than male caregivers, also find they have to give up meaningful employment (Carers UK 2014). An estimated 15 per cent of care-givers overall have to reduce their working hours in order to provide care beyond a low intensity, i.e less than an hour a day, every day (Triantafillou et al. 2010).

Gender proportions also vary according to ethnic minority background, although it can be difficult to ascertain whether figures are representative for ethnic minority groupings due to poor culturally appropriate service provision or access, or use of other care services in these groups (e.g. Carers UK 2014). Of the UK informal caregiver figures (6.5 million), approximately 600,000 UK caregivers are from Black, Asian and minority ethnic groups (BAME).

In the UK it is estimated that of the 6.5 million caregivers, almost 180,000 of them are under 18, which brings with it particular challenges as described in a later section addressing child or young caregivers. For the more typical caregiver, i.e. adult, middle-aged, it is worth noting that at this lifestage a significant minority of these carers will have their own health problems, as expected, given chronic disease prevalence within the general population. For example TILDA, the Irish Longitudinal Study on Ageing (Barrett et al. 2011) found that almost a third of their large, representative sample of the over-50s had a chronic health condition (for example, one in four had arthritis, and over a third reported being troubled by pain, 15 per cent by back pain specifically). Amongst carer samples, it has been estimated that the prevalence of long-standing health conditions, thought to be exacerbated by the caring role, lies between 60 and 70 per cent (e.g. GP Patient Survey 2013)

Expectancies of care

Gendered expectancies

Gender bias in the caring role may be a result of the greater life expectancies for women, as well as perhaps a questionable societal expectation of caring being a 'natural' role for women, who are 'expected' to find family-oriented roles fulfilling, even in the absence of financial reward, whereas men who often refrain from portraying an emotional, caring side are perceived as being more work-focused (Yee and Schulz 2000; Lee 1999, 2001; Ussher and Sandoval 2008). Gendered socialisation exists! The extent to which society places different expectations on males as compared to females is nothing new. We have described gender differences at various points throughout this textbook – starting with general beliefs about health, in health behaviours, in symptom identification and health-care use, including communication with health-care providers, and now in relation to providing care for a loved one. 'Provider' males and 'nurturer' females have led to an expectation of the care of a family member when ill falling to the female partner or relative. Whilst certainly there has been a shift, with more women being the 'main' earner within a family (thus when an elderly parent becomes ill, it may not be the daughter but the son who becomes responsible for their care), women do still dominate the caregiver statistics as we describe. Whether this results in different caregiving experiences is something we attend to in the following sections (see also the review by Pinquart and Sorensen 2006) and also 'In the spotlight'.

One example considers role identity among spousal caregivers in order to examine the effect of role discrepancies, i.e. where caregivers' behaviours were self-judged as being discrepant with their standards for spousal and caregiver roles on caregiver burden (Savundranayagam and Montgomery 2010). Those who cared for spouses with more problem behaviours (dressing wrongly, are agitated, forgetful, etc.) were more likely to exceed their role standards and as a result reported greater burden. Those involved in providing more assistance with patient activities of daily living less often reported exceeding their role standards, suggesting that this type of care may be seen as more 'fitting' of spousal obligation. Such findings suggest that caring becomes more stressful when it is judged as 'going beyond the call of duty' (p. 192), and thus identifying caregiver role expectations and in fact their perceived spousal obligations (e.g. familism; Parveen and Morrison 2009) is important.

Culture and caregiving expectancies

Most of the research examining cultural expectancies of care has been drawn from multicultural US populations, where Black Americans, Hispanic and Latino Americans are contrasted with White Americans (Pinquart and Sörensen 2005), or within Asia, mainly between Chinese and Hong Kong (e.g. Feng et al. 2013) or in the UK between White-British and British South Asian (this population comprises mainly four communities – Punjabi Sikh, Pakistani, Bangladeshi and Gujarati Hindu) (Katbamna 2004; Parveen and Morrison 2009). These studies highlight cultural variations in aspects of societal values such as collectivism (versus individualism), and in belief and value systems including familism and filial responsibility or piety - Filial piety (xiao, 孝) refers to the obligations of respecting, supporting and taking care of older family members (Tang 2006) and is a core cultural expectation in Asian nations, such as China, Korea and Japan (Feng et al. 2013).

In China, the one-child policy has meant that a typical three-generation family would consist of four elders, two adult children and one grandchild (a '4–2–1' family), where the adult children assume physical and emotional caring responsibilities for four elders and one child. If the elders need long-term care because of chronic illness, the caregiving burden to adult children can be dramatic (Liu and Cai 1997, as cited in Feng et al. 2013). The lack of siblings in this culture has significant implications for caregiver outcomes, given the lack of shared responsibility when a family member, typically an elder parent, becomes ill. Unlike in South Asian cultures where care expectancies tend to fall on female family members (daughters first, then daughters-in-law), in China filial obligation first extends to the eldest son (although, if married, his spouse will be expected to support the care role).

The issue of willingness to care

Studies of motivations or willingness to care have shown that the relationship between the potential caregiver and recipient, and intrinsic motivations to care (e.g. principles, caring nature) as opposed to extrinsic motivations (e.g. out of guilt or expectation) are crucial to caregiver well-being (Cahill 1999; Wells 1999; Lyonette and Yardley 2003; Sorensen et al. 2008; Williams et al. 2014). This small body of evidence highlight some key differences. In Williams and colleagues' qualitative study several caregivers reported being willing to provide care

Photo 15.2 Caregiving for an elder

Source: Fotolia.com/chuugo.

because they perceived their pre-illness relationship with the care recipient to have been a good one, where others provided care as the preferred alternative to feeling guilty for handing care over to a formal institution, e.g. a nursing home. Lyonette and Yardley, and Sorensen et al. (2008) report an effect of relationship quality on motivations to care, and Cahill (1999) further distinguished between relationship type, i.e between wives, daughters and daughters-in-law as she found that daughters and daughters-in-law reported more extrinsic motivations such as kinship obligations. This is consistent with findings from studies with ethnic minority caregivers (African-American, Hispanic and Asian-American caregivers; British Asian), where a greater emphasis on familism and filial responsibility is seen, born in part out of a sense of reciprocity for former parental care and support, but also out of emotional attachment (Pinquart and Sörensen 2005; Parveen and Morrison 2009).

These studies involved those who were already providing care and therefore motivations for caring are informed by the actual experience of care; however, Wells's study of hypothetical willingness to care found that men reported greater hypothetical willingness to care than women, and also, perhaps unrealistically, expected less burden to result from caregiving than did the women interviewed. More recently, in another interesting study with implications for the future (given how many of us may need to take on a caring role), Rohr and Lang (2014) addressed hypothetical willingness to care in relation to the gains or losses anticipated from the role. This study of 485 German adults (mean age 55 years, 77 per cent female) found that those who expressed willingness to provide care for a person in need, and those that were current caregivers, anticipated less losses and more gains than those who reported being unwilling to provide care. Those willing to provide future care also anticipated similar gains to the actual caregivers, which was significantly higher than anticipated by those unwilling to provide care or those who were undecided about providing care. Anticipating more gains and fewer losses, as well as older age and better subjective health were significant predictors of potential caregiving versus being undecided, whereas the anticipation of losses and low relationship satisfaction predicted potential unwillingness to care. The importance therefore of perceiving potential gains from caregiving is clear, and although these data are cross-sectional and don't address the complexities of carer type and relationship quality, further research is underway. This study finds willing potential caregivers to be similar to actual caregivers in expecting gains, and it may be that gain expectations will increase the likelihood of a person adopting the role in the future – longitudinal data is clearly required to explore further the predictors of transitions *into* caregiving. Gains from caregiving do exist, and so we discuss findings in this regard in the section on caregiving outcomes. It may also be the case that potential caregivers have preferences for providing some forms of care over others: for example, they may be willing to provide practical care but not assist with personal care tasks – this is another area requiring further research attention (Williams 2011).

Providing support to another can be considered a *prosocial behaviour*, with its characteristics of love, empathy, trust and altruism. The presence of the hormone **oxytocin** which acts on the peripheral and CNS and thus our behaviour, is influenced by our genetic make-up. It may be that those individuals who are willing to provide support to others differ in their oxytocin levels to those who are unwilling (Israel et al. 2012). This has been described by some as variations in 'tend and befriend' characteristics (e.g. Taylor 2006) and certainly it opens up an interesting line of research – are we genetically predisposed to the caregiving role – is there a 'neurogenics of niceness' (Poulin and Holman 2013; Poulin et al. 2013, and see Chapter 12 (☞). It is, however, unlikely to be the only explanation.

However, for many informal caregivers there may not be any clear options other than to provide the required care for their family member. For example, all five interviewees in Bolas's qualitative study of caregivers under the age of 18 years stated that they had 'no choice' in taking up the caring role, and admitted they would prefer not to have to do it. Feelings about it were often ambivalent: e.g. 'I don't know, I feel like it's something that I've got to do and I haven't got a choice really. I cannot not do it cos I'm not like that, I cannot watch, sit and watch the telly or play to by meself knowing that Leon is working me Nana, I cannot do that. I've got to help her if I know she's stresses, she gets stressed really a lot,

---

oxytocin

this hormone which also acts as a neurotransmitter in the brain appears to attenuate (reduce) autonomic stress responses and may be associated with affiliative social behaviour.

really lots.' Participants also felt the role was demanding but for some it was seen as inescapable.

Disability and dependence is increasing, not only among those considered 'elderly' but also in those in late middle age who may live for a further 10, 20 or 30 years in a dependent condition. More often societies are turning to families to provide a solution to these growing needs. Although the gender imbalance in terms of who provides care has shifted away from being predominantly female towards being more balanced, gender roles have generally changed hugely over the past century. Ask your mother or your grandmother about their views on staying at home to care for a sick or dependent relative; ask your father and your grandfather. Do the responses differ by generation? Do they differ by gender? Then consider your own situation and that of any siblings. Are you or they already, or likely to be facing in the future, the need to provide informal and unpaid care for a relative? How does this make you feel? How do you imagine you will balance your various life roles if you take on an additional caring role? Are your projected life goals likely to be constrained by these anticipated caring needs? Do you already worry about what will happen to your parents if they become chronically ill or develop dementia?

Questions such as these need to be asked, and answers need to be found. Are women, due to improved (albeit not yet perfect) gender equality in the workplace and an improved social status, less willing to care for a dependent, possibly ageing, family member than previous generations? Are men nowadays more open to the caregiving role than generations past? Do such matters have likely consequences for their mental and physical well-being if providing care becomes a necessity? What are the implications for the recipients of their care? What are the implications for health and social care policy? While such questions need social and political answers, they have significant psychological implications.

Family systems and family members

The families of people who develop an illness also need to adapt to changes that an illness brings. The diagnosis of serious illness and subsequent tests and/or treatments can have a significant impact on family coping and on their levels of certainty for the future, and life goals (Sherman and Simonton 2001). It is difficult to imagine any family that would not be affected by one of its members receiving a diagnosis of a long-term life-threatening, or disabling condition; however, it is probably even more distressing when the diagnosis is received by a child. As described in the previous chapter, staged theories of patient adjustment to illness (e.g. Morse and Johnson 1991) have been proposed. Bringing a similar way of thinking to those affected by stress (not necessarily illness) within the family, McCubbin and Patterson (1982) describe how pressures can disrupt or change the 'family system', with stages in a continuum of adaptation proposed:

1. *Stage of resistance:* where family members try to deny or avoid the reality of what has happened.

2. *Stage of restructuring:* where family members begin to acknowledge reality and start to reorganise their lives around the notion of a changed family.

3. *Stage of consolidation:* where newly adopted roles may have to become permanent, for example if recovery is not forthcoming; and where new ways of thinking (about life/health/behaviour) may emerge.

Relating this to illness more specifically, Rollands' Family-Systems Illness model (Rolland and Williams, 2005; Rolland 2012) offers a more systemic view of illness considering that, to be effective, a biopsychosocial approach to illness must acknowledge (a) the illness and its likely characteristics over time and (b) all persons involved in a family unit as they can 'in turn influence the course of an illness and the wellbeing of an affected person' (Rolland 2012: 453) (see Figure 15.1). Rolland observes the complexity of the mutual interactions between family members and suggests that positive and normative responses to illness in one of its members need to be explored instead of the more common narrower focus on pathological models of caregiving. The goal of a family is to understand the situation, and any likely changes in it (due to the health condition or treatments, for example), in a way that they can continue to function as a family. As Rolland points out, this also requires understanding of how they, as a family, function together and separately, with any gendered and cultural norms and expectations of caregiving also acknowledged. In this chapter we hope to address these points.

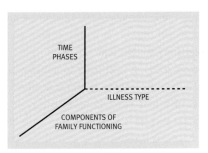

Figure 15.1 Three-dimensional model representing the relationship between illness type, time phases and family functioning

Source: Rolland (1987a, cited in Rolland 2012).

Three integrated dimensions of family system functioning have been highlighted by Olson and Stewart (1991): cohesion, adaptability and communication, with evidence that families who were balanced on these dimensions (i.e. they work together and are affiliated and emotionally bonded with each other; they adapt roles and rules in face of new situations, and they communicate effectively) experience better adaptation to life stressors, including illness. With regards to the impact of a disabling stroke, Palmer and Glass (2003) similarly identify the need for families to adjust to new patterns of relationship, roles and communication styles and 'to accommodate the stroke survivor's functional and social losses while continuing to meet the psychosocial needs of the entire family' (p. 256). Their review highlights that the process of recovery from stroke, from a family system perspective, is about support and collaboration from and between family members, and that the absence of these can have detrimental effects on the well-being of both the stroke sufferer and their family members.

Parents as caregivers

These broad dimensions of family system functioning have been reflected in many studies of parental coping. Studies highlight the importance of within-family communications, coping through the use of external social relationships, and coping through relationships with medical staff and parents of similarly affected children. Different coping responses are seen to have different implications for family functioning: for example, in relation to caring for a child with cystic fibrosis (McCubbin and Patterson 1983); in relation to supporting an adolescent

child with diabetes (Comeaux and Jaser 2010; Compas et al. 2012), where it is important for a parent to get the correct balance between providing care and making informed decisions on behalf of a younger child to allowing the child to develop, as appropriate to their age, some involvement in their illness management. Table 15.1 displays tasks faced by parental caregivers, described by parents of a child with cancer (Klassen et al. 2012), where it can be seen that potential tasks bring parents into contact with a range of authorities (health-care and educational, for example), requires a significant amount of time commitment, and efforts to retain normality for other members of the family. Whilst presenting these tasks as published, it is notable that several tasks listed as physical tasks have obvious emotional correlates: for example, dealing with child behavioural or emotional challenges, entertaining a sick child.

Does illness in a child influence parental coping with stress more generally? In a study comparing parental coping of 395 parents (224 mothers and 171 fathers) either of children with cancer who were undergoing or had completed cancer treatment (PCC) or of healthy children (PHC), perhaps surprisingly, coping did not differ between groups (Norberg et al. 2005). Within both parent groups, more frequent use of active problem focusing and less use of avoidance and passive reaction coping was associated with lower levels of parental anxiety and depression. There was a tendency for PCC to report greater use of passive reaction coping. Within the PCC parent group, coping was compared between those whose child had leukaemia (44 per cent) and those whose child had a brain tumour (14.9 per cent) and, although coping did not differ in itself, an interesting difference in what coping associated with was seen. Active problem-focused coping was associated with less emotional distress in parents of children with leukaemia, but not in those with brain tumours. Furthermore, whilst time since diagnosis did not influence coping overall, there was an interactive effect whereby avoidance coping was not related to anxiety or depression in the most recently diagnosed group but *was* related to both anxiety and depression in those diagnosed more than five years previously. This is consistent with what has been said elsewhere, i.e. avoidance coping may be adaptive only in the early post-diagnosis period in illness. Finally, in terms of mood, both state anxiety and state depression were higher among PCC than among PHC, and in both groups mothers scored higher than fathers. It is worth

Table 15.1 Caregiving tasks described by parents of a child with cancer

Emotional tasks	Physical tasks	Informational tasks
Dealing with people's responses to the cancer diagnosis and treatment	Accompanying child to and in hospital	Attending to educational needs of child
Encouraging child	Arranging childcare for child and siblings	Coordinating and scheduling healthcare appointments
Maintaining a new normal routine for child with cancer	Being vigilant	Filling out cancer-related paperwork
Maintaining composure for others	Caring for child (e.g., bathing, entertaining)	Keeping family, friends, school, and others informed
Providing emotional support for child, family, and other cancer families	Dealing with behavioural and emotional challenges of child and siblings	Learning about childhood cancer and its treatment
	Dealing with comorbid conditions	Learning how to navigate the healthcare system and access resources
	Food-related tasks	Learning to advocate
	Home care management	Seeking and sharing information with other cancer parents
	Managing symptoms and side effects of cancer treatment	Updating healthcare providers on child's medical condition
	Purchasing, preparing, and administering medication	
	Reducing risk of infection	

Source: Klassen et al. (2012).

noting in fact that 59 per cent of non-responders to this study were fathers and therefore perhaps the more distressed fathers did not participate. This is consistent with other studies and raises a question in need of further investigation – why do fathers seem to be more reluctant to talk about their child's illness and what consequences might this have for paternal well-being? There is some suggestion that some mothers 'gatekeep' the care of their child, resulting in some fathers feeling left on the periphery – this may help account for fathers' greater reporting of problem-focused coping and issues around their attempting to gain a sense of control over the situation (Hill et al. 2009, cited in Turner-Cobb 2014: 172).

Of course, it is not only when it is a child who is ill that families are affected. The incidence of most chronic and disabling conditions increases with age and therefore most recipients of informal care are adults. In a survey of six European countries, just over a fifth (22 per cent) of informal caregivers were spouses, and 60 per cent were either children or children-in-law (EUROFAMCARE 2006).

Spouses as caregivers

Spousal caregivers tend to live with the person they are providing care for, and this in itself explains why studies of the impact of caregiving commonly points to more deleterious effects of caregiving for this group than others (e.g adult daughters). By nature of co-habiting, spouses will provide more hours of support, spanning the range of needs over a day and night. In couples, support, whether practical, emotional or financial, tends to come from each other in the first instance and thus the supportive relationship is generally reciprocal, although most research has to date addressed the giving of support to patients by their carer spouses, and not the carer's own receipt of support (as discussed in Chapter 14 ☞). Typically in conditions with onset in middle age or amongst the young-old such as stroke or Parkinson's disease, the primary caregiver will be a partner or spouse, who themselves may have health problems and comorbidity (Adelman et al. 2015). Amongst the older- and oldest-old, however, many individuals, particularly females, will be widowed, thus care typically falls to an adult daughter. However, the gender gap in expected life expectancy after reaching aged 65 is not as wide as it used to be and so perhaps more male spouses will survive to face taking on a caring role (Triantifillou et al. 2010).

Child and adult-child caregivers

Children and young people (generally defined as under 18 years), and in fact middle-aged sons or daughters providing care for a parent, face particular issues when providing care atypical to that child–parent relationship – for example, it is not typical to help feed, dress or toilet your parent.

In terms of child caregivers more specifically, in the UK alone it is estimated that there are between 19,000 and 51,000 informal caregivers under the age of 18. Little is known about the full long-term impact of caregiving on these child caregivers, although some interesting qualitative findings suggest that for school-aged caregivers, their minds are distracted by thoughts of the caregiving demands and the care recipient even when they are away from the home. For example, Bolas et al. (2007) interviewed three female (aged 14, 16, 18) and two male caregivers (aged 14 and 16) about their caregiving experiences. One young man caring for his Mum said, 'Really you're a carer from when you wake up in the morning to when you go to sleep at night. Even if you're not in the house you're having still basically thinking about what've got to do when I get home, well really what I've got to do so it never really leaves me mind.' In such ways the academic performance of child caregivers and potentially their future potential is undermined. Socially, they also suffer. Interestingly, it has been observed that many young carers do not recognise themselves as carers at the time, responding simply to caregiving requests of their parent in a reciprocal manner for other forms of care received from the parent, and not perhaps knowing that such behaviour is not the norm (Smyth et al. 2011). Due to this, it may be hard to ascertain the true prevalence of young carers in a community.

The largest group of informal carers in the ageing population in Europe and globally comprises either adult children or children-in-law, who make up approximately 60 per cent of the total (EUROFAMCARE 2006). In a culture such as China, caring for an elder when needed is an expectation almost upheld by the constitution – the government lays the responsibility for care on the shoulders of the family, and filial obligation means that adult children are turned to to fulfil their caregiving responsibility (Feng et al. 2013). In China, this can often involve co-residing with the parent; however, in non-Eastern cultures it is more likely that the adult child will live elsewhere – which is why many studies report lower levels of caregiver burden in adult children compared to co-resident caregivers, usually spouses. Caring for a parent arises out of similar emotional investment as perhaps spouses have, but the potential for a reversal of roles – providing personal care for a parent where once it was received as a child, and the likelihood also of having to juggle other dependants – makes caring for a parent highly demanding. A recent qualitative study of Canadian adult-daughters in the context of providing care for a parent following a stroke highlights a sense of overload (Bastawrous et al. 2014). For these women, juggling multiple other roles on top of caregiving created strains in valued relationships with children and partner, and decreased participation in valued social activities (work and leisure).

There is evidence also that gender of the child caregiver may have an effect on the nature of caregiving tasks carried out, with sons more likely to provide practical support such as running errands, providing transport, than personal care or housework support (Pinquart and Sorensen 2006); however, this may depend on the gender of the care recipient, with evidence that female caregivers may also be more uncomfortable providing personal care to fathers. A large American study of almost 3,000 caregivers (Longitudinal Study of Aging) found that, over a two-year follow-up period, son caregivers were more likely to transition a parent with impairment in activities of daily living into residential care than a daughter caregiver (likewise did husbands more often than wives) (Allen et al. 2012).

Supportive relationships

There is a clear need to evaluate the nature and effects of supportive relationships, because the presence or absence of perceived and received social support from a loved one can significantly influence a person's response to, and outcomes of, stressful experiences, such as illness. As described in Chapter 12 (☞), there is consistent evidence as to the benefits of being part of a functional supportive network as opposed to being socially isolated.

Benefits of social support are to both the care recipient and the caregiver and include, for example:

- increased care recipient adherence to treatment and self-care (e.g. Lo 1999; Toljamo and Hentinen 2001);
- better caregiver emotional adjustment, including, for example, following spousal heart attack, or bereavement (e.g. Hallaråker et al. 2001; Balaswamy et al. 2004);
- improved marital relationships (e.g. O'Connor et al. 2008);
- reduced caregiver burden and isolation (Love et al. 2005);
- reduced mortality or increased survival (e.g. Berkman and Syme 1979; Aizer et al. 2013).

With regards to the latter point concerning the benefits of social support to survival, the classic findings of Berkman and Syme's nine-year follow-up study of 7,000 Californian residents with mixed health have been confirmed in many more specific populations (see Taylor 2004 for a review). More recently, Aizer's study of survival amongst over 734,000 American cancer patients found a consistent association between being married and surviving one's cancer, even after adjusting for demographics, cancer type and stage, and treatment provided (Aizer et al. 2013). The protective effects of marriage on health and health outcomes have been reported elsewhere, and generally point to greater 'gain' to husbands from wives' support during times of stress than married women seem to benefit from husband support (e.g. Cutrona 1996).

Consensus exists that it is not simply the absolute number of supports a person has available to them (structural) but the perceived quality and function of these supports (functional), whether support is provided willingly or reluctantly (e.g. Williams et al. 2011), and satisfaction with the received support that is critical in predicting such outcomes (e.g. Quick et al. 1996). However, social support is not always helpful, even if intended as such by the caregiver.

Helpful and unhelpful caring

Studies of caring for people with a range of illnesses, such as AIDS, chronic fatigue syndrome, diabetes and cancer, have found that there are common caring actions that are perceived as helpful – such as practical assistance and expressions of love, concern and understanding – and relative consistency in terms of actions considered to be unhelpful – for example, minimising the situation, being unrealistically cheerful, underestimating the illness effects on the patient, or being critical or overdemanding. Patients who perceived their caregivers' actions as unhelpful have been found to have more negative perceptions of themselves and their spouses, and greater depression (Clark and Stephens 1996; Romano et al. 2009; Band et al. 2015). Although helpful actions have generally been shown to occur more frequently than unhelpful actions, unhelpful actions appear to have a more strongly negative effect on well-being than helpful actions have a positive effect (e.g. Norris et al. 1990). Additionally, over caring or being overly helpful and solicitous (e.g. taking over a person's chores, encouraging them to rest) can act as a form of operant conditioning in which patients are rewarded for exhibiting 'sick role' behaviour (see Chapter 1 ☛). For example, among a sample of 119 patients with chronic fatigue syndrome and their significant other, 'over-helped' care recipients exhibited greater fatigue and pain than those receiving punishing (e.g. caregiver expresses irritation at patient) or distracting (e.g. caregiver involves patient in activities) caregiver responses (Schmaling et al. 2000). Over-protected patients may also experience reduced perceptions of self-efficacy, self-esteem and recovery motivation, and elevated depression (e.g. Thompson and Pitts 1992) and, among pain patients, increased disability (e.g. Williamson et al. 1997).

Several studies have identified social interactions that are unsupportive and detrimental to the care receiver's well-being. For example, a study of 271 individuals living with HIV identified four types of unsupportive interaction:

1. insensitivity;
2. disconnecting or disengaging behaviour;
3. blaming or fault-finding;
4. forced optimism.

The first three of these interaction types were significantly predictive of patient depression, above and beyond the prediction offered by patient physical functioning and positive social support (Ingram et al. 1999). Similarly, Kerns et al. (1990) found that what they termed 'punishing' spousal responses (such as ignoring the patient or expressing impatience or anger with them) was predictive

IN THE SPOTLIGHT

Caregivers' beliefs and behaviours matter!

In a systematic review of fourteen studies of the responses of significant others to chronic fatigue syndrome in a loved one (Band et al. 2015), it was evident that significant others' carers' beliefs have an affect on their caregiving behaviours and on patient outcomes. For example, making internal (patient) attributions of cause and responsibility for the illness and its symptoms was found to be associated with unhelpful caring responses, such as forced cheerfulness and encouraging the patient to rest (both typically found to be unhelpful to patient outcome), and with both caregiver and patient distress. In addition, in several studies reviewed, patients who perceived high levels of caring/solicitous behaviour reported more severe and frequent symptoms and increased help-seeking behaviour. However, the converse, i.e. perceiving caregiver responses to be negative or unhelpful, were also associated with poorer patient outcomes, including depression and anxiety. Finally, aspects of relationship quality such as relationship satisfaction was found to moderate some of the negative impact of over caring in a counter-intuitive manner – the negative impact of over-caring was heightened in those with higher relationship satisfaction. Being emotionally over-involved (EOI) was also associated with patient levels of distress. Reviews such as this provide further evidence that caregivers' beliefs and responses matter, and that interventions need to take account of significant others and relationship factors.

Given the range of caregiving tasks and caregiver characteristics, not surprisingly, significant research attention has also been given to the impact of caring on caregivers and on the factors that increase or decrease the likelihood of negative outcomes.

of increased distress and depressive symptoms. These types of findings highlight the need to assess positively perceived support separately from negatively perceived support, rather than assessing on a continuum of overall support without addressing how that support is evaluated. Given the evidence as to the presence of helpful and unhelpful caring actions, it is not perhaps surprising that, when initially faced with a caring role, care providers ask themselves questions such as, 'What is "good" care?' 'Am I suitably equipped to deal with the demands of the person I am caring for?' It may be that gender offers part of an answer to these questions.

In an interesting study, Neff and Karney (2005) explore the widely held assumption that women are better at providing support than men, a conclusion drawn in part from the aforementioned findings that married men benefited more from marriage than do women. Using both observational data and seven-day diaries obtained from 169 newly married couples without children, the authors concluded that it is not that men and women differ in the skills of giving support to their partner, or even in the amount of support provided day to day, but that women are more responsive to the changing needs of their husbands as indicated in their stress-indicative behaviours and therefore provided better and more positive support at times of greater need.

Consequences of caring for the caregiver

Unlike motherhood, a responsibility generally signalled by an expected event – childbirth – the informal caregiving role in the context of illness and disability is often one which emerges either suddenly or gradually but often unexpectedly out of a familial relationship. Like motherhood, however, there is generally little training for this role (Montgomery and Kosloski 2000)!

Providing care for, or helping others in an altruistic manner, for example through voluntary work, has generally been associated with social, emotional and possibly physical well-being of the helper, particularly among older adults (see Post 2007 for an overview). However, providing regular care in the context of illness in a loved one has been seen more often as a threat to well-being, possibly because of the emotional bonds that exist or because familial carers do more than just provide 'active help' on occasion, and instead are immersed in the role 24 hours a day (Poulin et al. 2010). Many different terms have been used to describe caregiver outcomes of providing care, and just as many different outcome measures are used, some of which assess mental health, some physical health and some global psychosocial well-being. A commonly employed term is that of 'caregiver burden', defined as the objective and subjective 'costs' of caring to the caregiver (e.g. Zarit et al. 1980). This term covers a broad-based outcome of caring that encompasses physical, psychological, financial and social costs of caring, and many studies have explored burden as an outcome, rather than focusing solely on emotional distress or physical outcomes (e.g. Schulz et al. 1995; Scholte op Reimer et al. 1998).

Emotional impact of caring

Research has suggested that up to three-quarters of caregivers for someone with chronic illness or disability experience clinically significant distress, a level significantly higher than that found in age-matched controls. Similarly, caregivers' physical health and life satisfaction are generally found to be lower than in non-caregivers. Feelings of loss, anxiety or depression are common among partners of those who have had a heart attack (e.g. Arefjord et al. 1998); and among those caring for a relative following a stroke, levels of depression have been shown to be two to three times that found in a comparable group of non-caregivers (Scholte op Reimer et al. 1998). See Table 15.2 for some common causes of caregiver distress.

Studies suggest that emotional distress is most marked among women caregivers (e.g. Kuenzler et al. 2010; Pinquart and Sörensen 2003; van den Heuvel et al. 2001), although some of the reported gender differences may be confounded by the fact that up to three-quarters of caregivers are women, which is reflected in study samples. In relation to caring for a sick child, it has also been suggested that fathers are less distressed by caregiving than are the mothers (above and beyond any gender effect on distress in general non-caregiving populations, see review and meta-analysis of Pinquhart and Sorenson

Table 15.2 Potential causes of caregiver distress

- The financial drain of caring caused by caring interference with employment
- The emotional demands of providing long-term care for a relative who often provides little in return
- The physically tiring nature of some caring roles
- The inability to replenish personal resources due to social isolation or poor utilisation of support resources and leisure time

Or more deep-seated, even unacknowledged sources of stress:

- Feelings of anger (e.g. with the person for becoming ill, for them being born handicapped)
- Feelings of guilt (e.g. that they may have directly/indirectly contributed to the situation)
- Feelings of grief (e.g. that they have 'lost' who they used to have)

These latter are indicative of extremely complex feelings that are difficult to voice, but if they are suppressed they can cause increased stress and distress.

2006), although differences do not appear huge. For example, 51 per cent of mothers and 39 per cent of fathers exhibited levels above the cut-off for emotional disorder in a study of parents of a child with cancer, and for both parents distress remained high even after cancer treatment had been completed, reflecting parental fears of recurrence (Sloper 2000). We raise the issue of whether masculine identity influences the appraisals men make of the caring role and their experiences of the role, in a later section and in 'In the spotlight'.

Young carers aged 14–18 years interviewed in a qualitative study (Bolas et al. 2007) reported feelings of isolation – sometimes due to not discussing or concealing their role so they were not seen by peers or social contacts as being 'different', or to avoid any stigma attached to the illness (more likely if their care recipient was suffering from a mental health condition). Although the young carers also reported positives in terms of enhanced self-regard and self-esteem, and pride was taken in performing caregiving tasks and feeling useful, such gains may not outweigh the negatives – unless, as one carer stated, they put this experience to good use in a future career as a carer for others. What is clear is that young caregivers, as reported in this study, are without doubt experiencing burden, and yet many chose not to trust the wider social world and got embroiled in secrecy both about their role and about the care recipient's condition for fear of rejection or stigmatisation. This isolation has clear implications for their own emotional well-being. Policy makers need to acknowledge the potential long-term personal and social consequences of child caregiving to a greater extent than is currently the case.

In a study of 442 carers aged under 16 years in Ireland (Cassidy et al. 2014), 36 per cent were found to exhibit clinical levels of distress (as assessed using the recommended caseness cut-offs of the General Health Questionnaire). Negative mental health was predicted by appraisals of burden, stress appraisals and benefit-finding (discussed in detail below). Low levels of support from family and friends, low levels of problem-focused coping and low levels of social recognition for their role were also predictive although these effects disappeared when all other variables had been entered into the analysis. However, it was clear from these data that negative mental health effects were present, and, surprisingly, these effects were not mediated by the young caregivers' resilience or, in other words, their ability to 'bounce back' from stress. We return to the important role personal resilience has been shown to have in other populations and in relation to other carer outcomes at a later point in this chapter.

Physical effects of caring

The stress of caring may also impact on some, but perhaps not all, people's physical health, ranging from sleep and weight disturbance (Klassen et al. 2011), through increased risk of physical health complaints (Kiecolt-Glaser et al. 2003), to actual health complaints such as back or joint pain (Triantafillou et al. 2010). Among cancer caregivers, for example, female caregivers experienced a decline in their own physical health in the six months following their partner's diagnosis of colorectal cancer, whereas male caregivers did not (Nijboer et al. 2001), perhaps relating to the higher levels of distress or lower levels of caregiver-perceived efficacy reported among women caregivers in other studies, although this study did not explore these issues. Interestingly, an extremely large study of the physical health, psychological well-being and quality of life of over eleven thousand Australian women aged from 70 to 75 (Lee 2001) did not find a significant difference in physical health between the 10 per cent identified as caregivers and the majority of the elderly sample. However, the caregivers did differ significantly in terms of their emotional well-being and perceived stress levels, supporting the reasonably consistent findings as to the emotional

impact of caring (see below). Wider quality of life is also affected, encompassing physical, social and emotional domains, for example. In the EUROFAMCARE study addressing carers in six European countries (as described earlier), carers in the UK and Sweden reported the highest quality of life (65 per cent and 67 per cent respectively), whilst those in Greece and Italy reported the lowest (50 per cent and 51 per cent respectively), which has been tentatively attributed to greater availability of services and active carer policies in the former countries (as cited in Triantafillou et al. 2010).

Immunological effects of caring

As described in Chapter 11 ☞, the nature, intensity, duration and frequency of stressor events have been found to influence the nature and extent of immune change in a dynamic manner, in part dependent on the state of the immune system at the time the stressor event occurs (Dantzer and Kelley 1989). There is a large body of evidence that points to immunosuppressant effects of long-term caring, and the effects can be exacerbated in older adults who may have pre-existing immune weaknesses (Graham et al. 2006, and see Chapter 12 ☞). In relation to caregiving stress, while immune effects are seen consistently in studies of older caregivers, findings among younger populations have been more inconsistent. For example, elderly caregivers of a spouse with Alzheimer's disease had lower immune function and reported more days of illness over the previous year than similarly aged healthy control subjects (Kiecolt Glaser et al. 1994), and the immuno-compromising effects of caring for a person with Alzheimer's has generally been confirmed (see reviews by Bourgeois et al. 1996; Kiecolt-Glaser et al. 2002). For example, Kiecolt-Glaser et al. (1996) conducted an early study where caregivers were given an influenza vaccination, and showed less appropriate immune responses to the vaccination than did the well-matched control participants. Differences were particularly evident when comparing those aged over 70 years (23.3 per cent of caregivers responded to the vaccine, compared to 60 per cent of controls) compared to those younger than 70 years (53.8 per cent of the caregivers responded compared to 70 per cent of the control subjects). Vedhara et al. (2002), however, found that caregivers of a spouse with multiple sclerosis did not differ in their immune responses following an influenza vaccination from non-caregivers. Multiple sclerosis is a condition equally as chronic as Alzheimer's but affecting a younger population, thus spousal caregivers are generally younger than spousal caregivers in the dementias. Vedhara's sample of younger caregivers did, however, also appear to be less distressed about their caring than that reported among other caregiver groups, which may in part explain their 'preserved' immune responses following vaccination. In another younger sample, parents of young children with a developmental disability, a reduced immune response both to influenza and pneumococcal vaccination was found, when compared to sex- and age-matched controls. In this study the reduced response to vaccination was greatest when parents were experiencing greater problem behaviours from the child (Gallagher et al. 2009). Together these findings suggest that immune responses to caregiving exist but that they may vary across populations and conditions, and that other factors are also likely to be at play.

An important point is that research into the physical consequences of carer stress have generally examined and found evidence of increased vulnerability to disease resulting from immune changes rather than actual disease development: for example, raised levels of the pro-inflammatory cytokine interleukin-6 found among caregivers is at a level considered a risk factor for cardiovascular disease (Kiecolt-Glaser et al. 2003). As described in Chapter 11 ☛ life stress has been shown to influence various inflammatory and immune responses (for example, the concentration of C-reactive protein and interleukin-6), with suggestions of these processes accelerating the development of age-related diseases (see Chapter 12, ☛). Kiecolt-Glaser and colleagues (2011) have also therefore examined the relationship between caregiving stress and the possibility of accelerated ageing by means of assessing telomere length – shorter **telomeres** had previously been associated with higher IL-6, and tumour necrosis factor-alpha (TNF-α) (Epel 2009). In their sample of Alzheimer's caregivers compared to controls (mean age 69.7 years overall), they found that caregivers had significantly shorter telomeres than controls. Furthermore, controlling for caregiver

---

telomeres

DNA clusters on the tip of our chromosomes, which prevent the DNA unravelling. Telomeres shorten naturally with age to the point where the cell cannot replicate.

---

status and other relevant factors, the experience of multiple early-life adversity was associated with higher IL-6 and shorter telomeres, which they claimed could translate into a 5–7 year difference in projected lifespan. Caregiving further magnified some of these relationships, reflecting the potential additive effects of stress.

In spite of the negative aspects of caring, studies have increasingly asked whether there are also positive aspects of the caring role.

Positive aspects of the caring role

Orbell et al. (1993) noted that caring 'may be appraised by the caregiver as negative, benign or positive. Caring may be appraised as an intrusion on personal lifeplans, but may also be appraised as positive, to the extent that it provides affirmation of valued aspects of the self' (p. 153). There are many reports of subjective feelings of satisfaction and rewards arising from the care role. For example, studies have identified caring satisfaction such as feeling a sense of fulfilment, feeling useful, increased feelings of closeness or increased day-to-day interactions as a result of patients and caregivers spending more leisure time together (e.g. Kinney et al. 1995; Kramer 1997; Parveen and Morrison 2012), and greater empathy and compassion amongst child caregivers than non-caregiving peers (Charles and Marshall 2012). In an early study, Kinney et al. (1995) investigated the daily hassles and uplifts (stresses and satisfactions) reported by 78 family caregivers of stroke patients and found that caregivers generally reported more uplifts (such as the care recipient cooperating with them, having pleasant interactions with care recipient) on a day-to-day basis than they did hassles (such as care recipient complaining or criticising, care recipient being unresponsive). However, this varied depending on the care recipient's level of impairment, with care recipients who had greater impairment generally having caregivers who reported more hassles. While hassles predicted poor caregiver well-being, when the overall number of uplifts outweighed the number of hassles, caregiver outcomes were improved (less depressed, better social relations). Such protective or buffering effects of uplifts, even in the face of concurrent hassles, highlights the importance of assessing both negative and positive aspects of caring and the interaction between them. Rapp and Chao (2000) in their study of dementia caregivers concluded that appraisals of strain and appraisals of gain exerted independent effects on negative affect (strain positively associated with NA, gain negatively associated). Interestingly, neither gain nor strain was associated with positive affect, which points to the fact that many factors influence caregiver affect, not only their appraisals of gain or strain. In a child caregiver sample, Cassidy et al. (2014) found that benefit-finding was explained primarily by perceived support from family and friends, and also by low perceived stress, the use of problem-focused coping, perceived social recognition of their role, and personal resilience. In turn, benefit-finding was associated with positive outcomes, as supported by longitudinal studies.

Furthermore, a recent review and reappraisal of the caregiving literature has led to questions as to whether caregiving is as generally negative as we have long supposed. This timely review in fact suggests that the positive experiences of caring have been downplayed, including longitudinal evidence from five large cohorts of caregivers and non-caregivers where a significant survival *advantage* has been found for caregivers in fact suggests that the positive experiences of caring have been downplayed (Roth et al. 2015). Such findings hold important implications for the future in terms of changing the population's expectations of taking on a caring role, and potentially enhancing willingness to take on the role if required. Nonetheless, whether outcomes are positive or negative, understanding is needed of the factors that act to increase or decrease the benefits of caregiving experienced.

Influences on caring outcomes

Features of the illness or of the cared-for

The illness or behavioural features of the care recipients have important but complex influences on caregiver outcome. Studies of caregivers of people with Alzheimer's disease, for example, have shown that distress is more clearly associated with demanding or disruptive behaviour than with the level of physical impairment or disability of the care recipient (e.g. Morrison 1999; Gaughler et al. 2000). Caregiver distress is subject to further fluctuations dependent on the care recipient's physical and mental well-being at any point in time (e.g. Beach et al. 2000).

Among caregivers of stroke survivors, while the severity of stroke impairment during the acute phase (i.e. approximately ten days post-stroke) predicted their future expectancies, it was their appraisals of the consequences of the illness and of their own coping resources that predicted their psychological well-being (Forsberg-Wärleby et al. 2001). The caregiver's subjective appraisals of the situation therefore differ from objective features of the illness including disability severity, in the extent to which they determine caregiver outcomes. To illustrate this further, again among those caring for stroke survivors, depression at six months was predicted primarily by an increase in negative characteristics of the care recipient (such as demanding behaviour), by reductions in caregivers perceiving that they had a reciprocal confiding relationship with the person they cared for, by the age and health of the care recipient (but not the caregiver's own age and health), and by income and a change in living standards. In contrast, caregiver burden was explained by the age of the caregiver (older caregivers were less burdened), a decline in the positive characteristics of the care recipient, reduced satisfaction with their own social contacts, and increased concern for future care (Schulz et al. 1988). This study, while somewhat dated, remains important because it examined changes in objective and subjective predictor variables over time, reflecting how the demands of caring are dynamic and fluctuating. It is worth noting that an increase in negative characteristics of the care recipient predicted caregiver depression, whereas a decrease in their positive characteristics predicted caregiver perceived burden. This reflects that burden is not equivalent to depression (as some studies imply) but is perhaps more tied up with the relationship between the caregiver and care recipient. It is increasingly evident that adjustment on the part of the caregiver (as well as the patient's own adjustment) is influenced by interpersonal processes, and, in the case of couples where one has an illness, the emotional, cognitive and behavioural responses of both parties to the situation. We address such dyadic factors in a later section.

The influence of caregiver characteristics and responses
Ethnicity and culture

Rapp and Chao (2000) found that the reported benefits of caregiving for a spouse or parent with dementia were greater in their small sample of black caregivers than their larger sample of white caregivers. It is possible that such differences are due to differences in the willingness of caregivers of different ethnicities or different cultural affiliations, to seek support outwith the family. Katbamnna and colleagues (2004) found that the fear of obligation to others reduced the likelihood of South Asian family caregivers making use of a wider social network to help provide care. This study did not find evidence of the oft-assumed willingness of extended family members to support the primary caregiver. However, in a review of 20 years of caring research, minority caregivers more often included extended family members than did White caregivers (non Hispanic) (Dilworth-Anderson et al. 2002). Related to this, Parveen and Morrison (2009) found higher levels of familism (feelings of loyalty and solidarity among family members, related to providing care) amongst British South Asian caregivers compared to White-British caregivers. This is consistent with other findings that familism is higher amongst African American, Asian and Latino caregivers compared to White caregivers (e.g. Knight et al. 2002). A study of South Asian caregivers living in Canada and providing care for their child with cancer (Klassen et al. 2012) provides qualitative evidence of distress compounded by a lack of support – consider this quote from a mother.

'I think I didn't deal with it too well at that time. That depression continues to this day . . . My depression kept getting worse. I was alone . . . I used to sometimes wish to tell more people, but my husband said, 'That won't be good, because the more you repeat these things to people, the more you'll think about them.' (p. 7).

The 'research focus' below describes further ethnic variations found in terms of coping strategies used and caregiving outcomes, and brings to the readers, attention the only theoretical model within the caregiving literature which explicitly considers the role culture plays in the stress-coping-outcome relationship – (The Sociocultural Stress and Coping Model, Aranda and Knight 1997; Knight and Sayegh 2010). An interesting and rare study of American Indian caregivers (Goins et al. 2011) highlights that few studies actually assess 'culture' in terms of the extent to which individuals identify with, and value, their own minority culture (reflected in use of their own language, rituals, or healing traditions, for example) as opposed to that of the dominant culture. Ethnicity is not the same as culture and it is important that caregiving research recognises that cultural identity may vary within those of a shared ethnicity, and therefore exert different influences on response to, and outcomes of, providing care.

RESEARCH FOCUS

Ethnicity, willingness to care and caregiver mood

Parveen, S., Morrison, V. and Robinson, C.A. (2013): Ethnicity, familism and willingness to care: Important influences on caregiver mood?, *Aging & Mental Health*, 17:1, 115-124.

Introduction

In a series of studies examining ethnic variations in both motivations to care, coping with caregiving, and caregiving outcomes, Parveen and colleagues have highlighted the importance of not assuming that models of illness cognition and coping hold for all cultures or even microcultures. Whilst both qualitative and quantitative data are available, and mood, quality of life and caregiver gains have been reported, here we focus on caregiver mood as the primary outcome as ethnic variations were significant and set the scene for subsequent study.

Aims and objectives

A total sample of 235 adult caregivers were recruited, of whom 162 were White-British (58 male, 104 female) and 73 were South Asian (6 male, 67 female). South Asian caregivers were more likely to be daughters (28.8 per cent), daughters-in-law (17.8 per cent) or wives (17.8 per cent). White-British caregivers were more likely to be wives (45.1 per cent), husbands (28.4 per cent) or daughters (13 per cent). Care recipients had varying diagnoses, with the largest groups comprising caregivers of those with dementia (65), multiple sclerosis (45), Parkinson's disease (35) and stroke (35). Participants completed a battery of self-report measures, including the Heller familism scale, Abell's willingness to care scale, the Brief IPQ, (Chapter 9 ☛), the Brief COPE, the SSQ social support questionnaire and the Hospital Anxiety and Depression scale (HADS)

Results

Unfortunately there were insufficient South Asian males to examine gender differences within this group, although White-British female caregivers were more anxious but not more depressed than White-British males. Many other differences between ethnic groups emerged. Exploring the influence of caregiver relationship type on mood (spouse, adult child (or child in-law) and others (parents or siblings)) revealed no effect within the White-British caregivers, but amongst British South Asian caregivers, spousal caregivers were both *less* anxious and *less* depressed than the adult-child or other type of caregiver. Similarly being in a married relationship, compared to a group comprising single, divorced or widowed individuals, was associated with less anxiety and depression in the British South Asian sample but made no difference to these scores in the White-British caregivers. The diagnosis of the care recipient made no difference to the mood of the British South Asian caregivers whereas amongst White-British caregivers those providing care for a loved one with dementia had significantly higher anxiety than caregivers in Parkinson's disease, MS, dementia or other diagnoses caregivers and significantly more depression than Parkinson's disease, MS, cancer or other caregivers.

Controlling for the effect of age (as British South Asian caregivers were younger), British South Asian caregivers had significantly higher levels of familism – although contrary to expectations familism was not significantly associated with mood amongst British South Asian caregivers but was associated with higher depression in the White-British caregiver. British South Asian caregivers used significantly more behavioural

disengagement and religious coping and reported significantly less support than White-British caregivers. When this latter correlation was explored further the difference lay in their greater use of friends and formal services for support, but did not differ from British South Asians in terms of support from family.

Whilst levels of willingness to care did not differ between the two caregiver groups, willingness to care and caregiver anxiety were related in opposing directions. Highly willing South Asian caregivers were more anxious, and highly willing White-British caregivers were less anxious. The authors suggest that this may be due to South Asian caregivers' willingness to care being related to the fulfillment of culturally valued obligations to care, thus leading to anxiety about failing to fulfil such obligations, whereas White-British caregivers were perhaps willing to provide care for more intrinsic reasons, including personal choice (Parveen et al. 2011).

When predicting anxiety using regression analyses amongst White-British caregivers, although 26 per cent of the variance was explained with a combination of demographic and coping variables and low satisfaction with social support (the strongest factor), none of the assessed variables remained significant. In contrast, in regressions within the British South Asian caregivers, 45 per cent of variance in anxiety was explained, predominantly demographics, willngness to care and a combination of coping strategies, particularly self-blame. Depression within White-British caregivers was explained totalling 29 per cent with demographics, coping (particularly substance use and low humour) and low satisfaction with support emerging. And finally, 38 per cent of the variance in depression amongst British South Asian caregivers, was explained predominantly by demographics and coping (self-blame). Notably, familism was not a predictor.

Discussion

Clear differences emerged in the characteristics of White-British and British South Asian caregivers and within each group clear differences in correlates of care-giver anxiety and depression. Differences in familism existed; however, this did not reflect in differences in willingness to care, with both groups reporting being equally willing. Perhaps feelings of filial obligation should not lead us to presuppose willingness, a suggestion supported by the author's own qualitative work (Parveen et al. 2011). Relationship type and marital status played a role for the South Asian caregivers, with married caregivers faring better than adult-child caregivers. The study, however, did not assess relationship quality, which as we have described elsewhere exerts a significant influence on caregiving outcomes.

Also, within the White-British sample diagnoses of the care recipient exerted an influence on caregiver mood, suggesting perhaps that White-British caregivers are more affected by the nature of the demands corresponding with different conditions than are British South Asians. This may be a consequence of differing motivations for care with differences in willingness to provide different forms of care (although the current data do not support this).

Overall, these findings only offered partial support for the hypotheses that (a) British South Asian caregivers will have higher levels of familism (supported), willingness to care (not supported) and lower use of support (supported), (b) that familism and willingness to care will be associated with anxiety and depression (not supported in regression analyses) and (c) that British South Asian caregivers will experience greater distress due to the differences outlined in (a) (not supported). In spite of this, there were several interesting findings regarding ethnic variations in motivations to care, coping responses and the use of support –sufficient to warrant further investigation. The authors therefore conducted a longitudinal study with a new caregiving sample (N=154, 123 of whom took part in three waves of data collection – baseline and a three-month and nine-month follow-up). Negative emotional outcomes have been examined as well as caregiver quality of life (in review) and caregiver gains (Parveen and Morrison 2012). Only through longitudinal study can changes in caregiving motivations, caregiving tasks, familism, illness perceptions, coping strategies and the use of social support be meaningfully examined in relation to caregiver outcomes (which themselves will likely change over time). In this longitudinal sample, familism declined over time, raising important questions as to what might bring this about and how, within ethnic minority caregivers, this shift in family loyalty is expressed.

Sociocultural models of caregiving stress, such as adopted in the studies reported here, provide a broader framework from which to explore caregiving variations within a multicultural context. By highlighting cultural variation in coping responses, including the use of social support, as well as potential differences in caregiving motivations, it is envisaged that support services will become more culturally appropriate.

Personality

Studies have highlighted the role of caregiver personality variables such as optimism (generally a positive resource) and neuroticism (generally a negative characteristic), showing that these characteristics had direct effects on caregiver mental health, as well as indirect effects via their influence on perceived stress, and on the perceptions and appraisals of the care recipient's level of impairment (e.g. Hooker et al. 1992; Shifren and Hooker 1995). More recently, research interest has turned to the construct of resilience – the ability to 'bounce back' in times of adversity, (Werner and Smith 1982, 1992), thought to be either a fixed trait or a stress-invoked adaptive response (Smith 2006) (see also Chapter 12 ☛). Cassidy et al. (2014), in their study of child caregivers, found that resilience was a small but significant predictor of life satisfaction and positive mental health (four and three per cent of the variance accounted for respectively), whereas resilience did not predict negative mental health and only explained one per cent of the variance in benefit-finding. It may be that, as these authors conclude, resilience is more important for developing positive health outcomes than it is for reducing negative outcomes.

Attachment

Pietromonaco et al. (2013) highlighted a need for health psychology research, particularly that attempting to understand processes of adjusting to illness within families, to better integrate relationship science and, in particular, attachment theory (cf Bowlby 1969, 1973). Attachments formed in childhood between a child and a parent (four protypical styles derived from two dimensions – anxiety and avoidance) are also seen in adult intimate relationships, and likely to be activated during periods of illness where one member takes on a caregiving role. Anxious attached individuals are governed by attending to distress and focus on their own distress and needs, with a fear of being rejected by others as a result of not being good enough. This anxiety is perhaps increased if the other person is absorbed in their own situation, such as is the case when a person is ill. Those with an avoidant attachment style, however, are characterised by a tendency to separate their thoughts from their emotions, and to be self reliant to the point of emotional detachment from others as perhaps a form of self-protection (from potential distress). Illness in a loved one, with consequent needs for the partner to emotionally invest in providing care, is thought to create a type of distancing. *Secure* adults are low in anxiety and avoidance, *preoccupied* adults are high in anxiety but low in avoidance, *fearful avoidant* individuals are high in both anxiety and avoidance, and *dismissing avoidant* individuals are low in anxiety but high in avoidance (Feeney and Collins 2001: 973).

A growing body of research is testing these theories in caregiver samples where the caregiver is spouse-partner (rather than an adult caring for a parent where adult-child attachments are present). For example, studies with cancer caregivers have found that having a secure attachment was related to autonomous motives for caregiving and for benefit-finding (both discussed in previous sections) (Kim et al. 2008). More recently Hasson-Ohayon and colleagues (2013) find an association between attachment style and finding meaning with an interesting gender difference – for men, finding meaning in caregiving was associated with low avoidance attachment, whereas for female caregivers finding meaning was positively associated with having social support. The authors propose that avoidant attachments may prevent those caregivers from accessing social interaction or, indeed, being emotionally involved in their caregiving role sufficiently to enable finding any meaning within it. In contrast, anxious attachment was not associated with finding meaning. Anxiously attached individuals by definition tend to be motivated more by addressing emotional needs and worries and therefore were hypothesised to experience more distress when required to take on the care of a loved one. This is supported in a study of cancer caregivers where an anxious attachment style was positively related to caregiver depression (Braun et al. 2007). Furthermore, among female caregivers of male partners admitted to hospital with acute coronary syndrome and assessed during the hospital stay and again six months later, there was a significantly stronger association between caregiver reported burden and depression in those with higher attachment anxiety (Vilchinsky et al. 2014).

Caregiver appraisals

It is generally accepted that the underlying source of caregiver distress or strain appears to result from subjective appraisals of an imbalance between the demands of caring and the resources perceived to be available to the caregiver (e.g. Orbell and Gillies 1993), which may include what Wallander and Varni (1998) refer to as 'resistance factors'. Resistance factors include intrapersonal factors such as personality, motivation, and self-efficacy beliefs, socio-ecological factors such as the caregiver's family environment and support resources, and stress-processing factors, which include an individual's cognitive appraisals of a situation and their coping responses (akin to Lazarus's theory, Chapter 11 (☞)).

The role of caregiver appraisal in predicting caregiver stress was highlighted in a rare prospective study of caregiver health carried out with 122 family caregivers of persons with Alzheimer's disease; in this sample, improvements in caregiver physical or mental health were not directly associated with a reduction in caring demands but with the caregiver's appraisal of the stressors as benign, with approach rather than avoidant coping, and with greater levels of the personal resource of social support (Goode et al. 1998).

Several studies point to a significant influence of care-giver perceptions of self efficacy, i.e. the extent to which they feel equipped to carry out caregiving tasks, on emotional outcomes and perceptions of strain or burden (e.g. van den Heuvel et al. 2001; Chronister and Chan 2006; Merluzzi et al. 2011). In this latter study, conducted within the context of palliative care, a caregiver efficacy inventory (CGI) was developed which produced four factors of perceived efficacy:

● in managing medical information;

● in caring for the care recipient;

● in caring for oneself;

● in managing difficult interactions and emotions.

In their study of 133 informal caregivers, the total CGI efficacy score was negatively associated with stress and burden, but in regression analyses the factors of caring for oneself and managing difficult interactions and emotions emerged as the most important to stress and burden. These are interesting findings worthy of further prospective examination and in caregivers of non-palliative populations where the need for carer self-care or the emotional experience may differ substantially.

Perceptions of the illness itself, rather than perceptions of caregiving, also play a role, as shown by McClenahan and Weinman (1998) where caregivers who had a chronic perceived timeline for the illness showed greater caregiver distress (see Chapter 9 ☞ for full discussion of illness perceptions). However, there is a larger body of work exploring the impact of carer illness perceptions on patient outcomes, as we also refer to when discussing dyadic beliefs later in the chapter, than there is currently in relation to caregivers' own outcomes.

There has also been a general tendency to expect males, firstly to take on less of a caring role, and, secondly, for those that do become a caregiver, for them to experience it differently to women due to taking on a non-socialised and less valued social role. The evidence, however, is not so clear-cut as may be expected, nor is it clear whether males appraise the role differently to females – see 'In the spotlight'.

IN THE SPOTLIGHT

Masculinity and caregiving

Stereotypical views of male gender is that, compared to females, males are less empathic, exhibit fewer emotional responses and more instrumental or practical coping responses in times of stress. Whilst gender is biologically determined, 'gender role' concerns issues of masculinity and femininity – identification of such are often socially determined (big boys don't cry, girls don't play with construction kits, etc., etc.), as defined by the World Health Organization (2014), where gender role concerns 'socially constructed roles, behaviors, activities and attributes that a given society considers appropriate for men and women'. It is expected that gender role expectations/norms therefore vary in different societies/cultures, and furthermore, as found in Pinquhart and Sorensen's (2006) review and meta-analysis, change over time as a result of social change, i.e. less gender variation in more recent studies compared to studies from earlier generations.

Gender role identity where measured, commonly categorised people on the basis of certain characteristics: e.g. masculine 'instrumental' traits include, for example, 'aggressive', 'dominant', whereas feminine 'expressive' traits include 'warm', 'sincere' (common scales used include the BEM Sex Role Inventory, Bem, 1979, and the Personal Attributes Questionnaire, Spence and Helmreich 1978, cited in Baker et al. 2010).

Until recently, there has been little exploration of how these self-identified traits are associated with coping appraisals generally, or for current interests, in relation to caregiving processes and outcomes. Hoyt (2009) describes how the usefulness of emotional approach coping, or the expressing and processing of emotion, for men, is unclear, and likely influenced by the extent to which a male subscribes to traditional male beliefs, and roles or experiences conflict with these. In his study of men with cancer, i.e. NOT caregivers, high gender role conflict was indeed related to low levels of emotional expression and in turn (as well as directly to) higher levels of distress. Taking this into the arena of caregiving, feeling conflicted with traditional gendered roles may also influence a caregiver's use of social support. For example, 'traditional' men value:

● success, power and competition, measured, for example, by recording extent of agreement with 'Winning is a measure of my value and personal worth';

● restricted expressions of emotionality, measured, for example, by recording extent of agreement with 'I do not like to show my emotions to other people';

● restricted affectionate behaviour between men (RABBM), measured, for example, by recording extent of agreement with 'Affection with other men makes me tense';

● conflict between work and family relations, measured, for example, by recording extent of agreement with 'I worry about failing and how it affects my doing well as a man'.

Compromised health has been shown to create role conflict, with illness described by some as a threat to masculinity (see Chapter 14 ☞). Similarly therefore, such feelings arising from the socialised male role may influence how men adapt to providing care for a loved one at home in a low-status role, where social support may be needed but not sought.

Baker et al. (2010) examined these associations in a sample of husbands caring for their wives who had been diagnosed with dementia. Both Masculine instrumentality and Feminine expressiveness were significantly and negatively correlated with personal strain, and Masculine instrumentality was significantly and negatively correlated with care role strain; however, none of those relationships persisted in multivariate regressions. Instead caregiver role strain was explained by caregiving situational characteristics (e.g. high duration of caregiving, negative reaction to recipients' memory and behaviour problems) and low conflict regarding restricting affectionate behaviour between men (i.e. they held a traditional view of this behaviour). Personal strain was explained by the same caregiver situation characteristics and also by RABBM, but in a different direction. i.e. high conflict/non-traditional beliefs around RABBM predicted personal strain. Poor self-rated caregiver health also added significantly to the explanation of personal strain. There was also no significant utility of gender identity

measures in explaining caregiver gain, with gain instead being predicted by lower educational attainment, conflict/ non-traditional views of success, power and competition, and RABBM (i.e. discomfort restricting affection between men). Contrary to expectations, restrictive emotionality was not associated with any outcome. The direction of effect of role conflict was the same for the experience of personal strain and for the experience of gain – rejecting or being conflicted with traditional non-affectionate behaviours between men led both to strain and also gain. Role strain in contrast was worse where traditional views on restricting affectionate behaviour with other men were upheld. It is important that studies next explore the social-support-seeking behaviours that are associated with such beliefs as gender role beliefs may socially constrain coping behaviours and potentially adjustment to caregiving.

One final thought: Baker and colleagues intriguingly propose that there may be a response bias at play whereby men may report feeling strained as caregiver as a means of distancing themselves from a role they perceive as fundamentally a feminine role and thus one they shouldn't be competent at! Conversely of course they may not want to report they are not coping out of concern that they will appear 'not "man enough" for the job' (p. 325). To explore these interesting issues further we need more studies to examine the interaction between gendered identity and care role appraisals, coping responses and outcomes and, ideally, also explore any perceived pressures or influences on reporting.

As described in Chapter 12 ☞, while perceiving control over outcome may not be always realistic, finding or retaining control over some aspects of an event or one's responses to it has generally been shown to be beneficial (Hagedoorn et al. 2002; Montpetit and Bergman 2007). Amongst married couples, it has even been shown that spouse caregivers' confidence in the recovery of their spouse following a stroke (Molloy et al. 2008), or in the patients own self-efficacy for managing their condition (arthritis, Gere et al. 2014) can be a significant longitudinal predictor of patient outcomes.

However, what effect do such beliefs have on carers' outcomes?

One example, Hagedoorn et al. (2002), in a comparison of male and female caregivers of a partner with cancer, found that elevated distress among female caregivers was found only in those who reported low levels of caregiver efficacy (not believing in one's ability to care effectively) and perceived challenges to their role identity resulting from a perception of not 'caring well'. Another study of cancer caregivers, however, found that perceived control over caregiving demands did not predict outcome, positive or negative (Fitzell and Pakenham 2010). They assessed caregiver appraisals of demand (stress, challenge) and resources (personal control, social support) in relation to both positive and negative caregiver adjustment, and while perceived control was not predictive, perceived stress (assessed using a single item) was. Perhaps surprisingly, scores on the more robust five-item measure of perceived challenge was predictive only of life satisfaction, illustrating that 'stress' is about more than just challenge – and indeed, the 'resource' variable of satisfaction with social support also added significantly to the prediction of all outcomes. The authors suggest that the lack of prediction of control beliefs (and also in fact of most of the coping subscales they assessed) may be due to using items which referred to control over caregiving challenges generally, rather than specific demands/caregiving tasks. This issue of whether to assess generically or specifically is an important one which we have addressed at various points throughout this text.

Use of social support

Shewchuck et al. (1998) found that adjustment to caring for a person with a spinal cord injury varied significantly over the first caring year and was influenced by patient and caregiver characteristics, such as age, the caregiver's own health, and also by the caregiver's behaviour in terms of their use of support. Using social support as a coping strategy has emerged as an important predictor of caregiver outcomes. For example, in a study of male heart attack patients and their spouses, Bennett and Connell (1999) found that the primary causes of caregiver anxiety were the perceived consequences of the heart attack, with many wives becoming hyper-vigilant, watching for signs that their partner may have a further MI, and that the lack of a confidante with whom they could discuss these concerns was an important factor in maintaining anxiety. Perceived social support, or the lack of it, also played a central role in the stress process model predicting QoL or burden in caregiving for a family member with traumatic brain injury (Chronister and Chan 2006). Following a longitudinal study of 88 couples where one partner has colorectal cancer, Hagedoorn et al. (2011) report findings whereby if past (pre-cancer) spousal support was perceived as being high, both patients and partners rated the quality of their relationship relatively high, regardless of their spouses' current

supportive behaviour. Although the measure of spousal supportiveness relies on retrospective reports of pre-cancer behaviour and thus may be prone to bias, such findings highlight the importance of having a supportive 'history' even if current support is less good – perhaps attributions for current low levels of active engagement or high levels of protective buffering are more sympathetic or more externally attributed, thus allowing relationship satisfaction to be maintained.

Protective buffering

Other caregiver behaviour, such as that made in response to the patient's situation, may also influence their emotional well-being: for example, spousal caregivers have been found to inhibit, deny or conceal negative information, thoughts or feelings, and yield to partners, in order to 'protect' their partners, although in doing so they may increase their own distress and even that of the patient partner (e.g. wives of heart attack patients, Coyne and Smith 1991; spouses of cancer patients, Langer et al. 2007; Manne et al. 2007). It may be that caregivers are dissatisfied with the relationship and therefore avoid engaging in discussions of emotions, for example; or it may be that their inhibition of expression creates dissatisfaction, or it may be that there is bidirectional flow! To examine these relationships longitudinally, Manne et al. (2007) assessed the protective buffering behaviours of both patients and spouses, and their distress and relationship satisfaction at three time points over an 18-month period following diagnosis of early-stage breast cancer. Buffering on the part of both patients and caregivers was found to decrease over time, whereas the high levels of relationship satisfaction remained relatively stable, suggesting that they are independent; however, buffering by either the patient or the partner contributed to patient distress and if buffering increased, so did distress. In Hagedoorn et al.'s (2011) study referred to above, longitudinal analyses found that in spousal carers high levels of protective buffering at baseline (of them by the patient) was associated with low levels of spousal relationship satisfaction, particularly where pre-cancer supportiveness from patients to carers was reported as having been relatively high. This is possibly because the buffering was seen to thwart their ability to carry out their caregiving role. Other relationship factors may also influence caregiver outcome as we now turn our attention to.

The relationship between caregiver and patient

Many studies have examined spousal caregivers, where the relationship is characterised by being full-time, interdependent and intimate (cf. Coyne and Fiske 1992) and thus uniquely supportive. Other studies have shown less control over the caregiver 'types' recruited to the study and have included informal caregivers with varying degrees of association – mothers, fathers, siblings, daughters, friends. Pinquart and Sörensen (2003) hypothesised that differences in psychological and physical health would be greater among spousal caregivers than non-spousal caregivers, for female rather than male caregivers, and for older rather than younger caregivers. While a study of caring for an older adult only, their results did support these hypotheses, and throughout this chapter we have highlighted gender or age where they have moderated findings. Poulin and colleagues (2010) found that active helping of a spouse predicted greater positive affect in caregivers when illness status, functional impairment and 'being on call' was controlled for, but particularly where there was a perceived interdependence with their spouse, i.e. where the caregivers agreed with statements such as 'I need my spouse as much as h/she needs me'. Helping and being on call generally predicted negative affect where interdependence was low. Such findings show that interdependence may 'buffer' any negative effects of helping behaviours in patient–carer dyads but also highlight that not all aspects of the caring role are negative. What is becoming increasingly clear is that, as well as the nature of the caregiver–patient relationship, the quality of the relationship between these individuals influences the outcomes of caring for both parties. Furthermore, coping together, described as 'dyadic coping', where both members of a partnership are engaged in coping with the stressor, even where it is only one that is directly affected, for example, with a cancer diagnosis, (Hagedoorn et al. 2008; Badr et al. 2010) has been found to increase adjustment outcomes including maintained relationship functioning (see review, Traa et al. 2015).

Relationship quality

De Vellis et al. (2003) stress that understanding the nature and processes in dyadic relationships is beneficial to our understanding of adjustment to illness. Social support research has not consistently explored the relationship between those studied in terms of the nature and quality of the interaction, and yet the reciprocal and interdependent relationships that people engage in are crucial. This reciprocity is represented in Figure 15.2, where the relationship depicted is that of a marriage. It has been observed that illness can cause a 'stress spill-over' effect by adding to existing marital challenges and introducing further opportunities for conflict and strain. In a daily diary study with 50 healthy couples in a long-term marriage, greater marital satisfaction was associated with both the expression and receipt of gratitude (Gordon et al. 2011), suggesting that even in long-standing relationships relatively simple gestures of thanks can be beneficial. In the context of caring for someone with illness or disability, feeling 'unappreciated' can be a frequent source of stress or burden (see later section). Working at maintaining a good relationship quality, or preventing it from becoming any worse (if it was not particularly good to begin with!) is extremely important if illness adjustment is to be optimal for both partners, and this may be particularly important where the threat to life is significant, for example in lung cancer (Badr and Taylor 2008).

Banthia et al. (2003) reported that the quality of a relationship can moderate the effects of individual coping, finding that prostate cancer patients in strong relationships experienced less distress than those in less strong relationships, even when they engaged in maladaptive coping strategies such as avoidant coping and intrusive thinking. Williamson et al. (1998) distinquish between depressed caregivers and resentful caregivers in

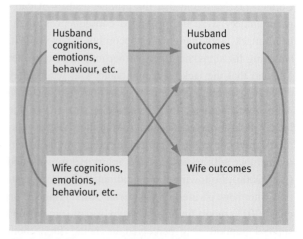

Figure 15.2 The interdependence model of couple adjustment

Source: DeVellis, Lewis and Sterba (2003: 263).

their cross-sectional study of 75 cancer caregivers: depressed caregivers reported close, communal and intimate relationships with the patient, and this closeness created the restrictions on their own activities (i.e. they wanted to be with the person they cared for), whereas resentful caregivers reported less close relationships and reported their activity restriction to be predicted by severity of patient symptoms (they were restricted out of the necessity to provide care). This important, but subtle, distinction between depressed and resentful caregivers may help to explain differences in longer-term caregiver outcomes. Thompson et al. (2002) also found that resentful caregivers tend to provide overly controlling and overprotective care, and they suggest that such caring styles may undermine patient autonomy and progress. More research that explores the causes of caregiver resentment is required as it may offer potential opportunites for intervention, to the benefit of both parties.

Relationship quality is also likely to interact with motivations to commence and to continue to provide care (see Lyonette and Yardley 2003). Badr and Taylor (2008) report how relationship maintenance behaviours, including strategies of positivity, providing assurance, using social networks, and sharing tasks, were greater in those who were less distressed (whether spousal carer or person with lung cancer) and that, over time, such behaviours, when carried out by both individuals, were beneficial to dyadic adjustment. Traa and colleagues (2015) echo this in their systematic review of 33 studies of dyadic coping in cancer, where open and constructive communications between the couple, supportive behaviours (in both), positive dyadic coping (for example, through joint information-seeking or sharing of feelings) and joint problem-solving, were related to better relationship functioning.

Couple identity

Another aspect that may mediate the stress of caregiving for a spouse is that of 'couple identity', whereby the relationship takes on its own identity, rather than being seen as two separate individuals. In a relatively new field of enquiry, Badr and colleagues (Badr et al. 2007) found that the extent to which a healthy spouse saw their relationship with their ill spouse as part of their self-concept (reflecting the importance to them of being part of a couple) partially mediated the effects of perceived overload, relational changes, and loss of independence and loss of 'self' on mental health scores. Although cross-sectional,

and involving relatively established caregivers (average of over five years), it is likely that this study will stimulate more research into this construct.

It is becoming clear from the research reviewed above that any stress experienced by a caregiver does not stem solely nor directly from what the caregivers *do* but rather from the meaning they ascribe to what they do (Dobbins 2007).

WHAT DO YOU THINK?

If you are in a relationship, what does it mean to you? Do your close personal relationships offer an implicit extension to how you see yourself? While research seems to suggest that couple identity is a positive factor when examining the mental health of members of the couple, can you think of any situations where there are possible risks to having a strong 'couple identity', perhaps at the expense of a strong sense of self? What about when the couple separates or one of the couple is widowed? What implications may there be then for well-being?

Dyadic perceptions, shared and discrepant beliefs

Given the individual nature of health and illness beliefs, stress appraisal and coping responses, it cannot be assumed that family caregivers and those they care for will exhibit similar beliefs and responses. A growing avenue of research is exploring whether differences in the beliefs and responses of informal caregivers and their partners, or other relatives, influence illness outcomes (e.g. Morrison 2001; Figueras and Weinman 2003; Sterba et al. 2008; Vilchinsky et al. 2011; Band et al. 2015).

Individuals in caring dyads may hold different and diverging beliefs about the illness itself: for example, the illness representations (see Chapter 9 ☞) of identity, timeline, causes, consequences and control/cure may differ between patients, caregiver spouses and significant others. Weinman et al. (2000) found that, following a heart attack, participation in rehabilitation exercises could be predicted more from spousal beliefs, particularly where the spouse attributed the heart attack to the patient's poor health habits (internal cause) than by the patient's own attributions. Figueiras and Weinman (2003) further examined the illness representations of 70 patient–partner dyads following a heart attack and distinguished between couples who shared 'similar positive' perceptions, 'similar negative' perceptions or 'conflicting' perceptions. The most negative perceptions and conflicting perceptions emerged in relation to perceptions of control/cure, with shared positive perceptions more evident in relation to the identity, timeline and consequences dimensions. Dyads with shared positive perceptions fared better in terms of lower disability, fewer sexual functioning difficulties, less health-related distress, greater vitality and better global adjustment than dyads with negative or conflicting perceptions.

As one might expect, caregivers provide support to an ill partner, parent, child or friend primarily because they think it is needed; however, as discussed above, this does not mean that care recipients will perceive the care and social support received as positive or helpful. This discrepancy is important: e.g. differences in perceived care needs between the caregiver and the care recipient may exist. Sarason et al. (1990) in fact noted that caregivers often perceive that they are giving more than the patients feel they are receiving, which has inevitable consequences for caregiver distress.

A study by Dagan and colleagues (Dagan et al. 2011) highlights how personal control beliefs can influence individuals' responsiveness to spousal behaviour perceived as either supportive or unsupportive. They hypothesised that people with relatively low personal control beliefs would be more responsive to both positively and negatively perceived support from their partner than people relatively high in personal control, because those high in perceived control 'need' the support less as they are better able to cope adaptively and independently. In support of this hypothesis is much research regarding the benefits of internal control beliefs (see elsewhere in this chapter and Chapter 12 ☞), and also people relatively low in control have been found to make more use of coping strategies such as social reliance (Elfström and Kreuter 2006). Additionally, those low in support may be more distressed by receiving supportive behaviours that they perceive as unhelpful, i.e. mismatched to their needs. Using a longitudinal design, 70 patients newly diagnosed with colorectal cancer and their partners (52 male patients, 18 female patients, thus 52 female partners and 18 male partners) were assessed at three months (baseline) and nine months (follow-up) following diagnosis, in terms of their perceived spousal supportive (SSL) behaviour (e.g. Can you talk with your partner openly and share your feelings with him/her?) and

unsupportive (SSL-N) behaviour (How often does your partner . . . make disapproving remarks towards you?). Participants also completed a measure of their sense of personal control (Pearlin and Schooler's seven-item Mastery list) and their depressive symptoms (Center for Epidemiologic Studies Depression Scale CES-D).

Higher personal control was moderately associated with lower levels of distress for both patients and partners. The hypothesised associations between patients' perceived supportive and unsupportive spousal behaviour and distress were not, however, significant. In contrast, carer partners' perceptions of supportive and unsupportive spousal behaviour were moderately associated with their distress. Furthermore, patients' perceptions of supportive and unsupportive spousal behaviour were moderately positively associated with partners' perceptions of spousal behaviour, reflecting congruence in the nature of support considered supportive or not supportive.

For both patients and partners, the interaction between perceived spousal supportive behaviour and personal control at baseline predicted follow-up distress. Patients and partners who perceived more spousal support reported less distress over time, but only if they were relatively low in personal control. In terms of unsupportive behaviour, partners who perceived more unsupportive spousal behaviour reported more distress, again only if they were relatively low in personal control. Patient data, however, did not show this relationship. This suggests perhaps that spousal partners low in control are more affected by unsupportive behaviour than are patients who are low in control and who perceive their carers as being unsupportive. Why this might be the case is unclear; however, it may be, the authors suggest, that for caregiving partners relatively low in control, perceiving unsupportive behaviour from the patients is interpreted as a sign that they are failing as caregivers, which may create increased distress for them in that role.

Such findings support the idea that those high in personal control beliefs possess coping skills required for their adaptation and are less reliant on others (although coping responses were not assessed and therefore this assumption is not testable in this study). However, the data do suggest that interventions to reduce distress should probably prioritise those people who are relatively low in personal control. Such findings also contribute to our understanding of who benefits from social support by showing that the effects of perceived spousal supportive and unsupportive behaviour on distress are qualified by personal control. By taking a dyadic approach, we can see in these data that patients and partners may perhaps respond differently to unsupportive spousal behaviours, even when gender is controlled for, and, if replicated, such a finding has important implications for when developing interventions or services.

This dyadic approach to coping with illness and caregiving research is growing. As described in Chapter 11 ☞, stress-coping theories have tended to focus on the individual; however, increasingly a more systems-led approach is being taken, in particular exploring patient–carer dyads within, typically, couples. A key proponent of this approach is Guy Bodenman who describes a systemic–transactional model (STM) of stress which develops the transactional model of stress-coping of Richard Lazarus (e.g. Lazarus and Folkman 1984) which was discussed fully in Chapter 11 ☞. The STM considers the interdependent relation between both members of a dyad and the reciprocal influence each has on the beliefs and outcomes of the other, and, crucially, acknowledges and enables measurement of the fact that the couples relationship can be both affected by, and a source of, stress (Bodenmann 1997; Falconier et al. 2015). This intradyadic stress, or relationship stress (Bodenmann et al. 2007) can further influence the effects of extra-dyadic stress, such as illness in one of the dyad. How members of the dyad cope, either separately or together, will also interact to influence outcome, such as was shown in a study of couples coping with metastatic breast cancer where shared positive coping benefited the adjustment of both, whereas shared negative coping was associated with greater distress, particularly amongst patient care recipients (Badr et al. 2010). In another study of long-term family caregivers (not all co resident and with wide variation in impairment of the care recipients), discrepancies between a caregiver and their care recipient in terms of appraisals of the caregiving role, specifically in terms of the difficulties encountered (caregivers reported more than care recipients), was predictive of caregiver, but not care recipient, perceived relationship strain (Lyons et al. 2002). It appears that discrepancy may differentially affect caregivers and care recipients, with further differences seen according to the outcome examined.

The importance of discrepancy exists in parent–child dyads as well as within spouse caregiver–recipient dyads. As reviewed in Chapter 14 ☞ parent–child dyads may converge and diverge in terms of their beliefs about an illness and its symptoms, depending on various factors, including the child's current health status. Parental over- or underestimation of a child's problem areas can have implications for parental caring behaviour. Furthermore, patient, partner or parent ratings also often diverge from health professionals' ratings of patient's QoL, activity or mood levels. This could lead to misunderstandings about treatment options or their usefulness, which may, as Janse et al. (2004) note, have implications for non-adherence. It may be that assessing both the 'patient' and a significant other will in fact give a more complete picture.

Longitudinal evidence is obviously needed which can explore causal relationships more fully. For example, using the IPQ-R (see Chapter 9 ☞) Sterba and colleagues (Sterba et al. 2008) found that, unlike in some of the conditions described above, couples shared similar beliefs about rheumatoid arthritis. Specifically where there was congruence concerning women's personal control over the illness and its cyclic nature, there was better psychological adjustment in women assessed four months later, even when controlling for their initial psychological adjustment, arthritis disability, education, years married, and global marriage rating. Similarly, although beliefs about chronic fatigue syndrome were found to be relatively congruent in a review of significant others and patients, significant other beliefs in their own right predicted both caregiver responses and patent outcomes (see review of Band et al. 2015, in 'In the spotlight', p. 448). In their own empirical study, the same authors (Band et al. 2014) found that, where significant other's were high on Expressed Emotion (both critical comments and emotional over involvement (EOI) parameters), the fatigue severity and depressive symptoms of the patient were worse when followed up after six months. Furthermore, EOI also predicted fatigue severity, and EOI was higher in parents than in partners. This supports earlier cross-sectional findings whereby playing down or minimising CFS and its consequences on the part of the spouses was associated with poorer patient outcomes (Heijmans et al. 1999). In this study, perhaps surprisingly, spouses being pessimistic about the illness timeline (i.e. thinking the illness was more chronic than patients thought it was) was associated with better patient outcomes.

In addressing perceptions of psychosocial adjustment to illness, it should not be surprising to find that any discrepancies in beliefs within a dyad are subject to fluctuations. This has been demonstrated, for example, in a study of 81 couples where the male had received a diagnosis of prostate cancer (Ezer et al. 2011). Exploring firstly whether belief incongruence existed, they found significant congruence in most domains of psychosocial adjustment (vocational, domestic, environmental, family relationships); however, incongruence in perceptions of health care received (wives more distressed by health care), psychological distress (husbands higher) and social activities (husbands more distressed about social relationships) existed at the time of diagnosis. Examining next whether (in)congruence changed over the first 12 months following diagnosis, at three months, wives continued to be more distressed by health-care expectations and men remained more psychologically distressed; however, men now also showed significantly discrepant and higher distress regarding sexual relationships. Men's

higher psychological distress and greater distress regarding sexual relationships persisted to the 12-month follow-up. This is consistent with other studies of prostate cancer, where challenges to sexual function have been shown to impact on a masculine identity, and it appears that spouses may be more able to accept changes in this life domain than the men themselves (Resendes and McCorkle 2006).

In concluding this section, it appears that as well as relationship type and quality playing a role in the caregiver (and care recipient) experience, the beliefs within a dyad concerning the illness with the giving and receiving of support, and the coping strategies which are used wthin a dyad, all have a contribution to make. Whilst it appears that shared perceptions and dyadic coping are more adaptive than discrepant and individual responses, there remains a need for further study, both within adult and parent–child dyads.

SUMMARY

This chapter has described the impact that illness in a significant other can have on individuals within a family, many of whom will find that they become primary caregivers. We have described what is meant by an informal caregiver as well as considering whether the label 'carer' is helpful to those involved or not, and we have presented evidence of a complex range of influences on the caregiving role and its possible outcomes. This complexity of influence places many challenges in front of a researcher or practitioner wishing to assess caregiver outcomes, and this is against a backdrop of an increased societal need for informal care, and improvements in carer-relevant policy and services. Relationship factors have to be considered as well as individual, social and cultural influences on caring uptake and the response to the caregiving role.

Importantly, we have highlighted that caring, or being ill, does not bring with it inevitable negative consequences. We have also addressed a new and important area of research that highlights that perceptions of illness and its consequences can vary in couples living with illness, and how such discrepancies and the interdependence in relationships can influence a range of outcomes. Acknowledging and identifying the consequences of caring enables interventions to be implemented for the benefit of caregivers and those they care for, as well as potentially for society in terms of reduced social and health-care costs of caring for caregivers who themselves experience significant stress, burden or ill health.

Further reading

Loewenthal, K.M. (2007). *Religion, Culture and Mental Health*. Cambridge: Cambridge University Press.

A review of the cognitive, emotional and behavioural aspects of religion and spirituality and their association with mental health across a range of differing cultures and religious groups: for example, Roman Catholicism, Judaism, Islam. Although not addressing physical health *per se*, this is worth a look if you are interested in religion, spirituality and well-being – a contributor to 'positive psychology'.

Key papers

Adelman, R.D., Tmanova, L.L., Delgado, D. et al. (2015). Caregiver burden: a clinical review. *JAMA*, 311: 1052–1059. doi:10.1001/jama.2014.304

A well-informed and timely review of evidence with clearly tabulated checklists for discussing and assessing caregiving responsibilities and caregiver needs. The crucial role of physicians in recognising and supporting caregivers in order to optimise caregiver health and that of the care recipient is highlighted alongside a summary of existing caregiver interventions.

Pinquart, M. and Sörensen, S. (2005). Ethnic differences in stressors, resources, and psychological outcomes of family caregiving: a meta-analysis. *The Gerontologist*, 45: 90–106.

This paper integrates the findings of 116 studies which have explored ethnicity in relation to caregiver demographics, filial obligation beliefs, coping and social support processes, and health outcomes. While the majority of studies compare African-American caregivers with White caregivers, interesting findings are also gathered from Hispanic, Asian and Native Americans.

Roth, D.L., Fredman, L. and Haley, W.E. (2015). Informal caregiving and its impact on health: a reappraisal from population-based studies, *The Gerontologist*, doi: 10.1093/geront/gnu177

A potentially important paper in that it questions the evidence as to negative impacts of caregiving and in doing so highlights the positive aspects, such as mortality and longevity gains.

Weblink

www.carersuk.org

Carers UK is a charity led by carers, for carers, but useful information for researchers can be downloaded from surveys and reports commissioned by the charity.

For open-access student resources specifically written to complement this textbook and support your learning, please visit **www.pearsoned.co.uk/morrison**

Chapter 16
Pain

Learning outcomes

By the end of this chapter, you should have an understanding of:

- different types of pain

- the prevalence of chronic pain

- psychological factors that influence the experience of pain

- the gate theory of pain

- the neuromatrix theory of pain

- behavioural and cognitive-behavioural treatments of acute and chronic pain

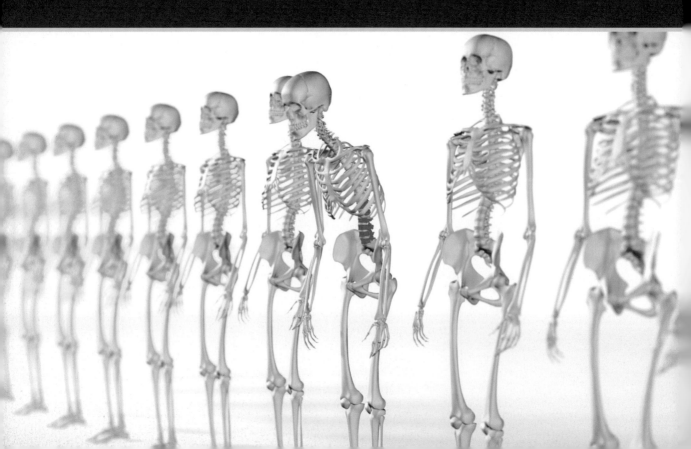

'It's good for women to suffer the pain of a natural birth', says medical chief

This headline in the *Guardian* e-newspaper went on to cite Dr Denis Walsh, 'one of the country's most influential midwives', that 'A large number of women want to avoid pain. Some just don't fancy the pain [of childbirth]. More women should be prepared to withstand pain. Pain in labour is a purposeful, useful thing, which has quite a number of benefits, such as preparing a mother for the responsibility of nurturing a newborn baby.' The *Guardian* began the article with a provocative summary of the argument: more women should endure the agony of labour because pain-relieving drugs, including epidural injections, carry serious medical risks, diminish childbirth as a rite of passage and under-mine the mother's bond with her child. This story instigated over 150 online comments – some accusing Dr Walsh of misogynist views (no man would endure this sort of pain), some (including many from women) supporting his arguments. But the issue strikes at the heart of the treatment of pain. We expect to be pain-free – and statements that medically related pain should be tolerated are controversial and against the grain. Taking medication for pain is the norm, rather than the exception. But do we seek out pharmacological or medical treatments too frequently? As we shall see in the chapter, psycho-logical processes are important both in the pain experience and in its treat-ment. Pain may not be desirable, but perhaps there should be an increasing focus on psychological approaches to pain control rather than seeking phar-macological treatments.

Source: headline from 'It's good for women to suffer the pain of a natural birth', The Guardian e-newspaper, 12/07/2009, © Guardian News & Media Ltd 2009; Denis Campbell.

Chapter outline

Pain occurs in a variety of medical conditions, and sometimes in the absence of any physical problems. So prevalent is this experience that we have taken an entire chapter to examine its aetiology and treatment. This chapter examines a number of physiological and psychological explanations for our differing experiences of pain. It first examines the experience of pain: how various types of pain are defined, how prevalent they are, and how we respond to acute and chronic pain. It then considers the role of emotion, cognitions and attention in mediating the experience of pain. The next section describes the gate theory of pain developed by Melzack and Wall, which explains how both biological and psychological factors combine to create our experience of pain. Finally, the chapter goes on to consider a number of psychological interventions used in the treatment of both acute and chronic pain. Additional or alternative treatments for many of these conditions are considered in Chapter 17 ☞, which may usefully be read in conjunction with this chapter if you are reading about the totality of psychological treatments that patients may encounter.

The experience of pain

Pain is a familiar sensation for most of us. It is functional. It is unpleasant, and it warns us of potential damage to the body. A reflex action when we feel pain is to pull away from its cause or to try and reduce it in some way. Pain may also signal the onset of disease, and is the symptom most likely to lead an individual to seeking medical help. The value of pain as a warning indicator is shown by the disadvantages experienced by those who feel no pain. People with a condition known as congenital universal insensitivity to pain (CUIP) usually die at a young age because they fail to respond to illnesses of which the main symptom is pain (such as appendicitis) or to avoid situations that risk their health (Nagasako et al. 2003). They could, for example, receive extensive burns by sitting too close to a hot fire without experiencing the warning signs that most of us take for granted.

Despite its survival benefits, when pain lasts a long time, it feels destructive and problematic. It can be so difficult to ignore that it takes over our lives. Chronic pain may be the result of long-term conditions such as rheumatoid arthritis. It may endure long after the time of

any physical damage, or even be experienced in areas of the body that no longer exist. Many people who have had an arm or leg amputated go on to experience **phantom limb pain**, in which they feel pain in their non-existent limb, sometimes for many years. Accordingly, pain can also be maladaptive and contribute to long-term problems for an affected individual.

Types of pain

Medical definitions have categorised various types of pain, including:

- *Acute pain*: despite most people's experience of acute pain as lasting only a few minutes, acute pain is defined as pain lasting less than three to six months. Some episodes of acute pain, usually involving some form of

---

phantom limb pain
a phenomenon that occurs following amputation of a limb, in which the individual feels like they still have their limb, and the limb is in pain.

injury, may occur only once, and generally the pain disappears once the damaged tissue has healed. However, acute pain may be recurrent. Conditions such as **migraine**, headaches or **trigeminal neuralgia** may involve repeated episodes of pain, each of which can be defined as 'acute' but which are also part of a longer-term condition.

● *Chronic pain:* this is pain that continues for more than three to six months. Chronic pain generally begins with an episode of acute pain that fails to improve over time. In this category, there are two broad types of pain: (1) pain with an identifiable cause such as rheumatoid arthritis or a back injury, and (2) pain with no identifiable cause. The latter is not unusual: 85 per cent of cases of back pain have no known physical cause (Deyo 1991). Chronic pain can, itself, be divided into two types:

1. *Chronic benign pain*: in which long-term pain is experienced to a similar degree over time. An example of this may be lower back pain.

2. *Chronic progressive pain*: here, the pain becomes progressively worse over time due to the progression of a disease such as rheumatoid arthritis.

Another way of thinking about types of pain is to think about the nature of the pain. Here, three dimensions of experience are frequently used:

1. *the type of pain*: including stabbing, shooting, throbbing, aching, piercing, sharp and hot;

2. *the severity of pain*: from mild discomfort to excruciating;

3. *the pattern of pain*: including brief, continuous and intermittent.

The prevalence of pain

It would be difficult to find many people who had not experienced some degree of acute pain in the last month

migraine
a headache with symptoms including nausea, vomiting or sensitivity to light. Associated with changes in vascular flow within the brain.

trigeminal neuralgia
a painful inflammation of the trigeminal nerve that causes sharp and severe facial pain.

or so, but chronic pain is also remarkably common. Currow et al. (2010) found that 18 per cent of a large Australian community sample reported some degree of chronic pain – and 5 per cent reported sufficient pain to interfere 'extremely' with activity. In an earlier study, the same group (Blyth et al. 2003) reported that the most frequently reported causes of pain were injury (38 per cent), sports injury (13 per cent) and a 'health problem' (29 per cent). Nearly 80 per cent of those who reported having chronic pain had consulted a doctor about it in the six months before the survey. Eriksen et al. (2003) reported similar prevalence levels in Denmark: 19 per cent of their community sample had some degree of chronic pain. Older people were more likely to report pain than younger people. Those who were divorced or separated were more likely to report having pain than married people. Not surprisingly, perhaps, people with jobs that involved 'high physical strain' were more likely to report chronic pain than those in more sedentary jobs. These high levels of pain appear to be a universal finding. Across Africa, 50 per cent of adults are likely to complain of lower back pain in any one year (Louw et al. 2007). Perhaps more alarming is the large numbers of young people that experience some degree of debilitating pain. Rathleff et al. (2013), for example, examined a sample of Danish schoolchildren aged between 12 and 19 years. Twenty per cent reported experiencing almost daily pain. More than half the sample reported pain or discomfort in their lower back; a quarter experienced a decreased function as a consequence of this pain. The pain appears to have been caused mainly by carrying a heavy satchel over one shoulder. Another way of looking at the prevalence of pain is to examine the use of analgesics within the general population. A Finnish study gives us some relevant data. Turunen et al. (2005) found that in a population sample of people aged 15–74 years old, 8.5 per cent used over-the-counter analgesics daily, and 13.6 per cent used analgesics at least several times a week.

Pain is a primary reason for visiting a doctor. Mantyselka et al. (2001), for example, reported that 40 per cent of primary care visits were the result of pain; 21 per cent of their sample who attended their doctor with a primary symptom of pain had experienced it for more than six months, and 80 per cent reported limited physical function due to their pain. The most common areas of pain were in the lower back, abdomen and head. Among particular patient groups, levels of pain can be even higher. Potter et al. (2003), for example, reported that 64 per cent of people receiving care from a hospice, the majority of whom had a diagnosis of terminal cancer, reported pain as one of their primary symptoms. The cost of pain is not only physical and psychological, but also economic. Maniadakis and Gray (2000) estimated the direct costs to the British health service of treating back pain in 1998 to be £1,632 million. The *indirect* costs of back pain to the economy in terms of days off sick, production losses in industry, the costs of 'informal' care of people with back pain, and so on, were even greater – an estimated £10,668 million.

Living with pain

To say that chronic pain is unpleasant is understating its potential effects. Pain can have a profound effect on an affected individual and those close to them, so much so that many people with chronic pain organise their day around their pain. They may be prevented from engaging in physical, social and even work activities. Some may even find looking after themselves on a day-to-day basis difficult. It may affect social and marital relationships, resulting in conflict between couples, which may itself exacerbate the pain (Leonard et al. 2006). It may also affect an individual's financial situation, as they may lose their job because of pain-related disability. It is noteworthy that people who have physically demanding jobs are more likely to experience pain than those in sedentary jobs – and most likely to lose them as a consequence of any physical limitations caused by pain (Eriksen et al. 2003). In an overview of qualitative exploration of the issue, Osborn and Rodham (2010) identified a number of psychological reactions to the presence of pain: confusion and worry, a feeling of 'assault on the self' and changes in self-identity, and being socially problematic. Clearly, there are more negative consequences than simply the experience of pain.

Not surprisingly, levels of depression are high among people with chronic pain (Nicholl et al. 2014). However, the direction of association between depression and pain is not always clear. Some people who are depressed may focus on bodily symptoms or minor aches and pains and be more likely to perceive them as painful 'symptoms' of disease than people who are not depressed. That is, depression may lead to high levels of reporting of pain symptoms. In other cases, the strain of living with pain and the restrictions on life that it imposes may lead to depression. There may indeed be a *reciprocal* relationship between depression and pain. People who are depressed may feel unable to cope with their pain and thus limit their activity to minimise any pain they experience. This lack of activity may lead to a stiffening of joints and muscles, which results in increased pain when they do attempt activities. This, in turn, may restrict their activity further and increase their depression. And so the cycle continues. The case of Mrs F provides an example of this.

An additional factor that may influence how people respond to pain comes from their interactions with their social environment. Pain brings a number of costs – it may also bring a number of (often unconscious) benefits to both the person in pain and those around them. Bokan et al. (1981) identified three kinds of 'gain' or reward associated with pain:

1. *primary (intrapersonal) gain:* occurs when expressions of pain (wincing, clutching painful areas, and so on) results in the cessation or reduction of an aversive consequence – for example, someone taking over a household chore that causes pain;

2. *secondary (interpersonal) gain:* occurs when pain behaviour results in a positive outcome, such as expressions of sympathy or care;

3. *tertiary gain:* the pleasure associated with helping an individual with pain.

Case history: Mrs F

I have a headache all the time. Some days are worse than others. When it's bad, its pounding and I cannot escape it. When I have a good day, I can feel it, but it is not so dominating. When I have a bad day, I don't want to do anything. I struggle to go to work as I do not want to lose my job. But I take 10 hours to do 5 hours' work. I can't concentrate, everything feels bad. I just want to lie down and not move. I don't want to do things at the weekend, but I know I must. But it really gets me down. I do things, but I'm not really all there . . . I don't enjoy them really. So, even when I do things I should enjoy I don't enjoy them like I used to . . . and knowing this makes me feel depressed, as I cannot see an end to the pain . . .

IN THE SPOTLIGHT

ETHNICITY AND PAIN

An anaesthetist who had worked in a variety of countries was describing the amount of anaesthetic he had to give to people having the same operation in different countries across Europe and the USA. He suggested that if the UK acted as a sort of 'baseline' against which to compare other countries, then people in the USA liked to be knocked out completely and not to experience any pain at all – so they needed more anaesthetic than people in the UK. By contrast, he suggested that people from Scandinavian countries expected to experience a reasonable amount of pain following surgery, so they needed less anaesthetic than people from the UK. Whether his story is true or not, it raises issues about whether there are differences in pain expectations and tolerance across countries and cultures.

A number of studies have examined similar issues, studying ethnic differences in the experience of both acute and chronic pain in the USA. Sheffield et al. (2000), for example, found that African-American participants in their study rated a series of thermal stimuli as more unpleasant and showed a tendency to rate their pain as more intense than white American participants. Incidentally, women also showed a tendency to rate the stimuli as more unpleasant and more intense than men. Similarly, Riley et al. (2002) found that African-American patients experiencing chronic pain reported significantly higher levels of pain unpleasantness, emotional response to pain and pain behaviour, but not pain intensity, than their white counterparts. In a similar study, Green et al. (2003) reported that African Americans with chronic pain reported more pain, sleep disturbance and depression than their white counterparts.

These data evoke a number of questions. The first question that has to be asked is: why are we interested in this type of issue? Why should we expect such differences, and what if anything do they tell us? Are any differences biological or genetic? Are they the result of sociocultural factors? Are they cognitively mediated? Are they the results of biased reporting of results – are there studies out there that have found no differences in pain experiences and responses between different social and ethnic groups that do not get reported? The data tell us very little about the origins of any between-group differences – and lead to dangers of ethnic stereotyping.

Ironically, these emerging stereotypes conflict with at least some health professionals' beliefs about ethnic differences in pain thresholds. What evidence there is suggests that African Americans are likely to be offered less analgesic than their white counterparts, at least in some US hospitals (see Chapter 2 ☞). But stereotypes do seem to influence our expectations of different social groups and how they are treated. Morris (1999), for example, noted that the least powerful groups within any culture are the most likely to experience disregard for their pain – and the most powerful are likely to have access to good pain relief should it be required. He cited historical examples of the disregard of pain among insane people in the eighteenth century, and black American women in the nineteenth century. One interesting belief noted by Morris was that in the eighteenth and nineteenth century labourers were thought to have 'coarse' nerves that freed them from pain while undertaking hard manual work, while upper class men and women were thought to have 'refined' nervous systems that would not allow them to engage in such labour without harm. Care should be taken not to establish more racial or ethnic stereotypes.

A further type of gain may stem from an individual's beliefs about their pain. If they believe that when they do certain things the pain they experience indicates they are causing themselves physical harm, the relief gained from avoiding that activity may also reinforce inaction and lack of activity.

These various reward systems can lead to considerable problems. If an individual in pain's expressions of pain are rewarded by outcomes they desire, and those around them gain satisfaction from providing them, this may result in them doing less and less to help themselves. This in turn may lead to increasing inactivity, muscle stiffness and wastage, which may exacerbate any problems they may have (see case history of Mr J).

Brena and Chapman (1983) described the so-called 'five Ds' that may result from such an environment:

1. dramatisation of complaints;

2. disuse through inactivity;

3. drug misuse as a result of over-medication in response to pain behaviour;

4. dependency on others due to learned helplessness and impaired use of personal coping skills;

5. disability due to inactivity.

By contrast, many people cope well with chronic pain for significant periods of time without encountering such problems, and many environments will encourage activity and minimise the pain experience. Evers et al. (2003), for example, found that patients with rheumatoid arthritis who had good social support reported less pain and better physical functioning than those who were less well supported. This may be the result of a number of factors. People who are well supported may be encouraged by friends to take part in activities which maintain function and prevent joint stiffening and other factors that contribute to pain. The emotional support that such people provide may also influence the experience of pain. Interestingly, patients with pain express similar levels of satisfaction with their partners whether they are too, inappropriately, 'supportive' or encourage independence and more positive coping strategies (Holtzman et al. 2004).

Biological models of pain

Perhaps the simplest biological theory of pain is that there are 'pain receptors' in the skin and elsewhere in the body that when activated transmit information to a centre in the brain that processes pain-related information. Once activated, this 'pain centre' produces the sensory experience of pain. This type of theory, known as a specificity theory, was first proposed in the third century BC by Epicurus and was taken up later by Descartes and others in the seventeenth century. Von Frey (1894; see Norrsell et al. 1999) added to this theory by suggesting that our skin includes three different types of nerve, each of which responds to touch, warmth or pain. These theories were further elaborated by Goldscheider (1884; see Norrsell et al. 1999), whose pattern theory of pain suggested that pain sensations occurred only when the degree of nerve stimulation crossed a certain threshold. These basic biological models of pain, with some elaboration, remained dominant until the 1960s. They were supported by the identification of nerves that were sensitive to different types of pain, and nerve tracts that led from the skin to the spine, where they linked with other nerves before leading to the brain (see below).

These theories have one common tenet: that the sensation of pain is a direct representation of the degree of physical damage or sensation sustained by the individual. This tenet has the benefit of simplicity. Unfortunately, it can easily be shown to be wrong. We have already hinted at a number of factors that influence our experience

---

Case history: Mr J

Mr J had experienced chronic backache for a number of months. Over this time, he found that certain activities increased his pain. Activities such as standing while raising his hands and lifting proved particularly difficult. Unfortunately, these activities corresponded to those involved in his usual task of preparing the evening meal. He worried that any pain he experienced was because of the position he was adopting while doing the cooking. As a result, although he did not complain about doing the cooking, he showed his pain through winces and an awkward stance at the worktop. His wife, alert to his non-verbal behaviour and not wishing her husband to be in pain, offered to do the cooking for him on a couple of occasions, and soon he stopped doing it altogether. As a result, Mr J felt better because he was avoiding his worries and a boring task, and Mrs J felt better because she cared about her husband and wanted to do the best she could for him. It seems like a win–win situation. However, both parties may eventually lose as a result of this process: Mr J because his increasing inactivity will lead to further back problems; Mrs J because she will potentially become overburdened and resentful of her role as a 'carer'.

of pain. Three other sets of evidence have been used to challenge these simple biological theories of pain:

1. pain in the absence of pain receptors;

2. 'pain receptors' that do not transmit pain;

3. the influence of psychological factors on the experience of pain.

Pain in the absence of pain receptors

Perhaps the most obvious evidence to counter these simple biological models is the evidence that many people experience pain in the absence of any nerve pain receptors. The most dramatic example of this phenomenon is known as 'phantom limb pain', which involves sensations, sometimes extremely painful, that feel located in a patient's missing limb following amputation. Up to 70 per cent of amputees report phantom limb pain a week after amputation, and over half of these people continue to experience phantom limb pain for many months or even years after their surgery (Dijkstra et al. 2002). Two years following amputation, nearly a third of patients who initially experienced phantom limb pain still experience significant pain despite using strong opiate medication (Mishra et al. 2007). Interestingly, people who have their upper limb amputated are far less likely to experience phantom limb pain than those who have had a leg amputated. Similar experiences are reported by people with spinal cord injuries and paralysis. Unfortunately, phantom limb pain is difficult to treat and can have a significant negative impact on those with the condition.

'Pain receptors' that do not transmit pain

A second physical phenomenon that presents problems for these early theories stems from the experiences of people with CUIP referred to above. Individuals with this condition may experience painless bone fractures and ulceration to their hands and feet, which may go unnoticed. They may also fail to identify pain as a symptom of severe disease and sustain dramatic injuries as a result of a failure to respond to danger signals. Some people with CUIP may even experience ulceration of the cornea of the eye as they fail to protect against strong sunlight (Nagasako et al. 2003). Individuals with CUIP appear to have intact pain

pathways, so they present the opposite problem to that posed by phantom limbs: a failure to perceive pain in the presence of an apparently intact pain pathway.

Psychological influences on pain

A number of psychological factors have been found to influence the experience of pain. Four of the key ones are:

1. *Mood*: anxiety and depression reduce pain tolerance and increase the reporting of pain.

2. *Attention*: focusing on pain increases the experience of pain.

3. *Cognitions*: expectations of increases or reductions in pain can be self-fulfilling.

4. *Social context*: the influence of others around us.

Mood and pain

Mood influences the perception of pain – and pain influences mood. Evidence of the influence of mood on the experience of pain can be found in studies in which participants are asked to rate or tolerate pain until their discomfort is too great to tolerate it any further. These have shown that people with chronic back pain who are depressed report the equivalent pain stimulus as more painful than people who are not experiencing low mood and tolerate pain for significantly less time (e.g. Tang 2008). In a classic example of this phenomenon, Fisher and Johnston (1996b) gave patients with lower back pain a simple mood induction procedure in which they were asked either about upsetting aspects of their condition or to report more positive aspects of their condition and how they were coping with it. Before and after this procedure, participants were given a plastic bag into which were placed as many packets of rice as they felt able to tolerate and then held the bag until it felt uncomfortable. In comparison with their performance at baseline, participants who reported the upsetting issues (and were therefore assumed to be more depressed) performed less well. By contrast, those whose mood was improved were able to hold the same weights for a longer period than baseline. This was an important study, as it used real patients faced with a task similar to their everyday activities.

Evidence of a reciprocal relationship between pain and mood has also been reported in a number of other studies. Magni et al. (1994), for example, followed over two thousand participants for a period of eight years. They found that participants who reported chronic pain at the begin-ning of the study were nearly three times more likely to become depressed over the follow-up period than those without this problem. By contrast, another group of people who were depressed and free of pain at the beginning of the study were over twice as likely to report having had a significant period of pain over the follow-up period. The authors speculated that depression may predict some 'pain conditions' while some 'pain conditions' may predict depression, although the nature of these two conditions was not clear. Suffice to say there is an interaction between pain and mood that can operate in both directions.

Attention and pain

One of the ways that mood may influence our perception of pain is by influencing the attention we pay to any pain sensations. Depressed or anxious people may pay more attention to pain sensations than other people, and this focus may significantly influence their experience of pain. Focusing on pain seems to increase its impact: focusing on other things seems to reduce it. For instance, many people who experience injuries while playing sports requiring effort and concentration do not notice the extent of any injuries until after the game has finished. Less anecdotally, there is evidence that fewer people experi-ence pain following physical trauma at times of intense stress, such as being on the battlefield, than when similar levels of injury are sustained in less stressful situations (Beecher 1946). This may be because of attentional factors – in the battlefield there are many important dis-tractions from one's own pain. However, other factors may also have been involved. It is possible, for example, that the soldiers were simply pleased to be alive following battle and thought that their injury would result in them being sent away from the battlefield. Civilians would be more likely to view their injuries as unwelcome and likely to interfere with their day-to-day activities. The issue here, therefore, may be the meaning ascribed to the injury and pain as much as the degree of attention paid to it.

Despite these alternative explanations, more con-trolled evaluations of the relationship between attention and pain have shown that the use of distraction can reduce pain, while experimental manipulations that increase attention to painful stimuli result in increased reporting of pain. James and Hardardottir (2002), for example, asked patients to place their lower arm in freezing cold water (an excruciatingly painful procedure known as the **cold pressor test**) and to either concentrate on a

> ### cold pressor test
> procedure in which participants place their arm in a mixture of water and ice maintaining the water temperature at between 0 and 3°C.

computer-based task or the pain sensations. Those who focused on the pain were least able to tolerate it and pulled their arm out of the water significantly earlier than those in the distraction task.

Attentional bias may also explain why some people with acute pain go on to develop chronic pain, while oth-ers do not. Vlaeyen et al. (1995) suggested that people who develop chronic pain in the absence of any clear physical injury or inflammation may respond to acute pain with a degree of fear, worry about its consequences and begin to check themselves for any pain sensations. Because they are now paying attention to a variety of aches and pains that may pass unnoticed in other people, they label their pain as symptomatic of an underlying problem. They may also stop engaging in activities that could trigger an episode of pain. In an experimental study that relates to this process, Nouwen et al. (2006) asked patients with chronic pain and individuals with no such problem to focus on the pain experienced during a cold pressor task (and therefore not related to the medical cause of their pain). Patients with chronic pain reported more pain and withdrew their hand from the water earlier than those in the control group. Further evidence of this process is provided by Dehghani et al. (2003). Their study, which used the dot probe task to explore attentional bias towards pain-related stimuli, found that people with chronic pain were more attentive to words describing the sensory expe-rience of pain than neutral words or words describing its emotional or behavioural consequences. Their results also indicated that people with high levels of fear of pain both attended to relevant words more quickly and then had dif-ficulty in focusing their attention away from them. Both results support the attentional hypothesis of chronic pain.

A number of theoretical models have elaborated on the role of attention in the experience of, and response to, pain. One example of this is Van Damme et al.'s (2010) motivational account of bias towards pain-related stimuli. This suggested we have an evolutionary bias towards automatically attending to pain, at the expense of paying attention to other goals; although, as we reported earlier in the chapter, this bias may be overrid-den at times. In addition, they argued that the individual may consciously elect to prioritise attempts at pain

Photo 16.1 The experience of pain differs according to context. Terry Butcher (in photograph) probably experienced no pain when clearly injured while playing football for England. After the match, it may have been a different story

Source: Getty Images/David Cannon.

control above other goals. With our limited attentional processing ability, this may mean increasing focus on pain reduction, and reduced attention to other life goals. A similar model was proposed by Eccleston and Crombez (1999) who identified three basic responses to pain. Firstly, the presence of pain initiates escape behaviours. Secondly, pain demands and captures attention. Thirdly, the ability of pain to capture attention and interrupt other ongoing activities is influenced by a number of characteristics of the pain: its intensity, novelty, and any emotion such as fear that it may be associated with. Pain interrupts other ongoing goal-related behaviour, with chronic pain resulting in the long-term interruption of attention towards other goals.

Cognition and pain

Mood may influence pain by influencing our thoughts about the nature and consequences of any pain. The types of thought that may influence the pain experience include:

- attributions concerning the cause of pain;
- beliefs about the ability to tolerate pain;
- beliefs about the ability to control pain;
- expectations of pain relief – the placebo effect.

A simple example of how attributions concerning the cause of pain may influence the pain experience was described by Cassell (1982) in a case report in which one patient's pain was easily controlled with codeine when they attributed it to **sciatica** but required strong opiate analgesia when they attributed the same pain to having cancer. Walsh and Radcliffe (2002) found that the beliefs of people with chronic back pain influenced their willingness to take part in an exercise programme. Those people who believed their pain was the result of physical damage to their spine were more reluctant to engage in exercise than those who attributed it to 'psychological' factors – because they were afraid that exercise would exacerbate their damaged back and increase their pain. Similarly, Murphy et al. (1997) found that the activities of people with lower back pain were more restricted by their expectations of pain than by the actual pain they experienced. They were most restricted when the pain they experienced exceeded the level of pain they expected – presumably because they considered this additional pain to indicate potential physical damage as a result of their exercise. Related to this, one particular cognitive response to pain, known as **catastrophising** (an exaggerated attribution of pain outcome: 'This pain means something is seriously wrong!') is consistently associated with poor outcomes, including reports of pre-operative pain (Roth et al. 2007), pain following physiotherapy (Hill et al. 2007), and restrictions in activity (Voerman et al. 2007). Unfortunately,

---

sciatica

pain down the leg, which is caused by irritation of the main nerve into the leg, the sciatic nerve. This pain tends to be caused where the nerves pass through and emerge from the lower bones of the spine (lumbar vertebrae).

catastrophising

the act of constructing **catastrophic thoughts.**

catastrophic thoughts

automatic thoughts that exaggerate the negative aspects of any situation.

when the cause of pain is particularly traumatic and the individual experiences high levels of stress or distress as a consequence, the experience of pain is likely to be magnified (Outcalt et al. 2014: see RESEARCH FOCUS)

People who feel able to tolerate or manage their pain are less restricted by it. Maly et al. (2007), for example, found that patients with osteoarthritis of the knee with high levels of belief in their ability to manage their pain walked more than those with less strong beliefs. Similarly, fit cyclists who believed in their ability to control or manage their pain allowed themselves to experience more painful exercise than those with lower control beliefs (Motl et al. 2007). Individuals with high control beliefs may also *experience* less pain. Jensen et al. (2001) found that among a group of patients with chronic pain involved in a pain management programme (which would not reduce the objective amount of pain experienced by the attenders), increased perceptions of control over pain were associated with reductions in reported pain. Experimental studies also provide support. In one such study, van den Hout et al. (2000) randomly assigned healthy participants to one of three preparatory conditions before they were given a cold pressor task. The preparatory conditions involved a task in which participants were given feedback either indicating high levels of control over the task, low levels of control, or no feedback. Despite the initial task being unrelated to pain, it seemed to have some carry-over to the cold pressor task, which was tolerated by the high control feedback for significantly longer than those who received low control feedback. Perceived control may also influence pain-related behaviour in patient populations. In a partial replication of their study of the effect of mood on pain behaviour described above, Fisher and Johnston (1996) allocated patients with chronic pain to conditions in which their perceptions of control over their pain were experimentally increased or decreased. Control was increased by asking patients to talk about times when they had been in control of their pain and decreased by asking them to recount periods when their control was low. Patients in the increased control condition performed their lifting task for longer than those in the decreased control condition.

Expectations of pain relief: the placebo response

One of the most fascinating phenomena associated with pain is known as the placebo response. If you were to give an inert tablet with no biochemical effects to people experiencing some degree of pain, *tell* them that it will have no effect, a percentage of those individuals (and probably quite a significant percentage) would report some relief from pain as a result of being given the 'tablet'. Red 'tablets' are more effective than blue 'tablets' in this context (Huskisson 1974). There appears some benefit to simply being given what appears to be treatment, whether this is a tablet, injection or more culturally diverse form of treatment. This phenomenon is known as the placebo effect.

A placebo (from the Latin, 'I please') is an inert preparation that has no pharmacological effects. In one of many studies of its impact, Verdugo and Ochoa (1994) examined the placebo response to an injection of saline (salt water) close to the area of maximum pain in patients with neuropathic pain – that is, pain that seems to be generated by the nerves themselves – which can be difficult to treat with conventional analgesia. Following this simple intervention, nearly two-thirds of the patients reported a 50 per cent or greater reduction in pain. In a similar study, Fine et al. (1994) tested a placebo injected into patients with chronic lower back pain. All participants in the study reported significant reductions in pain beginning between fifteen minutes and one hour after the injection and lasting up to several days. These are not unusual findings. Across a range of studies, the percentage of individuals to report at least a 50 per cent reduction in pain following being given a placebo ranges from a lowly 7 per cent to nearly 50 per cent across a variety of conditions and periods of time (McQuay and Moore 2005). Its effect is not limited to pain. The placebo effect can be found in inflammation, the speed of wound healing, immune responses to infection, and the treatment of conditions as diverse as angina, asthma and depression (Humphrey 2002). If a placebo is given following treatment with an active drug, the patient may not only show the degree of benefit in symptom reduction experienced during the active treatment, they may also experience the same side effects as they did while on the active drug (Suchman and Ader 1992).

Two key mechanisms through which the placebo effect is assumed to have its effect have been posited. The first involves a classical conditioned response, which has been implicated in immune and respiratory responses. A second process, particularly relevant to pain, involves our expectations of pain or pain relief (Price et al. 2008). We experience a reduction in pain because we expect a reduction in pain. The logic of this theory (and consistent with explanations of pain experiences described earlier in the chapter) is that if we can somehow change expectations about the efficacy or otherwise of a particular placebo treatment, then the effectiveness of that placebo treatment will also vary. In one of the few studies to attempt this, Fedele et al. (1989) found that repeated use of a placebo over several menstrual cycles in women suffering from painful periods resulted in a lowering of the placebo's success in controlling pain. Although they did not directly measure the beliefs and expectations of these women, such a finding is consistent with a gradual change of expectations in the effectiveness of the treatment leading to a reduction in placebo response. Of course, just as positive expectations can lead to a reduction in pain, negative expectations can lead to increases in pain – the nocebo response. Patients recently diagnosed as having a serious illness or patients who distrust their therapy, for example, are likely to report more pain than others (Benedetti et al. 2007).

On a slightly tangential note, the placebo effect is considered so important and pervasive that the best trials of the effectiveness of a new intervention involve a comparison with a placebo version of the intervention, for which trial participants have an equal expectation of effectiveness. To simply compare an intervention with no-treatment condition is no longer considered a good test of the effectiveness of an intervention. It must fare significantly better than a placebo to be considered an effective treatment. Medical placebos are relatively easy to construct – usually a tablet or injection identical to the real intervention. Psychological placebos are more difficult to construct, but typically involve as a minimum the same amount of time spent with the participants in some apparently 'psychological' act (e.g. a non-specific discussion of a problem) as the active therapy. Surprisingly, perhaps, despite the frequent use of placebos by medical practitioners (Howick 2013), there are few guidelines for their clinical use. Indeed, while Lichtenberg et al. (2004) produced some suggested guidelines, these or others appear not to have been formally assigned by any medical or statutory bodies. They suggested that:

- The intentions of the physician must be benevolent: their only concern should be the well-being of the patient.
- The placebo, when offered, must be given in the spirit of assuaging the patient's suffering, and not merely mollifying, silencing, or otherwise failing to address their distress.
- When proven ineffective, the placebo should be immediately withdrawn.
- The placebo cannot be given in place of another medication that the physician reasonably expects to be more effective. Administration of placebo should be considered when a patient is refractory to standard treatment, suffers from its side effects, or is in a situation where standard treatment does not exist.
- The physician should not hesitate to respond honestly when asked about the nature and anticipated effects of the placebo treatment he is offering.
- If the patient is helped by the placebo, discontinuing the placebo, in absence of a more effective treatment, would be unethical.

Socio-communication and pain

Pain is a personal experience, but it is made social through our communication of its presence to others. The chapter has already considered some of the outcomes of communicating pain in terms of behavioural gains. In a more wide-ranging model of what they termed socio-communication in pain, Hadjistavropoulos et al. (2011) examined the social influences on the experience and communcation of pain. They note that not only the expression of pain, but also its experience, can be modified by the presence of others. We can experience this on a daily basis, but more dramatically they cite the socially shared religious experiences around the world involving the intentional self-infliction of pain including self-flagellation, body piercing, and being carried on wooden frames held up by metal hooks, all of which occur in the absence of any experience of pain. By contrast, the *reported* experience of pain following observation of others experiencing pain and showing either low or high pain tolerance varies according to the condition observed, while males are likely to report less pain during the cold pressor task when in the presence of an attractive female experimenter than in the presence of a male equivalent. This reporting of pain may actually reflect 'actual' pain experiences, as they have been shown to influence not only reporting of pain but also activity in brain areas known to modulate the pain experience (Jackson et al. 2005).

Hadjistavropoulos et al. note also that the expression of pain can be deliberate or incidental. Verbal reporting

RESEARCH FOCUS

Outcalt, S.D., Ang, D.C., Jingwei, W. et al. (2014). Pain experience of Iraq and Afghanistan veterans with comorbid chronic pain and posttraumatic stress. *Journal of Rehabilitation Research and Development*, 51: 559-70.

Introduction

The authors note that both chronic pain and post-traumatic stress are significant health problems among military veterans. Around 19 per cent of veterans experience post-traumatic stress disorder (PTSD), and around 66 per cent them experience comorbid chronic pain. The study explored whether this co-occurrence of distress and pain results in a greater experience of pain and excess emotional and behavioural consequences among those with both conditions. They predicted that veterans with PTSD would experience greater catastrophising and less control over their pain than those with no distress, and therefore have a more debilitating pain experience.

Method

Participants were veterans involved in a randomised controlled trial of an intervention to improve functional and other pain-related outcomes in US military veterans with chronic musculoskeletal pain. All had participated in wars in Iraq and Afghanistan, had reported persistent musculoskeletal pain for at least three months and had at least 'moderate' functional limitation (a score of ≥7 on the Roland Morris Disability Scale). Those with severe medical or mental health problem conditions were excluded from participation.

Measures

Measures included those measuring: *post-traumatic stress* (Posttraumatic Stress Disorder Checklist-civilian); *pain-related disability* (Roland Morris Disability Questionnaire); *interference with behaviour due to pain* (Brief Pain Inventory); *pain catastrophising* (Pain Catastrophising Scale); *pain self-efficacy*, measuring the ability to 'handle' pain (Arthritis Self-Efficacy Scale); *pain centrality,* measuring how central is the pain to the experience of the individual's identity (Centrality of Pain Scale); depression and anxiety (the *Patient Health Questionnaire* and *Generalized Anxiety Disorder* instrument).

Mean and standard deviation of pain and affect scores in participants with and without PTSD. (All differences are significant at the p <.001 level).

Variable	PTSD	No PTSD
Pain characteristics		
Pain severity (GCPS)	72.30 ± 11.64	63.83 ± 13.76
Pain-related disability (Roland)	15.97 ± 4.26	13.06 ± 4.32
Pain interference (BPI)	6.88 ± 1.87	4.78 ± 2.05
Pain Cognitions		
Pain catastrophising (PCS)	28.59 ± 12.20	18.90 ± 11.24
Pain self-efficacy (ASES)	4.60 ± 2.20	5.95 ± 1.83
Pain centrality (CPS)	31.87 ± 7.75	25.68 ± 7.36
Affective distress		
Depression (PHQ-9)	16.32 ± 4.50	9.17 ± 5.14
Anxiety (GAD-7)	13.79 ± 4.04	6.85 ± 4.31

Results

The final sample comprised 241 participants, with an age range 21–73 years. Most were male (88.4 per cent) had served in the Army (66.4 per cent), and had recently been deployed to Iraq (75 per cent). They were now mainly employed or in training (73.4 per cent) and 'not comfortable' with their present income. Seventy-eight per cent screened positive for some degree of PTSD and 36 per cent had clinically significant symptoms. Comparisons were made between the mean scores (and their standard deviations) of those with clinical symptoms of PTSD and the rest of the sample using ANCOVA with covariates of age, gender, ethnicity, income and medical comorbidities (see table opposite).

Discussion and comment

This was a simple but powerful study that demonstrated that severe mood disturbance (in this case in the form of PTSD) is closely linked to a more severe pain experience. The study was cross-sectional, and, as always with this study design, the direction of causality between the various variables cannot indisputably be determined. The most plausible explanation for the findings is that exaggerated threat perceptions linked to pain (catastrophising), low pain self-efficacy and high pain centrality lead to increased perceptions of pain severity, disability, and interference with day-to-day activities. A further explanatory link not explored in the study was that the potential for high autonomic nervous system activation central to PTSD (people with the condition are continually on 'high alert' for danger) may also lead to a hypersensitivity to internal sensations, including those related to pain. This series of linkages was not explored in the study, but is consistent with several of the theories of pain introduced in this chapter. From a practical perspective, the study shows how important it is to consider any emotional comorbidity in people with chronic pain as it may contribute significantly to their pain experience and level of disability.

of pain usually involves self-awareness and attention being pain experience. It also allows construction of a desired response, whether this is to be honest in representing pain, or to dissemble to gain sympathy, social desirability and so on. Non-verbal responses are more likely to be unintentional (but may also carry deliberate messages). A common way of communicating pain is through our facial expression by, for example, lowering of brows, narrowing of the eyes, raising the upper lip, or parting the lips. These may be faked – although observers can frequently discriminate between genuine and faked responses – but cannot be completely hidden (Hill and Craig 2002). The ability to both express and understand pain may well be a process refined over time as it is of clear evolutionary benefit (Ickes and Decety 2009).

A psychobiological theory of pain

The evidence considered previously suggests that two sets of processes are involved in the experience of pain: one involving sensory information from the site of the painful stimulation, the other involving emotional and cognitive processes. The **gate control theory of pain** proposed by Melzack and Wall (e.g. 1965) takes both processes into account and is generally recognised as the best theoretical account of the experience of pain we now have. Melzack and Wall used the analogy of a gate to explain the pain experience. The essence of their gate control theory of pain is that the degree of pain we experience is the result of two sets of processes:

1. Pain receptors in the skin and organs transmit information about physical damage to a series of 'gates' in the spinal column (see Figure 16.1). Within the gates, these nerves link to other nerves along the spinal column that transmit information up to pain centres in the brain.

> **gate control theory of pain**
> a theory of pain developed by Melzack and Wall in which a 'gate' is used as a metaphor for the chemicals, including endorphins, that mitigate the experience of pain.

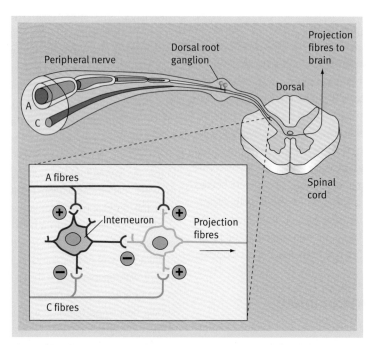

Figure 16.1 The transmission of information along the A and C fibres to the gelatinosa substantia in the spinal cord and upwards to the brain

Source: adapted from Rosenzweig, Leiman and Breedlove (1996: 272).

2. At the same time as we experience physical damage, we also experience related cognitions and emotions – fear, alarm, and so on. This information results in the activation of nerve fibres taking information from the brain down the spinal column to the gate at which the incoming pain signals enter the spinal column.

The degree of pain we experience is a result of differing levels of activation in these two systems. Activation of the sensory nerves from the site of the pain to the spinal column 'opens' the gate. This activates the nerves leading to the pain centres and is recognised as pain; that is the essence of the biological theories of pain described above. However, the downward pathways activated by emotional and cognitive factors can also influence the position of the gate. Anxious thoughts or focusing attention on pain 'open' the gate and increase our experience of pain; calming or distracting thoughts 'close' the gate. This, in effect, inhibits neural impulses travelling up through the spinal cord to the brain and reduces the experience of pain. The intensity of pain we experience at any time is a function of these two sometimes competing and sometimes complementary processes.

Pain sensations are transmitted from the site of an injury to the spinal gate by nerves known as nociceptors, three types of which have been identified:

● A delta fibres (types I and II):
  ○ respond to light touch, mechanical and thermal stimuli; carry information about brief sharp pain;
  ○ very strong noxious stimuli related to potential or actual damage to tissues; the experience is short-lasting.

● C polymodal fibres:
  ○ slow conducting; carry information about dull, throbbing, pain – which is experienced for a longer period than that from the A delta fibres.

Perhaps the most important characteristic of these different fibres is that they transmit information at different speeds. As a result, our response to injury usually involves two phases:

1. The first, mediated by A delta fibres, involves the experience of sharp pain.

2. This is followed by a more chronic throbbing pain mediated by the C polymodal fibres.

A second set of nerves, known as A beta fibres, also transmit tactile information, particularly related to gentle touch. These fibres can work to our advantage as they provide information that competes with the A delta and C fibres at the spinal column. When we receive an injury, activation of the A delta fibres is initiated and sends 'pain signals' via the spinal column to the brain. The first instinct we have following such an injury is to rub the site of the injury. This simple act reduces the amount of pain we experience. This occurs because rubbing the site of injury activates A beta fibres. Because they transmit information more quickly than C fibres, this information also reaches the brain more quickly and reduces the degree of activation that would have been triggered by the C fibres alone. Thus, in the terms of Melzack and Wall, activation of A beta fibres to touch and gentle stimuli can close the pain gate. Activation of A delta and C fibres to painful stimuli opens the gate.

The A and C fibres transmit information to areas in the spinal cord known as the substantia gelatinosa. These lie within the dorsal horn of each part of the spinal column (see Figure 16.1). Nerve impulses here trigger the release of a chemical known as substance P into the substantia gelatinosa. This, in turn, activates nerve fibres known as T(ransmitter) fibres, which transmit the sensation of pain to the brain:

● Information from A fibres is taken to the **thalamus** and on to the cortex, where the individual can plan and initiate action to remove them from the source of the pain.

● Information from the C fibres follows a pathway to the **limbic system**, **hypothalamus** and autonomic nervous system (see Chapter 8 ☛). Activity within the limbic system adds an emotional content, such as fear or alarm, to the experience of pain. The hypothalamus controls activity within the autonomic nervous system (see Chapter 8 ☛), which allows us to respond quickly to remove ourselves from harm.

The results of this neural activity are transmitted *down* the spinal column through nerve pathways known as reticulospinal fibres to the spinal gate mechanism (see Figure 16.2). These may trigger the release of a variety of chemicals into the 'soup' of chemicals in the substantia gelatinosa (and brain), the most important of which are naturally occurring opiate-like substances called endorphins. These 'close' the gate and moderate the degree of pain experienced. Activity in this system is mediated by a

> **thalamus**
>
> area of the brain that links the basic functions of the hindbrain and midbrain with the higher centres of processing, the cerebral cortex. Regulates attention and contributes to memory functions. The portion that enters the limbic system is involved in the experience of emotions.
>
> **limbic system**
>
> a series of structures in the brain, often referred to as the 'emotional computer' because of its role in coordinating emotions. It links sensory information to emotionally relevant behaviour, in particular responses to fear and anger. Includes the hippocampus, amygdala, anterior thalamic nuclei, septum and limbic cortex.
>
> **hypothalamus**
>
> area of the brain that regulates appetite, sexual arousal and thirst. Also appears to have some control over emotions.

number of factors, each of which influences the release of endorphins. These include:

● *Focusing on the pain*: worrying, or catastrophising, reduces the amount of endorphins released and opens the gate.

● *Emotional and cognitive factors*: feeling optimistic and unconcerned about the 'meaning' of the pain increases endorphin release and closes the gate – anxiety, worry, anger or depression opens the gate.

● *Physical factors*: relaxation increases endorphin release and lessens the experience of pain.

Pain medication will also 'close' the pain gate.

> **WHAT DO YOU THINK?**
>
> We have already identified a number of factors that influence our experience of pain. Think how you react to pain. Do these factors reflect your own experience of pain? And how do we come to respond to pain in the way we do? Do you rub yourself if you are bruised to ease the pain? If so, why? Did you learn to do it as a response to previous pain experiences – or were you told to do so by a parent or friend? Are you stoic in the face of pain? If so, is this a result of how others have expected you to respond? 'Big boys don't cry':

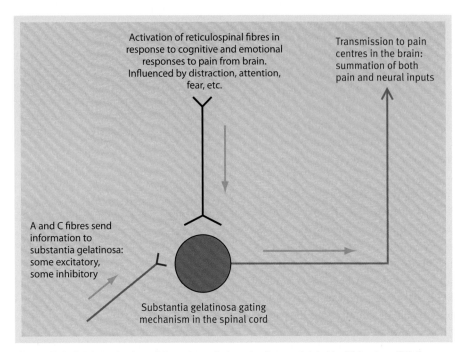

Activation of reticulospinal fibres in response to cognitive and emotional responses to pain from brain. Influenced by distraction, attention, fear, etc.

Transmission to pain centres in the brain: summation of both pain and neural inputs

A and C fibres send information to substantia gelatinosa: some excitatory, some inhibitory

Substantia gelatinosa gating mechanism in the spinal cord

Figure 16.2 A schematic view of the gate control mechanism postulated by Melzack and Wall

Cultural and childhood experiences may encourage different ways of expressing both emotional and physical pain in men and women. Do they affect how you respond to pain? Or do you respond in ways determined by your personality? People who are generally anxious may be more prone to respond to pain with catastrophic thinking, anxiety and high levels of physiological arousal – resulting in a relatively high experience of pain (and other labelling of bodily sensations as 'symptoms' of disease: see Chapter 9 (☞)). People who are more relaxed and optimistic may have a less emotional response to pain and experience relatively less pain. Is this the case for you?

Future understandings of pain: the neuromatrix

Despite the success of the gate theory of pain, it has still struggled to account for phantom limb pain: pain in the absence of stimulation by the A and C fibres. In response to these limitations, Melzack (2005) has developed a more complex theory of the mechanisms of pain that attempts to explain this mysterious phenomenon. His model has three key assumptions:

1. The same neural processes that are involved in pain perception in the intact body are involved in pain perception in the phantom limb.

2. All the qualities that we normally feel from the body, including pain, can be felt in the absence of inputs from the body.

3. The body is perceived as a unity and is identified as the 'self', distinct from other people and the surrounding world.

Melzack contended that the anatomical substrate of the 'body-self' is a large, widespread network of neurons linking the thalamus, cortex and limbic system in the brain. He termed this system the 'neuromatrix'. We process and integrate pain-related information within the neuromatrix. Related information about a pain experience (physical elements of the injury, emotional reactions to the injury, and so on) combine to form a 'neurosignature' or network of information about the nature and emotional reaction to a pain stimulus. Neurosignatures have two components:

1. *the body-self matrix*: processes and integrates incoming sensory and emotional information;

2. *the action neuromatrix*: develops behavioural responses in response to these networks.

Behavioural responses to pain can only occur after information about the nature of the pain, its cause, and physical and emotional consequences have been, at least, partially processed and integrated. We do not move away from a hot object, for example, until we realise that it is the cause of pain and that continuing to be near it will cause further pain and potential injury. We only become consciously aware of pain after this integrated network of information is then projected to what Melzack terms the 'sentient neural hub': the seat of consciousness. Here, the stream of nerve impulses is converted into a continually changing stream of awareness.

So far, Melzack's new theory does not explain the experience of phantom limb pain. This moves us from an explanation of how we feel pain from external sources to one explaining how we feel pain generated by the body itself. Melzack suggested that the neuromatrix is pre-wired to 'assume' that the limbs can move. Accordingly, in people who have had limbs removed, the body still sends signals to try to move them. When they do not move in response to these signals, stronger and more frequent messages may be sent to the muscles, and these are perceived as pain. Melzack's theory of pain is still relatively new and has only recently been subjected to empirical research. However, what data there are provide broad support for the existence of a neuromatrix, but we have yet to locate it within any particular brain area (Derbyshire 2000). That said, not all the phenomena of phantom limb pain can be explained by the neuromatrix. In particular, it fails to explain why the reduction or elimination of other sensations associated with the experience of the phantom limb is not accompanied by reductions in pain, how phantom limb pain can spontaneously cease, and why not all patients experience this type of pain (Giummarra et al. 2007).

Helping people to cope with pain

The first-line treatment for *acute* pain is generally some form of pharmacological treatment – varying in strength from aspirin to some form of opium derivative such as pethidine. Psychological interventions generally form a second-level intervention. The American Agency for Health Care Policy (1992), for example, suggested that these should be used for those who find this type of intervention 'appealing', where patients may benefit from reducing or avoiding pharmacological treatment, have high levels of anxiety, would need prolonged pain relief and/or who have incomplete pain relief following pharmacological intervention. By contrast, increasing numbers of patients with *chronic* pain resulting from conditions as varied as rheumatoid arthritis and lower back pain are being taught to manage their pain using psychological approaches in order to minimise the amount of painkilling medication they need to take and to maintain or improve their quality of life. It is important that the effectiveness of these interventions is evaluated as part of the day-to-day care of patients as well as in research studies. So, before we look at some of the approaches used to treat both acute and chronic pain, we examine some simple, and not so simple, ways of measuring pain.

Measuring pain

The simplest measure of pain involves the use of a simple linear visual analogue or numerical rating scales – typically varying from a score of 0, registering no pain, to 100, rating the most pain you could imagine. This type of measure is quick to administer and score and is frequently used in clinical settings. A limitation of the approach is that patients often find it quite difficult to consider pain in numerical terms. Another simple approach involves patients rating their pain on a series of adjectives denoting increasing pain: mild, distressing, excruciating, and so on. This has the advantage of being more easily comprehensible to patients than numeric scales – it uses concepts patients are more familiar with. However, this approach has its disadvantages, as many patients tend to rate themselves somewhere in the middle of such scales, making them less sensitive to subtle differences in pain than analogue scales.

One important limitation of these measures is that they simply measure the sensation of pain. However, we have already noted that the experience of pain is multidimensional. It involves emotional, cognitive and behavioural responses as well as sensory experiences. A number of measures have tried to address these inadequacies. Perhaps the best known of these is the McGill pain questionnaire (e.g. Melzack 1975). This is more complicated to administer and interpret than the simple scales described above. However, it provides a multidimensional understanding of the nature of the pain that an individual is experiencing. In its various forms, it measures:

- *the type of pain*: including throbbing, shooting, stabbing, cramping, gnawing, hot and tender, using a four-point scale from 'none' to 'severe';
- *the emotional response to the pain*: including tiring, exhausting, fearful and punishing;
- *the intensity of the pain*: on a scale from 'no pain' to 'worst possible pain';
- *the timing of pain*: whether it is brief, continuous or intermittent.

While this measure extends our assessment of pain, it does not address all the responses to it. It does not, for example, measure pain in relation to movement or measure an individual's behavioural response to pain. How much does it restrict their daily life? Can they walk up stairs, or lift heavy weights? These may all have to be measured separately. To remedy these deficits, Turk and Okifuji (1999) suggested that one can also measure:

- *verbal/vocalisations*: sighs, moans, complaints;
- *motor behaviour*: facial grimacing, distorted gait (limping), rigid or unstable posture, excessively slow or laboured movement, seek help/pain reducing behaviour;
- *treatment behaviours*: taking medication, use of protective device (e.g. cane, cervical collar), visit doctor;
- *functional limitations*: resting, reduced activity.

Each of these may become a target for some of the interventions discussed below.

Treating acute pain

A number of approaches have been used to help people to cope with acute pain. Any procedures used need to be relatively easy to learn and use. Accordingly, most approaches to acute pain control have focused on:

- increasing patients' sense of control over the pain experience and medical procedures that may be causing the pain;
- teaching coping skills, including distraction techniques and relaxation;
- hypnosis.

Some of these are discussed further in the context of preparing people for the experience of surgery in Chapter 10 ☛. Here, we address other ways of achieving these goals.

Increasing control: patient-controlled anaesthesia

The experience of pain following trauma or surgical operations can be made worse by patients' fears that they cannot control their pain. They may be frightened that when they are in significant pain the nurses may be too busy to give them painkillers, that the pain will be so bad that it will not be controlled by the type of painkiller they will be given, and so on. To alleviate such fears, patients may exaggerate reports of pain or pester healthcare professionals to give them painkillers in order to avoid periods of inadequate analgesia. This may result in them experiencing unnecessary anxiety and using more medication than necessary.

One way that each of these issues can be addressed is through the use of **patient-controlled analgesia (PCA)**. Using this method, the patient controls how much analgesic drug they receive through an intravenous drip – albeit with some controls built into the delivery system so they cannot exceed a specified dosage. It is assumed that because patients can control the timing of their pain relief, they will be less anxious about the control of their pain, be more satisfied with their analgesia and use less analgesic. Systematic reviews of this approach (e.g. Momeni et al. 2006) suggest that this is the case – and its use has even been advocated in patients with a pre-existing opioid dependency, as the overall amount of drug delivered by the system can be appropriately limited (Mehta and Langford 2006). Children can also use PCA systems. Birmingham et al. (2003) reported data from over a hundred children for whom PCA was used for acute postoperative pain control. Satisfactory analgesia was obtained in 90 per cent of cases, with no evidence of toxicity or serious adverse effects. It therefore

> **patient-controlled analgesia (PCA)**
> a technique through which small doses of analgesic drugs, usually opioids, are administered (usually by an intravenous drip and controlled by a pump) by patients themselves. It is mostly used for the control of postoperative pain.

seems a safe, beneficial form of treatment for a wide range of people.

Teaching coping skills

Distraction

We have already noted in the chapter that focusing on pain tends to increase the experience of pain, while distraction decreases it. Given the apparent simplicity of teaching distraction techniques, these would seem to be sensible strategies to teach patients who are in acute pain or who have to undergo painful procedures. The procedure seems to work. Callaghan and Li (2002), for example, taught women undergoing a hysterectomy to distract themselves from worrisome thoughts prior to their operation. Compared with women given only information about the procedure, they reported less pain and evidenced less distress after the operation. Fauerbach et al. (2002) also reported success after teaching distraction skills (in this case concentrating on music) – but only if patients actively focused on the music rather than simply trying not to think of the pain. More technologically based interventions, including the use of virtual reality games have also been shown to reduce the pain experienced during a number of medical procedures (Mott et al. 2008).

Relaxation

A second relatively simple approach that can be taught to patients is the use of relaxation. This involves teaching people to relax the muscles throughout their body, particularly those close to the site of the pain (see Chapter 13 ☞). This has a number of advantages. Firstly, it can be used to reduce any muscular tension that can contribute to the experience of pain. Secondly, because relaxation instructions may explicitly involve thinking about pleasant images, or at least images inconsistent with the painful situation, it may act as a form of distraction. The concentration involved in relaxing may also distract from pain sensations. Finally, there is evidence that relaxation promotes endorphin release and thus has a direct impact on the pain experience. There is ample evidence that relaxation procedures can help reduce levels of pain and distress associated with postoperative pain. Renzi et al. (2000), for example, reported that patients undergoing major bowel surgery who used relaxation experienced less pain, less distress and better sleep following surgery than a control group receiving 'standard care'. Similarly, Friesner et al. (2006) found

that relaxation combined with the use of opiate drugs was superior to opiate drugs alone during a short but painful surgical procedure involving removal of a tube inserted into the chest during coronary artery bypass surgery. The evidence in support of relaxation has been so consistent that the American National Institutes of Health consensus panel (National Institutes of Health Technology Assessment Panel 1996) concluded that relaxation procedures should be adopted for general use.

Hypnosis

Hypnosis is a procedure during which a health professional suggests that a patient experience changes in sensations, perceptions, thoughts or behaviour. The hypnotic context is generally established by an induction procedure. Although there are many different hypnotic inductions, most include suggestions for relaxation, calmness and well-being. Instructions to imagine or think about pleasant experiences are also commonly included in hypnotic inductions. It has been shown to have a reliable and significant effect on acute pain. Lang et al. (2006), for example, found self-hypnosis to reduce both pain and anxiety associated with having a needle breast biopsy. Not only can hypnosis reduce pain, but it may also aid patients' physical recovery. Ginandes et al. (2003) examined the effects of hypnosis on pain and wound healing following breast surgery. They allocated women to three interventions following surgery: usual care (normal analgesia); sessions with a counsellor providing unstructured support; and hypnosis, in which they focused on relaxation and 'accelerated wound healing' as part of the instructions ('Imagine your wound healing well'). They measured the women's pain and level of wound healing one week and seven weeks following the interventions and found that the wounds of the women in the hypnosis condition healed significantly more quickly than those in the others. They also experienced less pain over the course of their recovery. The benefits of self-hypnosis need not be restricted to adults (see Tomé-Pires and Miró 2012). Liossi et al. (2009) provide an example of the use of hypnosis in the control of pain during venipuncture (blood taken through a needle) in children aged between 6 and 16 years. The children were taught self-hypnosis techniques involving images including a switch to modulate the experience of pain, feelings of numbness, and the experience of anaesthesia across the hand. They were then encouraged to use this approach up to an hour before experiencing venipuncture. Those who received the hypnosis intervention experienced less anticipatory anxiety as well as less pain during the procedure itself.

Treating chronic pain

Transcutaneous electrical nerve stimulation (TENS)

Before examining psychological interventions to reduce chronic pain, we first consider a popular method of pain control, based on the electrical stimulation of A beta fibres in order to compete with the pain signals of pain-related nerves (see discussion earlier in the chapter) and stimulate C fibres to result in endorphin release. Transcutaneous electrical nerve stimulation (TENS) involves the use of a small electrical device, about the size of a personal stereo, that is connected by wires to electrodes, placed on the skin in the area of the pain. This allows a small, low-intensity electric charge to be passed across the area. Such stimulation devices are typically used for between 15 to 20 minutes, several times a day, and are controlled by the user. A Canadian review (Reeve et al. 1996) in which the authors examined the use of TENS across Canada, was broadly supportive of its use. They surveyed 50 hospitals with 200 or more beds, and estimated that over 450,000 uses of TENS took place in Canadian hospitals each year, with widespread use in the treatment of acute pain (used by 93 per cent of hospitals), pain associated with labour and delivery (43 per cent), and chronic pain (96 per cent).

Unfortunately, much of the evidence related to TENS is so poor, it does not provide a good basis for making judgements about its value and justifying its use. Al Smadi et al. (2003), for example, found that TENS was no better than TENS placebo in the treatment of low back pain in people with multiple sclerosis. However, they randomly allocated only five people to each treatment group – making any statistically significant treatment effect almost impossible to find. As a consequence of this limited evidence base, Nnoaham and Kumbang (2010) felt they could come to no conclusion about the effectiveness of TENS as a stand-alone treatment for acute pain, while Claydon et al. (2011) concluded there was strong evidence of a *lack* of effectiveness in all types of pain other than that associated with pressure.

Relaxation and biofeedback

Relaxation can be used to relax the whole body or to relax specific muscle groups such as those on the forehead or back, which contribute to headaches and back pain, respectively. The latter may be of particular benefit in some patients. Turk (1986), for example, noted that many patients who were taught general relaxation for the treatment of back pain generally reported reductions in pain. However, one small sub-group of individuals reported either no benefit or even an increase in pain following the intervention. Closer assessment revealed that, while many people in this group had been able to relax most of their muscles, they had been unable to relax the particular muscles in their back that were contributing to their pain. To do this, they needed guidance on relaxing these specific muscles. This can be achieved through the use of **biofeedback** techniques, including electromyographic biofeedback, galvanic skin response and thermal biofeedback:

- *Electromyographic (EMG) biofeedback:* measures the small amount of electrical current in the muscles. The voltage equates with muscle tension: higher voltage = higher tension. Uses electrodes stuck to the skin over specific muscles that contribute to pain, and provides the most direct and accurate form of feedback.

- *Galvanic skin response (GSR):* measures general tension in the body by measuring subtle changes in the moisture (sweat) typically of the hand. Increased sweat relates to increased general muscle tension – although the relationship is far from one-to-one.

- *Thermal biofeedback:* based on a theory that warming the skin can reduce the pain of headaches. Skin temperature is measured by a thermistor, often placed on the back of the fingers to avoid sweat and to provide a more accurate gauge of body temperature.

More recently, Shiri et al. (2013) investigated the effectiveness of 'virtual reality' feedback in which children practised relaxation wearing a virtual reality system and were able to achieve positive pain-free images of themselves.

> **biofeedback**
> technique of using monitoring devices to provide information regarding an autonomic bodily function, such as heart rate or blood pressure. Used in an attempt to gain some voluntary control over that function.

Whatever the mode of measurement, biofeedback helps patients to make changes (relax, increase finger temperature) guided by some form of feedback of any physiological changes they produce. In the case of auditory feedback, for example, a tone may become lower as the person relaxes their muscles. Visual feedback may involve moving an indicator along a scale as they do the same. In this way, changes in physiology that the patient may not recognise without feedback are made apparent and the patient can learn how to improve and replicate the response.

One particular problem in which biofeedback has been used with some success is in the treatment of chronic headaches (Andrasik 2010). Rains et al. (2005), for example, reported that biofeedback interventions resulted in between 35 per cent and 55 per cent improvements in migraine and tension-type headaches. These improvements are about three times as large as any gains following some form of placebo intervention, and the equivalent to gains achieved by medication. So effective is biofeedback in the treatment of tension headache, the European Federation of Neurological Sciences (Bendsten et al. 2010) guidelines recommended its use, noting at the same time that cognitive-behavioural interventions and relaxation are also 'likely' to be effective. However, while biofeedback may be an effective intervention in other forms of pain, it is generally no more effective than relaxation alone. As relaxation is both simpler and cheaper to implement, for these sorts of pain, relaxation rather than biofeedback, should perhaps be the first-line treatment, with biofeedback only used under particular circumstances, such as those identified by Turk earlier in this section. If relaxation techniques are to be augmented, it may be better to do so using strategies that address other aspects of the pain experience than the physiological ones.

One such alternative strategy has been to combine relaxation with antidepressant medication. No one has fully explained why antidepressant medication helps to reduce pain, but it has consistently been shown to do so. With this in mind, Holroyd et al. (2001) compared treatment with antidepressant medication, training in relaxation techniques, a combination of the two, and a placebo drug therapy. The results were encouraging for both

Photo 16.2 Biofeedback has proven to be an excellent treatment for specific pain due to muscle tension such as headache. However, in many cases, simple relaxation may prove as effective

Source: Science Photo Library/Will & Deni Mcintyre.

interventions. Both antidepressant and cognitive-behavioural techniques proved to be more effective than the placebo on measures including the frequency of head-aches, analgesic medication use and restrictions in activity as a result of the headache. Although both single active interventions were equally effective, patients who received the pharmacological medication experienced these changes more quickly than those in the cognitive-behavioural inter-vention. Nevertheless, the combined therapy proved the most effective. This resulted in clinically significant reduc-tions on a combined index of headache severity in 64 per cent of participants in this condition. This compared with 38 per cent of those in the antidepressant condition, 35 per cent of those receiving stress management, and 29 per cent of those in the placebo condition.

Behavioural interventions

The first modern psychological intervention for pain involved behavioural interventions, based on operant conditioning processes. The treatment model, initially developed by Fordyce (1976), is based on the premise that we cannot truly understand the pain experience of others; all we can do is observe 'pain behaviour'. Fordyce argued that this behaviour should, therefore, form the target of any intervention, not the unobservable inner experience. Operant theory states that pain behav-iour may be established and controlled not only by the experience of pain but also by how others respond to expressions of pain. Pain behaviour may be as subtle as gentle winces or as obvious as lying down unable to move as a result of apparently unbearable pain. It may be reinforced by expressions of sympathy, being 'let off' tasks about the home, given analgesia, and so on (see Bokan et al. 1981, earlier in the chapter).

The aim of behavioural interventions is to reduce dis-ability by changing the environmental contingencies that influence pain behaviour – to remove the individual from any reinforcement of their pain behaviour. Instead, non-pain-related, adaptive behaviour is reinforced. The methods used include:

- reinforcement of adaptive behaviour such as appro-priate levels of exercise;

- withdrawal of attention or other rewards that were previous responses to pain behaviour;

- providing analgesic medication at set times rather than in response to behaviour.

In this way, new forms of behaviour are encouraged through appropriate reinforcement, and older maladap-tive behaviour is extinguished through non-reinforce-ment. The approach may involve both health professionals and others with whom the patient interacts, including their partner or even friends.

Depending on the nature of the presenting problem, these processes may be added to by other interventions. In the case of lower back pain, for example, where dis-use may have resulted in a weakening of the back mus-cles, patients may take part in exercise programmes. In these, patients will typically engage in a number of exercise trials to identify their tolerance for various lift-ing activities and movements. The programme will then advance them through a series of progressively more difficult steps towards full mobility and strength. Success at each stage of the intervention is positively rewarded by the health-care professionals involved in the treat-ment programme.

Early studies of this approach were often case histo-ries, as the approaches used to treat individual cases were necessarily quite different. Fordyce (1976), for example, reported a case in which they moved a hospital patient who was engaging in excessive pain behaviour into a single room, the door of which could be closed if necessary. This prevented the patient trying to attract the attention of nurses in the ward. Rewards for non-pain behaviour and 'punishments' for pain-related behaviour were achieved by entering and leaving the room if the patient inappropriately demanded pain medication or staying for social chat if they did not do so. These vari-ous case reports indicated the potential for this type of treatment. More recently, the development of standard-ised behavioural programmes in the treatment of a vari-ety of disorders, including back pain, has meant that their effectiveness can be assessed using group designs. Back pain is frequently, and successfully, treated using behavioural methods, possibly because it is a common disorder that often has no obvious pathology but which can cause significant impairment. Van Tulder et al. (2003), for example, reported a meta-analysis of the effects of behavioural programmes on lower back pain, and concluded that there was strong evidence that behav-ioural treatments were of significant benefit on measures of reported pain, improvements in mobility and lifting capacity, and on behaviour away from the clinic. The shift from behavioural to cognitive-behavioural interventions in general has also been seen within pain treatment programmes, which now often combine behavioural and cognitive elements.

Cognitive-behavioural interventions

Behavioural interventions clearly work by changing behaviour, but these changes may also influence other parts of the pain experience. Active engagement in activities may distract patients from negative cognitive and emotional responses to pain. Re-engaging in activities previously stopped may increase self-efficacy beliefs and optimism ('Wow – I didn't think I was going to be able to do that. Perhaps I can do some other things I've stopped doing'). That is, behavioural programmes may *indirectly* change pain-related cognitions, and these changes may contribute to any improvements that patients make. Cognitive-behavioural approaches tackle these issues more directly. They focus on the cognitions mediating our emotional and behavioural responses to pain. Cognitions are seen as central to our experience of pain, and our reactions to it. As such, the model does not contradict the model of pain provided by the gate control model – it focuses on one group of variables that influence the gate. The goals of cognitive-behavioural therapy (CBT) for pain are threefold:

1. To help patients alter their beliefs that their problems are unmanageable. To help them to become 'resourceful problem solvers' and move away from feeling unable to cope with their pain.

2. To help patients identify the relationship between their thoughts, emotions and behaviour, and in particular how catastrophic or other negatively biased thoughts can lead to increased perceptions of pain, emotional distress and psychosocial difficulties.

3. To provide patients with strategies to manage their pain, emotional distress and psychosocial difficulties, and in particular to help them to develop effective and adaptive ways of thinking, feeling and behaving.

Cognitive-behavioural interventions can take the form of both individual and group interventions. Cognitive change is brought about in a number of stages (see also the discussion of stress management skill in Chapter 13 ☞). In these, patients are helped to identify any maladaptive thoughts that are increasing their experience of pain or their disability. This can be achieved by discussion in therapy sessions in which patients reflect back on periods of pain or when they have been frightened to engage in particular behaviour. Any thoughts that occurred at such times are identified and discussed. Patients may also be asked to monitor their thoughts during their day-to-day activities by completing a diary in which they record their level of pain, accompanying thoughts and mood.

Once patients have begun to identify how their thoughts influence the level of pain they experience, their behaviour and their mood, they are taught to change the nature of their thoughts to more adaptive ones. This may involve two types of cognitive intervention. The first is known as self-instruction training. In this, patients are taught to change the commentary in their head at times of worry or concern about their pain or activities to a more positive commentary. This can be pre-rehearsed and thought through with the therapist. Such thoughts include reassuring commentaries, such as *'I've had pain like this before and it didn't do me any harm in the long run'* or *'The pain only means I'm extending myself, not doing myself any damage'*. Other thoughts may involve reminders to use other strategies to help to control the pain: *'OK! When the pain starts, remember to relax so I don't add to it with tension'*, and so on.

A more complex cognitive process involves trying to identify the thoughts that are driving any emotional distress or inhibiting behaviour and challenging them. This involves treating them not as truths but as hypotheses, and challenging the hypotheses by looking for contrary evidence. In practice, these types of challenge may not be that different to the self-instructions, but they may be more targeted at particular worries or concerns:

> Oh no! My back's beginning to hurt again. I know that means I'm going to be in pain for hours – I'd better stop now and take it easy. Hang on! Remember the last time this happened; I didn't feel that bad, particularly after relaxing and slowing down a bit. So take it easy – keep going . . . I'll feel better in myself for trying.

These cognitive interventions are often accompanied by a programme of gradually increasing exercise. This may have a number of advantages. First, and most obviously, it will increase fitness and minimise restriction of activities. In addition, it allows patients to learn from their own experience that they will not be harmed by exercising – and therefore confirm some of the new beliefs that the cognitive therapy is trying to instil.

Other interventions may also be provided. One frequently used intervention involves teaching people to relax their muscles throughout their body and, particularly, close to the site of the pain (see above in the case of acute pain). Hanson and Gerber (1990) summarised a number of strategies for coping with periods of particularly intense pain that can be taught in a cognitive-behavioural programme, including:

- stop and ask myself if I can identify the pain trigger or learn anything from this pain;

- begin slow, deep breathing and remind myself to keep calm; review my alternatives;

- identify some distracting activities – a conversation with my partner about anything but the pain, a crossword puzzle, baking biscuits, etc.;

- take a long, hot shower;

- listen to relaxation or self-hypnosis tape;

- use positive self-talk – 'The pain won't last. I can handle this on my own';

- use pain-modification imagery – 'Imagine a block of ice resting on my back, see my endorphins working to counter the pain', and so on.

This section has been a long one, reflecting the wide use of cognitive-behavioural interventions in pain clinics throughout the world. It is therefore somewhat disappointing to end with the findings of a prestigious review of psychological therapies for the management of non-headache chronic pain, conducted by Williams et al. (2012) which arrived at a somewhat negative conclusion. Based on the findings of 35 studies with nearly 5,000 participants, they found no evidence of the effectiveness of behaviour therapy, and that cognitive-behaviour therapy was significantly more effective than no treatment on measures of disability, catastrophising, disability and mood in the short but not long term. However, there was little evidence of any advantage when compared with active or placebo interventions. That is, there was little evidence of a specific benefit directly attributable to the use of cognitive-behaviour therapy. More positively, the same group concluded that cognitive-behavioural interventions *are* effective in the treatment of both non-headache and headache pain in children (Eccleston et al. 2012) and we have already noted the benefits of biofeedback in the treatment of adult headache (Bendsten et al. 2010). Accordingly, behavioural or cognitive-behavioural interventions have the potential to be of benefit, but the likelihood of this is perhaps less than was originally

thought and hoped. One of the difficulties many patients who are referred for cognitive-behavioural therapy experience is that it presents a very different model of pain and its treatment to that which they are used to. Often because patients are frequently offered cognitive-behavioural therapy at the end of a long chain of medical or surgical treatments – most of which have failed, but which have emphasised the medical rather than psychological aspects of their condition (see Case history box), they may find it difficult to adopt this approach or find it disappointing that cognitive-behavioural interventions are not designed to reduce pain, but help people cope with it. Interviews with patients on a pain control programme conducted by Bair et al. (2009) found a number of other factors associated with low adherence including: lack of support from friends and family, limited resources, depression, ineffectiveness of pain-relief strategies, time constraints and other life priorities, physical limitations and poor patient–physician relationships. While adherence to any programme may be less than ideal, those that do adhere to programmes even when waiting for medical treatment do appear to benefit (McCracken et al. 2013). Perhaps future research needs to consider not just is cognitive-behaviour therapy for pain effective, but who benefits most from it.

Whatever the overall outcomes of cognitive-behavioural therapy, there is mounting evidence that cognitive change *is* an important mediator of change in therapy. In a relatively early study of this phenomenon, J. Burns et al. (2003) found that the cognitive changes patients made in the early stages of a cognitive-behavioural programme were strongly predictive of pain outcomes later in therapy. They took measures of catastrophising and pain at the beginning, end and middle of a four-week cognitive-behavioural pain management programme. Early changes on the measure of catastrophising were predictive of pain measures taken at the end of therapy. By contrast, early changes in pain did not predict changes in catastrophising. Turner et al. (2007) came to similar conclusions using data from patients with **temporomandibular disorder pain**. In this group,

---

temporomandibular disorder pain
a variety of conditions that cause tenderness and pain in the temporomandibular joint (hinge joint of the jaw).

Case history: Mr W

I came to this clinic [for cognitive-behavioural therapy] after years of looking for a treatment for my back pain. The doc sends you here, there, everywhere looking for the answer. I've had pain killers, TENS, physiotherapy, manipulation . . . and then surgery. Every time you go to the next treatment, you have that little ray of hope that this will provide the cure! I've even gone to the alternative people in the hope that they would help. The weirdest thing I have had was something called cranial manipulation . . . supposed to relieve the nerves or something. But every one you hope the pain will go . . . even if you don't believe it quite as strongly

with different treatments! But this has been different. Rather than trying to take the pain away, the course has focused on helping me cope with the pain. That was the first shock on the course – and it was disappointing. I expected that you could get rid of it, not keep it . . . and let me cope better! I was quite depressed for a few days when I learned this . . . but I guess I had to stick it out. I don't have much choice. But I must admit, as the course has gone on, it has helped. The relaxation really helps me. I can take myself away from the pain for a while if I imagine stuff. And at least I know I can cope with the pain, and won't let it stop me doing things like I used to...

changes in pain beliefs (control over pain, disability and pain signals harm), catastrophising and self-efficacy in relation to managing pain mediated the effects of cognitive-behavioural therapy on pain, activity interference and jaw-use limitations at one year.

Mindfulness-based interventions

As mindfulness-based interventions are becoming increasingly used in mental health settings, so are they in physical health settings – and with good effect. Meize Grochowski et al. (2015), for example, found that daily mindfulness meditation proved highly effective in reducing the pain associated with post herpetic neuralgia in a population of older adults.

An interesting uncontrolled study was reported by Rosenzweig et al. (2010), who as part of a larger study compared the effectiveness of mindfulness training in patients with a number of different types of pain and found marked differences in effectiveness. Most patients, with conditions as varied as back and neck pain, showed gains on measures of pain intensity and functional limitations. Patients with fibromyalgia, or tension or migraine headaches reported minimal benefit, while those with arthritis reported the greatest improvements. Of note was that increased use of meditation was not associated with greater gains on measures of pain or quality of life. Zautra et al. (2008) made a direct comparison of CBT and mindfulness in a group of patients with rheumatoid arthritis. Their outcome measures included a measure of pain and inflammation (interleukin 6). Overall, those in the CBT

group achieved the greatest changes in both measures. However, patients with a history of recurrent depression achieved greater changes on measures of joint tenderness and mood following the mindfulness training than did those in the CBT group. By contrast, Davis et al. (2015) found that, while mindfulness and CBT appeared to be of equal benefit in reducing pain, mindfulness proved superior in reducing catastrophic beliefs about the nature and implications of pain, morning disability and fatigue. These differing benefits, and lack of overall superiority of one approach over the other, is perhaps reflected in an increasing number of programmes that combine traditional CBT with mindfulness training (Day et al. 2014).

Some researchers are now evaluating innovative strategies to provide mindfulness-based interventions – in ways that are both effective and cost-effective. In one such study, Gardner-Nix et al. (2008) compared a mindfulness chronic pain intervention delivered using a group face-to-face format with the same intervention using a videoconferencing facility to patients in their own homes. Outcomes of these two active interventions were compared to those of a waiting list control group. Both groups made more gains on a measure of pain than those in the control condition. However, those who received the face-to-face intervention scored more highly than the remote group on measures of 'usual pain'. A second innovative approach was adopted by Johnston et al. (2008), who examined the impact of a self-help book related to acceptance and commitment therapy (see Chapter 13 ☞). Participants read the book and completed related exercises over a period of six weeks, with the support of weekly telephone calls. The intervention had a modest impact on pain, while also resulting in greater changes in acceptance, quality of life, and satisfaction with life.

Pain management clinics

So far, we have considered treatments for pain in isolation, without considering who provides the treatment or where patients may go for treatment. Nowadays, many hospitals provide services specifically for people with chronic pain – of whatever origin. These services will involve a number of people. Doctors, usually anaesthetists, provide expertise in the pharmacological and even surgical treatment of pain. Physiotherapists work with patients to develop exercise programmes that they can realistically expect to be able to engage in. Occupational therapists may work with patients to consider how they can improve their day-to-day activities around the home if their mobility is restricted. Specialist nurses may work with patients to develop pain management plans for individuals or groups of individuals. Psychologists may also contribute to and develop such programmes. Table 16.1 shows the outline of a typical outpatient pain management programme – conducted at the Gloucester Royal Hospital in the UK.

Table 16.1 Outline of a typical pain management programme, in this case run at the Gloucester Royal Hospital in the UK

WEEK 1	Welcome, introduction and housekeeping Pain management philosophy What is chronic pain? – questions answered Introduction to exercise – sitting and standing Pacing everyday activities The stress response and introduction to diaphragmatic breathing
WEEK 2	Recap pacing Goal setting and action plans Introduction to exercise – lying Sitting and chairs Introduction to stretch and relax Video patients doing exercises for comparison at end of group
WEEK 3	How pain works: the gate control theory of pain How pain works: pain pathways Thoughts and feelings about pain Exercises Stretch and relax Action plans
WEEK 4	Recommended use of medication for chronic pain Communication and relationships Pain management graduate perspective talk Exercises Introduction to relaxing your mind Action plans
WEEK 5	Lifting and bending Managing everyday activities Sexual relationships The benefits of exercise Exercise Relaxing your mind Action plans
WEEK 6	Introduction to fitness and fitness equipment Doctor's talk: medication, treatments and surgery for chronic pain, sleeping and beds/positions to ease pain Action plans Relaxation
WEEK 7	Flare-ups and setbacks Helpful sleep habits Video exercises and compare with the beginning of the course Introduction to brief relaxation techniques Reviewing progress, and setting goals for the follow-up sessions

SUMMARY

Pain is a widely prevalent phenomenon. Over 20 per cent of the general population are experiencing chronic pain at any one time, and the personal and social consequences of chronic pain are significant. Various types of pain have been identified:

● *acute:* lasting up to between three and six months;

● *chronic:* lasting more than three to six months; can be further categorised as chronic benign and chronic progressive pain.

Pain can also be defined in terms of its nature: its type, severity and pattern.

The experience of pain is moderated by a variety of physical and psychological factors, including:

- the degree of attention paid to the pain;
- the mood of the individual;
- the person's beliefs about the nature of the pain, including its cause and controllability.

Early specificity and pattern theories that did not take account of these psychological factors proved to be unsuccessful in explaining the various ways in which pain can be experienced. A more complex model developed by Melzack and Wall, known as the gate theory of pain, has superseded these models of pain. This suggests that pain is the outcome of a number of complementary or competing processes. Any model of pain has to take into account how psychological factors affect the perception of pain. The gate theory of pain suggests that:

- Afferent nerves carry pain messages up to the substantia gelatinosa and then through the spinal gate mechanism to the brain.
- At the same time, psychological processes influence the activity of nerves leading from the brain to the spinal gate.
- Activation of both systems results in a variety of chemicals being produced within the gate (substantia gelatinosa), some of which 'open' the pain gate, some of which 'close' it. The main chemicals

involved in reducing pain sensations in the substantia gelatinosa are endorphins.

Melzack has developed a more complex neurological model of pain, known as the neuromatrix, which accounts for phenomena previously difficult to account for by the gate theory (including phantom limb pain).

TENS is a physiological intervention based on the gate control theory of pain. Reliable evidence of its effectiveness is lacking.

Biofeedback interventions can help to reduce pain, but their overall effectiveness is often no greater than more general relaxation procedures. They may be best used when there are individual muscle groups contributing to the pain that are not relaxed following more general relaxation instructions, or for the treatment of headaches.

Both behavioural and cognitive-behavioural interventions have proved to be effective in the treatment of both acute and more chronic pain – but less than perhaps initially thought. Cognitive changes appear to mediate changes in the experience of pain. Mindfulness has also been shown to reduce pain, and (possibly to an even greater extent) quality of life and acceptance measures. Psychological interventions may be combined (at least in some cases) with antidepressant medication to provide maximal benefit.

Further reading

Jensen M.P. and Turk D.C. (2014). Contributions of psychology to the understanding and treatment of people with chronic pain: why it matters to ALL psychologists. *American Psychologist*, 69: 105-18.

An interesting take on the wider impact of pain research and interventions.

Melzack, R. and Wall, P.D. (2008). *The Challenge of Pain*. London: Penguin.

A classic. The most up-to-date text by the originators of the gate control theory – and over £200 cheaper than the more recent Wall and Melzack's *Textbook of Pain*. Written in a non-technical way for the interested 'lay' reader.

Williams, A., Eccleston, C. and Morley, S. (2012). Psychological therapies for the management of chronic pain (excluding headache) in adults. *Cochrane Database of Systematic Reviews*, Nov 14;11:CD007407.

Crombez, G., Eccleston, C., De Vlieger, P. et al. (2008). Is it better to have controlled and lost than never to have controlled at all? An experimental investigation of control over pain. *Pain*, 137: 631–9.

An interesting experimental study of what happens when you first provide control over pain, and then take it away.

Three differing theoretical psychosocial perspectives on pain:

Van Damme, S., Legrain, V., Vogt, J. et al. (2010). Keeping pain in mind: a motivational account of attention to pain. *Neuroscience and Biobehavioral Reviews*, 34: 204–13.

Eccleston, C. and Crombez, G. (1999). Pain demands attention: a cognitive-affective model of the interruptive function of pain. *Psychological Bulletin*, 125: 356–66.

Meredith, P., Ownsworth, T. and Strong, J. (2008). A review of the evidence linking adult attachment theory and chronic pain: presenting a conceptual model. *Clinical Psychology Review*, 28: 407–29.

A number of websites may also provide useful information:

www.jr2.ox.ac.uk/bandolier/booth/painpag/

www.painrelieffoundation.org.uk/

www.nlm.nih.gov/medlineplus/pain.html

www.psychnet-ukk.com/clinical_psychology/clinical_psychology_pain_management.htm

For open-access student resources specifically written to complement this textbook and support your learning, please visit **www.pearsoned.co.uk/morrison**

Chapter 17
Improving health and quality of life

Learning outcomes

By the end of this chapter, you should have an understanding of a number of psychological interventions that aim to:

- reduce distress: focusing on information provision, stress management training and providing social support

- improve disease management: focusing on information provision, self-management training, stress management training, facilitating family and social support, and the use of written emotional expression

- reduce the risk of future disease or disease progression: focusing on counselling, stress management and providing social support

Every hospital should have one . . . a psychology department, that is

Probably not a headline you will actually read. But it should be. Most general hospitals in most countries, even where there are well-established professions of clinical and health psychology, do not have access to psychologists. Read the research papers from countries such as the USA or UK, and you would believe that all hospitals are teaming with psychologists engaging in the interventions the empirical data show to be highly effective. But they are not. So why, if we know that psychology can 'make a difference', are so few hospitals actually employing professional psychologists? Perhaps physicians or surgeons do not think psychology has much, or anything, to offer? Well, many do. When one of the authors (PB) was working as a clinical psychologist in a general hospital, a number of physicians working in specialties including diabetes, gastroenterology and renal medicine asked for psychological input into their clinics. They were very keen . . . until they were asked to pay for the service of a psychologist from their budget! At which point, they were much less keen . . . and eventually most decided not to have the psychologist. So, psychology is seen as important, but not central to the provision of quality care. Therefore, when developing interventions, psychologists need to consider not only what is effective but also what is cost-effective. Health-care providers increasingly have to consider the bottom line: how much does it cost? Too much, and they will not pay. Something to consider as you read the chapter . . .

Chapter outline

This chapter focuses on a number of psychological interventions used to help people to cope with and manage serious illnesses. These interventions have a number of goals. Some seek to reduce the distress associated with having a serious illness. Others aim to help people to manage their illness as effectively as possible and to minimise its impact on their daily life. Yet others are designed to prevent the progression of an illness and minimise the risk of further health problems in the future. This chapter considers a number of interventions designed to achieve these goals in the context of chronic diseases, such as cancer, coronary heart disease and arthritis.

Coping with chronic illness

The onset of a serious illness has many implications for both the individual concerned and those around them (see also the discussion in Chapter 12 (☞). Following the onset of symptoms, the person with the illness may experience the anxiety of waiting for and being given a serious diagnosis, the possibility of having to come into hospital, with its associated discomfort and disruption of normal life. In the longer term, they may have to come to terms with restrictions or handicaps associated with their condition and the possibility of a gradual decline in health. They may have to learn how to manage their condition or take action to prevent their health deteriorating further. Having a chronic illness presents the individual with a number of 'tasks'. People who are HIV-positive have to take many drugs each day at carefully determined times; people with arthritis may benefit from engaging in a variety of exercises to maintain joint mobility; and so on. Other diseases, such as coronary heart disease (CHD), may or may not be apparent on a day-by-day basis. However, changing risk factors such as diet or smoking may help to prevent the disease progressing further. A third issue that patients often have to deal with is the significant emotional distress that may accompany a diagnosis of severe or chronic disease.

The interventions considered in this chapter aim to help people to cope with each of these challenges. This chapter examines the effectiveness of a number of approaches used to help people to reduce any distress they experience, to manage their disease and to prevent it developing further. The therapeutic approaches we consider include:

● providing relevant information;
● stress management training;
● the use of social support;
● self-management training;
● enhancing social support;
● the use of **written emotional expression**.

Each type of intervention may have multiple benefits. Improvements in mood, for example, may increase the likelihood of cardiac patients participating in an exercise programme, and therefore impact on both their well-being and their physical health. Conversely, taking part in such a programme may reduce depression or anxiety as the individual feels they are gaining control over their illness and their life. Stress management training may simultaneously reduce the distress associated with being HIV-positive and improve its prognosis through its positive impact on immune function. So, separating the specific outcomes of the various interventions is a little

---

written emotional expression

a writing technique in which participants write about upsetting incidents either in their past or related to specific issues.

artificial. Nevertheless, we try to tease out each of these multiple end points and consider how well each intervention achieves each of these separate goals.

Reducing distress

Information provision

Many people with serious illness experience significant levels of distress. They may have concerns about their prognosis and treatment, the potential effects of their illness on their quality of life, and so on. Levels of distress are perhaps highest in the early stages of an illness or at times when the nature of an illness changes. We discuss these issues in more detail in Chapter 12 ☞. However, as examples of the level of distress many patients experience, about a third of patients with cancer and a quarter of those who have had a myocardial infarction (MI) report clinically significant levels of distress at some time in the course of their illness (e.g. Lane et al. 2002b). This can be reduced by various types of information, including information about:

● the nature of a disease and/or its treatment;

● how to cope with disease and/or its treatment;

● how to change behaviour in order to reduce risk of disease or disease progression.

Perhaps the simplest form of information provision involves keeping patients informed about the progress of their condition and its treatment. Uncertainty can increase distress – providing information, even simple information, can reduce it. Wells et al. (1995), for example, found that giving information to people with cancer about their chemotherapy, showing them around the clinic where they were to receive the treatment, and giving them the opportunity to ask questions to a specialist counsellor was highly effective in reducing their levels of distress. A subsequent study reported by Deshler et al. (2006) found that patients preferred to be sent such information in the post prior to coming into hospital, and that those with high levels of trait anxiety benefited most from this type of intervention.

More complex information-based interventions may also be relevant at the beginning of a serious illness. One particular issue that needs to be dealt with particularly sensitively is telling patients and relatives when they have a disease with a poor or fatal prognosis – a process often known as 'breaking bad news'(see also Chapter 10 ☞). The way that this information is given at this time may have important implications for how people cope and come to terms with their prognosis. Clearly, the communication skills of the person giving the bad news are important in the success of this process. However, a simple informational strategy may also facilitate this process. Ong et al. (2000) gave patients an audiotape of the consultation in which they were given their 'bad news'. They were encouraged to play the tape in their own time to help them to recall the information given. This simple procedure resulted in higher levels of satisfaction and helped them to recall more information than a control group who did not receive the tape. In a different context, Cope et al. (2003) compared the effectiveness of a variety of communication strategies with women having a scan for a potential foetal abnormality. Two weeks after their consultation, women who received an audiotape or letter summarising the information given in the session reported less anxiety than the control group without this information. The groups did not differ on recall of information. Despite these encouraging findings, it should be noted that not all patients may benefit from this approach. McHugh et al. (1995) found that patients with a particularly poor prognosis who were given a tape recording of their bad news consultation were more likely to be depressed than those not given a tape.

Educational programmes whose primary intention is to help people to manage a disease or reduce risk of further disease may also impact on mood. Why this should happen is not clear. Such interventions may provide patients with a sense of control over their illness and reduce anxieties about their long-term health. They may also encourage participants not to overly restrict their lives as a result of their disease. Each may result in improved mood. An early but influential UK study of rehabilitation of people following an MI showed evidence of this effect. In this, Lewin et al. (1992) compared the effectiveness of a six-week home-based education package known as the *Heart Manual* with a placebo package of information and informal counselling. The *Heart Manual* focused on guiding patients through a progressive change of risk factors for CHD, including changes in diet, exercise and relaxation techniques. Patients followed the manual at home for a period of six weeks. Over this time, they also received three telephone calls from expert nurses to discuss their progress and any problems they were experiencing. Over the following year, participants who received the *Heart Manual* reported lower levels of anxiety and depression than those in the control group. They were also less likely than people in the control group to go to their doctor with concerns about their heart condition in the first six months following their discharge. The impact of this intervention on CHD-risk behaviours is discussed later in the chapter. In a similar type of programme, Hartford et al. (2002) used a telephone contact programme for patients who had had a coronary artery bypass graft and their partners. The programme provided information on a number of issues to aid recovery, including a graded activity and exercise plan as strategies to help cope with pain, and dealing with psychosocial problems, diet and medication use. The programme began with a meeting between a specialist nurse and the patient and their partner on the day of discharge, when they were provided with information about medication for pain, distances to walk, rest stops on the way home, the nurse's 24-hour telephone number, and a time when they would phone again. This was followed by six telephone calls at increasing intervals over the next seven weeks, during which problems were assessed and relevant information provided. Despite its emphasis on changing behaviour, it also proved effective in reducing both patient and partner levels of anxiety. New technologies may also be used to help the provision of information. Lo et al. (2010), for example, found a computer-based learning education programme given to Taiwanese patients who had experienced significant burns resulted in significant benefits on measures of knowledge, use of pressure garments and anxiety.

Stress management training

Stress management training involves teaching individuals directly how to cope with stress, using strategies including:

- *problem solving*: to prevent or minimise external problems that contribute to stress;
- *cognitive restructuring*: to identify and challenge stress-provoking thoughts which may initiate or exacerbate the stress response;
- *relaxation*: to reduce the physiological arousal that forms part of the stress response.

We discuss these approaches in more detail in Chapter 13 ☛. Given that these strategies are directly targeted at

reducing distress, one would hope that they are effective in doing so – and this does seem to be the case. A meta-analysis of 45 studies involving some form of stress management procedure across a wide range of health disorders (Meyer and Mark 1995) concluded that the average person was up to 60 per cent better off than those not receiving the intervention. The approach has proven effective at various stages in the process of care, including:

- waiting for a diagnosis;
- during treatment;
- coping with the emotional stress of living with a long-term illness.

Here, we consider examples of the effectiveness of stress management procedures in the context of cancer and heart disease.

One early study in people with cancer was reported by Fawzy et al. (1993), who compared a stress management programme with usual care in a group of patients with **malignant melanoma** whose tumours had been surgically excised. Only the active intervention group reported any improvements in mood both immediately after the intervention and at six-month follow-up. We discuss this study again later in the chapter when we consider the effects of this type of intervention on disease progression.

More recently, Antoni et al. (2001) found that a stress management programme was more effective than a one-day educational seminar in improving measures of depression and '**benefit-finding**' among women with early-stage breast cancer. Typical benefits included:

- a greater enthusiasm to live life to the full;
- making positive life choices as a result of illness;
- a greater appreciation of being alive;
- improved relationships with partner.

In the longer term, a study by the same research group (Stagl et al. 2014) found that women who received

---

malignant melanoma
a rare but potentially lethal form of skin cancer.

benefit-finding
a process of finding beneficial outcomes as a consequence of what is normally seen as a negative event, such as developing cancer or being infected with HIV.

stress management training following surgery for breast cancer experienced less depressive symptoms than those in a control group up to five years following the intervention. Similar gains have been made among men following medical treatment of prostate cancer (Penedo et al. 2006) and men and women during a course of radiotherapy (Krischer et al. 2007).

A second group in which we consider the effectiveness of stress management programmes is cardiac patients. Here, most interventions have proven effective (see, for example, Dickens et al. 2013), including one programme that involved only telephone contact with participants run from six Australian hospitals. O'Neil et al. (2014) found that twelve months following a combined cognitive-behavioural intervention for depression and a behavioural risk reduction programme delivered by telephone, participants who were depressed immediately following their infarction were significantly less likely to remain depressed and to have a better quality of life than those in a standard treatment control condition.

Other stress management programmes have targeted people with implantable cardioverter defibrillators (ICDs). These are small instruments placed in patients' chests with leads leading to the heart. They monitor the heart for potentially fatal changes in heart rhythm, which they correct firstly by 'pacing' the heart and, if necessary, shocking the heart. Pacing involves increasing the heart rate for a short time. The shock is similar to that from an external defibrillator. Patients may not notice the pacing, although many do. They certainly notice the shock, which has been described as similar to being punched hard in the chest. Although most patients never actually experience a shock, they are all aware that it can occur. As a consequence, many people avoid situations that they think may lead to an arrhythmia, such as engaging in exercise or potentially stressful situations. Those that have experienced a shock may experience classically conditioned fear in situations where this has occurred or those similar to it. ICDs are a relatively new technology, but are now being increasingly used, and studies helping people cope with them are now emerging. One such pilot study tested a stress management programme. Sears et al. (2007) compared two active stress management programmes following ICD implantation, one lasting a full day, the other involving six weekly sessions. Both interventions were associated with short-term reductions in anxiety and cortisol levels – although the lack of no-treatment control group allows the possibility that these

changes would have occurred naturally as patients adapted to having the ICD. The same research group subsequently found that a yoga-based stress management intervention can provide similar psychological benefits as well as reducing the frequency of heart arrhythmias that may trigger the ICD to fire (Toise et al. 2014).

Mindfulness

Mindfulness training can be considered a form of stress management, as it is often used to help patients manage any stress they are experiencing, and it is proving an effective and easy to learn skill. In a summary of all the research to date, Merkes (2010) identified 15 studies of the effectiveness of mindfulness-based stress reduction (MBSR: see Chapter 13 ☛) in reducing distress in patients with a variety of chronic diseases. They concluded that MBSR is likely to result in patients coping better with their symptoms, improved overall well-being and quality of life, as well as improved health status. Examples of this type of work include a study by Henderson et al. (2013), who examined the effectiveness of a mindfulness-based intervention on women in early-stage breast cancer receiving radiotherapy. It proved beneficial on a range of measures including meaningfulness, helplessness, cognitive avoidance, depression, paranoid ideation, hostility, anxiety, global severity, anxious preoccupation, and emotional control. Similarly, Gross et al. (2010) compared the effectiveness of MBSR with an education and no-treatment control conditions in patients who were sleeping poorly following organ transplantation. Following initial gains at two-month follow-up, by one year following the intervention, those in the MBSR group continued to report less anxiety and sleep problems than those in either of the other groups. A further example of a mindfulness based intervention is reported in the Research Focus box.

Enhancing social support

We discussed in Chapter 12 ☛ how social support can improve or maintain both mental and physical health. With this in mind, a number of studies have evaluated the impact of support groups designed to provide social support from people experiencing similar health problems. Many of these have been led by professionals and include an element of group therapy or working towards group goals. One of the first studies to evaluate the effectiveness of this approach was reported by Spiegel et al.

(1989). They randomly assigned women with breast cancer to either a usual treatment control or weekly support groups led by health professionals. These focused on a number of issues, including:

- building strong, supportive bonds;
- expressing emotions;
- dealing directly with fears of dying;
- improving relationships within the family;
- active involvement in decisions concerning treatment.

Only those in the active intervention evidenced any improvements on measures of depression and anxiety.

Subsequently, Giese-Davis et al. (2002) reported that women who went through the groups reported less suppression of negative moods while also showing less aggressive, inconsiderate, impulsive and irresponsible behaviour in comparison with the no-treatment group. They therefore concluded that this form of intervention can help women to become more expressive of their emotions without becoming more hostile. Supportive interventions appear to be of benefit to women across a variety of cultures, including Iranian (Montazeri et al. (2001) and Japanese (Fukui et al. 2000) women. With increasing access to the internet, the need for face-to-face support is changing, and some innovative work is now beginning to measure the benefits associated with online support groups. In one study of this approach, Vilhauer et al. (2010) found that 73 per cent of women with metastatic breast cancer invited to participate in the virtual group did so, and most continued to remain part of the group over a period of two months, accessing it on average six days a week. Although they did not measure mood, another study of this approach by the same group reported that the women reported benefits, including group cohesiveness, information exchange, feelings of being in the same situation as others, hope, catharsis and

altruism. Finally, although men may be relatively unwilling to attend support groups, they may still benefit from peer support. Weber et al. (2007), for example, found men who had experienced a **radical prostatectomy** benefited more, on measures of depression and self-efficacy from meeting with a fellow patient once a week for eight weeks to discuss any concerns they had and coping strategies they could use, than a control group.

Before leaving this issue, it is important to note that although socially based interventions have proven effective they may be less effective than other, individually based interventions, such as mindfulness (Carlson et al. 2013). In addition, Pollock et al. (2007) found that many patients preferred to turn to friends and families for support, and did not wish to attend more professionally organised support groups. This cautionary note supports an approach in which family and partner skills are strengthened, and provide the support given to the patient. Northouse and colleagues have conducted a number of evaluations of this type of intervention. In one study, they (Northouse et al. 2007) provided a couples-intervention addressing issues such as communication, coping with uncertainty, instilling hope, and symptom management. At four-month follow-up, the partners appeared to have benefited most, reporting less uncertainty, hopelessness, and symptom distress. In a previous study, in which they provided a similar intervention to couples in which the patient had recurrent breast cancer, Northouse et al. (2005) reported gains on measures of hopelessness and negative appraisal of illness among patients, and a signifi-

---

radical prostatectomy
otherwise known as a total prostatectomy, this involves using surgery to remove all of the prostate as a cure for prostate cancer.

RESEARCH FOCUS

Pbert, L., Madison, J.M., Druker, S. et al. (2012). Effect of mindfulness training on asthma quality of life and lung function: a randomised controlled trial. *Thorax*, 67: 769–776.

Introduction

The elevated stress experienced by many patients with asthma impacts negatively on their quality of life and can result in less than optimal medication adherence and poor asthma control. Stressed individuals tend to overestimate their shortness of breath and find it difficult to distinguish between symptoms of stress and asthma. This study evaluated the efficacy of a mindfulness training programme (mindfulness-based stress reduction (MBSR)) in improving asthma-related quality of life and lung function in patients with asthma.

Participants

The 83 participants were adult patients (mean age = 53 years), with three levels of asthma severity: mild, moderate or severe. People with intermittent asthma, smokers, and/or with other lung or heart diseases were excluded from the study. The mean number of years taking asthma medication was 13.3.

Method

Participants were randomly allocated to either an 8-week mindfulness-based stress reduction (MBSR) group-based programme or an educational 'Healthy living' programme. MBSR comprised eight weekly sessions and an all-day session in week six. Participants were taught: (i) body scan, in which attention is systematically moved through the body to bring awareness to sensations; (ii) sitting meditation, focusing on awareness of breathing, thoughts and feelings; and (iii) gentle stretching exercises to develop awareness during movement. Classes emphasised the integration of mindfulness into everyday life to support coping with symptoms and stress. Two CDs containing guided mindfulness exercises were provided to be practised for 30 minutes a day for six days per week. The health living course was similar in levels of contact and group format, and involved a series of lectures and discussion of self-care topics: healthy nutrition; physical activity; coping with stress (not including mindfulness); sleep hygiene; balancing work and personal life; and living a drug-free life.

Measures

Key outcome measures were the Asthma Quality of Life Questionnaire, Perceived Stress Scale and lung function, measured as 'morning peak expiratory flow', measuring airflow through the bronchi and the degree of obstruction in the airways due to asthmatic constriction.

They were measured at 10 weeks, 6 months and one year after the intervention.

Results

At 12-month follow-up, participants in the MBSR condition evidenced significant greater improvements on the Asthma Quality of Life Questionnaire score ($p<0.001$) and Perceived Stress Scale ($p = 0.001$) than the education condition.

From a medical perspective, although the percentage of people with well-controlled asthma rose in the MBSR group (from 7.3 per cent at baseline to 19.4 per cent) but not the education group (7.5 per cent at baseline to 7.9 per cent), the difference at 12-month follow-up was not significantly different. In addition, there was no evidence of improvements in lung function. Nevertheless, the percentage of participants in the intervention group using long-term controller medication fell from 80.5 per cent at baseline to 71.4 per cent at 12-month follow-up, while rising in the control condition from 74.4 per cent to 81.25 per cent (a marginally significant rate of change; $p = 0.06$). In addition, the MBSR group showed a significant decrease compared with the control group in the use of 'rescue' medications at 12 months ($p<0.001$).

Discussion and comment

Participation in an MBSR programme led to significant sustained improvements in quality of life and stress levels. In addition, there was modest evidence of improvements in asthma control despite less use of long-term and 'rescue' medications. The authors speculate that the latter finding may be a consequence of participants achieving more accurate discrimination between stress and true asthma symptoms and a reduced urgency and distress associated with mindfulness training. While findings of reductions in distress should be a sufficient justification for stress management interventions (this, after all is the primary target of the intervention), evidence (albeit self-report) of improvements in asthma control really do strengthen the justification of this form of intervention in people with asthma. Whether such interventions would be better targeted at specific groups, such as those reporting poor disease control and/or high levels of stress, remains to be seen.

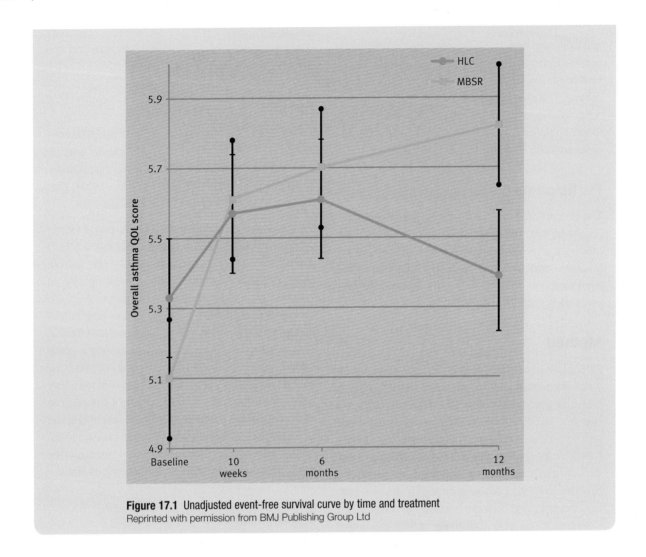

Figure 17.1 Unadjusted event-free survival curve by time and treatment
Reprinted with permission from BMJ Publishing Group Ltd

cantly lower negative appraisal of caregiving burden three months (but not six months) following such an intervention among their partners.

Managing illness

A second set of interventions can be used to help people to gain the skills and motivation to manage the symptoms of an illness as effectively as possible: to maintain an exercise and mobility programme in rheumatoid arthritis, an insulin regimen in type 1 diabetes, and so on. The goal of the intervention here is not to prevent the development of a disease but to minimise its negative impact on the affected individual.

Information provision

There is a significant body of evidence showing that patient education programmes can enhance knowledge about a condition or its management, at least in the short term (e.g. Gibson et al. 2000; van den Arend et al. 2000). However, even where increases in knowledge are achieved, they may not always impact on behaviour or symptom control. Indeed, a number of studies have found only a marginal relationship between educational programmes and behavioural change. In a systematic review of 11 such programmes for people with asthma, for example, Gibson et al. (2000) concluded that, while such programmes increased knowledge, there was no evidence that they impacted on measures of medication use, doctor visits, hospitalisation and lung function. However, the simple addition of an action plan (see discussion of problem-focused counselling and implementation intentions in Chapter 6 (☞) seemed to enhance their effectiveness (Powell and Gibson 2003).

The internet now provides a key source of information for many patients. This provides both formal 'official' sites and 'unofficial' sites, many of which advocate the use of a variety of treatment approaches or condemn them as dangerous and unacceptable. Given the plethora of, often contradictory, information on the internet, access to this information can both benefit patients and carry the potential for confusion and even harm. It also presents significant challenges for doctors when giving information about a particular condition. Witness one anecdotal story in which a UK doctor prescribed tamoxifen, a drug treatment known to significantly reduce the risk of cancer recurrence in women that have had breast cancer (see Buzdar 2004). In the consultation, he described both the benefits and the common side effects and health risks of taking the drug to one patient. With this knowledge, she decided to take the drug on a preventive basis. The next day she telephoned the doctor to say that she was no longer willing to take the drug as she had searched a number of US websites, and their descriptions of the health risks associated with the drug made her decide against its use. While in one way this may be seen as the power of truly informed consent, what had frightened this woman was reading a list of diseases that had occurred in women taking the drug. What she did not have was the data to contextualise this list, which included many conditions that may have occurred in only a very small percentage of those taking the drug, or they may not even have been the result of taking tamoxifen. Mindful of this, Kalichman et al. (2006) found that an eight-session training in the appropriate use of the internet given to people living with HIV/AIDS resulted in increased access to health information on the internet, and lower vulnerability to misinformation and fraud.

Another response to this issue has led health-care providers to set up their own web-based information that patients can easily access and that can provide appropriate information. One of many web-based health information sites is provided by the American Heart Association. Heart Profilers (www.americanheart.org/profilers) provides a web-based interactive tool through which patients can obtain a personalised report of 'scientifically accurate' treatment options, a list of questions to ask their doctor on their next visit (which has been shown to improve doctor–patient communication and patient satisfaction – see Chapter 10 (☞), and key information they need to participate in their treatment. In the site, menus lead to information related to heart failure and CHD, hypertension, high cholesterol and **atrial fibrillation**. The effectiveness of this type of intervention is difficult to assess. However, people who access health- and illness-related websites are generally more knowledgeable than those who do not (Kalichman et al. 2003), although this may be the result of better-informed people being most likely to access internet sites relevant to their illness. Nevertheless, these data suggest that the internet may prove a useful resource for people with many chronic conditions, and as we shall show later, can prove an effective medium of change.

Self-management training

Perhaps the best-known approach to helping patients to gain control over their illness is known as self-management training (Lorig 1996), and those who undertake this form of training are often referred to as 'expert patients'. The approach involves teaching affected individuals how to manage their illness in a way that maximises control over their symptoms and quality of life. It is based on social cognition theory (e.g. Bandura 2001), which suggests that patients can learn self-management skills from practice and watching others, and that success in achieving control leads, in turn, to increased confidence and continued application of new skills. Accordingly, the core of self-management training is a structured, progressive, skills-training programme that ensures success at each stage before progression to the next. Self-management programmes are usually, but not uniquely, run as group interventions, facilitating the process of learning from observation of others. The approach is specifically targeted at the effective management of disease. It does not focus on the emotional sequelae of disease; nor is it intended to be a preventive intervention. Self-management programmes began by

atrial fibrillation
a heart rhythm disorder (arrhythmia). It involves a very rapid heart rate, in which the atria (upper chambers of the heart) contract in a very rapid and disorganised manner and fail to pump blood effectively through the heart.

focusing on helping people cope with arthritis, typically addressing issues such as:

● exercising with arthritis;

● managing pain;

● eating healthily;

● preventing fatigue;

● protecting joints;

● taking arthritis medication;

● dealing with stress and depression;

● working with the doctor and health-care team;

● evaluating alternative treatments;

● outsmarting arthritis: problem solving.

These programmes proved extremely effective. An early review by SuperioCabuslay et al. (1996), for example, reported gains in excess of drug treatment alone of 20 to 30 per cent on measures of pain relief, 40 per cent in functional ability, and 60 to 80 per cent in the reduction in tender joint counts.

The original self-management programmes addressed all issues with all people. However, some issues they considered may be more or less relevant than others to differing programme recipients. As a result, a number of programmes have now moved from a 'one size fits all' approach to tailored programmes that provide a number of modules that participants can select according to their particular needs (Iversen et al. 2010). Evers et al. (2002) evaluated the effectiveness of one such programme targeted at people with rheumatoid arthritis. Modules included those targeted at helping people to cope with fatigue, negative mood and pain, and to maintain or improve social relationships. The programme resulted in mid- to long-term gains on a number of psychological measures, including the use of active coping strategies, mood, fatigue and helplessness in comparison with a no-treatment condition. Gains were also reported in an Australian study reported by Osborne et al. (2007) using the same approach. This study found significant reductions in pain and health distress, as well as increases in self-efficacy and exercise – changes which were sustained for at least two years. Adding an exercise component to a specific programme for people with osteoarthritic knee pain led Yip et al. (2007) to report significant gains in comparison to a no-treatment control group on measures of arthritis pain, fatigue, duration of weekly light exercise practice and knee flexion.

Following their success with arthritis, self-management programmes are now used to help people to manage a number of long-term conditions, with some success (Millard et al. 2013). Franek (2013), for example, reported the findings of a systematic review of self-management programmes, largely based on Lorig's model, across a range of conditions including arthritis and chronic pain, chronic respiratory diseases, diabetes, heart disease and stroke. When compared to usual care, the approach was associated with 'modest' improvements in pain, disability, fatigue, depression, health distress, self-rated health, and health-related quality of life. By contrast, the interventions did not reduce the number of visits to general practitioners' or Emergency Medical Units nor the number of admissions to hospital and time spent in hospital.

In one study of people living with HIV, Gifford et al. (1998) randomly assigned men to either a seven-session group self-management programme or usual care. The intervention used interactive methods to provide information about living with HIV/AIDS and a number of disease self-management skills, including symptom assessment and management, medication use (see Chapter 10 ☞), physical exercise and relaxation skills. Over the course of the study, participants who did not enter the programme reported increases in the number of 'troubling symptoms' they experienced and an increased feeling of loss of control over their health. By contrast, participants in the self-management condition reported more control over their health and fewer 'troubling symptoms'. Another programme (Inouye et al. 2001) reported short-term gains on measures of mood, including anger, and increases in perceived control over their condition following an HIV self-management intervention compared with a waiting-list control group.

A further example of a self-management programme involves the control of blood sugar levels in diabetes. Lorig et al. (2009) found a classic peer-led self-management intervention to be useful in improving a number of measures relative to a usual care condition. In comparison to this group, participants in the self-management group evidenced gains on measures of depression, symptoms of hypoglycaemia, communication with physicians, healthy eating immediately following the intervention. However, no change was found on a measure of long-term blood sugar (HbA1C), suggesting that day-to-day control over blood sugar had not improved.

An older, but interesting, study was reported by Langewitz et al. (1997), who provided what they termed 'intensified functional insulin therapy'. Not only did their intervention involve an educational component, but it also taught participants how factors such as additional exercise and eating meals with varying levels of carbohydrate may influence their blood sugar levels by allowing them to experience, and then cope with, these situations within the programme. This approach should provide more realistic learning than conventional approaches and therefore provide more benefit should problems arise. In comparison with baseline measures, participants in the intervention evidenced significant improvements in blood sugar levels and a reduction in the frequency with which they experienced **hypoglycaemic episodes** in the following year.

Self-management programmes need not be delivered 'live'. There are now several examples of graduated skills-based programmes that have translated key elements of the self-management process into written or computer-based form. The *Heart Manual*, which we described earlier in this chapter, provides a good example of this. The latest evaluation of this approach was reported by Jolly et al. (2007). They randomly allocated participants who had experienced an MI from inner-city, ethnically diverse, socially deprived areas of the West Midlands of England to receive either a hospital-based cardiac rehabilitation programme or the *Heart Manual* to be used at home. Both involved programmes including exercise, relaxation, education and lifestyle counselling. The *Heart Manual* followed the developmental approach of gradual change and skills learning suggested by Lorig. Significant improvements in total cholesterol, smoking status, self-reported physical activity and diet were seen in both conditions between baseline and the six-month follow-up. However, no clinically or statistically significant differences were seen between the home- and centre-based groups, suggesting that the home intervention is a viable and effective intervention.

Self-management programmes can also be implemented simply and cheaply using the internet or interactive programmes on computers. Devi et al. (2014), for example, found a six-week internet-delivered rehabilitation programme providing information about the prevention of further heart problems, and establishing user goals in terms of physical activity, diet, managing emotions and smoking to be more effective than normal care in a group of patients diagnosed with angina. Those using the programme logged in on average three times per week, and showed significant improvements relative to the normal care group on measures of daily steps walked, duration of 'sedentary activity', weight, emotion outcomes and frequency of angina. The health problem faced by participants in this study suggests older individuals are willing and able to engage in internet-based programmes. However, this may not always be the case. Several studies have shown younger people to enjoy and benefit from the use of such technology in managing illnesses such as diabetes (Pal et al. 2014) and asthma (e.g. van der Meer et al. 2007). Older populations, or those without computer literacy, may not feel comfortable with such an approach. In an ethnically diverse Californian sample, Sarkar et al. (2007), for example, found that 69 per cent of their respondents reported interest in telephone support, 55 per cent wanted group medical visits, while only 42 per cent would use the internet. Unsurprisingly, people who reported themselves as having poor literacy were more likely to be interested in telephone support than the alternative approaches.

Stress management training

A number of interventions have focused on teaching stress management procedures in an effort to control the symptoms of disorders as diverse as rheumatoid arthritis and **atopic dermatitis**. Some of the relevant literature is reviewed below, focusing on the treatment of irritable bowel syndrome (IBS), angina and diabetes.

---

hypoglycaemic episode

occurs when the body's glucose level is too low. It frequently occurs when too much insulin or oral diabetic medication is taken, not enough food is eaten, or following exercise without appropriate food intake. Symptoms include excessive sweating, paleness, fainting and eventually loss of consciousness.

---

atopic dermatitis

a number of conditions, including eczema, involving an inflammatory response of the skin.

Although the role attributable to stress in the aetiology of IBS has been downplayed recently (see Chapter 8 👉), a number of interventions using stress management techniques have been evaluated, and they seem to be reasonably effective – achieving similar outcomes to medical interventions whether conducted face to face (Spiller et al. 2007) or through the use of self-help material augmented by brief telephone contact (Moss-Morris et al. 2010). Taking the issue one step further, Kennedy et al. (2005) reported a study in which they examined whether stress management could add to the effectiveness of a drug that slows down the gut's activity and is generally used to treat IBS. All the people in the study were first given the drug treatment. Those who continued to have IBS symptoms six weeks later were either entered into a stress management programme or continued on their drug regimen in the hope that additional time on the drug would improve their symptoms. Patients in the cognitive-behavioural programme fared best, reporting significant improvements on a variety of measures of IBS symptoms as well as reductions in measures of emotional distress.

Episodes of angina may be triggered by emotional as well as by physical stresses (see Chapter 8 👉). Accordingly, a number of studies have explored the

> **treadmill test**
> a test of cardiovascular fitness in which participants gradually increase the level of exercise on a treadmill while having their heart monitored with an electrocardiogram.

potential benefits of stress management procedures in people with this condition, and, summarising the data to date, Kiseley et al. (2012) concluded that such interventions reduce the frequency of angina for up to three months post-intervention, followed by a diminishing benefit at one-year follow-up assessments. One of the first studies to conduct this type of intervention was reported by Bundy et al. (1994), who found that patients who took part in a stress management programme reported greater reductions in the frequency of angina symptoms, were less reliant on medication and performed better on a standardised exercise known as a **treadmill test** than a control group who did not receive the intervention. A much larger study, involving hundreds of participants, was reported by Gallacher et al. (1997), who compared a less intensive intervention, involving a stress management programme delivered in booklet form and three group meetings, with a no-treatment control condition. At

Case history: Mr P

Mr P provides an interesting case involving the use of stress management and angina. His problems began when he was admitted to hospital following an MI. As with most patients, he spent two days in the coronary care unit before being transferred to a medical ward, and was discharged a few days later following an uneventful time on that ward. Unfortunately, when he went home he developed the symptoms of angina, which on occasion mimicked the symptoms Mr P had experienced at the time of his initial infarction: chest pain, shortness of breath and feeling dizzy. The second of these episodes occurred following a major sale (he was a sales representative) leading to him feeling very excited, after which he walked out of a building into a freezing cold night to go to his car to drive home. The combination of adrenalin-fuelled excitement and sudden exposure to cold air triggered a significant episode of angina. Unfortunately, he found these symptoms

extremely frightening and interpreted them as indicating he was having a further MI. This resulted in him hyperventilating, exacerbating his physical symptoms, having a 'full-blown' panic attack, and then calling out an ambulance to be admitted to the same hospital. As on the first occasion, he was discharged from hospital the following day after being told that he had 'only' had an episode of angina.

In an attempt to stop this happening again, he was referred to a clinical psychologist. The challenges of therapy were to help Mr P distinguish (and then control) any panic symptoms from those of his heart disease, and to be able to distinguish any symptoms of angina from symptoms of a true MI. A mistake at any stage in this process could prove, literally, fatal. The intervention proved relatively simple, as Mr P was keen to adopt a psychological approach to managing his problems. The first stage involved working out exactly what was contributing to his feelings of panic. The key issue here was panicky thoughts, in particular thoughts that his heart disease was out of control and that he could die unless he got medical help. This led to increased sympathetic arousal, ironically placing more strain on his heart and increasing his angina, and hyperventilation which added to his feelings of being out of control, and dizziness.

The goal of therapy was to break this circle. This initially involved Mr P learning to relax and to use some simple breathing techniques he could use to slow his breathing when he became anxious. He practised these skills regularly until they became relatively easy to implement. Then, working with the psychologist, he developed a strategy to use if he experienced any angina symptoms. These were:

● Assume that the symptoms were angina, not a heart attack. Use positive self-talk to remind himself that

he had experienced the symptoms before and they were not a sign of impending death, that he could control them, and if he used his gtn [glyceryl trinitrate] spray (see Chapter 8 (☛)) they would soon go.

● Use relaxation and breathing exercises to bring his symptoms under control.

● Wait 5–10 minutes, to see whether the symptoms reduced as a result of these procedures.

● If they did not, to call an ambulance and seek medical help.

He talked this action plan through during a therapy session, and planned on its use at key times during the day. He used it twice, successfully, in the month following its development. In the next month, he did not experience any panic attacks, and was discharged from the psychology services. Another successful case!

---

six-month follow-up, patients in the intervention condition reported significantly fewer episodes of angina triggered by stress, but not exercise – a finding consistent with the intervention impacting directly on the stress mechanisms that led to the episodes of angina.

The potential benefits of stress management for the control of diabetes are perhaps less obvious than those related to angina. Nevertheless, there are reasons to presume that they could form an effective element in any programme of diabetes control. Stress often precedes periods of reduced adherence to self-care behaviour and may be associated with inappropriate changes in eating patterns (Snoek and Hogenelst 2008). In addition, high levels of stress hormones such as cortisol reduce the body's sensitivity to insulin and may be accompanied by elevations in blood sugar (Surwit and Schneider 1993). As a consequence, some studies have found relaxation to be an effective intervention in keeping blood sugar levels within the optimum range. Attari et al. (2006), for example, reported an Iranian study comparing the effectiveness of stress management versus no intervention in the long-term control of high blood sugar levels in people with type 1 diabetes. Their main outcome measure was a substance known as HbA(1c), which indicates levels of blood sugar over the previous three months. Over the course of the three-month intervention, participants in the stress management group had lower levels

of HbA(1c) than those in the no-intervention group. Similar gains have also been reported in people with type 2 diabetes (Surwit et al. 2002). Interestingly, they found that those people who reported the most stress did not benefit any more than those with lower levels of stress – perhaps because they found the stress management intervention more difficult to implement.

Perhaps the best interventions are those that combine teaching stress management techniques with other strategies to help to control diabetes. Grey et al. (2000), for example, compared an intensive diabetes management programme combined with a stress management programme with the diabetes management programme alone in young people with diabetes. By one-year follow-up, participants in the combined intervention had lower blood sugar levels and a higher belief in their ability to control diabetes and general health than those in the single condition. In addition, participants in the combined intervention were less likely to gain weight than those in the diabetes management programme, and women in this condition were least likely to report hypoglycaemic episodes. A similar combined intervention was reported by Safren et al. (2014) for people with uncontrolled type 2 diabetes, targeting both depression and adherence to medication. Gains were made on both levels of adherence and depression in the short term (three-month follow-up), and the gains on adherence

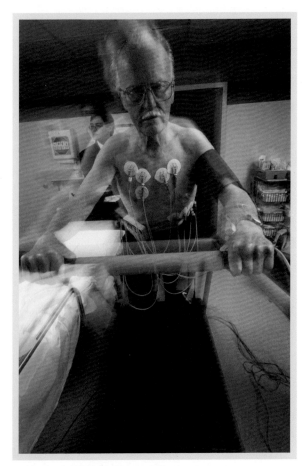

Photo 17.1 The treadmill can provide a good test of cardiac fitness while in the safety of a medical setting

Source: Getty Images/Alvis Upitis.

continued undiminished up to the year follow-up assessment. Less positively, gains on depression diminished over this time. Nevertheless, the potential health impact of increased medication adherence in this group is likely to be significant and this is an important gain.

Enhancing social and family support

Despite the widely acknowledged impact that family and friends of people with chronic illnesses may have on their behaviour and emotional well-being (see Chapter 12 ☞), relatively few interventions have targeted such individuals. Those that have, have generally had positive results – although among them are also some cautionary findings.

Some programmes have involved peers helping patients cope with chronic conditions. These may involve peer experts showing how best to manage a particular condition. One such programme reported the outcomes among a Hispanic community, with peers teaching strategies for managing a variety of chronic conditions – CHD, lung disease and type 2 diabetes. The intervention proved successful, with attenders reporting better health status, health behaviours and more confidence in their ability to manage their condition than controls who did not attend the sessions for up to one year after the end of the programme. Another project, described by Greco et al. (2001), reported outcomes of an intervention in which young people with diabetes and their best friends took part in a group intervention aimed at increasing diabetes-related knowledge in both participants and increasing the friend's support of the patient's diabetes care behaviour. The intervention achieved these goals. In addition, the young people's wider groups of friends understood more about diabetes, and parents reported less diabetes-related conflict. With the development of modern technology, support from peers or fellow patients need to always be live. The internet has become an important means of keeping in touch – although, as the results of Lindsay et al. (2009) indicated, if the goal is behavioural change, this is more likely to be achieved if an internet support group 'meeting' is moderated by a health professional or other informed individual. They evaluated the degree of risk behaviour change in cardiac patients living in an economically deprived area of the UK who were able to access professionally moderated then un-moderated online support groups. During the moderated phase, the group members achieved more changes in diet than a usual care control group. However, during the following un-moderated phase, they not only lost the behavioural gains they had made, but they also made *more* appointments with health-care staff than those in the control condition. Why this would happen is unclear, but the potential for an un-moderated group to spread worry and concern among its members rather than ameliorate is clear.

Involving partners in any intervention may also be of value – and may be done quite simply. Taylor et al. (1985), for example, compared the effects of wives' differing levels of involvement in an assessment of their husband's exercise capacity following an MI. The wives were allocated to one of three conditions: (i) no observation of the test, (ii) observing their partners taking part in a treadmill test to assess their cardiac fitness, (iii) observing their partners take the test and also taking part in it themselves. The key measure in the study was the wives' ratings of their partners' physical and cardiac efficiency. As may be predicted, the confidence the wives had in their husbands exercise capacity increased across each level of engagement in the exercise testing process. It is hoped that this confidence would result in the women being less restrictive of their partners' levels of exercise and less anxious when they did so. However, involving partners in educational programmes may not always be successful. Riemsma et al. (2003) reported that when both patients and their partners attended a cardiac group education programme, participants reported *decreases* in self-efficacy and increased fatigue. By contrast, patients participating in group education without partners showed *increases* in self-efficacy and decreased fatigue; perhaps because they had to take personal control and responsibility for their own care.

More complex family interventions have proven of benefit in helping people manage a range of chronic illnesses. Wysocki et al. (2007), for example, reported on the outcomes of a programme involving working with whole families to help young people cope with their diabetes. The intervention changed the family dynamics, for example, by reducing family conflict, and also changed condition-specific factors, such as improving adherence and long-term HbA(1c) levels. Similar benefits have been found in the treatment of other conditions that require young people to be actively involved in the management of their condition, such as asthma (Yorke and Shuldham 2005) and cystic fibrosis (Duff 2001). The intervention may also be of benefit to adult patients. Garcia-Huidobro et al. (2011), for example, found an intensive family intervention to be more effective than individual care in the treatment of uncontrolled type 2 diabetes in adults aged 18–70 years old living with at least one family member.

Emotional expression

Perhaps the most unexpected therapeutic approach now being developed for people with physical health problems is the variously termed narrative or written emotional expression. The work stems from the findings by Pennebaker in the 1980s (see Pennebaker et al. 1990) of the psychological effects of a writing task in which healthy participants, usually students, wrote about an event or issue from the past that had caused them upset or distress in a way that explored their emotional reaction to that event for about 15–20 minutes on three consecutive days. Typical instructions for this exercise were:

1. Find a place where you will not be disturbed. You can write by hand or on a computer – whatever you are most comfortable with. If you don't want to write, you can also talk into a tape recorder.

2. Plan on your writing for a minimum of three days and a minimum of 15 minutes a day. The only rule is that you write continuously. If you run out of things to say, simply repeat what you have already written.

3. Instructions: really let go and write about your very deepest thoughts and feelings about X. How does X relate to other parts of your life? For example, how do they tie into issues associated with your childhood, your relationship with your family and friends, and the life you have now? How might they be related to your future, your past, or who you are now? Why are you feeling the way you are and what other issues are being brought up by this?

4. You can write about the same general topic every day or a different one each day. Don't worry about spelling or grammar. Your writing is for you and you alone. Many people throw away their writing samples as soon as they are finished. Others keep them and even edit them.

5. Be your own experimenter. Try writing in different ways. If you find that you are getting too upset in your writing, then back off and change directions. Your goal here is to better understand your thoughts and feelings associated with X. See which approach to writing works best for you.

Following this process, participants typically reported short-term increases in depression or distress, but in the mid to long term experienced better mood and, importantly in this context, seemed to have better physical health as measured by immune function and the frequency of visiting a doctor (see Esterling et al. 1999). It took some time for this approach to be tested in patient populations. However, the interventions that have been conducted appear to show benefits. Smyth et al. (1999), for example, compared the effects of written expressed emotion and a neutral writing task in patients with rheumatoid arthritis (RA) and asthma. Those in the intervention condition were asked to write about the 'most stressful experience they had ever undergone'; those in the control group were asked to write about time-management issues as an exercise to reduce stress. Both types of patient in the intervention group fared better than their equivalents in the control group at four-month follow-up: patients with asthma showed improvements in lung function, while patients with RA showed improvements on a combined index measuring physician-rated factors such as disease activity, joint swelling and tenderness, and the presence and severity of joint deformities as well as patient reports of any constraints on daily living tasks. Accordingly, the gains reported cannot simply be attributed to changes in self-report of symptoms as a function of improved mood following the intervention: they appear to be 'objective' gains in disease activity. In a further examination of the role of emotional disclosure in RA reported by Lumley et al. (2011), gains were also made on variables including speed of walking, pain, swollen joints and physician-related disease activity six months following a written emotional expression intervention. Warner et al. (2006) also reported similar benefits for young people with asthma, and began to explore what elements of the writing task appeared to mediate the improvements they found. By analysing the content of the participants' writing, they noted that the greatest improvements in asthma were associated with improved insight into the issue the participants were writing about, and the expression of more negative emotions.

In a study evaluating both effectiveness of the written emotional expression approach and attempting to determine who benefits most from it, Stanton et al. (2002b) assigned participants, all of whom were in the early stages of breast cancer, to write about either: (a) their deepest thoughts and feelings regarding breast cancer (the emotional expression condition), (b) positive thoughts and feelings regarding breast cancer, or (c) facts about their experience of having breast cancer (the neutral task). Once again, the emotional expression seemed to be of benefit. In comparison with the neutral task, participants in the emotional expression condition reported fewer somatic symptoms and fewer visits to the doctor with worries about cancer or related medical conditions. Of interest was that women who typically did not use avoidant coping strategies appeared to benefit most from the emotional expression condition. The positive emotional expression task appeared to benefit those women who were typically avoidant, presumably because it did not force them to confront their fears and other issues raised by their disease.

WHAT DO YOU THINK?

The premise of the emotional expression paradigm is that it can be useful to think about, and somehow process, emotional issues. This has proved effective in a number of settings, but are there times when this may not be an optimal, or even a desirable, approach? It has been suggested that there may be times when the opposite approach may be of benefit. People waiting for medical information – some of which may have powerful implications for the individual, such as their HIV status or a diagnosis of cancer – may benefit more by being distracted from any worries they may have than dwelling on them. At this time, they have no information to process emotionally: rather, they are lacking any relevant information. At such times, it may be best to distract from any intrusive worries rather than focus on them, using the Pennebaker approach. This finding raises a frequently raised issue concerning the targeting of interventions at appropriate times and at individuals most likely to benefit from them. So what sort of conditions, situations or individuals may be best helped by emotional expression? Are there situations where this approach should be avoided, and other approaches considered?

Despite these positive results, it should be acknowledged that not all interventions involving written expression are effective. Harris et al. (2005), for example, found it did not benefit adults with asthma. Similarly, there may be some contexts in which the expression of emotions is actually counter-productive. Panagopoulou et al. (2006) found that women who were emotionally expressive were less likely to become pregnant while undergoing *in vitro* fertilisation than those who contained their emotions. The goal of the next phase of research into the written emotional expression is to find out with whom and in what context the approach works best (see the special section of the *British Journal of Health Psychology*, volume 13, part 1, 2008 for a series of papers that address this issue).

Preventing disease progression

Counselling

One particular form of counselling has been used with cardiac patients in an attempt to prevent disease progression, with somewhat mixed results. The Life Stress Monitoring Program (LSMP: Frasure-Smith and Prince 1985) targeted middle-aged men who had experienced an MI and who were struggling to cope in the year following their infarction. In the study, over four hundred and fifty patients were allocated into either a no-intervention control group or a low-contact 'counselling' intervention. In this, they received monthly telephone contact from a nurse for a period of one year, during which they completed a measure of psychological distress. If they scored above a criterion score, indicating significant stress, they were offered a home visit by the nurse. The action taken by this nurse could vary according to the circumstances they encountered: the majority of contacts involving teaching and providing reassurance by supplying information, but the intervention could involve changes in medication and referral to a cardiologist if necessary.

Half the participants in the intervention condition were visited by the nursing team over the period of the intervention, with an average of six hours contact per patient. By the end of the intervention, the total death rate in the control group was 9 per cent, while that of the intervention group was 5 per cent; a significant difference. Four years later, although a similar percentage of patients in the intervention and control groups had a further MI, patients in the intervention group were less likely to have died from their MI, suggesting a smaller but still significant long-term benefit from having taken part in the counselling intervention. Unfortunately, this finding may not be as exciting as it first appears. The proportion of white-collar workers in the intervention group was significantly greater than that in the control group. Accordingly, many of those in the intervention group may have been at less risk of re-infarction than those in the control group simply as a consequence of socio-economic differences (see Chapter 2 ☞). As a consequence of methodological constraints, these differences could not be statistically partialled out in their analyses, and the interpretation of the results must therefore be considered with some caution.

Such caution may be justified by the results of a later attempt to replicate these findings by the same team (Frasure-Smith et al. 1997). The Montreal heart attack readjustment trial (M-HART) study evaluated the same form of intervention, this time including interventions with women and an older population. Unfortunately, the intervention resulted in no benefits for men: re-infarction

rates in the first year were 2.4 per cent in the intervention group and 2.5 per cent in the control group. Worse, women in the intervention group proved to be *more* at risk of re-infarction than those in the control group, with re-infarction rates of 10.3 per cent and 5.4 per cent, respectively, an effect maintained up to five-year follow-up (Frasure-Smith et al. 2002). In retrospect, these findings may have been a consequence of inadequately trained nurses attempting to cope with extremely distressed individuals and exacerbating rather than moderating their problems. This hypothesis, suggested by Frasure-Smith herself, is supported by data indicating that those patients who reported benefiting from the counselling process evidenced lower rates of infarction than the control group.

Stress management training

The impact of more traditional cardiac rehabilitation programmes involving some form of stress management intervention has been explored in a number of studies. Unfortunately, these studies have rarely provided stress management interventions alone, and have often combined them with education and some form of **exercise programme** involving graded increases in activity. This combined form of intervention appears to be effective. Dusseldorp et al. (1999), for example, reported that psycho-educational interventions resulted in a 34 per cent reduction in cardiac mortality, a 29 per cent reduction in recurrence of MI, and significant positive effects on blood pressure, cholesterol, body weight, cigarette smoking, physical exercise and eating habits. In a later review of similar studies, Whalley et al. (2011) found gains on measures of emotion and a modest positive effect on cardiac mortality.

Perhaps the strongest evaluation of the specific effectiveness of stress management in the context of cardiac disease was provided by Friedman et al. (1986), who reported on a trial known as the Recurrent Coronary Prevention Program. This targeted men high on a

---

exercise programme
a key element of most cardiac rehabilitation, including a progressive increase in exercise usually starting in a gym, sometimes developing into exercise in the home and beyond.

measure of **Type A behaviour** who had experienced an MI. Participants were allocated to one of three groups: cardiac rehabilitation, cardiac rehabilitation plus Type A management, and a usual care control. The rehabilitation programme involved small group meetings over a period of four-and-half years, in which participants received information on medication, exercise and diet, as well as social support from the group. The Type A management group received the same information in addition to engaging in a sustained programme of behavioural change involving training in relaxation, cognitive techniques and specific behavioural change plans in which they reduced the frequency of their Type A behaviour. Evidence of the effectiveness of this process was compelling. Over the four-and-a-half years of the intervention, those in the Type A management programme were at half the risk of further infarction than those in the traditional rehabilitation programme, with total infarction rates over this time of 6 and 12 per cent in each group, respectively. This remains one of the most convincing studies of the effectiveness of stress management on survival following an MI (Schneiderman et al. 2001), although whether most health-care services could provide such an expensive long-term intervention is debatable.

Smaller studies have also shown positive gains following stress management interventions targeted at more general responses to stress. Blumenthal et al. (1997) assigned cardiac patients to either a 'usual care' group involving regular out-patient appointments with a cardiologist, a four-month programme of exercise, or a programme of stress management training. Those in the stress management group were least likely to have a cardiac event over the following year. In a second study examining these issues, the same team (Blumenthal et al. 2005) found both stress management and exercise to be equally effective in changing a number of psychological and physiological markers of disease. Meditation may also prove an effective intervention for people with CHD. Castillo-Richmond et al. (2000), for example, found evidence of a slowing in the development (and even perhaps a modest decrease) in the thickness of atherosclerosis in the carotid artery of hypertensive African

Americans who were taught meditation compared to controls who were not.

Depression substantially increases risk of infarction or re-infarction (see Frasure-Smith et al. 1995). Such a relationship suggests that interventions that reduce depression should reduce the risk of re-infarction. In one of the first studies to examine this issue, Black et al. (1998) allocated MI patients found to be experiencing significant distress to either usual care or to one to seven sessions of behavioural therapy. They found that 35 per cent of participants in the active intervention were hospitalised with cardiac symptoms in the following year, in comparison with 48 per cent of those in the usual care group. However, whether this difference was a consequence of physiological or psychological changes such as less anxiety over cardiac symptoms is not clear.

Unfortunately, evidence from the largest trial of any form of cardiac rehabilitation, known as the ENRICHD study (Berkman et al. 2003), suggests that interventions targeted at depression may not prove as effective as this early study suggested. The ENRICHD study was a large multicentre study involving 2,481 patients, providing an intervention lasting up to one year for people identified as depressed immediately following their MI. All participants in the active intervention arm received two or three treatment components, each aimed at improving their emotional state:

● group cognitive-behavioural therapy;
● social support enhanced by training participants in the social skills needed to develop their social support network;
● antidepressant medication for people who did not evidence any improvement in mood received.

A comparison group received the usual care provided by the institutions in which the study took place. Unfortunately, the results of the study were disappointing. Although the ENRICHD intervention did result in lower levels of depression than those achieved in the usual care condition, there were no differences in survival between the two groups over the two years following infarction. These data have led some to claim that there are no benefits to treating depression in MI patients – and they certainly seem to indicate this to be the case. However, the sheer size of the study meant that the investigators had limited control over the interventions received by patients in both arms of the study. This

---

Type A behaviour

time urgent easily angered behaviour associated with increased risk of coronary heart disease.

meant that the usual care received by some people in the control condition was, in fact, very similar to that provided by the ENRICHD study. In addition, attendance at the ENRICHD intervention was less than optimal, with most patients attending about eleven sessions – an attendance not that different to many of the control group interventions. Perhaps because of these factors, the differences in levels of depression between the two groups, although statistically significant, were not that great. Accordingly, it remains possible that the reductions in depression in the ENRICHD condition relative to the control condition were not sufficiently large to bring about reductions in risk for further MI.

If treating depression does not appear to result in health gains in cardiac patients, treating anxiety in patients with immune-system-mediated diseases does. One condition in which this issue has been explored is that of HIV/AIDS. Antoni et al. (2002), for example, followed the immunological outcomes in 25 HIV-positive men randomly allocated to either a ten-week stress management intervention or a waiting-list control condition. Their measures particularly focused on the impact of the intervention on CD4+ cells (see Chapter 8 ☞). Immediately following the intervention, those who took

part had higher CD4+ cell counts than those in the control group, despite there being no pre-treatment differences, suggesting that stress management may slow down the disease progress and reduce the risk of opportunistic infections.

A second set of studies has examined whether stress management procedures can influence the health outcomes of people with cancer. We know that stress management can improve immune function in the short term in this population (e.g. McGregor et al. 2004). The key question that then follows is whether these immune changes translate into health gains. The outcomes following the intervention conducted by Fawzy et al. (1993) described earlier in the chapter were encouraging. In a series of studies, they reported the percentage of people in a stress management group and a no-treatment control group to show progression of malignant melanoma six months, five–six years, and ten years after the intervention. At the first of the long-term follow-up periods, participants were significantly less likely to have died of cancer than those in the control group and were marginally more likely to have had a longer period free of disease. By the ten-year follow-up (Fawzy et al. 2003), these differential effects remained. By this time,

IN THE SPOTLIGHT

It's not just about saving lives . . .

Reading the report of the ENRICHD study, which was published in the prestigious *Journal of the American Medical Association*, it is clear that the readers of this journal had one interest. Did treating depression save lives? This is a question that has excited many health psychologists as well as medical doctors – and it is very important. But because it did not save lives, many psychologists consider the ENRICHD study to be a failure. But was it? Yes, from a biomedical stance, the results of the ENRICHD study were disappointing. But what about a more psychological perspective?

Depression is a potentially disabling condition that has significant implications for the quality of life and

rehabilitation outcomes of both patients and the people involved with them. While psychologists should be involved in the questions of the impact of disease on physiological processes, they should also be careful not to lose sight of other psychological questions and adopting too strong a biomedical stance in the questions they address. Changes in depression are an important outcome in themselves – not just a vehicle to reduce mortality. From this perspective, the ENRICHD intervention proved a costly one that fared moderately better than the care usually provided. As such, it provides a wealth of information about how to identify and treat depression in cardiac patients, with potentially significant benefits to future patients. We should be careful not to throw out the 'psychological baby' when we throw out the 'medical bath water'.

11 of the 34 people in the control group had had recurrences and had died of cancer; 3 others had had non-fatal recurrences. In the stress management group, 9 of 34 had died of cancer, and 2 had survived recurrences. Overall, these differences were not significantly different between the groups. However, after statistically controlling for differences in the severity of the presenting melanoma, more participants who took part in the stress management intervention survived up to ten years after their initial diagnosis than those in the control group. Similar gains following stress management training or similar interventions have been found in two large studies of patients with gastrointestinal cancer (Kuchler et al. 1999) and a mixture of cancers (McCorkle et al. 2000), although some smaller studies have reported null findings. Ross et al. (2002) pointed out that the effects of these interventions may have been stronger if patients had been selected for any of the studies as a result of their having some distress to ameliorate rather than simply having a diagnosis of cancer. 'Nevertheless, most of the emphasis of studies of psychosocial interventions in cancer is now focusing on quality of life rather than length of life'.

Enhancing social support

One of the earliest studies to examine the impact of increasing social support on disease outcomes was reported by Spiegel et al. (1981). In a study designed to improve the quality of life in cancer patients, they randomly assigned women with breast cancer to either an active treatment programme or a no-treatment control. The active intervention involved weekly support groups that emphasised building strong supportive bonds, expressing emotions, dealing directly with fears of dying, improving relationships within the family and active involvement in decisions concerning treatment. To the surprise of the investigators, women in this group lived an average of 18 months longer than those in the no-treatment control, despite being well matched for disease status at the beginning of the trial. These findings generated a great deal of excitement in the research and clinical community when published. Unfortunately, attempts at replication, including a study conducted by Spiegel himself (Spiegel et al. 2007), have failed to replicate this finding, and social support has yet to be convincingly shown to impact on illness outcomes in patients with cancer.

Photo 17.2 Social support can help you keep healthy. Sometimes by just having someone to talk to. Sometimes by supporting healthy behaviours – even in difficult circumstances!

SUMMARY

The chapter considered psychological interventions designed to achieve three interacting goals in patients with serious chronic diseases:

- to reduce distress;
- to improve disease management;
- to reduce risk of future disease or disease progression.

A number of approaches have been successfully used in each case.

Reductions in distress have been achieved by the use of:

- appropriate information (including information about a condition or coping strategies to minimise distress or improve control over the condition);
- stress management training while waiting for a diagnosis, during treatment and while coping with the emotional stress of living with a long-term illness;
- providing social support – often in the guise of professionally run support groups.

Improvements in the management of illness have been achieved by:

- providing information – particularly information that provides a structure to achieve symptom control rather than simply providing information about a condition or its treatment;
- training in self-management programmes, with emphasis shifting from the provision of general 'one size fits all' programmes to more bespoke

programmes specifically developed to suit participants' needs;

- stress management training in conditions in which stress is involved in their aetiology (e.g. IBS) or may exacerbate symptoms (e.g. angina, diabetes);
- improving social and family support;
- written emotional expression.

Finally, a number of interventions may impact on longer-term health:

- Counselling may be of benefit in cardiac patients, but results of the M-HART study have made people cautious in adopting this model.
- Stress management appears to be of benefit in improving health in a number of conditions, including CHD and HIV/AIDS.
- Treatment of depression in cardiac patients may impact on prognosis, although the ENRICHD study suggests that this approach should be viewed with caution.
- Social support may be of benefit, although the promise of some early studies has not been repeated in later studies.

Overall, there is significant evidence that psychological interventions can be of great value in helping people to come to terms with the emotional consequences of having a serious chronic illness. They may also be of benefit in aiding day-to-day symptoms and even longer-term prognoses in a more limited set of conditions.

Further reading

Antoni MH. (2013). Psychosocial intervention effects on adaptation, disease course and biobehavioral processes in cancer. *Brain, Behavior and Immunity,* 30 Suppl: S88–98.

Recent review of outcomes following primarily stress management interventions. Needs a bit of psychoneuroimmunology knowledge, so can be hard work. But worth the read.

Health Quality Ontario (2009). Behavioural interventions for type 2 diabetes: an evidence-based analysis. *Ontario Health Technology Assessment Service,* 9:1–45.

A detailed review of the impact of behavioural interventions in one, very important, disease. It's a slightly obscure publication series, but is free on the internet: http://www.ncbi.nlm.nih.gov/pmc/articles/PMC3377516/

Bradt, J., Dileo, C. and Potvin, N. (2013). Music for stress and anxiety reduction in coronary heart disease patients. *Cochrane Database of Systematic Reviews*, Dec 28; 12:CD006577.

A reminder that there are many ways to reduce stress and improve health in people with chronic disease.

Lumley M.A., Sklar E.R., Carty J.N. (2012) Emotional disclosure interventions for chronic pain: from the laboratory to the clinic. *Translational Behavioral Medicine,* 2:73–81.

The latest research on emotional disclosure: some positive, some negative findings.

Paul, C.L., Carey, M.L, Sanson-Fisher, R.W. et al. (2013). The impact of web-based approaches on psychosocial health in chronic physical and mental health conditions. *Health Education Research*, 28: 450–71.

Interesting paper considering the effectiveness of the internet as a means of intervention.

There are many expert patient websites. Some, such as the Stanford site, focus on research, and payment is required to access self-help materials. Others, such as the expert patient programme or the British Heart Foundation, offer a little more. The cardiac psychology site is particularly helpful.

www.expertpatients.co.uk/public/default.aspx?load=PublicHome

http://patienteducation.stanford.edu/

www.bhf.org.uk/

www.cardiacpsychology.com/page/page/4176374.htm

For open-access student resources specifically written to complement this textbook and support your learning, please visit **www.pearsoned.co.uk/morrison**

Part IV
Futures

Chapter 18
Futures

Learning outcomes

By the end of this chapter, you should have an understanding of:

- the need for theory-led practice

- how psychologists may influence practice, and some of the barriers to the effective development of practice

- the training and role of health psychologists in differing parts of the world

- influences on the uptake (or not) of recommended treatment approaches

Health psychology is the future

The most prevalent diseases, certainly across industrialised nations, are now frequently a consequence of how we behave: our lifestyle. Indeed, the World Bank considers the impact of one disease alone, type 2 diabetes, to have profound effects on the economy and cost of the provision of health care.

Their treatment often involves adherence to long-term medication and/or changes in lifestyle to manage symptoms or mitigate risk for increasing health problems. So, behaviour frequently causes diseases, and behavioural change is central to their treatment. But this is not the limit of the role or impact of health psychology in health care. Communication between health-care providers and patients, patients and health-care providers, influencing the use of frequently over-prescribed and abused drugs such as antibiotics, and increasing the psychological awareness of all health-care workers are all central to the discipline of health psychology and the practice of health psychologists. So, the future is exciting for health psychology. Or is it? Health psychologists have yet to obtain a strong professional presence in most health-care systems. The need for psychological skills, so easily recognised by health psychologists, is not necessarily recognised by others. Many health professionals feel they already have the relevant skills and there is no need for potentially expensive specialists. So, arguments for and against a role for health psychologists within a number of health-care systems are still being aired. And their conclusion remains in doubt. It is crucial that those involved in health psychology now spread the word and demonstrate their expertise to make it clear that we have a unique set of skills and abilities that health-care systems cannot afford to ignore. . .

Chapter outline

This chapter draws together a number of the strands of research and the practice of health psychology. It starts with a reminder of the need for health psychologists not only to develop the practice of health psychology, but also to develop and utilise theory in our practice of health psychology. It provides some examples of how theory may inform practice, before examining who may come to actually use interventions based on health psychology theory. The chapter considers some of the barriers to the dissemination of good health-care practice, whether based on health psychology or input from other disciplines. It also considers the development of health psychology as a health-care profession across a number of health-care settings.

The need for theory-driven practice

In this section we consider how health psychology theory can be applied in health-care settings. This book has outlined a wide range of contemporary evidence showing the importance of psychological and psychosocial factors in explaining health, health-related behaviour, and the outcomes of interventions to affect both. Key variables that influence behaviour have been integrated into coherent theories such as the theory of planned behaviour, social cognitive theory, and so on. More complex models, such as the health action process, have further integrated these theories into second-order theories of behavioural acquisition and change. These theories are developing and expanding as a direct result of the theoretical work conducted by many academic health psychologists: the theory of planned behaviour is now, for example, often considered in the context of additional variables such as moral norms and anticipated regret (see Chapter 5 ☞). However, such theories are not only of academic benefit to researchers and other psychologists but also of importance to a range of health-care practitioners, because they help identify which, out of the vast range of potential factors, are most likely to influence behaviour. They can help us construct interventions that are most likely to be effective in a variety of contexts.

An example of this can be found in work on smoking cessation. Ask many health professionals how to help someone stop smoking and they will probably say that the best way is to scare them into behavioural change. Empirical evidence suggests that such an approach will work for some, but not the majority of, smokers. Psychological theory provides a series of alternative factors that may be more influential:

● The *health belief model* suggests that not only do we need to convince smokers that smoking will result in serious illness and that they are at significant risk of developing such illnesses, but we also have to convince them that the benefits of stopping smoking (health, cost, fitness, etc.) outweigh the benefits of continued smoking (avoidance of withdrawal symptoms, loss of social camaraderie, 'It can't happen to me', etc.).

● The *theory of planned behaviour* further emphasises the role of attitudes and beliefs in behaviour change. It also indicates the potential role of peers and other important others in developing personal strategies in stopping smoking. It, and the *health action process*, also clearly indicate the benefit of planning behavioural change, not simply acting on impulse.

● *Social cognition theory* suggests that before people are motivated to stop smoking and/or to continue in any efforts to remain smoke-free, they have to believe they have the ability to do so. The principle of vicarious learning suggests we gain both skills and self-efficacy from observation of coping models – and these should form an integral part of smoking cessation programmes. The theory also suggests that, although health may be a long-term gain following smoking cessation, we are largely influenced by shorter-term benefits. Accordingly, smoking cessation programmes should highlight the short-term benefits of stopping smoking as well as the long-term health gains.

Finally, the emphasis of theory on the role of environmental triggers to behaviours such as smoking indicates the benefit of modifying the environment in the early days of smoking cessation to either minimise the number of cues to smoking a person may experience, or plan specific strategies on how to deal with any urges to smoke as a consequence of such cues should they occur. These factors have not designed an intervention programme, but they provide a good framework, based on first principles, on which to base any smoking cessation programme.

We now consider how two theories may inform our understanding of an individual's response to a set of symptoms and how they can determine the types of intervention we conduct. Some of the first theoretically driven interventions involved changing patients' inappropriate responses to their illness, and in particular the pain they were experiencing (see also Chapter 16 ☞). Seminal work by Fordyce (1982) was influenced by learning theory and used operant conditioning techniques to influence patients' pain-related behaviour. Fordyce argued that our response to pain is determined by both internal sensations of pain and the environmental contingencies any pain-related behaviour provokes. He noted that some individuals responded to pain with either an exaggerated response (groans of pain, winces, and so on) or an absence of behaviour (avoidance of behaviours that may result in pain). Both of these responses may result in poor outcomes. Exaggerated responses may result in over-medication, as carers and health professionals respond to these pain behaviours; avoidance behaviours may result in a reduction in physical capacity. Fordyce argued that rather than treat the pain, which we cannot see and evaluate, we should instead manage the pain-related behaviours by either administering pain relief on a regular basis, ignoring (not reinforcing) pain behaviours, and/or rewarding (reinforcing) appropriate behaviours such as engagement in physical activity. He showed in a series of elegant case reports how these simple interventions could significantly alter quite marked inappropriate use of pain medication.

More recent influences on the practice of health-care practitioners have been based on cognitive models of how we respond to and cope with serious illnesses. Leventhal's self-regulation theory (see Chapter 9 ☞), for example, suggests we generate a set of beliefs, or, more technically, we appraise the nature of our symptoms in terms of what illness they are associated with, its consequences, curability and so on. As in broader theories of emotion, this appraisal determines our emotional reaction to the illness. Although Leventhal does not specify specific appraisal–emotion links, other theories (e.g. Lazarus 1999) make these links for us. Appraisals of an illness as serious and out of our control may be associated with the emotions of anxiety and depression. Appraisals of an illness as serious but controllable may be associated with some anxiety, but also optimism and hope. Appraisals also determine our behavioural response to the illness. Appraisals that an illness is long-term and untreatable, for example, may result in different behaviours to appraisals that the illness will quickly go and is easily treatable. Self-regulation theory also suggests that coping is elicited by our emotional response to a situation, and in particular a negative emotional response. The coping strategies we adopt, whether emotion- or problem-focused, are designed to moderate these negative emotions. Accordingly, someone who has had a myocardial infarction may choose to exercise or stop smoking: behaviours that will both help reduce risk for disease progression and, by doing so, will reduce anxieties associated with such risk. Another individual may avoid exercise, as the sensations they experience while doing so remind them of their illness and the threat it carries to their health.

As we have seen in Chapter 11 ☞, where the coping responses match the reality of the situation, they are likely to be effective. Where there is a mismatch between appraisals and reality, inappropriate coping strategies may be evoked. Worse, inappropriate coping may lead to poor emotional and health states, and lead to a downward cycle of negative expectations and responses to illness. We need to know more about these various steps. However, the basic framework enables effective theoretically driven interventions. For example, we know that any intervention designed to optimise patients' responses to the onset of illness may benefit from a number of elements, including:

● Identification of illness beliefs and attempts to change them if they are either incomplete or incorrect: see, for example, the work of Petrie et al. with cardiac patients described in Chapter 17 ☞. The intervention may also involve the use of cognitive restructuring techniques described in Chapter 13 ☞.

● Teaching skills to help people cope more effectively with the stress of living with a serious illness. Encourage the use of problem-focused coping as appropriate in order to facilitate active attempts to enhance control over the illness and emotion-focused coping strategies or skills such as mindfulness to provide ways of reducing any emotional distress the individual may experience.

● Behavioural hypothesis testing (see Chapter 13 ☞) to disconfirm any inappropriate beliefs an individual may hold.

Again, theory does not provide an individualised intervention, but it does provide a structure around which any intervention may be designed.

The wider social and psychological environment may also be invaluable in facilitating and maintaining behavioural change. Such interventions draw on models of family dynamics, as we discuss in Chapter 15 ☞, and may involve a less individualised approach to behaviour change than is usually the case. These models may be particularly pertinent in the context of changing young people's behaviour (although we would argue that similar issues could usefully be considered in many interventions to adult behaviour). DiMatteo (2004a), for example, highlighted the following factors that should be considered when attempting to do so:

● building trust between health professional, young patient and parent through supportive and sensitive interactions and discussion of perspectives on treatment needs and goals;

● the consideration of specific beliefs and attitudes about treatment needs and goals, including areas of discrepancy between young person and parent, and in particular identifying the young person's health beliefs;

● identification and discussion of norms and expectations in relation to the desired behaviour that the young person is exposed to: for example, parental adherence behaviour and treatment anxieties, cultural and social norms of treatment adherence;

● gaining and encouraging family commitment to treatment and within-family communication if problems with treatment arise by providing social support, possibly via illness-specific support groups;

● working together to overcome barriers and increase belief in the ability of the young person to make any required behavioural changes (self-efficacy);

IN THE SPOTLIGHT

Who uses research?

As we discuss in the text, one of the key issues in health psychology is how to link theory to practice. This is a particularly salient issue in public health initiatives, as relatively few health psychologists work directly in health promotion. Furthermore, much of the research reported by health psychologists is in the journals they read. How much these journals are read by others, such as health promotion practitioners – and how much of what they read is translated into actual practice – is questionable.

This issue was highlighted in a paper published by Abraham et al. (2002), who performed a content analysis on safer-sex promotion leaflets used in the UK and Germany. They first identified the types of information that we know from theory and/or empirical data are likely to influence behaviour. They then examined the frequency with which these types of information were presented in their sample of safer-sex leaflets. Of the 20 categories of information they identified as influencing behaviour, only one-quarter of the leaflets used text that referred to more than ten. Two-thirds of the leaflets used two or less of these information categories. These data highlight a key issue facing health psychology – how to influence people involved in the health-care system, whether in prevention or treatment of illness. Without this influence, our research is of little or no benefit to health professionals and those they seek to care for.

GETTING EVIDENCE INTO PRACTICE | **525**

● tailoring wherever possible the treatment regime to the lifestyles of the family unit.

After reading this text, you may think that the issues raised here are obvious, and surely must be taken into account when health professionals develop their interventions in the 'real world'. But this is far from the case, as we highlight in IN THE SPOTLIGHT and in the following section. Thus, health psychology needs to continue developing relevant theories and interventions based upon them, and in particular interventions that are 'doable' within the context of busy health professionals (we return to this issue later) as well as considering ways in which the implementation of these interventions can be encouraged. We turn to this issue in the next section.

Getting evidence into practice

Having considered how psychological theory can guide the development of patient-focused and preventive interventions, we now consider how health psychologists and others may facilitate the application of these interventions with relevant client groups. Nowadays, clinicians of all types do not have the luxury of trying out or using interventions that they 'like' or 'feel' may be effective. Increasingly, we are constrained by guidelines and limits of acceptable interventions (see the relevant discussion in Chapter 6 ☞). All clinicians working within modern health-care systems necessarily engage in what is known as evidence-based practice. We use, or at least we should use, interventions or techniques for which there is good evidence of effectiveness. The intervention studies reported in this book have contributed to the knowledge upon which this evidence is based. But simply doing and reporting the research may not be sufficient for psychologists and others to make a contribution to health care. One key issue that all researchers need to address is how our research can effectively influence the process of health care.

The role and training of health psychologists

In the light of the significant research conducted by health psychologists, it would seem reasonable that health psychologists should be able to apply their theoretical and practical knowledge within the health-care system. The British Psychological Society (BPS) certainly thought so when it facilitated the development of the profession of health psychologists by first stimulating and then evaluating and accrediting training programmes in this emerging discipline. This oversight is now provided by a government body responsible for determining the standards of training for a variety of professions (the Health Care Professions Council), and the training of health psychologists is now at a level equivalent to a PhD. At the time of writing, this can be achieved in two ways, both of which involve an initial Master's level degree in health psychology (called the part 1 qualification). Following this, students must acquire the part 2 qualification in order to be able to act as a health psychology practitioner. This can be obtained through two differing routes, both of which involve trainees gaining the equivalent of two years' supervised practice in five areas of competence: (i) generic professional skills, (ii) behaviour change interventions, (iii) research, (iv) consultancy and, (v) teaching and training. In the so-called 'independent route' trainees keep a portfolio of experience which is assessed by an examiner appointed by the British Psychological Society. Trainees also undergo a *viva voce* examination to ensure their knowledge and competencies across a range of issues and contexts. Those following the university route complete the portfolio and also attend university at regular intervals. Examination of competence is carried out by the university. Unfortunately, at the time of writing, trainees on both routes have to organise their own work placements in which they gain the supervision and required skills. Dr Neil Coulson, past chair of the Division of Health Psychology, recently noted both the success of our training and its present weakness, stating:

> As we have developed and refined our models of training and have integrated them into BPS and HCPC systems and structures we are now in a position where we are enjoying a robust, evidence based, forward looking training curricula that will place health psychologists at the forefront of many responses to contemporary health challenges. However, in order to ensure that our discipline flourishes we need to address a number of key challenges including a) funding of stage 2 training places across

the entire UK and b) providing sufficient flexibility to cater for those who wish to pursue an academic career in health psychology as well as a practice-based career.

The BPS Division of Health Psychology identifies the key roles of health psychologists as people who apply psychological research and methods to:

● the promotion and maintenance of health;

● the prevention and management of illness;

● the identification of psychological factors contributing to physical illness;

● the improvement of the health-care system;

● the formulation of health policy.

They also note that the types of questions addressed by health psychologists include:

● How do people adapt to chronic illness?

● What factors influence healthy eating?

● How is stress linked to heart disease?

● Why do patients often not take their medication as prescribed?

Health psychologists work as applied psychologists, teachers, consultants and researchers within a variety of settings such as the NHS, higher education, health promotion, schools or industry. Prospects, the official UK graduate careers website, states that the typical work activities of health psychologists include:

● using psychological theories and interventions for primary prevention and health-related behaviour change in community and workplace settings to reduce health-damaging behaviour;

● encouraging the uptake of health-enhancing behaviour and psychological approaches to health promotion, improving communication between health-care professionals and patients;

● investigating cognitive processes, which mediate and determine health and illness behaviours;

● looking at the psychological impact of acute and chronic illness on individuals and their families to improve quality of life and reduce disability.

They also note that there has been a significant increase in the number of lectureships in health psychology, and growth in research into social and behavioural factors in health and health care. To gain a more detailed perspective on the role and type of job conducted by members of the Division of Health Psychology, the Division conducted a survey of all its members – of whom roughly one-quarter responded. A total of 58 per cent of the survey responders were chartered (i.e. professionally qualified), and one-quarter were also chartered to another discipline of psychology. Just over half the respondents were currently working within the university sector, while 9 per cent were in the NHS in secondary health-care services (usually hospitals) and clinical (direct patient contact) posts. A further 6 per cent of respondents were working in areas such as the prison service, charities, the civil service, research councils and self-employment. Of those working in the NHS, 37 per cent were consultant psychologists (of whom many were consultant *clinical* psychologists), 20 per cent were lower-grade qualified psychologists, while 12 per cent were trainees and 4 per cent were psychology assistants. The types of work individuals engaged in differed, of course, according to work setting and grade. Of those in the NHS, over two-thirds conducted a clinical service, mostly in chronic illness management, while others worked in health promotion, consultancy, education and training, health service research, public health and non-physical health-related practice (e.g. mental health, counselling, learning disabilities). Academics were largely involved in research and teaching.

Many of the more senior individuals in the NHS were probably clinical psychologists with joint membership of the divisions of clinical and health psychology. Many clinical psychologists work with patients who have physical health problems – often in the same ways as health psychologists. Clinical psychology is a well-established profession with a strong reputation within the NHS, and the emergence of the much newer profession of health psychologists, claiming the right to work in this clinical area, has not always been without causing tensions between the two professional groups. Nevertheless, Neil Coulson was optimistic about the role of the profession, particularly across a wide range of areas beyond immediate patient care:

In the past 5-8 years I believe health psychology as a field has made considerable progress with regards behaviour change and integrating evidence-based practice across a range of public health and health

Photo 18.1 Get down with it!

Source: Alamy Images/Tetra Images.

promotion settings. In addition, I believe even more progress has been made across a longer time period with regards self-management and supporting the psychosocial needs of people affected by long term conditions. That said, I believe both areas are yet to fully realise their full potential from a technology point of view. However, one area that I worry may be neglected going forward is the 'power of people' – arguably one of the greatest resources we can draw upon is that of others who may be living with a similar condition or trying to achieve a similar health behaviour change goal. We must not lose sight of this.

CASE STUDY

Health psychology in practice

These two job descriptions are examples of job descriptions recently undertaken by health psychologists.

1. Job title: Consultant health psychologist

● *Main roles*: Responsible for developing, leading, managing and providing the psychology service to Cardiac Medicine and Renal Medicine. Provides highly specialist psychological care (including individual and group interventions, consultative advice and supervision for colleagues, education of colleagues and service-based research) for patients with renal disease and coronary heart disease as part of the multidisciplinary teams. Provides supervision, teaching and training and consultation to other health-care staff and organisations. Supervises doctoral trainees and newly qualified Clinical and Health psychologists. Member of the Departmental Management Team which provides strategic and operational management of Health Psychology Services. Line-manages staff within the Renal and Cardiac Rehabilitation services. Participates in budgetary planning for the Renal and Cardiac Rehabilitation services.

2. Job title: Head of Stop Smoking Services

● *Main roles*: Managing and developing a stop smoking service. Applying research into practice. Determining levels of stop smoking treatment required according to local demand. Managing service budget. Ensuring that there is appropriate training available for health professionals and others regarding smoking cessation. Ensuring that trained staff receive appropriate ongoing professional development. Evaluating existing services and applying changes as necessary. Chairing the Primary Care Trust steering group for smoking cessation. Managing multi-disciplinary team of stop smoking advisers. Providing a health psychology input for other public health initiatives. Providing treatment services to people expressing an interest in stopping smoking. Liaising with other services within the Health Authority and Region to ensure exchange of information and coordinated service provision. Coordinating Continuing Professional Development (training)

● provision for stop smoking staff within the Health Authority. Working on Pan-London initiatives to promote stop smoking services.

The Australian Psychology Society (APS) Division of Health Psychology has a similar training and work type as in the UK. It notes that health psychologists have knowledge and skills in the following areas:

● the interaction between the physical systems of the body, psychological make-up and social networks of friends and family and how they influence health and illness;

● the amount and type of health problems experienced by various groups in Australia;

● the way that people behave, or the underlying attitudes that put their health at risk and how they might change these behaviours to prevent illness and promote health;

● strategies that people can learn to help them cope with illness or associated problems and how they can involve their friends and family to help them in their recovery; and

● the psychological impact of illness.

They identify the areas of specialism of health psychologists as:

● Health promotion:
  – development and provision of programmes that assist in the prevention of illnesses such as heart attacks, stroke, cancer, sexually transmitted diseases, smoking-related illness and dietary-related problems;
  – linking up with other health professionals to understand what behaviours might be contributing

to illness and how they might be changed, e.g. understanding why some people overeat or eat a high-fat diet;
  – identifying how behaviour is linked with the development of disease and injury;
  – designing public health education programmes in areas such as exercise and alcohol, cigarette and drug consumption;
  – determining the distribution of disease and the health needs of differing communities;
  – working with community members to improve their health.

● Clinical health:
  – developing therapy and education programmes to help people cope with health issues such as weight management, cancer and heart health;
  – using psychological treatment for problems that often accompany ill health and injury, such as anxiety, depression, pain, addiction, sleep and eating problems;
  – understanding how psychological factors such as stress, depression and anxiety might be contributing to illness;
  – helping people with the self-management of chronic illness;
  – understanding how people cope with diagnosis and medical treatment of acute health problems and how they obtain medical care;

- understanding how people cope with terminal illness, including the impact of grief, bereavement, death and dying;

- identifying how the relationship between health professionals, such as doctors, nurses and psychologists, and their patients can influence how well they recover from illness and injury;

- helping people cope with trauma, disability and rehabilitation.

Other countries have less developed professional roles for health psychologists. The Netherlands, for example, despite having a significant number of academic health psychologists, does not have a training programme for health psychologists – although they do have a two-year training programme for generic health professionals who may be involved in some of the work that health psychologists do in other countries. Similarly, in southern European countries such as Spain and Italy, while health psychology still remains a primarily academic subject, there is an increasing move to training health psychologists who can work in applied settings.

Other people 'do' psychology

Even where health psychologists *are* working in health-care systems, there are still far too few of them to provide a service to all those who may benefit from their work. In addition, many health-care professionals need to adopt psychologically sophisticated ways of working with patients. Accordingly, the application of the principles of care derived from health psychology research is frequently carried out by health professionals with no immediate alliance to psychology. In the absence of health psychologists, how can we ensure that the research conducted by health psychologists is considered by the wider health-care system?

One way this can be achieved is through a key role of health psychologists employed within any health-care system: teaching other professions about health psychology. But how else can this information be disseminated? Unfortunately, at the present time, the answer to this question has to be, 'with difficulty'. One acknowledged problem in influencing health professionals (including psychologists!) is the communication gap between researchers and practitioners; something that psychological research may particularly suffer from. Most health-care practitioners and managers rarely read journals which provide cutting-edge research on the delivery of health care even within their own discipline. But, for psychology the communication problem may be even more acute. Nurses tend to read nursing journals, doctors read medical journals, and so on. Walk through most hospital libraries and you will not see a psychology journal. Yet, most psychological research is published in psychology journals – not medical journals, and not nursing journals. As Richard Lazarus (2000: 667) noted, 'The lack of collaboration and communication between researcher and clinician . . . is a familiar and painful topic for most psychologists'. He went on to say that 'It is disheartening that so few researchers accept the responsibility of making the relevance of their research clear to the practitioner, and so few clinicians pay attention to such research even when it has implications for clinical practice'. Although Lazarus was referring primarily to the situation in the USA, his comments reflect the situation elsewhere in the world.

If reaching and influencing individual health-care professionals is difficult, how *can* psychology influence health care? One way is to publish in relevant journals. Another is through its influence on higher integrative policies. Health-care professionals provide care. But the type of care they provide is constrained by a number of bodies external to them. A number of national psychology and other professional bodies have produced guidelines on psychological care of people with physical health problems. Even more influential than these, though, may be guidelines for care produced by governments and government-sponsored organisations (to which we provide some useful internet links at the end of the chapter). In the United Kingdom, for example, the National Institute for Health and Care Excellence (NICE: www.nice.org.uk/) is responsible for producing treatment guidelines in relation to a variety of health conditions

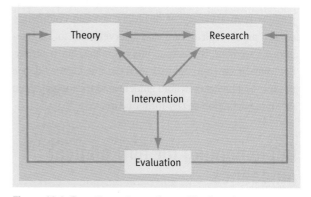

Figure 18.1 From theory to practice and back again

treated within the National Health Service. The NICE guidelines on strategies of behavioural change considered in Chapter 6 ☞ are a good example of this type of guideline. However, more general guidelines may also be influenced by health psychology. The first page of text of the NICE guidelines for the medical 'treatment of acutely ill patients in hospital', for example, runs as follows:

● This guideline offers best practice advice on the care of adult patients within the acute hospital setting. Treatment and care should take into account patients' needs and preferences. People with an acute illness should, if appropriate, have the opportunity to make informed decisions about their care and treatment, in partnership with their healthcare professionals.

● Good communication between healthcare professionals and patients is essential. It should be supported by evidence-based written information tailored to the patient's needs. Treatment and care, and the information patients are given about it, should be culturally appropriate. It should also be accessible to people with additional needs such as physical, sensory or learning disabilities, and to people who do not speak or read English.

● If the patient agrees, carers and relatives should have the opportunity to be involved in decisions about treatment and care. Carers and relatives should also be given the information and support they need.

The type of research reported in Chapter 10 ☞ has clearly contributed to this emphasis on good communication between health professionals and their patients. Health psychology has made a contribution, and an acknowledged contribution, to the care of critically ill patients through its influence on care guidelines. It has also contributed to more specific guidelines, including rehabilitation following myocardial infarction and implantation of ICDs (see Chapter 17 ☞). As guidelines develop for the care of patients with a variety of disorders, we can confidently expect psychological care and interventions to be integrated into them. But despite this optimism, our contribution may be far from optimal. And there is even evidence to show that inclusion within guidelines does not guarantee the implementation of any form of care.

Implementing (or not) clinical guidelines

Unfortunately, even when a fully informed evidence base and written guidelines of best practice exist, and

therefore the gap between research and practice has theoretically been bridged, there is no guarantee that they will actually be implemented by the health professions concerned. A starkly discouraging report by Bellbhudder and Stanfliet (2014), for example, reported that only 6.2 per cent of requests for blood tests to confirm a diagnosis of myocardial infarction made by a group of hospital doctors followed the correct guidelines. Less dramatically, Touzet et al. (2007) reported on the impact of new guidelines for French doctors on the primary care of **bronchiolitis**. This study showed only a slight increase in adherence to the guidelines for the use of non-validated drugs (6.6 per cent adherence before and 14.3 per cent after), provision of general advice (29.0 per cent adherence before and 57.1 per cent after) and physical therapy (91.9 per cent adherence before and 98.8 per cent after). This finding is by no means unique: even asking staff to engage in relatively simple tasks such as hand-washing following patient contact has proven extremely difficult. The NHS Centre for Reviews and Dissemination report, *Effective Health Care: Getting Evidence into Practice* (1999) noted that 'Unless research-based evidence and guidance is incorporated into practice, efforts to improve the quality of care will be wasted. Implementing evidence may require health professionals to change long-held patterns of behaviour' (NHS Centre for Reviews and Dissemination 1999: 1). They highlighted the following factors that may reduce the uptake of clinical guidelines:

● weaknesses in communicating the evidence base to practitioners;

● conflicting sources of information and opinion being available to practitioners (such as patient preferences, which can contradict global recommendations);

● difficulties in getting the right people to work together to implement change;

● resistance to change amplified by health professionals' stress levels.

> **bronchiolitis**
> inflammation of the bronchioles, the smallest air passages of the lungs. It is a common childhood disorder.

Other factors include:

- *personal attitudes and beliefs* regarding the *target behaviour* (their own and/or the patients' behaviour), the *treatment* (for example, attitudes towards HRT – hormone replacement therapy – chemotherapy, child immunisation, abortion) and the *condition* (e.g. obesity, drug use, heart disease, AIDS, chronic fatigue syndrome);

- *personal characteristics of the professional*: age, gender, and cultural values or norms may impact on the willingness to make any required changes;

- *information content*: any changes will not be implemented if they are not seen as credible or applicable to health professionals or patients;

- *information transfer*: deficient communication of information due to the problems of communication within large and complex organisations such as a hospital or health-care system;

- *transferability*: staff may argue that 'what works in research may not work in practice';

- *environmental/organisational issues*: staff may consider there not to be enough time, staff, or support in making any changes to their practice. They may also consider the changes to be too expensive.

Given the wide-ranging potential decision points at which any guidelines may fail, it is not surprising that efforts are being made to try to address this situation. Providing research information alone is insufficient to alter practitioner's health practice (Oxman et al. 1995). However, combining information with reminders about a new guideline can be of benefit. Doherty et al. (2007), for example, reported improvements in various aspects of the treatment of adults with asthma varying from 0 to 26 per cent (deliver therapy via a spacer device), 66 to 84 per cent (use systemic steroids), and 14 to 82 per cent (use written short-term plans) following a mail-out of guideline booklets, and placing posters with flow charts in clinical settings. No changes were found in a hospital which did not receive this intervention. These results show both the existing low levels of adherence to the guidelines and how a relatively simple intervention may markedly increase adherence.

The need for health psychologists to engage politically

Health psychologists need to engage in appropriate dissemination to health-care practitioners and, ideally, to policy makers; and need to become better at it. Having greater professional 'status' (as a consequence of rigorous training), and the increasing presence of health psychology 'practitioners' in health-care settings, will go some way towards making health psychology voices 'heard'. However, there is some concern that psychologists are reluctant to use their carefully collected evidence to provide 'guidelines' for practice. Johnson (1999) suggested that this wariness is due to psychologists' training in being critically aware of limitations in a knowledge base related to a particular type of care (for example, by discounting evidence of the successful implementation of psychological interventions as a consequence of less than perfect research designs). She concluded that: 'I sometimes think we spend more time criticizing each other than we do promoting our accomplishments. In the meantime, other health professionals are more than willing to write practice guidelines and identify standards of care in areas where psychology has greater expertise' (p. 330). To 'sell' our findings to practitioners and policy makers, we need to have confidence in both our findings and ourselves.

In addition to learning how to better 'sell' the findings of health psychology research to health professions and policy makers, Murray and Campbell (2003) argued that health psychologists need to engage more effectively at a socio-political level. To do so, they argued, health psychology needs to broaden its approaches to encompass sociocultural, economic and political aspects of health and health care. The perception of psychology, and by default, health psychology, is that we develop and test our theories and methods at an individual level. This traditional narrowness of focus has, Murray and Campbell argued, held back the effectiveness of strategies to improve health on a large scale (such as reducing HIV infection in sub-Saharan Africa, promoting healthier diets in the West), because salient aspects of the micro and macro socio-economic and political environment that act to maintain inequalities in health are ignored. They further noted that health psychology needs to engage in some reflection in order to move forward in a more 'actionable' manner. Schwarz and Carpenter (1999, cited in Davey-Smith et al. 2001) also noted that focusing on individual-level determinants of health instead of macro-level determinants (such as income or poverty levels) leads to individualised interventions that fail to address the question, or the solution, appropriately.

Photo 18.2 To make an increasing difference to the health of our nations, health psychologists need to disseminate their findings to a wide audience, including health professionals, educators and policy makers

Source: Shutterstock.com/hxdbzxy.

WHAT DO YOU THINK?

So, what do you think? How should psychology and psychologists attempt to influence key players both in health care and other spheres? What can individuals do to disseminate good psychological practice? And what should learned and professional bodies do to promote the discipline? Who are the key players psychologists should influence? Should they seek allies in other health professions, such as nurses or occupational therapists, disciplines for which psychology is a core element of their work? Should we influence politicians, leaders of health services, or others? Who would you target as people or positions to influence, and how would you set about this?

Keep it simple

One key element that has only briefly been touched upon in this chapter is that interventions are more likely to be implemented by both health professionals and their clients if they are relatively simple and easy to implement. One of the authors of this book (PB) was made acutely aware of this in a discussion with colleagues in an academic department of General Practice in which he was working at the time. He was thinking of evaluating the effectiveness of an intervention targeted at depressed cardiac patients to see whether it would reduce both depression and the incidence of recurrent myocardial infarction (see Chapter 17 ☞). The discussion revolved around whether it would be better to run the groups in the weeks immediately after the intervention (and therefore prevent any depression becoming chronic, but risk treating people who would naturally recover without any intervention) or wait for six months and treat people whose depression had become chronic (and potentially harder to treat). Unfortunately, the debate was rather cut short when one of the GPs noted that even if such an intervention were to work, there are so few psychologists who would be able to run such groups (and no likely funding within the NHS) that no GP would be able to send their patients to it! As a result of this discussion, PB went on to develop a highly effective one-page written intervention, based around active distraction, designed to reduce distress in women undergoing genetic risk assessment (Bennett et al. 2007).

Whatever the impact of this discussion on PB's career, the discussion held a key truth. Psychologists and others can develop many and complex interventions, but unless they are implementable within the context of a busy, and tightly resourced, health-care service (as they all are), they will not be taken up by health-care professionals, and managers will not fund them. Interventions such as the Recurrent Coronary Prevention Program (which worked) and the ENRICHD study (which didn't) described in Chapter 17 ☞ may show the potential impact of complex and extended psychological interventions on health. But even if both had proved enormously successful, neither would be implemented in most existing health services. Interventions such as establishing implementation intentions, as discussed in Chapter 6 ☞, or using simple distraction techniques to reduce worry may be less glamorous than these hugely expensive multi-factorial studies, but they may ultimately be of more benefit. The issue that has to be considered when developing any intervention is not only whether it is effective, but also whether it is *cost-effective*. Because only if it is cost-effective will both health-care providers and bodies that provide guidance to health-care providers (such as NICE) endorse the use of such interventions. Accordingly, health psychologists may usefully concentrate on this type of intervention if they want their interventions to be of value in the health-care system.

. . . and finally, be positive

While this textbook has highlighted many of the challenges faced by our discipline (such as definitional clarity, choice of assessment techniques and tools, inclusion and consideration of sociocultural influences on health and illness), it has highlighted the many domains in which health psychology has contributed significantly to understanding (e.g. health behaviour and behaviour change, stress and coping, illness processes and outcomes, psychosocial interventions). There is a lot to be positive about, but clearly not complacent, and many questions remain. For example, do implementation intentions work in clinical samples? Do stage-based activity interventions work in the long term? Does coping really make a difference? Much of health psychology tends to focus on problems – preventing illness, coping with illness, and so on. As well as being optimistic in ourselves, we can also learn from developments in the field of 'positive psychology' (e.g. Seligman and Csikszentmihalyi 2000), which bring with them many other opportunities for health psychology to strengthen its evidence base – see Chapters 11 and 12 ☞. Research in the 'positive psychology' tradition has shown that out of many potentially negative situations come positives (for example, reaffirmed love, or

the discovery of unknown personal strengths, caused by entering a spousal caring role), and that positive affect and the finding of 'meaning' in stressful situations can be adaptational (e.g. Folkman and Moscowitz 2000). Underlying many psychosocial interventions to improve adjustment or behavioural change has been the assumption that certain stressors (e.g. illness, caring) inevitably elicit negative affect and cognition, and that these need to be reduced in order to improve outcome. In contrast, positive psychology encourages thinking to turn to enhancement of positive affect (particularly that which is congruent with one's current situation), such as hope or optimism in a situation where goals are attainable, humour or positive reappraisal where goals are not so easily reached. A good example of how health psychology may provide a biased or distorted view of the impact of health problems can be found in the work examining the impact of cancer genetic risk identification. The work here has consistently found that around one-quarter of the women that undergo assessment for their risk of breast/ovarian cancer experience significant distress (see Chapter 6 ☞). However, a study of this group conducted by one of the authors (PB) found that the most highly endorsed emotional responses to this process included anxiety, but also included the more positive emotions related to hope, challenge and optimism. The neglect of such issues means we run the risk of pathologising many of the phenomena we study, and ignore many of the positive and human aspects they bring. Furthermore, in the area of preventive health, health psychology research has identified 'protective' factors for health as well as risk factors for morbidity. Think, for example, of the research supporting positive associations between social support, or optimism, and positive adjustment to stressful events. Such findings provide opportunities for interventions that are quite different in emphasis from those offered by the findings of negative associations between hostility, stress responses and coronary heart disease. We must not fall into the trap of assuming that we can only advise on 'what not to do'.

Health psychology will not stand still. Its contribution to the health of society is likely to grow as our knowledge base and our confidence in it grows, and as external bodies grow in confidence as to the important role psychology has to play in relation to health. Keep in touch via our website. New developments in the professional and academic practice of this discipline will be highlighted and updated annually on the companion website to this text: www.pearsoned.co.uk/morrison.

SUMMARY

This final chapter has attempted to draw together much of the work described in this book and to give the reader a picture of the ways in which health psychology research can contribute to health practice. Although health psychology is a theory-led discipline, its goals are applied, and we have attempted in this chapter to make the links between theory and practice evident. In addition, we have noted that there is a need for health psychologists to engage more politically and to 'sell' themselves and their (cost-effective) 'goods' more effectively to policy makers and health practitioners. In doing so, we would hope to maximise the impact of health psychology as a discipline upon health psychology as a practice. Our final aim should be to strengthen the links between health psychology and health professional practice in order to benefit all of us, who will at some point in our lives enter the health-care system.

Further reading

Michie, S., van Stralen, M.M. and West, R. (2011) The behaviour change wheel: a new method for characterising and designing behaviour change interventions. *Implementation Science*, 6: 42.

A freely accessible paper looking at Michie's 'behaviour change wheel' which provides a framework for the development of interventions at a range of 'levels' (e.g. individual, social, environmental, etc.). You can also access an online training programme on the specification of behaviour change techniques freely available (at the time of writing) at: www.bct-taxonomy.com.

The Improved Clinical Effectiveness through Behavioural Research Group (ICEBeRG) (2006). Designing theoretically-informed implementation interventions. *Implementation Science*, 1: 4.

A freely accessible paper examining issues in the translation of psychological theory to psychological practice.

Eccles, M., Grimshaw, J., Walker, A. et al. (2005). Changing the behavior of healthcare professionals: the use of theory in promoting the uptake of research findings. *Journal of Clinical Epidemiology*, 58, 107–12.

Another paper examining how to translate theory to practice in the context of health professional behaviour.

In addition to these static texts, it may be interesting to go to websites describing developments in the profession of health psychology. Some examples of such sites (extant in 2012) are:

The Australian Psychological Society:

www.psychology.org.au/community/specialist/health

The site provides a description of the role of health psychologists, as seen by the APS.

The British Psychological Society:

www.bps.org.uk/careers/accredited-courses/accredited-courses_home.cfm

This takes you to a description of a variety of UK postgraduate courses, including training in health psychology.

The European Health Psychology Society:

www.ehps.net/

This introductory page to EHPS leads to information about access to conferences and other potentially relevant information. Of particular note is that it also allows access to the EHPS's newsletter, *The European Health Psychologist*, which regularly presents updates on the professional developments in health psychology within Europe.

The International Society of Behavioral Medicine:

www.isbm.info/

According to the ISBM, 'Behavioral Medicine is the interdisciplinary field concerned with the development and integration of behavioral, psychosocial, and biomedical science knowledge and techniques relevant to the understanding of health and illness, and the application of this knowledge and these techniques to prevention, diagnosis, treatment and rehabilitation.' As such, it has much in common with the applied end of health psychology (and much that is different). The website may be of interest.

Some sources of published clinical guidelines. These are central government resourced guideline resources. Other guidelines may be produced by (usually) specific medical organisations involved in the treatment of specific disorders. Psychology guidelines tend to be more general, and not specific to conditions or types of intervention:

www.nhmrc.gov.au/publications/subjects/clinical.htm (Australia)

www.nice.org.uk/ (England)

www.sign.ac.uk/guidelines/published/index.html (Scotland)

www.guideline.gov/ (USA)

For open-access student resources specifically written to complement this textbook and support your learning, please visit www.pearsoned.co.uk/morrison

Glossary

A

acceptance coping: accepting the reality of a situation and that it cannot easily be changed.

ACE inhibitors: angiotensin II causes the muscles surrounding blood vessels to contract and thereby narrows the blood vessels. Angiotension Converting Enzyme (ACE) inhibitors decrease the production of angiotensin II, allowing blood vessels to dilate, and reduce blood pressure.

acetylcholine: a neurotransmitter that is released at the ends of nerve fibres in the parasympathetic nervous system and is involved in the transmission of nerve impulses in the body.

adrenal glands: endocrine glands, located above each kidney. Comprises the cortex, which secretes several steroid hormones, and the medulla, which secretes noradrenaline.

adrenaline: a neurotransmitter and hormone secreted by the adrenal medulla that increases physiological activity in the body, including stimulation of heart action and an increase in blood pressure and metabolic rate. Also known as epinephrine.

aetiology (etiology): the cause of disease.

affective: to do with affect or mood and emotions.

age-specific mortality: typically presented as the number of deaths per 100,000, per annum, according to certain age groups, for example comparing rates of death from cancer in 2001 between those aged 45–54 with those aged 55–64.

agonist: a drug that simulates the effects of neurotransmitters, such as the serotonin agonist fluoxetine, which induces satiety (reduces hunger).

Alcoholics Anonymous: a worldwide self-help organisation for people with alcohol-related problems. Based on the belief that alcoholism is a physical, psychological and spiritual illness and can be controlled by abstinence. The twelve steps provide a framework for achieving this.

ambivalence: the simultaneous existence of both positive and negative evaluations of an attitude object, which could be both cognitive and emotional.

ambulatory blood pressure: blood pressure measured over a period of time using an automatic blood pressure monitor which can measure blood pressure while the individual wearing it engages in their everyday activities.

angina: severe pain in the chest associated with a temporary insufficient supply of blood to the heart.

antibodies: immunoglobulins produced in response to an antigen.

antigen: unique protein found on the surface of a pathogen that enables the immune system to recognise that pathogen as a foreign substance and therefore produce antibodies to fight it. Vaccinations introduce specially prepared viruses or bacteria into a body, and these have antigens.

antioxidants: oxidation of low-density lipoprotein (LDL or 'bad') cholesterol has been shown to be important in the development of fatty deposits in the arteries; antioxidants are chemical properties (polyphenols) of some substances (e.g. red wine) thought to inhibit the process of oxidation.

antiretroviral drugs: drugs that prevent the reproduction of a type of virus known as a retrovirus. Most well known in the treatment of HIV.

aorta: the main trunk of the systemic arteries, carrying blood from the left side of the heart to the arteries of all limbs and organs except the lungs.

aphasia: impaired ability to understand or produce speech due to brain damage.

appraisals: interpretations of situations, events or behaviour that a person makes.

apraxia: an inability to execute purposive actions due to brain damage.

arteriosclerosis: loss of elasticity and hardening of the arteries.

atheroma: fatty deposit in the intima (inner lining) of an artery.

atherosclerosis: formation of fatty plaque in the arteries.

atopic dermatitis: a number of conditions, including eczema, involving an inflammatory response of the skin.

atrial fibrillation: a heart rhythm disorder (arrhythmia). It involves a very rapid heart rate, in which the atria (upper chambers of the heart) contract in a very rapid and disorganised manner and fail to pump blood effectively through the heart.

attention: generally refers to the selection of some stimuli over others for internal processing.

attributions: a person's perceptions of what causes beliefs, feelings, behaviour and actions (based on attribution theory).

autoimmune conditions: a group of diseases, including type 1 diabetes, Crohn's disease and rheumatoid arthritis, characterised by abnormal functioning of the immune system in which it produces antibodies against its own tissues – it treats 'self' as 'non-self'.

avoidant coping: a style of coping that involves emotional regulation by avoiding confrontation with a stressful situation. Analogous to emotion-focused coping.

B

bad news interview: conversation between health professional (usually a doctor) and patient in which they are told 'bad news', usually that their illness has a very poor prognosis and they may die.

baroreceptors: sensory nerve endings that are stimulated by changes in pressure. Located in the walls of blood vessels such as the carotid sinus.

B cell: a form of lymphocyte involved in destruction of antigens. Memory B cells provide long-term immunity against previously encountered pathogens.

behavioural immunogen: a behavioural practice considered to be health-protective, e.g. exercise.

behavioural pathogen: a behavioural practice thought to be damaging to health, e.g. smoking.

behaviourism: the belief that psychology is the study of observables and therefore that behaviour, not mental processes, is central.

benefit-finding: a process of finding beneficial outcomes as a consequence of what is normally seen as a negative event, such as developing cancer or being infected with the HIV.

beta-blockers: block the action of epinephrine and nor-epinephrine on β-adrenergic receptors, which mediate the 'fight or flight' response, within the heart and in muscles surrounding the arteries. In doing so, they reduce increases in blood pressure associated with sympathetic activation.

bile: a digestive juice, made in the liver and stored in the gallbladder. Involved in the digestion of fats in the small intestine.

biofeedback: technique of using monitoring devices to provide information regarding an autonomic bodily function, such as heart rate or blood pressure. Used in an attempt to gain some voluntary control over that function.

biomedical model: a view that diseases and symptoms have an underlying physiological explanation.

biopsy: the removal of a small piece of tissue for microscopic examination and/or culture, usually to help to make a diagnosis.

biopsychosocial: a view that diseases and symptoms can be explained by a combination of physical, social, cultural and psychological factors (cf. Engel 1977).

blunters: a general coping style that involves minimising or avoiding the source of threat or stress, i.e. avoiding threat-relevant information (as opposed to **monitors**).

body mass index: a measurement of the relative percentages of fat and muscle mass in the human body, in which weight in kilograms is divided by height in metres and the result used as an index of obesity.

bone marrow biopsy: usually performed under local anaesthetic by making a small incision into the skin. A biopsy needle is then pushed through the bone and takes a sample of marrow from the centre of the bone. Marrow contains platelets, phagocytes and lymphocytes.

bronchiolitis: inflammation of the bronchioles, the smallest air passages of the lungs. It is a common childhood disorder.

burnout: a psychological state characterised by long-term exhaustion and diminished interest in work.

C

carcinogenesis: the process by which normal cells become cancer cells (i.e. carcinoma).

cardiac arrest: situation in which the heart ceases to beat.

cardiac event: generic term for a variety of end points of coronary heart disease, including a myocardial infarction, angina and cardiac arrest.

cardiovascular: pertaining to the heart and blood vessels.

carotid artery: the main artery that takes blood from the heart via the neck to the brain.

carotid plaque: a plaque is a thick waxy coating which forms on blood vessel walls and restricts blood flow, in this instance in the carotid artery.

catastrophic thoughts: automatic thoughts that exaggerate the negative aspects of any situation.

catastrophising: the act of constructing **catastrophic thoughts.**

catecholamines: these chemical substances are brain neurotransmitters and include adrenaline and noradrenaline.

causal attribution: where a person attributes the cause of an event, feeling or action to themselves, to others, to chance or to some other causal agent.

CD4+ cells: otherwise known as helper T cells, these are involved in the proliferation of cytotoxic T cells as part of the immune response. HIV infection impairs their ability to provide this function.

cell suicide: a type of cell death in which the cell uses specialised cellular machinery to kill itself.

central nervous system: that part of the nervous system consisting of the brain and spinal cord.

cervical smear: smear of cells taken from the cervix to examine for the presence of cell changes indicating risk of cancer.

chronic bronchitis: an inflammation of the bronchi, the main air passages in the lungs, which persists for a long period or repeatedly recurs. Characterised by excessive bronchial mucus and a cough that produces sputum for three months or more in at least two consecutive years.

chronic obstructive airways disease: a persistent airway obstruction associated with combinations of chronic bronchitis, small airways disease, asthma and emphysema.

clot busters: drugs which dissolve clots associated with myocardial infarction and can prevent damage to the heart following such an event. Are best used within one hour of the infarction.

cognitive dissonance: a state in which conflicting or inconsistent cognitions produce a state of tension or discomfort (dissonance). People are motivated to reduce the dissonance, often by rejecting one set of beliefs in favour of the other.

cognitive restructuring: a reconsideration of automatic negative or catastrophic thoughts to make them more in line with reality.

cognitive schema (schemata): set of unconscious beliefs about the world and ourselves that shape more conscious cognitive responses to events that impinge on us.

cold pressor test: procedure in which participants place their arm in a mixture of water and ice maintaining the water temperature at between 0° and 3° C.

collectivist: a cultural philosophy that emphasises the individual as part of a wider unit and places emphasis on actions motivated by collective, rather than individual, needs and wants.

colonoscopy: a minor surgical procedure in which a small piece of bowel wall is cut from the colon. This can then be tested for the presence of malignant cells.

colostomy: a surgical procedure that creates an opening (stoma) in the abdomen for the drainage of stool from the large intestine (colon). It may be temporary or permanent.

colposcopy: a method used to identify cells that may develop into cancer of the cervix. Sometimes follows a cervical smear if abnormalities are found. A colposcope is a low-power microscope.

comparative optimism: initially termed 'unrealistic optimism', this term refers to an individual's estimate of their risk of experiencing a negative event compared with similar others (Weinstein and Klein 1996).

conditioning theory: the theory that behaviour is directly influenced by its consequences, positive and negative.

congestive heart failure: a disorder in which the heart loses its ability to pump blood efficiently. As a consequence, many organs do not receive enough oxygen and nutrients, leading to the potential for them to become damaged and, therefore, not work effectively.

coping self-efficacy: the belief that one can carry out a particular coping response in a given set of circumstances.

coronary angioplasty: a procedure where a small balloon is inserted into the blocked coronary artery of a person with **atheroma.**

coronary artery bypass graft: surgical procedure in which veins or arteries from elsewhere in the patient's body are grafted from the aorta to the coronary arteries, bypassing blockages caused by atheroma in the cardiac arteries and improving the blood supply to the heart muscle.

coronary heart disease: a narrowing of the blood vessels that supply blood and oxygen to the heart. Results from a build-up of fatty material and plaque (**atherosclerosis**). Can result in **angina** or **myocardial infarction.**

corticosteroids: powerful anti-inflammatory hormones (including cortisol) made naturally in the body or synthetically for use as drugs.

cortisol: a stress hormone that increases the availability of energy stores and fats to fuel periods of high physiological activity. It also inhibits inflammation of damaged tissue.

Crohn's disease: autoimmune disease that can affect any part of the gastrointestinal tract but most commonly occurs in the ileum (the area where the small and large intestine meet).

cross-sectional design: a study that collects data from a sample on one occasion only. Ideally, the sample should be selected to be representative of the population under study.

D

decisional balance: where the costs of behaviour are weighed up against the benefits of that behaviour.

defibrillator: a machine that uses an electric current to stop any irregular and dangerous activity of the heart's muscles. It can be used when the heart has stopped (**cardiac arrest**) or when it is beating in a highly irregular (and ineffective) manner.

denial response: taking a view that denies any negative implications of an event or stimulus. If subconscious, it is considered a defence mechanism.

diabetes (type 1 and 2): a lifelong disease marked by high levels of sugar in the blood and a failure to transfer this to organs that need it. It can be caused by too little insulin (type 1), resistance to insulin (type 2), or both.

diastolic blood pressure: the minimum pressure of the blood on the walls of the arteries between heartbeats (measured in relation to **systolic blood pressure**).

dispositional pessimism: having a generally negative outlook on life and a tendency to anticipate negative outcomes (as opposed to dispositional optimism).

distancing response: taking a detached view, often a scientific view, of an event or stimulus in order to reduce emotional activation.

diuretics: elevates the rate of bodily urine excretion, reducing the amount of fluid within the cardiovascular system, and reducing pressure within it.

drug abuse: involves use of a drug that results in significant social or work-related problems.

drug dependence: usually a progression from drug abuse. Involves dependence on the drug to achieve a desired psychological state, withdrawal symptoms in the absence of the drug, and social and work-related problems.

dualism: the idea that the mind and body are separate entities (cf. Descartes).

dysarthria: poor articulation of speech due to muscular problems.

dysphasia: an inability to generate speech, and sometimes to understand speech as a consequence of brain damage.

E

efficacy: Bandura's technical term analogous to confidence.

egocentric: self-centred, such as in the preoperational stage (age 2–7) of children, when they see things only from their own perspective (cf. Piaget).

emotion-focused coping: coping that seeks to manage the emotional response to the stressor.

empathy: an understanding of the situation from the individual's viewpoint.

emphysema: a late effect of chronic infection or irritation of the bronchial tubes. When the bronchi become irritated, some of the airways may be obstructed or the walls of the tiny air spaces may tear, trapping air in the lung beyond them. As a result, the lungs may become enlarged, at the same time becoming less efficient in exchanging oxygen for carbon dioxide.

empiricism: arising from a school of thought that all knowledge can be obtained through experience.

endocrine glands: glands that produce and secrete hormones into the blood or lymph systems. Includes the pituitary and adrenal glands, and the islets of

Langerhans in the pancreas. These hormones may affect one organ or tissue, or the entire body.

endorphins: naturally occurring opiate-like chemicals released in the brain and spinal cord. They reduce the experience of pain and can induce feelings of relaxation or pleasure. Associated with the so-called 'runner's high'.

epidemiology: the study of patterns of disease in various populations and the association with other factors such as lifestyle factors. Key concepts include mortality, morbidity, prevalence, incidence, absolute risk and relative risk. Type of question: Who gets this disease? How common is it?

erythrocyte: a mature blood cell that contains **haemoglobin** to carry oxygen to the bodily tissues.

exercise programme: a key element of most cardiac rehabilitation, including a progressive increase in exercise usually starting in a gym, sometimes developing into exercise in the home and beyond.

exogenous: relating to things outside the body.

expressed emotion: the disclosure of emotional experiences as a means of reducing stress; often achieved by describing the experience in writing.

F

factor analysis: A method of analysis which seeks to reduce relationships between a wide set of correlated items into meaningful groups, or factors.

false positive result: a situation in which an individual is told that they may have a disease or are at risk of disease, but subsequent tests show that they are not at risk or do not have the disease.

fine needle aspiration: entails placing a very thin needle into a mass within the breast and extracting cells for microscopic evaluation. It takes seconds, and the discomfort is comparable with that of a blood test.

fistulas: formation of small passages that connect the intestine with other organs or the skin.

G

gallbladder: a structure on the underside of the liver on the right side of the abdomen. It stores the bile that is produced in the liver before it is secreted into the intestines. This helps the body to digest fats.

gate control theory of pain: a theory of pain developed by Melzack and Wall in which a 'gate' is used as a metaphor for the chemicals, including **endorphins**, that mitigate the experience of pain.

general adaptation syndrome: a sequence of physiological responses to prolonged stress, from the alarm stage through the resistance stage to exhaustion.

H

haemoglobin: the main substance of the red blood cell. When oxygenated in the lungs, it is converted to oxy-haemoglobin, thus allowing the red blood cells to carry oxygen from the air in our lungs to all parts of the body.

HDL cholesterol: the so-called 'good' cholesterol.

health behaviour: behaviour performed by an individual, regardless of their health status, as a means of protecting, promoting or maintaining health, e.g. diet.

health differential: a term used to denote differences in health status and life expectancy across different groups.

health hardiness: the extent to which a person is committed to and involved in health-relevant activities, perceives control over their health and responds to health stressors as challenges or opportunities for growth.

health locus of control: the perception that one's health is under personal control; controlled by powerful others such as health professionals; or under the control of external factors such as fate or luck.

healthy life expectancy: the WHO provides a fairly vague definition of this phrase: the number of years that a person can expect to live in 'full health' (in contrast to life expectancy, which is how long one would expect to live) by taking into account years lived in less than full health due to disease and/or injury.

heart failure: a state in which the heart muscle is damaged or weakened and is unable to generate a cardiac output sufficient to meet the demands of the body.

hemianopia: loss of half the visual field, usually on one side of a vertical midline. People with the disorder may, for example, when asked only see or draw half a clock.

hemiparesis: weakness of one side of the body.

hemiplegia: paralysis of one side of the body.

high-density lipoprotein (HDL): lipoproteins are fat protein complexes in the blood that transport cholesterol, triglycerides and other lipids to various tissues. The main function of HDL appears to be to carry excess cholesterol to the liver for 're-packaging' or excretion in the bile. Higher levels of HDL seem to be protective against CHD, so HDL is sometimes referred to as 'good' cholesterol.

holistic: root word 'wholeness', holistic approaches are concerned with the whole being and its well-being, rather than addressing the purely physical or observable.

human papillomavirus (HPV): a family of over 100 viruses, of which 30 types can cause genital warts and be transmitted by sexual contact. While most genital HPV come and go over the course of a few years, some HPV infections may markedly elevate the risk for cancer of the cervix.

hypertension: a condition in which blood pressure is significantly above normal levels.

hypoglycaemic episode: occurs when the body's glucose level is too low. It frequently occurs when too much insulin or oral diabetic medication is taken, not enough food is eaten, or following exercise without appropriate food intake. Symptoms include excessive sweating, paleness, fainting and eventually loss of consciousness.

hypothalamus: area of the brain that regulates appetite, sexual arousal and thirst. Also appears to have some control over emotions.

I

illicit drugs: includes illegal substances, but also legal substances that are used in ways other than intended e.g. sniffing glue, injecting valium.

illness behaviour: behaviour that characterises a person who is sick and who seeks a remedy, e.g. taking medication. Usually precedes formal diagnosis, when behaviour is described as **sick role behaviour.**

illness cognition: the cognitive processes involved in a person's perception or interpretation of symptoms or illness and how they represent it to themselves (or to others) (cf. Croyle and Ditto 1990).

illness representations: beliefs about a particular illness and state of ill health – commonly ascribed to the five domains described by Leventhal: identity, timeline, cause, consequences and control/cure.

implicit attitude: attitudes that activate unintentionally in response to actual or symbolic presence of an attitude object (stimulus) and which therefore don't require the cognitive effort of explicit attitudes.

incidence: the number of new cases of disease occurring during a defined time interval – not to be confused with prevalence, which refers to the number of established cases of a disease in a population at any one time.

individual differences: aspects of an individual that distinguish them from other individuals or groups (e.g. age, personality).

individualistic: a cultural philosophy that places responsibility at the feet of the individual; thus behaviour is often driven by individual needs and wants rather than by community needs or wants.

inflammatory bowel disease: a group of inflammatory conditions of the large intestine and, in some cases, the small intestine. The main forms of IBD are **Crohn's disease** and **ulcerative colitis.**

irritable bowel syndrome: a disorder of the lower intestinal tract. Symptoms include pain combined with altered bowel habits resulting in diarrhoea, constipation or both. It has no obvious physiological abnormalities, so diagnosis is by the presence and pattern of symptoms.

ischaemic heart disease: a heart disease caused by a restriction of blood flow to the heart.

K

Kaposi's sarcoma: a malignant tumour of the connective tissue, often associated with AIDS. The tumours consist of bluish-red or purple lesions on the skin. They often appear first on the feet or ankles, thighs, arms, hands and face.

L

lay referral system: an informal network of individuals (e.g. friends, family, colleagues) turned to for advice or information about symptoms and other health-related matters. Often but not solely used prior to seeking a formal medical opinion.

life events: a term used to describe occurrences in a person's life which may be viewed positively or negatively but which inherently require some adjustment on the part of the person (e.g. marriage, loss of job). Such events are implicated in the experience of stress.

limbic system: a series of structures in the brain, often referred to as the 'emotional computer' because of its role in coordinating emotions. It links sensory information to emotionally relevant behaviour, in particular responses to fear and anger.

locus of control: a personality trait thought to distinguish between those who attribute responsibility for events to themselves (i.e. internal LoC) or to external factors (external LoC).

longitudinal (design): responses assessed in a study that have been taken on more than one occasion over time, either prospectively (future-oriented) or retrospectively (based on recall of past events). Prospective longitudinal studies are more powerful, and such methods are important to studies where assessment of change is important.

low-density lipoprotein (LDL): the main function of LDLs seems to be to carry cholesterol to various tissues throughout the body. LDLs are sometimes referred to as 'bad' cholesterol because elevated levels of LDL correlate most directly with **coronary heart disease.**

lower respiratory tract infection: infection of the parts of the respiratory system including the larynx, trachea, bronchi and lungs.

lumpectomy: a surgical procedure in which only the tumour and a small area of surrounding tissue are removed. Contrasts with mastectomy, in which the whole breast is removed.

lymphocyte: a type of white blood cell. Lymphocytes have a number of roles in the immune system, including the production of antibodies and other substances that fight infection and disease. Includes T and B cells.

M

malignant melanoma: a rare but potentially lethal form of skin cancer.

mammography: a low-dose X-ray procedure that creates an image of the breast. The X-ray image can be used to identify early stages of tumours.

mechanistic: a reductionist approach that reduces behaviour to the level of the organ or physical function. Associated with the **biomedical** model.

mediate/mediator: mediating variables explain how or why a relationship exists between two other variables: for example, the effects of age upon behaviour may be mediated by health beliefs; thus age effects would be said to be indirect, rather than direct.

melanoma: a form of skin cancer. Usually begins in a mole and has a poor prognosis unless treated early.

meta-analysis: a review and reanalysis of pre-existing quantitative datasets that combines the analysis so as to provide large samples and high statistical power from which to draw reliable conclusions about specific effects.

migraine: differs from other headaches because it involves symptoms such as nausea, vomiting or sensitivity to light. Their exact cause is not known. However, they appear to be related to problems with blood flow through parts of the brain. At the start of a migraine, blood vessels in certain areas of the brain constrict, leading to symptoms including visual disturbances, difficulty in speaking, weakness or numbness. Minutes to hours later, the blood vessels dilate, leading to increased blood flow in the brain and a severe headache.

mirroring: a key strategy in the process of reflection in which a health professional repeats key words or the last words spoken by a patient, which both show understanding and prompts further information provision.

moderator/moderation: moderating variables explains the conditions under which a relationship between two other variables may exist: for example, the relationship between individual beliefs and behaviour may be different depending on gender or health status.

monitors: a generalised coping style that involves attending to the source of stress or threat and trying to deal with it directly, e.g. through information gathering/attending to threat-relevant information (as opposed to **blunters**).

morbidity: costs associated with illness such as disability, injury.

mortality: death. Generally presented as mortality statistics, i.e. the number of deaths in a given population and/or in a given year ascribed to a given condition (e.g. number of cancer deaths among women in 2000).

motivation: memories, thoughts, experiences, needs and preferences that act together to influence (drive) the type, strength and persistence of our actions.

motivational interview: developed by Miller and Rollnick, a set of procedures designed to increase motivation to change behaviour.

multiple sclerosis: a disorder of the brain and spinal cord caused by progressive damage to the myelin sheath covering of nerve cells. This results in decreased nerve functioning, which can lead to a variety of symptoms, including weakness, paralysis, tremor, pain, tingling, numbness and decreased coordination.

myelin sheath: a substance that contains both protein and fat (lipid) and surrounds all nerves outside the brain. It acts as a nerve insulator and helps in the transmission of nerve signals.

myocardial infarction: death of the heart muscle due to a stoppage of the blood supply. More often known as a heart attack.

N

natural killer (NK) cells: cells move in the blood and attack cancer cells and virus-infected body cells.

negative affectivity: a dispositional tendency to experience persistent and pervasive negative or low mood and self-concept (related to **neuroticism**).

neophobia: a persistent and chronic fear of anything new (places, events, people, objects).

neuroticism: a personality trait reflected in the tendency to be anxious, feel guilty and experience generally negative thought patterns.

neurotransmitter: a chemical messenger (e.g. adrenaline, acetylcholine) used to communicate between neurons and other neurons and other types of cell.

nicotine replacement therapy (NRT): replacement of nicotine to minimise withdrawal symptoms following the cessation of smoking. Delivered in a variety of ways, including a transdermal patch placed against the skin, which produces a measured dose of nicotine over time.

noradrenaline: this **catecholamine** is a neurotransmitter found in the brain and in the **sympathetic nervous system**. Also known as norepinephrine.

O

objective: i.e. real, visible or systematically measurable (e.g. adrenaline levels). Generally pertains to something outside the body that can be seen by others (as opposed to **subjective**).

observational studies: research studies which evaluate the effects of an intervention (or a treatment) without comparison to a control group and thus such studies are more limited in their conclusions than randomised controlled trials.

operant conditioning: attributed to Skinner, this theory is based on the assumption that behaviour is directly influenced by its consequences (e.g. rewards, punishments, avoidance of negative outcomes).

oral hypoglycaemic agents: various drug types, all of which reduce circulating blood sugar.

outcome expectancies: the outcome that is expected to result from behaviour, e.g. exercise will make me fitter.

oxytocin: this hormone which also acts as a neurotransmitter in the brain appears to attenuate (reduce) autonomic stress responses and may be associated with affiliative social behaviour.

P

pain threshold: the minimum amount of pain intensity that is required before it is detected (individual variation).

pancreas: gland in which the islets of Langerhans produce insulin. Also produces and secretes digestive enzymes. Located behind the stomach.

parasympathetic nervous system: arm of the autonomic nervous system that is responsible for rest and recuperation.

pathogen: a collective name for a variety of challenges to our health and immune system, including bacteria and viruses.

patient-controlled analgesia (PCA): a technique through which small doses of analgesic drugs, usually opioids, are administered (usually by an intravenous drip and controlled by a pump) by patients themselves. It is mostly used for the control of postoperative pain.

perceived behavioural control: one's belief in personal control over a certain specific action or behaviour.

phagocyte: an immune system cell that can surround and kill micro-organisms and remove dead cells. Phagocytes include macrophages.

phantom limb pain: a phenomenon that occurs following amputation of a limb, in which the individual feels like they still have their limb, and the limb is in pain.

placebo intervention: an intervention designed to simulate a psychological intervention but not believed to be a specific therapy for the target condition.

platelets: tiny bits of protoplasm found in the blood that are essential for blood clotting. These cells bind together to form a clot and prevent bleeding at the site of injury.

post-traumatic growth: following a traumatic event, including serious illness, a person may experience positive psychological change, e.g. increased life appreciation, improved relations to self and others, new life values and priorities.

post-traumatic stress disorder: a disorder that forms a response to experiencing a traumatic event. The key elements are unwanted repetitive memories of the event, often in the form of flashbacks, attempts at avoidance of such memories, and a generally raised level of arousal.

predisposition: predisposing factors increase the likelihood of a person engaging in a particular behaviour, such as genetic influences on alcohol consumption.

premature mortality: death before the age it is normally expected. Usually set at deaths under the age of 75.

prevalence: the number of established cases of a disease in a population at any one time. Often described as a percentage of the overall population or cases per 100,000 people.

primary health promotion: health promotion targeted at preventing the onset of disease. Contrasts with secondary health promotion, which aims to prevent the further progression of disease.

primary prevention: intervention aimed at changing risk factors prior to disease development.

proactive coping: the process of anticipating potential stressors and acting in advance either to prevent them or to minimise their impact.

problem-focused coping: a style of coping that involves active planning and dealing with any source of stress.

problem-focused counselling: a counselling approach developed by Gerard Egan that attempts to foster a collaborative and structured approach between counsellor and client to solving life problems.

prognosis: the predicted outcome of a disease.

prosocial behaviour: behavioural acts that are positively valued by society and that may elicit positive social consequences, e.g. offering sympathy, helping others.

psychosocial: an approach that seeks to merge a psychological (more micro- and individually oriented) approach with a social approach (macro-, more community- and interaction-oriented), for example, to health.

pulmonary rehabilitation programme: a course attended by patients with chronic lung disease teaching strategies of disease management: relaxation, deep breathing, managing activity, and so on.

Q

qualitative methods: qualitative methods are concerned with describing (qualifying) the experience, beliefs and behaviour of a particular group of people. Data elicited is non-numerical, may or may not be generalisable to the wider population, but may generate themes of response that can be examined in further samples. The depth of material gained through qualitative work is great and allows insight into the meaning behind people's responses. Methods may include open-ended interviews, focus group discussions, taped transactions and conversations. Samples are generally small, given the time demands of data collection and analysis.

quantitative methods: unlike **qualitative methods**, quantitative methods are concerned with counting (quantifying), i.e. data describes the frequency with which a set of beliefs are held or behaviour actioned and means of scores can be obtained and compared statistically. Larger and more representative samples can be obtained, as the method of data collection is predominantly paper-based questionnaires that are self-completed (or can be completed in the presence of a researcher). Criticised for reducing data to numerical categories at the expense of breadth of illustrative meaning.

R

radical prostatectomy: otherwise known as a total prostatectomy, this involves using surgery to remove all of the prostate as a cure for prostate cancer.

reflection: the process of paraphrasing and restating both the feelings and words of the speaker in order to show empathy and understanding of what they are saying.

reinforcers: factors that reward or provide a positive response following a particular behaviour or set of behaviours (positive reinforcer), or enable the removal or avoidance of an undesired state or response (negative reinforcer).

repression: a defensive coping style that serves to protect the person from negative memories or anxiety-producing thoughts by preventing their gaining access to consciousness.

response shift: changes in subjective reports that may result from a reprioritisation of life expectations or recalibration of internal standards so that the construct being assessed is reconceptualised.

rheumatoid arthritis: a chronic autoimmune disease with inflammation of the joints and marked deformities. Something (possibly a virus) triggers an attack of the synovium in the joint by the immune system, which stimulates an inflammatory reaction that can lead to destruction of the joint.

risk ratio: a way of comparing whether the probability of a certain event is the same for two groups. A risk ratio of 1 implies that the event is equally likely in both groups. A risk ratio greater than 1 implies that the event is more likely in the first group. A risk ratio of less than 1 implies that the event is less likely in the first group.

S

salience: strength and importance.

sciatica: pain down the leg, which is caused by irritation of the main nerve into the leg, the sciatic nerve. This pain tends to be caused where the nerves pass through and emerge from the lower bones of the spine (lumbar vertebrae).

self-concept: those conscious thoughts and beliefs about yourself that allow you to feel that you are distinct from others and that you exist as a separate person.

self-determination theory: this theory considers the extent to which behaviour is self motivated (i.e. by intrinsic factors) and influenced by the core needs of autonomy, competence and psychological relatedness.

self-efficacy: the belief that one can perform particular behaviour in a given set of circumstances.

self-regulation: the process by which individuals monitor and adjust their behaviour, thoughts and emotions in order to maintain a balance or a sense of normal function.

self-talk: talking to oneself (internally). Can be negative and thus add to stress. Therapeutically, individuals are taught to use self-talk in a way that helps them to keep calm.

sensitivity (of a test): the ratio of true positive tests to the total number of positive cases expressed as a percentage; for example, a sensitive test may have 95 per cent success in detecting a disease among patients known to have that disease. A test with high sensitivity has few false negatives.

sick role behaviour: the activities undertaken by a person diagnosed as sick in order to try to get well.

social capital: feelings of social cohesion, solidarity and trust in one's neighbours.

social cognition theory (SCT): a model of social knowledge and behaviour that highlights the explanatory role of cognitive factors (e.g. beliefs and attitudes).

social comparison: the process by which a person or group of people compare themselves (their behaviour or characteristics) with others.

social desirability bias: the tendency to answer questions about oneself or one's behaviour in a way that is thought likely to meet with social (or interviewer) approval.

social identity: a person's sense of who they are at a group, rather than personal and individual, level (e.g. you are a student, possibly a female).

socialisation: the process by which a person learns – from family, teachers, peers – the rules, norms and moral codes of behaviour that are expected of them.

social learning theory: a theory that has at its core the belief that a combination of outcome expectancy and outcome value will shape subsequent behaviour. Reinforcement is an important predictor of future behaviour.

socio-economic status: a measure of the social class of an individual. Different measures use different indicators, including income, job type or years of education. Higher status implies a higher salary or higher job status.

Socratic dialogue: exploration of an individual's beliefs, encouraging them to question their validity.

specificity (of a test): the ratio of true negative tests to the total number of negative cases expressed as a percentage; for example healthy people are correctly identified as not having the condition being tested for. A test with high specificity has few false positives.

stages of change model: developed by Prochaska and di Clemente, this identifies five stages through which an individual passes when considering behavioural change: pre-contemplation, contemplation, preparation, change and maintenance/relapse.

statins: drugs designed to reduce cholesterol levels.

stem cell: a 'generic' cell that can make exact copies of itself indefinitely. In addition, such cells have the ability to produce specialised cells for various tissues in the body, including blood, heart muscle, brain and liver tissue. Found in the bone marrow.

stem cell transplant: procedure in which stem cells are replaced within the bone marrow following radiotherapy or chemotherapy or diseases such as leukaemia where they may be damaged.

stress inoculation training: a form of stress-reducing intervention in which participants are taught to control stress by rehearsing prior to going into stressful situations. Participants are taught to relax and use calming self-talk. The approach was developed by Donald Meichenbaum.

stress management training: a generic term for interventions designed to teach participants how to cope with stress.

stress reactivity: the physiological arousal, such as increased heart rate or blood pressure, experienced during a potentially stressful encounter.

stroke: damage to the brain either as a result of a bleed into the brain tissue or a blockage in an artery, which prevents oxygen and other nutrients reaching parts of the brain. More scientifically known as a cerebrovascular accident (CVA).

subjective: personal, i.e. what a person thinks and reports (e.g. excitement) as opposed to what is **objective**. Subjective is generally related to internal interpretations of events rather than observable features.

subjective expected utility (seu) theory: a decision-making model where an individual evaluates the expected utility (cf. desirability) of certain actions and their outcomes and selects the action with the highest seu.

subjective norm: a person's beliefs regarding whether important others (referents) would think that they should or should not carry out a particular action. An index of social pressure, weighted generally by the individual's motivation to comply with the wishes of others (see theory of planned behaviour).

sympathetic nervous system: the part of the autonomic nervous system involved in mobilising energy to activate and maintain arousal (e.g. increased heart rate).

synapse: junction between two neurons or between a neuron and target organ. Nerve impulses cross a synapse through the action of neurotransmitters.

systolic blood pressure: the maximum pressure of blood on the artery walls, which occurs at the end of the left ventricle output/contraction (measured in relation to **diastolic blood pressure**).

T

tachycardia: high heart rate – usually defined as greater than 100 beats per minute.

T cell: a cell that recognises antigens on the surface of a virus-infected cell, binds to that cell and destroys it.

telomeres: DNA clusters on the tip of our chromosomes, which prevent the DNA unravelling. Telomeres shorten naturally with age to the point where the cell cannot replicate.

temporomandibular disorder pain: a variety of conditions that cause tenderness and pain in temporomandibular joint (hinge joint of the jaw).

thalamus: area of the brain that links the basic functions of the hindbrain and midbrain with the higher centres of processing, the cerebral cortex. Regulates attention and contributes to memory functions. The portion that enters the limbic system is involved in the experience of emotions.

theory: a general belief or beliefs about some aspect of the world we live in or those in it, which may or may not be supported by evidence. For example, women are worse drivers than men.

thrombolytic: drugs that affect the blood clotting. Usually involves drugs that reduce the risk of clots forming.

transdermal patch: a method of delivering a drug in a slow release form. The drug is impregnated into a patch, which is stuck to the skin and gradually absorbed into the body.

transient ischaemic attacks: short periods of reduced blood flow to the brain, resulting in symptoms including short periods of confusion, weakness and other minor neurological symptoms.

treadmill test: a test of cardiovascular fitness in which participants gradually increase the level of exercise on a treadmill while having their heart monitored with an electrocardiogram.

trigeminal neuralgia: a painful inflammation of the trigeminal nerve that causes sharp and severe facial pain.

Type A behaviour (TAB): a constellation of characteristics, mannerisms and behaviour including competitiveness, time urgency, impatience, easily aroused hostility, rapid and vigorous speech patterns and expressive behaviour. Extensively studied in relation to the aetiology of coronary heart disease, where hostility seems central.

Type C personality: a cluster of personality characteristics manifested in stoic, passive and non-emotionally expressive coping responses. Thought to be associated with an elevated cancer risk.

Type D personality: a personality type characterised by high negative affectivity and social inhibition.

type 1 diabetes: see diabetes.

type 2 diabetes: see diabetes.

U

ulcerative colitis: a chronic inflammatory disease of the large intestine, characterised by recurrent episodes of abdominal pain, fever and severe diarrhoea.

ultrasound: the use of ultra high-frequency sound waves to create images of organs and systems in the body.

unrealistic optimism: also known as 'optimistic bias', whereby a person considers themselves as being less likely than comparable others to develop an illness or experience a negative event.

V

variable: (noun) something that can be measured or is reported and recorded as data, such as age, mood, smoking frequency or physical functioning.

vasospasm: a situation in which the muscles of artery walls in the heart contract and relax rapidly, resulting in a reduction of the flow of blood through the artery.

vicarious learning: learning from observation of others.

visual field loss: a loss of part of the usual field of vision. Does not include complete blindness in either one or two eyes.

volition: action or doing (the post-intentional stage high-lighted in the HAPA model of health behaviour change).

volitional: behaviour following deliberate or reflective processes rather than those which are automatic or impulsive.

W

well-being: the subjective evaluation of a person's overall life.

written emotional expression: a writing technique in which participants write about upsetting incidents either in their past or related to specific issues.

References

Aaronson, N.K., Ahmedzai, S., Bergman, B. et al. (1993). The European Organisation for Research and Treatment of Cancer QLQ-C30: a quality of life instrument for use in international clinical trials in oncology. *Journal of the National Cancer Institute*, 85: 365–76.

Abbott, S. (1988). Talking about AIDS. Report for AIDS Action Council, Canberra. *National Bulletin*, August, 24–7.

Abdullahi, A., Copping, J., Kessel, A. et al. (2009). Cervical screening: Perceptions and barriers to uptake among Somali women in Camden. *Public Health*, 123: 680–5.

Abraham, C., Krahé, B., Dominic, R. et al. (2002). Do health promotion messages target cognitive and behavioural correlates of condom use? A content analysis of safer sex promotion leaflets in two countries. *British Journal of Health Psychology*, 7: 227–46.

Abraham, C. and Michie, S. (2008). A taxonomy of behavior change techniques used in interventions. *Health Psychology*, 27: 379–87.

Abraham, S.C.S., Sheeran, P., Abrams, D. et al. (1996). Health beliefs and teenage condom use: a prospective study. *Psychology and Health*, 11: 641–55.

Abramsky, L. and Fletcher, O. (2002). Interpreting information: what is said, what is heard – a questionnaire study of health professionals and members of the public. *Prenatal Diagnosis* 22: 1188–94.

Absetz, P., Aro, A.R. and Sutton, S.R. (2003). Experience with breast cancer, pre-screening perceived susceptibility and the psychological impact of screening. *Psycho-Oncology*, 12: 305–18.

Aceijas, C. and Rhodes, T. (2007). Global estimates of the prevalence of HCV infection among injecting drug users. *International Journal of Drug Policy*, 18(5): 352–8.

Acharya, S.D., Elci, O.U., Sereika, S.M. et al. (2009). Adherence to a behavioral weight loss treatment program enhances weight loss and improvements in biomarkers. *Journal of Patient Preference and Adherence*, 3: 151–60.

Achat, H., Kawachi, I., Byrne, C. et al. (2000). Prospective study of job strain and risk of breast cancer. *International Journal of Epidemiology*, 29: 622–8.

Ackerman, K.D., Heyman, R., Rabin, B.S. et al. (2002). Stressful life events precede exacerbations of multiple sclerosis. *Psychosomatic Medicine*, 64: 916–20.

Ackerson, K. and Preston, S. (2009). A decision theory perspective on why women do or do not decide to have cancer screening: systematic review. *Journal of Advanced Nursing*, 65: 1130–40.

Adams, G. and Salter, P.S. (2009). Health psychology in African settings: a cultural-psychological analysis. *Journal of Health Psychology*, 12: 539–51.

Adams, J. and White, M. (2005). Why don't stage-based activity promotion interventions work? *Health Education Research*, 20: 237–43.

Addis, M. E. and Mahalik, J. R. (2003). Men, masculinity, and the contexts of help seeking. *American Psychologist*, 58, 5–14.

Adelman, R.D., Tmanova, L.L., Delgado, S. et al. (2015). Caregiver burden: a clinical review. *JAMA*, 311: 1052–9. doi:10.1001/jama.2014.304

Ader, R. (2001). Psychoneuroimmunology. *Current Directions in Psychological Science*, 10: 94–8.

Ader, R. (2007). *Psychoneuroimmunology*, 4th edn. New York: Academic Press.

Ader, R. and Cohen, N. (1993). Psychoneuroimmunology: conditioning and stress. *Annual Review of Psychology*, 44: 53–85.

Adler, N.E. and Matthews, K.A. (1994). Health psychology: why do some people get sick and some stay well? *Annual Review of Psychology*, 45: 229–59.

Adriaanse, M.A., Vinkers, C.D.W., deRidder, D.T.D. et al. (2011). Do implementation intentions help to eat a healthy diet? A systematic review and meta-analysis of the empirical evidence. *Appetite*, 56: 183–93.

Affleck, G., Tennen, H., Croog, S. et al. (1987). Causal attributions, perceived benefits, and morbidity after a heart attack: an 8-year study. *Journal of Consulting and Clinical Psychology*, 55: 29–35.

Affleck, G., Tennen, H., Zautra, A. et al. (2001). Women's pursuit of personal goals in daily life with fibromyalgia: a value-expectancy analysis. *Journal of Consulting and Clinical Psychology*, 69: 587–96.

Agency for Health Care Policy and Research (1992). *Acute Pain Management, Clinical Practice Guideline*. Silver Spring, MD: AHCPR.

Ager, A., Carr, S., Maclachlan, M. et al. (1996). Perceptions of tropical health risks in Mponda, Malawi: attributions of cause, suggested means of risk reduction and preferred treatment. *Psychology and Health*, 12: 23–31.

Ahmad, W. (2000) (ed.). *Ethnicity, Disability and Chronic Illness*. Buckingham: Open University Press.

Ai, A.L., Park, C.L., Huang, B. et al. (2007). Psychosocial mediators of religious coping styles: a study of short-term distress following cardiac surgery. *Personality & Social Psychology Bulletin*, 33: 867–82.

Aida, J., Kondo, K., Kawachi, I. et al. (2013) Does social capital affect the incidence of functional disability in older Japanese? A prospective population-based cohort study. *Journal of Epidemiology and Community Health*, 67: 42–7.

Aizer, A.A., Chen, M-H., McCarthy, E.P. et al. (2013). Marital status and survival in patients with cancer. *Journal of Clinical Oncology*, 31: 3869–76.

Ajzen, I. (1985). From intentions to actions: a theory of planned behavior. In J. Kuhl and J. Beckman (eds), *Action-control: From Cognition to Behavior*. Heidelberg: Springer Verlag.

Ajzen, I. (1991). The theory of planned behaviour. *Organizational Behavior and Human Decision Processes*, 50: 179–211.

Ajzen, I. and Fishbein, M. (1970). The prediction of behavior from attitudinal and normative beliefs. *Journal of Personality and Social Psychology*, 6: 466–87.

Ajzen, I. and Madden, T.J. (1986). Prediction of goal-directed behavior: attitudes, intentions, and perceived behavioral control. *Journal of Experimental Social Psychology*, 22: 453–74.

Akl, E.A., Oxman, A.D., Herrin J. et al. (2011). Framing of health information messages. *Cochrane Database of Systematic Reviews*, 12: CD006777.

Alaranta, H., Rytokoski, U., Rissanen, A. et al. (1994). Intensive physical and psychosocial training program for patients with chronic low back pain. *Spine*, 19: 1339–49.

Albarracín, D., Johnson, B.T., Fishbein, M. and Muellerleile, P. A. (2001). Theories of reasoned action and planned behaviour as models of condom use: a meta-analysis. *Psychological Bulletin*, 127:142–61.

Albarracín, D., Gillette, J.C., Earl, A.N. et al (2005). A test of major assumptions about behaviour change: a comprehensive look at the effects of passive and active HIV-prevention interventions since the beginning of the epidemic. *Psychological Bulletin*, 131: 856–97.

Aldridge, A.A., and Roesch, S.C. (2007). Coping and adjustment in children with cancer: a meta-analytic study. *Journal of Behavioral Medicine*, 30: 115–29.

Alexander, F. (1950). *Psychosomatic Medicine: Its Principles and Application*. New York: W.W. Norton.

Alexander, S.C., Keitz, S.A., Sloane, R. et al. (2006). A controlled trial of a short course to improve residents' communication with patients at the end of life. *Academic Medicine*, 81: 1008–12.

Allan, J.L., Farquharson, B., Choudhary, C. et al. (2009). Stress in telephone helpline nurses. *Journal of Advanced Nursing*, 65: 2208–15.

Allen, J.D., Stoddard, A.M., Mays, J. et al. (2001). Promoting breast and cervical cancer screening at the workplace: results from the Woman to Woman study. *American Journal of Public Health*, 91: 584–90.

Allen, S.M., Lima, J.C., Goldscheider, F.K. and Roy, J. (2012). Primary caregiver characteristics and transitions in community-based care. *The Journals of Gerontology, Series B: Psychological Sciences and Social Sciences*, 67(3), 362–71, doi:10.1093/geronb/gbs032.

Allied Dunbar National Fitness Survey (1992). *A Report on Activity Patterns and Fitness Levels*. London: Sports Council and Health Education Authority.

Alloy, L.B., Abramson, L.Y. and Francis, E.L. (1999). Do negative cognitive styles confer vulnerability to depression? *Current Directions in Psychological Science*, 8: 128–32.

Allport, G.W. (1920). The influence of the group upon association and thought. *Journal of Experimental Psychology*, 3: 159–82.

Allport, G.W. (1935). Attitudes. In C. Murchison (ed.), *Handbook of Social Psychology*. Worcester, MA: Clark University Press.

Allport, G.W. (1961). *Pattern and Growth in Personality*. New York: Holt, Rinehart & Winston.

Allport, G.W. (1966). Traits revisited. *American Psychologist*, 21: 1–10.

Al-Moamary, M.S. (2008). Experience with pulmonary rehabilitation program in a tertiary care center in Saudi Arabia. *Saudi Medical Journal*, 29: 271–6.

Aloise-Young, P.A., Hennigan, K.M. and Graham, J.W. (1996). Role of self-image and smoker stereotype in smoking onset during early adolescence: a longitudinal study. *Health Psychology*, 15: 494–7.

Al-Smadi, J., Warke, K., Wilson, I. et al. (2003). A pilot investigation of the hypoalgesic effects of transcutaneous electrical nerve stimulation upon low back pain in people with multiple sclerosis. *Clinical Rehabilitation*, 17: 742–9.

Amelang, M. and Schmidt-Rathjens, C. (1996). Personality, cancer and coronary heart disease: further evidence on a controversial issue. *British Journal of Health Psychology*, 1: 191–205.

American Agency for Health Care Policy (1992). *Acute Pain Management: Operative or Medical Procedures and Trauma. Clinical Practice Guideline No. 1*. Washington, DC: AAHCP.

American Cancer Society (2012). ACS Guidelines on Nutrition and Physical Activity for Cancer Prevention: Reducing the Risk of Cancer With Healthy Food Choices and Physical Activity. Kushi, L.H., Doyle, C., McCullough, M., et al. *CA Cancer Journal for Clinicians*, 62: 32–67.

American Heart Association (1995). *Heart and Stroke Facts: 1995 Statistical Supplement*. Dallas, TX: American Heart Association.

American Psychiatric Association (2000). *Diagnostic and Statistical Manual of Mental Disorders*, 4th edn with revised text. Washington, DC: American Psychiatric Association.

American Psychological Association (2015). *Stress in America: Paying with our Health*. Washington, DC: APA.

Ames, G.M. and Janes, C.R. (1987). Heavy and problem drinking in an American blue-collar population: implications for prevention. *Social Science and Medicine*, 25: 949–60.

Amirkhanian, Y.A., Kelly, J.A., Kabakchieva, E. et al. (2005). A randomized social network HIV prevention trial with young men who have sex with men in Russia and Bulgaria. *AIDS*, 19: 1897–905.

Andersen, R. and Newman, F. (1973). Societal and individual determinants of medical care utilization in the United States. *Millbank Memorial Fund Quarterly*, 51: 95–107.

Anderson, M.R., Drescher, C.W., Zheng, Y.Y. et al. (2007). Changes in cancer worry associated with participation in ovarian cancer screening. *Psycho-Oncology*, 16: 814–20.

Anderson, P. and Baumberg, B. (2006). *Alcohol in Europe: A Public Health Perspective*. London: Institute of Alcohol Studies.

Andersson, G. (1996). The benefits of optimism: a meta-analytic review of the Life Orientation Test. *Personality and Individual Differences*, 21: 719–25.

Andrasik F. (2010). Biofeedback in headache: an overview of approaches and evidence. *Cleveland Clinical Journal of Medicine,* 77 Suppl 3: S72–6.

André, M., Borgquist, L. and Molstad, S. (2002). Asking for 'rules of thumb': a way to discover tacit knowledge in general practice. *Family Practice*, 19: 617–22.

Andreassen, H.K., Bujnowska-Fedak, M.M., Chronaki, C.E. et al. (2007) European citizens use of e-health services: a study of seven countries. *BMC Public Health* 7(53).

Andreasson, S., Holder, H.D., Norström, T. et al. (2006). Estimates of harm associated with changes in Swedish alcohol policy: results from past and present estimates. *Addiction*, 101: 1096–105.

Annema, C.M., Luttik, M.L. and Jaarsma, T. (2009). Reasons for readmission in heart failure: perspectives of patients, caregivers, cardiologists and heart failure nurses. *Heart & Lung*, 38: 427–34.

Ansari, M., Shlipak, M.G., Heidenreich, P.A. et al. (2003). Improving guideline adherence: a randomized trial evaluating strategies to increase beta-blocker use in heart failure. *Circulation*, 107: 2799–804.

Antoni, M.H. (1987). Neuroendocrine influences in psycho-immunology and neoplasia: a review. *Psychology and Health*, 1: 3–24.

Antoni, M.H., Baggett, L., Ironson, G. et al. (1991). Cognitive behavioral stress management intervention buffers distress responses and immunological changes following notification of HIV-1 seropositivity. *Journal of Consulting and Clinical Psychology*, 59: 906–15.

Antoni, M.H., Cruess, D.G., Klimas, N. et al. (2002). Stress management and immune system reconstitution in symptomatic HIV-infected gay men over time: effects on transitional naive T-cells (CD4+CD45RA+CD29+). *American Journal of Psychiatry*, 159: 143–5.

Antoni, M.H., Lehman, J., Kilbourn, K. et al. (2001). Cognitive-behavioral stress management intervention decreases depression and enhances optimism and the sense of positive contributions among women under treatment for early-stage breast cancer. *Health Psychology*, 20: 20–32.

Antonovsky, A. (1987). *Unravelling the Mystery of Health: How People Manage Stress and Stay Well*. San Francisco, CA: Jossey-Bass.

Aoun, S.M., Bentley, B., Funk, L. et al. (2012). A 10-year literature review of family caregiving for motor neurone disease: moving from caregiver burden studies to palliative care interventions. *Palliative Medicine*, 27: 437–46.

Appels, A., Bar, F., Lasker, J. et al. (1997). The effect of a psychological intervention program on the risk of a new coronary event after angioplasty: a feasibility study. *Journal of Psychosomatic Medicine*, 43: 209–17.

Appleton, S., Watson, M., Rush, R. et al. (2004). A randomised controlled trial of a psychoeducational intervention for women at increased risk of breast cancer. *British Journal of Cancer*, 90: 41–7.

Aranda, M.P. and Knight, B.G. (1997). The influence of ethnicity and culture on the caregiver stress and coping process: a sociocultural review and analysis. *The Gerontologist*, 37: 342–54.

Arcaya, M., Glymour, M., Christakis, N.A. et al. (2014). Individual and spousal unemployment as predictors of smoking and drinking behavior. *Social Science & Medicine*, doi: 10.1016/j.socscimed.2014.03.034

Arefjord, K., Hallarakeri, E., Havik, O.E. and Maeland, J.G. (1998). Myocardial infarction: emotional consequences for the wife. *Psychology and Health*, 13: 135–46.

Arganini, C., Saba, A., Comitato, R. et al. (2012). Gender differences in food choice and dietary intake in modern Western societies. In J. Maddock (ed). *Public Health – Social and Behavioural Health*. Rijeka: InTech.

Arksey, H. and Glendinning, C. (2008). Combining work and care: carers' decision making in the context of competing policy pressures. *Social Policy & Administration*, 42:1–18.

Armitage, C.J. (2003). The relationship between multidimensional health locus of control and perceived behavioural control: how are distal perceptions of control related to proximal perceptions of control? *Psychology and Health*, 18: 723–38.

Armitage, C.J. (2009). Is there utility in the transtheoretical model? *British Journal of Health Psychology*, 14:195–210.

Armitage, C. and Conner, M. (1998). Extending the theory of planned behaviour: a review and avenues for further research. *Journal of Applied Social Psychology*, 28: 1429–64.

Armitage, C.J. and Conner, M. (2000). Social cognition models and health behaviour: a structured review. *Psychology & Health*, 15: 173–89.

Armitage, C.J. and Conner, M. (2002). Reducing fat intake: interventions based on the theory of planned behaviour. In D. Rutter and L. Quine (eds), *Changing Health Behaviour*. Buckingham: Open University Press.

Armitage, C.J., Conner, M., Loach, J. et al. (1999). Different perceptions of control: applying an extended theory of planned behaviour to legal and illegal drug use. *Basic and Applied Social Psychology*, 21: 301–16.

Aronson, E., Wilson, T.D. and Akert, A.M. (2005). *Social Psychology* (5th edn). Upper Saddle River, NJ: Prentice-Hall.

Arora, N.K. and McHorney, C.A. (2000). Patient preferences for medical decision making: who really wants to participate? *Medical Care*, 38: 335–41.

Arrigo, I., Brunner-LaRocca, H., Lefkovits, M. et al. (2008). Comparative outcome one year after formal cardiac rehabilitation: the effects of a randomized intervention to improve exercise adherence. *European Journal of Cardiovascular Prevention and Rehabilitation*, 15: 306 –11.

Arroyave, W.D., Clipp, E.C., Miller, P.E., et al. (2008). Childhood cancer survivors' perceived barriers to improving exercise and dietary behaviors. *Oncology Nursing Forum*, 35: 121–30.

Asamoah-Adu, A., Weir, S., Pappoe, M. et al. (1994). Evaluation of a targeted AIDS prevention intervention to increase condom use among prostitutes in Ghana. *AIDS*, 8: 239–46.

Ashton, L., Karnilowicz, W. and Fooks, D. (2001). The incidence and belief structures associated with breast self examination. *Social Behavior and Personality*, 29: 223–9.

Aspinwall, L.G. and Brunhart, S.M. (1996). Distinguishing optimism from denial: optimistic beliefs predict attention to health threats. *Personality and Social Psychology Bulletin*, 22: 993–1003.

Aspinwall, L.G. and Taylor, S.E. (1997). A stitch in time: self-regulation and proactive coping. *Psychological Bulletin*, 121: 417–36.

Astin, J.A. (1998). Why patients use alternative medicine: results of a national study. *Journal of the American Medical Association*, 279: 1548–53.

Aston Medical Adherence Study (AMAS) (2012) Establishing the extent of patient non-adherence to prescribed medication in the Heart of Birmingham teaching Primary Care Trust (HoBtPCT), Final Report, Heart of Birmingham teaching Primary Care Trust, R&D Programme, which is now part of NHS Birmingham and Solihull.

Astrom, M. (1996). Generalized anxiety disorder in stroke patients: a 3 year longitudinal study. *Stroke*, 17: 270–5.

Atkinson, R.M. (1994). Late onset problem drinking in older adults. *International Journal of Geriatric Psychiatry*, 9: 321–6.

Attari, A., Sartippour, M., Amini, M. et al. (2006). Effect of stress management training on glycemic control in patients with type 1 diabetes. *Diabetes Research and Clinical Practice*, 73: 23–8.

Audrain, J., Boyd, N.R., Roth, J. et al. (1997). Genetic susceptibility testing in smoking-cessation treatment: one-year outcomes of a randomized trial. *Addictive Behaviors*, 22: 741–51.

Aujoulat, I., Marcolongo, R., Bonadiman, L. and Deccache, A. (2008). Reconsidering patient empowerment in chronic illness: a critique of models of self-efficacy and bodily control. *Social Science & Medicine*, 66: 1228–39.

Austoker, J. (1994). Screening for ovarian, prostate and testicular cancers. *British Medical Journal*, 309: 315–20.

Australian Bureau of Statistics (2005). *The Health and Welfare of Australia's Aboriginal and Torres Strait Islander Peoples*. Canberra: Australian Bureau of Statistics.

Ayanian, J.Z., Cleary, P.D., Weissman, J.S. et al. (1999). The effect of patients' preferences on racial differences in access to renal transplantation. *New England Journal of Medicine*, 341: 1661–9.

Bacharach, S.B., Bamberger, P.A., Sonnenstuhl, W.J. et al. (2004). Retirement, risky alcohol consumption and drinking problems among blue-collar workers. *Journal of Studies in Alcohol*, 65: 537–45.

Bachiocco, V., Scesi, M., Morselli, A.M. et al. (1993). Individual pain history and familial pain tolerance models: relationships to post-surgical pain. *Clinical Journal of Pain*, 9: 266–71.

Back, A.L., Arnold, R.M., Baile, W.F. et al. (2007). Efficacy of communication skills training for giving bad news and discussing transitions to palliative care. *Archives of Internal Medicine*, 167: 453–60.

Badr, H., Acitelli, L.K. and Carmack Taylor, C.L. (2007). Does couple identity mediate the stress experienced by care-giving spouses? *Psychology & Health*, 22: 211–30.

Badr, H., Carmack, C.L., Kashy, D.A. et al. (2010). Dyadic coping in metastatic breast cancer. *Health Psychology*, 29:169–80.

Badr, H. and Taylor, C.L.C. (2008). Effects of relationship maintenance on psychological distress and dyadic adjustment among couples coping with lung cancer. *Health Psychology*, 27: 616–27.

Bagozzi, R.P. (1993). On the neglect of volition in consumer research: a critique and proposal. *Psychology and Marketing*, 10: 215–37.

Baider, L., Andritsch, E., Uziely, B. et al. (2003). Effects of age on coping and psychological distress in women diagnosed with breast cancer: review of literature and analysis of two different geographical settings. *Critical Reviews in Oncology/Hematology*, 46: 5–16.

Baile, W.F., Buckman, R., Lenzi, R. et al. (2000). SPIKES-A six-step protocol for delivering bad news: application to the patient with cancer. *The Oncologist*, 5: 302–11.

Bair, M.J., Matthias, M.S., Nyland, K.A. et al. (2009). Barriers and facilitators to chronic pain self-management: a qualitative study of primary care patients with comorbid musculoskeletal pain and depression. *Pain Medicine*, 10: 1280–90.

Bair, M.J., Robinson, R.L., Katon, W. et al. (2003). Depression and pain comorbidity: a literature review. *Archives of Internal Medicine*, 163: 2433–45.

Baird, B.M., Lucas, R.E. and Donnellan, M.B. (2010). Life satisfaction across the lifespan: findings from two nationally representative panel studies. *Social Indicators Research*, 99: 183–203. doi: 10.1007/s11205-010-9584-9

Baker, A.H. and Wardle, J. (2003). Sex differences in fruit and vegetable intake in older adults. *Appetite*, 40: 269–75.

Baker, K.L., Robertson, N., and Connelly, D. (2010). Men caring for wives or partners with dementia: Masculinity, strain and gain. *Aging & Mental Health*, 14: 319–27.

Bala, M., Strzeszynski, L. and Cahill, K. (2008). Mass media interventions for smoking cessation in adults. *Cochrane Database of Systematic Reviews*, 1: CD004704.

Balarajan, R. and Raleigh, V. (1993). *Ethnicity and Health in England*. London: HMSO.

Balaswamy, S., Richardson, V. and Price, C.A. (2004). Investigating patterns of social support used by widowers during bereavement. *The Journal of Men's Studies*, 13: 67–84.

Balldin, J., Berglund, M., Borg, S. et al. (2003). A 6-month controlled naltrexone study: combined effect with cognitive behavioral therapy in outpatient treatment of alcohol dependence. *Alcoholism Clinical and Experimental Research*, 27: 1142–9.

Baltes, P.B. and Baltes, M.M. (1990). *Successful Aging: Perspectives from the Behavioral Sciences*. New York: Cambridge University Press.

Band, R., Wearden, A., and Barrowclough, C. (2015) Patient outcomes in association with significant other responses to chronic fatigue syndrome: a systematic review of the literature, *Clinical Psychology: Science and Practice,* 22: 29-46 DOI: 10.1111/cpsp.12093

Bandolier (1999). Transcutaneous electrical nerve stimulation (TENS) in postoperative pain. *Bandolier*, July. Available from www.bandolier.com.

Bandolier (2003). Acute pain. *Bandolier* extra, February. Available from www.ebandolier.com.

Bandura, A. (1977). Self-efficacy: toward a unifying theory of behavioral change. *Psychological Review*, 84: 191–215.

Bandura, A. (1986). *Social Foundations of Thought and Action*. Upper Saddle River, NJ: Prentice Hall.

Bandura, A. (1997). *Self-Efficacy: The Exercise of Control*. New York: W.H. Freeman.

Bandura, A. (2001). Social cognitive theory: an agentic perspective. *Annual Review of Psychology*, 52: 1–26.

Banks, S.M., Salovey, P., Greener, S. et al. (1995). The effects of message framing on mammography utilization. *Health Psychology*, 14: 178–84.

Banthia, R., Malcarne, V.L., Varni, J.W. et al. (2003). The effects of dyadic strength and coping styles on psychological distress in couples faced with prostate cancer. *Journal of Behavioral Medicine*, 26: 31–52.

Barber, S.E., Clegg, A.P., Young, J.B. (2012). Is there a role for physical activity in preventing cognitive decline in people with mild cognitive impairment? *Age and Ageing*, 41: 5–8.

Bardel, A., Wallander, M.A., Wedel, H., and Svärdsudd, K. (2009). Age-specific symptom prevalence in women 35–64 years old: a population-based study. *BMC Public Health*, 9:37.

Bardia, A., Tleyjeh, I.M., Cerhan, J.R. et al. (2008). Efficacy of antioxidant supplementation in reducing primary cancer incidence and mortality: a systematic review and meta-analysis. *Mayo Clinic Proceedings*, 83: 23–34.

Barefoot, J.C., Dahlstrom, G. and Williams, R.B. (1983). Hostility, CHD incidence, and total mortality: a 25-year follow-up study of 255 physicians. *Psychosomatic Medicine*, 45: 59–63.

Barlow, J., Turner, A.P. and Wright, C.C. (2000). A randomised controlled study of the Arthritis Self-Management Programme in the UK. *Health Education Research Theory and Practice*, 15: 665–80.

Barlow, J.H., Wright, C., Sheasby, J. et al. (2002). Self-management approaches for people with chronic conditions: a review. *Patient Education and Counselling*, 48: 177–87.

Barnard, D., Street, A., Love, D.W. et al. (2006). Relationships between stressors, work support and burnout among cancer nurses. *Cancer Nursing*, 29: 338–45.

Barnett, M.M., Fisher, J.D., Cooke, H. et al. (2007). Breaking bad news: consultants' experience, previous education and views on educational format and timing. *Medical Education*, 41: 947–56.

Baron-Epel, O. and Kaplan, G. (2001). General subjective health status or age-related subjective health status: does it make a difference? *Social Science and Medicine*, 53: 1373–81.

Barrett, A., Savva, G., Timonen, V., and Kenny, R.A. (eds) (2011). *Fifty plus in Ireland 2011: First results from The Irish Longitudinal Study on Ageing (TILDA),* Dublin, Trinity College Dublin, May, 2011

Barrett, S. and Heubeck, B.G. (2000). Relationships between school hassles and uplifts and anxiety and conduct problems in Grades 3 and 4. *Journal of Applied Developmental Psychology*, 21: 537–54.

Barsdorf, A.I., Schiaffino, K.M., Imundo, L.F. and Levy, D.M. (2009). Pilot study of the Illness Perception Questionnaire-Revised (IPQ-R) in children with juvenile idiopathic arthritis (JIA) [abstract]. *Arthritis & Rheumatism*; 60 Suppl 10:237 DOI: 10.1002/art.25320

Barth, J., Schneider, S. and von Känel, R. (2010). Lack of social support in the etiology and the prognosis of coronary heart disease: a systematic review and meta-analysis. *Psychosomatic Medicine*, 72: 229–38.

Bartley, C.E. and Roesch, S.C. (2011). Coping with daily stress: the role of conscientiousness. *Personality and Individual Differences*, 50: 79–83.

Bartley, M., Sacker, A. and Clarke, P. (2004). Employment status, employment conditions, and limiting illness: prospective evidence from the British household panel survey 1991–2001. *Journal of Epidemiology and Community Health*, 58: 501–6.

Barton, M.B., Morley, D.S. and Moore, S. (2004). Decreasing women's anxieties after abnormal mammograms: a controlled trial. *Journal of the National Cancer Institute*, 96: 529–38.

Bastawrous, M., Gignac, M.A., Kapral, M.K., and Cameron, J.I. (2014). Adult daughters providing post-stroke care to a parent: a qualitative study of the impact that role overload has on lifestyle, participation and family relationships. *Clinical Rehabilitation*, September, e-pub, Doi:10.1177/0269215514552035

Baum, A. (1990). Stress, intrusive imagery and chronic distress. *Health Psychology*, 9: 665–75.

Baum, A., Garofalo, J.P. and Yali, A.M. (1999). Socioeconomic status and chronic stress. Does stress account for SES effects on health? *Annals of the New York Academy of Science*, 896: 131–44.

Baum, A., Gatchel, R.J. and Krantz, D.S. (1997). *An Introduction to Health Psychology*, 3rd edition, New York: McGraw-Hill.

Bauman, B. (1961). Diversities in conceptions of health and fitness. *Journal of Health and Human Behavior*, 2: 39–46.

Baumeister, R.F., Vohs, K.D., Aaker, J.L., and Garbinsky, E.N. (2013). Some key differences between a happy life and a meaningful life. *Journal of Positive Psychology*, 8: DOI: 10.1080/17439760.2013.830764

Beach, S.R., Schulz, R., Lee, J.L. et al. (2000). Negative and positive health effects of caring for a disabled spouse: longitudinal findings from the Caregiver Health Effects study. *Psychology and Aging*, 15: 259–71.

Beadsmoore, C.J. and Screaton, N.J. (2003). Classification, staging and prognosis of lung cancer. *European Journal of Radiology*, 45: 8–17.

Bean, D., Cundy, T. and Petrie, K. (2007) Ethnic differences in illness perceptions, self efficacy and diabetes self care. *Psychology and Health*; 22: 787–811.

Beasley, M., Thompson, T. and Davidson, J. (2003). Resilience in response to life stress: the effects of coping style and cognitive hardiness. *Personality and Individual Differences*, 34: 77–95.

Beaver, K., Bogg, J. and Luker, K.A. (1999). Decision-making role preferences and information needs: a comparison of colorectal and breast cancer. *Health Expectations*, 2: 266–76.

Beaver, K., Luker, K.A., Owens, R.G. et al. (1996). Treatment decision making in women newly diagnosed with breast cancer. *Cancer Nursing*, 19: 8–19.

Beck, A.T. (1976). *Cognitive Therapy and the Emotional Disorders*. New York: International Universities Press.

Beck, A. (1977). *Cognitive Therapy of Depression*. New York: Guilford Press.

Beck, A.T., Ward, C.H., Mendelson, M. et al. (1962). Reliability of psychiatric diagnoses: 2. A study of consistency of clinical judgements and ratings. *American Journal of Psychiatry*, 119: 351–7.

Beck, A.T., Wight, F.D., Newman, C.F. and Liese, B.S. (1993). *Cognitive Therapy for Substance Abuse*. New York: Guilford Press.

Becker, M.H. (ed.) (1974). The health belief model and personal health behavior, *Health Education Monographs*, 2: 324–508.

Becker, M.H., Haefner, D.P. and Maiman, L.A. (1977). The health belief model in the prediction of dietary compliance: a field experiment. *Journal of Health and Social Behavior*, 18: 348–66.

Becker, M.H. and Maiman, L.A. (1975). Socio-behavioral determinants of compliance with health and medical care recommendations. *Medical Care*, 13: 10–14.

Becker, M.H. and Rosenstock, I.M. (1984). Compliance with medical advice. In A. Steptoe and A. Mathews (eds), *Health Care and Human Behavior*. London: Academic Press.

Becker, M.H. and Rosenstock, I.M. (1987). Comparing social learning theory and the health belief model. In W.B. Ward (ed.), *Advances in Health Education and Promotion*. Greenwich, CT: JAI Press.

Beecher, H.K. (1946). Pain in men wounded in battle. *Annals of Surgery*, 123: 96–105.

Been, J.V., Nurmatov, U.B., Cox, B. et al. (2014). Effect of smoke-free legislation on perinatal and child health: a systematic review and meta-analysis. *The Lancet*, 383, 1549–60.

Belanger-Gravel, A., Godin, G. and Amireault, S. (2013). A meta-analytic review of the effect of implementation intentions on physical activity. *Health Psychology Review*, 7: 23–54.

Bell, D.E. (1982). Regret in decision-making under uncertainty. *Operations Research*, 21: 961–81.

Bellaby, P. (2003). Communication and miscommunication of risk: understanding UK parents' attitudes to combined MMR vaccination. *British Medical Journal*, 327: 725–8.

Bellbhudder U. and Stanfliet J.C. (2014). Clinicians ignore best practice guidelines: prospective audit of cardiac injury marker ordering in patients with chest pain. *South Africa Medical Journal*, 104: 305–6.

Belloc, N.B. and Breslow, L. (1972). Relationship between physical health status and health practices. *Preventive Medicine*, 1: 409–21.

Belsky, J. and Pluess, M. (2009). Beyond disthesis stress: differential susceptibilty to environmental influences. *Psychological Bulletin*, 135:885–908.

Bendsten, L., Evers, S., Linde, M. et al. (2010). EFNS guideline on the treatment of tension-type headache – report of an EFNS task force. *European Journal of Neurology*, 17: 1318–25.

Benedetti, F., Lanotte, M., Lopiano, L. et al. (2007). When words are painful: unraveling the mechanisms of the nocebo effect. *Neuroscience*, 147: 260–71.

Benight, C.C., Ironson, G., Klebe, K. et al. (1999). Conservation of resources and coping self-efficacy predicting distress following a natural disaster: a causal model analysis where the environment meets the mind. *Anxiety, Stress and Coping*, 12: 107–26.

Bennett, K.M. (2007). 'No sissy stuff': Towards a theory of masculinity and emotional expression in older widowed men. *Journal of Aging Studies*, 21:347–56.

Bennett, P. (2000). *Introduction to Clinical Health Psychology*. Oxford: Oxford University Press.

Bennett, P. (2003). *Abnormal and Clinical Psychology: An Introductory Text*. Buckingham: Open University Press.

Bennett, P. (2005a). Gastric and duodenal ulcers. In S. Ayers, A. Baum, C. McManus, et al. (eds), *Cambridge Handbook of Psychology, Health and Medicine*, 2nd edn. Cambridge: Cambridge University Press.

Bennett, P. (2005b). Irritable bowel syndrome. In S. Ayers, A. Baum, C. McManus, et al. (eds), *Cambridge Handbook of Psychology, Health and Medicine*, 2nd edn. Cambridge: Cambridge University Press.

Bennett, P. (2006). *Abnormal and Clinical Psychology: An Introductory Text*, 2nd edn. Buckingham: Open University Press.

Bennett, P. and Connell, H. (1999). Dyadic responses to myocardial infarction. *Psychology, Health and Medicine*, 4: 45–55.

Bennett, P. and Murphy, S. (1997). *Psychology and Health Promotion*. Buckingham: Open University Press.

Bennett, P., Owen, R.L., Koutsakis, S. et al. (2002). Personality, social context and cognitive predictors of post-traumatic stress disorder in myocardial infarction patients. *Psychology and Health*, 17: 489–500.

Bennett, P., Parsons, E., Brain, K. et al. (2010). Living at risk: a long-term follow-up study of women at intermediate risk of familial breast cancer. *Psycho-Oncology*, 19: 390–8.

Bennett, P., Phelps, C., Brain, K. et al. (2007). A randomised controlled trial of a brief self-help coping intervention designed to reduce distress when awaiting genetic risk information. *Journal of Psychosomatic Research*, 63, 59–64.

Bennett, P. and Smith, C. (1992). Parents' attitudinal and social influences on childhood vaccination. *Health Education Research: Theory and Practice*, 73: 341–8.

Bennett, P., Smith, P. and Gallacher, J.E.J. (1996). Vital exhaustion, neuroticism and symptom reporting in cardiac and non-cardiac patients. *British Journal of Health Psychology*, 1: 309–13.

Bennett, P., Wilkinson, C., Turner, J. et al. (2008) Psychological factors associated with emotional responses to receiving genetic risk information. *Journal of Genetic Counseling,* 17, 234–41.

Bennett, P., Williams, Y., Page, N. et al. (2004). Levels of mental health problems among UK emergency ambulance personnel. *Emergency Medical Journal*, 21: 235–6.

Bensing, J.M., Tromp, F., van Dulmen, S. et al. (2006). Shifts in doctor–patient communication between 1986 and 2002: a study of videotaped general practice consultations with hypertension patients. *BMC Family Practice*, 25: 62.

Benyamini, Y., Leventhal, E.A. and Leventhal, H. (2003). Elderly people's ratings of the importance of health-related factors to their self-assessments of health. *Social Science and Medicine*, 56: 1661–7.

Beran, M.S., Cunningham, W., Landon, B.E. et al. (2007). Clinician gender is more important than gender concordance in quality of HIV care. *Gender Medicine*, 4: 72–84.

Berenbaum, E. and Latimer-Cheung, A.E. (2014) Examining the link between framed physical activity ads and behavior among women. *Journal of Sport and Exercise Psychology*, 36: 271–80.

Berg, A.I., Hassing, L., McClearn, G.E. and Johansson, B. (2006). What matters for life satisfaction in the oldest-old? *Aging and Mental Health*, 10: 257–64.

Bergland, A., Nicolaisen, M., and Thorsen, K. (2013). Predictors of subjective age in people aged 40–79 years: a five-year follow-up study. The impact of mastery, mental and physical health. *Ageing and Mental Health*, 18: 653–61.

Berkman, L.F. (1984). Assessing the physical health effects of social networks and social support. *Annual Review of Public Health*, 5: 413–32.

Berkman, L.F., Blumenthal, J., Burg, M. et al. (2003). Effects of treating depression and low perceived social support on clinical events after myocardial infarction: the Enhancing Recovery in Coronary Heart Disease (ENRICHD) patients randomized trial. *Journal of the American Medical Association*, 289: 3106–16.

Berkman, L.F. and Syme, S.L. (1979). Social networks, lost resistance and mortality: a nine-year follow-up of Alameda County residents. *American Journal of Epidemiology*, 109: 186–204.

Bermingham, S.L., Cohen, A., Hague, J., and Parsonage, P. (2010). The cost of somatisation among the working-age population in England for the year 2008–09. *Mental Health in Family Medicine*, 7: 71–84.

Bernal, I., Domènech, E., Garcia-Planella, E. et al. (2006). Medication-taking behavior in a cohort of patients with inflammatory bowel disease. *Digestive Diseases and Sciences*, 51: 2165–9.

Bernstein, S.L., Cabral, L., Maantay, J. et al. (2009). Disparities in access to over-the-counter nicotine replacement products in New York City pharmacies. *American Journal of Public Health*, 99: 1699–704.

Bethune, G.R. and Lewis, H.J. (2009). Let's talk about smear tests: social marketing for the National Cervical Screening Programme. *Public Health*, 123 Suppl 1: e17–22.

BHF National Centre for Physical Activity and Health (2007). Active for later life: promoting physical activity with older people: A resource for agencies and organisations. Edinburgh:BHFNCPAH.

Bhopal, R., Hayes, L., White, M. et al. (2002). Ethnic and socio-economic inequalities in coronary heart disease, diabetes and risk factors in Europeans and South Asians. *Journal of Public Health Medicine*, 24: 95–105.

Bhopal, R., Unwin, N., White, M. et al. (1999). Heterogeneity of coronary heart disease risk factors in Indian, Pakistani, Bangladeshi, and European origin populations: cross-sectional study. *British Medical Journal*, 319: 215–20.

Bibace, R., Schmidt, L.R. and Walsh, M.E. (1994). Children's perceptions of illness. In G.N. Penny, P. Bennett and M. Herbert (eds), *Health Psychology: A Lifespan Perspective*. Switzerland: Harwood Academic Publishers.

Bibace, R. and Walsh, M.E. (1980). Development of children's conceptions of illness. *Pediatrics*, 66: 912–17.

Biddle, S. (1995). Exercise and psychosocial health. *Research Quarterly for Exercise and Sport*, 66: 292–7.

Biddle, S., Fox, K. and Boutcher, S. (2000). *Physical Activity and Psychological Wellbeing*. London: Routledge.

Biddle, S. and Murtrie, N. (1991). *Psychology of Physical Activity: A Health Related Perspective*. London: Springer Verlag.

Biddle, S.J.H. and Mutrie, N. (2008). *Psychology of Physical Activity: Determinants, Wellbeing and Interventions*, 2nd edn. London: Routledge.

Bieber, C., Müller, K.G., Blumenstiel, K. et al. (2006). Long-term effects of a shared decision-making intervention on physician–patient interaction and outcome in fibromyalgia: a qualitative and quantitative 1 year follow-up of a randomized controlled trial. *Patient Education and Counseling*, 63: 357–66.

Biener, L., McCallum-Keeler, G. and Nyman, A.L. (2000). Adults' response to Massachusetts anti-tobacco television advertisements: impact of viewer and advertisement characteristics. *Tobacco Control*, 9: 401–7.

Biggam, F.H., Power, K.G., MacDonald, R.R. et al. (1997). Self-perceived occupational stress and distress in a Scottish police force. *Work and Stress*, 11: 118–33.

Bigman, C.A., Cappella, J.N. and Hornik, R.C. (2010). Effective or ineffective: attribute framing and the human papillomavirus (HPV) vaccine. *Patient Education and Counseling*, 81(suppl.): S70–6.

Bijttebier, P., Vercruysse, T., Vertommen, H. et al. (2001). New evidence on the reliability and validity of the pediatric oncology quality of life scale. *Psychology and Health*, 16: 461–9.

Billings, A.G. and Moos, R.H. (1981). The role of coping responses and social resources in attenuating the stress of life events. *Journal of Behavioural Medicine*, 4: 139–57.

Billings, A.G. and Moos, R.H. (1984). Coping, stress, and resources among adults with unipolar depression. *Journal of Personality and Social Psychology*, 46: 877–91.

Bircher, J. (2005). Towards a dynamic definition of health and disease. *Medical Health Care Philosophy*, 8: 335–41.

Bird, J.E. and Podmore, V.N. (1990). Children's understanding of health and illness. *Psychology and Health*, 4: 175–85.

Birmingham Health Authority (1995). *Birmingham Annual Public Health Report: Closing the Gap*. Birmingham: Birmingham Health Authority.

Birmingham, P.K., Wheeler, M., Suresh, S. et al. (2003). Patient-controlled epidural analgesia in children: can they do it? *Anesthesia and Analgesia*, 96: 686–91.

Bishop, G.D. and Teng, C.B. (1992). Cognitive organization of disease information in young Chinese Singaporeans. Paper presented at First Asian Conference in Psychology, Singapore.

Bishop, R., Lau, M., Shapiro, S. et al. (2004). Mindfulness: a proposed operational definition. *Clinical Psychology: Science and Practice*, 11: 230–41.

Bjärehaed, J., Sarkohi, A. and Andersson, G. (2010). Less positive or more negative? Future-directed thinking in mild to moderate depression. *Cognitive Behavior Therapy*, 39, 37–45.

Bjordal, J.M., Johnson, M.I. and Ljunggreen, A.E. (2002). Transcutaneous electrical nerve stimulation (TENS) can reduce postoperative analgesic consumption: a meta-analysis with assessment of optimal treatment parameters for postoperative pain. *European Journal of Pain*, 7: 181–8.

Bjørge, T., Engeland, A., Tverdal, A. et al. (2008). Body mass index in adolescence in relation to cause-specific mortality: a follow-up of 230,000 Norwegian adolescents. *American Journal of Epidemiology*, 168: 30–7.

Black, J.L., Allison, T.G., Williams, D.E. et al. (1998). Effect of intervention for psychological distress on rehospitalization rates in cardiac rehabilitation patients. *Psychosomatics*, 39: 134–43.

Blair, S. and Brodney, S. (1999). Effects of physical inactivity and obesity on morbidity and mortality: current evidence and research issues. *Medicine and Science in Sports and Exercise*, 31(suppl.): S646–62.

Blakely, C., Blakemore, A., Hunter, C. et al. (2014). Does anxiety predict the use of urgent care by people with long term conditions? A systematic review with meta analysis. *Journal of Psychosomatic Research*, 77: 232–9.

Blalock, J.E. (1994). The syntax of immune-neuroendocrine communication. *Immunology Today*, 15: 504–11.

Blane, D., Higgs, P., Hyde, M. and Wiggins, R.D. (2004). Life course influences on quality of life in early old age. *Social Science and Medicine*, 58: 2171–9.

Blaxter, M. (1987). Evidence on inequality in health from a national survey, *The Lancet*, ii: 30–3.

Blenkinsop, S., Boreham, R. and McManus, S. (NFER) (2003). *Smoking, Drinking and Drug Use among Young People in England in 2002*. London: Stationery Office.

Blume, S. (2006). Anti-vaccination movements and their interpretations. *Social Science & Medicine*, 62: 628–42.

Blumenthal, J.A., Jiang, W., Babyak, M.A. et al. (1997). Stress management and exercise training in cardiac patients with myocardial ischemia. *Archives of Internal Medicine*, 157: 2213–17.

Blumenthal, J.A., Sherwood, A., Babyak, M.A. et al. (2005). Effects of exercise and stress management training on markers of cardiovascular risk in patients with ischemic heart disease: a randomized controlled trial. *Journal of the American Medical Association*, 293: 1626–34.

Blyth, F.M., March, L.M. and Cousins, M.J. (2003). Chronic pain-related disability and use of analgesia and health services in a Sydney community. *Medical Journal of Australia*, 179: 84–7.

Bodenmann, G. (1997). Dyadic coping –a systemic transactional view of stress and coping among couples: theory and empiricial findings. *European Review of Applied Psychology,* 47:137–40.

Bodenmann, G., Ledermann, T. and Bradbury, T. (2007). Stress, sex and satisfcaction in marriage. *Personal Relationships*, 14: 551–69.

Boersma, S.N., Maes, S. and van Elderen, T.M.T. (2005a). Goal disturbance predicts health-related quality of life and depression four months after myocardial infarction. *British Journal of Health Psychology*, 10: 615–30.

Boersma, S.N., Maes, S. and Joekes, K. (2005b). Goal disturbance in relation to anxiety, depression, and health-related quality of life after myocardial infarction. *Quality of Life Research*, 14: 2265–75.

Bogg, T. and Roberts, B.X. (2004). Conscientiousness and health-related behaviours: a meta-analysis of the leading behavioral contributors to mortality. *Psychological Bulletin*, 130: 887–919.

Boini, S., Briançon, S., Guillemin, F. et al. (2004). Impact of cancer occurrence on health-related quality of life: a longitudinal pre-post assessment. *Health and Quality of Life Outcomes*, 2: 4–19.

Bokan, J.A., Ries, R.K. and Katon, W.J. (1981). Tertiary gain and chronic pain. *Pain*, 10: 331–5.

Bolas, H., van Wersch, A. and Flynn, D. (2007). The well-being of young people who care for a dependent relative: an interpretative phenomenonological analysis. *Psychology & Health*, 22: 829–50.

Bolejko, A., Sarvik, C., Hagell, P. and Brinck, A. (2008). Meeting patient information needs before magnetic resonance imaging: development and evaluation of an information booklet. *Journal of Radiology Nursing*, 27: 96–102.

Bolejko A., Zackrisson S., Hagell P. et al. (2013). A roller coaster of emotions and sense – coping with the perceived psychosocial consequences of a false-positive screening mammography. *Journal of Clinical Nursing*, 23: 2053–62.

Bond, J., H.O. Dickinson, F. Matthews, C. Jagger and C. Brayne (2006). Self-rated health status as a predictor of death, functional and cognitive impairments: A longitudinal cohort study. *European Journal of Ageing*, 3: 193–206.

Boniol, M. and Autier, P. (2010). Prevalence of main cancer lifestyle risk factors in Europe in 2000. *European Journal of Cancer*, 46: 2534–44.

Booth, A.R., Norman, P., Harris, P.R. and Goyder, E. (2014). Using the theory of planned behaviour and self identity to explain chlamydia testing intentions in young people living in deprived areas. *British Journal of Health Psychology*, 19:101–12.

Booth-Kewley, S. and Friedman, H.S. (1987). Psychological predictors of heart disease: a quantitative review. *Psychological Bulletin*, 101: 343–62.

Booth-Kewley, S. and Vickers, R.R., Jr (1994). Associations between major domains of personality and health behaviour. *Journal of Personality*, 62: 281–98.

Boreham, R. and Shaw, A. (2001). *Smoking, Drinking and Drug Use Among Young People in England in 2000*. London: Stationery Office.

Borland, R. (1997). Tobacco health warnings and smoking related cognitions and behaviours. *Addiction*, 92(11): 1427–35.

Bosch, J.A., Fischer, J.E. and Fischer, J.C. (2009). Psychologically adverse work conditions are associated with CD8+ T cell differentiation indicative of immunesenescence. *Brain Behavior and Immunity*, 23: 527–34.

Bouhuys, A.L., Flentge, F., Oldehinkel, A.J. and van den Berg, M.D. (2004). Potential psychosocial mechanisms linking depression to immune function in elderly subjects. *Psychiatry Research*, 127: 237–45.

Bourbeau, J. and Bartlett, S.J. (2008). Patient adherence in COPD. *Thorax*, 63: 831–8.

Bourdeaudhuij, I. de. and Van Oost, P. (1998). Family characteristics and health behaviours of adolescents and families. *Psychology and Health*, 13: 785–804.

Bourdeaudhuij, I.D. (1997). Family food rules and healthy eating in adolescents. *Journal of Health Psychology*, 2: 45–56.

Bourgeois, M., Schulz, R. and Burgio, L. (1996). Interventions for caregivers of patients with Alzheimer's disease: a review and analysis of content, process and outcomes. *International Journal of Aging and Human Development*, 43: 35–92.

Bouteyre, E., Maurel, M. and Bernaud, J-L. (2007). Daily hassles and depressive symptoms among first year psychology students in France: the role of coping and social support. *Stress & Health*, 23: 93–9.

Bowden, A. and Fox-Rushby, J.A. (2003). A systematic and critical review of the process of translation and adaptation of generic health-related quality of life measures in Africa, Asia, Eastern Europe, the Middle East, South America. *Social Science and Medicine*, 57: 1289–306.

Bowland, L., Cockburn, J., Cawson, J. et al. (2003). Counselling interventions to address the psychological consequences of screening mammography: a randomised trial. *Patient Education and Counseling*, 49: 189–98.

Bowling, A. (1991). *Measuring Health: A Review of Quality of Life*. Buckingham: Open University Press.

Bowling, A. (1995a). *Measuring Disease: A Review of Disease-specific Quality of Life Measurement Scales*. Buckingham: Open University Press.

Bowling, A. (1995b). The most important things in life. Comparisons between older and younger population age groups by gender. Results from a national survey of the public's judgements. *International Journal of Health Sciences*, 6: 169–75.

Bowling, A. (2005). *Measuring Health: A Review of Quality of Life Scales*, 3rd edn. Milton Keynes: Open University Press.

Bowling, A. and Iliffe, S. (2006). Which model of successful ageing should be used? Baseline findings from a British longitudinal survey of ageing. *Age and Ageing*, 35: 607–14.

Brabin, L., Roberts, S.A., Farzaneh, F. et al. (2006). Future acceptance of adolescent human papillomavirus vaccination: a survey of parental attitudes. *Vaccine*, 24: 3087–94.

Bracken, P. and Thomas, P. (2002). Time to move beyond the mind–body split (editorial). *British Medical Journal*, 325: 1433–4.

Brain, K., Gray, J., Norman, P. et al. (2000). Randomized trial of a specialist genetic assessment service for familial breast cancer. *Journal of the National Cancer Institute*, 92: 1345–51.

Braithwaite, D., Emery, J., Walter, F. et al. (2004). Psychological impact of genetic counselling for familial cancer: a systematic review and meta-analysis. *Journal of the National Cancer Institute*, 96: 122–33.

Braithwaite, D., Sutton, S. and Steggles, N. (2002). Intention to participate in predictive genetic testing for hereditary cancer: the role of attitude toward uncertainty. *Psychology and Health*, 17: 761–72.

Bramson, H., Des Jarlais, D.C., Arasteh, K. et al. (2015). State laws, syringe exchange, and HIV among persons who inject drugs in the United States: history and effectiveness. *Journal of Public Health Policy* 36: 212–30.

Brändli, H. (1999). The image of mental illness in Switzerland. In J. Guimon, W. Fischer and N. Sartorius (eds), *The Image of Madness: The Public Facing Mental Illness and Psychiatric Treatment*. Basel: Karger, pp. 29–37.

Branney, P., Witty, K., and Eardley, I. (2014). Psychology, men and cancer. *The Psychologist*, 27: 410–14.

Brataas, H.V., Thorsnes, S.L. and Hargie, O. (2009). Themes and goals in cancer outpatient-cancer nurse consultations. *European Journal of Cancer Care*, 19: 184–91.

Bratzler, D.W., Oehlert, W.H. and Austell, A. (2002). Smoking in the elderly – It's never too late to quit. *Journal of the Oklahoma State Medical Association*, 95: 185–91.

Braun, M., Mikulincer, M., Rydall, A., et al. (2007). Hidden morbidity in cancer: spouse caregivers. *Journal of Clinical Oncology*, 25, 4829–34.

Braverman, M.T., Aarø, L.E. and Hetland, J. (2007). Changes in smoking among restaurant and bar employees following Norway's comprehensive smoking ban. *Health Promotion International*, 23: 5–15.

Brawley, O.W. and Freeman, H.P. (1999). Race and outcomes: is this the end of the beginning for minority health research? *Journal of the National Cancer Institute*, 91: 1908–9.

Brena, S.F. and Chapman, S.L. (1983). *Management of Patients with Chronic Pain*. Great Neck, NY: PMA Publications.

Brengman, M., Wauters, B., Macharis, C. et al. (2010). Functional effectiveness of threat appeals in exercise promotion messages. *Psicologica*, 31: 577–604.

Breslow, L. and Enstrom, J. (1980). Persistence of health habits and their relationship to mortality. *Preventive Medicine;* 9: 469–83.

Brewer, B.W., Manos, T.M., McDevitt, A.V. et al. (2000). The effect of adding lower intensity work on the perceived aversiveness of exercise. *Journal of Sport and Exercise Psychology*, 22: 118–30.

Brewer, N.T., Salz, T. and Lillie, S.E. (2007). Systematic review: the long-term effects of false-positive mammograms. *Annals of Internal Medicine*, 146: 502–10.

Brewin, C., Dalgleish, T. and Joseph, S. (1996). A dual representation theory of post-traumatic stress disorder. *Psychological Review*, 103: 670–86.

Brewin, C.R. and Holmes, E.A. (2003). Psychological theories of posttraumatic stress disorder. *Clinical Psychology Review*, 23: 339–76.

Bridle, C., Riemsma, R.P., Pattenden, J. et al. (2005). Systematic review of the effectiveness of health behavior interventions based on the transtheoretical model. *Psychology & Health*, 20: 283–301.

Brindle, R.C., Ginty, A.T., Phillips, A.C. and Carroll, D. (2014). A tale of two mechanisms: A meta-analytic approach toward understanding the autonomic basis of cardiovascular reactivity to acute psychological stress. *Psychophysiology*, 51: 964–76.

British Heart Foundation (2010). *The National Audit of Cardiac Rehabilitation. Annual Statistical Report*. London: British Heart Foundation.

British Heart Foundation (2012). *Coronary Heart Disease Statistics. A compendium of health statistics*, 2012 edition, British Heart Foundation Health Promotion Research Group Department of Public Health, University of Oxford.

British Medical Association (2003a). *Adolescent Health*. British Medical Association, Board of Science and Education: BMA Publications Unit.

British Medical Association (2003b). *Childhood Immunisation: A Guide for Healthcare Professionals*. British Medical Association, Board of Science and Education: BMA Publications Unit.

British Thoracic Society (1997). Guidelines for the management of chronic obstructive pulmonary disease. *Thorax*, 52(suppl. 5): 1–26.

Briviba, K., Pan, L. and Rechkemmer, G. (2002). Red wine polyphenols inhibit the growth of colon carcinoma cells and modulate the activation pattern of mitogen-activated protein kinases. *Journal of Nutrition*, 132: 2814–18.

Broadbent, E., Petrie, K.J., Alley, P.G. and Booth, R.J. (2003). Psychological stress impairs early wound repair following surgery. *Psychosomatic Medicine*, 65: 865–9.

Broers, S., Kaptein, A.A., Le Cessie, S. et al. (2000). Psychological functioning and quality of life following bone marrow transplantation: a 3-year follow-up study. *Journal of Psychosomatic Research*, 48: 11–21.

Bronfenbrenner, U. (1972). *Two Worlds of Childhood*. New York: Simon & Schuster.

Brose, L.S., Chong, C.B., Aspinall, E. et al. (2014). Effects of standardised cigarette packaging on craving, motivation to stop and perceptions of cigarettes and packs. *Psychology and Health*, 29: 849–60.

Brosschot, J.F., Gerin, W. and Thayer, J.F. (2006). Worry and health: the perseverative cognition hypothesis. *Journal of Psychosomatic Research*, 60: 113–24.

Brosschot, J.F., Pieper, S. and Thayer, J.F. (2005). Expanding stress theory: prolonged activation and perseverative cognition. *Psychoneuroendocrinology*, 30: 1043–9.

Brosschot, J.F. and Thayer, J.F. (1998). Anger inhibition, cardiovascular recovery, and vagal function: a model of the link between hostility and cardiovascular disease. *Annals of Behavioral Medicine*, 20: 326–32.

Brown, G.W. and Harris, T.O. (1989). Life events and measurement. In G.W. Brown and T.O. Harris (eds). *Life Events and Illness*. London (NY): The Guilford Press, pp. 3–45.

Brown, J., Cooper, C. and Kirkcaldy, B. (1996). Occupational stress among senior police officers. *British Journal of Psychology*, 87: 31–41.

Brown, J.S.L., Cochrane, R. and Hancox, T. (2000). Large-scale health promotion stress workshops for the general public: a controlled evaluation. *Behavioural and Cognitive Psychotherapy*, 28: 139–51.

Brown, L.F., and Kroenke, K. (2009). Cancer-related fatigue and its associations with depression and anxiety: a systematic review. *Psychosomatics*, 50:440–7.

Brown, R. (2004). Psychological mechanisms of medically unexplained symptoms: an integrative conceptual mode. *Psychological Bulletin*, 130: 793–813.

Brown, R.J. (2013). Explaining the unexplained. *The Psychologist*, 26: 868–72.

Bruce, J. and van Teijlingen, E. (1999). A review of the effectiveness of Smokebusters: community-based smoking prevention for young people. *Health Education Research*, 14: 109–20.

Brug, J., Conner, M., Harre, N. et al. (2005). The trans-theoretical model and stages of a change: a critique. Observations by five commentators on the paper by Adams, J. and White, M. Why don't stage-based activity promotion interventions work? *Health Education Research*, 20: 244–58.

Brunton, G., Harden, A., Rees, R. et al. (2003). *Children and Physical Activity: A Systematic Review of Barriers and Facilitators*. London: EPPI-Centre, Social Science Research Unit, Institute of Education, University of London.

Bryan, A.D., Aiken, L.S. and West, S.G. (1996). Increasing condom use: evaluation of a theory-based intervention to prevent sexually transmitted diseases in young women. *Health Psychology*, 15: 371–82.

Bryan, A.D., Aiken, L.S. and West, S.G. (1997). Young women's condom use: the influence of acceptance of sexuality, control over the sexual encounter, and perceived susceptibility to common STDs. *Health Psychology*, 16: 468–79.

Bryon, M. (1998). Adherence to treatment in children. In L.B. Myers and K. Midence (eds), *Adherence to Treatment in Medical Conditions*. Netherlands: Harwood Academic Publishers.

Budd, R.J. (1987). Response bias and the theory of reasoned action. *Social Cognition*, 5: 95–107.

Budd, R. and Rollnick, S. (1996). The structure of the readiness to change questionnaire: a test of Prochaska and di Clemente's transtheoretical model. *Health Psychology*, 15: 365–76.

Buglar, M.E., White, K.M. and Robinson, N.G. (2010). The role of self-efficacy in dental patients' brushing and flossing: testing an extended health belief model. *Patient Education & Counselling*, 78: 269–72.

Buick, D. and Petrie, K. (2002). 'I know just how you feel': the validity of healthy women's perceptions of breast cancer patients receiving treatment. *Journal of Applied Social Psychology*, 32: 110–23.

Bullen, K., Edwards, S., Marke, V., and Matthews, S. (2010). Looking past the obvious:experiences of altered masculinity in penile cancer. *Psycho-Oncology*, 19: 933–40.

Bullinger, M. (1997). The challenge of cross-cultural quality of life assessment. *Psychology and Health*, 12: 815–26.

Bundy, C., Carroll, D., Wallace, L. et al. (1994). Psychological treatment of chronic stable angina pectoris. *Psychology and Health*, 10: 69–77.

Burack, J.H., Barrett, D.C., Stall, R.D. et al. (1993). Depressive symptoms and CD4 lymphocyte decline among HIV infected men. *JAMA*, 270(21): 2568–73.

Burford, O., Jiwa, M., Carter, O. et al. (2013). Internet-based photoaging within Australian pharmacies to promote smoking cessation: randomized controlled trial. *Journal of Medical Internet Research*, 15: e64.

Burgess, C., Cornelius, V., Love, S. et al. (2005). Depression and anxiety in women with early breast cancer: five-year observational cohort study. *British Medical Journal*, 330: 702–5.

Burgoyne, R. and Renwick, R. (2004). Social support and quality of life over time among adults living with HIV in the HAART era. *Social Science and Medicine*, 58: 1353–66.

Burke, V., Beilin, L., Cutt, H. et al. (2007). Moderators and mediators of behaviour change in a lifestyle program for treated hypertensives: a randomized controlled trial (ADAPT). *Health Education Research*, B: 583–91.

Burns, J.W., Kubilus, A., Bruehl, S. et al. (2003). Do changes in cognitive factors influence outcome following multidisciplinary treatment for chronic pain? A cross-lagged panel analysis. *Journal of Consulting and Clinical Psychology*, 71: 81–91.

Burns, V.E., Carroll, D., Drayson, M. et al. (2003). Life events, perceived stress and antibody response to influenza vaccination in young, healthy adults. *Journal of Psychosomatic Research*, 55: 569–72.

Burell, G. (1996). Group psychotherapy in project New Life: treatment of coronary-prone behaviors for patients who had coronary bypass graft surgery. In S. Scheidt and R. Allan (eds), *Heart and Mind*. American Psychological Association.

Burton, D., Graham, J.W., Johnson, C.A. et al. (2010). Perceptions of smoking prevalence by youth in countries with and without a tobacco advertising ban. *Journal of Health Communication*, 15: 656–64.

Bury, J., Morrison, V. and MacLachlan, S. (1992). *Working with Women and AIDS: Medical, Social and Counselling Issues*. London: Routledge.

Bush, D.E., Ziegelstein, R.C., Tayback, M. et al. (2001). Even minimal symptoms of depression increase mortality risk after acute myocardial infarction. *American Journal of Cardiology*, 88: 337–41.

Busse, R., Blumel, M., Scheller-Kreinsen. and Zentner, A. (2010) *Tackling Chronic Disease in Europe: Strategies, Interventions and Challenges*. European Observatory on Health Systems and Policies, WHO, Regional Office for Europe.

Butow, P.N., Hiller, J., Price, M.A., et al. (2000). Empirical evidence for a relationship between life events, coping style and personality factors in the development of breast cancer. *Journal of Psychosomatic Research*, 49:169–81.

Buunk, B.P., Zurriaga, R. and González, P. (2006). Social comparison, coping and depression in people with spinal cord injury. *Psychology & Health*, 21: 791–807.

Buzdar, A.U. (2004). Hormonal therapy in early and advanced breast cancer. *Breast Journal*, 10(suppl. 1): S19–21.

Byrne, D.G. and Espnes, G.A. (2008). Occupational stress and cardiovascular disease. *Stress & Health*, 24: 231–8.

Byrne, D.G. and Mazanov, J. (2003). Adolescent stress and future smoking behaviour: a prospective investigation. *Journal of Psychosomatic Research*, 54: 313–21.

Byrne, P. and Long, B. (1976). *Doctors Talking to Patients: A Study of the Verbal Behaviour of General Practitioners Consulting in their Surgeries*. London: HMSO.

Cable, N., Bartley, M., Chandola, T. and Sacker, A. (2013). Friend are equally important to men and women, but family matters more for men's wellbeing. *Journal of Epidemiology and Community Health*, 67: 166–71.

Cacioppo, J.T., Andersen, B.L., Turnquist, D.C. et al. (1986). Psychophysiological comparison processes: interpreting cancer symptoms. In B.L. Andersen (ed.), *Women with Cancer: Psychosocial Perspectives*. New York: Springer Verlag.

Cacioppo, J.T., Andersen, B.L., Turnquist, D.C. et al. (1989). Psychophysiological comparison theory: on the experience, description and assessment of signs and symptoms. *Patient Education and Counselling*, 13: 257–70.

Cacioppo, J.T. and Patrick, B. (2008). *Loneliness: Human Nature and the Need for Social Connection*. New York: W.W. Norton.

Cacioppo, J.T., Poehlmann, K.M., Kiecolt-Glaser, J.K. et al. (1998). Cellular immune responses to acute stress in female caregivers of dementia patients and matched controls. *Health Psychology*, 17: 182–9.

Cahill, S.M. (1999). Caring in families: what motivates wives, daughters, and daughters-in law to provide dementia care? *Journal of Family Studies*, 5: 235–47.

Cai, Y., Hong, H., Shi, R. et al. (2008). Long-term follow-up study on peer-led school-based HIV/AIDS prevention among youths in Shanghai. *International Journal of STD and AIDS*, 19: 848–50.

Caldwell, T.M., Rodgers, B., Clark, C. et al. (2008). Life course socioeconomic predictors of midlife drinking patterns, problems and abstention: findings from the 1958 British Birth Cohort Study. *Drugs and Alcohol Dependence*, 95: 269–78.

Calhoun, L.G. and Tedeschi, R.G. (eds) (2007). *Handbook of Post-traumatic Growth: Research and Practice*. London: Lawrence Erlbaum Associates.

California Department of Health Services (2003). *Alcohol Use During Pregnancy*. Sacramento, CA: CDHS.

Callaghan, P. and Li, H.C. (2002). The effect of pre-operative psychological interventions on post-operative outcomes in Chinese women having an elective hysterectomy. *British Journal of Health Psychology*, 7: 247–52.

Calnan, M. (1987). *Health and Illness: The Lay Perspective*. London: Tavistock.

Cameron, L. (2008). Illness risk representations and motivations to engage in protective behavior: the case of skin cancer risk. *Psychology & Health*, 23: 91–112.

Cameron, L.D. and Leventhal, H. (eds) (2003). *The Self-regulation of Health and Illness Behaviour*. London: Routledge.

Campbell, J.D., Mauksch, H.O., Neikirk, H.J. and Hosokawa, M.C. (1990). Collaborative practice and provider styles in delivering health care. *Social Science and Medicine*, 30: 1359–65.

Campbell, M.K., Carr, C., Devellis, B. et al. (2009). A randomized trial of tailoring and motivational interviewing to promote fruit and vegetable consumption for cancer prevention and control. *Annals of Behavioral Medicine*, 38: 71–85.

Campbell, M.K., Tessaro, I., DeVellis, B. et al. (2002). Effects of a tailored health promotion program for female blue-collar workers: health works for women. *Preventive Medicine*, 4: 313–23.

Campbell, R., Starkey, F., Holliday, J. et al. (2008). An informal school-based peer-led intervention for smoking prevention in adolescence (ASSIST): a cluster randomised trial. *Lancet*, 371: 1595–602.

Canada, A., Fawzy, N. and Fawzy, F. (2005). Personality and disease outcome in malignant melanoma. *Journal of Psychosomatic Research*, 58: 19–27.

Cancer Research UK (2011): http://info.cancerresearchuk.org/cancerstats/types/prostate/screening

Cannon, W.B. (1932). *The Wisdom of the Body*. New York: W.W. Norton.

Cantril, H. (1967). *The Pattern of Human Concerns*. New Brunswick, NJ: Rutgers University Press.

Carballo, E., Cadarso-Suarez, I., Carrera, J. et al. (2010). Assessing relationships between health-related quality of life and adherence to antiretroviral therapy. *Quality of Life Research*, 13: 587–99.

Cardano, M., Costa, G. and Demaria, M. (2004). Social mobility and health in the Turin longitudinal study. *Social Science and Medicine*, 58: 1563–74.

Cardinal, B.J., Lee, J.Y., Kim, Y.H. et al. (2009). Behavioral, demographic, psychosocial, and sociocultural concomitants of stage of change for physical activity behavior in a mixed-culture sample. *American Journal of Health Promotion*, 23: 274–8.

Carels, R.A., Darby, L., Cacciapaglia, H.M. et al. (2007). Using motivational interviewing as a supplement to obesity treatment: a stepped-care approach. *Health Psychology*, 26: 369–74.

Carers UK (2014). *Facts About Carers*. [Brochure]. London: Carers UK.

Carers UK (2014). *State of Caring Survey*, London: Carers UK.

Carling, C.L., Kristoffersen, D.T., Oxman, A.D. et al. (2010). The effect of how outcomes are framed on decisions about whether to take antihypertensive medication: a randomized trial. *Public Library of Science One*, 5: e9469.

Carlson, L.E., Doll, R., Stephen, J. et al. (2013). Randomized controlled trial of Mindfulness-based cancer recovery versus supportive expressive group therapy for distressed survivors of breast cancer. *Journal of Clinical Oncology*, 31:3119–26.

Carlson, L.E., Taenzer, P., Koopmans, J. et al. (2003). Predictive value of aspects of the transtheoretical model on smoking cessation in a community-based, large-group cognitive behavioral program. *Addictive Behaviors*, 28: 725–40.

Carlson, N. (2003). *Physiology of Behaviour*, 8th edn. Boston, MA: Allyn and Bacon.

Caro, J.J., Speckman, J.L., Salas, M. et al. (1999). Effect of initial drug choice on persistence with antihypertensive therapy: the importance of actual practice data. *Canadian Medical Association Journal*, 160: 41–6.

Carod-Artal, J., Egido, J.A., González, J.L. et al. (2000). Quality of life among stroke survivors evaluated 1 year after stroke. *Stroke*, 31: 2995–3005.

Carr, A.J. and Higginson, I.J. (2001). Are quality of life measures patient centred? *British Medical Journal*, 322: 1357–60.

Carr, A.J., Gibson, B., and Robinson, P.G. (2001). Measuring quality of life: Is quality of life determined by expectations or experience? *British Medical Journal,* 322:1240–3.

Carr, D. (2003). A 'good death' for whom? Quality of spouse's death and psychological distress among older widowed persons. *Journal of Health and Social Behavior*, 44: 215–32.

Carrico, A.W., Antoni, M.H., Weaver, K.E. et al. (2005). Cognitive-behavioural stress management with HIV-positive homosexual men: mechanisms of sustained reductions in depressive symptoms. *Chronic Illness*, 1: 207–15.

Carroll, D., Davey-Smith, G. and Bennett, P. (1996a). Some observations on health and socioeconomic status. *Journal of Health Psychology*, 1: 1–17.

Carroll, D., Ebrahim, S., Tilling, K. et al. (2002). Admissions for myocardial infarction and World Cup football: database survey. *British Medical Journal*, 325: 1439–42.

Carroll, D., Tramèr, M., McQuay, H. et al. (1996b). Randomization is important in studies with pain outcomes: systematic review of transcutaneous electrical nerve stimulation in acute postoperative pain. *British Journal of Anaesthesia*, 77: 798–803.

Carroll, K.M., Libby, B., Sheehan, J. et al. (2001). Motivational interviewing to enhance treatment initiation in substance abusers: an effectiveness study. *American Journal of Addiction*, 10: 35–9.

Cartagena, R.G., Veugelers, P.J., Kipp, W. et al. (2006). Effectiveness of an HIV prevention program for secondary school students in Mongolia. *Journal of Adolescent Health*, 39: 9–16.

Carver, C.S. and Antoni, M.H. (2004). Finding benefit in breast cancer during the year after diagnosis predicts better adjustment 5–8 years after diagnosis. *Health Psychology* 26: 595–8.

Carver, C.S., Pozo, C., Harris, S.D. et al. (1993). How coping mediates the effect of optimism on distress: a study of women with early stage breast cancer. *Journal of Personality and Social Psychology*, 65: 375–90.

Carver, C.S. and Scheier, M.F. (1981). *Attention and Self-Regulation: A Control Theory Approach to Human Behavior*. New York: Springer.

Carver, C.S. and Scheier, M.F. (1998). *On the Self-regulation of Behaviour*. New York: Cambridge University Press.

Carver, C.S. and Scheier, M.F. (2000). Scaling back goals and recalibration of the affect system are processes in normal adaptive self-regulation: Understanding 'response shift' phenomena. *Social Science & Medicine*, 50:1715–22.

Carver, C.S. and Scheier, M.F. (2005). Optimism. In C.R. Snyder and S.J. Lopez (eds), *Handbook of Positive Psychology*. Oxford: Oxford University Press, pp. 231–43.

Carver, C.S., Scheier, M.F. and Pozo, C. (1992). Conceptualizing the process of coping with health problems. In H.S. Friedman (ed.), *Hostility, Coping and Health*. Washington: American Psychological Association.

Carver, C.S., Scheier, M.F. and Weintraub, J.K. (1989). Assessing coping strategies: a theoretically based approach. *Journal of Personality and Social Psychology*, 56: 267–83.

Casey, D., De Civita, M. and Dasgupta, K. (2010). Understanding physical activity facilitators and barriers during and following a supervised exercise programme in Type 2 diabetes: a qualitative study. *Diabetic Medicine*, 27: 79–84.

Casier, A., Goubert, L., Huse, D., et al. (2011). Acceptance and well being in adolescents and young adults with cystic fibrosis: a prospective study. *Journal of Pediatric Psychology,* 36:476–87.

Casier, A., Goubert, L., Gebhardt, W.A., de Baets, F., et al. (2013). Acceptance, well-being and goals in adolescents with chronic illness: a daily process analysis. *Psychology & Health*, 28: 1337–51.

Cassel, J. (1974). An epidemiological perspective of psychosocial factors in disease etiology. *American Journal of Public Health*, 64: 1040–3.

Cassell, E.J. (1976). Disease as an 'it': concepts of disease revealed by patients' presentation of symptoms. *Social Science and Medicine*, 10: 143–6.

Cassell, E.J. (1982). Paracetamol plus supplementary doses of codeine. An analgesic study of repeated doses. *European Journal of Clinical Pharmacology*, 23: 315–19.

Cassell, J.A., Mercer, C.H., Imriel, J. et al. (2006). Who uses condoms with whom? Evidence from national probability sample surveys. *Sexually Transmitted Infections*, 82: 467–73.

Cassidy, T., Giles, M., and McLaughlin, M. (2014). Benefit finding and resilience in child caregivers. *British Journal of Health Psychology*, 19: 606–18.

Cassileth, B.R., Lusk, E.J., Brown, L.L. and Cross, P.A. (1985). Psychosocial status of cancer patients and next of kin: normative data from the profile of mood states. *Journal of Psychosocial Oncology*, 3: 99–105.

Castillo-Richmond, A., Schneider, R.H., Alexander, C.N. et al. (2000). Effects of stress reduction on carotid atherosclerosis in hypertensive African Americans. *Stroke*, 31: 568–73.

Catz, S.L., Gore-Felton, C. and McClure, J.B. (2002). Psychological distress among minority and low-income women living with HIV. *Behavioral Medicine*, 28: 53–60.

Cella, D.F., Tulsky, D.S., Gray, G. et al. (1993). The Functional Assessment of Cancer Therapy scale: development and validation of the general measure. *Journal of Clinical Oncology*, 11: 570–9.

Centers for Disease Control and Prevention (1996). Community-level prevention of human immuno-deficiency virus infection among high-risk populations: the AIDS Community Demonstration Projects. *MMWR Morbidity and Mortality Weekly Reports*, 45(RR-6): 1–24.

The Centre for Social Justice, (2013). No quick fix: Exposing the depth of Britain's drug and alcohol problem Central Statistics Office. Population and Labour Force Projection 2006–2036. Dublin: Stationery Office; 2008.

Cesaroni, G., Forastiere, F., Agabiti, N. et al. (2008). Effect of the Italian smoking ban on population rates of acute coronary events. *Circulation*, 117: 1183–8.

Chacham, A.S., Maia, M.B., Greco, M. et al. (2007). Autonomy and susceptibility to HIV/AIDS among young women living in a slum in Belo Horizonte, Brazil. *AIDS Care*, 19(suppl. 1): S12–22.

Chadha, N.K. and Repanos, C. (2004). How much do healthcare professionals know about informed consent? A Bristol experience. *Surgeon*, 2: 328–33, 360.

Chadha, N.K. and Repanos, C. (2006). Patients' understanding of words used to describe lumps: a cross-sectional study. *Journal of Laryngology and Otology*, 120: 125–8.

Chaix, B., Rosvall, M. and Merlo, J. (2007). Neighborhood socioeconomic deprivation and residential instability: effects on incidence of ischemic heart disease and survival after myocardial infarction. *Epidemiology*, 18: 104–11.

Chalmers, B. (1996). Western and African conceptualisations of health. *Psychology and Health*, 12: 1–10.

Champion, V.L. (1990). Breast self-examination in women 35 and older: a prospective study. *Journal of Behavioural Medicine*, 13: 523–38.

Champion, V.L. and Miller, T.K. (1992). Variables related to breast self-examination. *Psychology of Women Quarterly*, 16: 81–96.

Chan, D.S., Callahan, C.W., Hatch-Pigott, V.B. et al. (2007). Internet-based home monitoring and education of children with asthma is comparable to ideal office-based care: results of a 1-year asthma in-home monitoring trial. *Pediatrics*, 119: 569–78.

Chan, D.S. and Fishbein, M. (1993). Determinants of women's intentions to tell their partner to use condoms. *Journal of Applied Social Psychology*, 23: 1455–70.

Chandrashekara, S., Jayashree, K., Veeranna, H.B. et al. (2007). Effects of anxiety on TNF-a levels during psychological stress. *Journal of Psychosomatic Research*, 63: 65–9.

Chapin, J. (2014). Adolescents and Cyber-bullying: The Precaution-Adoptions Process Model. *Education & Information Technology*, doi 10.1007/s.10639–014–9349–1

Chapman, S. and Martin, M. (2011). Attention to pain words in irritable bowel syndrome: increased orienting and speeded engagement. *British Journal of Health Psychology*, 16: 47–60.

Charles, G., Stainton, T., and Marshall, S. (2012). *Young Carers in Canada: The Hidden Costs and Benefits of Young Caregiving*. Ottawa, Canada:The Vanier Institute of the Family.

Charmaz, K. (1983). Loss of self: a fundamental form of suffering in the chronically ill. *Sociology of Health and Illness*, 5: 168–95.

Charmaz, K. (1991). *Good Days, Bad Days: The Self in Chronic Illness and Time*. New Brunswick, NJ: Rutgers University Press.

Charmaz, K. (1994). Identity dilemmas of chronically ill men. *Sociological Quarterly*, 35: 269–88.

Chartered Institute of Personnel Directors/Simplyhealth (2011). Absence Management Survey, CIPD.

Chassin, C., Presson, C.C., Rose, J.S. et al. (1996). The natural history of cigarettes from adolescence to adulthood: demographic predictors of continuity and change. *Health Psychology*, 15: 478–84.

Chatkin, J.M., Blanco, D.C., Scaglia, N. et al. (2006). Impact of a low-cost and simple intervention in enhancing treatment adherence in a Brazilian asthma sample. *Journal of Asthma*, 43: 263–6.

Cheing, G.L., Tsui, A.Y., Lo, S.K. et al. (2003). Optimal stimulation duration of TENS in the management of osteoarthritic knee pain. *Journal of Rehabilitation Medicine*, 35: 62–8.

Chen, J.Y., Fox, S.A., Cantrell, C.H. et al. (2007). Health disparities and prevention: racial/ethnic barriers to flu vaccinations. *Journal of Community Health*, 32: 5–20.

Chen, S.-L., Tsai, J.-C. and Lee, W.-L. (2008). Psychometric validation of the Chinese version of the Illness Perception Questionnaire-Revised for patients with hypertension. *Journal of Advanced Nursing*, 64: 524–34.

Chen, S.Y., Gibson, S., Katz, M.H. et al. (2002). Continuing increases in sexual risk behavior and sexually transmitted diseases among men who have sex with men: San Francisco, Calif., 1999–2001. *American Journal of Public Health*, 92: 1387–8.

Cheng, C. (2000). Seeking medical consultation: perceptual and behavioural characteristics distinguishing consulters and nonconsulters with functional dyspepsia. *Psychosomatic Medicine*, 62: 844–52.

Cheng, T.L., Savageau, J.A., Sattler, A.L. et al. (1993). Confidentiality in health care: a survey of knowledge, perceptions, and attitudes among high school students. *Journal of the American Medical Association*, 269: 1404–7.

Chesney, M.A. (2003). Adherence to HAART regimes. *AIDS Patient Care and STDs*, 17: 169–77.

Cho, H. and Salmon, C.T. (2006). Fear appeals for individuals in different stages of change: intended and unintended effects and implications on public health campaigns. *Health Communication*, 20: 91–9.

Chochinov, H.M., Hack, T., Hassard, T. et al. (2002). Dignity in the terminally ill: a cross-sectional, cohort study. *The Lancet*, 360: 2026–30.

Chochinov, H.M., Tataryn, D.J., Wilson, K.G. et al. (2000). Prognostic awareness and the terminally ill. *Psychosomatics*, 41: 500–4.

Choi, W.S., Harris, K.J., Okuyemi, K. et al. (2003). Predictors of smoking initiation among college-bound high school students. *Annals of Behavioral Medicine*, 26: 69–74.

Chowdury, R., Warnakula, S, Kunutsor, S., et l. (2014). Association of dietary, circulating, and supplement fatty acids with coronary risk: a systematic review and meta-analysis. *Annals of Internal Medicine,* 160: 398–406.

Christensen, A.J., Edwards, D.L., Wiebe, J.S. et al. (1996). Effect of verbal self-disclosure on natural killer cell activity: moderating influence of cynical hostility. *Psychosomatic Medicine*, 58: 150–5.

Christensen, C., Larson, J.R., Jr, Abbott, A. et al. (2000). Decision making of clinical teams: communication patterns and diagnostic error. *Medical Decision Making*, 20: 45–50.

Christie, D.and Khatun, H. (2012). Adjusting to life with chronic illness. *The Psychologist,* (Special feature on pediatric clinical psychology) 25:194–97.

Chronister, J. and Chan, F. (2006). A stress process model of caregiving for individuals with traumatic brain injury. *Rehabilitation Psychology*, 51: 190–201.

Chun, M., Knight, B.G. and Youn, G. (2007). Differences in stress and coping models of emotional distress among Korean, Korean American and White-American caregivers. *Aging and Mental Health*, 11: 20–9.

CIA Central Intelligence Agency (2008). *World Factbook, 2008*. Washington, DC: CIA.

Cioffi, D. (1991). Beyond attentional strategies: a cognitive-perceptual model of somatic interpretation. *Psychological Bulletin*, 109: 25–41.

Clare, P., Bradford, D., Courtney, R.J. et al. (2014) The relationship between socioeconomic status and 'hardcore' smoking over time – greater accumulation of hardened smokers in low-SES than high-SES smokers. *Tobacco Control*, 23: e85-e86.

Clark, A. (2003). 'It's like an explosion in your life …': lay perspectives on stress and myocardial infarction. *Journal of Clinical Nursing*, 12: 544–53.

Clark, D.B. and Sayette, M.A. (1993). Anxiety and the development of alcoholism: clinical and scientific issues. *American Journal on Addictions*, 2: 59–76.

Clark, K.L., Loscalzo, M., Trask, P.C. et al. (2010). Psychological distress in patients wth pancreatic cancer – an understudied group. *Psycho-Oncology*, 19: 1313–20.

Clark, R. and Gochett, P. (2006). Interactive effects of perceived racism and coping responses predict a school-based assessment of blood pressure in black youth. *Annals of Behavioral Medicine*, 32: 1–9.

Clark, S.L. and Stephens, M.A.P. (1996). Stroke patients' well-being as a function of caregiving spouses' helpful and unhelpful actions. *Personal Relationships*, 3: 171–84.

Clark-Carter, D. (2003). Effect sizes: the missing piece in the jigsaw. *The Psychologist*, 16: 636–8.

Clarke, R. (2000). Perceptions of interethnic group racism predict increased vascular reactivity to a laboratory challenge in college women. *Annals of Behavioral Medicine*, 22: 214–22.

Claydon L.S., Chesterton L.S., Barlas P. et al. (2011). Dose-specific effects of transcutaneous electrical nerve stimulation (TENS) on experimental pain: a systematic review. *Clinical Journal of Pain*, 27:635–47.

Clays, E., Leynen, F., De Bacquer, D. et al. (2007). High job strain and ambulatory blood pressure in middle-aged men and women from the Belgian job stress study. *Journal of Occupational and Environmental Medicine*, 49: 360–7.

Clayton, J.M., Butow, P.N., Tattersall, M.H. et al. (2007). Randomized controlled trial of a prompt list to help advanced cancer patients and their caregivers to ask questions about prognosis and end-of-life care. *Journal of Clinical Oncology*, 25: 715–23.

Clifford, S., Barber, N. and Horne, R. (2008). Understanding different beliefs held by adherers, unintentional non-adherers, and intentional non-adherers: application of the Necessity-Concerns Framework. *Journal of Psychosomatic Research*, 64: 41–6.

Cloute, K., Mitchell, A. and Yates, P. (2008). Traumatic brain injury and the constructuion of identitiy: a discursvive approach. *Neuropsychological Rehabilitation,* 18: 651–70.

Clow, A. (2001). The physiology of stress. In F. Jones and J. Bright (eds), *Stress: Myth, Theory and Research*. Harlow: Pearson, pp. 47–72.

Coates, T.J., McKusick, L., Kuno, R. et al. (1989). Stress management training reduced numbers of sexual partners but did not improve immune function in men infected with HIV. *American Journal of Public Health*, 79: 885–7.

Cobb, S. (1976). Social support as a moderator of life stress. *Psychosomatic Medicine*, 38: 300–14.

Coburn-Litvak, P.S., Pothakos, K., Tata, D.A. et al. (2003). Chronic administration of corticosterone impairs spatial reference memory before spatial working memory in rats. *Neurobiology, Learning & Memory*, 80: 11–23.

Cockburn, J., Paul, C., Tzelepis, F. et al. (2003). Delay in seeking advice for symptoms that potentially indicate bowel cancer. *American Journal of Health Behavior*, 27: 401–7.

Cocks, K., King, M.T., Velikova, G. et al. (2008). Quality, interpretation and presentation of European Organisation for Research and Treatment of Cancer quality of life questionnaire core data in randomised controlled trials. *European Journal of Cancer*, 44: 1793–8.

Cocquyt, V.F., Blondeel, P.N., Depypere, H.T. et al. (2003). Better cosmetic results and comparable quality of life after skin-sparing mastectomy and immediate autologous breast reconstruction compared to breast conservative treatment. *The British Association of Plastic Surgeons*, 56: 462–70.

Cohen, F. and Lazarus, R. (1979). Coping with the stresses of illness. In G.C. Stone, F. Cohen and N.E. Adler (eds), *Health Psychology: A Handbook*. San Francisco, CA: Jossey-Bass.

Cohen, H.J., Pieper, C.F., Harris, T. et al. (1997). The association of plasma IL-6 levels with functional disability in community-dwelling elderly. *Journal of Gerontology. A: Biological Science and Medical Science*, 52: M201–8.

Cohen, L.A. (1987). Diet and cancer. *Scientific American*, 102: 42–8.

Cohen, M., Hoffman, R.G., Cromwell, C. et al. (2002). The prevalence of distress in persons with human immunodeficiency virus infection. *Psychosomatics*, 43: 10–15.

Cohen, S. (1988). Psychosocial models of the role of social support in the etiology of physical disease. *Health Psychology*, 7: 269–97.

Cohen, S. (2004). Social relationships and health. *American Psychologist*, 59: 676–84.

Cohen, S. (2005). Keynote presentation at the eighth International Congress of Behavioral Medicine. *Journal of Behavioral Medicine*, 12: 123–1.

Cohen, S., Doyle, M.J., Skoner, D.P. et al. (1995). State and trait negative affect as predictors of objective and subjective symptoms of respiratory viral infections. *Journal of Personality and Social Psychology*, 68: 159–69.

Cohen, S., Doyle, W.J., Turner, R. et al. (2003). Sociability and susceptibility to the common cold. *Psychological Science*, 14: 389–95.

Cohen, S., Evans, G.W., Stokols, D. and Krantz, D.S. (1986). *Behavior, Health and Environmental Stress*. New York: Plenum.

Cohen, S., Frank, E., Doyle, W.J. et al. (1998). Types of stressors that increase susceptibility to the common cold in healthy adults. *Health Psychology*, 17: 214–23.

Cohen, S. and Herbert, T.B. (1996). Health psychology: psychological factors and physical disease from the perspective of human psychoneuroimmunology. *Annual Review of Psychology*, 47: 113–42.

Cohen, S. and Hoberman, H. (1983). Positive events and social support as buffers of life change stress. *Journal of Applied Social Psychology*, 13: 99–125.

Cohen, S., Kamarck, T. and Mermelstein, R. (1983). A global measure of perceived stress. *Journal of Health and Social Behaviour*, 24: 385–96.

Cohen, S., Tyrell, D.A. and Smith, A.P. (1993a). Life events, perceived stress, negative affect and susceptibility to the common cold. *Journal of Personality and Social Psychology*, 64: 131–40.

Cohen, S., Tyrell, D.A. and Smith, A.P. (1993b). Psychological stress and susceptibility to the common cold. *New England Journal of Medicine*, 325: 606–12.

Cohen, S. and Williamson, G.M. (1991). Stress and infectious disease in humans. *Psychological Bulletin*, 109: 5–24.

Cohen, S. and Wills, T.A. (1985). Stress, social support and the buffering hypothesis. *Psychological Bulletin*, 98: 310–57.

Cohn, M.A., and Fredrickson, B.L. (2009). Positive emotions. In S.J.Lopez and C.R. Snyder (eds), *Oxford Handbook of Positive Psychology*. Oxford University Press, pp.13–24.

Cole, S.W., Kemeny, M.E., Taylor, S.E. et al. (1996). Elevated physical health risk among gay men who conceal their homosexual identity. *Health Psychology*, 15: 23–51.

Coleman, D.L. (1979). Obesity genes: beneficial effects in heterozygous mice. *Science*, 203: 663–5.

Coleman, P.G. (1999). Identity management in later life. In R.T. Woods (ed.), *Psychological Problems of Ageing: Assessment, Treatment and Care*. Chichester: Wiley.

Collado, A., Felton, J.W., MacPherson, L. and Lejuez,C.W. (2014). Longitudinal trajectories of sensation seeking, risk taking propensity, and impulsivity across early to middle adolescence. *Additive Behaviors*, doi: 10.1016/j.addbeh.2014.01.024

Collicutt, J. (2011). Psychology, religion and spirituality. *The Psychologist*, 24: 250–1.

Collins, S. (2005). Explanations in consultations: the combined effectiveness of doctors' and nurses' communication with patients. *Medical Education*, 39: 785–96.

Comeaux, S.J. and Jaser, S.S. (2010). Autonomy and insulin in adolesecents with type 1 diabetes. *Pediatric Diabetes*, 11: 498–504.

COMMIT (1995). Community intervention trial for smoking cessation (COMMIT): II. Changes in adult cigarette smoking prevalence. *American Journal of Public Health*, 85: 193–200.

Committee on Understanding and Eliminating Racial and Ethnic Disparities in Health Care, Institute of Medicine, National Academy of Sciences, Smedley, B.D., Stith, A.Y. and Nelson, A.R. (eds) (2002). *Unequal Treatment: Confronting Racial and Ethnic Disparities in Health Care*. Washington, DC: National Academy Press.

Compas, B.E., Stoll, M.F., Thomsen, A.H. et al. (1999). Adjustment to breast cancer: age-related differences in coping and emotional distress. *Breast Cancer Research and Treatment*, 54: 195–203.

Compas, B.E., Jaser, S.S., Dunn, M.J. and Rodriguez, E.M. (2012). Coping with chronic illness in childhood and adolesecence. *Annual Review of Clinical Psychology*, 8: 455–80.

Conner, M. and Armitage, C.J. (1998). Extending the theory of planned behaviour: a review and avenues for further research. *Journal of Applied Social Psychology*, 28: 1429–64.

Conner, M. and Godin, G. (2007). Temporal stability of behavioural intention as a moderator of intention-health behaviour relationships. *Psychology & Health*, 22: 875–97.

Conner, M. and Higgins, A.R. (2010). Long-term effects of implementation intentions on prevention of smoking uptake among adolescents: a cluster randomized controlled trial. *Health Psychology*, 29: 529–38.

Conner, M. and Norman, P. (1996). *Predicting Health Behaviour: Research and Practice with Social Cognition Models*. Buckingham: Open University Press.

Conner, M. and Sparks, (2005). Theory of planned behaviour and health behaviour. In M. Conner and P. Norman (eds), *Predicting Health Behaviour*. London: Open University Press, pp.170–222.

Conner, M., Sutherland, E., Kennedy, F. et al. (2008). Impact of alcohol on sexual decision making: intentions to have unprotected sex. *Psychology & Health*, 23: 909–34.

Connor, J.L., Kypri, K., Bell, M.L. et al. (2010). Alcohol outlet density, levels of drinking and alcohol-related harm in New Zealand: a national study. *Journal of Epidemiology and Community Health*, 2010 Oct 14.

Connor-Smith, J.K., Compas, B.E., Wadsworth, M.E. et al. (2000). Responses to stress in adolescence: measurement of coping and involuntary stress responses. *Journal of Consulting and Clinical Psychology*, 68: 976–92.

Consedine, N.S., Horton, D., Magai, C. et al. (2007). Breast screening in response to gain, loss, and empowerment framed messages among diverse, low-income women. *Journal of Health Care for the Poor and Underserved*, 18: 550–66.

Constans, J.I., Mathews, A., Brantley, P.J. et al. (1999). Attentional reactions to an MI: the impact of mood state, worry, and coping style. *Journal of Psychosomatic Research*, 46: 415–23.

Cook, B.J. and Hausenblas, H.A. (2008). The role of exercise dependence for the relationship between exercise behavior and eating pathology: mediator or moderator? *Journal of Health Psychology*, 13: 495–502.

Cook, R.F., Billings, D.W., Hersch, R. et al. (2007). A field test of a web-based workplace health promotion program to improve dietary practices, reduce stress, and increase physical activity: randomized controlled trial. *Journal of Medical Internet Research*, 9: e17.

Cooper, C.L. and Payne, R. (eds) (1988). *Causes, Coping and Consequences of Stress at Work*. Chichester: Wiley.

Cooper, M.L., Agocha, V.S. and Sheldon, M.S. (2000). A motivational perspective on risky behaviours: the role of personality and affect regulatory processes. *Journal of Personality*, 68: 159–69.

Cope, C.D., Lyons, A.C., Donovan, V. et al. (2003). Providing letters and audiotapes to supplement a prenatal diagnostic consultation: effects on later distress and recall. *Prenatal Diagnosis*, 23: 1060–7.

Cordova, M., Andrykowski, M., Kenady, D. et al. (1995). Frequency and correlates of posttraumatic-stress-disorder-like symptoms after treatment for breast cancer. *Journal of Consulting and Clinical Psychology*, 63: 981–6.

Costa, P.T., Jr and McCrae, R.R. (1987). Neuroticism, somatic complaints and disease: is the bark worse than the bite? *Journal of Personality*, 55: 299–316.

Costa, P.T. and McCrae, R.R. (1992a). Four ways five factors are basic. *Personality and Individual Differences*, 13: 653–65.

Costa, P.T. and McCrae, R.R. (1992b). *Revised NEO Personality Inventory (NEO PI-R) and NEO Fivefactor Inventory (NEO FFI) Professional Manual*. Odessa, FL: Psychological Assessment Resources.

Costanzo, E.S., Lutgendorf, S.K. and Roeder, S. (2011). Common-sense beliefs about cancer and health practices among women completing treatment for breast cancer *Psycho-Oncology*, 20: 53–61.

Costanzo, E.S., Lutgendorf, S.K., Bradley, S.L., Rose, S. and Anderson, B. (2005). Cancer attributions, distress, and health practices among gynaecologic cancer survivors. *Psychosomatic Medicine*, 67: 972–80.

Costanzo, E.S., Lutgendorf, S.K., Mattes, M.L. et al. (2007) Adjusting to life after treatment: distress and quality of life following treatment for breast cancer, *British Journal of Cancer*. 97: 1625–31.

Cotman, C.W. and Engesser-Cesar, C. (2002). Exercise enhances and protects brain function. *Exercise Sport Science Reviews*, 30: 75–9.

Courtenay, W.H. (2000). Constructions of masculinity and their influence on men's well-being: a theory of gender and health. *Social Science and Medicine*, 50: 1385–401.

Covic, T., Adamson, B., Spencer, D. and Howe, G. (2003). A biopsychosocial model of pain and depression in rheumatoid arthritis: a 12-month longitudinal study. *Rheumatology*, 42: 176–85.

Cowburn, G. and Stockley, L. (2005). Consumer understanding and use of nutrition labelling: a systematic review. *Public Health & Nutrition*. 8: 21–8.

Cowburn, G. and Stockley, L. (2006). Consumer understanding and use of nutrition labelling: a systematic review. *Journal of the American Dietetic Association*, 106: 917–20.

Cox, D.D., Huppert, F.A. and Whichelow, M.J. (1993) The Health and lifestyle survey: seven years on: a longitudinal study of a nationwide sample, measuring changes in physical and mental health, attitudes and lifestyle. Dartmouth Pub Co.

Cox, D.S., Cox, A.D., Sturm, L. and Zimet, G. (2010). Behavioural interventions to Increase HPV Vaccination Acceptability Among Mothers of Young Girls. *Health Psychology*, 29: 29–39.

Cox, K. (2003). Assessing the quality of life of patients in phase I and II anti-cancer drug trials: interviews versus questionnaires. *Social Science and Medicine*, 56: 921–34.

Cox, K.L., Gorely, T.J., Puddey, I.B. et al. (2003). Exercise behaviour change in 40- to 65-year-old women: the SWEAT study (Sedentary Women Exercise Adherence Trial). *British Journal of Health Psychology*, 8: 477–95.

Cox, W.M. and Klinger, E. (2004). A motivational model of alcohol use: determinants of use and change. In W.M. Cox and E. Klinger (eds), *Handbook of Motivational Counselling: Concepts, Approaches, and Assessments*, Chichester: John Wiley, pp. 121–38.

Coyne, I. (2006). Children's experiences of hospitalization, *Journal of Child Health Care,* 10: 326–36.

Coyne, J. and Fiske, V. (1992). Couples coping with chronic and catastrophic illness. In T.J. Akamatsu, M.A.P. Stephens, S.E. Hobfoll and J.H. Crowther (eds), *Family Health Psychology*. Washington, DC: Hemisphere Publishing.

Coyne, J.C., Benazon, N.R., Rohrbaugh, M.J. et al. (2003). Patient and spousal attitude in couples living with chronic heart failure. Symposium paper presented at the 17th Conference of the European Health Psychology Society, September, Kos.

Coyne, J.C. and Racioppo, M.W. (2000). Never the twain shall meet? Closing the gap between coping research and clinical intervention research. *American Psychologist*, 55: 655–64.

Coyne, J.C. and Smith, D.A.F. (1991). Couples coping with a myocardial infarction: a contextual perspective on wives' distress. *Journal of Personality and Social Psychology*, 61: 404–12.

Coyne, J.C., Jaarsma, T., Luttik, M.L. et al (2011). Lack of prognostic value of type D personality for mortality in a large sample of heart failure patients. *Psychosomatic Medicine*, 73: 557–62.

Craft, I. and Landers, D.M. (1998). The effects of exercise on clinical depression and depression resulting from mental illness: A meta-regression analysis. *Journal of Sport & Exercise Psychology*, 20:339–57.

Cramer, J.A. (1998). Enhancing patient compliance in the elderly. Role of packaging aids and monitoring. *Drugs and Aging*, 12: 7–15.

Cramer, J.A. (2004). A systematic review of adherence with medications for diabetes. *Diabetes Care*, 27: 1218–24.

Cramp, F. and Daniel, J. (2008). Exercise for the management of cancer-related fatigue in adults. *Cochrane Database of Systematic Reviews*, issue 2, art. no.: CD006145. doi: 10.1002/14651858.CD006145.

Creed, F., Guthrie, E., Fink, P. et al (2010). Is there a better term than 'medically unexplained symptoms'? *Journal of Psychosomatic Research,* 68: 5–8.

Creed, F.H., Davis, I., Jackson, J. et al. (2012). The epidemiology of multiple somatic symptoms. *Journal of Psychosomatic Research,* 72: 311–17.

Crepaz, N., Pasin, W.F., Herbst, J.H. et al. (2008). Meta-analysis of cognitive behavioural interventions on HIV positive persons' mental health and immune functioning. *Health Psychology*, 27: 4–14.

Creuss, D.G., Antoni, M.H., McGregor, B.A. et al. (2000). Cognitive-behavioral stress management reduces serum cortisol by enhancing benefit finding among women being treated for early stage breast cancer. *Psychosomatic Medicine*, 62: 304–8.

Crisp, A., Sedgwick, P., Halek, C. et al. (1999). Why may teenage girls persist in smoking? *Journal of Adolescence*, 22: 657–72.

Crossley, M.L. (2000). *Rethinking Health Psychology*. Buckingham: Open University Press.

Crossley, M.L. and Small, N. (1998). Evaluation of HIV/AIDS Education Training Services Provided by London Lighthouse at St. Ann's Hospice. Stockport Health Authority.

Crowe, F.L., Key, T.J., Appleby, P.N. et al. (2008). Dietary fat intake and risk of prostate cancer in the European: prospective investigation into cancer and nutrition. *American Journal of Clinical Nutrition*, 87: 1405–13.

Croyle, R.T. and Barger, S.D. (1993). Illness cognition. In S. Maes, H. Leventhal and M. Johnston (eds), *International Review of Health Psychology*, Vol. II. Chichester: Wiley.

Croyle, R.T. and Ditto, P.M. (1990). Illness cognition and behavior: an experimental approach. *Journal of Behavioral Medicine*, 13: 31–52.

Csikszentmihalyi, M. (1997*). Finding Flow*. New York, Basic Books.

Csof, R.-M., Hood, R., Keler, B. et al. (2009). *Deconversion*. Goettingen: Vandenhoech & Ruprecht.

Cui, Z., Shah, S, Yan, L. et al. (2012) Effect of a school-based peer education intervention on physical activity and sedentary behaviour in Chinese adolescents: a pilot study. *BMJ Open* 2012; 2: e000721.

Culver, J.L., Arena, P.L., Antoni, M.H. and Carver, C.S. (2002). Coping and distress among women under treatment for early stage breast cancer: comparing African Americans, Hispanics and non-Hispanic whites. *Psycho-Oncology*, 11: 495–504.

Culver, J.L., Arena, P.L., Wimberly, S.R. et al. (2004). Coping among African American, Hispanic, and non-Hispanic white women recently treated for early stage breast cancer. *Psychology and Health*, 19: 157–66.

Cummings, J.H. and Bingham, S.A. (1998). Diet and the prevention of cancer. *British Medical Journal*, 317: 1636–40.

Curbow, B., Somerfield, M.R., Baker, F. et al. (1993). Personal changes, dispositional optimism, and psychological adjustment to bone marrow transplantation. *Journal of Behavioral Medicine*, 16: 423–43.

Currow, D.C., Agar, M., Plummer, J.L. et al. (2010). Chronic pain in South Australia – population levels that interfere extremely with activities of daily living. *Australia and New Zealand Journal of Public Health*, 34: 232–9.

Cutrona, C.E. (1996). *Social Support in Couples*. Thousand Oaks, CA: Sage.

Cutrona, C.E. and Russell, D.W. (1987). The provision of social relationships and adaptation to stress. In W.H. Jones and D. Perlman (eds), *Advances in Personal Relationships*, Vol. 1. Greenwich, CT: JAI Press.

Cutrona, C.E. and Russell, D.W. (1990). Type of social support and specific stress: toward a theory of optimal matching. In B.A. Sarason, I.G. Sarason and G.R. Pierce (eds), *Social Support: An Interactional View*. New York: Wiley.

Cutrona, C.E., Shaffer, P.A., Wesner, K.A. and Gardner, K.A. (2007). Optimally matching support and perceived spousal sensitivity, *Journal of Family Psychology*, 21: 754–8.

Dababneh, A.J., Swanson, N. and Shell, R.L. (2001). Impact of added rest breaks on the productivity and well being of workers. *Ergonomics*, 44: 164–74.

Dagan, M., Sanderman, R., Schokker, M.C. et al. (2011). Spousal support and changes in distress over time in couples coping with cancer: the role of personal control. *Journal of Family Psychology*, 25: 310–18.

Dallery J., Raiff B.R. and Grabinski M.J. (2013). Internet-based contingency management to promote smoking cessation: A randomized controlled study. *Journal of Applied Behavior Analysis*, 46:750–64.

Dalton, S.O., Boesen, E.H., Ross, L. et al. (2002). Mind and cancer: do psychological factors cause cancer? *European Journal of Cancer*, 38: 1313–23.

Daly, J.M., Hartz, A.J., Xu, Y. et al. (2009). An assessment of attitudes, behaviors, and outcomes of patients with type 2 diabetes. *Journal of the American Board of Family Medicine*, 22: 280–90.

Damjanovic, A.K., Yang, Y., Glaser, R. et al. (2007). Accelerated telomere erosion is associated with a declining immune function of caregivers of Alzheimer's disease patients. *Journal of Immunology*,179: 4249–54.

Dancey, C.P., Taghavi, M. and Fox, R.J. (1998). The relationship between daily stress and symptoms of irritable bowel: a time-series approach. *Journal of Psychosomatic Research*. 44(5): 537–45.

Danoff-Burg, S., and Revenson, TA. (2005). Benefit-finding among patients with rheumatoid arthritis:positive effects on interpersonal relationships. *Journal of Behavioral Medicine,* 28, 91–103.

Dantzer, R. and Kelley, K.W. (1989). Stress and immunity: an integrated view of relationships between the brain and the immune system. *Life Sciences*, 44: 1995–2008.

Darnley, S.E., Kennedy, T., Jones, R. et al. (2002). A randomised controlled trial of the addition of cognitive behavioural therapy (CBT) to antispasmodic therapy for irritable bowel syndrome (IBS) in primary care. *Gastroenterology*, 122: A-69.

Dauchet, L., Amouyel, P. and Dallongeville, J. (2009). Fruits, vegetables and coronary heart disease. *Nature Reviews Cardiology*, 6: 599–608.

Davey-Smith, G., Ebrahim, S. and Frankel, S. (2001). How policy informs the evidence: 'evidence-based' thinking can lead to debased policy making (editorial). *British Medical Journal*, 322: 184–5.

Davey-Smith, G., Wentworth, D., Neaton, J.D. et al. (1996). Socio-economic differentials in mortality risk among men screened for the Multiple Risk Factor Intervention Trial, 2: black men. *American Journal of Public Health*, 86: 497–504.

David, J.P. and Suls, J. (1996). Coping efforts in daily life: role of big five traits and problem appraisals. *Journal of Personality*, 67: 265–94.

Davidson, K.W., Gidron, Y., Mostofsky, E. and Trudeau, K.J. (2007). Hospitalization cost offset of a hostility intervention for coronary heart disease patients. *Journal of Consulting and Clinical Psychology*, 75: 657–62.

Davidson, K.W., MacGregor, M.E., Stuhr, J. et al. (2000). Constructive anger verbal behaviour predicts blood pressure in a population-based sample. *Health Psychology*, 19: 55–64.

Davidson, P.R. and Parker, K.C.H. (2001). Eye movement desensitization and reprocessing (EMDR): a meta-analysis. *Journal of Consulting and Clinical Psychology*, 69: 305–16.

Davies, J.B. and Baker, R. (1987). The impact of self-presentation and interviewer bias on self-reported heroin use. *British Journal of Addiction*, 82: 907–12.

Davies P., Walker A.E. and Grimshaw J.M. (2010). A systematic review of the use of theory in the design of guideline dissemination and implementation strategies and interpretation of the results of rigorous evaluations. *Implementation Science,* 5: 14.

Davis, J.L., Buchanan, K.L., Katz, R.V. and Green, B.L. (2012). Gender differences in cancer screening beliefs, behaviors, and willingness to participate: implications for health promotion. *American Journal of Men's Health*, 6, 211: DOI: 10.1177/1557988311425853

Davis, M.C., Zautra, A.J., Wolf, L.D. et al. (2015). Mindfulness and cognitive-behavioral interventions for chronic pain: differential effects on daily pain reactivity and stress reactivity. *Journal of Consulting and Clinical Psychology,* 83: 24–35.

Dawson, A.M., Brown, D.A., Cox, A. et al. (2014). Using motivational interviewing for weight feedback to parents of young children. *Journal of Paediatrics and Child Health*, 6: 461–70.

Day, M.A., Thorn, B.E. and Rubin, N.J. (2014). Mindfulness-based cognitive therapy for the treatment of headache pain: a mixed-methods analysis comparing treatment responders and treatment non-responders. *Complementary Therapy in Medicine,* 22: 278–85.

Deary, I.J., Clyde, Z. and Frier, B.M. (1997). Constructs and models in health psychology: the case of personality and illness reporting in diabetes mellitus. *British Journal of Health Psychology*, 2: 35–54.

DeBoer, M.F., Ryckman, R.M., Pruyn, J.F. et al. (1999). Psychosocial correlates of cancer relapse and survival: a literature review. *Patient Education and Counselling*, 37: 215–30.

deBruin, M. and Johnston, M. (2012). Methods in health psychology: how do we know what we really know? *The European Health Psychologist*, 14: 107–112.

Deci, E.L. and Ryan, R.M. (2000). The 'what' and 'why' of goal pursuits: human needs and the self-determination of behavior. *Psychological Inquiry*, 11: 227–68.

Deeg, D.J.H. and Kriegsman, D.M.W. (2003). Concepts of self-rated health: specifying the gender difference in mortality risk. *The Gerontologist*, 43: 376–86.

DeFriese, G. and Woomert, A. (1983). Self-care among the US elderly. *Research on Aging*, 5: 3–23.

De Haes, H. and Koedoot, N. (2003). Patient centered decision making in palliative cancer treatment: a world of paradoxes. *Patient Education and Counselling*, 50: 43–9.

Dehghani, M., Sharpe, L. and Nicholas, M.K. (2003). Selective attention to pain-related information in chronic musculoskeletal pain patients. *Pain*, 105: 37–46.

Deimling, G.T., Bowman, K.F., Sterns, S. et al. (2006) Cancer-related health worries and psychological distress among older adult long-term cancer survivors. *Psycho-Oncology*, 15: 306–20.

de Jongh T., Gurol-Urganci I., Vodopivec-Jamsek V. et al. (2012). Mobile phone messaging for facilitating self-management of long-term illnesses. *Cochrane Database of Systematic Reviews*, 12:CD007459.

de Lange, A.H., Taris, T.W., Kompier, M.A. et al. (2003). The very best of the millennium: longitudinal research and the demand–control–(support) model. *Journal of Occupational Health Psychology*, 8: 282–305.

Delaney-Black, V., Chiodo, L.M., Hannigan, J.H. et al. (2010). Just say 'I don't': lack of concordance between teen report and biological measures of drug use. *Pediatrics*, 126: 887–93.

De Longis, A., Folkman, S. and Lazarus, R.S. (1997). The impact of daily stress on health and mood: psychological and social resources as mediators. *Journal of Personality and Social Psychology*, 54: 486–95.

Dembrowski, T.M., MacDougall, J.M., Costa, P.T. et al. (1989). Components of hostility as predictors of sudden death and myocardial infarction in the Multiple Risk Factor Intervention Trial. *Psychosomatic Medicine*, 51: 514–22.

Demerouti, E., Bakker, A.B., Nachreiner, F. and Schaufeli, W.B. (2001). The job demands–resources model of burnout. *Journal of Applied Psychology*, 86: 499–512.

Dempster, M. and McCorry, N.K. (2011). The factor structure of the Revised Illness Perception Questionnaire in a population of oesophageal cancer survivors. *Psycho-Oncology*, doi: 10.1002/pon.1927.

De Moor, C., Sterner, J., Hall, M. et al. (2002). A pilot study of the effects of expressive writing on psychological and behavioral adjustment in patients enrolled in a phase II trial of vaccine therapy for metastatic renal cell carcinoma. *Health Psychology*, 21: 615–19.

De Neve, K.M. and Cooper, H. (1998). The happy personality: A meta-analysis of 137 personality traits and subjective wellbeing. *Psychological Bulletin*, 124: 197–229.

Denollet, J. (1998). Personality and coronary heart disease: the type-D scale-16 (DS16). *Annals of Behavioral Medicine*, 20: 209–15.

Denollet, J. and dePotter, B. (1992). Coping subtypes for men with coronary heart disease: relationship to well-being, stress and type-A behavior. *Psychological Medicine*, 22: 667–84.

Denollet, J., Pedersen, S.S., Vrints, C.J. and Conraads, V.M. (2006). Usefulness of Type D personality in predicting five-year cardiac events above and beyond concurrent symptoms of stress in patients with coronary heart disease. *The American Journal of Cardiology*, 97: 970e3.

Denollet, J., Sys, S.U., Stroobant, N. et al. (1996). Personality as an independent predictor of long-term mortality in patients with coronary heart disease. *The Lancet*, 347: 417–21.

Denscombe, M. (2001). Peer group pressure, young people and smoking: new developments and policy implications. *Drugs: Education, Prevention and Policy*, 8: 7–32.

de Nooijer, J., de Vet, E., Brug, J. and de Vries, N.K. (2006). Do implementation intentions help to turn good intentions into higher fruit intakes? *Journal of Nutrition Education and Behavior*, 38: 25–9.

de Nooijer, J., Lechner, L. and de Vries, H.A. (2001). Qualitative study on detecting cancer symptoms and seeking medical help: an application of Andersen's model of total patient delay. *Patient Education and Counseling*, 42: 145–57.

Department of Health (1991). *The Health of the Nation*. London: HMSO.

Department of Health (1992). *The Health of the Nation: A Strategy for Health in England*. London: HMSO.

Department of Health (1995). *Obesity: Reversing the Increasing Problem of Obesity in England*. Report from the Nutrition and Physical Activity Task Forces. London: HMSO.

Department of Health (1999) *Saving Lives: Our Healthier Nation*. London: Department of Health.

Department of Health (2000a). *Health Survey for England*. London: National Centre for Social Research & the National Foundation for Educational Research.

Department of Health (2000b) Statistics on smoking: England 1978 onwards. *Statistical Bulletin* 200/17. London: Department of Health.

Department of Health (2001a). *The 2000 Health Survey for England: The Health of Older People (aged 65+)*. London: Department of Health.

Department of Health (2001b). *The Expert Patient: A New Approach to Chronic Disease Management for the 21st Century*. London: Department of Health.

Department of Health (2001c). *Involving Patients and the Public in Healthcare*. Available from: www.dh.gov.uk/PolicyAndGuidance/OrganisationPolicy/PatientAndPublicInvolvement/InvolvingPatientsPublicHealthcare/fs/en.

Department of Health (2003). *Tackling Health Inequalities: A Programme for Action*. London: Department of Health.

Department of Health (2004). *At Least Five a Week: Evidence on the Impact of Physical Activity and its Relationship to Health*. A Report from the Chief Medical Officer. London: Department of Health.

Department of Health (2005). *Choosing Activity: A Physical Activity Action Plan*. London: UK Department of Health.

Department of Health (2007). *Tackling Health Inequalities: 2007 Status Report on the Programme for Action*. London: Department of Health.

Department of Health (2010). *Recognised, valued and supported: Next steps for the Carer's Strategy: Response to the call for views*. London: Department of Health.

Department of Health and Human Services (1996). Report of final mortality statistics, 1994. *Monthly Vital Statistics Report*, 45(3 suppl.). Hyattsville, MD: Public Health Service.

Department of Health and Human Services (1998). *Health, United States, 1998: Socio-economic Status and Health Chartbook*. Hyattsville, MD: National Center for Health Statistics.

Department of Transportation (2003). *National Survey of Pedestrian and Bicyclist Attitudes and Behaviors-Highlights Report*. National Highway Traffic Safety Administration and Bureau of Transportation Statistics.

Derbyshire, S.W. (2000). Exploring the pain 'neuro-matrix'. *Current Reviews of Pain*, 4: 467–77.

De Ridder, D., Fournier, M. and Bensing, J. (2004). Does optimism affect symptom report in chronic disease? What are its consequences for self-care behaviour and physical functioning? *Journal of Psychosomatic Research*, 56: 341–50.

DeRidder, D., Geenen, R., Kuijer, R., and van Middendorp, H. (2008). Psychological adjustment to chronic disease, *The Lancet*, 372: 246–55.

De Ridder, D. and Schreurs, K. (2001). Developing interventions for chronically ill patients: Is coping a helpful concept? *Clinical Psychology Review*, 21: 205–40.

Descartes, R. (1664). *Traite de l'homme*. Paris: Angot.

Deshler, A.M., Fee-Schroeder, K.C., Dowdy, J.L. et al. (2006). A patient orientation program at a comprehensive cancer center. *Oncology Nursing Forum*, 33: 569–78.

Detmar, S.B., Aaronson, N.K., Wever, L.D. et al. (2000). How are you feeling? Who wants to know? Patients' and oncologists preferences for discussing health-related quality of life issues. *Journal of Clinical Oncology*, 18: 3295–301.

Devanesen, D. (2000). Traditional Aboriginal medicine practice in the Northern Territory. In *International Symposium on Traditional Medicine*, Awaji Islands, Japan. Available from: www.nt.gov.au/health/comm_health/

abhealth_strategy?Traditional%20Aboriginal%20Medicine%20-%20Japan%20Paper.pdf.

De Vellis, R.F., Lewis, M.A. and Sterba, K.R. (2003). Interpersonal emotional processes in adjustment to chronic illness. In J. Suls and K.A. Wallston (eds), *Social Psychological Foundations of Health and Illness*. Malden, MA: Blackwell.

De Vet, E., De Nooijer, J., DeVries, N.K. and Brug, J. (2007). Comparing stage of change and behavioral intention to understand fruit intake. *Health Education Research*, 22: 599–608.

De Vet, E., Gebhardt, W.A., Sinnige, J. et al. (2011). Implementation intentions for buying, carrying, discussing and using condoms: the role of the quality of the plans. *Health Education Research*, 26: 443–55.

Devi, R., Powell, J. and Singh, S. (2014). A web-based program improves physical activity outcomes in a primary care angina population: randomized controlled trial. *Journal of Medical Internet Research*, 16: e186.

Devine, C.M., Jastran, M., Jabs, J. et al. (2006). 'A lot of sacrifices': work–family spillover and the food choice coping strategies of low-wage employed parents. *Social Science and Medicine*, 63: 2591–603.

Devins, G.M., Mendelssohn, D.C., Barré, P.E. et al. (2003). Predialysis psychoeducational intervention and coping styles influence time to dialysis in chronic kidney disease. *American Journal of Kidney Diseases*, 42: 693–703.

De Voogd, J.N., Sanderman, R., and Coyne, J.C. (2012). A meta-analysis of spurious assocations between type D personality and cardiovascular disease endpoints. *Annals of Behavioral Medicine*, 44: 136–7.

de Vries, H., Candel, M., Engles, R. et al. (2006). Challenges to the peer influence paradigm: results for 12–13 year olds from six European countries from the European Smoking Prevention Framework Approach study. *Tobacco Control*, 15: 83–9.

Dew, M.A., Di Martini, A.F., Dabbs, A., de V. et al. (2007). Rates and risk factors for nonadherence to the medical regimen after adults solid organ transplantation. *Transplantation*, 83: 858–73.

Dey, P., Bundred, N., Gibbs, A. et al. (2002). Costs and benefits of a one stop clinic compared with a dedicated breast clinic: randomised controlled trial. *British Medical Journal*, 324: 507.

Deyo, R.A. (1986). Early diagnostic evaluation of lower back pain. *Journal of General Internal Medicine*, 1: 328–38.

Deyo, R.A. (1991). Fads in the treatment of low back pain. *New England Journal of Medicine*, 325: 1039–40.

Deyo, R.A., Walsh, N.E., Martin, D.C. et al. (1990). A controlled trial of transcutaneous electrical nerve stimulation (TENS) and exercise for chronic low back pain. *New England Journal of Medicine*, 322: 1627–34.

Dickens, C., Cherrington, A., Adeyemi, I. et al. (2013). Characteristics of psychological interventions that improve depression in people with coronary heart disease: a systematic review and meta-regression. *Psychosomatic Medicine*, 75:211–21.

Dickens, C., Katon, W., Blakemore, A., et al. (2012) Does depression predict the use of urgent and uscheduled care by people with long term conditions? A systematic review with meta analysis. *Journal of Psychosomatic Research* 73:334–42.

di Clemente, C.C. and Prochaska, J.O. (1982). Self-change and therapy change of smoking behavior: a comparison of processes of change in cessation and maintenance. *Addictive Behaviours*, 7: 133–42.

di Clemente, C.C., Prochaska, J.O., Fairhurst, S.K. et al. (1991). The process of smoking cessation: an analysis of precontemplation, contemplation, and preparation stages of change. *Journal of Consulting and Clinical Psychology*, 59: 295–304.

di Clemente, C.C. and Velicer, W.F. (1997). The transtheoretical model of health behavior change. *American Journal of Health Promotion*, 12: 11–12.

Didlake, R.H., Dreyfus, K., Kerman, R.H. et al. (1988). Patient noncompliance: a major cause of late graft failure in cyclosporine-treated renal transplants. *Transplant Proceedings*, 20: 63–9.

Diefenbach, M.A., Leventhal, E.A., Leventhal, H. et al. (1995). Negative affect relates to cross-sectional but not longitudinal symptom reporting: data from elderly adults. *Health Psychology*, 15: 282–8.

Diener, E., Emmons, R.A., Larsen, R.J. and Griffen, S. (1985). The satisfaction with life scale. *Journal of Personality Assessment*, 49: 71–5.

Diener, E., Lucas, R.E. and Scollon, C.N. (2006). Beyond the hedonic treadmill: revising the adaptation theory of well-being. *American Psychologist*, 61(4): 305–14.

Diener, E., Oishi, S. and Lucas, R.E. (2009). Subjective well-being: the science of life happiness and life satisfaction. In: S.J. Lopez and C.R. Snyder (eds). *Oxford Handbook of Positive Psychology*. New York: Oxford University Press, pp. 187–94.

Diener., E. and Seligman, M.E.P. (2002). Very happy people. *Psychological Science*, 13: 81–4.

Digiusto, E. and Bird, K.D. (1995). Matching smokers to treatment: self-control versus social support. *Journal of Consulting and Clinical Psychology*, 63: 290–5.

Dijkstra, A., Conijn, B. and DeVries, H. (2006). A match–mismatch test of a stage model of behavior change in tobacco smoking. *Addiction*, 101: 1035–43.

Dijkstra, P.U., Geertzen, J.H., Stewart, R. et al. (2002). Phantom pain and risk factors: a multivariate analysis. *Journal of Pain Symptom Management*, 24: 578–85.

Dillay, J.W., McFarland, W., Woods, W.J. et al. (2002). Thoughts associated with unprotected anal intercourse among men at high risk in San Francisco 1997 –1999. *Psychology and Health*, 17: 235–46.

Dilworth-Anderson, P., Williams, I.C. and Gibson, B.E. (2002). Issues of race, ethnicitiy and culture in caregiving research: a 20-year review. *The Gerontologist*, 42: 237–72.

DiMatteo, M.R. (2004a). Variations in patients' adherence to medical recommendations: a quantitative review of 50 years of research. *Medical Care*, 42: 200–9.

DiMatteo, M.R. (2004b). The role of effective communication with children and their families in fostering adherence to pediatric regimes. *Patient Education and Counselling*, 55: 339–44.

DiMatteo, M.R., Haskard, K.B. and Williams, S.L. (2007). Health beliefs, disease severity, and patients adherence: a meta-analysis. *Medical Care*, 45: 521–8.

DiMatteo, M.R., Haskard-Zolnierek, K.B. and Martin, L.R. (2012). Improving patient adherence: a three-factor model to guide practice. *Health Psychology Review*, 6: 74–91.

DiMatteo, M.R., Lepper, H.D. and Croghan, T.W. (2000). Depression is a risk factor for non-compliance with medical treatment: meta-analysis of the effects of anxiety and depression on patient adherence. *Archives of Internal Medicine*, 160: 2101–7.

Ding, A. (2003). Youth are more sensitive to price changes in cigarettes than adults. *Yale Journal of Biology and Medicine*, 76: 115–24.

Ditto, P.H., Druley, J.A., Moore, K.A. et al. (1996). Fates worse than death: the role of valued life activities in health state evaluations. *Health Psychology*, 15: 332–43.

Ditto, T.T. and Jemmott, J.B., III (1989). From rarity to evaluative extremity: effects of prevalence information on evaluations of positive and negative characteristics. *Journal of Personality and Social Psychology*, 57: 16–26.

Dobbins, J.F. (2007). Connections of care: relationships and family caregiver narratives. In *The Meaning of Others: Narrative Studies of Relationships*, Josselson, R., Liblich, A. and McAdams, D.A. (eds). Washington, DC: American Psychological Association, pp. 189–211.

Dockray, S. and Steptoe, A. (2010). Positive affect and psychobiological processes. *Neuroscience and Behavioral Reviews*, 35: 69–75.

Dodds, J. and Mercey, D. (2002). *London Gay Men's Survey: 2001 Results*. London: Department of STDs, Royal Free and University College Medical School.

Doherty, S.R., Jones, P.D., Davis, L. et al. (2007). Evidence based implementation of adult asthma guidelines in the emergency department: a controlled trial. *Emergency Medicine Australasia*, 19: 31–8.

Dohrenwend, B.S. and Dohrenwend, B.P. (1981). Some issues in research on stressful life events. In I.G. Sarason and C.D. Spielberger (eds) *Stress and Anxiety*. Washington, DC: Hemisphere.

Dolan, P., Gudex, C., Kind, P. and Williams, A. (1996). Valuing health states: a comparison of methods. *Journal of Health Economics*, 15: 209–31.

Doll, R. and Hill, A.B. (1954). The mortality of doctors in relation to their smoking habits. *British Medical Journal*, 1: 1451–5.

Doll, R. and Peto, R. (1981). *The Causes of Cancer*. Oxford: Oxford University Press.

Doll, R., Peto, R., Boreham, J. and Sutherland, I. (2004). Mortality in relation to smoking: 50 years' observations on male British doctors. *British Medical Journal*, 328: 1519–28.

Doll, R., Peto, R., Hall, E. et al. (1994). Mortality in relation to consumption of alcohol: 13 years' observation on male British doctors. *British Medical Journal*, 309: 911–18.

Domchek, S.M., Bradbury, A., Garber, J.E. et al. (2013). Multiplex genetic testing for cancer susceptibility: out on the high wire without a net? *Journal of Clinical Oncology*, 31: 1267–70.

Donaghy, M. and Durward, B. (2000). *A report on the clinical effectiveness of physiotherapy in mental health*. Research and Clinical Effectiveness Unit, Chartered Society of Physiotherapy.

Donaldson, L (2009). *Guidance on the consumption of alcohol by children and young people*. Department of Health, London.

Dooley, D., Fielding, J. and Levi, L. (1996). Health and unemployment. *Annual Review of Public Health*, 17: 449–65.

Doyal, L. (2001). Sex, gender, and health: the need for a new approach. *British Medical Journal*, 323: 1061–3.

Dragano, N., Verde, P.E. and Siegrist, J. (2005). Organisational downsizing and work stress: testing synergistic health effects in employed men and women. *Journal of Epidemiology and Community Health*, 59: 694–9.

Dreyer, G., Hull, S., Aitken, Z. et al. (2009) The effect of ethnicity on the prevalence of diabetes and associated chronic kidney disease. *Quarterly Journal of Medicine;* 102: 261–9.

Droomers, M., Schrijvers, C.T.M. and Mackenbach, J.P. (2002). Why do lower educated people continue smoking? Explanations from the longitudinal GLOBE study. *Health Psychology*, 21: 263–72.

Drossaert, C.H., Boer, H. and Seydel, E.R. (1996). Health education to improve repeat participation in the Dutch breast cancer screening programme: evaluation of a leaflet tailored to previous participants. *Patient Education and Counselling*, 8: 121–31.

Drotar, D. and Bonner, M.S. (2009). Influences on adherence to pediatric asthma treatment: a review of correlates and predictors. *Journal of Developmental and Behavioral Pediatrics,* 30: 574–82.

Dua, R., Vassiliou, L. and Fan, K. (2013). Common maxillofacial terminology: do our patients understand what we say? *Surgeon*, 13: 1–4.

Duclos, M., Gouarne, C. and Bonnemaison, D. (2003). Acute and chronic effects of exercise on tissue sensitivity to glucocorticoids. *Journal of Applied Physiology*, 94: 869–75.

Duff, A.J. (2001). Psychological interventions in cystic fibrosis and asthma. *Paediatric Respiratory Reviews*, 2: 350–7.

Duffy, L.C., Zielezny, M.A., Marshall, J.R. et al. (1991). Relevance of major stress events as an indicator of disease activity prevalence in inflammatory bowel disease. *Behavioral Medicine*, Fall: 101–10.

Dundas, R., Morgan, M. and Redfern, J. (2001). Ethnic differences in behavioural risk factors for stroke: implications for health promotion. *Ethnicity and Health*, 6: 95–103.

Dunbar-Jacob, J., Burke, L.E. and Pucznski, S. (1995). Clinical assessment and management of adherence to medication regimens. In P.M. Nicassio and T.W. Smith (eds), *Managing Chronic Illness: A Bio-psychosocial Perspective*. Washington, DC: American Psychological Association.

Dunton, G.F. and Vaughan, E. (2008). Anticipated affective consequences of physical activity adoption and maintenance. *Health Psychology*, 27: 703–10.

Dusseldorp, F., van Elderen, T., Maes, S. et al. (1999). A meta-analysis of psycho-educational programs for coronary heart disease patients. *Health Psychology*, 18: 506–19.

Dutta-Bergman, M.J. (2003). A descriptive narrative of healthy eating: a social marketing approach using psychographics in conjunction with interpersonal, community, mass media and new media activities. *Health Marketing Quarterly*, 20: 81–101.

Dzewaltowski, D.A. (1989). Toward a model of exercise motivation. *Journal of Sport and Exercise Psychology*, 11: 251–69.

Eagly, A.H. and Chaiken, S. (1993). *The Psychology of Attitudes*. Orlando, FL: Harcourt Brace Jovanovich.

Eaker, E.D., Sullivan, L.M., Kelly-Hayes, M. et al. (2004). Does job strain increase the risk for coronary heart disease or death in men and women? *American Journal of Epidemiology*, 159: 950–8.

Earl, A. and Albarracín, D. (2007). Nature, decay, and spiraling of the effects of fear-inducing arguments and HIV counseling and testing: a meta-analysis of the short- and long-term outcomes of HIV-prevention interventions. *Health Psychology*, 26: 496–506.

Ebrahim, S., Taylor, F., Ward, K., Beswick, A. et al. (2011). Multiple risk factor interventions for primary prevention of coronary heart disease. *Cochrane Database of Systematic Reviews*, (1): CD001561.

Eccles, M.P., Grimshaw, J.M., MacLennan, G., et al. (2012). Explaining clinical behaviours using multiple theoretical models. *Implementation Science*, 7: 99–112

Eccleston, C. and Crombez, G. (1999). Pain demands attention: a cognitive-affective model of the interruptive function of pain. *Psychological Bulletin*, 125: 356–66.

Eccleston C., Palermo T.M., de C Williams A.C. et al. (2012). Psychological therapies for the management of chronic and recurrent pain in children and adolescents. *Cochrane Database of Systematic Reviews* 12: CD003968.

Eccleston C., Palermo T.M., Williams A.C. et al. (2014). Psychological therapies for the management of chronic and recurrent pain in children and adolescents. *Cochrane Database of Systematic Reviews* 5: CD003968.

Echabe, A.E., Guillen, C.S. and Ozamiz, J.A. (1992). Representations of health, illness and medicines: coping strategies and health promoting behaviour. *British Journal of Clinical Psychology*, 31: 339–49.

Echteld, M.A., Maes, S. and van Elderen, T.M.T. (1998). Predictors of quality of life in PTCA* patients: avoiding stressors increases quality of life. In R. Schwarzer (ed.), *Advances in Health Psychology Research*. Berlin: Berlin Free University. [*percutaneous transluminal coronary angioplasty]

Echteld, M.A., van Elderen, T.M.T. and van der Kamp, L.J.T. (2001). How goal disturbance, coping and chest pain relate to quality of life: a study among patients waiting for PTCA. *Quality of Life Research*, 10: 487–501.

Echteld, M.A., van Elderen, T. and van der Kamp, L.J.Th. (2003). Modeling predictors of quality of life after coronary angioplasty. *Annals of Behavioral Medicine*, 26: 49–60.

Edelmann, R. (1999). *Psychosocial Aspects of the Health Care Process*. Harlow: Prentice Hall.

Edwards, A. and Elwyn, G. (2009). *Shared Decision-making in Health Care. Achieving Evidence-based Patient Choice*. Oxford: Oxford University Press.

Edwards, A., Elwyn, G., Covey, J. et al. (2001). Presenting risk information: a review of the effects of 'framing' and other manipulations on patient outcomes. *Journal of Health Communication*, 6: 61–82.

Edwards, W. (1954). The theory of decision making. *Psychological Bulletin*, 51: 380–417.

Egan, G. (1998). *The Skilled Helper: Models, Skills, and Methods for Effective Helping*. Monterey, CA: Brooks/Cole.

Egan, G. (2013). *The Skilled Helper. A Problem-management and Opportunity Development Approach to Helping*. Belmont, CA: Brooks/Cole.

Eiser, C. (1985). *The Psychology of Childhood Illness*. New York: Springer Verlag.

Eiser, C. (1990). *Chronic Childhood Disease: An Introduction to Psychological Theory and Research*. Cambridge: Cambridge University Press.

Eiser, C. (2004). *Children with Cancer: Their Quality of Life*. NJ: Lawrence Erlbaum.

Eiser, C. and Havermans, T. (1992). Mothers' and fathers' coping with chronic childhood disease. *Psychology and Health*, 7: 249–57.

Eiser, C. and Morse, R. (2001). The measurement of quality of life in children: past and future perspectives. *Journal of Developmental and Behavioral Pediatrics*, 22: 248–56.

Eiser, C., Patterson, D. and Tripp, J.H. (1984). Diabetes and developing knowledge of the body. *Archives of Disease in Childhood*, 59: 167–9.

Eiser, J.R. (1996). Reconnecting the individual and the social in health psychology. *Psychology and Health*, 11: 605–18.

Ekkekakis, P., Hall, E.E. and Petruzello, S.J. (2008). The relationship between exercise intensity and affective responses demystified: to crack the 40-year-old nut, replace the 40-year-old nutcracker! *Annals of Behavioural Medicine*, 35: 136–49.

Elfström, M.L. and Kreuter, M. (2006). Relationships between locus of control, coping strategies, and emotional well-being in persons with spinal cord injury. *Journal of Clinical Psychology in Medical Settings*, 13: 93–103.

Ellaway, A., McKay, L., Macintyre, S., Kearns, A. and Hiscock, R. (2004). Are social comparisons of homes and cars related to psychosocial health? *International Journal of Epidemiology*, 33: 1065–71.

Ellington, L. and Wiebe, D.J. (1999). Neuroticism, symptom presentation, and medical decision making. *Health Psychology*, 18: 634–43.

Elliot, A. J., Sheldon, K. M. and Church, M. A. (1997). Avoidance personal goals and subjective well-being. *Personality and Social Psychology Bulletin*, 23, 915–27.

Elliot, A.J., Thrash, T.M. and Murayama, K. (2011). A longitudinal analysis of self-regulation and well-being: avoidance personal goals, avoidance coping, stress generation, and subjective well-being. *Journal of Personality*, 79: 3, DOI: 10.1111/j.1467–6494.2011.00694.x

Ellis, A. (1977). The basic clinical theory of rational–emotive therapy. In A. Ellis and R. Grieger (eds), *Handbook of Rational–Emotive Therapy*. New York: Springer Verlag.

Elmer, P.J., Grimm, R., Jr, Laing, B. et al. (1995). Lifestyle intervention: results of the Treatment of Mild Hypertension Study (TOMHS). *Preventive Medicine*, 24: 378–88.

Elstein A.S. and Schwartz, A. (2002) Clinical problem solving and diagnostic decision making: selective review of the cognitive literature, *BMJ* 2002 Mar 23; 324(7339): 729–32.

Elwyn, G., Edwards, A., Kinnersley, P. et al. (2000). Shared decision making and the concept of equipoise: the competences of involving patients in healthcare choices. *British Journal of General Practice*, 50: 892–9.

Elwyn, G., Frosch, D., Thomson, R. et al. (2012). Shared decision making: a model for clinical practice. *Journal of General Internal Medicine*, 27: 1361–7.

Emanuel, L., Bennett, K. and Richardson, V.E. (2007). The dying role. *Journal of Palliative Medicine*, 10: 159–68.

Emery, S., Wakefield, M.A., Terry-McElrath, Y. et al. (2007). Using message framing to promote acceptance of the human papillomavirus vaccine. *Health Psychology*, 26: 745–52.

Emler, N. (1984). Delinquency and reputation. *Progress in Experimental Personality Research*, 13: 174–230.

Endler, N.S. and Parker, J.D.A. (1993). The multi-dimensional assessment of coping: concepts, issues, measurement. In G.L. Van Heck, P. Bonaiuto, I.J. Deary and W. Nowack (eds), *Personality Psychology in Europe*, Vol. 4. Netherlands: Tilburg University Press.

Endler, N.S., Parker, J.D.A. and Summerfeldt, L.J. (1998). Coping with health problems: developing a reliable and valid multidimensional measure. *Psychological Assessment*, 10: 195–205.

Eng, J.J. and Martin-Ginis, K.A. (2007). Using the theory of planned behaviour to predict leisure time physical activity among people with chronic kidney disease. *Rehabilitation Psychology*, 52: 435–42.

Engbers, L.H., van Poppel, M.N., Chin, A. et al. (2006). The effects of a controlled worksite environmental intervention on determinants of dietary behavior and self-reported fruit, vegetable and fat intake. *BMC Public Health*, 6: 253.

Engel, G.L. (1977). The need for a new medical model: a challenge for biomedicine. *Science*, 196: 129–36.

Engel, G.L. (1980). The clinical application of the bio-psychosocial model. *American Journal of Psychiatry*, 137: 535–44.

Engler, M.B. and Engler, M.M. (2006). The emerging role of flavonoid-rich cocoa and chocolate in cardiovascular health and disease. *Nutrition Reviews*, 64: 109–18.

Epel, E.S. (2009). Telomeres in a life-span perspective: a new 'psychobiomarker'? *Current Directions in Psychological Science*, 18: 6–10.

Epton, T. and Harris, P.R. (2008). Self-affirmation promotes health behavior change, *Health Psychology*, 27: 746–52.

Erens, B., McManus, S., Prescott, A. et al. (2003). *National Survey of Sexual Attitudes and Lifestyles II: Reference Tables and Summary Report*. London: National Centre for Social Research.

Eriksen, H.R., Ihlebaek, C., Mikkelsen, A. et al. (2002). Improving subjective health at the worksite: a randomized controlled trial of stress management training, physical exercise and an integrated health programme. *Occupational Medicine*, 52: 383–91.

Eriksen, J., Jensen, M.K., Sjogren, P. et al. (2003). Epidemiology of chronic non-malignant pain in Denmark. *Pain*, 106: 221–8.

Erikson, E.H. (1959). Identity and the life cycle. *Psychological Issues*, 1: 1–171.

Erikson, E.H. (1980). *Identity and the Life Cycle: A Reissue*. New York: W.W. Norton.

Erikson, E.H., Erikson, J.M. and Kivnick, H.Q. (1986). *Vital Involvement in Old Age: The Experience of Old Age in Our Time*. New York: W.W. Norton.

Esterling, B.A., L'Abate, L., Murray, E.J. et al. (1999). Empirical foundations for writing in prevention and psychotherapy: mental and physical health outcomes. *Clinical Psychology Review*, 19: 79–96.

EUROFAMCARE (2006). *Services for Supporting Family Carers of Dependent Older People in Europe: the Trans-European Survey Report (TEUSURE)* – http://www.uke.de/extern/eurofamcare/deli.php.

European Commission (1999). *A Pan-EU Survey of Consumer Attitudes to Physical Activity, Body Weight and Health*. Luxembourg: EC. DGV/F.3.

European Commission (2006) FACTSHEET: Alcohol-related harm in Europe – key data. Brussels, European Communities.

European Commission (2008) *Long-term Care in the European Union*. Brussels: European Commission.

Euroqol Group (1990). Euroqol: a new facility for the measurement of health related quality of life. *Health Policy*, 16: 199–208.

Eurostat (2007). GP Utilisation. Retrieved from http://www.euphix.org

Evandrou, M. (2006). Inequalities among older people in London: the challenge of diversity. In V.R. Rodwin and M.K. Gusmano (eds), *Growing Older in World Cities: New York, London, Paris and Tokyo*. Nashville, TN: Vanderbilt University Press, pp. 173–98.

Evans, D. and Norman, P. (2002). Improving pedestrian road safety among adolescents: an application of the theory of planned behaviour. In D. Rutter and L. Quine (eds), *Changing Health Behaviour*. Buckingham: Open University Press.

Evans, G.W. and Stecker, R. (2004). Motivational consequences of environmental stress. *Journal of Environmental Psychology*, 24: 143–65.

Evans, R. E. C., Brotherstone, H., Miles, A., and Wardle, J. (2005). Gender differences in early detection of cancer. *Journal of Men's Health & Gender*, 2, 209–17.

Evans, S., Fishman, B., Spielman, L. and Haley, A. (2003). Randomized trial of cognitive behaviour therapy versus supportive psychotherapy for HIV-related peripheral neuropathic pain. *Psychosomatics*, 44: 44–50.

Evans-Whipp, T.J., Bond, L., Ukoumunne, O.C. et al. (2010). The impact of school tobacco policies on student smoking in Washington State, United States and Victoria, Australia. *International Journal of Environmental Research and Public Health*, 7: 698–710.

Evers, A.W., Kraaimaat, F.W., Geenen, R. et al. (2003). Pain coping and social support as predictors of long-term functional disability and pain in early rheumatoid arthritis. *Behaviour Research and Therapy*, 41: 1295–310.

Evers, A.W., Kraaimaat, F.W., van Legenveld, W., et al. (2001). Beyond unfavourable thinking:The Illness Cognition Questionnaire for chronic disease. *Journal of Consulting and Clinical Psychology*, 69: 1026–36.

Evers, A.W., Kraaimaat, F.W., van Riel, P.L. and de Jong, A.J. (2002). Tailored cognitive-behavioral therapy in early rheumatoid arthritis for patients at risk: a randomized controlled trial. *Pain*, 100: 141–53.

Everson, S.A., McKey, B.S. and Lovallo, W.R. (1995). Effects of trait hostility on cardiovascular responses to harassment in young men. *International Journal of Behavioral Medicine*, 2: 172–91.

Eves, F.F., Webb, O.J. and Mutrie, N. (2006). A workplace intervention to promote stair climbing: greater effects in the overweight. *Obesity (Silver Spring)*, 14: 2210–16.

Expert Group (2004). Research in the behavioural and social sciences to improve cancer control and care: a strategy for development. *European Journal of Cancer*, 40: 316–25.

Ey, S., Hadley, W., Allen, D.N. et al. (2005). A new measure of children's optimism and pessimism: the youth life orientation test. *Journal of Child Psychology & Psychiatry*, 46: 548–58.

Eysenck, H.J. (1970). *The Structure of Human Personality*, 3rd edn. London: Methuen.

Eysenck, H.J. (1982). *Personality, Genetics and Behaviour*. New York: Praeger.

Eysenck, H.J. (1985). Personality, cancer and cardiovascular disease: a causal analysis. *Personality and Individual Differences*, 6: 535–56.

Eysenck, H.J. (1991). Dimensions of personality: 16, 5, or 3? Criteria for a taxonomic paradigm. *Personality and Individual Differences*, 12: 773–90.

Eysenck, H.J. and Grossarth-Maticek, R. (1989). Prevention of cancer and coronary heart disease and the reduction in the cost of the National Health Service. *Journal of Social, Political and Economic Studies*, 14: 25–47.

Ezer, H., Chachamovich, J.L.R. and Chachamovich, E. (2011). Do men and their wives see it the same way? Congruence within couples during the first year of prostate cancer. *Psycho-Oncology*, 20: 155–64.

Fadardi, J.S. and Cox, W.M. (2009). Reversing the sequence: reducing alcohol consumption by overcoming alcohol attentional bias. *Drug & Alcohol Dependence*, 101: 137–45.

Fagerli, R.A., Lien, M.E. and Wandel, M. (2007). Health worker style and trustworthiness as perceived by Pakistani-born persons with type 2 diabetes in Oslo, Norway. *Health (London)*, 11: 109–29.

Fahrenwald, N.L. and Walker, S.N. (2003). Application of the transtheoretical model of behavior change to the physical activity behavior of WIC mothers. *Public Health Nursing*, 20: 307–17.

Falconier, M. K., Nussbeck, F. and Bodenmann, G. (2013). Dyadic coping in Latino couples: validity of the Spanish version of the Dyadic Coping Inventory. *Anxiety, Stress, & Coping,* 26, 446–66. doi: 10.1080/10615806.2012.699045

Falconier, M.K., Nussbeck, F., Bodenmann, G. et al. (2015). Stress from daily hassles in couples: its effects on intradyadic stress, relationship satisfaction, and physical and psychological well-being. *Journal of Marital & Family Therapy*, doi: 10.1111/jmft.12073

Faller, H. and Bülzebruck, H. (2002). Coping and survival in lung cancer: a 10-year follow-up. *American Journal of Psychiatry*, 159: 2105–7.

Faller, H., Schilleing, S. and Lang, H. (1995). Causal attribution and life threatening disease. *Journal of Psychosomatic Research* 39: 619–27.

Fallowfield, L.J., Hall, A., Maguire, G.P. et al. (1990). Psychological outcomes of different treatment policies in women with early breast cancer outside a clinical trial. *British Medical Journal*, 301: 575–80.

Fallowfield, L. and Jenkins, V. (2004). Communicating sad, bad, and difficult news in medicine. *Lancet*, 363: 312–19.

Fallowfield, L., Jenkins, V., Farewell, V. et al. (2002). Efficacy of a Cancer Research UK communication skills training model for oncologists: a randomised controlled trial. *The Lancet*, 359: 650–6.

Fallowfield, L., Ratcliffe, D., Jenkins, V. and Saul, J. (2001). Psychiatric morbidity and its recognition by doctors in patients with cancer. *British Journal of Cancer*, 84: 1011–15.

Family Heart Study Group (1994). Randomised controlled trial evaluating cardiovascular screening and intervention in general practice: principal results of British family heart study. *British Medical Journal*, 308: 313–20.

Farber, N.J., Urban, S.Y., Collier, V.U. et al. (2002). The good news about giving bad news to patients. *Journal of General Internal Medicine*, 17: 914–22.

Farquhar, J., Fortmann, S., Flora, J. et al. (1990a). Effects of community-wide education on cardiovascular disease risk factors. *Journal of the American Medical Association*, 264: 359–65.

Farquhar, J.W., Fortmann, S.P., Flora, J.A. et al. (1990b). Effects of community-wide education on cardiovascular disease risk factors. The Stanford Five-City Project. *Journal of the American Medical Association*, 264: 359–65.

Farquhar, J., Maccoby, N. and Wood, P. (1977). Community education for cardiovascular disease. *The Lancet*, 1: 1192–5.

Fauerbach, J.A., Lawrence, J.W., Haythornthwaite, J.A. and Richter, L. (2002). Coping with the stress of a painful medical procedure. *Behaviour Research and Therapy*, 40: 1003–15.

Faulkner, A. (1998). *When the News is Bad*. Cheltenham: Stanley Thorne.

Faulkner, A., Argent, J., Jones, A. and O'Keeffe, C. (1995). Improving the skills of doctors in giving distressing information. *Medical Education*, 29: 303–7.

Fawzy, F.I., Canada, A.L. and Fawzy, N.W. (2003). Malignant melanoma: effects of a brief, structured psychiatric intervention on survival and recurrence at 10-year follow-up. *Archives of General Psychiatry*, 60: 100–3.

Fawzy, F.I. and Fawzy, N.W. (1998). Psychoeducational interventions. In J. Holland (ed.), *Textbook of Psycho-Oncology*. New York: Oxford University Press.

Fawzy, F.I., Fawzy, N.W., Hyun, C.S., Elashoff, R. et al. (1993). Malignant melanoma: effects of an early structured psychiatric intervention, coping, and affective state on recurrence and survival 6 years later. *Archives of General Psychiatry*, 50: 681–9.

Fazio, R.H. and Olson, M.A. (2003). Implicit measures in social cognition research: their meaning and use. *Annual Review of Psychology*, 54: 297–327.

Fedele, L., Marchini, M., Acaia, B. et al. (1989). Dynamics and significance of placebo response in primary dysmenorrhea. *Pain*, 36: 43–7.

Feeney, B.C. and Collins, N.L. (2001). Predictors of caregiving in adult intimate relationships: an attachment theoretical perspective. *Journal of Personality and Social Psychology*, 80: 972–94.

Feldman, C.T., Bensing, J.M. and de Rujter, A. (2007). Worries are the mother of many diseases: general practitioners and refugees in the Netherlands on stress, being ill, and prejudice. *Patient Education and Counselling*, 65: 369–80.

Feldman, P.J., Cohen, S., Doyle, W.J. et al. (1999). The impact of personality on the reporting of unfounded symptoms and illness. *Journal of Personality and Social Psychology*, 77: 370–8.

Felsten, G. (2004). Stress reactivity and vulnerability to depressed mood in college students. *Personality and Individual Differences*, 36: 789–800.

Feng, Z., Liu, C., Guan, X. and Mor, V. (2013). China's rapidly aging population creates policy challenges in shaping a viable long-term care system. *Health Affairs,* 31: 2764–73.

Fenton, K.A., Korovessis, C., Johnson, A.M. et al. (2001). Sexual behaviour in Britain: reported sexually transmitted infections and prevalence of genital *Chlamydia trachomatir* infection. *The Lancet*, 358: 1851–4.

Ferguson, E. (2000). Hypochondriacal concerns and the five factor model of personality. *Journal of Personality*, 68: 705–24.

Ferguson, E (2013). Personality is of central concern to understand health: towards a theoretical model for health psychology. *Health Psychology Review*, 7: S32-S70. Doi: 10.1080/17437199.2010.547985

Ferguson, E. and Bibby, P.A. (2012). Openness to experience and all-cause mortality: a meta-analysis and r equivalent from risk ratios and odds ratios. *British Journal of Health Psychology*, 17: 85–102.

Ferguson, J., Bauld, L., Chesterman, J. and Judge, K. (2005). The English smoking treatment services: one year outcomes. *Addiction,* 100 (Suppl 2): 59–69.

Ferlay, J., Steliarova-Foucher, E., Lortet-Tieulent, J. et al. (2013). Cancer incidence and mortality patterns in Europe: Estimates for 40 countries in 2012. *European Journal of Cancer,* 49: 1374–1403.

Ferrie, J.E. (2001) Is job insecurity harmful to health? *Journal of the Royal Society of Medicine,* 94: 71–6.

Ferro, J.M. and Crespo, M. (1994). Prognosis after transient ischemic attack and ischemic stroke in young adults. *Stroke*, 25: 1611–16.

Ferruci, L., Baldasseroni, S., Bandinelli, D. et al. (2000). Disease severity and health-related quality of life across different chronic conditions. *Journal of the American Geriatrics Society*, 48: 1490–5.

Festinger, L. (1954). A theory of social comparison processes. *Human Relations*, 7: 117–40.

Festinger, L. (1957). *A Theory of Cognitive Dissonance*. Stanford, CA: Stanford University Press.

Figueiras, M.J. and Weinman, J. (2003). Do similar patient and spouse perceptions of myocardial infarction predict recovery? *Psychology and Health*, 18: 201–16.

Figueiras, M.J., Cortes, M.A., Marcelino, D. and Weinman, J. (2010). Lay views about medicines: the influence of the illness label for the use of generic versus brand. *Psychology & Health*, 25: 1121–8.

Filakti, H. and Fox, J. (1995). Differences in mortality by housing tenure and by car access from the OPCS Longitudinal Study. *Population Trends*, 81: 27–30.

Fine, P.G., Roberts, W.J., Gillette, R.G. and Child, T.R. (1994). Slowly developing placebo responses confound tests of intravenous phentolamine to determine mechanisms underlying idiopathic chronic low back pain. *Pain*, 56: 235–42.

Finkelstein, E.A., Khavjou, O. and Will, J.C. (2006). Cost-effectiveness of WISEWOMAN, a program aimed at reducing heart disease risk among low-income women. *Journal of Womens' Health*, 15: 379–89.

Finkelstein, D.M., Kubzansky, L.D., Capitman, J. et al. (2007). Socioeconomic differences in adolescent stress: the role of psychological resources. *Journal of Adolescent Health*, 40: 127–34.

Finnegan, J.R., Jr, Meischke, H., Zapka, J.G. et al. (2000). Patient delay in seeking care for heart attack symptoms: findings from focus groups conducted in five U.S. regions. *Preventive Medicine*, 31: 205–23.

Finney, L.J. and Iannotti, R.J. (2002). Message framing and mammography screening: a theory-driven intervention. *Behavioral Medicine*, 28: 5–14.

Fischer, M., Scharloo, M., Abbink, J. et al. (2010). The dynamics of illness perceptions: testing assumptions of Leventhal's common-sense model in a pulmonary rehabilitation setting. *British Journal of Health Psychology*, 15: 887–903.

Fishbein, M. (1967). Attitude and the prediction of behavior. In M. Fishbein (ed.), *Readings in Attitude Theory and Measurement*. New York: Wiley.

Fishbein, M. and Ajzen, I. (1985). *Belief, Attitude, Intention and Behavior: An Introduction to Theory and Research*. Reading, MA: Addison-Wesley.

Fishbein, M. and Ajzen, I. (2010). *Predicting and Changing Behavior: The Reasoned Action Approach*. New York: Psychology Press.

Fisher, J. and Chaudoir, S.R. (2010). The disclosure process model: understanding disclosure decision making and post disclosure outcomes among people living with a concealable stigmatized identity. *Psychological Bulletin*, 136: 236–56.

Fisher, J.D., Bell, P.A. and Baum, A. (1984). *Environmental Psychology*, 2nd edn. New York: Holt, Rinehart & Winston.

Fisher, K. and Johnston, M. (1996a). Emotional distress as a mediator of the relationship between pain and disability: an experimental study. *British Journal of Health Psychology*, 1: 207–18.

Fisher, K. and Johnston, M. (1996b). Experimental manipulation of perceived control and its effect on disability. *Psychology and Health*, 11: 657–69.

Fisher, K. and Johnston, M. (1998). Emotional distress and control cognitions as mediators of the impact of chronic pain on disability. *British Journal of Health Psychology*, 3: 225–36.

Fiske, S.T. and Taylor, S.E. (1991). *Social Cognition*, 2nd edn. New York: McGraw-Hill.

Fitzell, A. and Pakenham, K. (2010). Application of a stress-coping model to positive and negative adjustment outcomes in colorectal cancer caregiving. *Psycho-Oncology*, 19: 1171–8.

Flegal, K.M., Kit, B.K., Orpana, H. and Graubard, B.I. (2013). Association of all-cause mortality with overweight and obesity using standardized body mass index categories: a systematic review and meta-analysis. *JAMA*, 2,309: 71–82

Fleishman, J.A., Sherbourne, C.D., Cleary, P.D. et al. (2003). Patterns of coping among persons with HIV infection: configurations, correlates, and change. *American Journal of Community Psychology*, 32: 187–204.

Fletcher, S.W., Black, W., Harris, R. et al. (1993). Report of the international workshop on screening for breast cancer. *Journal of the National Cancer Institute*, 85: 1644–56.

Fletcher, S.W., Harris, R.P., Gonzalez, J.J. et al. (1993). Increasing mammography utilization: a controlled study. *Journal of the National Cancer Institute*, 20: 112–20.

Flor, H., Breitenstein, C., Birbaumer, N. and Fuerst, M. (1995). A psychophysiological analysis of spouse solicitousness towards pain behaviours, spouse interaction and physical consequences. *Behavior Therapy*, 26: 255–72.

Flynn, B.S., Worden, J.K., Bunn, J.Y. et al. (2007). Youth audience segmentation strategies for smoking-prevention mass media campaigns based on message appeal. *Health Education and Behavior*, 34: 578–93.

Flynn B.S., Worden J.K., Bunn J.Y. et al. (2011). Evaluation of smoking prevention television messages based on the elaboration likelihood model. *Health Education Research*, 26: 976–87.

Foa, E.B., Rothbaum, B.O., Riggs, D.S. and Murdock, T.B. (1991). Treatment of posttraumatic stress disorder in rape victims: a comparison between cognitive and behavioural procedures and counselling. *Journal of Consulting and Clinical Psychology*, 59: 715–23.

Fogarty, L., Roter, D., Larson, S. et al. (2002). Patient adherence to HIV medication regimens: a review of published and abstract reports. *Patient Education and Counseling* 46: 93–108.

Foley, E., Baillie, A., Huxter, M. et al. (2010). Mindfulness-based cognitive therapy for individuals whose lives have been affected by cancer: a randomized controlled trial. *Journal of Consulting and Clinical Psychology*, 78: 72–9.

Folkman, S. (1984). Personal control and stress and coping processes: a theoretical analysis. *Journal of Personality and Social Psychology*, 46: 839–52.

Folkman, S. (2008). The case for positive emotions in the stress process. *Anxiety, Stress and Coping*, 21: 3–14.

Folkman, S. (2010). Stress, coping and hope. *Psycho-Oncology*, 19: 901–8.

Folkman, S. and Chesney, M. (1995). Coping with HIV infection. In M. Stain and A. Baum (eds), *Chronic Diseases. Perspectives in Behavioral Medicine*. Hillsdale, NJ: Lawrence Erlbaum.

Folkman, S. and Lazarus, R.S. (1980). An analysis of coping in a middle-aged community sample. *Journal of Health and Social Behavior*, 21: 219–39.

Folkman, S. and Lazarus, R.S. (1985). If it changes it must be a process: study of emotion and coping during three stages of a college examination. *Journal of Personality and Social Psychology*, 48: 150–70.

Folkman, S. and Lazarus, R.S. (1988). *Manual for the Ways of Coping Questionnaire*. Palo Alto, CA: Consulting Psychologists Press.

Folkman, S.K. and Moskowitz, J.T. (2000). Positive affect and the other side of coping. *American Psychologist*, 55: 647–54.

Folkman, S. and Moskowitch, J.T. (2004). Coping: pitfalls and promise. *Annual Review of Psychology*, 55: 745–74.

Food Standards Agency (2000). *National Diet and Nutrition Survey: Young People Aged 4–18 Years*. London: Stationery Office.

Ford, S., Fallowfield, L. and Lewis, S. (1996). Doctor–patient interactions in oncology. *Social Science and Medicine*, 42: 1511–19.

Ford, S., Schofield, T. and Hope, T. (2003). What are the ingredients for a successful evidence-based patient choice consultation? A qualitative study. *Social Science and Medicine*, 56: 589–602.

Fordyce, W.E. (1976). *Behavioural Methods for Chronic Pain and Illness*. St Louis, MO: Mosby.

Fordyce, W.E. (1982). The modification of avoidance learning in pain behaviors. *Journal of Behavioral Medicine*, 5: 405–14.

Fordyce, W.E. (1986). Learning processes in pain. In R.A. Sternbach (ed.), *The Psychology of Pain*, 2nd edn. New York: Raven Press.

Forrest, G., Plumb, C., Ziebland, S. et al. (2006). Breast cancer in the family-children's perceptions of their mother's cancer and its initial treatment: qualitative study. *British Medical Journal*, 332: 998–1003.

Forsberg-Wärleby, G., Möller, A. and Blomstrand, C. (2001). Spouses of first-ever stroke patients: psychological well-being in the first phase after stroke. *Stroke*, 32: 1646–56.

Forwell, G.D. (1993). *Glasgow's Health: Old Problems – New Opportunities*. A report by the Director of Public Health. Glasgow: Department of Public Health.

Foster, D.W., Yeung, N. and Neighbors, C. (2013). I think I can't: drinking refusal self-efficacy as a mediator of the relationship between self-reported drinking identity and alcohol use. *Addictive Behaviors*, doi: 10.1016/jaddbeh.2013.10.009

Fournier, M., de Ridder, D. and Bensing, J. (2002). Optimism and adaptation to chronic disease: the role of optimism in relation to self-care options in type 1 diabetes mellitus, rheumatoid arthritis and multiple sclerosis. *British Journal of Health Psychology*, 7: 409–32.

Franek, J. (2013). Self-management support interventions for persons with chronic disease: an evidence-based analysis. *Ontario Health Technology Assessment Series*, 13: 1–60.

Frankl, V.E. (2006). *Man's Search for Meaning* (Lasch, I. Trans., 5th edn). Boston, MA: Bacon Press (original work published in 1946).

Franzkowiak, P. (1987). Risk taking and adolescent development. *Health Promotion*, 2: 51–60.

Frasure-Smith, N. (1991). In-hospital symptoms of psychological stress as predictors of long-term outcome after acute myocardial infarction in men. *American Journal of Cardiology*, 67: 121–7.

Frasure-Smith, N., Lespérance, F., Gravel, G. et al. (2000). Social support, depression, and mortality during the first year after myocardial infarction. *Circulation*, 101: 1919–24.

Frasure-Smith, N., Lespérance, F., Gravel, G. et al. (2002). Long-term survival differences among low-anxious, high-anxious and repressive copers enrolled in the Montreal heart attack readjustment trial. *Psychosomatic Medicine*, 64: 571–9.

Frasure-Smith, N., Lespérance, F., Prince, R.H. et al. (1997). Randomised trial of home-based psychosocial nursing intervention for patients recovering from myocardial infarction. *The Lancet*, 350: 473–9.

Frasure-Smith, N., Lespérance, F. and Talajic, M.E. (1995). Coronary heart disease/myocardial infarction: depression and 18-month prognosis after myocardial infarction. *Circulation*, 91: 999–1005.

Frasure-Smith, N. and Prince, R. (1985). The ischemic heart disease life stress monitoring program: impact on mortality. *Psychosomatic Medicine*, 47: 431–45.

Frattaroli, J. (2006). Experimental disclosure and its moderators: a meta-analysis. *Psychological Bulletin*, 132: 823–65.

Frayling, T.M., Timpson, N.J., Weedon, M.N. et al. (2007). A common variant in the FTO gene is associated with body mass index and predisposes to childhood and adult obesity. *Science*, 316: 889–94.

Freda, M.C. (2005). The readability of American Academy of Pediatrics patient education brochures. *Journal of Pediatric Health Care*, 19: 151–6.

Fredman, L., Hawkes, W.G., Black, S. et al. (2006). Elderly patients with hip fracture with positive affect have better functional recovery over 2 years. *Journal of the American Geriatric Society*, 54: 1074–81.

Fredrickson, B.L. (1998). What good are positive emotions? *Review of General Psychology*, 2: 300–19.

Fredrickson, B.L. (2001). The role of positive emotions in positive psychology: the broaden-and-build theory of positive emotions. *American Psychologist*, 56: 218–26.

Fredrickson, M. and Matthews, K.A. (1990). Cardiovascular responses to behavioral stress and hypertension: a meta-analytic review. *Annals of Behavioral Medicine*, 12: 30–9.

Freedland, K.E., Carney, R.M., Hance, M.L. et al. (1996). Cognitive therapy for depression in patients with coronary artery disease. *Psychosomatic Medicine*, 58: 93.

Freedman, L.S., Kipnis, V., Schatzkin, A. et al. (2008). Methods of epidemiology: evaluating the fat-breast cancer hypothesis: comparing dietary instruments and other developments. *Cancer Journals* 14: 69–74.

Freidson, E. (1961). *Patients' Views of Medical Practice*. New York: Russell Sage Foundation.

French, D.P. (2013). Editorial: The role of self-efficacy in changing health-related behaviour: cause, effect or spurious association? *British Journal of Health Psychology*, 18: 237–43.

French, D.P., Cooper, A. and Weinman, J. (2006). Illness perceptions predict attendance at cardiac rehabiltation following acute myocardial infarction: a systematic review with meta-analysis. *Journal of Psychosomatic Research*, 61: 757–67.

French, D.P., Senior, V., Weinman, J. and Marteau, T. (2001). Causal attributions for heart disease. *Psychology and Health*, 16: 77–98.

French, D.P., Marteau, T., Senior, V. et al. (2002). The structure of beliefs about the causes of heart attack: a network analysis. *British Journal of Health Psychology*, 7: 463–79.

French, J.R.P., Jr, Caplan, R.D. and Van Harrison, R. (1982). *The Mechanisms of Job Stress and Strain*. Chichester: Wiley.

French, S.A., Perry, C.L., Leon, G.R. and Fulkerson, J.A. (1994). Weight concerns, dieting behaviour, and smoking initiation among adolescents: a prospective study. *American Journal of Public Health*, 84: 1818–20.

Freud, S. and Breuer, J. (1895). Studies on hysteria. In J. Strachey (ed.), *The Standard Edition of the Complete Psychological Works of Sigmund Freud*. London: Hogarth Press.

Friedman, H.S. (2003). Healthy life-style across the lifespan: the heck with the Surgeon General! In J. Suls and K.A. Wallston (eds), *Social Psychological Foundations of Health and Illness*. Malden, MA: Blackwell.

Friedman, H.S. and Booth-Kewley, S. (1987). The 'disease-prone personality'. A meta-analytic view of the construct. *American Psychologist*, 42: 539–55.

Friedman, H.S., Tucker, J.S., Schwartz, J.E. et al. (1995). Childhood conscientiousness and longevity: health behaviors and cause of death. *Journal of Personality and Social Psychology*, 68: 696–703.

Friedman, M. and Rosenman, R.H. (1959). Association of specific overt behavior pattern with blood and cardiovascular findings. *Journal of American Medical Association*, 169: 1286–97.

Friedman, M. and Rosenman, R.H. (1974). *Type A Behavior and Your Heart*. New York: A.A. Knopf.

Friedman, M., Thoresen, C.E., Gill, J.J. et al. (1986). Alteration of Type A behavior and its effect on cardiac recurrences in post myocardial infarction patients: summary results of the Recurrent Coronary Prevention Project. *American Heart Journal*, 112: 653–65.

Friesner, S., Curry, D. and Moddeman, G. (2006). Comparison of two pain-management strategies during chest tube removal: relaxation exercise with opioids and opioids alone. *Heart and Lung*, 35 (4): 269–76.

Fromm, K., Andrykowski, M.A. and Hunt, J. (1996). Positive and negative psychosocial sequelae of bone marrow transplantation: implications for quality of life assessment. *Journal of Behavioral Medicine*, 19: 221–40.

Fuchs, F.D. (2011) Why do black Americans have higher prevalence of hypertension?: an enigma still unsolved. *Hypertension*, 57: 379–80.

Fukui, S., Kugaya, A., Okamura, H. et al. (2000). A psychosocial group intervention for Japanese women with primary breast carcinoma. *Cancer*, 89: 1026–36.

Fulkerson, J.A. and French, S.A. (2003). Cigarette smoking for weight loss or control among adolescents: gender and racial/ethnic differences. *Journal of Adolescent Health*, 32: 306–13.

Funk, S.C. (1992). Hardiness: a review of theory and research. *Health Psychology*, 11: 335–45.

Furnham, A. (1990). The Type A behaviour pattern and perception of self. *Personality and Individual Differences*, 11: 841–51.

Gadsby, J.G. and Flowerdew, M.W. (2000). Transcutaneous nerve stimulation and acupuncture-like transcutaneous nerve stimulation for chronic low back pain. In *The Cochrane Library*, issue 2. Oxford: Update Software.

Galavotti, C., Pappas-DeLuca, K.A. and Lansky, A. (2001). Modeling and reinforcement to combat HIV: the MARCH approach to behavior change. *American Journal of Public Health*, 91: 1602–7.

Gall, T.L. and Cornblatt, M.W. (2002). Breast cancer survivors give voice: a qualitative analysis of spiritual factors in long-term adjustment. *Psycho-Oncology*, 11: 524–35.

Gall, T.L., Miguez de Renart, R.M. and Boonstra, B. (2000). Religious resources in long-term adjustment to breast cancer. *Journal of Psychosocial Oncology*, 18: 21–37.

Gallacher, J.E.J., Hopkinson, C.A., Bennett, P. et al. (1997). Effect of stress management on angina. *Psychology and Health*, 12: 523–32.

Gallacher, J.E.J., Yarnell, J.W.G., Sweetnam, P.M. et al. (1999). Anger and incident heart disease in the Caerphilly study. *Psychosomatic Medicine*, 61: 446–53.

Gallagher, S., Phillips, A.C., Drayson, M.T., and Carroll, D. (2009a). Caregiving for children with developmental difficulties is associated with a poor antibody response to influenza vaccination. *Psychosomatic Medicine*, 71; 341–4.

Gallagher, S., Phillips, A.C., Drayson, M.T. and Carroll, D. (2009b). Parental caregivers of children with developmental difficulties mount a poor antibody response to pneumococcal vaccination. *Brain Behavior and Immunity*, 23: 338–46.

Gallo, W.T., Teng, H.M., Falba, T.A. et al. (2006).: The impact of late-career job loss on myocardial infarction and stroke: a 10 year follow-up using the health and retirement survey. *Occupational and Environmental Medicine*, 63: 683–7.

Gamble, J., Fitzsimons, D., Lynes, D. et al. (2007). Difficult asthma: people's perspectives on taking corticosteroid therapy. *Journal of Clinical Nursing*, 16: 59–67.

Gander, P.H., Merry, A., Millar, M.M. et al. (2000). Hours of work and fatigue-related error: a survey of New Zealand anaesthetists. *Anaesthetics and Intensive Care*, 28: 178–83.

Gannoni, A.F. and Shute, R.H. (2010). Parental and child perspectives on adaptation to childhood chronic illness. *Clinical Child Psychology and Psychiatry*, 15:39–53.

Garcia-Huidobro, D., Bittner, M., Brahm, P. et al. (2011). Family intervention to control type 2 diabetes: a controlled clinical trial. *Family Practice*, 28: 4–11.

Gardner, B. and Tang, V. (2014). Reflecting on non-reflective action : an exploratory think-aloud study of self-report habit measures. *British Journal of Health Psychology*, 19: 258–73.

Gardner-Nix, J., Backman, S., Barbati, J. et al. (2008). Evaluating distance education of a mindfulness-based meditation programme for chronic pain management. *Journal of Telemedicine and Telecare*, 14: 88–92.

Garratt, A., Schmidt, L., Mackintosh, A.M. and Fitzpatrick, R. (2002). Quality of life measurement: bibliographic study of patient assessed health outcome measures. *British Medical Journal*, 324: 1417–21.

Garssen, B. (2004). Psychological factors and cancer development. Evidence after 30 years of research. *Clinical Psychology Review*, 24: 115–338.

Gartland, N., O'Connor, D.B. and Lawton, R. (2012). The effects of conscientiousness on the appraisal of daily stressors. *Stress and Health*, 28: 80–6.

Gartland, N., O'Connor, D.B., Lawton, R. and Ferguson, E. (2014). Investigating the effects of conscientiousness on daily stress, affect and physical symptom processes: a daily diary study. *British Journal of Health Psychology*, 19: 311–28.

Gascoigne, P., Mason, M.D. and Roberts, E. (1999). Factors affecting presentation and delay in patients with testicular cancer: results of a qualitative study. *Psycho-Oncology*, 8: 144–54.

Gauce, A.M., Comer, J.P. and Schwartz, D. (1987). Long-term effect of a systems orientated school prevention program. *American Journal of Ortho-psychiatry*, 57: 127–31.

Gaughler, J.E., Davey, A., Pearlin, L.I. et al. (2000). Modeling caregiver adaptation over time: the longitudinal impact of behaviour problems. *Psychology and Aging*, 15: 437–50.

Gawande, A.A., Zinner, M.J., Studdert, D.M. et al. (2003). Analysis of errors reported by surgeons at three teaching hospitals. *Surgery*, 133: 614–21.

Geirdal, A.Ø., Reichelt, J.G., Dahl, A.A. et al. (2005). Psychological distress in women at risk of hereditary breast/ovarian or HNPCC cancers in the absence of demonstrated mutations. *Family Cancer*, 4: 121–6.

Gellert, G., Maxwell, R.M. and Siegel, B.S. (1993). Survival of breast cancer patients receiving adjunctive psychosocial support therapy: a 10-year follow-up study. *Journal of Clinical Oncology*, 11: 66–9.

General Medical Council (2002). *Tomorrow's Doctors, Recommendations on Undergraduate Medical Education*. London: General Medical Council.

Gerbert, B. (1984). Perceived likeability and competence of simulated patients: influence on physician's management plans. *Social Science and Medicine*, 18: 1053–60.

Gere, J., Martire, L.M., Keefe, F.J. et al. (2014). Spouse confidence in self-efficacy for arthritis management predicts improved patient health. *Annals of Behavioral Medicine*, 48: 337–46.

Gerend, M.A., Aiken, L.S. and West, S.G. (2004). Personality factors in older women's perceived susceptibility to diseases of aging. *Journal of Personality*, 72: 243–70.

Gerend, M.A. and Shepherd, J.E. (2007) Using message framing to promote acceptance of the human papillomavirus vaccine. *Health Psychology*, 26: 745–52.

German, J.B. and Walzem, R.L. (2000). The health benefits of wine. *Annual Review of Nutrition*, 20: 561–93.

Gibbons, C., Dempster, M. and Moutray, M. (2008). Stress and eustress in nursing students. *Journal of Advanced Nursing*, 61: 282–90.

Gibson, P.G., Coughlan, J., Wilson, A.J. et al. (2000). Limited (information only) patient education programs for adults with asthma. *Cochrane Database Systematic Review*, issue 1, art. no.: CD001005. doi: 10.1002/14651858. CD001005.

Giese-Davis, J., Koopman, C., Butler, L.D. et al. (2002). Change in emotion-regulation strategy for women with metastatic breast cancer following supportive – expressive group therapy. *Journal of Consulting and Clinical Psychology*, 70: 916–25.

Gifford, A.L., Laurent, D.D., Gonzales, V.M. et al. (1998). Pilot randomized trial of education to improve self-management skills of men with symptomatic HIV/AIDS. *Retrovirology*, 18: 136–44.

Gil, K.M., Keefe, F.J., Crisson, J.E. et al. (1987). Social support and pain behavior. *Pain*, 29: 209–17.

Gil, K.M., Williams, D.A., Keefe, F.J. et al. (1990). The relationship of negative thoughts to pain and psychological distress. *Behavior Therapy*, 21: 349–62.

Giles, M., McClenahan, C., Armour, C., et al. (2014). Evaluation of a theory of planned behaviour-based breastfeeding intervention in Northern Irish schools using a randomized cluster design. *British Journal of Health Psychology*, 19: 16–35.

Gill, P., Kaur, J.S., Rummans, T. et al. (2003). The hospice patient's primary caregiver. What is their quality of life? *Journal of Psychosomatic Research*, 55: 445–51.

Gillam, S., Jarman, B., White, P. and Law, R. (1989). Ethnic differences in consultation rates in urban general practice. *British Medical Journal*, 299: 953–7.

Gilliam, M.B. and Schwebel, D.C. (2013). Physical activity in child and adolescent cancer survivors: a review. *Health Psychology Review*, 7: 92–110.

Gillies, P.A. (1991). HIV infection, alcohol and illicit drugs. *Current Opinion in Psychiatry*, 4: 448–53.

Gilpin, E.A., Pierce, J.P., Johnson, M. et al. (1993) Physician advice to quit smoking: results from the 1990 California Tobacco Survey. *Journal of General Internal Medicine*, 8: 549–53.

Ginandes, C., Brooks, P., Sando, W. et al. (2003). Can medical hypnosis accelerate post-surgical wound healing? Results of a clinical trial. *American Journal of Clinical Hypnosis*, 45: 333–51.

Ginting, H., Näring, G. and Becker, E.S. (2013) Attentional bias and anxiety in individuals with coronary heart disease. *Psychology and Health,* 28: 1306–22.

Giummarra, M.J., Gibson, S.J., Georgiou-Karistianis, N. et al. (2007). Central mechanisms in phantom limb perception: the past, present, and future. *Brain Research Reviews*, 54: 219–32.

Glanz, K., Grove, J., Lerman, C. et al. (1999). Correlates of intentions to obtain genetic counseling and colorectal cancer gene testing among at-risk relatives from three ethnic groups. *Cancer Epidemiology Biomarkers and Prevention*, 8: 329–36.

Glanz, K., Lankenau, B., Foerster, S. et al. (1995). Environmental and policy approaches to cardiovascular disease prevention through nutrition: opportunities for state and local action. *Health Education Quarterly*, 22: 512–27.

Glaser, R. and Kiecolt-Glaser, J.K. (2005). Stress-induced immune dysfunction: implications for health. *National Reviews in Immunology*, 5: 243–51.

Glaser, R., Rice, J., Sheridan, J. et al. (1987). Stress-related immune suppression: health implications. *Brain, Behavior and Immunity*, 1: 7–20.

Glasgow, R.E., Boles, S.M., McKay, H.G. et al. (2003). The D-Net diabetes self-management program: long-term implementation, outcomes, and generalization results. *Preventive Medicine*, 36: 410–19.

Glasgow, R.E., Hollis, J.F., Ary, D.V. et al. (1993). Results of a year-long incentives based worksite smoking cessation program. *Addictive Behaviors*, 18: 209–16.

Glasgow, R.E., Toobert, D.J. and Hampson, S.E. (1996). Effects of a brief office-based intervention to facilitate diabetes dietary self-management. *Diabetes Care*, 19: 835–42.

Glenton, C. (2002). Developing patient-centred information for back pain sufferers. *Health Expectations*, 5: 319–29.

Goddard, M. and Smith, P. (1998). *Equity of Access to Health Care*. York: University of York.

Godin, G., Bélanger-Gravel, A., Eccles, M. and Grimshaw, J. (2008). Healthcare professionals' intentions and behaviours: a systematic review of studies based on social cognitive theories. *Implementation Science*, 3: 36.

Godin, G. and Kok, G. (1996). The theory of planned behavior: a review of its applications to health-related behaviours. *American Journal of Health Promotion*, 11: 87–98.

Godin, G., Lambert, L.-D., Owen, N. et al. (2004). Stages of motivational readiness for physical activity: a comparison of different algorithms of classification. *British Journal of Health Psychology*, 9: 253–67.

Godin, G., Sheeran, P., Conner, M. and Germain, M. (2008). Asking questions changes behavior: mere measurement effects on frequency of blood donation. *Health Psychology*, 27: 179–84.

Godin, G., Valois, P., Lepage, L. and Desharnais, R. (1992). Predictors of smoking behaviour: an application of Ajzen's theory of planned behaviour. *British Journal of Addiction*, 87: 1335–43.

Godinho, C.A., Alvarez, M-J., Lima, M.L.and Scwarzer, R. (2014). Will is not enough: coping planning and action control as mediators in the prediction of fruit and vegetable intake. *British Journal of Health Psychology*, 19: 856–70.

Goins, R.T., Spencer, S.M., McGuire, L.C. et al. (2011). Adult caregiving among American Indians: the role of cultural factors. *The Gerontologist*, 51: 310–20.

Gokee LaRose, J., Tate, D.F., Gorin, A.A. et al. Preventing weight gain in young adults: a randomized controlled pilot study. *American Journal of Preventive Medicine*, 39: 63–8.

Goldberg, D. (1997). *General Health Questionnaire (GHQ–12)*. Windsor: NFER-Nelson.

Goldberg, D. and Williams, P. (1988). *A User's Guide to the General Health Questionnaire*. Windsor: NFER-Nelson.

Goldberg, L.R. and Strycker, L.A. (2002). Personality traits and eating habits: the assessment of food preferences in a large community sample. *Personality and Individual Differences*, 32: 49–65.

Goldberg, R.J., Steg, P.G., Sadiq, I. et al. (2002). Extent of, and factors associated with, delay to hospital presentation in patients with acute coronary disease (the GRACE registry). *American Journal of Cardiology*, 89: 791–6.

Gollwitzer, P. M. (1993). Goal achievement: the role of intentions. *European Review of Social Psychology*, 4, 141–85.

Gollwitzer, P.M. (1999). Implementation intentions: strong effects of simple plans. *American Psychologist*, 54: 493–503.

Gollwitzer, P.M. and Brandstätter, V. (1997). Implementation intentions and effective goal pursuit. *Journal of Personality and Social Psychology*, 73: 186–99.

Gollwitzer, P.M. and Oettingen, G. (1998). The emergence and implementation of health goals. *Psychology and Health*, 13: 687–715.

Gollwitzer, P.M. and Oettingen, G. (2000). The emergence and implementation of health goals. In P. Norman and C. Abraham (eds), *Understanding and Changing Health Behaviour: From Health Beliefs to Self Regulation*. Amsterdam: Harwood Academic Press, pp. 229–60.

Gollwitzer, P.M. and Schaal, B. (1998). Metacognition in action: the importance of implementation intentions. *Personality and Social Psychology Review*, 2: 124–36.

Gollwitzer, P.M. and Sheeran, P. (2006). Implementation intentions and goal achievement: a meta-analysis of effects and processes. *Advances in Experimental Social Psychology*, 38: 69–119.

Gomel, M., Oldenburg, B., Simpson, J.M. et al. (1993). Work-site cardiovascular risk reduction: a randomized trial of health risk assessment, education, counseling, and incentives. *American Journal of Public Health*, 83: 1231–8.

Gomez, C.R., Nomellini, V., Faunce, D.E. and Kovacs, E.J. (2008). Innate immunity and aging. *Experimental Gerontology*, 43: 718–28.

Good, A. and Abraham, C. (2007). Measuring defensive responses to threatening messages: a meta-analysis of measures, *Health Psychology Review*, 1: 208–29.

Goode, K.T., Haley, W.E., Roth, D.L. et al. (1998). Predicting longitudinal changes in caregiver physical and mental health: a stress process model. *Health Psychology*, 17: 190–8.

Goodkin, K., Baldewicz, T.T., Asthana, D. et al. (2001). A bereavement support group intervention affects plasma burden of human immunodeficiency virus type 1. Report of a randomized controlled trial. *Journal of Human Virology*, 4: 44–54.

Goodkin, K., Feaster, D.J., Asthana, D. et al. (1998). A bereavement support group intervention is longitudinally associated with salutary effects on the CD4 cell count and number of physician visits. *Clinical and Diagnostic Laboratory Immunology*, 5: 382–91.

Goodwin, D., Boggs, S. and Graham-Pole, J. (1994). Development and validation of the Pediatric Oncology Quality of Life Scale. *Psychological Assessment*, 6: 321–8.

Goodwin, P.J., Leszcz, M., Ennis, M. et al. (2001). The effect of group psychosocial support on survival in metastatic breast cancer. *New England Journal of Medicine*, 345: 1719–26.

Gordon, C.L., Arnette, R.A.N.M. and Smith, R.E. (2011). Have you thanked your spouse today? Felt and expressed gratitude among married couples. *Personality and Individual Differences*, 50: 3339–43.

Gottlieb, B.H. and Bergen, A.E. (2010). Social support concepts and measures. *Journal of Psychosomatic Research*, 69: 511–20.

Gouin, J.P., Kiecol-Glaser, J.K., Malarkey, W.B. and Glaser, R. (2008). The influence of anger expression on wound healing. *Brain, Behavior and Immunity*, 22: 699–708.

Goyder, E.C., McNally, P.G. and Botha, J.L. (2000). Inequalities in access to diabetes care: evidence from a historical cohort study. *Quality in Health Care*, 9: 85–9.

Graber, M.L., Franklin, N. and Gordon, R. (2005). Diagnostic error in internal medicine. *Archives of Internal Medicine*, 165: 1493–9.

Gracey, F., Palmer, S., Rus, B. et al. (2008). 'Feeling part of things': personal construction of self after brain injury. *Neuropsychological Rehabilitation*, 18: 627–50.

Graham, H. (1994). Gender and class as dimensions of smoking behaviour in Britain: insights from a survey of mothers. *Social Science and Medicine*, 38: 691–8.

Graham, J., Ramirez, A., Love, S. et al. (2002). Stressful life experiences and risk of relapse of breast cancer: observational cohort study. *British Medical Journal*, 324: 1420–3.

Graham, J.E., Christian, L.M. and Kiecolt-Glaser, J.K. (2006). Stress, age and immune function: toward a lifespan approach. *Journal of Behavioral Medicine*, 29: 389–400.

Grana, E., Benowitz, N., Glantz, S.A. (2014). E-cigarettes- a scientific review. *Circulation*, May 13; 129: 1972–86. doi: 10.1161/CIRCULATIONAHA.114.007667

Gratton, L., Povey, R. and Clark-Carter, D. (2007). Promoting children's fruit and vegetable consumption: interventions using the Theory of Planned Behaviour as a framework. *British Journal of Health Psychology*, 12: 39–50.

Gray, S.E. and Rutter, D.R. (2007). Illness representations in young people with chronic fatigue syndrome. *Psychology and Health*, 22: 159–74.

Greaves, C. J., Sheppard, K. E., Abraham, C. et al. and The IMAGE Study Group. (2011). Systematic review of reviews of intervention components associated with increased effectiveness in dietary and physical activity interventions. *BMC Public Health*, 11,119–130. doi:10.1186/1471–2458–11–119

Greco, P., Pendley, J.S., McDonell, K. et al. (2001). A peer group intervention for adolescents with type 1 diabetes and their best friends. *Journal of Pediatric Psychology*, 26: 485–90.

Green, B.L., Rowland, J.H., Krupnick, J.L. et al. (1998). Prevalence of posttraumatic stress disorder in women with breast cancer. *Psychosomatics*, 39: 102–11.

Green, C.R., Baker, T.A., Sato, Y. et al. (2003). Race and chronic pain: a comparative study of young black and white Americans presenting for management. *Journal of Pain*, 4: 176–83.

Green, L. and Kreuter, M. (2005). *Health Program Planning: An Educational and Ecological Approach*, 4th edn. New York, NY: McGraw Hill.

Greenglass, E., Fiksenbaum, L. and Eaton, J. (2006). The relationship between coping, social support, functional disability and depression in the elderly. *Anxiety, Stress, and Coping*, 19: 5–31.

Greenhalgh, T., Collard, A., Campbell-Richards, D., et al. (2011). Storylines of self-management: narratives of people with diabetes from a multi-ethnic inner city population. *Health Services Research and Policy*, 16: 37–43.

Greenwald, A.G., McGhee, D.E and Schwartz, J.L.K. (1998). Measuring individual difference in implicit cognition: the implicit association test. *Journal of Personality and Social Psychology*, 74: 1464–80.

Greenwood, C.R., Carta, J.J. and Kamps, D. (1990). Teacher versus peer-mediated instruction: a review of educational advantages and disadvantages. In H. Foot, M. Morgan and R. Shute (eds), *Children Helping Children*. Chichester: Wiley.

Greenwood, D.C., Muir, K.R., Packham, C.J. et al. (1996). Coronary heart disease: a review of the role of psychosocial stress and social support. *Journal of Public Health Medicine*, 18: 221–31.

Greer, S. (1999). Mind–body research in psycho-oncology. *Advances in Mind–Body Medicine*, 15: 236–81.

Greer, S., Morris, T. and Pettingale, K. (1979). Psychological responses to breast cancer: effect on outcome. *The Lancet*, 2: 940–9.

Greer, S., Morris, T., Pettingale, K. and Haybittle, J. (1990). Psychological response to breast cancer and 15 year outcome. *The Lancet*, 335: 49–50.

Grey, M., Boland, E.A., Davidson, M. et al. (2000). Coping skills training for youths with diabetes mellitus has long-lasting effects on metabolic control and quality of life. *Journal of Pediatrics*, 137: 107–13.

Griffin-Blake, C.S. and DeJoy, D.M. (2006). Evaluation of social-cognitive versus stage-matched, self-help physical activity interventions at the workplace. *American Journal of Health Promotion*, 20: 200–9.

Griffith, G.L., Morrison, V., Williams, J.M.G. and Tudor Edwards, R. (2009). Can we assume that research participants are utility maximisers? *European Journal of Health Economics*, 10: 187–96.

Griffiths, L.J., Cortina- Borja, M., Sera, F. et al. (2013). How active are our children? Findings from the Millennium Cohort Study. *BMJ Open*, 3:e002893. doi:10.1136/bmjopen-2013- 002893

Grigsby, A.B., Anderson, R.J., Freedland, K.E. et al. (2002). Prevalence of anxiety in adults with diabetes. A systematic review. *Journal of Psychosomatic Research*, 53: 1053–60.

Griva, K. and Joekes, K. (2003). UK teachers under stress: can we predict wellness on the basis of characteristics of the teaching job? *Psychology & Health*, 18: 457–471.

Griva, K., Davenport, A., Harrison, M., and Newman, S.P. (2012). The impact of treatment transitions between dialysis and transplantation on illness cognitions and quality of life: a prospective study. *British Journal of Health Psychology*, 17: 812–27.

Griva, K., Myers, L.B. and Newman, S. (2000). Illness perceptions and self-efficacy beliefs in adolescents and young adults with insulin dependent diabetes mellitus. *Psychology and Health*, 15: 733–50.

Grodstein, F., Chen, J. and Willett, W.C. (2003). High-dose antioxidant supplements and cognitive function in community-dwelling elderly women. *American Journal of Clinical Nutrition*, 77: 975–84.

Gross, C.R., Kreitzer, M.J., Thomas, W. et al. (2010). Mindfulness-based stress reduction for solid organ transplant recipients: a randomized controlled trial. *Alternative Therapies in Health and Medicine*, 16: 36–44.

Grossardt, B.R., Bower, J.H., Geda, Y.E. et al. (2009). Pessimistic, anxious, and depressive personality traits predict all-cause mortality: the Mayo Clinic cohort study of personality and ageing. *Psychosomatic Medicine*, 71: 491–500.

Grossarth-Maticek, R., Bastiaans, J. and Kanazir, D.T. (1985). Psychosocial factors as strong predictors of mortality from cancer, ischemic heart disease and stroke: the Yugoslav prospective study. *Journal of Psychosomatic Research*, 29: 167–76.

Grundy, E. and Bowling, A. (1999). Enhancing the quality of extended life years: identification of the oldest old with a very good and very poor quality of life. *Aging and Mental Health*, 3: 199–212.

Grunfeld, E.A., Hunter, M.S., Ramirez, A.J. et al. (2003). Perceptions of breast cancer across the lifespan. *Journal of Psychosomatic Research*, 54: 141–6.

Gudbergsson, S.B., Fosså, S.D., Sanne, B. et al. (2007). A controlled study of job strain in primary-treated cancer patients without metastases. *Acta Oncologica*, 46: 534–44.

Gudmunsdottir, H., Johnston, M., Johnston, D. et al. (2001). Spontaneous, elicited and cued causal attributions in the year following a first myocardial infarction. *British Journal of Health Psychology*, 6: 81–96.

Gulland, A. (2002). BMA steps up call for ban on smoking in public places. *British Medical Journal*, 325: 1058.

Guthrie, R.M. (2001). The effects of postal and telephone reminders on compliance with pravastatin therapy in a national registry: results of the first myocardial infarction risk reduction program. *Clinical Therapeutics*, 23: 970–80.

Gutteling, J.J., Darlington, A-S.E., Janssen, H.L.A. et al. (2008). Effectiveness of health-related quality of life measurement in clinical practice: a prospective, randomized controlled trial in patients with chronic liver disease and their physicians. *Quality of Life Research*, 17: 195–205.

Haan, M.H. (2003). Can vitamin supplements prevent cognitive decline and dementia in old age? (editorial). *American Journal of Clinical Nutrition*, 77: 762–3.

Haan, M.N. and Kaplan, G.A. (1985). The contribution of socio-economic position to minority health. In M. Heckler (ed.), *Report of the Secretary's Task Force on Black and Minority Health: Crosscutting Issues in Health and Human Services*. Washington, DC: US Department of Health and Human Services.

Haas, D.C., Davidson, K.W., Schwartz, D.J. et al. (2005). Depressive symptoms are independently predictive of carotid atherosclerosis. *American Journal of Cardiology*, 95: 547–50.

Haberman, D. and Bloomfield, D.S.F. (1988). Social class differences in mortality in Great Britain around 1981. *Journal of the Institute of Actuaries*, 115: 495–517.

Habra, M.E., Linden, W., Anderson, J.C. et al. (2003). Type D personality is related to cardiovascular and neuroendocrine reactivity to acute stress. *Journal of Psychosomatic Research*, 55: 235–45.

Hack, T.F. and Degner, L.F. (2004). Coping responses following breast cancer diagnosis predicts psychological adjustment 3 years later. *Psycho-Oncology*, 13: 235–47.

Hadjistavropoulos T., Craig K.D,. Duck S. et al. (2011). A biopsychosocial formulation of pain communication. *Psychological Bulletin*, 137: 910–39.

Hagedoorn, M., Dagan, M., Puterman, E. et al. (2011). Relationship satisfaction in couples confronted with colorectal cancer: the interplay of past and current spousal support. *Journal of Behavioral Medicine* [Epub ahead of print]. doi:10.1007/s10865–010–9311–7.

Hagedoorn, M., Sanderman, R., Bolks, H.N. et al. (2008). Distress in couples coping with cancer: A meta-analysis and critical review of role and gender effects. *Psychological Bulletin*, 134: 1–30.

Hagedoorn, M., Sanderman, R., Buunk, B.P. et al. (2002). Failing in spousal caregiving: the 'identity-relevant stress' hypothesis to explain sex differences in caregiver distress. *British Journal of Health Psychology*, 7: 481–94.

Hagger, M. (2010). Editorial: Self-regulation: an important construct in health psychology research and practice. *Health Psychology Review*, 4: 57–65.

Hagger, M., Chatzisarantis, N., Biddle, S.J.H. et al. (2001). Antecedents of children's physical activity intentions and behaviour: predictive validity and longitudinal effects. *Psychology and Health*, 16: 391–407.

Hagger, M., Chatzisarantis, N., Biddle, S.J.H. (2002). A meta-analytic review of the theories of reasoned action and planned behavior in physical activity: predictive validity and the contribution of additional variables. *Journal of Sport and Exercise Psychology*, 24: 3–28.

Hagger, M.S. and Orbell, S. (2003). A meta-analytic review of the common-sense model of illness representations. *Psychology and Health*, 18: 141–84.

Hagger, M.S., Wood, C., Stiff, C. and Chatzisarantis, N.L.D. (2009). The strength model of self-regulation failure and health-related behaviour. *Health Psychology Review*, 3: 208–38.

Hagger, M., Wood, C., Stiff, C. and Chatzisarantis, N.L. (2010). Ego depletion and the strength model of self-control: a meta-analysis. *Psychological Bulletin*, 136: 495–525.

Hagger-Johnson, G.E., Sabia, G.E., Nabi, H. et al. (2013). Low conscientiousness and risk of all-cause, cardiovascular and cancer mortality over 17 years: Whitehall II cohort study. *Journal of Psychosomatic Research*, 73: 98103. Doi:10.1016/j.jsychores.2012.05.007.

Hajek, P., Taylor, T.Z. and Mills, P. (2002). Brief intervention during hospital admission to help patients to give up smoking after myocardial infarction and bypass surgery: randomised controlled trial. *British Medical Journal*, 324: 87–9.

Hakama, M., Coleman, M.P., Alexe, D.M. and Auvien, A. (2008). Cancer screening: evidence and practice in Europe 2008. *European Journal of Cancer*, 44: 1404–13

Hakim, A.A., Petrovitch, H., Burchfield, C.M. et al. (1998). Effects of walking on mortality among non-smoking retired men. *New England Journal of Medicine*, 338: 94–9.

Hale, G. (1996). The social construction of grief. In N. Cooper, C. Stevenson and G. Hale (eds), *Integrating Perspectives on Health*. Buckingham: Open University Press.

Hale, S., Grogan, S. and Willott, S. (2007). Patterns of self-referral in men with symptoms of prostate disease. *British Journal of Health Psychology*, 12: 403–19.

Hale, S., Grogan, S. and Willott, S. (2010) Male GPs' views on men seeking medical help: a qualitative study. *British Journal of Health Psychology*, 15: 697–713.

Halford, J.C.G. and Blundell, J.E. (2000). Serotonin drugs and the treatment of obesity. In T.G. Heffner and D.H. Lockwood (eds), *Obesity: Pathology and Therapy*. Berlin: Springer Verlag.

Hall, A.M., Kamper, S.J., Maher, C.G. et al. (2011). Symptoms of depression and stress mediate the effect of pain on disability, *Pain*, 152: 1044–51.

Hall, E.E., Ekkekakis, P. and Petruzzello, S.J. (2002). The affective beneficence of vigorous exercise revisited. *British Journal of Health Psychology*, 7: 47–66.

Hall, J.A., Roter, D.L. and Katz, N.R. (1988). Meta-analysis of correlates of provider behavior in medical encounters. *Medical Care*, 26: 657–75.

Hall, K.L. and Rossi, J.S. (2008). Meta-analytic examinations of the strong and weak principles across 48 health behaviours. *Preventive Medicine*, 46: 266–74.

Hall, P.A. and Fong, G.T. (2007). Temporal self-regulation theory: a model for individual health behavior. *Health Psychology Review*, 1: 6–52.

Hall, S.M., Humfleet, G.L., Muñoz, R.F. et al. (2009). Extended treatment of older cigarette smokers. *Addiction*, 104: 1043–52.

Hall, S. and Marteau, T.M. (2003). Causal attributions following serious unexpected negative events: a systematic review. *Journal of Social and Clinical Psychology*, 22: 515–36.

Hall, S.M., Tunstall, C., Rugg, D. et al. (1985). Nicotine gum and behavioral treatment in smoking cessation. *Journal of Consulting and Clinical Psychology*, 53: 256–8.

Hallal, P.C., Victora, C.G., Azevedo, M.R. et al. (2006). Adolescent physical activity and health: a systematic review. *Sports Medicine*, 36: 1019–30.

Hallaråker, E., Arefjord, K., Havik, O.E. and Maeland, J.G. (2001). Social support and emotional adjustment during and after a severe life event: a study of wives of myocardial infarction patients. *Psychology and Health*, 16: 343–56.

Halstead, M.T. and Fernsler, J.I. (1994). Coping strategies of long-term cancer patients. *Cancer Nursing*, 17: 94–100.

Hamer, M. and Karageorghis, C. (2007). Psychological mechanisms of exercise dependence. *Sports Medicine*, 37: 477–85.

Hamilton, J.G., Lobel, M. and Moyer, A. (2009). Emotional distress following genetic testing for hereditary breast and ovarian cancer: a meta-analytic review. *Health Psychology,* 28: 510–18.

Hamilton, K., Thomson, C.E. and White, K.M. (2013). Promoting active lifestyles in young children: investigating mothers' decisions about their child's physical activity and screen-time behaviours. *Maternal and Child Health Journal*, 17: 968–76.

Hammerfald, K., Eberle, C., Grau, M. et al. (2006). Persistent effects of cognitive-behavioral stress management on cortisol responses to acute stress in healthy subjects: a randomized controlled trial. *Psychoneuroendocrinology*, 31: 333–9.

Hämmig, O., Gutzwiller, F. and Bauer, G. (2009). Work–life conflict and associations with work- and nonwork-related factors and with physical and mental health outcomes: a nationally representative cross-sectional study in Switzerland. *BMC Public Health*, 30: 435.

Hampson, S.E., Glasgow, R.E. and Toobert, D.J. (1990). Personal models of diabetes and their relation to self-care activities. *Health Psychology*, 9: 632–46.

Hampson, S.E., Glasgow, R.E. and Zeiss, A. (1994). Personal models of osteoarthritis and their relation to self-management activities and quality of life. *Journal of Behavioural Medicine*, 17: 143–58.

Han, K.S. (2002). The effect of an integrated stress management program on the psychologic and physiologic stress reactions of peptic ulcer in Korea. *International Journal of Nursing Studies*, 39: 539–48.

Hankonen, N., Absetz, P., Ghisletta, P. et al. (2010). Gender differences in social cognitive determinants of exercise adoption. *Psychology & Health*, 25: 55–69.

Hanson, R.W. and Gerber, K.E. (1990). *Coping with Chronic Pain. A Guide to Patient Self-management*. New York: Guilford Press.

Harburg, E.J.C., Chape, C., Erfurt, J.C. et al. (1973). Socioecological stressor areas and black and white blood pressure: Detroit. *Journal of Chronic Disease*, 26: 595–611.

Harcourt, D., Ambler, N., Rumsey, N. et al. (1998). Evaluation of a one-stop breast lump clinic: a randomised controlled trial. *The Breast*, 7: 314–19.

Harcourt, D., Rumsey, N. and Ambler, N. (1999). Same-day diagnosis of symptomatic breast problems: psychological impact and coping strategies. *Psychology, Health & Medicine*, 4: 57–71.

Harding, S. and Maxwell, R. (1997). Differences in mortality of migrants. In F. Drever and M. Whitehead (eds), *Health Inequalities: Decennial Supplement*. London: HMSO.

Härkäpää, K., Järvikoski, A., Mellin, G. et al. (1991). Health locus of control beliefs and psychological distress as predictors for treatment outcome in low-back pain patients: results of a 3-month follow-up of a controlled intervention study. *Pain*, 46: 35–41.

Harland, J., White, M., Drinkwater, C. et al. (1999). The Newcastle Exercise Project: a randomised controlled trial of methods to promote physical activity in primary care. *British Medical Journal*, 319: 828–32.

Harris, A.H., Thoresen, C.E., Humphreys, K. et al. (2005). Does writing affect asthma? A randomized trial. *Psychosomatic Medicine*, 67: 130–6.

Harris, D.M. and Guten, S. (1979). Health-protective behaviour: an exploratory study. *Journal of Health and Social Behavior*, 20: 17–29.

Harris, P. and Middleton, W. (1994). The illusion of control and optimism about health: on being less at risk but no more in control than others. *British Journal of Social Psychology*, 33: 369–86.

Harris, T., Ferrucci, L., Tracy, R. et al. (1999). Associations of elevated interleukin-6 and C-reactive protein levels with mortality and the elderly. *American Journal of Medicine*, 106: 506–12.

Harrison, M.O., Koenig, H.G., Hays, J.C. et al. (2001). The epidemiology of religious coping: a review of recent literature. *International Reviews in Psychiatry*, 13: 86–93.

Hart, H., Bilo, H., Redekop, W. et al. (2003). Quality of life in patients with type 1 diabetes mellitus. *Quality of Life Research*, 12: 1089–97.

Hartford, K., Wong, C. and Zakaria, D. (2002). Randomized controlled trial of a telephone intervention by nurses to provide information and support to patients and their partners after elective coronary artery bypass graft surgery: effects of anxiety. *Heart and Lung*, 31: 199–206.

Haslam, D.W. and James, W.P.T. (2005). Obesity, *Lancet*, 366:1197–1209.

Hasson-Ohayon, I., Goldzweig, G., Sela-Oren, T. et al. (2013). Attachment style, social support and finding meaning among spouses of colorectal cancer pateints: gender differences. *Palliative and Supportive Care*, doi:10.1017/S1478951513000242

Haste, H. (2004). *My Body, My Self: Young People's Values and Motives about Healthy Living, Report 2*. London: Nestlé Social Research Programme.

Hatava, P., Olsson, G.L. and Lagerkranser, M. (2000). Preoperative psychological preparation for children undergoing ENT operations: a comparison of two methods. *Paediatric Anaesthesia*, 10: 477–86.

Hatchette, J.E., McGrath, P.J., Murray, M. and Finey, G.A. (2008). The role of peer communication in the socialization of adolescents' pain experiences: a qualitative investigation. *BMC Pediatrics*, 8: 2.

Hathaway, D. (1986). Effect of preoperative instruction on postoperative outcomes: a meta-analysis. *Nursing Research*, 35: 269–75.

Hausenblas, H.A. and Fallon, E.A. (2006). Exercise and body image: a meta-analysis. *Psychology & Health*, 21: 33–47.

Hausenblas, H.A. and Symons Downs, D. (2002). How much is too much? The development and validation of the Exercise Dependence Scale. *Psychology and Health*, 17: 387–404.

Havik, O.E. and Maeland, J.G. (1988). Changes in smoking behavior after a myocardial infarction. *Health Psychology*, 7: 403–20.

Hayes, L., White, M., Unwin, N. et al. (2002). Patterns of physical activity and relationship with risk markers for cardiovascular disease and diabetes in Indian, Pakistani, Bangladeshi and European adults in a UK population. *Journal of Public Health Medicine*, 24: 170–8.

Hayes, N. and Joseph, S. (2003). Big 5 correlates of three measures of subjective wellbeing. *Personality and Individual Differences*, 34: 723–7.

Hayes, S.C., Strosahl, K.D., Bunting, K. et al. (2004). What is acceptance and commitment therapy? In S.C. Hayes and K.D. Strosahl (eds), *A Practical Guide to Acceptance and Commitment Therapy*. New York: Springer.

Haynes, B. and Haines, A. (1998). Barriers and bridges to evidence-based clinical practice. *British Medical Journal*, 317: 273–6.

Haynes, R.B., Ackloo, E., Sahota, N. et al. (2008). Interventions for enhancing medication adherence. *Cochrane Database of Systematic Reviews*, issue 4, art. no.: CD000011. doi: 10.1002/14651858.CD000011.

Haynes, R.B., McKibbon, A. and Kanani, R. (1996). Systematic review of randomized trials of interventions to assist patients to follow prescriptions for medications. *The Lancet*, 384: 383–5.

Haynes, S.G., Feinleib, M. and Kannel, W.B. (1980). The relationship of psychosocial factors to coronary heart disease in the Framingham study. III. Eight year incidence of coronary heart disease. *American Journal of Epidemiology*, 111: 37–58.

Head K.J., Noar S.M., Iannarino N.T. et al. (2013). Efficacy of text messaging-based interventions for health promotion: a meta-analysis. *Social Science and Medicine*, 97:41–8.

Health and Social Care Information Centre (2013). *Smoking, Drinking and Drug Use Among Young People in England in 2012*. Retrieved August 4th 2014: http://www.hscic.gov.uk/catalogue/PUB11334/smok-drin-drug-youn-peop-eng-2012-repo.pdf

Health and Social Care Information Centre. *Health Survey for England – 2012: trend tables*. HSCIC, 2013.

Health Development Agency Magazine (2005). *Smoking Out Pregnant Teenagers*, Issue 25, Feb/March.

Health Education Authority (1998). *Young and Active? Policy Framework for Young People and Health – Enhancing Physical Activity*. London: Health Education Authority.

Health Promotion Authority for Wales (1996). *Lifestyle Changes in Wales. Health in Wales Survey 1996*, Technical Report no. 27. Cardiff: Health Promotion Authority for Wales.

Health Protection Agency (2010). *HIV in the United Kingdom: 2010 Report*. HPA. Also available online at: www.hpa.org.uk/topics/infectiousdiseases/infectionsAZ/HIV.

Health Survey for England (2004). Volume 1. *The Health of Ethnic Minority Groups*. The Health and Social Care Information Centre (HSCIC), 2006. http://www.hscic.gov.uk/pubs/hse04ethnic

Health Survey for England (2007). Leeds: Health and Social Care Information Centre (2008), available from www.ic.nhs.uk.

Health Survey for England (2008). Trend Tables. The NHS Information Centre, 2009. http://www.ic.nhs.uk/webfiles/publications/HSE/HSE08trends/Health_Survey_for_england_trend_tables_2008.pdf.

Health Utilisation Research Alliance (2006). Ethnicity, socio-economic deprivation and consultation rates in New Zealand general practice. *Journal of Health Service Research and Policy*, 11: 141–9.

Healy, C.M. and McKay, M.F. (2000). Nursing stress: the effects of coping strategies and job satisfaction in a sample of Australian nurses. *Journal of Advanced Nursing*, 31: 681–8.

Heather, N. and Robertson, I. (1997). *Problem Drinking*. Oxford: Oxford University Press.

Heaven, C.M. and Maguire, P. (1998). The relationship between patients' concerns and psychological distress in a hospice setting. *Psycho-Oncology*, 7: 502–7.

Hecimovic, K., Barrett, S.P., Darredeau, C. and Stewart, S.H. (2014). Cannabis use motives and personality risk factors. *Addictive Behaviors*, 39: 729–32.

Hedges, J.R., Mann, N.C., Meischke, H. et al. (1998). Assessment of chest pain onset and out-of-hospital delay using standardised interview questions: the REACT pilot study. *Academic Emergency Medicine*, 5: 773–80.

Heider, F. (1958). *The Psychology of Interpersonal Relations*. New York: Wiley.

Heijmans, M. (1998). Coping and adaptive outcome in chronic fatigue syndrome: importance of illness cognitions. *Journal of Psychosomatic Research*, 45: 39–51.

Heijmans, M. and de Ridder, D. (1998). Structure and determinants of illness representation in chronic disease: a comparison of Addison's disease and chronic fatigue syndrome. *Journal of Health Psychology*, 3: 523–37.

Heijmans, M., de Ridder, D. and Bensing, J. (1999). Dissimilarity in patients' and spouses' representations of chronic illness: explorations of relations to patient adaptation. *Psychology and Health*, 14: 451–66.

Heim, E., Augustiny, K., Blaser, A. and Burki, C. (1987). Coping with breast cancer: a longitudinal prospective study. *Psychotherapy and Psychosomatics*, 48: 44–59.

Heine, S.J. and Lehman, D.R. (1995). Cultural variation in unrealistic optimism: does the West feel more invulnerable than the East? *Journal of Personality and Social Psychology*, 68: 595–607.

Heitzler, C.D., Lytle, L.A., Erickson, D.J. et al. (2010). Evaluating a model of youth physical activity. *American Journal of Health Behavior*, 34: 593–606.

Heitzler, C.D., Martin, S.I., Duke, J. and Huhman, M. (2006). Correlates of physical activity in a national sample of children aged 9–13 years. *Preventive Medicine*, 42: 254–60.

Helder, D.I., Bakker, B., deHeer, P. et al. (2004). Quality of life in adults following bone marrow transplantation during childhood. *Bone Marrow Transplantation*, 33: 329–36.

Helgeson, V.S. (2010). Survivor centrality among breast cancer survivors: implications for wellbeing. *Psycho-Oncology*, doi:10.1002/pon.1750

Helgeson, V.S., and Novak, S.A. (2007). Illness centrality and well-being among male and female early adolescents with diabetes. *Journal of Pediatric Psychology*, 32: 260–272.

Helgeson, V.S., Reynolds, K.A. and Tomich, P.L. (2006). A meta-analytic review of benefit-finding and growth. *Journal of Consulting and Clinical Psychology*, 74: 797–816.

Helman, C. (1978). Feed a cold starve a fever: folk models of infection in an English suburban community and their relation to medical treatment. *Culture, Medicine and Psychiatry*, 2: 107–37.

Heloma, A. and Jaakola, M.S. (2003). Four-year follow-up of smoke exposure, attitudes and smoking behaviour following enactment of Finland's national smoke-free workplace law. *Addiction*, 98: 1111–17.

Hemingway, H. and Marmot, M. (1999). Psychosocial factors in the aetiology and prognosis of coronary heart disease: systematic review of prospective cohort studies. *British Medical Journal*, 318: 1460–7.

Henderson, L., Gregory, J. and Swan, G. (2002). *The National Diet and Nutrition Survey: Adults Aged 19 to 64 years*. London: HMSO.

Henderson V.P., Massion A.O., Clemow L. et al. (2013). A randomized controlled trial of mindfulness-based stress reduction for women with early-stage breast cancer receiving radiotherapy. *Integrated Cancer Therapy*, 12:404–13.

Hendry, L.B. and Kloep, M. (2002). *Lifespan Development: Resources, Challenges, Risks*. London: Thomson Learning.

Henkel, D. (2011). Unemployment and substance use: a review of the literature (1990–2010). Current Drug Abuse Reviews, 4: 4–27.

Henriksson, C., Larsson, M., Arnetz, J. *et al.* (2011). Knowledge and attitudes towards seeking medical care for AMI-symptoms. *International Journal of Cardiology*, 147:224–227.

Hennessy, D.A., Lanni-Manley, E. and Maiorana, N. (2006). The effects of fatal vision goggles on drinking and driving intentions in college students. *Journal of Drug Education*, 36: 59–72.

Hennrikus, D.J., Jeffery, R.W., Lando, H.A. et al. (2002). The SUCCESS project: the effect of program format and incentives on participation and cessation in worksite smoking cessation programs. *American Journal of Public Health*, 92: 274–9.

Henselmans, I., Fleer, J., de Vries, J. et al. (2010). The adaptive effect of personal control when facing breast cancer: cognitive and behavioural mediators. *Psychology & Health*, 25: 1023–40.

Herbert, T.B. and Cohen, S. (1993). Stress and immunity in humans: a meta-analytic review. *Psychosomatic Medicine*, 55: 364–79.

Herman, P.M. and Walsh, M.E. (2010). Hospital admissions for acute myocardial infarction, angina, stroke, and asthma after implementation of Arizona's comprehensive Statewide Smoking Ban. *American Journal of Public Health*, 101: 491–6.

Herman, P.M. and Walsh, M.E. (2010). Hospital admissions for acute myocardial infarction, angina, stroke, and asthma after implementation of Arizona's comprehensive Statewide Smoking Ban. *American Journal of Public Health*, 101: 491–6.

Herrman, C. and Wortman, C. (1985). Action control and the coping process. In J. Kuhl and J. Beckman (eds), *Action Control: From Cognition to Behavior*. New York: Springer-Verlag.

Herttua, K., Tabák, A.G., Martikainen, P. et al. (2013). Adherence to antihypertensive therapy prior to the first presentation of stroke in hypertensive adults: population based study. *European Heart Journal*, 34: 2933–9.

Herzlich, C. (1973). *Health and Illness: A Social Psychological Analysis*. London: Academic Press.

Herzog, T.A. (2008). Analysing the transtheoretical model using the framework of Weinstein, Rothman and Sutton (1998): the example of smoking cessation. *Health Psychology*, 27: 548–56.

Hewitt, D., McDonald, M., Portenoy, R. et al. (1997). Pain syndromes and etiologies in ambulatory AIDS patients. *Pain*, 70: 117–23.

Hibell, B., Guttormson, U., Ahlstrom, S., et al. (2012). *The 2011 ESPAD Report: Substance Use Among Students in 35 European countries*. The Swedish Council for Information on Alcohol and Other Drugs, Stockholm.

Hiemstra, M., Otten, R., van Schayck, O.C.and Engels, R.C. (2012). Smoking-specific communication and children's smoking onset: an extension of the theory of planned behaviour. *Psychology & Health,* 27: 1100–17.

Higgins, O., Sixsmith, J., Barry, M.M. and Domegan, C. (2011*). A Literature Review on Health Information-seeking Behaviour on the Web: A Health Consumer and Health Professional Perspective*. Stockholm: ECDC; 2011.

Higginson, I.J. and Carr, A.J. (2001). Using quality of life measures in the clinical setting. *British Medical Journal*, 322: 1297–300.

Hill, J.C., Lewis, M., Sim, J. et al. (2007). Predictors of poor outcome in patients with neck pain treated by physical therapy. *Clinical Journal of Pain*, 23: 683–90.

Hill, M.L. and Craig, K.D. (2002). Detecting deception in pain expressions: the structure of genuine and deceptive facial displays. *Pain*, 98: 135–44.

Hillier, S.M. and Jewell, J.A. (1983). *Health Care and Traditional Medicine in China, 1800–1982*. London: Routledge.

Hingson, R.M., Heeren, T., Winter, M.R. and Wechsler, H. (2003). Early age of first drunkenness as a factor in college students' unplanned and unprotected sex attributable to drinking. *Pediatrics*, 111: 34–41.

Hinkley, T., Crawford, D., Salmon, J., et al. (2008). Preschool children and physical activity: a review of correlates. *American Journal of Preventative Medicine*, 34: 435–41.

Hinton, J. (1999). The progress of awareness and acceptance of dying assessed in cancer patients and their caring relatives. *Palliative Medicine*, 13: 19–35.

Hittner, J.B. and Swickert, R. (2006). Sensation seeking and alcohol use: a meta-analytic review. *Addictive Behaviors*, 31: 1383–401.

Ho, S.M.Y., Chan, C.L.W. and Ho, R.T.H. (2004). Post-traumatic growth in Chinese cancer survivors. *Psycho-Oncology*, 13: 377–89.

Hoare, J. and Flatley, J. (2008). *Drug Misuse Declared: Findings from the 2007/08 British Crime Survey*. Home Office Statistical Bulletin 13/08. London: Home Office. Available from: http://www.homeoffice.gov.uk/rds/pdfs08/hosb1308.pdf.

Hobfoll, S.E. (1989). Conservation of resources: a new attempt at conceptualizing stress. *American Psychologist*, 44: 513–24.

Hobfoll, S. (1991). Traumatic stress: a theory based on rapid loss of resources. *Anxiety Research*, 4: 187–97.

Hobfoll, S.E. (2001). The influence of culture, community, and the nested-self in the stress processes: advancing conservation of resources theory. *Applied Psychology: An International Review*, 50: 337–421.

Hobfoll, S.E., Jackson, A.P., Lavin, J. et al. (1994). Women's barriers to safer sex. *Psychology and Health*, 9: 233–52.

Hobfoll, S.E. and Lilly, R.S. (1993). Conservation of resources; a new attempt at conceptualising stress. *American Psychologist*, 44: 513–24.

Hodgson, S. and Maher, E. (1999). *A Practical Guide to Human Cancer Genetics.* Cambridge: Cambridge University Press.

Hoffman, S., O'Sullivan, L.F., Harrison, A. et al. (2006). HIV risk behaviors and the context of sexual coercion in young adults' sexual interactions: results from a diary study in rural South Africa. *Sexually Transmitted Diseases*, 33: 52–8.

Hofmann, W., Friese, M. and Wiers, R.W. (2007). Impulsive versus reflective influences on health behavior: a theoretical framework and empirical review. *Health Psychology Review*, 2: 111–37.

Høie, M., Moan, I. and Rise. J. (2010). An extended version of the theory of planned behavour: Prediction of intentions to quit smoking using past behaviour as moderator. *Addiction Research & Theory*, 18: 572–85.

Holick, M.F. (2004). Sunlight and vitamin D for bone health and prevention of autoimmune disease, cancers and cardiovascular disease. *American Journal of Clinical Nutrition*, 80 (suppl.6), S1678–88.

Holland, J.C. and Gooen-Piels, J. (2000). Principles of psycho-oncology. In J.C. Holland and E. Frei (eds), *Psychological Care of the Patient with Cancer.* New York: Oxford University Press.

Holland, W.W. and Stewart, S. (2005). *Screening in Disease Prevention: What Works?* Oxford: Radcliffe.

Hollands, G.J. and Marteau,T.M. (2013). The impact of using visual images of the body within a personalized health risk assessment: an experimental study. *British Journal of Health Psychology*, 18: 263–78.

Hollis, J.F., Connett, J.E., Stevens, V.J. and Greenlick, M.R. (1990). Stressful life events, Type A behaviour, and the prediction of cardiovascular disease and total mortality over six years. *Journal of Behavioral Medicine*, 13: 263–81.

Holmbeck, G.N. (2002). A developmental perspective on adolescent health and illness: an introduction to the Special Issues. *Journal of Pediatric Psychology*, 27: 409–15.

Holmbeck, G.N., Johnson, S.Z., Wills, K.E. et al. (2002). Observed and perceived parental overprotection in relation to psychosocial adjustment in pre-adolescents with a physical disability: the meditational role of behavioral autonomy. *Journal of Consulting and Clinical Psychology*, 70: 96–110.

Holmes, E.A.F., Hughes, D.A. and Morrison, V. (2014). Predicting adherence to medications using health psychology theories: a systematic review of 20 years of empirical research. *Value in Health*, 17: 863–76.

Holmes, T.H. and Masuda, M. (1974). Life change and illness susceptibility. In B.S. Dohrenwend and B.P. Dohrenwend (eds), *Stressful Life Events: Their Nature and Effects*. New York: Wiley.

Holmes, T.H. and Rahe, R.H. (1967). The social readjustment rating scale. *Journal of Psychosomatic Research*, 11: 213–18.

Holroyd, K.A. and Lipchik, G.L. (1999). Psychological management of recurrent headache disorders: progress and prospects. In R.J. Gatchel and D.C. Turk (eds), *Psychosocial Factors in Pain*. New York: Guilford Press.

Holroyd, K.A., O'Donnell, F.J., Stensland, M. et al. (2001). Management of chronic tension-type headache with tricyclic antidepressant medication, stress management therapy, and their combination: a randomized controlled trial. *Journal of the American Medical Association*, 285: 2208–15.

Holt-Lunstad, J., Smith, T.B., and Layton, J.B. (2010). Social relationships and mortality risks. *PLoS Medicine*, 7(&) e0000316.

Holtzman, S., Newth, S. and DeLongis, A. (2004). The role of social support in coping with daily pain among patients with rheumatoid arthritis. *Journal of Health Psychology*, 9: 749–67.

Holzner, B., Kemmler, G., Cella, D. et al. (2004). Normative data for functional assessment of cancer therapy: general scale and its use for the interpretation of quality of life scores in cancer survivors. *Acta Oncologica*, 43: 153–60.

Hooker, K., Monahan, D., Shifren, K. et al. (1992). Mental and physical health of spouse caregivers: the role of personality. *Psychology and Aging*, 7: 367–75.

Hooper, L., Bartlett, C., Davey-Smith, G. et al. (2002). Systematic review of long-term effects of advice to reduce dietary salt in adults. *British Medical Journal*, 325: 628–32.

Hoorens, V. and Buunk, B.P. (1993). Social comparisons of health risks: locus of control, the person-positivity bias, and unrealistic optimism. *Journal of Applied Social Psychology*, 23: 291–302.

Hopwood, P. (1997). Psychological issues in cancer genetics: current research and future priorities. *Patient Education and Counselling*, 32: 19–31.

Horgan, R.P. and Kenny, L.C. (2007). Management of teenage pregnancy. *The Obstetrician and Gynaecologist*, 9: 153–8.

Horne, P.J., Hardman, C.A., Lowe, C.F. et al. (2009). Increasing parental provision and children's consumption of lunchbox fruit and vegetables in Ireland: the Food Dudes intervention. *European Journal of Clinical Nutrition*, 63: 613–18.

Horne, P.J., Tapper, K., Lowe, C.F. et al. (2004). Increasing children's fruit and vegetable consumption: a peer modelling and rewards-based intervention. *European Journal of Clinical Nutrition*, 58: 1649–60.

Horne, R. (1999). Patients' beliefs about treatment: the hidden determinant of treatment outcome? *Journal of Psychosomatic Research*, 47: 491–5.

Horne, R. (2001). Compliance, adherence and concordance. In K. Taylor and G. Harding (eds). *Pharmacy Practice*. London: Taylor & Francis, pp. 165–84.

Horne, R. and Weinman, J. (1999). Patients' beliefs about prescribed medicines and their role in adherence to treatment in chronic physical illness. *Journal of Psychosomatic Research*, 47: 555–67.

Horne, R. and Weinman, J. (2002). Self-regulation and self-management in asthma: exploring the role of illness perceptions and treatment beliefs in explaining non-adherence to preventer medication. *Psychology and Health*, 17: 17–32.

Hosking, S.G., Marsh, N.V. and Friedman, P.J. (1996). Post-stroke depression: prevalence, course and associated factors. *Neuropsychological Review*, 6: 107–33.

Hoth, K.F., Wamboldt, F.S., Bowler, R. et al. (2011). Attributions about cause of illness in chronic obstructive pulmonary disease. *Journal of Psychosomatic Research*, 70: 465–72.

Hotopf, M., Chidgey, J., Addington-Hall, J. and Ly, K.L. (2002). Depression in advanced disease: a systematic review. Part 1: Prevalence and case finding. *Palliative Medicine*, 16: 81–97.

Houck, C.D. Barker, D., Rizzo, C. et al. (2014). Sexting and sexual behavior in at-risk adolescents, *Pediatrics*, 133, e276 doi: 10.1542/peds.2013–1157

House, A., Dennis, M., Mogridge, L. et al. (1991). Mood disorders in the year after first stroke. *British Journal of Psychiatry*, 2: 211–21.

House, J.S. (1987). Chronic stress and chronic disease in life and work: conceptual and methodological issues. *Work and Stress*, 1: 129–34.

House, J.S., Kessler, R., Herzog, A.R. et al. (1991). Social stratification, age, and health. In K.W. Scheie, D. Blazer and J.S. House (eds), *Aging, Health Behaviours, and Health Outcomes*. Hillsdale, NJ: Lawrence Erlbaum.

House, J.S., Robbins, C. and Metzner, H.L. (1982). The association of social relationships and activities with mortality: prospective evidence from the Tecumseh Community Health Study. *American Journal of Epidemiology*, 116: 123–40.

Housman, J and Dorman, S. (2005). The Alameda County Study: a systematic, chronological review. *American Journal of Health Education*, 36: 302–8.

Houston, M. (2004). Commissioner denies plans for a Europe-wide smoking ban. *British Medical Journal*, 328: 544.

Howick, J., Bishop, F.I., Heneghan, C. et al. (2013). *Placebo Use in the United Kingdom: Results from a National Survey of Primary Care Practitioners*. PLoS One DOI: 10.1371/journal.pone.0058247.

Hoyt, M.A. (2009). Gender role conflict and emotional approach coping in men with cancer. *Psychology & Health*, 24: 981–96

Hu, F.B. (2003). Overweight and obesity in women: health risks and consequences. *Journal of Women's Health* 12: 163–72.

Hu, F.B., Willett, W.C., Colditz, G.A. et al. (1999). Prospective study of snoring and risk of hypertension in women. *American Journal of Epidemiology*, 150: 806–16.

Hu, F.B., Willett, W.C., Manson, J.E. et al. (2000). Snoring and risk of cardiovascular disease in women. *Journal of the American College of Cardiology*, 35: 308–13.

Hu, T.-W., Sung, H.-Y. and Keeler, T.E. (1995). Reducing cigarette consumption in California: tobacco taxes vs. an anti-smoking media campaign. *American Journal of Public Health*, 85: 1218–22.

Huang, T., Yang, B., Zheng, J. et al. (2012). Cardiovascular disease mortality and cancer incidence in vegetarians: a meta-analysis and systematic review, *Annals of Nutrition & Metabolism*, 60: 233–40.

Huber, M., Knottnerus, J.A., Green, L. et al. (2011). How should we define health? *British Medical Journal*, 343 doi: http://dx.doi.org/10.1136/bmj.d4163.

Huberty, J., Dodge, T., Peterson, K.R. et al. (2012). Creating a movement for active living via a media campaign. *American Journal of Preventive Medicine*, 43, Suppl 4: S390–1.

Huberty, J.L., Ransdell, L.B., Sidman, C. et al. (2008). Explaining long-term exercise adherence in women who complete a structured exercise program. *Research Quarterly for Exercise & Sport*, 79: 374–84.

Hudson, J.L., Bundy, C., Coventry, P.A. and Dickens, C. (2013). Exploring the relationship between cognitive illness representations and poor emotional health and their combined association with diabetes self-care. A systematic review with meta-analysis. *Journal of Psychosomatic Research*, 76: 265–74.

Hudson, M.M., Mertens, A.C., Yasui, Y. et al. (2003). Health status of adult long-term survivors of childhood cancer: a report from the Childhood Cancer Survivor Study. *JAMA*, 290: 1583–92.

Huerta, M.C. and Borgonovi, F. (2010). Education, alcohol use and abuse among young adults in Britain. *Social Science & Medicine*, 71: 143–51.

Hughes, G., Bennett, K.M. and Hetherington, M. (2004). Old and alone: barriers to healthy eating in older men living on their own. *Appetite*, 43: 269–76.

Hughes, N., Locock, L. and Ziebland, S. (2013). Personal identity and the role of 'carer' among relatives and friends of people with multiple sclerosis. *Social Science & Medicine*, 96: 78–85.

Huijbrechts, P., Duivenvoorden, H.J., Deckers, J.W. et al. (1996). Modification of smoking habits five months after myocardial infarction: relationship with personality characteristics. *Journal of Psychosomatic Research*, 40: 369–78.

Hulbert-Williams, N.J., Morrison, V., Wilkinson, C and Neal, R.D. (2013). Investigating the cognitive precursors of emotional response to cancer stress: re-testing Lazarus's transactional model. *British Journal of Health Psychology*, 18: 97–121.

Humphrey, N. (2002). Great expectations: the evolutionary psychology of faith-healing and the placebo effect. In C. von Hofsten and L. Bäckman (eds), *Psychology at the Turn of the Millennium, Vol. 2: Social, Developmental, and Clinical Perspectives*. Hove: Psychology Press.

Hunt, S.M. and Martin, C.J. (1988). Health related behaviour change: a test of a new model. *Psychology and Health*, 2: 209–30.

Hunt, S.M., McEwan, J. and McKenna, S.P. (1986). *Measuring Health Status*. Beckenham: Croom Helm.

Hunter, M.S., Grunfeld, E.A. and Ramirez, A.J. (2003). Help-seeking intentions for breast-cancer symptoms: a comparison of self-regulation model and the theory of planned behaviour. *British Journal of Health Psychology*, 8: 319–34.

Huskisson, E.C. (1974). Measurement of pain. *Lancet*, Nov 9; 2(7889): 1127–31.

Hyland, A., Wakefield, M., Higbee, C. et al. (2006). Anti-tobacco television advertising and indicators of smoking cessation in adults: a cohort study. *Health Education Research*, 21: 296–302.

Hyland, M.E., Bellesis, M., Thompson, P.J. and Keenyon, C.A.P. (1996). The constructs of asthma quality of life: psychometric, experimental and correlational evidence. *Psychology and Health*, 12: 101–21.

Ickes, W. and Decety, J. (eds). (2009). *The Social Neuroscience of Empathy*. Cambridge, MA: MIT Press.

Illinois Racial and Ethnic Health Disparities Council. http://app.idph.state.il.us/iphi/docs/DraftFinal.pdf.

Ingledew, D.K. and Ferguson, E. (2007). Personality and riskier sexual behaviour: motivational mediators. *Psychology & Health*, 22: 291–315.

Ingledew, D.K. and McDonagh, G. (1998). What coping functions are served when health behaviours are used as coping strategies? *Journal of Health Psychology*, 3: 195–213.

Ingraham, B.A., Bragdon, B. and Nohe, A. (2008). Molecular basis for the potential of vitamin D to prevent cancer. *Current Medical Research and Opinion*, 24: 139–49.

Ingram, K.M., Jones, D.A., Fass, R.J. et al. (1999). Social support and unsupportive social interactions: their association with depression among people living with HIV. *AIDS Care*, 11: 313–29.

Ingram, L., Morrison, V., Soulsby, J. et al. (2008). Mindfulness-based cognitive therapy for oncology outpatients and their family carers: a qualitative evaluation. Unpublished report based on Ingram, L, MSc University of Bath.

Inoue, S., Saeki, T., Mantani, T. et al. (2003). Factors related to patients' mental adjustment to breast cancer: patient characteristics and family functioning. *Support Care Cancer*, 11: 178–84.

Inouye, J., Flannelly, L. and Flannelly, K.J. (2001). The effectiveness of self-management training for individuals with HIV/AIDS. *Journal of the Association of Nurses in AIDS Care*, 12: 71–82.

Institute for Government (2010). *MINDSPACE; Influencing Behaviour Through Public Policy*. London: Institute for Government, the Cabinet Office.

International Obesity Taskforce and European Association for the Study of Obesity (2002). *Obesity in Europe: The Case for Action*. London: International Obesity Taskforce.

Iribarren, C., Darbinian, J.A., Lo, J.C. et al. (2006). Value of the sagittal abdominal diameter in coronary heart disease risk assessment: Cohort study in a large, multi-ethnic population. *American Journal of Epidemiology*, 164: 115–59.

Isikhan, V., Comez, T., Danis, M.Z. (2004). Job stress and coping strategies in health care professionals working with cancer patients, *European Journal of Oncology Nursing*, 8: 234–44.

Ison, E. (2009). The introduction of health impact assessment in the WHO European Healthy Cities Network. *Health Promotion International*, 24(suppl. 1): i64–i71.

Israel, S., Weisel, O., Ebstein, R.P. and Bornstein, G. (2012). Oxytocin, but not vasopressin, increases both parochial and universal altruism. *Psychoneuroendicrinology*, 37: 1341–4.

Iversen, M.D., Hammond, A. and Betteridge, N. (2010). Self-management of rheumatic diseases: state of the art and future perspectives. *Annals of Rheumatic Disease*, 69: 955–63.

Iwasaki, M., Otani, T., Sunaga, R. et al. (2002). Social networks and mortality based on the Komo–Ise cohort study in Japan. *International Journal of Epidemiology*, 31: 1208–18.

Jackson, P.L., Meltzoff, A.N. and Decety, J. (2005). How do we perceive the pain of others? A window into the neural processes involved in empathy. *NeuroImage*, 24: 771–9.

Jackson, R., Scragg, R. and Beaglehole, R. (1991). Alcohol consumption and risk of coronary heart disease. *British Medical Journal*, 303: 211–16.

Jacobs, D.R., Jr, Luepker, R.V., Mittelmark, M.B. et al. (1986). Community-wide prevention strategies: evaluation design of the Minnesota Heart Health Program. *Journal of Chronic Diseases*, 39: 775–88.

Jacobs, K., Titman, P. and Edwards, M. (2012). Bridging psychological and physical health care, (Special feature on pediatric clinical psychology) *The Psychologist,* 25: 190–3.

Jacobs, S.A., de Beer, H. and Larney, M. (2010). Adult consumers' understanding and use of information on food labels: a study among consumers living in the Potchefstroom and Klerksdorp regions, South Africa. *Public Health Nutrition*, 13: 1–13.

Jacobsen, P.B. and Hahn, D.M. (1998). Cognitive behavioral programmes. In J. Holland (ed.), *Textbook of Psycho-Oncology*. New York: Oxford University Press.

Jacobson, E. (1938). *Progressive Relaxation.* Chicago, IL: University of Chicago Press.

Jaffe, H. (1997). Dying for dollars. *Men's Health*, 12: 132–7.

Jaffe, L., Lutter, J.M., Rex, J. et al. (1999). Incentives and barriers to physical activity for working women. *American Journal of Health Promotion*, 13(4): 215–18.

Jago, R., Baranowski, T., Zakeri, I. et al. (2005). Observed environmental features and the physical activity of adolescent males. *American Journal of Preventive Medicine*, 29: 98–104.

James, J.E. (2004). Critical review of dietary caffeine and blood pressure: a relationship that should be taken more seriously. *Psychosomatic Medicine*, 66: 63–71.

James, J.E. and Hardardottir, D. (2002). Influence of attention focus and trait anxiety on tolerance of acute pain. *British Journal of Health Psychology*, 7: 149–62.

James, J., Thomas, P. and Kerr, D. (2007). Preventing childhood obesity: two year follow-up results from the Christchurch obesity prevention programme in schools (CHOPPS). *British Medical Journal*, 335: 841.

James, S.A., LaCroix, A.Z., Kleinbaum, D.G. and Strogatz, D.S. (1984). John Henryism and blood pressure differences among black men. II. The role of occupational stressors. *Journal of Behavioral Medicine*, 7: 259–75.

Janlert, U., Asplund, K. and Weinehall, L. (1992). Unemployment and cardiovascular risk indicators. Data from the MONICA survey in northern Sweden. *Journal of Social Medicine*, 20: 14–18.

Janse, A.J., Gemke, R.J.B.J., Uiterwaal, C.S.P.M. et al. (2004). Quality of life: patients and doctors don't always agree. *Journal of Clinical Epidemiology*, 57: 653–61.

Jansen, D.L., Heijmans, M.J.W.M., Rijken, M. et al. (2013). Illness perceptions and treatment perceptions of patients with chronic kidney disease: different phases, different perceptions? *British Journal of Health Psychology*, 18: 244–62.

Janz, N.K. and Becker, M.H. (1984). The health belief model: a decade later. *Health Education Quarterly*, 11: 1–17.

Janz, N.K., Zimmerman, M.A., Wren, P.A. et al. (1996). Evaluation of 37 AIDS prevention projects: successful approaches and barriers to program effectiveness. *Health Education Quarterly*, 23: 80–97.

Janzon, E., Hedblad, B., Berglund, G. and Engstrom, G. (2004). Changes in blood pressure and body weight following smoking cessation in women. *Journal of Internal Medicine*, 255: 266–72.

Jarvis, M.J. (2004). Why people smoke. *British Medical Journal*, 328: 277–9.

Jatoi, I., Zhu, K., Shah, M. et al. (2006). Psychological distress in U.S. women who have experienced false-positive mammograms. *Breast Cancer Research and Treatment*, 100: 191–200.

Jay, S.M., Elliott, C.H. and Fitzgibbons, I. (1995). A comparative study of cognitive behavior therapy versus general anaesthesia for painful medical procedures in children. *Pain*, 62: 3–9.

Jean-Pierre, P., Roscoe, J.A., Morrow, G.R. et al. (2010). Race-based concerns over understanding cancer diagnosis and treatment plan: A URCC CCOP Study. *Journal of the National Medical Association*, 102: 184–9.

Jellinek, E.M. (1960). *The Disease Concept of Alcoholism*. New Haven, CT: Hillhouse Press.

Jemmott, J.B., Croyle, R.T. and Ditto, P.H. (1988). Commonsense epidemiology: self-based judgements from laypersons and physicians. *Health Psychology*, 7(1): 55–73.

Jenkins, P.R., Jenkins, R.A., Nannis, E.D. et al. (2000). Reducing risk of sexually transmitted disease (STD) and human immunodeficiency virus infection in a military STD clinic: evaluation of a randomized preventive intervention trial. *Clinical Infectious Diseases*, 30: 730–5.

Jenkins, R.L., Lewis, G. and Bebbington, P. (1997). The National Psychiatric Morbidity Surveys of Great Britain: initial findings from the household survey. *Psychology and Medicine*, 27: 775–89.

Jenkinson, C., Fitzpatrick, R., Garrat, A. et al. (2001). Can item response theory reduce patient burden when measuring health status in neurological disorders? Results from

Rasch analysis of the SF36 physical functioning scale (PF-10). *Journal of Neurology, Neurosurgery and Psychiatry*, 71: 220–4.

Jensen, J.D. (2011). Can worksite nutritional interventions improve productivity and from profitablility? A literature review. *Perspectives in Public Health*, 131: 184–92.

Jensen, M.P., Turner, J.A. and Romano, J.M. (2001). Changes in beliefs, catastrophizing, and coping are associated with improvement in multidisciplinary pain treatment. *Journal of Consulting and Clinical Psychology*, 69: 655–62.

Jerant, A., Chapman, B., Duberstein, P. et al. (2011). Personality and medication non-adherence among older adults enrolled in a six-year trial. *British Journal of Health Psychology*, 16: 151–69.

Jerram, K.L. and Coleman, P.G. (1999). The big five personality traits and reporting of health behaviours and health problems in old age. *British Journal of Health Psychology*, 4: 181–92.

Jerusalem, M. and Schwarzer, R. (1992). Self-efficacy as a resource factor in stress appraisal process. In R. Schwarzer (ed.), *Self Efficacy: Thought Control of Action*. Washington, DC: Hemisphere.

Jessop, D.C., Herberts, C. and Soloman, L. (2005). The impact of financial circumstances on student mental health. *British Journal of Health Psychology*, 10: 421–39.

Jessor, R. and Jessor, S.L. (1977). *Problem Behavior and Psychosocial Development: A Longitudinal Study of Youth*. New York: Academic Press.

Jewell, J. and Hupp, S.D. (2005). Examining the effects of fatal vision goggles on changing attitudes and behaviors related to drinking and driving. *Journal of Primary Prevention*, 26: 553–65.

Jiang Y.Y., Yang Z.X., Ni R. et al. (2013) Effectiveness analysis on the physical activity and the health benefit of a community population based program. *Biomedical and Environmental Sciences*, 26: 468–73.

Jirojanakul, P., Skevington, S.M. and Hudson, J. (2003). Predicting young children's quality of life. *Social Science and Medicine*, 57: 1277–88.

Jobanputra, R. and Furnham, A. (2005). British Gujarati Indian immigrants' and British Caucasians' beliefs about health and illness. *International Journal of Social Psychiatry,* 51(4): 350–64.

Johnson, C.L. and Barer, B.M. (1997). *Life Beyond 85 Years: The Aura of Survivorship*. New York: Springer.

Johnson, J.V., Hall, E.M. and Theorell, T. (1989). Combined effects of job strain and social isolation on cardiovascular disease morbidity and mortality in a random sample of the Swedish male working population. *Scandinavian Journal of Work, Environment, and Health*, 15: 271–9.

Johnson, M.I. (2001). Transcutaneous electrical nerve stimulation (TENS) and TENS-like devices: do they provide pain relief? *Pain Reviews*, 8: 121–58.

Johnson, S.B. (1999). Commentary: psychologists' resistance to showcasing the profession's accomplishments: what is all the fuss about? *Journal of Pediatric Psychology*, 24: 329–30.

Johnson, W.D., Diaz, R.M., Flanders, W.D. et al. (2008) Behavioral interventions to reduce risk for sexual transmission of HIV among men who have sex with men. *Cochrane Database of Systematic Reviews*, 3 : CD001230.

Johnsson, K.O. and Berglund, M. (2003). Education of key personnel in student pubs leads to a decrease in alcohol consumption among patrons: a randomized controlled trial. *Addiction*, 98: 627–33.

Johnston, D.W. (2002). Acute and chronic psychological processes in cardiovascular disease. In K.W. Schaie, H. Leventhal and S.L. Willis (eds), *Effective Health Behavior in Older Adults*. New York: Springer, pp. 55–64.

Johnston, D.W. (2007). Emotions and the heart: psychological risk factors for cardiovascular disease. *European Health Psychologist*, 1: 9–11.

Johnston, L.D., O'Malley, P.M.,Bachman, J.G. and Schulenberg, J. (2009). *Monitoring the Future: National Survey Results on Drug Use 1975–2008: Vol 1. Secondary school students*. Bethesda, MD: National Institute on Drug Abuse.

Johnston, M., Bonetti, D., Joice, S. et al. (2007). Recovery from disability after stroke as a target for a behavioural intervention: results of a randomised controlled trial. *Disability and Rehabilitation*, 29: 1117–27.

Johnston, M., Foster, M., Shennan, J. et al. (2008). The effectiveness of an Acceptance and Commitment Therapy self-help intervention for chronic pain. *Clinical Journal of Pain*, 26: 393–402.

Johnston, M. and Kennedy, P. (1998). Editorial: special issue on clinical health psychology in chronic conditions. *Clinical Psychology and Psychotherapy*, 5: 59–61.

Johnston, M., Morrison, V., MacWalter, R. and Partridge, C. (1999). Perceived control, coping and recovery from disability following stroke. *Psychology and Health*, 14: 181–92.

Johnston, M. and Pollard, B. (2001). Consequences of disease: testing the WHO International Classification of Impairments, Disability and Handicap (ICIDH) model. *Social Science and Medicine*, 53: 1261–73.

Johnston, M., Pollard, B., Morrison, V. and MacWalter, R. (2004). Functional limitations and survival following stroke: psychological and clinical predictors of 3 year outcome. *International Journal of Behavioral Medicine*, 11: 187–96.

Johnston, M. and Vögele, C. (1993). Benefits of psychological preparation for surgery: a meta-analysis. *Annals of Behavioral Medicine,* 15: 245–56.

Joice, S., Johnston, M., Bonetti, D. et al. (2010) Stroke survivors' evaluations of a stroke workbook-based intervention designed to increase perceived control over recovery. *Health Education Journal*, doi: 10.1177/0017896910383555.

Joint Health Surveys Unit (2005). *Health Survey for England 2004: The Health of Minority Ethnic Groups*. London: HMSO.

Jokela, M., Batty, G.D., Nyberg, S.T. et al. (2013). Personality and all-cause mortality: individual-participant meta-analysis of 3,947 deaths in 76,150 adults. *American Journal of Epidemiology*, 178:667–675. Doi:10.1093/aje/kwt170

Jolly, K., Taylor, R., Lip, G.Y. et al. (2007). The Birmingham Rehabilitation Uptake Maximisation Study (BRUM). Home-based compared with hospital-based cardiac rehabilitation in a multi-ethnic population: cost-effectiveness and patient adherence. *Health Technology Assessment*, 11: 111–18.

Jonas, B.S. and Mussolino, M.E. (2000). Symptoms of depression as a prospective risk factor for stroke. *Psychosomatic Medicine*, 62: 463–71.

Jones, B.A., Reams, K., Calvocoressi, L. et al. (2007). Adequacy of communicating results from screening mammograms to African American and White women. *American Journal of Public Health*, 97: 531–8.

Jones, E. and Morrison, V. (2004). Patient–carer interactions following stroke: the effect on distress. BPS Division of Health Psychology Annual Conference, Edinburgh, September.

Jones, F.A., Burke, R.J. and Westman, M. (eds) (2006). *Work Life Balance: A Psychological Perspective*. New York: Psychology Press.

Jones, J.M., Haslam, S.A., Jetten, J. et al. (2011). That which doesn't kill us can make us stronger (and more satisfied with life): the contribution of personal and social changes to well-being after acquired brain injury. *Psychology & Health*, 26: 353–69.

Jones, M.A. and Johnston, D.W. (2000). A critical review of the relationship between perception of the work environment, coping and mental health in trained nurses, and patient outcomes. *Clinical Effectiveness in Nursing*, 4: 74–85.

Jones, M., Jolly, K., Raftery, J. et al. (2007). 'DNA' may not mean 'did not participate': a qualitative study of reasons for non-adherence at home- and centre-based cardiac rehabilitation. *Family Practice*, 24: 343–57.

Jones, J.R., Huxtable, C.S., Hodgson, J.T. et al. (2003). *Self-reported Illness in 2001/02: Results from a Household Survey*. London: Health and Safety Executive.

Jones, R., Pearson, J., McGregor, S. et al. (2002). Does writing a list help cancer patients ask relevant questions? *Patient Education and Counseling*, 47: 369–71.

Jones, R.A. (1990). Expectations and delay in seeking medical care. *Journal of Social Issues*, 46: 81–95.

Jørgensen, K.J. and Gøtzsche, P.C. (2004). Presentation on websites of possible benefits and harm from screening for breast cancer: a cross-sectional study. *British Medical Journal*, 328: 148–53.

Jousilahti, P., Vartiainen, E., Tuomilehto, J. et al. (1995). Effect of risk factors and changes in risk factors on coronary mortality in three cohorts of middle aged people in eastern Finland. *American Journal of Epidemiology*, 141: 50–60.

Joyce, C., Hickey, H., McGee, H. et al. (2003). A theory-based method for the evaluation of individual quality of life: the SEIQoL. *Quality of Life Research*, 12: 275–80.

Judge, T.A., Bono, J.E. and Locke, E.A. (2000). Personality and job satisfaction: the mediating role of job characteristics. *Journal of Applied Psychology*, 85: 237–49.

Julien, R.M. (1996). *A Primer of Drug Action: A Concise, Non-technical Guide to the Actions, Uses and Side Effects of Psychoactive Drugs*, 7th edn. New York: W.H. Freeman.

Kabat-Zinn, J. (2001). *Full Catastrophe Living: How to Cope with Stress, Pain and Illness Using Mindfulness Meditation*. London: Piatkus Books.

Kabat-Zinn, J. (2013*). Full Catastrophe Living, Revised Edition: How to Cope with Stress, Pain and Illness Using Mind-fulness.* London: Piatkus.

Kagee, A. and Deport, T. (2010). Barriers to adherence to antiretroviral treatment: the perspectives of patient advocates. *Journal of Health Psychology*, 15: 1001–11.

Kahn, K.L., Pearson, M.L., Harrison, E.R. et al. (1994). Health care for black and poor hospitalized Medicare patients. *Journal of the American Medical Association*, 271: 1169–74.

Kain Z.N., Caldwell-Andrews, A.A., Mayes, L.C. et al. (2007). Family-centered preparation for surgery improves perioperative outcomes in children: a randomized controlled trial. *Anesthesiology*, 106: 65–74.

Kalichman, S.C., Benotsch, E.G., Weinhardt, L. et al. (2003). Health-related internet use, coping, social support, and health indicators in people living with HIV/AIDS: preliminary results from a community survey. *Health Psychology*, 22: 111–16.

Kalichman, S.C., Cherry, C. and Browne-Sperling, F. (1999). Effectiveness of a video-based motivational skills-building HIV risk-reduction intervention for inner-city African American men. *Journal of Consulting and Clinical Psychology*, 67: 959–66.

Kalichman, S.C., Cherry, C., Cain, D. et al. (2006). Internet-based health information consumer skills intervention for people living with HIV/AIDS. *Journal of Consulting and Clinical Psychology*, 74: 545–54.

Kalnins, I.H.C., Ballantyne, P. and Quartaro, G. (1994). School-based community development as a health promotion strategy for children. *Health Promotion International*, 9: 269–79.

Kalra, L., Evans, A., Perez, I. et al. (2004). Training carers of stroke patients: randomised controlled trial. *British Medical Journal*, 328: 1099–104.

Kang, J.H., Cook, N.R., Manson, J.E. et al. (2009). Vitamin E, vitamin C, beta carotene, and cognitive function among women with or at risk of cardiovascular disease: the Women's Antioxidant and Cardiovascular Study. *Circulation*, 119: 2772–80.

Kanner, A.D., Coyne, J.C., Schaefer, C. and Lazarus, R.S. (1981). Comparison of two models of stress management: daily hassles and uplifts versus major life events. *Journal of Behavioral Medicine*, 4: 1–39.

Kanner, A.D., Feldman, S.S., Weinberger, D.A. and Ford, M. (1987). Uplifts, hassles, and adaptational outcomes in early adolescents. *Journal of Early Adolescence,* 7: 371–94.

Kaplan, G. and Baron-Epel, O. (2003). What lies behind the subjective evaluation of health status? *Social Science and Medicine*, 56: 1669–76.

Kaplan R.C., Bangdiwala S.I., Barnhart J.M. et al. (2014). Smoking among U.S. Hispanic/Latino adults: the Hispanic community health study/study of Latinos. *American Journal of Preventive Medicine*, 46: 496–506.

Kaplan, G.A. and Reynolds, P. (1988). Depression and cancer mortality and morbidity: prospective evidence from the Alameda County study. *Journal of Behavioral Medicine*, 11: 1–14.

Kaptein, A.A., Bijsterbosch, J., Scharloo, M. et al. (2010). Using the common-sense model of illness perceptions to examine osteoarthritis change: a 6-year longitudinal study. *Health Psychology*, 29: 56–64.

Karasek, R.A. (1979). Job demands, job decision latitude and mental strain: implications for job redesign. *Administrative Science Quarterly*, 24: 285–308.

Karasek, R. (1996). Lower health risk with increased job control among white collar workers. *Journal of Organizational Behavior*, 11: 171–85.

Karasek, R.A., Baker, D., Marxer, F. et al. (1981). Job decision latitude, job demands and cardiovascular disease: a prospective study of Swedish men. *American Journal of Public Health*, 71: 694–705.

Karasek, R.A. and Theorell, T. (1990). *Healthy Work: Stress, Productivity and the Reconstruction of Working Life.* New York: Basic Books.

Karasz, A. and McKinley, P.S. (2007). Cultural differences in conceptual models of fatigue. *Journal of Health Psychology*, 12: 613–26.

Karlamangla, A.S., Merkin, S.S., Crimmins, E.M. et al. (2010). Socioeconomic and ethnic disparities in cardiovascular risk in the United States, 2001–2006. *Annals of Epidemiology*, 20: 617–28.

Kasl, S.V. (1996). Theory of stress and health. In C.L. Cooper (ed.), *Handbook of Stress, Medicine and Health*. London: CRC Press.

Kasl, S.V. and Cobb, S. (1966a). Health behavior, illness behavior, and sick role behavior I. Health and illness behavior. *Archives of Environmental Health*, 12: 246–66.

Kasl, S.V. and Cobb, S. (1966b). Health behavior, illness behavior, and sick role behavior II. Sick role behavior. *Archives of Environmental Health*, 12: 531–41.

Katbamna, S., Ahmad, W., Bhakta, P. et al. (2004). Do they look after their own? Informal support for the South Asian carer. *Health & Social Care in the Community*, 12: 398–406.

Katon, W., Lin, E. and Kroenke, K. (2007). The association of depression and anxiety with medical symptom burden in patients with chronic medical illness. *General Hospital Psychiatry*, 29: 147–55.

Katz, M.H. (1997). AIDS epidemic in San Francisco among men who report sex with men: successes and challenges of HIV prevention. *Journal of Acquired Immune Deficiency Syndrome and Human Retrovirology*, 14: S38–S46.

Katz, D.L. and Meller, S. (2014). Can we say what diet is best for health? *Annual Review of Public Health*, 35: 83–103.

Kauff, N.D., Satagopan, J.M., Robson, M.E. et al. (2002). Risk-reducing Salpingo-oophorectomy in women with a BRCA1 or BRCA2 mutation. *New England Journal of Medicine*, 346: 1609–15.

Kearins, O., Walton, J., O'Sullivan, E. et al. (2009). Invitation management initiative to improve uptake of breast cancer screening in an urban UK Primary Care Trust. *Journal of Medical Screening*, 16: 81–4.

Keating, N.L., Guadagnoli, E., Landrum, M.B. et al. (2002). Treatment decision making in early-stage breast cancer: should surgeons match patients' desired level of involvement? *Journal of Clinical Oncology*, 20: 1473–9.

Keats, M.R., Culos-Reed, S.N., Courneya, K.S. et al. (2007). Understanding physical activity in adolescent cancer survivors: an application of the theory of planned behavior. *Psycho-Oncology*, 16: 448–57.

Keefe, F.J., Caldwell, D.S., Williams, D.A. et al. (1990). Pain coping skills training in the management of osteoarthritic knee pain – II: follow-up results. *Behavior Therapy*, 21: 435–47.

Keinan, G., Carmil, D. and Rieck, M. (1991). Predicting women's delay in seeking medical care after discovery of a lump in the breast: the role of personality and behaviour patterns. *Behavioral Medicine*, 17: 177–83.

Kelly, J.A., Murphy, D.A., Sikkema, K.J. et al. (1993). Psychological interventions to prevent HIV infection are urgently needed. *American Psychologist*, 48: 1023–34.

Kelly, J.A., Murphy, D.A., Sikkema, K.J. et al. (1997). Randomised, controlled, community-level HIV-prevention intervention for sexual-risk behaviour among homosexual men in US cities. *The Lancet*, 350: 1500–5.

Kelly, J.A., Murphy, D.A., Washington, C.D. et al. (1994). The effects of HIV/AIDS intervention groups for high-risk women in urban clinics. *American Journal of Public Health*, 84: 225–37.

Kelly, J.A., St Lawrence, J.S., Stevenson, L.Y. et al. (1992). Community AIDS/HIV risk reduction: the effects of endorsements by popular people in three cities. *American Journal of Public Health*, 82: 1483–9.

Kelly, J.M., Rowe, A.K., Onikpo, F. et al. (2007). Care takers' recall of Integrated Management of Childhood Illness counselling messages in Benin. *Tropical Doctor*, 37: 75–9.

Kelly, P.A. and Haidet, P. (2007) Physician overestimation of patient literacy: a potential source of health care disparities. *Patient Education and Counseling*, 66: 119–22.

Kemeny, M.E. (2003). The psychobiology of stress. *Current Directions in Psychological Science*, 12: 124–9.

Kemeny, M.E., Weiner, H., Taylor, S.E. et al. (1994). Repeated bereavement, depressed mood, and immune parameters in HIV seropositive and seronegative homosexual men. *Health Psychology*, 13: 14–24.

Kennedy, T., Jones, R., Darnley, S. et al. (2005). Cognitive behaviour therapy in addition to antispasmodic treatment for irritable bowel syndrome in primary care: randomised controlled trial. *British Medical Journal*, 331: 435.

Kentsch, M., Rodemerk, U., Muller-Esch, G. et al. (2002). Emotional attitudes toward symptoms and inadequate coping strategies are major determinants of patient delay in acute myocardial infarction. *Zeitschrift zu Kardiologie*, 91: 147–55.

Keogh E. and Cochrane M. (2002). Anxiety sensitivity, cognitive biases, and the experience of pain. *Journal of Pain*, 3: 320–9.

Kern, M.L. and Friedman, H.S. (2008). Do conscientious individuals live longer? A quantitative review. *Health Psychology*, 27: 505–12.

Kerns, R.D., Haythornwaite, J., Southwick, S. and Giller, E.L. (1990). The role of marital interaction in chronic pain and depressive symptom severity. *Journal of Psychosomatic Research*, 34: 401–8.

Kerr, T., Small, W., Buchner, C. et al. (2010). Syringe sharing and HIV incidence among injection drug users and increased access to sterile syringes. *American Journal of Public Health*, 100: 1449–53.

Khan AA, Khan A, Harezlak J, Tu W, Kroenke K. (2003). Somatic symptoms in primary care: etiology and outcome. *Psychosomatics* 2003; 44: 471–8.

Khantzian, E.J. (2003). Understanding addictive vulnerability: an evolving psychodynamic perspective. *Neuro-psychoanalysis*, 5: 3–35.

Khaw, K.T., Wareham, N., Bingham, S. et al. (2008). Combined impact of health behaviours and mortality in men and women: the EPIC-Norfolk prospective population study. *PLoS Medicine*, 5: e12.

Kickbusch, I. (2003). The contribution of the World Health Organization to a new public health and health promotion. *American Journal of Public Health*, 93: 383–8.

Kiechl, S., Egger, G., Mayr, M. et al. (2001). Chronic infections and the risk of carotid atherosclerosis: prospective results from a large population study. *Circulation*, 103: 1064–70.

Kiecolt-Glaser, J.K., Dura, J.R., Speicher, C.E. et al. (1991). Spousal caregivers of dementia victims: longitudinal changes in immunity and health. *Psychosomatic Medicine*, 53: 345–62.

Kiecolt-Glaser, J.K., Garner, W., Speicher, C. et al. (1984). Psychosocial modifiers of immunocompetence in medical students. *Psychosomatic Medicine*, 46: 7–14.

Kiecolt-Glaser, J.K. and Glaser, R. (1995). Psychological influences on immunity. *Psychosomatics*, 27: 621–4.

Kiecolt-Glaser, J.K. and Glaser, R. (1999). Psychoneuroimmunology and cancer: fact or fiction? *European Journal of Cancer*, 35: 1603–7.

Kiecolt-Glaser, J.K., Glaser, R., Gravenstein, S. et al. (1996). Chronic stress alters the immune response to influenza virus vaccination in older adults. *Proceedings of the National Academy of Science USA*, 93: 3043–7.

Kiecolt-Glaser, J.K., Glaser, R., Williger, D. et al. (1985). Psychosocial enhancement of immunocompetence in a geriatric population. *Health Psychology*, 4: 25–41.

Kiecolt-Glaser, J.K., Malarkey, W.B., Cacioppo, J.T. and Glaser, R. (1994). Stressful personal relationships: immune and endocrine function. In R. Glaser and J.K. Kiecolt-Glaser (eds), *Handbook of Human Stress and Immunity*. San Diego, CA: Academic Press.

Kiecolt-Glaser, J.K., Marucha, P.T., Malarkey, W.B. et al. (1995). Slowing wound healing by psychosocial stress. *The Lancet*, 4: 1194–6.

Kiecolt-Glaser, J.K., McGuire, L., Robles, T.F. et al. (2002). Psychoneuroimmunology: psychological influences on immune function and health. *Journal of Consulting and Clinical Psychology*, 70: 537–47.

Kiecolt-Glaser, J.K. and Newton, T.L. (2001). Marriage and health: his and hers. *Psychological Bulletin*, 127: 472–503.

Kiecolt-Glaser, J.K., Preacher, K.J., MacCallum, R.C. et al. (2003). Chronic stress and age-related increases in the pro-inflammatory cytokine IL-6. *Proceedings of the National Academy of Science*, 10: 9090–5.

Kiecolt-Glaser, J.P., Gouin, J.P., Weng, N. et al. (2011). Child-hood adversity heightens the impact of later-life care-giving stress on telomere length and inflammation. *Psychosomatic Medicine*, 73: 16–22.

Kiernan, P.J. and Isaacs, J.B. (1981). Use of drugs by the elderly. *Journal of the Royal Society of Medicine*, 74: 196–200.

Kim, H.S., Sherman, D.K. and Taylor, S.E. (2009). Culture and social support. *American Psychologist*, 63: 518–26.

Kim, Y., Carver, C.S., Deci, E.L., et al. (2008). Adult attachment and psychological well-being in cancer caregivers: The mediational role of spouses' motives for caregiving. *Journal of Health Psychology*, 27, S144–S154.

Kim, Y., and Evangelista, L.S. (2010). Relationship between illness perceptions, treatment adherence, and clinical outcomes in patients on maintenance hemodialysis. *Nephrology Nursing Journal*, 37: 271–80.

Kim, Y., Pavlish, C., Evangelista, L.S. et al. (2012). Racial/ethnic differences in illness perceptions in minority patients undergoing maintenance hemodialsis. *Nephrology Nursing Journal*, 39: 39–49

Kinman, G. and Jones, F. (2005). Lay representations of work stress: what do people really mean when they say they are stressed? *Work & Stress*, 19: 101–20.

Kinmonth, A.L., Woodcock, A., Griffin, S. et al. (1998). Randomised controlled trial of patient-centred care of diabetes in general practice: impact on current wellbeing and future disease risk. The Diabetes Care from Diagnosis Research Team. *British Medical Journal*, 317: 1202–8.

Kinney, J.M., Stephens, M.A.P., Franks, M.M. and Norris, V.K. (1995). Stresses and satisfactions of family caregivers to older stroke patients. *The Journal of Applied Gerontology*, 14: 3–21.

Kirby, S.D., Ureda, J.R., Rose, R.L. and Hussey, J. (1998). Peripheral cues and involvement level: influences on acceptance of a mammography message. *Journal of Health Communication*, 3: 19–35.

Kirkcaldy, B.D., Athanasou, J.A. and Trimpop, R. (2000). The idiosyncratic construction of stress: examples from medical work settings. *Stress Medicine*, 16: 315–26.

Kirkcaldy, B.D. and Cooper, C.L. (1992). Managing the stress of change: occupational stress among senior police officers in Berlin. *Stress Medicine*, 8: 219–31.

Kisely, S.R., Campbell, L.A., Yelland, M.J. et al. (2012). Psychological interventions for symptomatic management of non-specific chest pain in patients with normal coronary anatomy. *Cochrane Database of Systematic Reviews*, 6: CD004101.

Kitayama, S. and Cohen, D. (eds) (2007). *Handbook of Cultural Psychology*. New York: Guildford Press.

Kittleson, M.M., Meoni, L.A., Wang, N.Y. et al. (2006). Association of childhood socioeconomic status with subsequent coronary heart disease in physicians. *Archives of Internal Medicine*, 166: 2356–61.

Kivimäki, M., Elovainio, M., Kokko, K. et al. (2003). Hostility, unemployment and health status: testing three theoretical models. *Social Science and Medicine*, 56: 2139–52.

Kivimäki, M., Ferrie, J.E., Brunner, E. et al. (2005). Justice at work and reduced risk of coronary heart disease among employees: The Whitehall II Study. *Archives of Internal Medicine*, 165(19): 2245–51.

Kivimäki, M., Lawlor, D.A., Davey Smith, G. et al. (2007). Socioeconomic position, co-occurrence of behavior-related risk factors, and coronary heart disease: the Finnish Public Sector study. *American Journal of Public Health*, 97: 874–9.

Kivimäki, M., Leino-Arjas, P., Luukkonem, R. et al. (2002). Work stress and risk of cardiovascular mortality: prospective cohort study of industrial employées. *British Medical Journal*, 325: 857–60.

Kivimäki, M., Nyberg S.T., Batty, G.D. et al. (2012). Job strain as a risk factor for coronary heart disease: a collaborative meta-analysis of individual participant data. *The Lancet*, 380, 1491–7.

Kivimäki, M., Vahtera, J., Kosekenvuo, M. et al. (1998). Response of hostile individuals to stressful changes in their working lives: test of a psychosocial vulnerability model. *Psychological Medicine*, 28: 903–13.

Klassen, A.F., Gulati, S., Granek, L. et al. (2012). Understanding the health impact of caregiving: a qualitative study of immigrant parents and single parents of a child with cancer. *Quality of Life Research*, DOI 10.1007/s11136–011–0072–8

Klatsky, A.L. (2008). Alcohol, wine, and vascular diseases: an abundance of paradoxes. *American Journal of Physiology: Heart and Circulatory Physiology*, 63: 582–3.

Klein, C.T.F. and Helweg-Larsen, M. (2002). Perceived control and the optimistic bias: a meta-analytic review. *Psychology and Health*, 17: 437–46.

Klemenc-Ketiš, Z., Krizmaric, M. and Kersnik, J. (2013). Age- and gender-specific prevalence of self-reported symptoms in adults, *Central European Journal of Public Health*, 21: 160–4.

Kline, K.N. and Mattson, M. (2000). Breast self-examination pamphlets. A content analysis grounded in fear appeals research. *Health Communication*, 12: 1–21.

Kline, P. (1993). *Personality: the Psychometric View*. London: Routledge.

Klonoff, E.A. and Landrine, H. (1994). Culture and gender diversity in commonsense beliefs about the causes of six illnesses. *Journal of Behavioral Medicine*, 17: 407–18.

Kluger BM, Krupp LB, Enoka RM.. (2013). Fatigue and fatigability in neurologic illnesses: proposal for a unified taxonomy. *Neurology* (2013) 80(4):409–16.10.1212/WNL.0b013e31827f07be

Knapp, P., Raynor, D.K. and Jebar, A.H. et al. (2005). Interpretation of medication pictograms by adults in the UK. *Annals of Pharmacotherapy*, 39: 1227–33.

Knight, B.G., Robinson, G.S., Longmire, C.F., et al. (2002). Cross cultural issues in caregiving for persons with dementia: Do familism values reduce burden and distress? *Ageing International*, 27: 70–94.

Knight, B.G., and Sayegh, P. (2011). Cultural values and caregiving: the updated sociocultural stress and coping model. *Journal of Gerontology*: *Psychological Sciences* 65B: 5–13

Knott, C.S., Coombs, N, Stamatakis, E. and Biddolph, J.P. (2015). All cause mortality and the case for age specific alcohol consumption guidelines: pooled analyses of up to 10 population based cohorts, *British Medical Journal*; 350 doi: http://dx.doi.org/10.1136/bmj.h384

Knowler, W.C., Barrett-Connor, E., Fowler, S.E. et al. (2002). Reduction in the incidence of type 2 diabetes with lifestyle intervention or metformin. *New England Journal of Medicine*, 346: 393–403.

Kobasa, S.C. (1979). Stressful life events, personality and health: an inquiry into hardiness. *Journal of Personality and Social Psychology*, 37: 1–11.

Kobasa, S.C., Maddi, S. and Kahn, S. (1982). Hardiness and health: a prospective study. *Journal of Personality and Social Psychology*, 42: 168–77.

Koenig, H.G., George, L.K., Stangl, D. and Tweed, D.L. (1995). Hospital stressors experienced by elderly medical inpatients: developing a hospital stress index. *International Journal of Psychiatry in Medicine*, 25: 103–22.

Koenig, H.G., McCullough, M.E. and Larson, D.B. (2001). *Handbook of Religion and Health*. Oxford: Oxford University Press.

Koenig, H.G., Weslund, R.E., George, L.K., et al. (1993). Abbreviating the Duke Social Support Index for use in chronically ill elderly individuals, *Psychosoatics*, 34: 61–9.

Koffman, D.M., Lee, J.W., Hopp, J.W. et al. (1998). The impact of including incentives and competition in a workplace smoking cessation program on quit rates. *American Journal of Health Promotion*, 13: 105–11.

Koinis-Mitchell, D., McQuaid, E.L., Seifer, R. et al. (2009). Symptom perception in children with asthma: cognitive and psychological factors. *Health Psychology*, 28: 226–37.

Kok, G. and Schaalma, H. (1998). Theory-based and data-based health education intervention programmes. *Psychology and Health*, 13: 747–51.

Kole-Snijders, A.M.J., Vlaeyen, J.W.S. and Goossens, M.E.J. et al. (1999). Chronic low back pain: what does cognitive coping skills training add to operant behavioural treatment? Results of a randomized trial. *Journal of Consulting and Clinical Psychology*, 67: 931–44.

Kolk, A.M., Hanewald, G.J.F.P., Schagen, S. and Gijsbers van Wijk, C.M.T. (2003). A symptom perception approach to common physical symptoms. *Social Science and Medicine*, 57: 2343–54.

Konkolÿ Thege, B., Bachner, Y.G., Kushnir, T. and Kopp, M. (2009). Relationship between meaning in life and smoking status: results of a national representative survey. *Addictive Behaviours*, 34: 117–20.

Koob, G.F. (1999). Corticotropin-releasing factor, norepinephrine, and stress. *Biological Psychiatry*, 46: 1167–80.

Koopman, H.M., Baars, R.M., Chaplin, J. and Zwinderman, K.H. (2004). Illness through the eyes of a child: the development of children's understanding of the causes of illness. *Patient Education and Counselling*, 55: 363–70.

Koordeman R., Anschutz D.J. and Engels R.C. (2012). Alcohol portrayals in movies, music videos and soap operas and alcohol use of young people: current status and future challenges. *Alcohol and Alcoholism*, 47: 612–23.

Kop, N., Euwema, M. and Schaufeli, W. (1999). Burnout, job stress and violent behaviour among Dutch police officers. *Work and Stress*, 13: 3226–340.

Korfage I.J., Essink-Bot M.L., Westenberg S.M. et al. (2014). How distressing is referral to colposcopy in cervical cancer screening?: a prospective quality of life study. *Gynecologic Oncology*, 132: 142–8.

Kornblith, A.B., Herndon, J.E., II, Weiss, R.B. et al. (2003). Long-term adjustment of survivors of early-stage breast carcinoma, 20 years after adjuvant chemotherapy. *Cancer*, 98: 679–89.

Korotkov, D. and Hannah, T.E. (2004). The five factor model of personality: strengths and limitations in predicting health status, sick role and illness behaviour. *Personality and Individual Differences*, 36: 187–99.

Kosmider, S., Shedda, S., Jones, I.T. et al. (2009). Predictors of clinic non-attendance: opportunities to improve patient outcomes in colorectal cancer. *Internal Medicine Journal*, 40: 757–63.

Kosminder, S., Shedda, S., Jones, I. et al. (2010). Predictors of clinic non-attendance-opportunities to improve patient outcomes in colorectal cancer. *Internal Medicine Journal*, 40: 757–63.

Kouvonen, A., Kivimäki, M., Virtanen, M. et al. (2005). Work stress, smoking status, and smoking intensity: an observational study of 46 190 employees. *Journal of Epidemiology and Community Health*, 59: 63–9.

Kraft, P., Sutton, S. and McCreath-Reynolds, H. (1999). The transtheoretical model of behaviour change: are the stages qualitatively different? *Psychology and Health*, 14: 433–50.

Kramer, B.J. (1997). Gain in the caregiving experience. Where are we? What next? *The Gerontologist*, 37: 218–32.

Krantz, D.S., Glass, D.C., Shaeffer, M.A. and Davia, J.E. (1982). Behavior patterns and coronary disease: a critical evaluation. In J.T. Cacioppo and R.E. Petty (eds), *Perspectives in Cardiovascular Psycho-physiology*. New York: Guilford Press.

Krantz, D.S. and Manuck, S.B. (1984). Acute psychophysiological reactivity and risk of cardiovascular disease: a review and methodological critique. *Psychological Bulletin*, 96: 435–64.

Krantz, G. and Lundberg, U. (2006). Workload, work stress, and sickness absence in Swedish male and female white-collar employees. *Scandinavian Journal of Public Health*, 34: 238–46.

Krantz, G. and Orth, P. (2000). Common symptoms in middle-aged women: their relation to employment status, psychosocial work conditions and social support in a Swedish setting. *Journal of Epidemiology and Community Health*, 54: 192–9.

Krause, N.M. and Jay, G.M. (1994). What do global self-rated health items measure? *Medical Care*, 32: 930–42.

Krieger, N., Quesenberry, C. and Peng, T. (1999). Social class, race/ethnicity, and incidence of breast, cervix, colon, lung, and prostate cancer among Asian, black, Hispanic, and white residents of the San Francisco Bay area. *Cancer Causes Control*, 10: 525–37.

Krigsman, K., Nilsson, J.L. and Ring, L. (2007). Adherence to multiple drug therapies: refill adherence to concomitant use of diabetes and asthma/COPD medication. *Pharmacoepidemiology and Drug Safety*, 16: 1120–8.

Krischer, M.M., Xu, P., Meade, C.D. et al. (2007). Self-administered stress management training in patients undergoing radiotherapy. *Journal of Clinical Oncology*, 25: 4657–62.

Krohne, H.W. (1993). Vigilance and cognitive avoidance as concepts in coping research. In H.W. Krohne (ed.), *Attention and Avoidance: Strategies in Coping with Aversiveness*. Seattle, WA: Hogrefe and Huber.

Krol, Y., Grootenhuis, M.A., Destrée-Vonk, A. et al. (2003). Health-related quality of life in children with congenital heart disease. *Psychology and Health*, 18: 251–60.

Krones, T., Keller, H., Sönnichsen, A. et al. (2008). Absolute cardiovascular disease risk and shared decision making in primary care: a randomized controlled trial. *Annals of Family Medicine*, 6: 218–27.

Krueger, K.P., Berger, B.A. and Felkey, B. (2005). Medication adherence and persistence: a comprehensive review. *Advances in Therapy*, 22: 313–56.

Krukowski, R.A., Harvey-Berino, J. and Kolodinsky, J. (2006). Consumers may not use or understand calorie labeling in restaurants. *Journal of the American Dietetic Association*, 107: 33–4.

Kubler-Ross, E. (1969). *On Death and Dying*. New York: Macmillan.

Kuchler, T., Henne-Bruns, D., Rappat, S. et al. (1999). Impact of psychotherapeutic support on gastrointestinal cancer patients undergoing surgery: survival results of a trial. *Hepato-gastro-enterology*, 46: 322–35.

Kuenzler, A., Hodgkinson, K., Zindel, A. et al. (2010). Who cares, who bears, who benefits? Female spouses vicariously carry the burden after cancer diagnosis. *Psychology and Health*, 26: 337–52.

Kuntzleman, C.T. (1985). Enhancing cardiovascular fitness of children and youth: the Feelin' Good Program. In J.E. Zins, D.I. Wagner and C.A. Maher (eds), *Health Promotion in the Schools: Innovative Approaches to Facilitating Physical and Emotional Well-being*. New York: Hawthorn Press.

Kuper, H., Adams, H.O. and Trichopoulos, D. (2000). Infections as a major preventable cause of human cancer. *Journal of Internal Medicine*, 248: 171–83.

Kuper, H. and Marmot, M. (2003). Job strain, job demands, decision latitude, and risk of coronary heart disease within the Whitehall II study. *Journal of Epidemiology and Community Health*, 57: 147 53.

Kuper, H., Singh-Manoux, A., Siegrist, J. et al. (2002). When reciprocity fails: effort–reward imbalance in relation to coronary heart disease and health functioning within the Whitehall II study. *Occupational and Environmental Medicine*, 59: 777–84.

Kurtz, M.A., Kurtz, J.C., Given, C.W. and Given, B.A. (2008). Patient optimism and mastery – do they play a role in cancer patients' management of pain and fatigue? *Journal of Pain and Symptom Management*, 36: 1–10.

Kurtz, S. and Silverman, J. (1996). The Calgary–Cambridge observation guides: an aid to defining the curriculum and organising the teaching in communication training programmes. *Medical Education*, 30: 83–9.

Kyle, R.G., MacMillan, I., Forbat, L. et al. (2014). Scottish adolescents' sun-related behaviours, tanning attitudes and associations with skin cancer awareness: a cross-sectional study. *BMJ Open*, 4: e005137. doi: 10.1136/bmjopen-2014-005137

Kyngaes, H., Mikkonen, R., Nousiainen, E.M. et al. (2001). Coping with the onset of cancer. Coping strategies and resources of young people with cancer. *European Journal of Cancer Care*, 10: 6–11.

Laceulle, O.M., van Aken, M.A.G., Ormel, J. and Nederhof, E. (2014).Stress-sensitivity and reciprocal associations between stressful events and adolescenet temperament. *Personality & Individual Differences* http://dx.doi.org/10.1016/j.paid.2014.12.009

Lachman, M.E. and Weaver, S.L. (1998). The sense of control as a moderator of social class differences in health and well-being. *Journal of Personality and Social Psychology*, 74: 763–73.

Lahelma, E., Martikainen, P., Rahkonen, O. and Silventoinen, K. (1999). Gender differences in ill-health in Finland: patterns, magnitude and change. *Social Science and Medicine*, 48: 7–19.

Lai, D.T., Cahill, K., Qin, Y. et al. (2010). Motivational interviewing for smoking cessation. *Cochrane Database of Systematic Reviews*, issue 3, art. no.: CD006936. doi: 10.1002/14651858.CD006936.

Lally, P., Bartle, N. and Wardle, J. (2011). Social norms and diet in adolescents. *Appetite,* 57: 623–7.

Lamden, K.H. and Gemmell, I. (2008). General practice factors and MMR vaccine uptake: structure, process and demography. *Journal of Public Health*. 30: 251–7.

Lamers, S.M.A., Bolier, L., Westerhof, G.J. et al. (2012). The impact of emotional well-being on long-term recovery and survival in physical illness: a meta-analysis. *Journal of Behavioral Medicine*, 35: 538–47.

Lancaster, T., Silagy, C., Fowler, G. and Spiers, I. (1999).

Training health professionals in smoking cessation. In *The Cochrane Library*, issue 1. Oxford: Update Software.

Landmark, B.T. and Wahl, A. (2002). Living with newly diagnosed breast cancer: a qualitative study of 10 women with newly diagnosed breast cancer. *Journal of Advanced Nursing*, 49: 112–21.

Landolt, M.A., Vollrath, M., Ribi, K. et al. (2003). Incidence and associations of parental and child posttraumatic stress symptoms in pediatric patients. *Journal of Child Psychology and Psychiatry*, 44: 1199–207.

Lane, D., Beevers, D.G. and Lip, G.Y. (2002a). Ethnic differences in blood pressure and the prevalence of hypertension in England. *Journal of Human Hypertension*, 16: 267–73.

Lane, D., Carroll, D., Ring, C. et al. (2000). Effects of depression and anxiety on mortality and quality-of-life 4 months after myocardial infarction. *Journal of Psychosomatic Research*, 49: 229–38.

Lane, D., Carroll, D., Ring, C. et al. (2001). Predictors of attendance at cardiac rehabilitation after myocardial infarction. *Journal of Psychosomatic Research*, 51: 497–501.

Lane, D., Carroll, D., Ring, C. et al. (2002b). The prevalence and persistence of depression and anxiety following myocardial infarction. *British Journal of Health Psychology*, 7: 11–21.

Lane, R.D. (2014). Is it possible to bridge the Biopsychosocial and Biomedical models? *BioPsychoSocial Medicine*, 8: 3 doi: 10.1186/1751–0759–8-3

Lang, E.V., Berbaum, K.S., Faintuch, S. et al. (2006). Adjunctive self-hypnotic relaxation for outpatient medical procedures: a prospective randomized trial with women undergoing large core breast biopsy. *Pain*, 126: 155–64.

Lang, T., Nicaud, V., Slama, K. et al. (2000). Smoking cessation at the workplace. Results of a randomised controlled intervention study. Worksite physicians from the AIREL group. *Journal of Epidemiology and Community Health*, 54: 349–54.

Langer, S.L., Rudd, M.E. and Syrjala, K.L. (2007). Protective buffering and emotional desynchrony among spousal caregivers of cancer patients. *Health Psychology* 26: 635–43.

Langewitz, W.A., Loeb, Y., Nübling, M. et al. (2009). From patient talk to physician notes – comparing the content of medical interviews with medical records in a sample of outpatients in Internal Medicine. *Patient Education and Counseling*, 76: 336–40.

Langewitz, W., Wossmer, B., Iseli, J. and Berger, W. (1997). Psychological and metabolic improvement after an outpatient teaching program for functional intensified insulin therapy. *Diabetes Research and Clinical Practice*, 37: 157–64.

Larsen, R.J. and Kasimatis, M. (1991). Day-to-day physical symptoms: individual differences in the occurrence, duration, and emotional concomitants of minor daily illnesses. *Journal of Personality*, 59: 387–423.

Larson, J. (1999). The conceptualization of health. *Medical Care and Review*, 56: 123–236.

Larsson, G., Mattsson, E. and von Essen, L. (2010). Aspects of quality of life, anxiety and depression among persons diagnosed with cancer during adolescence: a long-term follow-up study. *European Journal of Cancer*, 46: 1062–8.

Larsson, M., Boëthius, G., Axelsson, S. et al. (2008). Exposure to environmental tobacco smoke and health effects among hospitality workers in Sweden: before and after the implementation of a smoke-free law. *Scandinavian Journal of Work, Environment & Health*, 34: 267–77.

Latimer, P. (1981). Irritable bowel syndrome: a behavioral model. *Behaviour Research and Therapy*, 19: 475–83.

Latimer, P., Sarna, S., Campbell, D. et al. (1981). Colonic motor and myoelectric activity: a comparative study of normal subjects, psychoneurotic patients and patients with the irritable bowel syndrome. *Gastro-enterology*, 80: 893–901.

Lau, R.R., Bernard, T.M. and Hartman, K.A. (1989). Further explorations of common sense representations of common illnesses. *Health Psychology*, 8(2): 195–219.

Lau, R.R. and Hartman, K.A. (1983). Common sense representations of common illnesses. *Health Psychology*, 2: 167–85.

Lauby, J.L., Smith, P.J., Stark, M. et al. (2000). A community-level HIV prevention intervention for inner-city women: results of the Women and Infants Demonstration Projects. *American Journal of Public Health*, 90: 216–22.

Laugesen, M. and Meads, C. (1991). Tobacco restrictions, price, income and tobacco consumption in OECD countries, 1960–1986. *British Journal of Addiction*, 86: 1343–54.

Laux, L. and Weber, H. (1991). Presentation of self in coping with anger and anxiety: an intentional approach. *Anxiety Research*, 3: 233–55.

Law, M.R., Wald, N.J. and Thompson, S.G. (1994). By how much and how quickly does reduction in serum cholesterol concentration lower risk of ischemic heart disease? *British Medical Journal*, 308: 367–72.

Lawlor, D.A., Ebrahim, S. and Davey Smith, G. (2002). Role of endogenous oestrogen in aetiology of coronary heart disease: analysis of age related trends in coronary heart disease and breast cancer in England and Wales and Japan. *British Medical Journal*, 325: 311–2.

Lawrence, D., Fagan, P., Backinger, C.L. et al. (2007). Cigarette smoking patterns among young adults ages 18–24 in the U.S. *Nicotine & Tobacco Research*, 9: 687–97.

Lawrence, E., Bunde, M., Barry, R.A. et al. (2008). Partner support and marital satisfaction: support amount, adequacy, provision and solicitation. *Personal Relationships*, 15: 445–63.

Lawrence, V., Murray, J., Samsi, K. and Banarjee, S. (2008). Attitudes and support needs of Black Caribbean, Asian and White British carers of people with dementia in the UK. *The British Journal of Psychiatry*, 193: 240–6.

Lawson, V.L., Lyne, P.A., Bundy, C. et al. (2007). The role of illness perceptions, coping and evaluation in care-seeking among people with type 1 diabetes. *Psychology and Health*, 22: 175–91.

Lazarus, R.S. (1966). *Psychological Stress and the Coping Process*. New York: McGraw-Hill.

Lazarus, R.S. (1984). Puzzles in the study of daily hassles. *Journal of Behavioral Medicine*, 7: 375–89.

Lazarus, R.S. (1991a). *Emotion and Adaptation*. New York: Oxford University Press.

Lazarus, R.S. (1991b). Psychological stress in the workplace. In P. Perrewe (ed.), *Handbook on Job Stress*. Special issue of *Journal of Social Behavior and Personality*, 6: 1–13.

Lazarus, R.S. (1993a). From psychological stress to the emotions: a history of changing outlooks. *Annual Review of Psychology*, 44: 1–21.

Lazarus, R.S. (1993b). Coping theory and research: past, present and future. *Psychosomatic Medicine*, 55: 234–47.

Lazarus, R.S. (1999). *Stress and Emotion: A New Synthesis*. New York: Springer Verlag.

Lazarus, R.S. (2000). Toward better research on stress and coping. *American Psychologist*, 55: 665–73.

Lazarus, R.S. and Folkman, S. (1984). *Stress, Appraisal, and Coping*. New York: Springer Verlag.

Lazarus, R.S., Kanner, A.D. and Folkman, S. (1980). Emotions: a cognitive-phenomenological analysis. In R. Plutchik and H. Kellerman (eds), *Theories of Emotions*. New York: Academic Press, pp. 189–217.

Lazarus, R.S. and Launier, R. (1978). Stress related transactions between person and environment. In L.A. Pervin and M. Lewis (eds), *Perspectives in International Psychology*. New York: Plenum.

Lazovitch, D. and Forster, J. (2005). Indoor tanning by adolescents: prevalence, practices and policies. *European Journal of Cancer*, 41: 20–7.

Lear, S.A. Ignaszewski, A., Linden, W. et al. (2003). The Extensive Lifestyle Management Intervention (ELMI) following cardiac rehabilitation trial. *European Heart Journal*, 24: 1920–7.

Lee, A., Cheng, F.F., Fung, Y. et al. (2006a). Can health promoting schools contribute to the better health and wellbeing of young people? The Hong Kong experience. *Journal of Epidemiology and Community Health*, 60: 530–6.

Lee, B.T., Chen, C., Yueh, J.H. et al. (2010). Computer-based learning module increases shared decision making in breast reconstruction. *Annals of Surgical Oncology*, 17: 738–43.

Lee, C. (1999). Health, stress and coping among women caregivers: a review. *Journal of Health Psychology*, 4: 27–40.

Lee, C. (2001). Experiences of family caregiving among older Australian women. *Journal of Health Psychology*, 6: 393–404.

Lee, E.-H., Chun, M., Kang, S. et al. (2004). Validation of the Functional Assessment of Cancer Therapy-General (FACT-G) scale for measuring the health-related quality of life in Korean women with breast cancer. *Japanese Journal of Clinical Oncology*, 34: 393–9.

Lee, I.-M., Rexrode, K.M., Cook, N.R. et al. (2001). Physical activity and coronary heart disease in women: is 'no pain, no gain' passé? *Journal of the American Medical Association*, 285: 1447–54.

Lee, S.J., Back, A.L., Block, S.D. and Stewart, S.K. (2002). Enhancing physician–patient communication. *Hematology*, 464–83.

Lee, V., Cohen, S.R., Edgar, L. et al. (2006b). Meaning-making intervention during breast and colorectal cancer treatment improves self-esteem, optimism, and self-efficacy. *Social Science & Medicine*, 62: 3133–45.

Leeks, K.D., Hopkins, D.P., Soler, R.E. et al. (2010). Worksite-based incentives and competitions to reduce tobacco use: a systematic review. *American Journal of Preventive Medicine*, 38(2 Suppl): S263–74.

Lefkowitz, R.J. and Willerson, J.T. (2001). Prospects for cardiovascular research. *Journal of the American Medical Association*, 285: 581–7.

Leigh, B.C. (2002). Alcohol and condom use: a meta-analysis of event level studies. *Sexually Transmitted Diseases*, 29: 476–82.

Leon, D.A. and McCambridge, J. (2006). Liver cirrhosis mortality rates in Britain from 1950 to 2002: an analysis of routine data. *The Lancet*, 367: 52–6.

Leonard, M.T., Cano, A. and Johansen, A.B. (2006). Chronic pain in a couples context: a review and integration of theoretical models and empirical evidence. *Journal of Pain*, 7: 377–90.

Lépine, J.P. and Briley, M. (2004). The epidemiology of pain in depression. *Human Psychopharmacology*, 19: S3–7.

Lerman, C. and Croyle, R. (1994). Psychological issues in genetic testing for breast cancer susceptibility. *Archives of Internal Medicine*, 154: 609–16.

Lerman, C., Hughes, C., Croyle, R.T. et al. (2000). Prophylactic surgery and surveillance practices one year following BRCA1/2 genetic testing. *Preventative Medicine*, 1: 75–80.

Lerman, C., Marshall, J. and Caminerio, A. (1996). Genetic testing for colon cancer susceptibility: anticipated reactions of patients and challenges to providers. *International Journal of Cancer*, 69: 58–61.

Leserman, J., Jackson, E.D., Petitto, J.M. et al. (1999). Progression to AIDS: The effects of stress, depressive symptoms, and social support. *Psychosomatic Medicine* 61(3): 397–406.

Leskin, G.A., Kaloupek, D.G. and Keane, T.M. (1998). Treatment for traumatic memories: review and recommendations. *Clinical Psychology Review*, 18: 983–1002.

Leslie, W.S., Hankey, C.R., Matthews, D. et al. (2004). A transferable programme of nutritional counselling for rehabilitation following myocardial infarction: a randomised controlled study. *European Journal of Clinical Nutrition*, 58: 778–86.

Leung, P.Y., Chan, C.L.W. and Ng, S.M. (2007). Tranquil acceptance coping: Eastern cultural beliefs as a source of strength among Chinese women with breast cancer. Paper presented at the International Psycho-Oncology Society (IPOS) conference, London, September 2007.

Leveälahti, H., Tishelman, C. and Öhlén, J. (2007). Framing the onset of lung cancer biographically: narratives of continuity and disruption. *Psycho-Oncology*, 16: 466–73.

Leventhal, E.A. and Crouch, M. (1997). Are there differences in perceptions of illness across the lifespan? In K.J. Petrie and J. Weinman (eds), *Perceptions of Health and Illness*. Amsterdam: Harwood Academic, pp. 77–102.

Leventhal, E.A., Hansell, S., Diefenbach, M., Leventhal, H. and Glass, D.C. (1996). Negative affect and self-report of physical symptoms: two longitudinal studies of older adults. *Health Psychology*, 15: 193–9.

Leventhal, H. and Coleman, S. (1997). Quality of life: a process view. *Psychology and Health*, 12: 753–67.

Leventhal, H. and Diefenbach, M. (1991). The active side of illness cognition. In J.A. Skelton and R.T. Croyle (eds), *Mental Representations in Health and Illness*. New York: Springer Verlag.

Leventhal, H., Diefenbach, M. and Leventhal, E. (1992). Illness cognition: using common sense to understand treatment adherence and effect cognitive interactions. *Cognitive Therapy and Research*, 16(2): 143–63.

Leventhal, H., Easterling, D.V., Coons, H. et al. (1986). Adaptation to chemotherapy treatments. In B. Anderson (ed.), *Women with Cancer*. New York: Springer Verlag.

Leventhal, H., Meyer, D. and Nerenz, D. (1980). The common sense model of illness danger. In S. Rachman (ed.), *Medical Psychology*, Vol. 2. New York: Pergamon.

Leventhal, H., Nerenz, D.R. and Steele, D.J. (1984). Illness representations and coping with health threats. In A. Baum, S.E. Taylor and J.E. Singer (eds), *Handbook of Psychology and Health: Social Psychological Aspects of Health*, Vol. 4. Hillsdale, NJ: Lawrence Erlbaum.

Leventhal, H., Patrick-Miller, L. and Leventhal, E.A. (1998). It's long-term stressors that take a toll: comment on Cohen et al. (1998). *Health Psychology*, 17: 211–13.

Leventhal, H. and Tomarken, A. (1987). Stress and illness: perspectives from health psychology. In S.V. Kasl and C.L. Cooper (eds), *Research Methods in Stress and Health Psychology*. London: Wiley.

Levine, R.M. and Reicher, S. (1996). Making sense of symptoms: self categorization and the meaning of illness/injury. *British Journal of Social Psychology*, 35: 245–56.

Levinson, D.J., Darrow, C.N., Klein, E.B. et al (1978). *The Seasons of a Man's Life*. New York: A.A. Knopf.

Levy, L., Patterson, R.E., Kristal, A.R. and Li, S.S. (2000). How well do consumers understand percentage daily value of food labels? *American Journal of Health Promotion*, 14: 157–60.

Lewin, B., Robertson, I.H., Irving, J.B. and Campbell, M. (1992). Effects of self-help post-myocardial-infarction rehabilitation on psychological adjustment and use of health services. *The Lancet*, 339: 1036–40.

Lewis, C.L. and Brown, S.C. (2002). Coping strategies of female adolescents with HIV/AIDS. *The Association of Black Nursing Faculty*, 13: 72–7.

Lewis, G., Bebbington, P., Brugha, T. et al. (1998). Socioeconomic status, standard of living, and neurotic disorder. *The Lancet*, 352: 605–9.

Lewis, S.C., Dennis, M.D., O'Rourke, S.J. and Sharpe, M. (2001). Negative attitudes among short-term stroke survivors predict worse long-term survival. *Stroke*, 32: 1640–5.

Ley, P. (1988). *Communicating with Patients. Improving Communication, Satisfaction, and Compliance*. London: Chapman Hall.

Ley, P. (1997). Compliance among patients. In A. Baum, S. Newman, J. Weinman, R. West and C. McManus (eds), *Cambridge Handbook of Psychology, Health and Medicine*. Cambridge: Cambridge University Press.

Lichtenberg, P., Heresco-Levy, U. and Nitzan, U. (2004). The ethics of the placebo in clinical practice. *Journal of Medical Ethics* 30: 551–4.

Lichtenstein, P. and Pedersen, N.L. (1995). Social relationships, stressful life events, and self-reported physical health: genetic and environmental influences. *Psychology and Health*, 10: 295–319.

Lim, A.S.H. and Bishop, G.D. (2000). The role of attitudes and beliefs in differential health care utilisation among Chinese in Singapore. *Psychology and Health*, 14: 965–77.

Lim, J., Maclurcan, M., Price, M., et al. (2004). Experiences of receiving genetic mutation status for women at increased risk for hereditary breast cancer. *Journal of Genetic Counselling*, 13: 113–15.

Lim, S.S., Vos, T., Flaxman, A.D. et al. (2013). A comparative risk assessment of burden of disease and injury attributable to 67 risk factors and risk factor clusters in 21 regions, 1990–2010: a systematic analysis for the Global Burden of Disease Study 2010. *Lancet* 380(9859): 2224–60.

Lin, E.H.B., Katon, W., von Korff, M. et al. (2004). Relationship of depression and diabetes self care, medication adherence and preventive care. *Diabetes Care*, 27: 2154–60.

Lincoln, K.D., Chatters, L.M. and Taylor, R.J. (2003). Psychological distress among Black and White Americans: differential effects of social support, negative interaction and personal control. *Journal of Health and Social Behavior*, 44: 390–407.

Linden, W., Gerin, W. and Davidson, K. (2003). Cardiovascular reactivity: status quo and a research agenda for the new millennium. *Psychosomatic Medicine*, 65: 5–8.

Linden, W., Stossel, C. and Maurice, J. (1996). Psychosocial treatment for cardiac patients: a meta-analysis. *Archives of Internal Medicine*, 156: 745–62.

Lindsay, S., Smith, S., Bellaby, P. et al. (2009). The health impact of an online heart disease support group: a comparison of moderated versus unmoderated support. *Health Education Research*, 24: 646–54.

Linegar, J., Chesson, C. and Nice, D. (1991). Physical fitness gains following simple environmental change. *American Journal of Preventive Medicine*, 7: 298–310.

Liossi, C., White, P., Franck, L. et al. (2007). Parental pain expectancy as a mediator between child expected and experienced procedure-related pain intensity during painful medical procedures. *The Clinical Journal of Pain*, 23: 392–9.

Liossi, C., White, P. and Hatira, P. (2006). Randomised clinical trial of a local anaesthetic versus a combination of self-hypnosis with a local anaesthetic in the management of paediatric procedure-related pain. *Health Psychology*, 25: 307–15.

Liossi, C., White, P. and Hatira, P. (2009). A randomized clinical trial of a brief hypnosis intervention to control venepuncture-related pain of paediatric cancer patients. *Pain*, 142: 255–63.

Lipton, A.A. and Simon, F.S. (1985). Psychiatric diagnosis in a state hospital: Manhattan state revisited. *Hospital and Community Psychiatry*, 36: 368–73.

Litt, M.D., Nye, C. and Shafer, D. (1995). Preparation for oral surgery: evaluating elements of coping. *Journal of Behavioral Medicine*, 18: 435–59.

Little, M. and Sayers, E.-J. (2004). While there's life … hope and the experience of cancer. *Social Science and Medicine*, 59: 1329–37.

Llewellyn, C.D., McGurk, M. and Weinman, J. (2007). The relationship between the Patient Generated Index (PGI) and measures of HR-QoL following diagnosis with head and neck cancer: are illness and treatment perceptions determinants of judgment-based outcomes? *British Journal of Health Psychology*, 12: 421–37.

Lo, B. (2006). HPV vaccine and adolescents' sexual activity. *British Medical Journal*, 332: 1106–7.

Lo, B. (2007). Human papillomavirus vaccination programmes. *British Medical Journal*, 335: 357–8.

Lo, R. (1999). Correlates of expected success at adherence to health regimen of people with IDDM. *Journal of Advanced Nursing*, 30: 418–24.

Lo, S.F., Hayter M., Hsu M. et al. (2010). The effectiveness of multimedia learning education programs on knowledge, anxiety and pressure garment compliance in patients undergoing burns rehabilitation in Taiwan: an experimental study. *Journal of Clinical Nursing*, 19: 129–37.

Lobb, E.A., Butow, P.N., Kenny, D.T. and Tattersall, M.H. (1999). Communicating prognosis in early breast cancer: do women understand the language used? *Medical Journal of Australia*, 171: 290–4.

Lobchuk, M.M. and Vorauer, J.D. (2003). Family care-giving, perspective-taking, and accuracy in estimating cancer patient symptom experiences. *Social Science and Medicine*, 57: 2379–84.

Lock, K., Pomerleau, J., Causer, L., Altmann, D.R. and McKee, M. (2005). The global burden of disease attributable to low consumption of fruit and vegetables: implications for the global strategy on diet. *Bulletin of the World Health Organization*, 83: 100–8.

Locke, E.A. and Latham, G.P. (2002). Building a practically useful theory of goal setting and task motivation: a 35-year odyssey. *American Psychologist*, 57: 705–17.

Locke E. A., Latham G. P. (2004). What should we do about motivation theory? Six recommendations for the 21st century. *Acad Manage Rev*; 29: 388–403.

Locke, G.R., III, Weaver, A.L., Melton, L.J., III and Talley, N.J. (2004). Psychosocial factors are linked to functional gastrointestinal disorders: a population based nested case-control study. *American Journal of Gastroenterology*, 99: 350–7.

Lodder, L., Frets, P.G., Trijsburg, R.W. et al. (2001). Psychological impact of receiving a BRCA1/BRCA2 test result. *American Journal of Medical Genetics*, 98: 15–24.

Loewenthal, K.M. (2007). *Religion, Culture and Mental Health*. Cambridge: Cambridge University Press.

Löf, M., Sardin, S. Lagiou. P. et al. (2007). Dietary fat and breast cancer risk in the Swedish women's lifestyle and health cohort. *British Journal of Cancer*, 97: 1570–6.

Logan, T.K., Cole, J. and Leukefeld, C. (2002). Women, sex, and HIV: social and contextual factors, meta-analysis of published interventions, and implications for practice and research. *Psychological Bulletin*, 128: 851–85.

Lok, C.F. and Bishop, G.D. (1999). Emotion control, stress, and health. *Psychology and Health*, 14: 813–27.

Lomas, J. (1991). Words without action? The production, dissemination, and impact of consensus recommendations. *Annual Reviews in Public Health*, 12: 41–65.

Longabaugh, R. and Morgenstern, J. (1999). Cognitive-behavioural coping-skills therapy for alcohol dependence. *Alcohol Research and Health*, 23: 78–85.

Longo, D.R., Johnson, J.C., Kruse, R.L. et al. (2001). A prospective investigation of the impact of smoking bans on tobacco cessation and relapse. *Tobacco Control*, 10: 267–72.

Lopez, S.J., Pedrotti, J.T. and Snyder, C.R. (eds) (2014). *Positive Psychology: The Scientific and Practical Exploration of Human Strengths*. 3rd edn. Los Angeles: Sage.

Lorentzen, C., Ommundsen, Y. and Hole, I. (2007). Psychosocial correlates of stages of change in physical activity in an adult community sample. *European Journal of Sports Science*, 7: 93–106.

Lorenz, F.O., Wickrama, K.A.S., Conger, R.D. and Elder, G.H. Jr. (2006). The short-term and decade-long effects of divorce on women's midlife health. *Journal of Health and Social Behavior*, 47: 111–25.

Lorig, K. (1996). *Patient Education: A Practical Approach*. Newbury Park, CA: Sage.

Lorig, K. and Holman, H. (1989). Long-term outcomes of an arthritis self-management study: effects of reinforcement efforts. *Social Science and Medicine*, 29: 221–4.

Lorig, K., Ritter, P.L., Villa, F.J. et al. (2009). Community-based peer-led diabetes self-management: a randomized trial. *Diabetes Education*, 35: 641–51.

Lorig, K., Sobel, D.S., Stewart, A.L. et al. (1999). Evidence suggesting that a chronic disease self-management program can improve health status while reducing hospitalisation. *Medical Care*, 37: 5–14.

Lotrean, L.M., Dijk, F., Mesters, I. et al. (2010). Evaluation of a peer-led smoking prevention programme for Romanian adolescents. *Health Education Research*, 25: 803–14.

Louria, D. (1988). Some concerns about educational approaches in AIDS prevention. In R. Schinazi and A. Nahmias (eds), *AIDS Children, Adolescents and Heterosexual Adults*. New York: Elsevier Science.

Louw, Q.A., Morris, L.D. and Grimmer-Somers, K. (2007). The prevalence of low back pain in Africa: a systematic review. *BMC Musculoskeletal Disorders*, 8: 105.

Lovallo, W.R. (1997). *Stress and Health: Biological and Psychological Interactions*. Newbury Park, CA: Sage.

Lovallo, W. R. (2011). Do low levels of stress reactivity signal poor states of health? *Biological Psychology*, 86, 121–128. doi: 10.1016/ j.biopsycho.2010.01.006

Lovallo, W.R., Pincomb, G.A., Brackett, D.J. et al. (1990). Heart rate reactivity as a predictor of neuroendocrine responses to aversive and appetitive challenges. *Psychosomatic Medicine*, 52: 17–26.

Love, A., Street, A., Rar, R. et al. (2005). Social aspectsof care-giving for people living with motor neurone disease:their relationships to carer wellbeing. *Palliative and Supportive Care*, 3: 33–8.

Lovegrove, E., Rumsey, N., Harcourt, D. et al. (2000). Factors implicated in the decision whether or not to join the tamoxifen trial in women at high familial risk of breast cancer. *Psycho-Oncology*, 9: 193–202.

Low, C.A., Stanton, A.L. and Danoff-Burg, S. (2006). Expressive disclosure and benefit finding among breast cancer patients: mechanisms for positive health effects. *Health Psychology*, 25: 181–9.

Lowe, C.F., Horne, P.J., Tapper, K. et al. (2004). Effects of a peer-modelling and rewards based intervention to increase fruit and vegetable consumption in children. *European Journal of Clinical Nutrition*, 58: 510–22.

Lowe, R., Norman, P. and Bennett, P. (2000). Coping, emotion and perceived health following myocardial infarction. *British Journal of Health Psychology*, 5: 337–50.

Lowe, R., Vedhara, K., Bennett, P. et al. (2003). Emotion-related primary and secondary appraisals, adjustment and coping associations in women awaiting breast disease diagnosis. *British Journal of Health Psychology*, 8: 377–91.

Lowes, J. and Tiggemann, M. (2003). Body dissatisfaction and dieting awareness in young children. *British Journal of Health Psychology*, 8: 135–47.

Lox, C.L., Martin Ginis, K.A. and Petruzzello, S.J. (2006). *The Psychology of Exercise: Integrating Theory and Practice*, 2nd edn. Scottsdale, AZ: Holcomb Hathaway.

Lucas, R.E. and Fujita, F. (2000). Factors influencing the relations between extraversion and pleasure affect. *Journal of Personality and Social Psychology*, 79: 1039–56.

Luck, A., Pearson, S., Maddern, G. et al. (1999). Effects of video information on pre-colonoscopy anxiety and knowledge: a randomised trial. *Lancet*, 354: 2032–5.

Lumley, M.A., Leisen, J.C.C., Partridge, R.T. et al. Does emotional disclosure about stress improve health in rheumatoid arthritis? Randomized, controlled trials of written and spoken disclosure. *Pain*, 152: 866–77.

Luszczynska, A., Diehl, M., Gutiérrez-Doña, B. et al. (2004). Measuring one component of dispositional self-regulation: attention control in goal pursuit. *Personality and Individual Differences*, 37: 555–66.

Luszczynska, A. and Cieslak, R. (2009). Mediated effects of social support for healthy nutrition: fruit and vegetable intake across 8 months after myocardial infarction. *Behavioral Medicine*, 35: 30–8.

Luszczynska, A., Gutiérrez-Doña, B. and Schwarzer, R. (2005). Self-efficacy in various domains of human functioning: evidence from five countries. *International Journal of Psychology*, 40: 80–9.

Luszczynska, A. and Schwarzer, R. (2003). Planning and self-efficacy in the adoption and maintenance of breast self-examination: a longitudinal study on self-regulatory cognitions. *Psychology and Health*, 18: 93–108.

Luszczynska, A., Sobczyk, A. and Abraham, C. (2007). Planning to lose weight: randomized controlled trial of an implementation intention prompt to enhance weight reduction among overweight and obese women. *Health Psychology*, 26: 507–12.

Lv, J., Liu, Q.M., Ren, Y.L. et al. (2014). A community-based multilevel intervention for smoking, physical activity and diet: short-term findings from the Community Interventions for Health programme in Hangzhou, China. *Journal of Epidemiology and Community Health*, 68: 333–9.

Lyle, R.G., MacMillan, I., Forbat, L., et al. (2014). Scottish adolescents' sun-related behaviours, tanning attitudes and associations with skin cancer awareness: a cross-sectional study. *BMJ Open*, 4:e005137. doi:10.1136/bmjopen-2014-005137

Lyonette, C. and Yardley, L. (2003). The influence on carer well-being of motivations to care for older people and the relationship with the care recipient. *Ageing & Society*, 23: 487–506.

Lyons, K.S., Zarit, S.H., Sayer, A.G. and Whitlatch, C.J. (2002). Caregiving as a dyadic process: perspectives from caregiver and receiver. *Journal of Gerontology: Psychological Sciences,* 57B: 195–204.

MacBryde, C.M. and Blacklow, R.S. (1970). *Signs and Symptoms: Applied Pathologic Physiology and Clinical Interpretation*, 5th edn. Philadelphia, PA: Lippincott.

Macdonald, S., McMillan, T.M. and Kerr, J. (2010). Readability of information leaflets given to attenders at hospital with a head injury. *Emergency Medicine Journal*, 27: 279–82.

MacInnes J. (2013). Relationships between illness representations, treatment beliefs and the performance of self-care in heart failure: a cross-sectional survey. *European Journal of Cardiovascular Nursing*, 12:536–43.

MacInnes, J. (2013a) An exploration of illness representations and treatment beliefs in heart failure. *Journal of Clinical Nursing*, 23: 1249–56.

Macintyre, S. (1986). The patterning of health by social position in contemporary Britain: directions for sociological research. *Social Science and Medicine*, 23: 393–415.

Macintyre, S. and Ellaway, A. (1998). *Ecological Approaches: Rediscovering the Role of the Physical and Social Environment*. Oxford: Oxford University Press.

Macintyre, S., Hunt, K and Sweeting, H (1996). Gender differences in health: are things really as simple as they seem? *Social Science & Medicine*, 42: 617–24.

MacKellar, D., Gallagher, K.M., Finlayson, T. et al. (2007). Surveillance of HIV risk and prevention behaviors of men who have sex with men – a national application of venue based, time-space sampling. *Public Health Reports*, 122 (Suppl.1), 39–47.

Mackenzie, J. (2006) 'Stigma and dementia—East European and South Asian family carers negotiating stigma in the UK', *Dementia: The International Journal of Social Research and Practice*, 5(2): 233–48.

MacNee, W. (2004). Guidelines for chronic obstructive pulmonary disease (editorial). *British Medical Journal*, 329: 361–3.

MacNicol, S.A.M., Murray, S.M. and Austin, E.J. (2003). Relationships between personality, attitudes and dietary behaviour in a group of Scottish adolescents. *Personality and Individual Differences*, 35: 1753–64.

Macrodimitris, D. and Endler, N.S. (2001). Coping, control, and adjustment in Type 2 diabetes. *Health Psychology*, 20: 208–16.

Maddern, L., Cadogan, J.C. and Emerson, M. (2006). 'Outlook': a psychosocial service for children with a different appearance. *Clinical Child Psychology & Psychiatry,* 11: 431–43.

Maddux, J.E. (2009). Self-efficacy: the power of believing you can. In S.J. Lopez and C.R. Snyder (eds), *Oxford Handbook of Positive Psychology*. New York: Oxford University Press, pp. 335–44.

Maes, S., Kittel, F., Scholten, H. and Verhoeven, C. (1990). Effects of the Brabantia project, a Dutch wellness-health programme at the worksite. *American Journal of Public Health*, 88: 1037–41.

Maes, S., Leventhal, H. and de Ridder, D.T. (1996). Coping with chronic disease. In M. Zeidner and N.S. Endler (eds), *Handbook of Coping*. New York: Wiley.

Maes, S. and van der Doef, M. (2004). Worksite health promotion. In A. Kaptein and J. Weinman (eds), *Health Psychology*. Oxford: BPS Blackwell, pp. 358–83.

Magar, E.C.E., Phillips, L.H. and Hosie, J.A. (2008). Self-regulation and risk-taking. *Personality & Individual Differences*, 45: 153–9.

Magarey, A., Daniels, L., Boulton, T. et al. (2003). Predicting obesity in early adulthood from childhood and parental obesity. *International Journal of Obesity*, 27: 505–13.

Magarey, A., Daniels, L.A. and Smith, A. (2001). Fruit and vegetable intakes of Australians aged 2 –18 years: an evaluation of the 1995 National Nutrition Survey data. *Australian and New Zealand Journal of Public Health*, 25: 155–61.

Magee, C. A. and Heaven, P. C. L. (2011). Big five personality factors, obesity and 2-year weight gain in Australian adults. *Journal of Research in Personality*, 45: 332–5.

Mager, W.M. and Andrykowski, M.A. (2002). Communication in the cancer 'bad news' consultation: patient perceptions and psychological adjustment. *Psycho-Oncology*, 11: 35–46.

Magklara, E., Burton, C. and Morrison, V. (2014) Does self-efficacy influence recovery and well-being in osteoarthritis patients undergoing joint replacement? A systematic review. *Clinical Rehabilitation,* DOI: 10.1177/0269215514527843

Magni, G., Moreschi, C., Rigatti-Luchini, S. and Merskey, H. (1994). Prospective study on the relationship between depressive symptoms and chronic musculoskeletal pain. *Pain*, 56: 289–97.

Magnusson, J.E. and Becker, W.J. (2003). Migraine frequency and intensity: relationship with disability and psychological factors. *Headache*, 43: 1049–59.

Magri, F., Cravello, L., Barili, L. et al. (2006). Stress and dementia: the role of the hypothalamic-pituitary-adrenal axis. *Aging & Clinical Experimental Research*, 18: 167–70.

Maguire, P. and Faulkner, A. (1988). How to improve the counselling skills of doctors and nurses in cancer care. *British Medical Journal*, 297: 847–9.

Maguire, P. and Pitceathly, C. (2002). Key communication skills and how to acquire them. *British Medical Journal*, 325: 697–700.

Mahalik, J.R., Burns, S.M. and Syzdek, M. (2007). Masculinity and perceived normative health behaviors as predictors of men's health behaviors. *Social Science & Medicine*, 64: 2201–9.

Mahler H.I.K., Kulik, J.A., Gerrard, M. and Gibbons, F.X. (2013). Effects of photoaging information and UV photo on sun protection intentions and behaviours: a cross-regional comparison. *Psychology & Health*, 28: 1009–32.

Maisto, S.A. and Connors, G.J. (1992). Using subject and collateral reports to measure alcohol consumption. In R.Z. Litten and J.P. Allen (eds), *Measuring Alcohol Consumption: Psychosocial and Biochemical Methods*. New Jersey: Humana Press.

Malfetti, J. (1985). Public information and education sections of the report of the Presidential Commission on Drunk Driving: a critique and a discussion of research implication. *Accident Analysis and Prevention*, 17: 347–53.

Maliski, S.L., Heilemann, M.V. and McCorkle, R. (2002). From 'death sentence' to 'good cancer': couples' transformation of a prostate cancer diagnosis. *Nursing Research*, 51: 391–7.

Malkin, C.J., Pugh, P.J., Morris, P.D. et al. (2010). Low serum testosterone and increased mortality in men with coronary heart disease. *Heart* 96: 1821–5.

Maly, M.R., Costigan, P.A. and Olney, S.J. (2007). Self-efficacy mediates walking performance in older adults with knee osteoarthritis. *Journal of Gerontology A: Biological Sciences and Medical Sciences*, 62: 1142–6.

Mandelblatt, J. and Kanesky, P.A. (1995). Effectiveness of interventions to enhance physician screening for breast cancer. *Journal of Family Practice*, 40: 162–71.

Maniadakis, N. and Gray, A. (2000). The economic burden of back pain in the UK. *Pain*, 84: 95–103.

Mann, T., de Ridder, D. and Fujita, K. (2013). Self regulation of health behavior: social psychological approaches to goal setting and goal striving. *Health Psychology*, 32: 487–98. Doi:10.1037/a0028533

Manne, S.L., Norton, T.R., Ostroff, J.S. et al. (2007). Protective buffering and psychological distress among couples coping with breast cancer: the moderating role of relationship satisfaction. *Journal of Family Psychology* 21: 380–8.

Manning, P.K. and Fabrega, H. (1973). The experience of self and body: health and illness in the Chiapas Highlands. In G. Psathas (ed.), *Phenomenological Sociology: Issues and Applications.* New York: Wiley.

Mannino, D.M. (2003). Chronic obstructive pulmonary disease: definition and epidemiology. *Respiratory Care*, 48: 1185–91.

Manstead, A.S.R. (2000). The role of moral norm in the attitude–behavior relationship. In D.J. Terry and M.A. Hogg (eds), *Attitudes, Behavior and Social Context: The Role of Norms and Group Membership*. Mahwah, NJ: Lawrence Erlbaum.

Mantyselka, P., Kumpusalo, E., Ahonen, R. et al. (2001). Pain as a reason to visit the doctor: a study in Finnish primary health care. *Pain*, 89: 175–80.

Marcell, A.V., Ford, C.A., Plock, J.H. et al. (2007). Masculine beliefs, parental communication, and male adolescents' health care use. *Pediatrics*, 119: 966–75.

Marcus, B.H., Rakowski, W. and Rossi, J.S. (1992). Assessing motivational readiness and decision-making for exercise. *Health Psychology*, 22: 3–16.

Marcus, B.H., Selby, V.C., Niaura, R.S. and Rossi, J.S. (1992). Self-efficacy and the stages of exercise behaviour change. *Research Quarterly in Exercise and Sport*, 63: 60–6.

Marewski J.N. and Gigerenzer G. (2012). Heuristic decision making in medicine. *Dialogues in Clinical Neuroscience*, 14: 77–89.

Marinus, J., Ramaker, C., van Hilten, J.J. and Stiggelbout, A.M. (2002). Health related quality of life in Parkinson's disease: a systematic review of disease specific instruments. *Journal of Neurology, Neurosurgery and Psychiatry*, 72: 241–8.

Markovitz, J.H., Matthews, K.A., Kannel, W.B. et al. (1993). Psychological predictors of hypertension in the Framingham study: is there tension in hypertension? *Journal of the American Medical Association*, 270: 2439–43.

Marks, D.F. (ed.) (2002). *The Health Psychology Reader*. London: Sage.

Marks, D.F., Murray, M., Evans, B. and Willig, C. (2000). *Health Psychology: Theory, Research and Practice*. London: Sage.

Marks, I., Lovell, K., Noshirvani, H. et al. (1998). Treatment of post-traumatic stress disorder by exposure and/or cognition restructuring. *Archives of General Psychiatry*, 55: 317–25.

Marks, J.T., Campbell, M.K., Ward, D.S. et al. (2006). A comparison of Web and print media for physical activity promotion among adolescent girls. *Journal of Adolescent Health*, 39: 96–104.

Marlatt, A. (1996). Taxonomy of high-risk situations for alcohol relapse: evolution and development of a cognitive-behavioral model. *Addiction*, 91: 37–50.

Marlatt, G.A., Baer, J.S., Donovan, D.M. and Kivlahan, D.R. (1986). Addictive behaviors: etiology and treatment. *Annual Review of Psychology*, 39: 223–52.

Marmot, M. (2005). Social determinants of health inequalities. *Lancet*, 365: 1099–104.

Marmot, M., Atinmo, T., Byers, T. et al. (2007). *Food, Nutrition, Physical Activity, and the Prevention of Cancer: A Global Perspective.* Washington, DC: American Institute for Cancer Research.

Marmot, M.G., Davey-Smith, G. and Stansfield, S. (1991). Health inequalities among British civil servants: the Whitehall Study II. *The Lancet*, 337: 1387–93.

Marmot, M.G., Fuhrer, R., Ettner, S.L. et al. (1998). Contribution of psychosocial factors to socioeconomic differences in health. *The Milbank Quarterly*, 76: 403–48.

Marmot, M.G. and Madge, N. (1987). An epidemiological perspective on stress and health. In S.V. Kasl and C.L. Cooper (eds), *Research Methods in Stress and Health Psychology*. London: Wiley.

Marmot, M., Ryff, C.D., Bumpass, L.L. et al. (1997). Social inequalities in health: next questions and converging evidence. *Social Science and Medicine*, 44: 901–10.

Marmot, M.G., Shipley, M.J. and Rose, G. (1984). Inequalities in health: specific explanations of a general pattern? *The Lancet*, i, 1003–6.

Marsh, A., Smith, L., Piek, J. and Saunders, B. (2003). The Purpose in Life scale: psychometric properties for social drinkers and drinkers in alcohol treatment. *Educational & Psychological Measurement*, 63: 859–71.

Marshall, A.L., Leslie, E.R., Bauman, A.E. et al. (2003). Print versus website physical activity programs: a randomized trial. *American Journal of Preventive Medicine*, 25: 88–94.

Marsland, A.L., Bachen, E.A., Cohen, S. et al. (2002). Stress, immune reactivity and susceptibility to infectious diseases. *Physiology & Behaviour*, 77: 711–16.

Marteau, T.M., Kidd, J., Cuddeford, L. and Walker, P. (1996). Reducing anxiety in women referred for colposcopy using an information booklet. *British Journal of Health Psychology*, 1: 181–9.

Marteau, T.M. and Kinmouth, A.L. (2002). Screening for cardiovascular risk: public health imperative or matter for individual informed choice? *British Medical Journal*, 325: 78–80.

Martin, F., Camfield, L., Rodham, K. et al. (2007). Twelve years' experience with the Patient Generated Index (PGI) of quality of life: a graded systematic review. *Quality of Life Research,* 16(4): 705–15.

Martin, J., Sabugal, G.M., Rubio, R. et al. (2001). Outcomes of a health education intervention in a sample of patients infected by HIV, most of them injection drug users: possibilities and limitations. *AIDS Care*, 13: 467–73.

Martin, L.M., Calle, E.E., Wingo, P.A. and Heath, C.W., Jr (1996). Comparison of mammography and Pap test use from the 1987 and 1992 National Health Interview Surveys: are we closing the gaps? *American Journal Preventive Medicine*, 12: 82–90.

Martin, P., Rosa, G., Siegler, I.C. et al. (2006). Personality and longevity: findings from the Georgia centenarian study. *Age*, 28: 343–52.

Martin, R. and Hewstone, M. (2003). Majority versus minority influence: When, not whether, source status instigates heuristic or systematic processing. *European Journal of Social Psychology,* 33: 313–30.

Martin, R., Lemos, C., Rothrock, N. et al. (2004). Gender disparities in common-sense models of illness among myocardial infarction victims. *Health Psychology*, 23: 345–53.

Martin, R. and Leventhal, H. (2004). Symptom perception and health-care seeking behavior. In J.M. Raczynski and L.C. Leviton (eds), *Handbook of Clinical Health Psychology*, Vol. 2. Washington, DC: American Psychological Association, pp. 299–328.

Martin, R., Rothrock, N., Leventhal, H. and Leventhal, E. (2003). Common sense models of illness: implications for symptom perception and health-related behaviours. In J. Suls and K.A. Wallston (eds), *Social Psychological Foundations of Health and Illness*. Oxford: Blackwell.

Martin Ginis, K.A., Burke, S.M. and Gauvin, L. (2007). Exercising with others exacerbates the negative effects of mirrored environments on sedentary women's feeling states. *Psychology & Health*, 22: 945–62.

Marucha, P.T., Kiecolt-Glaser, J.K. and Favgehi, M. (1998). Mucosal wound healing is impaired by examination stress. *Psychosomatic Medicine*, 60: 362–5.

Maslach, C. (1982). *Burnout: The Cost of Caring*. Englewood Cliffs, NJ: Prentice Hall.

Maslach, C. (1997). Burnout in health professionals. In A. Baum, S. Newman, J. Weinman, R. West and C. McManus (eds), *Cambridge Handbook of Psychology, Health and Medicine*. Cambridge: Cambridge University Press.

Massie, M.J. (2004). Prevalence of depression on patients with cancer. *Journal of the National Cancer Institute Monographs*, 32, 57–71.

Masui, Y., Gondo, Y., Inagaki, H. and Hirose, N. (2006). Do personality characteristics predict longevity? Findings from the Tokyo centenarian study. *Age*, 28: 353–61.

Matano, R.A., Futa, K.T., Wanat, S.F. et al. (2000). The Employee Stress and Alcohol Project: the development of a computer-based alcohol abuse prevention program for employees. *Journal of Behavioral Health Services Research*, 27: 152–65.

Matarazzo, J.D. (1980). Behavioral health and behavioral medicine: frontiers for a new health psychology. *American Psychologist*, 35: 807–17.

Matarazzo, J.D. (1984). Behavioral health: a 1990 challenge for the health sciences professions. In J.D. Matarazzo, N.E. Miller, S.M. Weiss, J.A. Herd and S.M. Weiss (eds), *Behavioral Health: A Handbook of Health Enhancement and Disease Prevention*. New York: Wiley.

Mathers, B.M., Degenhardt, L., Phillips, B., et al. (2008). Global epidemiology of injecting drug use and HIV among people who inject drugs: a systematic review. *The Lancet*, 372: 1733–45.

Mathes, T., Pieper, D., Antoine, S.L. et al. (2013) Adherence-enhancing interventions for highly active antiretroviral therapy in HIV-infected patients – a systematic review. *HIV Medicine*, 14: 583–95.

Mathews, C., Guttmacher, S.J., Coetzee, N. et al. (2002). Evaluation of a video based health education strategy to improve sexually transmitted disease partner notification in South Africa. *Sexually Transmitted Infections*, 78: 53–7.

Matthews, K.A., Siegel, J.M., Kuller, L.H. et al. (1983). Determinants of decision to seek medical treatment by patients with acute myocardial infarction symptoms. *Journal of Personality and Social Psychology*, 44: 1144–56.

Mattocks, C., Ness, A., Deere, K. et al. (2008). Early life determinants of physical activity in 11 to 12 year olds: cohort study. *British Medical Journal*, 336: 26–9.

Matza, L.S., Swensen, A.R., Flood, E.M. et al. (2004). Assessment of health-related quality of life in children: a review of conceptual, methodological, and regulatory issues. *Value in Health*, 7: 79–92.

Mayhew, A, Mullins T.L.K., Ding, L. et al. (2014). Risk perceptions and subsequent sexual behaviors after HPV vaccination in adolescents. *Pediatrics,* 133, 404–4011 DOI: 10.1542/peds.2013–2822

McCabe, K.M., Yeh, M., Lau, A. et al. (2005). Racial/ethnic differences in caregiver strain and perceived social support among parents of youth with emotional and behavioral problems. *Mental Health Services Research*, 5: 137–47.

McCaffery, J.M., Papandonatos, G.D., Stanton, C. et al. (2008). Depressive symptoms and cigarette smoking in twins from the National Longitudinal Study of Adolescent Health. *Health Psychology*, 27: S207–S215.

McCann, B.S., Retzlaff, B.M., Dowdy, A.A. et al. (1990). Promoting adherence to low-fat, low-cholesterol diets: review and recommendations. *Journal of the American Dietetic Association*, 90: 1408–14.

McCann, J., Stockton, D. and Goddard, S. (2002). Impact of false-positive mammography on subsequent screening attendance and risk of cancer. *Breast Cancer Research*, 4: R11.

McCarron, P., Davey-Smith, G. and Wormsley, J. (1994). Deprivation and mortality in Glasgow: changes from 1980 to 1992. *British Medical Journal*, 309: 1481–2.

McClenahan, R. and Weinman, J. (1998). Determinants of carer distress in non-acute stroke. *International Journal of Language and Communication Disorders*, 33: 138–43.

McCorkle, R., Strumpf, N., Nuamah, I. et al. (2000). A specialized home care intervention improves survival among older post-surgical cancer patients. *Journal of the American Geriatrics Society* 48(12): 1707–13.

McCracken, L.M. and Eccleston, C. (2003). Coping or acceptance: what to do about chronic pain? *Pain*, 105: 197–204.

McCracken, L.M., Sato, A. and Taylor, G.J. (2013). A trial of a brief group-based form of acceptance and commitment therapy (ACT) for chronic pain in general practice: Pilot outcome and process results. *Journal of Pain*, 14: 1398–406. 10.1016/j.jpain.2013.06.011 APA

McCrae, R.E. and Costa, P.T. (1987). Validation of the five-factor model of personality across instruments and observers. *Journal of Personality and Social Psychology*, 52: 81–90.

McCrae, R.E. and Costa, P.T. (1990). *Personality in Adulthood*. New York: Guilford Press.

McCrae, R.E., Costa, P.T., Ostendorf, F. et al. (2000). Nature over nurture: temperament, personality and life-span development. *Journal of Personality and Social Psychology*, 78: 173–86.

McCrae, R.R. (1990). Controlling neuroticism in the measurement of stress. *Stress Medicine*, 6: 237–40.

McCubbin, H.I. and Patterson, J.M. (1982). Family adaptations to crisis. In H.I. McCubbin, A. Cauble and J. Patterson (eds), *Family Stress, Coping and Social Support*. Springfield, IL: Charles Thomas.

McCubbin, H.I. and Patterson, J.M. (1983). The family stress process: the double ABCX model of adjustment and adaptation. In H.I. McCubbin, M.B. Sussman and J.M. Patterson (eds), *Social Stress and the Family: Advances and Developments in Family Stress Theory and Research*. New York: Haworth Press.

McDonald, H.P., Garg, A.X. and Haynes, R.B. (2002). Interventions to enhance patient adherence to medication prescriptions: scientific review. *Journal of the American Medical Association*, 288: 2868–79.

McElnay, J. and McCallion, C.R. (1998). Adherence and the elderly. In L.B. Myers and K. Midence (eds), *Adherence to Treatment in Medical Conditions*. Amsterdam: Harwood Academic.

McEwan, M.J., Espie, C.A. and Metcalfe, J. (2004). A systematic review of the contribution of qualitative research to the study of quality of life in children and adolescents with epilepsy. *Seizure*, 13: 3–14.

McEwen, B.S. (2008). Central effects of stress hormones in health and disease: understanding the protective and damaging effects of stress and stress mediators. *European Journal of Pharmacology*, 583: 174–85.

McGill, H.C. and Stern, M.P. (1979). Sex and athero-sclerosis. *Atherosclerosis Review*, 4: 157–248.

McGregor, B.A., Antoni, M.H., Boyers, A. et al. (2004). Cognitive-behavioral stress management increases benefit finding and immune function among women with early-stage breast cancer. *Journal of Psychosomatic Research*, 56: 1–8.

McGuire, W. (1985). Attitudes and attitude change. In G. Lindzey and E. Aronson (eds), *Handbook of Social Psychology*, Vol. 2. New York: Random House.

McHugh, P., Lewis, S., Ford, S. et al. (1995). The efficacy of audiotapes in promoting psychological well-being in cancer patients: a randomised, controlled trial. *British Journal of Cancer*, 71: 388–92.

McKee, H., Ntoumanis, N. and Smith, B. (2013). Weight maintenance: self-regulatory factors underpinning success and failure. *Psychology & Health*, 28: 1207–23.

McKenna, M.C., Zevon, M.A., Corn, B. and Rounds, J. (1999). Psychosocial factors and the development of breast cancer: a meta-analysis. *Health Psychology*, 18: 520–31.

McKenna, S.P. (2004). Assessing the quality of life in phases I and II anti-cancer drug trials: interviews versus questionnaires by Cox, K. (letter to the editor). *Social Science and Medicine*, 58: 659–60.

McKenna, S.P., Whalley, D. and Doward, L.C. (2000). Which outcomes are important in schizophrenia trials? *International Journal of Methods in Psychiatric Research*, 9 (suppl. 1): S58–67.

McKiernan, F.M. (1996). Bereavement and attitudes to death. In R.T. Woods (ed.), *Handbook of the Clinical Psychology of Ageing*. Chichester: Wiley.

McKirnan, D.J., Tolou-Shams, M., Courtenay-Quirk, C. et al. (2010). The treatment advocacy program: a randomized controlled trial of a peer-led safer sex intervention for

HIV-infected men who have sex with men. *Journal of Consulting and Clinical Psychology*, 78: 952–63.

McLeod, J.D. and Kessler, R.C. (1990). Socioeconomic status differences in vulnerability to undesirable life events. *Journal of Health and Social Behaviour*, 31: 162–72.

McManus, J. (2014) Promoting psychology in public health. *The Psychologist*, 27: 66.

McNair, D., Lorr, M. and Droppelman, L. (1971). *Manual for the Profile of Mood States*. San Diego, CA: Educational and Industrial Testing Service.

McNeill, L.H., Viswanath, K., Bennett, G.G. et al. (2007). Feasibility of using a web-based nutrition intervention among residents of multiethnic working-class neighborhoods. *Preventing Chronic Disease*, 4: A55.

McPherson, K.M., McNaughton, H. and Pentland, B. (2000). Information needs of families when one member of the family has a severe brain injury. *International Journal of Rehabilitation Research*, 23: 295–301.

McQuaid, E.L., Koinis-Mitchell, D., Walders, N. et al. (2007). Pediatric asthma morbidity: the importance of symptom perception and family response to symptoms. *Journal of Pediatric Psychology*, 32: 167–77.

McQuay, H.J. and Moore, R.A. (2005). Placebo. *Postgraduate Medical Journal*, 81: 155–60.

McVey, D. and Stapleton, J. (2000). Can anti-smoking television advertising affect smoking behaviour? Controlled trial of the Health Education Authority for England's anti-smoking TV campaign. *Tobacco Control*, 9: 273–82.

McVicar, A. (2003). Workplace stress in nursing: a literature review. *Journal of Advanced Nursing*, 44: 633–42.

Mead, G.E., Morley, W., Campbell, P. et al. (2009). Exercise for depression (intervention review). *Cochrane Library*, 2009, Issue 3.

Mechanic, D. (1962). The concept of illness behavior. *Journal of Chronic Disease*, 15: 189–94.

Mechanic, D. (1972). Social psychological factors affecting the presentation of bodily complaints. *New England Journal of Medicine*, 286: 1132–9.

Mechanic, D. (1978). *Medical Sociology*, 2nd edn. New York: Free Press.

Medley, A., Kennedy, C., O'Reilly, K. et al. (2009). Meta-analysis of peer education in developing countries. *AIDS Education and Prevention*, 21, 181–206.

Meechan, G., Collins, J. and Petrie, K. (2002). Delay in seeking medical care for self-detected breast symptoms in New Zealand women. *New Zealand Medical Journal*, 115: U257.

Meenan, R.F. and Mason, J.H. (1990). *AIMS2 Users Guide*. Boston University School of Medicine, Department of Public Health.

Meeske, K.A., Ruccione, K. and Globe, D.R. (2001). Post-traumatic stress, quality of life, and psychological distress in young adult survivors of childhood cancer. *Oncology Nursing Forum*, 28: 481–9.

Meeuwesen, L., Harmsen, J.A., Bernsen, R.M. et al. (2006). Do Dutch doctors communicate differently with immigrant patients than with Dutch patients? *Social Science and Medicine*, 63: 2407–17.

Mehta, V. and Langford, R.M. (2006). Acute pain management for opioid dependent patients. *Anaesthesia*, 61: 269–76.

Meichenbaum, D. (1985). *Stress Inoculation Training*. New York: Pergamon Press.

Meijer, S.A., Sinnema, G., Bijstra, J.O. et al. (2002). Coping style and locus of control as predictors for psychological adjustment of adolescents with a chronic illness. *Social Science and Medicine*, 54: 1453–61.

Meiser, B. (2005). Psychological impact of genetic testing for cancer susceptibility: an update of the literature. *Psycho-Oncology*, 14: 1060–74.

Meize-Grochowski, R., Shuster, G., Boursaw, B. et al. (2015). Mindfulness meditation in older adults with postherpetic neuralgia: A randomized controlled pilot study. *Geriatric Nursing*, 36: 154–60.

Melchior, M., Berkman, L.F., Niedhammer, I. et al. (2003). Social relations and self-reported health: a prospective analysis of the French Gazel cohort. *Social Science and Medicine*, 56: 1817–30.

Meldahl, M.L., Acaster, S. and Hayes, R.P. (2012). Exploration of oncologists' attitudes toward and perceived value of patient-reported outcomes. *Quality of Life Research*, 22: 725–31.

Mellins, C.A., Brackis-Cott, E., Dolezal, C. et al. (2004). The role of psychosocial and family factors in adherence to antiretroviral treatment in human immunodeficiency virus-infected children. *Pediatric Infectious Disease Journal*, 23: 1035–41.

Melzack, R. (1973). *The Puzzle of Pain*. London: Penguin Education.

Melzack, R. (1975). The McGill pain questionnaire: major properties and scoring methods. *Pain*, 1: 277–99.

Melzack, R. (1999). From the gate to the neuromatrix. *Pain*, suppl. 6: S121–6.

Melzack, R. (2005). Evolution of the neuromatrix theory of pain. The Prithvi Raj Lecture: presented at the third World Congress of World Institute of Pain, Barcelona 2004. *Pain Practice*, 5: 85–94.

Melzack, R. and Wall, P.D. (1965). Pain mechanisms: a new theory. *Science*, 50: 971–9.

Mendlowicz, M.V. and Stein, M.B. (2001). Quality of life in individuals with anxiety disorders. *American Journal of Psychiatry*, 157: 669–82.

Mendoza, S.A., Gollwitzer, P.M. and Amodio, D.M. (2010). Reducing the expression of implicit sterotypes: reflexive control through implementation intentions. *Personality and Social Psychology Bulletin*, 36: 512–23.

Mercken, L., Candel, M., Willems, P. and de Vries, H. (2007). Disentangling social selection and social influence effects on adolescent smoking: the importance of reciprocity of friendships. *Addiction*, 102: 1483–92.

Mercken, L., Candel, M., van Osch, L and de Vries, H. (2011). No smoke without fire: the impact of future friends on adolescent smoking behaviour. *British Journal of Health Psychology*, 16: 170–88.

Merkes, M. (2010). Mindfulness-based stress reduction for people with chronic diseases. *Australian Journal of Primary Health*, 16: 200–10.

Merluzzi, T.V., Philip, E.J., Dominic, O.V. and Heitzmann, C.A. (2011). Assessment of self-efficacy for caregiving: the critical role of self-care in caregiver stress and burden. *Palliative and Supportive Care*, 9: 15–24.

Merritt, M.M., Bennett, G.G., Williams, R.B. et al. (2004). Low educational attainment, John Henryism, and cardiovascular reactivity to and recovery from personally relevant stress. *Psychosomatic Medicine*, 66: 49–55.

Merzel, C. and D'Afflitti, J. (2003). Reconsidering community-based health promotion: promise, performance, and potential. *American Journal of Public Health*, 93: 557–74.

Meyer, J.M. and Stunkard, A.J. (1993). Genetics and human obesity. In A.J. Stunkard and T.A. Wadden (eds), *Obesity: Theory and Therapy*. New York: Raven Press.

Meyer, T.J. and Mark, M.M. (1995). Effects of psychosocial interventions with adult cancer patients: a meta-analysis of randomized experiments. *Health Psychology*, 12: 101–8.

Meyer-Weitz, A., Reddy, P., Van Den Borne, H.W. et al. (2000). The determinants of health care seeking behaviour of adolescents attending STD clinics in South Africa. *Journal of Adolescence*, 23: 741–52.

Michel, J.S., Kotrba, L.M., Mitchelson, J.K. et al. (2011). Antecedents of work-family conflict: A meta-analystic review. *Journal of Organizational Behavior*, 32: 689–725.

Michell, L. and Amos, A. (1997). Girls, pecking order, and smoking. *Social Science and Medicine*, 44: 1861–9.

Michie, S. and Prestwich, A. (2010) Are interventions theory-based? Development of a theory coding scheme. *Health Psychology*, 29: 1–8.

Michie, S., Ashford, S., Sniehotta, F.F. et al. (2011). A refined taxonomy of behaviour change techniques to help people change their physical activity and health eating behaviours: the CALO-RE. *Psychology and Health*, 26: 1479–98.

Michie, S., Dormandy, E. and Marteau, T.M. (2004). Increasing screening uptake among those intending to be screened: the use of action plans. *Patient Education and Counselling*, 55: 218–22.

Michie, S., Free, C. and West, R. (2012). Characterising the Txt2Stop smoking cessation text messaging intervention in terms of behaviour change techniques. *Journal of Smoking Cessation*, 7: 55–60.

Michie, S., Smith, J.A., Senior, V. and Marteau, T.M. (2003). Understanding why negative genetic test results sometimes fail to reassure. *American Journal of Medical Genetics*, 119A: 340–7.

Michielsen, H.J., DeVries, J. and van Heck. (2003). Psychometric qualities of a brief self-rated fatigue measure:the Fatigue Assessment Scale. *Journal of Psychosomatic Research*, 54: 345–52.

Mikkelsen, A. and Saksvik, P.O. (1999). Impact of a participatory organizational intervention on job characteristics and job stress. *International Journal of Health Services Research*, 29: 871–93.

Millard, T., Elliott, J. and Girdler, S. (2013). Self-management education programs for people living with HIV/AIDS: a systematic review. *AIDS Patient Care and STDs*, 27: 103–13.

Miller, G.E. and Cohen, S. (2001). Psychological interventions and the immune system: a meta-analytic review and critique. *Health Psychology*, 20: 47–63.

Miller, K.S., Vannatta, K., Compas, B.E. et al. (2009). The role of coping and temperament in the adjustment of children with cancer. *Journal of Pediatric Psychology*, 34: 1135–43.

Miller, R. and Miller, Y.D. (2003). Nifty after fifty: evaluation of a physical activity directory for older people. *Australia and New Zealand Journal of Public Health*, 27: 524–8.

Miller, S.M. (1987). Monitoring and blunting: validation of a questionnaire to assess styles of information seeking under threat. *Journal of Personality and Social Psychology*, 52: 345–53.

Miller, S.M., Brody, D.S. and Summerton, J. (1987). Styles of coping with threat: implications for health. *Journal of Personality and Social Psychology*, 54: 142–8.

Miller, S.M., Fang, C.Y., Manne, S.L. et al. (1999). Decision making about prophylactic oophorectomy among at-risk women: psychological influences and implications. *Gynaecological Oncology*, 75: 406–12.

Miller, S.M., Rodoletz, M., Mangan, C.E. et al. (1996). Applications of the monitoring process model to coping with severe long-term medical threats. *Health Psychology*, 15: 216–25.

Miller, T.Q., Smith, T.W., Turner, C.W. et al. (1996). A meta-analytic review of research on hostility and physical health. *Psychological Bulletin*, 119: 322–48.

Miller, W. and Rollnick, S. (2002). *Motivational Interviewing: Preparing People to Change Addictive Behaviour*. New York: Guilford Press.

Miller, W. and Rollnick, S. (2012). *Motivational Interviewing: Helping People Change*. New York: Guilford Press.

Miller, W., Rollnick, S. and Butler, C. (2008). *Motivational Interviewing in Health Care: Helping Patients Change Behavior*. New York: Guilford Press.

Milne, S., Welch, V., Brosseau, L. et al. (2001). Transcutaneous electrical nerve stimulation (TENS) for chronic low back pain. In *The Cochrane Library*, issue 4. Oxford: Update Software.

Mills, E.J., Nachega, J.B., Bangsberg, D.R. et al. (2006). Adherence to HAART: a systematic review of developed and developing nation patient-reported barriers and facilitators. *PLoS Medicine*, 3: e438.

Mindell, J. and Zaninotto, P. (2006) Cardiovascular disease and diabetes. In K. Sproston and J. Mindell (eds), *Health Survey for England 2004: The Health of Minority Ethnic Groups*. Leeds: The NHS Information Centre.

Ming, E.E., Adler, G.K., Kessler, R.C. et al. (2004). Cardiovascular reactivity to work stress predicts subsequent onset of hypertension: the Air Traffic Controller Health Change Study. *Psychosomatic Medicine*, 66: 459–65.

Ministry of Health (2003). *A Longer Healthy Life* (in Dutch). Den Haag: Ministry of Health, Welfare and Sport.

Mino, Y., Babazono, A., Tsuda, T. et al. (2006). Can stress management at the workplace prevent depression? A randomized controlled trial. *Psychotherapy and Psychosomatics*, 7: 177–82.

Mir, G. and Tovey, P. (2002). Cultural competency: profesional action and South Asian carers. *Journal of Management in Medicine*, 16: 7–19.

Mishra, S., Bhatnagar, S., Gupta, D. et al. (2007). Incidence and management of phantom limb pain according to World Health Organization analgesic ladder in amputees of malignant origin. *American Journal of Hospice and Palliative Care*, 24: 455–62.

Misra, R., Crist, M. and Burant, C.J. (2003). Relationships among life stress, social support, academic stressors, and reactions to stressors of international students in the United States. *International Journal of Stress Management*, 10: 137–57.

Mistry, R., McCarthy, W.J. and Yancey, A.K. (2009) Resilience and pattern of health risk behaviours in California adolescents. *Preventive Medicine*, 48: 291–7.

Mitchell, A.J. and Kakkadasam, V. (2011). Ability of nurses to identify depression in primary care, secondary care and nursing homes: a meta-analysis of routine clinical accuracy. *International Journal of Nursing Studies*, 48: 359–68.

Mitchell, A.J. and Kumar, M. (2002). Influence of psychological coping on survival: review is not systematic (letter to the editor). *British Medical Journal*, 326: 598.

Mitchell, J.B., Ballard, D.J., Matchar, D.B. et al. (2000). Racial variation in treatment for transient ischemic attacks: impact of participation by neurologists. *Health Services Research*, 34: 1413–28.

Moen, P., Fan, W. and Kelly, E.L. (2013). Team-level flexibility, work – home spillover, and health behavior. *Social Science and Medicine*, 84: 69–79.

Moens, V., Baruch, G. and Fearon, P. (2003). Opportunistic screening for chlamydia at a community based contraceptive service for young people. *British Medical Journal*, 326: 1252–5.

Moldofsky, H. and Chester, W.J. (1970). Pain and mood patterns in patients with rheumatoid arthritis: a prospective study. *Psychosomatic Medicine*, 32: 309–18.

Molloy, G.J., Dixon, D., Hamer, M. and Sniehotta, F.F. (2010). Social support and regular physical activity: does planning mediate this link? *British Journal of Health Psychology*, 15: 859–70.

Molloy, G.J., Johnston, M., Johnston, D.W. et al. (2008). Spousal caregiver confidence and recovery from ambulatory activity limitations in stroke survivors. *Health Psychology* 27: 286–90.

Molloy, G.J., O'Carroll, R.E. and Ferguson, E. (2014). Conscientiousness and medication adherence: a meta-analysis. *Annals of Behavioral Medicine*, 47: 92–101.

Molloy, G.J., Stamataki, E., Randall, G. and Harmerm, M. (2009). Marital status, gender, and cardiovascular mortality: behavioural, psychological distress and metabolic explanations. *Social Science & Medicine*, 69: 223–8.

Molyneux, A., Lewis, S., Leivers, U. et al. (2003). Clinical trial comparing nicotine replacement therapy (NRT) plus brief counselling, brief counselling alone, and minimal intervention on smoking cessation in hospital inpatients. *Thorax*, 58: 484–8.

Momeni, M., Crucitti, M. and De Kock, M. (2006). Patient-controlled analgesia in the management of postoperative pain. *Drugs*, 66: 2321–37.

Mommersteeg, P.M., Vermetten, E., Kavelaars, A. et al. (2008). Hostility is related to clusters of T-cell cytokines and chemokines in healthy men. *Psychoneuroendicrinology*, 33: 1041–50.

Montano, D., Hoven, H. and Siegrist, J. (2014). Effects of organisational-level interventions at work on employees' health: a systematic review. *BMC Public Health*, 14: 135.

Montazeri, A., Jarvandi, S., Haghighat, S. et al. (2001). Anxiety and depression in breast cancer patients before and after participation in a cancer support group. *Patient Education and Counseling*, 45: 195–8.

Montgomery, C., Lydon, A. and Lloyd, K. (1999). Psychological distress among cancer patients and informed consent. *Journal of Psychosomatic Research*, 46: 241–5.

Montgomery, G.H., Bovberg, D.H., Schnur, J.B. et al. (2007). A randomized clinical trial of a brief hypnosis intervention to control side effects in breast surgery patients. *Journal of the National Cancer Institute*, 99: 1304–12.

Montgomery, M. and McCrone, S.H. (2010). Psychological distress associated with the diagnostic phase for suspected breast cancer: a review. *Journal of Advanced Nursing*, 66: 2372–90.

Montgomery, R.J.V. and Kosloski, K.D. (2000). Family caregiving: change, continuity and diversity. In P. Lawton and R. Rubenstein (eds), *Alzheimer's Disease and Related Dementias: Strategies in Care and Research*. New York: Springer.

Montgomery, S., Udumyan, R., Magnuson, A. et al. (2013). Mortality following unemployment during an economic downturn: Swedish register-based cohort study. *BMJ Open*, 3: e003031.

Montpetit, M.A. and Bergeman, C.S. (2007). Dimensions of control: mediational analyses of the stress–health relationship. *Personality and Individual Differences*, 43: 2237–48.

Moodie, C.S. and Mackintosh, A.M. (2013). Young adult women smokers' response to using plain cigarette packaging: a naturalistic approach. *BMJ Open* 14: 812.

Moody, L.E. and McMillan, S. (2003). Dyspnoea and quality of life indicators in hospice patients and their caregivers, *Health and Quality of Life Outcomes*, 1: 9.

Moore, D., Aveyard, P., Connock, M. et al. (2009). Effectiveness and safety of nicotine replacement therapy assisted reduction to stop smoking: systematic review and meta-analysis. *British Medical Journal*, 338:b1024.

Moore, L. (2001). Are fruit tuck shops in primary schools effective in increasing pupils' fruit consumption? A randomised controlled trial. Abstract available from http://www.cf.ac.uk/socsi/whoswho/moore-tuckshop.html

Moore, L., Paisly, C.M. and Dennehy, A. (2000). Are fruit tuck shops in primary schools effective in increasing pupils' fruit consumption? A randomised controlled trial. *Nutrition and Food Science*, 30: 35–8.

Moore, S., Murphy, S., Tapper, K. et al. (2010). From policy to plate: barriers to implementing healthy eating policies in primary schools in Wales. *Health Policy*, 94: 239–45.

Moore, S. and Rosenthal, D. (1993). *Sexuality in Adolescence*. London: Routledge.

Moore, S.M., Barling, N.R. and Hood, B. (1998). Predicting testicular and breast self-examination behaviour: a test of the theory of reasoned action. *Behaviour Change*, 15: 41–9.

Moorey, S., Greer, S., Bliss, J. and Law, M. (1998). A comparison of adjuvant psychological therapy and supportive counselling in patients with cancer. *Psycho-Oncology*, 7: 218–28.

Moorey, S., Greer, S., Watson, M. (1994). Adjuvant psychological therapy for patients with cancer: outcome at one year. *Psycho-oncology*, 3: 39–46.

Moos, R.H. and Schaefer, A. (1984). The crisis of physical illness: an overview and conceptual approach. In R.H. Moos (ed.), *Coping with Physical Illness: New Perspectives*, Vol. 2. New York: Plenum.

Mor, V., Malin, M. and Allen, S. (1994). Age differences in the psychosocial problems encountered by breast cancer patients. *Journal of the National Cancer Institute Monographs*, 16: 191–7.

Morgan, J., Roufeil, L., Kaushik, S. et al. (1998). Influence of coping style and precolonoscopy information on pain and anxiety of colonoscopy. *Gastrointestinal Endoscopy*, 48: 119–27.

Moriarty, J., Sharif, N., Robinson, J. (2011) Black and minority ethnic people with dementia and their access to support and services, *Research Briefing* 35, SCIE Social Care Institute for Excellence, London. www.scie.org.uk/publications

Morley, S., Eccleston, C. and Williams, A. (1999). Systematic review and meta-analysis of randomized controlled trials of cognitive behaviour therapy and behaviour therapy for chronic pain in adults, excluding headache. *Pain*, 80: 1–13.

Morone, N.E., Greco, C.M. and Weiner, D.K. (2008). Mindfulness meditation for the treatment of chronic low back pain in older adults: a randomized controlled pilot study. *Pain*, 134: 310–19.

Morris, B.A. and Shakespeare-Finch, J. (2010). Rumination, post-traumatic growth, and distress: structural equation modelling with cancer survivors. *Psycho-Oncology*, doi: 10.1002/pon.1827.

Morris, C.D. and Carson, S. (2003). Routine vitamin supplementation to prevent cardiovascular disease: a summary of the evidence for the US Preventive Services Task Force. *Annals of Internal Medicine*, 139: 56–70.

Morris, D.B. (1999). Sociocultural and religious meanings of pain. In R.J. Gatchel and D.C. Turk (eds), *Psychosocial Factors in Pain*. New York: Guilford Press.

Morris, J.N., Clayton, D.G., Everitt, M.G. et al. (1990). Exercise in leisure time: coronary attack and death rates. *British Heart Journal*, 63: 325–34.

Morris, P.L.P., Robinson. R.G., Andrzejewski, P. et al. (1993). Association of depression with 10-year stroke mortality. *American Journal of Psychiatry*, 150: 124–9.

Morrison, M.F., Petitto, J.M., Ten Have, T. et al. (2002). Depressive and anxiety disorders in women with HIV infection. *American Journal of Psychiatry*, 159: 789–96.

Morrison, V. (1988). Observation and snowballing: useful tools for research into illicit drug use? *Social Pharmacology*, 2: 247–71.

Morrison, V. (1999). Predictors of carer distress following a stroke. *Reviews in Clinical Gerontology*, 9: 265–71.

Morrison, V. (2001). The need to explore discrepant illness cognitions when predicting patient outcomes. *Health Psychology Update*, 10: 9–13.

Morrison, V. (2003). Furthering the socio-cognitive explanation of addiction. *Neuro-Psychoanalysis*, 5: 39–42.

Morrison, V., Ager, A. and Willock, J. (1999). Perceived risk of tropical diseases in Malawi: evidence of unrealistic pessimism and the irrelevance of beliefs of personal control? *Psychology, Health and Medicine*, 4: 361–8.

Morrison, V., Henderson, B.J., Zinovieff, F. et al. (2011). Common, important, and unmet needs of cancer patients. *European Journal of Oncology Nursing*, doi:10.1016/j.ejon.2011.04.004.

Morrison, V., Johnston, M. and MacWalter, R. (2000b). Predictors of distress following an acute stroke: disability, control cognitions and satisfaction with care. *Psychology and Health*, 15: 395–407.

Morrison, V. and Plant, M.A. (1991). Licit and illicit drug initiations and alcohol related problems among illicit drug users in Edinburgh. *Drug and Alcohol Dependence*, 27: 19–27.

Morrison, V., Pollard, B., Johnston, M. and MacWalter, R. (2005). Anxiety and depression 3 years following stroke: demographic, clinical and psychological predictors. *Journal of Psychosomatic Research*, 59:209–13.

Morrison, V.L. (1991a). The impact of HIV upon injecting drug users: a longitudinal study. *AIDS Care*, 3: 197–205.

Morrison, V.L. (1991b). Starting, switching, stopping: users' explanations of illicit drug use. *Drug and Alcohol Dependence*, 27: 213–17.

Morrison, V., Holmes, E., Parveen, S., et al. (2015) Association of low self-efficacy and a high number of perceived barriers with non-adherence to antihypertensive medicines: A multi-national, cross-sectional survey. *Value Health*, 18(2): 206–16.

Morrison, V., Henderson, B., Taylor, C. et al. (2010). The impact of information order on intentions to undergo predictive genetic testing: an experimental study. *Journal of Health Psychology*, 15(7): 1082–92.

Morse, J.M. and Johnson, J.L. (1991). Towards a theory of illness. The illness constellation model. In J.M. Morse and J.L. Johnson (eds), *The Illness Experience: Dimensions of Suffering*. Newbury Park, CA: Sage.

Morse, S.R. and Fife, B. (1998). Coping with a partner's cancer: adjustment at four stages of the illness trajectory. *Oncology Nursing Forum*, 25: 751–60.

Morwitz, V.G., Johnson, E., Schmittlein, D. (1993). Does measuring intent change behavior? *Journal of Consumer Research*, 20: 46–61.

Moskowitz, J.T., Hult, J.R., Busolari, C. and Acree, M. (2009). What works in coping with HIV? A meta-analysis with implications for coping with serious illness. *Psychological Bulletin*, 135: 121–41.

Moss, S., Thomas, I., Evans, A. et al. (2005). Randomised controlled trial of mammographic screening in women from age 40: predicted mortality based on surrogate outcome measures. *British Journal of Cancer*, 92: 955–60.

Moss-Morris, R. and Chalder, T. (2003). Illness perceptions and levels of disability in patients with chronic fatigue syndrome and rheumatoid arthritis. *Journal of Psychosomatic Research*, 55: 305–8.

Moss-Morris, R., Deary, V., and Castell, B. (2013). Chapter 25: Chronic fatigue syndrome, *Handbook of Clinical Neurology*, 110: 303–14.

Moss-Morris, R., McAlpine, L., Didsbury, L.P. et al. (2010). A randomized controlled trial of a cognitive behavioural therapy-based self-management intervention for irritable bowel syndrome in primary care. *Psychological Medicine*, 40: 85–94.

Moss-Morris, R., Weinman, J., Petrie, K.J. et al. (2002). The revised Illness Perception Questionnaire (IPQ-R). *Psychology and Health*, 17: 1–16.

Motl, R.W., Gliottoni, R.C. and Scott, J.A. (2007). Self-efficacy correlates with leg muscle pain during maximal and submaximal cycling exercise. *Journal of Pain*, 8: 583–7.

Mott, J., Bucolo, S., Cuttle, L. et al. (2008). The efficacy of an augmented virtual reality system to alleviate pain in children undergoing burns dressing changes: a randomised controlled trial. *Burns*, 34: 803–8.

Mowery, R.L. (2007). The family, larger systems, and end-of-life decision making. In D. Balk, C. Wogrin, G. Thornton and D. Meagher (eds), *Handbook of Thanatology: The Essential Body of Knowledge for the Student of Death, Dying, and Bereavement*. Northbrook, IL: Association for Death Education and Counseling, pp. 93–102.

Mujtaba B.G. and Cavico F.J. (2013). Corporate wellness programs: implementation challenges in the modern American workplace. *International Journal of Health Policy and Management* 6: 193–9.

Munaf, M.R. and Johnstone, E.C. (2008). Genes and cigarette smoking. *Addiction*, 103: 893–904.

Murgraff, V., McDermott, M.R., White, D. et al. (1999). Regret is what you get: the effects of manipulating anticipated affect and time perspective on risky single occasion drinking. *Alcohol and Alcoholism*, 34: 590–600.

Murnaghan, D.A., Blanchard, C.M., Rodgers, W.M. et al. (2010). Predictors of physical activity, healthy eating and being smoke-free in teens: a theory of planned behaviour approach. *Psychology & Health*, 25: 925–41.

Murphy, D., Lindsay, S. and Williams, A.C. de C. (1997). Chronic low back pain: predictions of pain and relationship to anxiety and avoidance. *Behaviour Research and Therapy*, 35: 231–8.

Murphy, M.H., Nevill, A.M., Murtagh, E.M. and Holder, R.L. (2007). The effect of walking on fitness, fatness and resting blood pressure. *Preventive Medicine*, 44: 377–85.

Murray, C.J.L. and Lopez, A.D. (1997). Alternative projections of mortality and disability by cause 1990–2020: Global Burden of Disease Study. *The Lancet*, 349: 1498–504.

Murray, D.F., Marks, M., Evans, B. and Willig, C. (2000). *Health Psychology: Theory, Research and Practice*. London: Sage.

Murray, E., Pollack, L., White, M. et al. (2007). Clinical decision-making: physicians' preferences and experiences. *BMC Family Practice*, 8:10.

Murray, M. (1997). A narrative approach to health psychology: background and potential. *Journal of Health Psychology*, 2: 9–20.

Murray, M. and Campbell, C. (2003). Beyond the sidelines: towards a more politically engaged health psychology. *Health Psychology Update*, 12: 12–17.

Murrell, R. (2001). Assessing the quality of life of individuals with neurological illness. *Health Psychology Update*, 10.

Myers, L.B. (1998). Repressive coping, trait anxiety and reported avoidance of negative thoughts. *Personality and Individual Differences*, 24: 299–303.

Myers, L.B. and Reynolds, D. (2000). How optimistic are repressors? The relationship between repressive coping, controllability, self-esteem and comparative optimism for health-related events. *Psychology and Health*, 15: 677–87.

Myrtek, M. (2001). Meta-analyses of prospective studies on coronary heart disease, type A personality, and hostility. *International Journal of Cardiology*, 79: 245–51.

Nachega, J.B., Mugavero, M.J., Zeier, M. et al. (2010). Treatment simplification in HIV-infected adults as a strategy to prevent toxicity, improve adherence, quality of life and decrease healthcare costs. *Journal of Patient Preference and Adherence*, 5: 357–67.

Nagasako, E.M., Oaklander, A.L. and Dworkin, R.H. (2003). Congenital insensitivity to pain: an update. *Pain*, 101: 213–19.

Naish, J., Brown, J. and Denton, B. (1994). Intercultural consultations: investigation of factors that deter non-English speaking women from attending their general practitioners for cervical screening. *British Medical Journal*, 309: 1126–8.

Naliboff, B.D., Munakata, J., Chang, L. et al. (1998). Toward a biobehavioral model of visceral hypersensitivity in irritable bowel syndrome. *Journal of Psychosomatic Research*, 45: 485–93.

Nandi, A., Glymour, M.M. and Subramanian, S.V. (2014). Association among socioeconomic status, health behaviors, and all-cause mortality in the United States. *Epidemiology*, 25: 170–7.

Narevic, E. and Schoenberg, N.E. (2002). Lay explanations for Kentucky's 'Coronary Valley'. *Journal of Community Health*, 27: 53–62.

Nathan, J.P., Zerilli, T., Cicero, L.A. et al. (2007). Patients' use and perception of medication information leaflets. *Annals of Pharmacotherapy*, 41: 777–82.

National Collaborating Centre for Chronic Conditions (2004). Chronic obstructive pulmonary disease. National clinical guidelines on management of chronic obstructive pulmonary disease in adults in primary and secondary care. *Thorax*, 59(suppl. 1): 1–232.

National Diet and Nutrition Survey: Adults aged 19–64, Vol. 1 (2000). Carried out in 2000 on behalf of the Food Standards Agency and Department of Health by the Social Survey Division of the Office for National Statistics and Medical Research Council Human Nutrition Research. London: Stationery Office.

National Diet and Nutrition Survey Report. www.food.gov.uk/multimedia/pdfs/.../ndnsreport0809year1results.pdf.

National Institutes of Health Technology Assessment Panel (1996). Integration of behavioral and relaxation approaches into the treatment of chronic pain and insomnia. *Journal of the American Medical Association*, 276: 313–18.

Naughton, F., Jamison, J., Boase, S. et al. (2014). Randomized controlled trial to assess the short-term effectiveness of tailored web- and text-based facilitation of smoking cessation in primary care (iQuit in Practice). *Addiction,* 109: 1184–93.

Navas-Nacher, E.L., Colangelo, L., Beam, C. et al. (2001). Risk factors for coronary heart disease in men 18 to 39 years of age. *Annals of Internal Medicine*, 134: 433–9.

Nazroo, J.Y. (1998). *Genetic, Cultural or Socioeconomic Vulnerability? Explaining Ethnic Inequalities in Health*. Oxford: Blackwell.

Neal, R.D., Ali, N., Atkin, K. et al. (2006). Communication between South Asian patients and GPs: comparative study using the Roter Interactional Analysis System. *British Journal of General Practice*, 56: 869–75.

Neff, L.A. and Karney, B.R. (2005). Gender differences in social support: a question of skill or responsiveness? *Journal of Personality & Social Psychology*, 88: 79–90.

Nelson, D.V., Baer, P.E. and Cleveland, S.E. (1998). Family stress management following acute myocardial infarction: an educational and skills training intervention program. *Patient Education and Counseling*, 34: 135–45.

Ness, A.R., Frankel, S.J., Gunnell, D.J. et al. (1999). Are we really dying for a tan? *British Medical Journal*, 319: 114–16.

Ness, A.R. and Powles, J.W. (1997). Fruit and vegetables, and cardiovascular disease: a review. *International Journal of Epidemiology*, 26: 1–13.

New, S.J. and Senior, M. (1991). 'I don't believe in needles': qualitative aspects of a study into the uptake of infant immunisation in two English health authorities. *Social Science and Medicine*, 33: 509–18.

Newton, T.L., Watters, C.A., Philhower, C.L. et al. (2005). Cardiovascular reactivity during dyadic social interaction: the roles of gender and dominance. *International Journal of Psychophysiology*, 57: 219–28.

Ng, B., Dimsdale, J.E., Rollnick, J.D. and Shapiro, H. (1996). The effect of ethnicity on prescriptions for patient-controlled anaesthesia for post-operative pain. *Pain*, 66: 9–12.

NHS Centre for Reviews and Dissemination (1999). *Effective Healthcare: Getting Evidence into Practice*. NHS CRD, Vol. 5, No. 1. London: Royal Society of Medicine Press.

NHS Executive (1996). *Patient Partnership: Building a Collaborative Strategy*. Leeds: NHS Executive.

NICE (2007). National Institute for Health and Clinical Excellence. *Management of Depression in Primary and Secondary Care*. http://www.nice.org.uk/nicemedia/pdf/CG023fullguideline.pdf 2007

NICE (2009a). *Clinical Guideline 76: Medicines Adherence: Involving Patients in Decisions about Prescribed Medicines and Supporting Adherence*. London: National Institute for Health and Clinical Excellence.

NICE (2009b). *Costing Statement: Medicines Adherence: Involving Patients in Decisions about Prescribed Medicines and Supporting Adherence*. London: National Institute for Health and Clinical Excellence.

Nicholl, B.I., Mackay, D., Cullen, B. et al. (2014). Chronic multisite pain in major depression and bipolar disorder: cross-sectional study of 149,611 participants in UK Biobank. *BMC Psychiatry* 14: 350.

Nichols, K. (2003). *Psychological Care for the Ill and Injured: A Clinical Handbook*. Maidenhead: Open University Press.

Nicholson, N., Soane, E., Fenton-O'Creevy, M. et al. (2005). Personality and domain-specific risk-taking. *Journal of Risk Research*, 8: 157–76.

Nicolson, N.A. and van Diest, R. (2000). Salivary cortisol levels in vital exhaustion. *Journal of Psychosomatic Research*, 49: 335–42.

Niederhoffer, K.G. and Pennebaker, J.W. (2005). Sharing one's story: on the benefits of writing or talking about emotional experience. In C. Snyder and S.J. Lopez, *Handbook of Positive Psychology*. New York: Oxford University Press, pp. 573–83.

Niemcryk, S.J., Speer, M.A., Travis, L.B. et al. (1990). Psychosocial correlates of haemoglobin A1c in young adults with type I diabetes. *Journal of Psychosomatic Research*, 34: 617–27.

Niemi, M., Laaksonen, R., Kotila, M. and Waltimo, O. (1988). Quality of life 4 years after stroke. *Stroke*, 19: 1101–7.

Nijboer, C., Tempelaar, R., Triemstra, M. et al. (2001). Dynamics in cancer caregiver's health over time: gender-specific patterns and determinants. *Psychology and Health*, 16: 471–88.

Nimnuan C, Hotopf M, Wessely S. (2001). Medically unexplained symptoms: an epidemiological study in seven specialities. *Journal of Psychosomatic Research,* 51: 361–7.

Nnoaham, K.E. and Kumbang, J. (2010). Transcutaneous electrical nerve stimulation (TENS) for chronic pain. *Cochrane Database of Systematic Reviews*, issue 3, art. no.: CD003222. doi: 10.1002/14651858. CD003222.

Noble, L.M. (1998). Doctor–patient communication and adherence to treatment. In L.B. Myers and K. Midence (eds), *Adherence to Treatment in Medical Conditions*. Amsterdam: Harwood Academic.

Noblet, A.J. and LaMontagne, A. (2006). The role of workplace health promotion in addressing job stress. *Health Promotion International*, 21: 346–53.

Noguchi, K., Albarracín, D., Durantini, M.R. et al. (2007). Who participates in which health promotion programs? A meta-analysis of motivations underlying enrolment and retention in HIV-prevention interventions. *Psychological Bulletin*, 133: 955–75.

Nolen-Hoeksema, S. (1991). Responses to depression and their effects on the duration of depressive episodes. *Journal of Abnormal Psychology*, 100: 569–82.

Nolen-Hoeksema, S., Wisco, B.E. and Lyubomirsky, S. (2008). Rethinking rumination. *Perspectives on Psychological Science*, 3: 400–24.

Norberg, A.L., Lindblad, F. and Boman, K.K. (2005). Coping strategies in parents of children with cancer. *Social Science and Medicine*, 60: 965–75.

Nordstrom, C.K., Dwyer, K.M., Merz, C.N. et al. (2001). Work-related stress and early atherosclerosis. *Epidemiology*, 12: 180–5.

Norman, P. and Bennett, P. (1996). Health locus of control. In M. Conner and P. Norman (eds), *Predicting Health Behaviour*. Buckingham: Open University Press.

Norman, P., Bennett, P., Smith, C. and Murphy, S. (1998). Health locus of control and health behaviour. *Journal of Health Psychology*, 3: 171–80.

Norman, P. and Brain, K. (2005). An application of an extended health belief model to the prediction of breast self examination among women with a family history of breast cancer, *British Journal of Health Psychology*, 10: 1–16.

Norman, P., Conner, M. and Bell, S. (1999). The theory of planned behaviour and smoking cessation. *Health Psychology*, 18: 89–94.

Norman, P. and Smith, L. (1995). The theory of planned behaviour and exercise: an investigation into the role of prior behaviour, behavioural intentions and attitude variability. *European Journal of Social Psychology*, 25: 403–15.

Normandeau, S., Kalnins, I., Jutras, S. et al. (1998). A description of 5 to 12 year old children's conception of health within the context of their daily life. *Psychology and Health*, 13(5): 883–96.

Norris, S.L., McNally, K., Zang, X. et al. (2011). Published norms underestimate the health-related quality of life among persons with type 2 diabetes. *Journal of Clinical Epidemiology*, 64: 358–65.

Norris, V.K., Stephens, M.A. and Kinney, J.M. (1990). The influence of family interactions on recovery from stroke: help or hindrance? *The Gerontologist*, 30: 535–42.

Norrsell, U., Finger, S. and Lajonchere, C. (1999). Cutaneous sensory spots and the 'law of specific nerve energies': history and development of ideas. *Brain Research Bulletin*, 48: 457–65.

Norström, T. and Skog, O.J. (2005). Saturday opening of alcohol retail shops in Sweden: an experiment in two phases. *Addiction*, 100: 767–76.

Northouse, L., Kershaw, T., Mood, D. et al. (2005). Effects of a family intervention on the quality of life of women with recurrent breast cancer and their family caregivers. *Psycho-Oncology*, 14: 478–91.

Northouse, L.L., Mood, D.W., Schafenacker, A. et al. (2007). Randomized clinical trial of a family intervention for prostate cancer patients and their spouses. *Cancer*, 110: 2809–18.

Nouwen, A., Cloutier, C., Kappas, A. et al. (2006). The effects of focusing and distraction on cold-pressor induced pain in chronic back pain patients and controls. *Journal of Pain*, 7: 62–71.

Noyes, R., Jr (2001). Hypochondriasis: boundaries and comorbidities. In G.J.G. Asmundson, S. Taylor and B.J. Cox (eds), *Health Anxiety: Clinical and Research Perspectives on Hyponchondriasis and Related Conditions*. New York: John Wiley & Sons, pp. 132–60.

Nutbeam, D., Smith, C., Moore, L. et al. (1993). Warning! Schools can damage your health: alienation from school and its impact on child behaviour. *Journal of Paediatrics and Child Health*, 29(suppl. 1): S25–30.

Nyklícek, I. and Kuijpers, K.F. (2008). Effects of mindfulness-based stress reduction intervention on psychological well-being and quality of life: is increased mindfulness indeed the mechanism? *Annals of Behavioral Medicine*, 35: 331–40.

Oaten, M. and Cheng, K. (2006). Improved self-control: the benefits of a regular program of academic study. *Basic & Applied Social Psychology*, 28(1): 1–16.

Obieglo, I. Uchmanowicz, M. Wleklik, B. et al. (2015). The effect of acceptance of illness on the quality of life in patients with chronic heart failure. *European Journal of Cardiovascular Nursing*; DOI: 10.1177/1474515114564929

O'Boyle, C.A., McGee, H., Hickey, A. et al. (1992). Individual quality of life in patients undergoing hip replacement. *The Lancet*, 339: 1088–91.

O'Boyle, C.A., McGee, H., Hickey, A. et al. (1993). *The Schedule for the Evaluation of Individual Quality of Life (SEIQoL): Administration Manual*. Dublin: Department of Psychology, Royal College of Surgeons.

O'Brien, M.K., Petrie, K. and Raeburn, J. (1992). Adherence to medication regimens: updating a complex medical issue. *Medical Care Review*, 49: 435–54.

O'Carroll, R.E., Smith, K.B., Grubb, N.R. et al. (2001). Psychological factors associated with delay in attending hospital following a myocardial infarction. *Journal of Psychosomatic Research*, 51: 611–14.

O'Cleirigh, C., Ironson, G., Antoni, M. et al. (2003). Emotional expression and depth processing of trauma and their relation to long-term survival in patients with HIV/AIDS. *Journal of Psychosomatic Research*, 54: 225–35.

O'Connell, K., Skevington, S. and Saxena, S. et al. (2003). Preliminary development of the World Health Organization's Quality of Life HIV instrument (WHOQOL-HIV): analysis of the pilot version. *Social Science and Medicine*, 57: 1259–75.

O'Connor, A.P., Wicker, C.A. and Germino, B.B. (1990). Understanding the cancer patient's search for meaning. *Cancer Nursing*, 13: 167–75.

O'Connor, D.B. (2014). Health disclosure, *The Psychologist*, 28: 40–41.

O'Connor, D.B., Conner, M., Jones, F., McMillan, B., and Ferguson, E. (2009). Exploring the benefits of conscientiousness: an investigation of the role of daily stressors and health behaviors, *Annals of Behavioral Medicine*, 37:184–96.

O'Connor, D.B., Jones, F., Conner, M., McMilan, B. and Ferguson, E. (2008). Effects of daily hassles and eating styles on eating behavior, *Health Psychology*, 27(1): S20–S31.

O'Connor, E.J., McCabe, M.P. and Firth, L. (2008). The impact of neurological illness on marital relationships. *Journal of Sex and Marital Therapy*, 34: 115–132.

O'Connor, S.M., Jardine, A.G., and Millar, K. (2008). The prediction of self-care behaviors in end stage renal disease patients using Leventhal's Self Regulatory Model. *Journal of Psychosomatic Research*, 65: 191–200.

Odgers, P., Houghton, S. and Douglas, G. (1996). Reputation Enhancement Theory and adolescent substance use. *Journal of Child Psychology, Psychiatry and Allied Disciplines*, 37: 1015–22.

O'Donnell, L., San Doval, A., Duran, R. and O'Donnell, C.R. (1995). The effectiveness of video-based interventions in promoting condom acquisition among STD clinic patients. *Sexually Transmitted Diseases*, 22: 97–103.

O'Donovan, P.J. and Livingston, D.M. (2010). BRCA1 and BRCA2: breast/ovarian cancer susceptibility gene products and participants in DNA double-strand break repair. *Carcinogenesis*, 31: 961–7.

OECD (2012), Health at a Glance: Europe 2012, OECD Publishing. http://dx.doi.org/10.1787/9789264183896-en

OECD (2012a), OECD Health Data 2012, Online, OECD Publishing, Paris, available at: www.oecd.org/health/healthdata.

OECD (2014), Health Statistics 2014 http://www.oecd.org/els/health-systems/oecd-health-statistics-2014-frequently-requested-data.htm

O'Farrell, T.J. and Fals-Stewart, W. (2000). Behavioral couples therapy for alcoholism and drug abuse. *Journal of Substance Abuse Treatment*, 18: 51–4.

Office for National Statistics (1999). *Social Trends 29*. London: Stationery Office.

Office for National Statistics (2000). *Results from the 1998 General Household Survey*. London: Stationery Office.

Office for National Statistics (2001). *Smoking Related Behaviour and Attitudes*. Series OS No.17. London: ONS.

Office for National Statistics (2009). *Alcohol-related Deaths in the United Kingdom 1991–2007*. Statistical Bulletin, 28 January 2009. Cardiff: ONS.

Office for National Statistics (2009). *Population Trends, Autumn 2009*. Cardiff: ONS.

Office for National Statistics (2010). *Death Registrations by Cause in England and Wales 2009*. Statistical Bulletin. Cardiff: ONS.

Office for National Statistics (2010). *General Lifestyle Survey Overview*. A report on the 2010 General Lifestyle Survey, London: ONS.

Office for National Statistics (2011). *General Lifestyle Survey 2010*. Results published online at http://www.ons.gov.uk/ons/rel/ghs/general-lifestyle-survey/2010/index.html

Office for National Statistics (2012) *Measuring National Wellbeing, Health 2012* (Dunstan, S. ed.), London: ONS.

Office for National Statistics (2014). Infographic http://www.ons.gov.uk/ons/rel/vsob1/death-reg-sum-tables/2013/info-deaths-2013.html

Ogden, J. (2003). Some problems with social cognition models: a pragmatic and conceptual analysis. *Health Psychology*, 22: 424–8.

Ogden, J. and Clementi, C. (2011). The experience of being obese and the many consequences of stigma. *Journal of Obesity*, 429098, Open Access.

Ogden, J., Fuks, K., Gardner, M. et al. (2002). Doctors' expressions of uncertainty and patient confidence. *Patient Education and Counselling*, 48: 171–6.

Ogden, J., Veale, D. and Summers, Z. (1997). Development and validation of the exercise dependence questionnaire. *Addiction Research*, 5: 343–56.

O'Hara, L., Gough, B., Seymour-Smith, S. and Watts, S. (2013). 'It's not a disease, it's a nuisance': Controlling diabetes and achieving goals in the context of men with Type 1 diabetes. *Psychology & Health*, 28: 1227–45.

Ohayon, M.M., Guilleminault, C., Priest, R.G. et al. (2000). Is sleep-disordered breathing an independent risk factor for hypertension in the general population (13,057 subjects)? *Journal of Psychosomatic Research*, 48: 593–601.

Okamoto, K. (2006). Life expectancy at the age of 65 years and environmental factors: an ecological study in Japan. *Archives of Gerontology and Geriatrics*, 43: 85–91.

O'Keefe, D.J. and Jensen, J.D. (2007). The relative persuasiveness of gain-framed and loss-framed messages for encouraging disease prevention behaviors: a meta-analytic review. *Journal of Health Communication*, 12: 623–44.

Okelo, S.O., Wu, A.W., Merriman, B. et al. (2007). Are physician estimates of asthma severity less accurate in black than in white patients? *Journal of General Internal Medicine*, 22: 976–81.

Oldenburg, B. and Harris, D. (1996). The workplace as a setting for promoting health and preventing disease. *Homeostasis*, 37: 226–32.

Oliver, G., Wardle, J. and Gibson, E.L. (2000). Stress and food choice: a laboratory study. *Psychosomatic Medicine*, 2: 853–65.

Olson, D.H. and Stewart, K.L. (1991). Family systems and health behaviours. In H.E. Schroeder (ed.), *New Directions in Health Psychology Assessment*. New York: Hemisphere.

O'Malley, P.M., Johnston, L.D., Chaloupka, F.J. and Flay, B. (2005). Televised state-sponsored antitobacco advertising and youth smoking beliefs and behavior in the United States, 1999–2000. *Archives of Pediatric and Adolescent Medicine*, 159: 639–45.

O'Neil A., Taylor B., Hare D.L. et al. (2014). Long-term efficacy of a tele-health intervention for acute coronary syndrome patients with depression: 12-month results of the MoodCare randomized controlled trial. *European Journal of Preventive Cardiology*, 22: 1111–20.

O'Neill, M. and Simard, P. (2006). Choosing indicators to evaluate Healthy Cities projects: a political task? *Health Promotion International*, 21: 145–52.

Ong, J., Miller, P.S., Appleby, R. et al. (2009). Effect of a preoperative instructional digital video disc on patient knowledge and preparedness for engaging in postoperative care activities. *Nursing Clinics of North America*, 44, 103–15.

Ong L.M.L., Visser M.R.M., Lammes F.B. et al. (2000) Effect of providing cancer patients with the audiotaped initial consultation on satisfaction, recall, and quality of life: a randomised, double-blind study. *Journal of Clinical Oncology*, 18: 3052–60.

Onwuanyi, A.E., Clarke, A. and Vanderbush, E. (2003). Cardiovascular disease mortality. *Journal of the National Medical Association*, 95: 1146–51.

Onwuteaka-Phillipsen, B., van der Heide, A., Koper, D. et al. (2003). Euthanasia and other end-of-life decisions in The Netherlands in 1990, 1995 and 2001. *The Lancet*, 362: 395–9.

Orbell, S. and Gillies, B. (1993). What's stressful about caring? *Journal of Applied Social Psychology*, 23: 272–90.

Orbell, S., Hodgkins, S. and Sheeran, P. (1997). Implementation intentions and the theory of planned behaviour. *Personality and Social Psychology*, 23: 945–54.

Orbell, S., Hopkins, N. and Gillies, B. (1993). Measuring the impact of informal caregiving. *Journal of Community and Applied Social Psychology*, 3: 149–63.

Orbell, S. and Sheeran, P. (2002). Changing health behaviours: the role of implementation intentions. In D. Rutter and L. Quine (eds), *Changing Health Behaviour*. Buckingham: Open University Press.

Orford, J. (2001). *Excessive Appetites: A Psychological View of Addictions*, 2nd edn. Chichester: Wiley.

Ornish, D., Lin, J., Chan, J.M., et al. (2013). Effect of comprehensive lifestyle changes on telomerase activity and telomere length in men with biopsy-proven low-risk prostate cancer: 5-year follow-up of a descriptive pilot study. *The Lancet Oncology*, 14(11): 1112–20.

Orth-Gomér, K., Undén, A.-L. and Edwards, M.-E. (1988). Social isolation and mortality in ischemic heart disease. *Acta Medica Scandinavica*, 224: 205–15.

Orth-Gomér, K. and Undén, A.-L. (1990). Type A behaviour, social support, and coronary risk: interaction and significance for mortality in cardiac patients. *Psychosomatic Medicine*, 52: 59–72.

Osborn, M. and Rodham, K. (2010). Insights into pain: a review of qualitative research. *Reviews in Pain*, 4: 2–7.

Osborne, R.H., Wilson, T., Lorig, K.R. et al. (2007). Does self-management lead to sustainable health benefits in people with arthritis? A 2-year transition study of 452 Australians. *Journal of Rheumatology*, 34: 1112–17.

Osse, B.H.P., Myrra, J.F.J., Vernooj-Dassen, E.S. et al. (2002). Problems to discuss with cancer patients in palliative care: a comprehensive approach. *Patient Education and Counseling*, 47: 195–204.

Ossip-Klein, D.J., McIntosh, S. et al. (2000). Smokers aged 50+: who gets physician advice to quit? *Preventive Medicine*, 31: 364–9.

OXCHECK Study Group (1994). Effectiveness of health checks conducted by nurses in primary care: results of the OXCHECK study after one year. Imperial Cancer Research Fund OXCHECK Study Group. *British Medical Journal*, 308: 308–12.

OXCHECK Study Group (1995). Effectiveness of health checks conducted by nurses in primary care: final results of the OXCHECK study. Imperial Cancer Research Fund OXCHECK Study Group. *British Medical Journal*, 310: 1099–104.

Oxman, A.D., Davis, D., Haynes, R.B. et al. (1995). No magic bullets: a systematic review of 102 trials of interventions to improve professional practice. *Canadian Medical Association Journal*, 153: 1423–31.

Oyebode, O., Gordon-Dseagu, V., Walker, A. and Mindell, J.S. (2013). Fruit and vegetable consumption and all-cause, cancer and CVD mortality: analysis of Health Survey for England data. *Journal of Epidemiology & Community Health*, published March 31st, doi:10.1136/jech-2013- 203500

Pachter, L.M. (1994). Culture and clinical care: folk illness beliefs and behaviours and their implications for health care delivery. *Journal of the American Medical Association*, 7: 690–4.

Paffenbarger, R.S., Hyde, J.T., Wing, A.L. et al. (1986). Physical activity, all-cause mortality, and longevity of college alumni. *New England Journal of Medicine*, 314: 605–12.

Page, A.S., Cooper, A.R., Griew, P. et al. (2010). Independent mobility, perceptions of the built environment and children's participation in play, active travel and structured exercise and sport: the PEACH Project. *International Journal of Behavioral Nutrition and Physical Activity* 7:17.

Page-Shafer, K.A., Satariano, W.A., Winkelstein, W. Jr. (1996) Comorbidity and HIV disease progression in homosexual/bisexual men: the San Francisco Men's Health Study. *Annals of Epidemiology 1996*, 6: 420–30.

Painter, J.E., Sales, J.M., Pazol, K., et al. (2010). Psychosocial correlates of intention to receive an influenza vaccination among rural adolescents. *Health Education Research*, 25: 853–64.

Painter, J.E., Sales, J.M., Pazol, K. et al. (2011). Adolescent attitudes toward influenza vaccination and vaccine uptake in a school-based influenza vaccination intervention: a mediation analysis. *Journal of School Health*, 81: 304-12. doi: 10.1111/j.1746-1561.2011.00595.x

Pakenham, K.I., Pruss, M. and Clutton, S. (2000). The utility of sociodemographics, knowledge and health belief model variables in predicting reattendance for mammography screening: a brief report. *Psychology and Health*, 15: 585–91.

Pal, K., Eastwood, S.V., Michie, S. et al. (2014). Computer-based interventions to improve self-management in adults with type 2 diabetes: a systematic review and meta-analysis. *Diabetes Care*, 37: 1759–66.

Palesh, O., Butler, L.D., Koopman, C. et al. (2007). Stress history and breast cancer recurrence. *Journal of Psychosomatic Research*, 63: 233–9.

Palmer, S. and Glass, T.A. (2003). Family function and stroke recovery: a review. *Rehabilitation Psychology*, 48: 255–65.

Pampel, F.C., Krueger, P.M. and Denney, J.T. (2010). Socioeconomic disparities in health behaviors. *Annual Review of Sociology* 36: 349–70.

Pan, A., Sun, Q., Okereke, O.I. et al. (2011). Depression and risk of stroke morbidity and mortality: A meta-analysis and systematic review, *JAMA*, 306:1241–9.

Panagopoulou, E., Kersbergen, B. and Maes, S. (2002). The effects of emotional (non-) expression in (chronic) disease: a meta-analytic review. *Psychology and Health*, 17: 529–45.

Panagopoulou, E., Vedhara, K., Gaintarzti, C. et al. (2006). Emotionally expressive coping reduces pregnancy rates in patients undergoing in vitro fertilization. *Fertility and Sterility*, 86: 672–7.

Pandey, M., Sarita, G.P., Devi, N. et al. (2006). Distress, anxiety and depression in cancer patients undergoing chemotherapy. *World Journal of Surgical Oncology*, 4: 68.

Panter, J.R., Jones, A.P., van Sluijs, E.M.F. et al. (2010). Attitudes, social support and environmental perceptions as predictors of active commuting behaviour in school children. *Journal of Epidemiology and Community Health*, 64: 41–8.

Papanicolaou, D.A., Wilder, R.L., Manolagas, S.C. and Chrousos, G.P. (1998). The pathophysiologic roles of interleukin-6 in human disease. *Archives of Internal Medicine*, 128: 127–37.

Pargament, K.I., Koenig, H.G. and Perez, L.M. (2000). The many methods in religious coping: development and initial validation of the RCOPE. *Journal of Clinical Psychology*, 56: 519–43.

Paris, W., Muchmore, J., Pribil, A. et al. (1994). Study of the relative incidences of psychosocial factors before and after heart transplantation and the influence of post-transplantation psychosocial factors on heart transplantation outcome. *Journal of Heart Lung Transplantation*, 13: 424–30.

Park, C.L. (2010). Making sense of the meaning literature:an integrative review of meaning making and its effects on adjustment to stressful life events. *Psychological Bulletin*, 136: 257–301.

Park, C.L. (2006). Exploring relations among religiousness, meaning, and adjustment to lifetime and current stressful encounters in later life. *Anxiety, Stress, and Coping*, 19: 33–45.

Park, C.L. and Folkman, S. (1997). Meaning in the context of stress and coping. *Reviews in General Psychology*, 2: 115–44.

Park, C.L and Helgeson, V.S (2006). Introduction to the special section: growth following highly stressful life events – current status and future directions. *Journal of Consulting and Clinical Psychology*, 74: 791–6.

Park, C.L. and Lechner, S.C. (2007). Measurement issues in assessing growth following stressful life experiences. In L.G. Calhoun and R.G. Tedeschi (eds) (2007), *Handbook of Post-traumatic Growth: Research and Practice*. London: Lawrence Erlbaum Associates, pp. 47–67.

Park, D.C., Morrell, R.W., Frieske, D. et al. (1992). Medication adherence behaviors in older adults: effects of external cognitive supports. *Psychology and Aging*, 7: 252–6.

Park, H.I., Jacob, A.C., Wagner, S.H. and Baiden, M. (2014). Job control and burnout: a meta-analytic test of the con-

servation of resources model. *Applied Psychology: An International Journal*, 63: 607–42.

Park, J.E., Kim, K.I., Yoon, S.S. et al. (2010). Psycholgical distress as a negative survival factor for patients with hematologic malignancies who underwent allogeneic hematopoeitic stem cell transplantation. *Pharmacotherapy*, 30: 1239–46.

Park, P., Simmons, R.K., Prevost, A.T. et al. (2010). A randomized evaluation of loss and gain frames in an invitation to screening for type 2 diabetes: effects on attendance, anxiety and self-rated health. *Journal of Health Psychology*, 15: 196–204.

Parkes, K. (1984). Locus of control, cognitive appraisal, coping appraisal and coping in stressful episodes. *Journal of Personality and Social Psychology*, 46: 655–68.

Parle, M., Maguire, P. and Heaven, C. (1997). The development of a training model to improve health professionals' skills, self-efficacy and outcome expectancies when communicating with cancer patients. *Social Science and Medicine*, 44: 231–40.

Parsons, T. (1951). *The Social System*. New York: Free Press.

Partridge, C. and Johnston, M. (1989). Perceived control of recovery from physical disability: measurement and prediction. *British Journal of Clinical Psychology*, 28: 53–9.

Partridge, J and Pearson, A. (2008). 'Don't worry. . .it's the inside that counts.', *The Psychologist, (Special Issue on Visible Difference)* 21: 490–1.

Parveen, S. and Morrison, V. (2009). Predictors of familism in the caregiver role: a pilot study. *Journal of Health Psychology*, 14: 1135–43.

Parveen, S. and Morrison, V. (2012). Predicting caregiver gains: a longitudinal study. *British Journal of Health Psychology*, 17: 711–23.

Parveen, S., Morrison, V. and Robinson, C.A. (2011). Ethnic variations in the caregiver role: a qualitative study. *Journal of Health Psychology*, 16, 862–72.

Parveen, S., Morrison, V. and Robinson, C.A. (2013): Ethnicity, familism and willingness to care: important influences on caregiver mood?, *Aging & Mental Health*, 17:1 115–24

Parveen, S., Morrison, V. and Robinson, C.A. (2014). Does coping mediate the relationship between familism and caregiver outcomes, *Ageing & Mental Health,* http://dx.doi.org/10.1080/13607863.2013.827626

Parveen, S., Morrison, V. and Robinson, C. (2011). Ethnic variations in the caregiver role: a qualitative study. *Journal of Health Psychology*, doi: 10.1177/1359105310392416.

Pasterfield, D., Wilkinson, C., Finlay, I.G. et al. (2006). GPs' views on changing the law on physician-assisted suicide and euthanasia, and willingness to prescribe or inject lethal drugs: a survey from Wales. *British Journal of General Practice*, 56: 450–2.

Paton, A. (1999). Reflections on alcohol and the young. Invited commentary. *Alcohol and Alcoholism*, 34: 502–5.

Patterson, D.R. and Jensen, M.P. (2003). Hypnosis and clinical pain. *Psychological Bulletin*, 129: 495–521.

Patrick, D.L. and Peach, H. (1989). *Disablement in the Community*. Oxford: Oxford University Press.

Paunonen, S.V. and Ashton, M.C. (2001). Big five factors and facets and the prediction of behavior. *Journal of Personality and Social Psychology*, 91: 524–37.

Payne, N. (2001). Occupational stressors and coping as determinants of burnout in female hospice nurses. *Journal of Advanced Nursing*, 33: 396–405.

Payne, S. (2006). *The Health of Men and Women*. Buckingham: Open University Press.

Pbert, L., Osganian, S.K., Gorak, D. et al. (2006). A school nurse-delivered adolescent smoking cessation intervention: a randomized controlled trial. *Preventive Medicine*, 43: 312–20.

Pearlin, L.I. (1983). Role strains and personal stress. In H.B. Kaplan (ed.), *Psychosocial Stress: Trends in Theory and Research*. New York: Academic Press.

Pearlin, L.I. and Mullan, J.T. (1992). Loss and stress in ageing. In M.L. Wykle, E. Kahara and J. Kowal (eds), *Stress and Health among the Elderly*. New York: Springer Verlag.

Pearlin, L.I., Mullan, J.T., Semple, S.J. and Skaff, M.M. (1990). Caregiving and the stress process: an overview of concepts and their measures. *The Gerontological Society of America*, 30: 583–94.

Pearlin, L.I. and Schooler, C. (1978). The structure of coping. *Journal of Health and Social Behavior*, 19: 2–21.

Pearson, S., Maddern, G. and Hewett, P. (2005). Interacting effects of pre-operative information and patient choice in adaptation to colonoscopy: a randomised trial. *Diseases of the Colon and Rectum*. 48: 2047–54.

Peay, M.Y. and Peay, E.R. (1998). The evaluation of medical symptoms by patients and doctors. *Journal of Behavioral Medicine*, 21: 57–81.

Pederson-Fischer, A., Zacchariae, R. and Bovbjerg-Howard, D. (2009). Psychological stress and antibody response to influenza vaccination: a meta-analysis. *Brain, Behavior and Immunity*, 23: 427–33.

Pelosi, A.J. and Appleby, L. (1992). Psychological influences on cancer and ischaemic heart disease (for debate). *British Medical Journal*, 304: 1295–8.

Pelosi, A.J. and Appleby, L. (1993). Personality and fatal diseases. *British Medical Journal*, 306: 1666–7.

Peltola, H., Patja, A., Leinikkii, P. et al. (1998). No evidence for measles, mumps and rubella vaccine-associated inflammatory bowel disease or autism in a 14-year prospective study. *The Lancet*, 351: 1327–8.

Pendleton, D.A. (1983). Doctor–patient communication: a review. In D. Pendleton and J. Hasler (eds), *Doctor–Patient Communication*. London: Academic Press.

Pendleton, D., Schofield, T., Tate, P. and Havelock, P. (1984). *The Consultation: An Approach to Learning and Teaching*. Oxford: Oxford University Press.

Penedo, F.J., Molton, I., Dahn, J.R. et al. (2006). Randomized clinical trial of group-based cognitive-behavioral stress management in localized prostate cancer: development of stress management skills improves quality of life and benefit finding. *Annals of Behavioral Medicine*, 31: 261–70.

Penley, J.A. and Tmaka, J. (2002). Associations among the Big Five, emotional responses and coping with acute stress. *Personality and Individual Differences,* 32:1215–28.

Pennebaker, J.W. (1982). Social and perceptual factors affecting symptom reporting and mass psychogenic illness. In M.J. Colligan, J.W. Pennebaker and L.R. Murphy (eds), *Mass Psychogenic Illness: A Social Psychological Analysis*. Hillsdale, NJ: Lawrence Erlbaum.

Pennebaker, J.W. (1992). *The Psychology of Physical Symptoms*. New York: Springer Verlag.

Pennebaker, J.W. (1993). Putting stress into words: health, linguistic and therapeutic implications. *Behavioral Research Therapy*, 31: 539–48.

Pennebaker, J.W. and Beall, S. (1986). Confronting a traumatic event: toward an understanding of inhibition and disease. *Journal of Abnormal Psychology*, 95: 274–81.

Pennebaker, J.W., Colder, M. and Sharp, L.K. (1990). Accelerating the coping process. *Journal of Personality and Social Psychology*, 58: 528–37.

Pennebaker, J.W., Kiecolt-Glaser, J. and Glaser, R. (1988). Disclosure of trauma and immune function: health implications for psychotherapy. *Journal of Consulting and Clinical Psychology*, 56: 239–45.

Pennebaker, J.W. and Skelton, J.A. (1981). Selective monitoring of bodily sensations. *Journal of Personality and Social Behaviour*, 35: 167–74.

Penninx, B., Guralnik, J.M., Pahor, M. et al. (1998). Chronically depressed mood and cancer risk in older persons. *Journal of the National Cancer Institute*, 90: 1888–93.

Penninx, B.W.J.H., van Tilburg, T., Kriegsman, D.M.W. et al. (1999). Social network, social support, and loneliness in older persons with different chronic diseases. *Journal of Ageing and Health*, 11: 151–68.

Penwell, L.M. and Larkin, K.T. (2010). Social support and risk for cardiovascular disease and cancer: a qualitative review examining the role of inflammatory processes. *Health Psychology Review*, 4: 42–55.

Perkins, H.W., Haines, M.P. and Rice, R. (2005). Misperceiving the college drinking norm and related problems: a nationwide study of exposure to prevention information, perceived norms and student alcohol misuse. *Journal of Studies on Alcohol*, 66: 470–8.

Perna, F.M., Craft, L., Carver, C.S. and Antoni, M.H. (2008). Negative affect and barriers to exercise among early stage breast cancer patients. *Health Psychology*, 27: 275–9.

Perry, C.L. and Grant, M. (1988). Comparing peer-led to teacher-led youth alcohol education in four countries. (Australia, Chile, Norway and Swaziland). *Alcohol Health and Research World*, 12: 322–6.

Perry, K., Petrie, K.J., Ellis, C.J. et al. (2001). Symptom expectations and delay in acute myocardial infarction patients. *Heart*, 86: 91–2.

Perugini, M. and Bagozzi, R.P. (2001). The role of desires and anticipated emotions in goal-directed behaviours: broadening and deepening the theory of planned behaviour. *British Journal of Social Psychology*, 40: 79–98.

Peterson, T.R. and Aldana, S.G. (1999). Improving exercise behaviour: an application of the stages of change model in a worksite setting. *American Journal of Health Promotion*, 13: 229–32.

Peto, R., Darby, S., Deo, H. et al. (2000). Smoking, smoking cessation, and lung cancer in the UK since 1950: combination of national statistics with two case-control studies. *British Medical Journal*, 321: 323–9.

Peto, R. and Lopez, A.D. (1990). Worldwide mortality from current smoking patterns. In B. Durston and K. Jamrozik (eds), *Tobacco and Health 1990: The Global War*. Proceedings of the 7th World Conference on Tobacco and Health. Perth: Health Department of Western Australia.

Peto, R., Lopez, A.D., Borehan, J. et al. (1994). *Mortality from Smoking in Developed Countries 1950–2000*. Oxford: Oxford University Press.

Petrak, J.A., Doyle, A.-M., Smith, A. et al. (2001). Factors associated with self-disclosure of HIV serostatus to significant others. *British Journal of Health Psychology*, 6: 69–79.

Petrie, K.J., Buick, D.L., Weinman, J. and Booth, R.J. (1999). Positive effects of illness reported by myocardial infarction and breast cancer patients. *Journal of Psychosomatic Research*, 47: 537–43.

Petrie, K.J., Fontanilla, I., Thomas, M.G. et al. (2004). Effects of written emotional expression on immune function in patients with human immunodeficiency virus infection: a randomized trial. *Psychosomatic Medicine*, 66: 272–5.

Petrie, K.J., Jago, L.A. and Devcich, D.A. (2007). The role of illness perceptions in patients with medical conditions. *Current Opinion in Psychiatry*, 20: 163–7.

Petrie, K.J. and Weinman, J. (2003). More focus needed on symptom appraisal (editorial). *Journal of Psychosomatic Research*, 54: 401–3.

Petrie, K.J., Weinman, J., Sharpe, N. et al. (1996). Role of patients' view of their illness in predicting return to work and functioning after a myocardial infarction. *British Medical Journal*, 312: 1191–4.

Petrie, K.P., Cameron, L.D., Ellis, C.J. et al. (2002). Changing illness perceptions after myocardial infarction: an early intervention randomized controlled trial. *Psychosomatic Medicine*, 64: 580–6.

Petruzzello, S.J., Jones, A.C. and Tate, A.K. (1997). Affective responses to acute exercise: a test of opponent-process theory. *Journal of Sports Medicine and Physical Fitness*, 37: 205–11.

Petter, M., Blanchard, C., Kemp, K.A. et al. (2009). Correlates of exercise among coronary heart disease patients: review, implications and future directions. *European Journal of Cardiovascular Prevention and Rehabilitation*, 16: 515–26.

Petticrew, A., Fraser, J. and Regan, M. (1999). Adverse life events and risk of breast cancer: a meta-analysis. *British Journal of Health Psychology*, 4: 1–17.

Petticrew, M., Bell, R. and Hunter, D. (2002). Influence of psychological coping on survival and recurrence in people with cancer: a systematic review. *British Medical Journal*, 325: 1066.

Petty, R. and Cacioppo, J. (1986). The elaboration likelihood model of persuasion. In L. Berkowitz (ed.), *Advances in Experimental Social Psychology*, Vol. 19. Orlando, FL: Academic Press.

Petty, R.E. and Cacioppo, J.T. (1996). *Attitudes and Persuasion: Classic and Contemporary Approaches.* Boulder, CO: Westview Press.

Peveler, R., Carson, A. and Rodin, G. (2002). Depression in medical patients. *British Medical Journal*, 325: 149–52.

Pfeifer, G. (2009). Factors in food choice. *The Psychologist*, 22: 588–9.

Phelps, C., Bennett, P., Iredale, R. et al. (2005). The development of a distraction-based coping intervention for women waiting for genetic risk information: a phase 1 qualitative study. *Psycho-Oncology*, 15, 169–73.

Phillips, A.C., Der, G. and Carrolll, D. (2008). Stressful life-events exposure is associated with 17-year mortality, but it is health-related events that prove predictive. *British Journal of Health Psychology*, 13: 647–57.

Phillips, L.A., Leventhal, H. and Leventhal, E.A. (2013). Assessing theoretical predictors of long-term medication adherence: patients' treatment-related beliefs, experiential feedback and habit development. *Psychology & Health*, 28: 1135–51.

PHLS Communicable Disease Surveillance Centre (2002). *HIV and AIDS in the United Kingdom 2001. An Update: November 2002*. London: PHLS, ICH (London) and SCIEH.

Piaget, J. (1930). *The Child's Conception of Physical Causality*. London: Routledge and Kegan Paul.

Piaget, J. (1970). Piaget's theory. In P.H. Mussen (ed.), *Carmichael's Manual of Child Psychology*, 3rd edn, Vol. 1. New York: Wiley.

Pietromonaco, P.R., Uchino, B. and Dunkel Schetter, C. (2013) Close relationship processes and health: implications of attachment theory for health and disease. *Health Psychology*, 32: 499–513. http://dx.doi.org/10.1037/a0029349

Piette, J.D., Weinberger, M. and McPhee, S.J. (2000). The effect of automated calls with telephone nurse follow-up on patient-centered outcomes of diabetes care: a randomized controlled trial. *Medical Care*, 38: 218–30.

Pinel, J.P.J. (2003). *Biopsychology*, 5th edn. Boston, MA: Allyn and Bacon.

Pinel, J.P.J., Assanand, S. and Lehman, D.R. (2000). Hunger, eating and ill-health. *American Psychologist*, 55: 1105–16.

Pinquart, M. and Sörensen, S. (2003). Differences between caregivers and noncaregivers in psychological health and physical health: a meta-analysis. *Psychology and Aging*, 18: 250–67.

Pinquart, M. and Sörensen, S. (2005). Ethnic differences in stressors, resources, and psychological outcomes of family caregiving: a meta-analysis. *The Gerontologist*, 45: 90–106.

Pinquart, M. and Sörensen, S. (2006). Gender differences in caregiver stressors, social resources and health: an updated meta-analysis. *Journal of Gerontology: Psychological Sciences*, 61B: 33–45.

Pirozzo, S., Summerbell, C., Cameron, C. and Glasziou, P. (2003). Advice on low-fat diets for obesity. In *The Cochrane Library*, issue 1. Oxford: Update Software.

Pisinger, C. and DØssing, M. (2014). A systematic review of health effects of electronic cigarettes. *Preventive Medicine*, 69: 248–60.

Pisinger, C. and Jorgensen, T. (2007). Weight concerns and smoking in a general population: The Inter99 study. *Preventive Medicine*, 44: 283–9.

Pisters, M.F., Veenhof, C., de Bakker, D.H. et al. (2010). Behavioural graded activity results in better exercise adherence and more physical activity than usual care in people with osteoarthritis: a cluster-randomised trial. *Journal of Physiotherapy*, 56: 41–7.

Pitel, L., Geckova, A.M., van Dijk, J.P. et al. (2010). Gender differences in adolescent health-related behaviour diminished between 1998 and 2006. *Public Health*, 124: 512–18.

Plante, T.G. and Rodin, J. (1990). Physical fitness and enhanced psychological health. *Current Psychology Research and Reviews*, 9: 3–24.

Plassman, B.L., Williams, J.W., Burke, J.R. et al. (2010). Systematic review: factors associated with risk for and possible prevention of cognitive decline in later life. *Annals of Internal Medicine*, 153(3): 182–93.

Plotnikoff, R.C., Brunet, S., Courneya, K.S. et al. (2007). The efficacy of stage-matched and standard public health materials for promoting physical activity in the workplace: the Physical Activity Workplace Study (PAWS). *American Journal of Health Promotion*, 21: 501–9.

Plotnikoff, R.C., Lippke, S., Courneya, K. et al. (2010). Physical activity and diabetes: an application of the theory of planned behaviour to explain physical activity for type 1 and type 2 diabetes in an adult population sample. *Psychology & Health*, 25: 7–23.

Plotnikoff, R.C., Lubans, D.R., Penfold, C.M. and Courneya, K.S. (2014). Testing the utility of three social-cognitive models for predicting objective and self-report physical activity in adults with type 2 diabetes. *British Journal of Health Psychology*, 19: 329–46.

Plotnikoff, R.C., McCargar, L.J., Wilson, P.M. et al. (2005). Efficacy of an e-mail intervention for the promotion of physical activity and nutrition behavior in the workplace context. *American Journal of Health Promotion*, 19: 422–9.

Pollock, K., Wilson, E., Porock, D. et al. (2007). Evaluating the impact of a cancer supportive care project in the community: patient and professional configurations of need. *Health and Social Care in the Community*, 15: 520–9.

Polsky, D., Doshi, J.A., Marcus, S. et al. (2005). Long-term risk for depressive symptoms after a medical diagnosis. *Archives of Internal Medicine*, 165: 1260–6.

Pomp, S., Fleig, Schwarzer, R and Lippke, S. (2012). Depressive symptoms interfere with post-rehabilitation exercise: outcome expectancies and experience as mediators. *Psychology, Health and Medicine*, 17: 698–708.

Post, S.G. (ed.) (2007). *Altruism and Health: Perspectives From Empirical Research*. New York, NY: Oxford University Press.

Potter, J., Hami, F., Bryan, T. and Quigley, C. (2003). Symptoms in 400 patients referred to palliative care services: prevalence and patterns. *Palliative Medicine*, 17: 310–14.

Potter, J.D., Slattery, M.L., Bostick, R.M. and Gapstur, S.M. (1993). Colon cancer: a review of the epidemiology. *Epidemiological Review*, 15: 499–545.

Poulin, M.J., Brown, S.L., Dillard, A.J. and Smith, D.M. (2013). Giving to others and the association between stress and mortality. *American Journal of Public Health;* 103: 1649–55. doi: 10.2105/AJPH.2012.300876

Poulin, M.J., Brown, S.L., Ubel, P. et al. (2010). Does a helping hand mean a heavy heart? Helping behavior and well-being among spouse caregivers. *Psychology and Aging*, 25: 108–17.

Poulin M.J. and Holman, E.A. (2013). Helping hands, healthy body? Oxytocin receptor gene and prosocial behavior interact to buffer the association between stress and physical health. *Hormones and Behavior;* 63: 510–17, http://dx.doi.org/10.1016/j.yhbeh.2013.01.004

Pound, P., Bury, M., Gompertz, P. and Ebrahim, S. (1994). Views of survivors of stroke on the benefits of physiotherapy. *Quality in Health Care*, 3: 69–74.

Powell, H. and Gibson, P.G. (2003). Options for self-management education for adults with asthma. *Cochrane Database of Systematic Reviews*, CD004107.

Powell-Griner, E., Anderson, J.E. and Murphy, W. (1997). State and sex-specific prevalence of selected characteristics behavioural risk factor surveillance system, 1994 and 1995. *Morbidity and Mortality Weekly Report*, Centres for Disease Control, surveillance summaries, 46: 1–31.

Power, R., Koopman, C., Volk, J. et al. (2003). Social support, substance use, and denial in relationship to antiretroviral treatment adherence among HIV-infected persons. *AIDS Patient Care and STDs*, 17: 245–52.

Powers, J.R., Goodger, B. and Byles, J.E. (2004). Assessment of the abbreviated Duke Social Support Index in a cohort of older Australian women. *Australian Journal on Ageing*, 23: 71–6.

Pradhan, E.K., Baumgarten, M., Langenberg, P. et al. (2007). Effect of mindfulness-based stress reduction in rheumatoid arthritis patients. *Arthritis and Rheumatism*, 57: 1134–42.

Prentice, A.M. and Jebb, S.A. (1995). Obesity in Britain: gluttony or sloth. *British Medical Journal*, 311: 437–9.

Prescott-Clarke, P. and Primatesta, P. (1998). *Health Survey for England: The Health of Young People 1995–97*. London: The Stationery Office.

Price, D.D., Finniss, D.G. and Benedetti, F. (2008). A comprehensive review of the placebo effect: recent advances and current thought. *Annual Review of Psychology* 59: 565–90.

Price, M.A., Bell, M.L., Sommeijer, D.W. et al. (2013). Physical symptoms, coping styles and quality of life in recurrent ovarian cancer: a prospective population-based study over the last year of life, *Gynaecologic Oncology;* 130: 162–8 http://dx.doi.org/10.1016/j.ygyno.2013.03.031

Price, R.A. and Gottesman, I.I. (1991). Body fat in identical twins reared apart: roles for genes and environment. *Behavioral Genetics*, 21: 1–7.

Price, V.A. (1988). Research and clinical issues in treating Type A behavior. In B.K. Houston and C.R. Snyder (eds), *Type A Behavior Pattern: Research, Theory, and Practice*. New York: Wiley.

Prochaska, J.O. (1994). Strong and weak principles for progressing from precontemplation to action based on twelve problem behaviours. *Health Psychology*, 13: 47–51.

Prochaska, J.O. and di Clemente, C.C. (1984). *The Transtheoretical Approach: Crossing Traditional Boundaries of Therapy*. Homewood, IL: Dow Jones Irwin.

Prochaska, J.O. and di Clemente, C.C. (1986). Towards a comprehensive model of change. In B.K. Houston and N. Heather (eds), *Treating Addictive Behaviours: Processes of Change*. New York: Plenum.

Prochaska, J.O. and Marcus, B.H. (1994). The trans-theoretical model: applications to exercise. In R.K. Dishman (ed.), *Advances in Exercise Adherence*. Champaign, IL: Human Kinetics.

Prochaska, J.O., Norcross, J.C., Fowler, J.L. and Follick, M.J. (1992). Attendance and outcome in a worksite weight control program: processes and stages of change as process and predictor variables. *Addictive Behaviors*, 17: 35–45.

Prochaska, J.O. and Velicer, W.F. (1997). The Transtheoretical Model of health behavior change. *American Journal of Health Promotion*, 12: 38–48.

Prochaska, J.O., Velicer, W.F., Rossi, J.S. et al. (1994). Stages of change and decisional balance for 12 problem behaviours. *Health Psychology*, 13: 39–46.

Prohaska, T.R., Funch, D. and Blesch, K.S. (1990). Age patterns in symptom perception and illness behaviour among colorectal cancer patients. *Behavior, Health and Aging*, 1: 27–39.

Prohaska, T.R., Keller, M.L., Leventhal, E.A. et al. (1987). Impact of symptoms and aging attribution on emotions and coping. *Health Psychology*, 6: 495–514.

Project MATCH Research Group (1998). Matching alcoholism treatments to client heterogeneity: Project MATCH three-year drinking outcomes. *Alcoholism: Clinical and Experimental Research*, 22: 1300–11.

Ptacek, J.T.P. and Eberhardt, T.L. (1996). Breaking bad news: a review of the literature. *Journal of the American Medical Association*, 276: 496–502.

Ptacek, J.T., Ptacek, J.J. and Ellison, H. (2001). 'I'm sorry to tell you' – physicians' reports of breaking bad news. *Journal of Behavioral Medicine*, 24: 205–17.

Public Health England (2014). Evaluation of vaccine uptake during the 2013 MMR catch-up campaign in England, Report for the national measles oversight group, Public Health England, London.

Puccio, J.A., Belzer, M., Olson, J. et al. (2006). The use of cell phone reminder calls for assisting HIV-infected adolescents and young adults to adhere to highly active antiretroviral therapy: a pilot study. *AIDS Patient Care and STDS*, 20: 438–44.

Puska, P., Tuomilehto, J., Nissinen, A. et al. (1985). *The North Karelia Project: 20 Year Results and Experiences*. Helsinki: National Public Health Institutem.

Quah, S.-H. and Bishop, G.D. (1996). Seeking help for illness: the roles of cultural orientation and illness cognition. *Journal of Health Psychology*, 1: 209–22.

Quentin, W., Neubauer, S., Leidl, R. et al. (2007). Advertising bans as a means of tobacco control policy: a systematic literature review of time-series analyses. *International Journal of Public Health*, 52: 295–307.

Quick, J.D., Nelson, D.L., Matuszek, P.A.C. et al. (1996). Social support, secure attachments and health. In C.L. Cooper (ed.), *Handbook of Stress, Medicine and Health*. London: CRC Press.

Quinn, F., Johnston, M. and Johnston, D. (2013). Testing an integrated behavioural and biomedical model of disability in N-of-1 studies with chronic pain. *Psychology & Health*, 12: 1391–406.

Quinn, K., Kaufman, J.S., Siddiqi, A. and Yeatts, K.B. (2010). Stress and the city: housing stressors are associated with respiratory health among low socioeconomic status Chicago children. *Journal of Urban Health*, 87: 688–702.

Qureshi, M., Thacker, H.L., Litaker, D.G. et al. (2000). Differences in breast cancer screening rates: an issue of ethnicity or socioeconomics? *Journal of Women's Health and Gender Based Medicine*, 9: 1025–31.

Radley, A. (1994). *Making Sense of Illness: The Social Psychology of Health and Disease*. London: Sage.

Radley, A. (1996). Social psychology and health: framing the relationship. *Psychology and Health*, 11: 629–34.

Rafferty, Y., Friend, R. and Landsbergis, P.A. (2001). The association between job skill discretion, decision authority and burnout. *Work and Stress*, 15: 73–85.

Raftery, K.A., Smith-Coggins, R. and Chen, A.H. (1995). Gender-associated differences in emergency department pain management. *Annals of Emergency Medicine*, 26: 414–21.

Ragland, D.R. and Brand, R.J. (1988). Type A behaviour and mortality from coronary heart disease. *New England Journal of Medicine*, 318: 65–9.

Rahe, R. (1974). Life change and subsequent illness reports. In E.K.E. Gunderson and R. Rahe (eds), *Life Stress and Illness*. Springfield, IL: Charles Thomas.

Rahimi, A.R., Spertus, J.A., Reid, K.J. et al. (2007). Financial barriers to health care and outcomes after acute myocardial infarction. *Journal of the American Medical Association*, 297: 1063–72.

Rai, T, Clement, A., Bukach, C., et al. (2007). What influences men's decisions to have a prostate-specific antigen test? A qualitative study. *Family Practice*, 24: 365–71.

Rains, J.C., Penzien, D.B., McCrory, D.C. et al. (2005). Behavioral headache treatment: history, review of the empirical literature, and methodological critique. *Headache*, 45: S91–S108.

Ramel, W., Goldin, P.R., Carmona, P.E. and McQuaid, J.R. (2004). The effects of mindfulness meditation on cognitive processes and affect in patients with past depression. *Cognitive Therapy and Research*, 28: 433–55.

Ramirez, A., Craig, T., Watson, J. et al. (1989). Stress and relapse of breast cancer. *British Medical Journal*, 298: 291–3.

Ramirez, A.J., Westcombe, A.M., Burgess, C.C. et al. (1999). Factors predicting delayed presentation of symptomatic breast cancer: a systematic review. *The Lancet*, 353: 1119–26.

Ramnarayan, P., Roberts, G.C., Coren, M. et al. (2006). Assessment of the potential impact of a reminder system on the reduction of diagnostic errors: a quasi-experimental study. *BMC Medical Informatics and Decision Making*, 6: 22.

Ramo, D.E., Young-Wooolff, K.C. and Prochaska, J.J. (2015). Prevalence and correlates of electronic-cigarette use in young adults: Findings from three studies over five years. *Addictive Behaviors,* 41: 142–7.

Rampersaud, E., Mitchell, B.D., Pollin, T.I. et al. (2008). Physical activity and the association of common FTO gene variants with body mass index and obesity. *Archives of Internal Medicine*, 168: 1791–7.

Rand, C.S. and Wise, R.A. (1994). Measuring adherence to asthma medication regimens. *American Journal of Respiratory and Critical Care Medicine*, 149 (suppl.): 69–76.

Rao, G.A., Sutton, S.S., Hardin, J. et al. (2013) Impact of highly active antiretroviral therapy regimen on adherence and risk of hospitalization in veterans with HIV/AIDS. 53rd Interscience Conference on Antimicrobial Agents and Chemotherapy, Denver, abstract H-1464, 2013.

Rapp, S.R. and Chao, D. (2000). Appraisals of strain and of gain: effects on psychological wellbeing of caregivers of dementia patients. *Aging & Mental Health*, 4: 142–7.

Rasulo, D., Bajekal, M. and Yar, M. (2007). Inequalities in health expectancies in England and Wales: small area analysis from the 2001 Census. *Health Statistics Quarterly*, 34: 35–45.

Rathleff, M.S., Roos, E.M., Olesen, J.L. et al. (2013). High prevalence of daily and multi-site pain: a cross-sectional population-based study among 3000 Danish adolescents. *BMC Pediatrics*, 13: 191.

RCN (2002). Royal College of Nursing Congress 2002 Report summaries. *Nursing Standard*, 16: 4–9.

Reddy, D.M., Fleming, R. and Adesso, V.J. (1992). Gender and health. In S. Maes, H. Leventhal and M. Johnston (eds), *International Review of Health Psychology*, Vol. 1. Chichester: Wiley.

Reeve, J., Menon, D. and Corabian, P. (1996). Trans-cutaneous electrical nerve stimulation (TENS): a technology assessment. *International Journal of Technology Assessment in Health Care*, 12: 299–324.

Reich, J. and Schatzberg, A. (2010). Personality traits and medical outcome of cardiac illness. *Journal of Psychiatric Research*, 44: 1017–20.

Rennemark, M. and Hagberg, B. (1999). What makes old people perceive symptoms of illness? The impact of psychological and social factors. *Aging & Mental Health*, 3: 79–87.

Renner, B., Kwon, S., Yang, B.-H. et al. (2008). Social-cognitive predictors of dietary behaviors in South Korean men and women. *International Journal of Behavioral Medicine*, 15(1): 4–13.

Renner, B. and Schwarzer, R. (2003). Social-cognitive factors in health behaviour change. In J. Suls and K. Wallston (eds), *Social Foundations of Health and Illness*. Oxford: Blackwell.

Renner, B., Spivak, Y., Kwon, S. and Schwarzer, R. (2007). Does age make a difference? Predicting physical activity of South Koreans. *Psychology & Ageing*, 22: 482–93.

Renzi, C., Peticca, L. and Pescatori, M. (2000). The use of relaxation techniques in the perioperative management of proctological patients: preliminary results. *International Journal of Colorectal Diseases*, 15: 313–16.

Resendes, L.A. and McCorkle, R. (2006). Spousal responses to prostate cancer: an integrative review. *Cancer Investigations*, 24: 192–8.

Resnick, R.J. and Rozensky, R.H. (eds) (1997). *Health Psychology Through the Life Span: Practice and Research Opportunities*. Washington, DC: American Psychological Association.

Resnicow, K., Jackson, A., Wang, T. et al. (2001). Motivational interviewing intervention to increase fruit and vegetable intake through black churches: results of the Eat for Life trial. *American Journal of Public Health*, 91: 1686–93.

Rhodes, F. and Wolitski, B. (1990). Perceived effectiveness of fear appeals in AIDS education: relationship to ethnicity, gender, age and group membership. *AIDS Education and Prevention*, 2: 1–11.

Rhodes, R.E. and de Bruijn, G. (2013). How big is the physical activity intention-behaviour gap? A meta-analysis using the action control framework. *British Journal of Health Psychology*, 18: 296–309.

Rhodes, R.E. and Dickau, L. (2012). Meta-analysis of experimental evidence for the intention-behaviour relationship in the physical activity domain, *Health Psychology*, 31: 724–7.

Rhodewalt, F. and Zone, J.B. (1989). Appraisal of life change, depression, and illness in hardy and nonhardy women. *Journal of Personality and Social Psychology*, 56: 81–8.

Ricciardelli, L.A. and McCabe, M.P. (2001). Children's body image concerns and eating disturbance: a review of the literature. *Clinical Psychology Review*, 21: 325–44.

Rice, P.L. (1992). *Stress and Health*. Pacific Grove, CA: Brooks/Cole.

Richard, R., van der Pligt, J. and de Vries, N. (1996). Anticipated regret and time perspective: changing sexual risk-taking behaviour. *Journal of Behavioural Decision Making*, 9: 185–99.

Richards, J., Fisher, P. and Conner, F. (1989). The warnings on cigarette packages are ineffective. *Journal of the American Medical Association*, 261: 45.

Richards, M.A., Westcombe, A.M., Love, S.B. et al. (1999). Influence of delay on survival in patients with breast cancer: a systematic review. *The Lancet*, 353: 1119–26.

Richardson, J. (2000). The use of randomised control trials in complementary therapies: exploring the issues. *Journal of Advanced Nursing*, 32: 398–406.

Richardson, K.M. and Rothstein, H.R. (2008). Effects of occupational stress management intervention programs: a meta-analysis. *Journal of Occupational Health Psychology*, 13: 69–93.

Richmond, R.L., Kehoe, L. and de Almeida Neto, A.C. (1997). Effectiveness of a 24-hour transdermal nicotine patch in conjunction with a cognitive behavioural programme: one year outcome. *Addiction*, 92: 27–31.

Riemsma, R.P., Taal, E. and Rasker, J.J. (2003). Group education for patients with rheumatoid arthritis and their partners. *Arthritis and Rheumatism*, 49: 556–66.

Rigby, K., Brown, M., Anagnostou, P. et al. (1989). Shock tactics to counter AIDS: the Australian experience. *Psychology and Health*, 3: 145–59.

Riley, J.L., III, Wade, J.B., Myers, C.D. et al. (2002). Racial/ethnic differences in the experience of chronic pain. *Pain*, 100: 291–8.

Ringström, G., Abrahamsson, H., Strid, H. and Simrén, M. (2007). Why do subjects with irritable bowel syndrome seek health care for their symptoms? *Scandinavian Journal of Gastroenterology*, 42: 1194–203.

Rise, J. Sheeran, P. Skalle, S. (2006). The role of self-identity in the theory of planned behavior: a meta-analysis. Unpublished manuscript, Norwegian Institute for Alcohol and Drug Research, Oslo.

Rivis, A. and Sheeran, P. (2003). Social influences and the theory of planned behaviour: evidence for a direct relationship between prototypes and young people's exercise behaviour. *Psychology and Health*, 18: 567–83.

Rivis, A., Sheeran, P. and Armitage, C. (2010). Explaining adolescents' cigarette smoking: a comparison of four modes of action control and a test of the role of self-regulatory mode. *Psychology & Health*, 25: 893–909.

Robb, K.A., Bennett, M.I., Johnson, M.I. et al. (2008). Transcutaneous electric nerve stimulation (TENS) for cancer pain in adults. *Cochrane Database of Systematic Reviews*, 3: CD006276.

Robb, K., Oxberry, S.G., Bennett, M.I. et al. (2009). A Cochrane systematic review of transcutaneous electrical nerve stimulation for cancer pain. *Journal of Pain and Symptom Management*, 37: 746–53.

Roberts, C.S., Cox, C.E., Reintgen, D.S. et al. (1994). Influence of physician communication on newly diagnosed breast patients' psychologic adjustment and decision-making. *Cancer*, 74: 336–41.

Roberts, J. and Rowland, M. (1981). *Hypertension in Adults 25–74 Years of Age, United States, 1971–1975*. Hyattsville, MD: National Center for Health Statistics (Vital and Health Statistics, Series II: Data from the National Health Survey, No. 221). DHHS publication No. 81–1671.

Robertson, M., Moir, J., Skelton, J. et al. (2011). When the business of sharing treatment decisions is not the same as shared decision making: a discourse analysis of decision sharing in general practice. *Health (London)*, 15: 78–95.

Robinson, M.S. and Alloy, L.B. (2003). Negative cognitive styles and stress-reactive rumination interact to predict depression: a prospective study. *Cognitive Therapy and Research*, 27: 275–92.

Robinson, R.G. (1998). *The Clinical Neuropsychiatry of Stroke*. Cambridge: Cambridge University Press.

Roesch, S.C., Adams, L., Hines, A. et al. (2005). Coping with prostate cancer: a meta-analytic review. *Journal of Behavioural Medicine*, 28: 281–93.

Roesch, S.C. and Weiner, B. (2001). A meta-analytic review of coping with illness: do causal attributions matter? *Journal of Psychosomatic Research*, 50: 205–19.

Rogers, C.R. (1961). *On Becoming a Person*. Boston, MA: Houghton Mifflin.

Rogers, E. (1983). *Diffusion of Innovations*. New York: Free Press.

Rogers, G., Curry, M., Oddy, J. et al. (2003). Depressive disorders and unprotected casual anal sex among Australian homosexually active men in primary care. *HIV Medicine*, 4: 271–5.

Rogers, R.W. (1983). Cognitive and physiological responses to fear appeals and attitude change: a revised theory of protection motivation. In J.T. Cacioppo and R.E. Petty (eds), *Social Psychophysiology: A Source Book*. New York: Guilford Press.

Rogers, R.W. and Prentice Dunn, S. (1997). Protection motivation theory. In D.S. Goffman (ed.), *Handbook of Health Behavior Research 1: Personal and Social Determinants*. New York: Plenum, pp. 113–32.

Rohr, MK. and Lang, F.R. (2014). The role of anticipated gains and losses on preferences about future caregiving. *Journal of Gerontology, Series B: Psychological Sciences and Social Sciences*, doi:10.1093/geronb/gbu145

Rokach, A. (2011). From loneliness to belonging: A review. *Psychology Journal*, 8: 70–81.

Rokach, A. and Parvini, M. (2011). Experience of adults and children in hospitals. *Early Child Development and Care*, 18: 707–15.

Rolland, J.S. (2012). Mastering family challenges in serious illness and disability. In Walsh, F (ed.), *Normal Family Processes*, 4th edn, New York: Guilford Press, pp. 452–82.

Rolland, J.S. and Williams, J.K. (2005). Towards a biopsychosocial model for 21st century genetics. *Family Process*, 44: 3–24.

Romano, J. M., Jensen, M. P., Schmaling, K. B. et al. (2009). Illness behaviors in patients with unexplained chronic fatigue are associated with significant other responses. *Journal of Behavioral Medicine*, 32, 558–69. doi:10.1007/s10865–009–9234–3

Rook, K.S (2015). Social networks in later life: weighing positive and negative effects on health and wellbeing. *Current Directions in Psychological Science*, pp. 123–35.

Rook, K. S., August, K. J. and Sorkin, D. H. (2011). Social network functions and health. In R. Contrada and A. Baum (eds), *Handbook of Stress Science: Biology, Psychology, and Health*. NewYork, NY: Springer, pp. 123–35.

Ropka, M.E., Wenzel, J., Phillips, E.K. et al. (2006). Uptake rates for breast cancer genetic testing: a systematic review. *Cancer Epidemiology, Biomarkers and Prevention*, 15: 840–55.

Rosamond, W.D., Chambless, L.E., Heiss, G. et al. (2012) Twenty-two year trends in incidence of myocardial infarction, CHD mortality, and case-fatality in four US communities, 1987 to 2008. *Circulation*, 125: 1848–57.

Rosch, P.J. (1994). Can stress cause coronary heart disease? (Editorial). *Stress Medicine*, 10: 207–10.

Rosch, P.J. (1996). Stress and cancer: disorders of communication, control and civilization. In Cooper, C.L. (ed.), *Handbook of Stress, Medicine and Health*. Boca Raton, FL: CRC Press, pp. 27–60.

Rosco, J.A., Morrow, G.R., Aapro, M.S. et al. (2010). Anticipatory nausea and vomiting. *Supportive Care in Cancer*, doi: 10. 1007/s00520–010–0980–0.

Rose, J.S., Chassin, L., Presson, C.C. and Sherman, S.J. (1996). Prospective predictors of quit attempts and smoking cessation in young adults. *Health Psychology*, 15: 261–8.

Rose, S., Bisson, J. and Wessely, S. (2001). Psychological debriefing for preventing post traumatic stress disorder (PTSD). *Cochrane Database Systematic Review*, 3.

Rosenfeld, B., Breitbart, W., McDonald, M.V. et al. (1996). Pain in ambulatory AIDS patients II: impact of pain on psychological functioning and quality of life. *Pain*, 68: 323–8.

Rosengren, A., Hawken, S., Ounpuu, S. et al. (2004). Association of psychosocial risk factors with risk of acute myocardial infarction in 11119 cases and 1364 controls from 52 countries (the INTERHEART study): case-control study. *Lancet*, 364: 953–92.

Rosengren, A., Orth-Gomér, K., Wedel, H. and Wilhelmsen, L. (1993). Stressful life events, social support, and mortality in men born in 1933. *British Medical Journal*, 307: 1102–5.

Rosenman, R.H. (1978). Role of Type A pattern in the pathogenesis of ischaemic heart disease and modification for prevention. *Advances in Cardiology*, 25: 34–46.

Rosenman, R.H. (1996). Personality, behavior patterns, and heart disease. In C. Cooper (ed.), *Handbook of Stress, Medicine and Health*. Boca Raton, FL: CRC Press.

Rosenman, R.H., Brand, R.J., Jenkins, C.D. et al. (1975). Coronary heart disease in the Western Collaborative Group study; follow-up experience after 8 and a half years. *Journal of the American Medical Association*, 233: 872–7.

Rosenman, R.H., Brand, R.J., Sholtz, R.I. et al. (1976). Multivariate prediction of coronary heart disease during 8.5 year follow-up in the Western Collaborative Group study. *The American Journal of Cardiology*, 37: 903–10.

Rosenstock, I.M. (1966). Why people use health services. *Milbank Memorial Fund Quarterly*, 44: 94–124.

Rosenstock, I.M. (1974). The health belief model and preventive health behaviour. *Health Education Monographs*, 2: 354–86.

Rosenzweig, S., Greeson, J.M., Reibel, D.K. et al. (2010). Mindfulness-based stress reduction for chronic pain conditions: variation in treatment outcomes and role of home meditation practice. *Journal of Psychosomatic Research*, 68: 29–36.

Ross, D.A., Dick, B. and Ferguson, J. (eds) (2006*). Preventing HIV/AIDS in Young People. A Systematic Review of the Evidence from Developing Countries*. Geneva: World Health Organization.

Ross, L., Boesen, E.H., Dalton, S.O. and Johansen, C. (2002). Mind and cancer: does psychosocial intervention improve survival and psychological well-being? *European Journal of Cancer*, 38: 1447–57.

Rosser, B.A., McCracken. L.M., Velleman, S.C. et al. (2011). Concerns about medication and medication adherence in patients with chronic pain recruited from general practice. *Pain*, 152: 1201–5.

Roter, D.L. and Hall, J.A. (2004). Physician gender and patient-centered communication: a critical review of empirical research. *Annual Review of Public Health*, 25: 497–519.

Roth, D.L., Fredman, L. and Haley, W.E. (2015). Informal caregiving and its impact on health: a reappraisal from population-based studies. *The Gerontologist*, doi: 10.1093/geront/gnu177

Roth, M.L., Tripp, D.A., Harrison, M.H. et al. (2007). Demographic and psychosocial predictors of acute perioperative pain for total knee arthroplasty. *Pain Research and Management*, 12: 185–94.

Roth, S. and Cohen, L.J. (1986). Approach avoidance and coping with stress. *American Psychologist*, 41: 813–19.

Rothermund, K. and Brandstädter, J. (2003). Coping with deficits and losses in later life: from compensatory action to accommodation. *Psychology & Aging*, 18: 896–905.

Rotter, J.B. (1966). Generalized expectancies for the internal versus external control of reinforcement. *Psychological Monographs*, 90: 1–28.

Roussi, P. and Milller, S.M. (2014). Monitoring style of coping with cancer related threats: a review of the literature. *Journal of Behavioral Medicine*; 37: 931–54.

Rovelli, M., Palmeri, D., Vossler, E. et al. (1989). Noncompliance in organ transplant recipients. *Transplant Proceedings*, 21: 833–4.

Roy, R., Symonds, R.P., Kymar, D.M. et al. (2005). The use of denial in an ethnically diverse British cancer population: a cross-sectional study. *British Journal of Cancer*, 91: 1–5.

Royal College of Physicians (1995). *Alcohol and the Public Health*. London: Macmillan.

Royal College of Psychiatrists (2003). *The Mental Health of Students in Higher Education*. London: RCPsych.

Roye, C., Perlmutter Silverman, P. and Krauss, B. (2007). A brief, low-cost, theory-based intervention to promote dual method use by black and Latina female adolescents: a randomized clinical trial. *Health Education and Behavior*, 34: 608–21.

Ruberman, W., Weinblatt, E., Goldberg, J.D. et al. (1984). Psychosocial resilience and protective mechanisms. *American Journal of Orthopsychiatry*, 57: 316–30.

Rudat, K. (1994). *Black and Minority Ethnic Groups in England: Health and Lifestyles.* London: Health Education Authority.

Ruiter, R.A.C. and Kok, G. (2005). Saying is not (always) doing: cigarette warning labels are useless. *European Journal of Public Health*, 15: 329.

Ruiter, R.A.C. and Kok, G. (2006). Response to Hammond et al. Showing leads to doing, but doing what? The need for experimental pilot-testing. *European Journal of Public Health*, 16: 225.

Rumsey, N. and Harcourt, D. (2005). *The Psychology of Appearance*. Milton Keynes: Open University Press.

Russell, M.A., Wilson, C. and Baker, C.D. (1979). Effect of general practitioners' advice against smoking. *British Medical Journal*, 2: 231–5.

Rutledge, R.B., Skandali, N., Dayan, P. and Dolan, R.J. (2014). A computational and neural model of momentary subjective well-being. *Proceedings of the National Academy of Sciences*, 111: 2252–7, doi: 10.1073/pnas.1407535111

Rutter, D.R. (2000). Attendance and reattendance for breast cancer screening: a prospective 3-year test of the theory of planned behaviour. *British Journal of Health Psychology*, 2: 199–216.

Rutter, D.R., Steadman, L., Quine, L. (2006). An implementation intentions intervention to increase uptake of mammography. *Annals of Behavioral Medicine*, 32: 127–34.

Rutter, D. and Quine, L. (2002). *Changing Health Behaviour*. Buckingham: Open University Press.

Ryan, R.M. and Deci, E.L (2001). On happiness and human potential: a review of research on hedonic and eudaimonic wellbeing. *Annual Review of Psychology,* 52: 141–66.

Rystedt, L.W., Devereux, J. and Furnham, A.F. (2004). Are lay theories of work stress related to distress? A longitudinal study in the British workforce. *Work & Stress*, 18: 245–54.

Sabaté, E. (2003). *Adherence to Long-term Therapies: Evidence for Action*. Geneva: World Health Organization.

Sackett, D.L. and Haynes, R.B. (eds) (1976). *Compliance with Therapeutic Regimens*. Baltimore, MD: Johns Hopkins University Press.

Safer, M.A., Tharps, Q.J., Jackson, T.C. et al. (1979). Determinants of three stages of delay in seeking care at a medical setting. *Medical Care*, 7: 11–29.

Safren, S.A., Gonzalez, J.S., Wexler, D.J. et al. (2014). A randomized controlled trial of cognitive behavioral therapy for adherence and depression (CBT-AD) in patients with uncontrolled type 2 diabetes. *Diabetes Care*, 37: 625–33.

Safren, S.A., Otto, M.W. and Worth, J.L. (2001). Two strategies to increase adherence to HIV antiretroviral medication: Life-Steps and medication monitoring. *Behaviour Research and Therapy*, 39: 1151–62.

Safren, S.A., Radomsky, A.S., Otto, M.W. et al. (2002). Predictors of psychological well-being in a diverse sample of HIV-positive patients receiving highly active antiretroviral therapy. *Psychosomatics*, 43: 478–84.

Salander, P. (2007). Attributions of lung cancer: my own illness is hardly caused by smoking. *Psycho-Oncology*, 16: 587–92.

Salovey, P., Rothman, A.J., Detweiler, J.B. et al. (2000). Emotional states and physical health. *American Psychologist*, 55: 110–21.

Sallis, J.F., King, A., Sirard, J. and Albright, C. (2007). Perceived environmental predictors of physical activity over 6 months in adults: activity counseling trial. *Health Psychology*, 26: 701–9.

Sallis, J.F., Prochaska, J.J. and Taylor, W.C. (2000). A review of correlates of physical activity of children and adolescents. *Medicine & Science in Sports and Exercise*, 32: 963–75.

Samji, H., Cescon, A., Hogg, R.S. et al. (2013) Closing the gap: increases in life expectancy among treated HIV-positive individuals in the United States and Canada. *PLoS ONE* 8: e81355.

Samkoff, J.S. and Jacques, C.H. (1991). A review of studies concerning effects of sleep deprivation and fatigue on residents' performance. *Academic Medicine*, 66: 687–93.

Sandberg, T. and Conner, M. (2008). Anticipated regret as an additional preditor in the theory of planned behaviour: a meta-analysis. *British Journal of Social Psychology*, 47: 589–606.

Sandblom, G., Varenhorst, E., Rosell, J. et al. (2011). Randomised prostate cancer screening trial: 20 year follow-up. *British Medical Journal*, 342: d1539.

Sanders, S.H., Brena, S.F., Spier, C.J. et al. (1992). Chronic low back pain patients around the world: cross-cultural similarities and differences. *Journal of Clinical Pain*, 8: 317–23.

Sanderson, C. and Jemmott, J. (1996). Moderation and mediation of HIV-prevention interventions: relationship status, intentions, and condom use among college students. *Journal of Applied Social Psychology*, 26: 2076–99.

Sanderson, C.A. and Yopyk, D.J. (2007). Improving condom use intentions and behavior by changing perceived partner norms: an evaluation of condom promotion videos for college students. *Health Psychology*, 26: 481–7.

Sapolsky, R. (1986). Glucocorticoid toxicity in the hippocampus: reversal by supplementation with brain fuels. *Journal of Neuroscience*, 6: 2240–4.

Sapolsky, R.M. (1994). *Why Zebras Don't Get Ulcers*. New York: W.H. Freeman.

Sapolsky, R.M. (1996). Why stress is bad for your brain. *Science*, 273: 749–50.

Sapolsky, R.M., Krey, L.C. and McEwan, B.S. (1986). The neuroendocrinology of stress and ageing: the glucocorticoid cascade hypothesis. *Endocrine Reviews*, 7: 284–301.

Sapolsky, R.M., Romero, L.M. and Munck, A.U. (2000). How do glucocorticoids influence stress responses? Integrating permissive, suppressive, stimulatory, and preparative actions. *Endocrine Reviews*, 21: 55–89.

Sarason, B.R., Sarason, I.G. and Pierce, G.R. (1990). Traditional views of social support and their impact on assessment. In B.R. Sarason, I.G. Sarason and G.R. Pierce (eds), *Social Support: An Interactional View*. New York: Wiley.

Saremi, A., Hanson, R.L., Tulloch-Reid, M. et al. (2004). Alcohol consumption predicts hypertension but not diabetes. *Journal of Studies of Alcohol*, 65: 184–90.

Sargent-Cox, K.A., Anstey, K.J. and Luszcz, M.A. (2010). Patterns of longitudinal change in older adults' self-rated health: the effect of the point of reference. *Heath Psychology*, 29: 143–52.

Sargent, J.D., Dalton, M. and Beach, M. (2000). Exposure to cigarette promotions and smoking uptake in adolescents: evidence of a dose-response relation. *Tobacco Control*, 9: 163–8.

Sarkar, U., Piette, J.D., Gonzales, R. et al. (2007). Preferences for self-management support: findings from a survey of diabetes patients in safety-net health systems. *Patient Education and Counseling*, 70: 102–10.

Sarkeala, T., Heinavaara, S. and Anttila, A. (2008). Organised mammography screening reduces breast cancer mortality: a cohort study from Finland. *International Journal of Cancer*, 122: 614–19.

Sarkisian, C.A., Liu, H.H., Ensrud, K.E. et al. (2001). Correlates of attribution of new disability to 'old age'. *Journal of the American Geriatric Society*, 49: 134–41.

Saunders, C. and Baines, M. (1983). *Living with Dying: The Management of Terminal Disease.* Oxford: Oxford University Press.

Sausen, K.P., Lovallo, W.R., Pincomb, G.A. et al. (1992). Cardiovascular responses to occupational stress in medical students: a paradigm for ambulatory monitoring studies. *Health Psychology*, 11: 55–60.

Savage, R. and Armstrong, D. (1990). Effect of a general practitioner's consulting style on patients' satisfaction: a controlled study. *British Medical Journal*, 301: 968–70.

Savage, S.A. and Clarke, V.A. (1996). Factors associated with screening mammography and breast self-examination intentions. *Health Education Research*, 11: 409–21.

Savundranayagam, M.Y. and Montgomery, R.J.V. (2010). Impact of role discrepancies on caregiver burden among spouses. *Research on Aging*, 32: 175–99.

Scharloo, M., Baatenburg de Jong, R.J., Langeveld, T.P. et al. (2005). Quality of life and illness perceptions in patients with recently diagnosed head and neck cancer. *Head & Neck,* 27: 175–84.

Scharloo, M., Kaptein, A.A., Weinman, J. et al. (1998). Illness perceptions, coping and functioning in patients with rheumatoid arthritis, chronic obstructive pulmonary disease, and psoriasis. *Journal of Psychosomatic Research*, 44: 573–85.

Scheffler, R.M., Brown, T.T., Syme, L. et al. (2008). Community-level social capital and recurrence of acute coronary syndrome. *Social Science and Medicine*, 66: 1603–13.

Scheier, M.F. and Carver, C.S. (1985). Optimism, coping and health: assessment and implications of generalized outcome expectancies. *Health Psychology*, 4: 219–47.

Scheier, M.F. and Carver, C.S. (1992). Effects of optimism on psychological and physical well-being: theoretical overview and empirical update. *Cognitive Therapy Research*, 16: 201–28.

Scheier, M.F., Carver, C.S. and Bridges, M.W. (1994). Distinguishing optimism from neuroticism (and trait anxiety, self-mastery, and self-esteem): a reevaluation of the Life Orientation Test. *Journal of Personality & Social Psychology*, 67: 1063–78.

Scheier, M.F., Weintraub, J.K. and Carver, C.S. (1986). Coping with stress: divergent strategies of optimists and pessimists. *Journal of Personality and Social Psychology*, 51: 1257–64.

Scherwitz, L., Perkins, L., Chesney, M. et al. (1992). Hostility and health behaviours in young adults: the CARDIA study. *American Journal of Epidemiology*, 136: 136–45.

Schiaffino, K.M. and Cea, C.D. (1995). Assessing chronic illness representations: the implicit models of illness questionnaire. *Journal of Behavioral Medicine*, 18: 531–48.

Schiaffino, K.M. and Revenson, T.A. (1992). The role of perceived self-efficacy, perceived control, and causal attributions in adaptation to rheumatoid arthritis: distinguishing mediator vs moderator effects. *Personality and Social Psychology Bulletin*, 18: 709–18.

Schipper, K., Abma, T.A., Koops, C. et al. (2014). Sweet and sour after renal transplantation: a qualitative study about the positive and negative consequences of renal transplantation. *British Journal of Health Psychology*, 19: 580–91

Schlenk, E.A., Dunbar-Jacob, J. and Engberg, S. (2004). Medication non-adherence among older adults: a review of strategies and interventions for improvement. *Journal of Gerontological Nursing*, 30: 33–43.

Schmaling, K.B., Smith, W.R. and Buchwald, D.S. (2000). Significant other responses are associated with fatigue and functional status among patients with chronic fatigue syndrome. *Psychosomatic Medicine*, 62: 444–50.

Schmid Mast, M., Hall, J.A. and Roter, D.L. (2007). Disentangling physician sex and physician communication style: their effects on patient satisfaction in a virtual medical visit. *Patient Education and Counseling*, 68: 16–22.

Schneider, T.R. (2008). Evaluations of stressful transactions: What's in an appraisal. *Stress & Health*, 24: 151–8.

Schneiderman, N., Antoni, M.H. and Saab, P.G. (2001). Health psychology: psychosocial and bio-behavioral aspects of chronic disease management. *Annual Review of Psychology*, 52: 555–80.

Schnipper, H.H. (2001). Life after breast cancer. *Journal of Clinical Oncology*, 19: 3581–4.

Schofield, I., Kerr, S. and Tolson, D. (2007). An exploration of the smoking-related health beliefs of older people with chronic obstructive pulmonary disease, *Journal of Clinical Nursing*, 16: 1726–35.

Schofield, M.J., Lynagh, M. and Mishra, G. (2003). Evaluation of a Health Promoting Schools program to reduce smoking in Australian secondary schools. *Health Education and Research*, 18: 678–92.

Schofield, P.E., Butow, P.N., Thompson, J.F. et al. (2003). Psychological responses of patients receiving a diagnosis of cancer. *Annals of Oncology*, 14: 48–56.

Scholte op Reimer, J., de Haan, R.J., Rijners, P.T. et al. (1998). The burden of caregiving in partners of long-term stroke survivors. *Stroke*, 29: 1605–11.

Schou, I., Ekeberg, Ø. and Ruland, C.M. (2005). The mediating role of appraisal and coping in the relationship between optimism–pessimism and quality of life. *Psycho-Oncology*, 14: 718–27.

Schou, I., Ekeberg, O., Rulan, C.M. et al. (2004). Pessimism as a predictor of emotional morbidity one year following breast cancer surgery. *Psycho-Oncology*, 13: 309–20.

Schouten, B.C., Hoogstraten, J. and Eijkman, M.A. (2003). Patient participation during dental consultations: the influence of patients' characteristics and dentists' behavior. *Community and Dental Oral Epidemiology*, 31: 368–77.

Schrimshaw, E.W., Siegel, K. and Lekas, H.M. (2005). Changes in attitudes toward antiviral medication: a comparison of women living with HIV/AIDS in the pre-HAART and HAART Eras. *AIDS and Behavior*, 9: 267–9.

Schröder, C., Johnston, M., Morrison, V. et al. (2007). Health condition, impairment, activity limitations: relationship with emotions and control cognitions in people with disabling conditions. *Rehabilitation Psychology*, 52: 280–9.

Schroevers, M., Kraaij, V. and Garnefski, N. (2008). How do cancer patients manage unattainable personal goals and regulate their emotions? *British Journal of Health Psychology*, 13: 551–62.

Schulz, D.N., Kremers, S.P., Vandelanotte, C. et al. (2014). Effects of a web-based tailored multiple-lifestyle intervention for adults: a two-year randomized controlled trial comparing sequential and simultaneous delivery modes. *Journal of Medical Internet Research*, 16: e26.

Schulz, R., Bookwala, J., Knapp, J.E. et al. (1996). Pessimism, age, and cancer mortality. *Psychology and Aging*, 11: 304–9.

Schulz, R. and Quittner, A.L. (1998). Caregiving for children and adults with chronic conditions: introduction to the special issue. *Health Psychology*, 17: 107–11.

Schulz, R., Tompkins, C.A. and Rau, M.T. (1988). A longitudinal study of the psychosocial impact of stroke on primary support persons. *Psychology and Aging*, 3: 131–41.

Schulz, U. and Mohamed, N.E. (2004). Turning the tide: benefit finding after cancer surgery. *Social Science and Medicine*, 59: 653–62.

Schur, E.A., Sanders, M. and Steiner, H. (2000). Body dissatisfaction and dieting in young children. *International Journal of Eating Disorders*, 27: 74–82.

Schwartz, B.S., Stewart, W.F., Simon, D. et al. (1998). Epidemiology of tension-type headache. *Journal of the American Medical Association*, 279: 381–3.

Schwartz, C., Sprangers, M., Carey, A. et al. (2004). Exploring response shift in longitudinal data. *Psychology & Health*, 9: 161–80.

Schwartz, G.E. and Weiss, S. (1977). What is behavioral medicine? *Psychosomatic Medicine*, 36: 377–81.

Schwarzbold, M., Diaz, A., Martins, E.T. et al. (2008). Psychiatric disorders and traumatic brain injury. *Neuropsychiatric Disorders and Treatment,* 4: 797–816.

Schwarzer, R. (1992). Self efficacy in the adoption and maintenance of health behaviours: theoretical approaches and a new model. In R. Schwarzer (ed.), *Self Efficacy: Thought Control of Action*. Washington, DC: Hemisphere.

Schwarzer, R. (1994). Optimism, vulnerability, and self-beliefs as health-related cognitions: a systematic overview. *Psychology and Health*, 9: 161–80.

Schwarzer, R. (2001). Social-cognitive factors in changing health-related behavior. *Current Directions in Psychological Science*, 10: 47–51.

Schwarzer, R. and Hallum, S. (2008). Perceived teacher self-efficacy as a predictor of job stress and burnout-mediation analyses. *Applied Psychology: An International Review*, 57: 152–71.

Schwarzer, R., Jerusalem, M. and Hahn, A. (1994). Unemployment, social support and health complaints: a longitudinal study of stress in East German refugees. *Journal of Community and Applied Social Psychology*, 4: 31–45.

Schwarzer, R. and Knoll, N. (2007). Functional roles of social support within the stress and coping process: a theoretical and empirical overview. *International Journal of Psychology*, 42: 243–52.

Schwarzer, R. and Luszczynska, A. (2008). How to overcome health-compromising behaviours: the Health Action Process approach. *European Psychologist*, 13(2): 141–51.

Schwarzer, R., Luszczynska, A., Ziegelmann, P. et al. (2008). Social-cognitive predictors of physical exercise adherence: three longitudinal studies in rehabilitation. *Health Psychology*, 27: 854–63.

Schwarzer, R. and Renner, B. (2000). Social-cognitive predictors of health behavior: action self-efficacy and coping self-efficacy. *Health Psychology*, 19: 487–95.

Schwarzer, R., Schuz, B., Ziegelmann, J.P. et al. (2007). Adoption and maintenance of four health behaviors: theory-guided longitudinal studies on dental flossing, seat belt use, dietary behavior and physical activity. *Annals of Behavioral Medicine*, 33: 156–66.

Scollay, P., Doucett, M., Perry, M. et al. (1992). AIDS education of college students: the effect of an HIV-positive lecturer. *AIDS Education and Prevention*, 4: 160–71.

Scottish Executive (1999). *Fair Shares for All.* Report of the National Review of Resource Allocation for the NHS in Scotland, chaired by Professor Sir John Arbuthnott, principal and vice-chancellor of Strathclyde University. Edinburgh: HMSO.

Scully, J.A., Tosi, H. and Banning, K. (2000). Life events checklists: revisiting the Social Readjustment Rating Scale after 30 years. *Educational and Psychological Measurement*, 60: 864–76.

Seager, M. and Wilkins, D. (2014). Being a man – putting life before death. *The Psychologist,* 27: 404–5.

Seale, C. and Kelly, M. (1997). A comparison of hospice and hospital care for the spouses of people who die. *Palliative Care*, 11: 101–6.

Searle, A. and Bennett, P. (2001). Psychological factors and inflammatory bowel disease: a review of a decade of literature. *Psychology, Health and Medicine*, 6: 121–35.

Searle, B., Bright, J.E.H. and Bochner, S. (2001). Helping people to sort it out: the role of social support in the Job Strain Model. *Work and Stress*, 15: 328–46.

Sears, S.F., Sowell, L.D., Kuhl, E.A. et al. (2007). The ICD shock and stress management program: a randomized trial of psychosocial treatment to optimize quality of life in ICD patients. *Pacing and Clinical Electrophysiology*, 30: 858–64.

Segal, Z.V., Williams, J.M.G. and Teasdale, J.D. (2002). *Mindfulness-Based Cognitive Therapy for Depression: A New Approach to Preventing Relapse*. New York: Guilford.

Segan, C.J., Borland, R. and Greenwood, K.M. (2002). Do transtheoretical model measures predict the transition from preparation to action in smoking cessation? *Psychology and Health*, 17: 417–35.

Segerstrom, S.C. and Miller, G.E. (2004). Psychological stress and the human immune system: a meta-analytic study of 30 years of enquiry. *Psychological Bulletin*, 130: 601–30.

Segerstrom, S.C. and Smith, T.W. (2006). Physiological pathways from personality to health: the cardiovascular and immune systems. In M.E. Vollrath (ed.), *Handbook of Personality and Health*. Chichester: Wiley, pp. 175–94.

Segerstrom, S.C., Taylor, S.E., Kemeny, M.E. et al. (1998). Optimism is associated with mood, coping, and immune change in response to stress. *Journal of Personality and Social Psychology*, 74: 1646–55.

Seligman, M.E.P. (2003). Positive psychology: fundamental assumptions. *The Psychologist*, 16: 126–7.

Seligman, M.E.P. and Csikszentmihalyi, M. (2000). Positive psychology: an introduction. *American Psychologist*, 55: 5–14.

Selye, H. (1956). *The Stress of Life*. New York: McGraw-Hill.

Selye, H. (1974). *Stress without Distress*. Philadelphia, PA: Lipincott.

Selye, H. (1991). History and present status of the stress concept. In A. Monat and R.S. Lazarus (eds), *Stress and Coping*. New York: Columbia University Press.

Semmer, N.K. (2006). Personality, stress, and coping. In M.E. Vollrath (ed.), *Handbook of Personality and Health*. London: Wiley, pp. 73–113.

Serour, M., Alqhenaei, H., Al-Saqabi, S. et al. (2007). Cultural factors and patients' adherence to lifestyle measures. *British Journal of General Practice*, 57: 291–5.

Shahid, S., Bleam, R., Bessarab, D. and Thompson, S.C. (2010). 'If you don't believe it, it won't help you': use of bush medicine in treating cancer among Aboriginal people in Western Australia. *Journal of Ethnobiology and Ethnomedicine*, 6: 18.

Shakeshaft, A.P., Bowman, J.A. and Sanson-Fisher, R.W. (1999). A comparison of two retrospective measures of weekly alcohol consumption: diary and quantity/frequency index. *Alcohol and Alcoholism*, 34: 636–45.

Shankar, A., McMunn, A. and Steptoe, A. (2010). Health-related behaviors in older adults' relationships with socioeconomic status. *American Journal of Preventive Medicine*, 38: 39–46.

Sharpe, L. and Curran, L. (2006). Understanding the process of adjustment to illness. *Social Science & Medicine*, 62: 1153–66.

Shapiro, F. (1995*). Eye Movement Desensitisation and Reprocessing: Basic Principles*. New York: Guilford Press.

Shapiro, S.L., Oman, D., Thoresen, C.E. et al. (2008). Cultivating mindfulness: effects on well-being. *Journal of Clinical Psychology*, 64: 840–62.

Sharma, S., Malarcher, A.M., Giles, W.H. et al. (2004). Racial, ethnic and socioeconomic disparities in the clustering of cardiovascular disease risk factors. *Ethnicity and Disease*, 14: 43–8.

Sharp, T.J. (2001). Chronic pain: a reformulation of the cognitive-behavioural model. *Behaviour Research and Therapy*, 39: 787–800.

Sheeran, P. (2002). Intention–behaviour relations: a conceptual and empirical review. In M. Hewstone and W. Stroebe (eds), *European Review of Social Psychology*, Vol. 11. Chichester: Wiley.

Sheeran, P. and Abraham, C. (1996). The health belief model. In M. Conner and P. Norman (eds), *Predicting Health Behaviour*. Buckingham: Open University Press.

Sheeran, P., Abraham, C.S. and Orbell, S. (1999). Psychosocial correlates of heterosexual condom use: a meta-analysis. *Psychological Bulletin*, 125: 90–132.

Sheeran, P., Milne, S., Webb, T.L. and Gollwitzer, P.M. (2005). Implementation intentions and health behavior. In M Conner and P Norman (eds) *Predicting Health Behavior,* (2nd edn. Buckingham: Open University Press, pp. 276–323.

Sheeran, P. and Orbell, S. (1996). How confidently can we infer health beliefs from questionnaire responses? *Psychology and Health*, 11: 273–90.

Sheeran, P. and Orbell, S. (2000). Using implementation intentions to increase attendance for cervical cancer screening. *Health Psychology*, 19: 283–9.

Sheffield, D., Biles, P.L., Orom, H. et al. (2000). Race and sex differences in cutaneous pain perception. *Psychosomatic Medicine*, 62: 517–23.

Sheps, D.S. (2007). Psychological stress and myocardial ischemia: understanding the link and implications. *Psychosomatic Medicine*, 69: 491–2.

Sherbourne, C.D., Hays, R.D., Ordway, L. et al. (1992). Antecedents of adherence to medical recommendations: results from the Medical Outcomes Study. *Journal of Behavioral Medicine*, 15: 447–68.

Sherman, A.C. and Simonton, S. (2001). Coping with cancer in the family. *The Family Journal: Counselling and Therapy for Couples and Families*, 9: 193–200.

Sherman, K.A., Kasparian, N.A. and Mireskandari, S. (2010). Psychologcal adjustment among male partners in response to women's breast/ovarian cancer risk: a theoretical review of the literature. *Psycho-Oncology*, 19: 1–11.

Sherr, L. (1987). An evaluation of the UK government health education campaign on AIDS. *Psychology and Health*, 1: 61–72.

Sherr, L., Lampe, F.C., Clucas, C. et al. (2010). Self-reported non-adherence to ART and virological outcome in a multi-clinic UK study. *AIDS Care*, 23: 1–7.

Sherwood, A. and Turner, J.R. (1992). A conceptual and methodological overview of cardiovascular reactivity research. In J.R. Turner, A. Sherwood and K.C. Light (eds), *Individual Differences in Cardiovascular Responses to Stress*. New York: Plenum.

Shewchuck, R.M., Richards, J.S. and Elliott, T.R. (1998). Dynamic processes in health outcomes among caregivers of patients with spinal cord injuries. *Health Psychology*, 17: 125–9.

Shi, L., Liu, J., Fonseca, V. et al. (2010). Correlation between adherence rates measured by MEMS and self-reported questionnaires: a meta-analysis. *Health and Quality of Life Outcomes*, 8: 99 doi:10.1186/1477-7525-8-99

Shifren, K. and Hooker, K. (1995). Stability and change in optimism: a study among spouse caregivers. *Experimental Aging Research*, 21: 59–76.

Shilts, R. (2000). *And the Band Played on: Politics, People and the AIDS Epidemic*. New York: St Martin's Press.

Shinar, D., Schechtman, E. and Compton, R. (1999). Trends in safe driving behaviors and in relation to trends in health maintenance behaviors in the USA: 1985–1995. *Accident Analysis and Prevention*, 31: 497–503.

Shipley, B.A., Weiss, A., Der, G., Taylor, M.D. and Deary, I.J. (2007). Neuroticism, extraversion and mortality in the UK Health and Lifestyle Survey: a 21-year prospective cohort study. *Psychosomatic Medicine*, 69: 923–31.

Shiri, S., Feintuch, U., Lorber-Haddad, A. et al. (2012). Novel virtual reality system integrating online self-face viewing and mirror visual feedback for stroke rehabilitation: rationale and feasibility. *Topics in Stroke Rehabilitation*, 19(4): 277–86.

Siegel, K. and Gorey, E. (1997). HIV infected women: barriers to AZT use. *Social Science and Medicine*, 45: 15–22.

Siegel, K., Karus, D.G., Raveis, V.H. et al. (1996). Depressive distress among the spouses of terminally ill cancer patients. *Cancer Practice*, 4: 25–30.

Siegel, K. and Schrimshaw, E.W. (2005). Stress, appraisal, and coping: a comparison of HIV-infected women in the pre-HAART and HAART eras. *Journal of Psychosomatic Research*, 58: 225–33.

Siegel, K., Schrimshaw, E.W. and Dean, L. (1999). Symptom interpretation and medication adherence among late middle-age and older HIV-infected adults. *Journal of Health Psychology*, 4: 247–57.

Siegert, R.J. and Abernethy, D.A. (2005). Depression in multiple sclerosis: a review. *Journal of Neurology, Neurosurgery and Psychiatry*, 76: 469–75.

Siegman, A.W., Townsend, S.T., Civelek, A.C. and Blumenthal, R.S. (2000). Antagonistic behaviour, dominance, hostility and cornonary heart disease. *Psychosomatic Medicine*, 62: 248–57.

Siegrist, J., Dagmar Starke, D., Chandola, T. et al. (2004). The measurement of effort–reward imbalance at work: European comparisons. *Social Science and Medicine*, 58: 1483–99.

Siegrist, J., Peter, R., Junge, A. et al. (1990). Low status control, high effort at work and ischemic heart disease: prospective evidence from blue collar men. *Social Science and Medicine*, 35: 1127–34.

Sieverding, M., Weidner, G., von Volkmann, B. et al. (2005). Cardiovascular reactivity in a simulated job interview: the role of gender role self-concept. *International Journal of Behavioral Medicine*, 12: 1–10.

Siewert, K., Kubiak, T., Jonas, L. and Weber, H. (2013). The differential relations between perceived social support

and rumination-associated goals. *Journal of Social & Clinical Psychology*, 32: 1075–94.

Sikkema, K.J., Kelly, J.A., Winett, R.A. et al. (2000). Outcomes of a randomized community-level HIV-prevention intervention for women living in 18 low-income housing developments. *American Journal of Public Health*, 90: 53–7.

Silverman, D. (1987). *Communication and Medical Practice: Social Relations and the Clinic*. London: Sage.

Simmons, V.N., Heckman, B.W., Fink, A.C. et al. (2013). Efficacy of an experiential, dissonance-based smoking intervention for college students delivered via the Internet. *Journal of Consulting and Clinical Psychology*, 81: 810–20.

Simon, J.A., Carmody, T.P., Hudes, E.S. et al. (2003). Intensive smoking cessation counseling versus minimal counseling among hospitalized smokers treated with transdermal nicotine replacement: a randomized trial. *American Journal of Medicine*, 114: 555–62.

Simoni, J.M., Nelson, K.M., Franks, J.C. et al. (2011). Are peer interventions for HIV efficacious? A systematic review. *AIDS and Behavior*, 15: 1589–95.

Simoni, J.M., Pantalone, D.W., Plummer, M.D. et al. (2007). A randomized controlled trial of a peer support intervention targeting antiretroviral medication adherence and depressive symptomatology in HIV-positive men and women. *Health Psychology*, 26: 488–95.

Singh, R.B., Sharma, J.P., Rastogi, V. et al. (1997). Prevalence of coronary artery disease and coronary risk factors in rural and urban populations of north India. *European Heart Journal*, 18: 1728–35.

Singh, R.K., Panday, H.P. and Singh, R.H. (2003). Irritable bowel syndrome: challenges ahead. *Current Science*, 84: 1525–33.

Singh-Manoux, A., Marmot, M.G. and Adler, N.E. (2005) Does subjective social status predict health and change in health status better than objective status? *Psychosomatic Medicine*, 67: 855–61.

Sivell, S., Iredale, R., Gray, J. and Coles, B. (2007). Cancer genetic risk assessment for individuals at risk of familial breast cancer. *Cochrane Database of Systematic Reviews*, issue 2, art. no.: CD003721. doi 10.1002/14651858. CD003721.

Sjösten, N. and Kivelä, S-L. (2006). The effects of physical exercise on depressive symptoms among the aged: a systematic review. *Int J Geriatr Psychiatry*, 21: 410–18.

Skaalvik, E.M. and Skaalvik, S. (2009). Does school context matter? Relations with teacher burnout and job satisfaction. *Teaching and Teacher Education*, 25: 518–24.

Skarstein, J., Aass, N., Fossa, S.D. et al. (2000). Anxiety and depression in cancer patients: relation between the Hospital Anxiety and Depression Scale and the European Organization for Research and Treatment of Cancer Core Quality of Life Questionnaire. *Journal of Psychosomatic Research*, 49: 27–34.

Skelton, D.A., Young, A., Walker, A. et al. (1999). *Physical Activity in Later Life: Further Analysis of the Allied Dunbar*

National Fitness Survey and the Health Education Authority National Survey of Activity and Health. London: Health Education Authority.

Skevington, S.M. (1990). A standardised scale to measure beliefs about controlling pain (BPCQ): a preliminary study. *Psychology and Health*, 4: 221–32.

Skoffer, B. (2007). Low back pain in 15- to 16-year-old children in relation to school furniture and carrying of the school bag. *Spine*, 32: E713–7.

Skov-Ettrup, L.S., Dalum, P., Ekholm, O. et al. (2014). Reach and uptake of Internet- and phone-based smoking cessation interventions: results from a randomized controlled trial. *Preventive Medicine,* 62C: 38–43.

Slavin, S., Batrouney, C. and Murphy, D. (2007). Fear appeals and treatment side-effects: an effective combination for HIV prevention? *AIDS Care*, 19: 130–7.

Sloper, P. (2000). Predictors of distress in parents of children with cancer: a prospective study. *Journal of Pediatric Psychology*, 25: 79–92.

Smedslund, G. and Rundmo, T. (1999). Is Grossarth-Maticek's coronary prone type II an independent predictor of myocardial infarction? *Personality and Individual Differences*, 27: 1231–42.

Smee, C., Parsonage, M., Anderson, R. et al. (1992). *Effects of Tobacco Advertising on Tobacco Consumption: A Discussion Document Reviewing the Evidence.* London: Department of Health.

Smets, E.M., van Heijl, M., van Wijngaarden, A.K. et al. (2012) Addressing patients' information needs: a first evaluation of a question prompt sheet in the pretreatment consultation for patients with esophageal cancer. *Diseases of the Esophagus*, 25: 512–19.

Smith, A. and Roberts, K. (2003). Interventions for post-traumatic stress disorder and psychological distress in emergency ambulance personnel: a review of the literature. *Emergency Medical Journal*, 20: 75–8.

Smith, B.W., Shelley, B.M., Dalen, J. et al. (2008). A pilot study comparing the effects of mindfulness-based and cognitive-behavioral stress reduction. *Journal of Alternative and Complementary Medicine*, 14: 251–8.

Smith, C.A. and Lazarus, R.S. (1993). Appraisal components, core relational themes, and the emotions. *Cognition and Emotion*, 7: 233–69.

Smith, C.A., Wallston, K.A., Dwyer, K.A. et al. (1997). Beyond good or bad coping: a multi-dimensional examination of coping with pain in persons with rheumatoid arthritis. *Annals of Behavioral Medicine*, 19: 11–21.

Smith, D.A., Ness, E.M., Herbert, R. et al. (2005). Abdominal diameter index: a more powerful anthropometric measure for prevalent coronary heart disease risk in adult males. *Diabetes, Obesity and Metabolism*, 7: 370–80.

Smith, D.M., Loewenstein, G., Jankovic, A. and Ubel, P.A. (2009). Happily hopeless: adaptation to a permanent, but not to a temporary, disability. *Health Psychology*, 28: 787–91.

Smith, H., Gooding, S., Brown, R. et al. (1998). Evaluation of readability and accuracy of information leaflets in general practices for patients with asthma. *British Medical Journal*, 317: 264–5.

Smith, J.A. (1995). Semi-structured interviewing and qualitative analysis. In J.A. Smith, R. Harre and L. van Langerhove (eds). *Rethinking Methods in Psychology*. London: Sage, pp. 9–26.

Smith, J.A. (1996). Beyond the divide between cognition and discourse: using interpretative phenomenological analysis in health psychology. *Psychology and Health*, 11: 261–71.

Smith, L.A. and Foxcroft, D.R. (2009). The effect of alcohol advertising, marketing and portrayal on drinking behaviour in young people: systematic review of prospective cohort studies. *BMC Public Health*, 9: 51.

Smith, M.Y., Redd, W.H., Peyer, C. et al. (1999). Post-traumatic stress disorder in cancer: a review. *Psycho-Oncology*, 8: 521–37.

Smith, P.J., Humiston, S.G., Marcuse, E.K., et al. (2011). Parental delay or refusal of vaccine doses, childhood vaccination coverage at 24 months of age, and the Health Belief Model. *Public Health Report*, 126: 135–46.

Smith, T.W. (2006) Personality as risk and resilience in physical health. *Current Direction in Psychological Science* 15: 227–31.

Smith, T.W. (1994). Concepts and methods on the study of anger, hostility and health. In A.W. Siegman and T.W. Smith (eds), *Anger, Hostility and the Heart*. Hillsdale, NJ: Lawrence Erlbaum.

Smith, T.W., Gallo, L.C. and Ruiz, J.M. (2003). Toward a social psychophysiology of cardiovascular reactivity: interpersonal concepts and methods in the study of stress and coronary disease. In J. Suls and K. Wallston (eds), *Social Psychological Foundations of Health and Illness*. Oxford: Blackwell.

Smolderen, K.G. and Vingerhoets, A. (2010). Hospitalisation and stressful medical procedures. In D. French, K. Vedhara, A.A. Kaptein and J. Weinamn (eds), *Health Psychology*, 2nd edn. Chichester: Wiley, pp. 232–44.

Smyth, C., Blaxland, M. and Cass, B. (2011). 'So that's how I found out I was a young carer and that I had actually been a carer most of my life'. Identifying and supporting hidden young carers. *Journal of Youth Studies*, 14: 145–60.

Smyth, J.M., Stone, A.A., Hurewitz, A. and Kaell, A. (1999). Effects of writing about stressful experiences on symptom reduction in patients with asthma or rheumatoid arthritis: a randomized trial. *Journal of the American Medical Association*, 281: 1304–9.

Snell, J.L. and Buck, E.L. (1996). Increasing cancer screening: a meta analysis. *Preventive Medicine*, 25: 702–7.

Sniehotta, F. F. (2009). Towards a theory of intentional behaviour change: plans, planning, and self-regulation. *British Journal of Health Psychology*, 14, 261–73.

Sniehotta, F.F., Scholz, U., Schwarzer, R. (2005). Bridging the intention–behavior gap: planning, self-efficacy and action control in the adoption and maintenance of physical exercise. *Psychology & Health*, 20: 143–60.

Sniehotta, F.F., Scholz, U., Schwarzer, R. (2006). Action plans and coping plans for physical exercise: a longitudinal intervention study in cardiac rehabilitation. *British Journal of Health Psychology*, 11: 23–37.

Sniehotta, F.F., Scholz, U., Schwarzer, R. et al. (2005). Long-term effects of two psychological interventions on physical exercise and self-regulation following coronary rehabilitation. *International Journal of Behavioral Medicine*, 2: 244–55.

Snoek F.J., Hogenelst M.H. (2008). [Psychological implications of diabetes mellitus]. *Ned Tijdschr Geneeskd* [Dutch] 152: 2395–9.

Snoek, H.M., Engels, R.C., Janssen, J.M. et al. (2007). Parental behaviour and adolescents' emotional eating. *Appetite*, 49: 223–30.

Snow, P.C. and Bruce, D.D. (2003). Cigarette smoking in teenage girls: exploring the role of peer reputations, self concept and coping. *Health Education Research*, 18: 439–52.

Snyder, C. and Lopez, S.J. (2005). *Handbook of Positive Psychology*. New York: Oxford University Press.

Snyder, C.R., Harris, C., Anderson, J.R. et al. (1991a). The will and the ways: development and validation of an individual differences measure of hope. *Journal of Personality and Social Psychology*, 60: 570–85.

Snyder, C.R., Irving, L.M. and Anderson, J.R. (1991b). Hope and health. In D.R. Forsyth and C.R. Snyder (eds), *Handbook of Social and Clinical Psychology: The Health Perspective*. Elmsford, NY: Pergamon Press, pp. 285–305.

Snyder, C.R., Lehman, K.A., Kluck, B. et al. (2006). Hope for rehabilitation and vice versa. *Rehabilitation Psychology*, 51: 89–112.

Soames-Job, R.F. (1988). Effective and ineffective use of fear in health promotion campaigns. *American Journal of Public Health*, 78: 163–7.

Solberg Nes, L., Carlson, C.R., Crofford, L.J. et al. (2011). Individual difference and self-regulatory fatigue: optimism, conscientiousness, and self-consciousess. *Personality and Individual Differences*, 50: 475–80.

Solberg Nes, L. and Segestrom, S.C. (2006). Dispositional optimism and coping: a meta-analytic review. *Personality and Social Psychology Review*, 10: 235–51.

Solmes, M. and Turnbull, O.H. (2002). *The Brain and the Inner Mind: An Introduction to the Neuroscience of Subjective Wellbeing*. New York: Other Press/Karnac.

Solomon, R.L. (1977). Addiction: an opponent-process theory of acquired motivation: the affective dynamics of addiction. In J.D. Maser (ed.), *Psychopathology: Experimental Models*. San Francisco, CA: W.H. Freeman.

Soo, H., Burney, S. and Basten, C. (2009). The role of rumination in affective distress in people with a chronic physical illness: a review of the literature and theoretical formulation. *Journal of Health Psychology*, 14: 956–66.

Soons, P. and Denollet, J. (2009). Medical psychology services in Dutch general hospitals: state of the art developments and recommendations for the future. *Journal of Clinical Psychology in Medical Settings*, 16: 161–8.

Sorensen, G., Morris, D.M., Hunt, M.K. et al. (1992). Worksite nutrition intervention and employees' dietary habits: the Treatwell program. *American Journal of Public Health*, 82: 877–80.

Sorensen, G., Stoddard, A., Hunt, M.K. et al. (1998). The effects of a health promotion–health protection intervention on behavior change: the WellWorks Study. *American Journal of Public Health*, 88: 1685–90.

Sorensen, G., Stoddard, A., Peterson, K. et al. (1999). Increasing fruit and vegetable consumption through worksites and families in the Treatwell 5-a-day study. *American Journal of Public Health*, 89: 54–60.

Sorensen, G., Stoddard, A., Quintiliani, L. et al. (2010). Tobacco use cessation and weight management among motor freight workers: results of the gear up for health study. *Cancer Causes and Control*, 21(12): 2113–22.

Sorensen, S., Duberstein, P.R., Chapman, B. et al. (2008). How are personality traits related to preparation for future care needs in older adults? *The Journals of Gerontology, Series B:Psychological Sciences and Social Sciences*, 63: 328–36.

Sorensen T. (2008) *eHealth trends: WHO/European eHealth Consumer Trends Survey Final Report*. Luxembourg: Health & Consumer Protection Directorate General.

Soria, R., Legido, A., Escolano, C. et al. (2006). A randomised controlled trial of motivational interviewing for smoking cessation. *British Journal of General Practice*, 56: 768–74.

Sorkin, D.H., Mavadadi, S., Rook, K, et al. (2014). Dyadic collaboration in shared health behavior change: the effects of a randomized trial to test a lifestyle intervention for high-risk Latinas. *Health Psychology*, 33: 566–75.

Sorlie, P.D., Backlund, E. and Keller, J.B. (1995). US mortality by economic, demographic, and social characteristics: the National Longitudinal Mortality Study. *American Journal of Public Health*, 85: 949–56.

Soulsby, L. and Bennett, K. (2015). How relationships help us to age well. *The Psychologist*; 28: 110–113.

Sparks, P., Conner, M., James, R. et al. (2001). Ambivalence about health-related behaviours: an exploration in the domain of food choice. *British Journal of Health Psychology*, 6: 53–68.

Sparks, P. and Shepherd, R. (1992). Self-identity and the theory of planned behaviour: assessing the role of identification with green consumerism. *Social Psychology Quarterly*, 55: 388–99.

Speca, M., Carlson, L.E., Goodey, E. et al. (2000). A randomized wait-list controlled clinical trial: the effect of mindfulness meditation-based stress reduction program on mood and symptoms of stress in cancer patients. *Psychosomatic Medicine*, 62: 613–22.

Speisman, J.C., Lazarus, R.S., Mordkoff, A. et al. (1964). Experimental reduction of stress based on ego defense theory. *Journal of Abnormal and Social Psychology*, 68: 367–80.

Spence, M.J. and Moss-Morris, R. (2007). The cognitive behavioural model of irritable bowel syndrome: a prospective investigation of patients with gastroenteritis. *Gut*, 56: 1066–71.

Spiegel, D. (2001). Mind matters: coping and cancer progression. *Journal of Psychosomatic Research*, 50: 287–90.

Spiegel, D., Bloom, J.R., Kraemer, H.C. et al. (1989). Effect of psychosocial treatment on survival of patients with metastatic breast cancer. *The Lancet*, 14(2): 888–91.

Spiegel, D., Bloom, J.R. and Yalom, I. (1981). Group support for patients with metastatic cancer: a randomized outcome study. *Archives of General Psychiatry*, 38: 527–33.

Spiegel, D., Butler, L.D., Giese-Davis, J. et al. (2007). Effects of supportive-expressive group therapy on survival of patients with metastatic breast cancer: a randomized prospective trial. *Cancer*, 110: 1130–8.

Spiegel, D. and Giese-Davis, J. (2003). Depression and cancer: mechanisms and disease progression. *Biological Psychiatry*, 54: 269–82.

Spiller, R., Aziz, Q., Creed, F. et al. (2007). Clinical Services Committee of The British Society of Gastroenterology. Guidelines on the irritable bowel syndrome: mechanisms and practical management. *Gut*, 56: 1770–98.

Spolentini, I., Gianni, W., Repetto, L. et al. (2008). Depression and cancer: an unexplored and unresolved emergent issue in elderly patients. *Critical Reviews in Oncology/Hematology*, 65: 143–55.

Sreeramareddy, C.T., Shankar, R.P., Sreekumaran, B.V. et al. (2006). Care seeking behaviour for childhood illness: a questionnaire survey in western Nepal. *BioMedCentre International Health & Human Rights*, 6: 7. Published online 23 May 2006, doi: 10.1186/1472–698X-6–7.

Stagl, J.M., Bouchard, L.C., Lechner, S.C. et al. (2015). Long-term psychological benefits of cognitive-behavioral stress management for women with breast cancer: 11-year follow-up of a randomized controlled trial. *Cancer*, 121: 1873–81.

Stainton Rogers, W. (1991). *Explaining Health and Illness: An Exploration of Diversity*. London: Wheatsheaf.

Stamler, J., Daviglus, M.L., Garside, D.B. et al. (2000). Relationship of baseline serum cholesterol levels in 3 large cohorts of younger men to long-term coronary, cardiovascular and all-cause mortality, and to longevity. *Journal of the American Medical Association*, 19: 284(3): 311–18.

Stanczyk, N., Bolman, C., van Adrichem, M. et al. (2014) Comparison of text and video computer-tailored interventions for smoking cessation: randomized controlled trial. *Journal of Medical Internet Research*, 16: e69.

Stansfeld, S.A., Bosma, H., Hemingway, H. et al. (1998). Psychosocial work characteristics and social support as predictors of SF-36 health functioning: the Whitehall II study. *Psychosomatic Medicine*, 60: 247–55.

Stanton, A.L., Collins, C.A. and Sworowski, L.A. (2001). Adjustment to chronic illness: theory and research. In A. Baum, T.A. Revenson and J.E. Singer (eds), *Handbook of Health Psychology*. Maah, NJ: Lawrence Erlbaum, pp. 387–403.

Stanton, A.L., Danoff-Burg, S. and Huggins, M.E. (2002a). The first year after breast cancer diagnosis: hope and coping strategies as predictors of adjustment. *Psycho-Oncology*, 11: 93–102.

Stanton, A.L., Danoff-Burg, S., Sworowski, L.A. et al. (2002b). Randomized, controlled trial of written emotional expression and benefit finding in breast cancer patients. *Journal of Clinical Oncology*, 20: 4160–8.

Stanton, A.L., Ganz, P.A., Rowland, J.H. et al. (2005). Promoting adjustment after treatment for cancer. *Cancer*, 104: 2608–13.

Stanton, A.L., Kirk, K.B., Cameron, C.L. et al. (2000). Coping through emotional approach: scale construction and validation. *Journal of Personality and Social Psychology*, 78: 1150–69.

Stanton, A.L., Revenson, T.A. and Tennen, H. (2007). Health psychology: psychological adjustment to chronic disease. *Annual Review of Psychology*, 58: 565–92.

Stanton, A.L. and Snider, P.R. (1993). Coping with a breast cancer diagnosis: a prospective study. *Health Psychology*, 12: 16.

Starace, F., Bartoli, L., Aloisi, M.S. et al. (2000). Cognitive and affective disorders associated to HIV infection in the HAART era: findings from the NeuroICONA study. Cognitive impairment and depression in HIV/AIDS. *Acta Psychiatria Scandinavica*, 106: 20–6.

Stautz, K. and Cooper, A. (2013). Impulsivity-related personality traits and adolescent alcohol use: a meta-analytic review. *Clinical Psychology Review*, 33: 574–92.

Stead, L.F., Bergson, G. and Lancaster, T. (2008). Physician advice for smoking cessation. *Cochrane Database of Systematic Reviews*, 2: CD000165.

Steadman, L. and Quine, L. (2004). Encouraging young males to perform testicular self-examination: a simple, but effective, implementations intervention. *British Journal of Health Psychology*, 9: 479–88.

Steadman, L., Rutter, D.R. and Field, S. (2002). Individually elicited versus modal normative beliefs in predicting attendance at breast screening: examining the role of belief salience in the theory of planned behaviour. *British Journal of Health Psychology*, 7: 317–30.

Steffen, L.M., Arnett, D.K. and Blackburn, H. (2006). Population trends in leisure-time physical activity: Minnesota Heart Survey, 1980–2000. *Medicine and Science in Sports and Exercise*, 38: 1716–23.

Steinbrook, R. (2006). The potential of human papillomavirus vaccines. *New England Journal of Medicine*, 354: 1109–12.

Stenner, P.H.D., Cooper, D. and Skevington, S. (2003). Putting the Q into quality of life: the identification of subjective constructions of health-related quality of life using Q methodology. *Social Science and Medicine*, 57: 2161–72.

Stephen, J.E., Rahn, M., Verhoef, M. and Leis, A. (2007). What is the state of the evidence on the mind-cancer survival question, and where do we go from here? A point of view. *Supportive Care in Cancer*, 15: 923–30.

Stephens, C., Long, N. and Miller, N. (1997). The impact of trauma and social support on post traumatic stress disorder: a study of New Zealand police officers. *Journal of Criminal Justice*, 25: 303–14.

Stephens, M.R., Gaskell, A.L., Gent, C. et al. (2008). Prospective randomised clinical trial of providing patients with audiotape recordings of their oesophagogastric cancer consultations. *Patient Education and Counselling*, 72: 218–22.

Stephenson, J., Bauman, A., Armstrong, T. et al. (2000). *The Costs of Illness Attributable to Physical Inactivity in Australia: A Preliminary Study*. Canberra: Commonwealth Government of Australia.

Steptoe, A., Demakakos, P. and Oliveira, C de. (2012). The psychological wellbeing, health and functioning of older people in England. In Banks, J., Nazroo, J. and Steptoe, A. (eds). *The Dynamics of Ageing: Evidence from the English Longitudinal Study of Ageing 2002–10 (Wave 5)*. London: Institute for Fiscal Studies.

Steptoe, A., Doherty, S., Rink, E. et al. (1999). Behavioural counselling in general practice for the promotion of healthy behaviour among adults at increased risk of coronary heart disease: randomised trial. *British Journal of Medicine*, 319: 943–7.

Steptoe, A., O'Donnell, K., Marmot, M. and Wardle, J. (2008). Positive affect and psychosocial processes related to health. *British Journal of Psychology*, 99: 211–27.

Steptoe, A., Owen, N., Kunz-Ebrecht, S.R. and Brydon, L. (2004b). Loneliness and neuroendocrine, cardiovascular, and inflammatory stress responses in middle-aged men and women. *Psychoneuroendocrinology*, 29: 593–611.

Steptoe, A., Pollard, T. and Wardle, J. (1995). Development of a measure of the motives underlying the selection of food: the food choice questionnaire. *Appetite*, 25: 267–84.

Steptoe, A., Siegrist, J., Kirschbaum, C. and Marmot, M. (2004a). Effort–reward imbalance, overcommittment, and measures of cortisol and blood pressure over the working day. *Psychosomatic Medicine*, 66, 323–9.

Steptoe, A., Wardlaw, J. and Marmot, M. (2005). Positive affect and health-related neuroendocrine, cardiovascular, and inflammatory processes. *Proceedings of the National Academy of Sciences USA*, 102: 6508–12.

Steptoe, A., Willemsen, G., Owen, N. et al. (2001). Acute mental stress elicits delayed increases in circulating inflammatory cytokines. *Clinical Science* (London), 101: 185–92.

Sterba, K.R., DeVellis, R.F., Lewis, M. et al. (2008). Effect of couple illness perception congruence on psychological adjustment in women with rheumatoid arthritis. *Health Psychology*, 27: 221–9.

Sterling, P. and Eyer, J. (1988). Allostasis: a new paradigm to explain arousal pathology. In S. Fisher and J. Reason (eds), *Handbook of Life Stress, Cognition and Health*. Oxford: John Wiley, pp. 629–49.

Sterne, J.A.C. and Davey-Smith, G. (2001). Sifting the evidence – what's wrong with significance tests? *British Medical Journal*, 322: 226–31.

Stevenson, M., Palamara, P., Rooke, M. et al. (2001). Drink and drug driving: what's the skipper up to? *Australia and New Zealand Journal of Public Health*, 25: 511–13.

Stewart, A.L. and Ware, J.E. (eds) (1992). *Measuring Functioning and Well-being: The Medical Outcomes Study Approach*. Durham, NC: Duke University Press.

Stewart, M., Davidson, K., Meade, D. et al. (2000). Myocardial infarction: survivors' and spouses' stress, coping, and support. *Journal of Advanced Nursing*, 31: 1351–60.

Stewart-Knox, B.J., Sittlington, J., Rugkasa, J. et al. (2005). Smoking and peer groups: results from a longitudinal qualitative study of young people in Northern Ireland. *British Journal of Social Psychology*, 44: 397–414.

Stice, E., Presnell, K. and Sprangler, D. (2002). Risk factors for binge eating onset in adolescent girls: a 2-year prospective investigation. *Health Psychology*, 21: 131–8.

Stiegelis, H.E., Hagedoorn, M., Sanderman, R. et al. (2004). The impact of an informational self-management intervention on the association between control and illness uncertainty before and psychological distress after radiotherapy. *Psycho-Oncology*, 13: 248–59.

Stirling, A.M., Wilson, P. and McConnachie, A. (2001). Deprivation, psychological distress, and consultation length in general practice. *British Journal of General Practice*, 51: 456–60.

Stoate, H.G. (1989). Can health screening damage your health? *Journal of the Royal College of General Practitioners*, 39: 193–5.

Stocks, N.P., Ryan, P., McElroy, H. et al. (2004). Statin prescribing in Australia: socioeconomic and sex differences. A cross-sectional study. *Medical Journal of Australia*, 180: 229–31.

Stok, F.M., de Ridder, D.T.D., de Vet, E. and de Wit, J.B.F. (2014). Don't tell me what I should do, but what others do: the influence of descriptive and injunctive peer norms on fruit consumption in adolescents. *British Journal of Health Psychology*, 19: 52–64.

Stokols, D. (1992). Establishing and maintaining health environments. *American Psychologist*, 47: 6–22.

Stolzenberg, L. and D'Alessio, S.J. (2007). Is nonsmoking dangerous to the health of restaurants? The effect of California's indoor smoking ban on restaurant revenues. *Evaluation Review*, 31: 75–92.

Stone, A.A., Bovbjerg, D.H., Neale, J.M. et al. (1993). Development of common cold symptoms following experimental rhinovirus infection is related to prior stressful life events. *Behavioral Medicine*, 8: 115–20.

Stone, D.H. and Stewart, S. (1996). Screening and the new genetics: a public health perspective on the ethical debate. *Journal of Public Health Medicine*, 18: 3–5.

Stone, G.C. (1979). Health and the health system: a historical overview and conceptual framework. In G.C. Stone, F. Cohen and N.E. Adler (eds), *Health Psychology: A Handbook*. San Francisco, CA: Jossey-Bass.

Stone, L. (2014). Blame, shame and hopelessness: medically unexplained symptoms and the 'heartsink' experience [online]. *Australian Family Physician*, 43: 191–5.

Storch, M., Gaab, J., Küttel, Y. et al. (2007). Psychoneuroendocrine effects of resource-activating stress management training. *Health Psychology*, 26: 456–63.

Stone, S.V. and McCrae, R.R. (2007). Personality and health. In S. Ayers et al. (eds). *Cambridge Handbook of Psychology, Health and Medicine*, 2nd edn. Cambridge: Cambridge University Press, pp. 151–5.

Stoudemire, A. and Hales, R.E. (1991). Psychological and behavioral factors affecting medical conditions and DSM-IV: an overview. *Psychosomatics*, 32: 5–12.

Strack, F. and Deutsch, R. (2004). Reflective and impulsive determinants of social behavior. *Personality and Social Psychology Review*, 8:220–47.

Strang, S. and Strang, P. (2002). Questions posed to hospital chaplains by palliative care patients. *Journal of Palliative Medicine*, 5: 857–64.

Strauss, A. and Corbin, J. (1998). *Basics of Qualitative Research Techniques and Procedures for Developing Grounded Theory*, 2nd edn. London: Sage Publications.

Strauss, R.S. (2000). Childhood obesity and self esteem. *Pediatrics*, 105: e15.

Strecher, V.J., Champion, V.L. and Rosenstock, I.M. (1997). The health belief model and health behaviour. In D.S. Gochman (ed.), *Handbook of Health Behavior Research I: Personal and Social Determinants*. New York: Plenum.

Strecher, V.J. and Rosenstock, I.M. (1997). The health belief model. In A. Baum, S. Newman, J. Weinman, R. West and C. McManus (eds), *Cambridge Handbook of Psychology, Health and Medicine*. Cambridge: Cambridge University Press.

Street, R.L., O'Malley, K.J., Cooper, L.A. et al. (2008) Understanding concordance in patient–physician relationships: personal and ethnic dimensions of shared identity. *Annals of Family Medicine*, 6: 198–205.

Strike, P.C. and Steptoe, A. (2005). Behavioral and emotional triggers of acute coronary syndromes: a systematic review and critique. *Psychosomatic Medicine*, 67: 179–86.

Stroebe, W., Zech, E., Stroebe, M.D. et al. (2005). Does social support help in bereavement? *Journal of Social and Clinical Psychology*, 24: 1030–50.

Stronks, K., VandeMheen, H., VandenBos, J. et al. (1997). The interrelationship between income, health and employment status. *International Journal of Epidemiology*, 16: 592–600.

Strosahl, K.D., Hayes, S.C., Wilson, K.G. et al. (2004). An ACT primer. Core therapy processes, intervention strategies, and therapist competencies. In S.C. Hayes and K.D. Strosahl (eds), *A Practical Guide to Acceptance and Commitment Therapy*. New York: Springer.

Stuckey, S.J., Jacobs, A. and Goldfarb, J. (1986). EMG biofeedback training, relaxation training, and placebo for the relief of chronic back pain. *Perceptual and Motor Skills*, 63: 1023–36.

Stunkard, A.J. and Wadden, T. (1993). *Obesity: Theory and Therapy*, 2nd edn. New York: Raven Press.

Stürmer, T., Hasselbach, P. and Amelang, M. (2006). Personality, lifestyle, and risk of cardiovascular disease and cancer: follow-up of population based cohort. *British Medical Journal*, 332: 1359.

Suarez, E.C., Kuhn, C.M., Schanberg, S.M. et al. (1998). Neuro-endocrine, cardiovascular, and emotional responses of hostile men: the role of interpersonal challenge. *Psychosomatic Medicine*, 60: 78–88.

Suarez, E.C. and Williams, R.B. (1989). Situational determinants of cardiovascular and emotional reactivity in high and low hostile men. *Psychosomatic Medicine*, 51: 404–18.

Suchman, A.L. and Ader, R. (1992). Classic conditioning and placebo effects in crossover studies. *Clinical Pharmacology and Therapeutics*, 52: 372–7.

Suchman, C.A. (1965). Stages of illness and medical care. *Journal of Health and Social Behavior*, 6: 114–28.

Sullivan, M.J.L., Rodgers, W.M. and Kirsch, I. (2001). Catastrophizing, depression and expectancies for pain and emotional distress. *Pain*, 91: 147–54.

Suls, J. and Bunde, J. (2005). Anger, anxiety and depression as risk factors for cardiovascular disease: the problems and implications of overlapping affective dispositions. *Psychological Bulletin*, 131: 260–300.

Suls, J. and Fletcher, B. (1985). The relative efficacy of avoidant and nonavoidant coping strategies: a meta-analysis. *Health Psychology*, 4: 249–88.

Suls, J. and Martin, R. (2005). The daily life of the garden-variety neurotic: reactivity, stressors exposure, mood spillover, and maladaptive coping. *Journal of Personality*, 73: 1–25.

Suls, J. and Rittenhouse, J.D. (eds) (1987). Personality and Physical Health (Special Issue). *Journal of Personality*, 55: 155–393.

Suls, J., Wan, C.K. and Costa, P.T., Jr (1995). Relationship of trait anger to resting blood pressure: a meta-analysis. *Health Psychology*, 14: 444–56.

SuperioCabuslay, E., Ward, M.M. and Lorig, K.R. (1996). Patient education interventions in osteo-arthritis and rheumatoid arthritis: a meta-analytic comparison with nonsteroidal antiinflammatory drug treatment. *Arthritis Care and Research*, 9: 292–301.

Surtees, P.G., Wainwright, N.W.J., Luben, R.N. et al. (2008). Depression and ischemic heart disease mortality: evidence from the EPIC-Norfolk United Kingdom Prospective Cohort Study. *American Journal of Psychiatry*, 165: 515–23.

Surwit, R.S. and Schneider, M.S. (1993). Role of stress in the etiology and treatment of diabetes mellitus. *Psychosomatic Medicine*, 55: 380–93.

Surwit, R.S., van Tilburg, M.A., Zucker, N. et al. (2002). Stress management improves long-term glycemic control in type 2 diabetes. *Diabetes Care*, 25: 30–4.

Suter, P.B. (2002). Employment and litigation: improved by work, assisted by verdict. *Pain*, 100: 249–57.

Sutton, S. (1996). Can 'stages of change' provide guidance in the treatment of addictions? A critical examination of Prochaska and DiClemente's model. In G.E. Edwards and C. Dare (eds), *Psychotherapy, Psychological Treatments and the Addictions*. Cambridge: Cambridge University Press.

Sutton, S. (2000). A critical review of the trans-theoretical model applied to smoking cessation. In P. Norman, C. Abraham and M. Conner (eds), *Understanding and Changing Health Behaviour*. Amsterdam: Harwood Academic.

Sutton, S. (2001). Back to the drawing board? A review of applications of the transtheoretical model to substance use. *Addiction*, 96: 175–86.

Sutton, S. (2002). Using social cognition models to develop health behaviour interventions: problems and assumptions. In D. Rutter and L. Quine (eds), *Changing Health Behaviour*. Buckingham: Open University Press.

Sutton, S. (2004). Determinants of health-related behaviours: Theoretical and methodological issues. In S. Sutton, A. Baum and M. Johnston (eds). *The Sage Handbook of Health Psychology*. London: Sage, pp. 94–126.

Sutton, S. (2005). Another nail in the coffin of the transtheoretical model? A comment on West (2005). *Addiction*, 100: 1043–6.

Sutton, S. (2010). Using social cognition model to develop health behaviour interventions: the theory of planned behaviour as an example. In *Health Psychology*, 2nd edn. Oxford: BPS/Blackwell Publishing Ltd, pp. 122–34.

Sutton, S., Kinmouth, A., Hardeman, W. et al. (2014). Does electronic monitoring influence adherenec to medication? Randomized controlled trial of measurement reactivity. *Annals of Behavioral Medicine,* 48: 293–9.

Sutton, S., McVey, D. and Glanz, A. (1999). A comparative test of the theory of reasoned action and the theory of planned behaviour in the prediction of condom use intentions in a national sample of English young people. *Health Psychology*, 18: 72–81.

Suurmeijer, T.P.B.M., Reuvekamp, M.F. and Aldenkamp, B.P. (2001). Social functioning, psychological functioning, and quality of life in epilepsy. *Epilepsia*, 42: 1160–8.

Swami, V., Arteche, A., Chamorro-Premuzic, T. et al. (2009). Lay perceptions of current and future health, the causes of illness, and the nature of recovery: explaining health and illness in Malaysia. *British Journal of Health Psychology* 14: 519–40.

Swami, V., Furnham, A., Kannan, K. and Sinniah, D. (2008). Lay beliefs about schizophrenia and its treatment in Kota Kinabalu. Malaysia. *International Journal of Social Psychiatry*, 54: 164–79.

Swan, G.E., McClure, J.B., Jack, L.M. et al. (2010). Behavioral counseling and varenicline treatment for smoking cessation. *American Journal of Preventive Medicine*, 38: 482–90.

Swartz, L.H., Noell, J.W., Schroeder, S.W. et al. (2006). A randomised control study of a fully automated internet based smoking cessation programme. *Tobacco Control*, 15: 7–12.

Swartzman, L.C. and Lees, M.C. (1996). Causal dimensions of college students' perceptions of physical symptoms. *Journal of Behavioral Medicine*, 19(2): 85–110.

Szczepura A. (2005) Access to health care for ethnic minority populations. *Postgraduate Medical Journal,* 81: 141–7.

Taaffe, D.R., Harris, T.B., Ferrucci, L. et al. (2000). Cross-sectional and prospective relationships of interleukin-6 and C-reactive protein with physical performance in elderly persons: MacArthur Studies of Successful Aging. *Journal of Gerontology. A: Biological Science and Medical Science*, 55: M709–15.

Tak, N.I., Te Velde, S.J. and Brug, J. (2007). Ethnic differences in 1-year follow-up effect of the Dutch Schoolgruiten Project: promoting fruit and vegetable consumption among primary-school children. *Public Health Nutrition*, 10: 1497–507.

Tak, N.I., Te Velde, S.J. and Brug, J. (2009). Long-term effects of the Dutch Schoolgruiten Project: promoting fruit and vegetable consumption among primary-school children. *Public Health Nutrition*, 12: 1213–23.

Takao, S., Tsutsumi, A., Nishiuchi, K. et al. (2006). Effects of the job stress education for supervisors on psychological distress and job performance among their immediate subordinates: a supervisor-based randomized controlled trial. *Journal of Occupational Health*, 48: 494–503.

Takkouche, B., Regueira, C., Gestal-Otero, J.J. and Jesus, J. (2001). A cohort study of stress and the common cold. *Epidemiology*, 12: 345–9.

Tan, P.E.H. and Bishop, G.D. (1996). Disease representations and related behavioural intentions among Chinese Singaporeans. *Psychology and Health*, 11: 671–83.

Tang, N.K.Y., Salkovksis, P.M., Hodges, A. et al. (2008). Effects of mood on pain responses and pain tolerance: an experimental study in chronic back pain patients. *Pain*, 138: 392–401.

Tang, P.C. and Newcomb, C. (1998). Informing patients: a guide for providing patient health information. *Journal of the American Medical Informatics Association*, 5: 563–70.

Tang, Y. (2006). Obligation of filial piety, adult child caregiver burden, received social support and psychological wellbeing of adult child caregivers for frail elderly in Guangzhou, China (Unpublished doctoral dissertation). The University of Hong Kong, Hong Kong.

Tapper, K., Horne, P. and Lowe, C.F. (2003). The Food Dudes to the rescue! *The Psychologist*, 16: 18–21.

Targ, E.F. and Levine, E.G. (2002). The efficacy of a mind–body–spirit group for women with breast cancer: a randomized controlled trial. *General Hospital Psychiatry*, 24: 238–48.

Taylor, A., Chittleborough, C., Gill, T. et al. (2012) Relationship of social factors including trust, control over life decisions, problems with transport and safety, to psychological distress in the community. *Society of Psychiatry and Psychiatric Epidemiology*, 47: 465–73.

Taylor, B., Miller, E., Farrington, C.P. et al. (1999). Autism and measles, mumps and rubella vaccine: no epidemiological evidence for a causal association. *The Lancet*, 2026–9.

Taylor, B., Miller, E., Lingam, R. et al. (2002). Measles, mumps and rubella vaccination and bowel problems or developmental regression in children with autism: population study. *British Medical Journal*, 324: 393–6.

Taylor, C., Graham, J., Potts, H.W. et al. (2005). Changes in mental health of UK hospital consultants since the mid 1990s. *The Lancet*, 366: 742–4.

Taylor, C.B., Bandura, A., Ewart, C.K. et al. (1985). Exercise testing to enhance wives' confidence in their husbands' cardiac capability soon after clinically uncomplicated acute myocardial infarction. *American Journal of Cardiology*, 55: 635–8.

Taylor, S. (1983). Adjustment to threatening events: a theory of cognitive adaptation. *American Psychologist*, 38: 1161–73.

Taylor, S.E. (2006). Tend and befriend: biobehavioral bases of affiliation under stress. *Current Directions in Psychological Science*, 15: 273–7.

Taylor, S.E. (2007). Social support. In H.S. Friedman and R.C. Silver (eds), *Foundations of Health Psychology*. New York: Oxford University Press, pp. 145–71.

Taylor, S. (2011). Social support and health: a review. In Friedman, H.S. (ed.), *Oxford Handbook of Health Psychology*, Oxford Unversity Press, Chapter 9, pp. 189–214.

Taylor, S.E. and Armor, D.A. (1996). Positive illusions and coping with adversity. *Journal of Personality*, 64: 873–98.

Taylor, S.E., Klein, L.C., Grunewald, T.L. et al. (2003). Affiliation, social support, and biobehavioral responses to stress. In J. Suls and K.A. Wallston (eds), *Social Psychological Foundations of Health and Illness*. Oxford: Blackwell.

Taylor, S.E., Repetti, R.L. and Seeman, T. (1997). Health psychology: what is an unhealthy environment and how does it get under the skin? *Annual Reviews in Psychology*, 48: 411–47.

Taylor, S.E. and Seeman, T.E. (1999). Psychosocial resources and the SES–health relationship. *Annals of the New York Academy of Science*, 896: 210–25.

Taylor, S.E., Sherman, D.K., Kim, H.S. et al. (2004). Culture and social support: who seeks it and why? *Journal of Personality and Social Psychology*, 87: 354–62.

Taylor, S.E. and Stanton, A.L. (2008). Coping resources, coping processes, and mental health. *Annual Review of Clinical Psychology*, 3: 377–401.

Taylor, S.E., Welch, W., Kim, H.S. and Sherman, D.K. (2007). Cultural differences in the impact of social support on psychological and biological stress responses. *Psychological Science*, 18: 831–7.

Tedeschi, R.G. and Calhoun, L.G. (2004). Post-traumatic growth: conceptual foundations and empirical evidence. *Psychological Enquiry*, 15: 1–18.

Tedeschi, R.G. and Calhoun, L.G. (2008). Beyond the concept of recovery: growth and the experience of loss. *Death Studies*, 32: 27–39.

Temoshok, L. (1987). Personality, coping style, emotion and cancer: towards an integrative model. *Social Science and Medicine*, 20: 833–40.

Temoshok, L. and Dreher, H. (1993). *The Type C Connection: The Behavioral Links to Cancer and Your Health*. New York: Penguin.

Temoshok, L. and Fox, B.H. (1984). Coping styles and other psychosocial factors related to medical status and to prognosis in patients with cutaneous malignant melanoma. In B.H. Fox and B. Newberry (eds), *Impact of Psychoendocrine Systems in Cancer and Immunity*. Toronto: C.J. Hogrefe.

Tennant, C. (2002). Life events, stress and depression: a review of recent findings. *Australia and New Zealand Journal of Psychiatry*, 36: 173–82.

Tennen, H., Affleck, G., Armeli, S. et al. (2000). A daily process approach to coping: linking theory, research, and practice. *American Psychologist*, 55: 620–5.

Terracciano, A. and Costa, P.T. Jr (2004). Smoking and the five-factor model of personality. *Addiction*, 99: 472–81.

Terry, D.J. (1992). Stress, coping and coping resources as correlates of adaptation in myocardial infarction patients. *British Journal of Clinical Psychology*, 31: 215–25.

Thackeray, R., Crookston, B.T. and West, J.H (2013). Correlates of health-related social media use among adults, *Journal of Medical Internet research*, 15 doi:10.2196/jmir.2297

The Global Youth Tobacco Survey Collaborative Group (2002). Tobacco use among youth: a cross-country comparison. *Tobacco Control*, 11, 252–70.

Theisen, M.E., MacNeill, S.E., Lumley, M.A. et al. (1995). Psychosocial factors related to unrecognized acute myocardial infarction. *American Journal of Cardiology*, 75: 1211–13.

Theorell, T. and Karasek, R.A. (1996). Current issues relating to psychosocial job strain and cardiovascular disease research. *Journal of Occupational Health Psychology*, 1: 9–26.

Theunissen, N.C.M., de Ridder, D.T.D., Bensing, J.M. et al. (2003). Manipulation of patient–provider interaction: discussing illness representations or action plans concerning adherence. *Patient Education and Counselling*, 51: 247–58.

Theunissen, N.C.M., Vogels, T.G.C., Koopman, H.M. et al. (1998). The proxy problem: child report versus parent report in health-related quality of life research. *Quality of Life Research*, 7: 387–97.

Thoits, P.A. (1995). Stress, coping and social support processes. Where are we? What next? *Journal of Health and Social Behavior* (extra issue), 36: 53–79.

Thomas, D.B., Gao, D.L., Ray, R.M. et al. (2002). Randomized trial of breast self-examination in Shanghai – final results. *Journal of the National Cancer Institute*, 94: 1445–57.

Thomas, M., Walker, A., Wilmot, A. et al. (1998). *Living in Britain: Results from the 1996 General Household Survey*. London: Stationery Office.

Thompson, S.C. (1981). Will it hurt less if I can control it? A complex answer to a simple question. *Psychological Bulletin*, 90: 89–101.

Thompson, S.C., Galbraith, M., Thomas, C. et al. (2002). Caregivers of stroke patient family members: behavioural and attitudinal indicators of overprotective care. *Psychology and Health*, 17: 297–312.

Thompson, S.C. and Pitts, J.C. (1992). In sickness and in health: chronic illness, marriage and spousal caregiving. In S. Spacapan and S. Oskamp (eds), *Helping and Being Helped: Naturalistic Studies*. Newbury Park, CA: Sage.

Thompson, S.C., Sobolew-Shubin, A., Galbraith, M.E. et al. (1993). Maintaining perceptions of control: finding perceived control in low-control circumstances. *Journal of Personality and Social Psychology*, 64: 293–304.

Thompson, W.G., Longstreth, G. and Drossman, D.A. (2000). Functional bowel disorders and functional abdominal pain. In D.A. Drossman, E. Corazziari, N. Talley et al. (eds), *Rome II: The Functional Gastrointestinal Disorders*, 2nd edn. McLean, VA: Degnon Associates.

Thrasher, J.F., Hammond, D., Fong, G.T. et al. (2007). Smokers' reactions to cigarette package warnings with graphic imagery and with only text: a comparison between Mexico and Canada. *Salud Publica Mexico*, 49 Suppl 2: S233–40.

Thuné-Boyle, I.C.V., Stygall, J., Keshtgar, M.R.S. and Newman, S.P. (2006). Do religious/spiritual coping strategies affect illness adjustment in patients with cancer? A systematic review of the literature. *Social Science & Medicine*, 63: 151–64.

Thurstone, L.L. (1928). Attitudes can be measured. *American Journal of Sociology*, 33: 529–44.

Timperio, A., Ball, K., Salmon, J. et al. (2006). Personal, family, social and environmental correlates of active commuting to school. *American Journal of Preventive Medicine*, 30: 45–51.

Tjora, T., Hetland, J., AarØ, L.E. and Øverland, S. (2011). Distal and proximal family predictors of adolescents' smoking initiation and development: a longitudinal latent curve model analysis. *BMC Public Health*, 11: 911–20..

Tobias, M. and Yeh, L.C. (2006). Do all ethnic groups in New Zealand exhibit socio-economic mortality gradients? *Australian and New Zealand Journal of Public Health*, 30: 343–9.

Tobin, D.L., Holroyd, K.A., Baker, A. et al. (1988). Development and clinical trial of a minimal contact, cognitive-behavioral treatment for tension headache. *Cognitive Therapy and Research*, 12: 325–39.

Todorova, I.L., Falcón, L.M., Lincoln, A.K. et al. (2010). Perceived discrimination, psychological distress and health. *Sociology of Health and Illness*, 32: 843–61.

Toise S.C., Sears S.F., Schoenfeld M.H. et al. (2014). Psychosocial and cardiac outcomes of yoga for ICD patients: a randomized clinical control trial. *Pacing and Clinical Electrophysiology*, 37: 48–62.

Toljamo, M. and Hentinen, M. (2001). Adherence to self care and social support. *Journal of Clinical Nursing*, 10: 618–27.

Tomé-Pires C. and Miró J. (2012). Hypnosis for the management of chronic and cancer procedure-related pain in children. *International Journal of Clinical Experimental Hypnosis,* 60: 432–57.

Tomich, P.L. and Helgeson, V.S. (2004). Is finding something good in the bad always good? Benefit-finding among women with breast cancer. *Health Psychology*, 23: 16–23.

Touzet, S., Réfabert, L., Letrilliart, L. et al. (2007). Impact of consensus development conference guidelines on primary care of bronchiolitis: are national guidelines being followed? *Journal of Evaluation of Clinical Practice*, 13: 651–6.

Tov, W. and Diener, E. (2007). Culture and subjective well-being. In S. Kitayama and D. Cohen (eds), *Handbook of Cultural Psychology*. New York: Guilford Press, pp. 697–713.

Traa, M.J., de Vries, J., Bodenamnn, G. and den Oudsten, B.L. (2015). Dyadic coping and relationship functioning in couples coping with cancer: a systematic review. *British Journal of Health Psychology*, 20: 85–114.

Treviño, L.A., Baker, L., McIntosh, S. et al. (2014). Physical activity as a coping strategy for smoking cessation in mid-life and older adults, *Addictive Behaviors*, doi: 10.1016/j.addbeh.2014.01.014

Triandis, H.C. (1977). *Interpersonal Behavior*. Monterey, CA: Brooks/Cole.

Triantafillou, J., Naditch, M., Repkova, K. et al. (2010). *Informal Care in the Long Term Care System: European Overview Paper.* http://www.euro.centre.org/data/1278594816_84909.pdf.Downloaded 6/04/2015

Trichopoulou A., Bamia C., Trichopoulos D. (2009). Anatomy of health effects of Mediterranean diet: Greek EPIC prospective cohort study. *British Medical Journal*, 338: b2337.

Troiano, R.P., Berrigan, D., Dodd, K.W. et al. (2008). Physical activity in the United States measured by accelerometer. *Medicine & Science in Sports & Exercise,* 40: 181–8.

Tromp, D.M., Brouha, X.D.R., DeLeeuw, J.R.J. et al. (2004). Psychological factors and patient delay in patients with head and neck cancer. *European Journal of Cancer*, 40: 1509–16.

Troy, A.S., Wlhelm, F.H., Shallcross, A.J. and Mauss, I.B. (2010). Seeing the silver lining: cognitive reappraisal ability moderates the relationship between stress and depressive symptoms. *Emotion*, 10: 783–95.

Trufelli, D.C., Bensi, C.G., Garcia, J.B. et al. (2008). Burnout in cancer professionals: a systematic review and meta-analysis. *European Journal of Cancer Care*, 17: 524–31.

Tsarenko, Y. and Polonsky, M.J. (2011). 'You can spend your life dying or you can spend your life living': identity transition in people who are HIV-positive. *Psychology & Health*, 26: 465–83.

Tschuschke, V., Hertenstein, B., Arnold, R. et al. (2001). Associations between coping and survival time of adult leukaemia patients receiving allogenic bone marrow transplantation: results of a prospective study. *Journal of Psychosomatic Research*, 50: 277–85.

Tubiana-Rufi, N., Moret, L., Czernichow, P. et al. (1998). The association of poor adherence and acute metabolic disorders with low levels of cohesion and adaptability in families with diabetic children: the PEDIAB Collaborative Group. *Acta Paediatrica*, 87: 741–6.

Tudor-Smith, C., Nutbeam, D., Moore, L. et al. (1998). Effects of the Heartbeat Wales programme over five years on behavioural risks for cardiovascular disease: quasi-experimental comparison of results from Wales and a matched reference area. *British Medical Journal*, 316: 818–22.

Tunney, A.M. and Boore, J. (2013). The effectiveness of a storybook in lessening anxiety in children undergoing tonsillectomy and adenoidectomy in Northern Ireland. *Issues in Comprehensive Pediatric Nursing*, 36: 319–35.

Turk, D.C. (1986). *Workshop on Pain Management.* Birmingham, UK.

Turk, D.C., Litt, M.D., Salovey, P. et al. (1985). Seeking urgent pediatric treatment: factors contributing to frequency, delay and appropriateness. *Health Psychology*, 4: 43–59.

Turk, D.C. and Okifuji, A. (1999). Assessment of patients' reporting of pain: an integrated perspective. *The Lancet*, 353: 1784–8.

Turk, D.C., Rudy, T.E. and Salovey, P. (1986). Implicit models of illness. *Journal of Behavioral Medicine*, 9: 453–74.

Turner, J., Page-Shafer, K., Chin, D.P. et al. (2001). Adverse impact of cigarette smoking on dimensions of health-related quality of life in persons with HIV infection. *AIDS Patient Care and STDs*, 15: 615–24.

Turner, J.A. and Clancy, S. (1988). Comparison of operant behavioral and cognitive-behavioral group treatment for chronic low back pain. *Journal of Consulting and Clinical Psychology*, 56: 261–6.

Turner, J.A., Holtzman, S. and Mancl, L. (2007). Mediators, moderators, and predictors of therapeutic change in cognitive-behavioral therapy for chronic pain. *Pain*, 127: 276–86.

Turner, J.C. (1991). *Social Influence*. Bristol, England: Open University Press.

Turner, J.C., Hogg, M.A., Oakes, P.J. et al. (1987). *Rediscovering the Social Group: A Self-categorization Theory*. Oxford: Blackwell.

Turner-Cobb, J. (2014). *Child Health Psychology: A Biopsychosocial Perspective*. London: Sage.

Turner-Cobb, J.M., Gore-Felton, C., Marouf, F. et al. (2002). Coping, social adjustment, and attachment style as psychosocial correlates of adjustment in men and women with HIV/AIDS. *Journal of Behavioral Medicine*, 25: 337–53.

Turner-Cobb, J.M., Sephton, S.E., Koopman, C. et al. (2000). Social support and salivary cortisol in women with metastatic breast cancer. *Psychosomatic Medicine*, 62: 337–45.

Turunen, J.H., Mäntyselkä, P.T., Kumpusalo, E.A. et al. (2005). Frequent analgesic use at population level: prevalence and patterns of use. *Pain*, 115: 374–81.

Tyczynski, J.E., Bray, F., Aareleid, T. et al. (2004). Lung cancer mortality patterns in selected Central, Eastern and Southern European countries. *International Journal of Cancer*, 109: 598–610.

Uchino, B.N. (2006). Social support and health: a review of physiological processes potentially underlying links to disease outcomes. *Journal of Behavioral Medicine*, 29: 377–87.

UK Central Statistics Office (1980). A change in revenue from an indirect tax change. *Economic Trend*, March: 97–107.

UNAIDS (2008). http://www.unaids.org/en/.

United Nations, Department of Economic and Social Affairs, Population Division (2013). *World Population Ageing 2013*. ST/ESA/SER.A/348.

United Nations Office on Drugs & Crime (2014). World Drugs Report 2014, United Nations: New York. Downloaded on August 15th 2014: http://www.unodc.org/documents/wdr2014/World_Drug_Report_2014_web.pdf

United Nations Statistics Division (2014) Population and Vital Statistics Report, downloaded on March 6th 2014: http://unstats.un.org/unsd/demographic/products/vitstats/Sets/Series_A_2014.pdf

Unrod, M., Smith, M., Spring, B. et al. (2007). Randomized controlled trial of a computer-based, tailored intervention to increase smoking cessation counseling by primary care physicians. *Journal of General Internal Medicine*, 22: 478–84.

Uman, L.S., Chambers, C.T., McGrath, P.J. and Kisely, S. (2008). A systematic review of randomized controlled trials examining psychological interventions for needle-related procedural pain and distress in children and adolescents: an abbreviated Cochrane review. *Journal of Pediatric Psychology*, 33: 842–54.

Urquhart-Law, G. (2002). Dissimilarity in adolescent and maternal representations of type 1 diabetes: exploration of relations to adolescent well-being. *Child Health Care and Development*, 28: 369–78.

US Bureau of the Census (1999). *Statistical Abstracts of the United States: 1998*, 118th edn. Retrieved (2.10.2002) from: http://www.census.gov.

US Centers for Disease Control and Prevention (1996). Community-level prevention of human immuno-deficiency virus infection among high-risk populations: the AIDS Community Demonstration Projects. *MMWR Morbidity and Mortality Weekly Reports*, 45 (RR-6): 1–24.

US Department of Health and Human Services (1997). *Ninth Special Report to the U.S. Congress on Alcohol and Health, June 1997*. US Department of Health and Human Services, NIH, NIAAA.

US Department of Health and Human Services (2000). *Healthy People 2010*. Washington, DC: US Department of Health and Human Services.

US Department of Health and Human Services (2006). *The Health Consequences of Involuntary Exposure to Tobacco Smoke: A Report of the Surgeon General*. Atlanta, GA: US Department of Health and Human Services.

US Institute of Medicine (2002). *Unequal Treatment: Confronting Racial and Ethnic Disparities in Health Care*. Washington, DC: Institute of Medicine.

US Preventive Services Task Force (USPSTF) (2003). Routine vitamin supplementation to prevent cancer and cardiovascular disease: recommendations and rationale. *Annals of Internal Medicine*, 139: 51–5.

Ussher, J.M. and Sandoval, M. (2008). Gender differences in the construction and experience of cancer care. The consequence of gender positioning of carers. *Psychology and Health*, 23, 945–63.

Utz, R.L., Swenson, K.L., Caserta, M., Lund, D. and de Vries, B. (2013). Feeling lonely versus being alone: loneliness and social support among recently bereaved persons. *Journals of Gerontology Series B: Psychological Sciences and Social Sciences,* doi: 10.1093/geronb/gbt075.

Vaillant, G.E. (1998). Natural history of male psychological health XIV: relationship of mood disorder, vulnerability and physical health. *American Journal of Psychiatry*, 155: 184–91.

Valente, S.M. (2003). Depression and HIV disease. *Journal of Association of Nurses in AIDS Care*, 14: 41–51.

Valentine, A., Buchanan, H. and Knibb, R. (2010). A preliminary investigation of 4 to 11-year old children's knowledge and understanding of stress. *Patient Education and Counselling*, 79: 255–7.

Van Damme, S., Legrain, V., Vogt, J. et al. (2010). Keeping pain in mind: a motivational account of attention to pain. *Neuroscience and Biobehavioral Reviews*, 34: 204–13.

Van de Creek, L., Paget, S., Horton, R. et al. (2004). Religious and non-religious coping methods among persons with rheumatoid arthritis. *Arthritis and Rheumatology*, 51: 49–55.

Vandello, J.A. and Cohen. D. (1999) Patterns of individualism and collectivism across the United States. *Journal of Personality & Social Psychology*, 77: 279–92.

van den Arend, I.J., Stolk, R.P. et al. (2000). Education integrated into structured general practice care for type 2 diabetic patients results in sustained improvement of illness knowledge and self-care. *Diabetes Medicine*, 17: 190–7.

van den Heuvel, E.T.P., de Witte, L.P., Schure, L.M. et al. (2001). Risk factors for burn-out in caregivers of stroke patients, and possibilities for intervention. *Clinical Rehabilitation*, 15: 669–77.

van den Hout, J.H.C., Vlaeyen, J.W.S., Peters, M.L. et al. (2000). Does failure hurt? The effects of failure feedback on pain report, pain tolerance and pain avoidance. *European Journal of Pain*, 4: 335–46.

van der Doef, M. and Maes, S. (1998). The job demand–control(–support) model and physical health outcomes: a review of the strain and buffer hypotheses. *Psychology and Health*, 13: 909–36.

van der Doef, M. and Maes, S. (1999). The job demand–control(–support) model and psychological well-being: a review of 20 years empirical research. *Work and Stress*, 13: 87–114.

van der Geest, S. and Whyte, S. (1989). The charm of medicines: metaphors and metonyms. *Medical Anthropology Quarterly*, 3: 345–67.

van der Heide, A., Deliens, L., Faisst, K. et al. (2003). End-of-life decision-making in six European countries: descriptive study. *The Lancet*, 361: 345–50.

van der Meer, V., van Stel, H.F., Detmar, S.B. et al. (2007). Internet-based self-management offers an opportunity to achieve better asthma control in adolescents. *Chest*, 132: 112–19.

van der Pligt, J. and de Vries, N.K. (1998). Expectancy-value models of health behaviour: the role of salience and anticipated affect. *Psychology and Health*, 13: 289–305.

van der Velde, F.W., Hooykaas, C. and van der Pligt, J. (1992). Risk perception and behaviour: pessimism, realism and optimism about AIDS-related health behaviour. *Psychology and Health*, 6: 23–38.

van der Waerden, J.E., Hoefnagels C., et al. (2013). A randomized controlled trial of combined exercise and psycho-education for low-SES women: short- and long-term outcomes in the reduction of stress and depressive symptoms. *Social Science and Medicine*, 91: 84–93.

van Eck, M., Berkhof, H., Nicolson, N. et al. (1996). The effects of perceived stress, traits, mood states, and stressful daily events on salivary cortisol. *Psychosomatic Medicine*, 58: 508–14.

Vangeli, E. and West, R. (2008). Sociodemographic differences in triggers to quit smoking: findings from a national survey. *Tobacco Control*, 17: 410–15.

Van Hecke, A., Grypdonck, M. and Defloor, T. (2009). A review of why patients with leg ulcers do not adhere to treatment. *Journal of Clinical Nursing*, 18: 337–49.

van Koningsbruggen, G.M., Das, E. and Rosos-Ewoldse, D.R. (2009). How self-affirmation reduces defensive processing of threatening health information: evidence at the implicit level. *Health Psychology*, 28: 563–8.

van Stralen, M.M., De Vries, H., Mudde, A.N. et al. (2009). Determinants of initiation and maintenance of physical activity among older adults: a literature review. *Health Psychology Review*, 3: 147–207.

van Strien, T., Engels, R.C.M.E., van Leeuwe, J. and Snoek, H.M. (2005). The Stice model of overeating: tests in clinical and non-clinical samples. *Appetite*, 45: 205–13.

van Strien, T., Frijters, J.E.R., Bergers, G.P.A. and Defares, P.S. (1986). The Dutch Eating Behavior Questionnaire (DEBQ) for assessment of restrained, emotional and external eating behavior. *International Journal of Eating Disorders*, 5: 295–315.

van Strien, T., van de Laar, F.A., van Leeuwe, J.F.J. et al. (2007). The dieting dilemma in patients with newly diagnosed Type 2 diabetes: does dietary restraint predict weight gain 4 years after diagnosis? *Health Psychology*, 1: 105–12.

van't Riet, J., Ruiter, R.A., Werrij, M.Q. and de Vries, H. (2010). Investigating message-framing effects in the context of a tailored intervention promoting physical activity. *Health Education Research*, 25: 343–54.

van Tulder, M.W., Ostelo, R.W.J., Vlaeyen, J.W.S. et al. (2003). Behavioural treatment for chronic low back pain. In *The Cochrane Library*, issue 1. Oxford: Update Software.

van Vegchel, N., de Jonge, J., Bosma, H. and Schaufeli, W. (2005). Reviewing the effort–reward imbalance model: drawing up the balance of 45 empirical studies. *Social Science and Medicine*, 60: 1117–31.

van Wijk, C.M.T.G. and Kolk, A.M. (1997). Sex differences in physical symptoms: the contribution of symptom perception theory. *Social Science & Medicine*, 45: 231–46.

van Zuuren, F.J. and Dooper, R. (1999). Coping style and self-reported health promotion and disease detection behaviour. *British Journal of Health Psychology*, 4: 81–9.

Vaughan, P.W., Rogers, E.M., Singhal, A. et al. (2000). Entertainment-education and HIV/AIDS prevention: a field experiment in Tanzania. *Journal of Health Communication*, 5: 81–100.

Vaughn, L.M., Jacquez, F., Baker, R.C. (2009). Cultural health attributions, beliefs, and practices: effects on healthcare and medical education. *The Open Medical Education Journal,* 2: 64–74.

Vedhara, K., Cox, N.K.M., Wilcock, G.K. et al. (1999). Chronic stress in elderly carers of dementia patients and antibody responses to influenza vaccination. *The Lancet*, 353: 627–31.

Vedhara, K. and Irwin, M.R. (eds) (2005). *Human Psychoneuroimmunology*. Oxford: Oxford University Press.

Vedhara, K., McDermott, M.P., Evans, T.G. et al. (2002). Chronic stress in nonelderly caregivers. Psychological, endocrine and immune implications. *Journal of Psychosomatic Research*, 53: 1153–61.

Vedhara, K., Shanks, N., Anderson, S. et al. (2000). The role of stressors and psychosocial variables in the stress process: a study of chronic caregiver stress. *Psychosomatic Medicine*, 62: 374–85.

Vedhara, K., Tallon, D., Gale, L. et al. (2003). Psychological determinants of wound healing in diabetic patients with foot ulceration. Paper presented at the European Health Psychology conference, Kos, August 2003.

Vedhara, K., Wang, E.C.Y., Fox, J.D. et al. (2001). The measurement of stress-related immune dysfunction in humans: an introduction to psychoneuro-immunology. In *Assessments in Behavioural Medicine*. Hove: Brunner-Routledge, pp. 441–80.

Veenhoven, R. (2003). Happiness. *The Psychologist*, 16: 128–9.

Verbrugge, L.M. and Steiner, R.P. (1985). Prescribing drugs to men and women. *Health Psychology*, 4: 79–98.

Verdugo, R.J. and Ochoa, J.L. (1994). Sympathetically maintained pain. I. Phentolamine block questions the concept. *Neurology*, 44: 1003–10.

Vereecken, C., Rovner, A. and Maes, L.(2010). Associations of parenting styles, parental feeding practices and child characteristics with young children's fruit and vegetable consumption. *Appetite*, 55: 589–96.

Vermeire, E., Hearnshaw, H., Rätsep, A. et al. (2007) Obstacles to adherence in living with type-2 diabetes: an international qualitative study using meta-ethnography (EUROBSTACLE). *Primary Care Diabetes*, 1: 25–33.

Vestling, M., Tfvesson, B. and Iwarsson, S. (2003). Indicators for return to work after stroke and the importance of work for subjective well-being and life satisfaction. *Journal of Rehabilitation Medicine*, 35: 127–31.

Vickrey, B.G., Samuels, M.A. and Ropper, A.H. (2010). How neurologists think: a cognitive psychology perspective on missed diagnoses. *Annals of Neurology*, 67: 425–33.

Vikman, S., Airaksinen, K.E., Tierala, I. et al. (2004). Improved adherence to practice guidelines yields better outcome in high-risk patients with acute coronary syndrome without ST elevation: findings from nationwide FINACS studies. *Journal of Internal Medicine*, 256: 316–23.

Vilchinsky, N., Dekel, R., Leibowirtz, M., Reges, O., et al. (2011). Dynamics of support perceptions among couples coping with cardiac illness: the effect on recovery outcomes. *Health Psychology*, 230: 411–19

Vilchinsky, N., Dekel, R., Revenson, T.A. et al. (2014). Caregivers' burden and depressive symptoms: the moderational role of attachment orientations. *Health Psychology*, dx.doi.org/10.1037/hea0000121

Vilhauer, R.P., McClintock, M.K. and Matthews, A.K. (2010). Online support groups for women with metastatic breast cancer: a feasibility pilot study. *Journal of Psychosocial Oncology*, 28: 560–86.

Viner, R., McGrath, M. and Trudinger, P. (1996). Family stress and metabolic control in diabetes. *Archives of Diseases of Childhood*, 74: 418–21.

Viner, R. and Taylor, B. (2007). Adult outcomes of binge drinking in adolescence: findings from a UK national birth cohort. *Journal of Epidemiology and Community Health*, 61: 902–7.

Vingerhoets, A.J.J.M. and Perski, A. (2000). The psychobiology of stress. In A.A. Kaptein, A.W.P.M. Appels and K. Orth-Gomér (eds), *Psychology in Medicine*. Houten: Wolters Kluwer International, pp. 34–49.

Visser, M.J. (2007). HIV/AIDS prevention through peer education and support in secondary schools in South Africa. *Sahara Journal*, 4: 678–94.

Visser, de R.O. and Smith, J.A. (2007). Alcohol consumpton and masculine identity among young men. *Psychology & Health*, 22: 595–614.

Visser-Meily, A., van Heugten, C., Post, M. et al. (2005). Intervention studies for caregivers of stroke survivors: a critical review. *Patient Education and Counselling*, 56: 257–67.

Vitolins, M.Z., Rand, C.S., Rapp, S.R. et al. (2000). Measuring adherence to behavioral and medical interventions. *Controlled Clinical Trials*, 21(5 suppl.): 188S–94S.

Vlaeyen, J.W., Kole-Snijders, A.M., Boeren, R.G. et al. (1995). Fear of movement/(re)injury in chronic low back pain and its relation to behavioral performance. *Pain*, 62: 363–72.

Voerman, G.E., Sandsjö, L., Vollenbroek-Hutten, M.M. et al. (2007). Changes in cognitive-behavioral factors and muscle activation patterns after interventions for work-related neck–shoulder complaints: relations with discomfort and disability. *Journal of Occupational Rehabilitation*, 17: 593–609.

Vögele, C. (1998). Serum lipid concentrations, hostility and cardiovascular reactions to mental stress. *International Journal of Psycophysiology*, 28: 167–79.

Vögele, C., Jarvis, A. and Cheeseman, K. (1997). Anger suppression, reactivity, and hypertension risk: gender makes a difference. *Annals of Behavioral Medicine*, 19: 61–9.

Vögele, C. and Steptoe, A. (1993). Anger inhibition and family history as moderators of cardiovascular responses to mental stress in adolescent boys. *Journal of Psychosomatic Research*, 37: 503–14.

Vogt, T.M., Mullooly, J.P., Ernst, D. et al. (1992). Social networks as predictors of ischemic heart disease, cancer, stroke and hypertension: incidence, survival and mortality. *Journal of Clinical Epidemiology*, 45: 659–66.

Vollrath, M. (2006). *Handbook of Personality and Health*. Chichester: Wiley.

Vosvick, M., Koopman, C., Gore-Felton, C. et al. (2003). Relationship of functional quality of life to strategies for coping with the stress of living with HIV/AIDS. *Psychosomatics*, 44: 51–8.

Vrijens, B., De Geest, S., Hughes, D. et al. for the ABC project team (2012). A new taxonomy for describing and defining adherence to medications. *British Journal of Clinical Pharmacology*, 73: 691–705.

Wade, D.T. and Halligan, P.W. (2004). Do biomedical models of illness make for good healthcare systems? *British Medical Journal*, 329: 1398–401.

Wagenaar, A.C., Salois, M.J. and Komro, K.A. (2009). Effects of beverage alcohol price and tax levels on drinking: a meta-analysis of 1003 estimates from 112 studies. *Addiction*, 104: 179–90.

Wakefield, A.J., Murch, S.H., Anthony, A. et al. (1998). Ileal-lymphoid nodular hyperplasia, non-specific colitis and pervasive developmental disorder in children. *The Lancet*, 351: 637–41.

Wakefield, M.A., Chaloupka, F.J., Kaufman, N.J. et al. (2000). Effect of restrictions on smoking at home, at school, and in public places on teenage smoking: cross-sectional study. *British Medical Journal*, 321: 333–7.

Wakefield, M.A., Loken, B. and Hornik, R.C. (2010). Use of mass media campaigns to change health behaviour. *Lancet*, 376: 1261–71.

Walker, C., Papadopoulos, L., Lipton, M. et al. (2006). The importance of children's illness beliefs: the Children's Illness Perception Questionnaire (CIPQ) as a reliable assessment tool for eczema and asthma. *Psychology, Health & Medicine*, 11: 100–7.

Walker, J.G., Jackson, H.J. and Littlejohn, G.O. (2004). Models of adjustment to chronic illness: using the example of rheumatoid arthritis. *Clinical Psychology Review*, 24: 461–88.

Walker, L.G., Heys, S.D. and Eremin, O. (1999). Surviving cancer: do psychosocial factors count? *Journal of Psychosomatic Research*, 47: 497–503.

Walker, Z.A.K. and Townsend, J. (1999). The role of general practice in promoting teenage health: a review of the literature. *Family Practice*, 16: 164–72.

Wall, P.D. (1979). On the relation of injury to pain. The John J. Bonica Lecture. *Pain*, 6: 253–64.

Wallander, J.L. and Varni, J.W. (1998). Effects of pediatric chronic physical disorders on child and family adjustment. *Journal of Child Psychology and Psychiatry*, 39: 29–46.

Wallston, K.A. (1991). The importance of placing measures of health locus of control beliefs in a theoretical context. *Health Education Research*, 6: 251–2.

Wallston, K.A. and Smith, M.S. (1994). Issues of control and health: the action is in the interaction. In G. Penny, P. Bennett and M. Herbert (eds), *Health Psychology: A Lifespan Perspective*. London: Harwood Academic.

Wallston, K.A., Wallston, B.S. and deVellis, R. (1978). Development of the multidimensional health locus of control (MHLC) scale. *Health Education Monographs*, 6: 160–70.

Walsh, D.A. and Radcliffe, J.C. (2002). Pain beliefs and perceived physical disability of patients with chronic low back pain. *Pain*, 97: 23–31.

Walton, K.G., Schneider, R.H. and Nidich, S. (2004). Review of controlled research on the transcendental meditation program and cardiovascular disease: risk factors, morbidity, and mortality. *Cardiology Review*, 12: 262–6.

Wamala, S., Merlo, J., Bostrom, G. et al. (2007). Socioeconomic disadvantage and primary non-adherence with medication in Sweden. *International Journal for Quality in Health Care*, 19: 134–40.

Wang, H.W., Leineweber, C., Kirkeeide, R. et al. (2007). Psychosocial stress and atherosclerosis: family and work stress accelerate progression of coronary disease in women: the Stockholm Female Coronary Angiography Study. *Journal of Internal Medicine*, 261(3): 245–54.

Wang, J.L., Lesage, A., Schmitz, N. and Drapeau, A. (2008). The relationship between work stress and mental disorders in men and women: results from a population-based study. *Journal of Epidemiology and Community Health*, 62: 42–7.

Wang, X., Ouyang, Y., Liu, J. et al. (2014). Fruit and vegetable consumption and mortality from all causes, cardiovascular diseases and cancer: systematic review and dose-response metaanalysis of prospective studies, *BMJ* 2014;349:g4490 doi: 10.1136/bmj.g4490

Warburton, D.E.R., Charlesworth, S., Ivey, A. et al. (2010). A systematic review of the evidence for Canada's Physical Activity Guidelines for Adults, *International Journal of Behavioral Nutrition and Physical Activity*, 7: 39.

Warburton, D.M., Revell, A.D. and Thompson, D.H. (1991). Smokers of the future. Special issue: Future directions in tobacco research. *British Journal of Addiction*, 86: 621–5.

Ward, M.M., Mefford, I.N., Parker, S.D. et al. (1983). Epinephrine and norepinephrine responses in continuously collected human plasma to a series of stressors. *Psychosomatic Medicine*, 45: 471–86.

Ward, S.E., Leventhal, H. and Love, R. (1988). Repression revisited: tactics used in coping with a severe health threat. *Personality and Social Psychology Bulletin*, 14: 735–46.

Wardle, J., Cooke, L.J., Gibson, E.L. et al. (2003). Increasing children's acceptance of vegetables; a randomized trial of parent-led exposure. *Appetite*, 40: 155–62.

Wardle, J. and Johnson, F. (2002). Weight and dieting: examining levels of weight concern in British adults. *International Journal of Obesity*, 26: 1144–9.

Wardle, J. and Steptoe, A. (2003). Socioeconomic differences in attitudes and beliefs about healthy lifestyles. *Journal of Epidemiology and Community Health*, 57: 440–3.

Warner, B.J., Curnow, L.J., Polglase, A.L. and Debinski, H.S. (2005). Factors influencing uptake of genetic testing for colorectal cancer risk in an Australian Jewish population. *Journal of Genetic Counselling*, 14: 387–94.

Warner, L., Klausner, J.D., Rietmeijer, C.A. et al. (2008). Effect of a brief video intervention on incident infection among patients attending sexually transmitted disease clinics. *Public Library of Science Medicine*, 5: e135.

Warner, L.J., Lumley, M.A., Casey, R.J. et al. (2006). Health effects of written emotional disclosure in adolescents with asthma: a randomized, controlled trial. *Journal of Pediatric Psychology*, 31: 557–68.

Warren, L. and Hixenbaugh, P. (1998). Adherence and diabetes. In L. Myers and K. Midence (eds), *Adherence to Treatment in Medical Conditions*. The Netherlands: Harwood Academic.

Watson, D. and Clark, L.A. (1984). Negative affectivity: the disposition to experience aversive emotional states. *Psychological Bulletin*, 96: 465–90.

Watson, D., David, J.P. and Suls, J. (1999). Personality, affectivity, and coping. In C.R. Snyder (ed.), *Coping: The Psychology of What Works*. Oxford: Oxford University Press, pp. 119–40.

Watson, D. and Pennebaker, J.W. (1989). Health complaints, stress and distress: exploring the central role of negative affectivity. *Psychological Review*, 96: 234–54.

Watson, D. and Pennebaker, J.W. (1991). Situational, dispositional and genetic bases of symptom reporting. In J.A. Skelton and R.T. Croyle (eds), *Mental Representation in Health and Illness*. New York: Springer Verlag.

Watson, M., Buck, G., Wheatley, K. et al. (2004a). Adverse impact of bone marrow transplantation on quality of life in acute myeloid leukaemia patients: analysis of the UK Medical Research Council AML 10 Trial. *European Journal of Cancer*, 40: 971–8.

Watson, M., Davidson-Homewood, J., Haviland, J. et al. (2002). Influence of psychological coping on survival and recurrence: a response to the systematic review (letter to the editor). *British Medical Journal*, 325: 598.

Watson, M., Foster, C., Eeles, R. et al. (2004b). Psychosocial impact of breast/ovarian (BRCA1/2) cancer-predictive genetic testing in a UK multi-centre clinical cohort. *British Journal of Cancer*, 91: 1787–94.

Watson, M., Haviland, J.S., Greer, S. et al. (1999a). Influence of psychological response on survival in breast cancer: a population-based cohort study. *The Lancet*, 9187: 1331–6.

Watson, M., Homewood, J., Haviland, J. et al. (2005). Influence of psychological response on breast cancer survival: 10-year follow-up of a population-based cohort. *European Journal of Cancer*, 41: 1710–14.

Watson, M., Lloyd, S., Davidson, J. et al. (1999b). The impact of genetic counselling on risk perception and mental health in women with a family history of breast cancer. *British Journal of Cancer*, 79: 868–74.

Watson P.W. and McKinstry B. (2009). A systematic review of interventions to improve recall of medical advice in healthcare consultations. *Journal of the Royal Society of Medicine*, 102: 235–43.

Wearden, A.G., Dunn, G., Dowrick, C. and Morriss, R. (2012). Depressive symptoms and pragmatic rehabilitation for chronic fatigue syndrome. *British Journal of Psychiatry*, 201: 227–32.

Webb, J. (2013). 'Chose to be agents of change, not just victims', Austerity Psychology-Opinion. *The Psychologist*, 26: 645.

Webb, O.J. and Eves, F.F. (2007). Effects of environmental changes in a stair climbing intervention: generalization to stair descent. *American Journal of Health Promotion*, 22: 38–44.

Webb, O. J., Eves, F. F. and Smith, L. (2011) Investigating behavioural mimicry in the context of stair/escalator choice. *British Journal of Health Psychology*, 16: 373–85.

Webb T. L., Sheeran P. and Luszczynska A. (2009) Planning to break unwanted habits: habit strength moderates implementation intention effects on behavior change. *British Journal of Social Psychology*; 48: 507–23.

Webb, T.L., Sniehotta, F.F. and Michie, S. (2010). Using theories of behaviour change to inform interventions for addictive behaviours. *Addiction*, 105:1879–1892 doi:10.1111/j.1360–0443.2010.03028.x

Weber, A. and Lehnert, G. (1997). Unemployment and cardiovascular diseases: a causal relationship? *International Archives of Occupational and Environmental Health*, 70: 153–60.

Weber, B.A., Roberts, B.L., Yarandi, H. et al. (2007). The impact of dyadic social support on self-efficacy and depression after radical prostatectomy. *Journal of Aging and Health*, 19: 630–45.

Weber, M.A. and Julius, S. (1998). The challenge of very mild hypertension: should treatment be sooner or later? *American Journal of Hypertension*, 11: 1495–6.

Weiland, A., van de Kraats, R.E., Bllankenstein, A.H. et al. (2012). Encounters between medical specialists and patients with medially unexplained physical symptoms; influences of communication on patient outcomes and use of healthcare: a literature overview. *Perspectives in Medical Education*, 1: 192–206.

Weiner, B. (1986). *An Attributional Theory of Motivation and Emotion*. New York: Springer.

Weinman, J., Ebrecht, M., Scott, S. et al. (2008). Enhanced wound healing after emotional disclosure intervention. *British Journal of Health Psychology*, 13: 95–102.

Weinman, J. and Petrie, K.J. (1997). Illness perceptions: a new paradigm for psychosomatics? (editorial). *Journal of Psychosomatic Research*, 42: 113–16.

Weinman, J., Petrie, K.J., Moss-Morris, R. et al. (1996). The Illness Perception Questionnaire: a new method for assessing the cognitive representation of illness. *Psychology and Health*, 11: 431–55.

Weinman, J., Petrie, K.J., Sharpe, N. et al. (2000). Causal attributions in patients and spouses following first-time myocardial infarction and subsequent life changes. *British Journal of Health Psychology*, 5: 263–74.

Weinstein, N.D. (1982). Unrealistic optimism about susceptibility to health problems. *Journal of Behavioral Medicine*, 2: 125–40.

Weinstein, N. (1984). Why it won't happen to me: perceptions of risk factors and susceptibility. *Health Psychology*, 3: 431–57.

Weinstein, N. (1987). Unrealistic optimism about illness susceptibility: conclusions from a community-wide sample. *Journal of Behavioral Medicine*, 10: 481–500.

Weinstein, N.D. (1988). The precaution adoption process. *Health Psychology*, 7: 355–86.

Weinstein, N.D. (2003). Exploring the links between risk perception and preventive health behaviour. In J. Suls and K.A. Wallston (eds), *Social Psychological Foundations of Health and Illness*. Malden, MA: Blackwell.

Weinstein, N.D. and Klein, W.M. (1996). Unrealistic optimism: present and future. *Journal of Social and Clinical Psychology*, 15: 1–8.

Weinstein, N.D., Lyon, J.E., Sandman, P.M. and Cite, C.L. (1998). Experimental evidence for stages of precaution adoption. *Health Psychology*, 17: 445–53.

Weinstein, N.D., Rothman, A.J. and Sutton, S.R. (1998). Stage theories of health behavior: conceptual and methodological issues. *Health Psychology*, 17: 290–9.

Weinstein, N.D. and Sandman, P.M. (1992). A model of the precaution adoption process: evidence from home radon testing. *Health Psychology*, 11: 170–80.

Weinstein, N. and Sandman, P.M. (2002). Reducing the risk of exposure to radon gas: an application of the Precaution Adoption Process model. In D. Rutter and L. Quine (eds). *Changing Health Behaviour*. Buckingham: Open University Press, pp. 66–86.

Weinstein, N.D., Sandman, P.M. and Blalock, S.J. (2008). The precaution adoption process model. In K. Glanz, B.K. Rimer and K. Wiswanath (eds), *Health Behavior and Health Education: Theory, Research and Practice*, 4th edn. San Francisco, CA: Jossey-Bass, pp. 123–47.

Weisenberg, M., Raz, T. and Hener, T. (1998). The influence of film-induced mood on pain perceptions. *Pain*, 76: 365–75.

Weisse, C.S., Turbiasz, A.A. and Whitney, D.J. (1995). Behavioral training and AIDS risk reduction: overcoming barriers to condom use. *AIDS Education and Prevention*, 7: 50–9.

Weller, D. (2004). Behavioural and social science research in cancer: time for action (editorial comment). *European Journal of Cancer*, 40: 314–15.

Weller, S.C. and Davis-Beaty, K. (2007). Condom effectiveness in reducing heterosexual HIV transmission. *Cochrane Database of Systematic Reviews*, issue 4, art. no.: CD003255. doi: 10.1002/14651858.CD003255.

Wellings, K., Field, S., Johnson, A.M. et al. (1994). Studying sexual lifestyles. In K. Wellings, S. Field, A.M. Johnson and J. Wadsworth (eds), *Sexual Behaviour in Britain*. London: Penguin.

Wellings, K., Nanchahal, K., Macdowall, W. et al. (2001). Sexual behaviour in Britain: early heterosexual experience. *The Lancet*, 358/9296: 1843–50.

Wells, A. (2000) *Emotional Disorders and Metacognition: Innovative Cognitive Therapy*. Chichester: Wiley.

Wells, A. and Matthews, G. (1996). Modelling cognition in emotional disorder: the S-REF model. *Behaviour Research and Therapy*, 34: 881–8.

Wells, D. (2011). The value of pets for human health. *The Psychologist*, March: 172–6.

Wells, M.E., McQuellon, R.P., Hinkle, J.S. et al. (1995). Reducing anxiety in newly diagnosed cancer patients: a pilot program. *Cancer Practice*, 3: 100–4.

Wells, Y.D. (1999). Intentions to care for a spouse: gender differences in anticipated willingness to care and expected burden. *Journal of Family Studies*, 5: 220–34.

Wen, L.M., Thomas, M., Jones, H. et al. (2002). Promoting physical activity in women: evaluation of a 2-year community-based intervention in Sydney, Australia. *Health Promotion International*, 17: 127–37.

Wengreen, H.J., Madden, G.J., Aguilar, S.S. et al. (2013). Incentivizing children's fruit and vegetable consumption: results of a United States pilot study of the Food Dudes program. *Journal of Nutrition Education and Behavior*, 45: 54–9.

Werner, E.E. and Smith, R.S. (1982). *Vulnerable But Invincible: A Study of Resilient Children*. New York: McGraw Hill.

Werner, E.E. and Smith, R.S. (1992). *Overcoming The Odds: High Risk Children From Birth To Adulthood*. Ithaca, NY: Cornell University Press.

Wessely, S., Rose S. and Bisson, J. (1999). A systematic review of brief psychological interventions ('debriefing') for the treatment of immediate trauma related symptoms and the prevention of post-traumatic stress disorder. In *The Cochrane Library*. Oxford: Update Software.

West, R. (1992). Nicotine addiction: a re-analysis of the arguments. *Psychopharmacology*, 108: 408–10.

West, R. (2005). Time for a change: putting the transtheoretical (stages of change) model to rest. *Addiction*, 100: 1036–9.

West, R (2006). *Theory of Addiction*. Oxford: Blackwell.

West, R., Edwards, M. and Hajek, P.A. (1998). Randomized controlled trial of a 'buddy' system to improve success at giving up smoking in general practice. *Addiction*, 93: 1007–11.

West, R. and Shiffman, S. (2007). *Smoking Cessation*, 2nd edn. Oxford: Health Press.

Whalley, B., Rees, K., Davies, P. et al. (2011). Psychological interventions for coronary heart disease. *Cochrane Database of Systematic Reviews*, 10:CD002902.

White, A. (2007). A global projection of subjective well-being: a challenge to positive psychology? *Psychtalk* 56: 17–20.

White, A., Nicolaas, G., Foster, K. et al. (1993). *Health Survey for England 1991*. London: HMSO.

Whiteman, M.C. (2006). Personality, cardiovascular disease and public health. In M.E. Vollrath (ed.), *Handbook of Personality and Health*. Chichester: John Wiley & Sons, pp. 13–34.

Whooley, M. and Browner, W.S. (1998). Associations between depressive symptoms and mortality on older women. *Archives of Internal Medicine*, 158: 2129–35.

WHOQOL Group (1993). Study protocol for the World Health Organization project to develop a quality of life assessment instrument (WHOQOL). *Quality of Life Research*, 2: 153–9.

WHOQOL Group (1994). Development of the WHOQOL: rationale and current status. Monograph on quality of life assessment: cross-cultural issues 2. *International Journal of Mental Health*, 23: 24–56.

WHOQOL Group (1998). The World Health Organization Quality of Life Assessment (WHOQOL): development and psychometric properties. *Social Science and Medicine*, 46: 1569–85.

Widows, M.R., Jacobsen, P.B. and Fields, K.K. (2000). Relation of psychological vulnerability factors to posttraumatic stress disorder symptomatology in bone marrow transplant recipients. *Psychosomatic Medicine*, 62: 873–82.

Wiers, R.W. and Hofmann, W. (2010). Implicit cognition and health psychology: changing perspectives and new interventions. *The European Health Psychologist*, 12: 4–6.

Wilbert-Lampen, U., Leistner, D., Greven, S. et al. (2008). Cardiovascular events during World Cup soccer. *New England Journal of Medicine*, 358: 475–83.

Wild, S. and McKeigue, P. (1997). Cross sectional analysis of mortality by country of birth in England and Wales, 1970–92. *British Medical Journal*, 314: 705–10.

Wiles, R., Ashburn, A., Payne, S. et al. (2004). Discharge from physiotherapy following stroke: the management of disappointment. *Social Science and Medicine*, 59: 1263–73.

Wilkinson, M. (1992). Income distribution and life expectancy. *British Medical Journal*, 304: 165–8.

Wilkinson, R.G. (1990). Income distribution and mortality: a 'natural' experiment. *Sociology of Health and Illness*, 12: 391–412.

Wilkinson, R. and Pickett, K. (2010). *The Spirit Level: Why More Equal Societies Almost Always Do Better*. London: Penguin.

Wille, B., de Fruyt, F. and Feys, M. (2013). Big Five traits and intrinsic success in the new career era: A 15-year longitudinal study on employability and work – family conflict. *Applied Psychology: An International Review*, 62: 124–56.

William, S. and Copper, L. (2002). *Managing Workplace Stress*. Chichester: Wiley.

Williams, A.C., Eccleston, C. and Morley, S. (2012). Psychological therapies for the management of chronic pain (excluding headache) in adults. *Cochrane Database of Systematic Reviews*, 11: CD007407.

Williams, E.D., Stamatakis, E., Chandola, T. et al. (2011). Assessment of physical activity levels in South Asians in the UK: findings from the Health Survey for England. *Journal of Epidemiology & Community Health*, 65: 517–22.

Williams, J., Wake, M., Hesketh, K. et al. (2005). Health-related quality of life of overweight and obese children. *Journal of the American Medical Association*, 293: 1–5.

Williams, J.E., Paton, C.C., Siegler, I.C. et al. (2000). Anger proneness predicts coronary heart disease risk: prospective analysis from Atherosclerosis Risk in Communities (ARIC) study. *Circulation*, 1010: 2034–9.

Williams, K., Morrison, V. and Robinson, C. (2014) Exploring caregiving experiences: Caregiver coping and making sense of illness. *Ageing & Mental Health* http://dx.doi.org/10.1080/13607863.2013.860425

Williams, M.T. and Hord, H.G. (2005). The role of dietary factors in cancer prevention: beyond fruits and vegetables. *Nutrition in Clinical Practice*, 20: 451–9.

Williams, N.H., Hendry, M., France, B. et al. (2007). Effectiveness of exercise-referral schemes to promote physical activity in adults: systematic review. *British Journal of General Practitioners*, 57: 979–86.

Williams, P.G. (2006). Personality and illness behaviour. In M.E. Vollrath (ed.), *Handbook of Personality and Health*. Chichester: Wiley, pp. 157–73.

Williamson, D., Robinson, M.E. and Melamed, B. (1997). Pain behaviour, spouse responsiveness, and marital satisfaction in patients with rheumatoid arthritis. *Behavioral Modification*, 21: 97–118.

Williamson, G.M., Shaffer, D.R. and Schulz, R. (1998). Activity restriction and prior relationship history as contributors to mental health outcomes among middle-aged and older spousal caregivers. *Health Psychology*, 17: 152–62.

Williamson, S. and Wardle, J. (2002). Increasing participation with colorectal cancer screening: the development of a psychoeducational intervention. In D. Rutter and L. Quine (eds), *Changing Health Behaviour*. Buckingham: Open University Press.

Wills, T.A. (1981). Downward comparison principles in social psychology. *Psychological Bulletin*, 90: 245–71.

Wills, T.A. and Ainette, M.G. (2007). Social support and health. In S. Ayers et al. (eds), *Cambridge Handbook of Psychology, Health & Medicine*, 2nd edn. Cambridge: Cambridge University Press, pp. 202–7.

Wilsnack, R.W., Wilsnack, S.C., Kristjanson, A.F. et al. (2009). Gender and alcohol consumption: patterns from the multinational GENACIS project. *Addiction*, 104: 1487–500.

Wilson, J.F., Moore, R.W., Randolph, S. and Hanson, B.J. (1982). Behavioral preparation of patients for gastrointestinal endoscopy: information, relaxation and coping style. *Journal of Human Stress*, 8: 13–23.

Wilson, P.W.F., D'Agostino, R.B., Sullivan, L. et al. (2002). Overweight and obesity as determinants of cardiovascular risk. *Archives of Internal Medicine*, 162: 1867–72.

Wilson, T.D., Lindsey, S. and Schooler, T.Y. (2000). A model of dual attitudes. *Psychological Review*, 107: 101–26.

Wimbush, E., MacGregor, A. and Fraser, E. (1998). Impact of a national mass media campaign on walking in Scotland. *Health Promotion International*, 13: 45–53.

Windle, G. and Woods, R.T. (2004). Variations in subjective well-being: the mediating role of a psychological resource. *Ageing & Society*, 24: 583–602.

Winett, R.A., Anderson, E.S., Wojcik, J.R. et al. (2007). Guide to health: nutrition and physical activity outcomes of a group-randomized trial of an Internet-based intervention in churches. *Annals of Behavioral Medicine*, 33: 251–61.

Wing, R.R., Phelan, S. and Tate, D. (2002). The role of adherence in mediating the relationship between depression and health outcomes. *Journal of Psychosomatic Research*, 53: 877–81.

Winkleby, M., Fortmann, S. and Barrett, D. (1990). Social class disparities in risk factors for disease: eight year prevalence patterns by level of education. *Preventive Medicine*, 19: 1–12.

Wise, R.A. (1998). Drug activation of brain reward pathways. *Drug and Alcohol Dependence*, 51: 13–22.

Witham, M.D., Crighton, L.J. and McMurdo, M.E. (2007). Using an individualised quality of life measure in older heart failure patients. *International Journal of Cardiology*, 16: 40–5.

Witte, K. (1992). Putting the fear back into fear appeals: the extended parallel process model. *Communication Monographs*, 59: 329–49.

Witte, K. and Allen, M. (2000). A meta-analysis of fear appeals: implications for effective public health campaigns. *Health Education and Behavior*, 27: 591–615.

Woicik, P.B., Stewart, S.H., Pihl, P.O. and Conrod, P.J. (2009). The Substance Use Risk Profile Scale: A scale measuring traits linked to reinforcement-specific substance use profiles. *Addictive Behaviors*, 34: 1042–55.

Wolf, R.L., Lepore, S.J., Vandergrift, J.L. et al. (2008). Knowledge, barriers, and stage of change as correlates of fruit and vegetable consumption among urban and mostly immigrant black men. *Journal of the American Dietetic Association*, 108: 1315–22.

Wollin, S.D. and Jones, P.J. (2001). Alcohol, red wine and cardiovascular disease. *Journal of Nutrition*, 131: 1401–4.

Wong, C. and Mullan, B. (2009). Predicting breakfast consumption: an application of the theory of planned behaviour and the investigation of past behaviour and executive function. *British Journal of Health Psychology*, 14: 489–504.

Wong, Y.J., Ho, R.M., Shin, M. and Tsai, P. (2011). Chinese Singaporeans' lay beliefs, adherence to Asian values, and subjective well-being. *Personality and Individual Differences*, 50: 822–7.

Wood, F., Robling, M., Prout, H. et al. (2010). A question of balance: a qualitative study of mothers' interpretations of dietary recommendations. *Annals of Family Medicine*, 8: 51–7.

Wood, W. and Neal, D. T. (2009). The habitual consumer. *Journal of Consumer Psychology*; 19: 579–92.

Woods, R. (2008). Introduction. In R. Woods and L. Clare (eds), *Handbook of the Clinical Psychology of Ageing*, 2nd edn. London: Wiley, pp. 1–16.

Woods, R.T. (ed.) (1999). *Psychological Problems of Ageing: Assessment, Treatment and Care.* Chichester: Wiley.

Woodward, M., Oliphant, J., Lowe, G. et al. (2003). Contribution of contemporaneous risk factors to social inequality in coronary heart disease and all causes mortality. *Preventive Medicine*, 36: 561–8.

Woolf, S.H. (1996). Immunizations. In S.H. Woolf, S. Jonas and R.S. Lawrence (eds), *Health Promotion and Disease Prevention in Clinical Practice*. Baltimore, OH: Williams & Wilkins.

World Economic Forum (2008). *Working Towards Wellness – Practical Steps for CEOs* (World Economic Forum, Geneva 2008).

World Health Organization (1947). *Constitution of the World Health Organization.* Geneva: WHO.

World Health Organization (1980). *International Classification of Impairments, Disabilities and Handicaps (ICIDH). A Manual of Classification Relating to the Consequences of Disease.* Geneva: WHO.

World Health Organization (1981). *Global Strategy for Health for All by the Year 2000.* Geneva: WHO.

World Health Organization (1988). *Healthy Cities Project: Five Year Planning Framework.* Copenhagen: WHO Regional Office for Europe.

World Health Organization (1995). *World Health Report.* Geneva: WHO.

World Health Organization (1996). *Health Promoting Schools.* Report of a WHO Expert Committee on Comprehensive School Health Education and Promotion. Geneva: WHO.

World Health Organization (1999). *Health 21: Health for All in the 21st Century.* Copenhagen: WHO Regional Office for Europe.

World Health Organization (2000). *Obesity: Preventing and Managing the Global Epidemic.* Report of a WHO consultation. World Health Organization Technical Report Series 894, 1–253.

World Health Organisation (2001). *International Classification of Functioning, Disability and Health* (ICF). Geneva: WHO.

World Health Organization (2002a). *The World Health Report: Reducing Risks, Promoting Healthy Life.* Copenhagen: WHO Regional Office for Europe.

World Health Organization (2002b). *Towards a Common Language for Functioning, Disability and Health.* Geneva: WHO.

World Health Organization (2004). *Young People's Health in Context: Health Behaviour in School-aged Children (HBSC) Study.* International report from the 2001/2002 survey. C. Currie, C. Roberts, A. Morgan et al. (eds). Available from: www.euro.who.int.

World Health Organization (2008). *WHO Report on the Global Tobacco Epidemic: The MPOWER Report.* Geneva: WHO.

World Health Organization (2009a) *Global Health Risks: Mortality and Burden of Disease Attributable to Selected Major Risks.* Geneva: WHO.

World Health Organization (2009b) *Patient Adherence.* Retrieved from http://www.who.iny/topics/patient_adherence/en/index.html

World Health Organization (2010). *Global Recommendations on Physical Activity for Health.* Geneva: WHO.

World Health Organization (2012). *Measurement of Healthy Life Expectancy and Wellbeing.* www.who.int/healthinfo/SAGE_MeetingReport_Dec2012.pdf World Health Organization (2013). http://www.who.int/gho/publications/world_health_statistics/EN_WHS2013_Full.pdf

World Health Organization (2014, May 1st). *What do we Mean by "Sex" and "Gender"?*, retrieved, May 6th 2015 from http://www.who.int/gender/whatisgender/en/

World Health Organization Expert Committee (1990). *Cancer Pain Relief and Palliative Care*, Technical Report Series No. 84. Geneva: WHO.

World Health Report (2008). http://www.who.int/research/en/.

Wortley, P. and Fleming, P. (1997). AIDS in women in the United States: recent trends. *Journal of the American Medical Association*, 278: 911–16.

Wright, A.J. (2010). The impact of perceived risk on risk-reducing behaviours. In D. French, K. Vedhara, A.A. Kaptein and J. Weinman (eds), *Health Psychology*, 2nd edn. London: BPS Blackwell, pp. 111–21.

Wrosch, C. and Scheier, M.F. (2003). Personality and quality of life: the importance of optimism and goal adjustment. *Quality of Life Research*, 12 (S1): 59–72.

Wu, A.W., Snyder, C.F., Huang, I.C. et al. (2006). A randomized trial of the impact of a programmable medication reminder device on quality of life in patients with AIDS. *AIDS Patient Care and STDS*, 20: 773–81.

Wurm, S., Tomasik, M.J. and Tesch-Roemer, C. (2010). On the importance of a positive view on ageing for physical exercise among middle aged and older adults: cross-sectional and longitudinal findings. *Psychology & Health*, 25: 25–42.

Wysocki, T., Harris, M.A., Buckloh, L.M. et al. (2007). Randomized trial of behavioral family systems therapy for diabetes: maintenance of effects on diabetes outcomes in adolescents. *Diabetes Care*, 30: 555–60.

Yan, H. and Sellick, K. (2004). Quality of life of Chinese patients newly diagnosed with gastrointestinal cancer: a longitudinal study. *International Journal of Nursing Studies*, 41: 309–19.

Yang, L., Sahlqvist, S., McMinn, A. et al. (2010). Interventions to promote cycling: systematic review. *British Medical Journal*, Oct 18: 341.

Yardley, L. and Dibb, B. (2007). Assessing subjective change in chronic illness: an examination of response shift in health-related and goal-oriented subjective status. *Psychology & Health*, 22: 813–28.

Yates, T., Davies, M.J., Gray L.J. et al. (2010). Levels of physical activity and relationship with markers of diabetes and cardiovascular disease risk in 5474 white European and South Asian adults screened for type 2 diabetes. *Preventive Medicine*, 51: 290–4.

Ye, X.X., Huang, H., Li, S.H. et al. (2009). HIV/AIDS education effects on behaviour among senior high school students in a medium-sized city in China. *International Journal of STD and AIDS*, 20: 549–52.

Yee, J.L. and Schulz, R. (2000). Gender differences in psychiatric morbidity among family caregivers: a review and analysis. *The Gerontologist*, 40: 147–64.

Yip, Y.B., Sit, J.W., Fung, K.K. et al. (2007). Impact of an arthritis self-management programme with an added exercise component for osteoarthritic knee sufferers on improving pain, functional outcomes, and use of health care services: an experimental study. *Patient Education and Counseling*, 65: 113–21.

York Health Economics Consortium & University of London, (2010). *Evaluation of the Scale, Causes and Costs of Waste Medicines*. Final Report to Funders, York Health Economics Consortium & University of London ISBN 978 090 293 620 1.

Yorke, J. and Shuldham, C. (2005). Family therapy for chronic asthma in children. *Cochrane Database Systematic Review*, 2: CD000089.

Young, J.M., D'Este, C. and Ward, J.E. (2002). Improving family physicians' use of evidence-based smoking cessation strategies: a cluster randomization trial. *Preventive Medicine*, 35: 572–83.

Young, J.T. (2004). Illness behaviour: a selective review and synthesis. *Sociology of Health and Illness*, 26: 1–31.

Yurgelun-Todd, D. (2007). Emotional and cognitive changes during adolescence. *Current Opinion in Neurobiology*, 17: 251–7.

Yusuf, S., Hawken, S., Ôunpuu, S. et al. (2004). Effects of potentially modifiable risk factors associated with myocardial infarction in 52 countries (the INTERHEART study): case-control study. *The Lancet*, 364: 937–52.

Yzer, M.C., Fisher, J.D., Bakker, A.B. et al. (1998). The effects of information about AIDS risk and self-efficacy on women's intentions to engage in AIDS preventive behavior. *Journal of Applied Social Psychology*, 28: 1837–52.

Yzer, M.C., Siero, F.W. and Buunk, B.P. (2001). Bringing up condom use and using condoms with new sexual partners: intention or habitual? *Psychology and Health*, 16: 409–21.

Zabora, J., BrintzenhofeSzoc, K., Curbow, B. et al. (2001). The prevalence of psychological distress by cancer site. *Psycho-Oncology*, 10: 19–28.

Zachariae, R., Pedersen, C.G., Jensen, A.B. et al. (2003). Association of perceived physician communication style with patient satisfaction, distress, cancer-related self-efficacy, and perceived control over the disease. *British Journal of Cancer*, 88: 658–65.

Zakowski, S. (1995). The effects of stressor predictability on lymphocyte proliferation in humans. *Psychology and Health*, 10: 409–25.

Zakowski, S.G., Ramati, A., Morton, C. and Flanagan, R. (2004). Written emotional disclosure buffers the effects of social constraints on distress in cancer patients. *Health Psychology*, 23: 555–63.

Zakowski, S.G., McAllister, C.G., Deal, M. and Baum, A. (1992). Stress, reactivity, and immune function in healthy men. *Health Psychology*, 11: 223–32.

Zarit, S., Reever, K. and Bach-Peterson, J. (1980). Relatives of the impaired elderly: correlates of feelings of burden. *The Gerontologist*, 20: 649–55.

Zautra, A.J., Davis, M.C., Reich, J.W. et al. (2008). Comparison of cognitive behavioral and mindfulness meditation interventions on adaptation to rheumatoid arthritis for patients with and without history of recurrent depression. *Journal of Consulting and Clinical Psychology*, 76: 408–21.

Zaza, C. and Baine, N. (2002). Cancer pain and psychosocial factors: a critical review of the literature. *Journal of Pain and Symptom Management*, 24: 526–42.

Zborowski, M. (1952). Cultural components in response to pain. *Journal of Social Issues*, 8: 16–30.

Zeidner, M. and Saklofske, D. (1996). Adaptive and maladaptive coping. In M. Zeidner and N. Endler (eds), *Handbook of Coping: Theory, Research, Application*. New York: Wiley.

Zelter, L. and LeBaron, S. (1982). Hypnosis and nonhypnotic techniques for reduction of pain and anxiety during painful procedures in children and adolescents with cancer. *Journal of Pediatrics*, 101: 1032–5.

Zervas, I.M., Augustine, A. and Fricchione, G.L. (1993). Patient delay in cancer: a view for the crisis model. *General Hospital Psychiatry*, 15: 9–13.

Zhang, Y., Proenca, R., Maffie, M. et al. (1994). Positional cloning of the mouse obese gene and its human homologue. *Nature*, 372: 425–32.

Zimmer-Gembeck, M.J. and Skinner, E.A. (2011). Review: The development of coping across childhood and adolescence:

an integrative review and critique of research. *International Journal of Behavior Development*. 35: 1–17.

Zimmers, E., Privette, G., Lowe, R.H. and Chappa, F. (1999). Increasing use of the female condom through video instruction. *Perceptual and Motor Skills*, 88: 1071–7.

Zinovieff, F., Morrison, V., Coles, A. and Cartmell, R. (2005). Are the needs of cancer patients and their carers generic? Paper presented to the European Health Psychology Society annual conference, Galway, September.

Zohar, D. and Dayan, I. (1999). Must coping options be severely limited during stressful events: testing the interaction between primary and secondary appraisals. *Anxiety, Stress and Coping*, 12: 191–216.

Zola, I.K. (1973). Pathways to the doctor: from person to patient. *Social Science and Medicine*, 7: 677–89.

Zorrilla, E.P., McKay, J.R., Luborsky, L. and Schmidt, K. (1996). Relation of stressors and depressive symptoms to clinical progression of viral illness. *American Journal of Psychiatry*, 153(5): 626–35.

Zucker, A. (2007). Ethical and legal isues and end-of-life decision making. In D. Balk, C. Wogrin, G. Thornton and D. Meagher (eds), *Handbook of Thanatology: The Essential Body of Knowledge for the Student of Death, Dying, and Bereavement*. Northbrook, IL: Association for Death Education and Counseling, pp. 103–12.

Zucker, D., Hopkins, R.S., Sly, D.F. et al. (2000). Florida's 'truth' campaign: a counter-marketing, anti-tobacco media campaign. *Journal of Public Health Management Practice*, 6: 1–6.

Zuckerman, M., Eysenck, S.B. and Eysenck, H. J. (1978) Sensation seeking in England and America: cross-cultural, age and sex comparisons. *Journal of Consulting and Clinical Psychology*, 46: 139. Doi: 10.1037/0022–006X.46.1.139

Zuckerman, M. and Kuhlman, D.M. (2000). Personality and risk-taking: common biosocial factors. *Journal of Personality*, 68: 999–1029.

Index

ABC (Ascertaining Barriers to Compliance) group 89–90
academic health psychology 28
acceptance and commitment therapy (ACT) 381–2, 491–2
acceptance coping 407, 409, 421
ACE inhibitors 229
acetylcholine 168, 213, 222, 324
action control 130, 155
action planning 145, 155
action stage of behavioural change 150, 162
adaptation 417, 430
addiction
  disease concept of 71
  see also dependency problems
Addison's disease 255–6
adherence behaviour 88–95, 140, 142, 271, 288–95
  adherence rates 90
  behavioural change programmes 295–8
  definition and measurement 88–90
  maximising 291–4
  see also non-adherence behaviour
adjustment 430–1
adolescents see children and adolescents
adrenal cortex 213, 215
adrenal glands 213
adrenal medulla 213, 324
adrenaline (epinephrine) 105, 213, 215, 322, 324, 325, 333
adrenocorticotrophic hormone (ACTH) 213, 325
adulthood 20–1
advertising, tobacco and alcohol 188, 189
aetiology 5
affective response, and exercise 105–6
Africa/African cultures 15–16, 95
  HIV/AIDS 33, 196
  and life expectancy 33

age
  and delay behaviour 269
  and exercise 101
  and health behaviour 125
  and immune function 327
  and quality of life 22, 24, 413–17
  self-perceived 360
  and smoking 58–9
  and symptom perception 246
age-specific mortality 55, 58
ageing
  and cortisol 325
  and food choices 96
  and health 21–2
  population 21, 55, 415, 435
  social functioning model of 22
  successful 22, 24, 415–17
agonists 84
agreeableness 126, 128, 346, 349
AIDS see HIV/AIDS
Alameda County study 53, 362, 363, 366
alcohol consumption 11, 17, 35, 54, 55, 59–60, 64, 95
  beneficial effects of 53, 63–4
  binge drinking 62, 67, 190
  children and adolescents 59, 65
  dependency problems 66–8, 71, 72
  and educational attainment 67
  elderly groups 68
  and gender 47
  increasing cost of 191
  media influence on 189
  motivation 68, 131
  negative health effects of 61–2
  peer education 200
  prevalence of 59
  recommended daily limits 59–60
  and sexual activity 62, 70, 75
  and socio-economic status (SES) 66, 67
  standard measure or unit 59, 60

and student culture 62
and weight gain 65
Alcoholics Anonymous 71
allostatic load 325–6
alternative medicine 12, 16, 271
Alzheimer's disease 106
  caregivers 450, 451, 452, 456
ambivalence 132
ambulatory blood pressure 40, 42
American Psychological Society 28
American Society Cancer Prevention Study II 58
amniocentesis 111
amygdala 208–9
anger, and coronary heart disease risk 356
angina 79, 230, 232, 508–9
angioplasty 231–2, 423
antenatal screening 110, 111
anti-inflammatory cytokines 326, 327, 356
antibodies 214
anticipatory regret 144
antidepressant medication 487–8
antigens 116, 214, 326
antioxidants 96, 99, 100, 101
Antiretroviral Therapy (ART) 89, 91, 111, 217, 289–90, 291, 293, 294, 411
anxiety 259, 362, 363, 375, 398
  caregivers 444–5, 454–5
  and delay behaviour 271
  and dying patients 404
  and exercise 105
  and illness self-management 404
  and irritable bowel syndrome (IBS) 224
  preoperational 388–9, 403
  and quality of life 420–1
  as reaction to illness 399, 402
  and screening for risk 183–4
anxiety sensitivity (AS) 69–70
anxious attachment 456

aorta 226, 228
aphasia 210
appraisal theory of stress 255, 309–15, 322, 330
appraisals 309
  illness 523
approach-oriented coping 341, 342, 352, 421, 456
arbitrary inference 375
arteries 225–6, 228
arterioles 226
arteriosclerosis 78
arthritis
  self-management programmes 506
  see also rheumatoid arthritis
Asian cultures 15, 16
assisted suicide 420
associative learning 83
asthma
  education programmes 504–5
  medication 290, 291, 293
  mindfulness interventions 502–4
  treatment guidelines 531
  written emotional expression interventions 511–12
atheroma 37, 46, 229, 230, 232, 333
atherosclerosis 78, 230, 333
atopic dermatitis 507
atrial fibrillation 505
attachment 455–6
attention, and pain 473, 474–5
attentional control 130, 144
attentional model of symptom perception 242, 243–4
attitudes 131–2, 137–8, 139, 143, 144, 151, 185
attributional models *see* causal attributions
audience targeting 186–7
Australia
  ageing population 55
  fruit and vegetable intake 97
  health inequalities 36
  life expectancy 9–10
Australian Psychological Society (APS) 28, 528
autism 119
autogenic training 224
autoimmune conditions 53, 217–21
  see also diabetes; multiple sclerosis; rheumatoid arthritis
automatic negative thoughts (ANTs) 374
automaticity 144, 145–6
autonomic nervous system (ANS) 211–14, 222, 228, 322, 323–6, 481
avoidant attachment 456

avoidant coping 341, 345, 352, 408–9, 421, 444
avoidant strategies, smoking cessation 168

B cells 215, 228, 327
back pain 469, 473, 476, 488
bad news interviews 282–6, 499
  SPIKES model 282–3
baroreptors 228
basal ganglia 209
behaviour 132
  and health 11–12
  see also health behaviour
behavioural immunogens 52, 88
behavioural interventions
  pain management 488–9, 490, 523
  stress management 376, 378–9
behavioural medicine 267
behavioural pathogens 52
behaviourism 71
beliefs
  changing *see* cognitive interventions
  salient 136–7, 139–40
  subjective norm 137, 138, 139, 140, 143, 163
  see also health belief model
benefit-finding 405–8, 500
beta endorphins 326
beta-blockers 229
beta-carotene 95, 100
Big Five model of personality 126, 346–7
bile 221, 222
binge drinking 62, 67, 190
biofeedback 26, 486, 490
biological differences 46–7
biomedical models
  of ageing 22
  of illness 6–7, 17, 32, 110, 257
biopsychosocial model 8, 9, 27, 28
blood 228
blood donation 148
blood glucose 54
blood pressure 180, 208, 325
  ambulatory 40, 42
  diastolic 79, 228
  high 54, 79
  in hostile individuals 355–6
  problem-solving interventions to reduce 182–3
  and salt intake 79–80
  and stress 45, 47, 229, 318, 331, 332–3
  systolic 79, 228
  testing 109
  see also hypertension

blunting coping style 248, 342
bodily signs, and symptom perception 242–3
body dissatisfaction 84
body image 105
body mass index (BMI) 54, 78, 81, 83, 180
bone density screening 111
bone marrow biopsy 391
bowel disease 119, 223–5
  and stress 335
  see also colon cancer; colorectal cancer; inflammatory bowel disease
brain, behavioural anatomy of 208–11
BRCA1 and BRCA2 mutations 109, 113
breast cancer 14, 53, 64, 100
  and benefit-finding 406
  coping strategies 409
  and depression 399
  and fat intake 78, 79
  and illness perceptions 256
  lumpectomy 277
  and perceived control 358
  quality of life process 424
  response to symptoms 265
  and social support 367, 502, 516
  and stress 334–5, 500–1
  symptom perception 252
  treatment, emotional reactions to 403
  written emotional expression interventions 512
breast screening 186
  genetic testing 109, 114, 116, 148, 533
  mammography 110, 113, 139–40, 185
  self-examination 116, 135, 136, 139, 146
British Psychological Society (BPS) 28, 525–6
bronchiolitis 530
bronchitis, chronic 233, 234
bronchodilators 234
burnout 320, 385

calorific intake 79, 96
cancer 11, 14, 36, 207
  and alcohol consumption 64
  behavioural risk factors for 54
  benefit-finding 406–7
  breast *see* breast cancer
  caregivers 450, 454, 456, 458–9, 460–1
  cervical 74, 110, 117, 119, 123

cancer (*continued*)
colon   14, 53, 64, 100, 109
colorectal   14, 78, 110, 224–5, 265, 459
coping strategies   409
and depression   363, 398, 399
diagnosis, reactions to   398
and diet   78, 95
emotional responses   398, 403, 404
and ethnicity   44
and exercise   104
genes and cell proliferation in   225
illness perceptions   256
Kaposi's sarcoma   216
lung *see* lung cancer
and obesity   81
oral   119
ovarian   109, 112, 533
pancreatic   53, 399
prostate   14, 53, 79, 100, 110–11, 112, 409, 460, 464, 502
and quality of life   424, 425–6
screening programmes   45, 109–13, 139–40
skin   53, 115, 128, 131, 186, 283–4, 500
and social support   367, 447, 516
and stress   313–15, 334–5, 500–1, 515–16
survival, and quality of health care   38
testicular   78, 112, 115
treatment/end of treatment, emotional reactions to   403, 404
and type C personality   356–7
cannabis use   60, 64, 66, 69–70
and multiple sclerosis treatment   221
carcinogenesis   63–4
cardiac arrest   227
cardiac event   357
cardiovascular disease (CVD)   53, 54, 61, 95, 100, 104, 229–32, 320, 332
see also coronary (ischaemic) heart disease; heart disease; hypertension; myocardial infarction; stroke
cardiovascular reactivity, and stress   329–30, 333, 355, 367, 368
cardiovascular system   225–9, 332
care/caregivers, informal *see* informal care/caregivers
carotid artery   228
carotid plaques   364
Carstair's deprivation score   33, 34

cataclysmic events   316–18
catastrophic thoughts   375, 475
catastrophising   475, 490
catecholamines   105, 322, 327, 333
causal attributions   254, 261–2, 360, 475
CD4+ cells   215–16, 326
CD8+ cells   326
cell suicide   225
central nervous system (CNS)   322
cerebellum   308
cerebral cortex   208, 209, 322, 482
cerebrovascular accident (CVA) *see* stroke
cerebrum   209–10
cervical cancer   74, 110, 117, 119, 123
cervical screening   110, 112–13, 187
cervical smear   183
change4life campaign   187
checkpoint genes   225
children and adolescents
adherence to medication   290–1
alcohol consumption   59, 61, 62, 65
behavioural change   524–5
beliefs about health and illness   18–20
body dissatisfaction   84
as caregivers   438, 446, 449–50, 452, 455
and coping   342, 344
exercise behaviour   101, 102, 108, 139
food choices   97, 98, 99
fruit and vegetable consumption   98, *99*, 140–2
and health care-seeking behaviour   269
illicit drug use   60–1
and illness concept   19–20
obesity in   10, 78, 82
pain control   484, 485–6
parents and informal care of   444–5, 449
personality and risk behaviour   69
pregnancy   62, 66
preoperational stress management   390–1
quality of life and illness   413–15, 415, 429–30
risk behaviour   69, 125
self-concept and self-esteem   65–6
sexual activity   62, 119
and smoking   65, 66, 125
stress in   308, 318
and symptom interpretation   250–1
and symptom perception   245, 246

China
community-based interventions   194
informal care   437, 441, 446
chlamydia   72, 74
cholesterol   54, 78–9, 180, 230, 333
dietary   78
high-density lipoprotein (HDL or 'good')   47, 230
low-density lipoprotein (LDL or 'bad')   78, 96, 230
serum (blood)   78, 79
testing   109
cholesystokinin   22
chronic bronchitis   233, 234
chronic fatigue syndrome (CFS)   104, 244, 255–6, 398, 448, 463
chronic illness
definition of   408
financial cost of   207
chronic obstructive pulmonary disease (COPD)   11, 61, 233–4, 262
chronic pain   468, 469, 470, 483
attentional hypothesis of   474
and control beliefs   476
living with   470–2
medication and adherence in   92–4
and quality of life   421
treatment
antidepressant medication   487–8
behavioural interventions   488–9, 490
biofeedback   486–7, 490
cognitive-behavioural interventions   487, 488–91
mindfulness-based interventions   491–2
relaxation   486–8
transcutaneous electrical nerve stimulation (TENS)   486
city environments   172, 189
clinical health psychology   28
clinical psychology   27
clot busters   231, 265
cognition(s)   132
and pain   473, 475–6
surface   374–5, 378
and symptom perception   247–8
cognitive appraisal *see* appraisal
cognitive control   359
cognitive decline
and exercise   106
and vitamin supplements   101
cognitive defusion   381
cognitive development   17, 18–20
cognitive dissonance   132, 165

cognitive interventions 170–1
  stress management 376, 378, 500
cognitive re-labelling 168
cognitive regulation 130
cognitive restructuring 376, 378,
    407, 500, 524
cognitive schemata 253, 375, 378
cognitive-behavioural theories of
    stress 374–5, 376
cognitive-behavioural therapy
    (CBT) 224, 378, 379, 382,
    487, 488–91
cognitive—perceptual model of symptom
perception 242
cold pressor test 474
collectivism 16, 369–70, 407–8, 441
colon cancer 14, 53, 64, 100, 109
colonoscopy 390
colorectal cancer 14, 78, 110,
    224–5, 265, 459
colostomy 223
colposcopy 183
common cold, and stress 332
  'common-sense model' of
    illness 131, 253–4
communication problems, health
professional—patient 281
communication skills 17, 18
  health professionals 282–6
community intervention
    programmes 191–4
Community Intervention Trial for
    Smoking Cessation 193
comparative optimism 248
complementary medicine 12, 16, 271
compliance/concordance 88, 89, 288
  see also adherence behaviour
concrete operational stage of cognitive
    development 18, 19
conditioning theory 71
condom use/non-use 48, 70, 72,
    75, 77, 136, 143, 147, 162
conformity 69, 70
congenital universal insensitivity to
    pain (CUIP) 468, 473
congestive heart failure 364
conscientiousness 70, 126, 128,
    346, 346–51
consciousness 7
conservation of resources model of
    stress 316, 317–18, 321
contagion 19
contamination 19
contemplation stage of behavioural
    change 149, 150, 151, 162
control beliefs
  and caregiving behaviour 462–4

pain 476
  see also locus of control; perceived
    behavioural control (PBC);
    perceived control beliefs
coping 69, 70, 130, 254, 340–6
  acceptance 407, 409, 421
  adaptive 343–5
  approach-oriented 341, 342, 352,
    421, 456
  avoidant 341, 345, 352, 408–9,
    421, 444
  dyadic 460, 461, 464
  emotion-focused 311, 341, 342,
    343, 344–5, 359, 408, 409,
    523, 524
  flexibility 344
  goals 345–6
  with illness 405, 408–12, 523–4
  job stress 321
  meaning-focused 345
  with pain 343–4
  proactive 369
  problem-focused 311, 341, 342,
    343–4, 348, 359, 408, 409,
    444, 523, 524
  and quality of life (QoL) 421
  religious 409–10, 418, 454
  repressive 248
  smoking cessation 168
  with stress 340–6
coping planning 145, 147, 155
coping potential 311, 312
coping self-efficacy 154, 317
coping style 342, 343
  blunting 248, 342
  monitoring 248, 342
  and symptom perception 247–8
coronary angioplasty 231–2, 423
coronary artery bypass graft
    (CABG) 36, 232
coronary artery disease (CAD) see
    coronary (ischaemic) heart disease
    (CHD)
coronary (ischaemic) heart disease
    (CHD) 11, 35, 36, 37, 44, 54,
    78–9, 96, 230–2
  and alcohol consumption 63, 64
  anger as risk factor for 356
  community intervention
    programmes 191–4
  and depression 362–4, 399
  and diet 96
  distress reduction 499–500
  and ethnicity 44, 58
  gender differences 46–7
  hostility as risk factor for 355–6
  problem-focused interventions 182–3

and quality of life 418
  screening programmes 180–1, 181
  and sex hormones 46–7
  and smoking 61
  and stress 332–4, 501, 513–14
  and type A behaviour 354–5
  and type D personality 357–8
  workplace programmes 197
  see also angina; atherosclerosis;
    myocardial infarction (MI)
corpus callosum 209
corticosteroids 213–14, 234
corticotrophin-releasing factor
    (CRF) 325
cortisol 105, 214, 215, 325, 327,
    367
cost-effectiveness of
    interventions 533
counselling
  problem-focused 166–7, 377
  to prevent disease
    progression 512–13
critical health psychology 28
Crohn's disease 223, 335
cross-sectional studies 260
culture
  and beliefs about treatment 262–3
  and benefit-finding from
    illness 407–8
  and causal attributions 262
  and coping with illness 409
  and delay behaviour 268–9
  and health belief systems 15–17
  and illness perceptions 257
  and informal care 441, 452–5
  and medical consultations 281
  and medication non-adherence 91
  and quality of life 417–18, 427–8
  and social support 369–70
  and symptom interpretation 248–9
Cushing's disease 325
cystic fibrosis (CF) 109, 411
cytotoxic T cells 215, 219–20, 326

danger control 164
death see dying patients; mortality
decision-making see medical decision-
    making; treatment decisions
decisional balance 151
decisional control 359
deep muscle relaxation 377
defibrillators 227, 501
delay behaviour (in responding to
    symptoms) 265–72
  and age 269
  cultural influences on 268–9
  and emotions 271

delay behaviour (*continued*)
  gender differences 239
  influence of others on 270
  and location of symptom 268
  model of 266
  and personality 271–2
  and prevalence of symptoms 268
  and symptom type 267–8
  and treatment beliefs 270–1
dementia 11, 101, 106
  caregivers 451–2, 452–3
  see also Alzheimer's disease
demographic factors
  health behaviour 125
  informal caregivers 438, 440
denial 271, 309, 344, 353, 408–9
dependency problems
  alcohol consumption 66–8, 71, 72
  drug use 68, 72
  smoking 66, 67, 68
  treating 71–2
depletion model of illness 257
depression 398
  and cancer 363, 398, 399
  caregiver 444–5, 449, 454–5,
    460–1
  and coronary heart disease
    (CHD) 362–4, 399, 514–15
  and diabetes 258–9
  and dying patients 404
  and exercise 105, 106
  and hypertension 362
  and illness self-management 404
  and non-adherence behaviour 364
  and pain 470, 474
  and quality of life 421
  as reaction to illness 399, 402,
    404–5
descriptive norms 140–2, 163
developing countries
  fruit and vegetable intake 95
  mortality 33
developmental theories 17–18
diabetes 11, 63
  and anxiety 399
  illness acceptance 411
  self-management 399, 506–7
  social and family support 510, 511
  stress management 509–10
  type 1 109, 151, 179, 217,
    258–9, 266
  type 2 81, 82, 90, 104, 151, 179,
    217–18, 258–9, 418, 509–10
diagnosis 287–8
  computerised programmes
    for 288
  group decision-making 289

  and heuristics 287–8
  and hypothesis testing 287
  and pattern recognition 288
  reactions to 398
diarrhoeal diseases 11, 33
diet 5, 11, 54, 87
  adherence to changes in 296, 297
  food choices 83, 96–9
  healthy 95–9, 197–8, 296
  Mediterranean-style 87, 95
  unhealthy 78–81
diffusion of innovations theory 172
digestive system 221–2
  disorders of 222–5
  see also colon cancer; colorectal
  cancer
diptheria 117, 118, 119
disability 6, 7
  models of 8
disability-adjusted life years
    (DALYs) 55
disease
  and illness distinguished 241
  incidence of 11, 36
disease progression, prevention of
  counselling 512–13
  enhancing social support 516
  stress management training 513–16
disease prototypes 252–63
dispositional optimism 349, 352
dispositional pessimism 128, 351
distancing response 309
distraction techniques 485, 533
distress 311
  reduction of
  information provision 499–500
  social support 501–2, 504
  stress management training 500–1
Distress Thermometer 427
diuretics 229
DNA 107
dopamine 65, 67
Downs syndrome 109, 111
downward arrow technique 171,
    378
drinking *see* alcohol consumption
drug use 17, 33, 55, 60–1, 64, 65
  criminal model of 68
  dependency problems 68, 72
  motivational model of 68
  needle exchange schemes 190
  needle-sharing in 72, 73, 190
  prevalence of 60
  withdrawal symptoms 67
dualism 5–6
Duke Social Support Index 366
Dutch Eating Behaviours Questionnaire

  (DEBQ) 84
dyadic coping 460, 461, 464
dying patients 404
  quality of life 419–20
dynamic health assessment system
    (DYNHA) 427
dysarthria 210
dysphasia 210

e-cigarettes 56, 58, 169
eating behaviours 35, 83, 84, 96–9
eating disorders 84, 105
educational attainment
  and alcohol consumption 67
  and smoking cessation 70
efficacy 91
  see also self-efficacy
egocentric thinking 18
elaboration likelihood approach
    163–4, 185
elderly groups
  adherence to medication 291,
    294–5
  alcohol consumption 68
  and exercise 99, 101–2, 104, 105,
    108
  health care-seeking behaviour 269
  smoking among 58–9
electrocardiogram (ECG) 227
electromyographic (EMG)
  biofeedback 486
emotion-focused coping 311, 341,
    342, 343, 344–5, 359, 408,
    409, 523, 524
emotional disclosure 364
emotional eating 84
emotional expression, written 498,
    511–12
emotional impact of caring 449–50,
    454–5
emotional over-involvement
    (EOI) 448, 463
emotional reactions to illness 523
  negative 398–405
  positive 405–8
emotions 132, 144, 283
  and delay behaviour 271
  and stress 311–12, 313–14,
    362–4
  and symptom perception 246–7
emphysema 233–4
empiricism 25
enabling factors, and behavioural
change 160
end-of-life QoL 419–20
endocrine glands 213
endocrine processes 213–14, 367

endorphins   67, 105, 481, 485
beta   326
England *see* United Kingdom (UK)
English Longitudinal Study of
       Ageing   21–2, 41
ENRICHD study   514–15, 533
enteric nervous system   222
environment and health behaviour
       160, 161, 172, 188–91
   cues to action   188–9
   increasing costs of unhealthy
       behaviour   190–1
   minimising costs of health
       behaviour   189–90
environmental stress theory   316
epidemiology   21, 160–1
epilepsy   415, 421
epinephrine *see* adrenaline
erythrocytes   228
ethnic minorities   43–6
   access to health care   45–6
   and socio-economic status
       (SES)   44
ethnicity   32
   and adherence behaviour   91, 95
   and beliefs about treatment   262–3
   and coronary heart disease   44, 58
   and exercise   44, 102
   and fat intake   79
   and health behaviours   44, 125,
       142, 269
   and health differentials   32, 43–6
   and hypertension   231
   and informal care   440, 442, 452–5
   and medical consultations   281
   and pain   471
   and preventive behaviour   136
   and smoking prevalence   57–8
   and stress   45, 329
Europe
   cervical screening   113
   exercise levels   101–2
   immunisation   119
   mortality rates   10, 11
   overweight/obese population   82
   self-reported health status   23
European Health Psychology
       Society   28
European Organisation for Research
       and Treatment of Cancer
       (EORTC)   435–6
eustress   311
euthanasia   420
exam stress   318
exercise   22, 95, 99, 101–8
   adherence/non-adherence   296,
       297–8

audience targeting to promote   187
children and   99, 101, 102, 108, 139
environmental influences on   189–90
and ethnicity   44, 102
and gender   47, 101, 102
and genes   107
implementation intention (II)   147
internet-based interventions   202–3
lack of   54, 84
levels of   101–2, 103
media campaigns to promote   184
motivation to   297
motivational interviews   181
negative consequences of   107
and pain   475, 489
peer education   200
physical health benefits of   102,
       104–5
programmes   513
psychological benefits of   105–6
reasons for/for not exercising   108
recommendations to   99–102, 195
and socio-economic status
       (SES)   35
and theory of planned
       behaviour   139
existential theory   130
exogenous cells   228
expressed emotion (EE)   364, 463
extroversion   126, 128, 346, 348–9

Facebook   202–3
factor analysis   342
falvenol   63
family caregivers *see* informal
       care/caregivers
family history   109, 270
family influences
   on alcohol consumption and
       smoking   65, 67
   and children's adherence to
       medication   290–1
   see also parents
family support   510–11
family system and illness
       diagnosis   443–4
fat intake   78–9, 80, 95
fatigue
   as consequence of illness   397–8
   see also chronic fatigue syndrome
       (CFS)
Fatigue Assessment Scale   398
fear, and symptom perception   246
fear control   164
fear messages
   and behavioural change   164
   mass media   164, 185–6

fibre   95
fight or flight response   322–3, 324
fighting spirit   344, 345, 357
fistulas   223
five-factor model of personality   126,
       346–7
flavonoids   96
folic acid   100
food choices   83, 96–9
food diaries   76
Food Dudes programme (UK)   98
food labelling   188, 194
forebrain   208
formal operational stage of cognitive
       development   18, 19–20
framing of health messages   164,
       186, 281–2
Framingham Heart Study   66, 82,
       354, 362
frontal lobes   209
fruit intake   80, 81, 95–8, 199, 297
   adolescents   140–2
   guidelines   97, 195
   motivational interviews   181–2
functional disability (FD), social
support and   369
functional limitations profile (FLP)   427

gallbladder   221, 222
galvanic skin response (GSR)   486
gamma-interferon   219
gastric ulcer   222–3
gate control theory of pain   479–82,
       489
gender   32, 46–8
   and coronary heart disease
       (CHD)   46–7
   and delay behaviour   239, 269–70
   and exercise   47, 101, 102
   and health behaviour   47–8, 125,
       239
   of health professionals   270, 280–1
   and health-risk behaviour   65
   and hostility and health
       outcomes   355
   and informal caregiving   440–1,
       446, 448, 449, 457–8
   and life expectancy   9–10, 46
   and self-ratings of health (SRH)
       23, 46
   and smoking   47, 56
   and social support   366, 367, 369
   socialisation   245, 249
   and stress reactivity   47
   and symptom interpretation   249–50
   and symptom perception   239,
       245–6

gender role beliefs 457–8
general adaptation syndrome 323
general health questionnaire
(GHQ) 331
General Lifestyle Survey (UK,
2011) 59
general practitioners (GPs), patient
choice of 270
genes
and exercise 107
and proliferation of cancer
cells 225
and stress 307
genetic screening 108, 109–10, 113,
114, 116, 148, 533
genetics
and alcohol dependency 67
and obesity 83
and smoking 65
genital herpes 74
genital warts 74, 117
glucocorticoids 325, 327
goal-directed behaviour 129–30, 146
goals
coping 345–6
and quality of life 422
gonorrhoea 74
guided discovery 171, 378

habits 68, 144, 145–6
and behavioural change 298
haemoglobin 226, 233
happiness 362
hardiness 271, 353–4
headache pain 469, 487, 488, 490
health
and ageing 21–2
and behaviour 11–12
children's beliefs about 18–20
context-aware view of 15
cross-cultural perspectives on
14–17
historical overview 4–12
lay theories of 12–14
lifespan and perceptions of 17–24
and psychology 25–8
psychosocial models of 7–9
WHO definition of 14–15
health action process approach
(HAPA) 137, 153–5, 183, 297,
522
health behaviour 13, 52–3
age and 125
attitudes towards 131–2
coping functions 130
defined 52
distal influences on 124–31

demographic factors 125
goals and self-regulation of
behaviour 129–31
personality 125–8
social influences 128–9, 137, 139
and ethnicity 44, 125, 142, 269
and gender 47–8, 125, 239
measuring 76–7, 77–8
mediating variables 124
models of 131–4
moderating variables 124–5
motivation 128
and socio-economic status
(SES) 35, 124
see also health-protective
behaviour; health-risk behaviour
health behaviour change
adherence to 295–8
children and adolescents 524
cognitive interventions 170–1
diffusion of behaviours 172–3
enabling factors 160, 161
environmental factors 160, 161,
172, 188–91
guidelines for intervention
development 163, 173–4
implementation intention
approach 169
and mass media 184–5
modelling and practice 169–70
motivation see motivation to change
behaviour
predisposing factors 160, 161
problem-solving approaches
166–9, 173–4, 182–3
public health interventions 160–1,
191–200
reinforcing factors 160
and sociocognitive models of
behaviour change see health
belief model; social cognitive
theory; theory of planned behaviour
and stage models of behaviour
change 147, 149
see also health action process
approach (HAPA); precaution
adoption process model (PAPM);
transtheoretical model
strategies 162–74
workplace reward systems for 198
health belief model (HBM) 134–7,
172, 188, 291, 522
health care
access to 35–6, 45–6
quality of 38
Health and Care Professions
Council 28, 525

health cognitions 66
health differentials 32–43
and ethnicity 32, 43–6
evidence of 32–3
gender 46–8
and social deprivation
levels 33–4
socio-economic see socio-
economic
health differentials
health education 159, 171
health locus of control 127, 358–9
The Health of the Nation report
(UK) 79
health professionals
communication skills 282–6
ethnicity of 281
gender of 270, 280–1
style of interaction with
patients 280
work-related stress 383–5, 386–8
see also general practitioners (GPs)
health promotion 71, 528
see also public health interventions
health-protective behaviour 87–121
adherence behaviour 88–95
and health locus of control 127
health-screening 108–16
healthy diet 95–9
immunisation 116–20
and personality 126
see also preventive behaviour
health psychology 25, 27–8
clinical guidelines 529–31
evidence-based practice 525
implementability of
interventions 532–3
political engagement 531–2
positive approach to 533
research—practitioner gap 529
role and training of health
psychologists 525–9
theory-driven practice 522–5
health risk 52–3
health-risk behaviour 53–5
burden of ill-health attributed to 55
cessation 68, 70–1
and health belief model 136
and hostile individuals 355
and masculinity 125, 269
and personality 67, 69–70, 126
and planned behaviour, theory
of 142–3
primary prevention efforts 71
reasons for initiating 64–6, 125
secondary prevention efforts 71
social influences and 129

see also alcohol consumption; diet, unhealthy; drug use; sexual behaviour, unsafe/unprotected; smoking
health-screening 45, 108–16
  costs and benefits of 112–13
  criteria for establishing programmes 111–12
  for disease detection 108, 110–12
  making decisions about 114–15
  for risk factors 108, 109–10, 113, 114, 116, 180–1, 181, 183–4, 533
  self-screening 115, 116, 135, 136, 139, 146
  and theory of planned behaviour 139–40
  uptake 115–16, 185, 186, 187
health status 13
  differences in *see* health differentials
  self-reported 23–4
  and social support 366–70
Health Survey for England 57, 95, 97
Health Works for Women programme 198
Healthy Cities movement 172, 189
heart 226–8
heart attack *see* myocardial infarction (MI)
heart disease 10–11, 14, 36, 54, 207, 325
  behavioural risk factors for 54
  causal attributions 261
  and diet 95
  and ethnicity 44
  and exercise 104
  and overweight/obesity 78, 82
  see also coronary (ischaemic) heart disease
heart failure 229
Heart Manual 499–500, 507
heart rate 208, 211, 224, 325, 331
Heartbeat Wales programme 193–4
Helicobacter pylori 222–3, 224
helper T cells 215, 326, 327
hemianopia 211
hemiparesis 210
hemiplegia 210
hepatitis B 116
hepatitis C 64
heuristics, and diagnostic reasoning 287–8
hierarchy-health hypothesis 39
high-density lipoprotein (HDL) cholesterol 47, 230
hindbrain 208

hippocampus 208, 325
HIV/AIDS 11, 33, 54, 64, 75, 215–17
  coping responses 408, 411
  and depression and anxiety 402
  diagnosis, reactions to 398
  fear-based messages 185–6
  and informal care 447–8
  information campaigns 159, 162
  medication 216–17
    Antiretroviral Therapy (ART) 89, 91, 111, 217, 289–90, 291, 293, 294, 411
    non-adherence to medication for 89, 91
  peer education 195–6
  prevalence of 72–3
  public health programmes 194–6
  punishment beliefs 402
  and quality of life 421–2, 426
  screening 111
  self-management programmes 506
  and stress 335–6, 515
holistic approach 15, 16
homework tasks 171
homosexual sex 73, 187, 195
hope 360–1, 417
hopelessness/helplessness 344–5, 357, 409
hormones 213–14, 215
  appetite regulation 83
  sex 46–7
  stress 47, 105, 214, 247
hospices 419
hospital settings, minimising stress in 388–91
hospitalisation, emotional reactions to 403
hostility 355–6
Human Papilloma Virus (HPV) 74–5, 117, 119, 123, 142, 186
humoral theory of illness 4–5, 257
Huntington's disease 109, 113
hypertension 44, 78, 79, 82, 231, 325, 333
  anger as risk factor for 356
  and depression 362
  medication 229, 290, 291
hypnosis 485–6
hypochondriasis 247
hypoglycaemia 217, 507
hypothalamic–pituitary–adrenocortical (HPA) system 324–5, 326, 327, 368
hypothalamus 208, 211, 213, 222, 228, 322, 324, 325, 481

hypothesis testing, and diagnosis 287

illicit drug use *see* drug use
illness
  acceptance 411–12
  appraisals 523
  awareness of sensations of 240–1
  benefit-finding 405–8, 500
  biomedical model of 6–7, 17, 32, 110, 257
  biopsychosocial model of 9
  causal attributions 261–2
  children's beliefs about 18–20
  'common-sense model' of 253–4
  coping with 405, 408–12, 523–4
  depletion model of 257
  and disease distinguished 241
  emotional reactions to 523
  negative responses 398–405
  positive responses 405–8
  humoral theory of 4–5, 257
  impact of 396–408
  implicit models of 261
  managing 504–12
  information provision 504–5
  self-management 399, 404, 505–7
  social and family support 510–11
  stress management training 507–10
  written emotional expression 511–12
  physical consequences of 397–8
  and post-traumatic growth 405–8, 415
  psychogenic 26, 244
  psychosocial models of 7–9
  and quality of life *see* quality of life
  self-regulatory model of 253–4, 255, 258, 523
  stages of response approaches to 396–7, 443
  and stress *see* stress, and illness
illness behaviour 263
illness centrality 402–3
illness cognitions 253
illness experience
  measuring 427, 429–30
  and symptom interpretation 252
illness outcomes
  and illness representations 258–60
  measuring 427–8, 429–30
Illness Perception Questionnaire (IPQ and IPQ-R (revised)) 255–7, 261, 463

illness representations   14, 253, 254–5
  and adherence behaviour   291, 297
  and behavioural change   297
  and caring dyads   461–2
  and illness outcomes   258–60
  measurement of   255–7
  and treatment changes   260–1
illness/disease prototypes   252–63
image, and health-risk behaviour   65
immune dysfunction   215–17
  and stress   326–8
immune system   367
  caregivers   450–1
  central nervous systems links with   215
  components of   214–15
  illness and changes in   398
immunisation and vaccination   9, 54, 116–20, 135, 195
  costs and benefits of   118
  Human Papilloma Virus (HPV)   75, 110, 117, 119, 123, 142, 186
  influenza   117, 119, 136, 450
  MMR   116, 118, 119
  purpose of   116–17
  and theory of planned behaviour   142
immunoglobin A (IgA)   214
immunosenescence   327
implantable cardioverter defibrillators (ICDs)   501
implementability of interventions   532–3
implementation intentions (II)   131, 145, 146–7, 155, 169, 183
implicit attitudes   132
implicit models of illness approach   251
impulsivity   69, 70
incidence of disease   11, 36
income distribution, and mortality   38–9
individual differences
  and symptom interpretation   249–52
  and symptom perception   245–8
individualism   16, 369, 408, 441
individually targeted interventions   180–4
inflammatory bowel disease (IBD)   119, 223–4, 290, 335
influenza   54
  vaccination   117, 119, 136, 450
informal care/caregivers   435–65
  and attachment style   455–6

  and caregiver appraisals   456–9
  and caregiver—patient diverging beliefs and perceptions   461–4
  and caregiver—patient relationship   460–1
  children as   438, 446, 449–50, 452, 455
  consequences for caregiver   448–52
  and caregiver characteristics and responses   452–9
  emotional impact   449–50, 454–5
  and illness/behaviour of care recipients   452
  immunological effects   450–1
  physical effects   450
  positive aspects   451–2
  and culture   441, 452–4
  demographic characteristics of   438, 440
  and ethnicity   440, 442, 452–5
  and gender   440–1, 446, 448, 457–8
  helpful and unhelpful actions   447–8
  identity   438–9
  perceived control   359–60
  and personality   455
  prevalence of   437–8
  protective buffering   459
  resentment   460–1
  and social support   446–8, 456, 459
  spousal   440–1, 445–6, 458–9, 460–3
  strain/burden   320, 333, 449, 452, 456, 457
  tasks   437
  and willingness to care   441–3, 453–5
information framing   164, 186, 281–2
information provision   162–3, 173, 281–2
  and distress reduction   499–500
  and illness management   504–12
  online   114, 264–5
  and patient understanding and memory   292–3
informational control   359, 389
injunctive norms   140–2
insulin   217
intention   137–8, 139, 140, 142, 143, 150, 151
  implementation (II)   131, 145, 146–7, 155, 169, 183
intention—behaviour gap   143
INTER-HEART study   333

internalisation   19
International Classification of Functioning, Disability and Health   8, 9, 413
International Classification of Impairment, Disabilities and Handicaps (IC I-D-H) model   8, 413
International Conference on Global Health Challenges (2014)   3
internet
  as health information source   114, 264–5, 505
  health interventions via   200–3
  self-management programmes   507
  support groups   502, 510
  symptom checkers   264–5
interviews
  and health behaviour measurement   77
  motivational   164–6, 167, 181–2
introversion   69, 126
irritable bowel syndrome (IBS)   224, 335, 508
ischaemic heart disease see coronary (ischaemic) heart disease (CHD)
ischaemic pain   182

Kaposi's sarcoma   216
kidney disease patients   260–1
kidney transplantation, emotional reactions to   400–1

language
  and medical consultation   281
  skills   17, 18
  technical/medical   281
large intestine (colon)   222
lay model of ageing   22
lay referral systems   263, 264, 269, 270
lay theories
  of health   12–14
  of stress   315–16
leptin   83
life change units (LCU)   305–6
life events approach to stress   305–8, 330, 334
Life Events and Difficulties Scale (LEDS)   306
life expectancy   9–10
  country variations   9, 10, 33
  gender differences in   9–10, 46
  and income distribution   38
  and social deprivation   34
life hassles   307–8, 330
Life Orientation Test (LOT)   351, *352*

life stage
  and symptom interpretation 150–1
  and symptom perception 246
Life Stress Monitoring Program
      (LSMP) 513
lifespan 17–24
limbic system 208–9, 210, 211, 322,
      481, 482
liver disease, alcohol-related 61
locus of control 127–8, 138, 358–9,
      360
low-density lipoprotein (LDL)
cholesterol 78, 96, 230
lower respiratory tract infection 11, 33
lumpectomy 277
lung cancer 11, 33, 100, 234
  causal attributions 261–2
  and smoking 56–7, 61, 64, 68,
      234, 261, 262
  and vitamin D levels 53
lycopene 95, 96
lymph nodes 214
lymphatic system 214
lymphocytes 214, 215, 228, 325,
      326

McGill pain questionnaire 483–4
macrophages 214–15, 230
maintenance of health
      behaviour 150, 153, 162
malaria 11, 33
mammography 110, 113, 139–40,
      185
masculinity, and health-risk
      behaviour 125, 269
mass media campaigns 163–4,
      184–8
  anti-smoking 184–5
  audience targeting 186–8
  and awareness raising 184
  and behavioural change 184–5
  CHD-related behaviour 191–2,
      193–4
  fear messages 164, 185–6
  HIV/AIDS 185–6, 196
  information framing 186
mass psychogenic illness 244
meaning-focused coping 345
measles 10, 11, 116, 117, 118,
      119, 195
mechanistic viewpoint 6, 7
mediating variables 124
medical consultation 276–86
  factors influencing process
      of 279–86
  breaking bad news 282–6
  culture and language 281

gender of health professional 280–1
information given, type and
      framing of 281–2
  patient factors 282
  type of health professional 280
nature of the encounter 276
power relations 276–9
treatment decisions 277–9
medical decision-making 287–8
medical psychology 27
medical sociology 27
medically unexplained (physical)
symptoms (MU(P)S) 249–50
medication 288–95
  adherence to see adherence
      behaviour
  angina 232
  anti-hypertensive 229, 290, 291
  antidepressant 487–8
  asthma 290, 291, 293
  chronic pain 92–4
  cost and benefits of taking 291
  diabetes 218, 290
  gastric ulcer 223
  HIV 89, 91, 111, 216–17, 217,
      289–90, 291, 293, 294
  maximising use of 291–3
  MEMS systems 90, 293–4
  methods of dispensing 90
  overuse 93, 94
  rheumatoid arthritis 218
  side effects 93, 94, 291
  underuse 93, 94
meditation, mindfulness 379, 380,
      491
medulla oblongata 208, 211, 215
melanoma 115, 283–4, 500, 515
memory 208, 209–10, 418
  and patient-information
      provision 292–3
memory B cells 215
men
  alcohol consumption 59–60, 61,
      125
  as caregivers 442, 449, 457–8
  delay behaviour 239, 269–70
  food choices 96
  health-enhancing behaviour 125
  health-risk behaviour 125, 239,
      269
  symptom perception 239, 245–6
mental health 20, 27
meta-analysis 96
metabolic rate 83
metastasis 225
middle age 21
migraine 469

mind—body relationships 4–6, 7, 26
mindfulness-based
      interventions 363, 379–82,
      410, 491–2, 501, 502–4, 524
Minnesota Heart Health
      programme 193
minority groups 32
  see also ethnic minorities
mirroring 279
MMR vaccination 116, 118, 119
modal beliefs 139–40
modelling 65, 83
  behavioural change 169–70
moderating variables 124–5
monitoring coping style 248, 342
Montreal heart attack readjustment
trial (M-HART) study 513
mood 137
  and exercise 105–6
  and pain 473–4
  and symptom perception 246
moral norms 144, 163
morbidity 55, 81
mortality 10–12, 54
  age-specific 55, 58
  developing countries 33
  and income distribution 38–9
  and obesity 81, 82
  premature 35, 37, 39, 46
  risk factors for 54
  and social support 366
motivation 26, 131, 138, 297, 298
  intrinsic and extrinsic 128
  substance use 68
  to comply 137–8
motivation to change behaviour 150,
      153–4, 162–6
  elaboration likelihood approach
      163–4
  fear 164
  information framing 164
  information provision 162–3
  motivational interviewing 164–6,
      167, 181–2
motor neurons 222
MRFIT study 355
multidimensional health locus of
control (MHLC) scale 127, 358
multiple sclerosis (MS) 218–21, 397,
      404, 439, 450–1, 454
mumps 116
myelin sheath 220
myocardial infarction (MI) (heart
      attack) 46, 81, 104, 229,
      230–2, 333
  caregiver anxiety 459
  causal attributions 261

myocardial infarction (*continued*)
counselling interventions 512–13
and depression 363–4, 514–15
family interventions 510–11
and football spectatorship 388
response to symptoms 265
and self-management
programmes 507
stress management
interventions 513–14

National Diet and Nutrition Survey
(UK) 97
National Institute for Health and
Clinical Excellence
(NICE) 163, 529–30
National Longitudinal Study of
Adolescent Health (UK) 66
National Survey of Sexual Attitudes
and Lifestyles (UK) 75
natural disasters 316–18
natural killer (NK) cells 215, 325,
326, 327, 331, 398
negative affectivity (NA) 247, 251,
271, 357 and stress-illness
relationship 347-8, 363
negative responses to illness
398–405
neophobia 126
Netherlands
health policy documents 14
health psychologists 529
school-based interventions 199
neurological dysfunction 210–11
neuroticism 126, 128, 247, 249,
251, 271, 272, 346, 350, 354
caregiver 455
and stress-illness relationship 347–8
neurotransmitters 211, 213, 215, 222
neutrophils 214
nicotine 168
nicotine replacement therapy 36, 169
nocebo response 477
non-adherence behaviour 89
chronic pain sufferers 92–4
costs of 90
and depression 364
and misattributed cause of
illness/symptoms 262
reasons for 90–5, 290, 296–7
noradrenaline (norepinephrine) 105,
213, 222, 322, 323, 324, 325,
333
North Karelia project 192–3
Norwegian Longitudinal Health
Behaviour Study 64
nutritional information 188

obesity 10, 11, 78, 81–4, 95, 109
causes of 83–4
defining 81
interventions 83
negative health consequences
of 81, 82
prevalence of 82–3
objective signs of illness 242
observational learning 169–70
observational studies 100
occipital lobes 210
occupational stress *see* work-related
stress
oesophagus 221
oestrogen 46
oncogenes 225
online sources *see* internet
openness (to experience) 126, 346
operant conditioning 26, 488
opinion leaders 172
optimism 351–3, 361, 405, 407
caregiver 455
comparative 248
dispositional 351, 352
unrealistic (optimistic bias) 133,
148, 152, 271, 352–3, 359
oral cancers 119
oral hypoglaecemic agents 290
osteoarthritis 82
osteoporosis 53, 104, 111
outcome expectancies 129, 134,
150, 154
ovarian cancer 109, 112, 533
over-generalisation 375
OXCHECK Study Group 180
oxygen therapy 234
oxytocin 442
oxytocin receptor genotype
(OXTR) 368

pain 248–9, 467–94
and absence of pain
receptors 473
acute 468–9, 483, 484–6
biological models of 472–3
catastrophising and 475, 490
causal attributions 475
control beliefs 476
coping with 343–4
and endorphins 326, 481, 485
and ethnicity 471
and exercise 475, 489
gain/reward systems 470–1
gate control theory of 479–82,
489
ischaemic 182
living with 470–2

measuring 483–4
neuromatrix 482–3
and pain receptors that do not
transmit pain 473
phantom limb 7, 468, 473,
482, 483
placebo response 476–7
prevalence of 469–70
psychological influences on 473–9
and quality of life 421
and social support 472
socio-communication in 477, 479
thresholds 246
treatment 483, 484–92
antidepressant medication 487–8
behavioural interventions 488–9,
490, 523
biofeedback 486–7, 490
chronic *see* chronic pain
cognitive-behavioural
interventions 487, 488–91
distraction 485
hypnosis 485–6
mindfulness-based
interventions 491–2
patient-controlled analgesia
(PCA) 484–5
relaxation 485, 486–8
and theory-based practice 523
transcutaneous electrical nerve
stimulations (TENS) 486
types of 468–9
pain management clinics 492
palliative treatment 404, 419
pancreas 217, 222
pancreatic cancer 53, 399
parallel process model 164
parasympathetic nervous system
(PNS) 211, 213, 222, 322,
323, 329
parents
and alcohol consumption and
smoking 65, 67
as caregivers 444–5, 463
and child activity 108
coping responses 444–5
and food choices 98
parietal lobes 210
Parkinson's disease (PD) 418, 445,
454
past behaviour 144, 151
Patient Generated Index (PGI) as QoL
measure 426–7
patient-controlled analgesia
(PCA) 484–5
pattern recognition, and
diagnosis 287

peer education
HIV/AIDS prevention   195–6
school-based   200
peer influences   65, 125, 128–9
peer support   510
perceived behavioural control
(PBC)   127–8, 138, 139, 144,
147, 150, 151, 359
perceived control beliefs   358–61
caregivers   458–9
perceived stress scale   330, 331
peripheral processing   163
peristalsis   222
personal mastery beliefs   360, 405
personality   5, 26, 125–8, 332
caregiver   455
and coping strategy   343
and delay behaviour   271–2
five-factor model of   126, 346–7
locus of control   127–8, 358
and medication non-adherence   91
and risk behaviour   67, 69–70
and stress-illness processes   346–58
and symptom interpretation   251
and symptom perception   247
three-factor model of   126
pertussis (whooping cough)   117, 119
pessimism, dispositional   128, 351
phagocytes   214–15, 228, 325, 326
phantom limb pain   7, 468, 473,
482, 483
phenomenonism   19
physical activity *see* exercise
physical effects of caring   450
physiology   19
pineal gland   6
pituitary gland   213
placebo effect   7, 244, 476–7
placebo intervention   390, 487
planned behaviour *see* theory of
planned behaviour (TPB)
plasma B cells   215
platelets   228
pneumonia   54
polio   116, 117, 118
polyphenols   63–4, 95
pons   208
positive psychology   361–2, 533
positive responses to illness   405–8
post-traumatic growth   405–8, 415
post-traumatic stress disorder   317,
478–9
poverty   16, 32, 33
pre-actional self-efficacy   154
pre-contemplation stage of
behavioural
change   149, 150, 162

precaution adoption process model
(PAPM)   131, 152–3
PRECEDE—PROCEED model
160–1, 164, 172
predisposition   67, 160
pregnancy
antenatal screening   110, 111
condom use and prevention of   75
teenage   62, 66
unplanned   62, 66, 70
premature mortality   35, 37, 39, 46
preoperational stage of cognitive
development   18–19
preoperational stress
management   388–91
preparation stage of behavioural
change   149–50, 150, 151, 162
prevalence
of alcohol consumption   59
of disease   11, 36
and healthcare-seeking
behaviour   268
of HIV/AIDS   72–3
of illicit drug use   60
of obesity   82–3
of pain   469–70
of smoking   55, 56–9, 191
preventive behaviour
and health belief model   135–6
and planned behaviour, theory
of   139–40, 142
see also health-protective behaviour
primary attentional system (PAS)   244
primary prevention   71
see also health-screening
pro-inflammatory cytokines   326–7,
333, *356, 358, 364, 367, 451*
proactive coping   369
problem-focused coping   311, 341,
342, 343–4, 348, 359, 408,
409, 444, 523, 524
problem-focused counselling   166–7,
377
problem-solving approaches to
behavioural change   166–9, 173–4,
182–3
prognosis   225
PROMS (Patient-reported Outcome
Measures)   418, 420
prosocial behaviour   105, 366
prostate cancer   14, 53, 79, 100,
110–11, 112, 409, 460, 464, 502
protection motivation theory
(PMT)   137, 148, 164
PSA (Prostate Specific Antigen)
levels   111
psychogenic illness   26, 244

psychological resources model of
ageing   22
psychology
as a discipline   24–5
and health   25–8
psychopathology   67
psychophysiology   19, 26
psychosocial influences on QoL   420–1
psychosocial models   7–9
psychosocial vulnerability
hypothesis   355
psychosomatic medicine   7, 26
psychoticism   126, 346
public health   28
public health interventions   160–1,
191-200, 524
community programmes   191–4
coronary heart disease (CHD)
191–4
HIV/AIDS   194–6
school-based interventions   199–200
workplace   196–9
pulmonary rehabilitation   234, 296

quality of life (QoL)
and age   22, 24, 413–17
and aspects of illness   418
at end-of-life   419–20
of carers   450
and coping   421
and culture   417–18, 427–8
defined   412–13
domains   412–13, 424–5
and expectancies and
adaptation   417
and goals   422
measuring   423–31
generic versus specific
measures   424–6
illness experience and
outcomes   427–30
individualised measures   426–7
reasons for   423–4
response shift   428–9
social comparison   428–9
psychosocial influences on   420–1
and social support   421–2
and treatment   414, 418, 420, 423
quality-adjusted life years
(QALYs)   424
quantity/frequency index (QFI)   76
question ordering, and data
generation   148

reasoned action, theory of
(TRA)   137, 138, 148
recovery locus of control   358–9

recovery self-efficacy   154
Recurrent Coronary Prevention
        Program   533
red wine   63–4
reductionism   7
reflection   279
reinforcement   65, 150
reinforcers   83, 160, 161
relapse   150, 162, 298
relaxation training   376, 377, 485,
        486–8, 487, 500
religious beliefs   5, 17, 125, 263
   and causal attributions   262
   and non-adherence to
        medication   91
religious coping   409–10, 418, 454
repressive coping   248
resentment, caregiver   460–1
resilience   354
   caregiver   450, 455
resource loss, and stress   316,
        317–18
respiratory disease   10–11, 233–4
   see also asthma; chronic
        obstructive
   pulmonary disease (COPD); lung
        cancer
respiratory system   232–3
response shift   428–9, 431
retrospective control   359
retrospective diaries (RD)   76
rheumatoid arthritis (RA)   218, 219,
        409, 413, 463, 472
   CBT and mindfulness training   491
   models of adjustment   430
   self-management training   506
   written emotional expression
   interventions   511–12
risk factors, health-screening
        for   108, 109–10, 113, 114,
        116, 180–1, 181, 183–4, 533
risk perception   133, 134–5, 154, 155
risk ratios, male/female, premature
mortality   46
risk-taking propensity   66, 67, 69
road injury deaths   11
role models   195, 196
Royal Pharmaceutical Society of Great
Britain   89
rubella   116
rumination   363

salient beliefs   136–7, 139–40
salt intake   79–81, 95
   recommended levels of   80–1
saturated fats   80
school-based interventions   199–200

sciatica   475
screening see health-screening
secondary attentional system
        (SAS)   244
secondary prevention   71, 110
secretin   222
sedentary lifestyles   11, 84, 102
selective abstraction   375
self, loss of   402–3
self-concept   22, 65–6
self-determination theory   128
self-efficacy   68, 127, 133–4, 136,
        137, 138, 150, 163, 169, 298,
        360, 361, 367, 369
   caregiver   456–7, 458
   coping   154, 317
   for exercise   108, 139
   and health action process approach
        (HAPA)   151, 154
   initiative   154
   pre-actional   154
   recovery   154
   and theory of planned behaviour
        (TPB)   143, 144
self-esteem   65–6, 82, 105, 367
self-examination   115, 116, 135, 136,
        139, 146
self-identity   145, 402
   and symptom interpretation   251–2
self-instruction training   378, 489
self-management of illness   399, 404,
        505–7
self-monitoring   76–7, 150, 155, 298
self-presentation bias   77
self-ratings of health (SRH)   23–4, 46
self-regulation of behaviour   129–31,
        155, 297, 298
self-regulatory model of illness
        253–4, 255, 258, 523
self-report measures of behaviour   76
self-talk   378
sensation-seeking   67, 69, 70
sensitivity (of a test)   111
sensorimotor stage of cognitive
development   18–19
sensory neurons   222
serotonin   84
sex education   187, 200
sex hormones   46–7
sexual behaviour   47–8
   and alcohol consumption   62, 70, 75
   condom use/non-use   48, 70, 72,
        75, 77, 136, 143, 147, 162
   homosexual   73, 187, 195
   and HPV vaccination   119, 123
   media messages on   186
   safer   128, 136, 143, 195, 524

unsafe/unprotected   54, 62, 70,
        72–8, 142, 143, 162, 196
sexually transmitted diseases   48, 62,
        70, 72–5, 117, 119, 186, 269
   see also HIV/AIDS
sick role behaviour   12, 263, 272, 447
situation-outcomes
        expectancies   134
skin cancer   53, 115, 128, 131, 186,
        283–4, 500
small intestine   221, 222
smallpox   117
SMART goals   130
smoking   11, 14, 15, 17, 35, 54, 55,
        56–9, 95, 125, 131, 136
   age differences   58–9
   bans   56, 64–5, 191
   dependency development   66, 67,
        68
   and ethnicity   57–8
   and gender   47, 56
   health warnings on cigarette
        packets   188
   media campaigns against   184–5,
        191
   motivational model of   68
   negative health effects   61
   passive   61, 191
   peer education   200
   prevalence of   55, 56–9, 191
   reasons for   64–6, 68
   social influences and   128–9
   and socio-economic status
        (SES)   66
   and stress   66, 68
smoking cessation   68, 70–1
   adherence to programmes for   296
   avoidant strategies   168
   barriers to   70–1
   community interventions   193
   coping strategies   168
   and educational attainment   70
   individually targeted
        interventions   181
   and information provision   173
   internet-based programmes   201
   motivational interviews   181
   nicotine replacement therapy   36,
        169
   and planned behaviour, theory
        of   142–3, 144
   problem-solving approaches
        168–9, 173–4
   school-based programmes
        199–200
   and social support   367
   and socio-economic status (SES)   70

text messages and 201
and theory-based practice 522–3
and transtheoretical model 151
withdrawal symptoms 168, 169
workplace programmes 198
social capital 39–40
social causation and social
drift 34–5
social cognitive theory (SCT) 127,
129, 131, 134, 137, 169, 298,
505, 522–3
social comparison 407, 428–9
social context, and pain 473
social deprivation 33–4
social desirability bias 77, 132
social functioning model of
ageing 22
social identity 251
social influences
on health behaviour 128–9, 137,
139
on symptom perception 244–5
social inhibition (SI) 357
social isolation 48, 82, 365, 366,
402
social learning theory 65, 67, 71, 83,
127, 195, 358
social norms 128–9, 137
descriptive 140–2, 163
injunctive 140–2
social pressure 65
social readjustment rating scale
(SRRS) 305–6
social support 40, 43, 145, 147,
150, 198, 269, 320
actual received 365–6, 369
buffering effect of 367, 369
cultural differences in 369–70
definition, types and functions
of 365–6
detrimental effects of 370
direct effect of 367
and disease 366
and distress reduction 501–2, 504
and gender 366, 367, 369
health benefits of giving 368
and health status 366–70
and informal caregiving 446–8,
456, 459
and managing illness 510–11
and mortality 366
and pain 472
perceived 365, 369
and prevention of disease
progression 516
and quality of life (QoL) 421–2
and stress 339, 364–70

socialisation
and food choices 98
gender 245, 249
and smoking and drinking
behaviour 65
socio-economic health
differentials 32, 34–43, 44
access to health care 35–6
environmental factors 36–7
and gender 48
health behaviour 35
social causation versus social
drift 34–5
stress hypothesis 37–40, 42–3
socio-economic status (SES) 124
and alcohol consumption 66, 67
and exercise 35
and hypertension 231
and smoking 66, 70
sociocognitive models of behaviour
change see health belief model;
social cognitive theory; theory
of planned behaviour
Socratic dialogue 171, 378, 379
somatisation disorder 249–50
specificity (of a test) 111
SPIKES model 282–3
spina bifida 110, 111
'spiral' model of behaviour
change 150
spiritual beliefs, and non-adherence
to medication 91
spiritual well-being 15
spirituality 405, 406, 410, 418
spousal caregivers 440–1, 445–6,
458–9, 460–3
and couple identity 461
stage models of behaviour
change 147, 149
see also health action process
approach (HAPA); precaution
adoption process model (PAPM);
transtheoretical model
stages of change model see
transtheoretical model
Stanford Five City project 193
Stanford Three Towns project
191–2, 193
statins 36, 230
stem cell transplants 278
stem cells 228
stomach 221, 222
stress 32, 37–40, 215, 247,
303–37
acute 316–18
appraisal theory of 255, 309–15,
322, 330

and bad news interviews 282,
284–5
and blood pressure 45, 47, 229,
318, 331, 332–3
and cardiovascular reactivity
329–30, 333, 355, 367, 368
and cataclysmic events 316–18
in children 308, 318
chronic 318–22
cognitive-behavioural theories
of 374–5, 376
conservation of resources model
of 316, 317–18, 321
coping with 340–6
and emotions 311–12, 313–14,
362–4
and ethnicity 45, 329
exam 318
and football spectatorship 388
and gene sensitivity 307
general adaptation syndrome
model of 323
and illness 331–6
bowel disease 335
cancer 313–15, 334–5, 500–1,
515–16
common cold 332
coronary heart disease 332–4,
501, 513–14
direct route 331–2
gastric ulcer 222
HIV/AIDS 336–6, 515
indirect routes 332
and immune function
dysregulation 326–8
lay theories of 315–16
life events approach to 305–8,
330, 334
measurement of 330–1
patient—carer dyads 463
and personality 346–58
as physiological response
322–30, 331
and smoking 66, 68
and social support 339, 364–70
as a stimulus 304–8, 330
systemic—transactional model of
(STM) 463
as a transaction 308–15, 322,
340, 411
and work—life balance 43
work-related see work-related
stress
and wound healing 328
stress diaries 377, 378
stress hormones 47, 105, 214, 247
stress inoculation training 379

stress management 373–92
  behavioural interventions 376, 378–9
  changing triggers 376–7
  cognitive interventions 376, 378, 379, 500
  and distress reduction 500–4
  in managing illness 507–10
  mindfulness-based approaches 379–82, 501, 502–4
  preoperational 388–91
  relaxation training 376, 377, 500
  third wave therapies 379–82
  to prevent disease progression 513–16
  in the workplace 382–8
stress reactivity 318
stroke 11, 14, 44, 210–11
  and alcohol consumption 63
  behavioural risk factors for 54
  and depression 399
  and diet 95
  F.A.S.T. warning signs 210
  family system perspective and 444
  and fatigue 397
  and overweight 78
  symptoms 210
stroke carers 445, 449, 452
student culture, and alcohol consumption 62
subjective expected utility theory 137
subjective norm beliefs 137, 138, 139, 140, 143, 163
subjective signs of illness 242
sugar 95
sun exposure 53, 115, 131
surface cognitions 374–5, 378
surgery
  and anxiety 388–9, 403
  minimising stress prior to 388–91
swine flu 116
sympathetic nervous system (SNS) 105, 211, 213, 214, 222, 228–9, 322, 323, 324, 327, 375
sympathetic—adrenomedullary system (SAM) 324, 326, 327
symptom awareness 240
symptom interpretation 248–63
  causal attributions and 261–3
  cultural influences on 248–9
  gender differences in 249–50
  and illness experience 252
  and illness/disease prototypes 252–63

individual differences affecting 249–52
  and life stage 250–1
  and personality 251
  and self-identity 251–2
symptom perception 242–8
  attentional model of 242, 243–4
  bodily signs and 242–3
  and cognitions and coping style 247–8
  cognitive—perceptual model of 242
  and emotions 246–7
  gender differences in 239, 245–6
  individual differences affecting 245–8
  and life stage 246
  and personality 247
  social influences on 244–5
symptoms
  medically unexplained (physical) 249–50
  responding to 263–5
  delay behaviour see delay behaviour
synapses 211
systemic—transactional model of stress 463

T cells 215, 219–20, 228, 326, 327, 331
tachycardia 224
technology-based health interventions 90, 200–3, 265, 293–4
teenagers see children and adolescents
telomerase levels 107
telomeres 107, 451
temperomandibular disorder pain 490–1
temporal lobes 209–10
termination stage of behavioural change 150
testicular cancer 78, 112, 115
testicular self-examination 115, 116, 139
testosterone 46–7
tetanus 10, 119
text message health interventions 201, 265, 293
thalamus 208, 209, 481, 482
theory, defined 5
theory of planned behaviour (TPB) 131, 137–47, 151, 522
  extending 143–5
  limitations of 143
  and preventive behaviour 139–40, 142
  and risk behaviour 142–3

theory of reasoned action (TRA) 137, 138, 148
theory-led interventions 174–5
thermal biofeedback 486
three-factor model of personality 126
thrombolytic drugs 210
traditional medicine 268, 269, 271
trans-fatty acids 80
transactional model of stress 308–15, 322, 340, 411
  appraisal processes 309–15, 322
  criticism of 312
transcutaneous electrical nerve stimulations (TENS) 486
transient ischaemic attacks 287
transtheoretical model (or stages of change) 149–52
  and behavioural change 151, 162, 181
  limitations of 151–2
traumatic brain injury (TBI) 399
treadmill test 508
treatment
  adherence to see adherence behaviour
  changes in, and illness representations 260–1
  cost concerns 268, 414
  culture/ethnicity and beliefs about 262–3
  delay behaviour and beliefs about 270–1
  emotional reactions to 403
  end of, reactions to 403–4
  pain see under pain
  palliative 404, 419
  and quality of life 414, 418, 420, 423
  see also medication
treatment decisions 277–9
  joint decision-making 278, 288
  shared decision-making 277–8
Treatwell programme 198
trephination (trepanation) 4
trigeminal neuralgia 469
tuberculosis (TB) 10, 33, 398
tumour suppressor genes 225
type A behaviour 248, 347, 354–6, 375, 514
type B behaviour 354
type C personality 347, 356–7
type D personality 357–8
typhoid 10

ulcerative colitis 223–4, 335
ulcers, gastric 222–3
ultraviolet radiation (UVR) 53

unconscious   7
unemployment   43
    and ill health   308, 355
    and smoking and alcohol
        consumption   66
United Kingdom (UK)
    ageing population   21, 55
    alcohol consumption   59, 61
    cancer survival variation   38
    change4life campaign   187
    ethnicity and health   44
    exercise levels   101
    fruit and vegetable
        consumption   81, 97
    health care, access to   36, 45
    health policy documents   3, 14
    illicit drug use   60–1
    immunisation   117, 118, 119
    informal care   437–8, 440
    life expectancy   9, 46
    obesity   82
    premature mortality rates   37
    smoking in   56–8, 64–5
United States of America (USA)
    collectivist versus individualistic
        values in   16
    ethnicity and health   44
    fruit and vegetable intake   97, 98
    health care, access to
        35–6, 36
    life expectancy   33
unrealistic optimism (optimistic
        bias)   133, 148, 152, 271,
        352–3, 359

vaccination *see* immunisation and
        vaccination
vasospasm   232
vegetable intake   80, 81, 95–8,
        140–1, 199, 297

guidelines   97, 195
    motivational interviews   181–2
vegetarianism   96
veins   226
visual field loss   211
vitamin A   100
vitamin C   100, 101
vitamin D   53, 115
vitamin E   100, 101
vitamin supplements   99, 100–1
volitional behaviour   143, 146, 153,
        154–5, 155

waist circumference   81, 83
Ways of Coping scale   342
weight   83
    and alcohol consumption   66
    and fitness   104
    overweight   78, 81
    and smoking   66
    see also obesity
weight loss programmes, adherence
        to   296
Well Works programme   197–8
well-being   12, 14, 362, 416
    spiritual   15
Western Collaborative Group study
(WCGS)   354, 355
white blood cells   214–15, 228, 325,
        326
whooping cough (pertussis)   117, 119
withdrawal symptoms   67
    smoking cessation   168, 169
women
    alcohol consumption   59, 66
    as caregivers   440, 442, 449, 450
    and condom use   77
    and health care-seeking
        behaviour   269, 270
    and smoking   56, 57

symptom interpretation   249–50
symptom perception   245
work, fitness to   12
work—home spillover   43
work—life balance   43
work-related stress   40, 42–3,
        315–16, 318–22, 333, 334
    coping responses   321
    Effort/Reward Imbalance model
        of   43, 320, 386
    job demand—control (JDC) model of
        (job strain)   40, 42, 319–20, 334
    management of   382–8
    sources of   383
worksite public health   196–9
    coronary heart disease (CHD)
        risk   197
    healthy eating   197–8
    reward systems for behavioural
        change   198
    smoking cessation
        programmes   198
World Health Organization (WHO)   8,
        9, 14–15, 32–3, 52–3, 53–4
    definition of adherence   89
    on fruit and vegetable intake   95, 97
    health-promoting schools
        initiative   199
    Quality of Life (WHOQOL) working
        group   412–13, 424–5, 427
wound healing
    and hypnosis   485
    and stress   328
written emotional expression   498,
        511–12

Yerkes—Dodson law   318
yin and yang   16, 418
young people see children and
        adolescents